Get Instant Access
to thousands of editors and agents

WritersMarket.com
WHERE & HOW TO SELL WHAT YOU WRITE

Subscribe Today—No Risk or Obligation!

Sure, you already know **Novel & Short Story Writer's Market** is the essential tool for selling your fiction. And now, to complement your trusty *"writer's bible,"* you can try **WritersMarket.com** with absolutely no risk or obligation!

WritersMarket.com is loaded with practical, personalized features to help you publish your work. And as a purchaser of **2009 Novel & Short Story Writer's Market**, you're eligible for a 30-day free trial. There's absolutely no risk or obligation, so visit **WritersMarket.com** to sign up and see what it can do for your writing!

www.WritersMarket.com
The Ultimate Research Tool for Writers

Tear out your handy bookmark
for fast reference to symbols and abbreviations used in this book

---

N market new to this edition

A publisher accepts agented submissions only

C publisher of graphic novels and comics

Ø market is closed to submissions

actively seeking new writers

seeks both new and established writers

prefers working with established writers, mostly referrals

only handles specific types of work

award-winning market

Canadian market

market is located outside of the U.S. and Canada

imprint, subsidiary or division of major book publishing house (in book publishers section)

$ market pays (in magazine sections)

● comment from the editor of *Novel & Short Story Writer's Market*

ms, mss manuscript(s)

SASE self-addressed, stamped envelope

SAE self-addressed envelope

IRC International Reply Coupon, for use in countries other than your own

(For definitions of words and expressions relating specifically to writing and publishing, see the Glossary in the back of this book.)

—TEAR ALONG PERFORATION—

2009 NOVEL & SHORT STORY WRITER'S MARKET KEY TO SYMBOLS

 N market new to this edition

 A publisher accepts agented submissions only

 C publisher of graphic novels and comics

 market is closed to submissions

 actively seeking new writers

 seeks both new and established writers

 prefers working with established writers, mostly referrals

 only handles specific types of work

 award-winning market

 Canadian market

 market is located outside of the U.S. and Canada

 imprint, subsidiary or division of major book publishing house (in book publishers section)

$ market pays (in magazine sections)

● comment from the editor of *Novel & Short Story Writer's Market*

ms, mss manuscript(s)

SASE self-addressed, stamped envelope

SAE self-addressed envelope

IRC International Reply Coupon, for use in countries other than your own

(For definitions of words and expressions relating specifically to writing and publishing, see the Glossary in the back of this book.)

TEAR ALONG PERFORATION

Thank you for purchasing **Novel & Short Story Writer's Market**. Visit NSSWM.com to sign up for updates and access to other useful features.

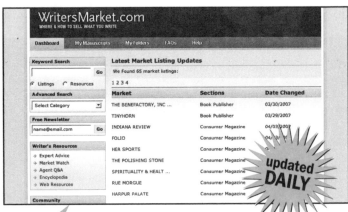
NSSM09

2009

NOVEL & SHORT STORY WRITER'S MARKET.®

From the Editors of Writer's Digest Books

WRITER'S DIGEST BOOKS
CINCINNATI, OH

Complaint Procedure

If you feel you have not been treated fairly by a listing in *Novel & Short Story Writer's Market*, we advise you to take the following steps:

- First try to contact the listing. Sometimes one phone call or a letter can quickly clear up the matter.

- Document all your correspondence with the listing. When you write to us with a complaint, provide the details of your submission, the date of your first contact with the listing and the nature of your subsequent correspondence.

We will enter your letter into our files and attempt to contact the listing. The number and severity of complaints will be considered in our decision whether or not to delete the listing from the next edition.

If you are a publisher of fiction and would like to be considered for a listing in the next edition of *Novel & Short Story Writer's Market*, send a SASE (or SAE and IRC) with your request for a questionnaire to *Novel & Short Story Writer's Market*—QR, 4700 East Galbraith Road, Cincinnati, Ohio 45236.

Editorial Director, Writer's Digest Books: Jane Friedman
Managing Editor, Writer's Digest Market Books: Alice Pope

Novel & Short Story Writer's Market Web page: www.nsswm.com
Writer's Market Web site: www.writersmarket.com
Writer's Digest Web site: www.writersdigest.com
F+W Publications Bookstore: http://fwbookstore.com

Distributed in Canada by Fraser Direct
100 Armstrong Ave.
Georgetown, ON, Canada L7G 5S4
Tel: (905) 877-4411

Distributed in the U.K. and Europe by David & Charles
Brunel House, Newton Abbot, Devon, TQ12 4PU, England
Tel: (+44) 1626 323200, Fax: (+44) 1626 323319
E-mail: postmaster@davidandcharles.co.uk

Distributed in Australia by Capricorn Link
P.O. Box 704, Windsor, NSW 2756, Australia
Tel: (02) 4577-3555

Distributed in New Zealand by David Bateman Ltd.
P.O. Box 100-242, N.S.M.C., Auckland 1330, New Zealand
Tel: (09) 415-7664, Fax: (09) 415-8892

Distributed in South Africa by Real Books
P.O. Box 1040, Auckland Park 2006, Johannesburg, South Africa
Tel: (011) 837-0643, Fax: (011) 837-0645
E-mail: realbook@global.co.za

ISSN: 0897-9790
ISBN-13: 978-1-58297-543-6
ISBN-10: 1-58297-543-4

Cover design by Claudean Wheeler
Interior design by Clare Finney
Production coordinated by Greg Nock
Photographs on selected pages © Frédéric Cirou/PhotoAlto

Attention Booksellers: This is an annual directory of F+W Publications. Return deadline for this edition is December 31, 2009.

Contents

CRAFT & TECHNIQUE

GETTING PUBLISHED

FOR MYSTERY WRITERS

FOR ROMANCE WRITERS

FOR SCIENCE FICTION, FANTASY & HORROR WRITERS

From the Editor

Often when I finish a great novel, I'm a tad exhausted from the journey. Characters enchant, plots rivet, settings envelop me, and I'm always amazed at what the author has achieved. The ability and drive to write a novel is one of those things that I really admire but don't ever imagine taking on myself, kind of like running a marathon.

In his interview in Premier Voices (page 36), debut novelist and experienced short story writer Gary Wilson reveals that it took him three years to finish *Sing, Ronnie Blue* and another year or so "tinkering with it" prior to publication. Just like a runner in training, Wilson paced himself. "It's important to maintain momentum," he says. "It's a long haul, and as Hemingway once said, when it hits, you have to have the legs to run with it. For me, writing a novel isn't a sprint, but a long-distance run, where when you fall into the right rhythm, you can go on forever."

Helen Schulman (interviewed on page 27) adds to that: "You never write books by giving up," she says. "You write them by going the distance, again and again. You really need to be a long-distance runner."

Sometimes, however, we all get in a creative funk, a time when words and ideas aren't flowing as freely as we'd like them to. At that point it might literally be time to run. Author Kelly James-Enger says running "is a great way to get away from the PC for a while. If I'm stuck on something work-related, I'll think about it while I'm running and often the 'answer' will pop into my head." (Read more about how exercise can enhance your writing life on page 14.)

Whatever you need to do to keep inspiration flowing, to keep yourself in shape for the writing long haul, do it. And when you've run the distance, turn to the 2009 *Novel & Short Story Writer's Market* to find the best markets for your work; whether you're writing novels or short fiction, whatever genre, we've got you covered. This edition offers the insights of authors like Pete Hautman (page 23), Elizabeth Moon (page 98), Patrick McGrath (page 31) and the late Edward D. Hoch (page 74). Read their interviews to learn how they've continued to pass the finish line in top form again and again. Then check out our many other features designed to keep you in tip top fiction form—like Roxanne St. Claire's article on juggling multiple projects and even multiple publishers (page 89), Laura Yeager's take on making the most of online fiction writing courses (page 43), and I.J. Schecter's piece on trimming deadweight from your manuscript (page 46)—no treadmill required.

Alice Pope
Managing Editor
Writer's Digest Market Books
nsswm@fwpubs.com

You've Got a Story

So What Now?

To make the most of *Novel & Short Story Writer's Market*, you need to know how to use it. And with more than 600 pages of fiction publishing markets and resources, a writer could easily get lost amid the information. This quick-start guide will help you wind your way through the pages of *Novel & Short Story Writer's Market*, as well as the fiction publishing process, and emerge with your dream accomplished—to see your fiction in print.

1. Read, read, read. Read numerous magazines, fiction collections and novels to determine if your fiction compares favorably with work currently being published. If your fiction is at least the same caliber as that you're reading, then move on to step two. If not, postpone submitting your work and spend your time polishing your fiction. Writing and reading the work of others are the best ways to improve craft.

For help with craft and critique of your work:

- You'll find advice and inspiration from best-selling authors and top fiction editors in the Writing Life section, beginning on page 5.
- You'll find articles on the craft and business aspects of writing fiction in the Craft & Technique section, beginning on page 43, and in the Getting Published section, beginning on page 52.
- If you're a genre writer, you will find information in For Mystery Writers, beginning on page 74, For Romance Writers, beginning on page 82 and For Science Fiction, Fantasy & Horror Writers, beginning on page 94.
- You'll find Contest listings beginning on page 431.
- You'll find Conference & Workshop listings beginning on page 491.

2. Analyze your fiction. Determine the type of fiction you write to best target markets most suitable for your work. Do you write literary, genre, mainstream or one of many other categories of fiction? For definitions and explanations of genres and subgenres, see the Glossary beginning on page 557 and the Genre Glossary beginning on page 564. There are magazines and presses seeking specialized work in each of these areas as well as numerous others.

For editors and publishers with specialized interests, see the Category Index beginning on page 594.

3. Learn about the market. Read *Writer's Digest* magazine (F+W Publications, Inc.); *Publishers Weekly*, the trade magazine of the publishing industry; and *Independent Publisher*, which contains information about small- to medium-sized independent presses. And don't forget the Internet. The number of sites for writers seems to grow daily, and among them you'll find www.writersmarket.com and www.writersdigest.com.

4. Find markets for your work. There are a variety of ways to locate markets for fiction. The periodicals sections of bookstores and libraries are great places to discover new journals and magazines that might be open to your type of short stories. Read writing-related magazines and newsletters for information about new markets and publications seeking fiction submissions. Also, frequently browse bookstore shelves to see what novels and short story collections are being published and by whom. Check acknowledgment pages for names of editors and agents, too. Online journals often have links to the Web sites of other journals that may publish fiction. And last but certainly not least, read the listings found here in *Novel & Short Story Writer's Market*.

Also, don't forget to utilize the Category Indexes at the back of this book to help you target your market for your fiction.

5. Send for guidelines. In the listings in this book, we try to include as much submission information as we can get from editors and publishers. Over the course of the year, however, editors' expectations and needs may change. Therefore, it is best to request submission guidelines by sending a self-addressed stamped envelope (SASE). You can also check each magazine's and press' Web site, which usually contains a page with guideline information. And for an even more comprehensive and continually updated online markets list, you can obtain a subscription to www.writersmarket.com.

6. Begin your publishing efforts with journals and contests open to beginners. If this is your first attempt at publishing your work, your best bet is to begin with local publications or those you know are open to beginning writers. Then, after you have built a publication history, you can try the more prestigious and nationally distributed magazines. For markets most open to beginners, look for the ◯ symbol preceding listing titles. Also, look for the ◪ symbol that identifies markets open to exceptional work from beginners as well as work from experienced, previously published writers.

7. Submit your fiction in a professional manner. Take the time to show editors that you care about your work and are serious about publishing. By following a publication's or book publisher's submission guidelines and practicing standard submission etiquette, you

---

EASY-TO-USE
REFERENCE
ICONS

E-MAIL
ADDRESSES
AND WEB
SITES

SPECIFIC
CONTACT
NAMES

$◪◪THE SOUTHERN REVIEW

Old President's House, Louisiana State University, Baton Rouge LA 70803. (225)578-5108. Fax: (225)578-5098. E-mail: southernreview@lsu.edu. Web site: www.lsu.edu/thesouthernreview. **Contact:** Bret Lott, editor. Magazine: 6¼ × 10; 240 pages; 50 lb. Glatfelter paper; 65 lb. #1 grade cover stock. Quarterly. Estab. 1935. Circ. 3,000.

• Several stories published in *The Southern Review* were Pushcart Prize selections.

Needs Literary. "We desire fiction that crystalizes immediately the author's voice and vision." Receives approximately 300 unsolicited mss/month. Accepts 6-7 mss/issue. Reading period: September-May. Publishes ms 6 months after acceptance. Agented fiction 1%. **Publishes 10-12 new writers/year.** Recently published work by Jill McCorkle, James Lee Burke, Robin Black, James Fowler. Also publishes literary essays, literary criticism, poetry.

DETAILED
SUBMISSION
GUIDELINES

How to Contact Send complete ms with cover letter and SASE. No queries. "Prefer brief letters giving information on author concerning where he/she has been published before, biographical info and what he/she is doing now." Responds in 2 months to mss. Sample copy for $8. Writer's guidelines online. Reviews fiction, poetry.

Payment/Terms Pays $30/page. Pays on publication for first North American serial rights. Sends galleys to author via e-mail. Sponsors awards/contests.

Advice "Careful attention to craftsmanship and technique combined with a compelling sense of the importance of story will always make us pay attention."

TIPS ON
APPROACHING
EACH
SPECIFIC
PUBLISHER

2009 NOVEL & SHORT STORY WRITER'S MARKET KEY TO SYMBOLS

- **N** market new to this edition
- **A** publisher accepts agented submissions only
- **Ø** market is closed to submissions
- **○** actively seeking new writers
- **◑** seeks both new and established writers
- **♥** prefers working with established writers, mostly referrals
- **◎** only handles specific types of work
- **▽** award-winning market
- **♦** Canadian market
- **⊕** market located outside of U.S. and Canada
- **◪** imprint, subsidiary or division of larger book publishing house (in book publishers section)
- **C** publisher of graphic novels or comics
- **$** market pays (in magazine sections)
- **•** comment from the editor of *Novel & Short Story Writer's Market*

ms, mss manuscript(s)

SASE self-addressed, stamped envelope

SAE self-addressed envelope

IRC International Reply Coupon, for use in countries other than your own

(For definitions of words and expressions relating specifically to writing and publishing, see the Glossary in the back of this book.)

Find a handy pull-out bookmark, a quick reference to the icons used in this book, right inside the front cover.

can increase your chances that an editor will want to take the time to read your work and consider it for publication. Remember, first impressions last, and a carelessly assembled submission packet can jeopardize your chances before your story or novel manuscript has had a chance to speak for itself. For help with preparing submissions read "The Business of Fiction Writing," beginning on page 65.

8. Keep track of your submissions. Know when and where you have sent fiction and how long you need to wait before expecting a reply. If an editor does not respond by the time indicated in his market listing or guidelines, wait a few more months and then follow up with a letter (and SASE) asking when the editor anticipates making a decision. If you still do not receive a reply from the editor within a month or two, send a letter withdrawing your work from consideration and move on to the next market on your list.

9. Learn from rejection. Rejection is the hardest part of the publication process. Unfortunately, rejection happens to every writer, and every writer needs to learn to deal with the negativity involved. On the other hand, rejection can be valuable when used as a teaching tool rather than a reason to doubt yourself and your work. If an editor offers suggestions with his or her rejection slip, take those comments into consideration. You don't have to automatically agree with an editor's opinion of your work. It may be that the editor has a different perspective on the piece than you do. Or, you may find that the editor's suggestions give you new insight into your work and help you improve your craft.

10. Don't give up. The best advice for you as you try to get published is be persistent, and always believe in yourself and your work. By continually reading other writers' work, constantly working on the craft of fiction writing, and relentlessly submitting your work, you will eventually find that magazine or book publisher that's the perfect match for your fiction. *Novel & Short Story Writer's Market* will be here to help you every step of the way.

GUIDE TO LISTING FEATURES

On page 3 you will find an example of the market listings contained in *Novel & Short Story Writer's Market* with call-outs identifying the various format features of the listings. (For an explanation of the symbols used, see the sidebar on this page.)

Blogs Writers Should Be Reading

by John Joseph Adams

The blogosphere is a wild and sometimes chaotic place, but in that vast sea of voices there are some people saying things that need to be heard. And since blogging is just a form of writing, there are naturally several blogs that dispense valuable writing advice. The benefits of interacting within the blogosphere can be great. Not only can you pick up free writing advice from professional writers who speak from personal experience or editors and agents who speak from their side of the desk, but you can also become part of your favorite writing community by reading the posts, then reacting to them either by posting comments or writing blog posts of your own.

Diving headfirst into the blogosphere is not without perils, however. If you have the tendency to spout off without really thinking through what you're saying, you can quickly develop a bad reputation as a troublemaker, or a troll, as such folks are known online. Reading a lot of blogs can also be a huge time-waster—time that might be better spent actually writing—so it's important to spend your blog-reading time wisely. Below is a list of some of the best blogs about writing and/or publishing, written by writers and other publishing professionals.

AUTHORS

When you're looking for advice about writing and how to get published, the obvious people to turn to are the ones who are making a living doing just that: published authors. Fortunately, these days many authors have active blogs on which they dispense valuable advice free of charge. Authors often talk about the process of writing, the pressure of deadlines, and the realities of life as a working writer. Additionally, most author blogs are at least in part an exercise in self-promotion; and while that's not generally intended as an instructional enterprise, you can learn a lot about promoting your own work by observing what works (and doesn't work) for them.

John Scalzi
scalzi.com/whatever

The author of several books, including non-fiction titles, such as *The Rough Guide to the* Universe, as well as novels, Scalzi has been online "taunting the tauntable" since 1998. His

JOHN JOSEPH ADAMS is the editor of the anthologies *Wastelands: Stories of the Apocalypse*, *Seeds of Change*, and *No More Room in Hell: Stories of the Living Dead*. He is also the assistant editor of *The Magazine of Fantasy & Science Fiction* and a freelance writer. His Web site is www.johnjosephadams.com.

blog, Whatever, covers numerous topics, treating them either humorously or seriously as the situation requires. His blog might be best known for his infamous "Bacon Cat" post, or for his moving essay on "Being Poor," but he writes about writing frequently enough that Subterranean Press published an entire book of his collected writings on writing, called *You're Not Fooling Anyone When You Take Your Laptop to a Coffeeshop*. Although it's available in handy book form, all of his writing-related articles are still online. And Whatever is a blog worth checking out whether you're interested in writing or not—it's one of the best blogs period.

Tess Gerritsen
tessgerritsen.com/blog

A doctor and best-selling author of medical thrillers such as *Harvest* and *Life Support*, Gerritsen's posts cover such topics as getting over receiving a bad review; how to decide whether or not to kill off a character; and how you can have all the action sequences in the world, but they're meaningless if there's no suspense. Almost every post is relevant to writing, making this a blog no writer should miss.

J.A. Konrath
jakonrath.blogspot.com

Titled "A Newbie's Guide to Publishing," this blog delivers what it promises. Konrath, author of the Lt. Jacqueline "Jack" Daniels thriller series, along with more than 50 articles and short stories, discusses subjects such as book promotion, publishing myths, the value of reviews, and the doubts associated with writing.

David Louis Edelman
davidlouisedelman.com

Edelman, author of the novels *Infoquake* and *MultiReal*, offers an informative blog on a variety of subjects. Of particular interest to writers are his posts on self-promotion. Starting with the sale of his first novel, you can follow Edelman's publicity plan, see what worked and what didn't.

Tobias S. Buckell
tobiasbuckell.com/weblog

A Caribbean-born science fiction writer and author of many short stories and the novels *Crystal Rain*, *Ragamuffin*, and *Sly Mongoose*, Buckell often discusses the issues surrounding race and ethnicity in fiction. Other useful writing posts focus on the business side of writing, such as his massive survey to calculate the average author advance for a first novel.

Jay Lake
jaylake.livejournal.com

Author of *Mainspring* and other novels, as well as more than 200 short stories, Lake posts so many blog entries one might wonder when he finds the time to write his fiction—but many of his posts are quite informative. He writes openly about the writing process—thinking out loud about what works and what doesn't, as well as discussing strategies for keeping yourself on track, such as his own decision to quit watching television.

GROUP BLOGS

If a single author's blog is good, then a blog by a group of authors is even better. Group blogs have the advantage of being more like a conversation between authors, rather than just one person's opinion—sort of like getting free admission to a symposium on writing. The other plus side about group blogs is that with multiple authors participating, the blog is usually updated quite often and the comment threads tend to be rather lively, since everyone participating has to have their say.

DeepGenre
deepgenre.com

Featuring authors Carol Berg, Constance Ash, David Louis Edelman, Kate Elliott, Katharine Kerr, Kevin Andrew Murphy, Laura J. Mixon, Lois Tilton, Madeleine Robins, and Sherwood Smith, DeepGenre is always on topic, delving into the definitions of genre, the business of writing, issues of craft (storytelling, characterization, style, etc.), as well as offering insights about why certain books do or don't work, and a variety other writing and publishing topics.

Writer Beware
accrispin.blogspot.com

Blog of Science Fiction Writers of America watchdog group Writer Beware. Led by authors A.C. Crispin and Victoria Strauss, Writer Beware seeks out and puts an end to writing scams by exposing fraudulent agents, highlighting bad contract language, and otherwise sticking up for the rights of writers.

EDITORS

Editors are, of course, the people you're trying to sell your work to, so an editorial blog would be one to watch. However, most editors have very little time to spend blogging (They all have lots of manuscripts to read, after all!), so real insight from acquiring editors in the blogosphere is a rare thing. While the following blogs are not written by acquiring editors, they provide insight into other aspects of publishing that, in the long run, can be equally as valuable.

Deanna Hoak
deannahoak.com

Written by a professional copyeditor specializing in science fiction and fantasy, this personal blog, often covers subjects other than writing and editing. But if you're looking for some insight into the copyediting process, look no further.

Rose Fox
rosefox.blogspot.com

Get behind-the-scenes information about *Publishers Weekly*—the publishing industry's top trade journal and review magazine—from the magazine's science fiction/fantasy/horror reviews editor. Fox helps authors understand when a review of their book might appear, and just what exactly is the value of a starred review.

LITERARY AGENTS

Like editors, you'd think that literary agents wouldn't really have time to blog, but there are several intrepid actual working agents who devote their time to helping out all you agent-seekers out there. Agents, of course, have to be a bit cautious what they write about, but agency blogs can be very helpful to writers because not only do they provide valuable advice about submission procedures, etiquette, and the like, they can also really help you learn what these agents in particular are looking for—above and beyond what their guidelines specify.

The Knight Agency
knightagency.blogspot.com

This agency specializes in romance and women's fiction with clients including best-selling authors Tommy Newberry, Don Piper & Cecil Murphey, and Karen Marie Monig. Also check out TKA agent Nephele Tempest's personal blog at nephele.livejournal.com.

Jennifer Jackson
arcaedia.livejournal.com

Jackson is an agent with the Donald Maass Literary Agency whose clients include best-selling fantasy writer Jim Butcher, Derringer-Award nominee C.M. Chan, and award-winning author Jo Ann Ferguson.

Book Ends Literary Agency
bookendslitagency.blogspot.com

Book Ends represents a wide variety of clients in the fields of spirituality, self-help, business, mystery, and romance. Their clients list include best-selling authors Elizabeth Joy Arnold, and Sally MacKenzie.

Rachel Vater
raleva31.livejournal.com

Vater is an agent with Folio Literary Management whose clients include best-selling authors Melissa Marr, and Jeaniene Frost.

Janet Reid
jetreidliterary.blogspot.com

Ried is an agent with FinePrint Literary Management, an agency specializing in crime fiction. Clients include authors Jeff Somers, Richard Gilbert, and Bill Cameron.

Dystel & Goderich Literary Management
dglm.blogspot.com

This agency represents everything from parenting and women's health books to literary and commercial fiction with clients including bestselling authors Cindy Adams, Jonathan Small, and David Morrell.

Kristen Nelson
pubrants.blogspot.com

Nelson is the founding agent of the Nelson Literary Agency whose clients include authors Linnea Sinclair, Sherry Thomas, and Marianne Mancusi.

THE ANONYMOUS PROFESSIONALS

Some agents and editors feel the need to blog, but prefer to do so anonymously—no doubt so that they can be brutally honest (and also perhaps so that their authors don't complain they're spending their time blogging, when they could be working on their manuscripts). These blogs tend to be more snarky and a bit more informal than their eponymous counterparts, but are equally (if not more) valuable for learning the answers to questions you may not have even thought to ask.

Miss Snark
misssnark.blogspot.com

Written by an anonymous literary agent, this is perhaps the first (and best) of this type of blog. Miss Snark has ceased updating, but the "snarkives" (blog archives) remain accessible, and there you'll find more than a whole book's worth of invaluable advice, including specific answers to reader questions.

Evil Editor
evileditor.blogspot.com

This anonymous book editor's regular features include ''Face Lift,'' in which Evil Editor revises query letters submitted by readers, and ''New Beginnings,'' in which authors post the first 150 words of their books and Evil Editor and ''his minions'' provide a brief continuation of the book and comment on the opening.

Editorial Anonymous
editorialanonymous.blogspot.com

An anonymous children's book editor posts excerpts of real query letters and phone calls—changing the names to protect the ignorant—for educational purposes. Posts also include insider essays about what really goes on in the publishing world. Most advice will apply in other realms of publishing as well, not just children's books.

The Rejecter
rejecter.blogspot.com

This blogger is an anonymous assistant at a literary agency, as well as a book author who claims to reject 95% of query letters immediately and put the other 5% in the ''maybe'' pile. Posts go over basic advice and answers reader questions.

This list is a good place to start, but don't stop here. Once you find some bloggers you like, check out the sidebars on their Web site to see if they have a blogroll—a list of other blogs they typically read and/or endorse—and start exploring from there. While many of these writers and publishing professionals are in the science fiction/fantasy field, writers of any genre should find these blogs useful. And if you look around, you should be able to find bloggers to learn from in whatever genre you prefer.

The Writing Life

L.A. Banks

Capturing Characters Through Dialogue

by Janice Gable Bashman

A symbiotic relationship between character and dialogue is key for L.A. Banks. With over 35 novels to her credit, 10 novellas, and numerous short stories in genres such as crime suspense, paranormal, romance, and women's fiction, Banks loves her characters.

It is no surprise that Banks—who writes under the pseudonyms L.A. Banks, Leslie Esdaile, Leslie E. Banks, Leslie Banks and Leslie Esdaile Banks—has written commercial fiction for five major publishers simultaneously. She is currently writing a 12-book paranormal fiction Vampire Huntress Legend series (*The Darkness*, February 2008 and *The Shadows*, July 2008) and a werewolf Crimson Moon series for St. Martin's Press (*Bad Blood*, April 2008 and *Cry Wolf*, October 2008). She also writes a crime/suspense series for Kensington/Dafina books (*Better Than*, June 2008). In addition, Banks has contributed to numerous anthologies, including *Hotter Than Hell* (June 2008) and *Amcestores* (September 2008), and wrote the novelization of the movie *Scarface* and a second book in that series, *Scarface: Point of No Return*.

You stated a symbiotic relationship is key between character and dialogue. "A character is captured by the dialogue and the dialogue is shaped by the character—these 'entities' are inextricably linked. Any disconnect between them is jarring for the reader." Explain.

Let's say a character is from an ethnic neighborhood in Southwest Philadelphia—his/her speech patterns should reflect the "norm" from that environment, just as though a kid from a South Boston neighborhood may have dialect idiosyncrasies that add dimension and "realness" to his/her character, or the speech patterns of a London banker would be vastly different than the two character types cited above. Without this texture, the characters read flat and are less believable.

How do you capture a character through dialogue, and how is the dialogue shaped by the character?

The dialogue "places" a character into recognizable patterns of personality and cultural identity. Do they speak in run-on sentences in their minds, but speak slowly and deliberately

JANICE GABLE BASHMAN has been a book reviewer for *Elle* magazine and the *Borzoi Reader*, completed multiple profiles for *Bucks* magazine, and wrote about Lisa See for the 2008 *Novel & Short Story Writer's Market*. She is an ongoing contributor to the *Wild River Review*, a literary e-zine that averages over a 150,000 hits a week and it a contributing editor for Bram Stoker award-winning author Jonathon Maberry's *The Crytopedia Magazine*. She's won multiple writing awards at the 2007 Philadelphia Writer's Conference.

in actual dialogue? Do they have regional slang? Is there a regional "twang" to it? Is their conversation deep and probing, or light and inane? The way your character communicates can tell us if he or she is nice, mean, arrogant, insecure, etc. It can also convey age (older characters use older slang references from years gone by). You must be sure that your character either speaks or thinks in the way that you have outwardly represented them. Here's an example—say you have a vampire, an evil predator, but he/she seems like "Joe regular" nice guy on the outside. His/her conversation may be nice, inviting, and blandly innocuous—but what is going on inside their mind (character's point of view) could be completely horrifying. This is how one uses the device of dialogue, whether internal to the character or external (between quotation marks when speaking in a scene) to thoroughly flesh-out that individual to make him/her more robust.

In my most recent novel, *The Shadows*, book 11 of the Vampire Huntress Legends series, and throughout the series, frankly, I play with all sorts of differences . . . age, gender, race, and belief systems throughout. So, there are always times when members of the same team (the Warriors of Light) might have the general goal that they need to prevail over the bad guys (evil, in this case), but there will always be a team debate about how to accomplish that. Some people will want to employ the conservative approach, some will want to just go for it, while still others will want more data before proceeding—and all of those different perspectives are based upon age, gender, basic personality, and past experiences (triumphs, failures, and fears). The way they argue their point will be characteristic of their personalities . . . one guy is a man of few but poignant words (think Mr. Spock type), another is data intense and overanalyzes everything, there's the group smart aleck, the group hothead, the peacemaker, the sage, etc.

When capturing a character and creating dialogue, what factors are important to know and why?

I think it's important to know where the person is from, ethnic/cultural background, age, hobbies and interests, and personality style (type A, a worrier, cool and collected), etc. The reason is that people tend to talk about what interests them or what they like or hate. They also draw colloquial references to pepper their conversations. The most mysterious of characters never speak about themselves, don't give any regional references, and only embellish upon what others around them are talking about. A great "ah ha" moment in a scene can be when another character suddenly realizes that "Joe" never says a word about where he's from, what he likes, or anything seemingly "normal." Thus, if you are going to have normal dialogue, you have to first get inside your characters' heads to know who they are, and reveal some of that in the things they talk about, the things they get passionate about, or just don't care about.

Explain the importance of a character's ethnicity, background, and stress in shaping dialogue and how you use these factors to capture a character's life.

I think a character's culture is an *amazing* tool, as is the stress they experience (which can subtly help bring that cultural identity to the fore.) Here's an example—take someone who grew up in the proverbial "Bible belt," who is culturally southern (pick any ethnicity) . . . if something scary jumps out of an alley at them, they might say, "Sweet Jesus!" (Or some variation on a theme.) A Latino person might say, "Madre d' Dios!" (Note: all of these are "mights" as there's no hard and fast rule—these are very broad strokes.) It's no different than point of view, too. For example, someone who grew up in Little Odessa (New York City) of impoverished Russian heritage might see something while watching television—let's make it a news broadcast while sitting in a grungy diner—and let's have them see wealthy American celebrities doing silly things, and think, "Rat bastards." Given the context of these people's circumstances and cultural backgrounds above, more definition beyond that scant dialogue isn't required. We, as readers, *know* more about these characters, and they feel more real to us after those short lines.

What elements affect the authenticity of a character's dialogue?

If you're going to do dialogue, you have to understand where the people you are writing about are coming from. You should sit for a bit discussing politics, religion, et al, with a person from the culture you're going to write about—or you might be off-base. When you put dialogue in a character's mouth that just rings so completely untrue from that ethnicity or culture, it's jarring. (Example—take a black kid from North Philly and have them say, "Whoa, dude far out." Trust me when I tell you that, your readers will stop believing from that point onward in the story). Your job as the writer is to make people "believe" while they are between your pages—no matter how fantastic a tale it is you're telling. Incorrect dialogue elements fracture belief. Do your homework and research. The same holds true for varying ages, genders, political backgrounds (conservative, liberal, apolitical, independent, conspiracy theorist—the list is long, but you need to know your character's viewpoint.) You simply have to have an understanding of human nature and the broad variations that come from different perspectives.

You stated that once a writer knows his characters, he should "trust [his] gut." Explain.

Trusting one's gut is like cooking. You've followed the recipe, but still "there's something missing." That's when you open the spice cabinet and begin experimenting. You're going to add "flavors" that are not in the general specs of the recipe . . . quirks, idiosyncrasies, drama that will perhaps make your character outside the norm of what one would expect. Here's a really crazy example—say you have that black kid from North Philly as a character in your story that I just mentioned, and you really want him to sound like a surfer dude because the lines are great and the timing is perfect. Okay, it's *your* story—all you have to do is justify it. So, go back into that character's past, give him a TV show, movie, comic or something that he loved the character in, and have his friends roll their eyes when he goes "surfer dude" on them . . . make me believe that this kid from "the 'hood" has an affinity to this "outside the box" (for him) language.

Maybe he was hooked on *Hawaii Five-O* reruns or something? Maybe some old surfer movie was the only thing that kept him sane when his old man beat his mother, you tell me, the reader. But make it real for me so that I buy the jarring disconnect between person and voice. It could add the craziest, most wonderful, unique blend to the story. That's where you trust your gut and "try" things out. That's where genius comes into the world you're building and unforgettable characters are made. If you can justify it and make it real, then go for it. Sometimes you won't know if something works until you try a little of it in the sauce, taste it while cooking, and then see what happens.

You have said that once you "figure who [your] characters are, [you] try to listen to their music, their pulse, and then work on their inner dialogue as though there was a melody to it." Explain how that happens. Also, describe a time when a character's music surprised you and how you reacted to it.

I call this "cultural immersion"—because dialogue, like music, has a cadence, a melody, a timing to it—a rhythm. Again, these are very broad strokes, and there is no one big stereotype for different kinds of people . . . but there are patterns. If you watch/listen to the general speech patterns of people who listen to rap, jazz, rock, country, etc., there are significant differences. These differences can come out in slang and dialogue, because music is culturally iconic. Take for example a McDonald's new slogan, "I'm loving it," comes out of that whole hip-hop, urban slang wave. Jill Scott (neo-soul artist) just came out with a new single, "Hate on Me," a derivation of "haters" — slang for people who are jealous of what another person has. Back in the day, a quickie saying was, "God bless the child," which meant, basically, you'd better get your own, and came out of the jazz movement's Billie Holiday theme, "God Bless the child (who has his own)." Therefore, if you listen to the music, you can catch on to the vibe and the slang a little bit, and then do some interpreting on the fly when creating your own inner dialogue for your characters.

One of the most surprising music things that happened while I was working on an urban heroine was, I had Celine Dion on as pure background noise (the CD changer was on auto pilot), but I was at a love scene juncture when Dion's sultry "I Surrender" came on . . . I recall sitting back, playing the song again and listening to the words and tempo, then shouting, Yes! Nothing else that I had in my collection worked to set the absolutely defenseless intention of that heroine at that moment. Go figure? I would have never normally paired "Damali" with Celine Dion—I just wouldn't have. So I learned something that night. It opened my mind and writing to really get creative with sampling new flavors and cross blends for even richer character development, if you will. What Dion was saying, the mood, and melody, everything worked for that scene. (I used it for *The Bitten*, a balcony scene in a vampire castle in Australia! Ya never know!)

You have said that you like "mixing folks up, causing collisions of culture, race, gender, and economic circumstances. It makes for a spicy, complex blend, a lot of tension, and leaves room for expanding one's knowledge about different threads within the fantastic tapestry of humanity." Explain how this occurs through dialogue and character, and the importance of this process in creating rich, three-dimensional characters.

Think of the movie, *Crash* . . . people seeing the same event from multiple angles. If you pit a man and a woman at odds over the same issue, you have it—a staunch Democrat versus a staunch Republican, an industrialist versus an environmentalist, a kid from "the 'hood" versus one from the suburbs, a Pro-Life supporter versus a Pro-Choice supporter, the list is endless. But when these characters collide, their passions on both sides of the table tell you who they are by what they say and think, and it will definitely make the sparks fly. If everyone is the same and agrees to everything, then it's boring. Your extremes also don't have to be "mega" extremes. It could be the quiet grounded soul versus the dare-devil, whereby the voice of reason in the group doesn't think doing something is a good idea and he/she finally bucks up against the group leader because of his/her convictions on the matter. The ways to illustrate this are endless, because people have such vastly different perspectives (if you build them that way).

The Writing Life

How Exercise Can Enrich Your Writing

by Eve Menezes Cunningham

Has too much writing or thinking about writing sapped your energy? Is your creativity low because you need some inspiration? Maybe spending time with your characters is the only interaction you've had for days and you're feeling lonely. Do you ever feel sluggish and out of shape after spending hours glued to your screen? These are all common problems for writers—but exercise can help you fix them.

Many writers wonder why they should take time away from their work to exercise, aside from the obvious heath reasons. "Writers desperately need to exercise. We need some way to counteract all the Cheetos and Twinkies we consume when we're working." says Lisa Daily, author of *Fifteen Minutes of Shame* (Plume). The need to exercise is about more than just your waistline; it's about giving your mind and body the ability to work efficiently.

Excuses to avoid the gym

While taking time away from writing is a concern, exercise is something writers can do without sacrificing as much time as expected. "I got into a 'must work, must earn money' rut. I work hard and the temptation is to sit at my machine for 10 hours a day," says Sue Moorcroft, author of *Uphill All the Way* (Transita) and *Family Matters* (Robert Hale). But she knows that this isn't healthy. Instead, Moorcroft attends three exercise classes a week during lunchtime and eats at her desk on those days. And when guilt about not writing comes up, she reminds herself, "I could do this if I worked in an office so I don't see why I shouldn't do it just because my office is at home."

Many writers have a problem getting started when looking at a blank page; they are paralyzed by the need to write something amazing, and the knowledge that whatever they finally start writing probably won't be. A similar fear often plagues first-time gym-goers. Feeling out of shape is completely understandable and getting there from square one can seem daunting. But don't psyche yourself out by dwelling on thoughts that are unlikely to motivate you to exercise. Instead, gather your self-discipline and get started. Whether it be writing or exercise, that self-discipline will help you get moving.

"Be prepared to build up slowly and go at your own pace, even if that pace is slow," says Moorcroft. "I feel a difference in my energy levels and a feeling of wellbeing. I had inflamed and clicky shoulders before I joined the gym and they're much better now." With more energy and less pain, even with the time away from her desk, exercise offers more writing time and greater efficiency.

EVE MENEZES CUNNINGHAM is a Business Coach for Writers. Sign up for free tips at www.coachingwriters.co.uk.

And keep in mind that just as it takes time and persistence to craft a successful work of fiction, it takes time for the exercise to make a difference. Kelly James-Enger, author of *Did You Get the Vibe?* and *White Bikini Panties* (both Kensington/Strapless), started running to get into shape. "Once you get over the hump (say, the first four to six weeks), you really will start to notice a difference in your energy levels and your attitude," she says. The greater overall fitness and wellbeing can lead to greater productivity.

But if you haven't found a kind of exercise you actually enjoy, your motivation levels are going to be low. You don't write in genres you don't like, so why exercise in unappealing ways? Moorcroft thought exercising meant forcing herself to go to the gym and "pounding about sweatily" until she felt ill. Now she enjoys the challenge of yoga and Pilates.

James-Enger stresses the need to find something that's fun. "You don't have to run if you hate it," she says. "Look for something you enjoy and can stick with. Consider what you like to do, not what you're 'supposed' to do." Moorcroft agrees: "The secret is to pick exercise that you really like and look forward to—a swim, a walk, a class. Remember that dancing is exercise, too."

Physical benefits

Physical well-being helps our mental health because of the way our body functions. When we exercise, our bodies produce endorphins. Strenuous exercise produces opioids. Endorphins are the body's natural "feel good" chemicals. Opioids have a similar effect to opiates (including morphine) and add to this feeling of wellbeing and stress relief.

"Running became a great stress-reliever for me," say James-Enger. "It still is. It got me through law school, five years of practice, and 10 + years of fulltime freelancing. It's a great way to get away from the PC for a while. Sometimes I listen to music; sometimes I veg and let my mind wander. If I'm stressed or wired, nothing makes me feel better than a decent run. Even the worst run is better than not running at all!"

Moorcroft says she often feels drowsy by the afternoon when she hasn't taken a class. But "in the afternoons following a lunch time class I never feel drowsy." She's not alone in finding that exercise actually creates more energy. This is great news for writers, especially if you're feeling blocked. Taking that time out for some exercise will help you come back refreshed so, while you've been away for an hour, you don't lose the whole afternoon.

James-Enger finds "the 45 minutes or so (plus cooling off, showering, cleaning up) is well worth the energy I get back from it. Writing is such a sedentary profession, it's critical to get up and do something. Even a quick walk or some stretches will boost your productivity and give you an energy boost."

When it comes to scheduling your exercise into your writing week, think about your natural body clock as well as your appointments. Many people find a walk, run or swim first thing in the morning energizes them for the day's writing. If exercise isn't your favourite thing to do, it can be a nice boost knowing that it's out of the way and you can check it off your list. If you choose a type of exercise you love, you can arrange to fit it in later as a reward for completing that complex chapter and make it work for you as motivation.

Mental benefits

As a writer, giving your conscious mind a rest might be just what you need to keep creativity flowing. Before you being exercise, think about something that's challenging you and ask your unconscious mind to work on it. Don't overwhelm yourself but pick one thing that would make a difference to the rest of your day. You may find that your unconscious mind suddenly comes up with the solution to that plot problem or character crisis in the middle of your workout when you least expected it. "If I'm stuck on something work-related, I'll think about it while I'm running and often the 'answer' will pop into my head," says James-Enger. When you're thinking about the exact same problem at your desk, it can be easy to creep from contemplation to obsessing. By doing something different, the quality of your thoughts changes so it is easier to find the answer. Take that pressure off and let inspiration flow.

"I get my best ideas when I'm moving. I'm not a fan of exercise in general, but it does

Quick Fixes

If you really don't even feel you have time to go for a quick walk or go to the gym, you can do these exercises at any time. Even at your desk.

Neck roll
Sitting or standing comfortably, gently roll your head backwards and slowly forwards towards your chest. Bringing it back up to centre, gently turn it to your left shoulder and then to your right shoulder. Repeat slowly and gently and you'll find that you are able to move it a little further each time as you loosen up.

Leg stretch, forward roll
Standing with your feet hip distance apart, slowly roll your chin and head down towards your chest and, vertebra by vertebra, all the way down as far as you can comfortably reach. If you can't touch your hands comfortably to the floor with your legs straight, bend your knees until you can. Hold for a few moments and feel the stretch in the back of your legs. When you're ready, slowly roll back up, vertebra by vertebra and bring your neck and head up last. Repeat a few times to loosen your spine and stretch your legs.

Shoulder easer
Shoulders put up with a lot when we're hunched over our computers all day writing. Take a little time out to stand with your feet hip distance apart. Clasp your wrists above your head and feel the stretch in your upper arms. Bring your hands back down and then repeat the lift but cross your other wrist over the top. Next, hold your wrist with the other hand behind your back and gently ease your arms backwards. Repeat on the other side for a lovely shoulder stretch.

Spinal rock
Sitting with your knees drawn in and your back straight, roll backwards as far as it is comfortable. Your spine is an excellent indicator of overall health and you may find that if you're run down, have a cold or are stressed, you aren't able to roll back as far. Spending a few moments each day doing this simple spinal rock can increase overall health and wellbeing as well as feeling like a lovely back massage. If this feels too strenuous, lie on your back with your knees pulled into your chest and gently rock from side to side so your lower back and hips get a massage.

Eye exercises
Choose a comfortable spot ahead of you and gently gaze at it. Without moving your face, slowly roll your eyes upwards as if to the 12 o'clock point of a clock. Roll them downwards to 6 o'clock. Take them to 9 o'clock. And then over to 3 o'clock. Repeat and feel free to add other "times" to roll your eyes towards as you develop more control. You may be surprised to find your eyes feel quite tired by this (they're muscles that need to be worked, too). If you ever find it hard to fall asleep pondering those plots, a couple of rounds of this can help you drop off.

get my brain going, says Daily. "I take a 40-minute walk every morning before I begin writing, and I head back out for another walk any time I get stuck." And when she's finishing up for the day, she does 15 minutes of T-Tapp exercise. All the shoulder rolls help her loosen up after spending the day at the computer.

Joining an class and making friends with other regulars or doing some sort of group activity can be a great way for writers to overcome isolation. Exercise classes often offer quite an unusual mix of people you might otherwise never meet. They can become inspiration for plots and fictional characters as well as being good company as you get to know them. Even if you keep to yourself, overheard snatches of conversation can trigger some surprising scenarios. "I enjoy mixing with other people because I work on my own most of the time," says Moorcroft.

So instead of dismissing exercise as unnecessary to improving your writing think again about the possible benefits and give it a shot for a few months. Do something different and get your blood flowing. It'll be worth it. For yourself and for your writing.

The Writing Life

Heidi Julavits & Gabrielle Zevin

Pushing the Limits of Narrative & Truth

by Kelcey Parker

In Gabrielle Zevin's novel *Margarettown*, Margaret Towne's husband wonders about a family of women he meets. The family includes Marge, May, Mia, Greta and Old Margaret, who explains that a witch placed "an enchantment" on newborn Margaret that "would split her into multiple ages until she found true love." Zevin literalizes the idea that a human being is a collection of selves. In doing so, she challenges fairy tale notions of true love: to love Margaret Towne is to love all of the Margarets in Margarettown. As Zevin explains, "I used fairy tale because I hoped it would speak to the gap between the narrator's and Margaret's experience of their marriage."

Heidi Julavits' most recent novel, *The Uses of Enchantment*, takes its title from Bruno Bettelheim's study of fairy tales and also delves into questions of identity. In the book's alternating narrative, Mary Veal is an adult woman returning home for her mother's funeral in 1999, a high school student who disappears briefly after field hockey practice in 1985, and the subject of a psychological study by a local therapist who treats her in the months following the (possible) abduction. "I love the challenge of establishing character in this post-identity era," Julavits says.

Heidi Julavits

Like their characters, Julavits and Zevin seem to exist as multiple selves: how else to explain how much they accomplish? Julavits has published two other novels, *The Mineral Palace* and *The Effect of Living Backward*; edits the literary and cultural magazine, *The Believer*; teaches at Columbia University; and raises a young daughter with her writer-husband Ben Marcus.

Zevin has written two books for teens, *Elsewhere* and *Memoirs of a Teenage Amnesiac*, which were described by the *New York Times* as sharing "a vision of wisdom rooted equally in loss and laughter." In a separate *Times* review, *Elsewhere* was compared to *A Wrinkle in Time* and *Tuck Everlasting* as one of those books with "a premise so fresh and arresting it seems to exist in a category all its own." Educated at Harvard, Zevin also writes screenplays, including *Conversations with Other Women*, which starred Helena Bonham Carter and Aaron Eckhart.

KELCEY PARKER's short stories have appeared or are forthcoming in *Image, Bellingham Review, Indiana Review, Western Humanities Review, Sycamore Review*, and other journals. She has a Ph.D. in creative writing and literature from the University of Cincinnati, and currently lives with her husband and daughter in Northern Indiana, where she is an assistant professor at Indiana University South Bend.

In this interview, Julavits and Zevin talk about how they got started, how they've evolved as writers, and how they structure both their lives and their novels.

Describe a typical week in your life. What sorts of activities and pursuits fill up your time?

Heidi Julavits: As I'm answering this I'm making lentil soup, guilting myself for not doing yoga (for the 675th day in a row), trying to write a magazine piece, trying to think up magazine pitches for a magazine I've never read before, writing apologetic e-mails to writers whose pieces are on submission to me at *The Believer* and that I have yet to read, doing a line edit on a *Believer* piece for the next issue, doing some Web research for my novel, cleaning the dead lily petals off my dining room table, guilting myself for not folding the laundry, thinking how much more time I have this week to not fold laundry now that I don't have any student stories to read (my semester just ended), thinking I should pay some bills, wondering where my check book is, wondering why I don't clean off my desk so that I don't have to work on the dining room table, wondering if I cleaned off my desk if my checkbook would reappear, hoping I can come by a bottle of wine before dinner time.

Gabrielle Zevin: Someone—I forget who—once said that the thing about writing is that it looks the same when you're doing it well as it does when you're doing it badly. I think of this pretty often.

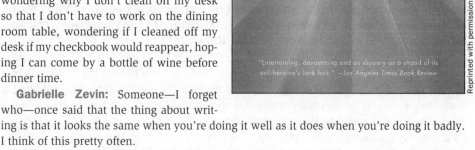

The Uses of Enchantment

Heidi Julavits

a novel

"Entertaining, devastating and as slippery as a strand of its anti-heroine's lank hair." —*Los Angeles Times Book Review*

Reprinted with permission.

I don't have to do anything but write for a living and so, this is what I do. I write and I discard—more of the latter. When a project is nearly done, I tend to stop checking my e-mail or answering my phone, but in general, I think it best to be in the world as much as possible. I've heard other writers talk about how they can't read or go to the movies or listen to music when they're writing, and I think that's a bit ridiculous. I do all those things.

How do other pursuits inform and infringe upon your novel-writing?

Julavits: I think many novel-writers seek out infringements upon their novel writing. See above. The "infringement-seeking" is part of my writing process. If I can concentrate on a single piece of writing (or activity) for longer than 30 minutes, that's some kind of a miracle. Remarkably, under these circumstances, things get done. Books eventually get written.

Zevin: They never infringe. I say no to much more than I say yes to. This might sound implausible, but I never make myself write anything. This, incidentally, is why I never contract to do books before I'm done with them—I only ever want to publish a book because I was done with it, not because the pub date was in November or whatever.

How did you go about getting your first books published?

Julavits: I had an agent. He sold my first book. Apparently the key to this selling was a story I had in *Esquire* magazine. I heard the phrase from someone in publishing, "strike while the iron is hot." Meaning, in my case, sell your book while the *Esquire* issue in which my story appeared was still on the stands. My agent did exactly that, and I was soon able to quit my waitressing job. But mind you I was 30 years old (to the day that I got my book deal), so there was a fair bit of worrying and Plan B thinking that preceded this. I went about getting my first books published by worrying a lot about what would happen if they didn't get published. This was, I think, healthy and not a complete waste of time, because it made me see how writing could and would be a part of my life given various future life configurations, not all of them so cheery.

Zevin: I put no thought into publishing until I was done with my first book and in retrospect, this was a tremendous advantage. I wrote the book I wanted to write and when I was finished, I asked everyone I knew if they knew any agents. I had a manager for screenwriting at the time who worked with another manager, and that other manager had gone to summer camp with a William Morris agent. I showed my manuscript to the erstwhile summer camp pal, and he agreed to represent it. He was the only agent to ever see the manuscript, and it sold to the first publisher who read it, too. All the hard parts came after. But I know I was very lucky.

Gabrielle Zevin

Both of you made a shift between your first and second books: Heidi in terms of structure; Gabrielle in terms audience and a move to the young adult market. What were some of the reasons behind the shift?

Julavits: I'd be suspicious of myself if I hadn't shifted between my first and second books, second and third, ad infinitum. I choose to see this shift as proof of artistic growth or failure to stagnate, though it could as easily be seen as aesthetic dilettantism. This shape-shifting is a way to keep myself intellectually engaged in the process of book writing, by changing the rules from book to book and throwing new obstacles in my own way.

Zevin: Well, actually I wrote (and sold) *Elsewhere* before *Margarettown*, but due to the vagaries of publishing—children's books tend to require a longer pre-publication lead time—*Margarettown* published first. Perhaps naively, I don't spend a great deal of time thinking about "category"—people (publishers, readers, critics) will categorize a writer/book without the writer having to do it herself.

What have you learned about the publishing business that you wish you would have known when you were starting out?

Julavits: I wish I had known how little say you have over how your book will look in its final book form. I was very into books as objects before I published my first book, but because of the opinions of people whose opinions will always trump yours, I've had to surrender that object relationship to a degree. But the fact that writers can still control the content of their books is something to rejoice. When I think of how little control I could have in the process, I'm thankful that my powerlessness stops at the cover.

Zevin: When I started, I was so grateful for any help I was given that I made the mistake of relying on others' judgment more than my own.

Gabrielle's latest book is *Memoirs of a Teenage Amnesiac*; Heidi's books take on the construction and reconstruction of memories. What interests you about the relationship between memory and identity?

Julavits: Without memories you're nobody, not even a new person. We've also pretty much decided, at this point in the culture, that memories are unreliable. Which means that identity is wildly subjective and ultimately unfixable, dependent upon something that we have learned to distrust. This logic influences how I create identities for my fictional people— i.e., in order to achieve what I consider ''verisimilitude'' my characters must appear in flux to themselves and everyone else, including the reader.

Zevin: With *Memoirs*, I wanted to explore the narrative dilemma that the main character posed—how do you tell a story when your memory is faulty? But, of course, this dilemma really applies to every character (and every person), amnesiac or not. On my recent book tour, I met an actual teenage amnesiac who thought the book was nonfiction and was really disappointed to find out it wasn't. But, from my point of view, all of my novels have been memoirs in a sense—not that they have been autobiographies or even autobiographical in detail—but they are me trying to order my experience at a given point in time. If I had a more interesting life, I'd probably write the ''straight'' kind of memoir. This is a roundabout way of saying that I probably write about memory and identity in my novels because the books are really sneaky self-portraits. In a way, I think all novels are.

Gabrielle's *Elsewhere* takes place in the after-life and hints of reincarnation, and *Margarettown* is about the multiple incarnations of one woman; Heidi has said her next novel is about reincarnation. What interests you about reincarnation?

Julavits: Reincarnation is a literal bodily way to shift identities while maintaining some sense of an essential self; what is essence and what is mutable, however, remains the question, and this question is what gets me excited as a writer.

Zevin: There was a nasty review of *Margarettown* that was syndicated into about 50 newspapers in the U.K. It said something like, ''Gabrielle Zevin believes that all women are schizophrenic and crazy.'' And well, no, I don't think anything like that. I think most of us are slightly, even imperceptibly different versions of ourselves—i.e. you are different at work than at home. But I also think we are different selves because life is very long and experience/time changes people and blah blah blah. This is to say, I play with ''multiple selves'' because I see it as a way to convey the truth of a person.

As for reincarnation? I'm not holding my breath for any particular version of the afterlife, including the one described in *Elsewhere*. The reason I wrote about the afterlife was because I wanted to make sense of this one.

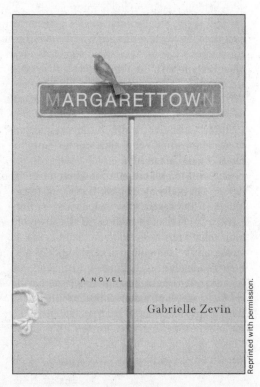

Reprinted with permission.

One of Heidi's three narrative frames in *The Uses of Enchantment* is titled "What Might Have Happened," and Gabrielle's main narrator in *Margarettown* is regularly corrected about all the details he is getting wrong in his letter to his daughter Jane. Both of you seem to experience a productive tension with the limits (and possibilities) of narrative and truth. What, for you, are the challenges and pleasures of narrative?

Julavits: I've extended [the challenge of establishing character] to narrative authority as well. Thus "the narrator" is someone who is equally suspect; a suspect narrator requires that the reader doesn't just absorb information, she becomes an essential part of the identity-making, the story-making, the sense-making.

Zevin: My main narrative challenge as a writer (as opposed to as a reader) is finding the best formal expression for a given story. I get the story from the characters, but I only know how to tell the story by figuring out the form—that probably sounds tautological, but it isn't. Determining the form involves a series of torturous decisions, at least for me. Something as simple as past or present tense can really change the whole nature of the narrative, including the novel's voice. So, knowing how much each of my decisions changes the narrative and changes the truth of the narrative, I rather like showing the novel's "seams" whenever it makes sense to.

Both of you have used single perspectives and multiple points of view. How—and how early in the process—do you decide how you will structure your novels?

Julavits: This is the fun puzzle part of writing a novel. I decide pretty early on what kind of structure I want, then the structure becomes an extra challenge to writing as well as a very helpful way to organize information.

Zevin: Usually, but not always, I extensively structure my novels before I start writing. And then, I'll write a draft in which I may (or may not) discover a bit about the characters/story along the way. Which can sometimes lead to me structuring all over again, and writing an entirely new draft. This is to say, it's pretty much different every time.

What are the advantages and limitations of writing for different audiences and in different genres and categories?

Julavits: To write in different genres becomes an extension of reading in different genres—it keeps me nimble and open-minded, and the limitations of one genre help me appreciate the freedoms of another.

Zevin: I think I've said this already—but the only audience I really write for is me. As a writer, I'm really a complete narcissist. (I'm a bit suspicious of any writer who isn't.) You asked about limitations? Well, the worst thing about publishing books for children is that some folks seem to get the idea that *everything* published for adults is somehow "better" than *anything* published for children. So, for me, the worst part of writing for different audiences/genres/categories can be the limitations that the audiences'/genres'/categories' expectations create.

I enjoy writing screenplays because they have strict rules, and I very much appreciate the rules of a screenplay when I'm stuck on a novel. Working on one gives you a sort of appreciation for the other, and I find that alternating between forms can even open you up creatively.

Pete Hautman

'Exploring the Various Literary Conceits' in YA

by T.E. Lyons

Minnesota novelist Pete Hautman made his mark in both adult and young adult fiction long before it was trendy for best-selling authors to attempt a YA crossover. Currently Hautman has published eight adult novels, most of which the author refers to as "crime novels." ("They are not about solving a mystery . . . I don't know what else to call them," he explains). He also has authored, co-authored, or edited 11 young-adult titles across a startling range in subject matter. Poker figures into several of the YA adventures, along with stories of science fiction, encounters with the horrible—and there is *Godless* (the 2004 National Book Award winner for Young People's Literature) the chronicle of several alienated teens who unite when one develops the concept for a new religion.

Although there may be different approaches for the two markets his books reach, Hautman is clear that he does not feel reined in by having to serve two masters. Instead, he relishes in his good fortune as well as the choices and discipline by which he has developed and maintained his career. He lives with Mary Logue, who collaborates with him on the "Bloodwater" series of teen mysteries. (As Hautman puts it, "I married my writing teacher.") He also participates in a monthly critique/support group in the Twin Cities area, and cites this as an important part of his writing process. "We discuss everything from very technical aspects to various sorts of complaining, which is very easy to do in this business," Hautman says. "And then we're also there to remind ourselves we're all doing what we wanted to do for a long time, and we're actually surviving doing it—and that's the good news."

In the 1990s, you were producing *New York Times* Notable Books with poker slang in the titles. *The Mortal Nuts* came out way before poker got its recent second- (or is it fifth?) legs as a cultural phenomenon.
Nobody knew what Texas Hold'em was in the general population at the time I wrote that book. I've written five poker-themed adult novels—my most recent one, *The Prop*, is about a professional poker player, so there's a lot of poker there. It was in some ways the most difficult book I've written. I took a tremendous amount of care with my action scenes, because I think it's the hardest kind of writing to do well. By "action" I'm not talking about shoot-

T.E. LYONS has published more than a thousand arts reviews, previews and features with newspapers in the Ohio Valley and Midatlantic regions—earning several awards from the Society of Professional Journalists along the way. In the last 15 years he's also sold several dozen pieces of short fiction to print and online publications. Galvanized and/or goaded by his children, nieces, and friends, he has learned to love the whole range of literary events and activities (most recently, speaking at 'cons'). And he's never met a genre he didn't like.

'em-up scenes, but just scenes where there are a lot of things physically happening, and the characters are interacting in ways other than conversation.

And it was difficult for me because I know a lot about poker. I'm not an expert poker player, but I'm a student of the game, and I've been playing for many years, and I play on a regular basis . . . and it's very difficult to write action scenes about something you know a great deal about. Because the tendency is to assume knowledge on the part of other people that they may not have. So it's hard to stand back from a poker game and say, "How do the readers who know nothing about poker perceive it?"

A nonfiction equivalent would be Jon Krakauer, who writes so that people who know nothing about mountain climbing feel they know what's going on. To write those scenes about poker so that someone who has no familiarity with the game can still follow the action and understand its significance and respond emotionally through the characters to what they're going through—it's a tough thing. But it was fun to do, and I think I pulled it off . . . poker players have appreciated the book because the poker's actually accurate.

My teen daughter was shocked at how well you nailed the voice of a Goth-inclined girl (including internal thoughts as well as external dialogue) in *Sweetblood*. How do you keep the voices of your YA character fresh and realistic?

I eavesdrop when I get a chance, but mostly it's memory work. The rhythm of teen talk is pretty much the same as it was 40 years ago. I don't try to duplicate exactly how present-day teens really talk, though. You'll notice very little use of current slang in my books—I don't want my books to feel dated five years from now.

How do you decide when a novel idea is YA or adult?

When I set out to write something, one of the first things I do is decide who is telling the story. If the story demands that my protagonist be a young person, then it follows that the concerns and challenges faced by that character are more likely to be relevant to younger readers.

Have there been any tough calls for you on this?

When I wrote *Mr. Was* [Edgar Award nominee, 1997], I started out with an adult protagonist, but after writing a hundred pages or so I realized that for most of the book (it's a time-travel story) my protagonist would have to be a teenager, so it became a YA novel. But generally I know which audience I'm writing for very early in the process.

Knowing what you're going for, especially with young adult fiction, would seem to be something that your editors want you to share with them.

And what I usually do is I give them a book. The last several books I've written for Simon & Schuster, they had no idea what they were getting. It was just a contract for an untitled novel. With the young adult fiction, I've been exploring the various literary conceits or chestnuts or stereotypes or genres or whatever you want to call them—one after another.

Hole in the Sky is of a subgenre I call the "After the Apocalypse" novel. Almost everyone in the world is dead. Cormac McCarthy's *The Road* fits into that, as does Richard Matheson's *I Am Legend*. For *Sweetblood* I wanted to explore the vampire novel, which has become its own subgenre in the last 30 years. *Godless* is a contemporary allegorical drama. *Invisible,* which I think is my best book technically, is also probably my funniest . . . it would be so horribly bleak if it wasn't funny. That's my take on the first-person unreliable narrator.

It's kinda fun, moving from thing to thing. I've given up on becoming fabulously wealthy in this business. Early on, I saw what a long shot that was, and I knew I didn't have the market and business sense to approach it the way of . . . a James Patterson, for instance. And so I try to write books that interest me and keep me interested in the writing process.

How is it working with editors when you *yet again* tell them, "Now I'm working on something different"?

Early on, all of my books were adult crime novels. The first [*Drawing Dead*] sold relatively quickly. Once I finished it, it took about a year and twenty-some rejections—which, in today's market, is relatively quickly for a first novel.

I was fortunate to have an editor who basically said, "write what you want to." I was *un*fortunate at the same time not to have an editor who said, "write this and we'll pay you huge fabulous sums of money for it." It's a philosophical and business decision taken by a lot of editors. If they perceive that you have some particular writing skills or some quirky something and they think they can sell some copy, they'll just say "Go." If they perceive you as being a workmanlike writer who can produce things on a reliable basis, and they need a certain type of book, they might approach you to do a book of that type. Different editors take different approaches.

In Simon & Schuster's Children's division, *Godless* was my fifth book. My editor and his cohorts were deliriously happy to have it win National Book Award. One of the things that they were congratulating themselves for was the fact that they had just let me do what I wanted and it had paid off for them. As opposed to saying, "Well, why don't you write some kind of cyberpunk or vampire novel, or" . . . directing me to write in a certain area. And it worked out. It doesn't always. It doesn't *usually*. I wrote the right book at the right time to get the attention of an award committee. Having been on a judging committee [National Book Award 2007] and gone through all those books, I realize how lucky I was to have it recognized that way.

Do you outline?

Yeah, but it doesn't matter. I tend to write starting with a scene and a character. Typically after I've been thinking about it for a few months, I'll start writing and I'll get between 30 and a hundred pages into it, and then I'll stop and look at it and then I'll make an outline. Then I'll continue with the writing, and by the time I'm another 20 or 30 pages further in, the outline has become completely irrelevant. Sometimes then I'll stop and make another outline. But the outline isn't something I do to provide a roadmap to myself. It's something I do to let me know where I am.

I've tried doing one of those extensive outlines before starting to write and it was too tedious. I've also tried to write an entire book without doing any outlining, and that actually works pretty well for the shorter books. *Invisible* was small enough that I could hold the whole thing in my head.

For *Mr. Was*, I had the whole wall covered with Post-It® notes. People were going back and forth in time—and it's also a historical novel, so I had to research the 1930s and '40s in

America and in South Pacific islands. That required . . . not *typical* outlining, but notes with little strings and arrows going between them to get the time-travel stuff right. Which is kind of an oxymoron, because time-travel stuff is always wrong—but I needed to make it plausible within the context of the tale.

You don't seem very interested in slam-bang endings for your young-adult work.
No. My adult novels tend to have more closure: you know where you are when they end. That reflects my taste in literature. As an adult, when I read for pleasure, I prefer books that end on a very clear note where justice is done, where I feel good and I can close the book and don't have to think about it anymore.

As a teen, I loved open ends. I loved books that I would sit down and wonder about. I loved books that allowed me to vicariously experience things I might never wish to experience in person—death, loss, horror—and also love and joy. It's one of the things that draws fiction readers to fiction, because it allows them to explore their own emotions through actions that aren't threatening to them physically.

To me, reading as a teen was very much about the journey and about the questions. I loved that little short story "The Lady and the Tiger," and thought that had the coolest ending. I also tend to treat subjects that I don't have answers for. For instance, in *Godless*, it's a book about the power of religion, but mostly it's about adolescents obtaining power and applying it for good and ill. At the end of that book it's very clear, from where Jason's left, how his acts have affected his relationships with his friends, and it's pretty clear what his options are, too. I certainly wasn't going to get to the end of that book and say, "So therefore, religion is bad" or "Therefore, religion is necessary" or anything like that. It was about the characters and their interactions.

Helen Schulman

Approaching Each Piece on Its Own Terms

by Travis Adkins

On the surface, these would seem to be difficult times for writers of literary fiction. In 2007, the National Endowment for the Arts conducted a survey that found that less than half of all Americans had reported reading any kind of literature—novel, poem, short story or play—within the previous year. Considering that the dwindling numbers of people who do still read tend to favor blockbusters over more thoughtful fare, it's an uphill battle for writers who value subtle, intimate glimpses of humanity over action-packed plots.

But there is still an audience for such writers. For proof of that, one need look no further than Helen Schulman.

The author of a short story collection, four novels and numerous screenplays, Schulman has won the admiration of critics and fellow writers, including Jennifer Egan, who calls her "one of the most gifted writers of our generation." Her fiction and nonfiction have appeared in *Vanity Fair*, *Time* and *The Paris Review*, among other publications.

In this genre-obsessed era of publishing, Schulman is a rarity, a successful writer who doesn't fit easily into a category. Her work spans the gamut from *Not a Free Show*, a collection of short stories that dealt with disaffected, drug-addicted youths, to *A Day at the Beach*, a novel that portrays a failing marriage against the backdrop of 9/11. Along the way she has written a comedy about lost loves and mysterious reincarnations (her novel *P.S.*, which was made into a movie), a tragedy about lives cut short (*Out of Time*) and—perhaps most daringly—a tragicomedy about a troubled doctor and his face-off with a Holocaust denier (*The Revisionist*).

While Schulman's subject matter is varied, what unites all of her work is an interest in people struggling with their imperfections, sometimes successfully, sometimes not. Here Schulman talks about her career, what interests her as a writer, and why writing is a long-distance race and not a sprint.

As a writer of literary fiction, as opposed to a writer of commercial or genre fiction, do you think it's harder to pitch your books to publishers, since you don't have an attention-grabbing sales hook? How do you get publishers interested?

I am thankful that I am not in the position of pitching anything. Most of my books have been sold as completed manuscripts—I have only once received a true advance for a partial novel,

---

TRAVIS ADKINS is a freelance writer and a frequent contributor to *Novel & Short Story Writer's Market*. He lives in Brooklyn, New York.

and that was with an editor I'd already worked with. It is my lovely agent's job to find my book an editorial home. He has always worked hard for me and I am totally indebted to him.

I would think that for a literary fiction writer, relationships with other writers are even more important than for commercial writers, given that it's a relatively small community. How important to you are your relationships with other writers?

Many of my friends are writers. And thankfully, many of my friends are not. I say thankfully not because writers make bad friends; they make the best. They are the ones who read your work (sometimes endlessly), make smart suggestions, lend you money, help you find jobs, and talk you off the roof in the wee hours of the morning. Writers need other writers simply because we need the support of people with the same passions, interests, trials and tribulations. But I also cherish my relationships with "civilians." It is nice to break free sometimes from that "relatively small community" and the truth is that the work of the world is often more compelling then a bunch of writers sitting around in sweatpants all day alone at their desks.

Do you think it's important for writers of literary fiction to have a champion, someone who will really go to bat for them, as their agent and their editor? Have you had people like that in your career? What else do you look for in an editor?

As I mentioned, I have been very fortunate to have a wonderful, smart, tough-minded and compassionate agent. He has steadfastly stood by my side during many bumps in the road. I feel graced by his presence. That said, I have had wonderful editors. My dream is always to maintain these relationships—I mate for life in most areas of my life. But illness, death and just plain artistic disagreement has made me a rather peripatetic author, much to my own disappointment. I have had three different editors on five works of fiction, all of them smart, talented people.

How did you break into screenwriting? How has that informed your work as a novelist?

When I was a graduate student at Columbia University I had a good friend—a very good writer named Chris Spain—who was writing screenplays. He asked me to work with him on a project and when we were done we got hired to write a screenplay together. A Writer's Guild strike followed and we got a bit derailed. After that we went our separate ways, but I really learned to write screenplays from Chris, and I'll always be grateful to him for that.

As for the second part of the question, screenwriting has really helped me to develop story. When I was first writing fiction, I was far more interested in language than narrative. Now, it's a toss up.

You've tackled some pretty fraught subjects in your writing—9/11 in *A Day at the Beach*, Holocaust denial in *The Revisionist*. What is it about those difficult subjects—other than their obvious dramatic appeal—that draws you as a writer, and what are some of the challenges of writing about them?

If I've learned anything about myself as a writer it is that I am interested in how the big issues, these world changing events, affect individual people. I am interested in the personal, the domestic and how this provides a specific lens when looking at the eruptions of the greater world. As a Jew, I felt that much of my own emotional make-up was predicated on inherited grief—my family had lost so much in their wild ride to America. As a New Yorker, I lived through 9/11 firsthand. Our lives have changed completely because of 9/11, in ways both subtle and overt. My feeling is that 9/11 has given birth to the worst period in American history, aside from slavery, and the ramifications of this point in time on the future are very frightening. I don't know how not to write about the time I'm in living in. Sometimes this alone causes problems—because the subject matter I'm dealing with changes before my eyes. This is the major problem of the new project I am working on—it is so zeitgeisty that each day that passes that it is *not* yet fully written makes it feel more and more dated.

You went from writing *The Revisionist*, which dealt with some very grim and painful themes, to writing *P.S.*, which was more of a lighthearted romantic story. Was that a deliberate choice? What was it like as a writer to make that transition?

It was absolutely deliberate. As my husband said, "Enough with the Holocaust." It was so hard to live in that place for so long. He threw up his hands when I wanted to go to visit the camps on a long postponed vacation. (I think we ended up in the Caribbean.) *P.S.* was fun and easy to write. My new book is again a departure from the painful process of writing *A Day at the Beach*. This new one was supposed to be the same kind of emotional palate cleanser for me that P.S. was—however, it's not proving to be that easy or fun to write. (Sigh). I'm not clear on whether a true pattern here is emerging or not. I think if I were writing full-time—my dream—it would make artistic sense to take on something big and hard and then follow with something slightly more comedic. But because I work so much as a teacher and an administrator and a freelancer, there may not be the time to indulge in all of this and still write the books I'm hoping to write. Perhaps a little mid-life angst has just crept into this last paragraph!

What gives you the most trouble as a writer? Does it differ from story to story, or do you find that you're generally grappling with the same technical problem with everything you write?

It is always hard for me to find the story. I write very long wind-ups, backstory, charactery kinds of things, this can go on for a 100 pages or more. There's nothing I've ever written, even after it's been published, that doesn't start too slow.

When do you know that it's time to give up on a story?

I give up when it drifts away from me, when the story itself never really starts.

You also teach fiction writing at The New School. As a teacher of writing, what's your philosophy?

I don't really have a philosophy. I like to approach each piece on its own terms. I do think that sometimes writing students need to be opened up to the pleasures of their medium. It amazes me sometimes how uninterested they are in language. I guess I like to awaken them to its complexities.

In *A Day at the Beach*, your character Gerhard Falktopf makes the criticism (referring obliquely to Raymond Carver) that "the author had relied too heavily on the bare bones of narrative, and narrative, inherently representational, was always second best to evocation . . ." Is that a view you share? Explain the difference between narrative and evocation?

As far as I am concerned, Gerhard Falktopf is a real person. He's not of course, I dreamed him up, but from the moment I met him on my own pages he'd simply defined himself. Gerhard is great lover of plotless abstraction, even though he is heavily drawn to the symbols alive in a culture and how they can be messed with (Jasper John's flags for instance, the surfer symbols that enliven Gerhard's own magnum opus "Day at the Beach," the dance he is choreographing to the music of Brian Wilson throughout the course of my novel). Gerhard is a great proponent of "high-low" (high culture and low culture). In this way we are linked, if slightly.

But back to evocation . . . Much of the best choreography of the past century to my mind was more evocative then it was narratively based. Certain movements evoke certain responses and emotions without being tied to specific representational meaning. Giselle, for example, is the story of a poor peasant girl who dies for love. You can follow the steps in her life that lead to her tragic demise. In a Balanchine ballet, like Jewels for example, there is no story to follow. And yet I find myself captivated by the sentences, the chains of movement always evoke enormous response. This is what Gerhard is drawn to. Personally, I am a great big fan of both. And since "A Day at the Beach" is only representational and relies heavily on a tight narrative structure, I am afraid it is not a novel that would much interest the great Gerhard Falktopf.

If you were to write a book called *Lessons for Writers*, what would you put down as the cardinal rule for beginning writers?

Read. Read literature. Read lots of it. Read slowly. What I really mean to say is read as a writer. Ask yourself why the writer made the choices that she has. Try to identify tactics. Look at how the words rub up against each other in a sentence. Think about your own response. Try to isolate the factors that evoked this response. Study your heroes. Emulate them, steal from them, try to get under their skin.

What's the best piece of writing advice you ever received?

John Irving visited Columbia when I was a grad student. I'm paraphrasing wildly, since this happened so long ago!—but what he said basically was that 10 years after teaching a class at the Iowa Workshop the writers that had succeeded in publishing books were not necessarily the ones whose talent had burned the brightest. They were the writers who could sit at their desks the longest. They were the ones who persevered, did not give up. It is hard to predict who these people may be—I know this as a fact now that I have been teaching so long myself. But a writer's life is hard. There is so much rejection, so little reward at times, it sometimes feels like the smart thing to do would be to give up. Perhaps it *is* the smart thing to do! Especially when thinking about the quality of one's life. But you never write books by giving up. You write them by going the distance, again and again. You really need to be a long-distance runner.

Patrick McGrath

'A Stern Mistress, the Novel'

by T.E. Lyons

The stories of Patrick McGrath have earned wide admiration for their precise observation, dark panache and a daring approach to narrative point of view. This author's prose carefully limns the shadowy corners of his character's lives—and especially their minds. Through seven novels and more than a dozen shorter works, McGrath has consistently demonstrated a willingness to make considerable demands of the reader.

McGrath's interest in the recesses and pathologies of the mind seems to have the most natural of histories—it is an inheritance, of sorts. When he was five years old, his father became medical superintendent of Broadmoor Hospital, a top-security mental institution in the south of England. The younger McGrath did not directly pursue the professional training of medicine and the mind—although work in a Canadian mental hospital was one of a variety of vocations and locations that led him to New York's Greenwich Village in the 1980s. But even his earliest published works show a keen interest in, and a quickly developing mastery of, themes that are important in his work to this day: psychology and psychiatry, family and class conflict, and the nature of artistic pursuits and erotic obsessions. Before his first novel was published, McGrath was already drawing attention for accomplishments in some of the more unusual facets of modern fiction. He experimented with unexpected point of view (in one story, the narrative is conveyed by a boot). He demonstrated a capacity to quickly saturate the reader in detailed setting and rich atmosphere. And he nimbly manipulated elements of the gothic storytelling tradition (e.g., disfigurement and apparitions) while maintaining the highest literary standards.

Blood and Water and Other Tales was his first book, hitting shelves in 1989. It was soon joined by *The Grotesque*, McGrath's first novel, which was also the first of his works to be adapted for film. Despite the acting contributions of Sting, Sir Alan Bates, and the author's wife Maria Aitken, the final product was one of which the author says, "I'm not surprised it's hard to find."

Spider, the author's second novel, arrived in 1990. As with its predecessor, *Spider*'s tale comes to the reader through the words of an unreliable narrator. Throughout his career, McGrath has continued to make thorough use of shaky points of view to offer perceptive

T.E. LYONS has published more than a thousand arts reviews, previews and features with newspapers in the Ohio Valley and Midatlantic regions—earning several awards from the Society of Professional Journalists along the way. In the last 15 years he's also sold several dozen pieces of short fiction to print and online publications. Galvanized and/or goaded by his children, nieces, and friends, he has learned to love the whole range of literary events and activities (most recently, speaking at 'cons'). And he's never met a genre he didn't like.

readers more than might be seen through clear and objective accounts. He has even gone so far as to present stories through multiple unreliable characters—as in *Port Mungo*, wherein a painter's feverish experiences from the remote Caribbean are presented on the page as from a self-deluded family member.

Asylum (1997) was a major success for McGrath. This tale of an affair between an institutionalized artist and an asylum director's wife was nominated for the Bram Stoker Award and became a motion picture starring Sir Ian McKellen (who also recorded the audiobook version of the novel). *Spider* was also adapted for the screen, with McGrath writing the screenplay himself and direction by David Cronenberg (*The Fly, A History of Violence*).

Reprinted with permission.

Among the author's other books are *Martha Peake: A Novel of the Revolution* (a *New York Times* Notable Book of 2000) and the collection of novellas *Ghost Town: Tales of Manhattan Now and Then*. His most recent novel is *Trauma*—a very direct merging of McGrath's interests in psychology and storytelling, narrated by a psychiatrist who has experienced tragedy at intersections of his personal and professional life.

Here, Patrick McGrath speaks about his experiences working in novels versus short story and film; how he employs unreliable narrators; benefits a writer can gain from a nurturing neighborhood environment and an understanding of psychology; and the consequence-laden role of labels in marketing novels.

The course of your career started with many short stories—but by the early '90s it seems that you were leaving that type of writing behind. What was the transition like? Do you recommend working on short stories to those who aspire to novel-writing?

Short stories are a very good way to acquire the basic skills such as characterization, dialogue, description of landscape, interiors, weather, architecture, etc., and plotting. I'd encourage any starting writer to work on stories. They're much easier to get published too, so you get that all-important early confirmation of your viability as a writer.

For me now a good idea suggests to me not that I write a story but that I discover the novelistic possibilities. Any idea really worth its salt will usually stand being explored at novel length, and this, for me at least, is the most satisfactory way of working—the long haul, the deep immersion, the growing obsessive focus on a single set of themes and characters.

Three of your works have been adapted for film. Have you learned anything from watching the process of adaptation to screen, and seeing audience reaction to your story in another medium, that you have brought back into your novel-writing?

I think the answer is no. The two activities—writing and adapting—and seeing the story onscreen—are for me sealed off in separate compartments. The reason for this is that writing a novel demands all one's attention and leaves no room for thoughts about reader reaction, filmic possibilities, etc. Nor do viewers' reactions to a film adaptation impinge on the composition of the next book. The logic, the rhythms, the tone, the precise unfolding of the narrative, these preoccupy me during the writing to the exclusion of all else. A stern mistress, the novel. Only masochists woo her.

You've written multiple times about the relationship between artists and sanity. Why have you found this to be worth revisiting?

I'm intrigued by artists first because their relationship to the world is such fertile territory for the novelist, in the sense that artists both interpret the world and express an emotional response to it; and second, because artists commonly assume skeptical or even subversive positions in relation to society. What this means, at least for a writer like me, is the opportunity to create characters who are flamboyant, violent, creative, disordered, rebellious or promiscuous, or some combination of all these traits. Artists also carry the heavy burden of being so closely identified with their work that failure or neglect can have deeply destructive consequences. So they're rich in dramatic potential for the sort of psychological narratives I tend to write.

How do you develop a story with an unreliable narrator? Do you trace the plot (i.e., with notes or on a database of some sort) both objectively *and* in the narrator's view?

Generally I begin with a rough idea of a story, or part of a story, and soon decide which of the characters will narrate it. As the writing goes forward I'm very alert to the relationship of this narrator to the story being told. Opportunities will occur for the narrator to present a given event or character in a way that reveals more about himself or herself than what's actually being described. Often the narrator will be unaware of what he's revealing, but the reader will not; and this is where the unreliability is first identified, and where the secondary or meta-story properly begins, that being the story of the flawed and uneasy relationship of teller to tale.

Your major projects have come out in a more-or-less even pace over the last 15 years. Is that coincidental or intentional? Do you ever have more than one novel in development at the same time?

The even pace of production just reflects the fact that I rarely pause between books. Even if I have no good idea for a new book, I get to work on a bad idea on the assumption that somewhere down the line a good idea will occur to me. But it won't occur unless I'm actually writing. With this approach, even given the many distractions life creates to slow the writer down, a book can be finished every two to three years.

What is your day-to-day writing process? Do you have a routine established once you have a firm idea for a novel? Same time of day? A particular place?

Pretty much. It'll vary depending on what stage of a book I'm at. When I'm writing first draft, I get to the desk pretty much first thing in the morning, and I set a target of a thousand words. And then there'll be the research that comes with the writing of the novel. I'll be reading whatever I need to be well-informed on aspects of the world that I'm imagining.

I've got an office in the apartment. That's where I go, that's my room. And I can close the door and I'm completely insulated from the world in there.

Do you keep it absolutely quiet?

I don't have music. I need silence . . . but I do answer the phone. I'm not completely "a monk in his cell."

Do you read and keep up with clinical psychology?

I wouldn't say in any seriously methodical way, but I keep my eyes and ears open. I basically will be drawn to a story in the *New York Times* rather than by leafing through the *Journal of American Psychiatry*. Once I do become interested in some psychiatric disorder, then I'll start looking for specialized literature . . . but I don't operate like a medical student.

Do you see that as a field of study that might help out an aspiring writer to understand character development?

From my point of view, I think it would be tremendously valuable. I have always found it fascinating to think about the psychological disorders that human beings can suffer from, and how that affects their relationships, the way they behave in the world, the way their minds work, the way they think, the way they feel. I've been enormously stimulated as a writer by reading Freud and by thinking about the psychiatric aspect of human nature.

You've attributed some of your development as a writer to the atmosphere and lifestyle of the East Village in the 1980s. Nowadays, there are online communities and more writers that seem to come from workshops. Your experience—an immersion in a great environment like that—is it now as important as it used to be? And do you think those places are now harder to find?

I'm not in touch so much with what sort of scene that younger writers have in New York. I would imagine it's more likely to be in Brooklyn these days than in Manhattan, because nobody can afford to live in Manhattan anymore—not, at least if you're a young struggling writer. But, what I found very valuable was . . . in the '80s in the East Village, there were places you could publish your work—a lot of small magazines that were very open to the work of people in the neighborhood. There were places you could *read* your work—cafes and bars that had open mics. There was a sense of a community of young writers—which brought not only mutual support, but it also brought a sense of competitiveness that I thought was very healthy.

We were all eager to be the first one to get a book contract. It's that sort of competitiveness that spurs you to work hard. I think there's nothing wrong with ambition and certainly to be in a big city, amongst a community of writers, is going to sharpen your ambitious instincts. It's going to make you work harder and be more productive, and this is all for the good.

Your work has been shelved ''mystery/suspense,'' probably even more frequently with ''horror,'' as well as with general literature. Are you disappointed with how stores/retailers/reviewers perceive your novels? Are you particularly disappointed with how your books have been categorized? Do you find it discouraging?

I don't like it, and the reason I don't like it is that once you do get these labels you lose readers. Or, rather, that people don't bother to read you because they've already made up their mind as a result of the way you've been labeled. Somebody will say, ''Oh, he's a Gothic writer. I don't read Gothic.''

It's an imprecise designation. There are Gothic elements in my work, but I'm not exclusively and comprehensively a Gothic whittler. I would much prefer to be just on the open shelves of fiction and literature, where people will not have preconceptions of the work conditioned by the labeling of bookstores and publishers.

If labels mean that people take for granted what is contained within the pages, does that mean that such categorization is less a problem for those who've not established themselves?

I would have thought that it was equally a problem for those who haven't established themselves. If you've written one or two books and someone has decided you're a crime writer or a Gothic writer or what have you—and that label sticks to you—you have a really tough job shaking that off. You'll find that reviewers will tend to accept this label.

It's a way of pigeonholing a writer, and it's often imprecise and unfair. It's probably *more* of a problem for a writer starting out, because it takes a lot of energy and time to shake off these facile classifications.

Premier Voices

Four Debut Novelists

Every author has a different story of how he or she got that first book contract. Some work on their first manuscript and it gets published rather quickly. Some write for years and years. Some have agents, some do not. Some first-time novelists have other writing credits under their belts, like newspaper columns or short stories. Some have had editorial positions or have taught fiction at the college level. Some take classes themselves. Some earns MFAs. Some earn fellowships. Some have mentors. Some win contests.

Each of these descriptions applies to one or more of the four debut novelists featured here. And though they all took different paths to publication, they all have one thing in common—their passion for fiction. "Process is its own reward, *Writing* is its own reward." says author Fiona Maazel. "Obviously it's great to get published, but it's best to think about that part as little as possible when you're doing the work."

Writing a novel *does* take work—and time and dedication. "It's a long haul, and as Hemingway once said, when it hits, you have to have the legs to run with it," says author Gary Wilson. But it's not just the writing and revising that takes work. There is also learning and submitting and persevering through the process of getting published. Read on to learn how the authors featured here worked on their craft, found the right home for their manuscripts, and made it onto bookstore shelves.

Camille DeAngelis
Mary Modern (Shaye Areheart Books)

Camille DeAngelis was walking by a bookstore in Atlanta when she noticed they had a very nice window display—of her book. "I had to take a picture of that. It's still surreal."

DeAngelis' whole publishing experience has been a bit surreal. She's never published a short story, and her novel *Mary Modern* was accepted for publication within a month of her agent sending out the manuscript. "The funny thing is that the main way the final version of the book is different is that there are more scenes in it; it's actually longer than the  first manuscript I submitted because they wanted me to flesh out the early scenes with Lucy and Gray, which definitely needed to be fleshed out."

Mary Modern is about biologist Lucy, who ends up cloning her grandmother, Mary. The problem is, Mary is in her early twenties, has memories from her earlier life, and doesn't understand what happened to her husband and how Lucy can be her granddaughter. Lucy and her boyfriend Gary try to deal with their relationship and help the displaced Mary.

While the book could be classified as science fiction, it's not primarily about the cloning. "It's using clones to explore the dynamics of this family, and this sort of weird identity crisis." DeAngelis needed something to enable a situation where grandmother and granddaughter were near the same age and fighting over the same guy, and cloning was just the thing to do that.

DeAngelis has always been writing. She began work on her first novel during college, at which point she was writing an opinion column in her college newspaper. She got an agent for it, but the novel didn't sell and her agent dropped her. DeAngelis found her current agent, "whom I'll hopefully have forever, or until she retires I guess," by checking for new agents at an agency her boss at HarperCollins wanted to work with. Kate Garrick took her on, and as Garrick is in her early thirties, DeAngelis hopes the two of them will be able to have their careers grow together. Garrick couldn't sell that first novel either.

While DeAngelis was disappointed at the time, now she's happy with how things went. "There are certain passages that I was so proud of at the time, and now I'm just like, wow, I'm really glad that book didn't sell. But it's funny because at the time you're really upset over it and your stomach is all in knots waiting to hear something, and then it doesn't turn out to be anything good, and then you're very frustrated . . . and I just decided I was going to work on another one."

Some time later, DeAngelis' aunt sent her a wedding portrait of her great-grandparents. DeAngelis fixated on her great-grandmother's face, "thinking about all of the really sad things that were going to happen to her in the future, after she walked out of that portrait studio. So I started ruminating on that and thinking—what would we say to one another if there was some sort of temporal blip and we could converse with one another. What would we have to say to one another? Over the course of a weekend the whole thing just sort of sprung up and I knew there was going to be a double love triangle and I knew all of the characters." She knew Mary's name from the beginning. "I had the name 'Mary Modern' in my head, and once I had the idea of having this conversation with my great-grandmother, and those two things kind of stuck together and I was like—Oh, 'Mary Modern.' "

The timing couldn't have worked out better as DeAngelis left her editorial position at HarperCollins a few months later to get her MFA in Galway, Scotland. Working

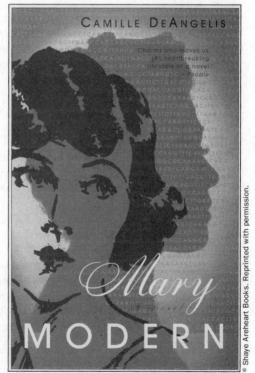

CAMILLE DeANGELIS

Charms and moves us. . . . [A] heartbreaking fairytale of a novel.
—*People*

Mary MODERN

© Shaye Areheart Books. Reprinted with permission.

on her MFA gave her the time to write, and going to Galway exposed her to authors at the right time to give her needed influence. Contemporary Irish novelist Kate O'Brian got DeAngelis thinking about "living in an ancestral home and having this really intense claustrophobia under the weight of all these family expectations and your family history." Gothic writer Joseph Sherridden Le Fanu's creepy stories influenced the tone of the book, and the name of the restaurant in *Mary Modern* is a reference to one of his short stories.

Mike McCormack served as her mentor at Galway. "He would sort of drop these pearls, not even realizing he was doing it." He recommended different writers to read, and told her

"Whatever you choose to write about, it has to be different, it has to grab the reader; you have to give them the feeling like they're reading something that they haven't read anything like before." Though said in an offhanded way, DeAngelis recognized how important this advice was and decided to take it to heart.

DeAngelis certainly succeeded in crafting something unique. She finished *Mary Modern* as the center piece of her MFA portfolio then sent the first 80 pages to her agent. Garrick's response was "Wow, this is weird, but it could be really awesome." After several months of working with Garrick on revisions, the manuscript was sent out and DeAngelis soon had an offer for her book.

Mary Modern would be a completely different book without her time in Scotland, says DeAngelis. "There are these things that you're exposed to by serendipity that just turn out to be exactly what you need at that time. So basically that whole year, that whole experience—outside and inside the classroom—really enabled me to write that book and it's a much better book for my having had that experience."

—Rachel McDonald

Fiona Maazel
Last Last Chance (Farrar, Straus & Giroux)

During her stint as Managing Editor at renowned journal *The Paris Review*, Fiona Maazel had more than just a chance to learn about the art of editing from one of the true literary legends, George Plimpton. She also had a crash-course in the business of the publishing world.

"There are a lot of great writers out there competing for a few venues that are themselves competing for an even smaller readership," says Maazel. "So I guess being at *The Paris Review* just taught me not to focus on that stuff, but to keep the pleasure of it all up front. Process is its own reward. *Writing* is its own reward. Obviously it's great to get published, but it's best to think about that part as little as possible when you're doing the work."

That insight paid off as Maazel wrote and sold *Last Last Chance*, the story of Lucy Clark, whose problems include a father suspected of unleashing a biological epidemic, a mother addicted to crack and a sister obsessed with Christian fundamentalism. "*Last Last Chance* started out as a short story," she says. "I gave it to my mother to read, and she thought it could work as the start of a book. I was pretty dejected at the time and not so keen on listening to my mother, but then this tends to be when mothers are most annoying, just for being right. So I started to look into it. And off I went. The story had an arc to it, so the goal was to fit an entire novel between where it finished and where it began. The book ended elsewhere, but that was the idea. It took about two years to get it done."

The novel was the second that she wrote. Maazel says that although she was "miserable" when her first novel didn't find a publisher—and she even questioned her commitment to writing a second—ultimately, sheer love of writing sustained her. "In the end, the question was moot because before I knew it, I was writing another book, wrestling with its challenges and enjoying the process all over again," she says. "There's no greater joy for me than sitting down to write, despite how hard it is. So what else was I going to do? First novel went in a drawer and I moved on. And I've been very lucky ever since."

Maazel says she was also fortunate to work with her editor at Farrar, Straus & Giroux, Paul Elie. "Paul is a terrific editor *and* writer," she says. "His book, *The Life You Save May Be Your Own*, is fierce in its intelligence and poise. My editorial experience with him might be every writer's dream. There was no over-hauling or massive revising, but we talked at length about subtleties so that the effect of our work together was cumulative. Pacing, tone, raising the temperature on X, lowering it on Y, and so on. He'd challenge me to do something and I'd have to step up. Some days we'd just talk about opening lines of stories we liked and why we liked them. It was all sort of nerdy—I love that—and also the collaborative process I needed. I came to trust his aesthetic and judgment and he seemed to trust mine, so the work went very well, and I know the book got better for having passed through his hands.''

Maazel, the recipient of the 2005 Lannan Fellowship for Fiction, also considers herself lucky to count among her mentors the critically acclaimed short-story writers Jim Shepard and Amy Hempel.

''I took my first fiction writing class with Jim Shepard in 1996 at Williams College, and it probably changed my life,'' she says. ''It was my first look at just how riveting talking about fiction could be. Fun, too. We all laughed a lot, and I started to write in earnest. Then I went to get my MFA, where I worked with Amy Hempel, among others, and this, too, was amazing. Amy was one of my heroes and a big reason I chose Bennington. She was encouraging and enthusiastic about my work, which speaks more to her generosity of spirit than the work itself. This is a difficult business, which is why I am so grateful to have friends with experience who can tell me what to do. I hope to be in a position one day to do the same for someone else.''

—*Travis Adkins*

Fiona Maazel

Last Last Chance

a novel

© Farrar, Straus & Giroux. Reprinted with permission.

Marcia Laycock
One Smooth Stone (Castle Quay Books)

Marcia Laycock heard about the Best New Canadian Author award and decided to submit her first novel, mostly just to get some input from industry professionals. She was surprised, and understandably excited, when she got the phone call saying her book had won. The prize? Publication of her manuscript.

After writing for 20 years, Laycock's persistence finally paid off. ''The key is to keep at it; just keep writing, keep submitting, keep learning. I think you never really arrive; there's always something to learn. I think perseverance is really one of the main features that a writer has to have if you want to get published in any genre, any kind of writing, you have to persevere. You have to keep at it, keep networking, keep meeting editors and publishers, meeting other writers, going to conferences as much as you can. Just keep doing it, and eventually that will bring success.''

Writing was something Laycock was used to, but writing a novel was a bit different. She has been writing an inspirational newspaper column in Alberta for years, and has self-published a few devotional books.

Laycock discovered the Alberta Christian Writers organization, joined them, and started

taking seminars and learning from the other members of the group. "I took any writing course I could find. There were other programs in the community and in the cities nearby that I could go up and take from time to time, so anything that I could I just devoured it and started to learn as much as I could."

A passing comment inspired the story for *One Smooth Stone*, and she soon starting filling it out. *One Smooth Stone* is a Christian suspense novel about a young man named Alex who struggles to come to grips with his unpleasant foster care upbringing and the revelation that his birth mother tried to abort him. Miscommunications and fear abound as Alex struggles to come to grips with his life.

All the experience with devotionals and speaking helped with crafting the novel. They're short pieces, so "you have to learn how to write tight, and I think that's a really good skill for any writer, no matter what you're writing." Writing the novel was very different from writing the devotionals. "You're creating your own world. You're creating characters, and even though you're building them out of your own experience—building them out of people you've known over the years—it's very different doing that than a piece of nonfiction which of course deals more truth and with things that actually happened."

The publishing process for *One Smooth Stone* was a bit different from what Laycock was used to. "With the self-publishing it was totally hands on. I made all the decisions basically. Whereas with *One Smooth Stone*, once it's handed over to the publisher it's out of your hands. They kind of do what they want with the book."

While Laycock is happy to have published her book and is working on the sequel, she tries to focus on something other than the next big contract. "I think that some people look at big publication contracts as the end-all and be-all of writing. But look at me—I've been writing for more than 20 years. When I look back over the body of work that I have had out there in one way or another, whether its been a paid contract or an article that's been in a magazine, or just something that I gave to friend, all of those things are valuable."

—*Rachel McDonald*

Gary Wilson
Sing, Ronnie Blue (Rager Media)

When he first finished his novel *Sing, Ronnie Blue*, Gary Wilson had an agent. "She was a wonderful and talented person, who strongly supported my writing," he says. "She was quite excited by the novel and the prospects for placing it. She tried for some time, and although she got many 'near misses,' there were no solid offers."

Wilson's agent eventually returned the novel to him, "with real regret," and suggested he could try to submit it on

his own. "I put the book away for a while, until one day I came across an ad, I think it was, for a new press called Rager Media, Inc. I checked out their Web site and liked the book list I saw and read samples of the writing they were publishing and wrote to them, asking if they were in the market for some good fiction."

Rager Media's editor-in-chief Chris White replied to Wilson right away and requested his manuscript, offering him a contract for *Sing, Ronnie Blue* two weeks later. "Chris called me to say that they definitely wanted to bring out my novel," says Wilson. "They were excited, too, by the prospects. Needless to say, so was I. It's been a marvelous fit. Though small, Rager gets around. My novel sold out its first press run the first month and has now twice appeared on the Small Press Distribution Best Selling Fiction list."

Before his debut novel hit bookstore shelves, Wilson had published dozens of short stories in journals like *Glimmer Train*, *The William and Mary Review*, and *Kansas Quarterly*, among others. He's also taught fiction writing at John Hopkins University and the University of Chicago. But all along, he's aspired to be a novelist. "I wrote two or three prior to *Sing, Ronnie Blue* that I still have in my file waiting their time to appear," he says. Wilson feels that novel and short story writing both employ the same basic techniques— character, conflict, narrative structure, voice, dialogue, setting, etc. "But they are also different, primarily, I think, in terms of focus. Someone once described novel writing as going into a house and examining all the rooms, the closets, the drawers, every nook and cranny, every hidden passage, while writing a story is settling on one room only and what happens there. Figuratively speaking, of course. The attention to language and voice, however, should be the same no matter what form of fiction one is writing. Strong language use, precise language use, is vital."

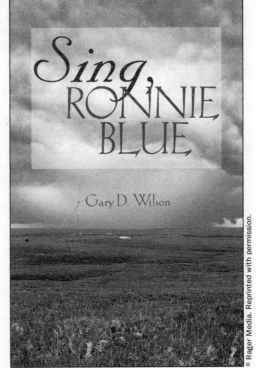

© Rager Media. Reprinted with permission.

In *Sing, Ronnie Blue*, Wilson chose to delve into the nooks and crannies of a small Kansas town, much like the one where he grew up. "I find small towns fascinating as microcosms of larger society," he says. "They have the same economic, social and cultural forces as any city but are, in some ways, easier to get your mind around."

Putting his characters in a place like Bartlett's Junction, he says, "given their histories there and with each other, a story seems naturally to evolve from that. It's interesting to me as well that Ronnie Blue and John Klein can be fast friends as teenagers but find that such a relationship is nearly impossible as adults. Something fundamental changes when the expectations of adulthood enter the picture. Maybe it's that the old rules suddenly appear as stronger, more indomitable forces."

Wilson's characters Ronnie Blue, son of the local junkyard owner, and John Klein, son of the president of the town's only bank, have drifted apart since being friends in high school. "Five years later, on the Fourth of July and his birthday, Ronnie Blue, who has become an itinerant grease monkey, crosses paths with his old friend, John Klein, who during that same five years has gone off to college and has come back to Bartlett's Junction, presumably to take over one day as president of the bank, just as his father did from his grandfather. So here we have two men at opposite ends of the American Dream coming together on Independence Day for a reunion that has tragic consequences for them both.''

It took Wilson three years to finish *Sing, Ronnie Blue* and another year or so ''tinkering with it'' prior to publication. ''I'm a slow writer, averaging maybe a page or two a day of finished copy. But over time, that adds up,'' he says. ''When I'm writing a novel, I try to pace myself and write four or five hours in the morning, have lunch and run errands, come back and maybe write a bit more, but usually tend to other things, like preparing for classes when I'm teaching and so on. It's important, I think, to maintain momentum, to write every day and stay in shape for that. It's a long haul, and as Hemingway once said, when it hits, you have to have the legs to run with it. For me, writing a novel isn't a sprint but a long-distance run, where when you fall into the right rhythm, you feel like you can go on forever.''

Wilson feels that ''if you are good enough and persistent enough, you probably will get published.'' He advises writers to be patient, learn, and keep sending manuscripts out. ''But don't do it just on a lark. Be serious and professional.''

For novice writers, ''and some professionals, too,'' he says, the most common obstacle to overcome is telling rather than showing in their writing. ''Many writers,'' says Wilson, ''have a tendency to explain to the reader what is happening in the story, rather than trusting that the reader will 'get it' on their own. Learn to trust your reader's intelligence and the power of your own language to evoke ideas and emotions. All writers—beginning and mature—need to read and read and read. Good work. The masters, old and new. It's from reading that we learn to write, I believe. Teachers can show technique and some skills, but no one can teach sensitivity to language and the talent to put that to use.''

—Alice Pope

CRAFT & TECHNIQUE

Making the Most of Online Fiction Writing Courses

by Laura Yeager

The fellow student in your fiction writing class who gives the best feedback happens to live in Greece. You live in Ames, Iowa. How is this possible?

You're in an online fiction writing class, working with people from all over the world.

In the last few years, the online fiction writing experience has become very popular. Three of the largest online fiction writing schools are Gotham Writers' Workshop (www.writingclas ses.com), Mediabistro (mediabistro.com/courses) and Writers Online Workshops (presented by Writer's Digest Books, www.writersonlineworkshops.com). All of these schools offer some form of fiction writing—short fiction, novel writing and/or both. At the schools listed above, fiction courses run, on average, about 10 weeks. Some of the topics discussed in these courses are plot, setting, character, point of view, theme, voice and dialogue. Most schools also touch on marketing your fiction. They all have the same goal: to help you become a better fiction writer.

Online fiction classes can do many things: give you deadlines, immerse you in a world where stories and novels matter, introduce you to others who love to write fiction, verify your hunches, help to eliminate bad habits, but the most important thing they give is an audience. In a fiction class, you're not writing in a vacuum. This audience factor is bound to make you a better writer.

Taking online fiction writing classes offers other advantages as well. One is convenience. You can study with a proven, published, perhaps, even *famous* writing teacher without having to travel to his or her place of employment. In fact, you don't even have to leave the comfort of your home. The computer and the Internet bring the teacher and the class members right to you.

Unlike "real world" fiction writing workshops, online classes are not intimidating. No facing your critics live, in the flesh. Online you have a kind of safety in that you never actually see the people in your class. You're working in the privacy of your study or a quiet café. The criticism is more indirect, consequently, and it's easier to take. And if someone makes you cry because he criticized your prized ending, no one ever has to know.

Another advantage to online classes is the cost. Most online fiction courses are reasonably priced (averaging about $400)—especially compared to in-person classes. You can also factor

LAURA YEAGER is a graduate of Oberlin College, Iowa State University and The University of Iowa. Her fiction has appeared in *The Paris Review, The Missouri Review, The North American Review, Ohio Short Fiction, Kaleidoscope* and bimagazine.org. She teaches Online Fiction Writing at Gotham Writers' Workshop, and Effective Speaking at Stark State College. She's currently looking for a publisher for three completed pre-teen novels.

in that you don't have to pay for gas to drive to the class or pay to park, you don't have to buy a brand new clothes to impress your classmates, you don't have to pay admission fees or take admission tests, and, in many instances, you don't need to buy a textbook. You simply pay for the class.

Online classes are also convenient and much easier to fit into your schedule than regular classes. If you have a day job, it may be difficult for you to physically go to school at night or on the weekends. The online fiction writing class lets you go to work, and take a class at your leisure. You do the work when you can fit it in.

Making the most of your class time

The first step is choosing a course. Be sure to pick one in your appropriate skill and experience level. If you're a beginner, don't register for an advanced class—be realistic and take the beginner level courses. Also try to pick a teacher who appeals to you. Read teacher bios online (if posted) at the school's Web site. Look at a teacher's publications. Perhaps, he's been published at one of your favorite magazines. Maybe she studied at a school you know and respect. Often, if you find a connection with the teacher, you'll have a more positive class experience.

You may want to ask the teacher for a recommended book list. All teachers have lists of favorite books, novels and short story collections that resonate for them in some way. Send your teacher an e-mail and ask for his personal book list. With this list, you can get a real feel for what the teacher likes and values in literature. This knowledge may help you understand his comments on your work.

Before you log in to your first online class session, be sure you have the necessary tools on hand. Of course, you're going to need a computer, an Internet connection and a word processing program. Check with the school you wish to attend to see what they require.

Also buy a good dictionary, thesaurus and a grammar handbook if you don't already have them. Most word processing programs have spell checkers as well as grammar checkers, but it's helpful to also have these tools in print form. In an online class, all the students and teacher see is your writing. You want to make a positive impact with your prose, so students and teacher respect your work and, yes, like you. I've found my writing becomes as clean as it can be with both "old fashioned" and "new fangled" spelling and grammar-checking resources.

One of the best things about studying online is that you don't have to do as much work as you do in the traditional classroom. You don't have to transport yourself to the class. Often, you don't have to read textbooks. Generally there are no tests and no question and answer sessions. Usually, all a writing student has to do is post her stories or novel excerpts on the writing school Web site and critique the other students' work. And these stories don't necessarily have to be generated during the duration of the course. So, writing courses can appear to be very easy. But don't be misguided into believing these courses are, indeed, a "piece of cake." You've enrolled in the course—be sure to do everything that's asked of you. If the teacher wants you to critique fellow students' work, do it. If the teacher asks you to produce two stories or three stories, do it. It's for your own good and the good of the class. Don't make the mistake of slacking off because you can "get away with it." That's a waste of money and a waste of an opportunity to improve your craft.

When you do post stories for an online class, which work should you present? One school of thought says put your best work forward. Show the world what you've got. Present a story that you feel is finished and is hot! Another school of thought says, put up the story that needs the most work, so that you can get feedback and advice for improving it. It all depends on how you want to use the class—as a "showcase" for your work or as more of a learning tool. For most of us, we're at the learning tool stage.

During your class time, don't be shy about asking the teacher to read rewrites of your stories. Often online fiction teachers will work with individual students on reworking this writing in subsequent drafts. In other words, the teacher might do more work for you if you ask him. Teachers get excited when a student is motivated to do more than is required. Ask the teacher many questions, and, if he is agreeable, show him more than one or two drafts of a story.

Giving & taking criticism

One of the hardest parts of taking any kind of writing "workshop" in which the students and teacher critique your work is knowing what feedback to take in and what to reject. You'll get better at this as you go along. You need to develop a critical eye. Is the student right when he says you need more character description? Is he right when he says your setting details aren't believable? Is the teacher right? For the beginner, I'd say it's safe to take most of the teacher's advice. That's what "beginner" means; you don't know much on your own. A more advanced student may have developed the critical skills to reject or accept what teacher comments he believes or doesn't believe in.

When critiquing fellow students' work, don't be catty. Be constructive. Always try to give positive feedback as well as negative. This courtesy should extend to the teacher as well. If you have a problem with the instructor or with the course, let the instructor know and give him the opportunity to rectify the situation. If a suitable solution is not found, *then* discuss the matter with his supervisor.

Online courses are good places to make fiction writing buddies. You may even make a lifelong friend. Pick the most astute students whose advice you agree with, whose vision you share. Send them an e-mail, and ask if they'd like to correspond with you and read your stories and offer to do the same for them.

Fiction writing is a difficult skill that takes years to master. Know that you're getting your feet wet with these courses, but that taking an online fiction writing course does not guarantee the creation of masterpieces and/or publication. This could take years. Enrolling in an online course is a step in the right direction.

Craft & Technique

Trimming the Deadweight in Your Manuscript

by I.J. Schecter

The hardest part of becoming a writer isn't learning how to write; it's learning how to un-write. No one wants to destroy, or even change, something they've created (with the possible exception of the *Gigli* production team), and even if we do summon the strength required for such wrenching acts, how can we be sure they're justified? Let's talk about five methods for determining whether acts of literary alteration are well founded.

Eliminate the pests

There are small bugs infecting your manuscript. They can be hard to get under control because they come in numerous forms and tend to spread themselves around, occupying every available nook and cranny. These bugs are called adjectives, and their subspecies, adverbs. Everyone from Strunk and White to Elmore Leonard has endorsed the importance of attacking these nuisances without prejudice, yet still they always seem to find their way into first drafts in abundance. Read the following sentence:

> "I can't live without you, Chloe," he said forcefully, gripping her slim shoulders with his broad hands.
> "Isn't that sweet?" she said coldly, sarcastically, brushing his large hands away, blithely pulling a compact from her purse and flipping it open with breezy, haughty contempt. "Now run along, won't you?"

Now compare it with this:

> "I can't live without you, Chloe," he said, gripping her shoulders.
> "Isn't that sweet?" she said, brushing his hands aside and flipping open her compact. "Now run along, won't you?"

Which packs more punch? Right—the second version.

There are two reasons adverbs and adjectives steal thunder from your manuscript. The first is a simple matter of swiftness. Excess words bog down sentences, making them sluggish. Crisp sentences, on the other hand, move nimbly, creating in the reader a feeling of lightness and ease.

I.J. SCHECTER's work has been nominated for Edgar Awards, won Story of the Year in *Eureka Literary Magazine* and appeared in *Alfred Hitchcock's Mystery Magazine*. His bestselling collection of golf essays, *Slices: Observations from the Wrong Side of the Fairway* (John Wiley & Sons), is available online or in bookstores. Visit his Web site, www.ijschecter.com.

The second reason has to do with a syndrome called Taking the Reader for Granted. When readers come across sentences like the first version of the example above, they often come away feeling insulted. The sentiment expressed in the dialogue above is obviously cold-hearted—there's no need to beat the reader over the head with explanation. Doing so is not only distracting, it's also offensive, and once a reader's relationship with you is soured, it can be hard to reverse the dynamic.

Remind yourself that it doesn't necessarily serve a purpose just because it's there

Eradicating adverbs and adjectives from your manuscript is a relatively painless exercise. Often it even produces a kind of exhilaration as you liberate your manuscript, bit by bit, from the extra weight.

Tearing out entire sentences, on the other hand, can be emotionally punishing. Some of them are just so lovely you can't imagine they don't belong. But look again and you'll realize they're only lovely on their own. As part of the overall story, they only serve to hold things back.

To counter the pain of removing whole sentences at a time, think about your appendix. At one point in human development—call it our early drafts—these organs served a necessary function, but no longer. Today we carry them around as evolutionary remnants that do nothing but occasionally cause people crippling pain until they're removed. Once our bodies are rid of them, they function as well as before—better, if the appendix was causing trouble. Don't focus on the part that's been discarded; focus on the improved state of the entity remaining.

The easiest exercise for determining which sentences should stay and which should go is also the most ruthless: Read the passage once with the sentence and once without. Usually the answer will be head-slappingly obvious, and toward those sentences that need to be exorcised you'll experience both annoyance at having included them in the first place and elation at the improvement you've made. Tear them out, give yourself a pat on the back, and move on.

Repeat after me

Every writer has certain stylistic tendencies, and few of us are good at recognizing our own. It is for this reason that you'll often find to your consternation that you've described hands similarly two times within the space of three pages, written five consecutive sentences with approximately the same number of words (a rhythmic no-no) or used a certain pet phrase on half a dozen occasions. In a retrospective assessment of his own work, Timothy Findley laments this syndrome:

> It came as something of a shock . . . to discover that for over 30 years of writing my attention has turned again and again to the same unvarying gamut of sounds and images. . . . The sound of screen doors banging; evening lamplight; music held at a distance—always being played on a gramophone; letters written on blue-tinted note paper; robins making forays onto summer lawns to murder worms; photographs in cardboard boxes; Colt revolvers hidden in bureau drawers and a chair that is always falling over.

Findley's self-effacement notwithstanding, as a writer you must keep your radar high to detect repeated images, syntactical choices or metaphorical leanings. Readers may not be able to identify this duplication as such, but they will still feel its effects: waning interest, predictability and a sensation of stagnancy in the language.

Think about bands whose songs, after a while, all begin to sound the same to you, causing you to migrate to other acts. Those bands have failed to keep your interest because they've gone on using the same instruments, the same musical hooks, the same keys and chord progressions, the same themes and lyrics over and over. This might work a handful of times, but sooner or later listeners—or, in your case, readers—are going to tire of the sameness.

Stylistic repetition is difficult to pick up during the writing process. Get your draft down first, then go back through the manuscript and focus only on fixing repetitive elements as needed by modifying sentence structure, varying your catalog of images and expanding your repertoire of metaphors and similes. Your manuscript will transform from a single ray of light into a prism.

Feel the rhythm

Effective pace and tempo are important, though elusive, goals for any writer. More important than the speed of your story or the volume of your voice is the consistency with which both are rendered. If a soft voice suddenly becomes shrill or a rapid pace suddenly slackens, the effect on the story is one of distension because the reader is being forced to make unexpected adjustments. Our tacit contract with readers says that they should be required only to read. Once we start demanding extra effort of them, they will be less inclined to invest time in our stories.

No concrete formula or simple exercise can be applied to assessing pace or tempo. There are only two ways to evaluate your manuscript's rhythmic consistency: a) read it, and b) have others read it. The latter option will provide you a more objective appraisal since you unavoidably carry biases about the story. Studies show us that even when we are presented with words lacking vowels, we'll still "see" the proper words. Since you're aware of your manuscript's ideal tempo, you may feel that tempo even if other readers don't. Ask friends, family members, professors, workshop classmates or anyone else you trust to read the story and give you the true dope on how fast or slow it moves, how softly or loudly it speaks, and, most important of all, whether these aspects periodically go awry.

Seal off all escape routes

As writers, we are all would-be kidnappers. Our ultimate aim is to snatch a person out of their reality and return them only once we're done. To abduct a reader successfully, you must not only execute the up-front capture but also ensure they have no way to leave—and no reason to want to.

That means making your manuscript lean and muscular from the first word to the last so the reader's attention doesn't drift for even a moment. Comb your manuscript in a search for two types of inadvertent escape valves: superfluous descriptions and accidental wake-ups.

Superfluous descriptions result from us walking ourselves through a scene and typically manifest in obvious action or unnecessary dialogue. Writing the scene, you see your protagonist walk over to answer the ringing phone—so you end up describing her hearing the ring, closing her magazine, walking over, picking up the receiver and greeting the other person. All you had to do—that is, all the reader needed from you—was to describe the phone ringing and heroine answering. All the other action is inferred.

Accidental wake-ups are moments in which we temporarily, but perilously, jolt the reader out of the story, usually with incongruous language, out-of-place imagery or perplexing character actions. If your villain suddenly and unaccountably behaves in a way inconsistent with the personality you've established for him, the reader's tether to your story begins to loosen. The same thing occurs if a gruesome murder abruptly interrupts what felt to the reader like a light romance. Hijack your readers, take them away, and don't give them any chance of escape—at least not until they've finished the book.

The Importance of Period Details

by I.J. Schecter

You've written a manuscript that really sings—especially that hilarious scene in the burger joint. But now that you think about it, was McDonald's around in 1948? It's time to do a little homework.

A serious effort is required to learn enough about a certain period that you can place a reader there, too. Let's talk about what it takes to sweep readers into another time and place without them having to leave their own couch.

Immerse yourself

You have a distinct advantage. You're writing in the Information Age, in which endless facts on virtually any setting or period are available. It wasn't long ago that writers had little choice but to write about the times and places they lived in if they wanted to be certain of authenticity, since people seldom had the opportunity to travel beyond their own borders and information remained far less accessible than it is today.

Still, you must become an expert on your temporal setting and location before trying to describe it to a reader. Dive into your research with both feet, gathering as much information as possible. Take a cue from Pulitzer Prize winner David McCullough: "I want the reader to feel—not just know—that other time and those other people. That's why it's so important to get inside the other time, inside the subject. I'm often asked if I'm working on a book, and I say, Yes I am. But what I really want to say is, No, I'm working *in* a book."

A word of caution: Though the Internet certainly makes research easier these days, the information it contains must be considered with a critical eye. Seek primary sources first: books written by credible parties, newspaper clippings, photographs, first-hand accounts. Treat Wikipedia and its ilk as secondary sources—useful for supplementing information or potentially filling in gaps—but never accept something you've taken from the Net as gospel unless you can corroborate it elsewhere.

Set the stage

Once you're happily swimming in facts and ready to begin writing, remind yourself that establishing period does not mean simply reciting lists of items or loosely appropriating

I.J. SCHECTER's work has been nominated for Edgar Awards, won Story of the Year in *Eureka Literary Magazine* and appeared in *Alfred Hitchcock's Mystery Magazine*. His bestselling collection of golf essays, *Slices: Observations from the Wrong Side of the Fairway* (John Wiley & Sons), is available online or in bookstores. Visit his Web site, www.ijschecter.com.

historical events; it means placing your characters within the setting so that readers can be transported via the connection they make with them. Consider the following three excerpts:

> On Sunday afternoon, after dinner, Father and Mother went upstairs and closed the bedroom door. Grandfather fell asleep on the divan in the parlor. The Little Boy in the sailor blouse sat on the screened porch and waved away the flies. Down at the bottom of the hill Mother's Younger Brother boarded the streetcar and rode to the end of the line.

> The apartment and furniture would have been nothing extraordinary as belonging to a homely, northern farmer, with a stubborn countenance, and stalwart limbs set out to advantage in knee-breeches and gaiters. Such an individual seated in his armchair, his mug of ale frothing on the round table before him, is to be seen in any circuit of five or six miles along these hills, if you go at the right time after dinner.

> After he returned from Europe the first time, he used the family landau drawn by two golden chestnuts, but when this was no longer practical he changed it for a Victoria and a single horse, and he continued to use it, with a certain disdain for fashion, when carriages had already begun to disappear from the world and the only ones left in the city were for giving rides to tourists and carrying wreaths at funerals.

The first passage is from E.L. Doctorow's *Ragtime*; the second, from Emily Brontë's *Wuthering Heights*; and the third from *Love in the Time of Cholera* by Gabriel García Márquez. Observe how all three authors subtly use period details to paint their characters' milieus. The details do not serve to distract us from the story; they serve to enrich it.

Make sense

Familiarizing yourself with the time and place of your story is the first step; bringing it to life is the next. Here, it's vital to avoid falling into a common trap. When we describe things to ourselves, we usually revert exclusively to visual imagery, since it's this sense that occurs to us most obviously. Visual narrative is undeniably crucial to a manuscript—it's like the chassis of a car. But without use of the other senses providing texture and richness, the story becomes as indistinct as any old car on the road.

Consider this opening from a *National Geographic* story on the mushrooming global problem of high-tech waste:

> June is the wet season in Ghana, but here in Accra, the capital, the morning rain has ceased. As the sun heats the humid air, pillars of black smoke begin to rise above the vast Agbogbloshie Market. I follow one plume toward its source, past lettuce and plantain vendors, past stalls of used tires, and through a clanging scrap market where hunched men bash on old alternators and engine blocks. Soon the muddy track is flanked by piles of old TVs, gutted computer cases, and smashed monitors heaped ten feet high. Beyond lies a field of fine ash speckled with glints of amber and green—the sharp broken bits of circuit boards.

The writer of this piece has brought us into the story not through sole visual description but by invoking multiple senses. Go back over the passage and count not only how many different senses are brought into play but also how smoothly they are woven together. When you lay out a scene, tell the reader what the period looked like—but don't forget also convey its smells, tastes and sounds, too.

Remember, setting is still just setting

Regardless whether your story is set in Ancient Egypt, Medieval France or the year 3019 on the planet Teknion-5, two things must power it: plot and character. The more research you do, the more knowledge you want to share—it's only natural. But time and place provide the framework for your story; they don't replace it.

Be aware of two specific pitfalls. The first is simple over-description. Readers are most impressed by understated expertise. Inundating them with every detail you've assembled about your story's setting will have at best a wearying effect and at worst an irritating one. Your goal is to use the knowledge to bring the reader into the world of your story—but don't forget that readers need things to happen. Get the story going, not a moment later than it should.

The second trapping to watch out for is didactic, or "show-off," writing—characterized by sentences that contain great bits of esoteric information but are there strictly to demonstrate how much the writer has learned. In these cases, the "I didn't know that" factor is not worth it weighed against potential reader annoyance. In other words, no one likes a show-off.

It's the details of *your* story that count

Say you want to write a story set in 18th-century Paris, but you're worried that people are already too familiar with descriptions of the click of horse's hooves on the cobblestone streets. Stop worrying. These are just the details that establish the skeleton of your story. While you still need to describe them properly, they aren't the ones that will set your manuscript apart. It's the details at the molecular level, the parts of *your* story within the context of the period, which make the difference. Certain images pepper stories about given periods because they provide reliable cues for the rest of us. Why are there so many saloons in Old West stories? Because saloons were where people gathered in the Old West. Why are Victorian Age stories pervaded by petticoats, crinolines and bodices? Because that's what the ladies wore. Think of it this way: When you look at a painting, is it the frame you notice first? No—it's the detail inside.

Even if a topic or period seems to have been covered to death, have faith that there's a way to communicate it in a fresh way. In the opening lines of the short story "Eisenheim the Illusionist" by Steven Millhauser, we are told that the art of magic flourished in the last years of the nineteenth century throughout Europe. This is common knowledge—however the manner in which Millhauser conveys the knowledge is special:

> In obscure villages of Moravia and Galicia, from the Istrian Peninsula to the mists of Bukovina, bearded and black-caped magicians in market squares astonished townspeople by drawing streams of dazzling silk handkerchiefs from empty paper cones, removing billiard balls from children's ears, and throwing into the air decks of cards that assumed the shapes of fountains, snakes, and angels before returning to the hand.

This is far from an ordinary depiction of magic. Read the passage again. In a single paragraph, we are dropped into a precise sliver of time in a particular region within a specific period. Time and place have been powerfully established, and at the same time we're excited about the specifics of the story to come.

Double-check—and then triple-check

You've researched conscientiously, woven period details into your story to provide context, and used all five senses to give the period true dimensionality. But you aren't done. Not yet. If you've ever written an article for a magazine, you're aware of the fact-checkers enlisted to confirm the veracity of every single word you've written. Before sending your manuscript anywhere, go back through it and be your own fact-checker, even confirming details you think couldn't possibly be inaccurate. Nail down all your facts, and there will be only one thing left for an editor to do: tumble willingly, and enthusiastically, into the world of your story.

Craft & Technique

Marketing Your Short Story Collection

by Jack Smith

Numerous journals and magazines, both print and online, provide markets for short fiction. Most of them are difficult markets to crack, many publishing as little as one to two percent of the submissions they receive. Even so, serious writers discover that persistence pays off: eventually, they are able to build a strong bio of short story publications. Soon it's time to gather a collection and get proposal packages "out there," circulating at a number of publishers. But now one often faces not only rigorous competition, but also marketing issues, which are of key importance to the publisher, especially commercial houses. After all, if publishers intend to stay afloat, they must sell books.

How well do collections sell?

Walter Cummins, long-time editor of *The Literary Review*, says that the marketability of the short story collection must be seen in terms of a larger context, that of the current marketability of fiction itself. "We're told that fiction sales overall, including novels, are down." This diminished fiction market has deep roots in the coming of television back in the 1950s, says Cummins, but most recently in "the growth in popularity of memoir and creative nonfiction. Personal confession has a cachet for many readers that apparently made-up stories lack. Writers transfer the techniques of short fiction to seeming presentations of 'fact' that has the appeal of gossip and eavesdropping on real lives. Consider, as a parallel, all the versions of confessional TV programs."

Memoir sales are up, fiction down—even novels. Given this market, how do short story collections fare?

COMMERCIAL PRESSES

Not well, says Fiona Inglis, literary agent with Curtis Brown: "We say no to short stories because publishers resist them because booksellers resist them because readers resist them . . . It's much more difficult to sell short stories than a full-length novel especially for newer writers." Jill Kneerim of the literary agency Kneerim & Williams also places the matter right in the hands of the consumer-reader: "The reason is easily found in your own book-

JACK SMITH's stories have been published in *North American Review*, *The Southern Review*, *Happy*, *In Posse Review*, *X-Connect*, *Night Train*, *NEO*, *Southern Ocean Review*, *B&A: New Fiction*, *Savoy*, and *Roswell Literary Review*, among others. He has stories upcoming in the *Texas Review* and *Word Riot*. He's published reviews in *X-Connect*, *RE:AL*, *Missouri Review*, *Texas Review*, *Prairie Schooner*, *Pleiades*, *Georgia Review*, and *Environment* magazine. He's also contributed eight articles to *Novel & Short Story Writer's Market*. His co-authored nonfiction book entitled *Killing Me Softly* was published by Monthly Review Press in 2002. Besides his writing, he co-edits *The Green Hills Literary Lantern*, published by Truman State University.

buying habits. Do you ever buy short story collections? I doubt it. Few readers do.'' And, adds Kneerim, ''Publishers are more and more pressured by their corporate owners to turn a profit rather than advance the cause of literature, so they can't afford to print and market a title that sells 5,000 copies. I don't think collections ever sold well, but in the days when publishers were owned by families the arithmetic was done differently and the latitude was far greater to publish valuable work even if unprofitable.''

The reader of a short story collection is viewed as the serious reader of literature—comprising a very limited market. ''Every story in a collection,'' says Walter Cummins, ''calls for a reorientation to a different fictional world with different characters and different issues.'' As a result, a story collection calls for ''much more effort'' than a novel of the same length. For Adam Chromy, of Artists and Artisans, ''A good analogy is music—most people like a good, commercial song produced professionally in a studio. Only serious music fans or other musicians really enjoy an experimental jam session.''

If commercial publishers do end up publishing a collection, says Chromy, they do so only to ''build buzz'' for a novel they're planning to publish with a specific audience in mind, an ''influential group of writers and serious readers that will be the only ones to buy it.''

SMALL PRESSES

The small press or ''indie'' might appear to be the refuge for the serious short story writer, whose intended audience is ''literary'' readers. This scenario may well be true for some small presses, but certainly not for all. The problem is that indies, like commercial houses, may have trouble marketing story collections, and when sales are crucial to keeping a press afloat, marketing dynamics must necessarily enter into publication decisions. When small presses don't take collections, why don't they?

Unbridled almost never publishes a collection because as Greg Michalson, co-editor, says, ''people just don't buy them.'' Exceptions might include a themed book ''that strikes a mass chord (though these are usually anthologies).'' Conceivably, a collection might get launched if ''the stories were contemporarily comic enough, or savage.'' But, says Michalson, the odds are stacked against most story collections produced by a single author: ''The quality, well-wrought story of literary magazine ilk by a relatively unknown or even respected mid-list author seems to me to be a complete crap shoot at best—no matter how deserving.''

If people don't buy collections, it's safe to conclude that book buyers are going to be reluctant to purchase them. This has been the experience of Ed Wilson, publisher of Absey & Co. Except for local writers, says Wilson, it's ''almost impossible to get Barnes & Noble to even consider placing a short story collection on the shelf.'' And it's the same, says Wilson, with Ingram, the distributor. ''For Ingram, it's all about numbers. It is a matter of shelf space. Only so many books can go in a store.'' These economic realities dictate what Wilson can do for writers: ''I get probably 50 to 100 queries for collections every month and I seldom even ask to see the entire collection because I know it will be so hard to market.''

Out of 24 titles published in 2008, Graywolf will publish only one short story collection. Rolph Blythe, Marketing Director, says one of the key problems is promotion. ''Print media reviews (the one consistently reliable, affordable means of promotion for publishers) tend to focus on novels, I believe, because there is often an easily-identifiable hook in the primary plot that lends itself to discussion and analysis.'' Novels can be linked more easily to a ''likely readership,'' says Blythe, whereas short story collections are hard to categorize with their ''range of settings and characters and time periods.'' As a result, ''Reviewers are often left grasping at straws for one overarching topic or theme.'' To say the writing is simply ''good'' isn't ''a terribly effective pitch.'' With these market constraints, Graywolf has to be careful about publishing collections; still, they do keep an eye out, Blythe says, for good collections to possibly catch a promising writer on ''the way up.''

UNIVERSITY PRESSES

Very few university presses publish fiction. If they do so, on the whole they tend to publish more novels than short story collections. A few presses do try to advance the cause of the short story form.

BkMk, a university-based press, for instance, publishes short story collections, along with poetry collections, in order "to serve these important literary genres that are increasingly squeezed out of commercial publishing." Two of their books are prize books. Ben Furnish, editor, does note definite problems with sales. Even though the literary quality of the work BkMk is publishing today is better than ever, sales of collections aren't increasing. In fact, library sales are down, and sales of books at readings are also down. Oddly enough, more and more students are enrolled in creative writing programs, and yet, says Furnish, "those numbers don't seem to translate into sales for new short-story collections. I fear that the simple truth is that more people are writing, but fewer people are reading." But the lack of sales is not a critical factor in book publication at BkMk.

Southern Methodist University Press also is not bound strictly by bottom line issues in making publishing decisions. Kathryn Lang, senior editor, states that the press does not let the issue of sales determine the genre published. They publish two to three collections per year. "For us, selling is less important than good critical notice. If we sell out a print run of 2,000-2,500 copies, we're pleased." The university, says Lang, supports their efforts to publish the highest quality fiction they can—they don't have to be "hot sellers." SMU's administration "understands that it is part of our mission to publish those good works that wouldn't stand a chance of publication otherwise." This policy has paid off, says Lang, in the case of one of SMU Press's backlist "bestsellers," *Alligator Dance*, a debut story collection by Janet Peery, published in 1993. Peery's work immediately gained national attention with a half-page review by Dorothy Allison in the *New York Times Book Review*, followed by a Whiting Award. Her professional life took off as well with her appointment to the prestigious Academy of Arts and Letters, a tenure-track position at Old Dominion University, and her pick of agents. "We probably went back to print on that book three times," says Lang. "We are proud that she's gone on to publish with St. Martin's Press a novel that was a National Book Award finalist, *The River Beyond the World*, based on one of the stories in *Alligator Dance*, and her most recent work, *What the Thunder Said*, a novella and stories, also an expansion of another of the stories in her first book."

If these two presses are given more latitude with regard to sales expectations in their publishing decisions, The University of Michigan Press is not—and since short story collections don't sell well, they can publish very few. For Chris Hebert, Acquisitions Editor, publishers who take on collections face the same problem noted by Rolph Blythe of Graywolf—the difficulty of developing a marketing pitch: "Given how much stories in collections can vary in all sorts of ways (storylines, characters), it's often tough to make a simple, compelling pitch to entice readers, which is why publishers often prefer collections that can be sold as 'linked stories' or 'novels in stories.' "

CONTESTS—A VIABLE ALTERNATIVE

Contests that include book publishing contracts for winners are a viable alternative to the ordinary publishing route. For the writer-contestant, the critical issue becomes the stiff competition only—not fierce competition *plus* marketability. Marketing-wise, the prestige of the award becomes a strong selling point for the press, lessening the concern with sales. Some contests include several genres—memoirs, novels, short novels, and collections. Three high-profile contests that focus on short story collections are the Flannery O'Connor Award, The Iowa Short Fiction Award, and the Drue Heinz Literature Prize.

• **The Flannery O'Connor Award.** "We like to think our series helps keep the art of short fiction alive and well—along with some other prizes and smaller trade houses devoted to short fiction," says John McLeod, Marketing and Sales Director, University of Georgia Press. "We see that as part of our mission." Another mission of the series "is to help launch literary careers by taking a chance on an unproven writer." Award-winning collections wouldn't sell enough to justify publication at the commercial presses, says McLeod, "so we're really helping to fill that void." Because of the Award's prestige, the press has been able to meet standard marketing challenges. First, over the past few years several winners have gained a "marketing boost" through reviews in such high-profile places as the *New York Times Book Review* and the *New York Review of Books*. Second, local print media have more of a "news hook" for contest winners than they would if the writer were simply local.

• **The Iowa Short Fiction Award.** "We are certainly not doing it for the money," says Holly Carver, who directs the contest. Supporting debut collections of short fiction is one of the publishing goals of the University of Iowa Press. "Launching—or helping to launch—a writer's career is important to us." Recent winners, says Carver, do seem to be more seasoned than previous ones—more "street-smart" and sophisticated, with agents and long-term career goals. "Perhaps now the award only enhances the status of a writer who has already worked long and hard in the field of the short story, whereas in earlier years the award shone a brighter spotlight on a writer who was not so well connected."

• **Drue Heinz Literature Prize.** This prize, sponsored by the University of Pittsburgh Press, offers an honorarium of $15,000. Cynthia Miller, the Director of the press, says that "over and over," the press has heard from winners "that the validation of winning the prize encouraged them to keep writing and to keep writing short stories." But secondly, winning a major prize like this "opens other publishing doors for our authors." It is the press's hope, Miller says, that media attention "will encourage more readers to read and buy short fiction." Writers entering the contest should know that the work of most recent winners has been published separately in literary magazines and journals.

SHORT STORY WRITERS SPEAK OUT

What do writers themselves say about putting together and selling collections? What about competition? What about marketing?

Robert Garner McBrearty, 2007 winner of the Sherwood Anderson Foundation Fiction Award for a new collection in progress (honorarium $15,000), had his earlier collection, *A Night at the Y*, published in 1999. He had initially shopped this collection around New York and to some of the major contests. Eventually he tried small presses and landed an acceptance. When *A Night at the Y* came out, John Daniel and Company was receiving over 5,000 submissions and queries per year and publishing about four collections. "One can see that the odds are long indeed." says McBrearty. "But even so, the publisher was very enthusiastic about the work itself and I think that's what it takes." It made a difference, McBrearty believes, that his collection was themed and that it was reasonably short—he cut it from 20 to 12 stories. The Anderson Award did much to boost his confidence, helping to convince him that his second collection, *Episode*—also relatively short and, like his first collection, filled with humorous, poignant stories—was worth completing and stood a good chance of finding a publisher. His instinct was right. He recently received an acceptance from Pocol Press.

Steven Wingate also believes in the contest route. "With competitions you know your work will get read, which can't always be said for commercial or indie presses." His collection, *Wifeshopping*, recently won a Bakeless Prize, sponsored by the Bread Loaf Writer's Conference at Middlebury College. "So much depends upon who judges a given competition, and if your work is strong, you have a chance." Before winning the Bakeless Prize, *Wifeshopping* was a finalist or semi-finalist in several competitions, including the Flannery O'Connor Award. This success encouraged Wingate to keep going. "Pursuing the competition route also gives you a built-in opportunity to refine your work over time: you polish, send out, put away, polish again. A first collection is more a beginning than a culmination. It gives you a chance to show the world your work, but after that you have to go back into uncertainty again and reinvent yourself as a writer.'' For Wingate, the Bakeless Prize has paid off. It means not only the prestige of winning the contest but publication of the collection by Houghton Mifflin.

If anyone knows about publishing short fiction, it's Gary Fincke, who has published a number of books in three genres—poetry, creative nonfiction, and short fiction. He finds it much more difficult to find a publisher for a short story collection than for the other two genres. Someone might get the idea, says Fincke, that his fiction isn't as strong as his work in other genres, but his stories have appeared in nationally-respected literary magazines and, to boot, he won the Flannery O'Connor Award. And so he concludes: ''I'm nearly certain it's the market, not the work.'' He's seen several signs of a shrinking fiction market: The University of Missouri Press, which published two of his story collections, no longer publishes fiction; Coffee House, which published an early collection of fiction, tried to niche market his work, and it's clear from their catalogue that they're moving generally in that direction; small presses as well as university presses are more open to nonfiction than to fiction. Fincke has recently been turning his attention to the commercial market, hoping to find an interested publisher for his next collection. But the market he's experiencing is unreceptive to this genre. ''The O'Connor Prize earned me an agent for my fiction, but she hasn't been able to sell a collection. All the houses that expressed an interest in my fiction asked to see a novel.''

Why put together short story collection at all if the odds against their being published are so tough? Ronald Frame, one of Scotland's most well-known writers, and author of several novels and commercial story collections, acknowledges that collections simply don't sell, but he adds: ''Nevertheless we story-writers persevere. Stories will continue to ferment in the brain, and they'll keep on demanding that they be written down.''

Until the market gets better—that is, until readers are purchasing short story collections in bookstores as much as they purchase novels—that may be as good as it gets for commercial publication and also for small press publication when sales really matter. Meanwhile, the collection's best bet may be a few university presses and a handful of contests sponsored by universities. For both venues, competition is indeed tough, but at least market considerations don't tend to be a significant determinant in final publication decisions.

25 Ways to Annoy Editors

(Without Even Knowing It)

by John Joseph Adams

All writers at some point in their careers make some kind of submission faux pas. It's embarrassing and you'll feel pretty dumb when it happens, but rest assured that there's almost certainly another writer out there who has done the same thing, or has done something even more obtuse.

Following standard manuscript format will take care of most of the problems you're likely to run into. But in my seven years experience as an editor at *The Magazine of Fantasy & Science Fiction*, I've come across a number of recurring mistakes that tend to get glossed over in guidelines, but are annoying nonetheless. Here are my top 25.

MANUSCRIPTS & SUBMISSION PACKAGES

1. The impenetrable envelope. Be careful about making your submission envelope too hard to open. Too much tape is the primary culprit. Don't tape up every gap in the envelope; leave some room for the letter opener.

2. Paper or plastic? Plastic envelopes are very hard to open, so don't use them. They seal quite securely, so they probably offer writers some measure of comfort, but it's a bit too secure—the letter opener doesn't work so well on them.

3. Confetti is for celebrations, not submissions. Never use those padded envelopes with the recycled confetti inside. They're not only messy, they're totally unnecessary. Your manuscript is made of *paper*, it's not going to break.

4. The world is not flat, but your manuscript should be. Always mail your manuscript flat. It doesn't matter if it's two pages and will fit nicely into a #10 envelope. Mail it flat. The editor will appreciate it.

5. One at a time, please. Don't bombard the same publication with more than one story at a time, and don't submit more than once a week, even if you get a rejection back in a few days. As a general rule of thumb, submit a story to a market, and then don't submit anything else to them until they've responded to your first submission.

6. The first rule of Write Club is *you do not staple your manuscript*. The pages of your manuscript should be loose, or bound only with a paperclip. Do not staple or otherwise bind your manuscript. This also goes for those clear, plastic folders you used to put your high school English papers in.

JOHN JOSEPH ADAMS is the editor of the anthologies *Wastelands: Stories of the Apocalypse, Seeds of Change,* and *No More Room in Hell: Stories of the Living Dead.* He is also the assistant editor of *The Magazine of Fantasy & Science Fiction* and a freelance writer. His Web site is www.johnjosephadams.com.

7. Unending ellipses. An ellipsis has three full stops. Always. (Occasionally, you will see what appears to be an ellipsis that is made of four dots, but in reality that's an ellipsis followed by a period because it ends a sentence). Never, under any circumstances, should an ellipsis ever have 5, 10, or 15 full stops, no matter how long a pause you're trying to indicate.

8. Ready for your close-up? Don't send headshots, no matter how good-looking you are. It doesn't help, and more often than not, it comes across as creepy, and the editorial staff will make fun of you at lunch.

9. Submission spam. If you're submitting to a market that accepts electronic submissions, double-check your submission to make sure it's the final draft before you click send. If you send three submissions in rapid succession explaining that *whoops, you messed up and sent the wrong file, use this one instead*, you're going to look silly and unprofessional.

10. Reading comprehension. If you're going to indicate that you've read the guidelines, make sure you follow them. For instance, don't send e-mail queries saying "I know you say not to query, but . . .," or instruct the editor to e-mail you his response even though the guidelines say to send an SASE.

SELF ADDRESSED STAMPED ENVELOPES (SASEs)

11. S is for "self." Remember that SASEs are *self*-addressed. Before you seal up your submission envelope, double-check to make sure your SASE isn't addressed back to the magazine or publisher you submitted to.

12. A place for everything. Be mindful of where you place your SASE in your submission envelope. Putting it too close to the top of the envelope sometimes results in it being damaged by the letter opener as the envelope is sliced open. Also, don't put your manuscript *inside* your SASE. That's almost like a pre-emptive rejection.

13. Does this envelope make me look fat? When you mail a manuscript flat, don't force the editor to cram your manuscript in a letter-size SASE to return your manuscript to you. Editors become conditioned to think *flat manuscript plus #10 envelope equals disposable manuscript*.

14. Recycle paper, not ink. A nifty way of avoiding the problem mentioned in #13 is to always send disposable manuscripts. It's easier for editors (and probably cheaper for you).

15. Return to sender. If you wanted your manuscript returned to you, but the publication doesn't return it, forget about it and try to make it more clear next time that you want it returned (or better yet, send disposable manuscripts.). If you write to the magazine asking them to return your manuscript, you're probably too late—it's almost certainly been recycled already.

16. Size matters. When sending disposable manuscripts, always use a #10 envelope for your SASE. Don't use a #7, #8, or #9, or the extra envelope you mistakenly grabbed when you bought that greeting card.

17. Format matters, too. Don't send postcards in lieu of envelope. Although they're cheaper to mail, most markets mail you a rejection letter (or form letter), so a postcard doesn't help.

18. Manuscript GPS. Speaking of postcards, if you want to be notified when your manuscript arrives, use USPS Delivery Confirmation rather than including a postcard with your submission. Why? Delivery Confirmation is automated and requires no extra work on behalf of the editor. Plus, if the slush pile gets backed up, a postcard might be sitting inside a sealed envelope for quite a while, so you'll be left in the dark as to its status. Note the distinction between Delivery Confirmation and Certified Mail—Delivery Confirmation requires no extra work from the recipient (and you check the status online), while Certified Mail requires a signature upon delivery, usually forcing the editorial staff to wait on line at the post office. (Don't send material Certified Mail.)

19. There can be only one. One SASE is always enough. Opening up a submission envelope and discovering not one but two SASEs is confusing, especially when one is large (for the return of a manuscripts) and the other is a #10.

20. Mailing 101. Know which side of the envelope the stamp goes on. You'd think everyone does, but sadly, that's not the case. (It goes in the upper right-hand corner.) And always affix your postage to your SASE. Don't paperclip it to the envelope or stick it inside the envelope. It's far too easy to lose that way, and it just creates extra work for the editorial staff.

COVER LETTERS

21. Page zero. Don't put your cover letter inside a separate envelope. It should just go on top of the first page of your manuscript. Think of it as "page zero."

22. Hello, my name is . . . Anything you want the editor to know should be in your cover letter; don't expect them to visit your Web site to learn anything about you. It's okay to mention your Web site, just don't assume the editor will go look at it, and whatever information you decide to share, keep it short and to the point.

23. Well, duh! Don't point out the obvious in your cover letter. For instance, don't point out that underlining equals italics, that underlining indicates character's thoughts, or that white space between paragraphs indicates a scene break.

MORTAL SINS

24. Rejecting rejections. Writing to an editor disagreeing with a rejection letter might help you blow off some steam, but it's never a good idea. Also be careful what you blog about or post to public message boards. If you badmouth an editor online, don't be surprised if it gets back to him or her.

25. The sting. Everyone knows—or *should* know—that plagiarism is wrong, but do keep in mind that it's still illegal even if you use it to prove a point. So, if you're thinking about setting up your own personal sting operation—by putting your name on a classic story and submitting it as your own—to prove that those mean editors don't really read your stories before rejecting them . . . don't do it; it won't prove anything anyway.

Keep in mind that the abovementioned dos and don'ts won't necessarily apply to every market; always check the guidelines. When in doubt, imagine that you're sitting in front of a stack of 100 or more submissions, and think about it from an editor's point of view.

By putting in a little extra time and thought into preparing your submissions, you can avoid these pitfalls (and avoid incurring an editor's wrath). And if you're consistently professional enough that the editor doesn't groan every time he or she sees one of your manuscripts, maybe you'll even avoid writing's biggest pitfall—rejection.

Getting Published

Writing as Real Estate?

Insider Advice on Selling in Buyers' Market

by Jude Tulli

The fiction market has many aspects in common with real estate. Think about it: writers develop properties, then attempt to solicit interest in them. Some estates, generally works of established authors, are sold on a blueprint or the merit of a prior holding, while others take years to find a buyer. An exclusive minority instigates high stakes bidding wars while many, it is painful to admit, find themselves annexed by a bedroom drawer.

Agents also carry over into the publishing industry, those business-savvy *sellerati* who stake their livelihoods on knowing what's "in" in the neighborhood of their clients' genres and how high to set the asking prices. The landscape speaks for itself: like building or renovating a house to sell, writing professionally isn't all about the art. It's true, a piece must be artfully (not necessarily *artistically*, mind you) conceived and executed. It needs a solid foundation and a distinct absence of plot leaks. But in addition to expert craftsmanship, a manuscript must also be deemed marketable to a publisher's existing or projected readership before an offer will be made.

The writer's perpetual dilemma: how to build the kinds of properties he or she loves *and* sell them. In this intellectual economy, every writer dreams of establishing a hotel on Boardwalk, yet for the unpublished even a doghouse on Mediterranean Avenue might not feel too shabby. Being an effective seller in a buyer's market isn't always easy, especially if you're unwilling to throw in your soul to sweeten the deal.

Yet it can be done. Many writers do find a path toward that elusive 5-bedroom, 3-bath on 20 acres with a private lake in the sky. Read on the hear from a few of them—bestselling novelists **Julianna Baggott**, **Sue Grafton** and **Gwynne Forster**; author and agent **Peter Miller**; and author and editor **Terri Windling**. It is my hope, dear reader, that the advice of these individuals successful in the construction (writing), inspection (slush pile prospecting/editing) and/or brokering (brokering) of manuscripts help to illuminate what treasures may loiter undiscovered in your own backyard.

JUDE TULLI has previously written for the *Novel & Short Story Writer's Market*, and wrote about screenwriting for novelists for the 2009 *Writer's Market*. He's had two short screenplays independently produced with a third currently in pre-production. He's currently shopping a fantasy novel manuscript which he expects will amass eager rejections from the industry's finest. He resides in the Sonoran Desert with his beloved wife Trish, their six cats and six fish but, sadly, no aquaritorium.

JULIANNA BAGGOTT

"I never thought I would be a novelist," bestselling author Julianna Baggott says with no greater emphasis than if she were telling me what she ate for breakfast. Rather, she started out wanting to be a playwright.

"The novel to me was a sellout to begin with." Ultimately, though, she fell in love with the "power trip," wherein you "don't need a collaborative effort" to breathe life into the work. More than that, she found the sheer square footage exhilarating. "Once you live in a mansion it's kind of hard to shove all your stuff back in an apartment."

Baggott writes both commercial and literary fiction, and offers a readily decipherable code for her readers to determine which works are which: the ones published under a pen name are commercial. So far she has two alter-egos: Bridget Asher, whose "debut" novel is entitled *My Husband's Sweethearts* (Bantam Dell), and the prolific children's writer N.E. Bode. And she reserves the right to create more. "I enjoy writing books for a big audience," she says, "and I enjoy having entertainment be what I'm trying to make and in the course of it art will happen."

Her prescription for commercial writing differs greatly from the necessities of composing literary fiction. Aspiring and established commercial authors, she says, are well-advised to "read *Publishers Weekly*, find out editors' tastes," and in essence gauge the market so they can write something the market will likely accept if not embrace. Toward that end, Baggott likes to keep an eye on the cultural climate. "Sometimes a book sort of snags the American psyche, and I'm always interested in 'Why that book?'"

If your goal is literary fiction, she says, you "should write the book. The need to tell a story doesn't come along every day." But when it does, "That's a gift. So you have to accept that gift." Her strategy for managing more ideas than she has time to develop is to "always write where the energy is, then if the novel in progress clams up on me, I let it sit for a while and go on to something else."

Yet even successfully published authors learn to choose their projects wisely. "I send novel ideas to my L.A. agent first," says Baggott, "and I learned that the hard way." In addition to routinely discussing ideas with her husband, she also garners feedback from her babysitter, who need not *say* a word. "I can tell whether she's interested in the story [or not]."

"I do more up-front work than I used to," Baggott says, which she equates with "feeling out the idea with other people" and not necessarily a little "man-handling of the plot." Still, all the preparedness in the world won't shield any writer from incoming rejection slips (even for manuscripts that go on to become bestsellers). "I have a very good relationship with rejection; we're palsy walsy. I offer it a beer, we watch a soap together and it goes on its way."

Ever-realistic about the industry, Baggott says that when she hears from another writer signing a first contract, "My stomach does a little flip-flop for it." She knows that a big deal is also an "opportunity to fail bigger!"

When she needs inspiration, "I go back to the books I love. Every book you love is a map, it contains a blueprint to write the book that you want to write. Any writer who has ever lived and published can teach you by what they left behind." Even books you hate, Baggott asserts, can be inspiring. But "you have to read as a writer," not just a fan. Like studying the mechanics of a clock, you have to "take it apart and find out how it works."

SUE GRAFTON

Sue Grafton knows more than a little something about catching hold of the collective imagination and running with it. Her bestselling Kinsey Millhone mystery series is on its *twentieth* installment, *T is for Trespass* (Putnam).

On the subject of improving one's odds for publication, Grafton says, "I think unpublished writers make two mistakes. The first is to imitate, consciously or unconsciously, the voice of a well-known writer, thinking this will insure a ready sale." If given the opportunity, would you rather live in a one-of-a-kind Frank Lloyd Wright or a cookie-cutter reproduction of the neighbors' neighbors' flat?

She continues, "The second big mistake many unpublished writers make is trying to second guess publishers. I've read query letters in which the writer sets about telling an agent or editor how pertinent his/her story is in today's market place and how fabulous the sales will be." In the modern real-estate market, it is considered wise to arrange your décor so that it tips off potential home-buyers as to which room is the formal dining room and which is the 20,000-gallon salt-water wave aquaritorium (don't forget to show them how to suit up before opening the door on the walk-through). Based on those unique selling points, you would know that your likely demographic consists of culinary home-snorkeling enthusiasts. But in the literary market, it's an editor's job to know his or her imprint's readership. Besides, you may sell your manuscript short if, for example, you call it a young adult mystery but it might appeal to adults, too.

Grafton recounts her response in one such instance: "I'm guessing you've never worked as a New York literary agent or an acquisitions editor for a publishing house. If I'm wrong about that, please pass right over this paragraph. If I'm correct, then the notion of your telling an agent or editor how to do their business is absurd on face of it. Since you're an unpublished writer, it's cheeky for you to address strategies for sales and marketing. You're implying that you know more about publishing than the professionals, which can't be the case. You probably read an article or took a writing class in which the instructor suggested such a letter as a sales technique." Grafton believes such advice, however well-meaning, is detrimental to one's first impression. "The move is not only silly, but will mark you as an amateur."

Amateur is not, technically, a four-letter word. But in publishing circles it may as well be.

GWYNNE FORSTER

Gwynne Forster is the award-winning and bestselling author of over 30 novels including *Getting Some of Her Own* (Dafina, 2007). She believes that publishers accept or reject manuscripts based on an estimation of their "sale value, taking into account the quality of writing, attractiveness of the story line and the drawing power of the writer's name." A supportive long-term relationship with an editor to run ideas by can help: "Every book that I have written has been published by a commercial publisher," she says, "However, two synopses have been rejected because the editor didn't think the storyline suitable or sufficiently interesting."

Forster prefers not to receive feedback from family or other writers on her works in progress. "The first person to read a text that I've written is my editor at Kensington, Harlequin or another of my publishers." She no longer participates in critique groups. "I belonged to a writers' club for a short while and I observed that when a writer presented work for comment, each person who commented, whether published or not, had a different and sometimes contrasting opinion. I noticed that the writer's original ideas tended to become polluted."

Likewise, she views trends as unreliable spectacles for a writer to survey ideas through. "I've learned not to count too heavily on trends. About two years elapse between the time I send a proposal to the editor and the date the book appears in stores. A trend can evaporate in two years."

Still, writers must adapt to certain market limitations. "I'm more comfortable writing longer books," says Forster, "but Harlequin wants shorter books now, and I find it challenging to construct a novel with strong characters in so few as 70,000 words." Other markets aren't as stringent. "My mainstream novels for Kensington shouldn't be more than 95,000 words, and I don't find that a problem . . . my first mainstream novels were hard cover, and sold well, but the book market sagged, and I settled for trade paperback, which is more affordable for the reader."

Forster knows firsthand that a debut novel need not define a writer or her entire career. If she were starting over again, however, "I would not have begun by writing a romance. Having done that, my general fiction novels are frequently referred to as romances and even reviewed as if they were. Yet, they are very different kinds of stories, in subject matter, construction and theme."

PETER MILLER

The "Literary Lion" of New York and writer of *Author! Screenwriter!* (Adams Media), Peter Miller has been working to turn art into creative commerce since 1973, when he founded what is now PMA Literary and Film Management, Inc. Despite the pride he takes in each sale, the reality of the business dictates, "I have to reject 99½% of the people who come to me."

Agents could not make a living in publishing if they were to spend their days acting as mentors to every aspirant. Both the numbers and Miller suggest that it behooves unpublished writers to seek out and soak in all the mentoring they need *before* submitting their manuscripts. Would you show a house in less than its peak condition and expect to attract an enthusiastic buyer? The trick is to polish your manuscript until it sparkles among the 0.5% that make the cut.

"It's tougher now to sell a novel than it's been in my over 30-year career," Miller says. For one thing, "Brand name writers take up a huge part of the market, occupying a lot of space in the bookstores because they print over a million copies in the first printing."

The most important thing for aspiring novelists to know about the market? "That it's changing." Over time, he says, "trends come and go, and genres come and go." For instance, "women's gothic horror doesn't exist anymore; chick lit is dying; supernatural romance is evolving into women's fiction; the western is no longer significant; thrillers are a tough sell right now," but, Miller contends, "A good love story, a *great* love story, is always going to have a market."

In reviewing material, Miller applies his own proven set of criteria. He asks himself of each manuscript: "Is the basic idea big enough, fresh enough, unique enough to be a book?" and "Does it have the architecture to be an entire book or is it just an article?" He analogizes showing vs. telling as "amateur vs. quality." Beyond the printed page, he also considers the writer's temperament and personality with key questions in mind: "Am I going to be friendly with my client?" and "Am I going to be passionate about representing him or her?"

The final test for him is one he recommends everyone employ. "Take yourself into the future three years from now and try to look back at what you've created in your life and aspire to greatness in ways that are completely out of the box." Miller prefers "long-term relationships with professional writers who desire to write a book every 10 months or year, who have tremendous passion, drive and talent." If he finds a synergy between what he wants to accomplish and the writer's own goals, he may make an offer of representation.

TERRI WINDLING

Award-winning writer, artist and co-director of the Endicott Studio for Mythic Arts, Terri Windling has published over 40 books that have been translated into as many as eight foreign languages. She has also worn the hats of a fantasy editor for Ace Books, an anthology editor and a consulting editor for Tor Books' fantasy line. "Reading fiction as an editor," she says, "is a very different process than reading privately for pleasure. I need to be more detached, interested not only in the plot but also in how skillfully the tale is told."

The ultimate deciding factors for publication are many and at times a work's fate rests solely upon the number of other saleable submissions inhabiting the same slush pile. The kind of story Windling will seriously consider is one in which "I find as I turn the pages that

I've stopped reading as an editor—I've slipped under the story's spell and I'm reading as a reader now, caught up and eager to find out what happens next.'' The antithesis, or insta-rejection? ''Clunky, sloppy, or cliché-ridden prose. No matter how good the idea behind a story is, if the writer doesn't have a feel for the rhythm of language, a good prose style, and a sound understanding of grammar, then I can't use it,'' she says. ''It always surprises me how many people submit stories, or even whole novels, before they've learned these basic aspects of their craft. It's like trying to play the violin at Carnegie Hall before you can even properly play scales.''

Windling believes that a writer's level of concern over market trends should be dictated by his or her objectives. ''If you see yourself as a commercial writer, and your primary goal is to be published soon and often, then keeping abreast of market trends makes good business sense.'' If you're a literary author who desires ''to create stories from your own heart's core, you might feel your creativity constrained if you're overly swayed by marketing concerns. Or, like many writers, you may be somewhere in the middle of this spectrum. The trick is finding what works best for you.''

Each path demands its own unique considerations. ''Sometimes if a certain form of fiction becomes fashionable, then everybody and her sister suddenly starts writing it, and your work can be lost in the pack.'' If you find ''there's not an easy marketing niche for your brand of work,'' Windling suggests, ''You might consider creating a new trend rather than changing your work to fit the old ones.'' Her own passion for mythic and fairy tale literature guided her to help build a market for it by creating various anthology and book series, and a web journal devoted to mythic arts. Her dedication paid off: ''Now you find mythic and fairy tale literature everywhere—but that's at least partially because a group of people worked hard and long to make this particular 'trend' happen.''

Likewise, Windling perceives that genre books are gaining greater credibility as ''writers like Susanna Clarke, Neil Gaiman, Philip Pullman, etc., are demonstrating that literary works can be created in all fields and genres.'' She sees this as a welcome evolution from when she was starting out and ''particularly in American publishing, genre and children's writers were most definitely second class citizens on the literary scene.''

Windling advocates remaining true to yourself as you navigate the publishing market. ''Don't write what you think you ought to write, but what you genuinely enjoy writing and are best suited to,'' she says. ''I've known authors who have tried to write literary works because they assumed that's what kind of writer they ought to be, only to find that they were actually happier creating commercial works. And I've known trendy, bestselling authors who were miserable because they were frustrated literary artists at heart.''

Getting Published

The Business of Fiction Writing

I t's true there are no substitutes for talent and hard work. A writer's first concern must always be attention to craft. No matter how well presented, a poorly written story or novel has little chance of being published. On the other hand, a well-written piece may be equally hard to sell in today's competitive publishing market. Talent alone is just not enough.

To be successful, writers need to study the field and pay careful attention to finding the right market. While the hours spent perfecting your writing are usually hours spent alone, you're not alone when it comes to developing your marketing plan. *Novel & Short Story Writer's Market* provides you with detailed listings containing the essential information you'll need to locate and contact the markets most suitable for your work.

Once you've determined where to send your work, you must turn your attention to presentation. We can help here, too. We've included the basics of manuscript preparation, along with information on submission procedures and how to approach markets. We also include tips on promoting your work. No matter where you're from or what level of experience you have, you'll find useful information here on everything from presentation to mailing to selling rights to promoting your work—the "business" of fiction.

APPROACHING MAGAZINE MARKETS

While it is essential for nonfiction markets, a query letter by itself is usually not needed by most magazine fiction editors. If you are approaching a magazine to find out if fiction is accepted, a query is fine, but editors looking for short fiction want to see *how* you write. A cover letter can be useful as a letter of introduction, but it must be accompanied by the actual piece. The key here is brevity. A successful cover letter is no more than one page (20 lb. bond paper). It should be single spaced with a double space between paragraphs, proofread carefully and neatly typed in a standard typeface (not script or italic). The writer's name, address and phone number appear at the top, and the letter is addressed, ideally, to a specific editor. (If the editor's name is unavailable, address to "Fiction Editor.")

The body of a successful cover letter contains the name and word count of the story, a brief list of previous publications if you have any, and the reason you are submitting to this particular publication. Mention that you have enclosed a self-addressed, stamped envelope or postcard for reply. Also let the editor know if you are sending a disposable manuscript that doesn't need to be returned. (More and more editors prefer disposable manuscripts that save them time and save you postage.) Finally, don't forget to thank the editor for considering your story. See the sample short story cover letter on page 67.

Note that more and more publications are open to receiving electronic submissions, both as e-mail attachments and through online submission forms. See individual listings for specific information on electronic submission requirements and always visit magazines' Web sites for up-to-date guidelines.

APPROACHING BOOK PUBLISHERS

Some book publishers do ask for queries first, but most want a query plus sample chapters or an outline or, occasionally, the complete manuscript. Again, make your letter brief. Include the essentials about yourself—name, address, phone number, e-mail and publishing experience. Include a 3 or 4 sentence ''pitch'' and only the personal information related to your story. Show that you have researched the market with a few sentences about why you chose this publisher. See the sample book query on page 68.

BOOK PROPOSALS

A book proposal is a package sent to a publisher that includes a cover letter and one or more of the following: sample chapters, outline, synopsis, author bio, publications list. When asked to send sample chapters, send up to three *consecutive* chapters. **An outline** covers the highlights of your book chapter by chapter. Be sure to include details on main characters, the plot and subplots. Outlines can run up to 30 pages, depending on the length of your novel. The object is to tell what happens in a concise, but clear, manner. **A synopsis** is a shorter summary of your novel, written in a way that expresses the emotion of the story in addition to just explaining the essential points. Evan Marshall, literary agent and author of *The Marshall Plan for Getting Your Novel Published* (Writer's Digest Books), suggests you aim for a page of synopsis for every 25 pages of manuscript. Marshall also advises you write the synopsis as one unified narrative, without section, subheads or chapters to break up the text. The terms synopsis and outline are sometimes used interchangeably, so be sure to find out exactly what each publisher wants.

A FEW WORDS ABOUT AGENTS

Agents are not usually needed for short fiction and most do not handle it unless they already have a working relationship with you. For novels, you may want to consider working with an agent, especially if you intend to market your book to publishers who do not look at unsolicited submissions. For more on approaching agents and to read listings of agents willing to work with beginning and established writers, see our Literary Agents section beginning on page 103 and refer to this year's edition of *Guide to Literary Agents*, edited by Chuck Sambuchino.

MANUSCRIPT MECHANICS

A professionally presented manuscript will not guarantee publication. But a sloppy, hard-to-read manuscript will not be read—publishers simply do not have the time. Here's a list of suggested submission techniques for polished manuscript presentation:

• **Use white, 8½ × 11 bond paper,** preferably 16 or 20 lb. weight. The paper should be heavy enough so it will not show pages underneath it and strong enough to take handling by several people.

• **Type your manuscript** on a computer and print it out using a laser or ink jet printer (or, if you must, use a typewriter with a new ribbon).

• **Proofread carefully.** An occasional white-out is okay, but don't send a marked-up manuscript with many typos. Keep a dictionary, thesaurus and stylebook handy and use the spellcheck function on your computer.

• **Always double space and leave a 1-inch margin** on all sides of the page.

• **For a short story manuscript,** your first page should include your name, address, phone number and e-mail address (single-spaced) in the upper left corner. In the upper right, indicate an approximate word count. Center the name of your story about one-third of the way down,

Short Story Cover Letter

Lauren Mosko
4700 East Galbraith Rd.
Cincinnati, OH 45236
Phone (513) 531-2690
Fax (513) 531-2687
lauren.mosko@fwpubs.com

March 2, 2008

Toni Graham
Cimarron Review
Oklahoma State University
205 Morrill Hall
Stillwater, OK 74078-0135

Dear Toni Graham:

I am submitting my short story, "Things From Which You Can Never Recover" (6,475 words), for your consideration in *Cimarron Review*.

I am currently an editor for Writer's Digest Books and my essays, interviews and reviews have been published in several books in the Writer's Market series, as well as *The Writer's Digest Handbook of Magazine Article Writing* (2nd ed.), *I.D. Magazine*, and the alt weeklies *Louisville Eccentric Observer* and (Cincinnati's now-defunct) *Everybody's News*.

Enclosed you will also find an SASE for your response; you may recycle the manuscript. This is a simultaneous submission.

Your listing in *Novel & Short Story Writer's Market* says you are seeking work with "unusual perspective, language, imagery and character," and I think my story fits this description. I hope you enjoy it. Thank you in advance for your time and consideration.

Sincerely,

Lauren Mosko

Encl: Short story, "Things From Which You Can Never Recover"
      SASE

This sample cover letter is professional, brief and succinct. It doesn't waste a second of the editor's time and allows the writer's work to speak for itself. The power is in the precise details: the name of the editor, the title of the story, the word count, the writer's publishing history, and attention to the journal's submission guidelines (noting that a SASE is enclosed, and that this is a simultaneous submission).

Query to Publisher: Novel

Teresa McClain
273 Chesterfield Lane
Sacramento, CA 99999
(714)555-6262
teresawriter@email.com

November 20, 1996 ————————————————— 1 line

Addressed to specific editor

Steven T. Murray, Editor-in-Chief
Fjord Press
P.O. Box 16349
Seattle, WA 98116 ————————————————— 1 line

Dear Mr. Murray: ————————————————— 1 line

Single-spaced text

Please consider reviewing a novel that I have completed concerning the emotional struggles a thirteen-year-old African-American boy endures when his mother declares that he must leave his native Harlem and move —— **Sounds good** down south (Florida) to live with a father he has never known. Entitled *Plenty Good Room*, the manuscript is written entirely from the viewpoint —— **She got me here!** of the thirteen-year-old (a la *Catcher in the Rye*) and is a first-person account replete with emotion and stingingly blunt dialogue. This book is not a children's book. The language is contemporary and often raw and —— **Got me again!** unrelenting. The book is, however, a timely exposé on a young black male growing up in a single-parent home where the parent is too young, too inexperienced, and too poor to adequately parent and where the father is not at all involved. ————————————————— 1 line

Now I'm hooked—got to read this

Good that she gives a clear idea of the overall structure of the novel

The manuscript is divided into three stages of the young man's life: His life in New York and the events that subsequently lead to his mother's insistence that his father shoulder the remaining responsibility of rearing him; the not so clear-cut path he takes to become a part of his father's life; and his life with his father and the ultimate unraveling of a dream he thought had come true.

Details enclosures in the body of the letter—perfectly fine

I have enclosed the first twenty pages of my thirteen-chapter manuscript. Please notify me if you are interested in reviewing my complete text for possible publishing considerations. I have also enclosed an SASE for your prompt response.

Sincerely,

Signature

Teresa McClain

Comments provided by Steven Murray of Fjord Press.

skip a line and center your byline (byline is optional). Skip four lines and begin your story. On subsequent pages, put last name and page number in the upper right hand corner.

• **For book manuscripts,** use a separate title page. Put your name, address, phone number and e-mail address in the lower right corner and word count in the upper right. If you have representation, list your agent's name and address in the lower right. (This bumps your name and contact information to the upper left corner.) Center your title and byline about halfway down the page. Start your first chapter on the next page. Center the chapter number and title (if there is one) one-third of the way down the page. Include your last name and the novel's title in all caps in the upper left and put the page number in the upper right of this page and each page to follow. Start each chapter with a new page.

• **Include a word count.** If you work on a computer, chances are your word processing program can give you a word count. (If you are using a typewriter, there are a number of ways to count the number of words in your piece. One way is to count the words in five lines and divide that number by five to find an average. Then count the number of lines and multiply to find the total words. For long pieces, you may want to count the words in the first three pages, divide by three and multiply by the number of pages you have.)

• **Always keep a copy.** Manuscripts do get lost. To avoid expensive mailing costs, send only what is required. If you are including artwork or photos but you are not positive they will be used, send photocopies. Artwork is hard to replace.

• **Suggest art where applicable.** Most publishers do not expect you to provide artwork and some insist on selecting their own illustrators, but if you have suggestions, please let them know. Magazine publishers work in a very visual field and are usually open to ideas.

• **Enclose a self-addressed, stamped envelope (SASE)** if you want a reply or if you want your manuscript returned. For most letters, a business-size (#10) envelope will do. Avoid using any envelope too small for an $8\frac{1}{2} \times 11$ sheet of paper. For manuscripts, be sure to include enough postage and an envelope large enough to contain it. If you are requesting a sample copy of a magazine or a book publisher's catalog, send an envelope big enough to fit.

• **Consider sending a disposable manuscript** that saves editors time and saves you money.

• **When sending electronic submissions** via e-mail or online submission form, check the publisher's Web site or contact them first for specific information and follow the directions carefully.

• **Keep accurate records.** This can be done in a number of ways, but be sure to keep track of where your stories are and how long they have been ''out.'' Write down submission dates. If you do not hear about your submission for a long time—about one to two months longer than the reporting time stated in the listing—you may want to contact the publisher. When you do, you will need an accurate record for reference.

MAILING TIPS
When mailing short correspondence or short manuscripts:
• Fold manuscripts under five pages into thirds and send in a business-size (#10) envelope.

• Mail manuscripts five pages or more unfolded in a 9×12 or 10×13 envelope.

• Mark envelopes in all caps, FIRST CLASS MAIL or SPECIAL FOURTH CLASS MANU-SCRIPT RATE.

• For return envelope, fold it in half, address it to yourself and add a stamp or, if going to a foreign country, International Reply Coupons (available at the main branch of your local post office).

• Don't send by certified mail. This is a sign of an amateur and publishers do not appreciate receiving unsolicited manuscripts this way.

• For the most current postage rates, visit the United States Postal Service online at www.usps.com.

When mailing book-length manuscripts:

First Class Mail over 11 ounces (about 65 8½×11 20 lb.-weight pages) automatically becomes **PRIORITY MAIL.**

Metered Mail may be dropped in any post office box, but meter strips on SASEs should not be dated.

The Postal Service provides, free of charge, tape, boxes and envelopes to hold up to two pounds for those using PRIORITY and EXPRESS MAIL. Requirements for mailing FOURTH CLASS and PARCEL POST have not changed.

Main branches of local banks will cash foreign checks, but keep in mind payment quoted in our listings by publishers in other countries is usually payment in their currency. Also note reporting time is longer in most overseas markets. To save time and money, you may want to include a return postcard (and IRC) with your submission and forgo asking for a manuscript to be returned. If you live in Canada, see "Canadian Writers Take Note" on page 345.

Important note about IRCs: Foreign editors sometimes find IRCs have been stamped incorrectly by the U.S. post office when purchased. This voids the IRCs and makes it impossible for foreign editors to exchange the coupons for return postage for your manuscript. When buying IRCs, make sure yours have been stamped correctly before you leave the counter. (Each IRC should be stamped on the bottom *left* side of the coupon, not the right.) More information about International Reply Coupons, including an image of a correctly stamped IRC, is available on the USPS Web site (www.usps.com).

RIGHTS

The Copyright Law states that writers are selling one-time rights (in almost all cases) unless they and the publisher have agreed otherwise. A list of various rights follows. Be sure you know exactly what rights you are selling before you agree to the sale.

• **Copyright** is the legal right to exclusive publication, sale or distribution of a literary work. As the writer or creator of a written work, you need simply to include your name, date and the copyright symbol © on your piece in order to copyright it. Be aware, however, that most editors today consider placing the copyright symbol on your work the sign of an amateur and many are even offended by it.

To get specific answers to questions about copyright (but not legal advice), you can call the Copyright Public Information Office at (202)707-3000 weekdays between 8:30 a.m. and 5 p.m. EST. Publications listed in *Novel & Short Story Writer's Market* are copyrighted *unless* otherwise stated. In the case of magazines that are not copyrighted, be sure to keep a copy of your manuscript with your notice printed on it. For more information on copyrighting your work see *The Copyright Handbook: How to Protect & Use Written Works*, 8th edition, by Stephen Fishman (Nolo Press, 2005).

Some people are under the mistaken impression that copyright is something they have to send away for, and that their writing is not properly protected until they have "received" their copyright from the government. The fact is, you don't have to register your work with the Copyright Office in order for your work to be copyrighted; any piece of writing is copyrighted the moment it is put to paper.

Although it is generally unnecessary, registration is a matter of filling out an application form (for writers, that's Form TX) and sending the completed form, a nonreturnable copy of the work in question and a check for $45 to the Library of Congress, Copyright Office, Register of Copyrights, 101 Independence Ave. SE, Washington DC 20559-6000. If the thought of paying $45 each to register every piece you write does not appeal to you, you can cut costs by registering a group of your works with one form, under one title for one $45 fee.

Most magazines are registered with the Copyright Office as single collective entities themselves; that is, the individual works that make up the magazine are *not* copyrighted individually in the names of the authors. You'll need to register your article yourself if you wish to have the additional protection of copyright registration.

For more information, visit the United States Copyright Office online at www.copyright.gov.

• **First Serial Rights**—This means the writer offers a newspaper or magazine the right to publish the article, story or poem for the first time in a particular periodical. All other rights to the material remain with the writer. The qualifier ''North American'' is often added to this phrase to specify a geographical limit to the license.

When material is excerpted from a book scheduled to be published and it appears in a magazine or newspaper prior to book publication, this is also called first serial rights.

• **One-time Rights**—A periodical that licenses one-time rights to a work (also known as simultaneous rights) buys the *nonexclusive* right to publish the work once. That is, there is nothing to stop the author from selling the work to other publications at the same time. Simultaneous sales would typically be to periodicals without overlapping audiences.

• **Second Serial (Reprint) Rights**—This gives a newspaper or magazine the opportunity to print an article, poem or story after it has already appeared in another newspaper or magazine. Second serial rights are nonexclusive; that is, they can be licensed to more than one market.

• **All Rights**—This is just what it sounds like. All rights means a publisher may use the manuscript anywhere and in any form, including movie and book club sales, without further payment to the writer (although such a transfer, or *assignment*, of rights will terminate after 35 years). If you think you'll want to use the material later, you must avoid submitting to such markets or refuse payment and withdraw your material. Ask the editor whether he is willing to buy first rights instead of all rights before you agree to an assignment or sale. Some editors will reassign rights to a writer after a given period, such as one year. It's worth an inquiry in writing.

• **Subsidiary Rights**—These are the rights, other than book publication rights, that should be covered in a book contract. These may include various serial rights; movie, television, audiotape and other electronic rights; translation rights, etc. The book contract should specify who controls these rights (author or publisher) and what percentage of sales from the licensing of these sub rights goes to the author.

• **Dramatic, Television and Motion Picture Rights**—This means the writer is selling his material for use on the stage, in television or in the movies. Often a one-year option to buy such rights is offered (generally for 10% of the total price). The interested party then tries to sell the idea to other people—actors, directors, studios or television networks, etc. Some properties are optioned over and over again, but most fail to become dramatic productions. In such cases, the writer can sell his rights again and again—as long as there is interest in the material. Though dramatic, TV and motion picture rights are more important to the fiction writer than the nonfiction writer, producers today are increasingly interested in nonfiction material; many biographies, topical books and true stories are being dramatized.

• **Electronic Rights**—These rights cover usage in a broad range of electronic media, from online magazines and databases to CD-ROM magazine anthologies and interactive games. The editor should specify in writing if—and which—electronic rights are being requested. The presumption is that unspecified rights are kept by the writer.

Compensation for electronic rights is a major source of conflict between writers and publishers, as many book publishers seek control of them and many magazines routinely include electronic rights in the purchase of print rights, often with no additional payment. Alternative ways of handling this issue include an additional 15 percent added to the amount to purchase first rights and a royalty system based on the number of times an article is accessed from an electronic database.

MARKETING AND PROMOTION

Everyone agrees writing is hard work whether you are published or not. Yet, once you achieve publication the work changes. Now, not only do you continue writing and revising your next project, you must also concern yourself with getting your book into the hands of readers. It becomes time to switch hats from artist to salesperson.

While even best-selling authors whose publishers have committed big bucks to marketing are asked to help promote their books, new authors may have to take it upon themselves to plan and initiate some of their own promotion, sometimes dipping into their own pockets. While this does not mean that every author is expected to go on tour, sometimes at their own expense, it does mean authors should be prepared to offer suggestions for promoting their books.

About Our Policies

Important

We occasionally receive letters asking why a certain magazine, publisher or contest is not in the book. Sometimes when we contact listings, the editors do not want to be listed because they:

- do not use very much fiction.
- are overwhelmed with submissions.
- are having financial difficulty or have been recently sold.
- use only solicited material.
- accept work from a select group of writers only.
- do not have the staff or time for the many unsolicited submissions a listing may bring.

Some of the listings do not appear because we have chosen not to list them. We investigate complaints of unprofessional conduct in editors' dealings with writers and misrepresentation of information provided to us by editors and publishers. If we find these reports to be true, after a thorough investigation, we will delete the listing from future editions.

There is no charge to the companies that list in this book. Listings appearing in *Novel & Short Story Writer's Market* are compiled from detailed questionnaires, phone interviews and information provided by editors, publishers, and awards and conference directors. The publishing industry is volatile and changes of address, editor, policies and needs happen frequently. To keep up with the changes between editions of the book, we suggest you check the market information on the *Writer's Market* Web site at www.writersmarket.com, or on the *Writer's Digest* Web site at www.writersdigest.com. Many magazine and book publishers offer updated information for writers on their Web sites. Check individual listings for those Web site addresses.

Organization newsletters and small magazines devoted to helping writers also list market information. Several offer online writers' bulletin boards, message centers and chat lines with up-to-the-minute changes and happenings in the writing community.

We rely on our readers, as well, for new markets and information about market conditions. E-mail us if you have any new information or if you have suggestions on how to improve our listings to better suit your writing needs.

Depending on the time, money and personal preferences of the author and publisher, a promotional campaign could mean anything from mailing out press releases to setting up book signings to hitting the talk-show circuit. Most writers can contribute to their own promotion by providing contact names—reviewers, hometown newspapers, civic groups, organizations—that might have a special interest in the book or the writer.

Above all, when it comes to promotion, be creative. What is your book about? Try to capitalize on it. Focus on your potential audiences and how you can help them to connect with your book.

Important Listing Information

- Listings are not advertisements. Although the information here is as accurate as possible, the listings are not endorsed or guaranteed by the editors of *Novel & Short Story Writer's Market*.

- *Novel & Short Story Writer's Market* reserves the right to exclude any listing that does not meet its requirements.

Getting Published

Edward D. Hoch

*Building Whodunits With
'What If?' and 'Then What?'*

by W.E. Reinka

The calendar scene above Edward D. Hoch's desk showed a quaint covered bridge. Staring at the photo, Hoch suddenly flashed on a story idea.

What if someone drove onto the covered bridge but never came out?

Minutes later he was composing one of his most famous stories, "The Problem of the Covered Bridge" in which buggy tracks in the snow lead into a covered bridge and stop half way. No tracks back out; no tracks beyond; no buggy.

More recently he was reading a newspaper article about a bird shelter in Arizona where cast-off pet birds could find sanctuary. Soon he was clacking his computer keys on "A Bird in Sand" in which a murder investigation leads to a discovery that homing pigeons are smuggling drugs from Mexico in tiny vials attached to their legs.

Writers typically flinch when asked "Where do you get your ideas?" Imagine how often Ed Hoch has been asked that given that he's been publishing stories for more than 50 years, which is just about how long he and his wife, Patricia, have been married. His published story count stands at around 955. He has contributed to every issue of *Ellery Queen's Mystery Magazine* for the last 35 years.

"Janet Hutchings, my editor at Ellery *Queen's Mystery Magazine*, figures I'm about five years away from reaching 1,000 published stories." And after he reaches 1,000? "I'll write number 1,001 and keep on going."

But, still, where does he get those ideas? Something—a calendar page, newspaper article, history book—plants a seed. That seed could be any number of things: a setting, a character or plot twist. He then nurtures that seed through a series of "what if?" questions to himself. Sometimes plots fall quickly into place. Other stories stump him until he works through them in hopefully not too convoluted fashion. "My wife sometimes complains that my stories get too complicated," he says with a chuckle.

He still remembers how his first published story germinated. "I was watching people at an amusement park pier walking down to the pier to meet the returning boat. They were strolling down group by group before the boat even arrived and I asked myself what if they all kept walking straight into the water?" He follows with more "what if" and "then what" questions to himself. People imitating lemmings are intriguing but not a story. Why are they jumping? Who or what is controlling them? How does the crime solver figure things out?

Case in point, in one of Hoch's most famous stories, "The Long Way Down," a man leaps

---

W.E. REINKA who frequently writes about books and authors, contributes essays, fiction and articles to publications nationwide.

from a skyscraper window but doesn't hit the pavement until three hours later. "Of course, I tried to capture the reader's attention with the supposed delayed landing. But, in order for the story to work, I also had to come up with a believable reason for the man to go out the window in the first place."

Chances are that when Hoch isn't writing, he's reading, including at mealtimes, "probably something my wife doesn't always appreciate." From his love of history he builds stories around historical events—the McKinley assassination or the way a flimflam man bilks a tiny western town on the day the nation switches to standardized time zones.

Speaking of reading, his first advice to aspiring writers is to "read, read, read." Just as tennis players seek matches with better players to improve their game, Hoch encourages writers to read "better writers than themselves." As for specific tips such as limiting the use of modifiers, Hoch says "doing lots of reading will cure all that."

Reading writers better than himself and writing almost every day helped him break through the rejection slips he started collecting when he was a high school junior until he published his first story at age 26. Even during his Army stint during the Korean War, Hoch continued to write. With no access to a typewriter during his Army days, he would write stories long hand and send them home to his mother who would type them for him.

Still, when he kept receiving one rejection slip after another, why didn't he give up? Maybe follow his father's footsteps and become a banker in his hometown of Rochester, New York.

After deciding in high school to become a writer, he simply never wavered in his determination. He's never had to force himself to write. Even when he still worked a day job writing press releases and advertising copy he still had no trouble coming home to write fiction at night. Besides, like a lot of writers approaching the brink of success, the pre-printed rejection slips eventually became more encouraging with hand-written compliments in the margins.

© Crippen & Landru Publishers. Reprinted with permission.

At one time, he had a backlog of about 100 unpublished stories. Eventually he sold them all. These days he figures he writes about 18 stories per year. No sooner does he finish one than he starts on the next—either the same day or the next morning.

"One of the things that bugs me about a lot of beginning writers is that they send out a story and wait for a reply. Let it go! Start the next one immediately."

Exactly how he starts the next story often depends on whether he's writing a stand-alone or using one of his series characters. Yes, if you've published almost 1,000 stories you can run series characters just as crime fiction novelists do.

Take Dr. Sam Hawthorne, a country doctor who ages over the years starting in 1922 when he establishes his practice. "The Problem of the Covered Bridge" is a Dr. Sam story. Dr. Sam solves "locked room" cases where a murder victim is found in a room (or caboose, windmill, lobster shack, etc.) with all the doors and windows locked from the inside. These are all "fair play" stories where the clues are laid out. No heretofore undiscovered secret panels, false floors or accomplices are part of the solution. The devoted Hoch reader learns that little gratuitous information seeps into the plot. If a handyman spills green paint on his coveralls or a widow takes a cherry pie to the church potluck, chances are that information is going to figure in the plot. The murder doesn't take place until well into the story after the clues are laid out.

Sometimes readers get sidetracked in impossible stories concentrating on how the murderer managed to set up the locked room. And, truly, that's one of the reasons that they're so much fun to read. However, impossible crimes still must contain all the essential elements of crime fiction. They are whodunits not just howdunits. "Part of writing an impossible story beyond the trickery is to establish motive and opportunity as with any other crime story—not only who killed the victim but why and when."

Stories featuring investigative detective Captain Leopold require an entirely different technique than Dr. Sam "impossible crime" stories because they're police procedurals. As such, they are front-weighted with the body turning up on the first page. Hoch won an Edgar, the "Oscar" of mysterydom, in 1968 for "The Oblong Room," a Captain Leopold story.

Nick Velvet, perhaps Hoch's most popular series character, is less frequently involved in murder. Velvet is a thief-for-hire (current fee $50,000 plus expenses) who will steal only valueless items. For example, in one story, he's hired to steal the four of spades from every deck of cards in a fortune teller's apartment to skew a scheduled clairvoyant reading. Of course, the stories always contain twists so that they're not so simple as whether Velvet successfully carries out his assignment.

Hoch has written a few novels over the years—crime fiction and science-fiction/fantasy. "But those were usually undertaken at an editor's commission. I always felt attracted to the short form. Novels take too long and start to bore me after a while." Obviously the short form suits him. Hoch is the only primarily short-story writer named as Grand Master by the Mystery Writers of America. He has also received Lifetime Achievement Awards at Bouchercon and the Private Eye Writers of America.

Hoch is well-traveled but not as well-traveled as his characters. That's where his research comes in. He writes in the bedroom he set aside as his writing office when he and his new bride moved into their house. Downstairs in the basement, thousands of books line the walls reflecting his interest in history and travel. After reading stories featuring Michael Vlado, the Gypsy Sleuth, readers would swear that Hoch knows Romania inside out but he's never been there.

Hoch's research into places he's never been reflects his no-excuses, sit-down, write-the-story approach to fiction. Perhaps this writer of impossible crimes owes his success to a lifelong attitude that nothing is impossible when it comes to his characters, his stories and his career. After all, who would ever believe that in today's world, one might make a living writing stories?

Editor's note: On January 17, 2008, not long after this interview was conducted, Edward D. Hoch passed at the age of 77. He published nearly 1,000 short stories and several novels throughout his long and celebrated career as a fiction writer.

Francine Mathews

Daring to Write

by Deborah Bouziden

Francine Mathews, also known as Stephanie Barron, began her writing career in 1992 on a dare. As a CIA analyst, Mathews was tired of working in an office all day. She had other aspirations.

"I told my husband I dreamed of working at home on my own, without a boss, and according to nobody's schedule," Mathews says. "He stared at me as if I were insane. 'You're paid to think,' he said. 'Do you know how rare that is in this country? You should be down on your knees thanking God for your job.'"

Mathews knew he was right—it *was* a dream job, but it wasn't *her* dream.

"So, we compromised," she said. "I would not quit my job simply to 'write' in poverty. in the suburbs. But if I could begin and complete a manuscript while continuing my salaried employment—and sell the manuscript to a real publisher—I could kiss the Agency goodbye. It was an immensely useful dare."

That dare gave Mathews a goal and an incentive. The next day, she set to work and in nine months completed *Death in the Off-Season*. Five months later, Mathews found an agent. With her book finished and in the capable hands of an agent, she went ahead and left her job as an analyst.

"He spent six weeks mailing the manuscript out before it found a home," Mathews said. "I had already quit my job and was in the process of moving from Washington, D.C. to Denver, Colorado. I got the news of the sale at a Stuckey's in Kansas."

Six months after that, her agent negotiated a two-book deal for her with Morrow/Avon. Mathews has come a long way since then. While she started out writing mysteries, she leaped into espionage thrillers with equal writing grace. However, that leap was not without momentary pause. When she left the CIA, Mathews had to sign a Secrecy Agreement, which obligated her to submit her written espionage work for review and clearance.

"(Working for the CIA) is indeed an obligation for life, but it has yet to prove a burdensome one," Mathews said. "I write fiction and fiction is inherently deniable. Many of my books have emerged utterly unchanged from the review process."

Writing as Stephanie Barron, Mathews has written nine Jane Austen mysteries. Casting Jane Austen as lead character in her books, Barron weaves stories of intrigue and murder while allowing Austen, the sleuth, to solve crimes.

Currently working on her nineteenth novel, Mathews is always finding new characters

DEBORAH BOUZIDEN has been writing and publishing articles and books since 1983. To read more about her and her work, visit her Web site, www.deborahbouziden.com.

and situations to write about. "I find, in general, that there are more stories than I have time to write—everything I encounter presents intriguing possibilities."

With your background in journalism, why did you decide to write novels?

I believe firmly that the ability to write well is a cognitive predisposition—that writers are born with the tendency to process life experience through words. We're verbal people, in short. I have always been someone who wrote to understand the things that happened to me. For years, that impulse took the form of journal entries, letters, poems, newspaper articles. In graduate school, it was academic papers. On the *Miami Herald*, crime reports. At the CIA, it found an outlet in predictive policy analysis. But fiction is a different animal—fiction begs the question of *art*. Fiction can be judged by complete strangers as unworthy of the paper it's printed on. Fiction is scary. And so writers avoid it. It's the ultimate test. And failing it means the loss of a lifelong dream. I couldn't attempt fiction much before the age of 30. I hadn't endured enough living, and I was too intimidated by the perceived need to produce art. I liberated my inner novelist when I decided to write suspense fiction—because however artful it might be, it is first and foremost *entertainment*. I felt I could attempt and achieve entertainment without terrifying myself into silence.

When you were presented with the challenge of writing the book, how did you decide which genre?

I deliberately chose a detective novel for my first book-length fiction, because I felt its underlying architecture—the puzzle plot—would provide a useful framework. A map, as it were, I could follow from page one to page 473. I sat down and analyzed five mysteries I particularly loved, and realized two things: They were tightly plotted and perfectly coherent despite their deliberately obscured plot; and each of them devoted a good deal of effort to the emotional growth of their characters. Both aspects were important to me. And so I set myself the task of crafting a watertight plot with compelling people as guides to the resolution. Finally, I recognized motive is the primary instigator of all action in a mystery plot. This is not to say it's the first element the reader encounters, or even the most compelling—but the writer has to know the reason death tears apart the lives of her characters. Only then does the rest of the book feel plausible.

Your books have many twists and turns. How do you keep the plots moving forward?

I'm a highly analytic person, and plotting is essential to my success as a writer. I always draft a narrative summary of the story before attempting to write; this is usually about 10 pages, double-spaced, rather than a strict encapsulation of each chapter. I also tend to do what I call sub-outlines, which nail down the specifics of each 100 pages of the manuscript; the first 100 has to accomplish a certain groundwork and movement in the plot that is entirely different from the middle 200 pages or the concluding 100 to 150. These sections of a book are as distinct as the acts of a screenplay or the movements of a piece of music, and sub-outlines help to keep them tight.

Why the choices to use first person in the Jane Austen novels and third in your others?

The question of voice is an important one. I prefer, frankly, to write from the omniscient third person—because it provides immense flexibility in plotting. One may reveal certain facts to the reader, through the actions of a secondary character, that are unknown to the protagonist of the novel; and this affords the reader a sense of privileged information, of investigating alongside of the protagonist with a unique set of tools. In the Austen novels, however, I employed the idea of "found" journals written by Jane—in an effort to lend authenticity to the series premise. I wanted to capture the first-person voice of her letters, which is freer, more intimate, more careless, more caustic than the contained narrative voice of her novels. Therefore, the books had to be written in the first person.

What are some of the main differences between writing mystery and writing espionage thrillers?

There is no question that suspense is more difficult to write than the classic mystery novel. Thrillers, even historical thrillers, have a broad cast of characters, simultaneously occurring subplots, and a tightness of pace designed to sustain suspense. This is an extraordinarily complex dance to choreograph. It cannot be done well in a single draft, and thus demands constant fine-tuning, revision, and self-editing. I spend perhaps eight weeks writing a Jane Austen mystery, which is straightforward narrative; I may spend eight months writing a suspense novel. I cannot say, however, I prefer one to the other. I love them both.

What has been the most difficult experience you've faced in your writing career?

Writing *Blown* was the most difficult thing I've ever done. It's a book about counterterrorism and political betrayal. I was immensely angry when I wrote it, and fierce agendas invariably get in the way of entertaining fiction. I wrote four distinct manuscripts over a period of two years before I got the book right. Only the third and fourth had anything to do with each other—and even then, the changes were immense. I shall never forget my editor at Bantam, Kate Miciak, telling me after she'd read the third manuscript: *This works. But your actual first chapter is Chapter 24.* I went back and cut the first two hundred pages, started page one at Chapter 24, and wrote the fourth version of that book.

If you had one piece of advice to give those who want to write but are perhaps putting it off because of their career, what would you tell them?

Sit down one rainy Saturday afternoon and write a one-page summary of your story. Try to capture the most compelling plot idea, the reason you *have to write* this book. It is essential, I should say, that you also know how the story *ends*; everyone knows how their story begins. Beginning is the easy part, which is why so many of us have 67 pages of five different novels sitting in our bedroom closets. The following week, sit down and expand that one page to five or seven, talking yourself through the action of the novel: beginning, middle, end. Main protagonist, main antagonist, essential conflict, resolution. Once you have this plot summary, write a page a day. A double-spaced page in 12-point font is a mere 250 words—something you could rattle off in a single cell phone call. Write a page a day, and you'll have a book in a year. The important thing is to start.

Resources

Where to Look for More Information

Below is a list of invaluable resources specifically for mystery writers. To order any of the Writer's Digest Books titles or to get a consumer book catalog, call (800)448-0915. You may also order Writer's Digest Books selections through www.fwbookstore .com, Amazon.com, or www.barnesandnoble.com.

MAGAZINES:

- *Mystery Readers Journal*, Mystery Readers International, P.O. Box 8116, Berkeley CA 94707. Web site: www.mysteryreaders.org.
- *Mystery News*, Black Raven Press, PMB 152, 105 E. Townline Rd., Vernon Hills IL 60061-1424. Web site: www.blackravenpress.com.
- *Mystery Scene*, 331 W. 57th St., Suite 148, New York NY 10019. Web site: www.mysterys cenemag.com.

BOOKS:

Howdunit series (Writer's Digest Books):

- *Modus Operandi: A Writer's Guide to How Criminals Work*, by Mauro V. Corvasce and Joseph R. Paglino
- *Missing Persons: A Writer's Guide to Finding the Lost, the Abducted and the Escaped*, by Fay Faron
- *Book of Poisons*, by Serita Stevens and Anne Bannon
- *Scene of the Crime: A Writer's Guide to Crime Scene Investigation*, by Anne Wingate, Ph.D.
- *Book of Police Procedure and Investigation*, by Lee Lofland

Other Writer's Digest Books for mystery writers:

- *The Criminal Mind, A Writer's Guide to Forensic Psychology*, by Katherine Ramsland
- *Writing Mysteries: A Handbook by the Mystery Writers of America*, edited by Sue Grafton
- *Writing and Selling Your Mystery Novel: How to Knock 'em Dead With Style*, by Hallie Ephron
- *You Can Write a Mystery*, by Gillian Roberts

ORGANIZATIONS & ONLINE:

- Crime Writers of Canada. Web site: www.crimewriterscanada.com.
- Crime Writers' Association. Web site: www.thecwa.co.uk.
- Mystery Writers of America, 17 E. 47th St., 6th Floor, New York NY 10017. Web site: www.mysterywriters.org

- The Private Eye Writers of America, 4342 Forest DeVille Dr., Apt. H, St. Louis MO 63129. Web site: http://hometown.aol.com/rrandisi/myhomepage/writing.html
- Sisters in Crime, P.O. Box 442124, Lawrence KS 66044-8933. Web site: www.sistersincrime.org
- Writer's Market Web site: www.writersmarket.com.
- Writer's Digest Web site: www.writersdigest.com.

Amanda Harte

Write What You Love to Read

by Mary Hagan

Most novelists do not sell the first book they write. Romance writer Amanda Harte was an exception—she sold her first novel, *Half Heart*, to Dell. This was a dream come true for Harte, who had decided to be a writer at the age of seven. However, when she graduated from Syracuse University with a degree in French, she was certain she couldn't make a living writing fiction. "Although I had a goal of being published before my 30 birthday, I didn't pursue it." She put her dream on hold and took a day job in Information Technology, for which she wrote "enough technical articles to cure insomnia in a medium-sized city."

Then 22 years after first deciding to be a writer, she made the decision to seriously pursue her dream. "I've since discovered that writing is as necessary to me as breathing," she says, "but at the time it was a horrible day job that convinced me it was time to make my dream come true. That was the impetus I needed to become a serious writer."

One month before her 29th birthday, she started a novel after seeing a TV commercial for Harlequin romances. "The ad intrigued me enough to buy one book from each line—at the time there were only two—and read them both. I was hooked." Her first book, *Half Heart*, for which she called on her experience studying in France, did not sell to Harlequin but did sell to Dell under the name Amanda Preble. The 50,000 word book is a highly emotional story about a woman who goes to France to recover from her fiancé's death in a plane crash.

CREATING COMPELLING CHARACTERS

Harte has gone on to write many more books, drawing readers into her romances with greatly flawed characters and an underlying theme of the healing power of love. Her characters' handicaps have ranged widely in severity and cause, from a little boy in *Stargazer* who's so traumatized by his mother's death that he's become mute, to the hero of *Whistling in the Dark* who has such poor eyesight the Army rejected him. Harte's current work-in-progress features a woman who walks with a limp. Harte does not possess a morbid fascination with handicaps, but rather loves books where characters overcome major obstacles.

To create such characters, Harte taps into her empathy, which helps her to draw realistic

MARY HAGAN lives in Ft. Collins, Colorado, where she's an avid skier, hiker and outdoor enthusiast. She has authored four nonfiction books, two on outdoor subjects and two on history. Her feature articles have appeared in local and national papers and magazines. Several of her children's stories have been published in leading magazines. Currently, she is revising a hiking guide and working on a novel.

portraits of people with problems—both emotional and physical. She can identify with her characters enough that she can be convincing in her descriptions, tapping into thoughts and feelings of those facing obstacles and problems that she's never personally experienced.

Harte compares writers to oysters. "We both create pearls, although not necessarily by choice. The oyster doesn't want to create a pearl; he does it in response to the irritation of sand inside his shell. For me, the irritations are those stories that take residence inside my head and demand to be written, or—in the case of my first book—it was a day job that demanded escape."

To Harte, the appeal of romance both as a writer and a reader is the happy ending. "In today's world where so much of news is depressing, I think readers get comfort from knowing—no matter what terrible things happen to the characters during the course of the book—there will be a happily-ever-after."

As a reader, Harte enjoys books with connected characters, so she often uses them in her work, with the main character in one book having a minor role in a second one. Historical romances *Midnight Sun* and *Rainbows at Midnight* (Leisure Books) take place in the same fictional Alaskan town and feature some of the same characters. She has loosely connected characters in the Unwanted Legacies romances with Avalon. Books in her Hidden Falls series (Avalon Books) are a mixture of contemporary/historical fiction that feature the carousel in the fictional town of Hidden Falls with continuing characters and a continuing plot line about how three children lives are affected by the death of their parents in a fire.

TACKLING HISTORICAL FICTION

Harte's War Brides trilogy, *Dancing in the Rain*, *Whistling in the Dark*, and *Laughing at Thunder* (Avalon) is her series that has attracted the most attention. Three sisters faced with World War I are featured as the heroines. "I was asked to write the series even though I was convinced it wasn't an interesting time period. Was I ever wrong. I now have plans for at least three more books set during The Great War."

With the exception of the War Brides books which she was asked to write, for Harte there is no pattern to what triggers an idea for a book. "A chance encounter with a carousel horse in—of all places—an Interstate rest stop led to *Carousel of Dreams*. A song piped through a restaurant in Phoenix led to *Bluebonnet Spring* (Avalon)." Her experiences in Europe when her husband was stationed there with the U.S. Army inspired her first historical novel set in France, *Silver Thorns* (Denise Little Presents, Kensington Publishing).

Harte says the most difficult novel she has written was a historical, *North Star*. Taking place during the era of the Underground Railroad, *North Star* features a deaf child and deals with the after effects of abuse. During the time the novel took place, not much was known about deafness, and abuse was swept under the carpet. "I find abuse extremely disturbing and wept as I wrote several of the scenes," she says, "but I thought it was a topic that needed to be addressed." Additionally, instead of the fictional towns she normally creates for her novels, this book takes place in historic Buffalo, New York, so she was worried about accuracy.

"I did a tremendous amount of research on the topics, but did take a few liberties with one procedure that I described as curing deafness. Mostly, because I was dealing with a real location, I lived with the fear that readers would send me hate mail, telling me that such and such a street wasn't cobblestoned at the time, or that the theater was in the wrong location. I got no such mail, but the concern did make the whole writing process more difficult."

When the book was finished, Harte was convinced it was mediocre. Others disagreed. *Affaire de Coeur* nominated it as Best American Historical that year, and her publisher felt so strongly about the book she sent it to Oprah. Oprah didn't select it for her book club, but Harte was both astonished and thrilled that Leisure Books thought it was special enough for consideration.

THE WRITING PROCESS

Harte begins her books with a setting or timeframe—sometimes both—and then finds characters who would live there. Plot evolves from both setting/timeframe and the characters who are put in a dramatic situation in that setting. She writes a synopsis, then a chapter-by-chapter outline, followed by the first draft, then a second, and then a final polishing. "Fellow writers shake their heads in dismay when they hear about my extremely organized method of writing, but it works for me."

During the time it takes her to write a book, Harte claims she grows to know her characters as well as she knows herself. She changes from being an onlooker watching them to actually being a part of them, living their emotions.

Harte writes in multiple genres—contemporary romance, historical romance, mysteries, women's fiction—all with a common denominator that "justice shall somehow prevail," a line from "Light One Candle," a favorite song by Peter, Paul and Mary. Because she is not comfortable writing explicit sex scenes, or explicit murder scenes, her romances are sweet and her mysteries cozies. In both cases, it's a matter of personal taste rather than prudery. She respects the authors who write more graphic books and the readers who enjoy them, but says, "They are not my cup of tea." For over a decade readers encouraged her to write for the inspirational market, but it wasn't until a dear friend died that she wrote proposals for two different series—historical romances and contemporary mysteries—in that genre.

As a writer, she thinks there is a challenge to changing genres. "It forces me to learn new things and keeps me from stagnating. It stretches me to grow and improve. Once the fundamentals of writing are learned, you take them with you, but you have to focus them differently, because each genre has different constraints and expectations."

Recently, Harte and her husband moved from New Jersey to Cheyenne, fulfilling a long-time dream to live in Wyoming. She has her own dedicated office space for the first time where she spends each morning and, if she hasn't finished her week's quota of chapters, afternoon writing. The office holds items that inspire her: a set of Lincoln bookends that were among her husband's grandfather's most prized possessions; a Waterford crystal paperweight, a gift from her husband to celebrate the millennium; a lamp shaped like the Eiffel Tower to remind her of the time she lived in France. Her computer faces one wall filled with framed covers of her books to inspire her when she reaches "the middle of the book doldrums" and to remind her she can finish the book she's writing.

When not working, she often speaks before writing and reading groups where it becomes obvious that Harte is a very organized and disciplined individual. She enjoys the personal contact and hopes she can help another writer along the path to publication or brighten a reader's day. "The biggest challenge facing romance writers is overcoming some readers' impressions of the romance genre," Harte says. "Unfortunately, there are people who've never read a romance but believe that they 1) are all about sex, 2) are all light and fluffy, 3) feature unrealistic characters. Not one of these is true, most definitely not about my books. I write about love, not sex."

To date, Harte has sold 25 novels, two nonfiction books, and numerous articles. Two novels are due out in 2008, and she has eight more under consideration. For years Harte sold her books without an agent. "I now have an agent. The reality is, many markets are closed to unagented writers, regardless of their publishing track record, so it's almost mandatory to have an agent. The notable exceptions are some Harlequin lines and some of the smaller publishers. The right agent can make a huge difference in a writer's career. The wrong agent . . . Let's not go there."

Because markets are constantly changing, Harte reads all the market news she can, but admits she doesn't always follow it. She believes each writer needs to find her niche with some following—or creating—trends, others writing the books they love.

"Writing is a demanding profession. There are no guarantees; the pay is frequently not commensurate with the time expended; rejection is a fact of life," Harte says. "But—on the other side of the scale and far outweighing those negatives—there's absolutely nothing that compares with seeing your book on the shelves or having a reader e-mail you that she stayed up all night because she loved your book so much."

For Romance Writers

Jo Beverley

'Writing Historicals Is Like Time Travel'

by Deborah Bouziden

J o Beverley has always been a writer. As a child she wrote stories and when she was a teenager she wrote a historical romance. In the early '80s she settled in to writing seriously and has stayed with it ever since. "I wanted to give people the same sort of pleasure I'd received from books and letting my imagination spin stories was addictive," Beverley says.

Her addiction has become profitable through the years. Her first sale was *Lord Wraybourne's Betrothed* in 1988 to Walker Books, a small New York publisher who publishes hardcover books for libraries. "I'm English by birth and raising," says Beverley "so a huge library user. I sent my regency romance to publishers I knew of, which were mostly those books in the library."

When she received the news of her first sale, she thought it was a rejection letter. Instead her editor had written a long letter requesting changes. When Beverley didn't respond, the editor called to follow up. Beverley feels fortunate as today that rarely happens. "I was clueless, but thrilled," she says about her introduction to the publishing business. Through the years, that naiveté has changed. Today, besides writing her books she maintains a strong professional oversight on the direction of her career.

Beverley writes a book a year and many of her earlier works have been reprinted. She is the author of more than 27 published books and numerous novellas. She has been the recipient of many awards including the Golden Leaf, the Award of Excellence, the National Readers Choice, and a two Career Achievement awards from Romantic Times. She has five Romance Writers of America RITA Awards and is listed in the RWA Hall of Fame and Honor Roll.

While Beverley has a dedicated group of readers, they are especially attached to her Malloren and Rogue series. With her well written, deeply researched and intriguing plots, who can blame them? She opens up a new world for readers and that's what she strives for. Beverley also seeks to bring new readers to her genre. "There is a constant stream of readers discovering romance novels," Beverley says. "I'm always getting e-mails from people saying, in effect, 'Why did I wait so long?' 'Why did I let prejudice block me from finding your books?' and 'They've brightened my life. I've rediscovered the joy of reading.'"

Beverley puts great effort into the research for each of her stories. At the end of most of her books, she gives readers additional historical information to chew on. On her Web site, she displays pictures of places where her stories have unfolded. One can walk into the Geor-

DEBORAH BOUZIDEN has been writing and publishing articles and books since 1983. To read more about her and her work, visit Web site, www.deborahbouziden.com.

gian world of the Mallorens, Devon, Cheltenham, or Brighton, England. If that isn't enough, readers can visit her research blog, http://minepast.blogspot.com. "It's where I put the stranger things I stumble across while writing."

In April 2008, her 28th book, *A Lady's Secret*—another romance in Malloren series, was released. This latest adventure features fun-loving Earls, cursing nuns, little white dogs, intrigue, and mysteries to be solved. But then what else is new? Writing, publishing, and selling are what Beverley does.

Describe how you build your books. About how long does it take you to write one?

I start with characters and their situation as they are when the book starts, but I'm a fly-into-the-mister, so what I know is often thin. I learn about them as I go. I'm usually writing in a period I already know from other books, so again I let the research needs grow from the story. For example, for the current book the characters insisted on being in Northern France rather than England, so I had to research travel in 18th century France. It takes me about a year to write a book, but I can work on more than one project at a time, in chunks.

Describe your research method. Any tricks of the trade you've learned through the years you could share with readers?

Read primary sources if you can—and these days there's a lot on the Net. From publications, letters, diaries, court records, etc., we get a true feel of how people thought at the time. Don't skimp. Writing historicals is like time travel. We need to be there to take our readers there. At the same time, don't info-dump. Just because we know something doesn't mean it needs to be in the story. Gather a ton of information and use an ounce.

You write in several different time periods. What fascinates you about them?

As my teenage romance was medieval, that's always been a love of mine, and I think it's a shame that somewhere along the line romances began to treat it either as grim or a place for farce. I think we need to recapture a bit of the tournaments and fair ladies magic, because it's wonderful.

Georgette Heyer inspired me to write Regency, and it's the wit and elegance that appeals there. As I see it, the new post-revolutionary restraint enveloped the pre-revolution wildness in a particularly interesting way. By Victorian times it was restraint without the brilliance beneath. But I dislike that period, so don't mind me.

Georgian is simply delicious, with excess in all directions, but including excess of ideas and free-thinking and experimentation. That's where the revolutions came from.

Tell me about the business of romance writing from your point of view.

Writing is a crazy sort of business, but perhaps many are. Most of us dance into it, free-spirited and creative, and then if we're commercially successful, we wake up one day to realize we're running a small business, or even a corporation! According to RWA statistics, romance fiction generated $1.37 billion in sales in 2006—almost twice as much as mystery and SF combined.

The huge numbers of romance readers mean that romance authors can make a good living, but that brings all the associated administrative tasks such as bookkeeping and paper filing. We also have to be or have a marketing and a PR department. Many of us have assistants, even if only part time.

The business side doesn't come naturally to many writers, and as I said, it's rarely what we expected when we started writing, but it is important. Some excellent writers have had careers implode simply because all this external stuff got out of hand. My main advice here is to be alert for the point when writing becomes a business and shift gears in some way. If it's really not your thing, spend the money to buy help. It'll be worth it in the end.

In your opinion, what are some misconceptions people have about writing and publishing, particularly about writing romance?

Some of them are hilarious, in a dark, twisted sort of way. I've had people say to me with a straight face that of course the books are all the same; we just change the names and locations. Or even that "all those Harlequins" are written by teams of men plugging variations into computer programs.

Such a brash display of ignorance, because if they'd read any they'd realize how impossible both scenarios are. This has led some people to disaster, however. One person did follow myth #1. She took a book, changed the names and locations and sold it. Of course, she soon had a plagiarism law suit heading her way and apparently complained that she'd been told it was all right to do that in romance.

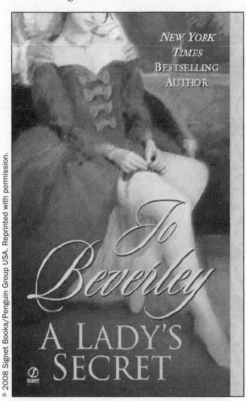

Less absurd, people will assume romance novels are easy to write. I think this is because they are easy to read, but that is our craft. Romances are popular fiction, and therefore the authors work to make the books pure pleasure. It's why so many people read so many of them.

What must a writer do to be successful?

I know it's trite, but—write a good book. I can expand on that, however. We are what we are, and as in everything, we aren't all brilliant, so we can only write the very best book we can. Embrace that or go crazy. However, we have full choice over what we write and our commitment to excellence.

Even the best writers can't write everything. I enjoy a good mystery, but I can't write them. I enjoy a lot of popular fiction that has little or no romance in it, but when I write anything it will become mostly a love story whether I want it to or not. Don't fight your natural flow and don't force yourself into writing something because you think it more respectable or more financially rewarding. Though writing is often challenging, there should always be that hum of satisfaction and bliss beneath it. Think of some sports. Marathons and rock climbing aren't always easy or comfortable, but people do them for a deep satisfaction and bliss, not out of duty or greed.

The other point is to always demand 100% of ourselves. A piece of work may not be perfect—perhaps no piece of work ever is perfect to the creator—but we have to know that it is the very best we can do at the time. We can't ask more of ourselves than that.

Write More, Write Well

How Authors Handle Multiple Books a Year

by Roxanne St. Claire

Once upon a time, not so very long ago, an author with a decent fan base and a supportive publisher was expected and encouraged to produce one book a year. More would saturate the market, and no respectable writer could possibly research, plot, and craft more than one fantastic book in a year. After all, creativity can't be forced and readers wouldn't take a writer seriously if he or she churned out a novel too quickly.

Once upon a time, unpublished authors were discouraged from querying about series or multiple books in their pitches to editors. Debut and midlist authors were thrilled to get a book slot once every 12 or 14 months. And publishing houses maintained a simple pattern with bestselling authors: a hard cover release, followed by a mass market version of the same book nine months later, followed by another hard cover release three months after that.

Once upon a time . . . meet Nora Roberts. Great books, in the hands of skilled (and highly disciplined) writers can most certainly be produced on a much more accelerated schedule. And, guess what? Readers buy them, love them, and demand more. Saturation doesn't occur; in fact, the "one-book-a-year" authors in the publishing genres of romance, mystery, science fiction, fantasy and young adult are now being asked by publishers and fans to write more, more, more. Better yet—from the reader's standpoint—those duets and trilogies are being released in consecutive months, and, even though they stand alone, include familiar, connected characters.

This monumental sea change in publishing has created both an opportunity and a new form of stress for even the most prolific writers. It isn't enough just to write terrific books, now you have to write them fast. Fear not. Many excellent writers have mastered the multiple books in a year career path, and their fan bases are growing because of the approach.

Keeping the pace, doing the math

But what about the writer? What gets sacrificed? Your personal life? Your hobbies? Your marketing programs? Your day job? Your laundry? Your sanity?

Some of the above, but not all. With focus and planning and the right type of novel in your heart and head, as well as support from your editor and publishing house, it is entirely possible to write two, three or more books in a year. This career path is not for the faint of heart, but it's achievable . . . as long as the writer has industrial-strength discipline.

ROXANNE ST. CLAIRE is a national bestselling author of *First You Run, Then You Hide* and *Now You Die*, a trilogy within her critically acclaimed "Bullet Catcher" series for Pocket Books, all released in 2008. The winner of the prestigious RITA Award as well as numerous other writing honors, she's had more than 20 titles published in the past five years and is a frequent speaker to writers and readers groups.

Like any job that requires high productivity, writing multiple books a year demands that the author be organized, structured, focused and prepared to work long hours for many days. And, frankly (this one is really hard for a lot of us), it might require some math. I once heard bestselling and critically acclaimed author Suzanne Brockmann describe her simple formula for meeting a deadline: she marked the due date on the calendar, estimated the page count, and divided that by the number of writing days she had before the deadline. This gave her precisely the number of pages she had to produce each day in order to turn a completed book in on time. Whether that number was two, five or 17, that's what she wrote.

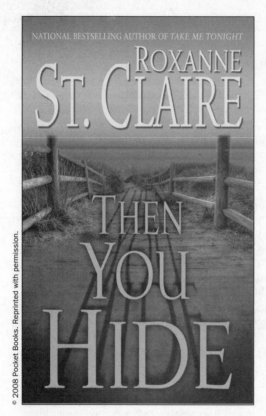

For those of us who are less mathematical, a poster-sized dry erase planning calendar can offer visual progress on a book. When I start a new book, I create a four month calendar and mark off any travel or personal time. Then I estimate how many pages I'll need to complete each week in order to complete the book in the allotted time and write the goal number at the end of every week. At the end of the week, I note actual pages against goal, getting an instant snapshot that shows if I'm off or on schedule.

A 400-page manuscript (approximately 100,000 words) can easily be researched, drafted, revised, and completed in four months with plenty of time to ponder and polish if you write 25 pages a week. That's only five pages a day, and many prolific authors can do twice that—leaving time for in-depth research, story development and revisions. And the occasional load of laundry.

Summoning the muse under pressure

But writing is a highly creative endeavor and no matter how disciplined a writer is, there is a muse who can be quite capricious and downright disdainful of anything requiring structure. Just ask *New York Times* bestselling author Carly Phillips.

"There is no secret for successfully publishing multiple books a year," Phillips says. "You write five pages a day five days a week and finish the book in two months. But, inevitably the *process* wreaks havoc with that ideal writing schedule."

The secret, according to Phillips, is to know and accept your process and make it work for you. She produces two novels a year that routinely catapult to the tops of the bestseller list, but she admits it isn't always a smooth trip. She says the writing goes right on schedule until page 100-125, the point when she's "introduced all the necessary threads and characters and gets that little 'click' in the brain that it will all work."

Then she sends what she's written to her editor for feedback and begins an in-depth revision and "layering" process that deepens the characters and enriches the story. Obviously, "simple math" falls by the wayside as the book takes its final shape, and page count becomes secondary to storytelling.

Phillips confesses that her system, while successful, is inefficient. "It's ugly and I have to accept the truth: it is how I write." And, based on the legions of fans that devour her books, this ugly process makes readers pretty happy.

For some writers, writing multiple books in a year requires the focus of working every single day. Lara Santiago is a bestselling superstar in the wild and wooly world of e-publishing, where fans are not just hungry for many books, they are ravenous, and used to instant Internet gratification. She has a record of five books written in one year, but is happiest with three or four.

Her technique? "Butt in chair, fingers on keyboard." Santiago writes every single day and maintains rigid "daily, weekly, monthly and yearly writing goals" that keep her on track. "One of my personal goals this year was to write at least 300,000 words and with less than a month left, I'm 7,000 words shy of that goal."

Obviously, the trick is to make these good, marketable, compelling stories that will leave the readers clamoring for more, as Lara has done many times over. One way to assure that happens is to create connected books—series with recurring characters and outstanding worldbuilding. This trend, which is growing to tsunami portions, is augmented by the release of two or three books within the series in one year, and very often they hit the bookstores in consecutive months, thrilling readers who don't want to wait for the next installment.

Turning out trilogies

One of publishing's biggest success stories with that approach is romantic thriller writer Allison Brennan, who burst on the scene a few years ago with a trilogy (*The Prey*, *The Hunt* and *The Kill*) from Ballantine and quickly hit the *USA Today* and *New York Times* bestseller lists. Publishers and readers took notice, as more and more related trilogies have followed suit. A mother of five who held a full time job as consultant to the California State Legislature when she sold her first book, Brennan's critically acclaimed dark thrillers prove that neither personal life nor creativity has to suffer in order to achieve great success with three blockbuster releases in a year.

Mindful of both the muse and her personal schedule, Brennan writes while her young children are in school and, as deadlines near, late into the night. She starts with a story premise and discovers her characters as she writes—and she writes quickly, usually in a Starbucks on a laptop, and conducts enormous amounts of primary research to be sure she has her facts correct.

"I begin a book with a situational premise and characters. Since I always believed that 'story is character,' they develop simultaneously." She also actively seeks premises that will sustain a trilogy, since that's what her fans have come to expect.

In order to deliver three books that will be published close together, many writers take a full year off with no new releases to meet the grueling deadlines of multiple books. This requires a very flexible and visionary publisher, and the support of the sales department who will be selling the concept into accounts. During that year, authors still have individual deadlines for each of the books, and are often pulled from one story back to an earlier book to review copy edits or galley proof pages. That year is long, but the payoff is a triple that, if done right, can vault an author into the stratosphere.

Juggling multiple publishers

Not all publishing houses can offer multiple slots in one year, and then a writer can consider writing for two houses at once. Usually, this means he or she will need to expand style and genre, and get the publishers to agree to "share" the author, but it is done often and successfully. Everyone benefits in the long run, as readers are treated to more than one type of book from their favorite authors, booksellers can see increased sales in two genres, and the author has the "safety net" of working for two publishers.

For Romance Writers

This career path requires delicate relationship and time management, since writing for more than one house is much like managing more than one boss—a balancing act of diplomacy and attention. Some writers even use different names so that readers don't confuse the two types of books, but still produce two, three, even four consistently good books each year for multiple publishers.

Not only can the multi-book per year schedule be done, some authors and editors say it *has* to be considered in today's highly competitive marketplace. If you can develop story ideas that can be connected or serialized and are adept at juggling multiple projects simultaneously, chances are you are cut out for success as a prolific writer. You need to be structured and disciplined, to understand how you write as well as you understand why you write, and you should be prepared for a very busy day and night.

Bottom line: you don't have to lose your mind, your muse or your mate to write multiple books in a year, but the laundry could take a hit.

Resources

Where to Look for More Information

Below is a list of invaluable resources specifically for romance writers. To order any of the Writer's Digest Books titles or to get a consumer book catalog, call (800)448-0915. You may also order Writer's Digest Books selections through www.fwbookstore.com, Amazon.com or www.barnesandnoble.com.

MAGAZINES:

- *Romance Writers Report*, Romance Writers of America, 16000 Stuebner Airline Rd., Suite 140, Spring TX 77379. (832)717-5200. Fax: (832)717-5201. E-mail: info@rwanational.org.
- *Romantic Times Bookclub Magazine*, 55 Bergen St., Brooklyn NY 11201. (718)237-1097. Web site: www.romantictimes.com.

BOOKS:

- *On Writing Romance: How to Craft a Novel That Sells*, by Leigh Michaels.
- *Writing Romances: A Handbook by the Romance Writers of America*, edited by Rita Clay Estrada and Rita Gallagher.
- *You Can Write a Romance*, by Rita Clay Estrada and Rita Gallagher (Writer's Digest Books)
- *Writing the Christian Romance*, by Gail Gaymer Martin

ORGANIZATIONS & ONLINE:

- Canadian Romance Authors' Network. Web site: www.canadianromanceauthors.com.
- Romance Writers of America, Inc. (RWA), 16000 Stuebner Airline Rd., Suite 140, Spring TX 77379. (832)717-5200. Fax: (832)717-5201. E-mail: info@rwanational.org. Web site: www.rwanational.org.
- Romance Writers of America regional chapters. Contact National Office (address above) for information on the chapter nearest you.
- The Romance Club. Web site: http://theromanceclub.com.
- Romance Central. Web site: www.romance-central.com. Offers workshops and forum where romance writers share ideas and exchange advice about romance writing.
- Writer's Market Web site: www.writersmarket.com.
- Writer's Digest Web site: www.writersdigest.com.

Speculative Fiction Editors Roundtable

by John Joseph Adams

What does it take to get out of the slush pile and into the table of contents? Here three top editors of short science fiction magazines weigh in.

Gordon Van Gelder is the editor and publisher of *The Magazine of Fantasy & Science Fiction*. He took over as editor of the magazine in January 1997, then took on the role of publisher as well in October 2000. As a teenager, Van Gelder published a number of short stories in anthologies such as *100 Great Fantasy Short-Short Stories* and *Bruce Coville's Book of Spine Tinglers*, putting his writing career on hold to pursue his editing career, which started with a summer internship with Bluejay Books. Later, he worked for 12 years as an editor at St. Martin's Press, and went on to edit several anthologies, including *In Lands That Never Were* and *Fourth Planet from the Sun*.

Gordon Van Gelder

Sheila Williams is the editor of *Asimov's Science Fiction*. She's been with the magazine since the summer of 1982, starting as an editorial assistant and taking over as editor in April 2004. She received her Master's degree in philosophy from Washington University, and moved to New York in 1981 to pursue a career in publishing. In addition to her experience at Asimov's, she is also the editor of more than two dozen anthologies, such as *A Woman's Liberation* and *Intergalactic Mercenaries*. She doesn't write fiction, and has no plans to do so in the future, but her editorial experience allows her keen insight into what works and what doesn't.

Susan Marie Groppi is the editor-in-chief of *Strange Horizons*. Groppi joined the staff as a fiction editor shortly after the magazine's launch in September 2000, and took over as editor-in-chief in 2003. In addition to her editorial work, she has a Ph.D. in History and is a lecturer at UC Berkeley. She doesn't write much fiction—she calls her one fiction publication in the magazine *Flytrap* an "aberration"—but she does often write critical nonfiction. Prior to joining *Strange Horizons*, Groppi worked as an editorial assistant at Circlet Press. She is the co-editor of the anthology *20 Epics* (with David Moles), and is currently one of the resident editors for the Online Writing Workshop (http://sff.onlinewritingworkshop.com).

JOHN JOSEPH ADAMS is the editor of the anthologies *Wastelands: Stories of the Apocalypse*, *Seeds of Change*, and *No More Room in Hell: Stories of the Living Dead*. He is also the assistant editor of *The Magazine of Fantasy & Science Fiction* and a freelance writer. His Web site is www.johnjosephadams.com.

What plots are you sick to death of seeing, and/or what would you like to see more of?

Gordon Van Gelder: Currently, the plot I'm seeing most often is: A previously unheard-of virus comes along, alters all of humanity in a way that has never before occurred, and one lucky person is immune. We've run a couple of stories with this plot already and it's quickly growing tiresome. I've also been getting lots of alternate history stories about different outcomes to the Civil War or to World War II.

What would I like to see more of? Well, if Santa got my list, this year I'll be getting more science fiction stories like "Finisterra" and "The Merchant at the Alchemist's Gate" that are really good *and* don't seem to follow the same paths as most of the other science fiction stories I'm reading these days.

Sheila Williams: I never know which plots I want to see more of until I see them, because they're the plots that do something I'm not expecting to see. I would definitely like to put a short-term moratorium on stories that lead off with exploding spaceships. Exploding spaceships that happen further into the story are currently OK, however.

Susan Marie Groppi: We've been seeing an awful lot of retold or reworked fairy tales. Of course, we've also bought a fair number of them, so I can see why people keep sending them, but at this point we're a little burnt out. Retellings are difficult, because on the one hand they can leverage a lot of emotional and narrative power by tapping into these familiar

Sheila Williams

images and plots, but authors really need to be thinking about whether they're bringing anything really new or meaningful to the retelling.

We also see a lot of what I've started calling the "foofy slipstreamy stories," pieces that are very lyrical, very image-driven, and sometimes very beautiful, but also kind of insubstantial, with no clear sense of what the dream-like magical images mean, or whether they're even real. Again, this is a type of story that we've developed a reputation for favoring, which is undoubtedly why we get so many of them, but I'm tired of them at this point.

Speaking just for myself, and not necessarily for my co-editors, I would *love* to see more science fiction. Something with robots, or quantum physics, or alien contact. I'm really a science fiction reader at heart, and not a fantasy reader.

What's the most common reason that a manuscript gets rejected?

Van Gelder: Reason #1 is because the story wasn't entertaining enough.

Williams: Exploding space ships and other predictable plot lines. Lazy plotting, i.e., the sense that the author isn't really sure of where he or she is going. Boring jobs and boring employees. Grim, detestable worlds and grim, detestable characters. Please note, though, that I have been known to buy stories that contain one or all of these plot devices (exception does not apply to lazy plotting, though).

Groppi: It just doesn't do anything special. The single most common reaction we have to submitted stories is "eh, it's fine, but it's nothing special." The special-ness can come from a number of different things—some really good use of language, a really great idea, or something in the pacing. It has to light up a circuit somewhere in my head, or it isn't going to stand out from the pack.

A new writer only has a few paragraphs to grab the editor's interest. What's the secret to writing strong beginnings?

Van Gelder: I can make two suggestions: 1) Introduce us to a character who's in an interesting situation and make us empathize with him/her/it. Kate Wilhelm is a master at this—I often tell students they should get one of Kate's collections or a handful of her novels and just read the opening pages of each one. 2) Cut the warm-ups. A lot of stories come in that feel like the author needed a few pages to warm up before the story starts rolling. That's fine from a writing point of view, but the warm-ups should be cut in revisions.

Williams: Figure out what your story is about and put the whole thing in the first sentence, but don't do it in such away that I can figure out what's coming from the information. Just be sure that the beginning is intriguing.

Susan Marie Groppi

Groppi: A strong beginning doesn't have to be action-packed, and it doesn't have to front-load whatever cool idea or concept is in the story, but I do think that the opening paragraphs of a story have to have something in them that makes me care. A hint that something cool is about to happen, or a sign that the character is interesting, or a feel for good language or good style. One of the things that's death for a manuscript is when I start reading it and there's nothing in the first paragraphs that I care about.

What kind of reading should aspiring writers be doing? Do you have any specific books on writing, or sterling examples of fiction to recommend?

Van Gelder: The usual advice is that an aspiring writer should read anything and everything. And that's true. But it often pays to read in a more focused way. For instance, if you're aspiring to write science fiction, try reading an anthology like *The Science Fiction Hall of Fame* and study each of the stories to see what techniques they use. I've heard several crime writers say they learned a lot by retyping an entire Elmore Leonard novel, start to finish.

On writing itself, I always recommend Damon Knight's *Creating Short Fiction* for studying the craft of the short story and Robin Wilson's *Those Who Can* anthology for aspiring science fiction writers. And Strunk & White's *Elements of Style* for everyone.

Williams: Read the magazines. Analyze the first paragraphs of stories that work. Read lots of stories in magazines and anthologies and analyze why they work.

Groppi: It all depends on what kind of writing you want to be doing. I'm going to echo the commonly-given advice, though, that writers should be readers, and should read as widely as possible. When you read something that makes you think, "Oh, I want to do *that*," then you should read it again, and maybe try to see if you can figure out what makes it tick.

What is it about a story that makes it right for your publication?

Van Gelder: I generally like to leave it to other people to try to answer this question because if I can ever answer it 100% correctly, that's when I should pack it in as an editor. One of the joys of editing *F&SF* is being able to surprise myself with stories we publish.

Williams: We run an eclectic assortment of stories at *Asimov's*. Love to see good science in a science fiction story. Not much horror—although there are exceptions. Most of these are situational rather than occult. Almost no high fantasy, but lots of strange tales where the explanation is just weird or fantastic.

Groppi: It's hard to say what makes something *right* for us, but it's a little easier to pin down what makes it likely to work for us. All three of us in the fiction department place a high priority on quality of prose, and a couple of us also have well-known weak spots for stories that deal with family dynamics or relationships. We're very interested in changing things up, though, and stories that feel different in some way from our norm are likely to get a little boost in the editorial process.

In what ways has the genre fiction marketplace changed over the past several years that new writers should be aware of?

Van Gelder: The biggest change in the last decade is the advent of electronic publications, but I don't know that there's much to say—in general, they're the same as print magazines in that you should check them out before submitting to them, follow their guidelines, etc. But one thing that *has* changed is that the Internet has made it easier to get information (and misinformation) quickly. There are more markets and more market guides than ever before and most of them are good, but it pays to do one's homework before submitting anything.

Williams: Exploding spaceship stories were probably easier to publish before editors started telling everyone that we had to be blown away by the opening paragraph. We still need to be blown away by the opening paragraph, but that doesn't mean the spaceships have to be blown up.

Groppi: The obvious first thing that comes to mind is that online publications have finally more-or-less bridged the respectability gap. Publishing in *Intergalactic Medicine Show* or *Jim Baen's Universe* or (if I can say this) *Strange Horizons* is, I think, unambiguously a "real" publishing credit now, as opposed to six or seven years ago, when online publications would be looked at a little bit askance (unless they were edited by Ellen Datlow). Magazines like *Clarkesworld* or the new online version of *Fantasy* have been able to hit the ground running, without needing the long slow ramp-up period of convincing the community that they're legit.

I also get the sense that the newer generation of writers, the ones who have entered into the short fiction market in the last five or 10 years, are much more likely than the veterans to be resigned to the fact that you can't make a living writing short fiction today. If you're good and prolific and dedicated, short fiction can provide a nice additional income stream, but it's not sustainable as a primary income stream, especially not if you're talking about genre fiction. This is mostly an effect *of* the marketplace, not an effect *on* the marketplace, but it's not without market effect. There's a rich and vibrant culture of small-press zines and anthologies, a culture that's based around the idea that you're never going to get paid a lot for this particular type of work, but you can be a part of something cool and creative. I don't want to overplay the benefits of this—I do think it's a shame that short fiction writers don't get paid more, and I see a lot of writers who have lowered their expectations and standards to a point that may be hurting their professional development. But it's fascinating to watch it happen, and I think we haven't seen the full implications of it yet.

Sci Fi/Fantasy/Horror

Elizabeth Moon

'The Work Itself Creates the Fire'

by Rachel McDonald

While known as a science fiction author, Elizabeth Moon's first trilogy was a fantasy with swords, elves and magic. Readers got to see Paksenarrion grow from a naïve mercenary recruit to an accomplished warrior battling dark gods. Soon after the books came out, Moon was approached to collaborate with Anne McCaffrey on Sassinak and Generation Warriors, stories that grew out of McCaffrey's Planet Pirates. There aren't any magic swords or elves in these books, but there are space ships, pirates and a conspiracy that needs to be stopped before it topples the government.

Moon has gone on from there to publish several science fiction series, The Serrano Legacy and Vatta's War, on her own. Her latest book, *Victory Conditions*, is the fifth book in the Vatta's War series. While all of the trappings of science fiction are there, Moon uses them to tap into larger issues, such as "the vulnerabilities (and efficiencies) created by the concentration of information/power into any monopoly."

Her stand-alone novels seem to garner the most critical acclaim, as *Remnant Population* was a finalist for the Hugo and *The Speed of Dark* won a Nebula. Both these books feature unconventional heroes, one an old woman who makes first contact with an alien species and the other a high functioning autistic man who must risk a "cure" for autism or losing his job.

Moon is going back to her fantasy roots and is currently working on a novel based in the world of Paksenarrion, but with a different protagonist. Here Moon talks about writing fantasy and science fiction and how things have changed over the years.

You won a Nebula for *The Speed of Dark* in 2004, and in 2007 you received the Robert A. Heinlein Award. How do you feel about winning awards like these?

Humbled. And happy of course, but both these awards were given by my peers, other writers in the field, and that's especially rewarding. Though the fan-based awards (the Compton Crook in 1989 for Sheepfarmer's Daughter and the Hugo nomination in 1997 for Remnant Population) were certainly thrilling.

RACHEL MCDONALD holds an MA in Comparative Literature, Professional Writing and Editing from the University of Cincinnati. She served as the prose editor for *Ellipsis . . . Literature and Art* and has contributed to several Writer's Digest Books titles including an interview with Rochelle Krich for a previous edition of *Novel & Short Story Writer's Market*.

Relatively early in your career you co-authored Sassinak and Generation Warriors with Anne McCaffrey. How did this come about? What were the effects of working with McCaffrey on your own writing?

McCaffrey's publisher for the Planet Pirates trio wanted to pair her with relatively new writers he thought would mix well with her style. Of course I was thrilled. In addition, I had a chance to learn from a master craftswoman—for instance, the projects required me to work with multiple major viewpoints, something I'd never done. It was an honor, a great learning experience, and a lot of fun.

You have mentioned that you don't much like the business side of writing. What parts do you avoid? What do you not mind so much?

I avoid getting involved in negotiations as much as possible: I was probably the only Brownie Scout in the history of Scouting who could not sell even one box of Girl Scout cookies. Luckily, I have a very good agent. The rest of it I can do, but it's still an interruption in the part I like best, which is the actual writing.

How have changes in technology affected your writing process?

As with any change in technology, there's "for better, for worse" to it. The downside is the need to keep adjusting to some idiot's bright idea of what I need in hardware or software . . . every change has a learning curve, and that learning curve takes time from productive work. In my experience, the "improvements" in the new software or hardware I must use in writing don't save me as much time or effort as they take to learn and do not offer me any bells and whistles I need. This is particularly true of operating system changes. The computer and word-processing software are tools, not toys—I'd like them to be as stable as a hammer or pair of pliers.

On the good side, compared to writing on a typewriter, writing on computer is much easier. I've always been a lousy typist, so being able to correct typos in the computer, move blocks of text around, and cut clumsy constructions without the help of bottles of white stuff and scissors is a great help. The ability to store a lot of data in a small space is great—the house is already full of books and paper, so it saves rummaging time when I can click from book to book, or look at the backstory data files, in the machine. Internet capability lets me work wherever I am and stay in touch with editors, agent, and so on. Instead of having to lug along a printer or find a print shop and then an express mail company in an unfamiliar city, I can simply e-mail the entire book, or revisions, to my editor. Digital photography lets me capture images—machines, topography, vegetation, wildlife, details of a location, clothing—that I can use in one or another book.

What are some other issues you would like to see science fiction writers deal with?

Whatever interests them. I could name a dozen issues I'd like people in my community, state, church, and nation to deal with in real life, but all of them have been dealt with in fiction (including science fiction) repeatedly. In general, I find fiction that's overtly issue-oriented much weaker than fiction centered on characters.

Serrano Legacy and Vatta's War both have themes that tie the series together (the effects of longevity and reliance on communication). Are you a plot-then-theme person, or vice versa?

Not really either. I'm a character-then-plot writer, with the theme emerging somewhere in the course of a project. It arises out of the characters and their concerns and often I have no idea what it is for a surprising length of time: one or more volumes in the multi-volume stories, and mid-book in the single-volume stories. When I've tried to write to a theme (for anthologies, for instance) I find I'm often writing oblique to the theme.

You began by writing fantasy but have spent most of your time writing science fiction. What's the difference for you between writing fantasy and science fiction? Are you going to write fantasy again?

Two things are different, one structural and one procedural. Structurally, science fiction "feels" as if it comes out of the front of my head and its deep layers are often at the meeting of technology and society: how will some imagined change affect society? It may go deeper but that connection to the technology/science issues must be there. Fantasy "feels" as if it comes out of the gut and its deep layers are fundamental human issues like courage, compassion, the nature of choice, etc.

Procedurally, I can't write book-length fantasy unless I have long stretches of uninterrupted time. Really uninterrupted—nobody coming down the hall to tell me about this neat thing they just read on the Internet, or asking what's for dinner, or mentioning that the taxes are due. I may need an hour alone just to get back through the mental gate between here and there. I can write—have written—shorter fantasy works when I have shorter periods of clear time, so since the last fantasy novel I've done quite a bit of short fantasy. Science fiction requires less complete mental submersion in the fictional universe, so I can write science fiction in shorter snatches—even 15 minutes at a time, if I have to.

One of the reasons I love Paksenarrion is she changes so much, and all of the change is believable; I love to see her grow.

Any advice for new writers on how they can get their characters to do the same?

To write realistic characters, writers need to observe the people around them with precision and compassion. It doesn't really matter how many people are available for observation—a village offers enough variety to the discerning writer, and a metropolis will provide inadequate characters for the unobservant. Quality of observation counts—noticing how people act, listening to them explain why (whether they're right or not is irrelevant), seeing how children and adolescents and adults grow and change (or don't.) Interaction is also necessary—the true hermit will never really intuit motivations and interactions of characters. Introspection—awareness of, and thinking about, one's own reactions to people and events, treating oneself as a subject of research—is another invaluable practice as long as the writer recognizes that his/her feelings and motivations are not universal. The better the quality of observation, the more data the writer has with which to develop characters.

In defining characters, ignore surface traits and give the character one to a few deep convictions/baseline traits. Put the character into enough multi-level peril—challenges that put stress on those beliefs/traits—so that change is inevitable. No one gets through a situation in which their deepest nature or beliefs are challenged without changing in some way. Then, sink into the character and follow him or her around in the story. If the character wanders away from the planned plot, so much the better—that character is beginning to develop autonomy. Let the character lead. A real character will change, and if not forced by an insensitive writer, will change believably. Unbelievable characters change for the author's reasons—to make a plot point that's on the outline, for instance, or to enact the writer's opinion on an issue. If a character goes stiff or limp, back off— that's a sign of over-control. Go back to where the character felt alive, and let the character take over again.

In previous interviews you've talked about your first writing gig as a newspaper columnist. Would you recommend fiction writers try writing nonfiction to hone their skills?

I recommend more writing (however much you're doing, write more). Nonfiction writing—especially for newspapers—teaches writers to stick to a topic, a word length, and a deadline. It's especially valuable for natural novelists, who are frustrated by short-story writing and may find they cannot finish a short story. Writing short nonfiction is a good way to learn how much "stuff" fits in 500 or 5,000 words. Another advantage is that there's usually less ego-involvement in nonfiction than in fiction. A weekly column on, say, quilting or school district news does not involve the personal exposure of a poem, short story, or novel. And since nonfiction is easier to sell, on average, nonfiction will build publishing credits, as well as experience in dealing with editors and rejection.

What's the biggest mistake you made when you started writing?

Listening to bad advice in my twenties. I was told by many people that you had to learn by writing short stories. I am not a natural short story writer; I'm a natural novelist. But for years, I would drop a story that grew too big, and start another—that also grew too big. I never finished anything because I thought it had to be short. Natural novelists need to go on and write that whole novel (and natural short story writers should go on writing short stories.) I did not write a publishable short story until I'd finished The Deed of Paksenarrion.

A second, almost-as-bad mistake was waiting for lightning. Before I committed the time and effort to getting serious about writing, I wanted some sign, some proof, that the time and effort would be worthwhile. It doesn't work that way. The proof comes later: Lightning does not strike the altar of talent until a lot of sacrificial hours have been piled up there and sweat-equity poured over them. Do the work. Do more of the work. Then . . . maybe lightning will strike. But the work itself creates the fire.

On the other hand, being a late bloomer meant that I had a lot more depth of knowledge—including people knowledge—when I finally did make it to market. That never hurts.

Sci Fi/Fantasy/Horror

Resources

Where to Look for More Information

Below is a list of invaluable resources specifically for science fiction, fantasy and horror writers. To order any of the Writer's Digest Books titles or to get a consumer book catalog, call (800)448-0915. You may also order Writer's Digest Books selections through www.fwbookstore.com, Amazon.com, or www.barnesandnoble.com.

MAGAZINES:
- *Locus*, P.O. Box 13305, Oakland CA 94661. E-mail: locus@locusmag.com. Web site: www.locusmag.com.
- *The Horror Writer*, P.O. Box 1188, Long Beach NY 11561. Web site: www.bloodmoonrisingmagazine.com/horrorwritermag.html.
- SPECFICME! (bimonthly PDF newsletter). Web site: www.specficworld.com.

BOOKS (by Writer's Digest Books):
- *How to Write Science Fiction & Fantasy*, by Orson Scott Card
- *The Writer's Complete Fantasy Reference*, from the editors of Writer's Digest Books
- *On Writing Horror*, edited by Mort Castle

ORGANIZATIONS & ONLINE:
- Fantasy-Writers.org. Web site: www.fantasy-writers.org.
- Horror Writers Association, P.O. Box 50577, Palo Alto CA 94303. Web site: www.horror.org.
- Science Fiction & Fantasy Writers of America, Inc., P.O. Box 877, Chestertown MD 21620. E-mail: execdir@sfwa.org. Website: www.sfwa.org/.
- SF Canada, 303-2333 Scarth St., Regina SK S4P 2J8. Web site: www.sfcanada.ca.
- SpecFicWorld. Web site: www.specficworld.com. Covers all 3 speculative genres (science fiction, fantasy and horror).
- Books and Writing Online. Web site: www.interzone.com/Books/books.html.
- Writer's Market Web site: www.writersmarket.com.
- Writer's Digest Web site: www.writersdigest.com.

Literary Agents

Many publishers are willing to look at unsolicited submissions but most feel having an agent is in the writer's best interest. In this section, we include agents who specialize in or represent fiction.

The commercial fiction field is intensely competitive. Many publishers have small staffs and little time. For that reason, many book publishers rely on agents for new talent. Some publishers are even relying on agents as "first readers" who must wade through the deluge of submissions from writers to find the very best. For writers, a good agent can be a foot in the door—someone willing to do the necessary work to put your manuscript in the right editor's hands.

It would seem today that finding a good agent is as hard as finding a good publisher. Yet those writers who have agents say they are invaluable. Not only can a good agent help you make your work more marketable, an agent also acts as your business manager and adviser, protecting your interests during and after contract negotiations.

Still, finding an agent can be very difficult for a new writer. If you are already published in magazines, you have a better chance than someone with no publishing credits. (Some agents read periodicals searching for new writers.) Although many agents do read queries and manuscripts from unpublished authors without introduction, referrals from their writer clients can be a big help. If you don't know any published authors with agents, attending a conference is a good way to meet agents. Some agents even set aside time at conferences to meet new writers.

Almost all the agents listed here have said they are open to working with new, previously unpublished writers as well as published writers. They do not charge a fee to cover the time and effort involved in reviewing a manuscript or a synopsis and chapters, but their time is still extremely valuable. Only send an agent your work when you feel it is as complete and polished as possible.

USING THE LISTINGS

It is especially important that you read individual listings carefully before contacting these busy agents. The first information after the company name includes the address and phone, fax, e-mail address (when available) and Web site. **Member Agents** gives the names of individual agents working at that company. (Specific types of fiction an agent handles are indicated in parentheses after that agent's name). The **Represents** section lists the types of fiction the agency works with. Reading the **Recent Sales** gives you the names of writers an agent is currently working with and, very importantly, publishers the agent has placed manuscripts with. **Writers' Conferences** identifies conferences an agent attends (and where you might possibly meet that agent). **Tips** presents advice directly from the agent to authors.

Also, look closely at the openness to submissions icons that precede most listings. They will indicate how willing an agency is to take on new writers.

THE AGENCY GROUP, LLC

1880 Century Park E., Suite 711, Los Angeles CA, 90068. (310)385-2800. E-mail: marcgerald@theage ncygroup.com. Website: www.theagencygroup.com. **Contact:** Marc Gerald, Caroline Greeven. Estab. 2002. Represents 50 clients. 10% of clients are new/unpublished writers. Currently handles: 60% nonfiction books; 30% novels; 10% multimedia.

- Prior to becoming an agent, Mr. Gerald owned and ran an independent publishing and entertainment agency.

Member Agents Marc Gerald; Caroline Greeven; Sarah Stephens.

Represents Nonfiction books, novels. **Considers these nonfiction areas:** Anthropology/archaeology; art/architecture/design; biography/autobiography; business/economics; child guidance/parenting; cooking/foods/nutrition; ethnic/cultural interests; government/politics/law; health/medicine; history; how-to; humor/satire; memoirs; money/finance; music/dance; nature/environment; popular culture; psychology; self-help/personal improvement; sports; true crime/investigative; interior design/decorating. **Considers these fiction areas:** All subjects except science fiction/fantasy.

- "While we admire beautiful writing, we largely represent recording artists, celebrities, authors, and pop culture and style brands with established platforms. When we represent fiction, we work almost exclusively in genre and in areas of expertise. We tend to take a non-linear approach to content—many of our projects ultimately have a TV/film or digital component." This agency is only taking on new clients through referrals.

How to Contact Considers simultaneous queries. Responds in 1 month to queries; 3 months to mss. Obtains most new clients through recommendations from others.

Recent Sales Sold 40 titles in the last year. *50 by 50*, by 50 Cent (Pocket); *Sew U*, by Wendy Mullin (Bullfinch); *Little Things*, by Jeffrey Brown (Fireside); *The Hustler's Wife #2*, by Nikki Turner (Random House); *One Red Paperclip*, by Kyle MacDonald (Three Rivers Press). Other clients include Tim McGraw, Eminem, Project Alabama, Wahida Clark, Steve Rinella, Meta Smith, Joy King, Merlin Bronques, Jim Limburgh, Chris Jericho.

Terms Agent receives 15% commission on domestic sales; 20% commission on foreign sales. Offers written contract. Charges clients for office fees (only for mss that have been sold).

THE AHEARN AGENCY, INC.

2021 Pine St., New Orleans LA 70118. E-mail: pahearn@aol.com. **Contact:** Pamela G. Ahearn. Estab. 1992. Member of MWA, RWA, ITW. Represents 35 clients. 20% of clients are new/unpublished writers. Currently handles: 10% nonfiction books; 90% novels.

- Prior to opening her agency, Ms. Ahearn was an agent for 8 years and an editor with Bantam Books. **Considers these nonfiction areas:** Animals; child guidance/parenting; current affairs; ethnic/cultural interests; gay/lesbian issues; health/medicine; history; popular culture; self-help/ personal improvement; theater/film; true crime/investigative; women's issues/studies. **Considers these fiction areas:** Action/adventure; contemporary issues; detective/police/crime; ethnic; family saga; feminist; glitz; historical; humor/satire; literary; mainstream/contemporary; mystery/suspense; psychic/supernatural; regional; romance; thriller.

- This agency specializes in historical romance and is also very interested in mysteries and suspense fiction. Does not want to receive category romance, science fiction or fantasy.

How to Contact Query with SASE. Accepts e-mail queries (no attachments). Considers simultaneous queries. Responds in 8 weeks to queries; 10 weeks to mss. Obtains most new clients through recommendations from others, solicitations, conferences.

Recent Sales *Red Chrysanthemum*, by Laura Joh Rowland; *Only a Duke Will Do*, by Sabrina Jeffries; *The Alexandria Link*, by Steve Berry.

Terms Agent receives 15% commission on domestic sales; 20% commission on foreign sales. Offers written contract, binding for 1 year; renewable by mutual consent.

Writers' Conferences Moonlight & Magnolias; RWA National Conference; Thriller Fest; Florida Romance Writers; Bouchercon; Malice Domestic.

Tips "Be professional! Always send in exactly what an agent/editor asks for—no more, no less. Keep query letters brief and to the point, giving your writing credentials and a very brief summary of your book. If one agent rejects you, keep trying—there are a lot of us out there!"

ALIVE COMMUNICATIONS, INC.

7680 Goddard St., Suite 200, Colorado Springs CO 80920. (719)260-7080. Fax: (719)260-8223. Website: www.alivecom.com. Estab. 1989. Member of AAR, Authors Guild. Represents 100+ clients. 5% of clients are new/unpublished writers. Currently handles: 50% nonfiction books; 35% novels; 5% novellas; 10% juvenile books.

Member Agents Rick Christian, president (blockbusters, bestsellers); Lee Hough (popular/commercial nonfiction and fiction, thoughtful spirituality, children's); Beth Jusino (thoughtful/inspirational nonfiction, women's fiction/nonfiction, Christian living).

Represents Nonfiction books, novels, short story collections, novellas. **Considers these nonfiction areas:** Biography/autobiography; business/economics; child guidance/parenting; how-to; memoirs; religious/inspirational; self-help/personal improvement; women's issues/studies. **Considers these fiction areas:** Action/adventure; contemporary issues; detective/police/crime; family saga; historical; humor/satire; literary; mainstream/contemporary; mystery/suspense; religious/inspirational; thriller.

> ⚬➤ This agency specializes in fiction, Christian living, how-to and commercial nonfiction. Actively seeking inspirational, literary and mainstream fiction, and work from authors with established track records and platforms. Does not want to receive poetry, young adult paperbacks, scripts or dark themes.

How to Contact Query with SASE. Be advised that this agency works primarily with well-established, bestselling, and career authors. Returns materials only with SASE. Obtains most new clients through recommendations from others.

Recent Sales Sold 300+ titles in the last year. A spiritual memoir, by Eugene Peterson (Viking); A biography of Rwandan president Paul Kagame, by Stephen Kinzer; *Ever After*, by Karen Klingsbury (Zondervan).

Terms Agent receives 15% commission on domestic sales; 15% commission on foreign sales. Offers written contract; 2-month notice must be given to terminate contract.

Tips "Rewrite and polish until the words on the page shine. Endorsements and great connections may help, provided you can write with power and passion. Network with publishing professionals by making contacts, joining critique groups, and attending writers' conferences in order to make personal connections and to get feedback. Alive Communications, Inc., has established itself as a premiere literary agency. We serve an elite group of authors who are critically acclaimed and commercially successful in both Christian and general markets."

MIRIAM ALTSHULER LITERARY AGENCY

53 Old Post Road N., Red Hook NY 12571. (845)758-9408. Website: www.miriamaltshulerliteraryage ncy.com. **Contact:** Miriam Altshuler. Estab. 1994. Member of AAR. Represents 40 clients. Currently handles: 45% nonfiction books; 45% novels; 5% story collections; 5% juvenile books.

> • Ms. Altshuler has been an agent since 1982.

Represents Nonfiction books, novels, short story collections, juvenile books. **Considers these nonfiction areas:** Biography/autobiography; ethnic/cultural interests; history; language/literature/criticism; memoirs; multicultural; music/dance; nature/environment; popular culture; psychology; sociology; theater/film; women's issues/studies. **Considers these fiction areas:** Literary; mainstream/contemporary; multicultural.

> ⚬➤ Does not want self-help, mystery, how-to, romance, horror, spiritual, fantasy, poetry, screenplays, science fiction or techno-thriller.

How to Contact Query with SASE, submit contact info with e-mail address. Prefers to read materials exclusively. No e-mail or fax queries. Considers simultaneous queries. Responds in 3 weeks to mss. Returns materials only with SASE. Obtains most new clients through recommendations from others.

Terms Agent receives 15% commission on domestic sales; 20% commission on foreign sales. Charges clients for overseas mailing, photocopies, overnight mail when requested by author.

Writers' Conferences Bread Loaf Writers' Conference; Washington Independent Writers' Conference; North Carolina Writers' Network Conference.

Tips See the Web site for specific submission details.

⦿ MARCIA AMSTERDAM AGENCY

41 W. 82nd St., Suite 9A, New York NY 10024-5613. (212)873-4945. **Contact:** Marcia Amsterdam. Estab. 1970. Signatory of WGA. Currently handles: 15% nonfiction books; 70% novels; 5% movie scripts; 10% TV scripts.

• Prior to opening her agency, Ms. Amsterdam was an editor.

Represents Novels, feature film, sitcom. **Considers these fiction areas:** Action/adventure; detective/police/crime; horror; mainstream/contemporary; mystery/suspense; romance (contemporary, historical); science fiction; thriller; young adult. **Considers these script subject areas:** Comedy; romantic comedy.

How to Contact Query with SASE. No e-mail or fax queries. Responds in 1 month to queries.

Recent Sales *Hidden Child*, by Isaac Millman (FSG); *Lucky Leonardo*, by Jonathan Canter (Sourcebooks).

Terms Agent receives 15% commission on domestic sales; 20% commission on foreign sales; 10% commission on dramatic rights sales. Offers written contract, binding for 1 year. Charges clients for extra office expenses, foreign postage, copying, legal fees (when agreed upon).

Tips "We are always looking for interesting literary voices."

⦿ ANDERSON LITERARY MANAGEMENT, LLC

12 W. 19th St., New York NY 10011. (212)645-6045. Fax: (212)741-1936. E-mail: kathleen@anderson literary.com; info@andersonliterary.com. Website: www.andersonliterary.com/. **Contact:** Kathleen Anderson. Estab. 2006. Member of AAR. Represents 100+ clients. 20% of clients are new/unpublished writers. Currently handles: 50% nonfiction books; 50% novels.

• Prior to her current position, Ms. Anderson was with Grinberg Literary. She has more than two decades of publishing experience.

Represents Nonfiction books, novels, short story collections, juvenile books. **Considers these nonfiction areas:** Anthropology/archaeology; art/architecture/design; biography/autobiography; current affairs; education; ethnic/cultural interests; gay/lesbian issues; government/politics/law; history; memoirs; music/dance; nature/environment; psychology; women's issues/studies. **Considers these fiction areas:** Action/adventure; ethnic; family saga; feminist; gay/lesbian; historical; literary; mystery/suspense; thriller; westerns/frontier; young adult; women's.

   ⚷ Specializes in commercial fiction (literary, women's, thriller, historical, young adult) and commercial nonfiction (investigative journalism, women's studies, biography, environmental studies, history, philosophy and religious studies) Does not want to receive genre fantasy, sci-fi or romance.

How to Contact Query with SASE, submit synopsis, first 3 sample chapter(s), proposal (for nonfiction). Accepts e-mail queries. No fax queries. Considers simultaneous queries. Responds in 12 weeks to queries; 12 weeks to mss. Returns materials only with SASE. Obtains most new clients through recommendations from others, solicitations, conferences.

Recent Sales Sold 20+ titles in the last year. *Vibes*, by Amy Ryan (Houghton Mifflin); *Another Faust*, by Daniel and Dina Nayeri (Candlewick); *The Assassins' Gate*, by George Packer; *17 Huntley Gardens*, by Richard Mason (Knopf); *The Reindeer People*, by Piers Vitebsky (Houghton Mifflin); *Maps for Lost Lovers*, by Nadeem Aslam (Knopf). Other clients include Emma Donoghue, Charles Bowden, Rafi Zabor, Marcia Willett, Jane Shaw, Molly Peacock, Anna Oliver, Conn Iggulden, Bella Bathurst, Kerry Hardie, Anna Beer, Janet Todd, Glen Hirshberg, Deanne Stillman, Chuck Wachtel, Barry Lyga, Craig Childs, Sarah Bilston.

Terms Agent receives 15% commission on domestic sales. Offers written contract.

Writers' Conferences Squaw Valley Conference.

⦿ ARTISTS AND ARTISANS INC.

104 W. 29th St., 11th Floor, New York NY 10001. Fax: (212)931-8377. E-mail: adam@artistsandartisa ns.com. Website: www.artistsandartisans.com. **Contact:** Adam Chromy. Estab. 2002. Represents 40 clients. 80% of clients are new/unpublished writers. Currently handles: 63% nonfiction books; 35% novels; 2% scholarly books.

• Prior to becoming an agent, Mr. Chromy was an entrepreneur in the technology field for nearly a decade.

Represents Nonfiction books, novels. **Considers these nonfiction areas:** Biography/autobiography; business/economics; child guidance/parenting; cooking/foods/nutrition; current affairs; ethnic/cultural interests; health/medicine; how-to; humor/satire; language/literature/criticism; memoirs; money/finance; music/dance; popular culture; religious/inspirational; science/technology; self-help/personal improvement; sports; theater/film; true crime/investigative; women's issues/studies; fashion/style. **Considers these fiction areas:** Confession; family saga; humor/satire; literary; mainstream/contemporary.

O→ "My education and experience in the business world ensure that my clients' enterprise as authors gets as much attention and care as their writing." Actively seeking working journalists for nonfiction books. Does not want to receive scripts.

How to Contact Query with SASE. Considers simultaneous queries. Responds in 2 weeks to queries; 2 weeks to mss. Returns materials only with SASE. Obtains most new clients through recommendations from others, solicitations, conferences.

Recent Sales Sold 12 titles in the last year. *Dr. Z on Scoring*, by Victoria Zdrok (Touchstone Fireside); *Winning Points with Your Woman*, by Jaci Rae (Touchstone); *From Binge to Blackout*, by Chris Volkmann and Toren Volkmann (NAL Penguin Group); *Modest Mouse*, by Alan Goldsher (Thomas Dunne Books); *Jewtopia*, by Brian Fogel and Sam Wolfson (Warner Books).

Terms Agent receives 15% commission on domestic sales; 25% commission on foreign sales. Offers written contract; 1-month notice must be given to terminate contract. "We only charge for extraordinary expenses (e.g., client requests check via FedEx instead of regular mail)."

Writers' Conferences ASJA Writers Conference.

Tips "Please make sure you are ready before approaching us or any other agent. If you write fiction, make sure it is the best work you can do and get objective criticism from a writing group. If you write nonfiction, make sure the proposal exhibits your best work and a comprehensive understanding of the market."

◙ AUTHENTIC CREATIONS LITERARY AGENCY

911 Duluth Hwy., Suite D3-144, Lawrenceville GA 30043. (770)339-3774. Fax: (770)339-7126. E-mail: ron@authenticcreations.com. Website: www.authenticcreations.com. **Contact:** Mary Lee Laitsch. Estab. 1993. Member of AAR, Authors Guild. Represents 70 clients. 30% of clients are new/unpublished writers. Currently handles: 60% nonfiction books; 40% novels.

Member Agents Mary Lee Laitsch; Ronald Laitsch; Jason Laitsch.

Represents Nonfiction books, novels, scholarly books. **Considers these nonfiction areas:** Anthropology/archaeology; biography/autobiography; child guidance/parenting; crafts/hobbies; current affairs; history; how-to; science/technology; self-help/personal improvement; sports; true crime/investigative; women's issues/studies. **Considers these fiction areas:** Action/adventure; detective/police/crime; family saga; literary; mainstream/contemporary; mystery/suspense; romance; sports; thriller.

How to Contact Query with SASE. No e-mail or fax queries. Considers simultaneous queries. Responds in 2 weeks to queries; 2 months to mss.

Recent Sales Sold 20 titles in the last year. *Secret Agent*, by Robyn Spizman and Mark Johnston (Simon & Schuster); *Beauchamp Beseiged*, by Elaine Knighton (Harlequin); *Visible Differences*, by Dominic Pulera (Continuum).

Terms Agent receives 15% commission on domestic sales; 15% commission on foreign sales. This agency charges clients for photocopying.

◖ AVENUE A LITERARY

419 Lafayette St., Third Floor, New York NY 10003. (212)624-5859. Fax: (212)228-6149. E-mail: submissions@avenuealiterary.com. Website: www.avenuealiterary.com. **Contact:** Jennifer Cayea. Estab. 2006. Represents 20 clients. 75% of clients are new/unpublished writers. Currently handles: 40% nonfiction books; 45% novels; 5% story collections; 10% juvenile books.

● Prior to opening her agency, Ms. Cayea was an agent and director of foreign rights for Nicholas Ellison, Inc., a division of Sanford J. Greenburger Associates. She was also an editor in the audio and large print divisions of Random House.

Represents Nonfiction books, novels, short story collections, juvenile books. **Considers these nonfiction areas:** Cooking/foods/nutrition; current affairs; ethnic/cultural interests; health/medicine; history; memoirs; music/dance; popular culture; self-help/personal improvement; sports; theater/film. **Considers these fiction areas:** Family saga; feminist; historical; literary; mainstream/contemporary; thriller; young adult; women's/chick lit.

○━ "Our authors are dynamic and diverse. We seek strong new voices in fiction and nonfiction, and are fiercely dedicated to our authors."

How to Contact Query with SASE, submit synopsis, publishing history, author bio, full contact info. Paste info in e-mail body. No attachments. Accepts e-mail queries. No fax queries. Considers simultaneous queries. Responds in 8 weeks to queries. Returns materials only with SASE. Obtains most new clients through recommendations from others, solicitations, conferences.

Recent Sales Two young adult novels, by Sofia Quintero (Knopf). Other clients include K.L. Cook, Dr. Raeleen D'Agostino, Elisha Miranda, Mario Bosquez, Jennifer Calderon, Daniel Serrano, Yasmin Davidds.

Terms Agent receives 15% commission on domestic sales; 15% commission on foreign sales. Offers written contract; 30-day notice must be given to terminate contract.

Tips "Build a résumé by publishing short stories if you are a fiction writer."

☑ BAKER'S MARK LITERARY AGENCY

P.O. Box 8382, Portland OR 97207. (503)432-8170. E-mail: info@bakersmark.com. Website: www.Bakersmark.com. **Contact:** Bernadette Baker or Gretchen Stelter. Estab. 2005. Currently handles: 35% nonfiction books; 25% novels; 40% graphic novels.

● Prior to becoming an agent, Ms. Baker received an M.S. in professional writing and publishing from Portland State University. She was the marketing director for Beyond Words Publishing—where she headed up marketing campaigns for two *New York Times* bestsellers. Ms. Stelter has worked as a freelance editor and writer for several Australian newspapers and Bond University; she also worked for Ooligan Press.

Represents Nonfiction books, novels, novellas, scholarly books, animation, anthologies, graphic novels (preferably with art). **Considers these nonfiction areas:** Anthropology/archaeology; biography/autobiography; business/economics; ethnic/cultural interests; gay/lesbian issues; government/politics/law; how-to; humor/satire; popular culture; true crime/investigative; women's issues/studies. **Considers these fiction areas:** Comic books/cartoon; detective/police/crime; erotica; ethnic; experimental; fantasy; feminist; gay/lesbian; glitz; historical; horror; humor/satire; literary; mainstream/contemporary; mystery/suspense; psychic/supernatural; regional (Pacific Northwest); thriller; women's; chick lit.

○━ "Baker's Mark specializes in graphic novels and popular nonfiction with an extremely selective taste in commercial fiction." Actively seeking graphic novels, nonfiction, fiction. Does not want to receive Western, poetry, sci-fi or children's.

How to Contact Query with SASE, submit proposal package, synopsis, 5 sample chapter(s), author bio, sample art and script for graphic novels. No fax queries. Considers simultaneous queries. Returns materials only with SASE. Obtains most new clients through recommendations from others, solicitations.

Recent Sales *City of Readers: A Book Lover's Guide to Portland, Oregon*, by Gabriel Boehmer (Tall Grass Press); *Unaffordable Nation: Searching for a Decent Life in America*, by Jeffrey D. Jones (Prometheus Books); *German Town* and *The Fielding Course*, both graphic novels, by Laurence Klavan and Susan Kim (:01 First Second Books); *The Wrenchies*, by Farel Dalrymple (:01 First Second Books).

Terms Agent receives 15% commission on domestic sales; 20% commission on foreign sales. Offers written contract, binding for 18 months; 30-day notice must be given to terminate contract.

Writers' Conferences New York Comic Convention, BookExpo of America, San Diego Comic Con, Stumptown Comics Fest, Emerald City Comic Con.

☑ BENNETT & WEST LITERARY AGENCY

1004 San Felipe Lane, The Villages FL 32159. (352)751-2314. E-mail: joanpwest@comcast.net. Website: www.bennettwestlit.com. **Contact:** Joan West or Lois Bennett. Estab. 2005; adheres to AAR canon of ethics. Represents 80 clients. 60% of clients are new/unpublished writers. Currently handles: 30% nonfiction books; 65% novels; 5% juvenile books.

● Prior to becoming an agent, Ms. West was a college professor and editor; Ms. Bennett was a psychologist and writer.

Member Agents Joan West (fiction, nonfiction, no juvenile or YA); Lois Bennett (YA and fiction, no nonfiction).

Represents Nonfiction books, novels, juvenile books (YA). **Considers these nonfiction areas:** Biography/autobiography; memoirs; military/war; New Age/metaphysics; self-help/personal improvement; sociology; sports; true crime/investigative; women's issues/studies. **Considers these fiction areas:** Action/adventure; detective/police/crime; family saga; fantasy; historical; juvenile; literary; mainstream/contemporary; mystery/suspense; psychic/supernatural; regional; romance; science fiction; sports; thriller; young adult.

O→ "We are sensitive to the writer's needs and friendly to new writers." Does not want to receive erotica, horror, screenplays, picture books or academic.

How to Contact Query with SASE, submit proposal package, outline/proposal, synopsis, 3 sample chapter(s), author bio, indication whether a reply via e-mail is acceptable. Query only, if contacting by e-mail. Submit all YA to Ms. Bennett and all nonfiction to Ms. West. Accepts e-mail queries. No fax queries. Considers simultaneous queries. Responds in 2-4 weeks to queries. Returns materials only with SASE. Obtains most new clients through recommendations from others.

Recent Sales *From the Depths*, by Gerry Doyle; *Into the Woods*, by RR Smythe; *Marie Antoinette, Diana and Alexandra: The Third*, by Alexandra Levin; *The Flame of Learning: The Life of Louise Pound*, by Marie Krohn.

Terms Agent receives 15% commission on domestic sales; 20% commission on foreign sales. Offers written contract, binding for 1 year; 30-day notice must be given to terminate contract. Charges for postage and copying fees (five cents per page) for material sent to publishers.

Writers' Conferences The Villages Literary Festival; Gulf Coast Writers' Conference; Florida First Coast Writers' Conference.

Tips "Proofread and edit your material. Be sure you have your submission in the proper format. Please reference our guidelines for format. Nonfiction writers must have appropriate credentials."

BENREY LITERARY

P.O. Box 812, Columbia MD 21044. (443)545-5620. Fax: (886)297-9483. E-mail: query@benreyliterary.com. Website: www.benreyliterary.com. **Contact:** Janet Benrey. Estab. 2006. Represents 35 clients. 20% of clients are new/unpublished writers. Currently handles: 50% nonfiction books; 50% novels.

● Prior to her current position, Ms. Benrey was with the Hartline Literary Agency.

Represents Nonfiction books, novels, scholarly books (narrow focus). **Considers these nonfiction areas:** How-to; religious/inspirational; self-help/personal improvement; true crime/investigative. **Considers these fiction areas:** Action/adventure; detective/police/crime; family saga; literary; mainstream/contemporary; mystery/suspense; religious/inspirational; romance; thriller; women's.

O→ This agency's specialties include romance, women's fiction, mystery, true crime, thriller (secular and Christian), as well as Christian living, church resources, inspirational. Actively seeking women's fiction, romance, mystery, suspense, Christian living, church resources. Does not want to receive fantasy, science fiction, Christian speculative fiction, erotica or paranormal.

How to Contact Query with SASE, submit proposal package, synopsis, 3 sample chapter(s), author bio. More submission details available online. Accepts e-mail queries. No fax queries. Considers simultaneous queries. Responds in 6 weeks to queries; 3 months to mss. Returns materials only with SASE. Obtains most new clients through recommendations from others, solicitations, conferences.

Recent Sales Sold 30 titles in the last year. *Hunt Club*, by Lisa Landolt (Avon); *Soldier on the Porch*, by Sharon Wildwind (Five Star); *In the Dead of Winter*, by Nancy Mehl (Barbour); *A Bird in the Hand*, by Nancy Mehl (Barbour). Agent receives 15% commission on domestic sales; 20% commission on foreign sales. Offers written contract; 30-day notice must be given to terminate contract. "We pass on the out-of-pocket costs of copying and shipping manuscripts for new clients until we have made their first sales."

Tips "Understand the market as best you can. Attend conferences and network. Don't create a new genre."

MEREDITH BERNSTEIN LITERARY AGENCY

2095 Broadway, Suite 505, New York NY 10023. (212)799-1007. Fax: (212)799-1145. Estab. 1981. Member of AAR. Represents 85 clients. 20% of clients are new/unpublished writers. Currently handles: 50% nonfiction books; 50% fiction.

● Prior to opening her agency, Ms. Bernstein served at another agency for 5 years.

Represents Nonfiction books, novels. **Considers these nonfiction areas:** Any area of nonfiction in which the author has an established platform. **Considers these fiction areas:** Literary; mystery/suspense; romance; thriller; women's.

○➤ This agency does not specialize. It is very eclectic.

How to Contact Query with SASE. No e-mail or fax queries. Considers simultaneous queries. Obtains most new clients through recommendations from others, conferences, developing/packaging ideas.

Recent Sales Three untitled thrillers, by Jordan Dane (Avon); Three untitled House of Night spinoff books, by PC Cast and Kristen Cast (St. Martin's Press); Untitled work, by Susan Shapiro (St. Martin's); *Home from the Honeymoon,* by Sharon Naylor (Stewart, Tabori & Chang).

Terms Agent receives 15% commission on domestic sales; 20% commission on foreign sales. Charges clients $75 disbursement fee/year.

Writers' Conferences Southwest Writers' Conference; Rocky Mountain Fiction Writers' Colorado Gold; Pacific Northwest Writers' Conference; Willamette Writers' Conference; Surrey International Writers' Conference; San Diego State University Writers' Conference.

ℕ BLISS LITERARY AGENCY INTERNATIONAL, INC.

1601 N. Sepulveda Blvd, #389, Manhattan Beach CA 90266. E-mail: query@blissliterary.com. Website: www.blissliterary.com. **Contact:** Jenoyne Adams. Estab. 2007.

Member Agents Prior to her current position, Ms. Adams was with Levine Greenberg Literary Agency.

Represents Nonfiction books, novels, juvenile books. **Considers these nonfiction areas:** Narrative nonfiction, women's, parenting. **Considers these fiction areas:** Literary; multicultural; commercial.

○➤ "Middle grade, YA fiction and nonfiction, young reader? Bring it on. We absolutely adore these categories. We are interested in developing and working on projects that run the gamut—fantasy, urban/edgy, serious, bling-blingy? SURE. We love it all. And we haven't found it yet, but with a deep appreciation for anime and martial arts flicks, we are looking for the perfect graphic novel."

How to Contact Query via e-mail or snail mail. Send query, synopsis, one chapter. No attachments. Responds in 8 weeks to queries.

Tips Non-query related matters can be addressed by e-mailing info@blissliterary.com.

ℕ ✪ BOOK CENTS LITERARY AGENCY, LLC

2011 Quarrier Street, Charleston WV 25311. (304)347-2330, ext. 1105. E-mail: cwitthohn@hotmail.com. Web site: www.bookcentsliteraryagency.com. **Contact:** Christine Witthohn. Estab. 2006.

○➤ Actively seeking single title romance (contemporary, romantic comedy, women's lit, paranormal, mystery/suspense), mainstream mystery/suspense, medical or legal fiction, espionage. Does not want to receive category romance, erotica, inspirational, historical, sci-fi/fantasy, horror/dark thrillers, screenplays.

✪ BOOKENDS, LLC

136 Long Hill Rd., Gillette NJ 07933. Website: www.bookends-inc.com; bookendslitagency.blogspot.com. **Contact:** Jessica Faust, Jacky Sach, Kim Lionetti. Estab. 1999. Member of AAR. Represents 50+ clients. 10% of clients are new/unpublished writers. Currently handles: 50% nonfiction books; 50% novels.

Member Agents Jessica Faust (fiction: romance, erotica, chick lit, women's fiction, mysterious and suspense; nonfiction: business, finance, career, parenting, psychology, women's issues, self-help, health, sex); Jacky Sach (mysteries, women's fiction, suspense, self-help, spirituality, alternative and mainstream health, business and career, addiction, chick-lit nonfiction).

Represents Nonfiction books, novels. **Considers these nonfiction areas:** Business/economics; child guidance/parenting; ethnic/cultural interests; gay/lesbian issues; health/medicine; how-to; money/finance; New Age/metaphysics; psychology; religious/inspirational; self-help/personal improvement; sex; spirituality; true crime/investigative; women's issues/studies. **Considers these fiction areas:** Detective/police/crime (cozies); mainstream/contemporary; mystery/suspense; romance; thriller; women's; chick lit.

○➤ BookEnds does not want to receive children's books, screenplays, science fiction, poetry, or technical/military thrillers.

How to Contact Review Web site for guidelines, as they change. Accepts e-mail queries. No fax queries.

Recent Sales *1,000 Wine Secrets,* by Carolyn Hammond (Sourcebooks); *Wolf Tales III,* by Kate Douglas (Kensington Aphrodisia); *Women at Ground Zero,* by Mary Carouba and Susan Hagen (Alpha Books).

BRADFORD LITERARY AGENCY

5694 Mission Center Road, #347, San Diego CA 92108. (619)521-1201. E-mail: laura@bradfordlit.c om. Website: www.bradfordlit.com. **Contact:** Laura Bradford. Estab. 2001. Represents 23 clients. 20% of clients are new/unpublished writers. Currently handles: 10% nonfiction books; 90% novels.

- Ms. Bradford started with her first literary agency straight out of college and has 13 years of experience as a bookseller in parallel.

Represents Nonfiction books, novels, novellas (within a single author's collection), anthology. **Considers these nonfiction areas:** Business/economics; child guidance/parenting; current affairs; government/politics/law; health/medicine; history; how-to; memoirs; money/finance; popular culture; psychology; religious/inspirational; self-help/personal improvement; women's issues/studies. **Considers these fiction areas:** Action/adventure; detective/police/crime; erotica; ethnic; family saga; historical; humor/satire; mainstream/contemporary; mystery/suspense; religious/inspirational; romance; thriller; young adult; women's (and chick lit); psychic/supernatural.

- Actively seeking romance (including category), romantica, women's fiction, mystery, thrillers and young adult. Does not want to receive poetry, short stories, children's books (juvenile) or screenplays.

How to Contact Query with SASE, submit cover letter, first 30 pages of completed ms., synopsis and SASE. Send no attachments via e-mail; only send a query. Accepts e-mail queries. No fax queries. Considers simultaneous queries. Responds in 10 weeks to queries; 10 weeks to mss. Returns materials only with SASE. Obtains most new clients through solicitations.

Recent Sales Sold 8 titles in the last year. *Witch Heart*, by Anya Bast (Berkley Sensation); *Hotter After Midnight*, by Cynthia Eden (Kensington Brava); *Sweet and Sinful*, by Jodi Lynn Copeland; *Every Night I'm Yours*, by Christia Kelley; *Grimspace*, by Ann Aguirre (Ace); *Hawk's Talons*, by Vonna Harper.

Terms Agent receives 15% commission on domestic sales; 25% commission on foreign sales. Offers written contract, binding for 2 years; 45-day notice must be given to terminate contract. Charges for photocopies, postage, extra copies of books for submissions.

Writers' Conferences RWA National Conference; Romantic Times Booklovers Convention.

BRANDT & HOCHMAN LITERARY AGENTS, INC.

1501 Broadway, Suite 2310, New York NY 10036. (212)840-5760. Fax: (212)840-5776. **Contact:** Gail Hochman. Estab. 1913. Member of AAR. Represents 200 clients.

Member Agents Carl Brandt; Gail Hochman; Marianne Merola; Charles Schlessiger; Bill Contardi.

Represents Nonfiction books, novels, short story collections, juvenile books, journalism. **Considers these nonfiction areas:** Biography/autobiography; current affairs; ethnic/cultural interests; government/politics/law; history; women's issues/studies. **Considers these fiction areas:** Contemporary issues; ethnic; historical; literary; mainstream/contemporary; mystery/suspense; romance; thriller; young adult.

How to Contact Query with SASE. No e-mail or fax queries. Considers simultaneous queries. Responds in 1 month to queries. Returns materials only with SASE. Obtains most new clients through recommendations from others.

Recent Sales *Season of Betrayal*, by Margaret Lowrie Robertson (Harcourt); *The Misremembered Man*, by Christina McKenna (Toby Press). Other clients include Scott Turow, Carlos Fuentes, Ursula Hegi, Michael Cunningham, Mary Pope Osborne, Julia Glass.

Terms Agent receives 15% commission on domestic sales; 20% commission on foreign sales. Charges clients for ms duplication or other special expenses agreed to in advance.

Tips "Write a letter which will give the agent a sense of you as a professional writer—your long-term interests as well as a short description of the work at hand."

[N] ☐ BRESSLER SCOGGINS LITERARY AGENCY

338 N. Elm St., Suite 308, Greensboro NC 27401. (336)553-3982; NY phone (646)688-5043. Fax: (336)553-0959. E-mail: becky@amplify-comm.com. Website: www.bresslerscoggins.com. **Contact:** Becky Scoggins. Estab. 2007. 80% of clients are new/unpublished writers. Currently handles: 10% nonfiction books; 70% novels; 20% juvenile books.

- Prior to becoming an agent, Ms. Scoggins spent several years in corporate sales and marketing for Borders Group.

Member Agents Becky Scoggins (fiction, juvenile, children's, picture); Jordan Bressler (fiction: romance, Southern, literary, mystery).

Represents Nonfiction books, novels, juvenile books. **Considers these nonfiction areas:** Child guidance/parenting; humor/satire; memoirs. **Considers these fiction areas:** Action/adventure; humor/satire; juvenile; literary; mainstream/contemporary; mystery/suspense; picture books; regional; romance; young adult; women's.

⚊ "We specialize in romance, Southern and literary fiction. We are an energetic and fun agency that acts as your advocate and team in the publishing industry." Actively seeking romance, Southern lit, juvenile and young adult. Does not want to receive poetry, business, historical nonfiction or short stories.

How to Contact Query with SASE, submit synopsis, 3 sample chapter(s). Accepts e-mail and fax queries. Considers simultaneous queries. Responds in 3 months to queries; 6 months to mss. Returns materials only with SASE. Obtains most new clients through recommendations from others, solicitations, conferences.

Terms Agent receives 15% commission on domestic sales; 20% commission on foreign sales. Offers written contract; 60-day notice must be given to terminate contract. This agency charges for copying of ms. and sometimes for shipping/postage.

Writers' Conferences South Carolina Book Festival; BookExpo America.

Tips "Read our submission guidelines carefully! Please be sure your manuscript is polished and completed. Have someone read it who can give you an honest opinion before sending it to an agent. In your query, be unique and eye-catching. Most of all, be patient."

▣ BRICK HOUSE LITERARY AGENTS

80 Fifth Ave., Suite 1101, New York NY 10011. Website: www.brickhouselit.com. **Contact:** Sally Wofford-Girand. Member of AAR.

Member Agents Sally Wofford-Girand; Jenni Ferrari-Adler; Melissa Sarver, assistant.

Represents Nonfiction books, novels. **Considers these nonfiction areas:** Ethnic/cultural interests; history; memoirs; women's issues/studies; biography; science; natural history. **Considers these fiction areas:** Literary.

⚊ Actively seeking history, memoir, women's issues, cultural studies, literary fiction and quality commerical fiction.

How to Contact Query via mail or e-mail.

▣ ANDREA BROWN LITERARY AGENCY, INC.

1076 Eagle Drive, Salinas CA 93905. E-mail: andrea@andreabrownlit.com. Website: www.andreabrownlit.com. **Contact:** Andrea Brown, president. Estab. 1981. 10% of clients are new/unpublished writers.

• Prior to opening her agency, Ms. Brown served as an editorial assistant at Random House and Dell Publishing and as an editor with Knopf.

Member Agents Andrea Brown; Laura Rennert; Michelle Andelman; Caryn Wiseman; Jennifer Jaeger; Jennifer Laughran, associate agent; and Jamie Weiss, associate agent.

Represents Nonfiction books, novels. **Considers these nonfiction areas:** Juvenile nonfiction; memoirs; young adult; narrative. **Considers these fiction areas:** Juvenile; literary; picture books; thriller; young adult; women's.

How to Contact For picture books, submit complete ms, SASE. For fiction, submit short synopsis, SASE, first 3 chapters. For nonfiction, submit proposal, 1-2 sample chapters. For illustrations, submit 4-5 color samples (no originals). We only accept queries via e-mail. Considers simultaneous queries. Obtains most new clients through referrals from editors, clients and agents.

Recent Sales *Chloe,* by Catherine Ryan Hyde (Knopf); Sasha Cohen Autobiography (HarperCollins); *The Five Ancestors,* by Jeff Stone (Random House).

Terms Agent receives 15% commission on domestic sales; 20% commission on foreign sales. Offers written contract. Charges clients for shipping costs.

Writers' Conferences SCBWI; Asilomar; Maui Writers' Conference; Southwest Writers' Conference; San Diego State University Writers' Conference; Big Sur Children's Writing Workshop; William Saroyan Writers' Conference; Columbus Writers' Conference; Willamette Writers' Conference; La Jolla Writers' Conference; San Francisco Writers' Conference; Hilton Head Writers' Conference.

▣ BROWNE & MILLER LITERARY ASSOCIATES

410 S. Michigan Ave., Suite 460, Chicago IL 60605-1465. (312)922-3063. E-mail: mail@browneandmiller.com. **Contact:** Danielle Egan-Miller. Estab. 1971. Member of AAR, RWA, MWA, Author's Guild.

Represents 150 clients. 2% of clients are new/unpublished writers. Currently handles: 25% nonfiction books; 75% novels.

Represents Nonfiction books, novels. **Considers these nonfiction areas:** Agriculture/horticulture; animals; anthropology/archaeology; biography/autobiography; business/economics; child guidance/parenting; cooking/foods/nutrition; crafts/hobbies; current affairs; ethnic/cultural interests; health/medicine; how-to; humor/satire; memoirs; money/finance; nature/environment; popular culture; psychology; religious/inspirational; science/technology; self-help/personal improvement; sociology; sports; true crime/investigative; women's issues/studies. **Considers these fiction areas:** Detective/police/crime; ethnic; family saga; glitz; historical; literary; mainstream/contemporary; mystery/suspense; religious/inspirational; romance (contemporary, gothic, historical, regency); sports; thriller; paranormal, erotica.

> **O—** "We are partial to talented newcomers and experienced authors who are seeking hands-on career management, highly personal representation, and who are interested in being full partners in their books' successes. We are editorially focused and work closely with our authors through the whole publishing process, from proposal to after publication." Actively seeking highly commercial mainstream fiction and nonfiction. Does not represent poetry, short stories, plays, screenplays, articles, or children's books.

How to Contact Query with SASE. *No unsolicited mss.* Prefers to read material exclusively. Put "submission" in the subject line. Send no attachments. Responds in 6 weeks to queries. Returns materials only with SASE. Obtains most new clients through referrals, queries by professional/marketable authors.

Terms Agent receives 15% commission on domestic sales; 20% commission on foreign sales. Offers written contract, binding for 2 years. Charges clients for photocopying, overseas postage, faxes, phone calls.

Writers' Conferences BookExpo America; Frankfurt Book Fair; RWA National Conference; CBA National Conference; London Book Fair; Bouchercon, regional writers conferences.

Tips "If interested in agency representation, be well informed."

⬛ CASTIGLIA LITERARY AGENCY

1155 Camino Del Mar, Suite 510, Del Mar CA 92014. (858)755-8761. Fax: (858)755-7063. Website: home.earthlink.net/ ~ mwgconference/id22.html. Estab. 1993. Member of AAR, PEN. Represents 50 clients. Currently handles: 55% nonfiction books; 45% novels.

Member Agents Julie Castiglia; Winifred Golden; Sally Van Haitsma; Deborah Ritchken.

Represents Nonfiction books, novels. **Considers these nonfiction areas:** Animals; anthropology/archaeology; biography/autobiography; business/economics; child guidance/parenting; cooking/foods/nutrition; current affairs; ethnic/cultural interests; health/medicine; history; language/literature/criticism; money/finance; nature/environment; psychology; religious/inspirational; science/technology; self-help/personal improvement; women's issues/studies. **Considers these fiction areas:** Ethnic; literary; mainstream/contemporary; mystery/suspense; women's.

> **O—** Does not want to receive horror, screenplays, poetry or academic nonfiction.

How to Contact Query with SASE. No fax queries. Returns materials only with SASE. Obtains most new clients through recommendations from others, solicitations, conferences.

Recent Sales Sold 29 titles in the last year. *Opium Season*, by Joel Havferstein (Lyons); *Bride of Casa Dracula*, by Marta Acosta (S&S); *Forever*, by Doug Keister (Gibbs Smith); *Orphan's Alliance*, by Robert Buettner (Little, Brown); *Waiting for the Apocalypse*, by Veronica Chater (Norton).

Terms Agent receives 15% commission on domestic sales; 25% commission on foreign sales. Offers written contract; 6-week notice must be given to terminate contract.

Writers' Conferences Santa Barbara Writers' Conference; Southern California Writers' Conference; Surrey International Writers' Conference; San Diego State University Writers' Conference; Willamette Writers' Conference.

Tips "Be professional with submissions. Attend workshops and conferences before you approach an agent."

⬛ ◎ THE CHUDNEY AGENCY

72 North State Road, Suite 501, Briarcliff Manor NY 10510. (914)488-5008. E-mail: mail@thechudney agency.com. Website: www.thechudneyagency.com. **Contact:** Steven Chudney. Estab. 2002. Member of SCBWI. 90% of clients are new/unpublished writers.

• Prior to becoming an agent, Mr. Chudney held various sales positions with major publishers.
Represents Novels, juvenile books. **Considers these nonfiction areas:** Juvenile nonfiction. **Considers these fiction areas:** Historical; juvenile; literary; mystery/suspense; young adult.

○━ This agency specializes in children's books, and wants to find authors who are illustrators as well. Actively seeking children's books. Does not want to receive board books or lift-the flap books, fables, folklore, or traditional fairytales, poetry or "mood pieces", stories for "all ages" (as these ultimately are too adult oriented), message-driven stories that are heavy-handed, didactic or pedantic.

How to Contact Query with SASE, submit proposal package, 4-6 sample chapter(s). For children's, submit full text and 3-5 illustrations. Accepts e-mail and fax queries. Considers simultaneous queries. Responds in 2-3 weeks to queries; 3-4 weeks to mss.

Recent Sales Sold 25 + titles in the last year. The Youngest Templar trilogy, by Michael Spradlin (Putnam); Do the Math series, by Wendy Lichtman (Greenwillow/HarperCollins); *Sir Ryan's Quest*, by Jason Deeble (Roaring Books Press); *Braless in Wonderland*, by Debbie Reed Fischer (Dutton Books/Penguin). Other clients include Barry Varela, Linda Johns, Dorian Cirrone, Leda Scubert, Deborah Lynn Jacobs, Shirley Harazin, Julie Sitegemeyer, Carol Baicker-McKee.

Terms Agent receives 15% commission on domestic sales; 20% commission on foreign sales. Offers written contract, binding for 1 year; 30-day notice must be given to terminate contract.

Tips "If an agent has a Web site, review it carefully to make sure your material is appropriate for that agent. Read lots of books within the genre you are writing; work hard on your writing; don't follow trends—most likely, you'll be too late."

▣ THE CREATIVE CULTURE, INC.

72 Spring St., Suite 304, New York NY 10012. (212)680-3510. Fax: (212)680-3509. Website: www.the creativeculture.com. **Contact:** Debra Goldstein. Estab. 1998. Member of AAR.

• Prior to opening her agency, Ms. Goldstein and Ms. Gerwin were agents at the William Morris Agency; Ms. Naples was a senior editor at Simon & Schuster.

Member Agents Debra Goldstein (self-help, creativity, fitness, inspiration, lifestyle); Mary Ann Naples (health/nutrition, lifestyle, narrative nonfiction, practical nonfiction, literary fiction, animals/vegetarianism); Laura Nolan (literary fiction, parenting, self-help, psychology, women's studies, current affairs, science); Karen Gerwin; Emmanuelle Alspaugh (romance, general nonfiction, fiction).

Represents Nonfiction books, novels.

○━ Does not want to receive children's, poetry, screenplays or science fiction.

How to Contact Query with bio, book description, 5-7 sample pages (fiction only), SASE. "We only reply if interested." Accepts e-mail queries. No fax queries. Responds in 2 months to queries.

Recent Sales *Dr. Neal Barnard's Program for Reversing Diabetes*, by Neil Barnard (Rodale); *The Power of Patience: How to Slow the Rush and Enjoy More Happiness, Success, and Peace of Mind Every Day*, by M.J. Ryan (Broadway Books); *The Secret Lives of Curious Virgins: My Life as a Reluctant Good Girl*, by Carlene Bauer (HarperCollins). Other clients include David Awbrey, Tom Hughes, Brenda McClain, Paula Chaffee Scardamalia.

Ⓝ ▣ DANIEL LITERARY GROUP

1701 Kingsbury Drive, Suite 100, Nashville TN 37215. (615)730-8207. E-mail: submissions@daniellit erarygroup.com. Website: www.danielliterarygroup.com. **Contact:** Greg Daniel. Estab. 2007. Represents 45 clients. 30% of clients are new/unpublished writers. Currently handles: 85% nonfiction books; 15% novels.

• Prior to becoming an agent, Mr. Daniel spent 10 years in publishing—six at the executive level at Thomas Nelson Publishers.

Represents Nonfiction books, novels. **Considers these nonfiction areas:** Biography/autobiography; business/economics; child guidance/parenting; current affairs; health/medicine; history; how-to; humor/satire; memoirs; nature/environment; popular culture; religious/inspirational; self-help/personal improvement; sports; theater/film; women's issues/studies. **Considers these fiction areas:** Action/adventure; contemporary issues; detective/police/crime; family saga; historical; humor/satire; literary; mainstream/contemporary; mystery/suspense; religious/inspirational; thriller. The agency currently accepts all fiction topics, except for children's, romance and sci-fi.

○━ "We take pride in our ability to come alongside our authors and help strategize about where they want their writing to take them in both the near and long term. Forging close relationships with our authors, we help them with such critical factors as editorial refinement, branding, audience, and marketing." The agency is open to submissions in almost every popular category of nonfiction, especially if authors are recognized experts in their fields. Does not want to receive screenplays, poetry or short stories.

How to Contact Query with SASE, submit publishing history, author bio, brief synopsis of work, key selling points. E-queries only. Send no attachments. For fiction, send first 5 pages pasted in e-mail. Accepts e-mail queries. No fax queries. Responds in 1-6 weeks to queries. Returns materials only with SASE.

Recent Sales Sold 25 titles in the last year. *Wild Things*, by Stephen James and David Thomas (Tyndale); *My Life as a Holy Roller*, by Julie Lyons (WaterBrook Multnomah); *40 Days Living the Jesus Creed*, by Scot McKnight (Paraclete); *The Sacredness of Questioning Everything*, by David Dark (Zondervan); *The Preacher*, by Darren Dillman (David C. Cook); *A New Kind of Human*, by Alex McManus (Zondervan).

Ⓝ Ⓐ DAVIS WAGER LITERARY AGENCY

419 N. Larchmont Blvd., #317, Los Angeles CA 90004. (323)962-7741. E-mail: timothy@daviswager.com. Website: www.daviswager.com/. **Contact:** Timothy Wager. Estab. 2004.

● Prior to his current position, Mr. Wager was with the Sandra Dijkstra Literary Agency, where he worked as a reader and associate agent.

Represents Nonfiction books, novels. **Considers these fiction areas:** Literary.

○━ Actively seeking: "literary fiction and general-interest nonfiction."

How to Contact Query with SASE, submit author bio, synopsis for fiction, book proposal or outline for nonfiction. Query via e-mail. No fax queries.

Ⓐ LIZA DAWSON ASSOCIATES

350 Seventh Ave., Ste. 2003, New York NY 10001. (212)465-9071. Fax: (212)947-0460. Website: www.lizadawsonassociates.com. Member of AAR, MWA, Women's Media Group. Represents 50+ clients. 15% of clients are new/unpublished writers. Currently handles: 60% nonfiction books; 40% novels.

● Prior to becoming an agent, Ms. Dawson was an editor for 20 years, spending 11 years at William Morrow as vice president and 2 years at Putnam as executive editor. Ms. Bladell was a senior editor at HarperCollins and Avon. Ms. Miller is an *Essence*-bestselling author and niche publisher. Ms. Olswanger is an author.

Member Agents Liza Dawson (plot-driven literary fiction, historicals, thrillers, suspense, parenting books, history, psychology—both popular and clinical—politics, narrative nonfiction and memoirs) Caitlin Blasdell (science fiction, fantasy—both adult and young adult—parenting, business, thrillers and women's fiction) Anna Olswanger (gift books for adults, young adult fiction and nonfiction, children's illustrated books, and Judaica) Havis Dawson (business books, how-to and practical books, spirituality, fantasy, Southern-culture fiction and military memoirs); David Austern (fiction and nonfiction, with an interest in young adult, pop culture, sports, and male-interest works).

Represents Nonfiction books, novels, novels and gift books (Olswanger only). **Considers these nonfiction areas:** Biography/autobiography; health/medicine; history; memoirs; psychology; sociology; women's issues/studies; politics; business; parenting. **Considers these fiction areas:** Fantasy (Blasdell only); historical; literary; mystery/suspense; regional; science fiction (Blasdell only); thriller; African-American (Miller only).

○━ This agency specializes in readable literary fiction, thrillers, mainstream historicals, women's fiction, academics, historians, business, journalists and psychology.

How to Contact Query with SASE. Individual query e-mails are query[agentfirstname]@lizadawsonassociates.com. Responds in 3 weeks to queries; 6 weeks to mss. Obtains most new clients through recommendations from others, conferences.

Recent Sales Sold 40 titles in the last year. *Going for It*, by Karen E. Quinones Miller (Warner); *Mayada: Daughter of Iraq*, by Jean Sasson (Dutton); *It's So Much Work to Be Your Friend: Social Skill Problems at Home and at School*, by Richard Lavoie (Touchstone); *WORDCRAFT: How to Write Like a Professional*, by Jack Hart (Pantheon); . . .*And a Time to Die: How Hospitals Shape the End of Life Experience*, by Dr. Sharon Kaufman (Scribner); *Zeus: A Biography*, by Tom Stone (Bloomsbury).

Terms Agent receives 15% commission on domestic sales; 20% commission on foreign sales. Offers written contract. Charges clients for photocopying and overseas postage.

THE JENNIFER DECHIARA LITERARY AGENCY

31 East 32nd St., Suite 300, New York NY 10016. (212)481-8484. E-mail: jenndec@aol.com. Website: www.jdlit.com. **Contact:** Jennifer DeChiara. Estab. 2001. Represents 100 clients. 50% of clients are new/unpublished writers. Currently handles: 50% nonfiction books; 25% novels; 25% juvenile books.

- Prior to becoming an agent, Ms. DeChiara was a writing consultant, freelance editor at Simon & Schuster and Random House, and a ballerina and an actress.

Represents Nonfiction books, novels, juvenile books. **Considers these nonfiction areas:** Biography/ autobiography; child guidance/parenting; cooking/foods/nutrition; crafts/hobbies; current affairs; education; ethnic/cultural interests; gay/lesbian issues; government/politics/law; health/medicine; history; how-to; humor/satire; interior design/decorating; juvenile nonfiction; language/literature/ criticism; memoirs; military/war; money/finance; music/dance; nature/environment; photography; popular culture; psychology; science/technology; self-help/personal improvement; sociology; sports; theater/film; true crime/investigative; women's issues/studies. **Considers these fiction areas:** Confession; detective/police/crime; ethnic; family saga; fantasy; feminist; gay/lesbian; historical; horror; humor/satire; juvenile; literary; mainstream/contemporary; mystery/suspense; picture books; regional; sports; thriller; young adult; chick lit; psychic/supernatural; glitz.

- "We represent both children's and adult books in a wide range of ages and genres. We are a full-service agency and fulfill the potential of every book in every possible medium—stage, film, television, etc. We help writers every step of the way, from creating book ideas to editing and promotion. We are passionate about helping writers further their careers, but are just as eager to discover new talent, regardless of age or lack of prior publishing experience. This agency is committed to managing a writer's entire career. For us, it's not just about selling books, but about making dreams come true. We are especially attracted to the downtrodden, the discouraged, and the downright disgusted." Actively seeking literary fiction, chick lit, young adult fiction, self-help, pop culture, and celebrity biographies. Does not want westerns, poetry, or short stories.

How to Contact Query with SASE. Considers simultaneous queries. Responds in 3-6 months to queries; 3-6 months to mss. Returns materials only with SASE. Obtains most new clients through recommendations from others, conferences, query letters.

Recent Sales Sold 30 titles in the last year. *I Was a Teenage Popsicle*, by Bev Katz Rosenbaum (Berkley/JAM); *Hazing Meri Sugarman*, by M. Apostolina (Simon Pulse); *The 10-Minute Sexual Solution* and *Virgin Sex: A Guy's Guide to Sex*, by Dr. Darcy Luadzers (Hatherleigh Press). ***Movie/ TV MOW script(s) optioned/sold:*** *Geography Club*, by Brent Hartinger (East of Doheny). Other clients include Adam Meyer, Herbie J. Pilato, Chris Demarest, Jeff Lenburg, Joe Cadora, Tiffani Amber Thiessen, Bonnie Neubauer.

Terms Agent receives 15% commission on domestic sales; 20% commission on foreign sales. Offers written contract.

SANDRA DIJKSTRA LITERARY AGENCY

1155 Camino del Mar, PMB 515, Del Mar CA 92014. (858)755-3115. Fax: (858)794-2822. E-mail: sdla@dijkstraagency.com. **Contact:** Taryn Fagerness. Estab. 1981. Member of AAR, Authors Guild, PEN West, Poets and Editors, MWA. Represents 100+ clients. 30% of clients are new/unpublished writers. Currently handles: 50% nonfiction books; 45% novels; 5% juvenile books.

Member Agents Sandra Dijkstra; Jill Marsal; Kevan Lyon; Taryn Fagerness; Elise Capron; Kelly Sonnack.

Represents Nonfiction books, novels. **Considers these nonfiction areas:** Americana; animals (pets); anthropology/archaeology; business/economics; child guidance/parenting; cooking/foods/nutrition; ethnic/cultural interests; gay/lesbian issues; government/politics/law; health/medicine; history; juvenile nonfiction; language/literature/criticism; memoirs; military/war; money/finance; nature/environment; psychology; regional; religious/inspirational; science/technology; self-help/ personal improvement; sociology; travel; women's issues/studies; Asian studies; art; accounting; biography; environmental studies; technology; transportation. **Considers these fiction areas:** Erotica; ethnic; fantasy; juvenile (YA middle grade and picture books); literary; mainstream/contemporary; mystery/suspense; picture books; science fiction; thriller; graphic novels.

○→ Does not want to receive Western, screenplays, short story collections or poetry.

How to Contact Submit for fiction, send brief synopsis and 50 sample pages double-spaced and single-sided, SASE. No e-mail or fax queries. Responds in 6 weeks to queries. Obtains most new clients through recommendations from others, solicitations, conferences.

Recent Sales

Terms Agent receives 15% commission on domestic sales; 20% commission on foreign sales. Offers written contract. Charges clients for expenses for foreign postage and copying costs if a client requests a hard copy submission to publishers.

Tips "Be professional and learn the standard procedures for submitting your work. Be a regular patron of bookstores, and study what kind of books are being published and will appear on the shelves next to yours. Read! Check out your local library and bookstores—you'll find lots of books on writing and the publishing industry that will help you. At conferences, ask published writers about their agents. Don't believe the myth that an agent has to be in New York to be successful. We've already disproved it!"

☑ ◎ JIM DONOVAN LITERARY

4515 Prentice St., Suite 109, Dallas TX 75206. E-mail: jdlqueries@sbcglobal.net. **Contact:** Melissa Shultz, agent. Estab. 1993. Represents 30 clients. 10% of clients are new/unpublished writers. Currently handles: 75% nonfiction books; 25% novels.

Member Agents Jim Donovan (history—particularly American, military and Western; biography; sports; popular reference; popular culture; fiction—literary, thrillers and mystery); Melissa Shultz (chick lit, parenting, women's issues, memoir).

Represents Nonfiction books, novels. **Considers these nonfiction areas:** Biography/autobiography; business/economics; child guidance/parenting; current affairs; government/politics/law; health/medicine; history; how-to; memoirs; military/war; money/finance; music/dance; nature/environment; popular culture; sports; true crime/investigative; women's issues/studies. **Considers these fiction areas:** Action/adventure; detective/police/crime; literary; mainstream/contemporary; mystery/suspense; thriller; women's.

○→ This agency specializes in commercial fiction and nonfiction. Does not want to receive poetry, children's, short stories, inspirational or anything else not listed above.

How to Contact For nonfiction, send query letter and SASE. For fiction, send 3 sample chapters, synopsis, SASE. Responds to e-queries only if interested. Accepts e-mail queries. No fax queries. Considers simultaneous queries. Responds in 3 weeks to queries; 1 month to mss. Returns materials only with SASE. Obtains most new clients through recommendations from others.

Recent Sales Sold 24 titles in the last year. *Born to be Hurt*, by Sam Staggs (St. Martin's Press); *The Last Great Season*, by Mike Shropshire (Grand Central); *To Hell on a Fast Horse*, by Mark Gardner (Morrow); *Live Fast, Die Young*, by Jeff Guinn (Simon and Schuster).

Terms Agent receives 15% commission on domestic sales; 20% commission on foreign sales. Offers written contract, binding for 1 year; 30-day notice must be given to terminate contract. This agency charges for things such as overnight delivery and manuscript copying. Charges are discussed beforehand.

Tips "Get published in short form—magazine reviews, journals, etc.—first. This will increase your credibility considerably, and make it much easier to sell a full-length book."

☑ DUNHAM LITERARY, INC.

156 Fifth Ave., Suite 625, New York NY 10010-7002. (212)929-0994. Website: www.dunhamlit.com. **Contact:** Jennie Dunham. Estab. 2000. Member of AAR. Represents 50 clients. 15% of clients are new/unpublished writers. Currently handles: 25% nonfiction books; 25% novels; 50% juvenile books.

● Prior to opening her agency, Ms. Dunham worked as a literary agent for Russell & Volkening. The Rhoda Weyr Agency is now a division of Dunham Literary, Inc.

Represents Nonfiction books, novels, short story collections, juvenile books. **Considers these nonfiction areas:** Anthropology/archaeology; biography/autobiography; ethnic/cultural interests; government/politics/law; health/medicine; history; language/literature/criticism; nature/environment; popular culture; psychology; science/technology; women's issues/studies. **Considers these fiction**

areas: Ethnic; juvenile; literary; mainstream/contemporary; picture books; young adult.

How to Contact Query with SASE. No e-mail or fax queries. Responds in 1 week to queries; 2 months to mss. Obtains most new clients through recommendations from others, solicitations.

Recent Sales *America the Beautiful*, by Robert Sabuda; *Dahlia*, by Barbara McClintock; *Living Dead Girl*, by Tod Goldberg; *In My Mother's House*, by Margaret McMulla; *Black Hawk Down*, by Mark Bowden; *Look Back All the Green Valley*, by Fred Chappell; *Under a Wing*, by Reeve Lindbergh; *I Am Madame X*, by Gioia Diliberto.

Terms Agent receives 15% commission on domestic sales; 20% commission on foreign sales.

◪ DYSTEL & GODERICH LITERARY MANAGEMENT

1 Union Square W., Suite 904, New York NY 10003. (212)627-9100. Fax: (212)627-9313. E-mail: miriam@dystel.com. Website: www.dystel.com. **Contact:** Miriam Goderich. Estab. 1994. Member of AAR. Represents 300 clients. 50% of clients are new/unpublished writers. Currently handles: 65% nonfiction books; 25% novels; 10% cookbooks.

  • Dystel & Goderich Literary Management recently acquired the client list of Bedford Book Works.

Member Agents Stacey Glick; Jane Dystel; Miriam Goderich; Michael Bourret; Jim McCarthy; Lauren Abramo; Adina Kahn.

Represents Nonfiction books, novels, cookbooks. **Considers these nonfiction areas:** Animals; anthropology/archaeology; biography/autobiography; business/economics; child guidance/parenting; cooking/foods/nutrition; current affairs; education; ethnic/cultural interests; gay/lesbian issues; government/politics/law; health/medicine; history; humor/satire; military/war; money/finance; New Age/metaphysics; popular culture; psychology; religious/inspirational; science/technology; true crime/investigative; women's issues/studies. **Considers these fiction areas:** Action/adventure; detective/police/crime; ethnic; family saga; gay/lesbian; literary; mainstream/contemporary; mystery/suspense; thriller.

  ○─ This agency specializes in cookbooks and commercial and literary fiction and nonfiction.

How to Contact Query with SASE. Considers simultaneous queries. Responds in 1 month to queries; 6 weeks to mss. Obtains most new clients through recommendations from others, solicitations, conferences.

Terms Agent receives 15% commission on domestic sales; 19% commission on foreign sales. Offers written contract. Charges for photocopying. Galley charges and book charges from the publisher are passed on to the author.

Writers' Conferences Whidbey Island Writers' Conference; Backspace Writers' Conference; Iowa Summer Writing Festival; Pacific Northwest Writers' Association; Pike's Peak Writers' Conference; Santa Barbara Writers' Conference; Harriette Austin Writers' Conference; Sandhills Writers' Conference; Denver Publishing Institute; Love Is Murder.

Tips "Work on sending professional, well-written queries that are concise and addressed to the specific agent the author is contacting. No dear Sirs/Madam."

Ⓝ ◯ EAMES LITERARY SERVICES

4117 Hillsboro Road, Suite 251, Nashville TN 37215. Fax: (615)463.9361. E-mail: info@eamesliterary .com; John@eamesliterary.com; Ahna@eamesliterary.com. Website: www.eamesliterary.com. **Contact:** John Eames.

Member Agents John Eames, Ahna Phillips.

Represents Nonfiction books, novels. **Considers these nonfiction areas:** Memoirs; religious/inspirational; young adult. **Considers these fiction areas:** Religious/inspirational; young adult.

  ○─ This agency specializes in the Christian marketplace. Actively seeking adult and young adult fiction that sparks the imagination, illuminates some angle of truth about the human condition, causes the reader to view the world with fresh eyes, and supports a Christian perspective on life in all its complexities. Stories might be redemptive, or tragic. Characters might be noble, or flawed. Situations might be humorous, or dark. And many manuscripts might contain some combination of all of the above. We also seek adult and young adult nonfiction that is anecdotal as well as instructional, utilizes a "show, don't tell" philosophy of writing, and offers a unique and biblically sound perspective on a given topic. If the submission is a nonfiction narrative (or memoir), the work should follow most of the same recommendations for a work of fiction, as listed above.

Recent Sales *Less is More Leadership: 8 Secrets to How to Lead and Still Have a Life*, by H. Dale Bourke (Harvest House Publishers); *Lessons from Lucy*, by Wendy Murray Zoba (NavPress).

⦿ ETHAN ELLENBERG LITERARY AGENCY

548 Broadway, #5-E, New York NY 10012. (212)431-4554. Fax: (212)941-4652. E-mail: agent@ethan ellenberg.com. Website: www.ethanellenberg.com. **Contact:** Ethan Ellenberg. Estab. 1983. Represents 80 clients. 10% of clients are new/unpublished writers. Currently handles: 25% nonfiction books; 75% novels.

- Prior to opening his agency, Mr. Ellenberg was contracts manager of Berkley/Jove and associate contracts manager for Bantam.

Represents Nonfiction books, novels, children's books. **Considers these nonfiction areas:** Current affairs; health/medicine; history; military/war; science/technology; narrative, biography. **Considers these fiction areas:** Commerical fiction—specializing in romance/fiction for women, science fiction and fantasy, thrillers, suspense and mysteries, children's books (all types: picture books, middle grade and YA).

- ⊶ This agency specializes in commercial fiction—especially thrillers, romance/women's, and specialized nonfiction. "We also do a lot of children's books." Actively seeking commercial fiction as noted above—romance/fiction for women, science fiction and fantasy, thrillers, suspense and mysteries. Our other two main areas of interest are children's books and narrative nonfiction. We are actively seeking clients, follow the directions on our Web site. Does not want to receive poetry, short stories, Western's, autobiographies or screenplays.

How to Contact For fiction, send introductory letter, outline, first 3 chapters, SASE. For nonfiction, send query letter, proposal, 1 sample chapter, SASE. For children's books, send introductory letter, up to 3 picture book mss, outline, first 3 chapters, SASE. No fax queries. Accepts e-mail queries (no attachments). Will only respond to e-mail queries if interested. Considers simultaneous queries. Responds in 4-6 weeks to mss. Returns materials only with SASE.

Recent Sales *Sleeping With the Fishes and Dead and Loving It*, by Maryjanice Davidson (Berkley); *The Summoner*, by Gail Martin (Solaris); *Empress of Mijak*, by Karen Miller (Harper Australia); *Hellgate: London*, by Mel Odom (Pocket Books); *The Last Colony* and *Android's Dream*, by John Scalzi (Tor Books); *General Winston's Daughter*, by Sharon Shinn (Ace Books); *Dead Sexy*, by Amanda Ashley (Kensington); *A Kitten Tale*, by Eric Rohmann (Knopf); *Howl at the Moon*, by Christine Warren. Other clients include Mel Odom, MaryJanice Davidson, Amanda Ashley, Rebecca York, Bertrice Small, Eric Rohmann.

Terms Agent receives 15% commission on domestic sales; 10% commission on foreign sales. Offers written contract. Charges clients (with their consent) for direct expenses limited to photocopying and postage.

Writers' Conferences RWA National Conference; Novelists, Inc; and other regional conferences.

Tips "We do consider new material from unsolicited authors. Write a good, clear letter with a succinct description of your book. We prefer the first 3 chapters when we consider fiction. For all submissions, you must include a SASE or the material will be discarded. It's always hard to break in, but talent will find a home. Check our Web site for complete submission guidelines. We continue to see natural storytellers and nonfiction writers with important books."

⦿ THE ELAINE P. ENGLISH LITERARY AGENCY

4701 41st St. NW, Suite D, Washington DC 20016. (202)362-5190. Fax: (202)362-5192. E-mail: elaine @elaineenglish.com. Website: www.elaineenglish.com. **Contact:** Elaine English. Member of AAR. Represents 16 clients. 25% of clients are new/unpublished writers. Currently handles: 100% novels.

- Ms. English has been working in publishing for more than 20 years. She is also an attorney specializing in media and publishing law.

Represents Novels. **Considers these fiction areas:** Historical; multicultural; mystery/suspense; romance (single title, historical, contemporary, romantic, suspense, chick lit, erotic); thriller; general women's fiction. The agency is slowly but steadily acquiring in all mentioned areas.

- ⊶ Actively seeking women's fiction, including single-title romances. Does not want to receive any science fiction, time travel, children's, or young adult.

How to Contact Prefers e-queries sent to queries@elaineenglish.com. If requested, submit synopsis, first 3 chapters, SASE. Accepts e-mail queries. No fax queries. Responds in 6-12 weeks to queries;

6 months to requested ms. Returns materials only with SASE. Obtains most new clients through recommendations from others, conferences, submissions.

Recent Sales *The Blue-Eyed Devil*, by Diane Whiteside (Kensington).

Terms Agent receives 15% commission on domestic sales; 20% commission on foreign sales. Offers written contract; 30-day notice must be given to terminate contract. Charges only for copying and postage; generally taken from proceeds.

Writers' Conferences RWA National Conference; SEAK Medical & Legal Fiction Writing Conference; Novelists, Inc; Malice Domestic; Washington Romance Writers Retreat, among others.

☑ FAIRBANK LITERARY REPRESENTATION

199 Mount Auburn St., Suite 1, Cambridge MA 02138-4809. (617)576-0030. Fax: (617)576-0030. E-mail: queries@fairbankliterary.com. Website: www.fairbankliterary.com. **Contact:** Sorche Fairbank. Estab. 2002. Represents 40 clients. 20% of clients are new/unpublished writers. Currently handles: 60% nonfiction books; 22% novels; 3% story collections; 15% illustrated.

Member Agents Sorche Fairbank; Matthew Frederick (sports, nonfiction, architecture, design).

Represents Nonfiction books, novels, short story collections. **Considers these nonfiction areas:** Agriculture/horticulture; art/architecture/design; biography/autobiography; cooking/foods/nutrition; crafts/hobbies; current affairs; ethnic/cultural interests; gay/lesbian issues; government/politics/law; how-to; interior design/decorating; memoirs; nature/environment; photography; popular culture; science/technology; sociology; sports; true crime/investigative; women's issues/studies. **Considers these fiction areas:** Action/adventure; feminist; gay/lesbian; literary; mainstream/contemporary; mystery/suspense; sports; thriller; women's; Southern voices.

    O➤ "I have a small agency in Harvard Square, where I tend to gravitate toward literary fiction and narrative nonfiction, with a strong interest in women's issues and women's voices, international voices, class and race issues, and projects that simply teach me something new about the greater world and society around us. We have a good reputation for working closely and developmentally with our authors and love what we do." Actively seeking literary fiction, international and culturally diverse voices, narrative nonfiction, topical subjects (politics, current affairs), history, sports, architecture/design and pop culture. Does not want to receive romance, poetry, science fiction, young adult or children's works.

How to Contact Query with SASE, submit author bio. Accepts e-mail queries. No fax queries. Considers simultaneous queries. Responds in 6 weeks to queries; 10 weeks to mss. Returns materials only with SASE. Obtains most new clients through recommendations from others, solicitations, conferences, ideas generated in-house.

Recent Sales Sold 19 titles in the last year. *Tale of Two Subs*, by Jonathan J. McCullough (Grand Central); *101 Things I Learned in Architecture School*, by Matthew Frederick (MIT Press); *Invisible Sisters*, by Jessica Handler (Public Affairs); *Bent Objects*, by Terry Border (Running Press); *To Full Term: A Mother's Triumph Over Miscarriage*, by Darci Hamilton-Klein (Berkley/Penguin); *Spirit of Summer: At Home in the Thousand Islands*, by Kathleen Quigley (Rizzoli); *The Uncommon Quilter*, by Jeanne Williamson (Potter Craft/Crown); *Solar Revolution*, by Travis Bradford (The MIT Press).

Terms Agent receives 15% commission on domestic sales; 20% commission on foreign sales. Offers written contract, binding for 12 months; 30-day notice must be given to terminate contract.

Writers' Conferences San Francisco Writers' Conference, Muse and the Marketplace/Grub Street Conference, Washington Independent Writers' Conference, Murder in the Grove, Surrey International Writers' Conference.

Tips "Be professional from the very first contact. There shouldn't be a single typo or grammatical flub in your query. Have a reason for contacting me about your project other than I was the next name listed on some Web site. Please do not use form query software! Believe me, we can get a dozen or so a day that look identical—we know when you are using a form. Show me that you know your audience—and your competition. Have the writing and/or proposal at the very, very best it can be before starting the querying process. Don't assume that if someone likes it enough they'll 'fix' it. The biggest mistake new writers make is starting the querying process before they—and the work—are ready. Take your time and do it right."

☑ THE FIELDING AGENCY, LLC

269 S. Beverly Drive, No. 341, Beverly Hills CA 90212. (323)461-4791. E-mail: wlee@fieldingagency.com. Website: www.fieldingagency.com. **Contact:** Whitney Lee. Estab. 2003. Currently handles: 25% nonfiction books; 35% novels; 35% juvenile books; 5% other.

• Prior to her current position, Ms. Lee worked at other agencies in different capacities.

Represents Nonfiction books, novels, short story collections, juvenile books. **Considers these non-fiction areas:** Animals; anthropology/archaeology; art/architecture/design; biography/autobiography; business/economics; child guidance/parenting; cooking/foods/nutrition; crafts/hobbies; current affairs; education; ethnic/cultural interests; gay/lesbian issues; government/politics/law; health/medicine; history; how-to; humor/satire; interior design/decorating; juvenile nonfiction; language/literature/criticism; memoirs; military/war; money/finance; nature/environment; popular culture; psychology; science/technology; self-help/personal improvement; sociology; sports; translation; true crime/investigative; women's issues/studies. **Considers these fiction areas:** Action/adventure; comic books/cartoon; detective/police/crime; ethnic; family saga; fantasy; feminist; gay/lesbian; glitz; historical; horror; humor/satire; juvenile; literary; mainstream/contemporary; mystery/suspense; picture books; romance; thriller; young adult; women's.

⚬⟃ "We specialize in representing books published abroad and have strong relationships with foreign co-agents and publishers. For books we represent in the U.S., we have to be head-over-heels passionate about it because we are involved every step of the way." Does not want to receive scripts for TV or film.

How to Contact Query with SASE, submit synopsis, author bio. Accepts queries by e-mail and snail mail. No fax queries. Considers simultaneous queries. Returns materials only with SASE. Obtains most new clients through recommendations from others.

Recent Sales *The Crows of Pearblossom*, by Aldous Huxley (Abrams); *It's Vintage, Darling!*, by Christa Weil (Hodder & Stoughton); *Thugs and Kisses*, by Sue Ann Jaffarian (Midnight Ink); *The Fine Art of Confident Conversation*, by Debra Fine (Piatkus/LB).

Terms Agent receives 15% commission on domestic sales; 20% commission on foreign sales. Offers written contract, binding for 9-12 months.

Writers' Conferences London Book Fair; Frankfurt Book Fair.

◩ DIANA FINCH LITERARY AGENCY

116 W. 23rd St., Suite 500, New York NY 10011. (646)375-2081. E-mail: diana.finch@verizon.net. **Contact:** Diana Finch. Estab. 2003. Member of AAR. Represents 45 clients. 20% of clients are new/unpublished writers. Currently handles: 65% nonfiction books; 25% novels; 5% juvenile books; 5% multimedia.

• Prior to opening her agency, Ms. Finch worked at Ellen Levine Literary Agency for 18 years.

Represents Nonfiction books, novels, scholarly books. **Considers these nonfiction areas:** Biography/autobiography; business/economics; child guidance/parenting; computers/electronic; current affairs; ethnic/cultural interests; government/politics/law; health/medicine; history; how-to; humor/satire; juvenile nonfiction; memoirs; military/war; money/finance; music/dance; nature/environment; photography; popular culture; psychology; science/technology; self-help/personal improvement; sports; theater/film; translation; true crime/investigative; women's issues/studies. **Considers these fiction areas:** Action/adventure; detective/police/crime; ethnic; historical; literary; mainstream/contemporary; thriller; young adult.

⚬⟃ Actively seeking narrative nonfiction, popular science, and health topics. Does not want romance, mysteries, or children's picture books.

How to Contact Query with SASE or via e-mail (no attachments). No phone or fax queries. Considers simultaneous queries. Returns materials only with SASE. Obtains most new clients through recommendations from others.

Recent Sales *Armed Madhouse*, by Greg Palast (Penguin US/UK); *The Bush Agenda*, by Antonia Juhasz; *Journey of the Magi*, by Tudor Parfitt (Farrar, Straus & Giroux); *Radiant Days*, by Michael FitzGerald (Shoemaker & Hoard); *The Queen's Soprano*, by Carol Dines (Harcourt Young Adult); *Was the 2004 Election Stolen?*, by Steven Freeman and Joel Bleifuss (Seven Stories); *An Iranian Memoir*, by Azadeh Moaveni (Random House); *Great Customer Connections*, by Rich Gallagher (Amacom). Other clients include Daniel Duane, Thomas Goltz, Hugh Pope, Owen Matthews, Dr. Robert Marion, Loretta Napoleoni.

Terms Agent receives 15% commission on domestic sales; 20% commission on foreign sales. Offers written contract. "I charge for photocopying, overseas postage, galleys, and books purchased, and try to recap these costs from earnings received for a client, rather than charging outright."

Tips "Do as much research as you can on agents before you query. Have someone critique your query letter before you send it. It should be only 1 page and describe your book clearly—and why you are writing it—but also demonstrate creativity and a sense of your writing style."

[N] FINEPRINT LITERARY MANAGEMENT

240 West 35th St., Suite 500, New York NY 10001. (212)279-1282. E-mail: (agentfirstname)@fineprin tlit.com. Website: www.fineprintlit.com. Estab. 2007. Member of AAR.

Member Agents Peter Rubie, CEO (nonfiction interests include narrative nonfiction, popular science, spirituality, history, biography, pop culture, business, technology, parenting, health, self help, music, and food; fiction interests include literate thrillers, crime fiction, science fiction and fantasy, military fiction and literary fiction); Stephany Evans, president (nonfiction interests include health and well-ness—especially women's health, spirituality, lifestyle, home renovating/decorating, entertaining, food and wine, popular reference, and narrative nonfiction; fiction interests include stories with a strong and interesting female protagonist, both literary and upmarket commercial—including chick lit, romance, mystery, and light suspense); June Clark (nonfiction: entertainment, self-help, parent-ing, reference/how-to books, teen books, food and wine, style/beauty, and prescriptive business titles); Diane Freed (nonfiction: health/fitness, women's issues, memoir, baby boomer trends, par-enting, popular culture, self-help, humor, young adult, and topics of New England regional interest); Meredith Hays (both fiction and nonfiction: commercial and literary; she is interested in sophisticated women's fiction such as urban chick lit, pop culture, lifestyle, animals, and absorbing nonfiction accounts); Gary Heidt (history, science, true crime, pop culture, psychology, business, military and some literary fiction); Janet Reid (mysteries and offbeat literary fiction); Amy Tipton (edgy fiction—gritty and urban, women's fiction, nonfiction/memoir, and YA).

Represents Nonfiction books, novels. **Considers these nonfiction areas:** Business/economics; child guidance/parenting; cooking/foods/nutrition; government/politics/law; health/medicine; history; how-to; humor/satire; interior design/decorating; memoirs; music/dance; psychology; science/tech-nology; self-help/personal improvement; spirituality; true crime/investigative; women's issues/stud-ies; young adult; narrative nonfiction, popular science. **Considers these fiction areas:** Detective/police/crime; fantasy; literary; military/war; mystery/suspense; romance; science fiction; young adult; women's.

How to Contact Query with SASE, submit synopsis and first two chapters for fiction; proposal for nonfiction. Do not send attachments or manuscripts without a request. Accepts e-mail queries. No fax queries. Returns materials only with SASE. Obtains most new clients through recommendations from others, solicitations.

Recent Sales *Baby Proof*, by Emily Giffin (St. Martin's Press); *Crossing Into Medicine Country*, by David Carson (Arcade); *Rollergirl: Totally True Tales From the Track*, by Melissa Joulwan (Simon & Schuster); *The Pirate Primer*, by George Choundras (Writer's Digest Books).

Terms Agent receives 15% commission on domestic sales; 20% commission on foreign sales.

[●] FIREBRAND LITERARY

701 President St., #4, Brooklyn NY 11215. (347)689-4762. Fax: (347)689-4762. E-mail: info@firebran dliterary.com. Website: www.firebrandliterary.com. **Contact:** Nadia Cornier. Estab. 2005. Repre-sents 30 clients. 50% of clients are new/unpublished writers. Currently handles: 10% nonfiction books; 85% novels; 5% novellas.

● Before becoming an agent, Ms. Cornier started her own publicity firm and currently channels her interest and skill in marketing into her work with authors.

Member Agents Nadia Cornier, nadia@firebrandliterary.com (young adult, adult commercial, adult genre romance, nonfiction, some middle grade); Ted Malawar; Michael Stearns (YA, middle grade, select picture books).

Represents Nonfiction books, novels, novellas, juvenile books. **Considers these nonfiction areas:** Business/economics; how-to; humor/satire; juvenile nonfiction; language/literature/criticism; money/finance. **Considers these fiction areas:** Erotica; fantasy; historical; juvenile; literary; main-stream/contemporary; romance; young adult; women's.

● "Firebrand endeavors to be a perfect fit for a few authors rather than a good fit for every author—we do so by working with our writers with editing and marketing direction alongside the usual responsibilities of selling their properties. Most of all, we want the author to be excited about what they're doing and what they're writing. While we in turn want to be excited to work with them. That kind of enthusiasm is contagious and we feel it is an important foundation to have when it comes to pitching an author's ideas not only to publishers and the industry, but to the world." Does not want to receive screenplays, poetry or anything about terrorists.

How to Contact This agency prefers its submissions made through the Web site form. See the site for all details. Send ms only by request. No e-mail or fax queries. Considers simultaneous queries. Responds in 2 weeks to queries; 2 months to mss. Returns materials only with SASE. Obtains most new clients through recommendations from others, solicitations.

Recent Sales *Austenland*, by Shannon Hale (Bloomsbury); *How To Get Suspended & Influence People*, by Adam Selzer (Random House/Delacorte); *Bitterwood*, by James Maxey (Solaris); Salem Witch Tryouts (series), by Kelly McClymer (Simon & Schuster).

Terms Agent receives 15% commission on domestic sales; 20% commission on foreign sales. Offers written contract; 30-day notice must be given to terminate contract.

Tips "Send a short query letter and let the work stand on its own."

☑ FOLIO LITERARY MANAGEMENT, LLC

505 Eighth Ave., Suite 603, New York NY 10018. Website: www.foliolit.com. Alternate address: 1627 K St. NW, Suite 1200, Washington DC 20006. Estab. 2006. Member of AAR. Represents 100+ clients.

• Prior to creating Folio Literary Management, Mr. Hoffman worked for several years at another agency; Mr. Kleinman was an agent at Graybill & English; Ms. Wheeler was an agent at Creative Media Agency; Ms. Fine was an agent at Vigliano Associates and Trident Media Group; Ms. Cartwright-Niumata was an editor at Simon & Schuster, HarperCollins, and Avalon Books; Ms. Becker worked as a copywriter, journalist and author.

Member Agents Scott Hoffman; Jeff Kleinman; Paige Wheeler; Celeste Fine; Erin Cartwright-Niumata, Laney K. Becker; Rachel Vater (fantasy, young adult, women's fiction).

Represents Nonfiction books, novels, short story collections. **Considers these nonfiction areas:** Animals (equestrian); business/economics; child guidance/parenting; history; how-to; humor/satire; memoirs; military/war; nature/environment; popular culture; psychology; religious/inspirational; science/technology; self-help/personal improvement; women's issues/studies; narrative nonfiction; art; espionage; biography; crime; politics; health/fitness; lifestyle; relationship; culture; cookbooks. **Considers these fiction areas:** Erotica; fantasy; literary; mystery/suspense; religious/inspirational; romance; science fiction; thriller (psychological); young adult; women's; Southern; legal; edgy crime.

How to Contact Query with SASE or via e-mail (no attachments). Read agent bios online for specific submission guidelines. Responds in 1 month to queries.

Recent Sales Sold more than 100 titles in the last year. *Finn*, by Jon Clinch (Random House); *A Killing Tide*, by P.J. Alderman (Dorchester); *The Inn on Half Moon Bay*, by Diane Tyrrel (Berkley); *The Biography of Kenny Chesney*, by Holly Gleason (Center Street); *Color of the Sea*, by John Hamamura (Thomas Dunne Books/St. Martin's Press); *The 30-Day Diabetes Miracle* (Perigee); *Meow Is for Murder*, by Linda O. Johnston (Berkley Prime Crime); *Wildlife's Scotland Yard*, by Laurel Neme (Joseph Henry Press); *Mockingbird*, by Charles J. Shields (Henry Holt); *Under the Mask*, by Heidi Ardizzone (Norton); *The Culture Code*, by Dr. Clotaire Rapaille (Doubleday).

Tips "Please do not submit simultaneously to more than one agent at Folio. If you're not sure which of us is exactly right for your book, don't worry. We work closely as a team, and if one of our agents gets a query that might be more appropriate for someone else, we'll always pass it along. Keep in mind, however, that although we do work closely together, we are all individuals, with specific tastes and preferences—as well as our own unique working styles. So it's important that you check each agent's bio page for clear directions as to how to submit, as well as when to expect feedback."

☑ THE GISLASON AGENCY

219 Main St. SE, Suite 506, Minneapolis MN 55414-2160. (612)331-8033. Fax: (612)331-8115. Website: www.thegislasonagency.com/default.html. **Contact:** Barbara J. Gislason. Estab. 1992. Member of Minnesota State Bar Association, American Bar Association, Art & Entertainment Law Section, Animal Law, Minnesota Intellectual Property Law Association Copyright Committee; Icelandic Association of Minnesota, American Academy of Acupuncture and Oriental Medicine. 80% of clients are new/unpublished writers. Currently handles: 10% nonfiction books; 90% novels.

- Ms. Gislason became an attorney in 1980, and continues to practice art and entertainment law. She has been nationally recognized as a Leading American Attorney and a Super Lawyer.

Represents Nonfiction books, novels. **Considers these nonfiction areas:** Animals; companion animals/pets, feral animals, working and service animals, domestic and farm animals, laboratory animals, caged animals and wild animals. **Considers these fiction areas:** Animals (companion animals/pets, feral animals, working and service animals, domestic and farm animals, laboratory animals, caged animals and wild animals).

○━ This agency is not taking submissions at this time. Check the Web site for updates.

How to Contact No e-mail or fax queries. Responds in 1 months to queries; 6 months to mss. Obtains most new clients through recommendations from others, conferences, *Guide to Literary Agents, Literary Market Place,* other reference books.

Terms Agent receives 15% commission on domestic sales; 20% commission on foreign sales. Offers written contract, binding for 1 year with option to renew. Charges clients for photocopying and postage.

Writers' Conferences Southwest Writers Conference; Willamette Writers Conference; Wrangling with Writing; other state and regional conferences.

Tips "We are looking for manuscripts for adults that express ideas and tell stories powerful enough to change people's views about animals, without overt sentimentality. Your cover letter should be well written and include a detailed synopsis (fiction) or proposal (nonfiction), the first 3 chapters, and author bio. Appropriate SASE required. If submitting nonfiction work, explain how the submission differs from and adds to previously published works in the field. Remember to proofread. If the work was written with a specific publisher in mind, this should be communicated."

✪ FRANCES GOLDIN LITERARY AGENCY, INC.

57 E. 11th St., Suite 5B, New York NY 10003. (212)777-0047. Fax: (212)228-1660. E-mail: agency@goldinlit.com. Website: www.goldinlit.com. Estab. 1977. Member of AAR. Represents over 100 clients.

Member Agents Frances Goldin, principal/agent; Ellen Geiger, agent (commercial and literary fiction and nonfiction, cutting-edge topics of all kinds); Matt McGowan, agent/rights director (innovative works of fiction and nonfiction); Sam Stoloff, agent (literary fiction, memoir, history, accessible sociology and philosophy, cultural studies, serious journalism, narrative and topical nonfiction with a progressive orientation); Josie Schoel, agent/office manager (literary fiction and nonfiction).

Represents Nonfiction books, novels. **Considers these nonfiction areas:** Serious, controversial nonfiction with a progressive political orientation. **Considers these fiction areas:** Adult literary.

○━ "We are hands on and we work intensively with clients on proposal and manuscript development." Does not want anything that is racist, sexist, agist, homophobic, or pornographic. No screenplays, children's books, art books, cookbooks, business books, diet books, self-help, or genre fiction.

How to Contact Query with SASE. No unsolicited mss or work previously submitted to publishers. Prefers hard-copy queries. Responds in 6 weeks to queries.

Recent Sales *Skin Deep*, by Dalton Conley (Pantheon); *Conned: How Millions Have Lost the Right to Vote*, by Sasha Abramsky (New Press); *Gotham II*, by Mike Wallace; *Animal, Vegetable, Miracle*, by Barbara Kingslover; an untitled memoir by Staceyann Chin.

⌀ IRENE GOODMAN LITERARY AGENCY

80 Fifth Ave., Suite 1101, New York NY 10011. E-mail: queries@irenegoodman.com. Website: www.irenegoodman.com. **Contact:** Irene Goodman, Miriam Kriss. Member of AAR.

Member Agents Irene Goodman; Miriam Kriss; Barbara Poelle.

Represents Nonfiction books, novels. **Considers these nonfiction areas:** History; parenting, social issues, francophilia, anglophilia, Judaica, lifestyles, cooking, memoir. **Considers these fiction areas:** Historical; literary; mystery/suspense; romance; thriller; young adult; women's; chick lit; modern urban fantasies.

○━ Specializes in "the finest in commercial fiction and nonfiction. We have a strong background in women's voices, including mysteries, romance, women's fiction, thrillers, suspense, and chick lit. Historical fiction is one of Irene's particular passions and Miriam is fanatical about modern urban fantasies. We are also very interested in young adult fiction, both literary and those with an edgy, chick-litty voice. In nonfiction, Irene is looking for topics on narrative history, social issues and trends, education, Judaica, Francophilia, Anglophilia, other cultures, animals, food, crafts, and memoir."

How to Contact Query with SASE, submit synopsis, first 10 pages. E-mail queries only! See the Web site submission page. No e-mail attachments. Responds in 2 months to queries.

Recent Sales *Beg For Mercy*, by Toni Andrews; *The Devil Inside*, by Jenna Black; *Hooking Up or Holding Out*, by Jamie Callan; *Seducing The Spy*, by Celeste Bradley.

Tips "We are receiving an unprecedented amount of e-mail queries. If you find that the mailbox is full, please try again in two weeks. E-mail queries to our personal addresses will not be answered."

☑ ASHLEY GRAYSON LITERARY AGENCY

1342 18th St., San Pedro CA 90732. Fax: (310)514-1148. E-mail: graysonagent@earthlink.net. Estab. 1976. Member of AAR. Represents 100 clients. 5% of clients are new/unpublished writers. Currently handles: 20% nonfiction books; 50% novels; 30% juvenile books.

Member Agents Ashley Grayson (fantasy, mystery, thrillers, young adult); Carolyn Grayson (chick lit, mystery, children's, nonfiction, women's fiction, romance, thrillers); Denise Dumars (mind/body/spirit, women's fiction, dark fantasy/horror); Lois Winston (women's fiction, chick lit, mystery).

Represents Nonfiction books, novels. **Considers these nonfiction areas:** Business/economics; computers/electronic; history; popular culture; science/technology; self-help/personal improvement; sports; true crime/investigative; mind/body/spirit; health; lifestyle. **Considers these fiction areas:** Fantasy; juvenile; multicultural; mystery/suspense; romance; science fiction; young adult; women's; chick lit.

> ⌐ "We prefer to work with published (traditional print), established authors. We will give first consideration to authors who come recommended to us by our clients or other publishing professionals. We accept a very small number of new, previously unpublished authors."

How to Contact As of early 2008, the agency was only open to fiction authors with publishing credits (no self-published). For nonfiction, only writers with great platforms will be considered.

Recent Sales *Ball Don't Lie*, by Matt de la Pena (Delacorte); *Heaven*, by Jack Cohen and Ian Stewart (Warner Books); *I Wish I Never Met You*, by Denise Wheatley (Touchstone/Simon & Schuster). Other clients include Isaac Adamson, John Barnes, Andrew Fox, Barb and J.C. Hendee, Geoffrey Landis, Bruce Coville, J.B. Cheaney, David Lubar and Christopher Pike.

Terms Agent receives 15% commission on domestic sales; 20% commission on foreign sales.

◻ JILL GRINBERG LITERARY AGENCY

244 Fifth Ave., Floor 11, New York NY 10011. (212)620-5883. Fax: (212)627-4725. E-mail: jillgrin@aol.com. Website: www.grinbergliterary.com.

> • Prior to her current position, Ms. Grinberg was at Anderson Grinberg Literary Management.

Member Agents Jill Grinberg; Kirsten Wolf (foreign rights).

Represents Nonfiction books, novels. **Considers these nonfiction areas:** Biography/autobiography; business/economics; current affairs; government/politics/law; health/medicine; history; multicultural; psychology; science/technology; spirituality; travel; women's issues/studies. **Considers these fiction areas:** Fantasy; historical; romance; science fiction; young adult; women's; literary fiction, commercial fiction, children's, middle grade.

How to Contact Query with SASE, submit Send a proposal and author bio for nonfiction; send a query, synopsis and the first 50 pages for fiction. No e-mail or fax queries.

Recent Sales *Red Sky in Mourning*, by Jill Grinberg (Hyperion); *Strange Angel*, by George Pendle (Harcourt); *Jesse James: Last Rebel of the Civil War*, by T.J. Stiles (Vintage); *Searching for El Dorado*, by Marc Herman (Nan A. Talese).

Tips "We prefer submissions by mail."

Ⓝ ☑ LAURA GROSS LITERARY AGENCY

75 Clinton Place, Newton MA 02459. (617)964-2977. Fax: (617)964-3023. E-mail: LGLitAg@aol.com. **Contact:** Laura Gross. Estab. 1988. Represents 30 clients. 75% of clients are new/unpublished writers. Currently handles: 40% nonfiction books; 50% novels; 10% scholarly books.

> • Prior to becoming an agent, Ms. Gross was an editor.

Represents Nonfiction books, novels. **Considers these nonfiction areas:** Biography/autobiography; child guidance/parenting; current affairs; ethnic/cultural interests; government/politics/law; health/

medicine; history; memoirs; popular culture; psychology; sports; women's issues/studies. **Considers these fiction areas:** Historical; literary; mainstream/contemporary; mystery/suspense; thriller.
How to Contact Query with SASE, submit author bio. Accepts e-mail queries. No fax queries. Obtains most new clients through recommendations from others.
Recent Sales Sold 10+ titles in the last year. This agency prefers not to share information on specific sales.
Terms Agent receives 15% commission on domestic sales; 20% commission on foreign sales. Offers written contract.

☑ REECE HALSEY NORTH

98 Main St., #704, Tiburon CA 94920. Fax: (415)789-9177. E-mail: info@reecehalseynorth.com. Website: www.reecehalseynorth.com. **Contact:** Kimberley Cameron. Estab. 1957 (Reece Halsey Agency); 1993 (Reece Halsey North). Member of AAR. Represents 40 clients. 30% of clients are new/unpublished writers. Currently handles: 75% fiction, 25% nonfiction.

- The Reece Halsey Agency has had an illustrious client list of established writers, including the estate of Aldous Huxley, and has represented Upton Sinclair, William Faulkner, and Henry Miller.

Member Agents Kimberley Cameron, Elizabeth Evans; Phil Lang; April Eberhardt.
Represents Nonfiction books, novels. **Considers these nonfiction areas:** Biography/autobiography; current affairs; history; language/literature/criticism; popular culture; science/technology; true crime/investigative; women's issues/studies. **Considers these fiction areas:** Action/adventure; contemporary issues; detective/police/crime; ethnic; family saga; historical; horror; literary; mainstream/contemporary; mystery/suspense; science fiction; thriller; women's.

O→ "We are looking for a unique and heartfelt voice that conveys a universal truth."
How to Contact Query with SASE, first 50 pages of novel. Please do not fax queries. Responds in 3-6 weeks to queries; 1 month to mss. Obtains most new clients through recommendations from others, solicitations.
Terms Agent receives 15% commission on domestic sales; 10% commission on dramatic rights sales. Offers written contract, binding for 1 year. Requests 6 copies of ms if representing an author.
Writers' Conferences Maui Writers Conference; Aspen Summer Words Literary Festival; Willamette Writers Conference, numerous others.
Tips "Always send a polite, well-written query and please include a SASE with it."

ℕ ☑ HALSTON FREEMAN LITERARY AGENCY, INC.

140 Broadway, 46th Floor, New York NY 10005. E-mail: queryhalstonfreemanliterary@hotmail.com. **Contact:** Molly Freeman, Betty Halston. Estab. 2007. Currently handles: 65% nonfiction books; 35% novels.

- Prior to becoming an agent, Ms. Halston was a marketing and promotion director for a local cable affiliate; Ms. Freeman was a television film editor and ad agency copywriter.

Member Agents Molly Freeman, Betty Halston.
Represents Nonfiction books, novels. **Considers these nonfiction areas:** Agriculture/horticulture; biography/autobiography; business/economics; child guidance/parenting; current affairs; ethnic/cultural interests; gay/lesbian issues; government/politics/law; health/medicine; history; how-to; humor/satire; memoirs; New Age/metaphysics; psychology; self-help/personal improvement; true crime/investigative; women's issues/studies. **Considers these fiction areas:** Action/adventure; detective/police/crime; ethnic; feminist; historical; horror; humor/satire; literary; mainstream/contemporary; mystery/suspense; romance; science fiction; thriller; westerns/frontier; women's.

O→ "We are a hands-on agency specializing in quality nonfiction and fiction. As a new agency, it is imperative that we develop relationships with good writers who are smart, hardworking and understand what's required of them to promote their books." Does not want to receive children's books, textbooks or poetry. Send no e-mail attachments.
How to Contact Query with SASE. For nonfiction, include sample chapters, synopsis, platform, bio and competitive titles. For fiction, include synopsis, bio and three sample chapters. No e-mail attachments. Accepts e-mail queries. No fax queries. Considers simultaneous queries. Responds in 2-6 weeks to queries; 1-2 months to mss. Obtains most new clients through recommendations from others, solicitations, conferences.
Terms Agent receives 15% commission on domestic sales; 20% commission on foreign sales. This agency charges clients for copying and postage directly related to the project.

🖊 THE JOY HARRIS LITERARY AGENCY, INC.

156 Fifth Ave., Suite 617, New York NY 10010. (212)924-6269. Fax: (212)924-6609. **Contact:** Joy Harris. Member of AAR. Represents more than 100 clients. Currently handles: 50% nonfiction books; 50% novels.

Represents Nonfiction books, novels. **Considers these fiction areas:** Ethnic; experimental; family saga; feminist; gay/lesbian; glitz; hi-lo; historical; humor/satire; literary; mainstream/contemporary; multicultural; multimedia; mystery/suspense; regional; short story collections; spiritual; translation; young adult; women's.

> **0→** No screenplays.

How to Contact Query with sample chapter, outline/proposal, SASE. No e-mail or fax queries. Considers simultaneous queries. Responds in 2 months to queries. Returns materials only with SASE. Obtains most new clients through recommendations from clients and editors.

Recent Sales This agency prefers not to share information on specific sales.

Terms Agent receives 15% commission on domestic sales; 20% commission on foreign sales. Charges clients for some office expenses.

🖊 HARTLINE LITERARY AGENCY

123 Queenston Dr., Pittsburgh PA 15235-5429. (412)829-2483. Fax: (412)829-2432. E-mail: joyce@hartlineliterary.com. Website: www.hartlineliterary.com. **Contact:** Joyce A. Hart. Estab. 1990. Represents 40 clients. 20% of clients are new/unpublished writers. Currently handles: 40% nonfiction books; 60% novels.

Member Agents Joyce A. Hart, principal agent; Andrea Boeshaar; Terry Burns; Tamela Hancock Murray; Diana Flegal; Erik Schmidgal.

Represents Nonfiction books, novels. **Considers these nonfiction areas:** Business/economics; child guidance/parenting; cooking/foods/nutrition; money/finance; religious/inspirational; self-help/personal improvement; women's issues/studies. **Considers these fiction areas:** Action/adventure; contemporary issues; family saga; historical; literary; mystery/suspense (amateur sleuth, cozy); regional; religious/inspirational; romance (contemporary, gothic, historical, regency); thriller.

> **0→** This agency specializes in the Christian bookseller market. Actively seeking adult fiction, self-help, nutritional books, devotional, and business. Does not want to receive erotica, gay/lesbian, fantasy, horror, etc.

How to Contact Submit summary/outline, author bio, 3 sample chapters. Accepts e-mail and fax queries. Considers simultaneous queries. Responds in 2 months to queries; 3 months to mss. Returns materials only with SASE. Obtains most new clients through recommendations from others.

Recent Sales *A Tendering in the Storm* and *A Mending at the Edge*, by Jane Kirkpatrick, (Waterbrook); *Jillian Dare*, by Melanie Jeschke, (Revell); *Gone to Glory*, by Ron & Janet Benrey (Steeple Hill); *A Candle in the Darkness* and *Through the Eyes of Love*, by Dorothy Clark (Steeple Hill); *A Cowboy Worth Marrying*, by Deborah Clopton (Steeple Hill); *Melodies for Murder*, Donn Taylor; *Right from the Start*, by Brenda Nixon (Revell).

Terms Agent receives 15% commission on domestic sales. Offers written contract.

🖊 RICHARD HENSHAW GROUP

22 West 23rd St., Fifth Floor, New York NY 10010. (212)414-1172. Fax: (212)414-1182. E-mail: submissions@henshaw.com. Website: www.rich.henshaw.com. **Contact:** Rich Henshaw. Estab. 1995. Member of AAR, SinC, MWA, HWA, SFWA, RWA. Represents 35 clients. 20% of clients are new/unpublished writers. Currently handles: 35% nonfiction books; 65% novels.

> • Prior to opening his agency, Mr. Henshaw served as an agent with Richard Curtis Associates, Inc.

Represents Nonfiction books, novels. **Considers these nonfiction areas:** Animals; biography/autobiography; business/economics; child guidance/parenting; computers/electronic; cooking/foods/nutrition; current affairs; gay/lesbian issues; government/politics/law; health/medicine; how-to; humor/satire; military/war; money/finance; music/dance; nature/environment; New Age/metaphysics; popular culture; psychology; science/technology; self-help/personal improvement; sociology; sports; true crime/investigative; women's issues/studies. **Considers these fiction areas:** Action/adventure; detective/police/crime; ethnic; family saga; fantasy; glitz; historical; horror; humor/satire; literary; mainstream/contemporary; mystery/suspense; psychic/supernatural; romance; science fiction; sports; thriller.

☯ This agency specializes in thrillers, mysteries, science fiction, fantasy and horror.

How to Contact Query with SASE. Responds in 3 weeks to queries; 6 weeks to mss. Obtains most new clients through recommendations from others, solicitations, conferences.

Recent Sales *Prepared For Rage*, By Dana Stabenow (St. Martin's Press); *The Girl With The Braided Hair*, by Margaret Coel (Berkley); *The History Of The Ancient World*, by Susan Wise Bauer (Norton); *The Art Of The Public Grovel*, By Susan Wise Bauer (Princeton University Press); *Three Sisters*, by James D. Doss (St. Martin's Press); *The Serpent Prince*, by Elizabeth Hoyt (Grand Central Publishing); *Hot*, by Julia Harper (Grand Central Publishing); *Dog Leg: Alternative Therapies For Animals*, by Lisa Preston (Alpine Publishing). Other clients include Jessie Wise, Peter van Dijk, Jay Caselberg, Judith Laik.

Terms Agent receives 15% commission on domestic sales; 20% commission on foreign sales. No written contract. 100% of business is derived from commissions on ms sales. Charges clients for photocopying and book orders.

Tips "While we do not have any reason to believe that our submission guidelines will change in the near future, writers can find up-to-date submission policy information on our Web site. Always include a SASE with correct return postage."

☑ HIDDEN VALUE GROUP

1240 E. Ontario Ave., Ste. 102-148, Corona CA, 92881. (951)549-8891. Fax: (951)549-8891. E-mail: bookquery@hiddenvaluegroup.com. Website: www.hiddenvaluegroup.com. **Contact:** Nancy Jernigan. Estab. 2001. Represents 40 clients. 20% of clients are new/unpublished writers.

Member Agents Jeff Jernigan, jjernigan@hiddenvaluegroup.com (men's nonfiction, fiction, Bible studies/curriculum, marriage and family); Nancy Jernigan, njernigan@hiddenvaluegroup.com (nonfiction, women's issues, inspiration, marriage and family, fiction).

Represents Nonfiction books, novels, juvenile books. **Considers these nonfiction areas:** Biography/autobiography; business/economics; child guidance/parenting; history; how-to; juvenile nonfiction; language/literature/criticism; memoirs; money/finance; psychology; religious/inspirational; self-help/personal improvement; women's issues/studies. **Considers these fiction areas:** Action/adventure; detective/police/crime; fantasy; literary; religious/inspirational; thriller; westerns/frontier; women's.

☯ "The Hidden Value Group specializes in helping authors throughout their publishing career. We believe that every author has a special message to be heard and we specialize in getting that message heard." Actively seeking established fiction authors, and authors who are focusing on women's issues. Does not want to receive poetry or short stories.

How to Contact Query with SASE, submit synopsis, 3 sample chapter(s), author bio. Accepts queries to bookquery@hiddenvaluegroup.com. Accepts e-mail queries. No fax queries. Considers simultaneous queries. Responds in 1 month to queries; 1 month to mss. Returns materials only with SASE. Obtains most new clients through recommendations from others, solicitations.

Recent Sales *Tilt*, by Erik Rees (Group Publishing); *Character Makeover*, by Katie Brazelton (Zondervan); *More Than a Match*, by Michael and Amy Smalley (Waterbrook Press); *Body, Beauty, Boys*, by Sarah Bragg; *The DNA of Relationships*, by Gary Smalley; *A Happier, Healthier You*, by Lorraine Bosse Smith.

Terms Agent receives 15% commission on domestic sales; 15% commission on foreign sales. Offers written contract.

Writers' Conferences Glorieta Christian Writers' Conference; CLASS Publishing Conference.

☑ FREDERICK HILL BONNIE NADELL, INC.

1842 Union St., San Francisco CA 94123. (415)921-2910. Fax: (415)921-2802. **Contact:** Elise Proulx. Estab. 1979. Represents 100 clients.

Member Agents Bonnie Nadell; Elise Proulx, associate.

Represents Nonfiction books, novels. **Considers these nonfiction areas:** Current affairs; health/medicine; history; language/literature/criticism; nature/environment; popular culture; science/technology; biography; government/politics, narrative. **Considers these fiction areas:** Literary; mainstream/contemporary.

How to Contact Query with SASE. Keep your query to one page. Send via snail mail. No e-mail or fax queries. Considers simultaneous queries. Returns materials only with SASE.

Recent Sales *It Might Have Been What He Said*, by Eden Collinsworth; *Consider the Lobster and Other Essays*, by David Foster Wallace; *The Underdog*, by Joshua Davis.

Terms Agent receives 15% commission on domestic sales; 20% commission on foreign sales; 15% commission on dramatic rights sales. Charges clients for photocopying and foreign mailings.

JABBERWOCKY LITERARY AGENCY

P.O. Box 4558, Sunnyside NY 11104-0558. (718)392-5985. Website: www.awfulagent.com. **Contact:** Joshua Bilmes. Estab. 1994. Member of SFWA. Represents 40 clients. 15% of clients are new/unpublished writers. Currently handles: 15% nonfiction books; 75% novels; 5% scholarly books; 5% other.

Represents Nonfiction books, novels, scholarly books. **Considers these nonfiction areas:** Biography/autobiography; business/economics; cooking/foods/nutrition; current affairs; gay/lesbian issues; government/politics/law; health/medicine; history; humor/satire; language/literature/criticism; military/war; money/finance; nature/environment; popular culture; science/technology; sociology; sports; theater/film; true crime/investigative; women's issues/studies. **Considers these fiction areas:** Action/adventure; contemporary issues; detective/police/crime; ethnic; family saga; fantasy; gay/lesbian; glitz; historical; horror; humor/satire; literary; mainstream/contemporary; psychic/supernatural; regional; science fiction; sports; thriller.

○⚷ This agency represents quite a lot of genre fiction and is actively seeking to increase the amount of nonfiction projects. It does not handle juvenile or young adult. Book-length material only—no poetry, articles, or short fiction.

How to Contact Query with SASE. Do not send mss unless requested. No e-mail or fax queries. Considers simultaneous queries. Responds in 3 weeks to queries. Returns materials only with SASE. Obtains most new clients through solicitations, recommendation by current clients.

Recent Sales Sold 30 US and 100 foreign titles in the last year. *From Dead to Worse*, by Charlaine Harris; *Victory Conditions*, by Elizabeth Moon; *Underground*, by Kat Richardson; Mistborn & Alcatraz series by Brandon Sanderson. Other clients include Simon Green, Tanya Huff, Tobias Buckell.

Terms Agent receives 15% commission on domestic sales; 20% commission on foreign sales. Offers written contract, binding for 1 year. Charges clients for book purchases, photocopying, international book/ms mailing.

Writers' Conferences Malice Domestic (May 2009); World Sci-Fi Convention (August 2008); full schedule on Web site.

Tips "In approaching with a query, the most important things to me are your credits and your biographical background to the extent it's relevant to your work. I (and most agents) will ignore the adjectives you may choose to describe your own work."

JELLINEK & MURRAY LITERARY AGENCY

HI 96822. E-mail: r.jellinek@verizon.net; jellinek@lava.net. **Contact:** Roger Jellinek. Estab. 1995. Represents 75 clients. 90% of clients are new/unpublished writers. Currently handles: 70% nonfiction books; 30% novels.

● Prior to becoming an agent, Mr. Jellinek was deputy editor, *New York Times Book Review* (1966-1974); editor-in-chief, New York Times Book Co. (1975-1981); editor/packager of book/TV projects (1981-1995); editorial director, Inner Ocean Publishing (2000-2003).

Member Agents Roger Jellinek; Eden Lee Murray. Literary Associates: Grant Ching; Lavonne Leong; Jeremy Colvin.

Represents Nonfiction books, novels, textbooks, movie scripts (from book clients), TV scripts (from book clients). **Considers these nonfiction areas:** Animals; anthropology/archaeology; art/architecture/design; biography/autobiography; business/economics; child guidance/parenting; computers/electronic; cooking/foods/nutrition; current affairs; ethnic/cultural interests; gay/lesbian issues; government/politics/law; health/medicine; history; how-to; memoirs; military/war; money/finance; nature/environment; New Age/metaphysics; popular culture; psychology; religious/inspirational; science/technology; self-help/personal improvement; travel; true crime/investigative; women's issues/studies. **Considers these fiction areas:** Action/adventure; confession; contemporary issues; detective/police/crime; erotica; ethnic; family saga; feminist; gay/lesbian; glitz; historical; horror; humor/satire; literary; mainstream/contemporary; multicultural; mystery/suspense; New Age; picture books; psychic/supernatural; regional (specific to Hawaii); thriller.

O— "Half our clients are based in Hawaii and half are from all over the world. We prefer submissions (after query) via e-mail attachment. We only send out fully-edited proposals and manuscripts." Actively seeking first-rate writing.

How to Contact Outline. Query with SASE, outline, author bio, 2 sample chapters, credentials/platform. Accepts e-mail and fax queries. Considers simultaneous queries. Responds in 2-3 weeks to queries; 2 months to mss. Returns materials only with SASE. Obtains most new clients through recommendations from others, solicitations, conferences.

Recent Sales Sold 10 titles and 1 script in the last year.

Terms Agent receives 15% commission on domestic sales; 25% commission on foreign sales. Offers written contract, binding for indefinite period; 30-day notice must be given to terminate contract. Charges clients for photocopies and postage. May refer to editing services if author asks for recommendation. "We derive no income from our referrals. Referrals to editors do not imply representation."

Writers' Conferences Mr. Jellinek manages the publishing program at the Maui Writers Conference.

Tips "Would-be authors should be well read and knowledgeable about their field and genre."

◉ CAREN JOHNSON LITERARY AGENCY

132 East 43rd St., No. 216, New York NY 10017. Fax: (718)228-8785. E-mail: cjohnson@johnsonlitagency.com. Website: www.carenjohnson.com. **Contact:** Caren Johnson. Estab. 2006. Represents 20 clients. 50% of clients are new/unpublished writers. Currently handles: 10% nonfiction books; 70% novels; 20% juvenile books.

• Prior to her current position, Ms. Johnson was with Firebrand Literary and the Peter Rubie Agency.

Represents Nonfiction books, novels. **Considers these nonfiction areas:** History; popular culture; science/technology. **Considers these fiction areas:** Detective/police/crime; erotica; ethnic; mainstream/contemporary; mystery/suspense; romance; young adult; women's.

O— Does not want to receive picture books, plays or screenplays/scripts.

How to Contact Query with SASE. Query via e-mail only, with query and up to one chaoter in the body of the e-mail. Considers simultaneous queries. Responds in 4-6 weeks to queries; 6-8 weeks to mss. Obtains most new clients through recommendations from others.

Recent Sales Sold 15 titles in the last year. This agency prefers not to share information on specific sales. Other clients include A.E. Roman, Kelley St. John, Dianna Love Snell, Caridad Pineiro, Barbara Ferrer, Irene Peterson, Karen Anders, Rob Preece, Stephanie Kuehnert, L. Faye Hughes, Anne Elizabeth, Terri Molina, Lori Avocato, Kelsey Timmerman, Marelene Wagman-Geller and Jennifer Echols.

Terms Agent receives 15% commission on domestic sales; 20% commission on foreign sales. Offers written contract; 30-day notice must be given to terminate contract. This agency charges for postage and photocopying, though the author is consulted before any charges are incurred.

Writers' Conferences RWA National; Romantic Times Conference; Backspace; BookExpo America; Moonlight and Magnolias.

◉ ELAINE KOSTER LITERARY AGENCY, LLC

55 Central Park W., Suite 6, New York NY 10023. (212)362-9488. Fax: (212)712-0164. **Contact:** Elaine Koster, Stephanie Lehmann. Member of AAR, MWA; Author's Guild, Women's Media Group. Represents 40 clients. 10% of clients are new/unpublished writers. Currently handles: 30% nonfiction books; 70% novels.

• Prior to opening her agency in 1998, Ms. Koster was president and publisher of Dutton-NAL, part of the Penguin Group.

Represents Nonfiction books, novels. **Considers these nonfiction areas:** Biography/autobiography; business/economics; child guidance/parenting; cooking/foods/nutrition; current affairs; ethnic/cultural interests; health/medicine; history; how-to; money/finance; nature/environment; popular culture; psychology; self-help/personal improvement; spirituality; women's issues/studies. **Considers these fiction areas:** Contemporary issues; detective/police/crime; ethnic; family saga; feminist; historical; literary; mainstream/contemporary; mystery/suspense; regional; thriller; young adult; chick lit.

O— This agency specializes in quality fiction and nonfiction. Does not want to receive juvenile, screenplays, or science fiction.

How to Contact Query with SASE, outline, 3 sample chapters. Prefers to read materials exclusively.

No e-mail or fax queries. Responds in 3 weeks to queries; 1 month to mss. Returns materials only with SASE. Obtains most new clients through recommendations from others.

Recent Sales *Stalking Susan*, by Julie Kramer (Doubleday); *Takeover*, by Lisa Black (Morrow); *One in a Million*, by Kimberla Lawson Roby.

Terms Agent receives 15% commission on domestic sales. Bills back specific expenses incurred doing business for a client.

Tips "We prefer exclusive submissions. Don't e-mail or fax submissions. Please include biographical information and publishing history."

KT PUBLIC RELATIONS & LITERARY SERVICES

1905 Cricklewood Cove, Fogelsville PA 18051. (610)395-6298. Fax: (610)395-6299. Website: www.kt publicrelations.com. **Contact:** Jon Tienstra. Estab. 2005. Represents 12 clients. 75% of clients are new/unpublished writers. Currently handles: 50% nonfiction books; 50% novels.

- Prior to becoming an agent, Kae Tienstra was publicity director for Rodale, Inc. for 13 years and then founded her own publicity agency; Mr. Tienstra joined the firm in 1995 with varied corporate experience and a master's degree in library science.

Member Agents Kae Tienstra (health, parenting, psychology, how-to, crafts, foods/nutrition, beauty, women's fiction, general fiction); Jon Tienstra (nature/environment, history, cooking/foods/nutrition, war/military, automotive, health/medicine, gardening, general fiction, science fiction/contemporary fantasy, popular fiction).

Represents Nonfiction books, novels. **Considers these nonfiction areas:** Agriculture/horticulture; animals; child guidance/parenting; cooking/foods/nutrition; crafts/hobbies; health/medicine; history; how-to; military/war; nature/environment; popular culture; psychology; science/technology; self-help/personal improvement; interior design/decorating. **Considers these fiction areas:** Action/adventure; detective/police/crime; family saga; fantasy (contemporary—no swords or dragons); historical; literary; mainstream/contemporary; mystery/suspense; romance; science fiction; thriller.

- "We have worked with a variety of authors and publishers over the years and have learned what individual publishers are looking for in terms of new acquisitions. We are both mad about books and authors and we look forward to finding publishing success for all our clients." Specializes in parenting, history, cooking/foods/nutrition, crafts, beauty, war, health/medicine, psychology, how-to, gardening, science fiction, fantasy, women's fiction, and popular fiction. Does not want to see unprofessional material.

How to Contact Query with SASE. Prefers snail mail queries. Will accept e-mail queries. Responds in 3 months to chapters; 6-9 months for mss. No fax queries. Considers simultaneous queries. Responds in 2 weeks to queries. Returns materials only with SASE.

Terms Agent receives 15% commission on domestic sales; 20% commission on foreign sales. Offers written contract. Charges clients for long-distance phone calls, fax, postage, photocopying (only when incurred). No advance payment for these out-of-pocket expenses.

MICHAEL LARSEN/ELIZABETH POMADA, LITERARY AGENTS

1029 Jones St., San Francisco CA 94109-5023. (415)673-0939. E-mail: larsenpoma@aol.com. Website: www.larsen-pomada.com. **Contact:** Mike Larsen, Elizabeth Pomada. Estab. 1972. Member of AAR, Authors Guild, ASJA, PEN, WNBA, California Writers Club, National Speakers Association. Represents 100 clients. 40-45% of clients are new/unpublished writers. Currently handles: 70% nonfiction books; 30% novels.

- Prior to opening their agency, Mr. Larsen and Ms. Pomada were promotion executives for major publishing houses. Mr. Larsen worked for Morrow, Bantam and Pyramid (now part of Berkley); Ms. Pomada worked at Holt, David McKay and The Dial Press. Mr. Larsen is the author of the third editions of *How to Write a Book Proposal* and *How to Get a Literary Agent* as well as the coauthor of *Guerilla Marketing for Writers: 100 Weapons for Selling Your Work*.

Member Agents Michael Larsen (nonfiction); Elizabeth Pomada (fiction, narrative nonfiction, nonfiction for women); Laurie McLean, laurie@agentsavant.com (fantasy, science, romance, middlegrade and YA fiction).

Represents Adult book-length fiction and nonfiction that will interest New York publishers or are irresistibly written or conceived. **Considers these nonfiction areas:** Anthropology/archaeology; art/architecture/design; biography/autobiography; business/economics; cooking/foods/nutrition; current affairs; ethnic/cultural interests; gay/lesbian issues; government/politics/law; health/medicine;

history; how-to; humor/satire; memoirs; money/finance; music/dance; nature/environment; New Age/metaphysics; popular culture; psychology; religious/inspirational; science/technology; self-help/personal improvement; sociology; sports; theater/film; travel; true crime/investigative; women's issues/studies; futurism. **Considers these fiction areas:** Action/adventure; contemporary issues; detective/police/crime; ethnic; experimental; family saga; fantasy; feminist; gay/lesbian; glitz; historical; humor/satire; literary; mainstream/contemporary; mystery/suspense; religious/inspirational; romance (contemporary, gothic, historical); chick lit.

O➔ "We have diverse tastes. We look for fresh voices and new ideas. We handle literary, commercial and genre fiction, and the full range of nonfiction books." Actively seeking commercial, genre and literary fiction. Does not want to receive children's books, plays, short stories, screenplays, pornography, poetry or stories of abuse.

How to Contact Query with SASE. Accepts e-mail queries. No fax queries. Responds in 2 weeks to queries. Responds in 8 weeks to pages or submissions.

Recent Sales Sold at least 15 titles in the last year. *Dangerous Touch*, by Jill Sorenson (Silhouette); *The Soul and the Scalpel: Surgery as a Path to Spiritual Transformation for Patients and Physicians*, by Allan Hamilton, M.D.(Tarcher/Penguin); *The Perfect SalesForce: The 6 Best Practices of the World's Best Sales Teams* by Derek Gatehouse (Portfolio/Penguin); *The Solemn Lantern Maker*, by Merlinda Bobis (Bantam); *Bitten to Death*, the fourth book in an urban fantasy series by J.D. Rardin (Laurie McLean) (Orbit/Grand Central).

Terms Agent receives 15% commission on domestic sales; 20% (30% for Asia) commission on foreign sales. May charge for printing, postage for multiple submissions, foreign mail, foreign phone calls, galleys, books, legal fees.

Writers' Conferences This agency organizes the annual San Francisco Writers' Conference (www.sfwriters.org).

Tips "We love helping writers get the rewards and recognition they deserve. If you can write books that meet the needs of the marketplace and you can promote your books, now is the best time ever to be a writer. We must find new writers to make a living, so we are very eager to hear from new writers whose work will interest large houses, and nonfiction writers who can promote their books. For a list of recent sales, helpful info, and three ways to make yourself irresistible to any publisher, please visit our Web site."

☑ LAZEAR AGENCY GROUP, INC.

431 Second St., Suite 300, Hudson WI 54016. (715)531-0012. Fax: (715)531-0016. E-mail: admin@lazear.com; info@lazear.com. Website: www.lazear.com. **Contact:** Editorial Board. Estab. 1984. 20% of clients are new/unpublished writers. Currently handles: 65% nonfiction books; 30% novels; 5% juvenile books.

● The Lazear Agency opened a New York office in September 1997.

Member Agents Jonathon Lazear; Christi Cardenas; Darrick Kline; Julie Mayo; Anne Blackstone; director of digital media Nate Roen.

Represents Nonfiction books, novels, short story collections, novellas, juvenile books, graphic novels. **Considers these nonfiction areas:** Agriculture/horticulture; americana; animals; anthropology/archaeology; art/architecture/design; biography/autobiography; business/economics; child guidance/parenting; computers/electronic; cooking/foods/nutrition; current affairs; education; ethnic/cultural interests; gardening; gay/lesbian issues; government/politics/law; health/medicine; history; how-to; humor/satire; interior design/decorating; juvenile nonfiction; language/literature/criticism; memoirs; military/war; money/finance; multicultural; music/dance; nature/environment; New Age/metaphysics; philosophy; photography; popular culture; psychology; recreation; regional; religious/inspirational; science/technology; self-help/personal improvement; sex; sociology; software; spirituality; sports; theater/film; travel; true crime/investigative; women's issues/studies; young adult; creative nonfiction. **Considers these fiction areas:** Action/adventure; confession; detective/police/crime; ethnic; family saga; fantasy; feminist; gay/lesbian; gothic; hi-lo; historical; humor/satire; juvenile; literary; mainstream/contemporary; military/war; multicultural; multimedia; mystery/suspense; New Age; occult; picture books; plays; poetry; poetry in translation; psychic/supernatural; religious/inspirational; romance; science fiction; short story collections; spiritual; sports; thriller; translation; westerns/frontier; young adult; women's.

○╼ Actively seeking new voices in commercial fiction and nonfiction. "It's all in the writing, no matter the subject matter." Does not want to receive horror, poetry, scripts and/or screenplays.

How to Contact Query with SASE, submit outline/proposal, synopsis, author bio, SASE. No phone calls or faxes. We prefer snail mail queries. Responds in 2 weeks to queries; 3 weeks to mss. Returns materials only with SASE. Obtains most new clients through recommendations from others, solicitations.

Recent Sales Sold more than 50 titles in the last year. *Dragonships*, by Margaret Weis and Tracy Hickman (Tor); Motorhead YA series, by Will Weaver (FSG); Untitled Book, by Henry Alford (Twelve); Untitled Book, by Jane Goodall and Thane Maynard (Hachette); *Gastroanomalies: Questionable Culinary Creations from the Golden Age of American Cookery*, by James Lileks (Crown).

Terms Agent receives 15% commission on domestic sales; 20% commission on foreign sales. Offers written contract. Charges clients for photocopying, international express mail, bound galleys, books used for subsidiary rights sales. No fees charged if book is not sold.

Tips "The writer should first view himself as a salesperson in order to obtain an agent. Sell yourself, your idea, your concept. Do your homework. Notice what is in the marketplace. Be sophisticated about the arena in which you are writing. Please note that we also have a New York office, but the primary office remains in Hudson, Wis., for the receipt of any material."

◙ PAUL S. LEVINE LITERARY AGENCY

1054 Superba Ave., Venice CA 90291-3940. (310)450-6711. Fax: (310)450-0181. E-mail: pslevine@ix.netcom.com. Website: www.paulslevine.com. **Contact:** Paul S. Levine. Estab. 1996. Member of the State Bar of California. Represents over 100 clients. 75% of clients are new/unpublished writers.

Represents Nonfiction books, novels, movie scripts, feature film, TV scripts, TV movie of the week, episodic drama, sitcom, animation, documentary, miniseries, syndicated material. **Considers these nonfiction areas:** Art/architecture/design; biography/autobiography; business/economics; child guidance/parenting; computers/electronic; cooking/foods/nutrition; crafts/hobbies; current affairs; education; ethnic/cultural interests; gay/lesbian issues; government/politics/law; health/medicine; history; how-to; humor/satire; interior design/decorating; language/literature/criticism; memoirs; military/war; money/finance; music/dance; nature/environment; New Age/metaphysics; photography; popular culture; psychology; religious/inspirational; science/technology; self-help/personal improvement; sociology; sports; theater/film; true crime/investigative; women's issues/studies; creative nonfiction. **Considers these fiction areas:** Action/adventure; comic books/cartoon; confession; detective/police/crime; erotica; ethnic; experimental; family saga; feminist; gay/lesbian; glitz; historical; humor/satire; literary; mainstream/contemporary; mystery/suspense; regional; religious/inspirational; romance; sports; thriller; westerns/frontier.

○╼ Actively seeking commercial fiction and nonfiction. Also handles children's and young adult fiction and nonfiction. Does not want to receive science fiction, fantasy, or horror.

How to Contact Query with SASE. Accepts e-mail and fax queries. Considers simultaneous queries. Responds in 1 day to queries; 2 months to mss. Returns materials only with SASE. Obtains most new clients through conferences, referrals, listings on various websites and in directories.

Recent Sales Sold 25 titles in the last year. This agency prefers not to share information on specific sales.

Terms Agent receives 15% commission on domestic sales; 20% commission on foreign sales. Offers written contract. Charges clients for messengers, long distance calls, postage (only when incurred). No advance payment necessary.

Writers' Conferences California Lawyers for the Arts Workshops; Selling to Hollywood Conference; Willamette Writers Conference; and many others.

◙ LINDSTROM LITERARY MANAGEMENT, LLC

871 N. Greenbrier St., Arlington VA 22205. Fax: (703)527-7624. E-mail: lindstromlit@aol.com. Website: www.lindstromliterary.com. **Contact:** Kristin Lindstrom. Estab. 1993. Member of Author's Guild. Represents 9 clients. 50% of clients are new/unpublished writers. Currently handles: 30% nonfiction books; 70% novels.

● Prior to her current position, Ms. Lindstrom was an editor of a monthly magazine in the energy industry, and an independent marketing and publicity consultant.

Represents Nonfiction books, novels. **Considers these nonfiction areas:** Animals; biography/autobiography; business/economics; current affairs; history; memoirs; popular culture; science/technology; true crime/investigative. **Considers these fiction areas:** Action/adventure; detective/police/crime; erotica; mainstream/contemporary; mystery/suspense; religious/inspirational; thriller; women's.

> ☞ "In 2006, I decided to add my more specific promotion/publicity skills to the mix in order to support the marketing efforts of my published clients." Actively seeking commercial fiction and narrative nonfiction. Does not want to receive juvenile or children's books.

How to Contact Query with SASE, submit author bio, synopsis and first four chapters if submitting fiction. For nonfiction, send the first 4 chapters, synopsis, proposal, outline and mission statement. Accepts e-mail queries. No fax queries. Considers simultaneous queries. Responds in 5 weeks to queries; 8 weeks to mss. Returns materials only with SASE. Obtains most new clients through recommendations from others, solicitations.

Recent Sales Sold 7 titles in the last year. *Perfect Circle* and *Prisoner*, by Carlos J. Cortes (Bantam Spectra); *Rain Song* and *Evening Peace*, by Alice Wisler (Bethany House); *Beach Trip* and a second book, by Cathy Holton (Ballantine); *7th Son: Descent*, by JC Hutchins (St. Martin's).

Terms Agent receives 15% commission on domestic sales; 20% commission on foreign sales. Offers written contract. This agency charges for postage, UPS, copies and other basic office expenses.

Tips "Do your homework on accepted practices; make sure you know what kind of book the agent handles."

◙ LIPPINCOTT MASSIE MCQUILKIN

80 Fifth Ave., Suite 1101, New York NY 10011. (212)337-2044. Fax: (212)352-2059. E-mail: info@lmqlit.com. Website: www.lmqlit.com. **Contact:** Molly Lindley, assistant. Estab. 2003. Represents 90 clients. 30% of clients are new/unpublished writers. Currently handles: 40% nonfiction books; 40% novels; 10% story collections; 5% scholarly books; 5% poetry.

Member Agents Maria Massie (fiction, memoir, cultural criticism); Will Lippincott (politics, current affairs, history); Rob McQuilkin (fiction, history, psychology, sociology, graphic material).

Represents Nonfiction books, novels, short story collections, scholarly books, graphic novels. **Considers these nonfiction areas:** Animals; anthropology/archaeology; art/architecture/design; biography/autobiography; business/economics; child guidance/parenting; current affairs; ethnic/cultural interests; gay/lesbian issues; government/politics/law; health/medicine; history; language/literature/criticism; memoirs; military/war; money/finance; music/dance; nature/environment; popular culture; psychology; religious/inspirational; science/technology; self-help/personal improvement; sociology; theater/film; true crime/investigative; women's issues/studies. **Considers these fiction areas:** Action/adventure; comic books/cartoon; confession; family saga; feminist; gay/lesbian; historical; humor/satire; literary; mainstream/contemporary; regional.

> ☞ LMQ focuses on bringing new voices in literary and commercial fiction to the market, as well as popularizing the ideas and arguments of scholars in the fields of history, psychology, sociology, political science, and current affairs. Actively seeking fiction writers who already have credits in magazines and quarterlies, as well as nonfiction writers who already have a media platform or some kind of a university affiliation. Does not want to receive romance, genre fiction or children's material.

How to Contact Send query via e-mail. Only send additional materials if requested. Considers simultaneous queries. Responds in 1 week to queries; 1 month to mss. Obtains most new clients through recommendations from others, solicitations, conferences.

Recent Sales Sold 27 titles in the last year. *The Abstinence Teacher*, by Tom Perrotta (St. Martins); *Queen of Fashion*, by Caroline Weber (Henry Holt); *Whistling Past Dixie*, by Tom Schaller (Simon & Schuster); *Pretty Little Dirty*, by Amanda Boyden (Vintage). Other clients include Peter Ho Davies, Kim Addonizio, Don Lee, Natasha Trethewey, Anatol Lieven, Sir Michael Marmot, Anne Carson, Liza Ward, David Sirota, Anne Marie Slaughter, Marina Belozerskaya, Kate Walbert.

Terms Agent receives 15% commission on domestic sales; 20% commission on foreign sales. Offers written contract; 30-day notice must be given to terminate contract. Only charges for reasonable business expenses upon successful sale.

◙ THE LITERARY GROUP INTERNATIONAL

51 E. 25th St., Suite 401, New York NY 10010. (212)274-1616. Fax: (212)274-9876. E-mail: fweimann @theliterarygroup.com. Website: www.theliterarygroup.com. **Contact:** Frank Weimann. Estab.

1985. 65% of clients are new/unpublished writers. Currently handles: 50% nonfiction books; 50% fiction.

Member Agents Frank Weimann; acquisitions editor Jaimee Garbacik.

Represents Nonfiction books, novels, graphic novels. **Considers these nonfiction areas:** Animals; anthropology/archaeology; biography/autobiography; business/economics; child guidance/parenting; crafts/hobbies; current affairs; education; ethnic/cultural interests; government/politics/law; health/medicine; history; how-to; humor/satire; juvenile nonfiction; language/literature/criticism; memoirs; military/war; money/finance; multicultural; music/dance; nature/environment; popular culture; psychology; religious/inspirational; science/technology; self-help/personal improvement; sociology; sports; theater/film; true crime/investigative; women's issues/studies; creative nonfiction. **Considers these fiction areas:** Action/adventure; contemporary issues; detective/police/crime; ethnic; family saga; fantasy; feminist; horror; humor/satire; mystery/suspense; psychic/supernatural; romance (contemporary, gothic, historical, regency); sports; thriller; westerns/frontier; young adult; experimental.

   O⟶ This agency specializes in nonfiction (memoir, military, history, biography, sports, how-to).

How to Contact Query with SASE, outline, 3 sample chapters. Prefers to read materials exclusively. Only responds if interested. Returns materials only with SASE. Obtains most new clients through referrals, writers' conferences, query letters.

Recent Sales Sold 90 titles in the last year. *The Magician*, by Michael Scott; *Dog & Bear: Two's Company*, by Laura Vaccaro Seeger; *101 Erotic Dares*, by Laura Corn; *Why Men Die First*, by Marianne Legato; *Bean's Books*, by Chudney Ross.

Terms Agent receives 15% commission on domestic sales; 20% commission on foreign sales. Offers written contract; 30-day notice must be given to terminate contract.

Writers' Conferences San Diego State University Writers' Conference; Maui Writers' Conference; Agents and Editors Conference, among others.

◪ LYONS LITERARY, LLC

116 West 23rd St., Suite 500, New York NY 10011. (212)851-8428. Fax: (212)851-8405. E-mail: info@lyonsliterary.com. Website: www.lyonsliterary.com. **Contact:** Jonathan Lyons. Estab. 2007. Member of AAR, The Author's Guild, American Bar Association, New York State Bar Associaton, New York State Intellectual Property Law Section. Represents 42 clients. 15% of clients are new/ unpublished writers. Currently handles: 60% nonfiction books; 40% novels.

Represents Nonfiction books, novels. **Considers these nonfiction areas:** Animals; biography/autobiography; cooking/foods/nutrition; crafts/hobbies; current affairs; ethnic/cultural interests; gay/ lesbian issues; government/politics/law; health/medicine; history; how-to; humor/satire; memoirs; military/war; money/finance; multicultural; nature/environment; popular culture; psychology; science/technology; sociology; sports; translation; travel; true crime/investigative; women's issues/ studies. **Considers these fiction areas:** Detective/police/crime; fantasy; feminist; gay/lesbian; historical; humor/satire; literary; mainstream/contemporary; mystery/suspense; psychic/supernatural; regional; science fiction; sports; thriller; women's; chick lit.

   O⟶ "With my legal expertise and experience selling domestic and foreign language book rights, paperback reprint rights, audio rights, film/TV rights and permissions, I am able to provide substantive and personal guidance to my clients in all areas relating to their projects. In addition, with the advent of new publishing technology, Lyons Literary, LLC is situated to address the changing nature of the industry while concurrently handling authors' more traditional needs."

How to Contact Query with SASE. Submit outline, synopsis, author bio. Accepts e-queries through online submission form. No fax queries. Considers simultaneous queries. Responds in 8 weeks to queries; 12 weeks to mss. Returns materials only with SASE. Obtains most new clients through recommendations from others. This agency prefers not to share information on specific sales.

Terms Agent receives 15% commission on domestic sales; 20% commission on foreign sales. Offers written contract.

Writers' Conferences Agents and Editors Conference.

Tips "Please submit electronic queries through our Web site submission form."

◖ DONALD MAASS LITERARY AGENCY

121 W. 27th St., Suite 801, New York NY 10001. (212)727-8383. E-mail: info@maassagency.com. Website: www.maassagency.com. Estab. 1980. Member of AAR, SFWA, MWA, RWA. Represents

more than 100 clients. 5% of clients are new/unpublished writers. Currently handles: 100% novels.

- Prior to opening his agency, Mr. Maass served as an editor at Dell Publishing (New York) and as a reader at Gollancz (London). He also served as the president of AAR.

Member Agents Donald Maass (mainstream, literary, mystery/suspense, science fiction); Jennifer Jackson (commercial fiction, romance, science fiction, fantasy, mystery/suspense); Cameron McClure (literary, mystery/suspense, urban, fantasy, narrative nonfiction and projects with multicultural, international, and environmental themes, gay/lesbian); Stephen Barbara (literary fiction, young adult novels, middle grade, narrative nonfiction, historical nonfiction, mainstream, genre).

Represents Novels. **Considers these nonfiction areas:** Young adult. **Considers these fiction areas:** Detective/police/crime; fantasy; historical; horror; literary; mainstream/contemporary; mystery/suspense; psychic/supernatural; romance (historical, paranormal, time travel); science fiction; thriller; women's.

- ⌐ This agency specializes in commercial fiction, especially science fiction, fantasy, mystery and suspense. Actively seeking to expand in literary fiction and women's fiction. Does not want to receive nonfiction, picture books, prescriptive nonfiction, or poetry.

How to Contact Query with SASE, synopsis, first 5 pages. Returns material only with SASE. Considers simultaneous queries. Responds in 2 weeks to queries; 3 months to mss.

Recent Sales *Afternoons With Emily*, by Rose MacMurray (Little, Brown); *Denial: A Lew Fonesca Mystery*, by Stuart Kaminsky (Forge); *The Shifting Tide*, by Anne Perry (Ballantine); *Midnight Plague*, by Gregg Keizer (G.P. Putnam's Sons); *White Night: A Novel of The Dresden Files*, by Jim Butcher (Roc).

Terms Agent receives 15% commission on domestic sales; 20% commission on foreign sales.

Writers' Conferences Donald Maass: World Science Fiction Convention; Frankfurt Book Fair; Pacific Northwest Writers Conference; Bouchercon. Jennifer Jackson: World Science Fiction Convention; RWA National Conference.

Tips "We are fiction specialists, also noted for our innovative approach to career planning. Few new clients are accepted, but interested authors should query with a SASE. Works with subagents in all principle foreign countries and Hollywood. No prescriptive nonfiction, picture books or poetry will be considered."

◖ MACGREGOR LITERARY

2373 N.W. 185th Ave., Suite 165, Hillsboro OR 97214. (503)277-8308. E-mail: submissions@macgregorliterary.com. Website: www.macgregorliterary.com. **Contact:** Chip MacGregor. Signatory of WGA. Represents 40 clients. 10% of clients are new/unpublished writers. Currently handles: 40% nonfiction books; 60% novels.

- Prior to his current position, Mr. MacGregor was the senior agent with Alive Communications. Most recently, he was associate publisher for Time-Warner Book Group's Faith Division, and helped put together their Center Street imprint.

Represents Nonfiction books, novels. **Considers these nonfiction areas:** Business/economics; current affairs; history; how-to; humor/satire; popular culture; religious/inspirational; self-help/personal improvement; sports; marriage, parenting. **Considers these fiction areas:** Detective/police/crime; historical; mainstream/contemporary; mystery/suspense; religious/inspirational; romance; thriller; women's/chick lit.

- ⌐ "My specialty has been in career planning with authors—finding commercial ideas, then helping authors bring them to market, and in the midst of that assisting the authors as they get firmly established in their writing careers. I'm probably best known for my work with Christian books over the years, but I've done a fair amount of general market projects as well." Actively seeking authors with a Christian worldview and a growing platform. Does not want to receive fantasy, sci-fi, children's books, poetry or screenplays.

How to Contact Query with SASE. Accepts e-mail queries. No fax queries. Considers simultaneous queries. Responds in 3 weeks to queries. Obtains most new clients through recommendations from others.

Recent Sales *Pop Culture Mom*, by Lynne Spears (Thomas Nelson); *Never Say Diet*, by Chantel Hobbs (Random House); The Amanda Bell Browne series, by Claudia Mair Burney (Simon & Schuster).

Terms Agent receives 15% commission on domestic sales; 15% commission on foreign sales. Offers written contract; 30-day notice must be given to terminate contract. Charges for "exceptional fees" after receiving authors' permission.

Writers' Conferences Blue Ridge Christian Writers' Conference; Write to Publish.

Tips "Seriously consider attending a good writers' conference. It will give you the chance to be face-to-face with people in the industry. Also, if you're a novelist, consider joining one of the national writers' organizations. The American Christian Fiction Writers (ACFW) is a wonderful group for new as well as established writers. And if you're a Christian writer of any kind, check into The Writers View, an online writing group. All of these have proven helpful to writers."

◎ THE DENISE MARCIL LITERARY AGENCY, INC.

156 Fifth Ave., Suite 625, New York NY 10010. (212)337-3402. Fax: (212)727-2688. Website: www.DeniseMarcilAgency.com. **Contact:** Denise Marcil, Maura Kye-Casella. Estab. 1977. Member of AAR.

- Prior to opening her agency, Ms. Marcil served as an editorial assistant with Avon Books and as an assistant editor with Simon & Schuster.

Member Agents Denise Marcil (women's commercial fiction, thrillers, suspense, popular reference, how-to, self-help, health, business, and parenting.

○→ This agency is currently not taking on new authors.

Recent Sales Sold 43 titles in the last year. *Welcome to Serenity*, by Sherryl Woods; *The Potable Pediatrician*; *Super Seniors*, by William Sears and Peter Sears; *In High Gear*, by Gina Wilkins; *The Anti-Alzheimers' Prescription*, by Vincent Fortanasce.

Terms Agent receives 15% commission on domestic sales; 20% commission on foreign sales. Offers written contract, binding for 2 years; 100% of business is derived from commissions on ms sales. Charges $100/year for postage, photocopying, long-distance calls, etc.

Writers' Conferences Pacific Northwest Writers' Conference; RWA National Conference.

Ⓝ ▢ SUSAN MARLANE LITERARY AGENCY

P.O. Box 4, Simi Valley CA 93062. Website: www.susanmarlaneliteraryagency.com. **Contact:** Susan Marlane. Estab. 2006. 80% of clients are new/unpublished writers. Currently handles: 90% nonfiction books; 10% novels.

Member Agents Prior to becoming an agent, Ms. Marlane was a freelance editor.

Represents Nonfiction books, novels. **Considers these nonfiction areas:** Biography/autobiography; business/economics; child guidance/parenting; cooking/foods/nutrition; crafts/hobbies; current affairs; education; government/politics/law; health/medicine; how-to; humor/satire; interior design/decorating; memoirs; music/dance; nature/environment; popular culture; psychology; religious/inspirational; science/technology; self-help/personal improvement; true crime/investigative; women's issues/studies; entertainment/film/celebrity, weight loss. **Considers these fiction areas:** Action/adventure; confession; detective/police/crime; family saga; historical; humor/satire; literary; mainstream/contemporary; mystery/suspense; religious/inspirational; romance; thriller; women's.

○→ Actively seeking nonfiction: self help, current affairs, popular culture, money/finance, weight loss and Christian works. Does not want to receive short stories, sexually explicit materials, fantasy or poetry.

How to Contact Query with SASE, submit a one-page query letter or book proposal. Include your plans for promoting the work. Snail mail queries only. Considers simultaneous queries. Responds in 4-8 weeks to queries; 1-3 months to mss. Returns materials only with SASE. Obtains most new clients through recommendations from others, solicitations.

Terms Agent receives 15% commission on domestic sales; 20% commission on foreign sales. Offers written contract; 30-day notice must be given to terminate contract.

Tips "Carefully proofread your work before sending. Make sure it's the best it can be. Be professional."

Ⓝ ◪ MAX AND CO., A LITERARY AGENCY AND SOCIAL CLUB

115 Hosea Ave., Cincinnati OH, 45220. (201)704-2483. E-mail: mmurphy@maxlit.com. Website: www.maxliterary.org. **Contact:** Michael Murphy. Estab. 2007.

- Prior to his current position, Mr. Murphy was with Queen Literary Agency. He has been in book publishing since 1981. His first 13 years were with Random House, where he was a vice president. Later, he ran William Morrow as their publisher, up until the company's acquisition & merger into HarperCollins. **Considers these nonfiction areas:** Humor/satire; memoirs; narrative nonfiction. **Considers these fiction areas:** Literary.

○━ Actively seeking narrative nonfiction, memoir, literary fiction, humor, and visual books. Does not want to receive genre fiction nor YA and children's books.

How to Contact E-queries preferred. Include brief synopsis, author bio and sample writing.

Recent Sales *Down and Out on Murder Mile*, by Tony O'Neill (HarperCollins); *Family Sentence*, by Jeanine Cornillot (Beacon Press); *Hero of the Underground*, by Jason Peter (St. Martin's); *Familial Ground* (Princeton Architectural)

⊘ MARGRET MCBRIDE LITERARY AGENCY

7744 Fay Ave., Suite 201, La Jolla CA 92037. (858)454-1550. Fax: (858)454-2156. E-mail: staff@mcbri delit.com. Website: www.mcbrideliterary.com. **Contact:** Michael Daley, submissions manager. Estab. 1980. Member of AAR, Authors Guild. Represents 55 clients.

• Prior to opening her agency, Ms. McBride worked at Random House, Ballantine Books, and Warner Books.

Represents Nonfiction books, novels. **Considers these nonfiction areas:** Biography/autobiography; business/economics; cooking/foods/nutrition; current affairs; ethnic/cultural interests; government/politics/law; health/medicine; history; how-to; money/finance; music/dance; popular culture; psychology; science/technology; self-help/personal improvement; sociology; women's issues/studies; style. **Considers these fiction areas:** Action/adventure; detective/police/crime; ethnic; historical; humor/satire; literary; mainstream/contemporary; mystery/suspense; thriller; westerns/frontier.

○━ This agency specializes in mainstream fiction and nonfiction. Does not want to receive screenplays, romance, poetry, or children's/young adult.

How to Contact Query with synopsis, bio, SASE. No e-mail or fax queries. Considers simultaneous queries. Responds in 4-6 weeks to queries; 6-8 weeks to mss. Returns materials only with SASE.

Terms Agent receives 15% commission on domestic sales; 25% commission on foreign sales. Charges for overnight delivery and photocopying.

◖ MENDEL MEDIA GROUP, LLC

115 West 30th St., Suite 800, New York NY 10001. (646)239-9896. Fax: (212)685-4717. E-mail: scott@mendelmedia.com. Website: www.mendelmedia.com. Estab. 2002. Member of AAR. Represents 40-60 clients.

• Prior to becoming an agent, Mr. Mendel was an academic. "I taught American literature, Yiddish, Jewish studies, and literary theory at the University of Chicago and the University of Illinois at Chicago while working on my PhD in English. I also worked as a freelance technical writer and as the managing editor of a healthcare magazine. In 1998, I began working for the late Jane Jordan Browne, a long-time agent in the book publishing world."

Represents Nonfiction books, novels, scholarly books (with potential for broad/popular appeal). **Considers these nonfiction areas:** Americana; animals; anthropology/archaeology; art/architecture/design; biography/autobiography; business/economics; child guidance/parenting; cooking/foods/nutrition; current affairs; education; ethnic/cultural interests; gardening; gay/lesbian issues; government/politics/law; health/medicine; history; how-to; humor/satire; language/literature/criticism; memoirs; military/war; money/finance; multicultural; music/dance; nature/environment; philosophy; popular culture; psychology; recreation; regional; religious/inspirational; science/technology; self-help/personal improvement; sex; sociology; software; spirituality; sports; true crime/investigative; women's issues/studies; Jewish topics; creative nonfiction. **Considers these fiction areas:** Action/adventure; contemporary issues; detective/police/crime; erotica; ethnic; feminist; gay/lesbian; glitz; historical; humor/satire; juvenile; literary; mainstream/contemporary; mystery/suspense; picture books; religious/inspirational; romance; sports; thriller; young adult; Jewish fiction.

○━ "I am interested in major works of history, current affairs, biography, business, politics, economics, science, major memoirs, narrative nonfiction, and other sorts of general nonfiction. Actively seeking new, major or definitive work on a subject of broad interest, or a controversial, but authoritative, new book on a subject that affects many people's lives. I also represent more light-hearted nonfiction projects, such as gift or novelty books, when they suit the market particularly well." Does not want queries about projects written years ago that were unsuccessfully shopped to a long list of trade publishers by either the author or another agent. "I am specifically not interested in reading short, category romances (regency, time travel, paranormal, etc.), horror novels, supernatural stories, poetry, original plays, or film scripts.''

How to Contact Query with SASE. Do not e-mail or fax queries. For nonfiction, include a complete, fully-edited book proposal with sample chapters. For fiction, include a complete synopsis and no more than 20 pages of sample text. Responds in 2 weeks to queries; 4-6 weeks to mss. Returns materials only with SASE. Obtains most new clients through recommendations from others.

Terms Agent receives 15% commission on domestic sales; 20% commission on foreign sales. Offers written contract, binding for 2 years; 1-month notice must be given to terminate contract. Charges clients for ms duplication, expedited delivery services (when necessary), any overseas shipping, telephone calls/faxes necessary for marketing the author's foreign rights.

Writers' Conferences BookExpo America; Frankfurt Book Fair; London Book Fair; RWA National Conference; Modern Language Association Convention; Jerusalem Book Fair.

Tips ''While I am not interested in being flattered by a prospective client, it does matter to me that she knows why she is writing to me in the first place. Is one of my clients a colleague of hers? Has she read a book by one of my clients that led her to believe I might be interested in her work? Authors of descriptive nonfiction should have real credentials and expertise in their subject areas, either as academics, journalists, or policy experts, and authors of prescriptive nonfiction should have legitimate expertise and considerable experience communicating their ideas in seminars and workshops, in a successful business, through the media, etc.''

⬤ HENRY MORRISON, INC.

105 S. Bedford Road, Suite 306A, Mt. Kisco NY 10549. (914)666-3500. Fax: (914)241-7846. **Contact:** Henry Morrison. Estab. 1965. Signatory of WGA. Represents 53 clients. 5% of clients are new/unpublished writers. Currently handles: 5% nonfiction books; 95% novels.

Represents Nonfiction books, novels. **Considers these nonfiction areas:** Anthropology/archaeology; biography/autobiography; government/politics/law; history. **Considers these fiction areas:** Action/adventure; detective/police/crime; family saga; historical.

How to Contact Query with SASE. Responds in 2 weeks to queries; 3 months to mss. Obtains most new clients through recommendations from others.

Recent Sales Sold 15 titles in the last year. *The Bourne Sanction*, by Eric Lustbader (Grand Central); *The Vampire of New York*, by R.L. Stevens (Signet); *The Cortez Mask*, by Paul Christopher (Signet); *City of God*, by Beverly Swerling (S&S); *Cold Plague*, by Dan Kalla (Forge); *Mausoleum*, by Justin Scott (Poisoned Press); *Spade & Archer*, by Joe Gores (Knopf); *Ghosts*, by Charles W. Henderson. Other clients include Daniel Cohen, Joel N. Ross, Dan Kalla, Christopher Hyde, Charles W. Henderson.

Terms Agent receives 15% commission on domestic sales; 25% commission on foreign sales. Charges clients for ms copies, bound galleys, finished books for submissions to publishers, movie producers and foreign publishers.

⬤ DEE MURA LITERARY

269 West Shore Drive, Massapequa NY 11758-8225. (516)795-1616. Fax: (516)795-8797. E-mail: query@deemuraliterary.com. **Contact:** Dee Mura, Karen Roberts, Bobbie Sokol, David Brozain. Estab. 1987. Signatory of WGA. 50% of clients are new/unpublished writers.

● Prior to opening her agency, Ms. Mura was a public relations executive with a roster of film and entertainment clients and worked in editorial for major weekly news magazines. **Considers these nonfiction areas:** Agriculture/horticulture; animals; anthropology/archaeology; biography/autobiography; business/economics; child guidance/parenting; computers/electronic; current affairs; education; ethnic/cultural interests; gay/lesbian issues; government/politics/law; health/medicine; history; how-to; humor/satire; juvenile nonfiction; memoirs; military/war; money/finance; nature/environment; science/technology; self-help/personal improvement; sociology; sports; travel; true crime/investigative; women's issues/studies. **Considers these fiction areas:** Action/adventure; contemporary issues; detective/police/crime (and espionage); ethnic; experimental; family saga; fantasy; feminist; gay/lesbian; glitz; historical; humor/satire; juvenile; literary; mainstream/contemporary; mystery/suspense; psychic/supernatural; regional; romance (contemporary, gothic, historical, regency); science fiction; sports; thriller; westerns/frontier; young adult; political. **Considers these script subject areas:** Action/adventure; cartoon/animation; comedy; contemporary issues; detective/police/crime (and espionage); family saga; fantasy;

feminist; gay/lesbian; glitz; historical; horror; juvenile; mainstream; mystery/suspense; psychic/supernatural; religious/inspirational; romantic comedy; romantic drama; science fiction; sports; teen; thriller; western/frontier.

O→ "Some of us have special interests and some of us encourage you to share your passion and work with us." Does not want to receive ideas for sitcoms, novels, films, etc., or queries without SASEs.

How to Contact Query with SASE. Accepts e-mail queries (no attachments). If via e-mail, put "query" and your genre in subject line. If via snail mail, include first few chapters or full proposal. No fax queries. Considers simultaneous queries. Only responds if interested; responds as soon as possible. Returns materials only with SASE. Obtains most new clients through recommendations from others, queries.

Recent Sales Sold more than 40 titles and sold 35 scripts in the last year.

Terms Agent receives 15% commission on domestic sales; 20% commission on foreign sales. Offers written contract. Charges clients for photocopying, mailing expenses, overseas/long distance phone calls/faxes.

Tips "Please include a paragraph on your background, even if you have no literary background, and a brief synopsis of the project."

☑ MUSE LITERARY MANAGEMENT

189 Waverly Place, #4, New York NY 10014. (212)925-3721. E-mail: museliterarymgmt@aol.com. Website: www.museliterary.com/. **Contact:** Deborah Carter. Estab. 1998. Member of MediaBistro, Author's Guild, SCBWI, International Thriller Writers. Represents 10 clients. 80% of clients are new/unpublished writers.

• Prior to starting her agency, Ms. Carter trained with an AAR literary agent and worked in the music business and as a talent scout for record companies in artist management. She has a BA in English and music from Washington Square University College at NYU.

Represents Novels, short story collections, novellas, juvenile books. **Considers these nonfiction areas:** Narrative-only nonfiction (memoir, outdoors, music, writing). Please query other narrative nonfiction subjects. **Considers these fiction areas:** Action/adventure; detective/police/crime; picture books; young adult; espionage; middle-grade novels; literary short story collections, literary fiction with popular appeal, mystery/suspense/thriller (no cozies).

O→ Specializes in manuscript development, the sale and administration of print, performance, and foreign rights to literary works, and post-publication publicity and appearances. Actively seeking progressive, African-American, and multicultural fiction for adults and children in the U.S. market. Does not want to receive category fiction (romance, chick lit, fantasy, science fiction, horror), or fiction/nonfiction with religious/spiritual matter, illness or victimhood.

How to Contact Query with SASE. Query via e-mail (no attachments). Discards unwanted queries. Responds in 2 weeks to queries; 2-3 weeks to mss. Obtains most new clients through recommendations from others, conferences.

Recent Sales Sold 2 titles in the last year. Untitled children's folktale collection, by Anne Shelby (UNC Press); foreign rights sales: *The Fund*, by Wes DeMott in Russian. Other clients include various new writers.

Terms Agent receives 15% commission on domestic sales; 20% commission on foreign sales. Offers written contract, binding for 1 year; 1-day notice must be given to terminate contract. Sometimes charges for postage and photocopying. All expenses are subject to client approval.

◖ JEAN V. NAGGAR LITERARY AGENCY, INC.

216 E. 75th St., Suite 1E, New York NY 10021. (212)794-1082. E-mail: jvnla@jvnla.com. Website: www.jvnla.com. **Contact:** Jean Naggar. Estab. 1978. Member of AAR, PEN, Women's Media Group, Women's Forum. Represents 80 clients. 20% of clients are new/unpublished writers. Currently handles: 35% nonfiction books; 45% novels; 15% juvenile books; 5% scholarly books.

• Ms. Naggar has served as president of AAR.

Member Agents Jean Naggar (mainstream fiction, nonfiction); Jennifer Weltz, director (subsidiary rights, children's books); Alice Tasman, senior agent (commercial and literary fiction, thrillers, narrative nonfiction); Mollie Glick, agent and director of contracts (specializes in literary fiction as well as narrative and practical nonfiction); Jessica Regel, agent (young adult fiction and nonfiction).

Represents Nonfiction books, novels. **Considers these nonfiction areas:** Biography/autobiography;

child guidance/parenting; current affairs; government/politics/law; health/medicine; history; juvenile nonfiction; memoirs; New Age/metaphysics; psychology; religious/inspirational; self-help/personal improvement; sociology; travel; women's issues/studies. **Considers these fiction areas:** Action/adventure; detective/police/crime; ethnic; family saga; feminist; historical; literary; mainstream/contemporary; mystery/suspense; psychic/supernatural; thriller.

> O→ This agency specializes in mainstream fiction and nonfiction and literary fiction with commercial potential.

How to Contact Query with SASE. Prefers to read materials exclusively. No e-mail or fax queries. Responds in 1 day to queries; 2 months to mss. Returns materials only with SASE. Obtains most new clients through recommendations from others.

Recent Sales *An Absolute Gentleman*, by Rose Marie Kinder; *Scot On The Rocks*, by Brenda Janowitz; *The Deporter*, by Ames Holbrook; *Love And Sex With Robots*, by David Levy; *You Must Be This Happy To Enter*, by Elizabeth Crane; *Night Navigation*, by Ginnah Howard; *After Hours At The Almost Home*, by Tara Yelen; *An Entirely Synthetic Fish: A Biography Of Rainbow Trout*, by Anders Halverson; *The Patron Saint Of Butterflies*, by Cecilia Galante; *6 Sick Hipsters*, by Rayo Casablanca; *Enola Holmes And The Case Of The Bizarre Bouquets*, by Nancy Springer; *Skin And Bones*, by Teri Coyne; *Dark Angels*, by Karleen Koen; *Wild Girls*, by Pat Murphy; *Executive Privilege*, by Phillip Margolin; *The Last Queen*, by C.W. Gortner; *Donkey-Donkey*, by Roger Duvoisin; *The Elephant Quilt*, by Susan Lowell; *Rhymes With Rufus*, by Iza Trapani.

Terms Agent receives 15% commission on domestic sales; 20% commission on foreign sales. Offers written contract. Charges for overseas mailing, messenger services, book purchases, long-distance telephone, photocopying—all deductible from royalties received.

Writers' Conferences Willamette Writers Conference; Pacific Northwest Writers Conference; Bread Loaf Writers Conference; Marymount Manhattan Writers Conference; SEAK Medical & Legal Fiction Writing Conference.

Tips "Use a professional presentation. Because of the avalanche of unsolicited queries that flood the agency every week, we have had to modify our policy. We will now only guarantee to read and respond to queries from writers who come recommended by someone we know. Our areas are general fiction and nonfiction—no children's books by unpublished writers, no multimedia, no screenplays, no formula fiction, and no mysteries by unpublished writers. We recommend patience and fortitude: the courage to be true to your own vision, the fortitude to finish a novel and polish it again and again before sending it out, and the patience to accept rejection gracefully and wait for the stars to align themselves appropriately for success."

▣ NELSON LITERARY AGENCY

1732 Wazee St., Suite 207, Denver CO 80202. (303)292-2805. E-mail: query@nelsonagency.com. Website: www.nelsonagency.com. **Contact:** Kristin Nelson. Estab. 2002. Member of AAR.

> ● Prior to opening her own agency, Ms. Nelson worked as a literary scout and subrights agent for agent Jody Rein.

Represents Novels, select nonfiction. **Considers these nonfiction areas:** Memoirs; narrative nonfiction. **Considers these fiction areas:** Literary; romance (includes fantasy with romantic elements, science fiction, fantasy, young adult); women's; chick lit (includes mysteries); commercial/mainstream.

> O→ NLA specializes in representing commercial fiction and high caliber literary fiction. Actively seeking Latina writers who tackle contemporary issues in a modern voice (think *Dirty Girls Social Club*). Does not want short story collections, mysteries (except chick lit), thrillers, Christian, horror, or children's picture books.

How to Contact Query by e-mail only.

Recent Sales *Schemes of Love*, by Sherry Thomas (Bantam Dell); *The Camelot Code*, by Mari Mancusi (Dutton Children's); *Magic Lost, Trouble Found*, by Lisa Shearin (Ace); *Magellan's Witch*, by Carolyn Jewel (Hachette/Warner); *No Place Safe*, by Kim Reid (Kensington); *Plan B*, by Jennifer O'Connell (MTV/Pocket Books); *Code of Love*, by Cheryl Sawyer (NAL/Penguin Group); *Once Upon Stilettos*, by Shanna Swendson (Ballantine); *I'd Tell You I Love You But Then I'd Have to Kill You*, by Ally Carter (Hyperion Children's); *An Accidental Goddess*, by Linnea Sinclair (Bantam Spectra). Other clients include Paula Reed, Becky Motew, Jack McCallum, Jana Deleon.

PARK LITERARY GROUP, LLC

270 Lafayette St., Suite 1504, New York NY 10012. (212)691-3500. Fax: (212)691-3540. E-mail: info@parkliterary.com. Website: www.parkliterary.com. Estab. 2005.

- • Prior to their current positions, Ms. Park and Ms. O'Keefe were literary agents at Sanford J. Greenburger Associates. Prior to 1994, she was a practicing attorney.

Member Agents Theresa Park (plot-driven fiction and serious nonfiction); Abigail Koons (quirky, edgy and commercial fiction, as well as superb thrillers and mysteries; adventure and travel narrative nonfiction, exceptional memoirs, popular science, history, politics and art).

Represents Nonfiction books, novels.

- ⚬ "The Park Literary Group represents fiction and nonfiction with a boutique approach: an emphasis on servicing a relatively small number of clients, with the highest professional standards and focused personal attention." Does not want to receive poetry or screenplays.

How to Contact Query with SASE, submit synopsis, 1-3 sample chapter(s), SASE. Send all submissions through the mail. No e-mail or fax queries. Responds in 4-6 weeks to queries.

Recent Sales

☒ ☐ ELLEN PEPUS LITERARY AGENCY

4200 Wisconsin Avenue, NW, #106-233, Washington DC 20016. (301)896-0185. Fax: (301)896-0185. E-mail: ellen@epliterary.com. Website: www.epliterary.com. **Contact:** Ellen Pepus; adheres to AAR canon of ethics. Represents 9 clients. 90% of clients are new/unpublished writers. Currently handles: 30% nonfiction books; 70% novels.

- • Prior to her current position, Ms. Pepus was employed at Graybill & English Literary Agency. She worked in foreign rights as well.

Represents Nonfiction books, novels. **Considers these nonfiction areas:** Animals; anthropology/archaeology; art/architecture/design; biography/autobiography; child guidance/parenting; cooking/foods/nutrition; crafts/hobbies; current affairs; ethnic/cultural interests; gay/lesbian issues; government/politics/law; health/medicine; history; how-to; humor/satire; interior design/decorating; language/literature/criticism; memoirs; military/war; money/finance; music/dance; nature/environment; New Age/metaphysics; photography; popular culture; psychology; science/technology; self-help/personal improvement; sociology; translation; true crime/investigative; women's issues/studies. **Considers these fiction areas:** Action/adventure; detective/police/crime; erotica; ethnic; family saga; fantasy; feminist; gay/lesbian; historical; literary; mainstream/contemporary; mystery/suspense; psychic/supernatural; romance; thriller; women's.

- ⚬ This agency specializes in fiction—both genre and literary. Narrative nonfiction is sought out, though Ms. Pepus will consider other nonfiction. Actively seeking literary and commercial fiction, narrative nonfiction. Does not want to receive children's, young adult, poetry, short stories, screenplays, science fiction or horror.

How to Contact Query with SASE, submit first 5 pages. E-queries are preferred. No fax queries. Considers simultaneous queries. Responds in 2 weeks to queries; 8 weeks to mss. Returns materials only with SASE. Obtains most new clients through recommendations from others, solicitations, conferences.

Terms Agent receives 15% commission on domestic sales; 20% commission on foreign sales. Offers written contract; 30-day notice must be given to terminate contract.

Writers' Conferences Washington Independent Writers, Society of Southwestern Authors, North Carolina Writers Network, Southern California Writers Conference, Space Coast Writers Guild Conference.

☒ L. PERKINS ASSOCIATES

5800 Arlington Ave., Riverdale NY 10471. (718)543-5344. Fax: (718)543-5354. E-mail: lperkinsagency@yahoo.com. Estab. 1990. Member of AAR. Represents 90 clients. 10% of clients are new/unpublished writers.

- • Ms. Perkins has been an agent for 20 years. She is also the author of *The Insider's Guide to Getting an Agent* (Writer's Digest Books), as well as three other nonfiction books. She has also edited two anthologies.

Represents Nonfiction books, novels. **Considers these nonfiction areas:** Popular culture. **Considers these fiction areas:** Erotica; fantasy; horror; literary (dark); science fiction.

o— Most of Ms. Perkins' clients write both fiction and nonfiction. "This combination keeps my clients publishing for years. I am also a published author, so I know what it takes to write a good book." Actively seeking a Latino *Gone With the Wind* and *Waiting to Exhale*, and urban ethnic horror. Does not want to receive anything outside of the above categories (westerns, romance, etc.).

How to Contact Query with SASE. Considers simultaneous queries. Responds in 12 weeks to queries; 3-6 months to mss. Returns materials only with SASE. Obtains most new clients through recommendations from others, solicitations, conferences.

Recent Sales Sold 100 titles in the last year. *How to Make Love Like a Porn Star: A Cautionary Tale*, by Jenna Jameson (Reagan Books); *Everything But ...?*, by Rachel Krammer Bussel (Bantam); *Dear Mom, I Always Wanted You to Know*, by Lisa Delman (Perigee Books); *The Illustrated Ray Bradbury*, by Jerry Weist (Avon); *The Poet in Exile*, by Ray Manzarek (Avalon); *Behind Sad Eyes: The Life of George Harrison*, by Marc Shapiro (St. Martin's Press).

Terms Agent receives 15% commission on domestic sales; 20% commission on foreign sales. No written contract. Charges clients for photocopying.

Writers' Conferences San Diego State University Writers' Conference; NECON; BookExpo America; World Fantasy Convention.

Tips "Research your field and contact professional writers' organizations to see who is looking for what. Finish your novel before querying agents. Read my book, *An Insider's Guide to Getting an Agent*, to get a sense of how agents operate. Read agent blogs—litsoup.blogspot.com and missnark.blogspot.com.

⊠ STEPHEN PEVNER, INC.

382 Lafayette St., Eighth Floor, New York NY 10003. (212)674-8403. Fax: (212)529-3692. E-mail: spevner@aol.com. **Contact:** Stephen Pevner.

Represents Nonfiction books, novels, feature film, TV scripts, TV movie of the week, episodic drama, animation, documentary, miniseries. **Considers these nonfiction areas:** Biography/autobiography; ethnic/cultural interests; gay/lesbian issues; history; humor/satire; language/literature/criticism; memoirs; music/dance; New Age/metaphysics; photography; popular culture; religious/inspirational; sociology; travel. **Considers these fiction areas:** Comic books/cartoon; erotica; ethnic; experimental; gay/lesbian; glitz; horror; humor/satire; literary; mainstream/contemporary; psychic/supernatural; thriller; urban. **Considers these script subject areas:** Comedy; contemporary issues; detective/police/crime; gay/lesbian; glitz; horror; romantic comedy; romantic drama; thriller.

o— This agency specializes in motion pictures, novels, humor, pop culture, urban fiction, and independent filmmakers.

How to Contact Query with SASE, submit outline/proposal. Prefers to read materials exclusively. No e-mail or fax queries. Responds in 2 weeks to queries; 1 month to mss. Obtains most new clients through recommendations from others.

Terms Agent receives 15% commission on domestic sales; 20% commission on foreign sales. Offers written contract, binding for 1 year; 6-week notice must be given to terminate contract. 100% of business is derived from commissions on ms sales.

Tips "Be persistent, but civilized."

Ⓝ ◻ PHENOMENON BOOKS AGENCY

10324 West 44th Ave., #3A, Wheat Ridge CO 80033. (720)210-3373. E-mail: phenomenonbooks@yahoo.com. Website: www.phenomenonbooks.com. **Contact:** Pamela Trayser. Estab. 2006. Currently handles: 2% nonfiction books; 98% novels.

• Prior to becoming an agent, Ms. Trayser was a writer.

Represents Novels. **Considers these fiction areas:** Fantasy; horror; juvenile (picture books to young adult); literary; thriller; young adult; psychic/supernatural; Christian, when dealing with marked genres.

o— Actively seeking picture books, middle grade fiction, political thrillers and literary work of the highest quality.

How to Contact Query with SASE, submit synopsis, 3 sample chapter(s). Consider submissions only from October to December, and March to May. Accepts e-mail queries. No fax queries. Considers simultaneous queries. Responds in 10 weeks to queries; 3 months to mss. Obtains most new clients through solicitations.

Terms Agent receives 15% commission on domestic sales; 20% commission on foreign sales.

N ✍ PLAINSMART PUBLISHING AGENCY

520 Kerr St., #20033, Oakville ON L6K 3C7, Canada. E-mail: query@plainsmart.com; info@plainsmart.com. Website: www.plainsmart.com/contactinfo.html. **Contact:** Curtis Russell. Estab. 2005. Represents 8 clients. 25% of clients are new/unpublished writers. Currently handles: 50% nonfiction books; 50% novels.

Represents Nonfiction books, novels, juvenile books. **Considers these nonfiction areas:** Biography/autobiography; business/economics; child guidance/parenting; cooking/foods/nutrition; current affairs; government/politics/law; health/medicine; how-to; humor/satire; memoirs; military/war; money/finance; nature/environment; popular culture; science/technology; self-help/personal improvement; sports; true crime/investigative; women's issues/studies. **Considers these fiction areas:** Action/adventure; detective/police/crime; erotica; ethnic; family saga; historical; horror; humor/satire; juvenile; literary; mainstream/contemporary; mystery/suspense; picture books; romance; sports; thriller; young adult; women's.

> ⚡ "We take on a very small number of clients per year in order to provide focused, hands-on representation. We pride ourselves in providing industry leading client service." Does not want to receive poetry or screenplays.

How to Contact Query with SASE, submit synopsis, author bio. Accepts e-mail queries. No fax queries. Considers simultaneous queries. Responds in 6 weeks to queries; 6 weeks to mss. Obtains most new clients through solicitations.

Recent Sales *World Famous*, by David Tyreman (AMACOM); *What Burns Within* and *The Frailty of Flesh*, by Sandra Ruttan; *The Road to a Nuclear al-qaeda*, by Al J. Venter (Potomac).

Terms Agent receives 15% commission on domestic sales; 25% commission on foreign sales. Offers written contract; 30-day notice must be given to terminate contract. This agency charges for postage/messenger services only if a project is sold.

Tips "Please review our Web site for the most up-to-date submission guidelines."

✍ PROSPECT AGENCY LLC

285 Fifth Ave., PMB 445, Brooklyn NY 11215. (718)788-3217. E-mail: esk@prospectagency.com. Website: www.prospectagency.com. **Contact:** Emily Sylvan Kim. Estab. 2005. Represents 15 clients. 50% of clients are new/unpublished writers. Currently handles: 66% novels; 33% juvenile books.

> • Prior to starting her agency, Ms. Kim briefly attended law school and worked for another literary agency.

Member Agents Emily Sylvan Kim; Becca Stumpf (adult and YA literary, mainstream fiction; nonfiction interests include narrative nonfiction, journalistic perspectives, fashion, film studies, travel, art, and informed analysis of cultural phenomena. She has a special interest in aging in America and environmental issues); Rachel Orr (fiction and nonfiction, particularly picture books, beginning readers, chapter books, middle-grade, YA novels).

Represents Nonfiction books, novels, juvenile books. **Considers these nonfiction areas:** Memoirs; science/technology; juvenile. **Considers these fiction areas:** Action/adventure; detective/police/crime; erotica; ethnic; family saga; juvenile; literary; mainstream/contemporary; mystery/suspense; picture books; romance; science fiction; thriller; westerns/frontier; young adult.

> ⚡ "We are currently looking for the next generation of writers to shape the literary landscape. Our clients receive professional and knowledgeable representation. We are committed to offering skilled editorial advice and advocating our clients in the marketplace." Actively seeking romance, literary fiction, and young adult submissions. Does not want to receive poetry, short stories, textbooks, or most nonfiction.

How to Contact Upload outline and 3 sample chapters to the Web site. Considers simultaneous queries. Responds in 3 weeks to queries; 1 month to mss. Obtains most new clients through recommendations from others, conferences, unsolicited mss.

Recent Sales *Love Potion #10*, by Janice Maynard (NAL); *Spectacular Now*, by Tim Tharp (Knopf Children). Other clients include Diane Perkins, Opal Carew, Marissa Doyle, Meagan Brothers, Elizabeth Scott, Bonnie Edwards, Susan Lyons, Rose Kent, Catherine Stine.

Terms Agent receives 15% commission on domestic sales; 20% commission on foreign sales. Offers written contract.

Writers' Conferences SCBWI Annual Winter Conference; Pikes Peak Writers Conference; RWA National Conference.

◢ RAINES & RAINES

103 Kenyon Road, Medusa NY 12120. (518)239-8311. Fax: (518)239-6029. **Contact:** Theron Raines (member of AAR); Joan Raines; Keith Korman. Represents 100 clients.

Represents Nonfiction books, novels. **Considers these nonfiction areas:** All subjects. **Considers these fiction areas:** Action/adventure; detective/police/crime; fantasy; historical; mystery/suspense; picture books; science fiction; thriller; westerns/frontier.

How to Contact Query with SASE. Responds in 2 weeks to queries.

Terms Agent receives 15% commission on domestic sales; 20% commission on foreign sales. Charges for photocopying.

◢ HELEN REES LITERARY AGENCY

376 North St., Boston MA 02113-2013. (617)227-9014. Fax: (617)227-8762. E-mail: reesagency@rees agency.com. **Contact:** Joan Mazmanian, Ann Collette, Helen Rees, Lorin Rees. Estab. 1983. Member of AAR, PEN. Represents more than 100 clients. 50% of clients are new/unpublished writers. Currently handles: 60% nonfiction books; 40% novels.

Member Agents Ann Collette (literary fiction, women's studies, health, biography, history); Helen Rees (business, money/finance/economics, government/politics/law, contemporary issues, literary fiction); Lorin Rees (business, money/finance, management, history, narrative nonfiction, science, literary fiction, memoir).

Represents Nonfiction books, novels. **Considers these nonfiction areas:** Biography/autobiography; business/economics; current affairs; government/politics/law; health/medicine; history; money/finance; women's issues/studies. **Considers these fiction areas:** Historical; literary; mainstream/contemporary; mystery/suspense; thriller.

How to Contact Query with SASE, outline, 2 sample chapters. No unsolicited e-mail submissions. No multiple submissions. No e-mail or fax queries. Responds in 3-4 weeks to queries. Obtains most new clients through recommendations from others, conferences, submissions.

Recent Sales Sold more than 35 titles in the last year. *Get Your Shipt Together*, by Capt. D. Michael Abrashoff; *Overpromise and Overdeliver*, by Rick Berrara; *Opacity*, by Joel Kurtzman; *America the Broke*, by Gerald Swanson; *Murder at the B-School*, by Jeffrey Cruikshank; *Bone Factory*, by Steven Sidor; *Father Said*, by Hal Sirowitz; *Winning*, by Jack Welch; *The Case for Israel*, by Alan Dershowitz; *As the Future Catches You*, by Juan Enriquez; *Blood Makes the Grass Grow Green*, by Johnny Rico; *DVD Movie Guide*, by Mick Martin and Marsha Porter; *Words That Work*, by Frank Luntz; *Stirring It Up*, by Gary Hirshberg; *Hot Spots*, by Martin Fletcher; *Andy Grove: The Life and Times of an American*, by Richard Tedlow; *Girls Most Likely To*, by Poonam Sharma.

Terms Agent receives 15% commission on domestic sales; 20% commission on foreign sales.

◢ REGAL LITERARY AGENCY

1140 Broadway, Penthouse, New York NY 10001. (212)684-7900. Fax: (212)684-7906. E-mail: Shann on@regal-literary.com. Website: www.regal-literary.com. **Contact:** Shannon Firth, Marcus Hoffmann. Estab. 2002. Member of AAR. Represents 100 clients. 20% of clients are new/unpublished writers. Currently handles: 48% nonfiction books; 46% novels; 6% poetry.

- Prior to becoming agents, Mr. Regal was a musician; Mr. Steinberg was a filmmaker and screenwriter; Ms. Reid and Ms. Schott Pearson were magazine editors; Mr. Hoffman worked in the publishing industry in London.

Member Agents Joseph Regal (literary fiction, science, history, memoir); Peter Steinberg (literary and commercial fiction, history, humor, memoir, narrative nonfiction, young adult); Bess Reed (literary fiction, narrative nonfiction, self-help); Lauren Schott Pearson (literary fiction, commercial fiction, memoir, narrative nonfiction, thrillers, mysteries); Markus Hoffmann (foreign rights manager, literary fiction, mysteries, thrillers, international fiction, science, music). Michael Psaltis of Psaltis Literary also works with Regal Literary agents to form the Culinary Cooperative—a joint-venture agency dedicated to food writing, cookbooks, and all things related to cooking. Recent sales include *Cooked* (William Morrow); *Carmine's Family Style* (St. Martin's Press); *Fish On a First-Name Basis* (St. Martin's Press); *The Reverse Diet* (John Wiley & Sons); and *The Seasoning of a Chef* (Doubleday/Broadway).

Represents Nonfiction books, novels, short story collections, novellas. **Considers these nonfiction areas:** Anthropology/archaeology; art/architecture/design; biography/autobiography; business/economics; cooking/foods/nutrition; current affairs; ethnic/cultural interests; gay/lesbian issues;

history; humor/satire; language/literature/criticism; memoirs; military/war; music/dance; nature/
environment; photography; popular culture; psychology; religious/inspirational; science/technol-
ogy; sports; translation; women's issues/studies. **Considers these fiction areas:** Comic books/car-
toon; detective/police/crime; ethnic; historical; literary; mystery/suspense; thriller; contemporary.

> O— "We have discovered more than a dozen successful literary novelists in the last 5 years. We
> are small, but are extraordinarily responsive to our writers. We are more like managers than
> agents, with an eye toward every aspect of our writers' careers, including publicity and other
> media." Actively seeking literary fiction and narrative nonfiction. Does not want romance,
> science fiction, horror, or screenplays.

How to Contact Query with SASE, 5-15 sample pages. No phone calls. No e-mail or fax queries.
Considers simultaneous queries. Responds in 2-3 weeks to queries; 4-12 to mss. Returns materials
only with SASE. Obtains most new clients through recommendations from others, unsolicited submissions.

Recent Sales Sold 20 titles in the last year. *The Stolen Child*, by Keith Donohue (Nan Talese/
Doubleday); *What Elmo Taught Me*, by Kevin Clash (HarperCollins); *The Affected Provincial's Com-
panion*, by Lord Breaulove Swells Whimsy (Bloomsbury); *The Three Incestuous Sisters*, by Audrey
Niffenegger (Abrams); *The Traveler*, by John Twelve Hawks (Doubleday). Other clients include
James Reston Jr., Tony Earley, Dennie Hughes, Mark Lee, Jake Page, Cheryl Bernard, Daniel Wallace,
John Marks, Keith Scribner, Cathy Day, Alicia Erian, Gregory David Roberts, Dallas Hudgens, Tim
Winton, Ian Spiegelman, Brad Barkley, Heather Hepler, Gavin Edwards, Sara Voorhees, Alex Abella.
Terms Agent receives 15% commission on domestic sales; 20% commission on foreign sales. No
written contract. Charges clients for typical/major office expenses, such as photocopying and foreign
postage.

☑ THE AMY RENNERT AGENCY

98 Main St., #302, Tiburon CA 94920. E-mail: queries@amyrennert.com. Website: www.amyrennert.
com. **Contact:** Amy Rennert.

Represents Nonfiction books, novels. **Considers these nonfiction areas:** Biography/autobiography;
health/medicine; history; memoirs; sports; lifestyle, narrative nonfiction. **Considers these fiction
areas:** General fiction, mystery.

> O— "The Amy Rennert Agency specializes in books that matter. We provide career management
> for established and first-time authors, and our breadth of experience in many genres enables
> us to meet the needs of a diverse clientele."

How to Contact Query via e-mail. For nonfiction, send cover letter and attach a Word file with
proposal/first chapter. For fiction, send cover letter and attach file with 10-20 pages.

Recent Sales *A Salty Piece of Land*, by Jimmy Buffett; *Maisie Dobbs*, by Jacqueline Winspear; *The
Prize Winner of Defiance, Ohio*, by Terry Ryan; *The Travel Detective*, by Peter Greenberg; *Offer of
Proof*, by Robert Heilbrun; *No Place to Hide*, by Robert O'Harrow; *The Poet of Tolstoy Park*, by Sonny
Brewer. Other clients include Elliot Jaspin, Beth Kephart, Kris Kristofferson, Adam Phillips, Don
Lattin, Kathryn Shevelow, Cynthia Kaplan, Frank Viviano, Amy Krouse Rosenthal, Kim Severson,
Pat Walsh, John Shannon, Brian Copeland, Tony Broadbent, Janis Cooke Newman.

Tips "Due to the high volume of submissions, it is not possible to respond to each and every one.
Please understand that we are only able to respond to queries that we feel may be a good fit with
our agency."

☑ JODIE RHODES LITERARY AGENCY

8840 Villa La Jolla Drive, Suite 315, La Jolla CA 92037-1957. **Contact:** Jodie Rhodes, president. Estab.
1998. Member of AAR. Represents 65 clients. 60% of clients are new/unpublished writers. Currently
handles: 45% nonfiction books; 35% novels; 20% juvenile books.

> ● Prior to opening her agency, Ms. Rhodes was a university-level creative writing teacher, work-
> shop director, published novelist, and vice president/media director at the N.W. Ayer Advertising
> Agency.

Member Agents Jodie Rhodes; Clark McCutcheon (fiction); Bob McCarter (nonfiction).

Represents Nonfiction books, novels. **Considers these nonfiction areas:** Biography/autobiography;
child guidance/parenting; ethnic/cultural interests; government/politics/law; health/medicine; history; memoirs; military/war; science/technology; women's issues/studies. **Considers these fiction**

areas: Ethnic; family saga; historical; literary; mainstream/contemporary; mystery/suspense; thriller; young adult; women's.

 o→ Actively seeking witty, sophisticated women's books about career ambitions and relationships; edgy/trendy YA and teen books; narrative nonfiction on groundbreaking scientific discoveries, politics, economics, military and important current affairs by prominent scientists and academic professors. Does not want to receive erotica, horror, fantasy, romance, science fiction, religious/inspirational, or children's picture books.

How to Contact Query with brief synopsis, first 30-50 pages, SASE. Do not call. Do not send complete ms unless requested. This agency does not return unrequested material weighing a pound or more that requires special postage. Include e-mail address with query. No e-mail or fax queries. Considers simultaneous queries. Responds in 3 weeks to queries. Returns materials only with SASE. Obtains most new clients through recommendations from others, agent sourcebooks.

Recent Sales Sold 40 titles in the last year. *The Ring*, By Kavita Daswani (HarperCollins); *Train To Trieste*, By Domnica Radulescu; *A Year With Cats And Dogs*, by Margaret Hawkins (Permanent Press); *Silence And Silhouettes*, by Ryan Smithson (Harpercollins); *Internal Affairs*, by Constance Dial (Permanent Press); *How Math Rules The World*, by James Stein (Harpercollins).

Terms Agent receives 15% commission on domestic sales; 20% commission on foreign sales. Offers written contract; 1-month notice must be given to terminate contract. Charges clients for fax, photocopying, phone calls, postage. Charges are itemized and approved by writers upfront.

Tips "Think your book out before you write it. Do your research, know your subject matter intimately, and write vivid specifics, not bland generalities. Care deeply about your book. Don't imitate other writers. Find your own voice. We never take on a book we don't believe in, and we go the extra mile for our writers. We welcome talented, new writers."

ANGELA RINALDI LITERARY AGENCY

P.O. Box 7877, Beverly Hills CA 90212-7877. (310)842-7665. Fax: (310)837-8143. E-mail: amr@rinald iliterary.com. Website: www.rinaldiliterary.com. **Contact:** Angela Rinaldi. Estab. 1994. Member of AAR. Represents 50 clients. Currently handles: 50% nonfiction books; 50% novels.

 • Prior to opening her agency, Ms. Rinaldi was an editor at NAL/Signet, Pocket Books and Bantam, and the manager of book development for *The Los Angeles Times*.

Represents Nonfiction books, novels, TV and motion picture rights (for clients only). **Considers these nonfiction areas:** Biography/autobiography; business/economics; health/medicine; money/finance; self-help/personal improvement; true crime/investigative; women's issues/studies; books by journalists and academics. **Considers these fiction areas:** Literary; commercial; upmarket women's fiction; suspense.

 o→ Actively seeking commercial and literary fiction. Does not want to receive scripts, poetry, category romances, children's books, Western's, science fiction/fantasy, technothrillers or cookbooks.

How to Contact For fiction, send first 3 chapters, brief synopsis, SASE. For nonfiction, query with SASE or send outline/proposal, SASE. Do not send certified or metered mail. Brief e-mail inquiries are OK (no attachments). Considers simultaneous queries. Please advise if it is a multiple submission. Responds in 6 weeks to queries. Returns materials only with SASE.

Recent Sales *Mother Love*, by Drusilla Campbell (Grand Central Publishing); *Put It in Writing*, by Deborah Hutchison (Sterling); *Global Warming Is Good for Business* (Quill Driver Books); *Zen Putting*, by Dr. Joseph Parent (Gotham Books).

Terms Agent receives 15% commission on domestic sales; 20% commission on foreign sales. Offers written contract. Charges clients for photocopying.

ANN RITTENBERG LITERARY AGENCY, INC.

30 Bond St., New York NY 10012. (212)684-6936. Fax: (212)684-6929. Website: www.rittlit.com. **Contact:** Ann Rittenberg, president. Estab. 1992. Member of AAR. Currently handles: 50% nonfiction books; 50% novels.

Represents Nonfiction books, novels. **Considers these nonfiction areas:** Biography/autobiography; history (social/cultural); memoirs; women's issues/studies. **Considers these fiction areas:** Literary.

 o→ This agent specializes in literary fiction and literary nonfiction. Does not want to receive Screenplays, genre fiction, Poetry, Self-help.

How to Contact Query with SASE, submit outline, 3 sample chapter(s), SASE. Query via snail mail *only*. No e-mail or fax queries. Considers simultaneous queries. Responds in 6 weeks to queries; 2 months to mss. Obtains most new clients through referrals from established writers and editors.

Recent Sales *Bad Cat*, by Jim Edgar (Workman); *A Certain Slant of Light*, by Laura Whitcomb (Houghton Mifflin); *New York Night*, by Mark Caldwell (Scribner); *In Plain Sight*, by C.J. Box (Putnam); *Improbable*, by Adam Fawer; *Colleges That Change Lives*, by Loren Pope.

Terms Agent receives 15% commission on domestic sales; 20% commission on foreign sales. Offers written contract. This agency charges clients for photocopying only.

Ⓝ Ⓐ LESLIE RIVERS, INTERNATIONAL (LRI)

P.O. Box 940772, Houston TX 77094-7772. (281)493-5822. Fax: (281)493-5835. E-mail: LRivers@Lesl ieRivers.com. Website: www.leslierivers.com. **Contact:** Judith Bruni. Estab. 2005; adheres to AAR's canon of ethics. Represents 20 clients. 80% of clients are new/unpublished writers. Currently handles: 25% nonfiction books; 70% novels; 5% scholarly books.

Member Agents Judith Bruni, literary agent and founder; Mark Bruni, consulting editor.

Represents Nonfiction books, novels, scholarly books, movie scripts, TV scripts, stage plays. **Considers these nonfiction areas:** Open to all genres, as long as the author is established with a platform. **Considers these fiction areas:** All fiction genres, but no children's fiction. **Considers these script subject areas:** Considers all script genres.

> ⊶ LRI collaborates with creative professionals and offers a customized, boutique service, based on the client's individual requirements. Send only your finest work. Actively seeking fiction— all subgenres. Does not want to receive children's books or poetry.

How to Contact Query with SASE, submit synopsis, author bio, 3 chapters or 50 pages, whichever is longer. Prefers an exclusive read, but will consider simultaneous queries. Accepts e-mail queries. No fax queries. Responds in 2 months to queries; 2 months to mss. Returns materials only with SASE. Obtains most new clients through recommendations from others, solicitations.

Terms Agent receives 15% commission on domestic sales; 25% commission on foreign sales. Offers written contract; 90-day notice must be given to terminate contract. This agency charges for postage, printing, copying, etc. If no sale is made, no charges are enforced.

Ⓐ B.J. ROBBINS LITERARY AGENCY

5130 Bellaire Ave., North Hollywood CA 91607-2908. (818)760-6602. E-mail: robbinsliterary@aol.c om. **Contact:** (Ms.) B.J. Robbins. Estab. 1992. Member of AAR. Represents 40 clients. 50% of clients are new/unpublished writers. Currently handles: 50% nonfiction books; 50% novels.

Represents Nonfiction books, novels. **Considers these nonfiction areas:** Biography/autobiography; current affairs; ethnic/cultural interests; health/medicine; how-to; humor/satire; memoirs; music/ dance; popular culture; psychology; self-help/personal improvement; sociology; sports; theater/film; travel; true crime/investigative; women's issues/studies. **Considers these fiction areas:** Detective/ police/crime; ethnic; literary; mainstream/contemporary; mystery/suspense; sports; thriller.

How to Contact Query with SASE, submit outline/proposal, 3 sample chapters, SASE. Accepts e-mail queries (no attachments). No fax queries. Considers simultaneous queries. Responds in 2-6 weeks to queries; 6-8 weeks to mss. Returns materials only with SASE. Obtains most new clients through conferences, referrals.

Recent Sales Sold 15 titles in the last year. *Getting Stoned with Savages*, by J. Maarten Troost (Broadway); *Hot Water*, by Kathryn Jordan (Berkley); *Between the Bridge and the River*, by Craig Ferguson (Chronicle); *I'm Proud of You*, by Tim Madigan (Gotham); *Man of the House*, by Chris Erskine (Rodale); *Bird of Another Heaven*, by James D. Houston (Knopf); *Tomorrow They Will Kiss*, by Eduardo Santiago (Little, Brown); *A Terrible Glory*, by James Donovan (Little, Brown); *The Writing on My Forehead*, by Nafisa Haji (Morrow); *Carry Me Home*, by John Hour Jr. (Simon & Schuster); *Lost on Planet China*, by J. Maarten Troost (Braodway).

Terms Agent receives 15% commission on domestic sales; 20% commission on foreign sales. Offers written contract; 3-month notice must be given to terminate contract. 100% of business is derived from commissions on ms sales. This agency charges clients for postage and photocopying (only after sale of ms).

Writers' Conferences Squaw Valley Writers Workshop; San Diego State University Writers' Conference; Santa Barbara Writers' Conference.

☑ THE ROSENBERG GROUP

23 Lincoln Ave., Marblehead MA 01945. (781)990-1341. Fax: (781)990-1344. Website: www.rosenbe rggroup.com. **Contact:** Barbara Collins Rosenberg. Estab. 1998. Member of AAR, recognized agent of the RWA. Represents 25 clients. 15% of clients are new/unpublished writers. Currently handles: 30% nonfiction books; 30% novels; 10% scholarly books; 30% college textbooks.

• Prior to becoming an agent, Ms. Rosenberg was a senior editor for Harcourt.

Represents Nonfiction books, novels, textbooks (college textbooks only). **Considers these nonfiction areas:** Current affairs; popular culture; psychology; sports; women's issues/studies; women's health; food/wine/beverages. **Considers these fiction areas:** Romance; women's.

⊶ Ms. Rosenberg is well-versed in the romance market (both category and single title). She is a frequent speaker at romance conferences. Actively seeking romance category or single title in contemporary chick lit, romantic suspense, and the historical subgenres. Does not want to receive inspirational or spiritual romances.

How to Contact Query with SASE. No e-mail or fax queries. Responds in 2 weeks to queries; 4-6 weeks to mss. Returns materials only with SASE. Obtains most new clients through recommendations from others, solicitations, conferences.

Recent Sales Sold 21 titles in the last year.

Terms Agent receives 15% commission on domestic sales; 15% commission on foreign sales. Offers written contract; 1-month notice must be given to terminate contract. Charges maximum of $350/year for postage and photocopying.

Writers' Conferences RWA National Conference; BookExpo America.

◑ JANE ROTROSEN AGENCY LLC

318 E. 51st St., New York NY 10022. (212)593-4330. Fax: (212)935-6985. E-mail: firstinitiallastname @janerotrosen.com. Estab. 1974. Member of AAR, Authors Guild. Represents over 100 clients. Currently handles: 30% nonfiction books; 70% novels.

Member Agents Jane R. Berkey; Andrea Cirillo; Annelise Robey; Margaret Ruley; Kelly Harms; Christina Hogrebe; Peggy Gordijn, director of translation rights.

Represents Nonfiction books, novels. **Considers these nonfiction areas:** Biography/autobiography; business/economics; child guidance/parenting; cooking/foods/nutrition; current affairs; health/medicine; how-to; humor/satire; money/finance; nature/environment; popular culture; psychology; self-help/personal improvement; sports; true crime/investigative; women's issues/studies. **Considers these fiction areas:** Action/adventure; detective/police/crime; family saga; historical; horror; mainstream/contemporary; mystery/suspense; romance; thriller; women's.

How to Contact Query with SASE. No e-mail or fax queries. Responds in 2 months to mss. Responds in 2 weeks to writers who have been referred by a client or colleague. Returns materials only with SASE. Obtains most new clients through referrals.

Recent Sales This agency prefers not to share information on specific sales.

Terms Agent receives 15% commission on domestic sales; 20% commission on foreign sales. Offers written contract, binding for 3-5 years; 2-month notice must be given to terminate contract. Charges clients for photocopying, express mail, overseas postage, book purchase.

☑ RUSSELL & VOLKENING

50 W. 29th St., #7E, New York NY 10001. (212)684-6050. Fax: (212)889-3026. Website: www.randvin c.com. **Contact:** Timothy Seldes, Jesseca Salky. Estab. 1940. Member of AAR. Represents 140 clients. 20% of clients are new/unpublished writers. Currently handles: 45% nonfiction books; 50% novels; 3% story collections; 2% novellas.

Represents Nonfiction books, novels, short story collections. **Considers these nonfiction areas:** Anthropology/archaeology; art/architecture/design; biography/autobiography; business/economics; cooking/foods/nutrition; current affairs; education; ethnic/cultural interests; gay/lesbian issues; government/politics/law; health/medicine; history; language/literature/criticism; military/war; money/finance; music/dance; nature/environment; photography; popular culture; psychology; science/technology; sociology; sports; theater/film; true crime/investigative; women's issues/studies; creative nonfiction. **Considers these fiction areas:** Action/adventure; detective/police/crime; ethnic; literary; mainstream/contemporary; mystery/suspense; picture books; sports; thriller.

⊶ This agency specializes in literary fiction and narrative nonfiction.

How to Contact Query with SASE, submit synopsis, several pages. No e-mail or fax queries. Responds in 4 weeks to queries.

Recent Sales *Digging to America*, by Anne Tyler (Knopf); *Get a Life*, by Nadine Gardiner; *The Franklin Affair*, by Jim Lehrer (Random House).

Terms Agent receives 15% commission on domestic sales; 20% commission on foreign sales. Charges clients for standard office expenses relating to the submission of materials.

Tips "If the query is cogent, well written, well presented, and is the type of book we'd represent, we'll ask to see the manuscript. From there, it depends purely on the quality of the work."

VICTORIA SANDERS & ASSOCIATES

241 Avenue of the Americas, Suite 11 H, New York NY 10014. (212)633-8811. Fax: (212)633-0525. E-mail: queriesvsa@hotmail.com. Website: www.victoriasanders.com. **Contact:** Victoria Sanders, Diane Dickensheid. Estab. 1993. Member of AAR; signatory of WGA. Represents 135 clients. 25% of clients are new/unpublished writers. Currently handles: 30% nonfiction books; 70% novels.

Represents Nonfiction books, novels. **Considers these nonfiction areas:** Biography/autobiography; current affairs; ethnic/cultural interests; gay/lesbian issues; government/politics/law; history; humor/satire; language/literature/criticism; music/dance; popular culture; psychology; theater/film; translation; women's issues/studies. **Considers these fiction areas:** Action/adventure; contemporary issues; ethnic; family saga; feminist; gay/lesbian; literary; thriller.

How to Contact Query by e-mail only.

Recent Sales Sold 20+ titles in the last year.

Terms Agent receives 15% commission on domestic sales; 20% commission on foreign sales. Offers written contract. Charges for photocopying, messenger, express mail. If in excess of $100, client approval is required.

Tips "Limit query to letter (no calls) and give it your best shot. A good query is going to get a good response."

SCHIAVONE LITERARY AGENCY, INC.

236 Trails End, West Palm Beach FL 33413-2135. (561)966-9294. Fax: (561)966-9294. E-mail: profsch ia@aol.com. New York office: 3671 Hudson Manor Terrace, No. 11H, Bronx, NY, 10463-1139, phone: (718)548-5332; fax: (718)548-5332; e-mail: jendu77@aol.com **Contact:** Dr. James Schiavone. CEO, corporate offices in Florida; Jennifer DuVall, president, New York office. Estab. 1996. Member of National Education Association. Represents 60+ clients. 2% of clients are new/unpublished writers. Currently handles: 50% nonfiction books; 49% novels; 1% textbooks.

- Prior to opening his agency, Dr. Schiavone was a full professor of developmental skills at the City University of New York and author of 5 trade books and 3 textbooks. Jennifer DuVall has many years of combined experience in office management and agenting.

Represents Nonfiction books, novels, juvenile books, scholarly books, textbooks. **Considers these nonfiction areas:** Animals; anthropology/archaeology; biography/autobiography; child guidance/parenting; current affairs; education; ethnic/cultural interests; gay/lesbian issues; government/politics/law; health/medicine; history; how-to; humor/satire; juvenile nonfiction; language/literature/criticism; military/war; nature/environment; popular culture; psychology; science/technology; self-help/personal improvement; sociology; spirituality (mind and body); true crime/investigative. **Considers these fiction areas:** Ethnic; family saga; historical; horror; humor/satire; juvenile; literary; mainstream/contemporary; science fiction; young adult.

- This agency specializes in celebrity biography and autobiography and memoirs. Does not want to receive poetry.

How to Contact Query with SASE. Do not send unsolicited materials or parcels requiring a signature. Send no e-attachments. Accepts e-mail queries. No fax queries. Considers simultaneous queries. Responds in 2 weeks to queries; 6 weeks to mss. Returns materials only with SASE. Obtains most new clients through recommendations from others, solicitations, conferences.

Terms Agent receives 15% commission on domestic sales; 20% commission on foreign sales. Offers written contract. Charges clients for postage only.

Writers' Conferences Key West Literary Seminar; South Florida Writers' Conference; Tallahassee Writers' Conference, Million Dollar Writers' Conference; Alaska Writers Conference.

Tips "We prefer to work with established authors published by major houses in New York. We will consider marketable proposals from new/previously unpublished writers."

◐ SCOVIL CHICHAK GALEN LITERARY AGENCY

276 Fifth Ave., Suite 708, New York NY 10001. (212)679-8686. Fax: (212)679-6710. E-mail: info@scgl it.com. Website: www.scglit.com. **Contact:** Russell Galen. Estab. 1992. Member of AAR. Represents 300 clients. Currently handles: 60% nonfiction books; 40% novels.

Member Agents Jack Scovil, jackscovil@scglit.com; Russell Galen, russellgalen@scglit.com (fiction novels that stretch the bounds of reality; strong, serious nonfiction books on almost any subject that teach something new; no books that are merely entertaining, such as diet or pop psych books; serious interests include science, history, journalism, biography, business, memoir, nature, politics, sports, contemporary culture, literary nonfiction, etc.); Anna Ghosh, annaghosh@scglit.com (strong nonfiction proposals on all subjects as well as adult commercial and literary fiction by both unpublished and published authors; serious interests include investigative journalism, literary nonfiction, history, biography, memoir, popular culture, science, adventure, art, food, religion, psychology, alternative health, social issues, women's fiction, historical novels and literary fiction); Ann Behar, annbehar@s cglit.com (juvenile books for all ages); Danny Baror, dannybaror@scglit.com (foreign rights).

Represents Nonfiction books, novels.

How to Contact E-mail queries preferred. Considers simultaneous queries.

Recent Sales *Nefertiti: A Novel*, by Michelle Moran (Crown); *The Making of the Fittest: DNA and the Record of Evolution*, by Sean B. Carroll; *Why Marines Fight*, by James Brady.

◖ SCRIBE AGENCY, LLC

5508 Joylynne Dr., Madison WI 53716. E-mail: queries@scribeagency.com. Website: www.scribeage ncy.com. **Contact:** Kristopher O'Higgins. Estab. 2004. Represents 8 clients. 50% of clients are new/ unpublished writers. Currently handles: 95% novels; 4% story collections; 1% novellas.

- "We have 17 years of experience in publishing and have worked on both agency and editorial sides in the past, with marketing expertise to boot. We love books as much or more than anyone you know. Check our website to see what we're about and to make sure you jive with the Scribe vibe."

Member Agents Kristopher O'Higgins; Jesse Vogel.

Represents Nonfiction books, novels, short story collections, novellas. **Considers these nonfiction areas:** Cooking/foods/nutrition; ethnic/cultural interests; gay/lesbian issues; humor/satire; memoirs; music/dance; popular culture; true crime/investigative; women's issues/studies. **Considers these fiction areas:** Action/adventure; comic books/cartoon; detective/police/crime; erotica; ethnic; experimental; fantasy; feminist; gay/lesbian; horror; humor/satire; literary; mainstream/contemporary; mystery/suspense; psychic/supernatural; science fiction; thriller; young adult.

O⌐ Actively seeking excellent writers with ideas and stories to tell.

How to Contact E-queries only. See the Web site for submission info, as it may change. Responds in 3-4 weeks to queries; 5 months to mss.

Recent Sales Sold 3 titles in the last year.

Terms Agent receives 15% commission on domestic sales; 20% commission on foreign sales. Offers written contract. Charges for postage and photocopying.

Writers' Conferences BookExpo America; The Writer's Institute; Spring Writer's Festival; WisCon; Wisconsin Book Festival; World Fantasy Convention.

◑ SERENDIPITY LITERARY AGENCY, LLC

305 Gates Ave., Brooklyn NY 11216. (718)230-7689. Fax: (718)230-7829. E-mail: rbrooks@serendipit ylit.com. Website: www.serendipitylit.com. **Contact:** Regina Brooks. Estab. 2000. Represents 50 clients. 50% of clients are new/unpublished writers. Currently handles: 50% nonfiction books; 50% fiction.

- Prior to becoming an agent, Ms. Brooks was an acquisitions editor for John Wiley & Sons, Inc. and McGraw-Hill Companies.

Member Agents Regina Brooks; Guichard Cadet (sports, pop culture, fiction, Caribbean writers).

Represents Nonfiction books, novels, juvenile books, scholarly books, children's books. **Considers these nonfiction areas:** Business/economics; current affairs; education; ethnic/cultural interests; history; juvenile nonfiction; memoirs; money/finance; multicultural; New Age/metaphysics; popular culture; psychology; religious/inspirational; science/technology; self-help/personal improvement; sports; women's issues/studies; health/medical; narrative; popular science, biography; politics; crafts/design; food/cooking; contemporary culture. **Considers these fiction areas:** Action/adventure; confession; ethnic; historical; juvenile; literary; multicultural; picture books; thriller; suspense; mystery; romance.

> ⚬⇌ African-American nonfiction, commercial fiction, young adult novels with an urban flair and juvenile books. No stage plays, screenplays or poetry.

How to Contact Prefers to read materials exclusively. For nonfiction, submit outline, 1 sample chapter, SASE. Responds in 2 months to queries; 3 months to mss. Obtains most new clients through conferences, referrals.

Recent Sales This agency prefers not to share information on specific sales. Recent sales available upon request.

Terms Agent receives 15% commission on domestic sales; 20% commission on foreign sales. Offers written contract; 2-month notice must be given to terminate contract. Charges clients for office fees, which are taken from any advance.

Tips "We are eagerly looking for young adult books. We also represent illustrators."

☑ THE SEYMOUR AGENCY

475 Miner St., Canton NY 13617. (315)386-1831. E-mail: marysue@slic.com. Website: www.theseymouragency.com. **Contact:** Mary Sue Seymour. Estab. 1992. Member of AAR, RWA, Authors Guild; signatory of WGA. Represents 50 clients. 5% of clients are new/unpublished writers. Currently handles: 50% nonfiction books; 50% fiction.

> • Ms. Seymour is a retired New York State certified teacher.

Represents Nonfiction books, novels. **Considers these nonfiction areas:** Business/economics; health/medicine; how-to; self-help/personal improvement; Christian books; cookbooks; any well-written nonfiction that includes a proposal in standard format and 1 sample chapter. **Considers these fiction areas:** Religious/inspirational (Christian books); romance (any type).

How to Contact Query with SASE, synopsis, first 50 pages for romance. Accepts e-mail queries. No fax queries. Considers simultaneous queries. Responds in 1 month to queries; 3 months to mss. Returns materials only with SASE.

Recent Sales Three books, by Beth Wiseman (Thomas Nelson); *The Everything Triathalon Book*, by Brent Manley (Adams); *The Everything Self-Hypnosis Book*, by Rene Bastarache (Adams).

Terms Agent receives 12-15% commission on domestic sales.

☑ WENDY SHERMAN ASSOCIATES, INC.

450 Seventh Ave., Suite 2307, New York NY 10123. (212)279-9027. Fax: (212)279-8863. Website: www.wsherman.com. **Contact:** Wendy Sherman. Estab. 1999. Member of AAR. Represents 50 clients. 30% of clients are new/unpublished writers. Currently handles: 50% nonfiction books; 50% novels.

> • Prior to opening the agency, Ms. Sherman worked for The Aaron Priest agency and served as vice president, executive director, associate publisher, subsidary rights director, and sales and marketing director in the publishing industry.

Member Agents Wendy Sherman; Michelle Brower; Emmanuelle Alspaugh.

Represents Nonfiction books, novels. **Considers these nonfiction areas:** Psychology; narrative; practical. **Considers these fiction areas:** Literary; women's (suspense).

> ⚬⇌ "We specialize in developing new writers, as well as working with more established writers. My experience as a publisher has proven to be a great asset to my clients."

How to Contact Query with SASE or send outline/proposal, 1 sample chapter. E-mail queries only for Ms. Brower and Ms. Alspaugh. Considers simultaneous queries. Responds in 1 month to queries. Returns materials only with SASE. Obtains most new clients through recommendations from others.

Recent Sales *The Measure of Brightness*, by Todd Johnson; *Supergirls Speak Out*, by Liz Funk; *Love in 90 Days*, by Diana Kirschner; *Pelican Road*, by Howard Bahr; *A Long, Long Time Ago and Essentially True*, by Brigid Pasulka; *Cooking and Screaming: A Memoir*, by Adrienne Kane.

Terms Agent receives 15% commission on domestic sales; 20% commission on foreign sales. Offers written contract.

Tips "The bottom line is: Do your homework. Be as well prepared as possible. Read the books that will help you present yourself and your work with polish. You want your submission to stand out."

JEFFREY SIMMONS LITERARY AGENCY

15 Penn House, Mallory St., London NW8 8SX England. (44)(207)224-8917. E-mail: jasimmons@btc onnect.com. **Contact:** Jeffrey Simmons. Estab. 1978. Represents 43 clients. 40% of clients are new/ unpublished writers. Currently handles: 65% nonfiction books; 35% novels.

• Prior to becoming an agent, Mr. Simmons was a publisher. He is also an author.

Represents Nonfiction books, novels. **Considers these nonfiction areas:** Biography/autobiography; current affairs; government/politics/law; history; language/literature/criticism; memoirs; music/ dance; popular culture; sociology; sports; theater/film; translation; true crime/investigative. **Considers these fiction areas:** Action/adventure; confession; detective/police/crime; family saga; literary; mainstream/contemporary; mystery/suspense; thriller.

⦿ This agency seeks to handle good books and promising young writers. "My long experience in publishing and as an author and ghostwriter means I can offer an excellent service all around, especially in terms of editorial experience where appropriate." Actively seeking quality fiction, biography, autobiography, showbiz, personality books, law, crime, politics, and world affairs. Does not want to receive science fiction, horror, fantasy, juvenile, academic books, or specialist subjects (e.g., cooking, gardening, religious).

How to Contact Submit sample chapter, outline/proposal, SASE (IRCs if necessary). Prefers to read materials exclusively. Responds in 1 week to queries; 1 month to mss. Obtains most new clients through recommendations from others, solicitations.

Terms Agent receives 10-15% commission on domestic sales; 15% commission on foreign sales. Offers written contract, binding for lifetime of book in question or until it becomes out of print.

Tips "When contacting us with an outline/proposal, include a brief biographical note (listing any previous publications, with publishers and dates). Preferably tell us if the book has already been offered elsewhere."

SPENCERHILL ASSOCIATES

P.O. Box 374, Chatham NY 12037. (518)392-9293. Fax: (518)392-9554. E-mail: ksolem@klsbooks. com; jennifer@klsbooks.com. **Contact:** Karen Solem or Jennifer Schober. Estab. 2001. Member of AAR. Represents 73 clients. 5% of clients are new/unpublished writers.

• Prior to becoming an agent, Ms. Solem was editor-in-chief at HarperCollins and an associate publisher.

Member Agents Karen Solem; Jennifer Schober.

Represents Novels. **Considers these fiction areas:** Detective/police/crime; historical; literary; mainstream/contemporary; religious/inspirational; romance; thriller; young adult.

⦿ "We handle mostly commercial women's fiction, historical novels, romance (historical, contemporary, paranormal), thrillers, and mysteries. We also represent Christian fiction." No poetry, science fiction, children's picture books, or scripts.

How to Contact Query jennifer@klsbooks.com with synopsis and first three chapters. E-queries preferred. No fax queries. Responds in 1 month to queries. Returns materials only with SASE.

Terms Agent receives 15% commission on domestic sales; 20% commission on foreign sales. Offers written contract; 3-month notice must be given to terminate contract.

THE SPIRIDON LITERARY AGENCY

P.O. Box 47594, 946 Lawrence Ave. E., Unit 2, Toronto ON M3C 1P0, Canada. E-mail: spiridon@roger s.com. **Contact:** Alethea Spiridon. Estab. 2007. Currently handles: 20% nonfiction books; 40% novels; 10% story collections; 30% juvenile books.

• Prior to becoming an agent, Ms. Spiridon was an editor for Harlequin Books in Toronto.

Represents Nonfiction books, novels, short story collections, novellas, juvenile books. **Considers these nonfiction areas:** Business/economics; child guidance/parenting; cooking/foods/nutrition; current affairs; health/medicine; history; how-to; juvenile nonfiction; language/literature/criticism; memoirs; nature/environment; popular culture; self-help/personal improvement; women's issues/ studies. **Considers these fiction areas:** Action/adventure; confession; experimental; family saga; fantasy; feminist; historical; humor/satire; juvenile; literary; mainstream/contemporary; mystery/ suspense; picture books; romance; young adult.

⦿ Actively seeking women's fiction, young adult, middle grade, nonfiction, literary fiction and commercial fiction.

How to Contact Submit outline/proposal, synopsis, author bio, 50 pages if submitting fiction, SASE.

Query with IRC, not SASE! Accepts e-mail queries. No fax queries. Considers simultaneous queries. Responds in 8 weeks to queries; 10 weeks to mss. Obtains most new clients through recommendations from others, solicitations.

Terms Agent receives 15% commission on domestic sales; 20% commission on foreign sales. Offers written contract; 1-month notice must be given to terminate contract. This agency charges for office expenses, such as postage and photocopies.

Tips "Think of the agent as your first reader. Do a meticulous self-edit of your work to ensure you present your best possible writing. Observe how other books are marketed by reading tons of back cover copy and then write a blurb for your own book. If you're struggling, you might not have a clear sense of direction for your work. You need to have a solid sense of your manuscript so you can present it seamlessly to agents (and then editors). Be clear. Be concise."

◙ PHILIP G. SPITZER LITERARY AGENCY, INC

50 Talmage Farm Ln., East Hampton NY 11937. (631)329-3650. Fax: (631)329-3651. E-mail: spitzer516@aol.com. **Contact:** Philip Spitzer, Lukas Ortiz. Estab. 1969. Member of AAR. Represents 60 clients. 10% of clients are new/unpublished writers. Currently handles: 35% nonfiction books; 65% novels.

- Prior to opening his agency, Mr. Spitzer served at New York University Press, McGraw-Hill, and the John Cushman Associates literary agency.

Represents Nonfiction books, novels. **Considers these nonfiction areas:** Biography/autobiography; business/economics; current affairs; ethnic/cultural interests; government/politics/law; health/medicine; history; language/literature/criticism; military/war; music/dance; nature/environment; popular culture; psychology; sociology; sports; theater/film; true crime/investigative. **Considers these fiction areas:** Detective/police/crime; literary; mainstream/contemporary; mystery/suspense; sports; thriller.

    ☐ This agency specializes in mystery/suspense, literary fiction, sports and general nonfiction (no how-to).

How to Contact Query with SASE, outline, 1 sample chapter. Responds in 1 week to queries; 6 weeks to mss. Obtains most new clients through recommendations from others.

Recent Sales *Suitcase City*, by Michael Connelly; *Acts of Nature*, by Jonathon King; *Last Call*, by Alafair Burke; *The Tin Roof Blowdown*, by James Lee Burke.

Terms Agent receives 15% commission on domestic sales; 20% commission on foreign sales. Charges clients for photocopying.

Writers' Conferences BookExpo America.

◙ NANCY STAUFFER ASSOCIATES

P.O. Box 1203, 1540 Boston Post Road, Darien CT 06820. (203)202-2500. Fax: (203)655-3704. E-mail: StaufferAssoc@optonline.net. **Contact:** Nancy Stauffer Cahoon. Estab. 1989. Member of Authors Guild. 5% of clients are new/unpublished writers. Currently handles: 15% nonfiction books; 85% novels. **Considers these nonfiction areas:** Current affairs; ethnic/cultural interests; creative nonfiction (narrative). **Considers these fiction areas:** Contemporary issues; literary; regional.

How to Contact Obtains most new clients through referrals from existing clients.

Recent Sales *The Absolutely True Diary of a Part-time Indian*, by Sherman Alexie; *West of Last Chance*, by Peter Brown and Kent Haruf.

Terms Agent receives 15% commission on domestic sales; 20% commission on foreign sales; 15% commission on dramatic rights sales.

◙ STEELE-PERKINS LITERARY AGENCY

26 Island Ln., Canandaigua NY 14424. (585)396-9290. Fax: (585)396-3579. E-mail: pattiesp@aol.com. **Contact:** Pattie Steele-Perkins. Member of AAR, RWA. Currently handles: 100% novels.

Represents Novels. **Considers these fiction areas:** Romance, genre and women's fiction, including multicultural and inspirational.

How to Contact Submit outline, 3 sample chapters, SASE. Considers simultaneous queries. Responds in 6 weeks to queries. Returns materials only with SASE. Obtains most new clients through recommendations from others, queries/solicitations.

Recent Sales This agency prefers not to share information on specific sales.

Terms Agent receives 15% commission on domestic sales. Offers written contract, binding for 1 year; 1-month notice must be given to terminate contract.

Writers' Conferences RWA National Conference; BookExpo America; CBA Convention; Romance Slam Jam.

Tips "Be patient. E-mail rather than call. Make sure what you are sending is the best it can be."

◐ STERNIG & BYRNE LITERARY AGENCY

2370 S. 107th St., Apt. #4, Milwaukee WI 53227-2036. (414)328-8034. Fax: (414)328-8034. E-mail: jackbyrne@hotmail.com. Website: www.sff.net/people/jackbyrne. **Contact:** Jack Byrne. Estab. 1950s. Member of SFWA, MWA. Represents 30 clients. 10% of clients are new/unpublished writers. Currently handles: 5% nonfiction books; 85% novels; 10% juvenile books.

Represents Nonfiction books, novels, juvenile books. **Considers these fiction areas:** Fantasy; horror; mystery/suspense; science fiction.

    ☞ Actively seeking science fiction/fantasy and mystery by established writers. Does not want to receive romance, poetry, textbooks, or highly specialized nonfiction.

How to Contact Query with SASE. Prefers e-mail queries (no attachments); hard copy queries also acceptable. Accepts e-mail queries. No fax queries. Responds in 3 weeks to queries; 3 months to mss. Returns materials only with SASE.

Terms Agent receives 15% commission on domestic sales; 20% commission on foreign sales. Offers written contract; 2-month notice must be given to terminate contract.

Tips "Don't send first drafts, have a professional presentation (including cover letter), and know your field. Read what's been done—good and bad."

◔ STRACHAN LITERARY AGENCY

P.O. Box 2091, Annapolis MD 21404. E-mail: query@strachanlit.com. Website: www.strachanlit.com. **Contact:** Laura Strachan.

    ● Prior to becoming an agent, Ms. Strachan was (and still is) an attorney.

Represents Nonfiction books, novels. **Considers these nonfiction areas:** Cooking/foods/nutrition; gardening; interior design/decorating; memoirs; photography; psychology; self-help/personal improvement; travel; narrative, parenting, arts. **Considers these fiction areas:** Literary; mystery/suspense; legal and psychological thrillers, children's.

    ☞ This agency specializes in literary fiction and narrative nonfiction. Actively seeking new, fresh voices.

How to Contact Query with cover letter outlining your professional experience and a brief synopsis. Send no e-mail attachments. Accepts e-mail queries. No fax queries.

Recent Sales *Serpent Box*, by Vincent Carrella (HarperPerennial); *Swan Town: The Secret Journal of Susanna Shakespeare*, by Michael Ortiz (HarperCollins Children's); *Little Star of Bela Lua*, by Luana Monteiro (Delphinium Books); *The Good Man*, by Ed Jae-Suk Lee (Bridge Works Publishing).

▦ ◔ THE SUSIJN AGENCY

64 Great Titchfield St., London W1W 7QH England, United Kingdom. (44)(207)580-6341. Fax: (44)(207)580-8626. Website: www.thesusijnagency.com. **Contact:** Laura Susijn, Nicola Barr. Currently handles: 25% nonfiction books; 75% novels.

    ● Prior to becoming an agent, Ms. Susijn was a rights director at Sheil Land Associates and at Fourth Estate; Ms. Barr was a commissioning editor at Flamingo (literary imprint of HarperCollins).

Represents Nonfiction books, novels. **Considers these nonfiction areas:** Biography/autobiography; memoirs; multicultural; popular culture; science/technology; travel. **Considers these fiction areas:** Literary.

    ☞ Does not want to receive romance, sagas, fantasy, children's/juvenile or screenplays.

How to Contact Submit outline, 2 sample chapters, SASE/IRC. Returns materials only with SASE. Obtains most new clients through recommendations from others.

Recent Sales Sold 120 titles in the last year. Clients include Dubravka Ugresic, Peter Ackroyd, Robin Baker, BI Feiyu, Jeffrey Moore, Podium, De Arbeiderspers, Van Oorschot.

Terms Agent receives 15% commission on domestic sales; 15-20% commission on foreign sales. Offers written contract; 6-week notice must be given to terminate contract. Charges clients for photocopying (only if sale is made).

EMMA SWEENEY AGENCY, LLC

245 East 80th St., Suite 7E, New York NY 10021. E-mail: queries@emmasweeneyagency.com; info@emmasweeneyagency.com. Website: www.emmasweeneyagency.com. **Contact:** Eva Talmadge. Estab. 2006. Member of AAR, Women's Media Group. Represents 50 clients. 5% of clients are new/unpublished writers. Currently handles: 30% nonfiction books; 70% novels.

• Prior to becoming an agent, Ms. Sweeney was a subsidiary rights assistant at William Morrow. Since 1990, she has been a literary agent, and was most recently an agent with Harold Ober Associates.

Member Agents Emma Sweeney, president; Eva Talmadge, rights manager; Lauren Carnali, editorial assistant (lauren@emmasweeneyagency.com).

Represents Nonfiction books, novels. **Considers these nonfiction areas:** Agriculture/horticulture; animals; biography/autobiography; cooking/foods/nutrition; memoirs. **Considers these fiction areas:** Literary; mystery/suspense; thriller; women's.

○— "We specialize in quality fiction and non-fiction. Our primary areas of interest include literary and women's fiction, mysteries and thrillers; science, history, biography, memoir, religious studies and the natural sciences." Does not want to receive romance and westerns or screenplays.

How to Contact See Web site for submission and contact information. No snail mail queries. Query by e-mail. Send no attachments. Accepts e-mail queries. No fax queries.

Recent Sales *Water for Elephants*, by Sara Gruen (Algonquin); *The Joy of Living*, by Yongey Mingyur Rinpoche (Harmony Books); *The River Wife*, by Jonis Agee (Random House).

Terms Agent receives 15% commission on domestic sales; 10% commission on foreign sales.

Writers' Conferences Nebraska Writers' Conference; Words and Music Festival in New Orleans.

THE SWETKY AGENCY

2150 Balboa Way, No. 29, St. George UT 84770. E-mail: fayeswetky@amsaw.org. Website: www.amsaw.org/swetkyagency/index.html. **Contact:** Faye M. Swetky. Estab. 2000. Member of American Society of Authors and Writers. Represents 40+ clients. 80% of clients are new/unpublished writers. Currently handles: 30% nonfiction books; 30% novels; 20% movie scripts; 20% TV scripts.

• Prior to becoming an agent, Ms. Swetky was an editor and corporate manager. She has also raised and raced thoroughbred horses.

Represents Nonfiction books, novels, short story collections, juvenile books, movie scripts, feature film, TV scripts, TV movie of the week, sitcom, documentary. **Considers these nonfiction areas:** All major nonfiction genres. **Considers these fiction areas:** All major fiction genres. **Considers these script subject areas:** Action/adventure; biography/autobiography; cartoon/animation; comedy; contemporary issues; detective/police/crime; erotica; ethnic; experimental; family saga; fantasy; feminist; gay/lesbian; glitz; historical; horror; juvenile; mainstream; multicultural; multimedia; mystery/suspense; psychic/supernatural; regional; religious/inspirational; romantic comedy; romantic drama; science fiction; sports; teen; thriller; western/frontier.

○— "We handle only book-length fiction and nonfiction and feature-length movie and television scripts. Please visit our Web site before submitting. All agency-related information is there, including a sample contract, e-mail submission forms, policies, clients, etc." Actively seeking young adult material. Do not send unprofessionally prepared mss and/or scripts.

How to Contact See Web site for submission instructions. Accepts e-mail queries only. Considers simultaneous queries. Response time varies. Obtains most new clients through queries.

Recent Sales *Zen and the Art of Pond Building*, by J.D. Herda (Sterling); *Solid Stiehl*, by D.J. Herda (Archebooks); *24/7*, by Susan Diplacido (Zumaya Publications); *House on the Road to Salisbury*, by Lisa Adams (Archebooks). ***Movie/TV MOW script(s) optioned/sold:*** *Demons 5*, by Jim O'Rear (Katzir Productions); *Detention* and *Instinct Vs. Reason*, by Garrett Hargrove (Filmjack Productions).

Terms Agent receives 15% commission on domestic sales; 20% commission on foreign sales; 20% commission on dramatic rights sales. Offers written contract, binding for 1 year; 30-day notice must be given to terminate contract.

Tips "Be professional. Have a professionally prepared product."

3 SEAS LITERARY AGENCY

P.O. Box 8571, Madison WI 53708. (608)221-4306. E-mail: queries@threeseaslit.com. Website: www.threeseaslit.com. **Contact:** Michelle Grajkowski, Cori Deyoe. Estab. 2000. Member of RWA, Chicago

Women in Publishing. Represents 40 clients. 10% of clients are new/unpublished writers. Currently handles: 5% nonfiction books; 80% novels; 15% juvenile books.

- Prior to becoming an agent, Ms. Grajkowski worked in both sales and purchasing for a medical facility. She has a degree in journalism from the University of Wisconsin-Madison. Prior to joining the agency in 2006, Ms. Deyoe was a multi-published author. She is excited to be part of the agency and is actively building her client list.

Member Agents Michelle Grajkowski; Cori Deyoe.

Represents Nonfiction books, novels, juvenile books, scholarly books.

- 3 Seas focuses on romance (including category, historical, regency, Western, romantic suspense, paranormal), women's fiction, mysteries, nonfiction, young adult and children's stories. No poetry, screenplays or short stories.

How to Contact E-mail queries **only** For fiction and young adult, query with first 3 chapters, synopsis, bio, SASE. For nonfiction, query with complete proposal, first 3 chapters, SASE. For picture books, query with complete ms. Considers simultaneous queries. Responds in 1 month to queries. Responds in 3 months to partials. Returns materials only with SASE. Obtains most new clients through recommendations from others, conferences.

Recent Sales Sold 75 titles in the last year. *Even Vampires Get the Blues* and *Light My Fire*, by Katie MacAlister (NAL); *Vamps in the City*, by Kerrelyn Sparks (Avon); *Date Me Baby, One More Time* and *Must Love Dragons*, by Stephanie Rowe (Warner); *From the Dark*, by Michelle Hauf (Harlequin Nocturne); *The Runaway Daughter*, by Anna DeStefano; *Calamity Jayne Rides Again*, by Kathleen Bacus (Leisure); *Daddy Daycare*, by Laura Marie Altom (Harlequin American); *Dark Protector*, by Alexis Morgan (Pocket); *Seduced By the Night*, by Robin T. Popp (Warner); *What Happens In Paris*, by Nancy Robards Thompson (Harlequin NEXT). Other clients include Naomi Neale, Brenda Mott, Winnie Griggs, Barbara Jean Hicks, Cathy McDavid, Lisa Mondello, R. Barri Flowers, Dyanne Davis, Catherine Kean, Pat White, Mary Buckham.

Terms Agent receives 15% commission on domestic sales; 20% commission on foreign sales. Offers written contract.

TRIADA U.S. LITERARY AGENCY, INC.

P.O. Box 561, Sewickley PA 15143. (412)401-3376. E-mail: uwe@triadaus.com. Website: www.triadaus.com. **Contact:** Dr. Uwe Stender. Estab. 2004. Represents 55 clients. 30% of clients are new/unpublished writers.

Member Agents Paul Hudson (science fiction, fantasy); Rebecca Post.

Represents Nonfiction books, novels, short story collections, juvenile books, scholarly books. **Considers these nonfiction areas:** Biography/autobiography; business/economics; child guidance/parenting; education; how-to; humor/satire; memoirs; popular culture; self-help/personal improvement; sports. **Considers these fiction areas:** Action/adventure; detective/police/crime; ethnic; fantasy; historical; horror; juvenile; literary; mainstream/contemporary; mystery/suspense; romance; science fiction; sports; thriller; young adult.

- "We are now focusing on self-help and how-to. Additionally, we specialize in literary novels and suspense. Education, business, popular culture, and narrative nonfiction are other strong suits. Our response time is fairly unique. We recognize that neither we nor the authors have time to waste, so we guarantee a 5-day response time. We usually respond within 24 hours." Actively looking for nonfiction, especially self-help, how-to, and prescriptive nonfiction. Deemphasizing fiction, although great writing will always be considered.

How to Contact E-mail queries preferred; otherwise query with SASE. Considers simultaneous queries. Responds in 1-5 weeks to queries; 2-6 weeks to mss. Returns materials only with SASE. Obtains most new clients through recommendations from others, conferences.

Recent Sales *The Sexual Solution*, by Joel Block and KD Neumann (Adams); *31 Days to Greatness*, by Kevin Elko and Bill Beausay (Amacom); *The Equation*, by Omar Tree (Wiley); *How to Survive Your Surgery*, by David Page and Pamela Rowland (Sterling).

Terms Agent receives 15% commission on domestic sales; 20% commission on foreign sales. Offers written contract; 30-day notice must be given to terminate contract.

Tips "I comment on all requested manuscripts that I reject."

TRIDENT MEDIA GROUP

41 Madison Ave., 36th Floor, New York NY 10010. Website: www.tridentmediagroup.com. **Contact:** Ellen Levine. Member of AAR.

Member Agents Kimberly Whalen, whalen.assistant@tridentmediagroup (commercial fiction and nonfiction, women's fiction, suspense, paranormal and pop culture); Jenny Bent, jbent@tridentmedi agroup.com (humor, literary fiction, women's commercial fiction, narrative nonfiction, biography, health, how-to); Eileen Cope, ecope@tridentmediagroup.com (narrative nonfiction, history, biography, pop culture, health, literary fiction and short story collections); Scott Miller, smiller@tridentmed iagroup.com (thrillers, crime, mystery, young adult, children's, narrative nonfiction, current events, military, memoir, literary fiction, graphic novels, pop culture); Paul Fedorko, pfedorko@tridentmedi agroup.com (commercial fiction, mysteries, thrillers, romantic suspense, business, sports, celebrity and pop culture); Alex Glass (aglass@tridentmediagroup, thrillers, literary fiction, crime, middle grade, pop culture, young adult, humor and narrative nonfiction); Melissa Flashman, mflashman@-tridentmediagroup.com (narrative nonfiction, serious nonfiction, pop culture, lifstyle); Alyssa Henkin, ahenkin@tridentmediagroup.com (juvenile, children's, YA)

Represents Nonfiction books, novels, short story collections, juvenile books. **Considers these nonfiction areas:** Biography/autobiography; current affairs; government/politics/law; humor/satire; memoirs; military/war; multicultural; popular culture; true crime/investigative; women's issues/studies; young adult. **Considers these fiction areas:** Detective/police/crime; humor/satire; juvenile; literary; military/war; multicultural; mystery/suspense; short story collections; thriller; young adult; women's.

O➡ Actively seeking new or established authors in a variety of fiction and nonfiction genres.

How to Contact Query with SASE or via e-mail. Check Web site for more details.

☐ VANGUARD LITERARY AGENCY

81 E. Jefryn Blvd., Suite E, Deer Park NY 11729. (718)710-3662. Fax: (718)504-4541. E-mail: sandylu @vanguardliterary.com. Website: www.vanguardliterary.com. **Contact:** Sandy Lu. Estab. 2006. Represents 15 clients. 60% of clients are new/unpublished writers. Currently handles: 20% nonfiction books; 80% novels.

• Prior to becoming an agent, Ms. Lu held managerial positions in commercial theater.

Represents Nonfiction books, novels, short story collections, novellas. **Considers these nonfiction areas:** Anthropology/archaeology; biography/autobiography; cooking/foods/nutrition; ethnic/cultural interests; gay/lesbian issues; history; memoirs; music/dance; popular culture; psychology; science/technology; sociology; translation; true crime/investigative; women's issues/studies. **Considers these fiction areas:** Action/adventure; confession; detective/police/crime; ethnic; historical; horror; humor/satire; literary; mainstream/contemporary; mystery/suspense; regional; thriller; women's (no chick lit).

O➡ "Very few agents in the business still edit their clients' manuscripts, especially when it comes to fiction. Vanguard Literary Agency is different. I care about the quality of my clients' works and will not send anything out to publishers without personally going through each page first to ensure that when the manuscript is sent out, it is in the best possible shape." Actively seeking literary and commercial fiction with a unique voice. Does not want to receive movie or TV scripts, stage plays or poetry; unwanted fiction genres include science fiction/fantasy, Western, YA, children's; unwanted nonfiction genres include self-help, how-to, parenting, sports, dating/relationship, military/war, religion/spirituality, New Age, gift books.

How to Contact Query with SASE, submit outline/proposal, synopsis, author bio, 10-15 sample pp. Accepts e-mail queries. No fax queries. Considers simultaneous queries. Responds in 2 weeks to queries; 6-8 weeks to mss. Returns materials only with SASE. Obtains most new clients through recommendations from others, solicitations, conferences.

Terms Agent receives 15% commission on domestic sales; 20% commission on foreign sales. Offers written contract, binding for 1 year; 30-day notice must be given to terminate contract. This agency charges for photocopying and postage, and discusses larger costs (in excess of $100) with authors prior to charging.

Tips "Do your research. Do not query an agent for a genre he or she does not represent. Personalize your query letter. Start with an interesting hook. Learn how to write a succinct yet interesting synopsis or proposal."

☑ VENTURE LITERARY

8895 Towne Centre Drive, Suite 105, #141, San Diego CA 92122. (619)807-1887. Fax: (772)365-8321. E-mail: submissions@ventureliterary.com. Website: www.ventureliterary.com. **Contact:** Frank R.

Scatoni. Estab. 1999. Represents 50 clients. 40% of clients are new/unpublished writers. Currently handles: 80% nonfiction books; 20% novels.

- Prior to becoming an agent, Mr. Scatoni worked as an editor at Simon & Schuster.

Member Agents Frank R. Scatoni (general nonfiction, biography, memoir, narrative nonfiction, sports, serious nonfiction, graphic novels, narratives); Jennifer de la Fuente (literary, commercial and women's fiction, women's nonfiction, pop culture).

Represents Nonfiction books, novels, graphic novels, narratives. **Considers these nonfiction areas:** Anthropology/archaeology; biography/autobiography; business/economics; current affairs; ethnic/cultural interests; government/politics/law; history; memoirs; military/war; money/finance; multicultural; music/dance; nature/environment; popular culture; psychology; science/technology; sports; true crime/investigative. **Considers these fiction areas:** Action/adventure; detective/police/crime; literary; mainstream/contemporary; mystery/suspense; sports; thriller; women's.

- ⚷ Specializes in nonfiction, sports, biography, gambling and nonfiction narratives. Actively seeking nonfiction, graphic novels and narratives.

How to Contact Considers e-mail queries only. *No unsolicited mss.* See Web site for complete submission guidelines. Obtains most new clients through recommendations from others.

Recent Sales *The 9/11 Report: A Graphic Adaptation*, by Sid Jacobson and Ernie Colon (FSG); *Untitled on Infertility*, by Cindy Margolis (Perigee/Penguin); *Phil Gordon's Little Blue Book*, by Phil Gordon (Simon & Schuster); *Super Critical*, by Todd Tucker (Free Press); *The Making of Michelle Wie*, by Eric Adelson (ESPN Books); *Online Ace*, by Scott Fischman (ESPN Books).

Terms Agent receives 15% commission on domestic sales; 20% commission on foreign sales. Offers written contract.

⊘ BETH VESEL LITERARY AGENCY

80 Fifth Ave., Suite 1101, New York NY 10011. (212)924-4252. E-mail: mlindley@bvlit.com. **Contact:** Molly Lindley, assistant. Estab. 2003. Represents 65 clients. 10% of clients are new/unpublished writers. Currently handles: 75% nonfiction books; 10% novels; 5% story collections; 10% scholarly books.

- Prior to becoming an agent, Ms. Vesel was a poet and a journalist.

Represents Nonfiction books, novels. **Considers these nonfiction areas:** Biography/autobiography; business/economics; ethnic/cultural interests; health/medicine; how-to; memoirs; psychology; self-help/personal improvement; true crime/investigative; women's issues/studies; cultural criticism. **Considers these fiction areas:** Detective/police/crime; literary; Francophone novels.

- ⚷ "My specialties include serious nonfiction, psychology, cultural criticism, memoir, and women's issues." Actively seeking cultural criticism, literary psychological thrillers, and sophisticated memoirs. No uninspired psychology or run-of-the-mill first novels.

How to Contact Query with SASE. Considers simultaneous queries. Responds in 2 weeks to queries; 1 month to mss. Returns materials only with SASE. Obtains most new clients through referrals, reading good magazines, contacting professionals with ideas.

Recent Sales Sold 10 titles in the last year. *James Brown's Body*, by Greg Tate (Riverhead); *Your Money or Your Life for the 21st Century*, by Vicki Robin (Penguin); *Beowulf on the Beach*, by Jack Murninghan (Three Rivers); *Shakespeare and Modern Culture*, by Marge Garber (Pantheon).

Terms Agent receives 15% commission on domestic sales; 20% commission on foreign sales. Offers written contract.

Writers' Conferences Squaw Valley Writers Workshop, Iowa Summer Writing Festival.

Tips "Try to find out if you fit on a particular agent's list by looking at his/her books and comparing yours. You can almost always find who represents a book by looking at the acknowledgements."

⊘ WALES LITERARY AGENCY, INC.

P.O. Box 9428, Seattle WA 98109-0428. (206)284-7114. Fax: (206)322-1033. E-mail: waleslit@waleslit.com. Website: www.waleslit.com. **Contact:** Elizabeth Wales, Neal Swain. Estab. 1988. Member of AAR, Book Publishers' Northwest, Pacific Northwest Booksellers Association, PEN. Represents 65 clients. 10% of clients are new/unpublished writers. Currently handles: 60% nonfiction books; 40% novels.

- Prior to becoming an agent, Ms. Wales worked at Oxford University Press and Viking Penguin.

Member Agents Elizabeth Wales; Neal Swain.

- ⚷ This agency specializes in narrative nonfiction and quality mainstream and literary fiction. Does not handle screenplays, children's literature, genre fiction, or most category nonfiction.

How to Contact Query with cover letter, SASE. No phone or fax queries. Prefers regular mail queries, but accepts 1-page e-mail queries with no attachments. Considers simultaneous queries. Responds in 3 weeks to queries; 6 weeks to mss. Returns materials only with SASE.

Recent Sales *The Floating World*, by Curtis Ebbesmeyer and Eric Scigliano (Smithsonian/HarperCollins); *Crow Planet*, by Lyanda Lynn Haupt (Little, Brown); *Shimmering Images*, by Lisa Dale Norton (St. Martin's); *A Grey Moon Over China*, by Thomas A. Day (Tor).

Terms Agent receives 15% commission on domestic sales; 20% commission on foreign sales.

Writers' Conferences Pacific Northwest Writers Conference; Willamette Writers Conference.

Tips "We are especially interested in work that espouses a progressive cultural or political view, projects a new voice, or simply shares an important, compelling story. We also encourage writers living in the Pacific Northwest, West Coast, Alaska, and Pacific Rim countries, and writers from historically underrepresented groups, such as gay and lesbian writers and writers of color, to submit work (but does not discourage writers outside these areas). Most importantly, whether in fiction or nonfiction, the agency is looking for talented storytellers."

CHERRY WEINER LITERARY AGENCY

28 Kipling Way, Manalapan NJ 07726-3711. (732)446-2096. Fax: (732)792-0506. E-mail: cherry8486 @aol.com. **Contact:** Cherry Weiner. Estab. 1977. Represents 40 clients. 10% of clients are new/ unpublished writers. Currently handles: 10-20% nonfiction books; 80-90% novels.

Represents Nonfiction books, novels. **Considers these nonfiction areas:** Self-help/personal improvement. **Considers these fiction areas:** Action/adventure; contemporary issues; detective/police/crime; family saga; fantasy; historical; mainstream/contemporary; mystery/suspense; psychic/supernatural; romance; science fiction; thriller; westerns/frontier.

> ⚪ Specializes in fantasy, science fiction, Western's, mysteries (both contemporary and historical), historical novels, Native-American works, mainstream and all genre romances.

How to Contact Query with SASE. Prefers to read materials exclusively. No fax queries. Responds in 1 week to queries; 2 months to mss. Returns materials only with SASE.

Recent Sales Sold 56 titles in the last year. This agency prefers not to share information on specific sales.

Terms Agent receives 15% commission on domestic sales; 15% commission on foreign sales. Offers written contract. Charges clients for extra copies of mss, first-class postage for author's copies of books, express mail for important documents/mss.

Tips "Meet agents and publishers at conferences. Establish a relationship, then get in touch with them and remind them of the meeting and conference."

WOLFSON LITERARY AGENCY

P.O. Box 266, New York NY 10276. E-mail: query@wolfsonliterary.com. Website: www.wolfsonliterary. com/. **Contact:** Michelle Wolfson. Estab. 2007. Adheres to AAR canon of ethics. Currently handles: 40% nonfiction books; 60% novels.

> ● Prior to forming her own agency, Michelle spent two years with Artists & Artisans, Inc. and two years with Ralph Vicinanza, Ltd.

Represents Nonfiction books, novels. **Considers these nonfiction areas:** Business/economics; child guidance/parenting; health/medicine; how-to; humor/satire; popular culture; self-help/personal improvement; women's issues/studies. **Considers these fiction areas:** Action/adventure; detective/police/crime; erotica; family saga; mainstream/contemporary; mystery/suspense; romance; thriller; young adult; women's.

> ⚪ Actively seeking commercial fiction, mainstream, mysteries, thrillers, suspense, women's fiction, romance, YA, practical nonfiction (particularly of interest to women), advice, medical, pop culture, humor, business.

How to Contact Query with SASE. E-queries only! Considers simultaneous queries. Responds in 2 weeks to queries; 3 months to mss. Obtains most new clients through recommendations from others, solicitations.

Terms Agent receives 15% commission on domestic sales; 25% commission on foreign sales. Offers written contract; 30-day notice must be given to terminate contract.

Writers' Conferences SDSU Writers' Conference; New Jersey Romance Writers of America Writers' Conference.

Tips "Be persistent."

◎ WORDSERVE LITERARY GROUP

10152 S. Knoll Circle, Highlands Ranch CO 80130. (303)471-6675. E-mail: rachelle@wordserveliterary.com. Website: www.wordserveliterary.com. **Contact:** Greg Johnson; Rachelle Gardner. Estab. 2003. Represents 70 clients. 20% of clients are new/unpublished writers. Currently handles: 30% nonfiction books; 40% novels; 10% story collections; 5% novellas; 10% juvenile books; 5% multimedia.

- Prior to becoming an agent in 1994, Mr. Johnson was a magazine editor and freelance writer of more than 20 books and 200 articles.

Member Agents Greg Johnson; Rachelle Gardner.

Represents Primarily religious books in these categories: nonfiction, fiction, short story collections, novellas. **Considers these nonfiction areas:** Biography/autobiography; child guidance/parenting; memoirs; religious/inspirational.

O⌐ Actively seeking materials with a faith-based angle.

How to Contact Query with SASE, proposal package, outline, 2-3 sample chapters. Considers simultaneous queries. Responds in 4 weeks to queries; 2 months to mss. Returns materials only with SASE. Obtains most new clients through recommendations from others.

Recent Sales Sold 1,500 titles in the last 15 years. Redemption series, by Karen Kingsbury (Tyndale); *Loving God Up Close*, by Calvin Miller (Warner Faith); *Christmas in My Heart*, by Joe Wheeler (Tyndale). Other clients include Steve Arterburn, Wanda Dyson, Catherine Martin, David Murrow, Leslie Haskin, Gilbert Morris, Calvin Miller, Robert Wise, Jim Burns, Wayne Cordeiro, Denise George, Susie Shellenberger, Tim Smith, Joe Wheeler, Athol Dickson, Bob DeMoss, Patty Kirk, John Shore.

Terms Agent receives 15% commission on domestic sales; 10-15% commission on foreign sales. Offers written contract; up to 60-day notice must be given to terminate contract.

Tips "We are looking for good proposals, great writing, and authors willing to market their books, as appropriate. Also, we're only looking for projects with a faith element bent. See the Web site before submitting."

◖ WRITERS HOUSE

21 W. 26th St., New York NY 10010. (212)685-2400. Fax: (212)685-1781. Website: www.writershouse.com. Estab. 1974. Member of AAR. Represents 440 clients. 50% of clients are new/unpublished writers. Currently handles: 25% nonfiction books; 40% novels; 35% juvenile books.

Member Agents Albert Zuckerman (major novels, thrillers, women's fiction, important nonfiction); Amy Berkower (major juvenile authors, women's fiction, art/decorating, psychology); Merrilee Heifetz (quality children's fiction, science fiction/fantasy, popular culture, literary fiction); Susan Cohen (juvenile/young adult fiction and nonfiction, Judaism, women's issues); Susan Ginsburg (serious and popular fiction, true crime, narrative nonfiction, personality books, cookbooks); Michele Rubin (serious nonfiction); Robin Rue (commercial fiction and nonfiction, young adult fiction); Jodi Reamer (juvenile/young adult fiction and nonfiction, adult commercial fiction, popular culture); Simon Lipskar (literary and commercial fiction, narrative nonfiction); Steven Malk (juvenile/young adult fiction and nonfiction); Dan Lazar (commercial and literary fiction, pop culture, narrative nonfiction, women's interest, memoirs, Judaica and humor); Rebecca Sherman (juvenile, young adult); Ken Wright (juvenile, young adult).

Represents Nonfiction books, novels, juvenile books. **Considers these nonfiction areas:** Animals; art/architecture/design; biography/autobiography; business/economics; child guidance/parenting; cooking/foods/nutrition; health/medicine; history; humor/satire; interior design/decorating; juvenile nonfiction; military/war; money/finance; music/dance; nature/environment; psychology; science/technology; self-help/personal improvement; theater/film; true crime/investigative; women's issues/studies. **Considers these fiction areas:** Action/adventure; contemporary issues; detective/police/crime; erotica; ethnic; family saga; fantasy; feminist; gay/lesbian; gothic; hi-lo; historical; horror; humor/satire; juvenile; literary; mainstream/contemporary; military/war; multicultural; mystery/suspense; New Age; occult; picture books; psychic/supernatural; regional; romance; science fiction; short story collections; spiritual; sports; thriller; translation; westerns/frontier; young adult; women's; cartoon.

O⌐ This agency specializes in all types of popular fiction and nonfiction. Does not want to receive scholarly, professional, poetry, plays, or screenplays.

How to Contact Query with SASE. No e-mail or fax queries. Responds in 1 month to queries. Obtains most new clients through recommendations from authors and editors.

Recent Sales Sold 200-300 titles in the last year. *Moneyball*, by Michael Lewis (Norton); *Cut and Run*, by Ridley Pearson (Hyperion); *Report from Ground Zero*, by Dennis Smith (Viking); *Northern Lights*, by Nora Roberts (Penguin/Putnam); Captain Underpants series, by Dav Pilkey (Scholastic); Junie B. Jones series, by Barbara Park (Random House). Other clients include Francine Pascal, Ken Follett, Stephen Hawking, Linda Howard, F. Paul Wilson, Neil Gaiman, Laurel Hamilton, V.C. Andrews, Lisa Jackson, Michael Gruber, Chris Paolini, Barbara Delinsky, Ann Martin, Bradley Trevor Greive, Erica Jong, Kyle Mills, Andrew Guess, Tim Willocks.

Terms Agent receives 15% commission on domestic sales; 20% commission on foreign sales. Offers written contract, binding for 1 year. Agency charges fees for copying mss/proposals and overseas airmail of books.

Tips "Do not send manuscripts. Write a compelling letter. If you do, we'll ask to see your work."

☑ ZACHARY SHUSTER HARMSWORTH

1776 Broadway, Suite 1405, New York NY 10019. (212)765-6900. Fax: (212)765-6490. E-mail: kfleury @zshliterary.com. Website: www.zshliterary.com. Alternate address: 535 Boylston St., 11th Floor. (617)262-2400. Fax: (617)262-2468. **Contact:** Kathleen Fleury. Estab. 1996. Represents 125 clients. 20% of clients are new/unpublished writers. Currently handles: 45% nonfiction books; 45% novels; 5% story collections; 5% scholarly books.

> ● "Our principals include two former publishing and entertainment lawyers, a journalist, and an editor/agent." Lane Zachary was an editor at Random House before becoming an agent.

Member Agents Esmond Harmsworth (commercial mysteries, literary fiction, history, science, adventure, business); Todd Shuster (narrative and prescriptive nonfiction, biography, memoirs); Lane Zachary (biography, memoirs, literary fiction); Jennifer Gates (literary fiction, nonfiction).

Represents Nonfiction books, novels. **Considers these nonfiction areas:** Animals; biography/autobiography; business/economics; current affairs; gay/lesbian issues; government/politics/law; health/medicine; history; how-to; language/literature/criticism; memoirs; money/finance; music/dance; psychology; science/technology; self-help/personal improvement; sports; true crime/investigative; women's issues/studies. **Considers these fiction areas:** Detective/police/crime; ethnic; feminist; gay/lesbian; historical; literary; mainstream/contemporary; mystery/suspense; thriller.

O→ Check the Web site for updated info.

How to Contact Query with SASE. No e-mail or fax queries. Obtains most new clients through recommendations from others.

Recent Sales *Can You Tell a Sunni from a Shiite?*, by Jeff Stein (Hyperion); *Christmas Hope*, by Donna Van Liere; *Female Chauvinist Pigs*, by Ariel Levy; *War Trash*, by Ha Jin; *Women Who Think Too Much*, by Susan Nolen-Hoeksema, PhD; *The Red Carpet*, by Lavanya Sankaran; *Grapevine*, by David Balter and John Butman.

Terms Agent receives 15% commission on domestic sales; 20% commission on foreign sales. Offers written contract, binding for 1 work only; 30-day notice must be given to terminate contract.

Literary Magazines

This section contains markets for your literary short fiction. Although definitions of what constitutes "literary" writing vary, editors of literary journals agree they want to publish the best fiction they can acquire. Qualities they look for in fiction include fully developed characters, strong and unique narrative voice, flawless mechanics, and careful attention to detail in content and manuscript preparation. Most of the authors writing such fiction are well read and well educated, and many are students and graduates of university creative writing programs.

Please also review our Online Markets section, page 293, for electronic literary magazines. At a time when paper and publishing costs rise while funding to small and university presses continues to be cut or eliminated, electronic literary magazines are helping generate a publishing renaissance for experimental as well as more traditional literary fiction. These electronic outlets for literary fiction also benefit writers by eliminating copying and postage costs and providing the opportunity for much quicker responses to submissions. Also notice that some magazines with Web sites give specific information about what they offer online, including updated writer's guidelines and sample fiction from their publications.

STEPPING STONES TO RECOGNITION

Some well-established literary journals pay several hundred or even several thousand dollars for a short story. Most, though, can only pay with contributor's copies or a subscription to their publication. However, being published in literary journals offers the important benefits of experience, exposure and prestige. Agents and major book publishers regularly read literary magazines in search of new writers. Work from these journals is also selected for inclusion in annual prize anthologies. (See next page for a list of anthologies.)

You'll find most of the well-known prestigious literary journals listed here. Many, including *The Southern Review* and *Ploughshares*, are associated with universities, while others like *The Paris Review* are independently published.

SELECTING THE RIGHT LITERARY JOURNAL

Once you have browsed through this section and have a list of journals you might like to submit to, read those listings again carefully. Remember this is information editors provide to help you submit work that fits their needs. You've Got a Story, starting on page 2, will guide you through the process of finding markets for your fiction.

Note that you will find some magazines that do not read submissions all year long. Whether limited reading periods are tied to a university schedule or meant to accommodate the capabilities of a very small staff, those periods are noted within listings (when the editors notify us). The staffs of university journals are usually made up of student editors and a managing editor who is also a faculty member. These staffs often change every year. Whenever possible, we indicate this in listings and give the name of the current editor and the length of that editor's term. Also be aware that the schedule of a university journal usually coincides with that university's academic year, meaning that the editors of most university publications are difficult or impossible to reach during the summer.

FURTHERING YOUR SEARCH

It cannot be stressed enough that reading the listings for literary journals is only the first part of developing your marketing plan. The second part, equally important, is to obtain fiction guidelines and to read with great care the actual journal you'd like to submit to. Reading copies of these journals helps you determine the fine points of each magazine's publishing style and sensibility. There is no substitute for this type of hands-on research.

Unlike commercial periodicals available at most newsstands and bookstores, it requires a little more effort to obtain some of the magazines listed here. The super-chain bookstores are doing a better job these days of stocking literaries, and you can find some in independent and college bookstores, especially those published in your area. The Internet is an invaluable resource for submission guidelines, as more and more journals establish an online presence. You may, however, need to send for a sample copy. We include sample copy prices in the listings whenever possible. In addition to reading your sample copies, pay close attention to the **Advice** section of each listing. There you'll often find a very specific description of the style of fiction the editors at that publication prefer.

Another way to find out more about literary magazines is to check out the various prize anthologies and take note of journals whose fiction is being selected for publication in them. Studying prize anthologies not only lets you know which magazines are publishing award-winning work, but it also provides a valuable overview of what is considered to be the best fiction published today. Those anthologies include:

- *Best American Short Stories*, published by Houghton Mifflin.
- *New Stories from the South: The Year's Best*, published by Algonquin Books of Chapel Hill.
- *The O. Henry Prize Stories*, published by Doubleday/Anchor.
- *Pushcart Prize: Best of the Small Presses*, published by Pushcart Press.

At the beginnings of listings, we include symbols to help you narrow your search. Keys to those symbols can be found on the inside covers of this book.

$✏ AFRICAN AMERICAN REVIEW

Saint Louis University, Humanities 317, 3800 Lindell Boulevard, St. Louis MO 63108-3414. (314)977-3688. Fax: (314)977-1514. E-mail: keenanam@slu.edu. Web site: aar.slu.edu. **Contact:** Joycelyn Moody, editor; Aileen Keenan, managing editor. Magazine: 7×10; 200 pages; 55 lb., acid-free paper; 100 lb. skid stock cover; illustrations; photos. "Essays on African-American literature, theater, film, art and culture generally; interviews; poetry and fiction by African-American authors; book reviews." Quarterly. Estab. 1967. Circ. 2,000.

- *African American Review* is the official publication of the Division of Black American Literature and Culture of the Modern Language Association. The magazine received American Literary Magazine Awards in 1994 and 1995.

Needs Ethnic/multicultural, experimental, feminist, literary, mainstream. "No children's/juvenile/young adult/teen." Receives 15 unsolicited mss/month. Accepts 16 mss/year. Publishes ms 1 year after acceptance. Agented fiction 10%. Recently published work by Solon Timothy Woodward, Eugenia Collier, Jeffery Renard Allen, Patrick Lohier, Raki Jones, Olympia Vernon. Length: 2,500-5,000 words; average length: 3,000 words. Also publishes literary essays, literary criticism, poetry. Sometimes comments on rejected mss.

How to Contact Responds in 1 week to queries; 3 months to mss. Sample copy for $12. Writer's guidelines online. Reviews fiction.

Payment/Terms Pays $25-75, 1 contributor's copy and 5 offprints. Pays on publication for first North American serial rights. Sends galleys to author.

$☺☑ AGNI

Boston University, 236 Bay State Rd., Boston MA 02215. (617)353-7135. Fax: (617)353-7134. E-mail: agni@bu.edu. Web site: www.agnimagazine.org. **Contact:** Sven Birkerts, editor. Magazine: 5³/₈×8¹/₂; 240 pages; 55 lb. booktext paper; art portfolios. "Eclectic literary magazine publishing first-rate poems, essays, translations and stories." Biannual. Estab. 1972. Circ. 4,000.

- Founding editor Askold Melnyczuk won the 2001 Nora Magid Award for Magazine Editing. Work from *AGNI* has been included and cited regularly in the *Pushcart Prize* and *Best American* anthologies.

Needs Translations, stories, prose poems. "No science fiction or romance." Receives 500 unsolicited mss/month. Accepts 3-5 mss/issue; 6-10 mss/year. Reading period September 1 through May 31 only. Publishes ms 6 months after acceptance. **Publishes 30 new writers/year.** Recently published work by Rikki Ducornet, Phong Nguyen, Jack Pulaski, David Foster Wallace, Lise Haines, Gania Barlow and Nicholas Montemarano.

How to Contact Responds in 2 weeks to queries; 4 months to mss. Accepts simultaneous submissions. Sample copy for $10 or online. Writer's guidelines for #10 SASE or online.

Payment/Terms Pays $10/page up to $150, 2 contributor's copies, 1-year subscription, and 4 gift copies. Pays on publication for first North American serial rights, rights to reprint in *AGNI* anthology (with author's consent). Sends galleys to author.

Advice "Read *AGNI* and other literary magazines carefully to understand the kinds of stories we do and do not publish. It's also important for artists to support the arts."

✏ THE AGUILAR EXPRESSION

1329 Gilmore Ave., Donora PA 15033-2228. (724)379-8019. E-mail: xyz0@access995.com. Web site: www.wordrunner.com/xfaguilar. **Contact:** Xavier F. Aguilar, editor. Magazine: 8¹/₂×11; 4-20 pages; 20 lb. bond paper; illustrations. "We are open to all writers of a general theme—something that may appeal to everyone." Publishes in October. Estab. 1986. Circ. 300.

Needs Adventure, ethnic/multicultural, experimental, horror, mainstream, mystery/suspense (romantic suspense), romance (contemporary). "No religious or erotic stories. Want more current social issues." Receives 15 unsolicited mss/month. Accepts 1-2 mss/year. Reading period: January, February, March. Publishes ms 1 month to 1 year after acceptance. **Publishes 2-4 new writers/year.** Recently published work by Ken Bennet. Length: 250-1,000 words; average length: 1,000 words. Also publishes poetry.

How to Contact Send a disposable copy of ms with SASE for reply. "We do not return any manuscripts and discard rejected works. If we decide to publish, we contact within 30 days." Responds in 1 month to mss. No simultaneous submissions. Sample copy for $8. Guidelines for first-class stamp.

Payment/Terms Pays 2 contributor's copies for lead story; additional copies at a reduced rate of $3. Acquires one-time rights. Not copyrighted.

Advice "We would like to see more social issues worked into fiction."

$⬛ ALASKA QUARTERLY REVIEW

ESB 208, University of Alaska-Anchorage, 3211 Providence Dr., Anchorage AK 99508. (907)786-6916. E-mail: ayaqr@uaa.alaska.edu. Web site: www.uaa.alaska.edu/aqr. **Contact:** Ronald Spatz, fiction editor. Magazine: 6×9; 232-300 pages; 60 lb. Glatfelter paper; 12 pt. C15 black ink or 4-color; varnish cover stock; photos on cover and photo essays. *AQR* "publishes fiction, poetry, literary nonfiction and short plays in traditional and experimental styles." Semiannual. Estab. 1982. Circ. 2,700.

● Two stories selected for inclusion in the 2004 edition of *The O'Henry Prize Stories*.

Needs Experimental, literary, translations, contemporary, prose poem. "If the works in *Alaska Quarterly Review* have certain characteristics, they are these: freshness, honesty and a compelling subject. What makes a piece stand out from the multitude of other submissions? The voice of the piece must be strong—idiosyncratic enough to create a unique persona. We look for the demonstration of craft, making the situation palpable and putting it in a form where it becomes emotionally and intellectually complex. One could look through our pages over time and see that many of the pieces published in the *Alaska Quarterly Review* concern everyday life. We're not asking our writers to go outside themselves and their experiences to the absolute exotic to catch our interest. We look for the experiential and revelatory qualities of the work. We will, without hesitation, champion a piece that may be less polished or stylistically sophisticated, if it engages me, surprises me, and resonates for me. The joy in reading such a work is in discovering something true. Moreover, in keeping with our mission to publish new writers, we are looking for voices our readers do not know, voices that may not always be reflected in the dominant culture and that, in all instances, have something important to convey." Receives 200 unsolicited mss/month. Accepts 7-18 mss/issue; 15-30 mss/year. Does not read mss May 10-August 25. Publishes ms 6 months after acceptance. **Publishes 6 new writers/year.** Recently published work by Howard Norman, Douglas Light, Courtney Angela Brkic, Alison Baker, Lindsay Fitz-Gerald, John Fulton, Ann Stapleton, Edith Pearlman. Publishes short shorts.

How to Contact Responds in 4 months to queries; 4 months to mss. Simultaneous submissions "undesirable, but will accept if indicated." Sample copy for $6. Writer's guidelines online.

Payment/Terms Pays $50-200 subject to funding; pays in contributor's copies and subscriptions when funding is limited. Honorariums on publication when funding permits. Acquires first North American serial rights. Upon request, rights will be transferred back to author after publication.

Advice "Professionalism, patience and persistence are essential. One needs to do one's homework and know the market. The competition is very intense, and funding for the front-line journals is generally inadequate, so staffing is low. It takes time to get a response, and rejections are a fact of life. It is important not to take the rejections personally, and also to know that editors make decisions for better or worse, and they make mistakes too. Fortunately there are many gatekeepers. *Alaska Quarterly Review* has published many pieces that had been turned down by other journals—including pieces that then went on to win national awards. We also know of instances in which pieces *Alaska Quarterly Review* rejected later appeared in other magazines. We haven't regretted that we didn't take those pieces. Rather, we're happy that the authors have made a good match. Disappointment should *never* stop anyone. Will counts as much as talent, and new writers need to have confidence in themselves and stick to it."

⬛ ◎ ALIMENTUM, The Literature of Food

P.O. Box 776, New York NY 10163. E-mail: submissions@alimentumjournal.com. Web site: www.alimentumjournal.com. **Contact:** Submissions editor. Literary magazine/journal: 6×7½, 128 pages, matte cover. Contains illustrations. "All of our stories, poems and essays have food or drink as a theme." Semiannual. Estab. 2005.

Needs Literary. Special interests: food related. Receives 100 mss/month. Accepts 20-24 mss/issue. Manuscript published one to two years after acceptance. **Publishes average of 2 new writers/year.** Published Mark Kurlansky, Oliver Sacks, Dick Allen, Ann Hood, Carly Sachs. Length: 4,500 words (max). Average length: 2,000-3,000 words. Publishes short shorts. Also publishes literary essays, poetry, spot illustrations. Rarely comments on/critiques rejected mss.

How to Contact Send complete ms with cover letter. Snail mail only. No previously published work. 5-poem limit per submission. Simultaneous submissions okay.'' Responds to queries and mss in 1-3 months. Send either SASE (or IRC) for return of ms or disposable copy of ms and #10 SASE for reply only. Sample copy available for $10. Guidelines available on Web site. Check for submission reading periods.

Payment/Terms Writers receive 1 contributor's copy. Additional contributor's copies $8. Pays on publication. Acquires first North American serial rights. Publication is copyrighted.

Advice ''Write a good story, no clichés, attention to style, strong voice, memorable characters and scenes.''

THE ALLEGHENY REVIEW, A National Journal of Undergraduate Literature

Box 32 Allegheny College, Meadville PA 16335. E-mail: review@allegheny.edu. Web site: http:// review.allegheny.edu. **Contact:** Senior editor. Magazine: 6×9; 100 pages; illustrations; photos. *"The Allegheny Review* is one of America's only nationwide literary magazines exclusively for undergraduate works of poetry, fiction and nonfiction. Our intended audience is persons interested in quality literature.'' Annual. Estab. 1983.

Needs Adventure, ethnic/multicultural, experimental, family saga, fantasy, feminist, gay, historical, horror, humor/satire, lesbian, literary, mainstream, military/war, mystery/suspense, New Age, psychic/supernatural/occult, religious/inspirational (general), romance, science fiction, western. No ''fiction not written by undergraduates—we accept nothing but fiction by currently enrolled undergraduate students. We consider anything catering to an intellectual audience.'' Receives 50 unsolicited mss/month. Accepts 3 mss/issue. Publishes ms 2 months after deadline. **Publishes roughly 90% new writers/year.** Recently published work by Dianne Page, Monica Stahl and DJ Kinney. Publishes short shorts (up to 20 pages). Also publishes literary nonfiction and poetry.

How to Contact Send complete mss with a cover letter. Accepts submissions on disk. Responds in 2 weeks to queries; 4 months to mss. Send disposable copy of ms and #10 SASE for reply only. Sample copy for $4. Writer's guidelines for SASE, by e-mail or on Web site.

Payment/Terms Pays 1 contributor's copy; additional copies $3. Sponsors awards/contests ; reading fee of $5.

Advice ''We look for quality work that has been thoroughly revised. Unique voice, interesting topic and playfulness with the English language. Revise, revise, revise! And be careful how you send it—the cover letter says a lot. We definitely look for diversity in the pieces we publish.''

ALLIGATOR JUNIPER

Prescott College, 220 Grove Ave., Prescott AZ 86301. (928)350-2012. Fax: (928)776-5137. E-mail: aj@prescott.edu. Web site: www.prescott.edu/highlights/alligatorjuniper/index.html. **Contact:** Rachel Yoder, managing editor. Literary magazine/journal: 7.5×10.5; 150 pages; photographs. *"Alligator Juniper* was founded with the intention of furthering the enviromental and experimental mission of Prescott College, its sponsoring institution, by featuring enviromentally-aware and socially-conscious writing and art. Since its premiere issue in 1995, *AJ* has provided local, national, and international artiists, both established and emerging, a forum in which to publish writing with timely, emotional themes. *AJ* is proud to showcase a perennially diverse range of artists.'' Annual. Estab. 1995. Circ. 1500. Member CLMP.

- *AJ* has received the AWP Director's Award for Content (2001 & 2003), annual funding from the Arizona Commission on the Arts and a Gregory Kolovakos Seed Grant from the Council of Literary Magazines and Presses (1997).

Needs Experimental, literary. Does not want genre fiction or children's literature. List of upcoming themes available on Web site. Accepts 5 mss/year. Does not read November-April. Ms published 3 months after acceptance.

How to Contact Only accepts submissions via annual *Alligator's Juniper* National Writing Contest. See seperate listing under Contests and Awards.

THE AMERICAN DRIVEL REVIEW, A Unified Field Theory of Wit

3561 SE Cora Drive, Portland OR 97202. (503)236-6377. E-mail: info@americandrivelreview.com. Web site: www.americandrivelreview.com. **Contact:** Tara Blaine and David Wester, editors. Magazine: 6×9; 90-100 pages; black and white illustrations and photos. *The American Drivel Review* is a journal of literary humor dedicated to formulating a Unified Field Theory of Wit. Estab. 2004. Circ. 200.

Needs "We are delighted to consider any categories, styles, forms or genres—real or imagined. We are interested in quality humorous writing in every conceivable form." Receives 75-100 unsolicited mss/month. Accepts 20-30 mss/issue; 60-80 mss/year. Publishes ms 2 months after acceptance. **Publishes 10-15 new writers/year.** Recently published work by Willie Smith, Laird Hunt, Matthew Summers-Sparks, Jack Collom, Richard Froude, Guy R. Beining, and Larry Fagin. Publishes short shorts. Also publishes literary essays, literary criticism, poetry.

How to Contact Send complete ms. Accepts submissions by e-mail, disk. Send SASE for return of ms. Responds in 2-3 months to queries. Accepts multiple submissions. No simultaneous submissions. Sample copy for $6.50. Writer's guidelines for #10 SASE, online or by e-mail.

Payment/Terms Pays 2 contributor's copies. Pays on publication for one-time rights.

Advice "We look primarily for sublime, funny, brilliant writing and a unique or experimental voice."

Ⓝ $Ⓐ AMERICAN SHORT FICTION

Badgerdog Literary Publishing, P.O. Box 301209, Austin TX 78703. (512)538-1305. Fax: (512)538-1306. E-mail: editors@americanshortfiction.org. Web site: www.americanshortfiction.org. **Contact:** Stacy Swann, Editor; Jill Meyers, Managing Editor. Literary magazine/journal: 6×9.5, 140 pages. Contains illustrations. Includes photographs. "*American Short Fiction* (ASF) strives to discover and publish new fiction in which transformations of language, narrative, and character occur swiftly, deftly, and unexpectedly. We are drawn to evocative language, unique subject matter, and an overall sense of immediacy. We target readers who love literary fiction, are drawn to independent publishing, and enjoy short fiction. *ASF* is one of the few journals that focuses solely on fiction." Quarterly. Estab. 1991. Circ. 2500. Member CLMP.

- ASF has had a selection included in Best Nonrequired Reading, 2007 and New Stories from the Southwest, 2008. Awards from the previous incarnation of ASF (when published by The University of Texas, 1991-1998) include selections in Best American Short Stories, The O. Henry Prize Stories, the Graywolf Annual, the Pushcart Prize anthology, and two time finalist for the National Magazine Award.

Needs Experimental, literary, translations. Does not want young adult fiction or genre fiction. "However, we are open to publishing mystery or speculative fiction if we feel it has literary value." Receives 200-300 mss/month. Accepts 5-6 mss/issue; 20-25 mss/year. Manuscript published 3 months after acceptance. Agented fiction 20%. **Publishes 2-3 new writers/year.** Published Maud Casey, Chris Bachelder, Vendela Vida, Benjamin Percy, Jack Pendarvis, Josh Magnuson, and Brian Leary. Length: 2000 words (min)-15000 words (max). Average length: 6,000 words. Publishes short shorts. Average length of short shorts: 500 words. Also publishes literary essays, literary criticism. Sometimes comments on/critiques rejected mss.

How to Contact Send complete ms with cover letter. Include estimated word count, brief bio. Responds to queries in 2 weeks. Responds to mss in 4-5 months. Send either SASE (or IRC) for return of ms or disposable copy of ms and #10 SASE for reply only. Considers simultaneous submissions. Sample copy available for $5. Guidelines available for SASE, via e-mail, on Web site.

Payment/Terms Writers receive $250-500, 2 contributor's copies, free subscription to the magazine. Additional copies $5. Pays on publication. Acquires first North American serial rights, electronic rights. Sends galleys to author. Publication is copyrighted. Sponsors Short Story Contest. See seperate listing or Web site.

Advice "We publish fiction that speaks to us emotionally, uses evocative and precise language, and takes risks in subject matter and/or form. Try to read an issue or two of *American Short Fiction* to get a sense of what we like. Also, to be concise is a great virtue."

Ⓝ Ⓐ AMOSKEAG, THE JOURNAL OF SOUTHERN NEW HAMPSHIRE UNIVERSITY

2500 N. River Road, Manchester NH 03106. (603)668-2211 x2376. E-mail: a.cummings@snhu.edu. **Contact:** Allison Cummings, Editor. Magazine has revolving editor. Editorial term: 3 yrs; 2007-2009. Literary magazine/journal. 6×9, 105-140 pages. Contains photographs. "We try to select work that will appeal to non-academic, general readers, while still holding interest for MFAs, writers, and academics. We accept work from writers nationwide, with a slight bias toward New England writers. We tend not to accept much experimental work, but the language of poetry or prose must nevertheless be dense, careful and surprising." Annual. Jouranal estab. 1983; literary journal since 2005. Circ.1,500.

Needs Ethnic/multicultural (general), experimental, feminist, gay, humor/satire, literary. Does not want genre fiction. Receives 200 mss/month. Accepts 10 prose mss and 15-20 poems/issue. Does not read December-August. Reading period is Sept-Dec. Ms published 5 months after acceptance. Published Jessica Bacal, Merle Drown, Pat Parnell, Octavio Quintanilla, Darryl Halbrooks, Simon Perchik and Baron Wormser. Length: 2,500 words (max). Average length: 1,250 words. Publishes short shorts. Average length of short shorts: 120 words. Also publishes poetry, creative nonfiction. Sometimes comments on/critiques rejected mss.

How to Contact Send complete ms with cover letter. Include brief bio, list of publications. Responds to queries in 1 month. Responds to mss in 4-7 months. Send either SASE (or IRC) for return of ms or disposable copy of ms and #10 SASE for reply only. Considers simultaneous submissions, multiple submissions. Sample copy available for $2. Guidelines available for SASE.

Payment/Terms Writers receive 3 contributor's copies. Additional copies $5. Pays on publication. Acquires one-time rights. Publication is copyrighted.

Advice "Stories need good pacing, believable characters and dialogue, as well as unusual subjects to stand out. Most stories we get are 'domestic fiction;' middle-class family dramas. We're drawn to stories about qypsies, the supernatural, travel, work, non-American perspectives, poverty or legends. Read the news, especially from other places and times, for inspiration. Try to entertain an editor who reads clever knock-offs ad nauseum."

$ 🖉 🖾 ANTIETAM REVIEW

Washington County Arts Council, 14 West Washington Street, Hagerstown MD 21740-5512. (301)791-3132. Fax: (240)420-1754. E-mail: antietamreview@washingtoncountyarts.com. Web site: www.washingtoncountyarts.com. **Contact:** Mary Jo Vincent, managing editor. Magazine: 8½×11; 75-90 pages; glossy paper; light card cover. A literary magazine of short fiction, poetry and black-and-white photography. Annual. Estab. 1982. Circ. 1,000.

Needs Condensed novels, ethnic/multicultural, experimental, literary ("short stories of a literary quality"), novel excerpts ("if works as an independent piece"), creative nonfiction, interviews, memoirs and book reviews. No religious, romance, erotic, confession or horror. Accepts 8-10 mss/year. Publishes ms 3-4 months after acceptance. **Publishes 2-3 new writers/year.** Recently published work by Stephen Dixon, Pinckney Benedict, Brad Barkley, Ellyn Bache, Joyce Kornblatt.

How to Contact Send complete ms. "Reading period September 1-December 1, annually. Queries accepted by mail, e-mail and phone. No electronic submissions. Manuscripts are not returned unless requested and sufficient postage and SASE is enclosed. Send #10 SASE for response only." Sample copy for $8.40 (current issue), $6.30 (back issue).

Payment/Terms Pays $50 and 2 contributor's copies. Pays on publication for first North American serial rights.

Advice "We seek high-quality, well-crafted work with significant character development and shift. No specific theme. We look for work that is interesting, involves the reader, and teaches us a new way to view the world. A manuscript stands out because of its energy and flow. Most of our submissions reflect the times more than industry trends. We also seek a compelling voice, originality, magic." Contributors are encouraged to review past issues before submitting.

$ 🖾 🖉 THE ANTIGONISH REVIEW

St. Francis Xavier University, P.O. Box 5000, Antigonish NS B2G 2W5 Canada. (902)867-3962. Fax: (902)867-5563. Web site: www.antigonishreview.com. **Contact:** Bonnie McIsaac, office manager. Literary magazine for educated and creative readers. Quarterly. Estab. 1970. Circ. 1,000.

Needs Literary, translations, contemporary, prose poem. No erotica. Receives 50 unsolicited mss/month. Accepts 6 mss/issue. Publishes ms 4 months after acceptance. **Publishes some new writers/year.** Recently published work by Arnold Bloch, Richard Butts and Helen Barolini. Sometimes comments on rejected mss.

How to Contact Send complete ms. Accepts submissions by fax. Accepts electronic (disk compatible with WordPerfect/IBM and Windows) submissions. Prefers hard copy with disk submission. Responds in 1 month to queries; 6 months to mss. No simultaneous submissions. Sample copy for $7 or online. Writer's guidelines for #10 SASE or online.

Payment/Terms Pays $100 per accepted story. Pays on publication. Rights retained by author.
Advice "Learn the fundamentals and do not deluge an editor."

$◪ ANTIOCH REVIEW

P.O. Box 148, Yellow Springs OH 45387-0148. E-mail: review@antioch.edu. Web site: www.review.a ntioch.edu. **Contact:** Fiction editor. Magazine: 6 × 9; 200 pages; 50 lb. book offset paper; coated cover stock; illustrations "seldom." "Literary and cultural review of contemporary issues, and literature for general readership." Quarterly. Estab. 1941. Circ. 5,000.

Needs Experimental, literary, translations, contemporary. No science fiction, fantasy or confessions. Receives 275 unsolicited mss/month. Accepts 5-6 mss/issue; 20-24 mss/year. No mss accepted June 1-September 1. Publishes ms 10 months after acceptance. Agented fiction 1-2%. **Publishes 1-2 new writers/year.** Recently published work by Edith Pearlman, Peter LaSalle, Nicholas Montemarano, Nathean Oates, Benjamin Percy.

How to Contact Send complete ms with SASE, preferably mailed flat. Responds in 4-6 months to mss. Sample copy for $7. Writer's guidelines online.

Payment/Terms Pays $15/printed page. Pays on publication.

Advice "Our best advice always is to *read* the *Antioch Review* to see what type of material we publish. Quality fiction requires an engagement of the reader's intellectual interest supported by mature emotional relevance, written in a style that is rich and rewarding without being freaky. The great number of stories submitted to us indicates that fiction still has great appeal. We assume that if so many are writing fiction, many must be reading it."

◪ APALACHEE REVIEW

Apalachee Press, P.O. Box 10469, Tallahassee FL 32302. (850)644-9114. Web site: http://apalacheere view.org/index.html. **Contact:** Michael Trammell, editor; Mary Jane Ryals, fiction editor. Literary magazine/journal: trade paperback size, 100-140 pages. Includes photographs. "At *Apalachee Review*, we are interested in outstanding literary fiction, but we especially like poetry, fiction, and nonfiction that addresses intercultural issues in a domestic or international setting/context." Annual. Estab. 1976. Circ. 500. Member CLMP.

Needs Ethnic/multicultural, experimental, fantasy/sci-fi (with a literary bent), feminist, historical, humor/satire, literary, mainstream, mystery/suspense, new age, translations. Does not want cliché-filled genre-oriented fiction. Receives 60-100 mss/month. Accepts 5-10 mss/issue. Manuscript published 1 yr after acceptance. Agented fiction 0.5%. **Publishes 1-2 new writers/year.** Recently published Lu Vickers, Joe Clark, Joe Taylor, Jane Arrowsmith Edwards, Vivian Lawry, Linda Frysh, Charles Harper Webb, Reno Raymond Gwaltney . Length: 600 words (min)-5,500 words (max). Average length: 3,500 words. Publishes short shorts. Average length of short shorts: 250 words. Also publishes literary essays, book reviews, poetry. Send review copies to Michael Trammell, editor. Sometimes comments on/critiques rejected mss.

How to Contact Send complete ms with cover letter. Include brief bio, list of publications. Responds to queries in 4-6 weeks. Responds to mss in 3-14 months. Send either SASE (or IRC) for return of ms or disposable copy of ms and #10 SASE for reply only. Considers simultaneous submissions. Sample copy available for $8 (current issue), $5 (back issue). Guidelines available for SASE, or check the Web site.

Payment/Terms Writers receive 2 contributors copies. Additional copies $5/each. Pays on publication. Acquires one-time rights, electronic rights. Publication is copyrighted.

◪ ◎ APPALACHIAN HERITAGE

CPO 2166, Berea KY 40404. (859)985-3699. Fax: (859)985-3903. E-mail: george-brosi@berea.edu. Web site: http://community.berea.edu/appalachianheritage/. **Contact:** George Brosi. Magazine: 6 × 9; 104 pages; 60 lb. stock; 10 pt. Warrenflo cover; drawings; b&w photos. "*Appalachian Heritage* is a Southern Appalachian literary magazine. We try to keep a balance of fiction, poetry, essays, scholarly works, etc., for a general audience and/or those interested in the Appalachian mountains." Quarterly. Estab. 1973. Circ. 750.

Needs Historical, literary, regional. "We do not want to see fiction that has no ties to Southern Appalachia." Receives 60-80 unsolicited mss/month. Accepts 2-3 mss/issue; 12-15 mss/year. Publishes ms 3-6 months after acceptance. **Publishes 8 new writers/year.** Recently published work by

Meridith Sue Willis, Lee Maynard, Bo Ball, Fred Chappell, Silas House, Ron Rash, and Lee Smith. Publishes short shorts. Occasionally comments on rejected mss.

How to Contact Send complete ms. Send SASE for reply, return of ms or send a disposable copy of ms. Responds in 1 month to queries; 6 weeks to mss. Sample copy for $6. Writer's guidelines free.

Payment/Terms Pays 3 contributor's copies; $6 charge for extras. Acquires first North American serial rights.

Advice "Get acquainted with *Appalachian Heritage*, as you should with any publication before submitting your work."

ⓝ ☑ ARGESTES LITERARY REVIEW

Collen Tree Press, 2941 170th St., South Amana IA 52334. (319)899-0994. E-mail: ctp_argestes@yahoo.com. **Contact:** Robert Bruce Kelsey, Fiction Editor. Literary magazine/journal. 100-150 pages. Contains illustrations. Includes photographs. "*Argestes* is a literary review of poetry and short story. We are a print-only journal. We are open to most forms of poetry and short story. We publish work of both established and new writers. We are an independent journal with no university affiliations." Semiannual. Estab. 1998. Circ. 200.

Needs Ethnic/multicultural (general), experimental, fantasy, feminist, gay, lesbian, literary, science fiction (soft/sociological), translations. Does not want gratuitous violence. Receives 30-60 mss/month. Accepts 3-6 mss/issue; 6-12 mss/year. Ms published 3-6 months after acceptance. **Publishes 3-6 new writers/year.** Published Joseph Hart, J. Cochran, Martin Galvin, Robert Parham, Tim Hurley and Joanne Lowery. Length: 2500 words (max). Average length: 1,700 words. Publishes short shorts. Average length of short shorts: 1,000 words. Also publishes literary essays, literary criticism, book reviews, poetry. Send review copies to Robert Bruce Kelsey-short story collections only. Sometimes comments on/critiques rejected mss.

How to Contact Send complete ms with cover letter. Include estimated word count, brief bio. Responds to queries in 4-8 weeks. Responds to mss in 4-8 weeks. Send disposable copy of ms and #10 SASE for reply only. Considers simultaneous submissions, multiple submissions. Sample copy available for $7. Guidelines available for SASE.

Payment/Terms Writers receive 2 contributor's copies. Additional copies $7. Pays on publication. Acquires first North American serial rights. Publication is copyrighted.

Advice "We look for a unique voice; an ear for language, dialogue; an obviously unique perception or emotional engagement with the subject matter. Read broadly and deeply, but craft your own stories in your own voice."

☑ ◎ ARKANSAS REVIEW, A Journal of Delta Studies

Department of English and Philosophy, P.O. Box 1890, Arkansas State University, State University AR 72467-1890. (870)972-3043. Fax: (501)972-3045. E-mail: tswillia@astate.edu. Web site: www.clt.astate.edu/arkreview. **Contact:** Tom Williams, fiction editor. Magazine: 8¼×11; 64-100 pages; coated, matte paper; matte, 4-color cover stock; illustrations; photos. Publishes articles, fiction, poetry, essays, interviews, reviews, visual art evocative of or responsive to the Mississippi River Delta. Triannual. Estab. 1996. Circ. 700.

Needs Literary (essays and criticism), regional (short stories). "No genre fiction. Must have a Delta focus." Receives 30-50 unsolicited mss/month. Accepts 2-3 mss/issue; 5-7 mss/year. Publishes ms 6-12 months after acceptance. Agented fiction 1%. **Publishes 3-4 new writers/year.** Recently published work by Susan Henderson, George Singleton, Scott Ely and Pia Erhart. Also publishes literary essays, poetry. Sometimes comments on rejected mss.

How to Contact Accepts submissions by e-mail, fax. Send SASE for reply, return of ms or send a disposable copy of ms. Responds in 1 week to queries; 4 months to mss. Sample copy for $7.50. Writer's guidelines for #10 SASE.

Payment/Terms Pays 3 contributor's copies; additional copies for $5. Acquires first North American serial rights.

Advice "We see a lot of stories set in New Orleans but prefer fiction that takes place in other parts of the Delta. We'd love more innovative and experimental fiction too but primarily seek stories that involve and engage the reader and evoke or respond to the Delta natural and/or cultural experience."

☑ THE ARMCHAIR AESTHETE

Pickle Gas Press, 31 Rolling Meadows Way, Penfield NY 14526. (585)388-6968. E-mail: bypaul@frontiernet.net or thearmchairaesthete@yahoo.com. **Contact:** Paul Agosto, editor. Magazine: 5½×8½;

60-75 pages; 20 lb. paper; 110 lb. card stock color cover and plastic spiral bound. *"The Armchair Aesthete* seeks quality writing that enlightens and entertains a thoughtful audience (ages 9-90) with a 'good read.' " Tri-annual. Estab. 1996. Circ. 100.

Needs Adventure, fantasy (science fantasy, sword and sorcery), historical (general), horror, humor/satire (satire), mainstream (contemporary), mystery/suspense (amateur sleuth, cozy, police procedural, private eye/hard-boiled, romantic suspense), science fiction (soft/sociological), western (frontier, traditional). "No racist, pornographic, overt gore; no religious or material intended for or written by children. Receives 90 unsolicited mss/month. Accepts 13-18 mss/issue; 60-80 mss/year. Publishes ms 1-12 months after acceptance. Agented fiction 5%. **Publishes 15-25 new writers/year.** Recently published work by Chris Brown, Laverne and Carol Frith, Lydia Williams, Andrew Bynom, and Douglas Empringham . Average length: 4,500 words. Publishes short shorts. Also publishes poetry. Sometimes comments on rejected mss.

How to Contact Accepts submissions by e-mail. Send SASE for reply, return of ms or send a disposable copy of ms. Responds in 2-3 weeks to queries; 3-6 months to mss. Accepts simultaneous, multiple submissions and reprints. Sample copy for $6.95 (paid to P. Agosto, Ed.) and 5 first-class stamps. Writer's guidelines for #10 SASE. No longer reviews fiction or poetry chapbooks.

Payment/Terms Pays 1 contributor's copy; additional copies for $6.95 (pay to P. Agosto, editor). Pays on publication for one-time rights.

Advice "Clever, compelling storytelling has a good chance here. We look for a clever plot, thought-out characters, something that surprises or catches us off guard. Write on innovative subjects and situations. Submissions should be professionally presented and technically sound."

THE BALTIMORE REVIEW

P.O. Box 36418, Towson MD 21286. Web site: www.baltimorereview.org. **Contact:** Susan Muaddi Darraj, managing editor. Magazine: 6×9; 150 pages; 60 lb. paper; 10 pt. CS1 gloss film cover. Showcase for the best short stories, creative nonfiction and poetry by writers in the Baltimore area and beyond. Semiannual. Estab. 1996.

Needs Ethnic/multicultural, literary, mainstream. "No science fiction, westerns, children's, romance, etc." Accepts 20 mss/issue; approx. 40 mss/year. Publishes ms 1-9 months after acceptance. **Publishes "at least a few" new writers/year.** Average length: 3,000 words. Publishes short shorts. Also publishes poetry.

How to Contact Send SASE for reply, return of ms or send a disposable copy of ms. Responds in 4-6 months to mss. Accepts simultaneous submissions. No e-mail or fax submissions. Sample copy online.

Payment/Terms Pays 2 contributor's copies. Acquires first North American serial rights.

Advice "We look for compelling stories and a masterful use of the English language. We want to feel that we have never heard this story, or this voice, before. Read the kinds of publications you want your work to appear in. Make your reader believe and care."

BATHTUB GIN

Pathwise Press, 2311 Broadway St, New Orleans, LA 70125. (812)327-2855. E-mail: pathwisepress@hotmail.com. Web site: www.pathwisepress.com. **Contact:** Fiction Editor. Magazine: 8½×5½; 60 pages; reycled 20-lb. paper; 80-lb. card cover; illustrations; photos. *"Bathtub Gin* is looking for work that has some kick to it. We are very eclectic and publish a wide range of styles. Audience is anyone interested in new writing and art that is not being presented in larger magazines." Semiannual. Estab. 1997. Circ. 250.

Needs Condensed novels, experimental, humor/satire, literary. "No horror, science fiction, historical unless they go beyond the usual formula." "We want more experimental fiction." Receives 20 unsolicited mss/month. Accepts 2-3 mss/issue. Reads mss for two issues June 1st-September 15th. "We publish in mid-October and mid-April." **Publishes 10 new writers/year.** Recently published work by J.T. Whitehead and G.D. McFetridge. Publishes short shorts. Also publishes literary essays, literary criticism, poetry. Often comments on rejected mss.

How to Contact Accepts submissions by e-mail. Send cover letter with a 3-5 line bio. Send SASE for reply, return of ms or send a disposable copy of ms. Responds in 1-2 months to queries. Accepts simultaneous, multiple submissions and reprints. Sample copy for $5. Writer's guidelines for #10 SASE. Reviews fiction.

Payment/Terms Pays 2 contributor's copies; discount on additional copies. Rights revert to author upon publication.

Advice "Please be advised that magazine is currently on hiatus and not accepting work until at least 2009."

☑ BAYOU

English Dept. University of New Orleans, 2000 Lakeshore Drive, New Orleans LA 70148. (504)280-7454. E-mail: bayou@uno.edu. Web site: http://cola.uno.edu/cww/bayou.htm. Magazine: 6×9; 150 pages; silk coated cover stock; photographs. Semiannual. Estab. 2002. Circ. 500.

Needs "From quirky nonfiction shorts to more traditional stories, we are committed to publishing solid work. Regardless of style, at Bayou we are always interested first in a well-told tale." Publishes ms 2-3 months after acceptance. Recently published work by Ben Brooks, Virgil Suarez, Marilyn Hacker, Sean Beaudoin, Tom Whalen, Mark Doty, Philip Cioffari Also publishes literary essays, poetry. Sometimes comments on rejected mss. Send fiction or nonfiction no more than 6,000 words. No more than 5 poems.

How to Contact Send complete ms. Send disposable copy of the ms and #10 SASE for reply only. Responds in 3-4 months to mss. Accepts simultaneous submissions. Sample copy for $7.

Payment/Terms Pays 2 contributor's copies and one year subscription. Pays on publication for first North American serial rights. Not copyrighted.

Advice "Do not submit in more than one genre at a time. Don't send a second submission until you receive a response to the first."

☐ BELLEVUE LITERARY REVIEW, A Journal of Humanity and Human Experience

Dept. of Medicine, NYU School of Medicine, 550 First Avenue, OBV-A612, New York NY 10016. (212)263-3973. Fax: (212)263-3206. E-mail: info@blreview.org. Web site: http://blreview.org. **Contact:** Ronna Wineberg, fiction editor. Magazine: 6×9; 160 pages. "The *BLR* is a literary journal that examines human existence through the prism of health and healing, illness and disease. We encourage creative interpretations of these themes." Semiannual. Estab. 2001. Member CLMP.

Needs Literary. No genre fiction. Receives 100 unsolicited mss/month. Accepts 9 mss/issue; 18 mss/year. Publishes ms 3-6 months after acceptance. Agented fiction 1%. **Publishes 3-6 new writers/year.** Recently published work by Amy Hempel, Sheila Kohler, Abraham Verghese, Stephen Dixon. Length: 5,000 words; average length: 2,500 words. Publishes short shorts. Also publishes literary essays, poetry. Sometimes comments on rejected mss.

How to Contact Submit online atwww.blreview.org (preferred). Also accepts mss via regular mail. Send complete ms. Send SASE (or IRC) for return of ms or disposable copy of the ms and #10 SASE for reply only. Responds in 3-6 months to mss. Accepts simultaneous submissions. Sample copy for $7. Writer's guidelines for SASE, e-mail or on Web site.

Payment/Terms Pays 2 contributor's copies, 1-year subscription and 1 year gift subscription; additional copies $5. Pays on publication for first North American serial rights. Sends galleys to author.

☑ BELLINGHAM REVIEW

Mail Stop 9053, Western Washington University, Bellingham WA 98225. (360)650-4863. E-mail: bhreview@cc.wwu.edu. Web site: www.wwu.edu/~bhreview. **Contact:** Fiction Editor. Magazine: 6×8¼; 150 pages; 60 lb. white paper; four-color cover." *Bellingham Review* seeks literature of palpable quality; stories, essays and poems that nudge the limits of form or execute traditional forms exquisitely. Semiannual. Estab. 1977. Circ. 1,600.

> ● The editors are actively seeking submissions of creative nonfiction, as well as stories that push the boundaries of the form. The Tobias Wolff Award in Fiction Contest runs December 1-March 15; see Web site for guidelines or send SASE.

Needs Experimental, humor/satire, literary, regional (Northwest). Does not want anything nonliterary. Accepts 3-4 mss/issue. Does not read ms February 2-September 14. Publishes ms 6 months after acceptance. Agented fiction 10%. **Publishes 10 new writers/year.** Recently published work by Patricia Vigderman, Joshua Rolnick, and A.G. Harmon. Publishes short shorts. Also publishes poetry.

How to Contact Send complete ms. Responds in 3 months to mss. Accepts simultaneous submissions. Sample copy for $7. Writer's guidelines online.

Payment/Terms Pays on publication when funding allows. Acquires first North American serial rights.

Advice "We look for work that is ambitious, vital and challenging both to the spirit and the intellect."

◢ ▨ BELLOWING ARK, A Literary Tabloid

P.O. Box 55564, Shoreline WA 98155. E-mail: bellowingark@bellowingark.org. **Contact:** Fiction Editor. Tabloid: $11\frac{1}{2} \times 17\frac{1}{2}$; 32 pages; electro-brite paper and cover stock; illustrations; photos. "We publish material we feel addresses the human situation in an affirmative way. We do not publish academic fiction." Bimonthly. Estab. 1984. Circ. 650.

• Work from *Bellowing Ark* appeared in the *Pushcart Prize* anthology.

Needs Literary, mainstream, serialized novels. "No science fiction or fantasy." Receives 30-70 unsolicited mss/month. Accepts 2-5 mss/issue; 700-1,000 mss/year. Publishes ms 6 months after acceptance. **Publishes 6-10 new writers/year.** Recently published work by Tom Cook, Diane Trzcinski, Myra Love, Shelley Uva, D.C. Taylor, and E.R. Romaine. Also publishes literary essays, literary criticism, poetry. Sometimes comments on rejected mss.

How to Contact Send complete ms and SASE. Responds in 6 weeks to mss. No simultaneous submissions. Sample copy for $4, $9\frac{1}{2} \times 12\frac{1}{2}$ SAE and $1.43 postage.

Payment/Terms Pays in contributor's copies. Acquires one-time rights.

Advice "*Bellowing Ark* began as (and remains) an alternative to the despair and negativity of the workshop/ academic literary scene; we believe that life has meaning and is worth living—the work we publish reflects that belief. Learn how to tell a story before submitting. Avoid 'trick' endings; they have all been done before and better. *Bellowing Ark* is interested in publishing writers who will develop with the magazine, as in an extended community. We find *good* writers and stick with them. This is why the magazine has grown from 12 to 32 pages."

◢ ▨ BELOIT FICTION JOURNAL

Box 11, 700 College St., Beloit College WI 53511. (608)363-2577. E-mail: bfj@beloit.edu. Web site: www.beloit.edu/ ~ english/bfjournal.htm. **Contact:** Chris Fink, editor-in-chief. Literary magazine: 6×9; 250 pages; 60 lb. paper; 10 pt. C1S cover stock; illustrations; photos on cover; ad-free. "We are interested in publishing the best contemporary fiction and are open to all themes except those involving pornographic, religiously dogmatic or politically propagandistic representations. Our magazine is for general readership, though most of our readers will probably have a specific interest in literary magazines." Annual. Estab. 1985.

• Work first appearing in *Beloit Fiction Journal* has been reprinted in award-winning collections, including the Flannery O'Connor and the Milkweed Fiction Prize collections, and has won the Iowa Short Fiction award.

Needs Literary, mainstream, contemporary. Wants more experimental and short shorts. Would like to see more "stories with a focus on both language and plot, unusual metaphors and vivid characters. No pornography, religious dogma, science fiction, horror, political propaganda or genre fiction." Receives 200 unsolicited mss/month. Accepts 20 mss/year. Publishes ms 9 months after acceptance. **Publishes 3 new writers/year.** Recently published work by Dennis Lehane, Silas House and David Harris Ebenbach. Length: 250-10,000 words; average length: 5,000 words. Sometimes comments on rejected mss.

How to Contact "Our reading period is from August 1st to December 1st only." No fax, e-mail or disk submissions. Responds in 2 weeks to queries; 2 months to mss. Accepts simultaneous submissions if identified as such. Please send one story at a time. Always include SASE. Sample copy for $10 (new issue), $8 (back issue, double issue), $6 (back issue, single issue). Writer's guidelines for #10 SASE or on Web site.

Payment/Terms Buys first North American serial rights only. Payment in copies.

Advice "Many of our contributors are writers whose work we had previously rejected. Don't let one rejection slip turn you away from our—or any—magazine."

◢ BERKELEY FICTION REVIEW

10B Eshleman Hall, University of California, Berkeley CA 94720. (510)642-2892. E-mail: bfictionrevie w@yahoo.com. Web site: www.OCF.Berkeley.EDU/ ~ bfr/. **Contact:** Rhoda Piland, editor. Magazine: $5\frac{1}{2} \times 8\frac{1}{2}$; 180 pages; perfect-bound; glossy cover; some b&w art; photographs. "The mission of *Berkeley Fiction Review* is to provide a forum for new and emerging writers as well as writers already established. We publish a wide variety of contemporary short fiction for a literary audience." Annual. Estab. 1981. Circ. 1,000.

Needs Experimental, literary, mainstream. "Quality, inventive short fiction. No poetry or formula fiction." Receives 70 unsolicited mss/month. Accepts 10-15 mss/issue. **Publishes 12-15 new writers/year.** Publishes short shorts. Occasionally comments on rejected mss.

How to Contact Responds in 3-9 months to mss. Accepts simultaneous, multiple submissions. Sample copy for $9.50. Writer's guidelines for SASE.

Payment/Terms Pays one contributor's copy. Acquires first rights. Sponsors awards/contests.

Advice "Our criteria is fiction that resonates. Voices that are strong and move a reader. Clear, powerful prose (either voice or rendering of subject) with a point. Unique ways of telling stories-these capture the editors. Work hard, don't give up. Don't let your friends or family critique your work. Get someone honest to point out your writing weaknesses, and then work on them. Don't submit thinly veiled autobiographical stories; it's been done before-and better. With the proliferation of computers, everyone thinks they're a writer. Not true, unfortunately. The plus side though is ease of transmission and layout and diversity and range of new work."

✒ 🔝 BIG MUDDY: A JOURNAL OF THE MISSISSIPPI RIVER VALLEY

Southeast Missouri State University Press, MS2650 English Dept., Southeast MO State University, Cape Girardeau MO 63701. E-mail: sswartwout@semo.edu. Web site: www6.semo.edu/universitypress/. **Contact:** Susan Swartwout, editor. Magazine: $8\frac{1}{2} \times 5\frac{1}{2}$ perfect-bound; 150 pages; acid-free paper; color cover stock; layflat lamination; illustrations; photos. "*Big Muddy* explores multidisciplinary, multicultural issues, people, and events mainly concerning the 10-state area that borders the Mississippi River, by people who have lived here, who have an interest in the area, or who know the River Basin. We publish fiction, poetry, historical essays, creative nonfiction, environmental essays, biography, regional events, photography, art, etc." Semiannual. Estab. 2001. Circ. 500.

Needs Adventure, ethnic/multicultural, experimental, family saga, feminist, historical, humor/satire, literary, mainstream, military/war, mystery/suspense, regional (Mississippi River Valley; Midwest), translations. "No romance, fantasy or children's." Receives 50 unsolicited mss/month. Accepts 7-10 mss/issue. Publishes ms 6 months after acceptance.

How to Contact Send SASE for return of ms or send a disposable copy of ms and #10 SASE for reply only. Responds in 10 weeks to mss. Accepts multiple submissions. Sample copy for $6. Writer's guidelines for SASE, e-mail, fax or on Web site. Reviews fiction.

Payment/Terms Pays 2 contributor's copies; additional copies $5. Acquires first North American serial rights.

Advice "In fiction manuscripts we look for clear language, avoidance of clichés except in necessary dialogue, a *fresh* vision of the theme or issue. Find some excellent and honest readers to comment on your work-in-progress and final draft. Consider their viewpoints carefully. Revise."

✒ THE BITTER OLEANDER

4983 Tall Oaks Dr., Fayettville NY 13066-9776. (315)637-3047. Fax: (315)637-5056. E-mail: info@bitteroleander.com. Web site: www.bitteroleander.com. **Contact:** Paul B. Roth. Zine specializing in poetry and short fiction: 6×9; 128 pages; 55 lb. paper; 12 pt. CIS cover stock; photos. "We're interested in the surreal; deep image particularization of natural experiences." Bi-annual. Estab. 1974. Circ. 1,500.

Needs Experimental, translations. "No pornography; no confessional; no romance." Receives 200 unsolicited mss/month. Accepts 4-5 mss/issue; 8-10 mss/year. Does not read in July. Publishes ms 4-6 months after acceptance. Recently published work by Daniel J. Doehr, V. Ulea, Emily Soto and Jeannette Ane Encinias . Max length: 2,500 words. Publishes short shorts. Also publishes literary essays, poetry. Always comments on rejected mss.

How to Contact Send SASE for reply, return of ms. Responds in 1 week to queries; 1 month to mss. Accepts multiple submissions. Sample copy for $8. Writer's guidelines for #10 SASE.

Payment/Terms Pays 1 contributor's copy; additional copies $8. Acquires first rights.

Advice "If within the first 100 words my mind drifts, the rest rarely makes it. Be yourself and listen to no one but yourself."

$✒ 🔝 BLACK WARRIOR REVIEW

P.O. Box 862936, Tuscaloosa AL 35486-0027. (205)348-4518. E-mail: bwr@ua.edu. Web site: www.bwr.ua.edu. **Contact:** Colleen Hollister, fiction editor. Magazine: 6×9; 160 pages; color artwork. "We publish contemporary fiction, poetry, reviews, essays and art for a literary audience. We publish the freshest work we can find." Semiannual. Estab. 1974. Circ. 2,000.

- Work that appeared in the *Black Warrior Review* has been included in the *Pushcart Prize* anthology, *Harper's Magazine*, *Best American Short Stories*, *Best American Poetry* and *New Stories from the South*.

Needs Literary, contemporary, short and short-short fiction. Wants "work that is conscious of form and well crafted. We are open to good experimental writing and short-short fiction. No genre fiction, please." Receives 300 unsolicited mss/month. Accepts 5 mss/issue; 10 mss/year. Unsolicited novel excerpts are not considered unless the novel is already contracted for publication. Publishes ms 6 months after acceptance. **Publishes 5 new writers/year.** Recently published work by Eric Maxon, Gary Parks, Gary Fincke, Anthony Varallo, Wayne Johnson, Jim Ruland, Elizabeth Wetmore, Bret Anthony Johnston, Rick Bass, Sherri Flick. Length: 7,500 words; average length: 2,000-5,000 words. Occasionally comments on rejected mss.

How to Contact Send complete ms with SASE (1 story per submission). Responds in 4 months to mss. Accepts simultaneous submissions if noted. Sample copy for $10. Writer's guidelines online.

Payment/Terms Pays up to $100, copies, and a 1-year subscription. Pays on publication for first rights.

Advice "We look for attention to language, freshness, honesty, a convincing and sharp voice. Send us a clean, well-printed, proofread manuscript. Become familiar with the magazine prior to submission."

⬭ ◎ BLUE MESA REVIEW

University of New Mexico, MSC03 2170, 1 University of New Mexico, Albuquerque NM 87131-0001. Fax: (505)277-5573. E-mail: bmrinfo@unm.edu. Web site: www.unm.edu/~bluemesa. **Contact:** Skye Pratt. Magazine: 6×9; 300 pages; 55 lb. paper; 10 pt CS1 photos. *Blue Mesa Review* publishes the best/most current creative writing on the market. Annual. Estab. 1989. Circ. 1,000.

Needs Literary fiction, including but not limited to ethnic/multicultural, experimental, feminist, gay, historical, humor/satire, lesbian, literary, mainstream, regional, western themes. Accepts 25 mss/year. Accepts mss year round; all submissions must be post marked by October 1; reads mss September-March; responds in 3-6 months. Publishes ms 5-6 months after acceptance. Also publishes literary essays, poetry, author interviews, and book reviews.

How to Contact Send SASE for reply. Sample copy for $12. Writer's guidelines online.

Payment/Terms Pays 2 contributor's copies. Acquires first North American serial rights.

◪ ◎ BLUELINE

125 Morey Hall, Department of English and Communication, SUNY Potsdam, Postdam NY 13676. (315)267-2043. E-mail: blueline@potsdam.edu. Web site: http://www2.potsdam.edu/blueline/blue.html. **Contact:** Fiction Editor. Magazine: 6×9; 200 pages; 70 lb. white stock paper; 65 lb. smooth cover stock; illustrations; photos. "*Blueline* is interested in quality writing about the Adirondacks or other places similar in geography and spirit. We publish fiction, poetry, personal essays, book reviews and oral history for those interested in Adirondacks, nature in general, and well-crafted writing." Annual. Estab. 1979. Circ. 400.

Needs Adventure, humor/satire, literary, regional, contemporary, prose poem, reminiscences, oral history, nature/outdoors. No urban stories or erotica. Receives 8-10 unsolicited mss/month. Accepts 6-8 mss/issue. Does not read January-August. Publishes ms 3-6 months after acceptance. **Publishes 2 new writers/year.** Recently published work by Joan Connor, Laura Rodley and Ann Mohin. Length: 500-3,000 words; average length: 2,500 words. Also publishes literary essays, poetry. Occasionally comments on rejected mss.

How to Contact Accepts simultaneous submissions. Sample copy for $6.

Payment/Terms Pays 1 contributor's copy; charges $7 each for 3 or more copies. Acquires first rights.

Advice "We look for concise, clear, concrete prose that tells a story and touches upon a universal theme or situation. We prefer realism to romanticism but will consider nostalgia if well done. Pay attention to grammar and syntax. Avoid murky language, sentimentality, cuteness or folkiness. We would like to see more good fiction related to the Adirondacks and more literary fiction and prose poems. If manuscript has potential, we work with author to improve and reconsider for publication. Our readers prefer fiction to poetry (in general) or reviews. Write from your own experience, be specific and factual (within the bounds of your story) and if you write about universal features such as love, death, change, etc., write about them in a fresh way. Triteness and mediocrity are the hallmarks of the majority of stories seen today.''

🎯 BOGG, Journal of Contemporary Writing

Bogg Publications, 422 N. Cleveland St., Arlington VA 22201-1424. E-mail: boggmag@aol.com. **Contact:** John Elsberg, US editor. Magazine: 6×9; 56 pages; 70 lb. white paper; 70 lb. cover stock; line illustrations. ''Poetry (to include prose poems, haiku/tanka and experimental forms), experimental short fiction, reviews.'' Published 2 or 3 times a year. Estab. 1968. Circ. 800.

Needs Very short experimental fiction and prose poems. Receives 25 unsolicited prose mss/month. Accepts 4-6 mss/issue. Publishes ms 3-18 months after acceptance. **Publishes 40-80 new writers/ year.** Recently published work by Linda Bosson, Brian Johnson, Katrina Holden Bronson, Karen Rosenberg, Carla Mayfield , and Elizabeth Bernays. Also occasionally publishes interviews and essays on small press history. Rarely comments on rejected mss.

How to Contact Responds in 1 week to queries; 2 weeks to mss. Sample copy for $4 or $6 (current issue). Reviews fiction. Does not consider e-mail or simultaneous submissions.

Payment/Terms Pays 2 contributor's copies; reduced charge for extras. Acquires one-time rights.

Advice ''We look for voice and originality. Read magazine first. *Bogg* is mainly a poetry journal, and we look for prose poems and short experimental or wry fiction that works well with the poetry .''

🌐 ▢ BOOK WORLD MAGAZINE

Christ Church Publishers Ltd., 2 Caversham Street, London England SW3 4AH United Kingdom. 0207 351 4995. Fax: 0207 3514995. E-mail: leonard.holdsworth@btopenworld.com. **Contact:** James Hughes. Magazine: 64 pages; illustrations; photos. ''Subscription magazine for serious book lovers, book collectors, librarians and academics.'' Monthly. Estab. 1971. Circ. 6,000.

Needs Also publishes literary essays, literary criticism.

How to Contact Query. Send IRC (International Reply Coupon) for return of ms. Responds in 3 months to queries; 3 months to mss. Accepts simultaneous submissions. Sample copy for $7.50. Writer's guidelines for IRC.

Payment/Terms Pays on publication for one-time rights.

Advice ''Always write to us before sending any mss.''

$▢ BOULEVARD

Opojaz, Inc., 6614 Clayton Rd., PMB 325, Richmond Heights MO 63117. (314)862-2643. Fax: (314)862-2982. E-mail: ballymon@hotmail.com. Web site: www.richardburgin.com. **Contact:** Richard Burgin, editor; Edmund de Chasca, senior editor. Magazine: 5½×8½; 150-250 pages; excellent paper; high-quality cover stock; illustrations; photos. ''*Boulevard* is a diverse literary magazine presenting original creative work by well-known authors, as well as by writers of exciting promise.'' Triannual. Estab. 1985. Circ. 11,000.

Needs Confessions, experimental, literary, mainstream, novel excerpts. ''We do not want erotica, science fiction, romance, western or children's stories.'' Receives over 600 unsolicited mss/month. Accepts about 10 mss/issue. Does not accept manuscripts between May 1 and October 1. Publishes ms 9 months after acceptance. **Publishes 10 new writers/year.** Recently published work by Joyce Carol Oates, Floyd Skloot, Alice Hoffman, Stephen Dixon and Frederick Busch. Length: 9,000 words maximum; average length: 5,000 words. Publishes short shorts. Also publishes literary essays, literary criticism, poetry. Sometimes comments on rejected mss.

How to Contact Send complete ms. Accepts submissions on disk. SASE for reply. Responds in 2 weeks to queries; 3-4 months to mss. Accepts multiple submissions. No simultaneous submissions. Sample copy for $9. Writer's guidelines online.

Payment/Terms Pays $50-700. Pays on publication for first North American serial rights.

Advice ''We pick the stories that move us the most emotionally, stimulate us the most intellectually, are the best written and thought out. Don't write to get published—write to express your experience and vision of the world.''

🎯 THE BRIAR CLIFF REVIEW

Briar Cliff University, 3303 Rebecca St., Sioux City IA 51104-0100. (712)279-5477. E-mail: curranst@ briarcliff.edu. Web site: www.briarcliff.edu/bcreview. **Contact:** Phil Hey or Tricia Currans-Sheehan, fiction editors. Magazine: 8½×11; 120 pages; 70 lb. 100# Altima Satin Text; illustrations; photos.

"*The Briar Cliff Review* is an eclectic literary and cultural magazine focusing on (but not limited to) Siouxland writers and subjects. We are happy to proclaim ourselves a regional publication. It doesn't diminish us; it enhances us." Annual. Estab. 1989. Circ. 750.

Needs Ethnic/multicultural, feminist, historical, humor/satire, literary, mainstream, regional. "No romance, horror or alien stories." Accepts 5 mss/year. Reads mss only between August 1 and November 1. Publishes ms 3-4 months after acceptance. **Publishes 10-14 new writers/year.** Recently published work by Jenna Blum, Brian Bedard, Christian Michener, Rebecca Tuch, Scott H. Andrews, and Josip Novakovich. Length: 2,500-5,000 words; average length: 3,000 words. Also publishes literary essays, literary criticism, poetry. Sometimes comments on rejected mss.

How to Contact Send SASE for return of ms. Does not accept electronic submissions (unless from overseas). Responds in 4-5 months to mss. Accepts simultaneous submissions. Sample copy for $12 and 9×12 SAE. Writer's guidelines for #10 SASE. Reviews fiction.

Payment/Terms Pays 2 contributor's copies; additional copies available for $9. Acquires first rights.

Advice "So many stories are just telling. We want some action. It has to move. We prefer stories in which there is no gimmick, no mechanical turn of events, no moral except the one we would draw privately."

☑ ◎ BRILLANT CORNERS, A Journal of Jazz & Literature

Lycoming College, Williamsport PA 17701. (570)321-4279. Fax: (570)321-4090. E-mail: feinstein@lycoming.edu. **Contact:** Sascha Feinstein, editor. Journal: 6×9; 100 pages; 70 lb. Cougar opaque, vellum, natural paper; photographs. "We publish jazz-related literature—fiction, poetry and nonfiction." Semiannual. Estab. 1996. Circ. 1,200.

Needs Condensed novels, ethnic/multicultural, experimental, literary, mainstream, romance (contemporary). Receives 10-15 unsolicited mss/month. Accepts 1-2 mss/issue; 2-3 mss/year. Does not read mss May 15-September 1. Publishes ms 4-12 months after acceptance. Publishes short shorts. Also publishes literary essays, literary criticism, poetry. Rarely comments on rejected mss.

How to Contact SASE for return of ms or send a disposable copy of ms. Accepts unpublished work only. Responds in 2 weeks to queries; 1-2 months to mss. Sample copy for $7. Reviews fiction.

Payment/Terms Acquires first North American serial rights. Sends galleys to author when possible.

Advice "We look for clear, moving prose that demostrates a love of both writing and jazz. We primarily publish established writers, but we read all submissions carefully and welcome work by outstanding young writers."

ⓝ ☐ THE BROADKILL REVIEW, A JOURNAL OF LITERATURE

John Milton and Company Quality Used Books, 104 Federal Street, Milton DE 19968. (302)684-0174. E-mail: the_broadkill_review@earthlink.net. **Contact:** Jamie Brown, Publisher/Editor. PDF Literary magazine/journal. Contains illustrations, photographs. "Quality is the most important factor. This isn't to suggest that we are snobs, for I'm not talking about subject matter, but about the bell-like resonance of the work (evoked within the reader) and clarity. I want the reader left with the feeling that it matters to the reader personally that they read the story. Writing is the first interactive medium, after all, and although 100% communication cannot ever be achieved, owing to all sorts of internal and unconscious filters and the differences between two peoples' perceptions of the same thing, the stories I like are those that understand that and which encourage a kind of divestiture of the self and an investment in the story with whatever they, the reader, can bring to it of an emotional commitment. I am a fan of John Gardner's *On Becoming a Novelist*, and firmly believe in establishing 'the waking dream' as the responsibility of the author." Bimonthly. Estab. 2007. Circ. 12,000. Member CLMP, Delaware Press Assn.

Needs Literary. Does not want anything gratuitous. List of upcoming themes available for SASE, on Web site. Receives 8-20 mss/month. Accepts 1-4 mss/issue; 16-20 mss/year. Manuscript published 1-3 months after acceptance. **Publishes 30 new writers/year**. Published Thom Wade Myers, Chad Clifton, Tina Hession, Joshua D. Isard, Maryanne Khan, Richard Myers Peabody, H. A. Maxson, Bob Yearick, Gaylene Carbis, Louise D'Arcy, and Andee Jones. Length: 6000 words (max). Average length: 3300 words. Publishes short shorts. Also publishes literary essays, literary criticism, book reviews, poetry. Send review copies to Editor, The Broadkill Review, 104 Federal Street, Milton, DE 19968. Sometimes comments on/critiques rejected mss.

How to Contact Send complete ms with cover letter. Prefers submissions by e-mail. Include estimated word count, brief bio, list of publications. Responds to queries in 1 week. Responds to mss in 4-26 weeks. Send either SASE (or IRC) for return of ms or disposable copy of ms and #10 SASE for reply only. Considers simultaneous submissions, multiple submissions. Sample copy free upon request. Guidelines available via e-mail.

Payment/Terms Writers receive contributor's copy. Pays on publication. Acquires first rights. Publication is copyrighted.

Advice "Finish the work. Getting to the end of your first draft may be emotionally satisfying and physically enervating, but that is the point where the WORK of writing begins. Don't stint on the effort it may take you to revise your work. We are interested in publishing in our pages that which rises above the ordinary. We are not, on the other hand, interested in stories about your three-headed cat, zombies, flesh-eating bacteria, BEMs from outer-space, or psychopathic axe murderers. In short, your stories and poems should not rely on the unusual circumstance in place of actually having work which is finely crafted, insightful of the human condition, or which manages to make the reader continue to think about it after they have finished reading it. We are open to almost everything that does what Literature should do, which is to exact a price greater than the effort required to read it. The selection process is entirely subjective. We are not representative of the whole world. We publish what moves US."

$⬛ BYLINE

P.O. Box 111, Albion NY 14411. (585)355-8172. E-mail: robbi@bylinemag.com. Web site: www.bylinemag.com. **Contact:** Robbi Hess. Magazine "aimed at encouraging and motivating all writers toward success, with special information to help new writers. Articles center on how to write better, market smarter, sell your work." Monthly. Estab. 1981.

Needs Literary, genre, general fiction. "Does not want to see erotica or explicit graphic content. No science fiction or fantasy." Receives 100-200 unsolicited mss/month. Accepts 1 mss/issue; 11 mss/year. Publishes ms 3 months after acceptance. **Publishes many new writers/year.** Recently published work by Ami Elizabeth Reeves, David Dumitru, William Eisner. Also publishes poetry.

How to Contact No cover letter needed. Responds in 10-12 weeks to mss. Accepts simultaneous submissions "if notified." Writer's guidelines for #10 SASE or online.

Payment/Terms Pays $50 and 3 contributor's copies. Pays on publication for first North American serial rights.

Advice "We look for good writing that draws the reader in; conflict and character movement by story's end. We're very open to new writers. Submit a well-written, professionally prepared ms with SASE. No erotica or senseless violence; otherwise, we'll consider most any theme. We also sponsor short story and poetry contests. Read what's being published. Find a good story, not just a narrative reflection. Keep submitting."

Ñ ⬛ CAIRN: The New St. Andrews Review

St. Andrews College Press, 1700 Dogwood Mile, Laurinburg NC 28352. (910)277-5310. Fax: (910)277-5020. E-mail: pressemail@sapc.edu. Web site: www.sapc.edu/sapress.html. **Contact:** Fiction Editor. Magazine: 50-60 lb. paper. "*Cairn* is a nonprofit, national/international literary magazine which publish es established as well as emerging writers ." Estab. 1969. Member CLMP and AWP.

Needs Literary, short stories and short-short fiction. "We're looking for original, imaginative short fiction with style and insight." **Publishes 10-15 new writers/year.**

How to Contact Accepts no submissions by e-mail. Send only snail-mail disposabel copy of ms with SASE for reply only. Responds in 3-4 months to mss. Accepts simultaneous submissions with notice.

Payment/Terms Pays 3 contributor's copies.

⬛ ◎ ⬛ CALLALOO, A Journal of African-American and African Diaspora Arts and Letters

Dept. of English, TAMU 4227, Texas A&M University, College Station TX 77843-4227. (979)458-3108. Fax: (979)458-3275. E-mail: callaloo@tamu.edu. Web site: http://callaloo.tamu.edu. **Contact:** Charles H. Rowell, editor. Magazine: 7×10; 250 pages. "Devoted to publishing fiction, poetry, drama of the African diaspora, including North, Central and South America, the Caribbean, Europe and Africa. Visually beautiful and well-edited, the journal publishes 3-5 short stories in all forms and styles in each issue." Quarterly. Estab. 1976. Circ. 2,000.

● One of the leading voices in African-American literature, *Callaloo* has recieved NEA literature grants. Several pieces every year are chosen for collections of the year's best stories, such as *Beacon's Best* John Wideman's "Weight" from *Callaloo* won the 2000 O. Henry Award.

Needs Ethnic/multicultural (black culture), feminist, historical, humor/satire, literary, regional, science fiction, serialized novels, translations, contemporary, prose poem. "No romance, confessional. Would like to see more experimental fiction, science fiction and well-crafted literary fiction particularly dealing with the black middle class, immigrant communities and/or the black South." Accepts 3-5 mss/issue; 10-20 mss/year. **Publishes 5-10 new writers/year.** Recently published work by Charles Johnson, Edwidge Danticat, Thomas Glave, Nallo Hopkinson, John Edgar Wideman, Jamaica Kincaid, Percival Everett and Patricia Powell. Also publishes poetry.

How to Contact Generally accepts unpublished work, rarely accepts reprints. Responds in 2 weeks to queries; 6 months to mss. Accepts multiple submissions. Sample copy for $12. Writer's guidelines online.

Payment/Terms Pays in contributor's copies. Aquires some rights. Sends galleys to author.

Advice "We look for freshness of both writing and plot, strength of characterization, plausibilty of plot. Read what's being written and published, especially in journals such as *Callaloo*."

CALYX, A Journal of Art & Literature by Women

Calyx, Inc., P.O. Box B, Corvallis OR 97339. (541)753-9384. Fax: (541)753-0515. E-mail: calyx@proaxis.com. Web site: www.calyxpress.org. **Contact:** Editor. Magazine: 6×8; 128 pages per single issue; 60 lb. coated matte stock paper; 10 pt. chrome coat cover; original art. Publishes prose, poetry, art, essays, interviews and critical and review articles. "*Calyx* exists to publish fine literature and art by women and is committed to publishing the work of all women, including women of color, older women, working class women and other voices that need to be heard. We are committed to discovering and nurturing beginning writers." Biannual. Estab. 1976. Circ. 6,000.

Needs Receives approximately 1,000 unsolicited prose and poetry mss when open. Accepts 4-8 prose mss/issue; 9-15 mss/year. Reads mss October 1-December 31; submit only during this period. Mss received when not reading will be returned. Publishes ms 4-12 months after acceptance. **Publishes 10-20 new writers/year.** Recently published work by M. Evelina Galang, Chitrita Banerji, Diana Ma , Catherine Brady. Also publishes literary essays, literary criticism, poetry.

How to Contact Responds in 4-12 months to mss. Accepts simultaneous submissions. Sample copy for $ 10 plus $4 postage. Include SASE.

Payment/Terms "Combination of free issues and 1 volume subscription.

Advice Most mss are rejected because "The writers are not familiar with *Calyx*. Writers should read *Calyx* and be familar with the publication. We look for good writing, imagination and important/ interesting subject matter."

THE CARIBBEAN WRITER

The University of the Virgin Islands, RR 1, Box 10,000-Kinghill, St. Croix 00850 Virgin Islands. (340)692-4152. Fax: (340)692-4026. E-mail: info@thecaribbeanwriter.org. Web site: www.thecaribbeanwriter.org. **Contact:** Quilin B. Mars, managing editor. Magazine: 6×9 inches; 304 pages; 60 lb. paper; glossy cover stock; illustrations; photos. "*The Caribbean Writer* is an international magazine with a Caribbean focus. The Caribbean should be central to the work, or the work should reflect a Caribbean heritage, experience or perspective." Annual. Estab. 1987. Circ. 1,500.

• Work published in *The Caribbean Writer* has received two Pushcart Prizes and Quenepon Award.

Needs Historical (general), humor/satire, literary, mainstream, translations, contemporary and prose poem. Receives 65 unsolicited mss/month. Accepts 60 mss/issue. **Publishes approximately 20% new writers/year.** Recently published work by Jacqueline Johnson, E. A. Markham And Mcdonald Dixon. Also publishes literary essays, fiction, translations, plays, and book reviews.

How to Contact Accepts submissions by e-mail. "Blind submissions only. Send name, address and title of manuscript on separate sheet. Title only on manuscript. Accepts simultaneous, multiple submissions. Sample copy for $7 and $4 postage.

Payment/Terms Pays 2 contributor's copies. Annual prizes for best story ($400); for best poem ($300); $200 for first time publication; best work by Caribbean Author ($500); best work by Virgin Islands author ($200). Acquires one-time rights.

Advice Looks for "work which reflects a Caribbean heritage, experience or perspective."

CAROLINA QUARTERLY

Greenlaw Hall CB #3520, University of North Carolina, Chapel Hill NC 27599-3520. (919)962-0244. Fax: (919)962-3520. E-mail: cquarter@unc.edu. Web site: www.unc.edu/depts/cqonline. **Contact:**

Elena Oxman, editor-in-chief. Literary journal: 80-100 pages; illustrations. Publishes fiction for a "general literary audience." Triannual. Estab. 1948. Circ. 900-1,000.

● Work published in *Carolina Quarterly* has been selected for in inclusion in *Best American Short Stories*, in *New Stories for the South: The Year's Best*.

Needs Literary. "We would like to see more short/micro-fiction and more stories by minority/ethnic writers." Receives 150-200 unsolicited mss/month. Accepts 4-5 mss/issue; 14-16 mss/year. Does not read mss May-August. Publishes ms 4 months after acceptance. **Publishes 5-6 new writers/ year.** Recently published work by Pam Durban, Elizabeth Spencer, Brad Vice, Wendy Brenner, and Nanci Kincaid. Publishes short shorts. Also publishes literary essays, poetry. Occasionally comments on rejected mss.

How to Contact Responds in 3 months to queries; 6 months to mss. Does not accept e-mail submissions. No simultaneous submissions. Sample copy for $6. Writer's guidelines for SASE.

Payment/Terms Pays in contributor's copies. Acquires first rights.

○ CC&D, CHILDREN, CHURCHES & DADDIES MAGAZINE: THE UNRELIGIOUS, NONFAMILY-ORIENTED LITERARY AND ART MAGAZINE

Scars Publications and Design, 829 Brian Court, Gurnee IL 60031-3155. (847)281-9070. E-mail: ccand d96@scars.tv. Web site: http://scars.tv. **Contact:** Janet Kuypers, editor in chief. Literary magazine/ journal: 5×7, 60 lb paper. Contains illustrations & photographs. Monthly. Estab. 1993.

Needs "Our biases are works that relate to issues such as politics, sexism, society, and the like, but are definitely not limited to such. We publish good work that makes you think, that makes you feel like you've lived through a scene instead of merely reading it. If it relates to how the world fits into a person's life (political story, a day in the life, coping with issues people face), it will probably win us over faster. We have received comments from readers and other editors saying that they thought some of our stories really happened. They didn't, but it was nice to know they were so concrete, so believable people thought they were nonfiction. Do that to our readers." Interested in many topics including adventure, ethnic/multicultural, experimental, feminist, gay, historical, lesbian, literary, mystery/suspense, new age, psychic/supernatural/occult, science fiction. Does not want religious or rhyming or family-oriented material. Manuscript published 1 yr after acceptance. Published Mel Waldman, Kenneth DiMaggio, Pat Dixon, Robert William Meyers, Troy Davis, G.A. Scheinoha, Ken Dean. Average length: 1,000 words. Publishes short shorts, essays and stories. Also publishes poetry. Always comments on/critiques rejected mss if asked.

How to Contact Send complete ms with cover letter or query with clips of published work. Prefers submissions by e-mail. "If you have email and send us a snail-mail submission, we will accept writing only if you email it to us." Responds to queries in 2 weeks; mss in 2 weeks. "Responds much faster to e-mail submissions and queries." Send either SASE (or IRC) for return of ms or disposable copy of ms and #10 SASE for reply only, but if you have e-mail PLEASE send us an electronic submission instead. (If we accept your writing, we'll only ask for you to e-mail it to us anyway.) Considers simultaneous submissions, previously published submissions, multiple submissions. Sample copy available for $6. Guidelines available for SASE, via e-mail, on Web site. Reviews fiction, essays, journals, editorials, short fiction.

◙ CENTER, A Journal of the Literary Arts

University of Missouri, 202 Tate Hall, Columbia MO 65211-1500. (573)882-4971. E-mail: cla@missou ri.edu. Web site: http://center.missouri.edu. **Contact:** Fiction editor. Magazine: 6×9; 125-200 pages; perfect bound, with 4-color card cover. *Center*'s goal is to publish the best in literary fiction, poetry and creative nonfiction by previously unpublished and emerging writers, as well as more established writers. Annual. Estab. 2000. Circ. 500.

Needs Ethnic/multicultural, experimental, humor/satire, literary. Receives 30-50 unsolicited mss/ month. Accepts 3-5 mss/year. Reads mss from July 1-December 1 only. Publishes ms 6 months after acceptance. **Publishes 25% new writers/year.** Recently published work by William Eisner and Kim Chinquee. Publishes short shorts. Also publishes literary essays, poetry. Sometimes comments on rejected mss.

How to Contact Send SASE (or IRC) for return of ms or send a disposable copy of ms and #10 SASE for reply only. Responds in 1 month to queries; 3-4 months to mss. Accepts simultaneous, multiple submissions. Sample copy for $3, current copy $6. Writer's guidelines for SASE.

Payment/Terms Pays 2 contributor's cop ies; additional copies $3. Pays on publication for one-time rights.

☑ CHAFFIN JOURNAL

English Department, Eastern Kentucky University, Case Annex 467, Richmond KY 40475-3102. (859)622-3080. E-mail: robert.witt@eku.edu. Web site: www.english.eku.edu/chaffin_journal. **Contact:** Robert Witt, editor. Magazine: $8 \times 5^{1}/_{2}$; 120-130 pages; 70 lb. paper; 80 lb. cover. "We publish fiction on any subject; our only consideration is the quality." Annual. Estab. 1998. Circ. 150.

Needs Ethnic/multicultural, historical, humor/satire, literary, mainstream, regional (Appalachia). "No erotica, fantasy." Receives 20 unsolicited mss/month. Accepts 6-8 mss/year. Does not read mss October 1 through May 31. Publishes ms 6 months after acceptance. **Publishes 2-3 new writers/ year.** Recently published work by Meridith Sue Willis, Marie Manilla, Raymond Abbott, Marjorie Bixler, Chris Helvey. Length: 10,000 words; average length: 5,000 words.

How to Contact Send SASE for return of ms. Responds in 1 week to queries; 3 months to mss. Accepts simultaneous, multiple submissions. Sample copy for $6. Writer's guidelines for SASE, or e-mail submissions are online.

Payment/Terms Pays 1 contributor's copy; additional copies $6. Pays on publication for one-time rights.

Advice "All manuscripts submitted are considered."

$⊕ CHAPMAN

Chapman Publishing, 4 Broughton Place, Edinburgh Scotland EH1 3RX United Kingdom. (+44)131 557 2207. E-mail: chapman-pub@blueyonder.co.uk. Web site: www.chapman-pub.co.uk. **Contact:** Joy Hendry, editor. "*Chapman*, Scotland's quality literary magazine, is a dynamic force in Scotland—publishing poetry; fiction; criticism; reviews; articles on theatre, politics, language and the arts. Our philosophy is to publish new work, from known and unknown writers, mainly Scottish, but also worldwide." Published three times a year. Estab. 1970. Circ. 2,000.

Needs Experimental, historical, humor/satire, literary, Scottish/international. "No horror, science fiction." Accepts 4-6 mss/issue. Publishes ms 6 months after acceptance. **Publishes 50 new writers/ year.**

How to Contact No simultaneous submissions. Writer's guidelines by e-mail or send SASE/IRC.

Payment/Terms Pays by negotiation. Pays on publication for first rights.

Advice "Keep your stories for six months and edit carefully. We seek challenging work which attempts to explore difficult/new territory in content and form, but lighter work, if original enough, is welcome."

☑ CHICAGO QUARTERLY REVIEW

Monadnock Group Publishers, 517 Sherman Ave., Evanston IL 60202-2815. **Contact:** Syed Afzal Haider and Lisa McKenzie, editors. Magazine: 6×9; 125 pages; illustrations; photos. Annual. Estab. 1994. Circ. 300.

Needs Literary. Receives 30-40 unsolicited mss/month. Accepts 6-8 mss/issue; 8-16 mss/year. Publishes ms 1 year after acceptance. Agented fiction 10%. **Publishes 8-10 new writers/year.** Length: 5,000 words; average length: 2,500 words. Publishes short shorts. Also publishes literary essays, poetry. Sometimes comments on rejected mss.

How to Contact Send a disposable copy of ms and #10 SASE for reply only. Responds in 2 months to queries; 6 months to mss. Accepts simultaneous submissions. Up to 5 poems in a single submission; does not accept multiple short story submissions. Sample copy for $9.

Payment/Terms Pays 4 contributor's copies; additional copies $9. Pays on publication for one-time rights.

Advice "The writer's voice ought to be clear and unique and should explain something of what it means to be human. We want well-written stories that reflect an appreciation for the rhythm and music of language, work that shows passion and commitment to the art of writing."

Ⓝ $⊕ ☑ ◎ ☑ CHROMA, AN INTERNATIONAL QUEER LITERARY JOURNAL

P.O. Box 44655, London, England N16 0WQ. +44-20-7193-7642. E-mail: editor@chromajournal.co. uk. Web site: www.chromajournal.co.uk. **Contact:** Shaun Levin, editor. Literary magazine/journal. 52 pages. Contains illustrations. Includes photographs. "*Chroma* is the only international queer literary and arts journal based in Europe. We publish poetry, short prose and artwork by lesbian, gay, bisexual and transgendered writers and artists. We are always looking for new work and encourage work in translation. Each issue is themed, so please check the Web site for details. Past themes have included: Foreigners, Beauty, Islands, and Tormented." Semiannual. Estab. 2004. Circ. 1,000. **Needs** Comics/graphic novels, erotica, ethnic/multicultural, experimental, feminist, gay, lesbian, literary. Receives 100 mss/month. Accepts 12 mss/issue; 24 mss/year. Ms published 3 months after acceptance. **Publishes 20 new writers/year.** Length: 2,000 words (min)-5,000 words (max). Average length: 3,000 words. Publishes short shorts. Average length of short shorts: 1,000 words. Also publishes book reviews, poetry. Send review copies to Eric Anderson, books editor. Sometimes comments on/critiques rejected mss.

How to Contact Send complete ms with cover letter. Include brief bio. Responds to queries in 1 month via email. Considers simultaneous submissions, multiple submissions. Guidelines available on Web site.

Payment/Terms Writers receive up to $150. Additional copies $7. Pays on publication. Acquires first rights. Publication is copyrighted. "The *Chroma* International Queer Writing Competition runs every two years. The first was in 2006. Check guidelines on our Web site."

Advice "We look for a good story well told. We look for writers doing interesting things with language, writers who are not afraid to take risks in the stories they tell and the way they tell them. Read back issues. If you like what we do, send us your work."

$⬛ 🖉 ◎ CHRYSALIS READER

1745 Gravel Hill Road, Dillwyn VA 23936. (434)983-3021. E-mail: chrysalis@hovac.com. Web site: www.swedenborg.com /chrysalis. **Contact:** Robert Tucker, fiction editor. Book series: 7½×10; 192 pages; coated cover stock; illustrations; photos." *The Chrysalis Reader* audience includes people from numerous faiths and backgrounds. Many of them work in psychology, education, religion, the arts, sciences, or one of the helping professions. The style of writing may be humorous, serious, or some combination of these approaches. Essays, poetry, and fiction that are not evangelical in tone but that are unique in addressing the *Chrysalis Reader* theme are more likely to be accepted. Our readers are interested in expanding, enriching, or challenging their intellects, hearts, and philosophies, and many also just want to enjoy a good read. For these reasons the editors attempt to publish a mix of writings. Articles and poetry must be related to the theme; however, you may have your own approach to the theme not written in our description ." Estab. 1985. Circ. 3,000.

● This journal explores contemporary questions of spirituality from the perspective of Swedenborgian theology .

Needs Adventure, experimental, historical, literary, mainstream, mystery/suspense, science fiction, fiction (leading to insight), contemporary, spiritual, sports. No religious works. Upcoming theme: "Renewal" (Fall 2008). Receives 50 unsolicited mss/month. Accepts 20-40 mss/year. Publishes ms 9 months after acceptance. **Publishes 10 new writers/year.** Recently published work by Robert Bly, William Kloefkorn, Raymond Moody, Virgil Suárez, Carol Lem, Alan Magee, John Hitchcock. Also publishes literary essays, literary criticism, poetry. Sometimes comments on rejected mss.

How to Contact Query with SASE. Accepts submissions by e-mail. Responds in 1 month to queries; 4-6 months to mss. No simultaneous submissions, previously published work. Sample copy for $10 and 8½×11 SAE. Writer's guidelines and themes for issues for SASE or online.

Payment/Terms Pays $25-100. Pays at page-proof stage. Acquires first rights, makes work-for-hire assignments. Sends galleys to author.

Advice Looking for "1: Quality; 2. appeal for our audience; 3. relevance to/illumination of an issue's theme."

🖉 CIMARRON REVIEW

Oklahoma State University, 205 Morrill Hall, Stillwater OK 74078-0135. (405)744-9476. Web site: http://cimarronreview.okstate.edu. **Contact:** Toni Graham, fiction editor. Magazine: 6×9; 110 pages. "Poetry and fiction on contemporary themes; personal essays on contemporary issues that cope with life in the 21st century. We are eager to receive manuscripts from both established and less experienced writers who intrigue us with their unusual perspective, language, imagery and character." Quarterly. Estab. 1967. Circ. 600.

Needs Literary-quality short stories and novel excerpts. No juvenile or genre fiction. Accepts 3-5 mss/issue; 12-15 mss/year. Publishes ms 2-6 months after acceptance. **Publishes 2-4 new writers/ year.** Recently published work by Adam Braver, Gary Fincke, Catherine Brady, Nona Caspers, David Ryan. Also publishes literary essays, literary criticism, poetry.

How to Contact Send complete ms with SASE. Responds in 2-6 months to mss. Accepts simultaneous submissions. Sample copy for $7. Reviews fiction.

Payment/Terms Pays 2 contributor's copies. Acquires first North American serial rights.

Advice "In order to get a feel for the kind of work we publish, please read an issue or two before submitting."

$ ☑ THE CINCINNATI REVIEW

P.O. Box 210069, Cincinnati OH 45221-0069. (513)556-3954. E-mail: editors@cincinnatireview.com. Web site: www.cincinnatireview.com. **Contact:** Brock Clarke, fiction editor. Magazine: 6×9; 180-200 pages; 60 lb. white offset paper. "A journal devoted to publishing the best new literary fiction and poetry as well as book reviews, essays and interviews." Semiannual. Estab. 2003.

Needs Literary. Does not want genre fiction. Accepts 13 mss/year. Reads submissions September 1-May 31. Manuscripts arriving during June, July and August will be returned unread.

How to Contact Send complete ms with SASE. Does not consider e-mail submissions. Responds in 2 weeks to queries; 6 weeks to mss. Accepts simultaneous submissions with notice. Sample copy for $9, subscription $15. Writer's guidelines online or send SASE.

Payment/Terms Pays $25/page. Pays on publication for first North American serial, electronic rights. All rights revert to author upon publication.

⬕ ◻ ◎ THE CLAREMONT REVIEW, The Contemporary Magazine of Young Adult Writers

The Claremont Review Publishers, 4980 Wesley Rd., Victoria BC V8Y 1Y9 Canada. (250)658-5221. Fax: (250)658-5387. E-mail: editor@theClaremontReview.ca. Web site: www.theClaremontReview. ca. **Contact:** Lucy Bashford (managing editor), Susan Stenson, Janice McCachen, Terence Young, editors. Magazine: 6×9; 110-120 pages; book paper; soft gloss cover; b&w illustrations. "We are dedicated to publishing emerging young writers aged 13-19 from anywhere in the English-speaking world, but primarily Canada and the U.S." Biannual. Estab. 1992. Circ. 700.

Needs Young adult/teen ("their writing, not writing for them"). No science fiction, fantasy. Receives 20-30 unsolicited mss/month. Accepts 10-12 mss/issue; 20-24 mss/year. Publishes ms 3 months after acceptance. **Publishes 100 new writers/year.** Recently published work by Danielle Hubbard, Kristina Lucas, Taylor McKinnon. Length: 5,000 words; average length: 1,500-3,000 words. Publishes short shorts. Also publishes poetry. Always comments on rejected mss.

How to Contact Responds in 3 months to mss. Accepts multiple submissions. Sample copy for $10.

Payment/Terms Pays 1 contributor's copy. Additional copies for $6. Acquires first North American serial, one-time rights. Sponsors awards/contests.

Advice Looking for "good concrete narratives with credible dialogue and solid use of original detail. It must be unique, honest and have a glimpse of some truth. Send an error-free final draft with a short cover letter and bio. Read us first to see what we publish."

◻ COAL CITY REVIEW

Coal City Press, University of Kansas, Lawrence KS 66045. E-mail: coalcity@sunflower.com. **Contact:** Mary Wharff, fiction editor. Literary magazine/journal: 8½×5½, 124 pages, heavy cover. Includes photographs. Annual. Estab. 1990. Circ. 200.

Needs Experimental, literary. Does not want erotica, horror, romance, mystery. Receives 10-20 mss/month. Accepts 8-10 mss/issue. Does not read November-March. Manuscript published up to 1 year after acceptance. Agented fiction 0%. **Publishes 5-10 new writers/year.** Published Daniel A. Hoyt, Bill Church, Laurie Martin-Frydman (debut), Tasha Haas, Marc Dickinson (debut), Elspeth Wood. Length: 50 words (min)—4,000 words (max). Average length: 2,000 words. Publishes short shorts. Average length of short shorts: 250 words. Also publishes literary criticism, poetry. Sometimes comments on/critiques rejected manuscripts.

How to Contact Submit via e-mail to coalcity@sunflower.com. Attach Word file. Include estimated word count, brief bio, list of publications. Responds to mss in 4 months. Send disposable copy of ms and #10 SASE for reply only. Considers simultaneous submissions. Sample copy available for $7. Guidelines available via e-mail.

Payment/Terms Writers receive 2 contributor's copies. Additional copies $5. Pays on publication. Acquires one-time rights. Publication is copyrighted.

Advice "We are looking for artful stories—with great language and great heart. Please do not send work that has not been thoughtfully and carefully revised or edited."

$ ☑ COLORADO REVIEW

Center for Literary Publishing, Department of English, 9105 Campus Delivery, Colorado State University, Fort Collins CO 80523. (970)491-5449. E-mail: creview@colostate.edu. Web site: http://colorad oreview.colostate.edu. **Contact:** Stephanie G'Schwind, editor. Literary journal: 224 pages; 60 lb. book weight paper. Estab. 1956. Circ. 1,100.

Needs Ethnic/multicultural, experimental, literary, mainstream, contemporary. "No genre fiction." Receives 1,000 unsolicited mss/month. Accepts 4-5 mss/issue. Does not read mss May-August. Publishes ms within 1 year after acceptance. Recently published work by Paul Mandelbaum, Ann Hood, Kent Haruf, Charles Baxter, and Bret Lott. Also publishes poetry.

How to Contact Send complete ms. Responds in 2 months to mss. Sample copy for $10. Writer's guidelines online. Reviews fiction.

Payment/Terms Pays $5/page plus two contributor's copies. Pays on publication for first North American serial rights. Rights revert to author upon publication. Sends galleys to author.

Advice "We are interested in manuscripts that show craft, imagination and a convincing voice. If a story has reached a level of technical competence, we are receptive to the fiction working on its own terms. The oldest advice is still the best: persistence. Approach every aspect of the writing process with pride, conscientiousness—from word choice to manuscript appearance. Be familiar with the *Colorado Review*; read a couple of issues before submitting your manuscript."

COLUMBIA: A JOURNAL OF LITERATURE AND ART

2960 Broadway, 415 Dodge Hall, New York NY 10027. Fax: (212)854-7704. E-mail: columbiajournal @columbia.org. Web site: www.columbiajournal.org. **Contact:** Editor-in-Chief. Magazine: 6×9; 176 pages; glossy cover; illustrations; photos. "We publish the very best contemporary poetry, fiction and creative nonfiction from emerging and established writers." Annual. Estab. 1977. Circ. 2,000.

Needs Ethnic/multicultural, experimental, historical, humor/satire, literary, translations. "We are not interested in children's literature or genre pieces, unless they can be considered to transcend the genre and be of interest to the general reader." Receives 50+ unsolicited mss/month. Publishes ms 1-12 months after acceptance. Agented fiction 70%. **Publishes 2-4 new writers/year.** Recently published work by Rebecca Curtis, Aimee Bender, Etgar Keret, Jonathan Lethem, Deb Olin Unferth. Length: 5,000 words; average length: 3,000 words. Publishes short shorts. Rarely comments on rejected mss.

How to Contact Send complete ms. Responds in 3 months to queries. Accepts simultaneous, multiple submissions. Sample copy for $8. Writer's guidelines online.

Payment/Terms Acquires first North American serial rights. Sponsors awards/contests.

CONCHO RIVER REVIEW

Angelo State University, English Dept., Box 10894 ASU Station, San Angelo TX 76904. (325)942-2269, ext. 230. Fax: (325)942-2208. E-mail: me.hartje@angelo.edu. Web site: www.angelo.edu/dept/english/concho_river_review.htm. **Contact:** Terry Dalrymple, fiction editor. Magazine: 6½×9; 100-125 pages; 60 lb. Ardor offset paper; Classic Laid Color cover stock; b&w drawings. "We publish any fiction of high quality—no thematic specialties." Semiannual. Estab. 1987. Circ. 300.

Needs Ethnic/multicultural, historical, humor/satire, literary, regional, western. Also publishes poetry, nonfiction, book reviews. "No erotica; no science fiction." Receives 10-15 unsolicited mss/month. Accepts 3-6 mss/issue; 8-10 mss/year. Publishes ms 4-6 months after acceptance. **Publishes 4 new writers/year.** Recently published work by Gordon Alexander, Riley Froh, Gretchen Geralds, Kimberly Willis Holt. Length: 1,500-5,000 words; average length: 3,500 words.

How to Contact Send electric copy upon acceptance. Responds in 3 weeks to queries. Accepts simultaneous submissions (if noted). Sample copy for $4. Writer's guidelines for #10 SASE. Reviews fiction.

Payment/Terms Pays in contributor's copies; $5 charge for extras. Acquires first rights.

Advice "We prefer a clear sense of conflict, strong characterization and effective dialogue."

Ⓝ ☑ CONTROLLED BURN

Kirtland Community College, 10775 N. St. Helen Rd. Roscommon MI 48653. (989)275-5000, ext. 386. E-mail: cburn@kirtland.edu. **Contact:** Carol Finke. Literary magazine/journal: 150 pages. "Our job is to take the best writing we get without regard to style, subject matter or form." Annual. Estab. 1995. Circ. 600.

Needs Literary fiction, whether serious or humorous. Does not want badly written work. Receives 100 mss/month. Accepts 3-5 mss/issue; 3-5 mss/year. Reads mss from May 1 through December 1. Manuscript published 4-6 months after acceptance. **Publishes 4-5 new writers/year.** Published Jim Daniels, Dennis Hinrichsen, David Dodd Lee, Brenda Flanagan. Length: 100-8,000. Average length: 5,000. Publishes short shorts. Average length of short shorts: 500. Also publishes poetry.

How to Contact Send complete ms with cover letter. Include brief bio, list of publications. Responds to queries in 4-6 weeks. Responds to mss in 4-6 weeks. Send disposable copy of ms and #10 SASE for reply only. Also accepts email submissions. Considers multiple submissions if identified as such. Sample copy available for $3. Guidelines available for SASE.

Payment/Terms Writers receive 2 contributors copies. Pays on publication. Acquires one-time rights.

Advice "Read our magazine to get a feel for what we publish. Then send us your best work."

COTTONWOOD

Box J, 400 Kansas Union, University of Kansas, Lawrence KS 66045-2115. (785)864-2516. Fax: (785)864-4298. E-mail: tlorenz@ku.edu. **Contact:** Tom Lorenz, fiction editor. Magazine: 6×9; 100 pages; illustrations; photos. "*Cottonwood* publishes high quality prose, poetry and artwork and is aimed at an audience that appreciates the same. We have a national scope and reputation while maintaining a strong regional flavor." Semiannual. Estab. 1965. Circ. 500.

Needs "We publish literary prose and poetry." Receives 25-50 unsolicited mss/month. Accepts 5-6 mss/issue; 10-12 mss/year. Publishes ms 6-18 months after acceptance. Agented fiction 10%. **Publishes 1-3 new writers/year.** Recently published work by Connie May Fowler, Oakley Hall, Cris Mazza. Length: 1,000-8,000 words; average length: 2,000-5,000 words. Publishes short shorts. Also publishes literary essays, literary criticism, poetry.

How to Contact SASE for return of ms. Responds in 6 months to mss. Accepts simultaneous submissions. Sample copy for $8.50, 9×12 SAE and $1.90. Reviews fiction.

Payment/Terms Acquires one-time rights.

Advice "We're looking for depth and/or originality of subject matter, engaging voice and style, emotional honesty, command of the material and the structure. *Cottonwood* publishes high quality literary fiction, but we are very open to the work of talented new writers. Write something honest and that you care about and write it as well as you can. Don't hesitate to keep trying us. We sometimes take a piece from a writer we've rejected a number of times. We generally don't like clever, gimmicky writing. The style should be engaging but not claim all the the attention itself."

$ CRAB ORCHARD REVIEW, A Journal of Creative Works

Dept. of English, Faner Hall 2380-Mail Code 4503, Southern Illinois University Carbondale, 1000 Faner Dr. , Carbondale IL 62901-4503. (618)453-6833. Fax: (618)453-8224. E-mail: jtribble@siu.edu. Web site: www.siu.edu/~crborchd **Contact:** Jon Tribble, managing editor. Magazine: 5½×8½; 275 pages; 55 lb. recycled paper, card cover; photo on cover. "We are a general interest literary journal published twice/year. We strive to be a journal that writers admire and readers enjoy. We publish fiction, poetry, creative nonfiction, fiction translations, interviews and reviews." Estab. 1995. Circ. 2,500.

- *Crab Orchard Review* has won Illinois Arts Council Literary Awards and a 2007 Program Grant from the Illinois Arts Council.

Needs Ethnic/multicultural, literary, excerpted novel. No science fiction, romance, western, horror, gothic or children's. Wants more novel excerpts that also stand alone as pieces. List of upcoming themes available on Web site. Receives 9 00 unsolicited mss/month. Accepts 15-20 mss/issue; 20-40 mss/year. Reads February- April and August - October. Publishes ms 9-12 months after acceptance. Agented fiction 1%. **Publishes 2 new writers/year.** Recently published work by Sally Bellerose, Midge Raymond, Terez Rose, Donna Hemans, Melanie Jennings. Length: 1,000-6,500 words; average length: 2,500 words. Also publishes literary essays, poetry. Rarely comments on rejected mss.

How to Contact Send SASE for reply, return of ms. Responds in 3 weeks to queries; 9 months to mss. Accepts simultaneous submissions. Sample copy for $10 . Writer's guidelines for #10 SASE.

Payment/Terms Pays $100 minimum; $20/page maximum, 2 contributor's copies and a year subscription. Acquires first North American serial rights.

Advice "We look for well-written, provocative, fully realized fiction that seeks to engage both the reader's senses and intellect. Don't submit too often to the same market, and don't send manuscripts that you haven't read over carefully. Writers can't rely on spell checkers to catch all errors. Always include a SASE. Read and support the journals you admire so they can continue to survive.''

$CRAZYHORSE

College of Charleston, Dept. of English, 66 George St., Charleston SC 29424. (843)953-7740. E-mail: crazyhorse@cofc.edu. Web site: http://crazyhorse.cofc.edu. **Contact:** Anthony Varallo, fiction editor. Literary magazine: 8³/₄×8¹/₄; 150 pages; illustrations; photos. "*Crazyhorse* publishes writing of fine quality regardless of style, predilection, subject. Editors are especially interested in original writing that engages in the work of honest communication." Raymond Carver called *Crazyhorse* "an indispensable literary magazine of the first order." Semiannual. Estab. 1961. Circ. 2,000.

• Richard Jackson's "This" won a 2004 Pushcart Prize for *Crazyhorse*.

Needs All fiction of fine quality. Receives 200 unsolicited mss/month. Accepts 8-10 mss/issue; 16-20 mss/year. Publishes ms 6-12 months after acceptance. Recently published work by Luke Blanchard, Karen Brown, E. V. Slate, Melanie Rae Thon, Lia Purpura, Carolyn Walker. Length: 25 pages; average length: 15 pages. Publishes short shorts. Also publishes literary essays, poetry.

How to Contact Send SASE for return of ms or disposable copy of ms and #10 SASE for reply only. Responds in 1 week to queries; 3 months to mss. Accepts simultaneous submissions. Sample copy for $5; year subscription for $16. Writer's guidelines for SASE or by e-mail.

Payment/Terms Pays $20 per page and 2 contributor's copies; additional copies $5. Acquires first North American serial rights. Sends galleys to author.

Advice "Write to explore subjects you care about. Clarity of language; subject is one in which something is at stake."

THE CREAM CITY REVIEW

University of Wisconsin-Milwaukee, Box 413, Milwaukee WI 53201. (414)229-4708. E-mail: info@creamcityreview.org. Web site: www.creamcityreview.org. **Contact:** Monica Rausch and Ann Stewart, fiction editors. Magazine: 5¹/₂×8¹/₂; 150-300 pages; 70 lb. offset/perfect bound paper; 80 lb. cover stock; illustrations; photos. "General literary publication—an eclectic and electric selection of the best fiction we can find." Semiannual. Estab. 1975. Circ. 2,000.

Needs Ethnic/multicultural, experimental, literary, regional, translations, flash fiction, literary humor, magical realism, prose poem. "Would like to see more quality fiction. No horror, formulaic, racist, sexist, pornographic, homophobic, science fiction, romance." Receives 300 unsolicited mss/month. Accepts 6-10 mss/issue. Does not read fiction, nonfiction or poetry April-September. **Publishes 10 new writers/year.** Recently published work by Ben Percy, Yannick Murphy, Michael Martone, Stuart Dybek, Laurence Goldstein, Harold Jaffe, Bradford Morrow, Gordon Weaver, Gordon Henry, Louis Owens, Arthur Boozhoo, George Makana Clark, Kyoko Mori. Publishes short shorts. Also publishes literary essays, book reviews, literary criticism, poetry, memoir, comics.

How to Contact Responds in 6 months to mss. Accepts simultaneous, multiple submissions. Sample copy for $7 (back issue), $12 (current issue). Reviews fiction.

Payment/Terms Pays 1-year subscription. Acquires first rights. Rights revert to author after publication. Sponsors awards/contests.

Advice "The best stories are those in which the reader doesn't know what is going to happen or what the writer is trying to do. Avoid formulas. Surprise us with language and stunning characters."

CUTBANK

English Dept., University of Montana, Missoula MT 59812. (406)243-6156. E-mail: cutbank@umontana.edu. Web site: www.cutbankonline.org. **Contact:** Fiction Editor. Magazine: 5¹/₂×8¹/₂; 115-230 pages. "Publishes serious-minded and innovative fiction and poetry from both well known and up-and-coming authors." Semiannual. Estab. 1973. Circ. 1,000.

Needs No "science fiction, fantasy or unproofed manuscripts." "Innovative, challenging, well-written stories. We're always on the look-out for a boldness of form and a rejection of functional fixedness." Receives 200 unsolicited mss/month. Accepts 6-12 mss/year. Does not read mss March 1-September 30. Publishes ms 6 months after acceptance. **Publishes 4 new writers/year.** Recently published work by Kellie Wells and Danielle Dutton. Occasionally comments on rejected mss.

How to Contact SASE. Responds in 4 months to mss. Accepts simultaneous submissions. Sample copy for $4 (current issue $10). Writer's guidelines for SASE or on Web site.

Payment/Terms Pays 2 contributor's copies. Rights revert to author upon publication, with provision

Cutbank receives publication credit. Awards the Montana Prize for Fiction in the spring, as selected by the magazine's editors and an annual guest judge. Contest submissions accepted December-February. $13 entry fee includes subscription.

Advice "Familiarity with the magazine is essential. *Cutbank* is very open to new voices—we have a legacy of publishing acclaimed writers early in their careers—but we will consider only your best work."

CUTTHROAT, A JOURNAL OF THE ARTS

P.O. Box 2414, Durango CO 81302. (970)903-7914. E-mail: cutthroatmag@gmail.com. Web site: www.cutthroatmag.com. **Contact:** Donley Watt, fiction editor for print edition, Beth Alvarado, Fiction editor for online edition. Literary magazine/journal and online magazine: 6×9, 130+ pages, fine cream paper, slick cover. Includes photographs. "We publish only high quality fiction and poetry. We are looking for the cutting edge, the endangered word, fiction with wit, heart, soul and meaning." Annual. Estab. 2005. Member CCLMP.

Needs Ethnic/multicultural, experimental, feminist, humor/satire, literary, mainstream. Does not want romance, horror, historical, fantasy, religious, teen, juvenile. List of upcoming themes available on Web site. Receives 100+ mss/month. Accepts 6 mss/issue; 10-12 mss/year. Does not read from October 1st-March 1st and from June 1st-July 15th. **Publishes 5-8 new writers/year.** Published Summer Wood, Peter Christopher, Jamey Genna, Doug Frelke, Sally Bellerose, Marc Levy. Length: 500 words (min)-5000 words (max). Publishes short shorts. Also publishes book reviews. Send review copies to Pamela Uschuk. Sometimes comments on/critiques rejected mss.

How to Contact Send complete ms with cover letter. Accepts submissions by e-mail. Include estimated word count, brief bio. Responds to queries in 1-2 weeks. Responds to mss in 12-16 weeks. Send either SASE (or IRC) for return of ms or disposable copy of ms and #10 SASE for reply only. Considers simultaneous submissions, multiple submissions. Sample copy available for $10. Guidelines available for SASE, on Web site.

Payment/Terms Writers receive contributor's copies. Additional copies $10. Pays on publication. Acquires first North American serial rights. Sends galleys to author. Publication is copyrighted. "Sponsors the Rick DeMarinis Short Fiction Prize. See separate listing and Web site for more information."

Advice "Read our magazine and see what types of stories we've published. The piece must have heart and soul, excellence in craft."

DESCANT, Ft. Worth's Journal of Fiction and Poetry

Texas Christian University, TCU Box 297270, Ft. Worth TX 76129. (817)257-6537. Fax: (817)257-6239. E-mail: descant@tcu.edu. Web site: www.descant.tcu.edu. **Contact:** Dave Kuhne, editor. Magazine: 6×9; 120-150 pages; acid free paper; paper cover. "*descant* seeks high quality poems and stories in both traditional and innovative form." Annual. Estab. 1956. Circ. 500-750. Member CLMP.

● Offers four cash awards: The $500 Frank O'Connor Award for the best story in an issue; the $250 Gary Wilson Award for an outstanding story in an issue; the $500 Betsy Colquitt Award for the best poem in an issue; the $250 Baskerville Publishers Award for outstanding poem in an issue. Several stories first published by *descant* have appeared in *Best American Short Stories*.

Needs Literary. "No horror, romance, fantasy, erotica." Receives 20-30 unsolicited mss/month. Accepts 25-35 mss/year. Publishes ms 1 year after acceptance. **Publishes 50% new writers/year.** Recently published work by William Harrison, Annette Sanford, Miller Williams, Patricia Chao, Vonesca Stroud, and Walt McDonald. Length: 1,000-5,000 words; average length: 2,500 words. Publishes short shorts. Also publishes poetry.

How to Contact Send complete ms with cover letter. Include estimated word count and brief bio. Responds in 6-8 weeks to mss. Accepts simultaneous submissions. Sample copy for $10. SASE, e-mail or fax.

Payment/Terms 2 Contributor's copies, additional copies $6. Pays on publication for one-time rights. Sponsors awards/contests.

Advice "We look for character and quality of prose. Send your best short work."

THE DOS PASSOS REVIEW

Briery Creek Press, 201 High St., Farmville VA 23909.434-395-2113. E-mail: carrollhackettma@longwood.edu. **Main Contact:** Mary Carroll-Hackett, editor. Literary magazine/journal: digest-sized, 122

pages, 70 lb opaque paper, 80 lb linen cover. Semiannual. Estab. 2004. Member CLMP.
Needs Ethnic/multicultural (general), feminist, gay, lesbian, literary, mainstream, Does not want genre. Receives 50 mss/month. Accepts 10 mss/issue; 21 mss/year. Does not read August 1-January 31. Manuscript published 2 months after acceptance. Publishes 3 new writers/year. Length: 3,000 words (max). Publishes short shorts. Also publishes literary essays, poetry. Never comments on/critiques rejected manuscripts.
How to Contact Send complete ms with cover letter. Include estimated word count, brief bio, list of publications, SASE. Send disposable copy of ms and #10 SASE for reply only. Considers simultaneous submissions, previously published submissions, multiple submissions. Sample copy available for $6.50. Guidelines available for SASE, via e-mail, on Web site.
Payment/Terms Writers receive 2 contributor's copies. Additional copies $6.50. Pays on publication. Acquires first North American serial rights. Publication is copyrighted.
Advice "When selecting fiction, unified ideas, actions, and cohesive character arcs make a manuscript stand out. Proofread."

ECLIPSE, A Literary Journal

Glendale College, 1500 N. Verdugo Rd., Glendale CA 91208. (818)240-1000. Fax: (818)549-9436. E-mail: eclipse@glendale.edu. **Contact:** Bart Edelman, editor. Magazine: 8½ × 5½; 150-200 pages; 60 lb. paper. "*Eclipse* is committed to publishing outstanding fiction and poetry. We look for compelling characters and stories executed in ways that provoke our readers and allow them to understand the world in new ways." Annual. Circ. 1,800. CLMP.
Needs Ethnic/multicultural, experimental, literary. "Does not want horror, religious, science fiction or thriller mss." Receives 50-100 unsolicited mss/month. Accepts 10 mss/year. Publishes ms 6-12 months after acceptance. **Publishes 8 new writers/year.** Recently published work by Amy Sage Webb, Ira Sukrungruang, Richard Schmitt, George Rabasa. Length: 6,000 words; average length: 4,000 words. Publishes short shorts. Also publishes poetry. Sometimes comments on rejected mss.
How to Contact Send complete ms. Responds in 2 weeks to queries; 4-6 weeks to mss. Accepts simultaneous submissions. Sample copy for $8. Writer's guidelines for #10 SASE or by e-mail.
Payment/Terms Pays 2 contributor's copies; additional copies $ 7. Pays on publication for first North American serial rights.
Advice "We look for well crafted fiction, experimental or traditional, with a clear unity of elements. A good story is important, but the writing must transcend the simple act of conveying the story."

EMRYS JOURNAL

The Emrys Foundation, P.O. Box 8813, Greenville SC 29604. E-mail: ldishman@charter.net. Web site: www.emrys.org. **Contact:** L.B. Dishman. Catalog: 9 × 9¾; 120 pages; 80 lb. paper. "We publish short fiction, poetry and creative nonfiction. We are particularly interested in hearing from women and other minorities." Annual. Estab. 1984. Circ. 400.
Needs Literary, contemporary. No religious, sexually explicit or science fiction mss. Accepts approx 18 mss/issue. Reading period: August 1-November 1, no ms will be read outside the reading period. Publishes mss in April. **Publishes several new writers/year.** Recently published work by Jessica Goodfellow and Ron Rash. Length: 5,000 words; average length: 3,500 words. Publishes short shorts.
How to Contact Send complete ms with SASE. Responds after end of reading period. Does not accept simultaneous submissions. Accepts multiple submissions. Sample copy for $15 and 7 × 10 SAE with 4 first-class stamps. Writer's guidelines for #10 SASE.
Payment/Terms Pays in contributor's copies. Acquires first rights.
Advice Looks for previously unpublished literary fiction.

EUREKA LITERARY MAGAZINE

300 E. College Ave., Eureka College, Eureka IL 61530-1500. (309)467-6591. E-mail: elm@eureka.edu. **Contact:** Eric Freeze, editor. Magazine: 6 × 9; 120 pages; 70 lb. white offset paper; 80 lb. gloss cover; photographs (occasionally). "We seek to be open to the best stories that are submitted to us. Our audience is a combination of professors/writers, students of writing and literature, and general readers." Semiannual. Estab. 1992. Circ. 500.
Needs Adventure, ethnic/multicultural, experimental, fantasy (science), feminist, historical, humor/satire, literary, mainstream, mystery/suspense (private eye/hard-boiled, romantic), psychic/supernatural/occult, regional, romance (historical), science fiction (soft/sociological), translations. Would

like to see more "good literary fiction stories, good magical realism, historical fiction. We try to achieve a balance between the traditional and the experimental. We look for the well-crafted story, but essentially any type of story that has depth and substance to it is welcome." Receives 100 unsolicited mss/month. Accepts 10-12 mss/issue; 20-30 mss/year. Does not read mss in summer (May-August). **Publishes 5-6 new writers/year.** Recently published work by Jane Guill, Sarah Strickley, Ray Bradbury, Patrick Madden, Virgil Suarez, Cynthia Gallaher, Wendell Mayo, Tom Noyes, and Brian Doyle. Length: 4,000-6,000 words; average length: 5,000 words. Also publishes short shorts, flash fiction and poetry.

How to Contact Accepts submissions by e-mail. Send SASE for reply, return of ms or send disposable copy of ms. Responds in 2 weeks to electronic queries; 4 months to mss. Accepts simultaneous, multiple submissions. Sample copy for $7.50.

Advice "Do something that hasn't been done a thousand times already. Give us unusual characters in unusual conflicts—clear resolution isn't always necessary, but it's nice. We don't hold to hard and fast rules about length, but most stories could do with some cutting. Make sure your title is relevant and eye-catching. Please do not send personal gifts or hate mail. We're a college-operated magazine, so we do not actually exist in summer. If we don't take a submission, that doesn't automatically mean we don't like it—we try to encourage authors who show promise to revise and resubmit. Order a copy if you can."

EVANSVILLE REVIEW

University of Evansville, 1800 Lincoln Ave., Evansville IN 47722. (812)488-1042. **Contact:** Fiction editor. Magazine: 6×9; 180 pages; 70 lb. white paper; glossy full-color cover; perfect bound. Annual. Estab. 1989. Circ. 1,000.

Needs Does not want erotica, fantasy, experimental or children's fiction. "We're open to all creativity. No discrimination. All fiction, screenplays, nonfiction, poetry, interviews and anything in between." Receives 70 unsolicited mss/month. Does not read mss January-August. Agented fiction 2%. **Publishes 20 new writers/year.** Recently published work by John Updike, Arthur Miller, X.J. Kennedy, Jim Barnes, Rita Dove. Also publishes literary essays, poetry.

How to Contact Send SASE for reply, or send a disposable copy of ms. Responds in 1 month to queries; 3 months to mss. Accepts simultaneous, multiple submissions and reprints. Sample copy for $5. Writer's guidelines free.

Payment/Terms Pays 2 contributor's copies. Pays on publication for one-time rights. Not copyrighted.

Advice "Because editorial staff rolls over every 1-2 years, the journal always has a new flavor."

FAULTLINE, Journal of Art and Literature

Dept. of English and Comparative Literature, University of California Irvine, Irvine CA 92697-2650. (949)824-1573. E-mail: faultline@uci.edu. Web site: www.humanities.uci.edu/faultline. **Contact:** Editors change in September each year. Literary magazine: 6×9; 200 pages; illustrations; photos. "We publish the very best of what we recieve. Our interest is quality and literary merit." Annual. Estab. 1992.

Needs Translations, literary fiction, nonfiction up to 20 pages. Receives 150 unsolicited mss/month. Accepts 6-9 mss/year. Does not read mss April-September. Publishes ms 9 months after acceptance. Agented fiction 10-20%. **Publishes 30-40% new writers/year.** Recently published work by Maile Meloy, Aimee Bender, David Benioff, Steve Almond, Helen Maria Viramontes, Thomas Keneally. Publishes short shorts. Also publishes literary essays, poetry.

How to Contact Send SASE for reply, return of ms or send a disposable copy of ms. Responds in 2 weeks to queries; 4 months to mss. Accepts simultaneous submissions. Sample copy for $5. Writer's guidelines for business-size envelope.

Payment/Terms Pays 2 contributor's copies. Pays on publication for one-time rights.

Advice "Our commitment is to publish the best work possible from well-known and emerging authors with vivid and varied voices."

FEMINIST STUDIES

0103 Taliaferro, University of Maryland, College Park MD 20742-7726. (301)405-7415. Fax: (301)405-8395. E-mail: creative@feministstudies.org. Web site: www.feministstudies.org. **Contact:** Minnie Bruce Pratt, creative writing editor. Magazine: journal-sized; about 200 pages; photographs. "We are interested in work that addresses questions of interest to the feminist studies audience, particularly work that pushes past the boundaries of what has been done before. We look for creative work that is intellectually challenging and aesthetically adventurous, that is complicated in dialogue with feminist ideas and concepts, and that shifts our readers into new perspectives on women/gender.'' Triannual. Estab. 1974. Circ. 7,500.

Needs Ethnic/multicultural, feminist, LGBT, contemporary. Receives 20 unsolicited mss/month. Accepts 2-3 mss/issue. "We review fiction and poetry twice a year. Deadline dates are May 1 and December 1. Authors will recieve notice of the board's decision by July 15 and February 15, respectively." Recently published work by Grace M. Cho, Dawn McDuffie, Susanne Davis, Liz Robbins, Maria Mazziotti Gillan, Cathleen Calbert, and Mary Ann Wehler. Sometimes comments on rejected mss.

How to Contact No simultaneous submissions. Sample copy for $17. Writer's guidelines at Web site.

Payment/Terms Pays 2 contributor's copies and 10 tearsheets.

$☑ ☒ FICTION

Department of English, The City College of New York, 138th St. & Convent Ave., New York NY 10031. (212)650-6319. E-mail: fictionmagazine@yahoo.com. Web site: www.fictioninc.com. **Contact:** Mark J. Mirsky, editor. Magazine: 6×9; 150-250 pages; illustrations; occasionally photos. "As the name implies, we publish only fiction; we are looking for the best new writing available, leaning toward the unconventional. *Fiction* has traditionally attempted to make accessible the unaccessible, to bring the experimental to a broader audience." Semiannual. Estab. 1972. Circ. 4,000.

• Stories first published in *Fiction* have been selected for inclusion in the *Pushcart Prize, Best of the Small Presses* anthologies and more recently *Best American Short Stories*.

Needs Experimental, humor/satire (satire), literary, translations, contemporary. No romance, science fiction, etc. Receives 200 unsolicited mss/month. Accepts 12-20 mss/issue; 24-40 mss/year. Reads mss September 15-April 15. Publishes ms 1 year after acceptance. Agented fiction 10-20%. Recently published work by Joyce Carol Oates, John Barth, Robert Musil, Romulus Linney. Publishes short shorts. Sometimes comments on rejected mss.

How to Contact Send complete ms with cover letter and SASE. No e-mail submissions. Responds in 3 months to mss. Accepts simultaneous submissions. Sample copy for $5. Writer's guidelines online.

Payment/Terms Pays $75 plus subscription. Acquires first rights.

Advice "The guiding principle of *Fiction* has always been to go to *terra incognita* in the writing of the imagination and to ask that modern fiction set itself serious questions, if often in absurd and comical voices, interrogating the nature of the real and the fantastic. It represents no particular school of fiction, except the innovative. Its pages have often been a harbor for writers at odds with each other. As a result of its willingness to publish the difficult, experimental, unusual, while not excluding the well known, *Fiction* has a unique reputation in the U.S. and abroad as a journal of future directions."

Ⓝ $☒ ☑ THE FIDDLEHEAD

University of New Brunswick, Campus House, Box 4400, Fredericton NB E3B 5A3 Canada. (506)453-3501. Web site: www.lib.und.ca/texts/fiddlehead. **Contact:** Mark A. Jarman, fiction editor. Magazine: 6×9; 128-160 pages; ink illustrations; photos. "No criteria for publication except quality. For a general audience, including many poets and writers." Quarterly. Estab. 1945. Circ. 1,000.

Needs Literary. Receives 100-150 unsolicited mss/month. Accepts 4-5 mss/issue; 20-40 mss/year. Publishes ms 1 year after acceptance. Agented fiction: small percentage. **Publishes high percentage of new writers/year.** Recently published work by Eric Miller, Ed O'Connor, Jan Conn, Alexander Jackson, and Young Smith. Average length: 3,000 words. Publishes short shorts. Occasionally comments on rejected mss.

How to Contact Send SASE and *Canadian* stamps or IRCs for return of mss. Responds in 6 months to mss. No simultaneous submissions. Sample copy for $15 (US).

Payment/Terms Pays $20 (Canadian)/published page and 1 contributor's copy. Pays on publication for first or one-time rights.

Advice "Less than 5% of the material received is published."

☑ FIRST CLASS

Four-Sep Publications, P.O. Box 86, Friendship IN 47021. E-mail: christopherm@four-sep.com. Web site: www.four-sep.com. **Contact:** Christopher M, editor. Magazine: 4¼×11; 48-60+ pages; 24 lb./60 lb. offset paper; craft cover; illustrations; photos. "*First Class* features short fiction and poetics fr om the cream of the small press and killer unknowns—mingling before your very hungry eyes. I publish plays, too." Biannual. Estab. 1995. Circ. 200-400.

Needs Erotica, literary, science fiction (soft/sociological), satire, drama. "No religious or traditional poetry, or 'boomer angst'—therapy-driven self loathing." Receives 50-70 unsolicited mss/month. Accepts 4-6 mss/issue; 10-12 mss/year. Publishes ms 1 month after acceptance. **Publishes 10-15 new writers/year.** Recently published work by Gerald Locklin, John Bennnet, B.Z. Niditch. Length: 5,000-8,000; average length: 2,000-3,000 words. Publishes short shorts. Also publishes poetry. Sometimes comments on rejected mss.

How to Contact Send SASE or send a disposable copy of ms and #10 SASE for reply only. Responds in 3-5 week to queries. Accepts simultaneous submissions and reprints. Sample copy for $6. Writer's guidelines for #10 SASE. Reviews fiction.

Payment/Terms Pays 1 contributor's copy; additional copies $5. Acquires one-time rights.

Advice "Don't bore me with puppy dogs and the morose/sappy feeling you have about death. Belt out a good, short, thought-provoking, graphic, uncommon piece."

$☑ ⯅ FIVE POINTS, A Journal of Literature and Art

P.O. Box 3999, Georgia State University, Atlanta GA 30302 . (404)463-9484. Fax: (404)651-3167. E-mail: msexton@gsu.edu. Web site: www.webdelsol.com/Five_Points. **Contact:** Megan Sexton, associate editor. Magazine: 6×9; 200 pages; cotton paper; glossy cover; photos. *Five Points* is "committed to publishing work that compels the imagination through the use of fresh and convincing language." Triannual. Estab. 1996. Circ. 2,000.

- Fiction first appearing in *Five Points* has been anthologized in *Best American Fiction*, Pushcart anthologies, and *New Stories from The South*.

Needs List of upcoming themes available for SASE. Receives 250 unsolicited mss/month. Accepts 4 mss/issue; 15-20 mss/year. Does not read mss April 30-September 1. Publishes ms 6 months after acceptance. **Publishes 1 new writer/year.** Recently published work by Frederick Busch, Ursula Hegi, Melanie Rae Thon. Average length: 7,500 words. Publishes short shorts. Also publishes literary essays, poetry. Sometimes comments on rejected mss.

How to Contact Send SASE for reply to query. No simultaneous submissions. Sample copy for $7.

Payment/Terms Pays $15/page minimum ($250 maximum) , free subscription to magazine and 2 contributor's copies; additional copies $4. Acquires first North American serial rights. Sends galleys to author. Sponsors awards/contests.

Advice "We place no limitations on style or content. Our only criteria is excellence. If your writing has an original voice, substance and significance, send it to us. We will publish distinctive, intelligent writing that has something to say and says it in a way that captures and maintains our attention."

☑ ◎ FLINT HILLS REVIEW

Dept. of English, Box 4019, Emporia State University, Emporia KS 66801-5087. (620)341-6916. Fax: (620)341-5547. E-mail: webbamy@emporia.edu. Web site: www.emporia.edu/fhr/. **Contact:** Kevin Rabas, co-editor. Magazine: 9×6; 115 pages; 60 lb. paper; glossy cover; illustrations; photos. "*FHR* seeks work informed by a strong sense of place or region, especially Kansas and the Great Plains region. We seek to provide a publishing venue for writers of the Great Plains and Kansas while also publishing authors whose work evidences a strong sense of place, writing of literary quality, and accomplished use of language and depth of character development." Annual. Estab. 1996. Circ. 300. CLMP.

Needs Ethnic/multicultural, gay, historical, regional (Plains), translations. "No religious, inspirational, children's." Want to see more "writing of literary quality with a strong sense of place." List of upcoming themes online. Receives 5-15 unsolicited mss/month. Accepts 2-5 mss/issue; 2-5 mss/year. Does not read mss April-December. Publishes ms 4 months after acceptance. **Publishes 4 new writers/year.** Recently published work by Kim Stafford, Elizabeth Dodd, Bart Edelman, and Jennifer Henderson. Length: 1 page-5,000; average length: 3,000 words. Publishes short shorts. Also publishes literary essays, literary criticism, poetry.

How to Contact Send a disposable copy of ms and #10 SASE for reply only. Responds in 5 weeks to queries; 6 months to mss. Accepts simultaneous, multiple submissions. Sample copy for $5.50. Writer's guidelines for SASE, by e-mail, fax or on Web site. Reviews fiction.

Payment/Terms Pays 2 contributor's copies; additional copies $5.50. Acquires one-time rights.

Advice "Strong imagery and voice, writing that is informed by place or region, writing of literary quality with depth of character development. Hone the language down to the most literary depiction that is possible in the shortest space that still provides depth of development without excess length."

◪ FLORIDA REVIEW

Dept. of English, University of Central Florida, P.O. Box 161346, Orlando FL 32816-1346. (407)823-2038. E-mail: flreview@mail.ucf.edu. Web site: www.english.ucf.edu/~flreview. **Contact:** Susan Fallows, editor. Magazine: 6×9; 160 pages; semi-gloss full color cover, perfect bound. "We publish fiction of high 'literary' quality—stories that delight, instruct and take risks. Our audience consists of avid readers of fiction, poetry and creative nonfiction." Semiannual. Estab. 1972. Circ. 1,500.

Needs Experimental, literary. "We aren't particularly interested in genre fiction (sci-fi, romance, adventure, etc.) but a good story can transcend any genre." Receives 500 unsolicited mss/month. Accepts 5-7 mss/issue; 10-14 mss/year. Publishes ms 4 months after acceptance. **Publishes 3-5 new writers/year.** Recently published work by Billy Collins, David Huddle, Wendell Mayo, Virgil Suarez. Length: 2,000-7,000 words; average length: 5,000 words. Publishes short shorts. Also publishes creative nonfiction, poetry. Rarely comments on rejected mss.

How to Contact Send complete ms. Send SASE (or IRC) for return of the ms or send disposable copy of the ms and #10 SASE for reply only. Responds in 2 weeks to queries; 2 months to mss. Accepts simultaneous submissions. Sample copy for $6. Writer's guidelines for #10 SASE or online.

Payment/Terms Rights held by UCF, revert to author after publication.

Advice "We're looking for writers with fresh voices and original stories. We like risk."

◪ FLYWAY, A Literary Review

Iowa State University, 206 Ross Hall, Ames IA 50011. (515)294-8273. Fax: (515)294-6814. E-mail: flyway@iastate.edu. Web site: www.flyway.org. **Contact:** Stephen Pett, editor. Literary magazine: 6×9; 64 pages; quality paper; cover stock; some illustrations; photos. "We publish quality fiction with a particular interest in place as a component of 'story,' or with an 'enviromental' sensibility. Our stories are accompanied by brief commentaries by their authors, the sort of thing a writer might say introducing a piece at a reading." Biannual. Estab. 1995. Circ. 500.

Needs Literary. Receives 50 unsolicited mss/month. Accepts 2-5 mss/issue; 10-12 mss/year. Reads mss September 1-May. Publishes ms 5 months after acceptance. **Publishes 7-10 new writers/year.** Recently published work by Naomi Shihab Nye, Gina Ochsner, Ted Kooser. Length: 5,000; average length: 3,500 words. Publishes short shorts. Often comments on rejected mss.

How to Contact Send SASE. Sample copy for $8. Writer's guidelines for SASE.

Payment/Terms Pays 2 contributor's copies; additional copies $6. Acquires one-time rights.

Advice "Quality, originality, voice, drama, tension. Make it as strong as you can."

FOG CITY REVIEW

Fog City Writers, 350 Bay Street, Suite 100-348, San Francisco CA 94133-1966. E-mail: info@fogcitywriters.com. Web site: http://www.fogcitywriters.com. **Contact:** Steven Fichera, Editor. Literary magazine/journal: 6×9; 150-200 pages. "Presently we publish most genres. We look for stories, poems and essays that have a bite to them; be it surprise, shock, sadness, happiness or just gritty." Annual. Estab. 2008.

Needs Adventure, experimental, family saga, fantasy, feminist, gay, historical, horror, humor/satire, lesbian, literary, mainstream, military/war, mystery, new age, religious, romance, science fiction, thriller/espionage, translations, western. Does not want erotica or children's fiction. Receives 100 mss/month. Accepts 10-20 mss/issue. Does not read September-April. Ms published 3-4 months after acceptance. **Publishes 10-15 new writers/year.** Published Michael John Paul Pope, Valerie J. Stokes, Angela Kriger, Gilda Haber, Piero Scaruffi and J. D. Blair. Length: 5000 words (max). Average length: 4,000 words. Also publishes literary essays, literary criticism, poetry. Rarely comments on/critiques rejected mss.

How to Contact Send complete ms with cover letter. Accepts submissions by e-mail, through Web site (preferred), on disk. Include estimated word count, brief bio, list of publications, e-mail address. Responds to queries in 2 months. Send either SASE (or IRC) for return of ms or disposable copy of ms and #10 SASE for reply only. Considers simultaneous submissions. Sample copy available. Guidelines available for SASE, via e-mail, on Web site.

Payment/Terms Writers receive $100-200. Pays on acceptance. Acquires first rights. Publication is copyrighted. "Occasionally sponsors contests. See Web site for details."

Advice "Obviously the writing must be good, but the story must have some meaning or worth. As long as you submit your work with an email address and the proper length, our advice is to go for it. Do not be afraid."

FOLIATE OAK LITERARY MAGAZINE, Foliate Oak Online

University of Arkansas-Monticello, MCB 113, Monticello AR 71656. (870)460-1247. E-mail: foliateoak @uamont.edu. Web site: www.foliateoak.uamont.edu. **Contact**: Diane Payne, faculty advisor. Magazine: 6×9; 80 pages. Monthly. Estab. 1980. Circ. 500.

Needs Adventure, comics/graphic novels, ethnic/multicultural, experimental, family saga, feminist, gay, historical, humor/satire, lesbian, literary, mainstream, science fiction (soft/sociological). No religious, sexist or homophobic work. Receives 80 unsolicited mss/month. Accepts 20 mss/issue; 50 mss/year. Does not read mss May-August. Publishes ms 1 month after acceptance. **Publishes 130 new writers/year.** Recently published work by David Barringer, Thom Didato, Joe Taylor, Molly Giles, Patricia Shevlin, Tony Hoagland. Length: 50- 2,500 words; average length: 1,500 words. Publishes short shorts. Also publishes literary essays, literary criticism, poetry. Rarely comments on rejected mss.

How to Contact Send complete ms as an e-mail attachment (Word or RTF). Postal submissions will not be read. Please include author's name and title of story/poem/essay in e-mail header. In the e-mail, please send contact information and a short bio. Responds in 4 weeks. Only accepts submissions August through April. Accepts simultaneous submissions and multiple submissions. Please contact ASAP if work is accepted elsewhere. Sample copy for SASE and 6×8 envelope. Writer's guidelines online. Reviews fiction.

Payment/Terms Pays contributor's copy. Acquires electronic rights. Sends galleys to author. Not copyrighted.

Advice "We're open to honest, experimental, offbeat, realistic and surprising writing, if it has been edited. Limit poems to five per submission, and one short story or creative nonfiction (less than 2,500 words. You may send up to three flash fictions. PLease put your flash fiction in one attachment. Please don't send more writing until you hear from us regarding your first submission. We are also looking for artwork sent as .jpg or .gif files."

FREEFALL MAGAZINE

The Alexandra Writers' Centre Society, 922 Ninth Ave. SE, Calgary AB T2G 0S4 Canada. (403)264-4730. E-mail: freefallmagazine@yahoo.com. Web site: www.freefallmagazine.ca. **Contact:** Michel ine Maylor, editor-in-chief; Lynn Fraser, managing editor. Magazine: 8½×5¾; 100 pages; bond paper; bond stock; b&w illustrations; photos. "*FreeFall* features the best of new, emerging writers and gives them the chance to get into print along with established writers. Now in its 18th year, *FreeFall* seeks to attract readers looking for well-crafted stories, poetry and artwork." Semiannual. Estab. 1990. Circ. 650. Alberta Magazine Publishers Association (AMPA). Canadian Magazines.

Needs Literary fiction, poetry, nonfiction, artwork, photography, and reviews. Accepts 3-5 mss/ issue; 6-10 mss/year. Reads July and January. Publishes ms 4-6 months after acceptance. **Publishes 40% new writers/year.** Length: 500-3,000 words.

How to Contact Send SASE (or IRC) for return of ms, or send a disposable copy of ms with e-mail address or #10 SASE for reply only. Responds in 3 months to mss. Sample copy for $10 (US). Writer's guidelines for SASE, e-mail or on Web site.

Payment/Terms Pays 1 contributor's copy; additional copies $10 (US). Acquires first North American serial, one-time rights.

Advice "We look for thoughtful word usage, craftmanship, strong voice and unique expression coupled with clarity and narrative structure. Professional, clean presentation of work is essential. Carefully read *FreeFall* guidelines before submitting. Do not fold manuscript, and submit 9×11 envelope. Include SASE/IRC for reply and/or return of manuscript. You may contact us by e-mail after initial hardcopy submission. For accepted pieces a request is made for disk or e-mail copy. Strong Web presence attracts submissions from writers all over the world."

☐ FRESH BOILED PEANUTS

E-mail: freshboiledpress@gmail.com. Web site: www.freshboiledpeanuts.com. "We embrace the fact that literary magazines are a dime a dozen. We have no grand illusions of money or fame. We publish for the sake of the work itself. So it better be good." Semiannual. Estab. 2004.

Needs "Open to all fiction categories." Also publishes literary essays, literary criticism, poetry. Sometimes comments on rejected mss.

How to Contact Send complete ms. Accepts submissions by e-mail only (must be a .doc file or .txt file). Responds in 2-3 months to mss. Accepts simultaneous, multiple submissions. Sample copy available online. Writer's guidelines online.

Payment/Terms Pays 1 contributor's copy. Acquires one-time rights.

Advice "Please be sure to visit our Web site for up-to-date submission guidelines."

⚎ ☑ FRONT & CENTRE

Black Bile Press, 573 Gainsborough Ave., Ottawa ON K2A 2Y6 Canada. (613)729-8973. E-mail: firth@istar.ca. Web site: www.ardentdreams.com/bbp. **Contact:** Matthew Firth, editor. Magazine: half letter-size; 40-50 pages; illustrations; photos. "We look for new fiction from Canadian and international writers—bold, aggressive work that does not compromise quality." Three issues per year. Estab. 1998. Circ. 500.

Needs Literary ("contemporary realism/gritty urban"). "No science fiction, horror, mainstream, romance or religious." Receives 20 unsolicited mss/month. Accepts 6-7 mss/issue; 10-20 mss/year. Publishes ms 6 months after acceptance. Agented fiction 10%. **Publishes 8-9 new writers/year.** Recently published work by Len Gasparini, Katharine Coldiron, Salvatore Difalco, Gerald Locklin, Amanda Earl, Tom Johns. Length: 50-4,000 words; average length: 2,500 words. Publishes short shorts. Always comments on rejected mss.

How to Contact Send SASE (from Canada) (or IRCs from USA) for return of ms or send a disposable copy of ms with #10 SASE for reply only. Responds in 2 weeks to queries; 4 months to mss. Accepts multiple submissions. Sample copy for $5. Writer's guidelines for SASE or by e-mail. Reviews fiction.

Payment/Terms Acquires first rights. Not copyrighted.

Advice "We look for attention to detail, unique voice, not overtly derivative, bold writing, not pretentious. We should like to see more realism. Read the magazine first—simple as that!"

$☑ FUGUE

200 Brink Hall, University of Idaho, P.O. Box 441102, Moscow ID 83844-1102. (208)885-6156. Fax: (208)885-5944. E-mail: fugue@uidaho.edu. Web site: www.uidaho.edu/fugue. **Contact:** Fiction editor. Magazine: 6×9; 175 pages; 70 lb. stock paper. By allowing the voices of established writers to lend their authority to new and emerging writers, *Fugue* strives to provide its readers with the most compelling stories, poems, essays, interviews and literary criticism possible. Semiannual. Estab. 1990. Circ. 1,400.

● Work published in *Fugue* has won the Pushcart Prize and has been cited in *Best American Essays*.

Needs Ethnic/multicultural, experimental, humor/satire, literary. Receives 80 unsolicited mss/month. Accepts 6-8 mss/issue; 12-15 mss/year. Does not read mss May 1-August 31. Publishes ms 6 months after acceptance. **Publishes 4-6 new writers/year.** Recently published work by Kent Nelson, Marilyn Krysl, Cary Holladay, Padgett Powell, Dean Young, W.S. Merwin, Matthew Vollmer. Publishes short shorts. Also publishes literary essays, literary criticism, poetry. Sometimes comments on rejected mss.

How to Contact Send complete ms. Send SASE (or IRC) for return of the ms or disposable copy of the ms and #10 SASE for reply only. Responds in 3-4 months to mss. Accepts simultaneous submissions. Sample copy for $8. Writer's guidelines for SASE or on Web site.

Payment/Terms Pays $10 minimum and 1 contributor copy as well as a one-year subscription to the magazine; additional copies $5. Pays on publication for first North American serial, electronic rights.

Advice "The best way, of course, to determine what we're looking for is to read the journal. As the name *Fugue* indicates, our goal is to present a wide range of literary perspectives. We like stories that satisfy us both intellectually and emotionally, with fresh language and characters so captivating that they stick with us and invite a second reading. We are also seeking creative literary criticism which illuminates a piece of literature or a specific writer by examining that writer's personal experience."

⬤ GARGOYLE

3819 N. 13th St., Arlington VA 22201. (703)525-9296. E-mail: gargoyle@gargoylemagazine.com. Web site: www.gargoylemagazine.com. **Contact:** Richard Peabody and Lucinda Ebersole, editors. Literary magazine: 5½×8½; 200 pages; illustrations; photos. *"Gargoyle Magazine* has always been a scallywag magazine, a maverick magazine, a bit too academic for the underground and way too underground for the academics. We are a writer's magazine in that we are read by other writers and have never worried about reaching the masses." Annual. Estab. 1976. Circ. 2,000.

Needs Erotica, ethnic/multicultural, experimental, gay, lesbian, literary, mainstream, translations. "No romance, horror, science fiction." Wants "edgy realism or experimental works. We run both." Wants to see more Canadian, British, Australian and Third World fiction. Receives 50-200 unsolicited mss/month. Accepts 10-15 mss/issue. Accepts submissions during June, July, and Aug. Publishes ms 6-12 months after acceptance. Agented fiction 5%. **Publishes 2-3 new writers/year.** Recently published work by Naomi Ayala, Toby Barlow, Laura Chester, Pat MacEnulty, Toby Olson, Kit Reed, Megan Elizabeth Swades and Paul West. Length: 30 pages maximum; average length: 5-10 pages. Publishes short shorts. Also publishes literary essays, literary criticism, poetry. Sometimes comments on rejected mss.

How to Contact We prefer electronic submissions. Please send in the body of a letter. For snail mail, send SASE for reply, return of ms or send a disposable copy of ms. Responds in 2 weeks to queries; 3 months to mss. Accepts simultaneous submissions. Sample copy for $12.95.

Payment/Terms Pays 1 contributor's copy; additional copies for ½ price. Acquires first North American serial, and first British rights. Sends galleys to author.

Advice "We have to fall in love with a particular fiction."

◻ GEORGETOWN REVIEW

G and R Publishing, Box 227, 400 East College St., Georgetown KY 40324. (502)863-8308. Fax: (502)868-8888. E-mail: gtownreview@georgetowncollege.edu. Web site: http://georgetownreview. georgetowncollege.edu. **Contact:** Steven Carter, editor. Literary magazine/journal: 6×9, 192 pages, 20 lb. paper, four-color 60 lb. glossy cover. "We publish the best fiction we receive, regardless of theme or genre." Annual. Estab. 1993. Circ. 1,000. Member CLMP.

Needs Ethnic/multicultural (general), experimental, literary. Does not want adventure, children's, fantasy, romance. Receives 100-125 mss/month. Accepts 8-10 mss/issue; 15-20 mss/year. Does not read March 16-August 31. Manuscript published 1 month-2 years after acceptance. Agented fiction 0%. **Publishes 3-4 new writers/year.**Published Liz Funk (debut), Laura Selby, Sallie Bingham, David Romtvedt, Carla Panciera. Average length: 4,000 words. Publishes short shorts. Average length of short shorts: 500-1,500 words. Also publishes literary essays, poetry. Sometimes comments on/critiques rejected manuscripts.

How to Contact Send complete ms with cover letter. Include brief bio, list of publications. Responds to queries in 1 month. Responds to mss in 1-3 months. Send either SASE (or IRC) for return of ms or disposable copy of ms and #10 SASE for reply only. Considers simultaneous submissions. Sample copy available for $6.50. Guidelines available on Web site.

Payment/Terms Writers receive 2 contributor's copies, free subscription to the magazine. Additional copies $5. Pays on publication. Acquires first North American serial rights. Publication is copyrighted. "Sponsors annual contest with $1,000 prize. Check Web site for guidelines."

Advice "We look for fiction that is well written and that has a story line that keeps our interest. Don't send a first draft, and even if we don't take your first, second, or third submission, keep trying."

$◻ ⬤ THE GEORGIA REVIEW

The University of Georgia, 012 Gilbert Hall, University of Georgia, Athens GA 30602-9009. (706)542-3481. Fax: (706)542-0047. Web site: www.uga.edu/garev. **Contact:** Stephen Corey, editor. Journal: 7×10; 208 pages (average); 50 lb. woven old-style paper; 80 lb. cover stock; illustrations; photos. "Our readers are educated, inquisitive people who read a lot of work in the areas we feature, so they expect only the best in our pages. All work submitted should show evidence that the writer is at least as well educated and well-read as our readers. Essays should be authoritative but accessible to a range of readers." Quarterly. Estab. 1947. Circ. 4,000.

● Stories first published in *The Georgia Review* have been anthologized in *Best American Short Stories*, *Best American Mystery Stories*, *New Stories from The South* and the *Pushcart Prize Collection*. *The Georgia Review* won the National Magazine Award in essays in 2007.

Needs "Ordinarily we do not publish novel excerpts or works translated into English, and we strongly discourage authors from submitting these." Receives 300 unsolicited mss/month. Accepts 3-4 mss/issue; 12-15 mss/year. Does not read unsolicited mss May 5-August 15. Publishes ms 6 months after acceptance. **Publishes some new writers/year.** Recently published work by Lee K. Abbot, Kevin Brockmeier, Mary Hood, Joyce Carol Oates, George Singleton. Also publishes literary essays, literary criticism, poetry. Occasionally comments on rejected mss.

How to Contact Send complete ms. Responds in 2 weeks to queries; 2-4 months to mss. No simultaneous submissions. Sample copy for $7. Writer's guidelines online.

Payment/Terms Pays $50/published page. Pays on publication for first North American serial rights. Sends galleys to author.

$⊘ ▨ THE GETTYSBURG REVIEW

Gettysburg College, Gettysburg PA 17325. (717)337-6770. Fax: (717)337-6775. Web site: www.gettysburgreview.com. **Contact:** Peter Stitt, editor. Magazine: 6¹/₄×10; 170 pages; acid free paper; full color illustrations. "Our concern is quality. Manuscripts submitted here should be extremely well written." Reading period September-May. Quarterly. Estab. 1988. Circ. 4,000.

- Work appearing in *The Gettysburg Review* has also been included in *Prize Stories: The O. Henry Awards*, *Pushcart Prize* anthology, *Best American Fiction*, *New Stories from The South*, *Harper's* and elsewhere. It is also the recipient of a Lila Wallace-Reader's Digest grant and NEA grants.

Needs Experimental, historical, humor/satire, literary, mainstream, novel excerpts, regional, serialized novels, contemporary. "We require that fiction be intelligent and esthetically written." Receives 350 unsolicited mss/month. Accepts 15-20 mss/issue; 60-80 mss/year. Publishes ms within 1 year after acceptance. **Publishes 1-5 new writers/year.** Recently published work by Robert Olen Butler, Joyce Carol Oates, Naeem Murr, Tom Perrotta, Alison Baker, Alice Fulton. Length: 2,000-7,000 words; average length: 3,000 words. Publishes short shorts. Also publishes literary essays, literary criticism, poetry. Sometimes comments on rejected mss.

How to Contact Send complete ms with SASE. Responds in 1 month to queries; 3-6 months to mss. Accepts simultaneous submissions. Sample copy for $7. Writer's guidelines online.

Payment/Terms Pays $30/page. Pays on publication for first North American serial rights.

Advice "Reporting time can take more than three months. It is helpful to look at a sample copy of *The Gettysburg Review* to see what kinds of fiction we publish before submitting."

⊘ GINOSKO

P.O. Box 246, Fairfax CA 94978. Web site: www.GinoskoLiteraryJournal.com. **Contact**: Paul Cesaretti, editor. Magazine. Ghin-oce-koe: to perceive, understand, come to know; knowledge that has an inception, an attainment; the recognition of truth by personal experience. "Writing that lifts up the grace and beauty of human frailty yet carries with it the strength and veracity of humility, compassion, belief." Published semiannually. Estab. 2003. Circ. 2,000 +.

Needs Short fiction, poetry, creative nonfiction; download issues off Web site for tone & style. Receives 80- 100 unsolicited mss/month. **Publishes 4 new writers/year.** Recently publi shed work by Lisa Harris, Stephanie Dickinson, Michael Hettich, Leonore Wilson, Gayle Elen Harvey, Martin Steele, Devin Wayne Davis. Selects work from ezine for printed anthology.

How to Contact Send complete ms. Accepts submissions by e-mail (ginoskoeditor@aol.com) and snail mail. Responds in 1-3 months to mss. Accepts simultaneous and reprints submissions.

Payment/Terms Not copyrighted.

Advice "Between literary vision and spiritual realities."

$⊘ ▨ GLIMMER TRAIN STORIES

Glimmer Train Press, Inc., 1211 NW Glisan St. #207, Portland OR 97209. (503)221-0836. Fax: (503)221-0837. E-mail: eds@glimmertrain.org. Web site: www.glimmertrain.org. **Contact:** Susan Burmeister-Brown and Linda B. Swanson-Davies. Magazine: 7¹/₄×9¹/₄; 225 pages; recycled; acid-free paper; 12 photographs. "We are interested in literary short stories published by new and established writers." Quarterly. Estab. 1991. Circ. 16,000.

- The magazine also sponsors a short story contest for new writers, a very short fiction (under 3000 words) contest and a family-themed contest.

Needs Literary. Receives 4,000 unsolicited mss/month. Accepts 10 mss/issue; 40 mss/year. Publishes ms up to 18 months after acceptance. Agented fiction 5%. **Publishes 15 new writers/year.**

Recently published work by Judy Budnitz, Nancy Reisman, Herman Carrillo, Andre Dubus III, William Trevor, Alberto Rios, Alice Mattison. Sometimes comments on rejected mss.

How to Contact Submit work online atwww.glimmertrain.org. Different submission categories are open each month of the year. Accepted work published in *Glimmer Train Stories*. Responds in 2 months to mss. Accepts simultaneous submissions. Sample copy for $12 on Web site. Writer's guidelines online.

Payment/Terms Pays $700 for standard submissions, up to $2,000 for contest winning stories. Pays on acceptance for first rights.

Advice "When a story stays with us after the first reading, it gets another reading. Those stories that simply don't let us set them aside get published."

☑ GLOBAL CITY REVIEW

City College of New York, 138th St. and Convent Ave., New York NY 10031. E-mail: globalcityreview @ccny.cuny.edu. Web site: www.webdelsol.com/globalcityreview. **Contact:** Linsey Abrams. Magazine: 140 pages; stock paper; cardstock cover. "The perspective of *GCR* is feminist—women are an important focus, as are writers who write from a gay and lesbian or minority position, culturally decentralized voices because of age or culture, international perspectives, the silenced, the poor, etc. The point is an opening of literary space." Semiannual. Estab. 1993. Circ. 500. CLMP.

Needs Ethnic/multicultural (general), experimental, feminist, gay, lesbian, literary, translations. "No genre fiction." Receives 25-30 unsolicited mss/month. Accepts 4-6 mss/issue; 8-12 mss/year. Publishes short shorts. Also publishes literary essays, literary criticism, poetry.

How to Contact Send a disposable copy of ms and #10 SASE for reply only. Responds in 2-6 months to mss. Accepts simultaneous submissions. Sample copy for $8.50. Writer's guidelines for SASE or on Web site. Reviews fiction.

Payment/Terms Pays 2 contributor's copies; additional copies $8.50. Acquires one-time rights.

$ ☑ ☑ GRAIN LITERARY MAGAZINE

Saskatchewan Writers Guild, P.O. Box 67, Saskatoon SK S7K 3K1 Canada. (306)244-2828. Fax: (306)244-0255. Web site: www.grainmagazine.ca. **Contact:** Kent Bruyneel, editor. Literary magazine: 6×9; 128 pages; Chinook offset printing; chrome-coated stock; some photos. "*Grain* publishes writing of the highest quality, both traditional and innovative in nature. *Grain* aim: To publish work that challenges readers; to encourage promising new writers; and to produce a well-designed, visually interesting magazine." Quarterly. Estab. 1973. Circ. 1,500.

Needs Experimental, literary, mainstream, contemporary, prose poem, poetry. "No romance, confession, science fiction, vignettes, mystery." Receives 80 unsolicited mss/month. Accepts 8-12 mss/ issue; 32-48 mss/year. Publishes ms 11 months after acceptance. Recently published work by Yann Martel, Tom Wayman, Lorna Crozier. Also publishes poetry. Occasionally comments on rejected mss.

How to Contact Send complete ms with SASE (or IRC) and brief letter. Accepts queries by e-mail, mail, fax, phone. Responds in 1 month to queries; 4 months to mss. No simultaneous submissions. Sample copy for $13 or online. Writer's guidelines for #10 SASE or online.

Payment/Terms Pays $50-225. Pays on publication for first Canadian serial rights.

Advice "Submit a story to us that will deepen the imaginative experience of our readers. *Grain* has established itself as a first-class magazine of serious fiction. We receive submissions from around the world. Do not use U.S. postage stamps on your return envelope. Without sufficient Canadian postage or an International Reply Coupon, we *will not* read or reply to your submission. We look for attention to detail, credibility, lucid use of language and metaphor and a confident, convincing voice. Make sure you have researched your piece, that the literal and metaphorical support one another."

☐ GRANTA, The Magazine of New Writing

Granta Publications, 12 Addison Ave., London England W11 4QR United Kingdom. (44)(020)7 605 1360. E-mail: editorial@granta.com. Web site: www.granta.com. **Contact:** Jason Cowley, editor. Magazine: paperback, 256 pages approx; photos. "*Granta* magazine publishes fiction, reportage, biography and autobiography, history, travel and documentary photography. It does not publish 'writing about writing.' The realistic narrative—the story—is its primary form." Quarterly. Estab. 1979. Circ. 80,000.

Needs Literary, novel excerpts. No genre fiction. Themes decided as deadline approaches. Receives 100 unsolicited mss/month. Accepts 0-1 mss/issue; 1-2 mss/year. **Publishes 1-2 new writers/year.**
How to Contact Send SAE and IRCs for reply, return of ms or send a disposable copy of ms. Responds in 3 months to mss. Accepts simultaneous submissions. Sample copy for $14.95. Writer's guidelines online.
Payment/Terms Payment varies. Pays on publication. Buys world English language rights, first serial rights (minimum). "We hold more rights in pieces we commission." Sends galleys to author.
Advice "We are looking for the best in realistic stories; originality of voice; without jargon, connivance or self-conscious 'performance'—writing that endures."

GRASSLIMB

Grasslimb, P.O. Box 420816, San Diego CA 92142. E-mail: editor@grasslimb.com. Web site: www.grasslimb.com. **Contact:** Valerie Polichar, editor. Magazine: 14×20; 8 pages; 60 lb. white paper; illustrations. "*Grasslimb* publishes literary prose, poetry and art. Fiction is best when it is short and avant-garde or otherwise experimental." Semiannual. Estab. 2002. Circ. 200.
Needs Ethnic/multicultural, experimental, gay, literary, mystery/suspense (crime), regional, thriller/espionage, translations. Does not want romance or religious writings. Accepts 2-4 mss/issue; 4-8 mss/year. Publishes ms 3-6 months after acceptance. **Publishes 4 new writers/year.** Recently published work by Grá Linnaea, Kuzhali Manickavel, Park Dorris. Length: 500-2,000 words; average length: 1,500 words. Publishes short shorts. Also publishes poetry. Rarely comments on rejected mss.
How to Contact Send complete ms. Send SASE for return of ms or disposable copy of ms and #10 SASE for reply only. Responds in 4 months to mss. Accepts simultaneous and reprints, multiple submissions. Sample copy for $2.50. Writer's guidelines for SASE, e-mail or on Web site. Reviews fiction.
Payment/Terms Writers receive $5 minimum; $50 maximum, and 2 contributor's copies; additional copies $3. Pays on acceptance for first print publication serial rights.
Advice "We publish brief fiction work that can be read in a single sitting over a cup of coffee. Work can be serious or light, but is generally 'literary' in nature, rather than mainstream. Experimental work welcome. Remember to have your work proofread and to send short work. We cannot read over 2,500 and prefer under 2,000 words. Include word count."

GREEN MOUNTAINS REVIEW

Johnson State College, Johnson VT 05656. (802)635-1350. E-mail: gmr@jsc.vsc.edu. Web site: http://greenmountainsreview.jsc.vsc.edu. **Contact:** Leslie Daniels, fiction editor. Magazine: digest-sized; 160-200 pages. Semiannual. Estab. 1975. Circ. 1,700.
   ● *Green Mountains Review* has received a Pushcart Prize and Editor's Choice Award.
Needs Adventure, experimental, humor/satire, literary, mainstream, serialized novels, translations. Receives 100 unsolicited mss/month. Accepts 6 mss/issue; 12 mss/year. "Manuscripts received between March 1 and September 1 will not be read and will be returned." Publishes ms 6-12 months after acceptance. **Publishes 0-4 new writers/year.** Recently published work by Howard Norman, Debra Spark, Valerie Miner, Peter LaSalle. Publishes short shorts. Also publishes literary criticism, poetry. Sometimes comments on rejected mss.
How to Contact Send complete ms and SASE. Responds in 1 month to queries; 6 months to mss. Accepts simultaneous submissions if advised. Sample copy for $7.
Payment/Terms Pays contributor's copies, 1-year subscription and small honorarium, depending on grants. Acquires first North American serial rights. Rights revert to author upon request.

THE GREENSBORO REVIEW

3302 Hall for Humanities and Research Administration, UNC Greensboro, P.O. Box 26170, Greensboro NC 27402-6170. (336)334-5459. E-mail: jlclark@uncg.edu. Web site: www.greensbororeview.org. **Contact:** Jim Clark, editor. Magazine: 6×9; approximately 128 pages; 60 lb. paper; 80 lb. cover. Literary magazine featuring fiction and poetry for readers interested in contemporary literature. Semiannual. Circ. 800.
   ● Stories for *The Greensboro Review* have been included in *Best American Short Stories*, *The O. Henry Awards Prize Stories*, *New Stories from The South*, and *Pushcart Prize*.
Needs Accepts 6-8 mss/issue; 12-16 mss/year. Unsolicited manuscripts must arrive by September

15 to be considered for the spring issue and by February 15 to be considered for the fall issue. Manuscripts arriving after those dates may be held for the next consideration. **Publishes 10% new writers/year.** Recently published work by Robert Morgan, George Singleton, Robert Olmstead, Brock Clarke, Dale Ray Phillips, Kelly Cherry.

How to Contact Responds in 4 months to mss. Accepts multiple submissions. No simultaneous submissions. Sample copy for $5.

Payment/Terms Pays in contributor's copies. Acquires first North American serial rights.

Advice "We want to see the best being written regardless of theme, subject or style."

THE GRIFFIN

Gwynedd-Mercy College, P.O. Box 901, 1325 Sumneytown Pike, Gwynedd Valley PA 19437-0901. (215)646-7300, ext. 256. Fax: (215)641-5517. E-mail: allego.d@gmc.edu. **Contact:** Donna Allego, editor. Literary magazine: $8\frac{1}{2} \times 5\frac{1}{2}$; 112 pages. "*The Griffin* is a literary journal sponsored by Gwynedd-Mercy College. Its mission is to enrich society by nurturing and promoting creative writing that demonstrates a unique and intelligent voice. We seek writing which accurately reflects the human condition with all its intellectual, emotional and ethical challenges." Annual. Estab. 1999. Circ. 500.

Needs Short stories, essays and poetry. Open to genre work. "No slasher, graphic violence or sex." Accepts mss depending on the quality of work submitted. Receives 20-30 unsolicited mss/month. Publishes ms 6-9 months after acceptance. **Publishes 10-15 new writers/year.** Length: 2,500 words; average length: 2,000 words. Publishes short shorts. Also publishes literary essays, poetry.

How to Contact Send complete ms. All submissions must be on disk and include a hard copy. Send disposable copy of ms, disk and #10 SASE for reply only. Responds in 2-3 months to queries; 6 months to mss. Accepts simultaneous submissions "if notified." Sample copy for $8.

Payment/Terms Pays 2 contributor's copies; additional copies for $8.

Advice "Looking for well-constructed works that explore universal qualities, respect for the individual and community, justice and integrity. Check our description and criteria. Rewrite until you're sure every word counts. We publish the best work we find regardless of industry needs."

GUD MAGAZINE

Greatest Uncommon Denominator Publishing, P.O. Box 1025, Acton CA 93510-1025. (603)397-3843. E-mail: editor@gudmagazine.com. Web site: www.gudmagazine.com. **Contact:** Kaolin Fire, founding editor. Literary magazine/journal. "*GUD Magazine* transcends and encompasses the audiences of both genre and literary fiction. Published twice a year in an attractive 5" ×8" perfect bound, 200+ page format, *GUD* features fiction (from flash to 15,000 word stories), art, poetry, essays and reports and short drama. See Web site for more." Estab. 2006.

Needs Adventure, erotica, ethnic/multicultural, experimental, fantasy, horror, humor/satire, literary, science fiction, why. Accepts 40 mss/year. Manuscript published 6 months after acceptance. Length: 15,000 words (max).

How to Contact Submit via online form only. Responds to mss in up to 6 months. Considers simultaneous submissions, previously published submissions, and multiple submissions. Guidelines available on Web site.

Advice "Be warned: We read a lot. We've seen it all before. We are not easy to impress. Is your work original? Does it have something to say? Read it again. If you genuinely believe it to be so, send it. But first read the guidelines."

◪ GULF STREAM MAGAZINE

Florida International University, English Dept., Biscayne Bay Campus, 3000 N.E. 151st St., N. Miami FL 33181-3000. (305)919-5599. E-mail: gulfstreamfiu@yahoo.com. **Contact:** Corey Ginsberg, editor. Magazine: $5\frac{1}{2} \times 8\frac{1}{2}$; 124 pages; recycled paper; 80 lb. glossy cover; cover illustrations. "We publish *good quality*—fiction, nonfiction and poetry for a predominately literary market." Semiannual. Estab. 1989. Circ. 1,000.

Needs Literary, mainstream, contemporary. Does not want romance, historical, juvenile or religious work. Receives 250 unsolicited mss/month. Accepts 5 mss/issue; 10 mss/year. Does not read mss during the summer. Publishes ms 3-6 months after acceptance. **Publishes 2-5 new writers/year.** Recently published work by Leonard Nash, Jesse Millner, Lyn Millner, Peter Meinke, Susan Neville. Length: 7,500 words; average length: 5,000 words. Publishes short shorts. Also publishes poetry.

How to Contact Responds in 6 months to mss. Accepts simultaneous submissions "if noted." Sample copy for $5. Writer's guidelines for #10 SASE.

Payment/Terms Pays in gift subscriptions and contributor's copies. Acquires first North American serial rights.

Advice "Looks for fresh, original writing—well plotted stories with unforgettable characters, fresh poetry and experimental writing. Usually longer stories do not get accepted. There are exceptions, however."

ℕ Ⓓ HAPA NUI, READER-DRIVEN CONTENT

967 Garden Street, East Palo Alto CA 94303. E-mail: editors@hapanui.com. Web site: www.hapanui.com. **Contact:** Julianne Bonnet, editor. Print and online literary magazine/journal. Size: 4.25×5.5, 200 pages. Contains illustrations. Includes photographs. "In Hawaiian, 'hapa nui' means majority or large part. The concept of the reader-driven lit mag is at the heart of what we see as a new movement in literature. One part on-line venue and one part print journal, *Hapa Nui* is a placce where readers determine through a democratic voting process what they like and, ultimately, which work makes it into print. Submit your work or just come back and vote to participate in this new literary revolution." Annual. Estab. 2008. Circ. 250. Member CLMP.

Needs Ethnic/multicultural (general), experimental, family saga, feminist, gay, historical (general), humor/satire, lesbian, literary, mainstream, mystery. Does not want space fantasy, sword and sorcery, religious, overly spiritual or children's/juvenile. Receives 100 mss/month. Accepts up to 52 mss/year. Ms published 1-12 months after acceptance. **Publishes 37% new writers/year.** Published Joyce Nower, Changming Yuan and Rob Carney. Length: 2,500 words (max). Average length: 1,500 words. Publishes short shorts. Average length of short shorts: 250 words. Also publishes literary essays, poetry. Sometimes comments on/critiques rejected mss.

How to Contact Send complete ms with cover letter by e-mail. Include estimated word count, brief bio. Responds to mss in 12 weeks. Considers previously published submissions, multiple submissions. Sample copy available for $5. Guidelines available on Web site.

Payment/Terms Writers receive 2 contributer's copies. Additional copies $5. Pays on publication. Acquires first North American serial rights, anthology rights. Sends galleys to author. Publication is copyrighted.

Advice "The first paragraph really needs to pull the reader in. The ending has to support a conclusion to everything leading up to that point. We tend to look for work that really speaks to the human struggle-no matter what the circumstances or surroundings. Read the publication or visit the Web site often to get a idea for editorial preferences."

$Ⓓ HAPPY

46 St. Paul's Avenue, Jersey City, NJ 07306. E-mail: bayardx@gmail.com. **Contact:** Bayard, fiction editor. Magazine: 5½×8; 150-200 pages; 60 lb. text paper; 150 lb. cover; perfect-bound; illustrations; photos. Quarterly. Estab. 1995. Circ. 500.

Needs Erotica, ethnic/multicultural, experimental, fantasy, feminist, gay, horror, humor/satire, lesbian, literary, novel excerpts, psychic/supernatural/occult, science fiction, short stories. No "television rehash or religious nonsense." Wants more work that is "strong, angry, empowering, intelligent, God-like, expressive." Receives 300-500 unsolicited mss/month. Accepts 30-40 mss/issue; 100-150 mss/year. Publishes ms 6-12 months after acceptance. **Publishes 25-30 new writers/year.** Length: 6,000 words maximum; average length: 1,000-3,500 words. Publishes short shorts. Often comments on rejected mss.

How to Contact Send complete ms. Include estimated word count. Send SASE for reply, return of ms or send a disposable copy of ms. Responds in 1 month to queries. Accepts simultaneous submissions. Sample copy for $20. Writer's guidelines for #10 SASE.

Payment/Terms Pays 1-5¢/word. Pays on publication for one-time rights.

Advice "Excite me!"

Ⓓ HARPUR PALATE, A Literary Journal at Binghamton University

English Department, P.O. Box 6000, Binghamton University, Binghamton NY 13902-6000. E-mail: harpur.palate@gmail.com. Web site: http://harpurpalate.binghamton.edu. **Contact:** Kathryn Henion, editor. Magazine: 6×9; 180-200 pages; coated or uncoated paper; 100 lb. coated cover; 4-color art portfolio insert. "We have no restrictions on subject matter or form. Quite simply, send us your highest-quality prose or poetry." Semiannual. Estab. 2000. Circ. 600.

Needs Adventure, ethnic/multicultural, experimental, historical, humor/satire, mainstream, mystery/suspense, novel excerpts, literary, fabulism, magical realism, metafiction, slipstream. Receives 400 unsolicited mss/month. Accepts 5-10 mss/issue; 12-20 mss/year. Publishes ms 1-2 months after acceptance. **Publishes 5 new writers/year.** Recently published work by Lee K. Abbott, Jaimee Wriston Colbert, Joan Connor, Stephen Corey, Viet Dinh, Andrew Farkas, Timothy Liu, Mary Ann Mohanraj, Maura Stanton, Michael Steinberg, Martha Witt. Length: 250-8,000 words; average length: 2,000-4,000 words. Publishes short shorts. Also publishes poetry. Sometimes comments on rejected mss.

How to Contact Send complete ms with a cover letter. Include e-mail address on cover. Include estimated word count, brief bio, list of publications. Send a disposable copy of ms and #10 SASE for reply only. Responds in 1-3 week to queries; 4- 8 months to mss. Accepts simultaneous submissions if stated in the cover letter. Sample copy for $10. Writer's guidelines online.

Payment/Terms Pays 2 copies. Pays on publication for first North American serial, electronic rights. Sponsors awards/contests.

Advice "*Harpur Palate* accepts submissions between July 15 and November 15 for the winter issue, between December 15 and April 15 for the summer issue. *Harpur Palate* sponsors a fiction contest for the summer issue and a poetry contest for the winter issue. We do not accept submissions via e-mail. Almost every literary magazine already says this, but it bears repeating: Look at a recent copy of our publication to get an idea of the kind of writing published."

⬤ HARVARD REVIEW

Harvard University, Lamont Library, Cambridge MA 02138. (617)495-9775. E-mail: harvrev@fas.har vard.edu. Web site: http://hcl.harvard.edu/harvardreview. **Contact:** Christina Thompson, editor. Magazine: 6×9; 192-240 pages; illustrations; photographs. Semiannual. Estab. 1992. Circ. 2,000.

Needs Literary. Receives 200 unsolicited mss/month. Accepts 4 mss/issue; 8 mss/year. Publishes ms 3-6 months after acceptance. **Publishes 3-4 new writers/year.** Recently published work by Joyce Carol Oates, Alice Hoffman, William Lychack, Jim Crace, and Karen Bender. Length: 1,000-7,000 words; average length: 3,000-5,000 words. Publishes short shorts. Also publishes literary essays, literary criticism, poetry, and plays. Sometimes comments on rejected mss.

How to Contact Send SASE for return of ms or disposable copy of ms and SASE for reply only. Responds within 6 months to queries. Accepts simultaneous submissions. Writer's guidelines online.

Payment/Terms Pays 2 contributor's copies; additional copies $7. Pays on publication for first North American serial rights. Sends galleys to author.

⬤ HAWAI'I PACIFIC REVIEW

Hawai'i Pacific University, 1060 Bishop St., Honolulu HI 96813. (808)544-1108. Fax: (808)544-0862. E-mail: pwilson@hpu.edu. Web site: www.hpu.edu. **Contact:** Patrice M. Wilson, editor. Magazine: 6×9; 100 pages; glossy coated cover. "*Hawai'i Pacific Review* is looking for poetry, short fiction and personal essays that speak with a powerful and unique voice. We encourage experimental narrative techniques and poetic styles, and we welcome works in translation." Annual.

Needs Ethnic/multicultural (general), experimental, fantasy, feminist, historical (general), humor/satire, literary, mainstream, regional (Pacific), translations. "Open to all types as long as they're well done. Our audience is adults, so nothing for children/teens." Receives 30-50 unsolicited mss/month. Accepts 5-10 mss/year. Does not read mss January-August each year. Publishes ms 10 months after acceptance. **Publishes 1-2 new writers/year.** Recently published work by Wendell Mayo, Elizabeth Crowell, Janet Flora. Publishes short shorts. Also publishes literary essays, poetry. Sometimes comments on rejected mss.

How to Contact Send SASE for return of ms or send a disposable copy of ms and SASE for reply only. Responds in 2 weeks to queries; 15 weeks to mss. Accepts simultaneous submissions but must be cited in the cover letter. Sample copy for $5.

Payment/Terms Pays 2 contributor's copies; additional copies $7. Pays on publication for first North American serial rights.

Advice "We look for the unusual or original plot; prose with the texture and nuance of poetry. Character development or portrayal must be unusual/original; humanity shown in an original insightful way (or characters); sense of humor where applicable. Be sure it's a draft that has gone through substantial changes, with supervision from a more experienced writer, if you're a beginner. Write about intense emotion and feeling, not just about someone's divorce or shaky relationship. No soap-opera-like fiction."

☑ ☒ HAYDEN'S FERRY REVIEW

The Virginia G. Piper Center for Creative Writing at Arizona State University, Box 875002, Arizona State University, Tempe AZ 85287-5002. (480)965-1337. E-mail: hfr@asu.edu. Web site: www.hayde nsferryreview.org. **Contact:** Beth Staples. Editors change every 1-2 years. Magazine: 6³/₄ × 9³/₄; 150 pages; fine paper; illustrations; photos. "*Hayden's Ferry Review* publishes best quality fiction, poetry, and creative nonfiction from new, emerging and established writers." Semiannual. Estab. 1986. Circ. 1,300.

• Work from *Hayden's Ferry Review* has been selected for inclusion in *Pushcart Prize* anthologies and *Best Creative Nonfiction*.

Needs Ethnic/multicultural, experimental, humor/satire, literary, regional, slice-of-life vignettes, contemporary, prose poem. Possible special fiction issue. Receives 250 unsolicited mss/month. Accepts 5 mss/issue; 10 mss/year. Publishes ms 6 months after acceptance. Recently published work by Joseph Heller, Ron Carlson, Norman Dubie, John Updike, Richard Ford, Yusef Komunyakaa, Joel-Peter Witkin, Ai, David St. John, Gloria Naylor, Tess Gallagher, Ken Kesey, Naomi Shihab Nye, Allen Ginsberg, T.C. Boyle, Raymond Carver, Rita Dove, Chuck Rosenthal, Rick Bass, Charles Baxter, Pam Houston, and Denise Duhamel. Publishes short shorts. Also publishes literary criticism.

How to Contact Send complete ms. SASE. Responds in 2 weeks to queries; 5 months to mss. Accepts simultaneous submissions. Sample copy for $7.50. Writer's guidelines online.

Payment/Terms Pays $25-100. Pays on publication for first North American serial rights. Sends galleys to author.

☑ ◎ HEAVEN BONE

Heaven Bone Press, 62 Woodcock Mtn. Dr. Washingtonvile, NY 10992. (845)496-4109. E-mail: heave nbone@hvc.rr.com. **Contact:** Steven Hirsch and Kirpal Gordon, editors. Magazine: 8¹/₂ × 11; 96-116 pages; 60 lb. recycled offset paper; full color cover; computer clip art, graphics, line art, cartoons, halftones and photos scanned in .tif format. "Expansive, fine surrealist and experimental literary, earth and nature, spiritual path. We use current reviews, essays on spiritual and esoteric topics, creative stories. Also: reviews of current poetry releases and expansive literature." Readers are "scholars, surrealists, poets, artists, muscians, students." Annual. Estab. 1987. Circ. 2,500.

Needs Experimental, fantasy, regional, esoteric/scholarly, spiritual. "No violent, thoughtless, exploitive or religious fiction." Receives 45-110 unsolicited mss/month. Accepts 5-15 mss/issue; 12-30 mss/year. Publishes ms 2 weeks-10 months after acceptance. **Publishes 3-4 new writers/year.** Recently published work by Keith Abbot and Stephen-Paul Martin. Length: 1,200-5,000 words; average length: 3,500 words. Publishes short shorts. Also publishes literary essays, literary criticism, poetry. Sometimes comments on rejected mss.

How to Contact Send SASE for reply or return of ms. Responds in 3 weeks to queries; 10 months to mss. Accepts reprints submissions. Sample copy for $10. Writer's guidelines for SASE. Reviews fiction.

Payment/Terms Pays in contributor's copies; charges for extras. Acquires first North American serial rights. Sends galleys to author.

Advice "Read a sample issue first. Our fiction needs are temperamental, so please query first before submitting. We prefer shorter fiction. Do not send first drafts to test them on us. Please refine and polish your work before sending. Always include SASE. We are looking for the unique, unusual and excellent."

☒ $☑ HOBART, ANOTHER LITERARY JOURNAL

PO Box 1658, Ann Arbor MI 48106. (206)399-0410. E-mail: aaron@hobartpulp.com. Web site: http:// www.hobartpulp.com. **Contact:** Aaron Burch, Editor. Literary magazine/journal. 6×9, 200 pages. Contains illustrations. Includes photographs. "We publish non-stuffy, unpretentious, high quality fiction that never takes itself too serious and always entertains." Semiannual. Estab. 2002. Circ. 1000. Member CLMP.

• Inclusion in *Best American Nonrequired Reading* and *Best American Fantasy*, as well as multiple notable mentions in *Best American Nonrequired Reading* and *Best American Essays*.

Needs Literary. Receives 200 mss/month. Accepts 20 mss/issue; 40 mss/year. Ms published 2-8 months after acceptance. **Publishes 2-5 new writers/year.** Published Benjamin Percy, Tod Goldberg, Chris Bachelder, Sheila Heti, Stephany Aulenback, Catherine Zeidler and Ryan Call. Length: 1000 words (min)-7000 words (max). Average length: 3000 words. Publishes short shorts. Also publishes literary essays. Sometimes comments on/critiques rejected mss.

How to Contact Send complete ms with cover letter. Accepts submissions by e-mail. Responds to queries in 2 weeks. Responds to mss in 1-4 months. Send disposable copy of ms and #10 SASE for reply only. Considers simultaneous submissions. Sample copy available for $2. Guidelines available for SASE, via e-mail, on Web site.

Payment/Terms Writers receive $50-150, 2 contributor's copies, free subscription to the magazine. Additional copies $5. Pays on publication. Acquires first rights. Publication is copyrighted.

Advice "We'd love to receive fewer run-of-the-mill relationship stories and more stories concerning truck drivers, lumberjacks, carnival workers, and gunslingers. In other words: surprise us. Show us a side of life rarely depicted in literary fiction."

HOME PLANET NEWS

Home Planet Publications, P.O. Box 455, High Falls NY 12440. (845)687-4084. **Contact:** Donald Lev, editor. Tabloid: 11½×16; 24 pages; newsprint; illustrations; photos. "*Home Planet News* publishes mainly poetry along with some fiction, as well as reviews (books, theater and art) and articles of literary interest. We see *HPN* as a quality literary journal in an eminently readable format and with content that is urban, urbane and politically aware." Triannual. Estab. 1979. Circ. 1,000.

• *HPN* has received a small grant from the Puffin Foundation for its focus on AIDS issues.

Needs Ethnic/multicultural, experimental, feminist, gay, historical, lesbian, literary, mainstream, science fiction (soft/sociological). No "children's or genre stories (except rarely some science fiction)." Publishes special fiction issue or anthology. Receives 12 unsolicited mss/month. Accepts 1 mss/issue; 3 mss/year. Publishes ms 1 year after acceptance. Recently published work by Hugh Fox, Walter Jackman, Jim Story. Length: 500-2,500 words; average length: 2,000 words. Publishes short shorts. Also publishes literary criticism.

How to Contact Send complete ms. Send SASE for reply, return of ms or send a disposable copy of the ms. Responds in 6 months to mss. Sample copy for $4. Writer's guidelines for SASE.

Payment/Terms Pays 3 contributor's copies; additional copies $1. Acquires one-time rights.

Advice "We use very little fiction, and a story we accept just has to grab us. We need short pieces of some complexity, stories about complex people facing situations which resist simple resolutions."

$ THE IDAHO REVIEW

Boise State University, English Dept., 1910 University Dr., Boise ID 83725. (208)426-1002. Fax: (208)426-4373. E-mail: mwieland@boisestate.edu. **Contact:** Mitch Wieland, editor. Magazine: 6×9; 180-200 pages; acid-free accent opaque paper; coated cover stock; photos. "A literary journal for anyone who enjoys good fiction." Annual. Estab. 1998. Circ. 1,000. Member CLMP.

• Recent stories reprinted in *The Best American Short Stories, The O. Henry Prize Stories, The Pushcart Prize,* and *New Stories from The South.*

Needs Experimental, literary. "No genre fiction of any type." Receives 150 unsolicited mss/month. Accepts 5-7 mss/issue; 5-7 mss/year. "We do not read from May 1-August 31." Publishes ms 1 year after acceptance. Agented fiction 5%. **Publishes 1 new writers/year.** Recently published work by Rick Bass, Melanie Rae Thon, Ron Carlson, Joy Williams, Madison Smartt Bell, Carolyn Cooke. Length: open; average length: 7,000 words. Publishes short shorts. Also publishes literary essays, poetry. Sometimes comments on rejected mss.

How to Contact Send SASE for return of ms or send a disposable copy of ms and #10 SASE for reply only. Responds in 3-5 months to mss. Accepts simultaneous, multiple submissions. Sample copy for $8.95. Writer's guidelines for SASE. Reviews fiction.

Payment/Terms Pays $100 when funds are available plus 2 contributor's copies; additional copies $5. Pays on publication for first North American serial rights. Sends galleys to author.

Advice "We look for strongly crafted work that tells a story that needs to be told. We demand vision and intlligence and mystery in the fiction we publish."

ILLUMINATIONS, An International Magazine of Contemporary Writing

Dept. of English, College of Charleston, 66 George St., Charleston SC 29424-0001. (843)953-1920. Fax: (843)953-1924. E-mail: lewiss@cofc.edu. Web site: www.cofc.edu/illuminations. **Contact:** Simon

Lewis, editor. Magazine: 5×8; 80 pages; illustrations. "*Illuminations* is one of the most challengingly eclectic little literary magazines around, having featured writers from the United States, Britain and Romania , as well as Southern Africa." Annual. Estab. 1982. Circ. 500.

Needs Literary. Receives 5 unsolicited mss/month. Accepts 1 mss/year. **Publishes 1 new writer/ year.** Recently published work by John Michael Cummings. Also publishes poetry. Sometimes comments on rejected mss.

How to Contact Send SASE for reply, return of ms or send a disposable copy of ms. Responds in 2 weeks to queries; 2 months to mss. No simultaneous submissions. Sample copy for $10 and 6×9 envelope. Writer's guidelines free.

Payment/Terms Pays 2 contributor's copies of current issue; 1 of subsequent issue. Acquires one-time rights.

$ ✐ ◎ IMAGE, Art, Faith, Mystery

3307 Third Ave. W, Seattle WA 98119. (206)281-2988. E-mail: image@imagejournal.org. Web site: www.imagejournal.org. **Contact:** Gregory Wolfe. Magazine: 7×10; 136 pages; glossy cover stock; illustrations; photos. "*Image* is a showcase for the encounter between religious faith and world-class contemporary art. Each issue features fiction, poetry, essays, memoirs, an in-depth interview and articles about visual artists, film, music, etc. and glossy 4-color plates of contemporary visual art." Quarterly. Estab. 1989. Circ. 4,500. Member CLMP.

Needs Literary, translations. Receives 100 unsolicited mss/month. Accepts 2 mss/issue; 8 mss/year. Publishes ms 1 year after acceptance. Agented fiction 5%. Recently published work by Annie Dillard, David James Duncan, Robert Olen Butler, Bret Lott, Melanie Rae Thon. Length: 4,000-6,000 words; average length: 5,000 words. Also publishes literary essays, poetry.

How to Contact Send SASE for reply, return of ms or send disposable copy of ms. Responds in 1 month to queries; 3 months to mss. Sample copy for $16. Reviews fiction.

Payment/Terms Pays $10/page and 4 contributor's copies; additional copies for $6. Pays on acceptance. Sends galleys to author.

Advice "Fiction must grapple with religious faith, though the settings and subjects need not be overtly religious."

$ ✐ ☒ INDIANA REVIEW

Indiana University, Ballantine Hall 465, 1020 E. Kirkwood, Bloomington IN 47405-7103. (812)855-3439. Web site: www.indianareview.org. **Contact:** Fiction editor. Magazine: 6×9; 160 pages; 50 lb. paper; Glatfelter cover stock. "*Indiana Review*, a nonprofit organization run by IU graduate students, is a journal of previously unpublished poetry and fiction. Literary interviews and essays also considered. We publish innovative fiction and poetry. We're interested in energy, originality and careful attention to craft. While we publish many well-known writers, we also welcome new and emerging poets and fiction writers." Semiannual. Estab. 1976. Circ. 2,000.

● Work published in *Indiana Review* received a Pushcart Prize (2001) and was included in *Best New American Voices* (2001). *IR* also received an Indiana Arts Council Grant and a NEA grant.

Needs Ethnic/multicultural, experimental, literary, mainstream, novel excerpts, regional, translations. No genre fiction. Receives 300 unsolicited mss/month. Accepts 7-9 mss/issue. Reads year round, but refer to web site for closed submission periods. Publishes ms an average of 3-6 months after acceptance. **Publishes 6-8 new writers/year.** Recently published work by Stuart Dybek, Marilyn Chin, Ray Gonzalez, Abby Frucht. Also publishes literary essays, poetry.

How to Contact Send complete ms. Accepts submissions by e-mail. Cover letters should be *brief* and demonstrate specific familiarity with the content of a recent issue of *Indiana Review*. Include SASE. Responds in 4 months to mss. Accepts simultaneous submissions if notified *immediately* of other publication. Sample copy for $9. Writer's guidelines online.

Payment/Terms Pays $5/page, plus 2 contributor's copies. Pays on publication for first North American serial rights. Sponsors awards/contests.

Advice "Because our editors change each year, so do our literary preferences. It's important that potential contributors are familiar with our most recent issue of *Indiana Review* via library, sample copy or subscription. Beyond that, we look for prose that is well crafted and socially relevant. Dig deep. Don't accept your first choice descriptions when you are revising. Cliché and easy images sink 90% of the stories we reject. Understand the magazines you send to—investigate!"

INKWELL MAGAZINE

Manhattanville College, 2900 Purchase St., Purchase NY 10577. (914)323-7239. E-mail: inkwell@mvi lle.edu. Web site: www.inkwelljournal.org. **Contact:** Fiction editor. Literary Journal: 5½×7½; 120-170 pages; 60 lb. paper; 10 pt C1S, 4/c cover; illustrations; photos. *"Inkwell Magazine* is committed to presenting top quality poetry, prose and artwork in a high quality publication. *Inkwell* is dedicated to discovering new talent and to encouraging and bringing talents of working writers and artists to a wider audience. We encourage diverse voices and have an open submission policy for both art and literature." Annual. Estab. 1995. Circ. 1,000. Member CLMP.

Needs Experimental, humor/satire, literary. "No erotica, children's literature, romance, religious." Receives 120 unsolicited mss/month. Accepts 45 mss/issue. Does not read mss December-July. Publishes ms 2 months after acceptance. **Publishes 3-5 new writers/year.** Recently published work by Alice Quinn, Margaret Gibson, Benjamin Cheever, Paul Muldoon, Pablo Medina, Carol Muske-Dukes. Length: 5,000 words; average length: 3,000 words. Publishes short shorts. Also publishes poetry.

How to Contact Send a disposable copy of ms and #10 SASE for reply only. Responds in 1 month to queries; 4-6 months to mss. Sample copy for $6. Writer's guidelines for SASE.

Payment/Terms Pays contributor's copies and sends complimentary copies; additional copies $8. Acquires first North American serial, first rights. Sponsors awards/contests.

Advice "We look for well-crafted original stories with a strong voice."

$ THE IOWA REVIEW

308 EPB, The University of Iowa, Iowa City IA 52242. (319)335-0462. Fax: (319)335-2535. Web site: www.iowareview.org. **Contact:** Fiction Editor. Magazine: 5½×8½; 200 pages; first-grade offset paper; Carolina CS1 10-pt. cover stock. "Stories, essays, poems for a general readership interested in contemporary literature." Triannual magazine. Estab. 1970. Circ. 2,500.

Needs "We are open to a range of styles and voices and always hope to be surprised by work we then feel we need." Receives 600 unsolicited mss/month. Accepts 4-6 mss/issue; 12-18 mss/year. Does not read mss January-August. Publishes ms an average of 12-18 months after acceptance. Agented fiction less than 2%. **Publishes some new writers/year.** Recently published work by Benjamin Chambers, Pierre Hauser, Stellar Kim. Also publishes literary essays, literary criticism, poetry.

How to Contact Send complete ms with cover letter. "Don't bother with queries." SASE for return of ms. Responds in 3 months to queries; 3 months to mss. "We discourage simultaneous submissions." Sample copy for $9 and online. Writer's guidelines online. Reviews fiction.

Payment/Terms Pays $25 for the first page and $15 for each additional page, plus 2 contributor's copies; additional copies 30% off cover price. Pays on publication for first North American serial, nonexclusive anthology, classroom, online serial rights.

Advice "We have no set guidelines as to content or length; we look for what we consider to be the best writing available to us and are pleased when writers we believe we have discovered catch on with a wider range of readers. It is never a bad idea to look through an issue or two of the magazine prior to a submission."

$ ISOTOPE

A Journal of Literary Nature and Science Writing, 3200 Old Main Hill, Logan UT 84322-3200. (435)797-3697. Fax: (435)797-3797. E-mail: lbrown@cc.usu.edu. Web site: isotope.usu.edu. **Contact:** Charles Waugh, fiction editor. Literary magazine/journal: 8½×11, 52 pages. Contains illustrations. Includes photographs. "Focus on nature and science writing that meditates on and engages in the varied and complex relations among the human and non-human worlds." Semiannual. Estab. 2003. Circ. 1,000. Member CLMP.

Needs Experimental, humor/satire, literary, translations. Special interests: nature and science. Receives 10 mss/month. Accepts 1-2 mss/issue; 2-4 mss/year. Does not read October 16 through June 30. Manuscript published 6-18 months after acceptance. **Publishes 2 new writers/year.** Published Jill Stegman, Emily Doak, Janette Fecteau. Length: 250-7,500. Average length: 5,000. Publishes short shorts. Average length of short shorts: 500. Also publishes literary essays, poetry. Rarely comments on/critiques rejected mss.

How to Contact Send complete ms with cover letter. Include brief bio, list of publications. Send either SASE (or IRC) for return of ms or disposable copy of ms and #10 SASE for reply only. Considers simultaneous submissions, multiple short submissions. Sample copy available for $5. Guidelines available on Web site.

Payment/Terms Writers receive $100 per story, 4 contributor's copies, free subscription to the magazine. Additional copies $4. Pays on publication. Acquires first North American serial rights. Sends galleys to author. Publication is copyrighted.

ⓝ ⍉ ◎ J JOURNAL: New Writing on Justice

Dept. of English, John Jay College of Criminal Justice, 619 West 54th Street, 7th Floor, New York NY 10019. E-mail: journal@jjay.cuny.edu. **Contact:** Adam Berlin and Jeffrey Heiman, editors. Literary magazine/journal: 6×9; 120 pages; 60 lb paper; 80 lb cover. "*J* is a literary journal publishing fiction, poetry and creative nonfiction on the subjects of crime, criminal justice, law and law enforcement. While the themes are specific, they need not dominate the work. We're interested in questions of justice from all perspectives." Semiannual. Estab. 2008.

Needs Experimental, gay, historical (general), literary, military/war, mystery, regional. Receives 100 mss/month. Accepts 5 mss/issue; 10 mss/year. Does not read July and August. Ms published 6 months after acceptance. Length: 750-6,000 words. Average length: 4,000 words. Also publishes poetry. Sometimes comments on/critiques rejected mss.

How to Contact Send complete ms with cover letter. Include estimated word count, brief bio, list of publications. Responds to queries in 4 weeks; mss in 12 weeks. Send disposable copy of ms and #10 SASE for reply only. Considers simultaneous submissions. Sample copy available for $10. Guidelines available via e-mail.

Payment/Terms Writers receive 2 contributor's copies. Additional copies $10. Pays on publication. Acquires first rights. Publication is copyrighted.

Advice "We're looking for literary fiction with some connection to the subject of justice."

⍉ THE JABBERWOCK REVIEW

Mississippi State University, Drawer E, Dept. of English, Mississippi State MS 39762. (662)325-3644. E-mail: jabberwock@org.msstate.edu. Web site: www.msstate.edu/org/jabberwock. **Contact:** fiction editor (revolving editorship). Magazine: 8½×5½; 120 pages; glossy cover; illustrations; photos. "We are located in the South—love the South—but we publish good writing from anywhere and everywhere. And from anyone. We respect writers of reputation—and print their work—but we take great delight in publishing new and emerging writers as well." Semiannual. Estab. 1979. Circ. 500.

Needs Ethnic/multicultural, experimental, feminist, gay, literary, mainstream, regional, translations. "No science fiction, romance." Receives 150 unsolicited mss/month. Accepts 7-8 mss/issue; 15 mss/year. "We do not read March 15 to September 1." Publishes ms 4-6 months after acceptance. **Publishes 1-5 new writers/year.** Recently published work by Robert Morgan, Charles Harper Webb, Ted Kooser, Alison Baker, Alyce Miller, Lorraine Lopez, J.D. Chapman. Length: 250-5,000 words; average length: 4,000 words. Publishes short shorts. Also publishes literary essays, poetry. Sometimes comments on rejected mss.

How to Contact Send SASE (or IRC) for return of ms. Responds in 5 months to mss. Accepts simultaneous submissions "with notification of such." Sample copy for $6. Writer's guidelines for SASE.

Payment/Terms Pays 2 contributor's copies. Sponsors awards/contests.

Advice "It might take a few months to get a response from us, but your manuscript will be read with care. Our editors enjoy reading submissions (really!) and will remember writers who are persistent and commited to getting a story 'right' through revision."

$⍉ THE JOURNAL

The Ohio State University, 164 W. 17th Ave., Columbus OH 43210. (614)292-4076. Fax: (614)292-7816. E-mail: thejournal@osu.edu. Web site: http://english.osu.edu/journals/the_journal.cfm/. **Contact:** Kathy Fagan (poetry); Michelle Herman (fiction). Magazine: 6×9; 150 pages. "We're open to all forms; we tend to favor work that gives evidence of a mature and sophisticated sense of the language." Semiannual. Estab. 1972. Circ. 1,500.

Needs Novel excerpts, literary short stories. No romance, science fiction or religious/devotional. Receives 100 unsolicited mss/month. Accepts 2 mss/issue. Publishes ms 1 year after acceptance. Agented fiction 10%. **Publishes some new writers/year.** Recently published work by Michael Mar-

tone, Gregory Spatz and Stephen Graham Jones. Sometimes comments on rejected mss.
How to Contact Send complete ms with cover letter and SASE. Responds in 2 weeks to queries; 2 months to mss. Accepts simultaneous submissions. No electronic submissions. Sample copy for $7 or online. Writer's guidelines online.
Payment/Terms Pays $20. Pays on publication for first North American serial rights. Sends galleys to author.
Advice "Manuscripts are rejected because of lack of understanding of the short story form, shallow plots, undeveloped characters. Cure: Read as much well-written fiction as possible. Our readers prefer 'psychological' fiction rather than stories with intricate plots. Take care to present a clean, well-typed submission."

🖊 📝 KARAMU

English Dept., Eastern Illinois University, 600 Lincoln Ave., Charleston IL 61920. (217)581-6297. E-mail: cfoxa@eiu.edu. **Contact:** Fiction Editor. Literary magazine: 5×8; 132-150 pages; illustrations. "*Karamu* is a literary magazine of ideas and artistic expression independently produced by the faculty members and associates of Eastern Illinois University. We publish writing that captures something essential about life, which goes beyond superficial, and which develops voice genuinely. Contributions of creative nonfiction, fiction, poetry and artwork of interest to a broadly educated audience are welcome." Annual. Estab. 1966. Circ. 500.
  • *Karamu* has received three Illinois Arts Council Awards.
Needs Adventure, ethnic/multicultural, experimental, feminist, gay, historical, humor/satire, lesbian, literary, mainstream, regional. "No pornographic, science fiction, religious, political or didactic stories—no dogma or proselytizing." List of upcoming editorial themes available for SASE. Receives 80-90 unsolicited mss/month. Accepts 10-15 mss/issue. Does not read February 16-September 1. Publishes ms 1 year after acceptance. **Publishes 3-6 new writers/year.** Recently published work by Paul Pekin, Kathryn Henion, Justin Nicholes, JoeAnn Hart, Michael Phillipps and Kathleen Spivack. Publishes short shorts. Also publishes poetry. Sometimes comments on rejected mss.
How to Contact Send SASE for reply. Responds in 1 week to queries. Does not accepts simultaneous submissions. Sample copy for $8 or 2 for $6 for back issues. Writer's guidelines for SASE.
Payment/Terms Pays 1 contributor's copy; additional copies at discount. Acquires one-time rights.
Advice Looks for "convincing, well-developed characters and plots expressing aspects of human nature or relationships in a perceptive, believable and carefully considered and written way."

$ 🖊 📝 THE KENYON REVIEW

Walton House, 104 College Dr., Gambier OH 43022. (740)427-5208. Fax: (740)427-5417. E-mail: kenyonreview@kenyon.edu. Web site: www.kenyonreview.org. **Contact:** Fiction Editor. An international journal of literature, culture and the arts dedicated to an inclusive representation of the best in new writing (fiction, poetry, essays, interviews, criticism) from established and emerging writers. Estab. 1939. Circ. 6,000.
  • Work published in the *Kenyon Review* has been selected for inclusion in *The O. Henry Prize Stories*, *Pushcart Prize* anthologies, *Best American Short Stories*, and *Best American Poetry*.
Needs Excerpts from novels, condensed novels, ethnic/multicultural, experimental, feminist, gay, historical, humor/satire, lesbian, literary, mainstream, translations, contemporary. Receives 900 unsolicited mss/month. Unsolicited mss typically read only from September 1-January 31. Publishes ms 1 year after acceptance. Recently published work by Alice Hoffman, Beth Ann Fennelly, Romulus Linney, John Koethe, Albert Goldbarth, Erin McGraw.
How to Contact Only accepting mss via online submissions program. Please visit Web site for instructions. Do not submit via e-mail or snail mail. No simultaneous submissions. Sample copy $12 single issue, includes postage and handling. Please call or e-mail to order. Writer's guidelines online.
Payment/Terms Pays $15-40/page. Pays on publication for first rights.
Advice "We look for strong voice, unusual perspective, and power in the writing."

📖 ◎ KEREM, Creative Explorations in Judaism

Jewish Study Center Press, Inc., 3035 Porter St. NW, Washington DC 20008. (202)364-3006. E-mail: langner@erols.com. Web site: www.kerem.org. **Contact:** Sara R. Horowitz and Gilah Langner, editors. Magazine: 6×9; 128 pages; 60 lb. offset paper; glossy cover; illustrations; photos. "*Kerem* publishes Jewish religious, creative, literary material—short stories, poetry, personal reflections, text study, prayers, rituals, etc." Estab. 1992. Circ. 2,000.

Needs Jewish: feminist, humor/satire, literary, religious/inspirational. Receives 10-12 unsolicited mss/month. Accepts 1-2 mss/issue. Publishes ms 2-10 months after acceptance. **Publishes 2 new writers/year.** Also publishes literary essays, poetry.

How to Contact Prefers submissions by e-mail. Send SASE for reply, return of ms or send disposable copy of ms. Responds in 2 months to queries; 5 months to mss. Accepts simultaneous, multiple submissions. Sample copy for $8.50. Writer's guidelines online.

Payment/Terms Pays free subscription and 2-10 contributor's copies. Acquires one-time rights.

Advice "Should have a strong Jewish content. We want to be moved by reading the manuscript!"

$⬚ THE KIT-CAT REVIEW

244 Halstead Ave., Harrison NY 10528. (914)835-4833. E-mail: kitcatreview@gmail.com. **Contact:** Claudia Fletcher, editor. Magazine: $8^1/2 \times 5^1/2$; 75 pages; laser paper; colored card cover stock; illustrations. "*The Kit-Cat Review* is named after the 18th Century Kit-Cat Club, whose members included Addison, Steele, Congreve, Vanbrugh and Garth. Its purpose is to promote/discover excellence and originality." *The Kit-Cat Review* is part of the collections of the University of Wisconsin (Madison) and State University of New York (Buffalo). Quarterly. Estab. 1998. Circ. 500.

Needs Ethnic/multicultural, experimental, literary, novel excerpts, slice-of-life vignettes. No stories with "O. Henry-type formula endings. Shorter pieces stand a better chance of publication." No science fiction, fantasy, romance, horror or new age. Receives 40 unsolicited mss/month. Accepts 6 mss/issue; 24 mss/year. Publishes ms 6-12 months after acceptance. **Publishes 14 new writers/ year.** Recently published work by Chayym Zeldis, Michael Fedo, Louis Phillips, Elisha Porat. Length: 5,000 words maximum; average length: 2,000 words. Publishes short shorts. Also publishes literary essays, literary criticism, poetry.

How to Contact Send complete ms. Accepts submissions by disk. Send SASE (or IRC) for return of ms, or send disposable copy of ms and #10 SASE for reply only. Responds in 1 week to queries; 2 months to mss. Accepts simultaneous, multiple submissions. Sample copy for $7 (payable to Claudia Fletcher). Writer's guidelines not available.

Payment/Terms Pays $25-200 and 2 contributor's copies; additional copies $5. Pays on publication for first rights.

▦ ◎ LA KANCERKLINIKO

% Laurent Septier, 162 rue Paradis, P.O. Box 174, 13444 Marseille Cantini Cedex France. (33)2-48-61-81-98. Fax: (33)2-48-61-81-98. E-mail: lseptier@hotmail.com. **Contact:** Laurent Septier. "An Esperanto magazine which appears 4 times annually. Each issue contains 32 pages. *La Kancerkliniko* is a political and cultural magazine." Quarterly. Circ. 300.

Needs Science fiction, short stories or very short novels. "The short story (or the very short novel) must be written only in Esperanto, either original or translation from any other language." Wants more science fiction. **Publishes 2-3 new writers/year.** Recently published work by Mao Zifu, Manuel de Sabrea, Peter Brown and Aldo de'Giorgi.

How to Contact Accepts submissions by e-mail, fax. Accepts disk submissions. Accepts multiple submissions. Sample copy for 3 IRCs from Universal Postal Union.

Payment/Terms Pays in contributor's copies.

◪ LAKE EFFECT, A Journal of the Literary Arts

Penn State Erie, Humanities and Social Sciences, 5091 Station Rd., Erie PA 16563-1501. (814)898-6281. Fax: (814)898-6032. E-mail: goL1@psu.edu. **Contact:** George Looney, editor-in-chief. Magazine: $5^1/2 \times 8^1/2$; 136-150 pages; 55 lb. natural paper; 12 pt. C1S cover. "In addition to seeking strong, traditional stories, *Lake Effect* is open to more experimental, language-centered fiction as well." Annual. Estab. as *Lake Effect*, 2001; as *Tempest*, 1978. Circ. 500. Member CLMP.

Needs Experimental, literary, mainstream. "No children's/juvenile, fantasy, science fiction, romance or young adult/teen." Receives 120 unsolicited mss/month. Accepts 5-9 mss/issue. Publishes ms 1 year after acceptance. **Publishes 6 new writers/year.** Recently published work by Edith Pearlman, Francois Camoin, Cris Mazza, Joan Connor, Rick Henry, Joanna Howard. Length: 4,500-5,000 words; average length: 2,600-3,900 words. Publishes short shorts. Also publishes literary essays, poetry.

How to Contact Send SASE for return of ms or send a disposable copy of ms and #10 SASE for reply only. Responds in 3 weeks to queries; 4-6 months to mss. Accepts simultaneous submissions. Sample copy for $6. Writer's guidelines for SASE.

Payment/Terms Pays 2 contributor's copies; additional copies $2. Acquires first, one-time rights. Not copyrighted.

Advice "We're looking for strong, well-crafted stories that emerge from character and language more than plot. The language is what makes a story stand out (and a strong sense of voice). Be sure to let us know immediately should a submitted story be accepted elsewhere."

ⓝ LAND-GRANT COLLEGE REVIEW

P.O. Box 1164, New York NY 10159-1164. E-mail: editors@lgcr.org. Web site: www.lgcr.org. **Contact:** Fiction Submission. Magazine: 6×9; 196 pages; 70 lb. Natural Stock paper; 12 point cover stock. "The *Land-Grant College Review* is a nationally distributed literary journal. Recent contributors include Aimee Bender, Josip Novakovich, Robert Olmstead, Ron Carlson and Stephen Dixon." Annual. Estab. 2002. Circ. 4,000.

• Recent Stories in the magazine have been included in *O. Henry Prize Stories* and *Best American Non-Required Reading*.

Needs Literary. No genre fiction, humor for its own sake, or anything "cutesy-pooh." Accepts 16 mss/issue. Publishes ms 3-4 months after acceptance. Agented fiction 10%. **Publishes 2 new writers/year.** Recently published work by Aimee Bender, Josip Novakovich, Robert Olmstead, Ron Carlson, Arthur Bradford, Alan Chuese. Average length: 2,750 words. Publishes short shorts.

How to Contact Send complete ms. Responds in 6-8 months to mss. Accepts simultaneous submissions. Sample copy for $12. Writer's guidelines online.

Payment/Terms Pays in copies. Acquires first North American serial rights.

Advice "Read the magazine first and familiarize yourself with stories we've selected in the past. Send only your absolute best work."

⊕ LANDFALL/OTAGO UNIVERSITY PRESS

Otago University Press, P.O. Box 56, Dunedin New Zealand. Fax: (643)479-8385. E-mail: landfall@otago.ac.nz. **Contact:** Landfall Editor.

Needs Publishes fiction, poetry, commentary and reviews of New Zealand books.

How to Contact Send copy of ms with SASE. Sample copy not available.

Advice "We concentrate on publishing work by New Zealand writers, but occasionally accept work from elsewhere."

☑ ◎ LE FORUM, Supplement Littéraire

Franco-American Research Opportunity Group, University of Maine, Franco American Center, Orono ME 04469-5719. (207)581-3764. Fax: (207)581-1455. E-mail: lisa_michaud@umit.maine.edu. Web site: www.francomaine.org. **Contact:** Lisa Michaud, managing editor. Magazine: 56 pages; illustrations; photos. Publication was founded to stimulate and recognize creative expression among Franco-Americans, all types of readers, including literary and working class. This publication is used in classrooms. Circulated internationally. Quarterly. Estab. 19 72. Circ. 5,000.

Needs "We will consider any type of short fiction, poetry and critical essays having to with Franco-American experience. They must be of good quality in French or English. We are also looking for Canadian writers with French-North American experiences." Receives 10 unsolicited mss/month. Accepts 2-4 mss/issue. **Publishes some new writers/year.** Length: 750-2,500 words; average length: 1,000 words. Occasionally comments on rejected mss.

How to Contact Include SASE. Responds in 3 weeks to queries; 1 month to mss. Accepts simultaneous submissions and reprints. Sample copy not available.

Payment/Terms Pays 3 copies. Acquires one-time rights.

Advice "Write honestly. Start with a strongly felt personal Franco-American experience. If you make us feel what you have felt, we will publish it. We stress that this publication deals specifically with the Franco-American experience."

☑ THE LEDGE MAGAZINE

40 Maple Ave., Bellport NY 11713-2011. (631)286-5252. E-mail: tkmonaghan@aol.com. Web site: www.theledgemagazine.com. **Contact:** Tim Monaghan, publisher. Literary magazine/journal: 6×9,

192 pages, offset paper, glossy stock cover. *"The Ledge Magazine* publishes cutting-edge contemporary fiction by emerging and established wirters."* Annual. Estab. 1988. Circ. 1,000.

Needs Erotica, ethnic/multicultural (general), literary. Receives 60 mss/month. Accepts 3-4 mss/ issue. Manuscript published 6 months after acceptance. Published Xujun Eberlein, Franny French, Clifford Garstang, Richard Jespers, Al Sims. Length: 2,500 words (min)-7,500 words (max). Average length: 6,000 words. Also publishes poetry. Rarely comments on/critiques rejected mss.

How to Contact Send complete ms with cover letter. Include estimated word count, brief bio. Responds to queries in 4 weeks. Responds to mss in 6 months. Send SASE (or IRC) for return of ms. Considers simultaneous submissions. Sample copy available for $10. Subscription: $20 (2 issues), $36 (4 issues). Guidelines available for SASE.

Payment/Terms Writers receive 1 contributor's copy. Additional copies $6. Pays on publication. Acquires first North American serial rights. Sends galleys to author. Publication is copyrighted.

Advice "We seek stories that utilize language in a fresh, original way. Truly compelling stories are especially appreciated. We dislike sloppy or hackneyed writing."

LICHEN, Arts & Letters Preview

234-701 Rossland Road East, Whitby ON L1N 9K3 Canada. E-mail: info@lichenjournal.ca. Web site: www.lichenjournal.ca. **Contact:** Ruth E. Walker and Gwynn Scheltema, fiction editors. Magazine: 5¼×8¼; 144 pages; text/illustrations black ink on Rolland Opaque, Natural 60 lb. 8 page photos black on 80 lb. Coated White paper. *"Lichen* publishes fiction, poetry, plays, essays, reviews, interviews, black & white art and photography by local, Canadian and international writers and artists. We present a unique mix of city and country, of innovation and tradition to a broad spectrum of readers."* Semiannual. Estab. 1999. Circ. 1,000.

• *Lichen* was named runner-up for "Favourite Literary Magazine" in *Write Magazine's* National 2000 Reader Poll.

Needs Literary. "No work that is obtuse, bigoted, banal, or hate-mongering. We will consider almost any subject or style if the work shows clarity and attention to craft." Receives 12-24 unsolicited mss/month. Accepts 5-8 mss/issue; 10-16 mss/year. Publishes ms 2-12 months after acceptance. **Publishes 4-7 new writers/year.** Recently published work by Nancy Holmes, Stan Rogal, J.J. Steinfeld, Brad Smith, George Elliott Clarke. Length: 250-3,000 words; average length: 1,000-2,500 words. Publishes short shorts. Also publishes literary essays, literary criticism, poetry. Sometimes comments on rejected mss.

How to Contact Send complete ms. Accepts submissions by e-mail. Include estimated word count, brief bio and list of publications. Send SASE for return of ms or disposable copy of ms and #10 SASE for reply only. For submissions outside Canada, include IRC with SASE. Responds in 1-4 weeks to queries; 3-6 months to mss. Sample copy for $12. Writer's guidelines online.

Payment/Terms 1 contributor's copy and a 1-year subscription. Pays on publication for first North American serial rights.

Advice "We look for exceptional writing that engages the reader, professional presentation in standard ms format, and an indication of knowledge of the type of writing we publish, as well as knowledge of our submission guidelines. Keep your cover letter brief, not cute."

THE LISTENING EYE

Kent State University Geauga Campus, 14111 Claridon-Troy Rd., Burton OH 44021. (440)286-3840. E-mail: grace_butcher@msn.com. **Contact:** Grace Butcher, editor. Magazine: 5½×8½; 60 pages; photographs. "We publish the occasional very short stories (750 words/3 pages double spaced) in any subject and any style, but the language must be strong, unusual, free from cliché and vagueness. We are a shoestring operation from a small campus but we publish high-quality work." Annual. Estab. 1970. Circ. 250.

Needs Literary. "Pretty much anything will be considered except porn." Reads mss January 1-April 15 only. Publishes ms 3-4 months after acceptance. Recently published work by Elizabeth Scott, Sam Ruddick, H.E. Wright. Publishes short shorts. Also publishes poetry. Sometimes comments on rejected mss.

How to Contact Send SASE for return of ms or disposable copy of ms with SASE for reply only. Responds in 4 weeks to queries; 4 months to mss. Accepts reprint submissions. Sample copy for $3 and $1 postage. Writer's guidelines for SASE.

Payment/Terms Pays 2 contributor's copies; additional copies $3 with $1 postage. Pays on publication for one-time rights.

Advice "We look for powerful, unusual imagery, content and plot. Short, short."

▢ ▨ THE LITERARY REVIEW, An International Journal of Contemporary Writing

Fairleigh Dickinson University, 285 Madison Ave., Madison NJ 07940. (973)443-8564. Fax: (973)443-8364. E-mail: tlr@fdu.edu. Web site: www.theliteraryreview.org. **Contact:** Walter Cummins, editor-in-chief. Magazine: 6×9; 160 pages; professionally printed on textpaper; semigloss card cover; perfect-bound. "Literary magazine specializing in fiction, poetry and essays with an international focus. Our audience is general with a leaning toward scholars, libraries and schools." Quarterly. Estab. 1957. Circ. 2,000.

● Work published in *The Literary Review* has been included in *Editor's Choice, Best American Short Stories* and *Pushcart Prize* anthologies.

Needs Works of high literary quality only. Does not want to see "overused subject matter or pat resolutions to conflicts." Receives 90-100 unsolicited mss/month. Accepts 20-25 mss/year. Does not read submissions February 1-September 1. Publishes ms 1½-2 years after acceptance. Agented fiction 1-2%. **Publishes 80% new writers/year.** Recently published work by Irvin Faust, Todd James Pierce, Joshua Shapiro, Susan Schwartz Senstadt. Also publishes literary essays, literary criticism, poetry. Occasionally comments on rejected mss.

How to Contact Responds in 3-4 months to mss. Submit online atwww.theliteraryreview.org/submit. html only. Accepts multiple submissions. Sample copy for $7. Writer's guidelines for SASE. Reviews fiction.

Payment/Terms Pays 2 contributor's copies; $3 discount for extras. Acquires first rights.

Advice "We want original dramatic situations with complex moral and intellectual resonance and vivid prose. We don't want versions of familiar plots and relationships. Too much of what we are seeing today is openly derivative in subject, plot and prose style. We pride ourselves on spotting new writers with fresh insight and approach."

▢ THE LONG STORY

18 Eaton St., Lawrence MA 01843. (978)686-7638. E-mail: rpburnham@mac.com. Web site: http://web.mac.com/rpburnham/iWeb/Site/LongStory.html. **Contact:** R.P. Burnham. Magazine: 5½×8½; 150-200 pages; 60 lb. cover stock; illustrations (b&w graphics). For serious, educated, literary people. Annual. Estab. 1983. Circ. 1,200.

Needs Ethnic/multicultural, feminist, literary, contemporary. "No science fiction, adventure, romance, etc. We publish high literary quality of any kind but especially look for stories that have difficulty getting published elsewhere—committed fiction, working class settings, left-wing themes, etc." Receives 30-40 unsolicited mss/month. Accepts 6-7 mss/issue. Publishes ms 3 months to 1 year after acceptance. **Publishes 90% new writers/year.** Length: 8,000-20,000 words; average length: 8,000-12,000 words.

How to Contact Include SASE. Responds in 2 months to mss. Accepts simultaneous submissions "but not wild about it." Sample copy for $7.

Payment/Terms Pays 2 contributor's copies; $5 charge for extras. Acquires first rights.

Advice "Read us first and make sure submitted material is the kind we're interested in. Send clear, legible manuscripts. We're not interested in commercial success; rather we want to provide a place for long stories, the most difficult literary form to publish in our country."

▢ ▣ LOUISIANA LITERATURE, A Review of Literature and Humanities

Southeastern Louisiana University, SLU 792, Hammond LA 70402. (985)549-5022. Fax: (504)549-5021. E-mail: ngerman@selu.edu. Web site: www.louisianaliterature.org. **Contact:** Norman German, fiction editor. Magazine: 6×9; 150 pages; 70 lb. paper; card cover; illustrations. "Essays should be about Louisiana material; preference is given to fiction and poetry with Louisiana and Southern themes, but creative work can be set anywhere." Semiannual. Estab. 1984. Circ. 400 paid; 500-700 printed.

Needs Literary, mainstream, regional. "No sloppy, ungrammatical manuscripts." Receives 100 unsolicited mss/month. May not read mss June-July. Publishes ms 6-12 after acceptance. **Publishes 4 new writers/year.** Recently published work by Anthony Bukowski, Tim Parrish, Robert Phillips,

Andrew Otis Haschemeyer. Length: 1,000-6,000 words; average length: 3,500 words. Also publishes literary essays, literary criticism, poetry. Sometimes comments on rejected mss.

How to Contact Include SASE. Responds in 3 months to mss. Sample copy for $8. Reviews fiction.

Payment/Terms Pays usually in contributor's copies. Acquires one-time rights.

Advice "Cut out everything that is not a functioning part of the story. Make sure your manuscript is professionally presented. Use relevant specific detail in every scene. We love detail, local color, voice and craft. Any professional manuscript stands out."

◎ THE LOUISIANA REVIEW

Division of Liberal Arts, Louisiana State University at Eunice, P.O. Box 1129, Eunice LA 70535. (337)550-1315. E-mail: bfonteno@lsue.edu. **Contact:** Dr. Billy Fontenot, editor. Magazine: 8½×5½ bound; 100-200 pages; b&w illustrations. "We are looking for excellent work by Louisiana writers as well as those outside the state who tell us their connection to it." Annual. Estab. 1999. Circ. 300-600.

Needs Ethnic/multicultural (Cajun or Louisiana culture), historical (Louisiana-related or setting), regional (Louisiana, Gulf Coast). Receives 25 unsolicited mss/month. Accepts 5-7 mss/issue. Reads year-round. Publishes ms 6-12 months after acceptance. Recently published work by Tom Bonner, Laura Cario, Sheryl St. Germaine. Length: up to 9,000 words; average length: 2,000 words. Publishes short shorts. Also publishes poetry and b&w artwork. Sometimes comments on rejected mss.

How to Contact Send SASE for return of ms. Responds in 5 weeks to queries; 10 weeks to mss. Accepts multiple submissions. Sample copy for $5.

Payment/Terms Pays 1 contributor's copy. Pays on publication for one-time rights. Not copyrighted but has an ISSN number.

Advice "We do like to have fiction play out visually as a film would rather than static and undramatized. Louisiana or Gulf Coast settings and themes preferred."

◨ THE LOUISVILLE REVIEW

Spalding University, 851 S. Fourth St., Louisville KY 40203. (502)585-9911, ext. 2777. E-mail: louisvillereview@spalding.edu. Web site: www.louisvillereview.org. **Contact:** Sena Jeter Naslund, editor. Literary magazine. "We are a literary journal seeking original stories with fresh imagery and vivid language." Semiannual. Estab. 1976.

Needs Literary. Receives 200+ unsolicited mss/month. Accepts 4-6 fiction mss/issue; 8-12 fiction mss/year. Publishes ms 6 months after acceptance. **Publishes 8-10 new writers/year.** Recently published work by Scott Russell Sanders, Lawrence Millman, Aleda Shirley, Bill Roorbach, and Piotr Florczyk. Publishes essays, fiction, nonfiction and poetry.

How to Contact Send a disposable copy of ms and #10 SASE for reply only. Responds in 6 months to queries; 6 months to mss. Accepts multiple submissions.

Payment/Terms Pays 2 contributor's copies.

LULLWATER REVIEW

Emory University, P.O. Box 22036, Atlanta GA 30322. (404)727-6184. E-mail: lullwaterreview@yahoo.com. (for inquiries only, *NO electronic submissions*). **Contact:** Editors-in-chief. Magazine: 6×9; 100 pages; 60 lb. paper; photos. "*Lullwater Review* seeks submissions that are strong and original. We require no specific genre or subject." Semiannual. Estab. 1990. Circ. 2,000. Member, Council of Literary Magazines and Presses.

Needs Adventure, condensed novels, ethnic/multicultural, experimental, fantasy, historical, humor/satire, mainstream, mystery/suspense, novel excerpts, religious/inspirational, science fiction, slice-of-life vignettes, suspense, western. "No romance or science fiction, please." Receives 75-115 unsolicited mss/month. Accepts 3-7 mss/issue; 6-14 mss/year. Does not read mss in June, July, August. Publishes ms 1-2 months after acceptance. **Publishes 25% new writers/year.** Recently published work by Greg Jenkins, Thomas Juvik, Jimmy Gleacher, Carla Vissers and Judith Sudnolt. Also publishes poetry.

How to Contact Send complete ms. Accepts submissions by postal mail only. Responds in 1-3 months to queries; 3-6 months to mss. Accepts simultaneous submissions. Sample copy for $5. Writer's guidelines for #10 SASE.

Payment/Terms Pays 3 contributor copies. Pays on publication for first North American serial rights. Sponsors awards/contests.

Advice "We at the *Lullwater Review* look for clear cogent writing, strong character development and an engaging approach to the story in out fiction submissions. Stories with particularly strong voices and well-developed central themes are especially encouraged. Be sure that your manuscript is ready before mailing it off to us. Revise, revise, revise!"

$□ LUNCH HOUR STORIES

Lunch Hour Publications, 22833 Bothell-Everett Hwy, STE 110-PMB 1117, Bothell WA 98021. (425)246-3726. Fax: (425)424-8859. E-mail: editor@lunchhourbooks.com. Web site: www.lunchhourstories.com. **Contact:** Nina Bayer, editor. Literary magazine/journal: $5^{1}/_{2} \times 8^{1}/_{2}$, 20 pages, natural linen paper, natural linen cover. "*Lunch Hour Stories* publishes only short stories and distributes them only to paid subscribers. *Lunch Hour Stories* are thin, easy-to-carry booklets that contain one short story each. They are designed to fit easily into a purse or briefcase and be read in less than 60 minutes. They are distributed by mail 16 times per year (minimum of one issue per month). Estab. Jan 2007.

Needs Literary, mainstream. Special interests: "Literary only." Does not want genre (romance, sci-fi, fantasy, etc.); experimental; religious; children's/young adult; feminist/gay; erotica. Accepts 1 mss/issue; 16 mss/year. Manuscript published 6-18 months after acceptance. Length: 4,000 words (min)-8,000 words (max). Average length: 6,000 words. Also publishes annual anthology of very short stories (less than 500 words). See Web site for full submissions guidelines. Often comments on/critiques rejected mss.

How to Contact Send one printed copy with a cover letter. Include word count, brief bio, contact information, SASE, synopsis of 100 words. Responds to mss in 3-6 months. Send disposable copy of ms and #10 SASE for reply only. Considers multiple and simultaneous submissions. Sample copy $2.50 in US, $4 worldwide with SASE (6 × 9). Guidelines and annual contest information available on Web site.

Payment/Terms Writers receive $50 flat-rate payment, 10 contributor's copies, and free one-year subscription to the magazine. Additional copies $2.50 in US, $4 worldwide. Pays on publication. Acquires first worldwide English language serial rights. All stories must be previously unpublished. Rights revert back to author following publication, with some limitations for the first year. Sends galleys to author. Publication is copyrighted.

Advice "Stories should be well written and carefully edited. They should be engrossing, humorous, warm or moving. They should make us want to read them more than once and then share them with a friend. We encourage new writers to step out and take a chance! Do your best work, share it with a critique group, and then share it with us."

☑ THE MACGUFFIN

Schoolcraft College, Department of English, 18600 Haggerty Rd., Livonia MI 48152-2696. (734)462-4400, ext. 5327. Fax: (734)462-4679. E-mail: macguffin@schoolcraft.edu. Web site: www.schoolcraft.edu/macguffin/. **Contact:** Steven A. Dolgin, editor; Nausheen S. Khan, managing editor; Elizabeth Kircos, fiction editor; Carol Was, poetry editor. Magazine: 6 × 9; 164 + pages; 60 lb. paper; 110 lb. cover; b&w illustrations; photos. "The *MacGuffin* is a literary magazine which publishes a range of material including poetry, creative nonfiction and fiction. Material ranges from traditional to experimental. We hope our periodical attracts a variety of people with many different interests." Triannual. Estab. 1984. Circ. 600.

Needs Adventure, ethnic/multicultural, experimental, historical (general), humor/satire, literary, mainstream, translations, contemporary, prose poem. "No religious, inspirational, juvenile, romance, horror, pornography." Receives 35-55 unsolicited mss/month. Accepts 10-15 mss/issue; 30-50 mss/year. Does not read mss between July 1-August 15. Publishes ms 6 months to 2 years after acceptance. Agented fiction 10-15%. **Publishes 30 new writers/year.** Recently published work by Gerry LaFemina, Gail Waldstein, Margaret Karmazin, Linda Nemec Foster, Laurence Lieberman, Conrad Hilberry, Thomas Lux and Vivian Shipley. Length: 100-5,000 words; average length: 2,000-2,500 words. Publishes short shorts. Also publishes literary essays. Occasionally comments on rejected mss.

How to Contact Send SASE or e-mail. Responds in 4-6 months to mss. Sample copy for $6; current issue for $9. Writer's guidelines free.

Payment/Terms Pays 2 contributor's copies. Acquires one-time rights.

Advice "We want to give promising new fiction writers the opportunity to publish alongside recognized writers. Be persistent. If a story is rejected, try to send it somewhere else. When we reject a story, we may accept the next one you send us. When we make suggestions for a rewrite, we may accept the revision. There seems to be a great number of good authors of fiction, but there are far too few places for publication. However, this is changing. Make your characters come to life. Even the most ordinary people become fascinating if they live for your readers."

☑ THE MADISON REVIEW

Department of English, Helen C. White Hall, 600 N. Park St., University of Wisconsin, Madison WI 53706. (608)263-0566. E-mail: madisonreview@yahoo.com. Web site: madisonreview.org. **Contact:** Miles Johnson and Angela Voras-Hills, fiction editors. Magazine: 6×9; 180 pages. "We are an independent literary journal featuring quality fiction, poetry, artwork and interviews. Both established and emerging writers are encouraged to submit." Semiannual. Estab. 1978. Circ. 1,000.

Needs "Well-crafted, compelling fiction featuring a wide range of styles and subjects." Receives 300 unsolicited mss/period. Accepts 6 mss/issue. Does not read May-September. Publishes ms 4 months after acceptance. **Publishes 4 new writers/year.** Recently published work by Anne Germanacos and Kate Reuther. Average length: 4,000 words. Also publishes poetry.

How to Contact Responds in 4 months to mss. Accepts multiple submissions. Sample copy for $4 via postal service or e-mail.

Payment/Terms Pays 2 contributor's copies; $5 charge for extras. Acquires first North American serial rights.

$☒ ☑ ☒ THE MALAHAT REVIEW

The University of Victoria P.O. Box 1700, STN CSC, Victoria BC V8W 2Y2 Canada. (250)721-8524. E-mail: malahat@uvic.ca. Web site: www.malahatreview.ca. **Contact:** John Barton, editor. "We try to achieve a balance of views and styles in each issue. We strive for a mix of the best writing by both established and new writers." Quarterly. Estab. 1967. Circ. 1,000.

• *The Malahat Review* has received Canada's National Magazine Award for poetry and fiction.

Needs "General ficton and poetry." Accepts 3-4 fiction mss/issue. Publishes ms within 6 months after acceptance. **Publishes 4-5 new writers/year.** Recently published work by Steven Hayward, Pauline Holdstock, Pasha Malla, Anne Sanow, J.M. Villaverde, Terrence Young.

How to Contact Send complete ms. "Enclose proper postage on the SASE (or send IRC)." Responds in 2 weeks to queries; 3 months to mss. No simultaneous submissions. Sample copy for $16.45 (US). Writer's guidelines online.

Payment/Terms Pays $40 CAD/magazine page. Pays on acceptance for second serial (reprint), first world rights.

Advice "We do encourage new writers to submit. Read the magazines you want to be published in, ask for their guidelines and follow them. Check Web site for information on *Malahat*'s novella competition and *Far Horizons for Short Fiction* award contest."

$☑ ☒ MANOA, A Pacific Journal of International Writing

English Dept., University of Hawaii, Honolulu HI 96822. (808)956-3070. Fax: (808)956-3083. E-mail: mjournal-l@hawaii.edu. Web site: http://manoajournal.hawaii.edu. **Contact:** Frank Stewart, editor. Magazine: 7×10; 240 pages. "High quality literary fiction, poetry, essays, personal narrative, reviews. Most of each issue devoted to new work from Pacific and Asian nations. Our audience is primarily in the U.S., although expanding in Pacific countries. U.S. writing need not be confined to Pacific settings or subjects." Semiannual. Estab. 1989. Circ. 2,000 print; 1,000 digital.

• *Manoa* has received numerous awards, and work published in the magazine has been selected for prize anthologies.

Needs Literary, mainstream, translations (from U.S. and nations in or bordering on the Pacific), contemporary, excerpted novel. No Pacific exotica. Accepts 1-2 mss/issue. Agented fiction 10%.

Publishes 1-2 new writers/year. Recently published fiction by Wang Ping, Larissa Behrendt, Tony Birch, Roger McDonald, Alexis Wright, Prafulla Roy. Also publishes poetry.

How to Contact Please query first before sending in mss. Include SASE. Does not accept submissions by e-mail. Responds in 3 weeks to queries; 1 month to poetry mss; 6 months to fiction to mss. Accepts simultaneous submissions. Sample copy for $10 (U.S.). Writer's guidelines online. Reviews fiction.

Payment/Terms Pays $100-500 normally ($25/printed page). Pays on publication for first North American serial, non-exclusive, one-time print rights. Sends galleys to author.

N 💿 MARGINALIA

Communication Arts, Language and Literature Department of Western State College of Colorado, 115 Taylor Hall, Western State College of Colorado, Gunnison CO 81231. (970)943-2436. Fax: (970)943-7069. E-mail: marginalia@western.edu. Web site: www.western.edu/marginalia. **Contact:** Alicita Rodriguez, editor. Literary magazine/journal and online magazine: 6×9, 150 pages, 100 lb paper. "At *Marginalia,* we are interested in the interplay between the contained text and its surrounding negative space. For this reason, we encourage work that demonstrates mastery of any given genre, as well as work that transgresses or blurs established forms. We encourage work that transgresses generic boundaries, such as short shorts and prose poems." Annual. Estab. 2005. Circ. 1,000.
Needs Experimental, literary. Does not want mainstream or genre fiction. List of upcoming themes available on Web site. Receives 40 mss/month. Accepts 10 mss/issue; 15 mss/year. Ms published 6 months after acceptance. **Publishes 15% new writers/year.**Published Mark Irwin, Andrea Jonahs, Steve Katz, Alex Lemon, Gina Ochsner, Contessa Riggs, George Singleton, Abdelkrim Tabal, Wendy Walker and Tom Whalen. Average length: 3,000 words. Publishes short shorts. Also publishes literary essays, book reviews, poetry. Send review copies towww.western.edu/marginalia/submit.php. Sometimes comments on/critiques rejected mss.
How to Contact Submit full ms via online submissions. Include estimated word count, brief bio, list of publications. Responds to mss in 9 weeks. Considers simultaneous submissions, multiple submissions. Sample copy available for $9. Sample copy, guidelines available on Web site.
Payment/Terms Writers receive 3 contributor's copies. Additional copies $5. Pays on acceptance. Acquires first rights. Sends galleys to author. Publication is copyrighted. "For contest info, check online atwww.western.edu/marginalia/contest.php"
Advice "In selecting fiction, we look for crisp, unique diction and interesting syntax. We want excellent sentence-level writing. We are not interested in stories that stress plot or conceit over language. Beginning fiction writers should be professional. Do not write clever or long cover letters. Never explain what your story intends to do: the work should speak for itself. Start your stories at an interesting point. The biggest reason why we reject fiction is because the stories don't really begin until page four or five."

$ 💿 💟 THE MASSACHUSETTS REVIEW

South College, University of Massachusetts, Amherst MA 01003-9934. (413)545-2689. Fax: (413)577-0740. E-mail: massrev@external.umass.edu. Web site: www.massreview.org. **Contact:** Fiction Editor. Magazine: 6×9; 172 pages; 52 lb. paper; 65 lb. vellum cover; illustrations; photos. Quarterly. Estab. 1959. Circ. 1,200.
  • Stories from *The Massachusetts Review* have been anthologized in the *100 Best American Short Stories of the Century* and the *Pushcart Prize* anthology.
Needs Short stories. Wants more prose less than 30 pages. Does not read fiction mss May 1-September 1. Publishes ms 18 months after acceptance. Agented fiction Approximately 5%. **Publishes 3-5 new writers/year.** Recently published work by Ahdaf Soueif, Elizabeth Denton, Nicholas Montemarano. Also publishes poetry. Sometimes comments on rejected mss.
How to Contact Send complete ms. No returned ms without SASE. Responds in 3 months to mss. Accepts simultaneous, multiple submissions. Sample copy for $8. Writer's guidelines online.
Payment/Terms Pays $50. Pays on publication for first North American serial rights.
Advice "Shorter rather than longer stories preferred (up to 28-30 pages)." Looks for works that "stop us in our tracks." Manuscripts that stand out use "unexpected language, idiosyncrasy of outlook and are the opposite of ordinary."

💿 METAL SCRATCHES

P.O. Box 685, Forest Lake MN 55025. E-mail: metalscratches@aol.com. **Contact:** Kim Mark, editor. Magazine: 5½×8½; 35 pages; heavy cover-stock. "*Metal Scratches* focuses on literary fiction that examines the dark side of humanity. We are not looking for anything that is 'cute' or 'sweet'." Semiannual. Estab. 2000.
Needs Experimental, horror (psychological), literary. "No poetry, science fiction, rape, murder or horror as in gore." Receives 20 unsolicited mss/month. Accepts 5-6 mss/issue; 20 mss/year. Pub-

lishes ms 6 months after acceptance. **Publishes 3 new writers/year.** Length: 3,500 words; average length: 3,000 words. Publishes short shorts. Sometimes comments on rejected mss.

How to Contact Send complete ms. Accepts submissions by e-mail. (No attachments.) Send disposable copy of ms and #10 SASE for reply only. Responds in 1 month to mss. Accepts simultaneous, multiple submissions. Sample copy for $3. Writer's guidelines for SASE or by e-mail.

Payment/Terms Pays 2 contributor's copies and one year subscription; additional copies for $2.50. Pays on publication for one-time rights. Not copyrighted.

Advice "Clean manuscripts prepared according to guidelines are a must. Send us something new and inventive. Don't let rejections from any editor scare you. Keep writing and keep submitting."

$ ☑ MICHIGAN QUARTERLY REVIEW

3574 Rackham Bldg., 915 E. Washington, University of Michigan, Ann Arbor MI 48109-1070. (734)764-9265. E-mail: mqr@umich.edu. Web site: www.umich.edu/ ~ mqr. **Contact:** Fiction Editor. "An interdisciplinary journal which publishes mainly essays and reviews, with some high-quality fiction and poetry, for an intellectual, widely read audience." Quarterly. Estab. 1962. Circ. 1,500.

- Stories from *Michigan Quarterly Review* have been selected for inclusion in *The Best American Short Stories*, *The O. Henry Prize Stories* and *Pushcart Prize* volumes.

Needs Literary. "No genre fiction written for a market. Would like to see more fiction about social, political, cultural matters, not just centered on a love relationship or dysfunctional family." Receives 200 unsolicited mss/month. Accepts 2 mss/issue; 8 mss/year. Publishes ms 1 year after acceptance. **Publishes 1-2 new writers/year.** Recently published work by Robert Boyers, Herbert Gold, Alice Mattison, Joyce Carol Oates, Vu Tran. Length: 1,500-7,000 words; average length: 5,000 words. Also publishes literary essays, poetry.

How to Contact Send complete ms. "I like to know if a writer is at the beginning, or further along, in his or her career. Don't offer plot summaries of the story, though a background comment is welcome." Include SASE. Responds in 2 months to queries; 6 weeks to mss. No simultaneous submissions. Sample copy for $4. Writer's guidelines online.

Payment/Terms Pays $10/published page. Pays on publication. Buys first serial rights. Sponsors awards/contests.

Advice "There's no beating a good plot, interesting characters and a fresh use of the English language. (Most stories fail because they're written in such a bland manner, or in TV-speak.) Be ambitious, try to involve the social world in the personal one, be aware of what the best writing of today is doing, don't be satisfied with a small slice-of-life narrative but think how to go beyond the ordinary."

☑ ☑ MID-AMERICAN REVIEW

Department of English Box W, Bowling Green State University, Bowling Green OH 43403. (419)372-2725. Fax: (419)372-6805. Web site: www.bgsu.edu/midamericanreview. **Contact:** Ashley Kaine, fiction editor. Magazine: 6×9; 232 pages; 60 lb. bond paper; coated cover stock. "We try to put the best possible work in front of the biggest possible audience. We publish serious fiction and poetry, as well as critical studies in contemporary literature, translations and book reviews." Semiannual. Estab. 1981.

Needs Experimental, literary, translations, memoir, prose poem, traditional. "No genre fiction. Would like to see more short shorts." Receives 700 unsolicited mss/month. Accepts 4-8 mss/issue. Publishes ms 6 months after acceptance. Agented fiction 5%. **Publishes 4-8 new writers/year.** Recently published work by Rebecca Barry, George Singleton and Jean Thompson. Also publishes literary essays, poetry. Occasionally comments on rejected mss.

How to Contact Send complete ms with SASE. Responds in 4 months to mss. Sample copy for $9 (current issue), $5 (back issue); rare back issues $10. Writer's guidelines online. Reviews fiction.

Payment/Terms Pays $10/page up to $50, pending funding. Pays on publication when funding is available. Acquires first North American serial, one-time rights. Sponsors awards/contests.

Advice "We look for well-written stories that make the reader want to read on past the first line and page. Cliché themes and sloppy writing turn us off immediately. Read literary journals to see what's being published in today's market. We tend to publish work that is more non-traditional in style and subject, but are open to all literary non-genre submissions."

☑ THE MINNESOTA REVIEW, A Journal of Committed Writing

Dept. of English, Carnegie Mellon University, Pittsburgh PA 15213. (412)268-9825. E-mail: editors@theminnesotareview.org. Web site: http://theminnesotareview.org. **Contact:** Jeffrey Williams, editor.

Magazine: $5^{1}/_{4} \times 7^{1}/_{2}$; approximately 200 pages; some illustrations; occasional photos. "We emphasize socially and politically engaged work." Semiannual. Estab. 1960. Circ. 1,500.

Needs Experimental, feminist, gay, historical, lesbian, literary. Receives 50-75 unsolicited mss/month. Accepts 3-4 mss/issue; 6-8 mss/year. Publishes ms 6-12 months after acceptance. **Publishes 3-5 new writers/year.** Recently published work by E. Shaskan Bumas, Carlos Fuentes, Maggie Jaffe, James Hughes. Publishes short shorts. Also publishes literary essays, literary criticism, poetry. Occasionally comments on rejected mss.

How to Contact Include SASE. Responds in 3 weeks to queries; 3 months to mss. Accepts simultaneous, multiple submissions. Sample copy for $15. Reviews fiction.

Payment/Terms Pays in contributor's copies. Charge for additional copies. Acquires first rights.

Advice "We look for socially and politically engaged work, particularly short, striking work that stretches boundaries."

Ⓝ ☑ MINNETONKA REVIEW

Minnetonka Review Press, LLC, P.O. Box 386, Spring Park MN 55384. E-mail: query@minnetonkarev iew.com. Web site: www.minnetonkareview.com. **Contact:** Troy Ehlers, Editor-in-Chief. Literary magazine/journal: 6×9, 200 pages, recycled natural paper, glossy cover. Contains illustrations. Includes photographs. "We publish work of literary excellence. We are particularly attracterd to fiction with careful prose, engaging and tension filled stories, and new perspectives, forms and styles." Semiannual. Estab. 2007. Circ. 1,000.

Needs Literary, mainstream. Receives 100 mss/month. Accepts 7 mss/issue; 15 mss/year. Does not read during the summer between May 15th and October 15th. Ms published 6-8 months after acceptance. **Publishes 6 new writers/year.** Published Bev Jafek, Daniel DiStasio, Nathan Leslie, Robin Lippincott, Megan Cass, Arthur Saltzman and Arthur Winfield Knight. Length: 1,200 words (min)-6,000 words (max). Average length: 4,000 words. Publishes short shorts. Average length of short shorts: 1,200 words. Also publishes literary essays, poetry. Rarely comments on/critiques rejected mss.

How to Contact Send complete ms with cover letter. Accepts submissions by e-mail. Include brief bio. Responds to queries in 2 weeks. Responds to mss in 4 months. Send either SASE (or IRC) for return of ms or disposable copy of ms and #10 SASE for reply only. Considers simultaneous submissions. Sample copy available for $9. Guidelines available for SASE, via e-mail, on Web site.

Payment/Terms Writers receive 3 contributor's copies. Additional copies $7. Pays on publication. Acquires first North American serial rights. Publication is copyrighted. "Two authors from each issue recieve a $150 Editor's Prize. Other contests with $1,000 prize are held from time to time. Details are available on our Web site"

Advice "The trick seems to be holding our attention, whether via novelty, language, style, story, good descriptions or tension. Always be honing your craft, reading and writing. And when you read, it helps to be familiar with what we publish, but in general, you should be reading a number of literary journals and anthologies. Think of your work as a contribution to a greater literary dialogue."

☻ MISSISSIPPI REVIEW

University of Southern Mississippi, 118 College Dr. #5144, Hattiesburg MS 39406-0001. (601)266-4321. Fax: (601)266-5757. E-mail: rief@mississippireview.com. Web site: www.mississippireview.c om. **Contact:** Rie Fortenberry, managing editor. Semiannual. Estab. 1972. Circ. 1,500.

Needs Annual fiction and poetry competition. $1,000 awarded in each category plus publication of all winners and finalists. Fiction entries 5,000 words or less. Poetry entry equals 1-3 poems, page limit is 10. $15 entry fee includes copy of prize issue. No limit on number of entries. Deadline October 1. No mss returned. **Publishes 25-30 new writers/year.**

How to Contact Sample copy for $8. Writer's guidelines online.

Payment/Terms Acquires first North American serial rights.

$ ☑ ☻ THE MISSOURI REVIEW

1507 Hillcrest Hall, University of Missouri, Columbia MO 65211. (573)882-4474. Fax: (573)884-4671. E-mail: question@missourireview.com. Web site: www.missourireview.com. **Contact:** Speer Morgan, editor; Evelyn Somers, associate editor. Magazine: $6^{3}/_{4} \times 10$; 200 pages. "We publish contemporary fiction, poetry, interviews, personal essays, cartoons, special features for the literary and the general reader interested in a wide range of subjects." Estab. 1978. Circ. 5,500.

● This magazine had stories anthologized in the *Pushcart Prize*, *Best American Short Stories*, *The O. Henry Prize Stories*, *Best American Essays*, *Best American Mystery Stories*, *Best American Nature and Science Writing*, *Best American Erotica*, and *New Stories from The South*.

Needs Literary fiction on all subjects, novel excerpts. No genre fiction. Receives 500 unsolicited mss/month. Accepts 5-7 mss/issue; 16-20 mss/year. **Publishes 6-10 new writers/year.** Recently published work by Ed Falco, Lauren Slater, Jacob M. Appel, Fan Wu. Also publishes literary essays, poetry. Often comments on rejected mss.

How to Contact Send complete ms. May include brief bio and list of publications. Send SASE for reply, return of ms or send disposable copy of ms. Online submissions via Web site. Responds in 2 weeks to queries; 12 weeks to mss. Sample copy for $8 or online. Writer's guidelines online.

Payment/Terms Pays $30/printed page up to $750. Offers signed contract. Sponsors awards/contests.

☑ MOBIUS, The Journal of Social Change

505 Christianson, Madison WI 53714. (608)242-1009. E-mail: fmschep@charter.net. Web site: www. mobiusmagazine.com. **Contact:** Fred Schepartz, editor. Magazine: 8½×11; 16-24 pages; 60 lb. paper; 60 lb. cover. "Looking for fiction which uses social change as either a primary or secondary theme. This is broader than most people think. Need social relevance in one way or another. For an artistically and politically aware and curious audience." Quarterly. Estab. 1989. Circ. 1,500.

Needs Ethnic/multicultural, experimental, fantasy, feminist, gay, historical, horror, humor/satire, lesbian, literary, mainstream, science fiction, contemporary, prose poem. "No porn, no racist, sexist or any other kind of -ist. No Christian or spirituality proselytizing fiction." Wants to see more science fiction, erotica "assuming it relates to social change." Receives 15 unsolicited mss/month. Accepts 3-5 mss/issue , "however we are now doubling as a webzine, which means a dramatic change in how we operate. Any work considered suitable will first be published in the web version and will be held for further consideration for the print version." Publishes ms 3-9 months after acceptance. **Publishes 10 new writers/year.** Recently published work by Margaret Karmazin, Benjamin Reed, John Tuschen, Ken Byrnes. Length: 500-5,000 words; average length: 3,500 words. Publishes short shorts. Always comments on rejected mss.

How to Contact Include SASE. Responds in 4 months to mss. Accepts simultaneous, multiple submissions and reprints. Sample copy for $2, 9×12 SAE and 3 first class stamps. Writer's guidelines for SASE.

Payment/Terms Pays contributor's copies. Acquires one-time rights, electronic rights for www version.

Advice "Note that fiction and poetry may be simultaneously published in e-version of *Mobius*. Due to space constraints of print version, some works may be accepted in e-version, but not print version. We like high impact, we like plot and character-driven stories that function like theater of the mind. Looks for first and foremost, good writing. Prose must be crisp and polished; the story must pique my interest and make me care due to a certain intellectual, emotional aspect. Second, *Mobius* is about social change. We want stories that make some statement about the society we live in, either on a macro or micro level. Not that your story neeeds to preach from a soapbox (actually, we prefer that it doesn't), but your story needs to have *something* to say."

Ⓝ ☑ THE MOCHILA REVIEW

Hignell Book Printing. Web site: www.missouriwestern.edu/EFLJ /mochila. **Contact:** Bill Church, editor. Magazine: 9×6; 120-160 pages; photos. "Good readership, no theme." Annual. Estab. 2000.

Needs Literary. Does not accept genre work, erotica. Receives 25 unsolicited mss/month. Accepts 5-10 mss/issue. Does not read mss December-July. Publishes ms 6 months after acceptance. **Publishes 2-3 new writers/year.** Length: 5,000 words (max); average length: 3,000 words. Publishes short shorts; average 500 words. Also publishes literary essays, poetry. Rarely comments on rejected mss.

How to Contact Send complete disposable copy of ms with cover letter and #10 SASE for reply only. Include estimated word count, brief bio and list of publications. Responds in 3-5 months to mss. Accepts simultaneous submissions. Sample copy for $7 . Writer's guidelines for SASE or on Web site.

Payment/Terms Pays 2 contributor's copies; additional copies $5 . Acquires first rights. Publication not copyrighted.

Advice "Manuscripts with fresh language, energy, passion and intelligence stand out. Study the craft and be entertaining and engaging."

NATURAL BRIDGE

English Department, University of Missouri-St. Louis, One University Boulevard, St. Louis MO 63121-4400. (314)516-7327. Fax: (314)516-5781. E-mail: natural@umsl.edu. Web site: www.umsl.edu/~natural. **Contact:** Steven Schreiner, founding editor. Magazine: 6×9; 250 pages; 60 lb. opaque recycled paper; 12 pt. matte cover. "*Natural Bridge* is published by the UM-St. Louis MFA Program. Faculty and graduate students work together in selecting manuscripts, with a strong emphasis on originality, freshness, honesty, vitality, energy, and linguistic skill." Semiannual. Estab. 1999. Circ. 1,000. CLMP.

Needs Literary. List of upcoming themes available for SASE or online. Receives 900 unsolicited mss/submission period. Accepts 35 mss/issue; 70 mss/year. Submit only July 1-August 31 and November 1-December 31. Publishes ms 9 months after acceptance. **Publishes 12 new writers/year.** Recently published work by Tayari Jones, Steve Stern, Jamie Wriston Colbert, Lex Williford, and Mark Jay Mirsky. Also publishes literary essays, poetry. Sometimes comments on rejected mss.

How to Contact Send SASE for return of ms or send a disposable copy of ms and #10 SASE for reply only. Responds in 6 months to mss. Accepts simultaneous submissions. Sample copy for $8. Writer's guidelines for SASE, e-mail or on Web site.

Payment/Terms Pays 2 contributor's copies and a one-year subscription; additional copies $5. Acquires first North American serial rights.

Advice "We look for fresh stories, extremely well written, on any subject. We publish mainstream literary fiction. We want stories that work on first and subsequent readings—stories, in other words, that both entertain and resonate. Study the journal. Read all of the fiction in it, especially in fiction-heavy issues like numbers 4 and 11."

NEW DELTA REVIEW

Louisiana State University, Dept. of English, 214 Allen Hall, Baton Rouge LA 70803-5001. (225)578-4079. E-mail: new-delta@lsu.edu. Web site: http://www.lsu.edu/newdeltareview/. **Contact:** Editors change every year. Check Web site. Magazine: 6×9; 75-125 pages; high quality paper; glossy card cover; color artwork. "We seek vivid and exciting work from new and established writers. We have published fiction from writers such as Stacy Richter, Mark Poirier and George Singleton." Semiannual. Estab. 1984. Circ. 500.

- *New Delta Review* also sponsors the Matt Clark Prizes for fiction and poetry. Work from the magazine has been included in the *Pushcart Prize* anthology.

Needs Humor/satire, literary, mainstream, translations, contemporary, prose poem. "No Elvis stories, overwrought 'Southern' fiction, or cancer stories." Receives 150 unsolicited mss/month. Accepts 3-4 mss/issue; 6-8 mss/year. Reads from August 15-April 15. **Publishes 1-3 new writers/year.** Average length: 15 ms pages. Publishes short shorts. Also publishes poetry. Rarely comments on rejected mss.

How to Contact SASE (or IRC). Responds in 3 weeks to queries; 3 months to mss. Accepts simultaneous submissions only when stated in the cover letter. Sample copy for $7.

Payment/Terms Pays in contributor's copies. Charge for extras. Acquires first North American serial, electronic rights. Sponsors awards/contests.

Advice "Our staff is open-minded and youthful. We base decisions on merit, not reputation. The manuscript that's most enjoyable to read gets the nod. Be bold, take risks, surprise us."

NEW ENGLAND REVIEW

Middlebury College, Middlebury VT 05753. (802)443-5075. Fax: (802)443-2088. E-mail: nereview@middlebury.edu. Web site: http://go.miiddlebury.edu/nereview. **Contact:** Stephen Donadio, editor. Magazine: 7×10; 180 pages; 50 lb. paper; coated cover stock. Serious literary only. Reads September 1 to May 31 (postmarked dates). Quarterly. Estab. 1978. Circ. 2,000.

Needs Literary. Receives 550 unsolicited mss/month. Accepts 20 mss/issue; 80 mss/year. Does not accept mss June-August. Publishes ms approx 2-6 months after acceptance. Agented fiction less than 5%. **Publishes approx. 10 new writers/year.** Recently published work by Carl Phillips, Janet Kauffman, Mark Rudman, Lucia Perillo, Christopher Sorrentino. Publishes short shorts and translations. Sometimes comments on rejected mss.

How to Contact "Send complete mss with cover letter, hard copy only. Will consider simultaneous submissions, but must be stated as such and you must notify us immediately if the manuscript is accepted for publication elsewhere." No poetry simultaneous submissions please. SASE. Responds in 2 weeks to queries; 3 months to mss. Sample copy for $8, add $5 for overseas. Writer's guidelines online. No electronic submissions.

Payment/Terms Pays $10/page ($20 minimum), and 2 copies. Pays on publication for first North American serial, first, second serial (reprint) rights. Sends galleys to author.

Advice "Please wait to hear back about one ms before submitting again."

$⬭ ⬭ NEW LETTERS

University of Missouri-Kansas City, University House, 5101 Rockhill Road, Kansas City MO 64110-2499. (816)235-1168. Fax: (816)235-2611. E-mail: newletters@umkc.edu. Web site: www.newletters .org. **Contact:** Robert Stewart, editor. Magazine: 6×9, 14 lb. cream paper; illustrations. "*New Letters* is intended for the general literary reader. We publish literary fiction, nonfiction, essays, poetry. We also publish art." Quarterly. Estab. 1934. Circ. 2,500.

Needs Ethnic/multicultural, experimental, humor/satire, literary, mainstream, translations, contemporary. No genre fiction. Does not read mss May 1-October 1. Publishes ms 5 months after acceptance. Recently published work by Thomas E. Kennedy, Sheila Kohler, Charlotte Holmes, Rosellen Brown, Janet Burroway. Publishes short shorts.

How to Contact Send complete ms. Do not submit by e-mail. Responds in 1 month to queries; 3 months to mss. No simultaneous submissions. Sample copy for $10 or sample articles on Web site. Writer's guidelines online.

Payment/Terms Pays $30-75 for fiction and $15 for single poem. Pays on publication for first North American serial rights. Sends galleys to author. $4,500 awarded annually in writing contest for short fiction, essay, and poetry. Visitwww.newletters.org for contest guidelines.

Advice "Seek publication of representative chapters in high-quality magazines as a way to the book contract. Try literary magazines first."

⬭ NEW MADRID

Murray State University, 7C Faculty Hall, Murray KY 42071. (270)809-4713, (270)809-2401. Fax: (270)809-4545. E-mail: newmadrid@murraystate.edu. Web site: http://murraystate.edu/newmadr id. **Contact:** Ann Neelon, fiction editor. Literary magazine/journal: 166 pages; contains illustrations & photographs. "*New Madrid* takes its name from the fault in the earth's crust in the middle of the United States. We are especially interested in work by writers in what some call 'the flyover zone.'" Semiannual. Estab. 1980. Circ.1,500.

Needs Literary. List of upcoming themes available on Web site. "We have two reading periods, one from October to mid-November, and one during February and March." Also publishes literary essays, literary criticism, poetry. Rarely comments on/critiques rejected mss.

How to Contact Send complete ms with cover letter. Accepts submissions by Online Submissions Manager only. Include brief bio, list of publications. Considers multiple submissions. Guidelines available via e-mail, on Web site.

Payment/Terms Pays 1 contributor copy on publication. Acquires first North American serial rights. Publication is copyrighted.

Advice "Quality is the determining factor for breaking into *New Madrid*. We are looking for excellent work in a range of genres, forms and styles."

⬭ $⬭ NEW MILLENNIUM WRITINGS

New Messenger Writing and Publishing, P.O. Box 2463, Knoxville TN 37901. Phone/fax: (865)428-0389. E-mail: donwilliams7@charter.net. Web site: http://newmillenniumwritings.com. **Contact:** Don Williams, editor. Annual anthology. 6×9, 204 pages, 60 lb. white paper, glossy 4-color cover. Contains illustrations. Includes photographs. "Superior writing is the sole criterion." Annual. Estab. 1996. Circ. 3,000. Received Golden Presscard Award from Sigma Delta Chi (1997)

Needs All types of fiction. Receives 100 mss/month. Accepts 10 mss/year. Does not read June-Feb. (except for contests). Manuscript published 6 months after acceptance. Agented fiction 0%. Publishes 2 new writers/year. Published Allen Wier, Marilyn Kallet, Don Williams, Ted Kooser. Length: 500 words (min)-6,000 words (max). Average length: 4,000 words. Publishes short shorts. Also publishes literary essays, poetry. Rarely comments on/critiques rejected manuscripts.

How to Contact Accepts ms through biannual *New Millennium Writing* Awards only.
Payment/Terms See listing for *New Millennium Writing* Awards in Contests & Awards section.
Advice "Looks for originality, accessibility, musicality, psychological insight, moral sensibility. E-mail for list of writing tips or send SASE. No charge."

☑ ☒ NEW ORLEANS REVIEW

Box 195, Loyola University, New Orleans LA 70118. (504)865-2295. Fax: (504)865-2294. E-mail: noreview@loyno.edu. Web site: www.loyno.edu/ ~ noreview/. **Contact:** Christopher Chambers, editor. Journal: 6×9; perfect bound; 200 pages; photos. "Publishes poetry, fiction, translations, photographs, nonfiction on literature, art and film. Readership: those interested in contemporary literature and culture." Biannual. Estab. 1968. Circ. 1,500.

 • Work from the *New Orleans Review* has been anthologized in *New Stores from the South* and the *Pushcart Prize Anthology. Best American Non required reading, Best American Poetry, O. Henry Prize Anthology*.

Needs "Quality fiction from conventional to experimental." **Publishes 12 new writers/year.** Recently published work by Gordon Lish, Michael Martone, Dylan Landis, Stephen Graham Jones, Carolyn Sanchez and Josh Russell.
How to Contact Responds in 4 months to mss. Accepts simultaneous submissions "if we are notified immediately upon acceptance elsewhere." Sample copy for $6. Reviews fiction.
Payment/Terms Pays $25-50 and 2 copies. Pays on publication for first North American serial rights.
Advice "We're looking for dynamic writing that demostrates attention to the language, and a sense of the medium, writing that engages, surprises, moves us. We're not looking for genre fiction, or academic articles. We subscribe to the belief that in order to truly write well, one must first master the rudiments: grammar and syntax, punctuation, the sentence, the paragraph, the line, the stanza. We recieve about 3,000 manuscripts a year, and publish about 3% of them. Check out a recent issue, send us your best, proofread your work, be patient, be persistent."

$☑ ◎ THE NEW QUARTERLY, Canadian Writers and Writing

St. Jerome's University, 290 University Ave. North, Waterloo ON N2L 3G3 Canada. (519)884-8111, ext. 290. E-mail: editor@ tnq. ca. Web site: www .tnq.ca. **Contact:** Kim Jernigan, editor. " Publishes Canadian writing only, fiction and poetry plus essays on writing. Emphasis on emerging writers and genres, but we publish more traditional work as well if the language and narrative structure are fresh." Quarterly. Estab. 1981. Circ. 1,000.
Needs Publishes ms 4 months after acceptance.
How to Contact Send complete ms. Does not accept submissions by e-mail. Responds in 2 weeks to queries; 3-6 months to mss. Accepts simultaneoues submissions if indicated in cover letter. Sample copy for $15 (cover price, plus mailing). Writer's guidelines for #10 SASE or online.
Payment/Terms Pays $200/story, $30/poem. Pays on publication for first Canadian rights.

☑ NEW SOUTH

(Formerly GSU Review) Georgia State University, Campus P.O. Box 1894, MSC 8R0322 Unit 8, Atlanta GA 30303-3083. (404)413-5874. Fax: (404)413-5830. Web site: www.review.gsu.edu. **Contact:** Prose Editor. Literary journal. "*New South* is a biannual literary magazine publishing poetry, fiction, creative nonfiction, and visual art. We're looking for original voices and well-written manuscripts. No subject or form biases." Biannual.
Needs Literary fiction and creative nonfiction. Receives 200 unsolicited mss/month. Publishes and welcomes short shorts.
How to Contact Include SASE for notification. Responds in 3-5 months. Sample copy for $5. Writer's guidelines for SASE or on Web site.
Payment/Terms Pays in contributor's copy. Acquires one-time rights.

▥ NEW WELSH REVIEW

P.O. Box 170, Aberystwyth, Ceredigion Wales SY23 1 WZ United Kingdom. 01970-628410. Fax: 01970-628410. E-mail: editor@newwelshreview.com. Web site: www.newwelshreview.com. Editor: Francesca Rhydderch. **Contact:** Fiction Editor. "*NWR*, a literary quarterly ranked in the top five of British literary magazines, publishes stories, poems and critical essays. The best of Welsh writing in English, past and present, is celebrated, discussed and debated. We seek poems, short stories, reviews, special features/articles and commentary." Quarterly.

Needs Short fiction. Accepts 8 mss/year. **Publishes 20% new writers/year.** Recently published work by Peter Ho Davies.

How to Contact Send hard copy only with SASE or international money order for return.

Payment/Terms Pays "cheque on publication and one free copy."

THE NEW WRITER

P.O. Box 60, Cranbrook TN17 2ZR United Kingdom. 01580 212626. Fax: 01580 212041. E-mail: editor@the newwriter.com. Web site: www.thenewwriter.com. **Contact:** Suzanne Ruthven, editor. Magazine: A4; 56 pages; illustrations; photos. Contemporary writing magazine which publishes "the best in fact, fiction and poetry." Publishes 6 issues per annum. Estab. 1996. Circ. 1,500.

Needs "We will consider most categories apart from stories written for children. No horror, erotic or cosy fiction." Accepts 4 mss/issue; 24 mss/year. Publishes ms 1 year after acceptance. Agented fiction 5%. **Publishes 12 new writers/year.** Recently published work by Sally Zigmond, Lorna Dowell, Wes Lee, Amy Licence, Cathy Whitfield, Katy Darby, Clio Gray. Length: 2,000-5,000 words; average length: 3,500 words. Publishes short shorts. Also publishes literary essays, literary criticism, poetry. Often comments on rejected mss.

How to Contact Query with published clips. Accepts submissions by e-mail, fax. Send SASE (or IRC) for return of ms or send a disposable copy of ms and #10 SASE for reply only. "We consider short stories from subscribers only but we may also commission guest writers." Responds in 2 months to queries; 4 months to mss. Accepts simultaneous submissions. Sample copy for SASE and A4 SAE with IRCs only. Writer's guidelines for SASE. Reviews fiction.

Payment/Terms Pays £10 per story by credit voucher; additional copies for £1.50. Pays on publication for one-time rights. Sponsors awards/contests.

Advice "Hone it—always be prepared to improve the story. It's a competitive market."

NIMROD, International Journal of Prose and Poetry

University of Tulsa, 600 S. College Ave., Tulsa OK 74104-3189. (918)631-3080. Fax: (918)631-3033. E-mail: nimrod@utulsa.edu. Web site: www.utulsa.edu/nimrod/. **Contact:** Gerry McLoud, fiction editor. Magazine: 6×9; 192 pages; 60 lb. white paper; illustrations; photos. "We publish one thematic issue and one awards issue each year. A recent theme was 'Crossing Borders,' a compilation of poetry and prose from all over the world. We seek vigorous, imaginative, quality writing. Our mission is to discover new writers and publish experimental writers who have not yet found a 'home' for their work." Semiannual. Estab. 1956. Circ. 3,000.

Needs "We accept contemporary poetry and/or prose. May submit adventure, ethnic, experimental, prose poem or translations. No science fiction or romance." Receives 120 unsolicited mss/month. **Publishes 5-10 new writers/year.** Recently published work by Felicia Ward, Ellen Bass, Jeanette Turner Hospital , Kate Small. Also publishes poetry.

How to Contact SASE for return of ms. Accepts queries by e-mail. Does not accept submissions by e-mail unless the writer is living outside the U.S. Responds in 5 months to mss. Accepts simultaneous, multiple submissions.

Payment/Terms Pays 2 contributor's copies.

Advice "We have not changed our fiction needs: quality, vigor, distinctive voice. We have, however, increased the number of stories we print. See current issues. We look for fiction that is fresh, vigorous, distinctive, serious and humorous, unflinchingly serious, ironic—whatever. Just so it is quality. Strongly encourage writers to send #10 SASE for brochure for annual literary contest with prizes of $1,000 and $2,000."

NITE-WRITER'S INTERNATIONAL LITERARY ARTS JOURNAL

3845 Dalewood Street, Pittsburgh PA 15227. (412)668-0691. E-mail: cxpression@msn.com. Web site: www.nitewriters.com. **Contact:** Editor/Publisher: John A. Thompson, Sr. or Fiction Editor: Bree Orner-Thompson. Online literary journal. Nite-Writers International Literary Arts Journal is "dedicated to the emotional intellectual with a creative perception of life." Quarterly. Estab. 1993. Will begin publishing as an online journal in January 2009.

Needs: Literary mainstream, historical, adventure, erotica, humor/satire, inspirational, senior citizen/retirement, sports. Average length: 2,500 words. Also publishes literary essays, literary criticism, photography, poetry, haiku/senryu, acrostic poetry, flash fiction. Recently published work by Julia Klatt Singer, Jean Oscarson Schoell, Lawrence Keough, S. Anthony Smith.

How to Contact: If submitting by snail mail, enclose SASE for return of mss. Responds within 6 months to mss. Accepts simultaneous submissions and previously published work (let us know when & where). Send SASE for writer's guidelines or go to www.nitewriters.com for guidelines.

Payment/Terms: Does not pay. Will offer a print on demand service quarterly. Copyright reverts to author upon publication. Retains First North American Serial rights.

Advice: " Read a lot of what you write - study the market. Don't fear rejection, but use it as learning tool to strengthen your work before resubmitting."

$ ◎ ⬇ THE NORTH AMERICAN REVIEW

University of Northern Iowa, Cedar Falls IA 50614-0516. (319)273-6455. Fax: (319)273-4326. Web site: www.webdelsol.com/NorthAmReview/NAR/. **Contact:** Grant Tracey, fiction editor. "The *NAR* is the oldest literary magazine in America and one of the most respected. Though we have no prejudices about the subject matter of material sent to us, our first concern is quality." Bimonthly. Estab. 1815. Circ. under 5,000.

• Works published in *The North American Review* have won the Pushcart Prize.

Needs Open (literary). "No flat narrative stories where the inferiority of the character is the paramount concern." Wants to see more "well-crafted literary stories that emphasize family concerns. We'd also like to see more stories engaged with environmental concerns." Reads fiction mss all year. Publishes ms an average of 1 year after acceptance. **Publishes 2 new writers/year.** Recently published work by Lee Ann Roripaugh, Dick Allen, Rita Welty Bourke.

How to Contact Accepts submissions by USPS mail only. Send complete ms with SASE. Responds in 3 months to queries; 4 months to mss. No simultaneous submissions. Sample copy for $5. Writer's guidelines online.

Payment/Terms Pays $5/350 words; $20 minimum, $100 maximum. Pays on publication for first North American serial, first rights.

Advice "Stories that do not condescend to the reader or their character are always appealing to us. We also like stories that have characters doing things (acting upon the world instead of being acted upon). We also like a strong narrative arc. Stories that are mainly about language need not apply. Your first should be your second best line. Your last sentence should be your best. Everything in the middle should approach the two."

◎ NORTH CAROLINA LITERARY REVIEW, A Magazine of North Carolina Literature, Literary History and Culture

English Dept., East Carolina University, Greenville NC 27858-4353. (252)328-1537. Fax: (252)328-4889. E-mail: bauerm@ecu.edu. Web site: www.ecu.edu/nclr. "Articles should have a North Carolina literature slant. First consideration is always for quality of work. Although we treat academic and scholarly subjects, we do not wish to see jargon-laden prose; our readers, we hope, are found as often in bookstores and libraries as in academia. We seek to combine the best elements of a magazine for serious readers with the best of a scholarly journal." Annual. Estab. 1992. Circ. 750.

Needs Regional (North Carolina). Must be North Carolina related—either a North Carolina-connected writer or set in North Carolina. Publishes ms 1 year after acceptance.

How to Contact Query. Accepts queries by e-mail. Responds in 1 month to queries; within 6 months to mss. Sample copy for $10-25. Writer's guidelines online.

Payment/Terms Pays on publication for first North American serial rights. Rights returned to writer on request.

◻ ◎ NORTH CENTRAL REVIEW, YOUR UNDERGRADUATE LITERARY JOURNAL

North Central College, 30 N. Brainard St., CM #235, Naperville IL 60540. (630)637-5291. Fax: (630)637-5221. E-mail: nccreview@noctrl.edu. **Contact:** Dr. Anna Leahy, advisor. Magazine has revolving editor. Editorial term: Editor changes each year in the Fall. Literary magazine/journal: $5^{1}/_{2} \times 8^{1}/_{2}$, 120 pages, perfect binding, color card-stock cover. Includes photographs. "The *North Central Review* is an undergraduate literary journal soliciting fiction, poetry, nonfiction and drama from around the country and the globe—but only from college students. This offers undergraduates a venue for sharing their work with their peers." Semiannual. Estab. 1936, undergraduate focus as of 2005. Circ. 500-750, depending on funding.

Needs Considers all categories. Deadlines: February 15 and October 15. Does not read February 15-August 15. Accepts 4-8 mss/issue; 8-16 mss/year. Manuscript published 2-3 months after acceptance. Agented fiction 0%. **Publishes "at least half, probably more" new writers/year.**Length: 5,000 words (max). Average length: 2,000 words. Publishes short shorts. Average length of short shorts: 100-700 words. Also publishes literary essays, poetry. Rarely comments on/critiques rejected manuscripts.

How to Contact Send complete ms with cover letter. Accepts submissions by e-mail. Include student (.edu) e-mail address or copy of student ID with ID number marked. Responds to queries in 2 weeks. Responds to mss in 4 months. Send disposable copy of ms and #10 SASE for reply only. Considers multiple submissions. Sample copy free upon request (older issue) or available for $5 (most recent issue). Guidelines available at http://blogs.noctrl.edu/review, for SASE, via e-mail.

Payment/Terms Writers receive 2 contributors copies. Additional copies $5. Pays on publication. Acquires one-time rights.

Advice "The reading staff changes year to year (and sometimes from one academic term to the next) so tastes change. That said, at least three readers evaluate each submission, and there's usually a widespread agreement on the best ones. While all elements need to work together, readers take notice when one element—maybe setting or character—captivates and even teaches the reader something new. Don't send something you just drafted and printed. Give your work some time, revise it, and polish what you plan to send us. That said, don't hesitate to submit and submit again to the *North Central Review*. Undergraduates are beginners, and we welcome new voices."

☑ ☒ NORTH DAKOTA QUARTERLY

University of North Dakota, Merrifield Hall Room 110, 276 Centennial Drive Stop 7209 Grand Forks ND 58202-7209. (701)777-3322. Fax: (701)777-2373. E-mail: ndq@und.edu. Web site: www.und.no dak.edu/org/ndq. **Contact:** Robert W. Lewis, editor. Magazine: 6×9; 200 pages; bond paper; illustrations; photos. "*North Dakota Quarterly* is a literary journal publishing essays in the humanities; some short stories, some poetry. Occasional special topic issues." General audience. Quarterly. Estab. 1911. Circ. 600.

- Work published in *North Dakota Quarterly* was selected for inclusion in *The O. Henry Prize Stories*, *The Pushcart Prize Series*, and *Best American Essays*.

Needs Ethnic/multicultural, experimental, feminist, historical, literary, Native American. Receives 125-150 unsolicited mss/month. Accepts 4 mss/issue; 16 mss/year. Publishes ms 2 years after acceptance. **Publishes 4-5 new writers/year.** Recently published work by Louise Erdrich, Robert Day, Karen Alpha and Jason Courter. Average length: 3,000-4,000 words. Also publishes literary essays, literary criticism, poetry. Sometimes comments on rejected mss.

How to Contact SASE. Responds in 3 months to mss. Sample copy for $10. Reviews fiction.

Payment/Terms Pays 2-4 contributor's copies; 30% discount for extras. Acquires one-time rights. Sends galleys to author.

$☑ NORTHWOODS JOURNAL, A Magazine for Writers

Conservatory of American Letters, P.O. Box 298, Thomaston ME 04861. (207)226-7528. E-mail: cal@americanletters.org. Web site: www.americanletters.org. Magazine: 5½×8½; 32-64 pages; white paper; 8 pt. glossy, full color cover; digital printing; some illustrations; photos. "No theme, no philosophy—for writers and for people who read for entertainment." Quarterly. Estab. 1993. Circ. 100.

Needs Adventure, experimental, fantasy (science fantasy, sword and sorcery), literary, mainstream, mystery/suspense (amateur sleuth, police procedural, private eye/hard-boiled, romantic suspense), psychic/supernatural/occult, regional, romance (gothic, historical), science fiction (hard science, soft/sociological), western (frontier, traditional), sports. "Would like to see more first-person adventure. No porn or evangelical." Publishes annual *Northwoods Anthology*. Receives 20 unsolicited mss/month. Accepts 12-15 mss/year. **Publishes 15 new writers/year.** Recently published work by J.F. Pytko, Richard Vaughn, Kelley Jean White. Also publishes literary criticism, poetry.

How to Contact Send SASE for reply, return of ms or send a disposable copy of ms. Responds in 2 days to queries; by next deadline plus 5 days to mss. No simultaneous submissions or electronic submissions. Sample copy for $6.50 next issue, $10 current issue, $14.50 back issue, all postage paid. Or send 7×10 SASE with $1.35 postage affixed and $6.50. Writer's guidelines for #10 SASE. Reviews fiction. Reviews editor J. R. Clifford 1537 Oakhurst Dr, Mt Pleasant, SC 29464. Send SASE

for rules of submission. Accepts books for review or reviews of small press and self published books.
Payment/Terms Varies "but is generally 1 cent per word or more, based on experience with us. Pays an advance (non refundable) based on sales we can attribute to your influence." Pays on acceptance for first North American serial rights. 50/50 split of additional sales.
Advice "Read guidelines, read the things we've published. Know your market. Anyone submitting to a publication he/she has never seen deserves whatever happens to them."

$ 🖉 🔽 NOTRE DAME REVIEW

University of Notre Dame, 840 Flanner Hall, Notre Dame IN 46556. (574)631-6952. Fax: (574)631-8209. Web site: www.nd.edu/~ndr/review.htm. **Contact:** William O'Rourke, fiction editor. Literary magazine: 6×9; 200 pages; 50 lb. smooth paper; illustrations; photos. "The *Notre Dame Review* is an indepenent, noncommercial magazine of contemporary American and international fiction, poetry, criticism and art. We are especially interested in work that takes on big issues by making the invisible seen, that gives voice to the voiceless. In addition to showcasing celebrated authors like Seamus Heaney and Czelaw Milosz, the *Notre Dame Review* introduces readers to authors they may have never encountered before, but who are doing innovative and important work. In conjunction with the *Notre Dame Review*, the online companion to the printed magazine engages readers as a community centered in literary rather than commercial concerns, a community we reach out to through critique and commentary as well as aesthetic experience." Semiannual. Estab. 1995. Circ. 1,500.

● Pushcart prizes in fiction and poetry. Best American Short stories; Best American Poetry.

Needs No genre fiction. Upcoming theme issues planned. Receives 75 unsolicited mss/month. Accepts 4-5 mss/issue; 10 mss/year. Does not read mss November-January or April-August. Publishes ms 6 months after acceptance. **Publishes 1 new writer/year.** Recently published work by Ed Falco, Jarda Cerverka, David Green. Publishes short shorts. Also publishes literary criticism, poetry.
How to Contact Send complete ms with cover letter. Include 4-sentence bio. Send SASE for response, return of ms, or send a disposable copy of ms. Responds in 6 months to mss. Accepts simultaneous submissions. Sample copy for $6. Writer's guidelines online. Mss sent during summer months will be returned unread.
Payment/Terms Pays $5-25. Pays on publication for first North American serial rights.
Advice "We're looking for high quality work that takes on big issues in a literary way. Please read our back issues before submitting."

🖉 OASIS, A Literary Magazine

P.O. Box 626, Largo FL 33779-0626. (727)345-8505. E-mail: dasislit@aol.com. **Contact:** Neal Storrs, editor. Magazine: 70 pages. "The only criterion is high literary quality of writing." Quarterly. Estab. 1992. Circ. 300.
Needs High-quality writing. Also publishes translations. Receives 150 unsolicited mss/month. Accepts 6 mss/issue; 24 mss/year. Publishes ms 4 months after acceptance. **Publishes 2 new writers/year.** Recently published work by Wendell Mayo, Jim Meirose, Al Masarik and Mark Wisniewski. Also publishes literary essays, poetry. Occasionally comments on rejected mss.
How to Contact Send complete ms. Accepts submissions by e-mail, disk. Send SASE for reply, return of ms or send a disposable copy of ms. Responds in 1-3 days to mss. Accepts simultaneous and reprints, multiple submissions. Sample copy for $7.50. Writer's guidelines for #10 SASE.
Payment/Terms Pays in contributor's copies.
Advice "If you want to write good stories, read good stories. Cultivate the critical ability to recognize what makes a story original and true to itself."

🖉 ◎ OHIO TEACHERS WRITE

Ohio Council of Teachers of English Language Arts, 644 Overlook Dr., Columbus OH 43214. E-mail: rmcclain@bright.net. **Contact:** Scott Parsons, editor. Editors change every 3 years. Magazine: 8½×11; 50 pages; 60 lb. white offset paper; 65 lb. blue cover stock; illustrations; photos. "The purpose of the magazine is three fold: (1) to provide a collection of fine literature for the reading pleasure of teachers and other adult readers; (2) to encourage teachers to compose literary works along with their students; (3) to provide the literate citizens of Ohio a window into the world of educators not often seen by those outside the teaching profession." Annual. Estab. 1995. Circ. 1,000. Submissions are limited to Ohio Educators.
Needs Adventure, ethnic/multicultural, experimental, fantasy (science fantasy), feminist, gay, his-

torical, humor/satire, lesbian, literary, mainstream, regional, religious/inspirational, romance (contemporary), science fiction (hard science, soft/sociological), western (frontier, traditional), senior citizen/retirement, sports, teaching. Receives 2 unsolicited mss/month. Accepts 7 mss/issue. "We read only in May when editorial board meets." Recently published work by Lois Spencer, Harry R. Noden, Linda J. Rice, June Langford Berkley. Publishes short shorts. Also publishes poetry. Often comments on rejected mss.

How to Contact Send SASE with postage clipped for return of ms or send a disposable copy of ms. Accepts multiple submissions. Sample copy for $6.

Payment/Terms Pays 2 contributor's copies; additional copies $6. Acquires first rights.

N: ☑ ◎ ONE LESS, ART ON THE RANGE

One Less Press, 6 Village Hill Road, Williamsburg MA 01096-9706. E-mail: onelessartontherange@yahoo.com. Web site: www.onelessmag.blogspot.com. **Contact:** David Gardner, co-editor. Literary magazine/journal: 6×9, 100-200 pages, 60 lb. white paper, 10 pt. cover. Contains illustrations and photographs. "*One Less* publishes work that challenges artistic conventions and modes of expression. Accepted forms: poetry, prose, short stories, novel excerpts, play excerpts, comics, photography, painting, film stills, drawing and mixed media." Annual. Estab. 2005.

● 2004 Northampton Arts Council/Massachusetts Cultural Council Grant Recipient.

Needs Comics/graphic novels, ethnic/multicultural, experimental, historical, literary. Does not want erotica, romance, religious, young adult/teens, new age, family saga, sports, children's/juvenile. Receives 1 mss/month. Accepts 5-10 mss/issue; 10-15 mss/year. Manuscript published 3-4 months after acceptance. **Publishes 1-2 new writers/year.** Published Anne Waldman, Lisa Jarnot, Bruce Covey, Elizabeth Robinson, and Ken Rumble. Length: 1 word (min)-1,500 words (max). Average length: 1,200 words. Publishes short shorts. Also publishes literary essays, literary criticism, poetry. Never comments on/critiques rejected manuscripts.

How to Contact Query first. Accepts submissions by e-mail. Include estimated word count, brief bio, list of publications. Responds to queries in 1 week. Responds to mss in 2 months. Send either SASE (or IRC) for return of ms or disposable copy of ms and #10 SASE for reply only. Sample copy available for $10. Guidelines available for SASE, via e-mail, on Web site.

Payment/Terms Writers receive 1 contributor's copy. Additional copies $10. Pays on publication. Acquires all rights, revert back to writer/artist upon publication. Publication is copyrighted.

Advice "Obtain a copy of our magazine and become familiar with the fiction we publish."

▦ ☑ OPEN WIDE MAGAZINE

40 Wingfield Road, Lakenheath, Brandon, Suffolk IP27 9HR United Kingdom. E-mail: contact@openwidemagazine.co.uk. Web site: www.openwidemagazine.co.uk. **Contact:** Liz Roberts. Literary magazine/journal: A5, 80 pages. Quarterly. Estab. 2001. Circ. 1,700.

Needs Adventure, ethnic/multicultural, experimental, feminist, gay, horror, humor/satire, lesbian, mainstream, mystery/suspense, principle beat. Receives 100 mss/month. Accepts 25 mss/issue. Manuscript published 3 months after acceptance. **Publishes 30 new writers/year.** Length: 500-4,000. Average length: 2,500. Publishes short shorts. Also publishes poetry also reviews (music, film, art) and interviews. Rarely comments on/critiques rejected mss.

How to Contact Accepts submissions by e-mail. Include estimated word count, brief bio. Send either SASE (or IRC) for return of ms or disposable copy of ms and #10 SASE for reply only.

Payment/Terms Copies $10. Acquires one-time rights. Publication is copyrighted.

☑ PACIFIC COAST JOURNAL

French Bread Publications, P.O. Box 56, Carlsbad CA 92018. E-mail: paccoastj@frenchbreadpublications.com. Web site: www.frenchbreadpublications.com/pcj. **Contact:** Stephanie Kylkis, fiction editor. Magazine: 5½×8½; 40 pages; 20 lb. paper; 67 lb. cover; illustrations; b&w photos. "Slight focus toward Western North America/Pacific Rim." Quarterly. Estab. 1992. Circ. 200.

Needs Ethnic/multicultural, experimental, feminist, historical, humor/satire, literary, science fiction (soft/sociological, magical realism). "No children's, religious, or hard sci-fi." Receives 150unsolicited mss/month. Accepts 3-4 mss/issue; 10-12 mss/year. Publishes ms 6-18 months after acceptance. Length: 4,000 words; average length: 2,500 words. Publishes short shorts. Also publishes literary essays, poetry. Sometimes comments on rejected mss.

How to Contact Send SASE for reply, return of ms or send a disposable copy of ms. Also accepts e-mail address for response instead of SASE. Responds in 6-9 months to mss. Accepts simultaneous submissions and reprints. Sample copy for $3, 6×9 SASE and 3oz. postage. Reviews fiction.

Payment/Terms Pays 1 contributor's copy. Acquires one-time rights.

Advice *"PCJ* is an independent magazine and we have a limited amount of space and funding. We are looking for experiments in what can be done with the short fiction form. The best stories will entertain as well as confuse."

N 🗌 🗌 PACKINGTOWN REVIEW

University of Illinois, Chicago. E-mail: editors@packingtownreview.com. Web site: www.packingto wnreview.com. **Contact:** Tasha Fouts and Snezana Zabic, Editors-in-Chief. Magazine has revolving editor. Editorial term: 3 years. Next term: 2011. Literary magazine/journal: 8½×11, 250 pages. *"Packingtown Review* publishes imaginative and critical prose by emerging and established writers. We welcome submissions of poetry, scholarly articles, drama, creative nonfiction, fiction, and literary translation, as well as genre-bending pieces." Annual. Estab. 2008.

Needs Comics/graphic novels, ethnic/multicultural (general), experimental, feminist, gay, glitz, historical (general), literary, mainstream, military/war, translations. Does not want to see uninspired or unrevised work. "We also would like to avoid fantasy, science fiction, overtly religious, or romantic pieces." Ms published max of nine months after acceptance. Length: 3,000 words (min)-8,000 words (max). Publishes short shorts. Also publishes literary essays, literary criticism, book reviews, poetry. Send review copies to Tasha Fouts or Snezana Zabic (Editors-in-Chief). Sometimes comments on/critiques rejected mss.

How to Contact Send complete ms with cover letter. Include estimated word count, brief bio. Responds to queries in 3 weeks. Responds to mss in 3 months. Considers simultaneous submissions. Sample copy available for $14. Guidelines available for SASE, via e-mail.

Payment/Terms Writers receive 2 contributor's copies. Pays on publication. Acquires first North American serial rights. Sends galleys to author. Publication is copyrighted.

Advice "We are looking for well crafted prose. We are open to most styles and forms. We are also looking for prose that takes risks and does so successfully. We will consider articles about prose."

N 🗌 🗌 PADDLEFISH

1105 W. 8th Street, Yankton SD 5708. (605)688-1362. E-mail: james.reese@mtmc.edu. Web site: www.mmcpaddlefish.com. **Contact:** Dr. Jim Reese, editor. Literary magazine/journal: 6×9, 150 pages. Includes photographs. "We publish unique and creative pieces." Annual. Estab. 2007.

Needs Adventure, children's/juvenile, comics/graphic novels, erotica, ethnic/multicultural, experimental, family saga, fantasy, feminist, gay, glitz, historical, horror, humor/satire, lesbian, literary, mainstream, military/war, mystery, new age, psychic/supernatural/occult, religious, romance, science fiction, thriller/espionage, translations, western, young adult/teen. Does not want excessive or gratuitous language, sex or violence. Receives 50 mss/month. Accepts 10 mss/year. Submission period is Nov 1-Feb 28. Ms published 3-9 months after acceptance. **Publishes 5-10 new writers/ year.** Published David Lee, William Kloefkorn, David Allen Evans, Jack Anderson and Maria Mazzi-otti Gillan. Length: 2,500 words (max). Publishes short shorts. Also publishes literary essays, poetry. Rarely comments on/critiques rejected mss.

How to Contact Send complete ms with cover letter. Include estimated word count, brief bio, list of publications. Send disposable copy of ms and #10 SASE for reply only. Guidelines available for SASE.

Payment/Terms Writers receive 1 contributor's copy. Additional copies $8. Pays on publication. Acquires one-time rights. Sends galleys to author. Publication is copyrighted. "Cash prizes are award to Mount Marty students."

🗌 🗌 PALO ALTO REVIEW, A Journal of Ideas

Palo Alto College, 1400 W. Villaret, San Antonio TX 78224. (210)921-5021. Fax: (210)921-5008. E-mail: eshull@accd.edu. **Contact:** Ellen Shull, editor. Magazine: 8½×11; 64 pages; 60 lb. gloss white paper; illustrations; photos. More than half of each issue is devoted to articles and essays. "We select stories that we would want to read again. Not too experimental nor excessively avant-garde, just good fiction." Semiannual. Estab. 1992. Circ. 500.

• *Palo Alto Review* was awarded the Pushcart Prize for 2001.

Needs Adventure, ethnic/multicultural, experimental, fantasy, feminist, historical, humor/satire, literary, mainstream, mystery/suspense, regional, romance, science fiction, translations, western.

Upcoming themes available for SASE. Receives 100-150 unsolicited mss/month. Accepts 2-3 mss/issue; 4-6 mss/year. Does not read mss April -May and October-December when putting out each issue. Publishes ms 2-15 months after acceptance. **Publishes 20 new writers/year.** Recently published work by Char Miller, Naveed Noori, E.M. Schorb, Louis Phillips, Tom Filer, Jo Lecoeur, H. Palmer Hall. Publishes short shorts. Also publishes poetry, essays, articles, memoirs, book reviews. Always comments on rejected mss.

How to Contact Send SASE for reply, return of ms or send a disposable copy of ms. "Request sample copy and guidelines." Accepts submissions by e-mail only if outside the US. Responds in 4 months to mss. Accepts simultaneous submissions. Sample copy for $5. Writer's guidelines for #10 SASE or e-mail to eshull@accd.edu.

Payment/Terms Pays 2 contributor's copies; additional copies for $5. Acquires first North American serial rights.

Advice "Good short stories have interesting characters confronted by a dilemma working toward a solution. So often what we get is 'a moment in time,' not a story. Generally, characters are interesting because readers can identify with them. Edit judiciously. Cut out extraneous verbiage. Set up a choice that has to be made. Then create tension—who wants what and why they can't have it."

⬛ ☑ PAPER STREET

P.O. Box 14786, Pittsburgh PA 15234-0768. (412)951-1581. E-mail: editor@paperstreetpress.org. Web site: http://paperstreetpress.org. **Contact:** Dory Adams, Fiction Editor. Literary magazine/journal. 6×9, 120 pages. "Paperstreet Press is a non-profit, independent literary publisher producing a semi-annual literary journal featuring both local and national writers." Semiannual. Estab. Spring 2004. Circ. 500. Member CLMP.

● Honorable Mention, Pushcart Prize 2004, 2005

Needs Historical (general), literary, translations. Does not want fantasy, horror or religious. Receives 60 mss/month. Accepts 3-6 mss/issue; 6-12 mss/year. Does not read Sept-May. Mss published 12-18 months after acceptance. **Publishes 20% new writers/year.** Published Erin Malone, Terry Dubow, Lori Wilson and Krista Mann. Publishes short shorts. Also publishes book reviews, poetry. Send review copies to Attn: Editor. Rarely comments on/critiques rejected mss.

How to Contact Send complete ms with cover letter. Include brief bio, list of publications, and full contact information: address, email, phone number and name. Responds to mss in 3-9 months. Send disposable copy of ms and #10 SASE for reply only. Considers simultaneous submissions. Sample copy available for $9. Guidelines available for SASE, via e-mail, on Web site.

Payment/Terms Writers receive 1 contributor's copy, free subscription to the magazine. Additional copies $9 each. Pays on publication. Acquires first North American serial rights. Publication is copyrighted.

Advice "In the best fiction there is a moment that occures when the story, the writer and the reader leave the usual path and experience a stepping off, an exhilarating lift or transcendence, that occurs when the writing moves forward, unafraid of the unexpected turn and fresh territory. We seek to provide that connection between readers and writers who love well-crafted stories that are driven by character, rooted in place, and value humor, language and imagery. Avoid sentimentality and clichè. Show us something new."

$⬜ ◎ ⬛ PARADOX, THE MAGAZINE OF HISTORICAL AND SPECULATIVE FICTION

Paradox Publications, P.O. Box 22897, Brooklyn NY 11202-2897. E-mail: editor@paradoxmag.com. Web site: www.paradoxmag.com. **Contact:** Christopher M. Cevasco, editor/publisher. Literary magazine/journal. 8½×11, 57 pages, standard white paper with b&w interior art, glossy color cover. Contains illustrations. Includes photographs. "Paradox is the only English-language print magazine exclusively devoted to historical fiction in either its mainstream or genre forms." Semiannual. Estab. 2003. Circ. 600. Member Speculative Literature Foundation Small Press Co-operative. Awards: 6 honorable mentions (2003) and 3 honorable mentions (2004) in *Year's Best Fantasy & Horror*, edited by Ellen Datlow, Kelly Link and Gavin Grant; 2 honorable mentions (2004) in *Year's Best Science Fiction*, edited by Gardner Dozois.

Needs Fantasy (historical), horror (historical), military/war, historical mystery/suspense, science fiction (historical, e.g. time travel and alternate history), western (historical). Does not want children's stories, gratuitous erotica, vampires, werewolves. Receives 75 mss/month. Accepts 6-8 mss/issue; 12-16 mss/year. Manuscript published 6 months after acceptance. Agented fiction 5%. **Pub-**

lishes 1-2 new writers/year.Published Jack Whyte, Sarah Monette, Adam Stemple, Paul Finch, Eugie Foster, Darron T. Moore (debut). Length: 2,000 words (min)-15,000 words (max). Average length: 6,000 words. Publishes short shorts. Average length of short shorts: 1,200 words. Also publishes literary essays, book reviews, poetry. Send review copies to Christopher M. Cevasco. Always comments on/critiques rejected manuscripts.

How to Contact Send complete ms with cover letter. Include estimated word count. Responds to mss in 4 months. Send either SASE (or IRC) for return of ms or disposable copy of ms and #10 SASE for reply only. Sample copy available for $7.50 (includes postage), or for $8 to Canada, or for $11 elsewhere. Guidelines available on Web site.

Payment/Terms Writers receive 3-5¢/word, 4 contributor's copies. Additional copies ⅓ off cover price. Pays on publication. Acquires first world English-language rights. Sends galleys to author. Publication is copyrighted. ''Offers periodic fiction writing contests; details posted in magazine and on Web site.''

☑ ☒ THE PARIS REVIEW

62 White St., New York NY 10013. Web site: www.theparisreview.org. **Contact:** Fiction Editor. Philip Gourevitch, editor. Magazine: about 192 pages; illustrations; photography portfolios (unsolicited artwork not accepted). Fiction, nonfiction and poetry of superlative quality. ''Our contributors include prominent as well as previously unpublished writers. The Writers at Work interview series features important contemporary writers discussing their own work and the craft of writing.'' Published quarterly.

Needs Fiction, nonfiction, poetry. Receives 2,000 unsolicited mss/month. Recently published work by Gish Jen, Benjamin Percy, Etgar Keret, Karl Taro Greenfeld, Andre Aciman, Mary Kinzie, Uzodinma Iweala, and Richard Price.

How to Contact Send complete ms and SASE. Responds in 2 months to fiction mss; 6 months for poetry. Accepts simultaneous, multiple submissions. Sample copy for $12. Writer's guidelines online.

Payment/Terms Payment varies depending on length. Pays on publication for first English-language rights. Sends galleys to author. Sponsors awards/contests.

☒ ☑ ◎ PASSAGER

Passager Press, % The University of Baltimore, Baltimore MD 21201. (410)837-6047. E-mail: passager @saysomethingloudly.com. Web site: www.passagerpress.com. **Contact**: Editors. Literary magazine/journal: 8¼×8¼, 84 pages, recycled paper. ''*Passager* has a special focus on older writers. Its mission is to encourage, engage and strengthen the imagination well into old age and to give mature readers oppertunities that are sometimes closed off to them in our youth-oriented culture. We are dedicated to honoring the creativity that takes hold in later years and to making public the talents of those over the age of 50.'' Semiannual. Estab. 1990. Circ. 1,500. Member CLMP.

Needs Literary. Receives 20 mss/month. Accepts 4 mss/issue; 4 mss/year. Does not read Sept.15 through Feb 15th. Ms published 4 months after acceptance. Publishes 2-3 new writers/year. Published Miriam Karme, Lucille Schulberg Warner, Sally Bellerose and Craig Hartglass. Length: 4,000 words (max). Publishes short shorts. Also publishes poetry and memoir. Never comments on/ critiques rejected mss.

How to Contact Send complete ms with cover letter. Check Web site for guidelines. Include estimated word count, brief bio, list of publications. Responds to mss in 5 months. Send either SASE (or IRC) for return of ms or disposable copy of ms and #10 SASE for reply only. Considers simultaneous submissions. Sample copy available for $10. Guidelines available for SASE, on Web site.

Payment/Terms Writers receive 1 contributor's copy. Additional copies $7. Pays on publication. Acquires first North American serial rights. Publication is copyrighted.

Advice ''Stereotyped images of old age will be rejected immediately. Write humorous, tongue-in-cheek essays. Read the publication, or at least visit the Web site.''

☑ PASSAGES NORTH

Northern Michigan University, Department of English, Gries Hall, Rm 229, Marquette MI 49855. (906)227-1203. Fax: (906)227-1096. E-mail: passages@nmu.edu. Web site: http://myweb.nmu.edu/ ~passages. **Contact:** Kate Myers Hanson, Editor-in-Chief. Magazine: 7×10; 200-300 pgs; 60 lb. paper. ''*Passages North* publishes quality fiction, poetry and creative nonfiction by emerging and established writers.'' Annual. Estab. 1979. Circ. 1,500.

Needs Ethnic/multicultural, literary, short-short fiction. No genre fiction, science fiction, "typical commercial press work." Receives 200 unsolicited mss/month. Accepts 12-15 mss/year. Reads mss September 1-April 15. **Publishes 10% new writers/year.** Recently published work by John McNally, Steve Almond, Tracy Winn and Midege Raymond. Length: 5,000 words (max). Average lenth 3,000 words. Publishes short shorts. Average length: 1,000 words. Also publishes literary essays, poetry. Comments on rejected mss when there is time.

How to Contact Send complete ms with cover letter. Responds in 2-4 months to mss. Accepts simultaneous submissions. Sample copy for $3-7. Guidelines for SASE, e-mail, on Web site.

Payment/Terms Pays 2 contributor's copies. Rights revert to author upon publication. Publication is copyrighted. Occasionally sponsors contests; check Web site for details.

Advice "We look for voice, energetic prose, writers who take risks. We look for an engaging story in which the author evokes an emotional response from the reader through carefully rendered scenes, complex characters, and a smart, narrative design. Revise, revise. Read what we publish."

THE PATERSON LITERARY REVIEW

Passaic County Community College, One College Blvd., Paterson NJ 07505. (973)684-6555. Fax: (973)523-6085. E-mail: mgillan@pccc.edu. Web site: www.pccc.edu/poetry. **Contact:** Maria Mazziotti Gillan, editor. Magazine: 6×9; 400 pages; 60 lb. paper; 70 lb. cover; illustrations; photos. Annual.

• Work for *PLR* has been included in the *Pushcart Prize* anthology and *Best American Poetry*.

Needs Ethnic/multicultural, literary, contemporary. "We are interested in quality short stories, with no taboos on subject matter." Receives 60 unsolicited mss/month. Publishes ms 6-12 months after acceptance. **Publishes 5% new writers/year.** Recently published work by Robert Mooney and Abigail Stone. Also publishes literary essays, literary criticism, poetry.

How to Contact Send SASE for reply or return of ms. "Indicate whether you want story returned." Accepts simultaneous submissions. Sample copy for $13 plus $1.50 postage. Reviews fiction.

Payment/Terms Pays in contributor's copies. Acquires first North American serial rights.

Advice Looks for "clear, moving and specific work."

PEARL, A Literary Magazine

3030 E. Second St., Long Beach CA 90803-5163. (562)434-4523. E-mail: pearlmag@aol.com. Web site: www.pearlmag.com. **Contact:** Marilyn Johnson, editor. Magazine: 5½×8½; 96 pages; 60 lb. recycled, acid-free paper; perfect bound; coated cover; b &w drawings and graphics. "We are primarily a poetry magazine, but we do publish some *very short* fiction. We are interested in lively, readable prose that speaks to *real* people in direct, living language; for a general literary audience." Biannual. Estab. 1974. Circ. 600.

Needs Humor/satire, literary, mainstream, contemporary, prose poem. "We will consider short-short stories up to 1,200 words. Longer stories (up to 4,000 words) may only be submitted to our short story contest. All contest entries are considered for publication. Although we have no taboos stylistically or subject-wise, obscure, predictable, sentimental, or cliché-ridden stories are a turn-off." Publishes an all-fiction issue each year. Receives 30-40 unsolicited mss/month. Accepts 15-20 mss/issue; 12-15 mss/year. Submissions accepted January-June *only*. Publishes ms 6-12 months after acceptance. **Publishes 1-5 new writers/year.** Recently published work by James D. McCallister, Heidi Rosenberg, W. Joshua Heffernan, Suzanne Greenberg, Fred McGavran, Gerald Locklin, Robert Perchan, Lisa Glatt. Length: 500-1,200 words; average length: 1,000 words. Also publishes poetry.

How to Contact Include SASE. Responds in 2 months to mss. Accepts simultaneous, multiple submissions. Sample copy for $8 (postpaid). Writer's guidelines for #10 SASE.

Payment/Terms Pays 1 contributor's copy. Acquires first North American serial rights. Sends galleys to author. Sponsors awards/contests.

Advice "We look for vivid, *dramatized* situations and characters, stories written in an original 'voice,' that make sense and follow a clear narrative line. What makes a manuscript stand out is more elusive, though—more to do with feeling and imagination than anything else."

$ PEEKS & VALLEYS, A Fiction Journal

E-mail: editor@peeksandvalleys.com. Web site: http://peeksandvalleys.com/. **Contact:** Mary Anne DeYoung, editor. "*Peeks & Valleys* is a fiction journal that seeks traditional, character driven fiction.

Our goal is to encourage and offer an outlet for both accomplished and new writers and to cause contemplation on the part of the reader.'' Quarterly. Estab. 1999.

Needs ''Please no sci-fi, formulaic, interview/profile or erotica.'' Receives 40 unsolicited mss/month. Accepts 7-8 mss/issue; 28-32 mss/year. Publishes ms 8 months after acceptance. **Publishes 80% new writers/year.** Length: 5000 words max; average length: 1,500 words. Also publishes poetry.

How to Contact Send complete ms. Accepts submissions by e-mail. Check Web site for writer's guidelines. Responds in 4 months to mss. Accepts simultaneous submissions and reprints. Sample copy for $5.75. Writer's guidelines online.

Payment/Terms Pays $ 10.00 plus 2 contriubter's copies. Pays on publication for one-time, second serial (reprint) rights.

Advice ''Follow submission guidelines, and don't exceed the recommended length. Study the journal to get a clear idea of what is needed. Be sure to check the Web site for information on the annual flash fiction contest.''

☐ PENNSYLVANIA ENGLISH

Penn State DuBois, College Place, DuBois PA 15801. (814)375-4814. Fax: (814)375-4784. E-mail: ajv2@psu.edu. ''Mention *Pennsylvania English* in the subject line.'' **Contact:** Antonio Vallone, editor. Magazine: 5¼×8¼; up to 200 pages; perfect bound; full color cover featuring the artwork of a Pennsylvania artist. ''Our philosophy is quality. We publish literary fiction (and poetry and nonfiction). Our intended audience is literate, college-educated people.'' Annual. Estab. 1985. Circ. 300.

Needs Literary, mainstream, contemporary. ''No genre fiction or romance.'' Reads mss during the summer. Publishes ms up tp 12 months after acceptance. **Publishes 4-6 new writers/year.** Recently published work by Dave Kress, Dan Leone and Paul West. Publishes short shorts. Also publishes literary essays, literary criticism, poetry. Sometimes comments on rejected mss.

How to Contact SASE. Does not normally accept electronic submissions. ''We are creating Pennsylvania English Online —www.pennsylvaniaenglish.com— for electronic submissions and expanded publishing oppurtunities.'' Responds in up to 12 months to mss. Accepts simultaneous submissions. Does not accept previously published work. Sample copy for $10.

Payment/Terms Pays in 2 contributor's copies. Acquires first North American serial rights.

Advice ''Quality of the writing is our only measure. We're not impressed by long-winded cover letters detailing awards and publications we've never heard of. Beginners and professionals have the same chance with us. We receive stacks of competently written but boring fiction. For a story to rise out of the rejection pile, it takes more than the basic competence.''

☑ PEREGRINE

Amherst Writers & Artists Press, 190 University Drive, Amherst MA 01002. (413)253-3307. E-mail: peregrine@amherstwriters.com. Web site: www.amherstwriters.com. **Contact:** Nancy Rose, editor. Magazine: 6×9; 100 pages; 60 lb. white offset paper; glossy cover. ''Peregrine has provided a forum for national and international writers since 1983, and is committed to finding excellent work by new writers as well as established authors. We welcome work reflecting diversity of voice. We like to be surprised. We look for writing that is honest, unpretentious, and memorable. We like to be surprised. All decision are made by the editors.'' Annual. Member CLMP.

Needs Poetry and prose. ''No previously published work. No children's stories.'' Short pieces have a better chance of publication. No electronic submissions. Accepts 6-12 mss/issue. Reads January-March . Publishes ms 4 months after acceptance. **Publishes 8-10 new writers/year.** Recently published work by Linda Lee Benanti, Steven Riel, David Lunden, Elisabeth Carter, Aaron Zimmerman, Colette Volkema DeNooyer, Peter Schneider . Publishes short shorts.

How to Contact Enclose sufficiently stamped SASE for return of ms; if disposable copy, enclose #10 SASE for response. Deadline for submission: March 31. Accepts simultaneous submissions. Sample copy for $12. Writer's guidelines for #10 SASE or Web site.

Payment/Terms Pays contributor's copies. All rights return to writer upon publication.

Advice ''Check guidelines before submitting your work. Familiarize yourself with Peregrine. We look for heart and soul as well as technical expertise. Trust your own voice.''

☑ PHANTASMAGORIA

Century College English Dept., 3300 Century Ave. N, White Bear Lake MN 55110. (651)779-3410. E-mail: allenabigail@hotmail.com. **Contact**: Abigail Allen, editor. Magazine: 5½×8½; 140-200 pages.

"We publish literary fiction, poetry and essays (no scholarly essays)." Semiannual. Estab. 2001. Circ. 1,000. Member CLMP.

Needs Experimental, literary, mainstream. "No children's stories or young adult/teen material." Receives 120 unsolicited mss/month. Accepts 20-40 mss/issue; 40-80 mss/year. Publishes ms 6 months after acceptance. Publishes 5-10 new writers/year. Recently published work by Greg Mulcahy, Hiram Goza, Kim Chinquee, Louis E. Bourgeois. Length: 4,000 words; average length: 2,500 words. Publishes short shorts. Also publishes literary essays, poetry.

How to Contact Send SASE (or IRC) for return of ms or send a disposable copy of ms and #10 SASE for reply only. Responds in 2 weeks to queries. Sample copy for $9. Writer's guidelines for SASE. Reviews fiction.

Payment/Terms Pays 2 contributor's copies. Acquires first North American serial rights.

N ☑ ◎ PHILADELPHIA STORIES

Fiction/Art/Poetry of the Delaware Valley, 2021 S. 11th Street, Philadelphia PA 19148. (215)551-5889. Fax: (215)635-0195. E-mail: info@philadelphiastories.org. Web site: www.philadelphiastories. org. **Contact**: Carla Spataro, Fiction Editor/Co-Publisher. Literary magazine/journal. 8½×11; 24 pages; 70# Matte Text, all four-color paper; 70# Matte Text cover. Contains illustrations., photographs. "*Philadelphia Stories Magazine* publishes fiction, poetry, essays and art written by authors living in, or originally from, Pennsylvania, Delaware, or New Jersey." Quarterly. Estab. 2004. Circ. 10,000. Member CLMP.

Needs Experimental, literary, mainstream. "We will consider anything that is well written but are most inclined to publish literary or mainstream fiction. We are NOT particularly interested in most genres (sci fi/fantasy, romance, etc.)." List of upcoming themes available for SASE, on Web site. Receives 45-80 mss/month. Accepts 3-4 mss/issue for print, additional 1-2 online; 12-16 mss/year for print, 4-8 online. Ms published 1-2 months after acceptance. **Publishes 50% new writers/ year.** Published Justin St. Germain, Christine, Tim Zatzariny Jr., Lee W. Doty, Shantee' Cherese, Marguerite, Victoria Sprow. Length: 5,000 words (max). Average length: 4,000 words. Publishes short shorts. Average length of short shorts: 800 words. Also publishes literary essays, book reviews, poetry. Send review queries to: info@philadelphiastories.org. Rarely comments on/critiques rejected mss.

How to Contact Send complete ms with cover letter via online submission form only. Include estimated word count, list of publications, affiliation to the Philadelphia area. Responds to mss in 12 weeks. Considers simultaneous submissions. Sample copy available for $5, on Web site. Guidelines available on Web site.

Payment/Terms Writers receive 2+ contributor's copies. Pays on publication. Acquires one-time rights. Publication is copyrighted. "Occasionally sponsores contests; visit our Web site for opportunities"

Advice "All work is screened by three editorial board members, who rank the work. These scores are processed at the end of the quarterly submission period, and then the board meets to decide which pieces will be published in print and online. We look for exceptional, polished prose, a controlled voice, strong characters and place, and interesting subjects. Follow guidelines. We cannot stress this enough. Read every guideline carefully and thoroughly before sending anything out. Send out only polished material. We reject many quality pieces for various reasons; try not to take rejection personally. Just because your piece isn't right for one publication doesn't mean it's bad. Selection is an extremely subjective process."

☑ THE PINCH

(formerly *River City*) Dept. of English, The University of Memphis, Memphis TN 38152. (901)678-4591. E-mail: thepinch@memphis.edu. Web site: www.thepinchjournal.com or ww.mfainmemphis. com. **Contact:** Kristen Iversen, Editor-in-Chief. Magazine: 7×10; 150 pages. Semiannual. Estab. 1980. Circ. 1,500.

Needs Short stories, poetry, creative nonfiction, essays, memoir, travel, nature writing, photography, art. **Publishes some new writers every year.** Recently published work by Chris Fink, Bill Roorbach, Stephen Dunn, Denise Duhamel, Robert Morgan, and Beth Ann Fennelly.

How to Contact Send complete ms. Responds in 2 months to mss. Sample copy for $10.

Payment/Terms Pays 2 contributor's copies. Acquires first North American serial rights.

Advice "We have a new look and a new edge. We're soliciting work from writers with a national or international reputation as well as strong, interesting work from emerging writers. The Pinch Writing Award (previously River City Writing Award) in Fiction offers a $1,500 prize and publication. Check our Web site for details.''

⊿ PINYON

Mesa State College, Dept. of Languages, Lit and Comm, 1100 North Avenue, Grand Junction CO 81501-3122. E-mail: pinyonpoetry@hotmail.com. **Contact:** fiction editor. Literary magazine/journal: $8^{1}/_{2} \times 5^{1}/_{2}$, 120 pages, heavy paper. Contains illustrations and photographs. Annual. Estab. 1996. Circ. 200.

Needs Literary. Receives 16-20 mss/month. Accepts 3-4 mss/issue; 3-4 mss/year. Does not read mss January-August. Manuscript published 6 months after acceptance. Length: 1,500 words (min)-5,000 words (max). Average length: 2,500 words. Publishes short shorts. Average length of short shorts: 500 words. Also publishes poetry.

How to Contact Send complete ms with cover letter. Include brief bio. Responds to queries in 1 month. Responds to mss in 6 months. Send either SASE (or IRC) for return of ms or disposable copy of ms and #10 SASE for reply only. Considers simultaneous submissions, multiple submissions. Sample copy available for $4.50. Send SASE for guidelines.

Payment/Terms Writers receive 2 contributor's copies. Acquires one-time rights. Publication is copyrighted.

Advice ''Ask yourself if the work is something you would like to read in a publication.''

◻ PISGAH REVIEW

Department of Humanities, Brevard College, Brevard NC 28712. (828)586-1969. E-mail: jubaltara@yahoo.com. Web site: www.pisgahreview.com. **Contact:** Jubal Tiner or Lonnie Busch, co-editors. Literary magazine/journal: $5^{1}/_{2} \times 8^{1}/_{2}$, 120 pages. Includes cover photograph. ''*Pisgah Review* publishes primarily literary short fiction, creative nonfiction and poetry. Our only criteria is quality of work; we look for the best. The magazine does give a small preference to work that is based evocatively on place, but we will look at any work of quality.'' Semiannual. Estab. 2005. Circ. 200.

Needs Ethnic/multicultural, experimental, literary, mainstream. Special interests: stories rooted in the theme of place—physical, psychological, or spiritual. Does not want genre fiction or inspirational stories. Receives 30 mss/month. Accepts 6-8 mss/issue; 12-15 mss/year. Manuscript published 6 months after acceptance. **Publishes 5 new writers/year.** Published Ron Rash, Thomas Rain Crowe, Joan Conner. Length: 2,000 words (min)-7,500 words (max). Average length: 4,000 words. Publishes short shorts. Average length of short shorts: 1,000 words. Also publishes poetry and creative nonfiction. Sometimes comments on/critiques rejected mss.

How to Contact Send complete ms with cover letter. Accepts submissions by e-mail. Responds to mss in 4-6 months. Send either SASE (or IRC) for return of ms or disposable copy of ms and #10 SASE for reply only. Considers simultaneous submissions. Sample copy available for $7. Guidelines available for SASE, via e-mail.

Payment/Terms Writers receive 2 contributor's copies. Additional copies $7. Pays on publication. Acquires first North American serial rights. Sends galleys to author. Publication is copyrighted.

Advice ''We select work only of the highest quality. Grab us from the beginning and follow through. Engage us with your language and characters. A clean manuscript goes a long way toward acceptance. Stay true to the vision of your work, revise tirelessly, and submit persistently.''

$⊿ ▼ PLEIADES

Pleiades Press, Department of English & Philosophy, University of Central Missouri, Martin 336, Warrensburg MO 64093. (660)543-4425. Fax: (660)543-8544. E-mail: kdp8106@yahoo.com. Web site: www.ucmo.edu/englphil/pleiades. **Contact:** G.B. Crump , Matthew Eck, Phong Nguyen, Prose editors. Magazine: $5^{1}/_{2} \times 8^{1}/_{2}$; 250 pages; 60 lb. paper; perfect-bound; 8 pt. color cover. ''We publish contemporary fiction, poetry, interviews, literary essays, special-interest personal essays, reviews for a general and literary audience.'' Semiannual. Estab. 1991. Circ. 3,000.

• Work from *Pleiades* appears in recent volumes of *The Best American Poetry*, *Pushcart Prize* and *Best American Fantasy and Horror*.

Needs Ethnic/multicultural, experimental, feminist, gay, humor/satire, literary, mainstream, novel excerpts, regional, translations, magical realism. No science fiction, fantasy, confession, erotica. Receives 100 unsolicited mss/month. Accepts 8 mss/issue; 16 mss/year. ''We're slower at reading manuscripts in the summer.'' Publishes ms 9 months after acceptance. **Publishes 4-5 new writers/ year.** Recently published work by Sherman Alexie, Edith Pearlman, Joyce Carol Oates, James Tate. Length: 2,000-6,000 words; average length: 3,000-6,000 words. Also publishes literary essays, literary criticism, poetry. Sometimes comments on rejected mss.

How to Contact Send complete ms. Include 75-100 word bio and list of publications. Send SASE for reply, return of ms or send a disposable copy of ms. Responds in 2 months to queries; 2 months to mss. Accepts simultaneous submissions. Sample copy for $5 (back issue), $6 (current issue). Writer's guidelines for #10 SASE.

Payment/Terms Pays $10. Pays on publication for first North American serial, second serial (reprint) rights. Occasionally requests rights for TV, radio reading, Web site.

Advice Looks for ''a blend of language and subject matter that entices from beginning to end. Send us your best work. Don't send us formula stories. While we appreciate and publish well-crafted traditional pieces, we constantly seek the story that risks, that breaks form and expectations and wins us over anyhow.''

Ⓝ◑◎Ⓖ PMS, POEMMEMOIRSTORY

University of Alabama at Birmingham, HB 217, 1530 3rd Avenue South, Birmingham AL 35294-4450. (205)934-5380; (205)934-4250. Fax: (205)975-8125. E-mail: lfrost@uab.edu. Web site: http://www.pms-journal.org. **Contact:** Linda Frost, editor-in-chief. Literary magazine/journal: 6×9; 120 pages; recycled white; matte paper; cover photos. ''We print one issue a year, our cover price is $7, and our journal publishes fine creative work by women writers from across the nation (and beyond) in the three genres listed in the title. One of our distinctive features is a memoir that we feature in each issue written by a woman who has experienced something of historic, national import but who would not necessarily call herself a writer. Our first issue, for instance, featured a piece by Emily Lyons, the nurse who was critically injured in the 1998 bombing of the Birmingham New Woman All Women clinic. We've published a wide range of these featured pieces including a memoir by a woman who was in the World Trade Center on 9-11, another by a woman who was serving in Iraq, another by a student who lived through Katrina in New Orleans, and another by a woman who married her lesbian partner in a wedding in Boston during that initial window of opportunity. *PMS 8* was our first special issue, guest edited by Honorée Fanonne Jeffers and featuring all African-American women writers. We are currently distributed by Ingram Periodicals, Inc.'' Annual. Estab. 2001. Circ. 1,500. Member Council of Literary Magazines and Presses and the Council of Editors of Learned Journals.

● Work from PMS has been reprinted in a number of award anthologies: *New Stories from the South 2005*, *The Best Creative Nonfiction 2007 and 2008*, *Best American Poetry 2003 and 2004*, and *Best American Essays 2005 and 2007*.

Needs Comics/graphic novels, ethnic/multicultural (general), experimental, feminist, literary, translations. ''We don't do erotic, mystery work, and most popular forms, per se. We publish short stories and essays including memoirs and other brands of creative nonfiction.'' Receives 30 mss/month. Accepts 4-6 mss/issue. As of 2009, reading period is January 1 through March 30. Ms published within 6 months after acceptance. **Publishes 5 new writers/year.** Published Vicki Covington, Kim Aubrey, Patricia Brieschke, Gaines Marsh. Length: 4,500 words (max). Average length: 3,500-4,000 words. Publishes short shorts. Average length of short shorts: 300-350 words. Also publishes literary essays, poetry. Rarely comments on/critiques rejected mss.

How to Contact Send complete ms with cover letter. Include list of publications. Responds to queries in 1 month. Responds to mss in 1-4 months. Send disposable copy of ms and #10 SASE for reply only. Considers simultaneous submissions, multiple submissions. Sample copy available for $7. Guidelines available for SASE, on Web site.

Payment/Terms Writers receive 2 contributor's copies. Additional copies $7. Pays on publication. Acquires one-time rights. Publication is copyrighted.

Advice ''Send your best work; excellent work with a strong eye for detail and a sense of a fresh use of the language. Read a lot, write a lot, and get into the habit of sending your work out a lot.''

◑ POINTED CIRCLE

Portland Community College-Cascade, 705 N. Killingsworth St., Portland OR 97217. (503)978-5251. E-mail: kimball@pcc.edu. **Contact:** Cynthia Kimball, English instructor, faculty advisor. Magazine:

80 pages; b&w illustrations; photos. "Anything of interest to educationally/culturally mixed audience." Annual. Estab. 1980.

Needs Ethnic/multicultural, literary, regional, contemporary, prose poem. "We will read whatever is sent, but encourage writers to remember we are a quality literary/arts magazine intended to promote the arts in the community. No pornography. Be mindful of deadlines and length limits." Accepts submissions only October 1-March 1, for July 1 issue.

How to Contact Accepts submissions by e-mail, fax. Submitted materials will not be returned; SASE for notification only. Accepts multiple submissions. Writer's guidelines for #10 SASE.

Payment/Terms Pays 2 copies. Acquires one-time rights.

Advice "Looks for quality—topicality—nothing trite. The author cares about language and acts responsibly toward the reader, honors the reader's investment of time and piques the reader's interest."

POLYPHONY H.S., A Student-Run National Literary Magazine for High School Writers

Polyphony H.S., % Educational Endeavors, 1535 N. Dayton, Chicago IL 60622. (312)266-0123. Fax: (312)643-1036. E-mail: billylombardo@comcast.net. Web site: www.polyphonyhs.com. **Contact:** Billy Lombardo, managing editor. Literary magazine/journal: 9X6, 70-120 pages, silk finish 80 lb. white paper, silk finish 100 lb. cover. "Our goal is to seek out the finest high school writers in the country, to work with them to grow as writers, and to exhibit their fiction before a national audience. Every submission is edited, commented upon, by at least three high school editors from around the country. Students who are interested in national editorial positions can contact Billy Lombardo at the above E-ddress." Annual. Estab. 2005. Circ. 2,000.

Needs: Poetry, fiction, and creative nonfiction. Receives 250-500mss/year. Accepts 20-40 mss/issue. Publishes 20-40 new writers/year. Length: 3,000 words (max). Average length: 2,000 words. Always comments on/critiques rejected mss.

How to Contact: See Web site. Only accepts E-submissions. Send complete mss as Word attachment and also paste within the e-mail text. Type title of piece, author's name in Subject line of e-mail. Include brief bio, name of school. Deadline: third Saturday in February. Responds to mss within 6 weeks. Considers simultaneous submissions. Sample copy available for $7 + $2 shipping/handling.

Payment/Terms Writers receive 2 contributor's copies. Additional copies $3.50. Pays on publication. Acquires first rights. Publication is not copyrighted.

Advice "If you want to hear what your intelligent, thoughtful peers from around the country have to say about your poetry, fiction, and creative nonfiction, send us a little something."

PORTLAND REVIEW

Portland State University, Box 347, Portland OR 97207-0347. (503)725-4533. E-mail: phaas@pdx.e du. Web site: www.portlandreview.org. **Contact:** Patrick Haas, editor. Magazine: 9×6; 100 pages; b&w art and photos. Triannual. Estab. 1956. Circ. 500.

Needs Experimental, historical, humor/satire, novel excerpts, regional, slice-of-life vignettes. Wants more humor. No fantasy, detective, western, or science fiction. Receives 100 unsolicited mss/month. Accepts 10-12 mss/issue; 30-40 mss/year. Publishes ms 3-6 months after acceptance. Recently published work by Katy Williams, Tina Boscha, Kathryn Ma, and Brian Turner.

How to Contact Send complete ms. Send SASE for return of ms. Responds in 6 weeks to queries; 2-4 months to mss. Accepts simultaneous submissions. Sample copy for $9. Writer's guidelines online.

Payment/Terms Pays contributor's copies. Acquires first North American serial rights.

POST ROAD

P.O. Box 600725, Newtown MA 02460. E-mail: mary@postroadmag.com. Web site: www.postroadm ag.com. **Contact:** Mary Cotton. Literary magazine/journal. 8½×11½, 240 pages, 60 lb. opaque paper, gloss cover. "*Post Road* is a nationally distributed literayy magazine based out of New York and Boston that publishes work in the following genres: art, criticism, fiction, nonfiction, and poetry. *Post Road* also features two innovations: the Recommendations section, where established writers write 500-1,000 words on a favorite book(s) or author(s); and the Etcetera section, where we publish interviews, profiles, translations, letters, classic reprints, documents, topical essays, travelogues, etc." Estab. 2000. Circ. 2,000.

● Work from *Post Road* has received the following honors: honorable mention in the 2001 O. Henry Prize Issue guest-edited by Michael Chabon, Mary Gordon, and Mona Simpson; the Pushcart Prize; honorable mention in *The Best American Nonfiction* series; and inclusion in the *Best American Short Stories* 2005.

Needs Literary. Receives 100 mss/month. Accepts 4-6 mss/issue; 8-12 mss/year. Does not read mss March 16-May 31 and September 2-January 14. Manuscript published 6 months after acceptance. Published Brian Booker, Louis E. Bourgeois, Becky Bradway, Adam Braver, Ashley Capps, Susan Choi, Lisa Selin Davis, Rebecca Dickson, Rick Moody. Average length: 5,000 words. Average length of short shorts: 1,500 words. Also publishes literary essays, literary criticism, poetry. Sometimes comments on/critiques rejected manuscripts.

How to Contact Accepts submissions by e-mail. Electronic submissions only. Include brief bio. Responds to mss in 1 months. Send SASE (or IRC) for return of ms. Considers simultaneous submissions. Guidelines available on Web site.

Payment/Terms Writers receive 2 contributor's copies. Pays on publication. Acquires first North American serial rights. Sends galleys to author. Publication is not copyrighted.

Advice "Looking for interesting narrative, sharp dialogue, deft use of imagery and metaphor. Be persistent and be open to criticism."

☑ POTOMAC REVIEW, The Journal for Arts & Humanities

Montgomery College, Paul Peck Humanities Institute, 51 Mannakee St., Rockville MD 20850. (301)251-7417. Fax: (301)738-1745. E-mail: potomacrevieweditor@montgomerycollege.edu. Web site: www.montgomerycollege.edu/potomacreview. **Contact:** Julie Wakeman-Linn, editor. Magazine: 5½×8½; 175 pages; 50 lb. paper; 65 lb. color cover. Potomac Review "reflects a view of our region looking out to the world, and in turn, seeks how the world views the region." Bi-annual. Estab. 1994. Circ. 750.

Needs "Stories and poems with a vivid, individual quality that get at 'the concealed side' of life." Essays and creative nonfiction pieces welcome. No themes. Recieves 300 + unsolicited mss/month. Accepts 40-50 mss/issue. Publishes ms within 1 year after acceptance. Recently published work by Jim Tomilson, Tim Wendel, Rose Solari, Moira Egan, Martin Galvin, Elizabeth Murawski, Richard Peabody, Jeff Hardin, and Nancy Naomi Carlson. Length: 5,000 words; average length: 2,000 words.

How to Contact Send SASE with adequate postage for reply and/or return of ms. Responds in 3 -6 months to mss. Accepts simultaneous submissions. Sample copy for $10. Writer's guidelines on Web site.

Payment/Terms Pays 2 or more contributor's copies; additional copies for a 40% discount.

Advice "Send us interesting, well crafted stories. Have something to say in an original, prov ocative voice. Read recent issue to get a sense of the journal's new direction."

☑ ☑ PRAIRIE SCHOONER

University of Nebraska, English Department, 201 Andrews Hall, P.O. Box 880334, Lincoln NE 68588-0334. (402)472-0911. Fax: (402)472-9771. Web site: http://prairieschooner.unl.edu. **Contact:** Hilda Raz, editor. Magazine: 6×9; 200 pages; good stock paper; heavy cover stock. "A fine literary quarterly of stories, poems, essays and reviews for a general audience that reads for pleasure." Estab. 1926. Circ. 3,000.

● *Prairie Schooner*, one of the oldest publications in this book, has garnered several awards and honors over the years. Work appearing in the magazine has been selected for anthologies including the *Pushcart Prize* anthology and *Best American Short Stories*.

Needs Good fiction (literary). Receives 500 unsolicited mss/month. Accepts 4-5 mss/issue. Mss are read September through May only. **Publishes 5-10 new writers/year.** Recently published work by Robert Olen Butler, Janet Burroway, Aimee Phan, Valerie Sayers, Daniel Stern. Also publishes poetry.

How to Contact Send complete ms with SASE and cover letter listing previous publications—where, when. Responds in 4 months to mss. Sample copy for $6. Writer's guidelines and excerpts online. Reviews fiction.

Payment/Terms Pays in contributor's copies and prize money awarded. Will reassign rights upon request after publication. Sponsors awards/contests.

Advice "*Prairie Schooner* is eager to see fiction from beginning and established writers. Be tenacious. Accept rejection as a temporary setback and send out rejected stories to other magazines. *Prairie Schooner* is not a magazine with a program. We look for good fiction in traditional narrative modes as well as experimental, meta-fiction or any other form or fashion a writer might try. Create striking detail, well-developed characters, fresh dialogue; let the images and the situations evoke the stories' themes. Too much explication kills a lot of otherwise good stories. Be persistent. Keep writing and sending out new work. Be familiar with the tastes of the magazines where you're sending. We are receiving record numbers of submissions. Prospective contributors must sometimes wait longer to receive our reply."

$ ⬚ ◺ ◿ PRISM INTERNATIONAL

Department of Creative Writing, Buch E462-1866 Main Mall, University of British Columbia, Vancouver BC V6T 1Z1 Canada. (604)822-2514. Fax: (604)822-3616. E-mail: prism@interchange.ubc.ca. Web site: http://prismmagazine.ca. **Contact:** Editor. Magazine: 6×9; 80 pages; Zephyr book paper; Cornwall, coated one-side cover; artwork on cover. "An international journal of contemporary writing—fiction, poetry, drama, creative nonfiction and translation." Readership: "public and university libraries, individual subscriptions, bookstores—a worldwide audience concerned with the contemporary in literature." Quarterly. Estab. 1959. Circ. 1,200.

• *Prism International* has won numerous magazine awards, and stories first published in *Prism International* have been included in the *Journey Prize Anthology* every year since 1991.

Needs Experimental, traditional. New writing that is contemporary and literary. Short stories and self-contained novel excerpts (up to 25 double-spaced pages). Works of translation are eagerly sought and should be accompanied by a copy of the original. Would like to see more translations. "No gothic, confession, religious, romance, pornography, or sci-fi." Also looking for creative nonfiction that is literary, not journalistic, in scope and tone. Receives over 100 unsolicited mss/month. Accepts 70 mss/year. "PRISM publishes both new and established writers; our contributors have included Franz Kafka, Gabriel García Márquez, Michael Ondaatje, Margaret Laurence, Mark Anthony Jarman, Gail Anderson-Dargatz and Eden Robinson." Publishes ms 4 months after acceptance. **Publishes 7 new writers/year.** Recently published work by Ibi Kaslik, Melanie Little, Mark Anthony Jarman. Publishes short shorts. Also publishes poetry.

How to Contact Send complete ms by mail. "Keep it simple. U.S. contributors take note: Do not send SASEs with U.S. stamps, they are not valid in Canada. Send International Reply Coupons instead." Responds in 4 months to queries; 3-6 months to mss. Sample copy for $11 or on Web site. Writer's guidelines online.

Payment/Terms Pays $20/printed page of prose, $40/printed page of poetry, and 1-year subscription. Pays on publication for first North American serial rights. Selected authors are paid an additional $10/page for digital rights. Cover art pays $300 and 4 copies of issue. Sponsors awards/contests, including annual short fiction and nonfiction contests.

Advice "Read several issues of our magazine before submitting. We are committed to publishing outstanding literary work. We look for strong, believeable characters; real voices; attention to language; interesting ideas and plots. Send us fresh, innovative work which also shows a mastery of the basics of good prose writing."

⊕ ◺ QUALITY WOMEN'S FICTION, Extending the Boundaries of Women's Fiction

QWF, 234 Brook St., Unit 2, Waukesha WI 53188. E-mail: qwfsubmissionsusa@yahoo.comWeb site: www.allwriters.org. (click on QWF) **Contact:** Kathie Giorgio, Editor. Magazine: A5; 100 pages; glossy paper. "Whether a story is about a woman's highest point in her life, or her lowest, the stories must resonate with an emotional chord. All QWF stories must have impact." Published twice a year. Estab. 1994. Circ. 1,000.

Needs Accepts all genres, as long as the main characters are women and the stories are written by women. Receives 200 unsolicited mss/reading period. Accepts 25 mss/issue; 50 mss/year. Only reads during reading periods. Publishes ms in next issue after acceptance. Publishes new writers. Length: up to 5,000 words; average length: 2,500 words. Publishes short shorts. Always comments on rejected mss.

How to Contact Send complete ms. Accepts submissions by e-mail only. Send complete ms as Word document. Responds in 2 months to queries; 2 months to mss. Simultaneous submissions okay, but not preferred. Back issues available for sale on Web site.Payment/Terms Pays in copies. Acquires first rights.

Advice "Evoking emotion is the most important characteristic of a QWF story. There is no room for a dry reporting of the facts here. Rather, the stories should present the expanse that is every woman's emotional lifetime and experience."

Literary Magazines

⬛ ◎ QUARTER AFTER EIGHT, A Journal of Prose and Community

QAE, Ellis Hall, Ohio University, Athens OH 45701. (740)593-2827. E-mail: editor@quarteraftereight. org. Web site: www.quarteraftereight.org. **Contact:** Wendy Walker, co-editor-in-chief. Magazine: 6×9; 200 pages; 20 lb. glossy cover stock; photos. "We look to publish work which challenges boundaries of genre, style, idea, and voice." Annual.

Needs Condensed novels, ethnic/multicultural, experimental, gay, humor/satire, lesbian, literary, mainstream, translations. "No traditional, conventional fiction." Receives 150-200 unsolicited mss/ month. Accepts 40-50 mss/issue. Does not read mss mid-March-mid-September. Publishes ms 6-12 months after acceptance. **Publishes 20-30 new writers/year.** Recently published work by Virgil Suárez, Maureen Sexton, John Gallagher and Amy England. Length: 10,000 words; average length: 3,000 words. Publishes short shorts. Also publishes literary essays, literary criticism, prose poetry. Occasionally comments on rejected mss.

How to Contact Send SASE for return of ms or send a disposable copy of ms. Responds in 3-5 months to mss. Accepts simultaneous, multiple submissions. Sample copy for $10, 8×11 SAE and $1.60 postage. Writer's guidelines for #10 SASE. Reviews fiction.

Payment/Terms Pays 2 contributor's copies; additional back copies $7. Acquires first North American serial rights. Rights revert to author upon publication. Sponsors awards/contests.

Advice "We look for fiction that is experimental, exploratory, devoted to and driven by language—that which succeeds in achieving the QAE aesthetic. Please subscribe to our journal and read what is published. We do not publish traditional lined poetry or straightforward conventional stories. We encourage writers to submit after they have gotten acquainted with the QAE aesthetic."

$⬛ ◩ QUARTERLY WEST

University of Utah, 255 S. Central Campus Dr., Dept. of English, LNCO 3500, Salt Lake City UT 84112-9109. (801)581-3938. E-mail: quarterlywest@yahoo.com. Web site: www.utah.edu/quarterlywest. **Contact:** Rachel Marston and Pam Balluck. Magazine: 7×10; 50 lb. paper; 4-color cover stock. "We publish fiction, poetry, and nonfiction in long and short formats, and will consider experimental as well as traditional works." Semiannual. Estab. 1976. Circ. 1,900.

• *Quarterly West* was awarded First Place for Editorial Content from the American Literary Magazine Awards. Work published in the magazine has been selected for inclusion in the *Pushcart Prize* anthology and *The Best American Short Stories* anthology.

Needs Ethnic/multicultural, experimental, humor/satire, literary, mainstream, novel excerpts, slice-of-life vignettes, translations, short shorts, translations. No detective, science fiction or romance. Receives 300 unsolicited mss/month. Accepts 6-10 mss/issue; 12-20 mss/year. Reads mss between September 1 and May 1 only. "Submissions received between May 2 and August 31 will be returned unread." Publishes ms 6 months after acceptance. **Publishes 3 new writers/year.** Recently published work by Steve Almond, Linh Dinh.

How to Contact Send complete ms. Brief cover letters welcome. Send SASE for reply or return of ms. Responds in 6 months to mss. Accepts simultaneous submissions if notified. Sample copy for $7.50. Writer's guidelines online.

Payment/Terms Pays $15-50, and 2 contributor's copies. Pays on publication for first North American serial rights.

Advice "We publish a special section of short shorts every issue, and we also sponsor a biennial novella contest. We are open to experimental work—potential contributors should read the magazine! We solicit occasionally, but tend more toward the surprises—unsolicited. Don't send more than one story per submission, and wait until you've heard about the first before submitting another."

⬛ RAINBOW CURVE

P.O. Box 93206, Las Vegas NV 89193-3206. E-mail: rainbowcurve@sbcglobal.net. Web site: www.rai nbowcurve.com. **Contact:** Daphne Young and Julianne Bonnet, editors. Magazine: 5½×8½; 100 pages; 60 lb. paper; coated cover. "*Rainbow Curve* publishes fiction and poetry that dabble at the edge; contemporary work that evokes emotion. Our audience is interested in exploring new worlds of experience and emotion; raw, visceral work is what we look for." Semiannual. Estab. 2002. Circ. 500.

Needs Ethnic/multicultural, experimental, feminist, gay, lesbian, literary. "No genre fiction (romance, western, fantasy, sci-fi)." Receives 60 unsolicited mss/month. Accepts 10-15 mss/issue; 20-30 mss/year. Publishes ms 6 months after acceptance. Agented fiction 1%. **Publishes 80% new**

writers/year. Recently published work by Jonathan Barrett, Trent Busch, Rob Carney, Peter Fontaine, Bridget Hoida, and Karen Toloui. Length: 500-10,000 words; average length: 7,500 words. Publishes short shorts. Sometimes comments on rejected mss.

How to Contact Send SASE for return of ms or send a disposable copy of ms and #10 SASE for reply only. Responds in 3 months to mss. Accepts simultaneous submissions. Sample copy for $6. Writer's guidelines for SASE or on Web site.

Payment/Terms Pays 1 contributor's copy; additional copies $5. Acquires one-time rights. Sends galleys to author.

Advice "Unusual rendering of usual subjects and strong narrative voice make a story stand out. Unique glimpses into the lives of others—make it new."

$⬤ THE RAMBLER

Rambler Publications, LLC, P.O. Box 5070, Chapel Hill NC 27514-5001. (919)545-9789. Fax: (919)545-0921. E-mail: editor@ramblermagazine.com. Web site: www.ramblermagazine.com. **Contact:** Elizabeth Oliver, Managing Editor. Magazine: 8⅛×10⅞, 64 pages, full color. Contains illustrations. Includes photographs. *"The Rambler,* a magazine of personal expression, features in-depth interviews with artists, writers and performers as well as selections of fiction, poetry and essays." Bimonthly. Estab. Jan/Feb 2004. Circ. 4,000.

Needs Literary. Does not want any kind of genre fiction. Receives 150 mss/month. Accepts 1-2 mss/issue; 6-12 mss/year. Manuscript published 6-18 months after acceptance. Agented fiction 5%. **Publishes 15 new writers/year.** Published Marjorie Kemper, Lawrence Naumoff, Christopher Locke, Catherine McCall, Kathryn Hughes, and Marianne Gingher. Length: 8,000 words max. Average length: 4,000 words. Publishes short shorts. Average length of short shorts: 300-1,000 words. Also publishes nonfiction, poetry. Sometimes comments on/critiques rejected manuscripts.

How to Contact Send complete ms with cover letter. Include estimated word count, brief bio, list of publications. Prose submissions may also be sent by e-mail to fiction@ramblermagazine.com or nonfiction@ramblermagazine.com. Responds to queries in 2 months. Responds to mss in 4-6 months. Send either SASE (or IRC) for return of ms or disposable copy of ms and #10 SASE for reply only. Considers multiple submissions. Sample copy available for $7. Guidelines available for SASE, on Web site.

Payment/Terms Writers receive $25-$50 flat-rate payment, 1 contributors copy, complimentary one-year subscription to the magazine. Additional copies $6. Pays on publication. Acquires first North American serial rights. Sends galleys to author. Publication is copyrighted.

Advice "We're looking for stories that are well written with well-developed characters, believable dialogue and satisfying plots. A story that moves us in some way, connects us to something larger. Something that stays with us long after the story is finished. Send us your best work."

⬤ RATTAPALLAX

Rattapallax Press, 532 La Guardia Place, Suite 353, New York NJ 10012. E-mail: info@rattapallax.com. Web site: www.rattapallax.com. **Contact:** Alan Cheuse, fiction editor. Literary magazine: 9×12; 128 pages; bound; some illustrations; photos. "General readership. Our stories must be character driven with strong conflict. All accepted stories are edited by our staff and the writer before publication to ensure a well-crafted and written work." Semiannual. Estab. 1999. Circ. 2,000.

Needs Literary. Receives 15 unsolicited mss/month. Accepts 3 mss/issue; 6 mss/year. Publishes ms 3-6 months after acceptance. Agented fiction 15%. **Publishes 3 new writers/year.** Recently published work by Stuart Dybek, Howard Norman, Molly Giles, Rick Moody. Length: 1,000-10,000 words; average length: 5,000 words. Publishes short shorts. Also publishes poetry. Often comments on rejected mss.

How to Contact Send SASE for return of ms. Responds in 3 months to queries; 3 months to mss. Sample copy for $7.95. Writer's guidelines for SASE or on Web site.

Payment/Terms Pays 2 contributor's copies; additional copies for $7.95. Pays on publication for first North American serial rights. Sends galleys to author.

Advice "Character driven, well crafted, strong conflict."

$⬤ THE RAVEN CHRONICLES, A Magazine of Transcultural Art, Literature and the Spoken Word

The Raven Chronicles, Warren Building, 909 NE 43rd Street, Seattle WA 98105-6020. (206)364-2045.

E-mail: editors@ravenchronicles.org. Web site: www.ravenchronicles.org. **Contact:** Fiction editor. Magazine: 8½×11; 96 pages; 50 lb. book; glossy cover; b&w illustrations; photos. *"The Raven Chronicles* is designed to promote transcultural art, literature and the spoken word.*"* Bi-annual. Estab. 1991. Circ. 2,500-5,000.

Needs Ethnic/multicultural, literary, regional, political, cultural essays. "No romance, fantasy, mystery or detective." Receives 300-400 unsolicited mss/month. Accepts 35-60 mss/issue; 105-150 mss/year. Publishes ms 12 months after acceptance. **Publishes 50-100 new writers/year.** Recently published work by David Romtvedt, Sherman Alexie, D.L. Birchfield, Nancy Redwine, Diane Glancy, Greg Hischak , Sharon Hashimoto. Length: 2,500 words (but negotiable); average length: 2,000 words. Publishes short shorts. Also publishes literary essays, literary criticism, poetry. Sometimes comments on rejected mss.

How to Contact Send SASE for return of ms. Does not accept unsolicited submissions by e-mail (except foreign submissions). Responds in 3 months to mss. Does not accept simultaneous submissions. Sample copy for $6.50. Writer's guidelines for #10 SASE.

Payment/Terms Pays $10-40 and 2 contributor's copies; additional copies at half cover cost. Pays on publication for first North American serial rights. Sends galleys to author.

Advice Looks for "clean, direct language, written from the heart , and experimental writing. Read sample copy, or look at *Before Columbus* anthologies and *Greywolf Annual* anthologies."

Ⓝ Ⓐ THE RED CLAY REVIEW

M. A. in Professional Writing Program, Dept of English, Bldg. #27, Kennesaw State University, Kennesaw GA 30144-5591. E-mail: julie_redclayreview@yahoo.com. Web site: http://rcr.kaitopia.com. **Contact:** Dr. Jim Elledge, Director M.A. in Professional Writing Program or student Editor-in-Chief. Magazine has revolving editor. Editorial term: 1 year. Literary magazine/journal. 8½×5½, 80-120 pages, 60# white paper, 10 pt matte lam. cover. *"The Red Clay Review* is dedicated to publishing only the most outstanding graduate literary pieces. It has been established by members of the Graduate Writers Association at Kennesaw State University. It is unique because it only includes the work of graduate writing students. We publish poems (must be limited to 300 words, double spaced, 12 pt. font, 3-5 poems per submission), fiction/nonfiction pieces (must not exceed 10 pages, double spaced, 12 pt. font), and 10 minute plays/scenes (should be limited to 11 total pages since the first page will usually be mostly taken up by character listing/setting description.)" Annual. Estab. 2008.

Needs "We do not have any specific themes or topics, but keep in mind that we are a literary publication. We will read whatever is sent in. We will publish whatever we deem to be great literary writing. So in essence, every topic is open to submission, and we are all interested in a wide variety of subjects. We do not prohibit any topic or subject matter from being submitted. As long as submissions adhere to our guidelines, we are open to reading them. However, subject matter in any area that is too extreme may be less likely to be published because we want to include a broad collection of literary graduate work, but on the other hand, we cannot morally reject great writing." Receives 12 mss/month. Does not read November 1- June 1. Ms published 6 months after acceptance. Length: 2,500 words (min)-8,000 words (max). Publishes short shorts. Also publishes literary essays, poetry. Never comments on/critiques rejected mss.

How to Contact Send complete ms with cover letter. Include brief bio, list of publications, and an e-mail address must be supplied for the student, as well as the student's advisor's contact information (to verify student status). Responds to mss in 12-16 weeks. Considers simultaneous submissions, multiple submissions. Guidelines available on Web site.

Payment/Terms Writers receive 2 contributor's copies. Pays on publication. Acquires first rights. Publication is copyrighted.

Advice "Because the editors of *RCR* are graduate student writers, we are mindful of grammatical proficiency, vocabulary, and the organizational flow of the submissions we receive. We appreciate a heightened level of writing from fellow graduate writing students; but we also hold it to a standard to which we have learned in our graduate writing experience. Have your submission(s) proofread by a fellow student or professor."

Ⓐ RED ROCK REVIEW

Community College of Southern Nevada, 3200 E. Cheyenne Ave. N., Las Vegas NV 89030. (702)651-4094. Fax: (702)651-4639. E-mail: richard_logsdon@ccsn.nevada.edu. Web site: www.ccsn.edu/english/redrockreview/index/html. **Contact:** Dr. Richard Logsdon, senior editor. Magazine: 5×8;

125 pages. "We're looking for the very best literature. Stories need to be tightly crafted, strong in character development, built around conflict. Poems need to be tightly crafted, characterised by expert use of language." Semiannual. Estab. 1995. Circ. 250.

Needs Experimental, literary, mainstream. Receives 350 unsolicited mss/month. Accepts 40-60 mss/issue; 80-120 mss/year. Does not read mss during summer. Publishes ms 3-5 after acceptance. **Publishes 5-10 new writers/year.** Recently published work by Charles Harper Webb, Mary Sojourner, Mark Irwin. Length: 1,500-5,000 words; average length: 3,500 words. Publishes short shorts. Also publishes literary essays, literary criticism, poetry. Sometimes comments on rejected mss.

How to Contact Send SASE (or IRC) for return of ms. Responds in 2 weeks to queries; 3 months to mss. Accepts simultaneous, multiple submissions. Sample copy for $5.50. Writer's guidelines for SASE, by e-mail or on Web site.

Payment/Terms Pays 2 contributor's copies. Pays on acceptance for first rights.

RED WHEELBARROW

De Anza College, 21250 Stevens Creek Blvd., Cupertino CA 95014-5702. (408)864-8600. E-mail: splitterrandolph@fhda.edu. Web site: www.deanza.edu/redwheelbarrow. **Contact:** Randolph Splitter, editor-in-chief, or fiction editor. Magazine: 200-275 pages; photos. "Contemporary poetry, fiction, creative nonfiction, b&w graphics, comics and photos." Annual. Estab. 1976 as *Bottomfish*; 2000 as *Red Wheelbarrow*. Circ. 250-500.

Needs "Thoughtful, meaningful writing. We welcome submissions of all kinds, and we seek to publish a diverse range of styles and voices from around the country and the world." Receives 75 unsolicited mss/month. Accepts 30-50 mss/issue. Reads mss September through February. Submission deadline: January 31; publication date: Spring or Summer. Publishes ms 2-4 months after acceptance. Agented fiction 1%. **Publishes 0-2 new writers/year.** Recently published work by Joan Connor, Brian Friesen, Caroline Marwitz, Gary Craig Powell, Chad Simpson. Length: 4,000 words; average length: 2,500 words. Publishes short shorts. Also publishes poetry.

How to Contact Accepts submissions by e-mail. Responds in 2-4 months to mss. Accepts simultaneous submissions. Sample copy for $10; back issues $2.50. Writer's guidelines online.

Payment/Terms Pays 1 contributor's copy. Acquires first North American serial rights.

Advice "Write freely, rewrite carefully. Resist clichés and stereotypes. We are not affiliated with Red Wheelbarrow Press or any similarly named publication."

REED MAGAZINE

San Jose State University, Dept. of English, One Washington Square, San Jose CA 95192-0090. (408)927-4458. E-mail: reed@email.sjsu.edu. Web site: www.sjsu.edu/reed. **Contact:** Nick Taylor, editor. Literary magazine/journal: 9×5.75, 200 pages, semi-gloss paper, card cover. Contains illustrations. Includes photographs. "*Reed Magazine* is one of the oldest student-run literary journals west of the Mississippi. We publish outstanding fiction, poetry, nonfiction and art as a service to the South Bay literary community." Annual. Estab. 1944. Circ. 3,500. Member CLMP.

Needs Ethnic/multicultural (general), experimental, feminist, gay, historical (general), humor/satire, lesbian, literary, mainstream, regional (northern California). Does not want children's, young adult, fantasy, or erotic. Receives 30 mss/month. Accepts 5-7 mss/issue. Does not read Nov 2-May 31. Ms published 6 months after acceptance. Publishes 3-4 new writers/year. Published Tommy Mouton, Alan Soldofsky, Gwen Goodkin and Al Young. Length: 2,000 words (min)-6,000 words (max). Average length: 3,500 words. Also publishes literary essays, book reviews, poetry. Send review copies to Nick Taylor, Editor. Never comments on/critiques rejected mss.

How to Contact Submit online. Include estimated word count, brief bio. Responds to mss in 6 months. Considers simultaneous submissions, multiple submissions. Sample copy available for $8. Guidelines available on Web site.

Payment/Terms Writers receive free subscription to the magazine. Additional copies $5. Pays on publication. Acquires first North American serial rights. Sends galleys to author. Publication is copyrighted. "Sponsors the Steinbeck Award, given annually for the best short story. The prize is $1,000 and there's a $15 entry fee."

Advice "Well-writen, original, clean grammatical prose is essential. Keep submitting! The readers are students and change every year."

⊿ REFLECTIONS LITERARY JOURNAL
Piedmont Community College, P.O. Box 1197, Roxboro NC 27573. (336)599-1181. E-mail: reflect@pi edmontcc.edu. **Contact:** Dawn Langley, editor. Magazine: 100-150 pages. Annual. Estab. 1999. Circ. 250.
Needs Literary. "Accepts mss from NC authors only (residents or natives) and from authors we've previously published. If time and space permit, we'll consider submissions from Southeastern U.S. authors." Publishes mss 6-10 months after acceptance. **Publishes 3-5 new writers/year.** Recently published work by Maureen Sherbondy, Dainiel Green, Betty Moffett, Lian Gouw, Sejal Badani Ravani, Donna Conrad. Max Length: 4,000 words; average length: 2,500 words. Publishes short shorts. Also publishes poetry and essays.
How to Contact Send SASE for return of ms or #10 SASE for reply only. Sample copy for $5. Writer's guidelines for SASE or by e-mail.
Payment/Terms Pays 1 contributor's copy; additional copies $6 pre-publication; $7 post-publication. Acquires first North American serial rights. Sponsors awards/contests.
Advice "We look for good writing with a flair, which captivates an educated lay audience. Don't take rejection letters personally. We turn away many submissions simply because we don't have room for everything we like. For that reason, we're more likely to accept shorter well-written stories than longer stories of the same quality. Also, stories containing profanity that doesn't contribute to the plot, structure or intended tone are rejected immediately."

$⊿ THE REJECTED QUARTERLY, A Journal of Quality Literature Rejected at Least Five Times
P.O. Box 1351, Cobb CA 95426. E-mail: bplankton@juno.com. **Contact:** Daniel Weiss, Jeff Ludecke, fiction editors. Magazine: 8½×11; 36-44 pages; 60 lb. paper; 10 pt. coated cover stock; illustrations. "We want the best literature possible, regardless of genre. We do, however, have a bias toward the unusual and toward speculative fiction. We aim for a literate, educated audience. *The Rejected Quarterly* believes in publishing the highest quality rejected fiction and other writing that doesn't fit anywhere else. We strive to be different, but will go for quality every time, whether conventional or not." Semiannual. Estab. 1998.
Needs Experimental, fantasy, historical, humor/satire, literary, mainstream, mystery/suspense, romance (futuristic/time travel only), science fiction (soft/sociological), sports. Accepts poetry about being rejected. Receives 30 unsolicited mss/month. Accepts 3-6 mss/issue; 8-12 mss/year. Publishes ms 1-12 months after acceptance. **Publishes 2-4 new writers/year.** Recently published work by Sharon Ellis, Hannah Gersen and John C. Carter. Length: 8,000 words. Publishes short shorts (literature related), literary criticism, rejection-related poetry. Often comments on rejected mss.
How to Contact Send SASE for reply, return of ms or send a disposable copy of ms. No longer accepting email submissions. Responds in 2-4 weeks to queries; 1-9 months to mss. Accepts reprint submissions. Sample copy for $6 (IRCs for foreign requests). Reviews fiction.
Payment/Terms Pays $12.50 and 1 contributor's copy; additional copies $5. Pays on acceptance for first rights.
Advice "We are looking for high-quality writing that tells a story or expresses a coherent idea. We want unique stories, original viewpoints and unusual slants. We are getting far too many inappropriate submissions. Please be familiar with the magazine. Be sure to include your rejection slips! Send out quality rather than quantity."

Ⓝ ⊿ RIVER OAK REVIEW
Elmhurst College, 190 Prospect Ave, Elmhurst IL 60126-3296. (630)617-3137. Fax: (630)617-3609. E-mail: riveroak@elmhurst.edu. Web site: www.riveroakreview.org. **Contact:** Ron Wiginton, editor. Literary magazine/journal: 6×9, 195 pages; perfect bound paper; glossy, 4 color cover. "We try with each issue to showcase many voices of America, loud and soft, radical and sublime. Each piece we publish, prose or poetry, is an attempt to capture a part of 'us', with the notion that it is through our art that we are defined as a culture." Estab. 1993. Circ. 500.
Needs Ethnic/multicultural (general), experimental, literary, mainstream, translations. Does not want genre fiction or "lessons of morality; 'idea' driven stories usually do not work." Receives 50-75 mss/month. Accepts 7-8 mss/issue; 14-16 mss/year. Ms published 3 months after acceptance. Agented fiction 1%. **Publishes 2-3 new writers/year.** Published Adam Lichtenstein, Robert Moulthrop, J. Malcom Garcia and Laura Hope-Gill. Length: 250 words (min)-7,000 words (max). Average

length: 3,000 words. Publishes short shorts. Average length of short shorts: 750 words. Also publishes literary essays, book reviews, poetry. Send review copies to Ron Wiginton, Editor. Sometimes comments on/critiques rejected mss.

How to Contact Send complete ms with cover letter. Accepts submissions by e-mail. Include list of publications. Responds to mss in 6 months. Send disposable copy of ms and #10 SASE for reply only. Considers simultaneous submissions. Sample copy available for $5. Guidelines available for SASE, via e-mail, on Web site, via fax.

Payment/Terms Writers receive 2 contributor's copies. Additional copies $10. Pays on publication. Acquires first North American serial rights. Publication is copyrighted.

Advice "The voice is what we notice first. Is the writer in command of the language? Secondly, does the story have anything to say? It's not that 'fluff' cannot be good, but we note our favorites stories tend to have meaning beyond the surface of the plot. Thirdly, the story must by populated by 'real' peoples who are also interesting, characters, in other words, who have lives underneath the storyline. Finally, look before you leap."

⬤ ⬛ RIVER STYX

Big River Association, 3547 Olive Street, Suite 107, St. Louis MO 63117. (314)533-4541. Fax: (314)533-3345. Web site: www.riverstyx.org. **Contact:** Richard Newman, editor. Magazine: 6×9; 100 pages; color card cover; perfect-bound; b&w visual art. "*River Styx* publishes the highest quality fiction, poetry, interviews, essays, and visual art. We are an internationally distributed multicultural literary magazine." Mss read May-November. Estab. 1975.

● *River Styx* has had stories appear in *New Stories from the South* and has been included in *Pushcart* anthologies.

Needs Ethnic/multicultural, experimental, feminist, gay, lesbian, literary, mainstream, novel excerpts, translations, short stories, literary. "No genre fiction, less thinly veiled autobiography." Receives 350 unsolicited mss/month. Accepts 2-6 mss/issue; 6-12 mss/year. Reads only May through November. Publishes ms 1 year after acceptance. **Publishes 20 new writers/year.** Recently published work by Julianna Baggott, Philip Graham, Katherine Min, Richard Burgin, Nancy Zafris, and Eric Shade. Publishes short shorts. Also publishes poetry. Sometimes comments on rejected mss.

How to Contact Send complete ms. SASE required. Responds in 4 months to mss. Accepts simultaneous submissions "if a note is enclosed with your work and if we are notified immediately upon acceptance elsewhere." Sample copy for $8. Writer's guidelines online.

Payment/Terms Pays 2 contributor copies, plus 1-year subscription; $8/page if funds are available. Pays on publication for first North American serial, one-time rights.

Advice "We want high-powered stories with well-developed characters. We like strong plots, usually with at least three memorable scenes, and a subplot often helps. No thin, flimsy fiction with merely serviceable language. Short stories shouldn't be any different than poetry—every single word should count. One could argue every word counts more since we're being asked to read 10 to 30 pages."

⬤ THE ROCKFORD REVIEW

The Rockford Writers Guild, P.O. Box 858, Rockford IL 61105. E-mail: daveconnieross@aol.com. Web site: http://writersguild1.tripod.com. **Contact:** David Ross, editor. Magazine: 100 pages; perfect bound; color illustrations; b&w photos. "We look for prose and poetry with a fresh approach to old themes or new insights into the human condition." Semiannual. Estab. 1971. Circ. 600.

Needs Ethnic/multicultural, experimental, fantasy, humor/satire, literary, regional, science fiction (hard science, soft/sociological). "No graphic sex, translations or overly academic work." Recently published work by James Bellarosa, Sean Michael Rice, John P. Kristofco, L.S. Sedishiro. Also publishes literary essays.

How to Contact Include SASE. Responds in 2 months to mss. Accepts simultaneous, multiple submissions. Sample copy for $9. Writer's guidelines for SASE or online.

Payment/Terms Pays contributor's copies. "Two $25 editor's choice cash prizes per issue." Acquires first North American serial rights.

Advice "We're wide open to new and established writers alike—particularly short satire."

⬤ THE SARANAC REVIEW

Suny Plattsburgh, Dept. of English, Champlain Valley Hall, Plattsburgh NY 12901. (518)564-5151. Fax: (518)564-2140. E-mail: saranacreview@plattsburgh.edu. Web site: http://research.plattsburgh.edu/

saranacreview/. **Contact**: fiction editor. Magazine: $5^{1}/_{2} \times 8^{1}/_{2}$; 180-200 pages; 80 lb. cover/70 lb. paper; glossy cover stock; illustrations; photos. *"The Saranac Review* is committed to dissolving boundaries of all kinds, seeking to publish a diverse array of emerging and established writers from Canada and the U.S. *The Saranac Review* aims to be a textual clearing in which a space is opened for cross-pollination between American and Canadian writers. In this way the magazine reflects the expansive bright spirit of the etymology of it's name, Saranac, meaning 'cluster of stars.'' Annual. Estab. 2004.

Needs Ethnic/multicultural, historical, literary. Publishes ms 8 months after acceptance. Publishes flash fiction. Also publishes poetry and literary/creative nonfiction. Sometimes comments on rejected mss.

How to Contact Send complete ms. Send SASE (or IRC) for return of ms or send disposable copy of the ms and #10 SASE for reply only. Responds in 4 months to mss. Accepts simultaneous submissions. Sample copy for $6. Writer's guidelines online, or by e-mail. "Please send one story at a time." Maximum length: 7,000 words.

Payment/Terms Pays 2 contributor's copies; discount on extras and free subscription for following issue. Pays on publication for first North American serial, first rights.

Advice "We publish serious, generous fiction."

SCRIVENER, Creative Review

Scrivener Press, 853 Sherbrooke St. West, Montreal QC H3A 2T6 Canada. E-mail: info@scrivenerrevi ew.com. Web site: www.scrivenerreview.com. **Contact:** Justin Scherer, fiction editor. "Scrivener is eclectic. We publish the best in prose, poetry, art and photography from contributors around the world. Our twenty-five year history includes works by and interviews with Margaret Atwood, Leonard Cohen, Lawrence Ferlinghetti, Timothy Findley, Carol Shields, Seamus Heaney, and Winslaw Syzmborska.'' Annual. Estab. 1981. Circ. 400. Member: CMPA.

Needs Comix/graphic shorts, experimental, humor/satire, literary, mainstream, translations, transgressive, slipstream. Receives 20 unsolicited mss/month. Accepts 3-6 mss/issue. Publishes ms 1 month after acceptance. **Publishes 2-4 new writers/year**. Length: up to 10,000 words; average length: 5,000 words. Publishes short shorts. Also publishes poetry. Rarely comments on rejected mss.

How to Contact Send complete ms. Prefers submissions by e-mail to fiction@scrivenerreview.com. Send SASE (or IRC) for return of the ms or send a disposable copy of the ms and #10 SASE for reply only. Responds in 3 weeks to queries; 6 months to mss. Does not accept previously published work. Accepts multiple submissions. If a contributor chooses to submit their work to multiple publications they must immediately notify the review of any acceptances. Sample copy for $ 10 Canadian and $2 shipping. Writer's guidelines online.

Payment/Terms Pays 1 contributor's copy on publication. Acquires first North American serial rights, and an option for first electronic rights.

Advice "While Scrivener welcomes all forms of writing and visual art we are particularly interested in experimental pieces. Originality is our prime criterion. Disregard the conventions of form and content, and send us material that is challenging and transgressive. Both new and established contributors are encouraged to subit.''

$SHENANDOAH, The Washington and Lee University Review

Washington and Lee University, Mattingly House, 2 Lee Avenue, Washington and Lee University, Lexington VA 24450-2116. (540)458-8765. E-mail: shenandoah@wlu.edu. Web site: http://shenand oah.wlu.edu. Triannual. Estab. 1950. Circ. 2,000.

Needs Mainstream, novel excerpts. No sloppy, hasty, slight fiction. Publishes ms 10 months after acceptance.

How to Contact Send complete ms. Responds in 2 months to mss. Sample copy for $10. Writer's guidelines online.

Payment/Terms Pays $25/page. Pays on publication for first North American serial, one-time rights.

SLEEPINGFISH

Calamari Press. E-mail: white@sleepingfish.net. Web site: www.sleepingfish.net. **Contact:** Derek White, editor. Literary magazine/journal: 6×8, 160 pages, 60 lb. vellum paper, card stock cover. Contains illustrations. Includes photographs. *"Sleepingfish* publishes an eclectic mix of flash fiction, prose and visual poetry, experimental texts, text/image and art." Published every 9 months. Estab. 2003. Circ. 500.

Needs Adventure, comics/graphic novels, ethnic/multicultural, experimental, literary. Does not want to see any fiction or writing that fits into a genre or that is written for any other reason except for the sake of art. Receives 250 mss/month. Accepts 25 mss/issue; 25 mss/year. Manuscript published less than 3 months after acceptance. **Publishes 2-3 new writers/year.** Published Norman Lock, Peter Markus, Kevin Sampsell, Christian Peet, Brian Evenson, Thurston Moore, Kim Chinquee, and Danielle Dutton. Length: 1 word (min)-5,000 words (max). Average length: 1,000 words. Publishes short shorts. Average length of short shorts: 500 words. Rarely comments on/critiques rejected mss.

How to Contact Send complete ms with cover letter. Only accepts submissions by e-mail. Include brief bio. Responds to queries in 2 weeks. Responds to mss in 2 months. Send SASE (or IRC) for return of ms. Considers simultaneous submissions, multiple submissions. Guidelines available on Web site.

Payment/Terms Writers receive 1 contributor copy. Additional copies half price. Pays on publication. Acquires first rights. Sends galleys to author. Publication is copyrighted.

Advice "Write or create what's true to yourself and find a publication where you think your work honestly fits in."

☑ ◎ SO TO SPEAK, A Feminist Journal of Language and Art

George Mason University, 4400 University Dr., MS 2 C5, Fairfax VA 22030. (703)993-3625. E-mail: sts@gmu.edu. Web site: www.gmu.edu/org/sts. **Contact:** Caroline Zuschek; Amy Amoroso, fiction editor. Magazine: $5^{1}/_{2} \times 8^{1}/_{2}$; approximately 100 pages. "We are a feminist journal of language and art." Semiannual. Estab. 1993. Circ. 1,000.

Needs Ethnic/multicultural, experimental, feminist, lesbian, literary, mainstream, regional, translations. "No science fiction, mystery, genre romance." Receives 100 unsolicited mss/month. Accepts 3-5 mss/issue; 6-10 mss/year. Publishes ms 6 months after acceptance. **Publishes 5 new writers/year.** Length: For fiction, up to 5,000 words; for poetry, 3-5 pages per submission; average length: 5,000 words; for poetry, 2-5 poems per submission. Publishes short shorts , nonfiction up to 4,000 words and art words. Also publishes literary essays, literary criticism, poetry.

How to Contact Send complete ms. Include bio (50 words maximum) and SASE for return of ms or send a disposable copy of ms. Responds in 6 months to mss. Accepts simultaneous submissions. Sample copy for $7. Reviews fiction.

Payment/Terms Pays contributor copies. Acquires first North American serial rights. Sponsors awards/contests.

Advice "We do not read between March 15 and August 15. Every writer has something they do exceptionally well; do that and it will shine through in the work. We look for quality prose with a definite appeal to a feminist audience. We are trying to move away from strict genre lines. We want high quality fiction, nonfiction, poetry, art, innovative and risk-taking work."

Ⓝ $☐ SOFA INK QUARTERLY

Gray Sunshine, P.O. Box 625, American Fork, UT 84003. E-mail: acquisitions@sofaink.com. Web site: www.sofaink.com. **Contact:** David Cowsert, editor-in-chief. Literary magazine/journal. "The magazine is distributed primarily to waiting rooms and lobbies of medical facilities. All our stories and poetry have positive endings. We like to publish a variety of genres with a focus on good storytelling and word mastery that does not include swearing, profaning deity, gore, excessive violence or gratuitous sex." Quarterly. Estab. 2005. Circ. 650.

Needs Adventure, ethnic/multicultural, experimental, fantasy, historical, humor/satire, mainstream, mystery/suspense, romance, science fiction, slice-of-life vignettes, western. Does not want erotic or religious. Accepts 12-20 mss/year. Manuscript published 3 months after acceptance. Length: 7,500 words (max). Also publishes poetry.

How to Contact Send complete ms with cover letter. Accepts submissions by e-mail. Responds to queries in 1-3 months. Responds to mss in 1-3 months. Considers simultaneous submissions. Sample copy available for $6. Guidelines available for SASE, on Web site.

Payment/Terms Writers receive $5 flat-rate payment. **Pays on acceptance.** Acquires first North American serial rights. Publication is copyrighted.

Advice "Follow our content guidelines. Electronic submissions should be in a Word attachment rather than in the body of the message."

SONORA REVIEW

University of Arizona's Creative Writing MFA Program, University of Arizona, Dept. of English, Tucson AZ 85721. E-mail: sonora@email.arizona.edu. Web site: www.coh.arizona.edu/sonora. **Contact:** PR Griffis, Amy Knight, editors. Magazine: 6×9; approx. 100 pages; photos. "We look for the highest quality poetry, fiction, and nonfiction, with an emphasis on emerging writers. Our magazine has a long-standing tradition of publishing the best new literature and writers. Check out our Web site for a sample of what we publish and our submission guidelines, or write us for a sample back issue." Semiannual. Estab. 1980. Circ. 500.

Needs Ethnic/multicultural, experimental, literary, mainstream, novel excerpts. Receives 200 unsolicited mss/month. Accepts 2-3 mss/issue; 6-8 mss/year. Does not read in the summer (June-August). Publishes ms 3-4 months after acceptance. **Publishes 1-3 new writers/year.** Recently published work by Antonya Nelson, Steve Almond. Also publishes literary essays, literary criticism, poetry. Sometimes comments on rejected mss.

How to Contact Send complete ms. Send disposable copy of the ms and #10 SASE for reply only. Responds in 2-5 weeks to queries; 3 months to mss. Accepts simultaneous, multiple submissions. Sample copy for $6. Writer's guidelines online. Reviews fiction.

Payment/Terms Pays 2 contributor's copies; additional copies for $4. Pays on publication for first North American serial, one-time, electronic rights.

Advice "Send us your best stuff."

SOUTH CAROLINA REVIEW

611 Strode Tower Box 340522, Clemson University, Clemson SC 29634-0522. (864)656-5399. Fax: (864)656-1345. E-mail: cwayne@clemson.edu. Web site: www.clemson.edu/caah/cedp. **Contact:** Wayne Chapman, editor. Magazine: 6×9; 200 pages; 60 lb. cream white vellum paper; 65 lb. cream white vellum cover stock. Semiannual. Estab. 1967. Circ. 500.

Needs Literary, mainstream, poetry, essays, reviews. Does not read mss June-August or December. Receives 50-60 unsolicited mss/month. Recently published work by Ronald Frame, Dennis McFadden, Dulane Upshaw Ponder, and Stephen Jones. Rarely comments on rejected mss.

How to Contact Send complete ms. Requires text on disk upon acceptance in WordPerfect or Microsoft Word in PC format. Responds in 2 months to mss. Sample copy for $15 includes postage. Reviews fiction.

Payment/Terms Pays in contributor's copies.

SOUTH DAKOTA REVIEW

Dept. of English, University of South Dakota, 414 E. Clark St., Vermillion SD 57069. (605)677-5184. Fax: (605)677-5298. E-mail: sdreview@usd.edu. Web site: www.usd.edu/sdreview. **Contact:** fiction editor. Magazine: 6×9; 120-140 pages; book paper; glossy cover stock; photos on cover. "Literary magazine for university and college audiences and their equivalent. Emphasis is often on the American West and its writers, but will accept mss from anywhere. Issues are usually personal essay, fiction and poetry with some literary essays." Quarterly. Estab. 1963. Circ. 550.

● *Pushcart* and *Best American Essays* nominees.

Needs Ethnic/multicultural, literary, mainstream, regional. "We like very well-written, thematically ambitious, character-centered short fiction. Contemporary Western American setting appeals, but not required if they story has a good sense of place. No formula stories, horror, or adolescent 'I' narrator." Receives 100 unsolicited mss/month. Accepts 30 mss/year. Publishes ms 1-6 months after acceptance. **Publishes 3-5 new writers/year.** Recently published work by Gary Fincke, Grace Bauer, William Kloefkorn.

How to Contact Send complete ms. "We like cover letters that are not boastful and do not attempt to sell the stories, but rather provide some personal information about the writer which can be used for a contributor's note." Responds in 10-12 weeks to mss. Sample copy for $8.

Payment/Terms Acquires first, second serial (reprint) rights.

Advice Rejects mss because of "careless writing; often careless typing; stories too personal ('I' confessional); aimlessness of plot; unclear or unresolved conflicts; subject matter that editor finds clichéd, sensationalized, pretentious or trivial. We are trying to use more fiction and more variety."

◙ THE SOUTHEAST REVIEW

English Department, Florida State University, Tallahassee FL 32306-1036. (850)644-2773. E-mail: southeastreview@english.fsu.edu. Web site: www.english.fsu.edu/southeastreview. **Contact:** Jessica Pitchford, senior editor. Magazine: 6×9; 160 pages; 70 lb. paper; 10 pt. Krome Kote cover; photos. *The Southeast Review* publishes literary fiction, poetry, and nonfiction. Biannual. Estab. 1979. Circ. 1,000.

Needs "The mission of The Southeast Review is to present emerging writers on the same stage as well-established ones. In each semi-annual issue, we publish literary fiction, creative nonfiction, poetry, interviews, book reviews and art. With nearly 60 members on our editorial staff who come from throughout the country and the world, we strive to publish work that is representative of our diverse interests and aesthetics, and we celebrate the eclectic mix this produces." We receive approximately 400 submissions per month and we accept less than 1-2% of them. We will comment briefly on rejected mss when time permits. Publishes ms 2-6 months after acceptance. **Publishes 4-6 new writers/year.** Recently published work by Susanna Childress, Natalie Diaz, Robert Morgan, Dan Pope, Andrew Sage, and Kevin Wilson.

How to Contact Send complete ms. Responds in 3-5 months to mss. Sample copy for $6.

Payment/Terms Pays 2 contributor's copies. Acquires first North American serial rights which then revert to author.

Advice "Avoid trendy experimentation for its own sake (present-tense narration, observation that isn't also revelation). Fresh stories, moving, interesting characters and a sensitivity to language are still fiction mainstays. We also publish the winner and runners-up of the World's Best Short Story Contest, Poetry Contest, and, for the first time in 2008, Narrative Nonfiction Contest."

◙ SOUTHERN CALIFORNIA REVIEW

(formally Southern California Anthology), Master of Professional Writing, 3501 Trousdale Parkway, Mark Taper Hall, THH 355J, University of Southern California, Los Angeles CA 90089-4034. (213)740-3253. Fax: (213)740-5775. E-mail: scr@college.usc.edu. Web site: www.usc.edu/dept/LAS/mpw/students/sca.php. **Contact**: fiction editor. Magazine: 150 pages; semiglosss cover stock. "Formerly known as the Southern California Anthology, Southern California Review (SCR) is the literary journal of the Master of Professional Writing program at the University of Southern California. It has been publishing fiction and poetry since 1982 and now also accepts submissions of creative nonfiction, plays, and screenplays. Printed every October and April with original cover artwork, every issue contains new, emerging, and established authors." Semiannual. Estab. 1983. Circ. 1,000.

Needs "We accept short shorts but rarely use stories more than 8,000 words. Novel excerpts are acceptable if they can stand alone. We do consider genre work (horror, mystery, romance, sci-fi) if it transcends the boundaries of the genre." Receives 120 unsolicited mss/month. Accepts 10-15 mss/issue. Publishes ms 4 months after acceptance. **Publishes 20-30 new writers/year.** Recently published work by James Ragan, James Tate, Alice Fulton, John Updike, Joyce Carol Oates, Hubert Selby Jr., Marge Piercy, Stephen Dunn, Ruth Stone, Gay Talese. Publishes short shorts.

How to Contact Send complete, typed, double-spaced ms. Cover letter should include list of previous publications. Address to the proper editor (Fiction, Poetry, etc.). Please include a cover letter. Be sure your full name and contact information (address, phone, and email) appear on the first page of the manuscript. Response time for submissions is 3 to 6 months. No electronic or email submissions are accepted. Every submission must include a self-addressed stamped envelope (SASE). Sample copy for $10. Writer's guidelines for SASE and on Web site.

Payment/Terms Pays in 2 contributor copies. Acquires first rights.

Advice "The Anthology pays particular attention to craft and style in its selection of narrative writing."

$◙ ◙ THE SOUTHERN REVIEW

Old President's House, Louisiana State University, Baton Rouge LA 70803. (225)578-5108. Fax: (225)578-5098. E-mail: southernreview@lsu.edu. Web site: www.lsu.edu/thesouthernreview. **Contact:** Bret Lott, editor. Magazine: 6¼×10; 240 pages; 50 lb. Glatfelter paper; 65 lb. #1 grade cover stock. Quarterly. Estab. 1935. Circ. 3,000.

● Several stories published in *The Southern Review* were *Pushcart Prize* selections.

Needs Literary. "We select fiction that conveys a unique and compelling voice and vision." Receives approximately 300 unsolicited mss/month. Accepts 4-6 mss/issue. Reading period: September-May.

Publishes ms 6 months after acceptance. Agented fiction 1%. **Publishes 10-12 new writers/year.**
Recently published work by Jill McCorkle, James Lee Burke, Robin Black, James Fowler. Also publishes literary essays, literary criticism, poetry and book reviews.

How to Contact Mail hard copy of ms with cover letter and SASE. No queries. "Prefer brief letters
giving author's prefessional information, including recent or notable publcations. Biographical info
not necessary." Responds within 10 weeks to mss. Sample copy for $8. Writer's guidelines online.
Reviews fiction, poetry.

Payment/Terms Pays $30/page. Pays on publication for first North American serial rights. Sends
page proof to author via e-mail. Sponsors awards/contests.

Advice "Careful attention to craftsmanship and technique combined with a developed sense of the
creation of story will always make us pay attention."

◪ SOUTHWEST REVIEW

P.O. Box 750374, Dallas TX 75275-0374. (214)768-1037. Fax: (214)768-1408. E-mail: swr@mail.smu.
edu. Web site: www.smu.edu/southwestreview. **Contact:** Jennifer Cranfill, Senior Editor. Magazine:
6×9; 150 pages. "The majority of our readers are well read adults who wish to stay abreast of the
latest and best in contemporary fiction, poetry, and essays in all but the most specialized disciplines."
Quarterly. Estab. 1915. Circ. 1,600.

Needs "High literary quality; no specific requirements as to subject matter, but cannot use sentimental, religious, western, poor science fiction, pornographic, true confession, mystery, juvenile or
serialized or condensed novels." Receives 200 unsolicited mss/month. Publishes ms 6-12 months
after acceptance. Recently published work by Alice Hoffman, Sabina Murray, Alix Ohlin. Also publishes literary essays, poetry. Occasionally comments on rejected mss.

How to Contact Mail complete ms or submit on line. Responds in 1-4 months to mss. Accepts
multiple submissions. Sample copy for $6. Writer's guidelines for #10 SASE or on Web site.

Payment/Terms Pays negotiable rate and 3 contributor copies. Acquires first North American serial
rights. Sends galleys to author.

Advice "Despite the title, we are not a regional magazine. Before you submit your work, it's a good
idea to take a look at recent issues to familiarize yourself with the magazine. We strongly advise all
writers to include a cover letter. Keep your cover letter professional and concise and don't include
extraneous personal information, a story synopsis, or a resume. When authors ask what we look
for in a strong story submission the answer is simple regarless of graduate degrees in creative writing,
workshops, or whom you know. We look for good writing, period."

◪ ◎ SOUTHWESTERN AMERICAN LITERATURE

Center for the Study of the Southwest, Texas State University-San Marcos, 601 University Drive, San
Marcos TX 78666. (512)245-2224. Fax: (512)245-7462. E-mail: mb13@txstate.edu. Web site: http://
swrhc.txstate.edu/cssw/. **Contact:** Twister Marquiss, assistant editor; Mark Busby, co-editor; Dick
Maurice Heaberlin, co-editor. Magazine: 6×9; 125 pages; 80 lb. cover stock. "We publish fiction,
nonfiction, poetry, literary criticism and book reviews. Generally speaking, we want material covering the Greater Southwest or material written by Southwest writers." Biannual. Estab. 1971. Circ.
300.

Needs Ethnic/multicultural, literary, mainstream, regional. "No science fiction or romance." Receives 10-15 unsolicited mss/month. Accepts 1-2 mss/issue; 4-5 mss/year. Publishes ms 6 months
after acceptance. **Publishes 1-2 new writers/year.** Recently published work by Greg Garrett, Michelle Brooks, Donald Lucio Hurd, Walt McDonald, Carol Hamilton, Larry D. Thomas. Length:
6,250 words; average length: 4,000 words. Also publishes literary essays, literary criticism, poetry.
Sometimes comments on rejected mss.

How to Contact Send complete ms. Include cover letter, estimated word count, 2-5 line bio and list
of publications. Does not accept e-mail submissions. Responds in 3-6 months to mss. Sample copy
for $8. Writer's guidelines free.

Payment/Terms Pays 2 contributor copies. Acquires first rights.

Advice "We look for crisp language, an interesting approach to material; a regional approach is
desired but not required. Read widely, write often, revise carefully. We are looking for stories that
probe the relationship between the tradition of Southwestern American literature and the writer's
own imagination in creative ways. We seek stories that move beyond stereotype and approach the
larger defining elements and also ones that, as William Faulkner noted in his Nobel Prize acceptance

speech, treat subjects central to good literature—the old verities of the human heart, such as honor and courage and pity and suffering, fear and humor, love and sorrow.''

☐ ◎ SPEAK UP

Speak Up Press, P.O. Box 100506, Denver CO 80250. (303)715-0837. Fax: (303)715-0793. Web site: www.speakuppresss.org. **Contact:** Senior editor. Magazine: $5^{1}/_{2} \times 8^{1}/_{2}$; 128 pages; 55 lb. Glat. Supple Opaque Recycled Natural paper; 12 CIS cover; illustrations; photos. *''Speak Up* features the original fiction, nonfiction, poetry, plays, photography and artwork of young people 13-19 years old. *Speak Up* provides a place for teens to be creative, honest and expressive in an uncensored environment.'' Annual. Estab. 1999. Circ. 2,900.

Needs Teen writers. Receives 30 unsolicited mss/month. Accepts 30 mss/issue; 30 mss/year. Publishes ms 3-12 months after acceptance. **Publishes 20 new writers/year.** Length: 5,000 words; average length: 500 words. Publishes short shorts. Also publishes literary essays, poetry.

How to Contact Send complete ms. Accepts submissions by e-mail, fax. Responds in 3 months to queries; 3 months to mss. Accepts simultaneous, multiple submissions and reprints. Sample copy free. Please include required submission forms. See Web site for submission guidelines.

Payment/Terms Pays 2 contributor copies. Acquires first North American serial, one-time rights.

☑ ☑ SPINDRIFT

Shoreline Community College, 16101 Greenwood Ave. North, Seattle WA 98133. (206)546-5864. E-mail: spindrift@shoreline.edu. Web site: http://success.shoreline.edu/spindrift/home.html. **Contact:** Debby Handrich, Literary Editor. Magazine: 125 pages; quality paper; photographs; b&w artwork. ''We publish a variety of short fiction and poetry, most of which would be considered literary. Authors are from all over the map, but we give priority to writers from our community.'' Released in May of each year. Estab. 1966. Circ. 500.

• *Spindrift* has received awards for ''Best Literary Magazine'' from the Community College Humanities Association both locally and nationally and awards from the Pacific Printing Industries.

Needs Multicultural, experimental, historical, literary, mainstream, regional, serialized novels, translations, prose poem. ''No detective, science fiction, romance, religious/inspirational. We look for fresh, original work that is not forced or 'straining' to be literary.'' Publishes ms 3-4 months after acceptance. **Publishes 5-6 new writers/year.** Recently published work by Ed Harkness and Virgil Suarez.

How to Contact Send complete ms. Do not place name on ms, and please indicate multiple submissions in cover letter. Submit by Feb. 1. Responds by March 15 if SASE is included. Accepts multiple submissions. Sample copy for $10, 9×11 SAE and $2 postage; sample back issues for $4.

Payment/Terms Pays contributor's copies. Acquires first rights. Not copyrighted.

Advice ''Let the story tell itself; don't force or overdo the language. Show the reader something new about people, situations, life itself.''

Ⓝ ☐ Ⓖ SPOUT

Spout Press, P.O. Box 581067, Minneapolis MN 55458-1067.E-mail: editors@spoutpress.org. Web site: www.spoutpress.org. **Contact:** Carrie Eidem, fiction editor. Literary magazine/journal: $5^{3}/_{4} \times 8^{1}/_{2}$, 60 pages. Contains illustrations. Includes photographs. ''With *Spout* we strive to publishsh experimental writing. We don't focus on any certain style, tone or approach for the stories we publish. *Spout* also has an annual fiction story of the year contest. Please see Web site for details.'' Semiannual. Estab. 1989. Member CLMP.

Needs Adventure, comics/graphic novels, ethnic/multicultural (general), experimental, feminist, gay, science fiction. Does not want children's fiction. Receives 15-20 mss/month. Accepts 3-5 mss/ issue; 6-10 mss/year. Ms published 1-2 months after acceptance. **Publishes 6-10 new writers/year.** Published Jeri Blazek, Ryan Van Cleave and Mike Tuohy. Length: 500 words (min)-7,000 words (max). Average length: 5,000 words. Publishes short shorts. Average length of short shorts: 500 words. Also publishes poetry. Rarely comments on/critiques rejected mss.

How to Contact Send complete ms with cover letter. Include estimated word count, brief bio. Responds to queries in 2 weeks. Responds to mss in 6 weeks. Send either SASE (or IRC) for return of ms or disposable copy of ms and #10 SASE for reply only. Considers simultaneous submissions, multiple submissions. Sample copy available for $5. Guidelines available for SASE, via e-mail, on Web site.

Payment/Terms Writers receive 1 contributor copy. Additional copies $5. Pays on publication. Acquires one-time rights. Publication is not copyrighted. "We take submissions from the fall to spring for our Story of the Year contest. See Web site for details."
Advice "Please look at our *Spout* to see if your submissions will fit our journal."

N ☑ THE SPUR
4528 Pine St, Philadelphia PA 19143. (919)618-3852. E-mail: editors@spurjournal.com. Web site: http://www.spurjournal.com. **Contact**: Asher Spiller, editor. Literary magazine/journal: 8½×11, 44 pages. Contains illustrations. Includes photographs. "Based out of West Philadelphia, *The Spur* is a biannual literary magazine that prides itself on its ability to cut directly to the heart of contemporary dilemmas without posing its own agenda. Withholding judgment, our fiction, poetry, and essays trace the social, ethical, and political problems facing our local and global communities and offer readers the space to pause and consider where we stand. We seek to emphasize the relevance of the words we publish, finding that the best work, whether it be in the form of poetry, fiction or an essay, always speaks to its own time." Semiannual. Estab. 2007. Circ. 1,000.
Needs Ethnic/multicultural, experimental, feminist, gay, historical (general), humor/satire, lesbian, literary, military/war, translations. Receives 40-60 mss/month. Accepts 8-12 mss/issue; 16-24 mss/year. Ms published 3 months after acceptance. Published Adam Bloom, Ian Grody, Samanta Schweblin (Trans. by Brendan Lanctot), and Scott Sheppard. Length: 5,000 words (max). Average length: 3,500 words. Publishes short shorts. Also publishes literary essays, literary criticism, book reviews, poetry. Send review copies to editors@spurjournal.com. Sometimes comments on/critiques rejected mss.
How to Contact Send complete ms with cover letter. E-mail submissions preferred. Include estimated word count, brief bio. Responds to queries in 1 week. Responds to mss in 2-3 months. Considers simultaneous submissions, previously published submissions, multiple submissions. Sample copy available for $5. Guidelines available on Web site.
Payment/Terms Writers receive 4 contributor's copies. Additional copies $5. Pays on publication. Acquires one-time rights. Sends galleys to author. Publication is not copyrighted.
Advice "We are looking for work that stands out as relevant. Writers of fiction and poetry often use the versatility of these genres to avoid coming to grips with the dilemmas facing themselves and those around them. We want work that engages timely issues. We invite experimental work but are weary of experiments that are not well edited. Submissions should be clean, crisp, and stylistically effective. Do not over-extend yourself. Writing well does not mean you have to conquer the world in one short story."

STAND MAGAZINE
North American Office: Department of English, VCU, Richmond VA 23284-2005. (804)828-1331. E-mail: dlatane@vcu.edu. Web site: www.standmagazine.org. "*Stand Magazine* is concerned with what happens when cultures and literatures meet, with translation in its many guises, with the mechanics of language, with the processes by which the policy receives or disables its cultural makers. *Stand* promotes debate of issues that are of radical concern to the intellectual community worldwide." Quarterly. Estab. 1952 in Leeds UK. Circ. 3,000 worldwide.
Needs "No genre fiction." Publishes ms 10 months after acceptance.
How to Contact Send complete ms. Responds in 6 weeks to queries; 3 months to mss. Sample copy for $12. Writer's guidelines for #10 SASE with sufficient number of IRCs or online.
Payment/Terms Payment varies. Pays on publication. Aquires first world rights.

$☐ ◎ ☑ STONE SOUP, The Magazine by Young Writers and Artists
Children's Art Foundation, P.O. Box 83, Santa Cruz CA 95063-0083. (831)426-5557. Fax: (831)426-1161. Web site: www.stonesoup.com. **Contact:** Ms. Gerry Mandel, editor. Magazine: 7×10; 48 pages; high quality paper; photos. Audience is children, teachers, parents, writers, artists. "We have a preference for writing and art based on real-life experiences; no formula stories or poems. We only publish writing by children ages 8 to 13. We do not publish writing by adults." Bimonthly. Estab. 1973. Circ. 20,000.
  • This is known as "the literary journal for children." *Stone Soup* has previously won the Ed Press Golden Lamp Honor Award and the Parent's Choice Award.
Needs Adventure, ethnic/multicultural, experimental, fantasy, historical, humor/satire, mystery/

suspense, science fiction, slice-of-life vignettes, suspense. "We do not like assignments or formula stories of any kind." Receives 1,000 unsolicited mss/month. Accepts 10 mss/issue. Publishes ms 4 months after acceptance. **Publishes some new writers/year.** Also publishes literary essays, poetry.
How to Contact Send complete ms. "We like to learn a little about our young writers, why they like to write, and how they came to write the story they are submitting." Please do not include SASE. Do not send originals. Responds only to those submissions being considered for possible publication. "If you do not hear from us in 4 to 6 weeks it means we were not able to use your work. Don't be discouraged! Try again!" No simultaneous submissions. Sample copy for $5 or online. Writer's guidelines online.
Payment/Terms Pays $40 for stories. Authors also receive 2 copies, a certificate, and discounts on additional copies and on subscriptions. Pays on publication.
Advice Mss are rejected because they are "derivatives of movies, TV, comic books, or classroom assignments or other formulas. Go to our Web site, where you can see many examples of the kind of work we publish."

$ 🖳 ☑ STORIE, All Write

Leconte Press, Via Suor Celestina Donati 13/E, Rome 00167 Italy. (+39)06 614 8777. Fax: (+39)06 614 8777. E-mail: storie@tiscali.it. Web site: www.storie.it. **Contact**: Gianluca Bassi, editor; Barbara Pezzopane, assistant editor; George Lerner, foreign editor. Magazine: 186 pages; illustrations; photographs. "*Storie* is one of Italy's leading literary magazines. Committed to a truly crossover vision of writing, the bilingual (Italian/English) review publishes high quality fiction and poetry, interspersed with the work of alternative wordsmiths such as filmmakers and musicians. Through writings bordering on narratives and interviews with important contemporary writers, it explores the culture and craft of writing." Bimonthly. Estab. 1989. Circ. 20,000.
Needs Literary. Receives 150 unsolicited mss/month. Accepts 6-10 mss/issue; 30-50 mss/year. Does not read mss in August. Publishes ms 2 months after acceptance. Publishes 20 new writers/year. Recently published work by Joyce Carol Oates, Haruki Murakami, Paul Auster, Robert Coover, Raymond Carver, T.C. Boyle, Ariel Dorfman, Tess Gallagher. Length: 2,000-6,000 words; average length: 1,500 words. Publishes short shorts. Also publishes literary essays, literary criticism, poetry. Sometimes comments on rejected mss.
How to Contact Accepts submissions by e-mail or on disk. Include brief bio. Send complete ms with cover letter. "Manuscripts may be submitted directly by regular post without querying first; however, we do not accept unsolicited manuscripts via e-mail. Please query via e-mail first. We only contact writers if their work has been accepted. We also arrange for and oversee a high-quality, professional translation of the piece." Responds in 1 month to queries; 6 months to mss. Accepts multiple submissions. Sample copy for $ 10. Writer's guidelines online.
Payment/Terms Pays $30-600 and 2 contributor's copies. Pays on publication for first (in English and Italian) rights.
Advice "More than erudite references or a virtuoso performance, we're interested in the recording of human experience in a genuine, original voice. *Storie* reserves the right to include a brief review of interesting submissions not selected for publication in a special column of the magazine."

☑ 🛇 STORYQUARTERLY

P.O. Box 29272, San Francisco CA 94129. Web site: www.storyquarterly.com. **Contact:** Fiction Editors. Magazine: An all-story online literary journal with print editions. "*StoryQuarterly*, publishes American and international literature of high quality in a full range of styles and forms— outstanding writing and unusual insights." Estab. 1975. Circ. 40,000.
  • *StoryQuarterly* received recognitions in *New Stories form the South*, *Best American Mystery Stories*, O. Henry Prize Stories, Best American Short Stories, Best American Essays and Pushcart Prize Collection.
Needs "Well-written stories, serious or humorous, that get up and go from the first page." Receives 1,500 unsolicited mss/month. Accepts 40-50 mss/yr. **New and emerging authors especially encouraged.** Published established authors include J.M. Coetzee, Robert Olen Butler, T.C. Boyle, Stuarte Dybek, Alice Hoffman, and Charles Johnson.
How to Contact Submissions accepted online through Web site: www.storyquarterly.com. "Online submissions site notifies receipt of submissions, and online file tracks status. We decide in about

two months; Payment ranges: $150- $750. Plus annual prizes of more than $18,000 awarded.
Advice Long on and study magazine online. *SQ* fiction is selected for literary quality.

☐ STRAYLIGHT

UW-Parkside, English Dept., 900 Wood Rd., P.O. Box 2000, Kenosha WI 53141. (262)595-2139. Fax: (262)595-2271. E-mail: straylight@litspot.net. Web site: www.litspot.net/straylight. **Contact:** fiction editor. Magazine has revolving editor. Editorial term: 1 years. Literary magazine/journal: $6^{1}/_{4} \times 9^{1}/_{2}$, 75 pages, quality paper, uncoated index stock cover. Contains illustrations. Includes photographs. "*Straylight* is a new literary journal. We are interested in publishing high quality, character-based fiction of any style. We tend not to publish strict genre pieces, though we may query them for future special issues. We do not publish erotica." Biannual with special issues. Estab. 2005.
Needs Ethnic/multicultural (general), experimental, gay, lesbian, literary, mainstream, regional. Special interests: genre fiction in special theme issues. Accepts 5-7 mss/issue; 10-14 mss/year. Does not read May-August. Manuscript published 6 months after acceptance. Agented fiction 0%. Length: 1,000 words (min)-5,000 words (max). Average length: 2,500 words. Publishes short shorts. Also publishes poetry. Rarely comments on/critiques rejected mss.
How to Contact Send complete ms with cover letter. Accepts submissions by e-mail. Include brief bio, list of publications. Responds to queries in 2 weeks. Responds to mss in 2 months. Send either SASE (or IRC) for return of ms or disposable copy of ms and #10 SASE for reply only. Sample copy available for $6. Guidelines available for SASE, on Web site.
Payment/Terms Writers receive 2 contributor's copies. Additional copies $3. Pays on publication. Acquires first North American serial rights. Publication is copyrighted.
Advice "We tend to publish character-based and inventive fiction with cutting-edge prose. We are unimpressed with works based on strict plot twists or novelties. Read a sample copy to get a feel for what we publish."

☑ STRUGGLE, A Magazine of Proletarian Revolutionary Literature

Detroit MI 48213-0261. (213)273-9039. E-mail: timhall11@yahoo.com. **Contact:** Tim Hall, editor. Magazine: $5^{1}/_{2} \times 8^{1}/_{2}$; 36-72 pages; 20 lb. white bond paper; colored cover; illustrations; occasional photos. Publishes material related to "the struggle of the working class and all progressive people against the rule of the rich—including their war policies, repression, racism, exploitation of the workers, oppression of women and general culture, etc." Quarterly. Estab. 1985.
Needs Ethnic/multicultural, experimental, feminist, historical, humor/satire, literary, regional, science fiction, translations, young adult/teen (10-18), prose poem, senior citizen/retirement. "The theme can be approached in many ways, including plenty of categories not listed here. Readers would like fiction about anti-globalization, the fight against racism, prison conditions, neo-conservatism and the Iraq War. Would also like to see more fiction that depicts life, work and struggle of the working class of every background; also the struggles of the 1930s and '60s illustrated and brought to life. No romance, psychic, mystery, western, erotica, religious." Receives 10-12 unsolicited mss/ month. Recently published work by Gregory Alan Norton, Paris Smith, Keith Laufenberg. Length: 4,000 words; average length: 1,000-3,000 words. Publishes short shorts. Normally comments on rejected mss.
How to Contact Send complete ms. Accepts submissions by e-mail. "Tries to" report in 3-4 months to queries. Accepts simultaneous, multiple submissions and reprints. Sample copies for $3; $5 for double-size issues; subscriptions $10 for 4 issues; make checks payable to Tim Hall, Special Account, not to *Struggle*.
Payment/Terms Pays 1 contributor's copy. No rights acquired . Not copyrighted.
Advice "Write about the oppression of the working people, the poor, the minorities, women and, if possible, their rebellion against it—we are not interested in anything which accepts the status quo. We are not too worried about plot and advanced technique (fine if we get them!)—we would probably accept things others would call sketches, provided they have life and struggle. For new writers: just describe for us a situation in which some real people confront some problem of oppression, however seemingly minor. Observe and put down the real facts. Experienced writers: try your 'committed'/experimental fiction on us. We get poetry all the time. We have increased our fiction portion of our content in the last few years. The quality of fiction that we have published has continued to improve. If your work raises an interesting issue of literature and politics, it may get discussed in letters and in my editorial. I suggest ordering a sample."

$ ⬜ ⬜ SUBTERRAIN, Strong words for a polite nation

P.O. Box 3008, MPO, Vancouver BC V6B 3X5 Canada. (604)876-8710. Fax: (604)879-2667. E-mail: subter@portal.ca. Web site: www.subterrain.ca. **Contact:** Fiction editor. Magazine: 8¼×10⅞; 46-52 pages; gloss stock paper; color gloss cover stock; illustrations; photos. "Looking for unique work and perspectives from Canada and beyond." Triannual. Estab. 1987. Circ. 3,000.

Needs Literary. Does not want genre fiction or children's fiction. Receives 100 unsolicited mss/month. Accepts 4 mss/issue; 10-15 mss/year. Publishes ms 4 months after acceptance. Recently published work by John Moore. Also publishes literary essays, literary criticism. Rarely comments on rejected mss.

How to Contact Send complete ms. Include disposable copy of the ms and #10 SASE for reply only. Responds in 2-4 months to mss. Accepts multiple submissions. Sample copy for $5. Writer's guidelines online.

Payment/Terms Pays $25 per page for prose. Pays on publication for first North American serial rights.

Advice "Read the magazine first. Get to know what kind of work we publish."

Ⓝ $ ⬜ ◎ SUBTROPICS

P. O. Box 112075, Turlington Hall, Univ. of FL, Gainesville FL 32611-2075. (352)392-6650, ext. 234. Fax: (352)392-0860. E-mail: subtropics@english.ufl.edu. Web site: http://www.english.ufl.edu/subt ropics. **Contact:** David Leavitt, fiction editor. Literary magazine/journal: 9×6, 160 pages. Includes photographs. "*Subtropics*—headed by fiction editor David Leavitt, poetry editor Sidney Wade, and managing editor Mark Mitchell—is committed to publishing the best new fiction, poetry, literary nonfiction, and translation by emerging and established writers. In addition to new work, *Subtropics* also, from time to time, republishes important and compelling stories, essays, and poems that have lapsed out of print." Triannual. Estab. 2006. Circ. 3,500. Member CLMP.

● Stories included in *Best American Short Stories 2007* and *The O. Henry Prize Stories 2007*. Poems included in *Best American Poetry 2006 and 2007*.

Needs Literary. Does not want genre fiction. Receives 1,000 mss/month. Accepts 5-6 mss/issue; 15-18 mss/year. Does not read between May 1 and August 31. Ms published 3-6 months after acceptance. Agented fiction 33%. **Publishes 1-2 new writers/year.** Published John Barth, Ariel Dorfman, Tony D'Souza, Allan Gurganus, Frances Hwang, Kuzhali Manickavel, Eileen Pollack, Padgett Powell, Nancy Reisman, Jarret Rosenblatt, Joanna Scott, and Olga Slavnikova. Average length: 5,000 words. Publishes short shorts. Average length of short shorts: 400 words. Also publishes literary essays, poetry. Rarely comments on/critiques rejected mss.

How to Contact Send complete ms with cover letter. Responds to mss in 2-6 weeks. Send disposable copy of ms. Replies via e-mail only. Do not include SASE. Considers simultaneous submissions. Sample copy available for $12.95. Guidelines available on Web site.

Payment/Terms Writers receive $500-1,000, 2 contributor's copies. Additional copies $12.95. Pays on acceptance. Acquires first North American serial rights. Publication is copyrighted.

Advice "Please read the guidelines and at least one issue of the magazine before submitting."

$ ⬜ THE SUN

The Sun Publishing Co., 107 N. Roberson St., Chapel Hill NC 27516. (919)942-5282. Fax: (919)932-3101. Web site: www.thesunmagazine.org. **Contact:** Sy Safransky, editor. Magazine: 8½×11; 48 pages; offset paper; glossy cover stock; photos. "We are open to all kinds of writing, though we favor work of a personal nature." Monthly. Estab. 1974. Circ. 72,000.

Needs Literary. Open to all fiction. Receives 800 unsolicited mss/month. Accepts 20 short stories/year. Publishes ms 3-12 months after acceptance. Recently published work by Alex Mindt, John Tait, April Wilder, Theresa Williams. Also publishes poetry and nonfiction.

How to Contact Send complete ms. Accepts reprint submissions. Sample copy for $5. Writer's guidelines online.

Payment/Terms Pays $300-1,000. Pays on publication for first, one-time rights.

Advice "We favor honest, personal writing with an intimate point of view."

⬜ SYCAMORE REVIEW

Purdue University, Department of English, 500 Oval Drive, West Lafayette IN 47907. (765)494-3783. Fax: (765)494-3780. E-mail: sycamore@purdue.edu. Web site: www.sycamorereview.com. **Contact:**

Editor-in-Chief. Magazine: 8×8; 100-150 pages; heavy, textured, uncoated paper; heavy laminated cover. "Journal devoted to contemporary literature. We publish both traditional and experimental fiction, personal essay, poetry, interviews, drama and graphic art. Novel excerpts welcome if they stand alone as a story." Semiannual. Estab. 1989. Circ. 1,000.

Needs Experimental, humor/satire, literary, mainstream, regional, translations. "We generally avoid genre literature but maintain no formal restrictions on style or subject matter. No romance, children's." Would like to see more experimental fiction. Publishes ms 11 months after acceptance. Recently published work by Lucia Perillo, June Armstrong, W.P. Osborn, William Giraldi. Also publishes poetry. Sometimes comments on rejected mss.

How to Contact Send complete ms with SASE, cover letter with previous publications and address. Responds in 4 months to mss. Accepts simultaneous submissions. Sample copy for $5. Writer's guidelines for #10 SASE or online.

Payment/Terms Acquires one-time rights.

Advice "We publish both new and experienced authors but we're always looking for stories with strong emotional appeal, vivid characterization and a distinctive narrative voice; fiction that breaks new ground while still telling an interesting and significant story. Avoid gimmicks and trite, predictable outcomes. Write stories that have a ring of truth, the impact of felt emotion. Don't be afraid to submit, send your best."

$⍯ TAMPA REVIEW

University of Tampa Press, 401 W. Kennedy Blvd., Tampa FL 33606. (813)253-6266. Fax: (813)258-7593. Web site: tampareview.ut.edu. **Contact:** Lisa Birnbaum and Kathleen Ochshorn, fiction editors. Magazine: 7½×10½; hardback; approximately 100 pages; acid-free paper; visual art; photos. An international literary journal publishing art and literature from Florida and Tampa Bay as well as new work and translations from throughout the world. Semiannual. Estab. 1988. Circ. 500.

Needs Ethnic/multicultural, experimental, fantasy, historical, literary, mainstream, translations. "We are far more interested in quality than in genre. Nothing sentimental as opposed to genuinely moving, nor self-conscious style at the expense of human truth." Accepts 4-5 mss/issue. Reads September-December; reports January-May. Publishes ms 10 months after acceptance. Agented fiction 20%. Recently published work by Elizabeth Spencer, Lee K. Abbott, Lorrie Moore, Gordon Weaver, Tim O'Brien. Publishes short shorts. Also publishes literary essays, poetry.

How to Contact Send complete ms. Include brief bio. Responds in 5 months to mss. Accepts multiple submissions. Sample copy for $7. Writer's guidelines online.

Payment/Terms Pays $10/printed page. Pays on publication for first North American serial rights. Sends galleys to author.

Advice "There are more good writers publishing in magazines today than there have been in many decades. Unfortunately, there are even more bad ones. In T. Gertler's *Elbowing the Seducer*, an editor advises a young writer that he wants to hear her voice completely, to tell (he means 'show') him in a story the truest thing she knows. We concur. Rather than a trendy workshop story or a minimalism that actually stems from not having much to say, we would like to see stories that make us believe they mattered to the writer and, more importantly, will matter to a reader. Trim until only the essential is left, and don't give up belief in yourself. And it might help to attend a good writers' conference, e.g. Wesleyan or Bennington."

⍯ TAPROOT LITERARY REVIEW

Taproot Writer's Workshop, Inc., Box 204, Ambridge PA 15003. (724)266-8476. E-mail: taproot10@aol.com. **Contact:** Tikvah Feinstein, editor. Magazine: 5½×8½; 93 pages; 20 lb. paper; hardcover; attractively printed; saddle-stitched. "We select on quality, not topic. Variety and quality are our appealing features." Annual. Estab. 1987. Circ. 500.

Needs Literary. "No pornography, religious, popular, romance fiction. Wants more stories with multicultural themes, showing intensity, reality and human emotions that readers can relate to, learn from, and most importantly—be interesting." The majority of ms published are received through annual contest. Receives 20 unsolicited mss/month. Accepts 6 mss/issue. **Publishes 2-4 new writers/year.** Recently published work by Jennifer Stephanie Kaplan Cohen, Rebecca J. Foust, Vicky Tachau, Rosalia Scalia, Alena Horowitz, Lonnie Goldman, Shirley Barasch. Publishes short shorts. Also publishes poetry. Sometimes comments on rejected mss.

How to Contact Accepts submissions by e-mail. Send for guidelines first. Send complete ms with a cover letter. Include estimated word count and bio. Responds in 6 months to mss. No simultaneous submissions. Sample copy for $5, 6×12 SAE with 5 first-class stamps. Writer's guidelines for #10 SASE.

Payment/Terms Awards $25 in prize money for first place fiction and poetry winners each issue; certificate for 2nd and 3rd place; 1 contributor's copy. Additionally, *Taproot* offers a coveted literary prize, promotion, and $15 for the winner. Acquires first rights. Sponsors awards/contests.

Advice *"Taproot* is getting more fiction submissions, and every one is read entirely. This takes time, so response can be delayed at busy times of year. Our contest is a good way to start publishing. Send for a sample copy and read it through. Ask for a critique and follow suggestions. Don't be offended by any suggestions—just take them or leave them and keep writing. Looks for a story that speaks in its unique voice, told in a well-crafted and complete, memorable style, a style of signature to the author. Follow writer's guidelines. Research markets. Send cover letter. Don't give up."

◙ THE TEXAS REVIEW

Texas Review Press at Sam Houston State University, P.O. Box 2146, Huntsville TX 77341-2146. (936)294-1992. Fax: (936)294-3070 (inquiries only). E-mail: eng_pdr@shsu.edu. Web site: www.shsu. edu/~www_trp/. **Contact:** Paul Ruffin, editor. Magazine: 6×9; 148-190 pages; best quality paper; 70 lb. cover stock; illustrations; photos. "We publish top quality poetry, fiction, articles, interviews and reviews for a general audience." Semiannual. Estab. 1976. Circ. 1,200. A member of the Texas A&M University Press consortium.

Needs Humor/satire, literary, mainstream, contemporary fiction. "We are eager enough to consider fiction of quality, no matter what its theme or subject matter. No juvenile fiction." Receives 40-60 unsolicited mss/month. Accepts 4 mss/issue; 6 mss/year. Does not read mss May-September. Publishes ms 6-12 months after acceptance. **Publishes some new writers/year.** Recently published work by George Garrett, Ellen Gilchrist, Fred Chappell. Also publishes literary essays, literary criticism, poetry. Sometimes comments on rejected mss.

How to Contact Send complete ms. No mss accepted via fax. Send disposable copy of ms and #10 SASE for reply only. Responds in 2 weeks to queries; 3-6 months to mss. Accepts multiple submissions. Sample copy for $5. Writer's guidelines for SASE and on Web site.

Payment/Terms Pays contributor's copies and one year subscription. Pays on publication for first North American serial, one-time rights. Sends galleys to author.

Advice "Submit often; be aware that we reject 90% of submissions due to overwhelming number of mss sent."

$◙ THEMA

Box 8747, Metairie LA 70011-8747. (504)940-7156. **Contact:** Virginia Howard, editor. Magazine: 5½×8½; 150 pages; Grandee Strathmore cover stock; b&w illustrations. *"Thema* is designed to stimulate creative thinking by challenging writers with unusual themes, such as 'rage over a lost penny.' Appeals to writers, teachers of creative writing, and general reading audience." Estab. 1988. Circ. 350.

Needs Adventure, ethnic/multicultural, experimental, fantasy, historical, humor/satire, literary, mainstream, mystery/suspense, novel excerpts, psychic/supernatural/occult, regional, religious/inspirational, science fiction, slice-of-life vignettes, western, contemporary, sports, prose poem. "No erotica." 2008 themes were *"Everybody Quit"* (March 1); *"Henry's Fence"* (July 1); *"When Things Get Back to Normal"* (November 1). Write for 2009 themes (listed on web site: http://members.cox. net/thema). Publishes ms within 6 months after acceptance. **Publishes 9 new writers/year.** Recently published work by Madonna Dries Christensen, Robert Raymer, Sandra Maddux-Creech, and June Freeman Baswell. Publishes short shorts. Also publishes poetry. Sometimes comments on rejected mss.

How to Contact Send complete ms with SASE, cover letter, include "name and address, brief introduction, specifying the intended target issue for the mss." SASE. Responds in 1 week to queries; 5 months to mss. Accepts simultaneous, multiple submissions and reprints. Does not accept e-mailed submissions. Sample copy for $10. Writer's guidelines for #10 SASE.

Payment/Terms Pays $10-25. Pays on acceptance for one-time rights.

Advice "Do not submit a manuscript unless you have written it for a specified theme. If you don't know the upcoming themes, send for guidelines first before sending a story. We need more stories told in the Mark Twain/O. Henry tradition in magazine fiction."

◨ ▨ THIRD COAST

Dept. of English, Western Michigan University, Kalamazoo MI 49008-5331. (269)387-2675. Fax: (269)387-2562. E-mail: editors@thirdcoastmagazine.com. Web site: www.thirdcoastmagazine.com. Editor: Rachel Swearingen. **Contact:** Jessi Phillips and James Miranda, fiction editors. Magazine: 6×9; 176 pages. "We will consider many different types of fiction and favor those exhibiting a freshness of vision and approach." Twice-yearly. Estab. 1995. Circ. 2,875.

- *Third Coast* has received Pushcart Prize nominations. The section editors of this publication change with the university year.

Needs Literary. "While we don't want to see formulaic genre fiction, we will consider material that plays with or challenges generic forms." Receives 200 unsolicited mss/month. Accepts 6-8 mss/issue; 15 mss/year. Recently published work by Keith Banner, Peter Ho Davies, Moira Crone, Lee Martin, John McNally, and Peter Orner. Also publishes literary essays, poetry, one-act plays. Sometimes comments on rejected mss.

How to Contact Visit our Web site at http://www.thirdcoastmagazine.com for guidelines. *Third Coast* only accepts submissions submitted to its online submission manager. All hard copy submissions will be returned unread. Reads mss from August through May of each year.

Payment/Terms Pays 2 contributor's copies as well as a 1 year subscription to the publication; additional copies for $4. Acquires first North American serial rights.

Advice "We seek superior fiction from short-shorts to 30-page stories."

▧ $◨ THIRD WEDNESDAY, A LITERARY ARTS MAGAZINE

174 Greenside Up, Ypsilanti, MI 48197. (734)434-2409. E-mail: submissions@thirdwednesday.org. Web site: http://thirdwednesday.org. **Contact:** Laurence Thomas, editor. Literary magazine/journal. 60-65 pages. Contains illustrations. Includes photographs. "*Third Wednesday* publishes quality (a subjective term at best) poetry, short fiction and artwork by experienced writers and artists. We welcome work by established writers/artists, as well as those who are not yet well known, but headed for prominence." Quarterly. Estab. 2007.

Needs Experimental, fantasy, humor/satire, literary, mainstream, romance, translations. Does not want "purely anecdotal accounts of incidents, sentimentality, pointless conclusions, or stories without some characterization or plot development." Receives 5-10 mss/month. Accepts 3-5 mss/issue. Ms published 3 months after acceptance. Length: 1,500 words (max). Average length: 1,000 words. Publishes short shorts. Also publishes poetry. Sometimes comments on/critiques rejected mss.

How to Contact Send complete ms with cover letter. Accepts submissions by e-mail. Include estimated word count, brief bio. Responds to mss in 6-8 weeks. Considers simultaneous submissions. Sample copy available for $8. Guidelines available for SASE, via e-mail.

Payment/Terms Writers receive $3, 1 contributor's copy. Additional copies $8. Pays on acceptance. Acquires first rights.

Advice "Of course, originality is important along with skill in writing, deft handling of language and meaning which goes hand in hand with beauty, whatever that is. Short fiction is specialized and difficult, so the writer should read extensively in the field."

▨ ◻ TICKLED BY THUNDER, Helping Writers Get Published Since 1990

Tickled By Thunder Publishing Co., 14076 86A Ave., Surrey BC V3W 0V9 Canada. (604)591-6095. E-mail: info@tickledbythunder.com. Web site: www.tickledbythunder.com. **Contact:** Larry Lindner, publisher. Magazine: digest-sized; 24 pages; bond paper; bond cover stock; illustrations; photos. "*Tickled By Thunder* is designed to encourage beginning writers of fiction, poetry and nonfiction." Quarterly. Estab. 1990. Circ. 1,000.

Needs Fantasy, humor/satire, literary, mainstream, mystery/suspense, science fiction, western. "No overly indulgent horror, sex, profanity or religious material." Receives 25 unsolicited mss/month. Accepts 3 mss/issue; 12 mss/year. Publishes ms 3-9 months after acceptance. **Publishes 10 new writers/year.** Recently published work by Rick Cook and Jerry Shane. Length: 2,000 words; average length: 1,500 words. Also publishes literary essays, literary criticism, poetry.

How to Contact Send complete ms. Include estimated word count and brief bio. Send SASE or IRC for return of ms; or send disposable copy of ms and #10 SASE for reply only. No e-mail submissions. Responds in 3 months to queries; 6 months to mss. Accepts simultaneous, multiple submissions and reprints. Writer's guidelines online.

Payment/Terms Pays on publication for first, second serial (reprint) rights.
Advice "Make your characters breathe on their own. Use description with action."

▨ ◎ ▨ TRANSITION, An International Review

104 Mount Auburn St., 3R, Cambridge MA 02138. (617)496-2845. Fax: (617)496-2877. E-mail: transiti on@fas.harvard.edu. Web site: www.transitionmagazine.com. **Contact:** Laurie Calhoun, director of publications. Magazine: $9^1/_2 \times 6^1/_2$; 150-175 pages; 70 lb. Finch Opaque paper; 100 lb. White Warren Lustro dull cover; illustrations; photos. "*Transition* magazine is a quarterly international review known for compelling and controversial writing from and about Africa and the dispora. This prestigious magazine is edited at Harvard University, and editorial board members include such heavy-hitters as Toni Morrison, Jamaica Kincaid and bell hooks. The magazine also attracts famous contributors such as Spike Lee, Philip Gourevitch and Carolos Fuentes." Quarterly. Estab. 1961. Circ. 3,000.

• Four-time winner fo the Alternative Press Award for international reporting, (2001, 2000, 1999, 1995); finalist in the 2001 National Magazine Award in General Excellence category.

Needs Ethnic/multicultural, historical, humor/satire, literary, regional (African diaspora, Third World, etc.). Receives 40 unsolicited mss/month. Accepts 2-4 mss/year. Publishes ms 6-8 months after acceptance. Agented fiction 30-40%. **Publishes 5 new writers/year.** Recently published work by Wole Soyinka, Henry French, George Makana Clark, Brent Edwards, and Emily Raboteau. Length: 4,000-8,000 words; average length: 7,000 words. Also publishes literary essays, literary criticism. Sometimes comments on rejected mss.

How to Contact Query with published clips or send complete ms. Include brief bio and list of publications. Send disposable copy of ms and #10 SASE for reply only. Responds in 2 months to queries; 6 months to mss. Accepts simultaneous submissions. Sample copy not available. Writer's guidelines for #10 SASE.

Payment/Terms 4 contributor's copies. Sends galleys to author.

Advice "We look for a non-white, alternative perspective, dealing with issues of race, ethnicity and identity in an upredictable, provocative way."

▨ ▨ TRIQUARTERLY

629 Noyes St., Northwestern University, Evanston IL 60208-4170. (847)491-7614. Fax: (847)467-2096. Web site: www.triquarterly.com. **Contact:** Susan Firestone Hahn, editor. Magazine: $6 \times 9^1/_4$; 240-272 pages; 60 lb. paper; heavy cover stock; illustration; photos. "A general literary quarterly. We publish short stories, novellas or excerpts from novels, by American and foreign writers. Genre or style is not a primary consideration. We aim for the general but serious and sophisticated reader. Many of our readers are also writers." Triannual. Estab. 1964. Circ. 5,000.

• Stories from *Triquarterly* have been reprinted in *The Best American Short Stories*, *Pushcart Prizes* and *O. Henry Prize* Anthologies.

Needs Literary, translations, contemporary. "No prejudices or preconceptions against anything *except* genre fiction (romance, science fiction, etc.)." Receives 500 unsolicited mss/month. Accepts 10 mss/issue; 30 mss/year. Does not read or accept mss between April 1 and September 30. Publishes ms 1 year after acceptance. Agented fiction 10%. **Publishes 1-5 new writers/year.** Recently published work by John Barth, Chaim Potok, Joyce Carol Oates and Robert Girardi. Publishes short shorts.

How to Contact Send complete ms with SASE. Responds in 3 months to queries; 3 months to mss. No simultaneous submissions. Sample copy for $5. Writer's guidelines for #10 SASE.

Payment/Terms Payment varies depending on grant support. Pays on publication for first North American serial rights. Nonexclusive reprint rights. Sends galleys to author.

▨ ▨ UNDER HWY 99, Showcasing the Untold Story

Seattle WA. E-mail: info@underhwy99.com. Web site: http://underhwy99.com. **Contact:** Erica Goodkind, editor. Literary magazine/journal: $8^1/_2 \times 11$; 25-35 pages; 60# paper; 80# glossy cover. Contains illustrations, photographs. "The 'untold story' is the story that is most important to you—the one you feel most compelled to tell. This is a publication for people who like a good read, and for those who have an undying devotion to and special knack for writing." Triannual. Estab. 2008. Circ. 300.

Needs Adventure, ethnic/multicultural (general), historical (general), humor/satire, literary, mainstream. Special interests: slice-of-life, music inspired prose. Does not want horror, romance, science ficiton, Evangelic. Receives 20-30 mss/month. Accepts 5-10 mss/issue; 15-25 mss/year. Manuscript published 2-4 months after acceptance. **Publishes 75% new writers/year.** Length: 3,500 words (max). Average length: 2,500 words. Publishes short shorts. Average length of short shorts: 500 words. Rarely comments on/critiques rejected mss.

How to Contact Send complete ms with cover letter. Accepts submissions by e-mail only. Include estimated word count, brief bio. Responds to queries in 4 weeks; mss in 2 months. Considers simultaneous submissions, multiple submissions. Sample copy available for $4.95. Guidelines available on Web site.

Payment/Terms Writers receive 1 contributor's copy. Additional copies $4.95. Pays on publication. Acquires first rights, electronic rights. Publication is not copyrighted.

Advice "We have weakness for smart, imaginative pieces that bring out the uniqueness in any given situation. We tend to find stories that cast ordinary things in an unusal light and unusual things in an ordinary light particularly irresistible. Pieces should balance all othe usual elements of any good piece of literature: character, setting, theme, voice, pacing, etc."

UPSTREET

Ledgetop Publishing, P.O. Box 105, Richmond MA 01254-0105. (413)441-9702. E-mail: submissions @upstreet-mag.org. Web site: http://www.upstreet-mag.org. **Contact:** editor. Literary magazine/ journal. 7 × 8.5, 224 pages, 60# white offset paper. "A literary annual containing the best new fiction, poetry, and creative nonfiction available. First three issues feature interviews with Jim Shepard, Lydia Davis, and Wally Lamb. Independently owned and published, nationally distributed. Founded by Vivian Dorsel, former managing editor of *The Berkshire Review* for eight years, who selected the members of the editorial staff for their love of the written word, their high standards of literary judgment, and their desire to offer a voice to prose writers and poets who might not find publication opportunities in more mainstream journals." Annual. Estab. 2005. Circ. 4,000. Member CLMP.

Needs Ethnic/multicultural (general), experimental, humor/satire, literary, mainstream. Does not want juvenile/YA, religious, or "any genre fiction that is not 'literary' (i.e., imaginative, sophisticated, innovative)." Does not read March-June. Ms published 2 months after acceptance. Length: 5,000 words (max). Publishes short shorts. Also publishes literary essays, poetry. Rarely comments on/critiques rejected mss.

How to Contact Send complete ms with cover letter. Accepts submissions by e-mail. Include estimated word count, brief bio, contact information. Considers simultaneous submissions, multiple submissions. Sample copy available for $8.50 plus postage. Guidelines available via e-mail.

Payment/Terms Writers receive 1 contributor's copy. Additional copies $10. Pays on publication. Acquires first North American serial rights. Publication is copyrighted.

VERSAL

Wordsinhere, Amsterdam, The Netherlands. E-mail: versal@wordsinhere.com. Web site: http://versal.wordsinhere.com. **Contact:** Robert Glick, fiction editor. Literary magazine/journal: 20 cm × 20 cm, 100 pages, offset, perfect bound, acid free color cover. Includes artwork. "*Versal* is the only English-language literary magazine in the Netherlands and publishes new poetry, prose and art from around the world. We publish writers with an instinct for language and line break, content and form that is urgent, involved and unexpected." Annual. Estab. 2002. Circ. 750.

Needs Experimental, literary. Receives 20 mss/month. Accepts 8 mss/year. Does not read mss January 16-September 14. Manuscript published 3 months after acceptance. **Publishes 2 new writers/year.** Published Russell Edson, Alissa Nutting, Tye Pemberton, Rhonda Waterfall. Length: 3,000 words (max). Publishes short shorts. Average length of short shorts: 1,500 words. Also publishes poetry. Sometimes comments on/critiques rejected mss.

How to Contact Send complete ms with cover letter. Accepts submissions electronically only. Include brief bio. Responds to queries in 1 week. Responds to mss in 3 months. Considers simultaneous submissions. Guidelines available on Web site.

Payment/Terms Writers receive 1 contributor copy and subscription discount. Additional copies $15. Pays on publication. Acquires one-time rights. Sends galleys to author. Publication is copyrighted.

Advice "We are drawn to good pacing, varied tone and something out of the ordinary. Above all, we look for surprise and richness of detail in representing this surprise. We especially love something written in an unusual voice that also contains depth in content. For more traditional voices, we look for surprise within the story, either by giving us an unusual situation or by having characters surprise us with their actions. Nasty sex and drug adventures don't really shock us, so unless there's a fantastic twist to the tale, they don't provide a jump out of the slush pile. In flash fiction, we are less inclined to the purely anecdotal than to work that somehow manages to convey depth and/or tension.''

◙ ⊻ VESTAL REVIEW, A flash fiction magazine

2609 Dartmouth Dr., Vestal NY 13850. E-mail: submissions@vestalreview.net. Web site: www.vestal review.net. **Contact:** Mark Budman, publisher/editor. Magazine: $8^{1}/_{2} \times 5^{1}/_{2}$; 45 pages; heavy cover stock; illustrations. ''*Vestal Review* is the magazine specializing in flash fiction (stories under 500 words). We accept only e-mail submissions.'' Quarterly Web version; semi-annual print version. Circ. 1,500.

- *Vestal Review* received a Golden Web Award in 2002-2003.

Needs Ethnic/multicultural, horror, literary, mainstream, speculative fiction. Receives 60-100 unsolicited mss/month. Accepts 7-8 mss/issue; 28-32 mss/year. Does not read mss March, June, September and December. Publishes ms 2-3 months after acceptance. **Publishes 2-3 new writers/year.** Recently published work by Steve Almond, Katharine Weber, Aimee Bender, Sam Lipsyte, Kirk Nesset, Judith Cofer, Robert Boswell, Bruce Holland Rogers, Pamela Painter, and Michelle Richmond. Publishes only short shorts of 500 words or less. Sometimes comments on rejected mss.

How to Contact Send complete ms with a cover letter via e-mail only. Include estimated word count, brief bio and list of publications. Responds in 1 week to queries; 3 months to mss. Accepts simultaneous, multiple submissions. A sample copy is $10 (add $2 for postage, $4 for foreign address). Writer's guidelines online.

Payment/Terms Pays 3¢-10¢/word and 1 contributor's copy; additional copies $10. Pays on publication for first North American serial, electronic rights. Sends galleys to author.

Advice ''We like literary fiction, with a plot, that doesn't waste words. Don't send jokes masked as stories. Read guidelines on Web site.''

$◙ VIRGINIA QUARTERLY REVIEW

University of Virginia, One West Range, P.O. Box 400223, Charlottesville VA 22904-4223. (434)924-3124. Fax: (434)924-1397. Web site: www.vqronline.org. **Contact:** Ted Genoways, editor. ''A national journal of literature and discussion, featuring nonfiction, fiction, and poetry for both educated general readers and the academic audience.'' Quarterly. Estab. 1925. Circ. 6,000.

Needs Ethnic/multicultural, feminist, historical, humor/satire, literary, mainstream, mystery/suspense, novel excerpts, serialized novels, translations. Accepts 3 mss/issue; 20 mss/year. Publishes ms 3-6 months after acceptance.

How to Contact Send complete ms. SASE. No queries. Responds in 3-4 months to mss. Sample copy for $14. Writer's guidelines online.

Payment/Terms Pays $100/page maximum. $5 per line for poetry. Pays on publication for first North American rights and nonexclusive online rights. Submissions only accepted online.

Ⓝ $WHR: THE SOUND OF INNOVATIVE WRITING

Western Humanities Review, University of Utah, English Department, 255 S. Central Campus Dr., Room 3500, Salt Lake City UT 84112-0494. (801)581-6070. E-mail: whr@mail.hum.utah.edu. Web site: www.hum.utah.edu/whr. **Contact:** PJ Carlisle, managing editor or Lance Olsenh, fiction editor. Biannual. Estab. 1947. Circ. 1,300.

Needs Experimental and innovative fiction. Does not want genre (romance, sci-fi, etc.). Receives 100 mss/month. Accepts 5-6 mss/issue; 6-8 mss/year. Does not read April-September. Publishes ms up to 1 year after acceptance. **Publishes 3-5 new writers/year.** Recently published work by Michael Martone, Steve Almond, Craig Dworkin, Benjamin Percy, Francois Camoin, Kate Bernheimer, Lidia Yuknavitch. Publishes short shorts. Also innovative literary criticism and poetry. Rarely comments on rejected mss.

How to Contact Send one story per reading period. No email submissions or queries. Sample copy for $10. Writer's guidelines online.

Payment/Terms Pays $5/published page when available — or one comp. copy of the issue/pg. Pays on publication.

◙ WHISKEY ISLAND MAGAZINE

Dept. of English, Cleveland State University, Cleveland OH 44115-2440. (216)687-2056. Fax: (216)687-6943. E-mail: whiskeyisland@csuohio.edu. Web site: www.csuohio.edu/whiskey_island. Editors change each year. Magazine of fiction, creative nonfiction, theater writing, poetry and art. "We provide a forum for new writers, for themes and points of view that are both traditional and experimental." Semiannual. Estab. 1978. Press run: 750.

Needs "Would like to see more short shorts, flash fiction." Receives 100 unsolicited mss/month. Accepts 46 mss/issue. **Publishes 5-10 new writers/year.** Recently published work by Nin Andrews, Robert Pope and Karen Kotrba. Also publishes poetry.

How to Contact Send complete ms. Accepts submissions by e-mail. Responds in 6 months. Sample copy for $6. Subscription $12.

Payment/Terms Pays 2 contributor copies and 1-year subscription. Acquires one-time rights. Sponsors annual prose contest with $500 prize and publication. $10 per entry.

Advice "We read manuscripts year round. We seek engaging writing of any style."

Ⓝ ⊕ ◙ Ⓖ WHITE FUNGUS, An Experimental Arts Magazine

P.O. Box 6173, Wellington, Aotearoa, New Zealand. (64)4 382 9113. E-mail: whitefungusmail@yahoo.com. Web site: www.whitefungus.com. **Contact:** Ron Hanson, Editor. Literary magazine/journal. Oversize A5, 104 pages, matte paper, matte card cover. Contains illustrations, photographs. "*White Fungus* covers a range of experimental arts including literature, poetry, visual arts, comics and music. We are interested in material that is bold, innovative and well-researched. Independence of thought and meaningful surprises are a high priority." Semiannual. Estab. 2004. Circ. 2,000.

Needs Comics/graphic novels, ethnic/multicultural, experimental, feminist, gay, historical (general), humor/satire, lesbian, literary, science fiction. "*White Fungus* considers submissions on the basis of quality rather than genre." Receives 20 mss/month. Accepts 3 mss/issue; 6 mss/year. Ms published 1-12 months after acceptance. **Publishes 2 new writers/year.** Published Hamish Low, Cyril Wong, Aaron Coyes, Hamish Wyn, Tim Bollinger, Kate Montgomery, Tessa Laird and Tobias Fischer. Average length: 1,200 words. Publishes short shorts. Average length of short shorts: 1,000 words. Also publishes literary criticism, poetry. Sometimes comments on/critiques rejected mss.

How to Contact Query with clips of published work. Accepts submissions by e-mail, on disk. Include brief bio, list of publications. Responds to queries in 1 week. Responds to mss in 1 week. Send either SASE (or IRC) for return of ms or disposable copy of ms and #10 SASE for reply only. Considers simultaneous submissions, multiple submissions. Sample copy available for $10. Guidelines available via e-mail.

Payment/Terms Writers receive 10 contributor's copies, free subscription to the magazine. Additional copies $6. Pays on publication. Acquires first rights. Publication is copyrighted.

Advice "We like writing that explores the world around it rather than being self-obsessed. We're not interested in personal fantasies or self-projections, just an active critical response to one's enviroment. Be direct, flexible and consider how your work might be considered in an international context. What can you contribute or shed light on?"

◙ WILLARD & MAPLE, The Literary Magazine of Champlain College

163 South Willard Street, Freeman 302, Box 34, Burlington VT 05401. (802)860-2700 ext. 2462. E-mail: willardandmaple@champlain.edu. **Contact:** fiction editor. Magazine: perfect bound; 125 pages; illustrations; photos. "*Willard & Maple* is a student-run literary magazine from Champlain College that publishes a wide array of poems, short stories, creative essays, short plays, pen and ink drawings, black and white photos, and computer graphics. We now accept color." Annual. Estab. 1996.

Needs We accept all types of mss. Receives 20 unsolicited mss/month. Accepts 1 mss/year. Does not read mss March 31-September 1. Publishes ms within 1 year after acceptance. **Publishes 10 new writers/year.** Recently published work by Morgan Merrihew, John Grey, Suki Fredericks, Ginger Vieira, and Devin Beliveau. Length: 5,000 words; average length: 2,500 words. Publishes short shorts. Also publishes literary essays, poetry. Sometimes comments on rejected mss.

How to Contact Send complete mss. Send SASE for return of ms or send disposable copy of mss and #10 SASE for reply only. Responds in 6 months to queries; 6 months to mss. Accepts simultaneous, multiple submissions. Sample copy for $8. Writer's guidelines for SASE or send e-mail. Reviews fiction.

Payment/Terms Pays 2 contributor's copies; additional copies $12. Pays on publication for one-time rights.

Advice "The power of imagination makes us infinite."

◪ THE WILLIAM AND MARY REVIEW

The College of William and Mary, Campus Center, P.O. Box 8795, Williamsburg VA 23187-8795. (757)221-3290. E-mail: review@wm.edu. Web site: www.wm.edu/so/wmreview. **Contact:** Address all prose submissions ATTN: Prose Editor. Magazine: 6×9; 96 pages; coated paper; 4-color card cover; photos. "Our journal is read by a sophisticated audience of subscribers, professors, and university students." Annual. Estab. 1962. Circ. 1,600.

Needs Experimental, family saga, historical, horror (psychological), humor/satire, literary, mainstream, science fiction, thriller/espionage, short stories. "We do not want to see typical genre pieces. Do not bother sending fantasy or erotica." Receives 35 unsolicited mss/month. Accepts 4-5 mss/year. Does not read mss from February to August. Publishes ms 1-2 months after acceptance. **Publishes 1-2 new writers/year.** Length: 250-7,000 words; average length: 3,500 words. Publishes short shorts. Also publishes poetry. Rarely comments on rejected mss.

How to Contact Send complete ms. Send SASE (or IRC) for return of the mss or send disposable copy of the ms and #10 SASE for reply only. Include a cover letter. Responds in 5-6 months to queries. Accepts simultaneous, multiple submissions but requires identification of those that are simultaneous and notification if they are accepted elsewhere. Sample copy for $5.50.

Payment/Terms Pays 5 contributor's copies; additional copies $5. Pays on publication for first North American serial rights.

Advice "We do not give much weight to prior publications; each piece is judged on its own merit. New writers should be bold and unafraid to submit unorthodox works that depart from textbook literary tradition. We would like to see more quality short shorts and nonfiction works. We receive far too many mediocre genre stories."

WILLOW REVIEW

College of Lake County, 19351 W. Washington, Grayslake IL 60030. (847)543-2956. E-mail: com426 @clcillinois.edu. Web site: www.clcillinois.edu/community/willowreview.asp. **Contact:** Michael Latza, editor. Literary magazine/journal. 6×9, 110 pages. Annual. Estab. 1969. Circ. 800.

Needs Literary. Receives 10 mss/month. Accepts 3-5 mss/issue. Does not read mss May 1-September 1. Publishes 2-3 new writers/year. Published Patricia Smith, Tim Joycek. Length: 7,500 words (max). Publishes short shorts. Average length of short shorts: 500 words. Also publishes literary criticism. Rarely comments on/critiques rejected manuscripts.

How to Contact Send complete ms with cover letter. Include estimated word count, brief bio, list of publications. Responds to mss in 3-4 months. Send either SASE (or IRC) for return of ms or disposable copy of ms and #10 SASE for reply only. Considers simultaneous submissions, multiple submissions. Sample copy available for $5. Guidelines available for SASE, via e-mail.

Payment/Terms Writers receive 2 contributors copies. Additional copies $7. Pays on publication. All rights revert to author upon publication.

Ⓝ $◪ ◎ Ⓖ WITHERSIN MAGAZINE, DARK, DIFFERENT; THE PLEASANTLY SINISTER

30318 Deer Meadow Rd, Temecula CA 92591. (951)795-5498. Fax: (951)699-0486. E-mail: withersin @hotmail.com. Web site: http://www.withersin.com. **Contact:** Misty L. Gersley, Editor-in-Chief. Literary magazine/journal: 6×9, 100 pages. Contains illustrations. Includes photographs. "A literary chimera, *Withersin* explores the bittersweet stain of the human condition. Comprised of an impressive array of original razor wire fiction, oddments and incongruities, obscure historical footnotes, unconventional research articles, delectable interviews, highlights, reviews and releases in film, music and print; all sewn together with threads of deviant art." Triannual. Estab. 2007. Circ. 600.

Needs Comics/graphic novels, experimental, historical (general), horror, literary, psychic/supernatural/occult, regional (specific and unique places; legends and lore). Does not want romance, erotica (read: pornography), or politically charged pieces. List of upcoming themes available for SASE, on Web site. Receives 100-300 mss/month. Accepts 3-5 mss/issue; 9-15 mss/year. Does not read July-March. Ms published 9-18 months after acceptance. **Publishes 5 new writers/year.** Published David Bain, Robert Heinze, Edward Morris, Michael Pignatella, M.W. Anderson, Sunil Sadanand, David Sackmyster, Mark Allan Gunnells and Chet Gottfried. Length: 500 words (min)-3,000 words (max).

Average length: 2,000 words. Publishes short shorts. Average length of short shorts: 500 words. Also publishes literary essays, literary criticism, book reviews, poetry. Send review copies to *Withersin* Reviews, P.O. Box 892665 Temucula, CA 92589-2665 or *Withersin* Reviews 30318 Deer Meadow Rd, Temecula CA 92591. Often comments on/critiques rejected mss.

How to Contact Send complete ms with cover letter. Accepts submissions by e-mail, on disk. Include estimated word count, brief bio. Responds to queries in 2-3 weeks. Responds to mss in 4-6 weeks. Send either SASE (or IRC) for return of ms or disposable copy of ms and #10 SASE for reply only. Considers previously published submissions (reprints have different pay scale), multiple submissions. Sample copy available for $7.25, on Web site. Guidelines available for SASE, via e-mail, on Web site.

Payment/Terms Writers receive 1-5¢ per word, 3000 word payment cap, 1 contributor's copy. Additional copies $7.25. Pays on publication. Acquires first North American serial rights, one-time rights. Publication is copyrighted. Occasionally sponsors contests, check Web site for details. "We also sponsor videography contests on www.youtube.com/withersin."

Advice "Beyond an interesting plot structure and ideology, we definitely look for 'complete' pieces i.e. short works that have a distinct beginning, middle and end—Emphasis on END. It is actually difficult to complete a work of short fiction with all of these elements present, and it is important to continue to work and rework your piece until this comes to fruition. Your work should be free of errors, and each sentence should flow well into the next. Stand out works feature looking at the world from an odd, oblique angle. Make us think. Look outside the box, and tell us what you see— Elements of horror can always be presented in a non-traditional, yet still somehow gut-wrenching and unsettling way. Stay away from cliché. Before turning in your manuscript, read it aloud. Then have someone else unfamiliar with the piece read it aloud to you. This will highlight any unintentional snafus in grammar, spelling, sentence structure and flow. It will also allow you some great feedback. Look for open endings and correct them. Remember, you must articulate your writing so the reader can understand your message."

$⬚ WORKERS WRITE!

Blue Cubicle Press, LLC, P.O. Box 250382, Plano TX 75025-0382.(972)824-0646. E-mail: info@workerswritejournal.com. Web site: www.workerswritejournal.com. **Contact:** David LaBounty, editor. Literary magazine/journal: 100-164 pages, 20 lb. bond paper paper, 80 lb. cover stock cover. "We publish stories that center on a particular workplace." Annual.

Needs Ethnic/multicultural (general), humor/satire, literary, mainstream, regional. Receives 100 mss/month. Accepts 12-15 mss/year. Manuscript published 3-4 months after acceptance. **Publishes 1 new writer/year**. Length: 500 words (min)-5,000 words (max). Average length: 3,000 words. Publishes short shorts. Also publishes poetry. Often comments on rejected mss.

How to Contact Send complete ms with cover letter. Accepts submissions by e-mail. Responds to queries in 1 weeks. Responds to mss in 2-3 months. Send either SASE (or IRC) for return of ms or disposable copy of ms and #10 SASE for reply only. Considers simultaneous submissions, previously published submissions, multiple submissions. Sample copy available for $8. Guidelines available for SASE, via e-mail, on Web site.

Payment/Terms Pays $50 maximum and contributor's copies. Additional copies $4. Pays on publication.

Advice "We publish stories from the worker's point of view."

◨ WRITER'S BLOC

Texas A&M University-Kingsville, Dept. of Language & Literature, MSC 162 Fore Hall Room 110, Kingsville TX 78363. (361)593-2514. E-mail: kfmcd00@tamuk.edu. **Contact:** Dr. Cathy Downs. Magazine: 6×9; 100 pages; illustrations; photos. "*Writer's Bloc* fills approximately half of its pages with work from South Texas, a bilingual and bicultural area. Our policy is to create a magazine of quality that is entertaining, handsome, and thought-filled." Annual. Circ. 300.

Needs Ethnic/multicultural, experimental, literary, regional, translations. No pornography. No genre fiction. No work by children. Accepts about 6 mss/year. Does not read mss February-September. Length: 3,500 words; average length: 2,500 words. Publishes short shorts. Also publishes literary essays, poetry.

How to Contact Send complete ms and diskette. Send SASE for reply only. Sample copy for $6. Writer's guidelines for #10 SASE.

Payment/Terms Pays 1 contributor's copy. Pays on publication for one-time rights.

⊘ THE YALOBUSHA REVIEW, The Literary Journal of the University of Mississippi

Dept. of English, P.O. Box 1848, University MS 38677. (662)915-3175. Fax: (662)915-7419. E-mail: yreditor@yahoo.com. Web site: www.olemiss.edu/yalobusha. **Contact:** Danielle Sellers, editor. Magazine: 5×10; 125 pages; illustrations; photos. Annual. "Literary journal seeking quality submissions from around the world." Estab. 1995. Circ. 1,000.

Needs Experimental, family saga, historical, humor/satire, literary, mainstream, genre. Does not want sappy confessional or insights into parenthood. Receives 100 unsolicited mss/month. Accepts 8-10 mss/issue. Reading period: July 15-November 15. Publishes ms 4 months after acceptance. **Publishes 3-4 new writers/year.** Recently published work by Steve Almond, Shay Youngblood, Dan Chaon. Length: 500-5,000 words; average length: 4,000 words. Publishes short shorts. Also publishes nonfiction, poetry.

How to Contact Send complete ms. Include a brief bio. Does not accept electronic submissions unless from outside the U.S. Accepts simultaneous submissions. Send disposable copy of ms and #10 SASE for reply only. Responds in 2-4 months to mss. Reading period is July 15-November 15. Sample copy for $5. Writer's guidelines for #10 SASE.

Payment/Terms Pays 2 contributor's copies. Pays honorarium when funding available. Acquires first North American serial rights.

Advice "We look for writers with a strong, distinct voice and good stories to tell. Thrill us."

Ⓝ $◻ ZEEK, A JEWISH JOURNAL OF THOUGHT AND CULTURE

Metatronics Inc., 104 West 14th St., 4th Floor, New York NY 10011. E-mail: zeek@zeek.net. Web site: www.zeek.net. **Contact:** Dan Friedman, fiction editor. Literary magazine/journal, online magazine: 96 pages, card cover. Contains illustrations. Includes photographs. "*Zeek* is a new Jewish journal of thought and culture. Our mission is to present alternative Jewish voices of criticism, literature and religious thought, in an intelligent, but non-academic, context. *Zeek* exists both online and in print, in semi-annual journal form. *Zeek* believes in expansive definitions of what constitutes Jewish writing and culture, and is dedicated toward enriching those definitions within its pages. While it would be reductive to label any writing produced by Jews as 'Jewish writing,' *Zeek* believes that vibrant Jewish writing embraces a wide variety of media, opinions and perspectives that often express their Jewishness in subtle and unexpected ways, and often presents Jewish readings of non-Jewish culture. This may mean, for example, expressing an ethical/humanist sensibility in art criticism, or engaging the alterity of Jewishness with that of queer sexuality, or immersing oneself in the many diasporic cultures of Jewish character, from New York's Broadway to Marxism. Sometimes it may mean content that grapples with explicitly Jewish cultural themes, and sometimes it may mean Jews interacting with other cultures in a way in which Jewishness is relevant and informative." Semiannual. Estab. 2003. Circ. 2,000. Member IPA.

Needs Comics/graphic novels, ethnic/multicultural (general, Jewish), feminist, gay, historical (general, Jewish), humor/satire, lesbian, literary, religious (Jewish), translations. Does not want "cynical, inspirational. No ethnocentric writing or simplistic ranting. If someone else can say it, let them; define new boundaries." Receives 20 mss/month. Accepts 2-4 (with more online) mss/issue; 4-8 (with more online) mss/year. Manuscript published 4 months after acceptance. Agented fiction 0%. **Publishes 5-7 new writers/year.** Published David Ehrlich, Dalia Rosenfeld, Rebecca Mostov (debut), Joshua Henkin, Hayyim Obadiah. Length: 750-2,500 words. Average length: 1,500 words. Publishes short shorts. Average length of short shorts: 500 words. Also publishes literary essays, literary criticism, book reviews, poetry. Send review copies to Review Editor. Often comments on/critiques rejected mss.

How to Contact Accepts submissions by e-mail. Send ms attachment and cover letter to zeek@zeek.net. Include estimated word count, brief bio, list of publications. Responds to queries in 4 weeks. Responds to mss in 8 weeks. Send disposable copy of ms and #10 SASE for reply only, but strongly prefers e-mail submissions. Considers simultaneous submissions, multiple submissions. Guidelines available on Web site.

Payment/Terms Writers receive $25-$50 flate-rate payment, contibutor's copies, free subscription to the magazine. Additional copies $7/each. Pays on publication. Acquires first rights. Publication is copyrighted.

Advice "Seeks quality, freshness of perspective. Something intangibly Jewish and questioning of Jewish mores. Read the online archives. Ask yourself what questions your fiction poses."

$◎ ZYZZYVA, The Last Word: West Coast Writers & Artists

P.O. Box 590069, San Francisco CA 94159-0069. (415)752-4393. Fax: (415)752-4391. E-mail: editor@ zyzzyva.org. Web site: www.zyzzyva.org. **Contact:** Howard Junker, editor. "We feature work by writers currently living on the West Coast or in Alaska and Hawaii only. We are essentially a literary magazine, but of wide-ranging interests and a strong commitment to nonfiction." Estab. 1985. Circ. 3,500.

Needs Ethnic/multicultural, experimental, humor/satire, mainstream. Receives 300 unsolicited mss/ month. Accepts 10 mss/issue; 30 mss/year. Publishes ms 3 months after acceptance. Agented fiction 1%. **Publishes 15 new writers/year.** Recently published work by Amanda Field, Katherine Karlin, Margaret Weatherford. Publishes short shorts. Also publishes literary essays, poetry.

How to Contact Send complete ms. Responds in 1 week to queries; 1 month to mss. Sample copy for $7 or online. Writer's guidelines online.

Payment/Terms Pays $50. Pays on acceptance for first North American serial and one-time anthology rights.

Small Circulation Magazines

This section of *Novel & Short Story Writer's Market* contains general interest, special interest, regional and genre magazines with circulations under 10,000. Although these magazines vary greatly in size, theme, format and management, the editors are all looking for short stories. Their specific fiction needs present writers of all degrees of expertise and interests with an abundance of publishing opportunities. Among the diverse publications in this section are magazines devoted to almost every topic, every level of writing, and every type of writer. Some of the markets listed here publish fiction about a particular geographic area or by authors who live in that locale.

Although not as high-paying as the large-circulation consumer magazines, you'll find some of the publications listed here do pay writers 1-5¢/word or more. Also, unlike the big consumer magazines, these markets are very open to new writers and relatively easy to break into. Their only criteria is that your story be well written, well presented and suitable for their particular readership.

In this section you will also find listings for zines. Zines vary greatly in appearance as well as content. Some paper zines are photocopies published whenever the editor has material and money, while others feature offset printing and regular distribution schedules. A few have evolved into very slick four-color, commercial-looking publications.

SELECTING THE RIGHT MARKET

First, zero in on those markets most likely to be interested in your work. Begin by looking at the Category Index starting on page 594. If your work is more general—or conversely, very specialized—you may wish to browse through the listings, perhaps looking up those magazines published in your state or region. Also check the Online Markets section for other specialized and genre publications.

In addition to browsing through the listings and using the Category Index, check the openness icons at the beginning of listings to find those most likely to be receptive to your work. This is especially true for beginning writers, who should look for magazines that say they are especially open to new writers (◻) and for those giving equal weight to both new and established writers (◪). For more explanation about these icons, see the inside covers of this book.

Once you have a list of magazines you might like to try, read their listings carefully. Much of the material within each listing carries clues that tell you more about the magazine. You've Got a Story, starting on page 2, describes in detail the listing information common to all the markets in our book.

The physical description appearing near the beginning of the listings can give you clues about the size and financial commitment to the publication. This is not always an indication of quality, but chances are a publication with expensive paper and four-color artwork on the cover has more prestige than a photocopied publication featuring a clip-art cover. For more information on some of the paper, binding and printing terms used in these descriptions, see Printing and Production Terms Defined on page 555.

FURTHERING YOUR SEARCH

It cannot be stressed enough that reading the listing is only the first part of developing your marketing plan. The second part, equally important, is to obtain fiction guidelines and read the actual magazine. Reading copies of a magazine helps you determine the fine points of the magazine's publishing style and philosophy. There is no substitute for this type of hands-on research.

Unlike commercial magazines available at most newsstands and bookstores, it requires a little more effort to obtain some of the magazines listed here. You may need to send for a sample copy. We include sample copy prices in the listings whenever possible. See The Business of Fiction Writing on page 65 for the specific mechanics of manuscript submission. Above all, editors appreciate a professional presentation. Include a brief cover letter and send a self-addressed, stamped envelope for a reply. Be sure the envelope is large enough to accommodate your manuscript, if you would like it returned, and include enough stamps or International Reply Coupons (for replies from countries other than your own) to cover your manuscript's return. Many publishers today appreciate receiving a disposable manuscript, eliminating the cost to writers of return postage and saving editors the effort of repackaging manuscripts for return.

Most of the magazines listed here are published in the U.S. You will also find some English-speaking markets from around the world. These foreign publications are denoted with a ⊕ symbol at the beginning of listings. To make it easier to find Canadian markets, we include a 🔷 symbol at the start of those listings.

Small Circulation

⊕ ☑ ◎ **THE ABIKO ANNUAL WITH JAMES JOYCE, Finnegans Wake Studies**
ALP Ltd., % T. Hamada, Hananoi 1787-28, Kashiwa-shi 277-0812, Japan. (011)81-471-69-8036. E-mail: hamada-tatsuo@jcom.home.ne.jp. Web site: http://members.jcom.home.ne.jp/hamada-tatsuo/. **Contact:** Tatsuo Hamada. Magazine: A5; 350 pages; illustrations; photos. "We primarily publish James Joyce *Finnegans Wake* essays from writers here in Japan and abroad." Annual. Estab. 1989. Circ. 300.
Needs Experimental (in the vein of James Joyce), literary, inspirational. Also essays on James Joyce's *Finnegans Wake* from around the world. Receives very few unsolicited mss/month. Also publishes literary essays, literary criticism, poetry. Always comments on rejected mss.
How to Contact Send a disposable copy of ms or e-mail attachment. Responds in 1 week to queries; 3 months to mss. Accepts multiple submissions. Sample copy for $20. Guidelines for SASE. Reviews fiction.
Payment/Terms Pays 1 contributor's copy; additional copies $25. Copyright reverts to author upon publication.
Advice "We require camera-ready copy. The writer is welcome to accompany it with appropriate artwork."

Ⓝ **$□ AEON SPECULATIVE FICTION**
Quintamid, LLC., 600 First Ave, Ste 526, Seattle WA 98104. Web site: http://aeonmagazine.com. **Contact:** Bridget McKenna, editor. Magazine: 80-120 pages, downloadable electronic formats. Contains illustrations. "Aeon publishes science fiction, fantasy and horror with strong character-based stories or outstanding stylistic sensibilities." Quarterly. Estab. 2004. Circ. 1,500.
Needs Fantasy classic, contemporary/urban, magical realism, horror (dark fantasy, futuristic), science fiction hard sf/ soft/sociological, alternate history), young adult/teen (fantasy/science fiction), and poetry with science fiction or fantasy content." tories must have discernable speculative element." Receives 150 mss/month. Accepts 6-8 mss/issue; 25-30 mss/year. Ms published 3-6 months

after acceptance. Publishes 10-12 new writers/year. Length: 7,500 words (max). Average length: 4,000 words. Publishes short shorts. Average length of short shorts: 1,000 words. Sometimes comments on/critiques rejected mss.

How to Contact Send complete ms. Responds to queries in 2-3 weeks. Responds to mss in 1-3 months. Send disposable copy of ms.

Payment/Terms Writers receive 6¢/word, 1 contributor's copy. Pays on publication. Acquires first electronic rights. Sends galleys to author. Publication is copyrighted.

Advice "Originality, a strong, confident and unique voice, compelling story and characters make a manuscript stand out. Read widely, create from your heart, and understand Strunk & White."

$ 🌐 ◨ ◎ ALBEDO ONE, The Irish Magazine of Science Fiction, Fantasy and Horror

Albedo One, 2 Post Rd., Lusk, Co Dublin Ireland. (+353)1-8730177. E-mail: bobn@yellowbrickroad. ie. Web site: www.albedo 1.com. **Contact:** editor, *Albedo One*. Magazine: A4; 64 pages. "We hope to publish interesting and unusual fiction by new and established writers. We will consider anything, as long as it is well written and entertaining, though our definitions of both may not be exactly mainstream. We like stories with plot and characters that live on the page. Most of our audience are probably committed genre fans, but we try to appeal to a broad spectrum of readers." Triannual. Estab. 1993. Circ. 900.

Needs Experimental, fantasy, horror, literary, science fiction. Receives more than 80 unsolicited mss/month. Accepts 15-18 mss/year. Publishes ms 1 year after acceptance. **Publishes 6-8 new writers/year.** Length: 2,000- 9,000 words; average length: 4,000 words. Also publishes literary criticism. Sometimes comments on rejected mss.

How to Contact Responds in 3 months to mss. PDF—electronic—sample cop ies are available for download at a reduced price of €2 each. Guidelines available by e-mail or on Web site. Reviews fiction.

Payment/Terms Pays €3 per 1,000 words, and 1 contributor's copy; additional copies $5 plus p&p. Pays on publication for first rights.

Advice "We look for good writing, good plot, good characters. Read the magazine, and don't give up."

Ⓝ ◨ THE ALEMBIC

Providence College, English Dept., Providence College, Providence RI 01918. (401)865-2751. E-mail: cdeniord@providence.edu. **Contact:** Magazine has revolving editor. Editorial term: one year. Magazine: 6×9, 80 pages. Contains illustrations, photographs. "We publish strong work from both emerging and established writers." Annual. Estab. 1940. Circ. 600.

Needs "We are open to all styles of fiction." Receives 200 mss/month. Accepts 5 mss/issue; 5 mss/ year. Does not read January-September. Ms published 6 months after acceptance. **Publishes 15 new writers/year.** Published Bruce Smith, Robin Behn, Rane Arroyo, Sharon Dolin, Jeff Friedman, Khalid Mattawa. Length: 20 pages or words (min)-6000 words (max). Average length: 5000 words. Publishes short shorts. Average length of short shorts: 200 words. Also publishes literary essays, literary criticism, book reviews, poetry. Send review copies to Chard deNiord. Never comments on/critiques rejected mss.

How to Contact Send complete ms with cover letter. Include brief bio. Responds to queries in 1 month; mss in 8 months. Send SASE (or IRC) for return of ms. Considers simultaneous submissions. Sample copy available for $12. Guidelines available for SASE, via e-mail.

Payment/Terms Writers receive 2 contributor's copies. Additional copies $12. Pays on publication. Acquires first rights. Publication is not copyrighted.

Advice "We're looking for stories that are wise, memorable, grammatical, economical, poetic in the right places, and end strongly. Take Heraclitus' claim that 'character is fate' to heart and study the strategies, styles and craft of such masters as Anton Chekov, J. Cheever, Flannery O'Connor, John Updike, Rick Bass, Phillip Roth, Joyce Carol Oates, William Treavor, Lorrie Moore and Ethan Canin."

◨ ANY DREAM WILL DO REVIEW, Short Stories and Humor from the Secret Recesses of our Minds

Any Dream Will Do, Inc., 1830 Kirman Ave., C1, Reno NV 89502-3381. (775)786-0345. E-mail: cassjmb@i ntercomm.com. Web site: www.willigocrazy.org/Ch08.htm. **Contact:** Dr. Jean M. Bradt, editor and publisher. Magazine: 5½×8½; 52 pages; 20 lb. bond paper; 12pt. Carolina cover stock.

"The *Any Dream Will Do Review* showcases a new literary genre, Fiction In The Raw, which attempts to fight the prejudice against consumers of mental-health services by touching hearts, that is, by exposing the consumers' deepest thoughts and emotions. In the *Review*'s stories, accomplished authors honestly reveal their most intimate secrets. Seewww. willigocrazy.org/Ch09a.htm for detai led instructions on how to write Fiction In The Raw." Published every 1 or 2 years. Estab. 2001. Circ. 200.

Needs Adapted ethnic/multicultural, mainstream, psychic/supernatural/occult, romance (contempo rary), science fiction (soft/sociological), all of which must follow the guidelines at Web site. No pornography, true-life stories, black humor, political material, testimonials, experimental fiction, or depressing accounts of hopeless or perverted people. Accepts 10 mss/issue; 20 mss/year. Publishes ms 12 months after acceptance. **Publishes 10 new writers/year.** Publishes short shorts. Often comments on rejected mss.

How to Contact Send complete ms. Accepts submissions by e-mail (cassjmb@i ntercomm.com). Please submit by e-mail. If you must submit by hardcopy, please send disposable copies. No queries, please. Responds in 8 weeks to mss. Sample copy for $4 plus postage. Writer's guidelines online.

Payment/Terms Pays in contributor's copies; additional copies $4 plus postage. Acquires first North American serial rights.

Advice "Read several stories on www.willigocrazy.org before starting to write. Proof your story many times before submitting. Make the readers think. Above all, present people (preferably diag-nosed with mental illness) realistically rather than with prejudice." Now publishing booklets; check Web site for more info.

$☑ APEX SCIENCE FICTION AND HORROR DIGEST

Apex Publications, P.O. Box 24323, Lexington KY 40524. (859)312-3974. E-mail: jason@apexdigest.c om. Web site: www.apexdigest.com. **Contact:** Jason Sizemore, editor-in-chief. Magazine: 5$\frac{1}{2}$×8$\frac{1}{2}$, 128 pages, 70 lb. white offset paper, glossy #120 cover. Contains illustrations. "We publish dark sci-fi with horror elements. Our readers are those that enjoy speculative fiction with dark themes." Quarterly. Estab. 2005. Circ. 3,000.

Needs Dark science fiction. "We're not fans of 'monster' fiction." Receives 150-250 mss/month. Accepts 8 mss/issue; 32 mss/year. Manuscript published 3 months after acceptance. Publishes 10 new writers/year. Published Ben Bova, William F. Nolan, Tom Piccirilli, M.M. Buckner, JA Rourath, and James P. Hogan. Length: 200 words (min)-10,000 words (max). Average length: 4,000 words. Publishes short shorts. Average length of short shorts: 500 words. Also publishes literary essays. Often comments on/critiques rejected manuscripts.

How to Contact Send complete ms with cover letter. Include estimated word count, brief bio. Re-sponds to queries in 3-4 weeks. Responds to mss in 3-4 weeks. Prefers submissions by e-mail, or send disposable copy of ms and #10 SASE for reply only. Considers previously published submis-sions; "must query, however." Sample copy available for $6. Guidelines available via e-mail, on Web site.

Payment/Terms Writers receive 2.5¢/word and two comp copies of magazine. Additional copies $4. Pays on publication. Acquires first North American serial rights. Publication is copyrighted.

Advice "Be professional. Be confident. Remember that any criticisms offered are given for your benefit."

Ⓝ $☐ ◎ ☑ THE APUTAMKON REVIEW, VOICES FROM DOWNEAST MAINE AND THE CANADIAN MARITIMES (OR THEREABOUTS)

the WordShed, LLC, P.O. Box 190, Jonesboro MA 04648. (207)434-5661. Fax: (207)434-5661. E-mail: thewordshed@tds.net. **Contact:** Les Simon, Publisher. Magazine. Approx. 160 pages. Contains illustrations. Includes photographs. "All age groups living in downeast Maine and the Canadian Maritimes, or thereabouts, are invited to participate. *The Aputamkon Review* will present a mismash of truths, half truths and outright lies, including but not limited to short fiction, tall tales, creative nonfiction, essays, (some) poetry, haiku, b&w visual arts, interviews, lyrics and music, quips, quirks, quotes that should be famous, witticisms, follies, comic strips, cartoons, jokes, riddles, recipes, puzzles, games...Stretch your imagination. Practically anything goes." Annual. Estab. 2006. Circ. 500. Member Maine Writers and Publishers Alliance.

Needs Adventure, children's/juvenile, comics/graphic novels, ethnic/multicultural, experimental, family saga, fantasy, glitz, historical, horror, humor/satire, literary, mainstream, military/war, mystery, psychic/supernatural/occult, religious, romance, science fiction, thriller/espionage, translations, western, young adult/teen. Does not want mss which are heavy with sex or religion. Receives 1-20 mss/month. Accepts 10-20 mss/year. Ms published max of 12 months after acceptance. Length: 250 words (min)-4,000 words (max). Average length: 500 words. Publishes short shorts. Also publishes literary essays, literary criticism, poetry. Rarely comments on/critiques rejected mss.

How to Contact Send complete ms with cover letter. Accepts submissions by e-mail, on disk. Include age if under 18, and a bio will be requested upon acceptance of work. Responds to queries in 2-4 weeks. Responds to mss in 1-6 months. Send SASE (or IRC) for return of ms or a disposable copy of ms and #10 SASE for reply only. Considers simultaneous submissions, multiple submissions. Sample copy available for $12 plus s/h . Guidelines available for SASE, via e-mail, via fax.

Payment/Terms Writers receive $10-35 depending on medium. Pays on acceptance. Acquires first North American serial rights. Publication is copyrighted.

Advice "Be colorful, heartfelt and honest, not mainstream. Write what you want and then submit."

THE BINNACLE

University of Maine at Machias, 9 O'Brien Ave., Machias ME 04654. E-mail: ummbinnacle@maine.edu. Web site: www.umm.maine.edu/binnacle. "We are looking for the fresh voices of people who know what dirt under their fingernails, a belly laugh, and hard luck feel like , and of writers who are not afraid to take a chance." Semiannual, plus annual Ultra-Short Competion editon. Estab. 1957. Circ. 300.

Needs Ethnic/multicultural, experimental, humor/satire, mainstream, slice-of-life vignettes. No extreme erotica, fantasy, horror, or religious, but any genre attuned to a general audience can work. Publishes ms 3 months after acceptance.

How to Contact Submissions by e-mail preferred. Responds in 1 month to queries; 3 months to mss. Accepts simultaneous submissions. Sample copy for $7. Writer's guidelines online at Web site or by e-mail.

Payment/Terms $300 in prizes for Ultra-Short. $50 per issue for one work of editor's choice. Acquires one-time rights.

$☐ ◎ BLACK LACE

BLK Publishing CO., P.O. Box 83912, Los Angeles CA 90083-0912. (310)410-0808. Fax: (310)410-9250. E-mail: newsroom@blk.com. Web site: www.blacklace.org. **Contact:** Fiction Editor. Magazine: $8^{1}/_{8} \times 10^{5}/_{8}$; 48 pages; book stock; color glossy cover; illustrations; photos. "*Black Lace* is a lifestyle magazine for African-American lesbians. Its content ranges from erotic imagery to political commentary." Quarterly. Estab. 1991.

Needs Ethnic/multicultural, lesbian. "Avoid interracial stories of idealized pornography." Accepts 4 mss/year. Recently published work by Nicole King, Wanda Thompson, Lynn K. Pannell, Sheree Ann Slaughter, Lyn Lifshin, JoJo and Drew Alise Timmens. Publishes short shorts. Also publishes literary essays, literary criticism, poetry.

How to Contact Query with published clips or send complete ms. Send a disposable copy of ms. No simultaneous submissions. Accepts electronic submissions. Sample copy for $7. Writer's guidelines free.

Payment/Terms Pays $50 and 2 contributor's copies. Acquires first North American serial rights. Right to anthologize.

Advice "*Black Lace* seeks erotic material of the highest quality. The most important thing is that the work be erotic and that it feature black lesbians or themes. Study the magazine to see what we do and how we do it. Some fiction is very romantic, other is highly sexual. Most articles in *Black Lace* cater to black lesbians between two extremes."

◎ BREAD FOR GOD'S CHILDREN

Bread Ministries, Inc., P.O. Box 1017, Arcadia FL 34265. (863)494-6214. Fax: (863)993-0154. E-mail: bread@breadministries.org. "An interdenominational Christian teaching publication published 6-8 times/year written to aid children and youth in leading a Christian life." Estab. 1972. Circ. 10,000.

Needs No fantasy, science fiction, or nonChristian themes. Publishes ms 6 months after acceptance.

How to Contact Send complete ms. Responds in 6 months to mss. Accepts simultaneous submissions. Three sample copies for 9×12 SAE and 5 first-class stamps. Writer's guidelines for #10 SASE.

Payment/Terms Pays $40-50. Pays on publication for first rights.

Advice "We are looking for writers who have a solid knowledge of Biblical principles and are concerned for the youth of today living by those principles. Our stories must be well written, with the story itself getting the message across—no preaching, moralizing, or tag endings."

N ⚅ BROKEN PENCIL

P.O. Box 203 STN P, Toronto ON M5S 2S7 Canada. (416)204-1700. E-mail: editor@brokenpencil.com. Web site: www.brokenpencil.com. **Contact:** Hal Niedzviecki, fiction editor. Magazine. "Founded in 1995 and based in Toronto, Canada, *Broken Pencil* is a Web site and print magazine published four times a year. It is one of the few magazines in the world devoted to underground culture and the independent arts. We are a great resource and a lively read. A cross between the *Utne Reader*, an underground *Reader's Digest*, and the now defunct *Factsheet15*, *Broken Pencil* reviews the best zines, books, Web sites, videos, and artworks from the underground and reprints the best articles from the alternative press. Also, ground-breaking interviews, original fiction, and commentary on all aspects of the independent arts. From the hilarious to the perverse, *Broken Pencil* challenges conformity and demands attention." Quarterly. Estab. 1995. Circ. 5,000.

Needs Adventure, erotica, ethnic/multicultural, experimental, fantasy, historical, horror, humor/satire, amateur sleuth, romance, science fiction. Accepts 8 mss/year. Manuscript published 2-3 months after acceptance. Length: 500-3,000 words.

How to Contact Accepts submissions by e-mail.

Payment/Terms Acquires first rights.

Advice "Write to receive a list of upcoming themes and then pitch us stories based around these themes. If you keep your ear to the ground in alternative and underground arts communities, you will be able to find content appropriate for *Broken Pencil*."

N ⚄ ◎ CEMETARY MOON

Fortress Publishing, Inc., 3704 Hartzdale Dr., Camp Hill PA 17011. (717)350-8760. E-mail: cemetarymoon@yahoo.com. Web site: www.fortresspublishinginc.com. **Contact:** Chris Pisano, Editor-in-Chief. Zine: $5^{1}/_{2} \times 8^{1}/_{2}$, 48 pages, 24 lb paper, glossy cover. Contains illustrations, photographs. "We're tired of slasher stories filled with profanity. We'd like to bring back the stylings of Poe and Lovecraft." Quarterly. Estab. 2007. Circ. 100.

Needs Horror (dark fantasy, futuristic, psychological, supernatural, gothic). "As long as there are horror, suspense, and/or gothic elements in the story, we'll look at it." Receives 10-20 mss/month. Accepts 4-8 mss/issue; 16-32 mss/year. Ms published 3-9 months after acceptance. **Publishes 1-10 new writers/year.** Published Kristine Ong Muslim, Barry J. House, Christopher Hivner, Ken Goldman. Length: 500-5,000 words. Average length: 2,000 words. Publishes short shorts. Also publishes poetry. Sometimes comments on/critiques rejected mss.

How to Contact Send complete ms with cover letter by e-mail only. Include estimated word count, brief bio, list of publications. Responds to queries in 2 weeks. Responds to mss in 1-10 weeks. Considers simultaneous submissions, previously published submissions, multiple submissions. Sample copy available for $4 or on Web site. Guidelines available via e-mail.

Payment/Terms Writers receive 1 contributor copy. Additional copies $2.50. Pays on publication. Acquires one-time rights. Publication is copyrighted.

Advice "We want compelling stories—if we stop reading your story, so will the reader. We don't care about trick or twist endings; we're more concerned about how you take us there. Don't try to reinvent the wheel. Listen to advice with an open mind. Read your story, reread it, then read it again before you send it anywhere."

$ ◎ CHARACTERS, Kids Short Story Outlet

Davis Publications, P.O. Box 708, Newport NH 03773. (603)863-5896. Fax: (603)863-8198. E-mail: hotdog@nhvt.net. **Contact:** Cindy Davis, editor. Magazine: $5^{1}/_{2} \times 8^{1}/_{2}$; 45 pages; saddle bound cover stock; illustrations. "We want to give kids a place to showcase their talents." Quarterly. Estab. 2003.

Needs "We accept all subjects of interest to kids. Particularly would like to see humor, mystery and adventure." Max length: 2,000 words. Receives 60 unsolicited mss/month. Accepts 8-12 mss/issue; 36-48 mss/year. Publishes ms 1-6 months after acceptance. Publishes short shorts. Comments on rejected mss.

How to Contact Send complete ms. Accepts submissions by e-mail, fax. Send disposable copy of the ms and #10 SASE or e-mail address for reply. Responds in 2-4 weeks to mss. Accepts simultaneous submissions and reprints. Sample copy for $5. Writer's guidelines for #10 SASE, or by e-mail.

Payment/Terms Pays $5 and contributor's copy. Pays on publication for one-time rights. Not copyrighted.

Advice ''We like stories with characters who're faced with a dilemma, be it physical or emotional, and find a way to work through it.''

ℕ $◪ CONCEIT MAGAZINE

P.O. Box 8544, Emeryville CA 94662. (415)401-8370. Fax: (415)401-8370. E-mail: conceitmagazine20 07@yahoo.com. Web site: www.myspace.com/conceitmagazine. **Contact:** Perry Terrell, Editor. Magazine: 8½×5½, 44 pages, copy paper paper. Contains illustrations, photographs. ''If it's on your mind, write it down and send it to Perry Terrell at *Conceit Magazine*. Writing is good therapy.'' Monthly. Estab. 2007. Circ. 300 + .

Needs Adventure, children's/juvenile, ethnic/multicultural, experimental, family saga, fantasy, feminist, gay, historical, horror (futuristic, psychological, supernatural), humor/satire, lesbian, literary, mainstream, military/war, mystery, new age, psychic/supernatural/occult, religious, romance (contemporary, futuristic/time travel, historical, regency, suspense), science fiction (soft/sociological), thriller/espionage, translations, western, young adult/teen (adventure, easy-to-read, fantasy/science fiction, historical, mystery/suspense, problem novels, romance, series, sports, western). Does not want profanity, porn, gruesomeness. List of upcoming themes available for SASE, on Web site. Receives 40-50 mss/month. Accepts 20-22 mss/issue; up to 264 mss/year. Ms published 3-10 months after acceptance. **Publishes 150 new writers/year.** Published Cindy Rosmus, Dr. C. David Hay, D. Neil Simmons, Tamara Nahistadt, Zachary Nahistadt. Length: 100 words (min)-3,000 words (max). Average length: 1,500-2,000 words. Publishes short shorts. Average length of short shorts: 50-500 words. Also publishes literary essays, literary criticism, book reviews, poetry. Send review copies to Perry Terrell. Sometimes comments on/critiques rejected mss.

How to Contact Query first or send complete ms with cover letter. Accepts submissions by e-mail, by fax, on disk. Include estimated word count, brief bio, list of publications. Responds to queries in 1-2 weeks. Responds to mss in 1-4 weeks. Send either SASE (or IRC) for return of ms or disposable copy of ms and #10 SASE for reply only. Considers simultaneous submissions, previously published submissions, multiple submissions. Sample copy free with SASE. Guidelines available for SASE, via e-mail, on Web site, via fax.

Payment/Terms Writers receive 1 contributor copy and subscribers vote on who receives a $100 monthly stipend. Additional copies $4.50. Pays on publication. Acquires one-time rights. Publication is copyrighted. ''Occassionly sponsors contests. Send SASE or check blog on Web site for details.''

Advice ''Uniqueness and creativity make a manuscript stand out. Be brave and confident. Let me see what you created.''

$◪ ◎ THE COUNTRY CONNECTION

Pinecone Publishing, P.O. Box 100, Boulter ON K0L 1G0 Canada. (613)332-3651. E-mail: editor@pine cone.on.ca. Web site: www.pinecone.on.ca. ''*The Country Connection* is a magazine for true nature lovers and the rural adventurer. Building on our commitment to heritage, cultural, artistic, and environmental themes, we continually add new topics to illuminate the country experience of people living within nature. Our goal is to chronicle rural life in its many aspects, giving 'voice' to the countryside.'' Estab. 1989. Circ. 5,000.

Needs Ontario history and heritage, humor/satire, nature, environment, the arts, country living. ''Canadian material by Canadian authors only.'' Publishes ms 4 months after acceptance.

How to Contact Send complete ms. Accepts submissions by e-mail, disk. Sample copy for $ 6.68. Writer's guidelines online.

Payment/Terms Pays 10¢/word. Pays on publication for first rights.

◻ CREATIVE WITH WORDS PUBLICATIONS

Creative With Words Publications, P.O. Box 223226, Carmel CA 93922. Fax: (831)655-8627. E-mail: geltrich@mbay.net. Web site: members.tripod.com/CreativeWithWords. **Contact:** Brigitta Geltrich, general editor.

Needs Ethnic/multicultural, humor/satire, mystery/suspense (amateur sleuth, private eye), regional (folklore), young adult/teen (adventure, historical). ''Do not submit essays.'' No violence or erotica, overly religious fiction or sensationalism. ''Once/twice a year we publish an anthology of the writings of young writers, titled "We are Poets and Writers, Too! Once/twice a year we publish the *Eclectics* written by adults only (20 and older); throughout the year we publish thematic anthologies written by all ages." List of upcoming themes available for SASE. Limit poetry to 20 lines or less, 46 characters per line or less. Receives 50-200 unsolicited mss/month. Accepts 50-80 mss/anthology. Publishes ms 1-2 months after acceptance. Recently published work by Najwa Salam Brax, Sirock Brighton, Roger D. Coleman, Antoinette Garrick and Maria Dickerhof. Sometimes comments on rejected mss.

How to Contact Send complete ms with a cover letter with SASE. Include estimated word count. Responds in 2 weeks to queries; 2 months to mss. Sample copy for $7. Writer's guidelines for #10 SASE.

Payment/Terms 20% reduction cost on 1-9 copies ordered, 30% reduction on 10 to 19 copies, 40% reduction on each copy on order of 20 or more. Acquires one-time rights.

Advice "We offer a great variety of themes. We look for clean family-type fiction/poetry. Also, we ask the writer to look at the world from a different perspective, research topic thoroughly, be creative, apply brevity, tell the story from a character's viewpoint, tighten dialogue, be less descriptive, proofread before submitting and be patient. We will not publish every manuscript we receive. It has to be in standard English, well written, proofread. We do not appreciate receiving manuscripts where we have to do the proofreading and the correcting of grammar."

DAN RIVER ANTHOLOGY

Conservatory of American Letters, P.O. Box 298, Thomaston ME 04861. (207)226-7528. Web site: www.americanletters.org. **Contact:** R.S. Danbury III, editor. Book: 6×9; 192 pages; 60 lb. paper; gloss 10 pt. full-color cover. Deadline every year is March 31, with acceptance/rejection by May 15, proofs out by June 15, and book released December 7. Annual. Estab. 1984. Circ. 750.

Needs Adventure, ethnic/multicultural, experimental, fantasy, historical, horror, humor/satire, literary, mainstream, psychic/supernatural/occult, regional, romance (contemporary and historical), science fiction, suspense, western, contemporary, prose poem, senior citizen/retirement. "Virtually anything but porn, evangelical, juvenile. Would like to see more first-person adventure." Reads "mostly in April." Length: 800-3,500 words; average length: 2,000-2,400 words. Also publishes poetry.

How to Contact Send complete ms. No simultaneous submissions. Submit disk in rich text format (.RTF), disk must be single spaced, do not justify, do not indent paragraphs. Be sure sase is large enought if you want your disk back. Send cd or floppy. We can not accept anything not on disk. Nothing previously published. Sample copy for $16.95 paperback, $39.95 cloth, plus $3.50 shipping. Writer's guidelines available for #10 SASE or online.

Payment/Terms Payment "depends on your experience with us, as it is a nonrefundable advance against royalties on all sales that we can attribute to your influence. For first-timers, the advance is about 1¢/word." Pays on acceptance for first rights.

Advice "Read an issue or two, know the market. Don't submit without reading guidelines on the Web or send #10 SASE."

DARK DISCOVERIES

Dark Discoveries Publications, 142 Woodside Drive, Longview WA 98632. (360)425-5796. E-mail: info@darkdiscoveries.com. Web site: www.darkdiscoveries.com. **Contact:** James R. Beach, Editor-in-Chief/Publisher. Magazine: 8½×11, 64 pages. Contains illustrations. Includes photographs. "We publish dark fiction in the horror/fantasy realm with a lean towards the psychological side. We do publish mystery and supernatural as well. We also feature interviews, articles and reviews." Quarterly. Estab. 2004. Circ. 3,000.

• Two stories published in *Dark Discoveries* have been Honorable Mentions in the *Year's Best Fantasy & Horror* and two stories have been nominated for the Bram Stoker Awards.

Needs Horror (dark fantasy). Does not want straight science fiction or mystery, "but will look at hybrid horror stories with elements of each. No straight sword and socery or fantasy either." Receives 50-70 mss/month. Accepts 25 mss/year. Ms published within 12 months after acceptance. **Publishes 2-4 new writers/year.** Published Elizabeth Engstrom, Kealan Partick Burke, Jay Lake, Tony Richards, John Maclay, John Everson, Tim Waggoner, Cindy Foster, Stephen Mark Raingy, CN Pitts and Brian Knight. Length: 1,000-5,000 words. Average length: 4,000 words. Publishes short shorts. Average length of short shorts: 1,000 words. Also publishes literary essays, literary criticism, book reviews. Send review copies to James R. Beach. Often comments on/critiques rejected mss.

How to Contact Send complete ms with cover letter. Accepts submissions by e-mail. Include estimated word count, brief bio, list of publications. Responds to queries in 1-2 weeks. Responds to mss in 6-7 months. Send either SASE (or IRC) for return of ms or disposable copy of ms and #10 SASE for reply only. Considers simultaneous submissions, previously published submissions if you query first. Sample copy available for $6.99. Guidelines available for SASE, via e-mail, on Web site.

Payment/Terms Writers receive 1-2¢ per word, 2 contributor's copies. Additional copies at 40% of cover price. Pays on publication. Acquires one-time rights. Publication is copyrighted. "Occasionally sponsors contests. Check the Web site for details."

Advice "I look for well-written and thought provoking tales. I don't like to see the same well-tread themes. Be it a new or established writer, I like to see the writer's voice show through. Take our suggestions to heart, and if you don't succeed at catching our eye at first keep trying."

⊞ ◎ DARK HORIZONS

36 Town End, Cheadle, Staffordshire, ST 10 1PF United Kingdom. E-mail: darkhorizons@britishfanta sysociety.org.uk. Web site: www.britishfantasysociety.org.uk. **Contact:** Peter Coleborn and Jan Edwards, editors. "We are a small press fantasy magazine. Our definition of fantasy knows no bounds, covering science, heroic, dark and light fantasy and horror fiction." Biannual. Circ. 500.

Needs "We prefer material that touches on fantasy, supernatural, horror or the weird, rather than hard SF. Our preferred length is 3,000-5,000 words. We publish nonfiction and poetry."

How to Contact Send complete ms with brief cover letter and IRCs or e-mail address. Accepts submissions by mail only.

Payment/Terms Contributor's copies.

Advice "We look for a well-written story with good characters. No gratuitous violence, please."

Ⓝ $⊞ ◪ ◎ DARK TALES

Dark Tales, P.O. Box 681, Worcester, UK WR3 8WB. E-mail: sean@darktales.co.uk. Web site: www.d arktales.co.uk. **Contact:** Sean Jeffery, editor. Magazine: contains illustrations. "We publish horror and speculative short fiction from anybody, anywhere, and the publication is professionally illustrated throughout." Estab. 2003. Circ. 350+.

Needs Horror (dark fantasy, futuristic, psychological, supernatural), science fiction (soft/sociological). Receives 25+ mss/month. Accepts 10-15 mss/issue; 25-40 mss/year. Ms published 6 months after acceptance. **Publishes 20 new writers/year.** Published Davin Ireland, Niall McMahon, David Robertson, Valerie Robson, K.S. Dearsley and Mark Cowley. Length: 500-3,500 words. Average length: 2,500 words. Publishes short shorts. Average length of short shorts: 500 words. Sometimes comments on/critiques rejected mss. Has occasional contests; see Web site for details.

How to Contact Send complete ms with cover letter. Include estimated word count, list of publications. Responds to queries in 1 week. Responds to mss in 12 weeks. Send disposable copy of ms and #10 SASE for reply only. Sample copy available for $3. Guidelines available on Web site.

Payment/Terms Writers receive $5 per thousand words. Additional copies $7.10. Pays on publication. Acquires first British serial rights. Sends galleys to author. Publication is copyrighted.

Advice "Have a believable but inspiring plot, sympathetic characters, an original premise, and a human heart no matter how technical or disturbing a story. Read a copy of the magazine! Make sure you get your writing basics spot-on. Don't rehash old ideas—if you must go down the werewolf/vampire route, put a spin on it."

◻ DOWN IN THE DIRT, The Publication Revealing all your Dirty Little Secrets

Scars Publications and Design, 829 Brian Court, Gurnee IL 60031-3155. (847)281-9070. E-mail: alexra nd@scars.tv. Web site: scars.tv. **Contact:** Alexandria Rand, editor. Magazine: 5½ × 8½; 60 lb. paper; illustrations; photos. Monthly. Estab. 2000.

Needs Adventure, ethnic/multicultural, experimental, fantasy, feminist, gay, historical, horror, lesbian, literary, mystery/suspense, New Age, psychic/supernatural/occult, science fiction. No religious or rhyming or family-oriented material. Publishes ms within 1 year after acceptance. Recently published work by Simon Perchik, Jim Dewitt, Jennifer Connelly, L.B. Sedlacek, Aeon Logan, Helena Wolfe. Average length: 1,000 words. Publishes short shorts. Also publishes poetry. Always, if asked, comments on rejected mss.

How to Contact Query with email submission. Prefers submissions only by e-mail. If you choose to send us a snail mail submission, please send SASE (or IRC) for return of the ms or disposable copy of the ms and #10 SASE for reply only. "If you have e-mail, please send electronic submissions instead." Responds in 1 month to queries; 1 month to mss. Accepts simultaneous, multiple submissions and reprints. Sample copy for $6. Writer's guidelines for SASE, e-mail or on the Web site.

$ DREAMS & VISIONS, Spiritual Fiction

Skysong Press, 35 Peter St. S., Orillia ON L3V 5A8 Canada. (705)329-1770. E-mail: skysong@bconnex .net. Web site: www.bconnex.net/~skysong. **Contact:** Steve Stanton, editor. Magazine: $5^1/2 \times 8^1/2$; 60 pages; 20 lb. bond paper; glossy cover. "Innovative literary fiction for adult Christian readers." Semiannual. Estab. 1988. Circ. 300.

Needs Experimental, fantasy, humor/satire, literary, mainstream, mystery/suspense, novel excerpts, religious/inspirational, science fiction, slice-of-life vignettes. "We do not publish stories that glorify violence or perversity. All stories should portray a Christian worldview or expand upon Biblical themes or ethics in an entertaining or enlightening manner." Receives 20 unsolicited mss/month. Accepts 5 mss/issue; 10 mss/year. Publishes ms 4-8 months after acceptance. **Publishes 3 new writers/year.** Recently published work by Fred McGavran, Steven Mills, Donna Farley, and Michael Vance. Length: 2,000-6,000 words; average length: 2,500 words.

How to Contact Send complete ms. Responds in 3 weeks to queries; 3 months to mss. Accepts simultaneous submissions and reprints. Sample copy for $ 5.95. Writer's guidelines online.

Payment/Terms Pays 1¢/word (Canadian). Pays on publication for one-time rights.

Advice "In general we look for work that has some literary value, that is in some way unique and relevant to Christian readers today. Our first priority is technical adequacy, though we will occasionally work with a beginning writer to polish a manuscript. Ultimately, we look for stories that glorify the Lord Jesus Christ, stories that build up rather than tear down, that exalt the sanctity of life, the holiness of God, and the value of the family."

$ THE FIRST LINE

Blue Cubicle Press, LLC, P.O. Box 250382, Plano TX 75025-0382. (972)824-0646. E-mail: submission @thefirstline.com. Web site: www.thefirstline.com. **Contact:** Robin LaBounty, manuscript coordinator. Magazine: 8×5; 64-72 pages; 20 lb. bond paper; 80 lb. cover stock. "We only publish stories that start with the first line provided. We are a collection of tales—of different directions writers can take when they start from the same place. Quarterly. Estab. 1999. Circ. 1,000.

Needs Adventure, ethnic/multicultural, fantasy, gay, humor/satire, lesbian, literary, mainstream, mystery/suspense, regional, romance, science fiction, western. Receives 200 unsolicited mss/month. Accepts 12 mss/issue; 48 mss/year. Publishes ms 1 month after acceptance. **Publishes 6 new writers/year.** Length: 300-3,000 words; average length: 1,500 words. Publishes short shorts. Also publishes literary essays, literary criticism. Often comments on rejected mss.

How to Contact Send complete ms. Accepts submissions by e-mail. Send SASE for return of ms or disposable copy of the ms and #10 SASE for reply only. Responds in 1 week to queries; 3 months to mss. Accepts multiple submissions. No simultaneous submissions. Sample copy for $3.50. Writer's guidelines for SASE, e-mail or on Web site. Reviews fiction.

Payment/Terms Pays $20 maximum and contributor's copy; additional copy $2. Pays on publication.

Advice "Don't just write the first story that comes to mind after you read the sentence. If it is obvious, chances are other people are writing about the same thing. Don't try so hard. Be willing to accept criticism."

IRREANTUM, Exploring Mormon Literature

The Association for Mormon Letters, P.O. Box 970874, Orem UT 84097-0874. (801)582- 2090. Web site: www.mormonletters.org/irreantum/. **Contact:** Managing Editor. Magazine or Zine: $8^1/2 \times 7^1/2$; 100-120 pages; 20 lb. paper; 20 lb. color cover; illustrations; photos. "While focused on Mormonism, Irreantum is a cultural, humanities-oriented magazine, not a religious magazine. Our guiding principle is that Mormonism is grounded in a sufficiently unusual, cohesive, and extended historical and cultural experience that it has become like a nation, an ethnic culture. We can speak of Mormon literature at least as surely as we can of a Jewish or Southern literature. Irreantum publishes stories, one-act dramas, stand-alone novel and drama excerpts, and poetry by, for, or about Mormons (as well as author interviews, essays, and reviews). The magazine's audience includes readers of any or no religious faith who are interested in literary exploration of the Mormon culture, mindset, and worldview through Mormon themes and characters. Irreantum is currently the only magazine devoted to Mormon literature.'' Biannual. Estab. 1999. Circ. 300.

Needs Adventure, ethnic/multicultural (Mormon), experimental, family saga, fantasy, feminist, historical, horror, humor/satire, literary, mainstream, mystery/suspense, New Age, psychic/supernatural/occult, regional (Western USA/Mormon), religious/inspirational, romance, science fiction, thriller/espionage, translations, young adult/teen. Receives 5 unsolicited mss/month. Accepts 3 mss/issue; 6 mss/year. Publishes ms 3-12 months after acceptance. **Publishes 3 or more new writers/year.** Recently published work by Anne Perry, Brady Udall, Brian Evenson and Robert Kirby. Length: 1,000-5,000 words; average length: 5,000 words. Publishes short shorts. Also publishes literary essays, literary criticism, poetry. Sometimes comments on rejected mss. Annual fiction contest and annual personal essay contest with cash prizes.

How to Contact Accepts submissions by e-mail only to irreantum@mormonletters.org, in Microsoft Word or WordPerfect file format. Short pieces (such as Poetry or Readers Write) may be included in the body of the e-mail message. Please include the category of work you are submitting in the subject line (e.g., Poetry submission, Critical Essay submission). Writers will receive a copy of the Irreantum issue in which their work appears (Readers Write contributors excepted). Send complete ms with cover letter. Include brief bio and list of publications. Responds in 2 weeks to queries; 2 months to mss. Accepts simultaneous and reprints, multiple submissions. Sample copy for $8. Writer's guidelines at http://www.mormonletters.org/irreantum/submit.html. Reviews fiction.

Payment/Terms Pays $0-100. Pays on publication for one-time rights.

Advice ''Irreantum is not interested in didactic or polemical fiction that primarily attempts to prove or disprove Mormon doctrine, history or corporate policy. We encourage beginning writers to focus on human elements first, with Mormon elements introduced only as natural and organic to the story. Readers can tell if you are honestly trying to explore the human experience or if you are writing with a propagandistic agenda either for or against Mormonism. For conservative, orthodox Mormon writers, beware of sentimentalism, simplistic resolutions, and foregone conclusions.''

✍ ◎ ITALIAN AMERICANA

URI/CCE, 80 Washington Street, Providence RI 02903-1803. (401)277-5306. Fax: (401)277-5100. E-mail: bonomoal@etal.uri.edu. Web site: www.italianamericana.com. **Contact:** C.B. Albright, editor. Magazine: 6×9; 240 pages; varnished cover; perfect bound; photos. ''*Italian Americana* contains historical articles, fiction, poetry and memoirs, all concerning the Italian experience in the Americas.'' Semiannual. Estab. 1974. Circ. 1,200.

Needs Literary, Italian American. No nostalgia. Wants to see more fiction featuring ''individualized characters.'' Receives 10 unsolicited mss/month. Accepts 3 mss/issue; 6-7 mss/year. Publishes ms up to 1 year after acceptance. Agented fiction 5%. **Publishes 2-4 new writers/year.** Publishing 2 issues a year of historical articles, fiction, memoir, poetry and reviews. Award winning authors in all categories, such as Mary Caponegro, Sal La Puma, Dana Gioia (past poetry editor).

How to Contact Send complete ms (in duplicate) with a cover letter. Include 3-5 line bio, list of publications. Responds in 1 month to queries; 2 months to mss. No simultaneous submissions. Sample copy for $7. Writer's guidelines for #10 SASE. Reviews fiction.

Payment/Terms 1 contributor's copy; additional copies $7. Acquires first North American serial rights.

Advice ''Please individualize characters, instead of presenting types (i.e., lovable uncle, etc.). No nostalgia.''

✍ KELSEY REVIEW

Mercer County College, P.O. Box B, Trenton NJ 08690. (609)586-4800. Fax: (609)586-2318. E-mail: kelsey.review@mccc.edu. Web site: www.mccc.edu. **Contact**: Ed Carmien, Holly-Katherine Mathews, editors. Magazine: 7×14; 98 pages; glossy paper; soft cover. ''Must live or work in Mercer County, NJ.'' Annual. Estab. 1988. Circ. 2,000.

Needs Regional (Mercer County, NJ only), open. Receives 10 unsolicited mss/month. Accepts 24 mss/issue. Reads mss only in May. **Publishes 10 new writers/year.** Recently published work by Thom Beachamps, Janet Kirk, Bruce Petronio. Publishes short shorts. Also publishes literary essays, poetry.

How to Contact SASE for return of ms. Responds in June to mss. Accepts multiple submissions. Sample copy free.

Payment/Terms 5 contributor's copies. Rights revert to author on publication.
Advice Look for "quality, intellect, grace and guts. Avoid sentimentality, overwriting and self-indulgence. Work on clarity, depth and originality."

$ ☑ Ⓖ LADY CHURCHILL'S ROSEBUD WRISTLET

Small Beer Press, 150 Plesant St., #306, Easthampron MA 01017. E-mail: info@lcrw.net. Web site: www.lcrw.net/lcrw. **Contact:** Gavin Grant, editor. Zine: half legal size; 60 pages; 60 lb. paper; glossy cover; illustrations; photos. Semiannual. Estab. 1996. Circ. 1,000.

Needs Comics/graphic novels, experimental, fantasy, feminist, literary, science fiction, translations, short story collections. Receives 25 unsolicited mss/month. Accepts 4-6 mss/issue; 8-12 mss/year. Publishes ms 6-12 months after acceptance. **Publishes 2-4 new writers/year.** Recently published work by Amy Beth Forbes, Jeffrey Ford, Carol Emshwiller and Theodora Goss. Length: 200-7,000 words; average length: 3,500 words. Also publishes literary essays, poetry. Sometimes comments on rejected mss.

How to Contact Send complete ms with a cover letter. Include estimated word count. Send SASE (or IRC) for return of ms, or send a disposable copy of ms and #10 SASE for reply only. Responds in 4 weeks to queries; 3-6 months to mss. Sample copy for $5. Writer's guidelines online. Reviews fiction.

Payment/Terms Pays 1¢/word, $20 minimum and 2 contributor's copies; additional copies contributor's discount 40%. Pays on publication for first, one-time and electronic rights.
Advice "I like fiction that tends toward the speculative."

Ⓖ LEADING EDGE, Magazine of Science Fiction and Fantasy

4087 JKB, Provo, UT 84602. E-mail: fiction@leadingedgemagazine.com. Web site: www.leadingedge magazine.com. **Contact:** Fiction Director. Magazine specializing in science fiction and fantasy. *Leading Edge* is dedicated to helping new writers make their way into publishing. "We send back critiques with every story. We don't print anything with explicit language, graphic violence or sex." Semiannual. Estab. 1981.

Needs Fantasy and science fiction short stories, poetry, and artwork. Receives 50 unsolicited mss/month. Accepts 8 mss/issue; 16 mss/year. Publishes ms 1-6 months after acceptance. **Publishes 9-10 new writers/year.** Have published work by Orson Scott Card, Brandon Sanderson, and Dave Wolverton. Max length: 15,000; average length: 10,000 words.

How to Contact Send complete ms with cover letter and SASE. Include estimated word count. Send #10 SASE for reply only if disposable ms. Responds in 3 months to mss. Sample copy for $5.95. Writer's guidelines on Web site or send a SASE.

Payment/Terms 1¢/word for fiction; $10 for first 4 pages of poetry, $1.50 for each subsequent page; 2 contributor's copies; additional copies $4.95. Pays for publication for first North American serial rights. Sends galleys to author.

Advice "Buy a sample issue to know what is currently selling in our magazine. Also, make sure to follow the writer's guidelines when submitting."

Ⓖ LEFT CURVE

P.O. Box 472, Oakland CA 94604-0472. (510)763-7193. E-mail: editor@leftcurve.org. Web site: www. leftcurve.org. **Contact:** Csaba Polony, editor. Magazine: 8½×11; 144 pages; 60 lb. paper; 100 pt. C1S gloss layflat lamination cover; illustrations; photos. "*Left Curve* is an artist-produced journal addressing the problem(s) of cultural forms emerging from the crises of modernity that strive to be independent from the control of dominant institutions, based on the recognition of the destructiveness of commodity (capitalist) systems to all life." Published irregularly. Estab. 1974. Circ. 2,000.

Needs Ethnic/multicultural, experimental, historical, literary, regional, science fiction, translations, contemporary, prose poem, political. "No topical satire, religion-based pieces, melodrama. We publish critical, open, social/political-conscious writing." Receives 50 unsolicited mss/month. Accepts 3-4 mss/issue. Publishes ms 6-12 months after acceptance. Recently published work by Mike Standaert, Ilan Pappe, John Gist . Length: 500-5,000 words; average length: 1,200 words. Publishes short shorts. Sometimes comments on rejected mss.

How to Contact Send complete ms. Accepts submissions by e-mail (editor@leftcurve.org). Send complete ms with cover letter. Include "statement of writer's intent, brief bio and reason for submitting to *Left Curve*." Accepts electronic submissions; "prefer 3½ disk and hard copy, though we do accept e-mail submissions." Responds in 6 months to mss. For $10, 9×12 SAE and $1.42 postage. Writer's guidelines for 1 first-class stamp.

Payment/Terms Contributor's copies. Rights revert to author.

Advice "We look for continuity, adequate descriptive passages, endings that are not simply abandoned (in both meanings). Dig deep; no superficial personalisms, no corny satire. Be honest, realistic and gouge out the truth you wish to say. Understand yourself and the world. Have writing be a means to achieve or realize what is real."

$▣ THE LONDON MAGAZINE, Review of Literature and the Arts

The London Magazine, 32 Addison Grove, London England W4 1ER United Kingdom. (00)44 0208 400 5882. Fax: (00)44 0208 994 1713. E-mail: admin@thelondonmagazine.net. Web site: www.thelondonmagazine.ukf.net. Bimonthly. Estab. 1732. Circ. 1,000.

Needs Adventure, confessions, erotica, ethnic/multicultural, experimental, fantasy, historical, humor/satire, mainstream, mystery/suspense, novel excerpts, religious/inspirational, romance, slice-of-life vignettes, suspense. Publishes ms 4 months after acceptance.

How to Contact Send complete ms. Include SASE. Responds in 1 month to queries; 4 months to mss. Accepts simultaneous submissions. Sample copy for £8.75. Writer's guidelines free.

Payment/Terms Pays minimum £20; maximum rate is negotiable. Pays on publication for first rights.

N $▨ ▣ ◎ ▼ MOM WRITER'S LITERARY MAGAZINE, MOM WRITERS WHO HAVE SOMETHING TO SAY

Mom Writer's Productions, LLC., P.O. Box 447, St. Johnsbury, VT 05719. (877)382-6771. E-mail: publisher@momwriterslitmag.com. Web site: www.momwriterslitmag.com. **Contact:** Samantha Gianulis, Editor-in-Chief. Online and print literary magazine. Print: 8×10, 52 pages. Contains illustrations. Includes photographs. *"Mom Writer's Literary Magazine* is a publication written by moms for moms across the globe who come together to share their stories. We publish creative nonfiction essays, fiction, columns, book reviews, profiles about mom writers and visual art. *Mom Writer's Literary Magazine* seeks writing that is vivid, complex and practical. We are not looking for 'sugar-coated' material. We believe the art of Motherhood is deserving of literary attention. We are a literary magazine for mothers with something to say. We're proud to have published essays that are emotionally moving, smart, raw and, sometimes, humorous. *Mom Writer's Literary Magazine* honors the fulfilling and tedious work that women do by making their stoires visible through print." Quarterly. Estab. 2005-Online, 2007-Print. Circ. 6,000. Member Mom Writers Publishing Cooperative.

● *Mom Writer's Literary Magazine* was picked by *Writer's Digest* magazine as one of the Best Web Sites for Writers in 2006 & 2007

Needs Adventure, ethnic/multicultural, family saga, feminist, literary, mainstream, romance (contemporary, suspense). Special interests: motherhood. Does not want children/juvenile, religious, horror, or western. Receives 20-30 mss/month. Accepts 2 mss/issue; 8 mss/year. Ms published 1-4 months after acceptance. **Publishes 2 new writers/year.** Length: 800-1,500 words. Average length: 1,400 words. Publishes short shorts. Average length of short shorts: 1,200 words. Also publishes literary essays, book reviews, poetry. Send review copies to Jennifer Brown, Reviews Editor. Rarely comments on/critiques rejected mss.

How to Contact Send complete ms with cover letter. Accepts submissions by e-mail. Include estimated word count, brief bio. Responds to mss in 1-3 months. Considers simultaneous submissions. Guidelines available on Web site.

Payment/Terms Writers receive $100 max., 1 contributor's copy. Additional copies $5. Pays on publication. Acquires one-time rights. Publication is copyrighted.

Advice "May be any genre. Story must flow smoothly and really get our attention (all editors). Must be within the word limits and submitted correctly. Also, please have a title for your story."

N $▨ ◎ NECROLOGY MAGAZINE, WHERE REALITY IS JUST A STATE OF MIND

Isis International, P.O. Box 510232, St. Louis MO 62151. (314)315-5200. E-mail: editor@necrologymag.com. Web site: www.necrologymag.com. **Contact:** John Ferguson, editor. Magazine: 8.5×5.5, 70 pages. Contains illustrations. Includes photographs. "We publish horror, sci-fi and fantasy. We look for Lovecraft-type fiction, but it is not required. While fiction represents most of our needs, we also publish articles, artwork, poetry and photos. Our intended audience are those who love a good story.

Let your imagination run wild; we like bizarre and unique fiction with a dark and deathly ring." Quarterly. Estab. 2006. Circ. 1,500.

Needs Fantasy (space fantasy, sword and sorcery), horror (dark fantasy, futuristic, psychological, supernatural), science fiction (hard science/technological, soft/sociological). "We publish mostly horror and related material. While we do accept sci-fi and fantasy, we would like it to contain a hint of horror. We do not want to see 'hack and slash' type horror." Receives 70-100 mss/month. Accepts 5-6 mss/issue; 20-25 mss/year. Ms published 3-9 months after acceptance. Agented fiction 25%. **Publishes 5-8 new writers/year.** Published Josheph DeRepentigny, David R. Beshears, Mark Sant and Melissa Sihan Mutlu. Length: 500-15,000 words (max). Average length: 8,000 words. Publishes short shorts. Average length of short shorts: 1,000 words. Also publishes literary essays, literary criticism, book reviews, poetry. Send review copies to John Ferguson, editor. Often comments on/critiques rejected mss.

How to Contact Send complete ms with cover letter. Accepts submissions by e-mail, on disk. Responds to queries in 2 weeks. Responds to mss in 2 months. Send either SASE (or IRC) for return of ms or disposable copy of ms and #10 SASE for reply only. Sample copy available for $4. Guidelines available for SASE, via e-mail, on Web site.

Payment/Terms Writers receive $10-25, 1 contributor's copy. Additional copies $4. Pays on acceptance. Acquires first North American serial rights. Publication is copyrighted.

Advice "We look for unique twists, unusual plots and bizarre realities. Don't duplicate other's work. Read work by H.P. Lovecraft, Robert E. Howard, Stephen King, Edgar Allen Poe; these are some of the masters of horror. They created their own style, so create your own, too."

◎ NEW METHODS, The Journal of Animal Health Technology

P.O. Box 952, Willits CA 95490. E-mail: norwal3@yahoo.com. Web site: www.geocities.com/norwal 13photos.yahoo.com/norwal13. **Contact:** Ronald S. Lippert, publisher. Newsletter & E-mail: 8½ ×11; 2-4 pages; 20 lb. paper; illustrations; "rarely photos." Network service for mostly professionals in the animal field; e.g., animal health technicians. Monthly. Estab. 1976. Circ. 5,608.

Needs Animals: contemporary, experimental, historical, mainstream, regional. No stories unrelated to animals. Receives 12 unsolicited mss/month. Accepts 1 mss/issue; 12 mss/year. Publishes short shorts. Occasionally comments on rejected mss. Recently published by animal rights group; Recently comments sought on San Francisco Zoo tiger killings.

How to Contact Query first with theme, length, expected time of completion, photos/illustrations, if any, biographical sketch of author, all necessary credits, or send complete ms. Responds in up to 4 months to queries. Accepts simultaneous, multiple submissions. Sample copy and back issues available. Writer's guidelines for SASE.

Payment/Terms Acquires one-time rights. Sponsors awards/contests.

Advice "Emotion, personal experiences—make the person feel it. We are growing."

• Protect, preserve, and restore environment of all life forms.

☑ ◎ NEW WITCH, not your mother's broomstick

BBI, Inc., P.O. Box 687, Forest Grove, OR 97116. (503)430-8817. E-mail: meditor@newwitch.com. Web site: www.newwitch.com. **Contact:** Kenaz Filan, managing editor. Magazine. "Witch is dedicated to Witches, Wiccans, Neo-Pagans, and various other earth-based, ethnic, pre-christian, shamanic and magical practitioners. We hope to reach not only those already involved in what we cover, but also the curious and completely new as well." Quarterly. Estab. 2002. Circ. 15,000.

Needs Adventure, erotica, ethnic/multicultural, fantasy, historical, horror, humor/satire, mainstream, mystery, religious, romance. Special interests: Pagan/Earth Religion material. Does not accept fictionalized retellings of real events. Avoid gratuitous sex and violence: in movie rating terms think PG-13. Also avoid gratuitous sentimentality and Pagan moralizing: don't beat our readers with the Rede or the Threefold Law. Accepts 3-4 mss/year. Length: 1,000-5,000 words.

How to Contact Prefers submissions by e-mail. Responds to queries in 1-2 weeks. Responds to mss in 1 months. Sample copy available with 9×12 SASE with sufficient postage for 8 ounces to your location. Guidelines available on Web site.

Advice "Read the magazine, do your research, write the piece, send it in. That's really the only way to get started as a writer: Everything else is window dressing."

☑ NEWN

(formerly New England Writers' Network) P.O. Box 483, Hudson MA 01749-0483. (978)562-2946. E-mail: NEWNeditor@aol.com. Web site: www.newnmag.net. **Contact:** Glenda Baker, fiction editor. Magazine: 8½×11; 24 pages; coated cover. "We are devoted to helping new writers get published and to teaching through example and content. We are looking for well-written stories that grab us from the opening paragraph." Quarterly. Estab. 1994. Circ. 300.

Needs Adventure, condensed novels, ethnic/multicultural, humor/satire, literary, mainstream, mystery/suspense, religious/inspirational, romance. "We will consider anything except pornography or extreme violence." Accepts 5 mss/issue; 20 mss/year. Publishes ms 4-12 months after acceptance. **Publishes 10-12 new writers/year.** Recently published work by Alan Gould, L. Carroll Kiser, William Parsons, Barry Judson Lohnes . Publishes short shorts. Also publishes poetry. Sometimes comments on rejected mss.

How to Contact Send complete ms with cover letter. Include estimated word count. Bio on acceptance. Reads mss only from January 1 to March 1. No simultaneous submissions. Sample copy for $5.50. Writer's guidelines free. Subscription: $24 for one year; $45 for 2 years.

Payment/Terms Pays $10 for fiction, $5 for personal essays, $5 per poem and 1 contributor's copy. Pays on publication for first North American serial rights. Sponsors awards/contests.

Advice "We are devoted to helping new writers get published and to teaching through example and content. Give us a try! Please send for guidelines and a sample."

☑ ◎ ☒ NIGHT TERRORS

1202 W. Market Street, Orrville OH 44667-1710. (330)683-0338. E-mail: editor@night-terrors-publications.com. Web site: www.night-terrors-publications.com. **Contact:** D.E. Davidson, editor/publisher. Magazine: 8½×11; 52 pages; 80 lb. glossy cover; illustrations; photos. "*Night Terrors* publishes quality, thought-provoking horror fiction for literate adults." Quarterly. Estab. 1996. Circ. 1,000.

● *Night Terrors* has had 24 stories listed in the Honorable Mention section of *The Year's Best Fantasy and Horror, Annual Colletions.*

Needs Horror, psychic/supernatural/occult. "*Night Terrors* does not accept stories involving abuse, sexual mutilation or stories with children as main characters. We publish traditional supernatural/psychological horror for a mature audience. Our emphasis is on literate work with a chill." Wants to see more psychological horror. Receives 50 unsolicited mss/month. Accepts 12 mss/issue; 46 mss/year. Publishes ms 6-12 months after acceptance. **Publishes 16 new writers/year.** Recently published work by John M. Clay, Ken Goldman and Barbara Rosen. Length: 2,000-5,000 words; average length: 3,000 words. Often comments on rejected mss.

How to Contact Send complete ms with cover letter. Include estimated word count, 50-word bio and list of publications. Send a #10 SASE or larger SASE for reply or return of ms. Responds in 1 week to queries; 3 months to mss. Accepts simultaneous submissions. Sample copy for $6 (make checks payable to Night Terrors Publications). Writer's guidelines for #10 SASE.

Payment/Terms "Pays 2 contributor's copies for nonprofessional writers; additional copies for $4.50. Pays by arrangement with professional writers." Pays on publication for first North American serial rights. Sends galleys to author.

Advice "I publish what I like. I like stories which involve me with the viewpoint character and leave me with the feeling that his/her fate could have been or might be mine. Act professionally. Check your work for typos, spelling, grammar, punctuation, format. Send your work flat in a 9×12 envelope. And if you must, paper clip it, don't staple."

☐ ◎ THE NOCTURNAL LYRIC, Journal of the Bizarre

The Nocturnal Lyric, P.O. Box 542, Astoria OR 97103. E-mail: nocturnallyric@melodymail.com. Web site: www.angelfire.com/ca/nocturnallyric. **Contact:**Susan Moon, editor. Magazine: 8½×11; 40 pages; illustrations. "Fiction and poetry submitted should have a bizarre horror theme. Our audience encompasses people who stand proudly outside of the mainstream society." Annual. Estab. 1987. Circ. 400.

Needs Horror (dark fantasy, futuristic, psychological, supernatural, satirical). "No sexually graphic material—it's too overdone in the horror genre lately." Receives 25-30 unsolicited mss/month. Accepts 10-11 mss/issue; 10-11 mss/year. Publishes ms 1 year after acceptance. **Publishes 20 new writers/year.** Recently published work by Kendall Evans, Tim Scott, Cyrus Gray, Richard Pitaniello and Karla Ungurean. Length: 2,000 words maximum; average length: 1,500 words. Publishes short shorts. Also publishes literary essays, poetry. Rarely comments on rejected mss.

How to Contact Send complete ms with cover letter. Include estimated word count. Responds in 3 month to queries; 8 months to mss. Accepts simultaneous , multiple submissions and reprints. Sample copy for $2 (back issue); $3 (current issue). Writer's guidelines online.

Payment/Terms Pays with discounts on subscriptions and discounts on copies of issue. Pays on acceptance Not copyrighted.

Advice "A manuscript stands out when the story has a very original theme and the ending is not predictable. Don't be afraid to be adventurous with your story. Mainstream horror can be boring. Surreal, satirical horror is what true nightmares are all about."

$ ☒ ☑ ON SPEC

P.O. Box 4727, Station South, Edmonton AB T6E 5G6 Canada. (780)413-0215. Fax: (780)413-1538. E-mail: onspec@onspec.ca. Web site: www.onspec.ca/. **Contact:** Diane L. Walton, editor. Magazine: $5^{1}/_{4} \times 8$; 112-120 pages; illustrations. "We publish speculative fiction by new and established writers, with a strong preference for Canadian authored works." Quarterly. Estab. 1989. Circ. 2,000.

Needs Fantasy, horror, science fiction, magic realism. No media tie-in or shaggy-alien stories. No condensed or excerpted novels, Religious/inspirational stories, fairy tales. "We would like to see more horror, fantasy, science fiction—well-developed stories with complex characters and strong plots." Receives 100 unsolicited mss/month. Accepts 10 mss/issue; 40 mss/year. "We read manuscripts during the month after each deadline: February 28/May 31/August 31/November 30." Publishes ms 6-18 months after acceptance. **Publishes 10-15 new writers/year.** Recently published work by Mark Shainblum, Hugh Spencer and Leah Bobet. Length: 1,000-6,000 words; average length: 4,000 words. Also publishes poetry. Often comments on rejected mss.

How to Contact Send complete ms. Accepts submissions by disk. SASE for return of ms or send a disposable copy of ms plus #10 SASE for response. Include Canadian postage or IRCs. No e-mail or fax submissions. Responds in 2 weeks to queries; 4 months after deadline to mss. Accepts simultaneous submissions. Sample copy for $8. Writer's guidelines for #10 SASE or on Web site.

Payment/Terms Pays $50-180 for fiction. Short stories (under 1,000 words): $50 plus 1 contributor's copy. Pays on acceptance for first North American serial rights.

Advice "We're looking for original ideas with a strong SF element, excellent dialogue, and characters who are so believable, our readers will really care about them."

☑ ☑ ORACLE STORY & LETTERS

Rising Star Publishers, 7510 Lake Glen Drive, Glen Dale MD 20769. (301)352-233. Fax: (301)352-2529. E-mail: hekwonna@aol.com. **Contact:** Obi H. Ekwonna, publisher. Magazine: $5^{1}/_{2} \times 8^{1}/_{2}$; 60 lb. white bound paper. Quarterly. Estab. 1989. Circ. 1,000.

Needs Adventure, children's/juvenile (adventure, fantasy, historical, mystery, series), comics/graphic novels, ethnic/multicultural, family saga, fantasy (sword and sorcery), historical, literary, mainstream, military/war, romance (contemporary, historical, suspense), thriller/espionage, western (frontier saga), young adult/teen (adventure, historical). Does not want gay/lesbian or erotica works. Receives 10 unsolicited mss/month. Accepts 7 mss/issue. Publishes ms 4 months after acceptance. **Publishes 5 new writers/year.** Recently published work by Joseph Manco, I.B.S. Sesay. Publishes short shorts. Also publishes literary essays, literary criticism, poetry. Rarely comments on rejected mss.

How to Contact Send complete ms. Accepts submissions by disk. Send SASE (or IRC) for return of the ms, or send a disposable copy of the ms and #10 SASE for reply only. Responds in 1 month to mss. Accepts multiple submissions. Sample copy for $10. Writer's guidelines for #10 SASE, or by e-mail.

Payment/Terms Pays 1 contributor's copy. Pays on publication for first North American serial rights.

Advice "Read anything you can lay your hands on."

◎ PARADOXISM

University of New Mexico, 200 College Rd., Gallup NM 87301. Fax: (503)863-7532. E-mail: smarand @unm.edu. Web site: www.gallup.unm.edu/ ~ smarandache/a/paradoxism.htm. **Contact:** Dr. Florentin Smarandache. Magazine: $8^{1}/_{2} \times 11$; 100 pages; illustrations. "*Paradoxism* is an avant-garde movement based on excessive use of antinomies, antitheses, contraditions, paradoxes in the literary creations set up by the editor in the 1980s as an anti-totalitarian protest." Annual. Estab. 1993. Circ. 500.

Needs Experimental, literary. "Contradictory, uncommon, experimental, avant garde." Plans specific themes in the next year. Publishes annual special fiction issue or anthology. Receives 5 unsolicited mss/month. Accepts 10 mss/issue. Recently published work by Mircea Monu, Doru Motoc and Patrick Pinard. Publishes short shorts. Also publishes literary essays, literary criticism, poetry. Sometimes comments on rejected mss.

How to Contact Send a disposable copy of ms. Responds in 2 months to mss. Accepts simultaneous submissions. Sample copy for $19.95 and 8½×11 SASE. Writer's guidelines online.

Payment/Terms Pays subscription. Pays on publication. Not copyrighted.

Advice "We look for work that refers to the paradoxism or is written in the paradoxist style. The Basic Thesis of the paradoxism: everything has a meaning and a non-meaning in a harmony with each other. The Essence of the paradoxism: a) the sense has a non-sense, and reciprocally B) the non-sense has a sense. The Motto of the paradoxism: 'All is possible, the impossible too!' The Symbol of the paradoxism: a spiral—optic illusion, or vicious circle."

Ⓝ 🄾 PLAIN SPOKE

Amsterdam Press, 6199 Steubenville Road SE, Amsterdam OH 43903. (740)543-4333. E-mail: plainspoke@gmail.com. Web site: www.plainspoke.net. **Contact:** Joshua Diamond. Magazine: digest-sized; 36-52 pages; heavy paper; card cover. "We publish work that has a sense of word economy, strong voice, Americana appeal, tightness, and shies away from the esoteric and expositional. We like to be surprised." Quarterly. Estab. 2007.

Needs Comics, experimental, humor/satire, literary, mainstream, western (frontier saga), Americana, flash fiction, metafiction. Does not want science fiction, furry, cliché, plot-driven, formulaic. Receives 80 mss/month. Accepts 2-3 mss/issue; 10-12 mss/year. Length: 1,500-3,000 words. Average length: 1,750 words. Publishes short shorts. Average length of short shorts: 1,000 words. Also publishes literary essays, literary criticism, book reviews, poetry. Send review copies to reviews editor. Often comments on/critiques rejected manuscripts.

How to Contact Send complete ms with cover letter. Accepts submissions by e-mail and on disk. Include estimated word count, brief bio in 3rd person, list of publications, "limit publication credits to 6." Responds to mss in 1-4 months. Send disposable copy of ms and #10 SASE for reply only. Considers simultaneous submissions, multiple submissions. Guidelines available for SASE, via e-mail, on Web site.

Payment/Terms Writers receive 1 contributor copy; additional copies $3. Pays on publication. Acquires first North American serial rights. Publication is copyrighted.

Advice "Work that surprises us stands out. We don't like the predictable. We don't want to feel like we're reading a story, pull us in. Make every word count and don't rely on adverbs."

$🄾 THE POST

Publishers Syndication International, P.O. Box 6218, Charlottesville VA 22906-6218. E-mail: asamuels@publisherssyndication.com. Web site: www.publisherssyndication.com. **Contact:** A.P. Samuels, editor. Magazine: 8½×11; 32 pages. Monthly. Estab. 1988.

Needs Adventure, mystery/suspense (private eye), romance (romantic suspense, historical, contemporary), western (traditional). "No explicit sex, gore, weird themes, extreme violence or bad language." Receives 35 unsolicited mss/month. Accepts 1 mss/issue; 12 mss/year. Agented fiction 10%. **Publishes 1-3 new writers/year.** Average length: 10,000 words.

How to Contact Send complete ms with cover letter. Responds in 5 weeks to mss. Sample copy not available. Writer's guidelines for #10 SASE.

Payment/Terms 1-2¢/word. Pays on acceptance.

Advice "Manuscripts must be for a general audience."

◻ 🄾 PRAYERWORKS, Encouraging God's people to do real work of ministry—intercessory prayer

The Master's Work, P.O. Box 301363, Portland OR 97294-9363. (503)761-2072. E-mail: vannm1@aol.com. Web site: www.prayerworksnw.org. **Contact**: V. Ann Mandeville, editor. Newsletter: 5½×8; 4 pages; bond paper. "Our intended audience is 70% retired Christians and 30% families. We publish 350-500 word devotional material—fiction, nonfiction, biographical, poetry, clean quips and quotes.

Our philosophy is evangelical Christian serving the body of Chirst in the area of prayer.'' Estab. 1988. Circ. 1,100.

Needs Religious/inspirational. ''No nonevangelical Christian. Subject matter may include anything which will build relationship with the Lord—prayer, ways to pray, stories of answered prayer, teaching on a Scripture portion, articles that will build faith, or poems will all work.'' We even use a series occasionally. Publishes ms 2-6 months after acceptance. **Publishes 30 new writers/year.** Recently published work by Allen Audrey and Petey Prater. Length: 350-500 words; average length: 350-500 words. Publishes short shorts. Also publishes poetry. Often comments on rejected mss.

How to Contact Send complete ms with cover letter. Include estimated word count and a very short bio. Responds in 1 month to mss. Accepts simultaneous , multiple submissions and reprints. Writer's guidelines for #10 SASE.

Payment/Terms Pays free subscription to the magazine and contributor's copies. Pays on publication. Not copyrighted.

Advice Stories ''must have a great take-away—no preaching; teach through action. Be thrifty with words—make them count.''

$◻ PURPOSE

616 Walnut Ave., Scottdale PA 15683-1999. (724)887-8500. Fax: (724)887-3111. E-mail: horsch@mph.org. Web site: www.mph.org. **Contact**: James E. Horsch, editor. Magazine: $5^3/_8 \times 8^3/_8$; 8 pages; illustrations; photos. Weekly. Estab. 1968. Circ. 8,500.

Needs Historical (related to discipleship theme), humor/satire, religious/inspirational. No militaristic, narrow patriotism, or racist themes. Receives 150 unsolicited mss/month. Accepts 3 mss/issue; 140 mss/year. Publishes ms 1 year after acceptance. **Publishes 15-25 new writers/year.** Length: 600 words; average length: 400 words. Occasionally comments on rejected mss.

How to Contact Send complete ms. Send all submissions by Word attachment via e-mail. Responds in 3 months to queries. Accepts simultaneous submissions, reprints, multiple submissions. Sample copy and writer's guidelines for $2, 6×9 SAE and 2 first-class stamps. Writer's guidelines online.

Payment/Terms Pays up to 7¢/word for stories, and 2 contributor's copies. Pays on acceptance for one-time rights.

Advice ''Many stories are situational, how to respond to dilemmas. Looking for first-person storylines. Write crisp, action moving, personal style, focused upon an individual, a group of people, or an organization. The story form is an excellent literary device to help readers explore discipleship issues. The first two paragraphs are crucial in establishing the mood/issue to be resolved in the story. Work hard on the development of these.''

$▨ ◻ ◎ QUEEN'S QUARTERLY, A Canadian Review

Queen's Quarterly, 144 Barrie St. Kingston ON K7L 3N6 Canada. (613)533-2667. Fax: (613)533-6822. E-mail: queens.quarter ly@queensu.ca. Web site: www.queensu.ca/quarterly. **Contact**: Boris Castel, editor. Magazine: 6×9; 800 pages/year; illustrations. ''A general interest intellectual review, featuring articles on science, politics, humanities, arts and letters. Book reviews, poetry and fiction.'' Quarterly. Estab. 1893. Circ. 3,000.

Needs Historical, literary, mainstream, novel excerpts, short stories, women's. ''Special emphasis on work by Canadian writers.'' Accepts 2 mss/issue; 8 mss/year. Publishes ms 6-12 months after acceptance. **Publishes 5 new writers/year.** Recently published work by Gail Anderson-Dargatz, Tim Bowling, Emma Donohue, Viktor Carr, Mark Jarman, Rick Bowers and Dennis Bock. Also publishes literary essays, literary criticism, poetry.

How to Contact ''Send complete ms with SASE and/or IRC. No reply with insufficient postage.'' Responds in 2-3 months to queries. Sample copy online. Writer's guidelines online. Reviews fiction.

Payment/Terms Pays $100-300 for fiction, 2 contributor's copies and 1-year subscription; additional copies $5. Pays on publication for first North American serial rights. Sends galleys to author.

ℕ $◪ ◎ RENARD'S MENAGERIE, The Journal of Anthropomorphic Fiction

Water Dreams Productions LLC, P.O. Box 6212, Bellevue WA 98008-0212. (425)444-7463. E-mail: editors@RenardsMenagerie.com. Web site: http://www.renardsmenagerie.com. **Contact**: Fox Cutter, publisher & editor. Magazine: 6×9; 60 pages; glossy cover; illustrations. ''*Renard's Menagerie* is a fiction magazine focusing on anthropomorphic stories. In this case, anthropomorphic means more then just furry stories. We accept all type of anthropomorphic stories and characters. From werewolves to talking cat mysteries, they all come under the umbrella of anthropomorphic." Quarterly. Estab. 2007. Circ. 50.

Needs Adventure, ethnic/multicultural, experimental, family saga, fantasy, feminist, gay, historical, horror, humor/satire, lesbian, literary, mainstream, military/war, mystery, new age, psychic/supernatural/occult, romance, science fiction, thriller/espionage, western, young adult/teen. "We avoid stories of an 'adult' nature. We ask that sex and violence be limited to what you might see on Prime Time Television." Receives 15-20 mss/month. Accepts 4 mss/issue; 20 mss/year. Ms published 3-6 months after acceptance. **Publishes 5-6 new writers/year.** Published Phil Geusz, Julie Frost, Gerri Leen, Laurie Tom, Donald Jacob Uitvlugt, Jane Chirgwin, Kevin Andrew Murphy. Length: 2000-10,000 words. Average length: 4,000 words. Also publishes book reviews. Send review copies to Fox Cutter. Rarely comments on/critiques rejected mss.

How to Contact Send complete ms with cover letter. Accepts submissions by e-mail. Include list of publications. Responds to queries in 2 weeks; mss in 8 weeks. Send disposable copy of ms and #10 SASE for reply only. Sample copy, guidelines available on Web site.

Payment/Terms Writers receive 1¢ per word, 3 contributor's copies. Additional copies $5.50. Pays on publication. Sends galleys to author. Publication is copyrighted.

Advice "We're looking for a good story with well written characters that are worth reading about. The characters must make decisions and the decisions must have an effect on the story. Learn to use your word processor, it will help you with a lot of the little issues that come up with document formatting."

✔ ROSEBUD, The Magazine For People Who Enjoy Good Writing

Rosebud, Inc., N3310 Asje Rd., Cambridge WI 53523. (608)423-9780. Fax: (608)423-9976. E-mail: jrodclark@smallbytes.net. Web site: www.rsbd.net;www.hyperionstudio.com/rosebud. **Contact:** Roderick Clark, editor. Magazine: 6½×9½; 136 pages; 50 lb. matte; 100 lb. cover; illustrations. Quarterly. Estab. 1993. Circ. 7,000.

Needs Adventure, ethnic/multicultural, experimental, historical (general), literary, mainstream, novel excerpts, psychic/supernatural/occult, regional, romance (contemporary), science fiction (soft/sociological), slice-of-life vignettes, translations. "No formula pieces." Receives 120 unsolicited mss/month. Accepts 20 mss/issue; 60 mss/year. Publishes ms 1-4 months after acceptance. **Publishes 70% new writers/year.** Recently published work by Ray Bradbury, XJ Kennedy and Nikki Giovanni. Publishes short shorts. Also publishes literary essays. Often comments on rejected mss.

How to Contact Send complete ms. Include SASE for return of ms and $1 handling fee. Responds in 3 months to mss. Accepts simultaneous and reprints submissions. Sample copy for $6.95 or sample articles online. Writer's guidelines for SASE or on Web site.

Payment/Terms Pays for poems in issues only. Pays $30 and 3 contributor's copies; additional copies 45. Pays on publication for for first, one-time, second serial (reprint) rights.

Advice "Each issue will have six or seven flexible departments (selected from a total of sixteen departments that will rotate). We are seeking stories; articles; profiles; and poems of: love, alienation, travel, humor, nostalgia and unexpected revelation. Something has to 'happen' in the pieces we choose, but what happens inside characters is much more interesting to us than plot manipulation. We like good storytelling, real emotion and authentic voice."

Ⓝ $✔ SCYWEB BEM, Science Fiction & Fantasy Audiozine

Riamac Group, P.O. Box 691298, Charlotte NC 28227. (704)545-8844. E-mail: editor@scywebbem.com. Web site: www.scywebbem.com. **Contact:** Cameron Harne, Editor. Audiozine. CDROM format; comes in Standard Audio and MP3 Audio; both versions are approx 4 hours. "*SCYWEB BEM* is a science fiction/fantasy audio publication that draws primarily upon the talents of new, unknown, 'up-and-coming' authors, as well as established authors." Triannual. Estab. 2006. Circ. 3,000.

Needs Fantasy (space fantasy, sword and sorcery), horror (dark fantasy, futuristic, supernatural), science fiction (hard science/technological, soft/sociological). Does not want stories that hinge on overt sexual contact. *SCYWEB BEM* only publishes horror in its Halloween (October) edition. *SCYWEB BEM*'s 2009 winter edition will focus on Christmas themes. Deadlines and issue dates will be posted on the Web site as they become available. List of upcoming themes available on Web site. Receives 25-100 mss/month. Accepts 6 mss/issue; 24 mss/year. Ms published 3-6 months after acceptance. Agented fiction 1%. **Publishes 16 new writers/year.** Published Amy Cullen St. Claire, Colin Tyler Auld, A.J. Kenning, Michael Cregan, Roman Semonova, Hank Quense, Joan E.R. Johnson, Patrick Keating, Rodrigo Cuadra and Linda Zhu. Length: 3,000-17,000 words. Average length: 8,500 words. Often comments on/critiques rejected mss.

How to Contact Send complete ms with cover letter. Accepts submissions on disk. Include estimated word count, brief bio, list of publications. Responds to queries in 3 weeks; mss in 2 months. Send either SASE (or IRC) for return of ms or disposable copy of ms and #10 SASE for reply only. Sample copy and guidelines available for on Web site.

Payment/Terms Writers receive $10-100, 2 contributor's copies. Additional copies $6.95. Pays on acceptance. Acquires first rights, first North American serial rights, electronic rights. Publication is copyrighted.

Advice "It is almost impossible to define criteria for selecting fiction. In the end, it all comes down to a simple question: Was the story enjoyable and the ending satisfying? Check our Web site for tips on exactly what we're looking for."

◘ SILENT VOICES

Ex Machina Press, LLC, P.O. Box 11180, Glendale CA 91226.(818)244-7209. E-mail: exmachinapag@ aol.com. Web site: www.exmachinapress.com. **Contact:** Peter Balaskas, editor. Literary magazine/ journal. "*Silent Voices* is an annual literary anthology whose purpose is to publish fiction of a variety of styles and genres. By taking stories of a diverse nature and placing them in a specific order, we produce a creative mosaic that tells a larger story." Annual. Estab. 2004. Circ. 1,000.

Needs Adventure, erotica, ethnic/multicultural, experimental, fantasy, historical, horror, humor/ satire, mainstream, mystery, religious, romance, science fiction, western. Manuscript published 4-5 months after acceptance. Length: 10,000 words.

How to Contact Send complete ms with cover letter via e-mail only. Considers simultaneous submissions. Guidelines available on Web site. Please read Web site guidelines before submitting.

Payment/Terms Pays 2 contributor's copies. Acquires first North American serial rights.

◘ ◎ SLATE & STYLE, Magazine of the National Federation of the Blind Writers Division

NFB Writer's Division, 2704 Beach Drive, Merrick NY 11566. (516)868-8718. E-mail: loristay@aol.c om. **Contact**: Lori Stayer, editor. Quarterly magazine: 28-32 print/40 Braille pages; e-mail, cassette and large print. "Articles of interest to writers, and resources for blind writers." Estab. 1982. Circ. 200.

Needs Adventure, fantasy, humor/satire, contemporary, blindness. No erotica. "Avoid theme of death." Does not read mss in June or July. **Publishes 2 new writers/year**. Recently published work by Jana Simms Moynihan, Ann Chiapetta, and Bill Harper. Publishes short shorts. Also publishes literary criticism, poetry. Sometimes comments on rejected mss.

How to Contact Accepts submissions by e-mail. Responds in 3-6 weeks to queries; 3-6 weeks to mss. Sample copy for $3.

Payment/Terms Pays in contributor's copies. Acquires one-time rights. Sponsors awards/contests.

Advice "The best advice I can give is to send your work out; manuscripts left in a drawer have no chance at all."

◎ SOLEADO

IPFW, CM 267 2101 E. Coliseum Blvd., Fort Wayne IN 46805.(260)481-6630. Fax: (260)481-6985. E-mail: summersj@ipfw.edu. Web site: www.soleado.org. **Contact:** Jason Summers, editor. Magazine. "We are looking for good literary writing in Spanish, from Magical Realism á la García Márquez, to McOndo-esque writing similiar to that of Edmundo Paz-Soldá and Alberto Fuguet, to Spanish pulp realism like that of Arturo Pérez-Reverte. Testimonials, experimental works like those of Diamela Eltit, and women's voices like Marcela Serrano and Zoé Valdés are also encouraged. We are not against any particular genre writing, but such stories do have to maintain their hold on the literary, as well as the genre, which is often a difficult task. Please do not send anything in English. We publish a very limited selection of work in Spanglish—Do not send us anything without having read what we have already published." Annual. Estab. 2004.

Needs Children's/juvenile, ethnic/multicultural, experimental, fantasy, historical, humor/satire, mainstream, mystery, science fiction. Accepts 2-6 mss/year. Length: 8,000 words (max).

How to Contact Send complete ms with cover letter. Accepts submissions by e-mail. Responds to queries in 2 weeks. Responds to mss in 3 months. Guidelines available on Web site.

Payment/Terms Acquires first rights, first North American serial rights, one-time rights, electronic rights.

SPACE AND TIME MAGAZINE, THE MAGAZINE OF FANTASY, HORROR, AND SCIENCE

HDi Consulting, Inc., 1308 Centennial Ave, Ste 101, Piscataway, NJ 08854. (732)512-8789. E-mail: fictioneditor@spaceandtimemagazine.com. Web site: http://spaceandtimemagazine.com. **Fiction Contact:** Gerard Houarner, fiction editor. Magazine: 8½×11, 48 pages, matte paper, glossy cover. Contains illustrations. "We love stories that blend elements—horror and science fiction, fantasy with SF elements, etc. We challenge writers to try something new and send us their unclassifiable works—what other publications reject because the work doesn't fit in their 'pigeonholes.'" Quarterly. Estab. 1966. Circ. 2,000.

Needs Fantasy (high, sword and sorcery, modern), horror (dark fantasy, futuristic, psychological, supernatural), romance (futuristic/time travel), science fiction (hard science/technological, soft/sociological). Does not want anything without some sort of speculative element. Receives 250 mss/month. Accepts 8 mss/issue; 32 mss/year. Closes periodically due to backlog. Check Web site to see if submissions are open. Ms published 3-6 months after acceptance. **Publishes 2-4 new writers/year.** Published PD Cacek, AR Morlan, Jeffrey Ford, Charles De Lint and Jack Ketchum. Length: 1,000-10,000 words. Average length: 6,500 words. Publishes short shorts. Average length of short shorts: 1,000 words. Also publishes poetry, occasional book reviews. Send review copies to Publisher Hildy Silverman, hildy@spaceandtimemagazine.com. Sometimes comments on/critiques rejected mss.

How to Contact Send complete ms with cover letter. Accepts submissions by e-mail. Include estimated word count, brief bio, list of publications. Responds to queries in 4-6 weeks. Responds to mss in 4-6 weeks. Send disposable query letter and #10 SASE for reply only if unable to email submission. Sample copy available for $5. Guidelines available via e-mail, on Web site.

Payment/Terms Writers receive 1¢ per word, 2 contributor's copies. Additional copies $ 5. Pays on publication. Acquires first North American serial rights, one-time rights. Publication is copyrighted.

Advice "Be well written—that means proper grammar, punctuation and spelling. Proofread! The greatness of your story will not supersede sloppy construct. Strong internal logic no matter how 'far out' the story. New twists on familiar plots or truly unique offerings will make your manuscript stand out. Blend genre elements in a new and interesting way, and you'll get our attention."

STEAMPUNK MAGAZINE, PUTTING THE PUNK BACK INTO STEAMPUNK

Strangers In A Tangled Wilderness. E-mail: strangers@riseup.net. Web site: http://www.steampunkmagazine.com. **Contact:** Magpie Killjoy, editor. Magazine/online magazine: 8.5×11", 80 pages, recycled paper. Contains illustrations. "*SteamPunk Magazine* is involved in supporting the SteamPunk subculture, a subculture that offers a competing vision of humanity's interaction with technology, a subculture that wears too many goggles." Quarterly. Estab. 2007. Circ. 600 print; 50,000 online.

Needs Adventure, comics/graphic novels, ethnic/multicultural, experimental, fantasy (space fantasy), feminist, horror (dark fantasy, supernatural), humor/satire, literary, military/war, mystery, romance (gothic, historical), science fiction, western. Special interests: steampunk. "We are not interested in promoting misogynist, nationalistic, pro-colonial, monarchical, homophobic, or otherwise useless text." List of upcoming themes available on Web site. Receives 5-12 mss/month. Accepts 2-4 mss/issue; 8-16 mss/year. Manuscript published 2 months after acceptance. **Publishes 6-10 new writers/year.** Published John Reppion, Margaret Killjoy, GD Falksen, Will Strop, Catastraphone Orchestra and Olga Izakson. Length: 500-6,000 words. Average length: 3,500 words. Publishes short shorts. Average length of short shorts: 800 words. Also publishes literary essays, literary criticism, book reviews. Send review copies to Magpie Killjoy. Sometimes comments on/critiques rejected mss.

How to Contact Send complete ms with cover letter. Accepts submissions by e-mail only. Include brief bio, list of publications. Responds to queries in 2 weeks. Responds to mss in 2 months. Considers simultaneous submissions, previously published submissions, multiple submissions. Sample copy available for $3, on Web site. Guidelines available on Web site.

Payment/Terms Writers receive 2 contributor's copies. Additional copies $1.45. Pays on publication.

Advice "We want work that does not simply repeat the stereotypical steampunk genre ideas; work that offers something tangible other than shiny brass thing-a-mabobs. Don't write about a steampowered robot, unless you really have to."

$☐ THE STORYTELLER, A Writer's Magazine

2441 Washington Road, Maynard AR 72444. (870)647-2137. Fax: (870)647-2454. E-mail: storyteller1 @hightowerco m.com. Web site: www.thestorytellermagazine.com. **Contact**: Regina Cook Williams, editor. Tabloid: 8½×11; 72 pages; typing paper; glossy cover; illustrations. "This magazine is open to all new writers regardless of age. I will accept short stories in any genre and poetry in any type. Please keep in mind, this is a family publication." Quarterly. Estab. 1996.

 • Offers *People's Choice Awards* and nominates for a *Pushcart Prize*.

Needs Adventure, historical, humor/satire, literary, mainstream, mystery/suspense, religious/inspirational, romance, western, young adult/teen, senior citizen/retirement, sports. "I will not accept pornography, erotica, science fiction, new age, foul language, graphic horror or graphic violence." No children's stories. Wants more well-plotted mysteries. Publishes ms 3-9 months after acceptance. **Publishes 30-50 new writers/year.** Recently published work by Jodi Thomas, Jory Sherman, David Marion Wilkinson, Dusty Richards and Tony Hillerman. Publishes short shorts. Also publishes literary essays, poetry. Sometimes comments on rejected mss. Word length 2,500.

How to Contact Send complete ms with cover letter. Include estimated word count and 5-line bio. Submission by mail only. Responds in 1-2 weeks to mss. No queries. Accepts simultaneous submissions and reprints. Sample copy for $6. Writer's guidelines for #10 SASE.

Payment/Terms Pays ¼¢ per word. Sponsors awards/contests.

Advice "Follow the guidelines. No matter how many times this has been said, writers still ignore this basic and most important rule." Looks for "professionalism, good plots and unique characters. Purchase a sample copy so you know the kind of material we look for." Would like more "well-plotted mysteries and suspense and a few traditional westerns. Avoid sending anything that children or young adults would not (or could not) read, such as really bad language."

▦ ◪ STUDIO, A Journal of Christians Writing

727 Peel Street, Albury 2640. Australia. (+61)26021-1135. E-mail: studio00@bigpond.net.au. **Contact**: Paul Grover, managing editor. Quarterly. Circ. 300.

Needs "*Studio* publishes prose and poetry of literary merit, offers a venue for new and aspiring writers, and seeks to create a sense of community among Christians writing." Accepts 30-40 mss/year. **Publishes 40 new writers/year.** Recently published work by Andrew Lansdown and Benjamin Gilmour.

How to Contact Accepts submissions by e-mail. Send SASE. "Overseas contributors must use International postal coupons in place of stamped envelope." Responds in 1 month to mss. Sample copy for $10 (Aus).

Payment/Terms Pays in copies; additional copies are discounted. Subscription $60 (Australian) for 4 issues (1 year). International draft in Australian dollars and IRC required, or Visa and Mastercard facilities available. "Copyright of individual published pieces remains with the author, while each collection is copyright to *Studio*."

◪ TALEBONES, Fiction on the Dark Edge

Fairwood Press, 21528 104th Street Court East, Bonney Lake WA 98391. (253)269-2640. E-mail: info@talebones.com. **Contact**: Patrick Swenson, editor. Magazine: digest size; 100 pages; standard paper; glossy cover stock; illustrations; photos. "We like stories that have punch, but still entertain. We like science fiction and dark fantasy, humor, psychological and experimental works." Published 2-3 times a year. Estab. 1995. Circ. 1,000.

Needs Fantasy (dark), humor/satire, science fiction (hard science, soft/sociological, dark). "No straight slash and hack horror. No cat stories or stories told by young adults." "Would like to see more science fiction." Receives 200 unsolicited mss/month. Accepts 8-10 mss/issue; 16-30 mss/year. Publishes ms 3-4 months after acceptance. **Publishes 2-3 new writers/year.** Recently published work by William F. Nolan, Nina Kiriki Hoffman, Anne Harris, Darrell Schweitzer, and James Van Pelt . Length: 1,000-6,000 words; average length: 3,000-4,000 words. Publishes short shorts. Also publishes poetry.

How to Contact Send complete ms with cover letter. Include estimated word count and 1-paragraph bio. Responds in 1 week to queries; 1-2 months to mss. Sample copy for $7. Writer's guidelines for #10 SASE. Reviews fiction.

$ ▱ ◎ ▾ TALES OF THE TALISMAN

Hadrosaur Productions, P.O. Box 2194, Mesilla Park NM 88047-2194. E-mail: hadrosaur@zianet.com. Web site: www.talesofthetalisman.com. **Contact:** David L. Summers, editor. Zine specializing in science fiction: 8½ × 10½; 90 pages; 60 lb. white stock; 80 lb. cover. *"Tales of the Talisman* is a literary science fiction and fantasy magazine published 4 times a year. We publish short stories, poetry, and articles with themes related to science fiction and fantasy. Above all, we are looking for thought-provoking ideas and good writing. Speculative fiction set in the past, present, and future is welcome. Likewise, contemporary or historical fiction is welcome as long as it has a mythic or science fictional element. Our target audience includes adult fans of the science fiction and fantasy genres along with anyone else who enjoys thought-provoking and entertaining writing." Quarterly. Estab. 1995. Circ. 200.

 • Received an honorable mention in *The Year's Best Science Fiction* 2004 edited by Gardner Dozois.

Needs Fantasy (space fantasy, sword and sorcery), horror, science fiction (hard science/technological, soft/sociological). "We do not want to see stories with graphic violence. Do not send 'mainstream' fiction with no science fictional or fantastic elements. Do not send stories with copyrighted characters, unless you're the copyright holder." Receives 60 unsolicited mss/month. Accepts 7-10 mss/issue; 21-30 mss/year. Publishes ms 9 months after acceptance. **Publishes 8 new writers/year.** Recently published work by Michael D. Turner, Rick Novy, David Boop, Carol Hightshoe, Lyn Lifshin, and Deborah P. Kolodji. Length: 1,000-6,000 words; average length: 4,000 words. Also publishes poetry. Often comments on rejected mss.

How to Contact Send complete ms. Accepts submissions by e-mail (hadrosaur@zianet.com). Include estimated word count, brief bio and list of publications. Send SASE (or IRC) for return of ms or send a disposable copy of ms and #10 SASE for reply only. Responds in 1 week to queries; 1 month to mss. Accepts reprint submissions. No simultaneous submissions. Sample copy for $8. Writer's guidelines online.

Payment/Terms Pays $6-10. Pays on acceptance for one-time rights.

Advice "First and foremost, I look for engaging drama and believable characters. With those characters and situations, I want you to take me someplace I've never been before. The story I'll buy is the one set in a new world or where the unexpected happens, but yet I cannot help but believe in the situation because it feels real. Read absolutely everything you can get your hands on, especially stories and articles outside your genre of choice. This is a great source for original ideas."

▱ ◎ TEA, A MAGAZINE

Olde English Tea Company, Inc., 3 Devotion Road P.O. Box 348, Scotland CT 06264. (860)456-1145. Fax: (860)456-1023. E-mail: teamag@teamag.com. Web site: www.teamag.com. **Contact:** Jobina Miller, assistant to the editor. Magazine. "An exciting quarterly magazine all about tea, both as a drink and for its cultural significance in art, music, literature, history and society." Quarterly. Estab. 1994. Circ. 9,500.

Needs Needs fiction that is tea related.

How to Contact Send complete ms with cover letter. Responds to mss in 6 months. Guidelines available for SASE.

Payment/Terms Pays on publication. Acquires all rights.

$ ▱ TIMBER CREEK REVIEW

P.O. Box 16542, Greensboro NC 27416. E-mail: timber_creek_review@hoopsmail.com. **Contact:** John M. Freiermuth, editor; Willa Schmidt, associate editor. Newsletter: 5½ × 8½; 76-80 pages; computer generated on copy paper; saddle-stapled with colored paper cover; some illustrations. "Fiction, humor/satire, poetry and travel for a general audience." Quarterly. Estab. 1992. Circ. 130-150.

Needs Adventure, ethnic/multicultural, feminist, historical, humor/satire, literary, mainstream, mystery/suspense, regional, western, literary nonfiction, and one-act plays. "No religious, children's, gay, modern romance, and no reprints please!" Receives 50 unsolicited mss/month. Accepts 30-36 stories and 75-85 poems a year. Publishes ms 2-6 months after acceptance. Length: 3,500-6,000 words. **Publishes 0-3 new writers/year.** Recently published work by Patricia Schultheis, Jim Meirose, Beau Boudreaux, Mitchel LesCarbeau, Eugene R. Baker, James Longstaff, Aaron W. Hillman, Iain S. Baird, Channing Wagg, Jeff lacy, Michael Fessler, and Kevin McKelvey.

How to Contact Cover letter expected. Accepts simultaneous submissions. Sample copy for $5.00, subscription $18. Overseas mail add $2 for postage.

Payment/Terms Pays $10-40, plus subscription. Acquires first North American serial rights. Not copyrighted.

Advice "Stop watching TV and read that literary magazine where your last manuscript appeared. There are no automatons here, so don't treat us like machines. We may not recognize your name at the top of the manuscript. Include a statement that the mss have previously not been published on paper nor on the internet, nor have they been accepted by others. A few lines about yourself breaks the ice, the names of three or four magazines that have published you in the last year or two would show your reality, and a bio blurb of 27 words including the names of 2 or 3 of the magazines you send the occasional subscription check (where you aspire to be?) could help. If you are not sending a check to some little magazine that is supported by subscriptions and the blood, sweat and tears of the editors, why would you send your manuscript to any of them and expect to receive a warm welcome? No requirement to subscribe or buy a sample, but they're available and are encouraged. There are no phony contests and never a reading fee. We read all year long, but may take 3-8 months to respond."

☐ ◎ TRAIL OF INDISCRETION

Fortress Publishing, Inc., 3704 Hartzdale Dr., Camp Hill PA 17011. (717)350-8760. E-mail: fortresspu blishinginc@yahoo.com. Web site: www.fortresspublishinginc.com. **Contact:** Brian Koscienski, editor in chief. Zine specializing in genre fiction: digest ($5\frac{1}{2} \times 8\frac{1}{2}$), 48 pages, 24 lb. paper, glossy cover. "We publish genre fiction—sci-fi, fantasy, horror, etc. We'd rather have a solid story containing great characters than a weak story with a surprise 'trick' ending." Quarterly. Estab. 2006. Circ. 100.

Needs Adventure, fantasy (space fantasy, sword and sorcery), horror (dark fantasy, futuristic, psychological, supernatural), humor/satire, psychic/supernatural/occult, science fiction (hard science/technological, soft/sociological). Does not want "touchy-feely 'coming of age' stories or stories where the protagonist mopes about contemplating his/her own mortality." Accepts 5-7 mss/issue. Manuscript published 3-9 months after acceptance. **Publishes 2-10 new writers/year.** Published Cliff Ackman (debut), Roger Arnold, Susan Kerr (debut), Kristine Ong Muslim, Tala Bar, CJ Henderson, Danielle Ackley-McPhail. Length: 5,000 words (max). Average length: 3,000 words. Publishes short shorts. Sometimes comments on/critiques rejected mss.

How to Contact Send complete ms with cover letter. Accepts submissions by e-mail. Include estimated word count, brief bio, list of publications. Responds to queries in 1-2 weeks. Responds to mss in 1-10 weeks. Send either SASE (or IRC) for return of ms or disposable copy of ms and #10 SASE for reply only. Considers simultaneous submissions, previously published submissions. Sample copy available for $4 or on Web site. Guidelines available for SASE, via e-mail, on Web site.

Payment/Terms Writers receive 1 contributor copy. Additional copies $2.50. Pays on publication. Acquires one-time rights. Publication is copyrighted.

Advice "If your story is about a 13-year-old girl coping with the change to womanhood while poignantly reflecting the recent passing of her favorite aunt, then we *don't* want it. However, if your story is about the 13-year-old daughter of a vampire cowboy who stumbles upon a government conspiracy involving unicorns and aliens while investigating the grizzly murder of her favorite aunt, then we'll look at it. Please read the magazine to see what we want. Love your story, but listen to advice."

Ⓝ $◩ ◎ WATERMEN

Fine & Finer Graphic, 2428 Gramercy Ave, Torrance CA 90501. (310)850-6431. E-mail: tomlockie@sb cglobal.net. Web site: http://freedivingfilms.com/watermen.htm. **Contact:** Tom Lockie, editor. Magazine: 8.5×11, 32 pages. Contains illustrations. Includes photographs. "*Watermen* is a term referring to the lifeguarding, bodysurfing, surfing, spearfishing, SCUBA diving lifestyle. The magazine is dedicated to the ocean lifestyle, arts, fashion and sports: diving, surfing, kayaking, paddleboating, underwater photography. We publish stories and articles dealing with adventure travel and above all ecological issues—protecting oceans and water health. Also publishes medical articles, travel articles, poems and short stories." Semiannual. Estab. 2006. Circ. 5,000.

Needs Adventure, humor/satire, literary, mainstream. Special interests: watersport stories. Receives 10-12 mss/month. Accepts 2-3 mss/issue; 4-6 mss/year. Ms published 1-5 months after acceptance. Agented fiction 10%. **Publishes 1-2 new writers/year.** Published Brian Donahue and Matteo Verna.

Length: 500-1,500 words. Average length: 1,200 words. Publishes short shorts. Average length of short shorts: 400-500 words. Also publishes book reviews, poetry. Send review copies to Tom Leckie; has to be watersport based. Sometimes comments on/critiques rejected mss.

How to Contact Accepts submissions by e-mail only. Please query first. Include brief bio. Responds to queries in 3 weeks. Responds to mss in 1 months. Sample copy free with 8½×11 SASE and $2.60 postage. Guidelines available via e-mail.

Payment/Terms Writers receive $20 per page. Additional copies $5 & $1.90 postage. Pays on publication. Acquires electronic rights, archive rights. Publication is not copyrighted.

Advice "Writer must be seriously involved in watersports to stand out. Pay some heavy dues in the water."

$ ☑ ◎ ☑ WEBER, THE CONTEMPORARY WEST

1214 University Circle, Ogden UT 84408-1214. (801)626-6473. E-mail: weberjournal@weber.edu. Web site: weber journal.weber.edu. **Contact**: Michael Wutz, editor. Magazine: 7½×10; 120-140 pages; coated paper; 4-color cover; illustrations; photos. "We seek the following themes: preservation of and access to wilderness, environmental cooperation, insight derived from living in the West, cultural diversity, changing federal involvement in the region, women and the West, implications of population growth, a sense of place, etc. We love good writing that reveals human nature as well as natural environment." Triannual. Estab. 1984. Circ. 1,000.

Needs Adventure, comics/graphic novels, ethnic/multicultural, experimental, feminist, historical, humor/satire, literary, mainstream, military/war, mystery/suspense, New Age, psychic/supernatural/occult, regional (contemporary western US), translations, western (frontier sage, tradtional, contemporary), short story collections. No children's/juvenile, erotica, religious or young adult/teen. Receives 50 unsolicited mss/month. Accepts 3-6 mss/issue; 9-18 mss/year. Publishes ms up to 18 months after acceptance. **Publishes "few" new writers/year.** Recently published work by Gary Gildner, Stephen Dunn, Ron McFarland and Carolyn Forché. Publishes short shorts. Also publishes literary essays, poetry, art. Sometimes comments on rejected mss.

How to Contact Send complete ms with a cover letter. Include estimated word count, bio (if necessary), and list of publications (not necessary). Responds in 3 months to mss. Accepts multiple submissions. Sample copy for $10.

Payment/Terms Pays $150-300. Pays on publication for first, electronic rights. Requests electronic archive permission. Sends galleys to author.

Advice "Is it true? Is it new? Is it interesting? Will the story appeal to educated readers who are concerned with the contemporary western United States? Declining public interest in reading generally is of concern. We publish both print media and electronic media because we believe the future will expect both options. The Dr. Neila C. Seshachari Fiction Award, a $500 prize, is awarded annually to the best fiction appearing in *Weber* each year."

$ ☑ WEIRD TALES

Business Office: 9710 Traville Gateway Drive #234, Rockville MD 20850. Editorial address (all fiction submissions): P.O. Box 38190, Tallahassee FL 32315. E-mail: weirdtales@gmail.com. Web site: www.weirdtales.net. **Contact:** Ann VanderMeer, fiction editor. Magazine: 8½×11; 80-96 pages; white, newsprint paper; glossy 4-color cover; illustrations and comics. "We publish fantastic fiction, supernatural horror for an adult audience." Published 6 times a year. Estab. 1923. Circ. 5,000.

Needs Fantasy (sword and sorcery), horror, psychic/supernatural/occult, translations. No hard science fiction or non-fantasy. "Looking for darkly fantastical fiction, work that is unique and unusual. Stories that are recognized as Weird Tales for the 21st Century." Receives 1,200 unsolicited mss/month. Accepts 8 mss/issue; 48 mss/year. Publishes ms 6-18 months after acceptance. Agented fiction 10%. **Publishes 8 new writers/year.** Recently published work by Michael Moorcock, Tanith Lee, Thomas Ligotti, Darrell Schweitzer, Sarah Monette and Michael Boatman. Length: up to 10,000 words, but very few longer than 8,000; average length: 4,000 words. Publishes short shorts.

How to Contact Send complete ms. You must include SASE for reply and return of ms or send a disposable copy of ms with SASE. Responds in 6-8 weeks to mss. Accepts simultaneous submissions. No multiple submissions. Also accepts email submissions to weirdtales@gmail.com. If sending via e-mail please note: have the first 3-4 paragraphs pasted into the body of the email and the entire document attached, either as a PC Word document or an RTF file. Sample copy for $6. Writer's guidelines for #10 SASE or by e-mail. Reviews books of fantasy fiction.

Payment/Terms Pays 3-4¢/word and 2 contributor's copies on acceptance. Acquires first North American serial, plus anthology option rights.

Advice "Traditional fantasy tropes are fine as long as it's a new and different take on the genre. Do not send any familiar story lines and do not send any pastiches of Lovecraft."

[N] $[✑] [◎] THE WILLOWS

2436 Federal Ave #4, Los Angeles CA 90064. E-mail: editor@thewillowsmagazine.com. Web site: www.thewillowsmagazine.com. **Contact:** Ben Thomas, lead editor. Literary magazine/journal. 8½×11, 70-90 pages, matte paper, matte cover. Contains illustrations. "Founded to give voice to a unique but neglected corner of horror literature, *The Willows* strives to publish only the best in true classic-style weird fiction. We pride ourselves on our gentlemanly aesthetic, as well as our love of mad science, strange monstrosities, and ethereal wonder. Our readers share our passion for this bygone age, and the scientific romances of its greatest literary minds." Bimonthly. Estab. 2007. Circ. 50.

Needs Horror (dark fantasy, supernatural). Special interests: classic-style weird fiction. Does not want gory horror, slashers, splatterpunk, or "anything not fitting to be told over brandy in a gentleman's lounge in 1920s London." Receives 50-60 mss/month. Accepts 10 mss/issue; 60 mss/year. Manuscript published 2-4 months after acceptance. **Publishes 5 new writers/year.** Published Paul Melniczek, Charles Muir, Paul Marlowe, Nike Bourke, Nickolas Cook, G.W. Thomas, Lawrence Dagstine, Kristine Ong Muslim, G.D. Falksen and Tara Kolden. Length: 1,000-5,500 words. Average length: 3,500 words. Publishes short shorts. Average length of short shorts: 500 words. Also publishes literary essays, literary criticism, poetry. Often comments on/critiques rejected mss.

How to Contact Send complete ms with cover letter. Accepts submissions by e-mail. Include estimated word count, brief bio, list of publications, expression of interest in the classic weird tale genre. Responds to queries in 2 weeks. Responds to mss in 1 month. Considers previously published submissions. Guidelines available on Web site.

Payment/Terms Writers receive $25. Additional copies $3.50 each. Pays on publication. Acquires first North American serial rights. Sends galleys to author. Publication is copyrighted.

Advice "We love work set in Victorian times, in the European countryside, in a twisted fairyland, in the underbelly of an enchanted city, or in the ruins of an undiscovered civilization. We want tales of cosmic fright; eerie fireside memories of nature's deadly mystery; adventures among the aether, the hemera, the spirit realm; tragedies of mad academics who take science too far; warnings of monstrosities that lurk in the sea, in the air, beneath the ground; stories of strange mechanical devices with unholy purposes; or anything else fitting the classic weird motifs. We do not accept stories set in postmodern times. This means nothing after the 1940s. In fact, we prefer stories that are timeless, or at least set in Victorian or Edwardian times. Weird fiction does not merely mean 'stories that are weird.' Weird Fiction refers to a specific genre, and if this genre is one with which you are unfamiliar, we ask that you not submit here until you have become sufficiently familiar."

[N] $[✑] [◎] WRONG WORLD, The World of Unitended Consequences

QWAND LLC, 7437 Village Square Drive, Suite 210, Castle Rock CO 80108. (303)719-0037 ext. 112. Fax: (303)537-3212. E-mail: editor@wrongworld.com. Web site: http://www.wrongworld.com. **Contact:** Susan Tingle, Editor. Contains illustrations. Online DVD store featuring short stories produced on DVD for TV. " 'Our marketing model is similar to NetFlix and Blockbuster's,' says *Wrong World* creator Mike Tingle. 'Customers select and order DVD rentals online. We then mail their selections to them. When finished with the DVD, the customer mails it back to us in the postage prepaid return envelope we provided. The rental period is two weeks.' At this time, *Wrong World* stories are produced and distributed exclusively on DVD. Customers rent or buy *Wrong World* stories and read them on your TV just like watching a movie. Discover an exciting new media for the world's best writers of horror, supernatural, fantasy, paranormal, suspense, thriller and science fiction. In the tradition of classic shows like *The Twilight Zone*, *Alfred Hitchcock Presents*, *Outer Limits* and *One Step Beyond*, every story includes an opening and closing narration presented by *Wrong World* host Dr. Lyle Merrick." Quarterly. Estab. 2007.

Needs "*Wrong World* readers want new-fashioned scary stories (any genre) that are (including, but not in any order) creepy, suspenseful, thrilling, menacing, troubled (individuals or people), the last cliffhanger hanging (survivor stories), terrifying, mystifying, paranormal, magical, otherworldly (outer space, ghost and other dimensions), danger filled, disturbing (mildly), monsters/monstrous, aliens, catastrophes, world(s) ending events, natural disasters, cults, abandonment/isolation, serial-anything, chillers, psychotic, sociopathic, phobic, neurotic, life and death, supernatural/horrific, nonstop flight and chase, forbidden (anything), and all sorts of traps/trapped, and hunters/hunted. Flat out, the *Wrong World* target market wants scary." Does not want stories that don't meet PG13 standards or reprints. Stories must be original, never published. Upcoming themes include *Teachers*—Reading, Writing and Repeating. Submissions deadline December 5, 2008, for release on DVD/Video January 10, 2009. *Hospital*—Healthscares. Submissions deadline April 5, 2009 for release on DVD/Video May 10, 2009. Additional 2009 collection themes and deadlines will be announced on Web site at www.wrongworld.com. Accepts 3 mss/issue; 12 mss/year. Ms published 6 months after acceptance. Published Melanie Tem, Mike Tingle. Length: 2,500-3,500 words. Average length: 3,000 words. Sometimes comments on/critiques rejected mss.

How to Contact Submit via online form. Accepts submissions through Web site only. Include estimated word count, brief bio. Responds to mss in 6 weeks. Considers multiple submissions. Sample copy available on Web site. Guidelines available on Web site.

Payment/Terms Writers receive 7½¢ per word. Pays on acceptance.

Advice "Every story is rated on ten subjective specifications. Each category is worth ten points. The highest possible score is 100 points. Stories are rated on Originality, Length and Fit, Twists, Characters, Commerciality, Writing, Guidelines, Educational Merit, Readability and Editing. Read the *Wrong World* Submissions page carefully. This document is available to read and print on our Submissions page. Read the story excerpts on the Web site and listen to the narrations to see the type of stories we publish."

$⬛ ZAHIR, A Journal of Speculative Fiction

Zahir Publishing, 315 South Coast Hwy. 101, Suite U8, Encinitas CA 92024. E-mail: stempchin@zahirtales.com. Web site: www.zahirtales.com. **Contact:** Sheryl Tempchin, editor. Magazine: Digest-size; 80 pages; heavy stock paper; glossy, full color cover stock. "We publish literary speculative fiction." Triannual. Estab. 2003.

Needs Fantasy, literary, psychic/supernatural/occult, science fiction, surrealism, magical realism. No children's stories, excessive violence or pornography. Accepts 6-8 mss/issue; 18-24 mss/year. Publishes ms 2-12 months after acceptance. **Publishes 6 new writers/year.** Sometimes comments on rejected mss.

How to Contact Send complete ms. Send SASE (or IRC) for return of ms, or send disposable copy of the ms and #10 SASE for reply only. E-mail queries okay. No e-mail mss except from writers living outside the U.S. Responds in 1-2 weeks to queries; 1-3 months to mss. Accepts reprints submissions. No simultaneous submissions. Sample copy for $8 (US), $8.50 (Canada) or $10.50 (International). Writer's guidelines for #10 SASE, by e-mail, or online.

Payment/Terms Pays $10 and 2 contributor's copies. Pays on publication for first, second serial (reprint) rights.

Advice "The stories we are most likely to buy are well written, have interesting, well-developed characters and/or ideas that fascinate, chill, thrill, or amuse us. They must have some element of the fantastic or surreal."

Online Markets

As production and distribution costs go up and the number of subscribers falls, more and more magazines are giving up print publication and moving online. Relatively inexpensive to maintain and quicker to accept and post submissions, online fiction sites are growing fast in numbers and legitimacy. Jason Sanford, editor of *storySouth*, explains, "Online journals reach far greater audiences than print journals with far less cost. I have a friend who edits a print literary journal and he is constantly struggling to cover the cost of printing 500 copies twice a year. At *storySouth*, we reach 1,000 individual readers every single day without having to worry that we're going to break the bank with our printing budget. The benefit for writers is that your stories tend to gain more attention online than in small literary journals. Because small journals have print runs of 500-1,000 copies, there is a limit on how many people will read your work. Online, there is no limit. I've been published in both print and online literary journals, and the stories I've published online have received the most attention and feedback."

Writers exploring online opportunities for publication will find a rich and diverse community of voices. Genre sites are strong, in particular those for science fiction/fantasy and horror. (See *Alienskin* and *DargonZine*.) Mainstream short fiction markets are also growing exponentially. (See *Toasted Cheese* and *Paperplates*, among many others.) Online literary journals range from the traditional (*The Barcelona Review*, *The Green Hills Literary Lantern*) to those with a decidedly more quirky bent (*Timothy McSweeney's Internet Tendency*, *The Absinthe Literary Review*). Writers will also find here more highly experimental and multimedia work. (See *Convergence* and *Diagram*.)

Online journals are gaining respect for the writers who appear on their sites. As Jill Adams, publisher and editor of *The Barcelona Review*, says: "We see our Internet review, like the small independent publishing houses, as a means of counterbalancing the big-business mentality of the multi-national publishing houses. At the same time, we want to see our writers 'make it big.' Last year we heard from more and more big houses asking about some of our new writers, wanting contact information, etc. So I see a healthy trend in that big houses are finally—after being skeptical and confused—looking at it seriously and scouting online."

While the medium of online publication is different, the traditional rules of publishing apply to submissions. Writers should research the site and archives carefully, looking for a match in sensibility for their work. They should then follow submission guidelines exactly and submit courteously. True, these sites aren't bound by traditional print schedules, so your work theoretically may be published more quickly. But that doesn't mean online journals have a larger staff, so exercise patience with editors considering your manuscript.

Also, while reviewing the listings in this market section, notice they are grouped differently from other market listings. In our literary magazines section, for example, you'll find primarily only publications searching for literary short fiction. But Online Markets are grouped by medium, so you'll find publishers of mystery short stories listed next to those looking for horror next to those specializing in flash fiction, so review with care. In addition, online markets with print counterparts, such as *North American Review*, can be found listed in the print markets sections.

A final note about online publication: Like literary journals, the majority of these markets are either nonpaying or very low paying. In addition, writers will not receive print copies of the publications because of the medium. So in most cases, do not expect to be paid for your exposure.

$ ☑ THE ABSINTHE LITERARY REVIEW

P.O. Box 328, Spring Green WI 53588. E-mail: staff@absinthe-literary-review.com. Web site: www.absinthe-literary-review.com. **Contact:** Charles Allen Wyman, editor-in-chief. Electronic literary magazine. "*ALR* publishes short stories, novel excerpts, poems, book reviews, and literary essays. Our target audience is the literate individual who enjoys creative language use, character-driven fiction and the clashing of worlds—real and surreal, poetic and prosaic, sacred and transgressive."
Needs "Transgressive works dealing with sex, death, disease, madness, and the like; the clash of archaic with modern-day; archetype, symbolism; surrealism, philosophy, physics; existential, and post-modern flavoring; experimental or flagrantly textured (but not sloppy or casual) fiction; intense crafting of language from the writer's writer. Anathemas: mainstream storytellers, 'Oprah' fiction, high school or beginner fiction, poetry or fiction that contains no capital letters or punctuation, 'hot' trends, genre, and utterly normal prose or poetry; first, second or third drafts, pieces that exceed our stated word count (5,000 max.) by thousands of words." **Publishes 3-6 new writers/year.** Recently published work by Bruce Holland Rogers, David Schneiderman, Virgil Suarez, John Tisdale, James Reidel and Dan Pope.
How to Contact *ALR* will cease publishing for an indefinite period including all of the 2008 calendar year. Check online guidelines for updates on future submission periods. Questions? E-mail the *ALR* staff at staff@absinthe-literary-review.com.
Payment/Terms Pays $2-10 for fiction and essays; $1-10 for poetry.
Advice "Submit elsewhere for now."

☑ THE ADIRONDACK REVIEW

Black Lawrence Press, 8405 Bay Parkway #C8, % Diane Goettel, Brooklyn NY 11214. E-mail: tar@blacklawrencepress.com. Web site: http://adirondackreview.homestead.com. **Contact:** Diane Goettel, editor. Online literary magazine/journal. Contains illustrations & photographs. Estab. 2000.
Needs Adventure, experimental, family saga, gay, historical (general), psychological, translations. Does not want SciFi, fantasy. Receives over 200 mss/month. Accepts 5-10 mss/issue; 20-30 mss/year. Manuscript published 1-5 months after acceptance. Agented fiction 5%. **Publishes 15% new writers/year.** Published Frank Haberie, Steve Gillis, Melinda Misrala, Kate Swoboda. Length: 700-8,000 words. Average length: 3,000 words. Publishes short shorts. Average length of short shorts: 800 words. Also publishes literary essays, literary criticism, book reviews, poetry. Send review copies to Diane Goettel. Rarely comments on/critiques rejected mss.
How to Contact Send complete ms with cover letter. Accepts submissions by e-mail. Include estimated word count, brief bio, list of publications, and "how they learned about the magazine." Responds to queries in 1-2 months. Responds to mss in 2-4 months. Send either SASE (or IRC) for return of ms or disposable copy of ms and #10 SASE for reply only. Considers simultaneous submissions, multiple submissions.
Payment/Terms Acquires first rights. Sponsors contests. See Web site for details.

$ ☑ ALIENSKIN MAGAZINE, An Online Science Fiction, Fantasy & Horror Magazine

Froggy Bottom Press, P.O. Box 495, Beaver PA 15009. E-mail: alienskin@alienskinmag.com. Web site: www.alienskinmag.com. **Contact:** Feature fiction: Kay Patterson; Flash fiction: Phil Adams. Online magazine. "Our magazine was created for, and strives to help, aspiring writers of SFFH. We endeavor to promote genre writers." Bimonthly. Estab. 2002. Circ. 1, 900 + internet.
Needs Fantasy (dark fantasy, sword and sorcery), horror (dark fantasy, futuristic, psychological,

psychic/supernatural/occult), science fiction (hard science/technological, soft/sociological). ''No excessive blood, gore, erotica, vulgarity or child abuse. No experimental or speculative fiction that does not use basic story elements of character, conflict, action and resolution. No esoteric ruminations.'' Receives 150-250 unsolicited mss/month. Accepts 30-37 mss/issue; 200-222 mss/year. Publishes ms 30-60 days after acceptance. **Publishes 18-42 new writers/year.** Recently published work by Michael A. Kechula, Gordon Ross Lanser, Andrew Knighton and Brensa Cooper. Length: 1,000-3,500 words; average length: 2,200 words. Publishes micro and flash fiction. Always comments on rejected mss.

How to Contact Send complete ms. Accepts submissions by e-mail only. Include estimated word count, brief bio, name, address, and e-mail address. Responds in 1-2 weeks to queries; 2 months to mss. Accepts multiple submissions. Sample copy online. Writer's guidelines online.

Payment/Terms ½¢/word for 1,001-3,500 words; $5 flat pay for 500-1,000 words. Exposure only for 150 word micro fiction. Pays on publication for first, electronic rights. Sponsors a pro-payment contest each year.

Advice ''We look for interesting stories, offer ing something unique; stories that use basic story elements of character, conflict, action and resolution. We like the dark, twisted side of SFFH genres. Read our guidelines and follow the rules. Treat the submission process as a serious business transaction. Only send stories that have been spell-checked, and proofread at least twice. Try to remember: editors who offer a critique on manuscripts do so to help you as a writer, not to hamper or dissuade you as a writer.''

$☐ ◎ ⚑ ALLEGORY, Tri-Annual Online Magazine of SF, Fantasy & Horror

(formerly Peridot Books), 1225 Liberty Bell Dr., Cherry Hill NJ 08003. E-mail: submissions@allegorye zine.com. Web site: www.allegoryezine.com. **Contact:** Ty Drago, editor. Online magazine specializing in science fiction, fantasy and horror. ''We are an e-zine by writers for writers. Our articles focus on the art, craft and business of writing. Our links and editorial policy all focus on the needs of fiction authors.'' Triannual. Estab. 1998.

• Peridot Books won the Page One Award for Literary Contribution.

Needs Fantasy (space fantasy, sword and sorcery, sociological), horror (dark fantasy, futuristic, supernatural), science fiction (hard science/technological, soft/sociological). ''No media tie-ins (Star Trek, Star Wars, etc., or space opera, vampires).'' Receives 150 unsolicited mss/month. Accepts 8 mss/issue; 24 mss/year. Publishes ms 1-2 months after acceptance. Agented fiction 5%. **Publishes 10 new writers/year.** Length: 1,500-7,500 words; average length: 4,500 words. Also publishes literary essays, literary criticism. Often comments on rejected mss.

How to Contact Send complete ms with a cover letter, electronic only. Include estimated word count, brief bio, list of publications and name and e-mail address in the body of the story. Responds in 8 weeks to mss. Accepts simultaneous, multiple submissions and reprints. Writer's guidelines online.

Payment/Terms $15/story-article. Pays on publication for one-time, electronic rights.

Advice ''Give us something original, preferably with a twist. Avoid gratuitous sex or violence. Funny always scores points. Be clever, imaginative, but be able to tell a story with proper mood and characterization. Put your name and e-mail address in the body of the story. Read the site and get a feel for it before submitting.''

ℕ ◐ ⚑ ANDERBO.COM

Anderbo Publishing, 341 Lafayette St. #974, New York NY 10012-2417. (917)705-4081. Fax: (212)777-3400. E-mail: editors@anderbo.com. Web site: www.anderbo.com. **Contact:** Rick Rofihe, editor-in-chief. Online literary magazine/journal. ''Quality fiction, poetry, 'fact' and photography on a Web site with 'print-feel' design.'' Estab. 2005. Member CLMP.

• Received the Best New Online Magazine or Journal, *storySouth* Million Writers Award in 2005.

Needs Literary. Does not want any genre literature. ''We're interested only in literary fiction, poetry, and literary 'fact.' '' Receives 100 mss/month. Accepts 12 mss/year. Ms published one month after acceptance. **Publishes 6 new writers/year.** Published Lisa Margonelli, Lucille Lang Day, Martha Wilson and Susan Breen. Length: 3,500 words (max). Average length: 2,600 words. Publishes short shorts. Average length of short shorts: 1,400 words. Also publishes literary essays, poetry. Rarely comments on/critiques rejected mss.

How to Contact Send complete ms with cover letter. Accepts submissions by e-mail. Include brief bio, list of publications. Responds to queries in 2 months. Responds to mss in 2 months. Considers simultaneous submissions. Guidelines available on Web site.

Payment/Terms Acquires first rights, first North American serial rights, one-time rights, electronic rights. Publication is copyrighted.

Advice "We are looking for fiction that is unique, urgent, accessible and involving. Look at our site and read what we've already published."

⬛ ◪ APPLE VALLEY REVIEW, A JOURNAL OF CONTEMPORARY LITERATURE

Queen's Postal Outlet, Box 12, Kingston ON K7L 3R9 Canada. E-mail: editor@leahbrowning.net. Web site: www.applevalleyreview.com. **Contact:** Leah Browning, editor. Online literary magazine. Includes photographs/artwork on cover. "Each issue features a selection of beautifully crafted poetry, short fiction and essays. We prefer work that has both mainstream and literary appeal. As such, we avoid erotica, work containing explicit language and anything violent or extremely depressing. Our audience includes teens and adults of all ages." Semiannual. Estab. 2005. Member CLMP.

Needs Ethnic/multicultural (general), experimental, humor/satire, literary, mainstream, regional (American South, Southwest), translations, literary women's fiction (e.g. Barbara Kingsolver, Anne Tyler, Lee Smith, Elinor Lipman, Perri Klass). Does not want genre fiction, erotica, work containing explicit language, or anything violent or extremely depressing. Receives 50+ mss/month. Accepts 1-3 mss/issue; 2-12 mss/year. Manuscript published 3-6 months after acceptance. Published Miriam Sagan, Barry Jay Kaplan, Jenny Steele, Kerri Quinn, Patricia Gosling. Length: 100-3,000 words. Average length: 2,000 words. Publishes short shorts. Average length of short shorts: 1,200 words. Also publishes literary essays, poetry. Sometimes comments on/critiques rejected mss.

How to Contact Send complete ms with cover letter. Accepts submissions only via e-mail. Include estimated word count, brief bio. Responds to mss in 1 week-3 months. Considers multiple submissions. Guidelines available on Web site. Sample copy on Web site.

Payment/Terms Acquires first rights, right to archive online. Publication is copyrighted.

Advice "Excellent writing always makes a manuscript stand out. Beyond that, I look for stories and poems that I want to read again, and that I want to give to someone else to read—work so interesting for one reason or another that I feel compelled to share it. Please read at least some of the previously published work to get a feel for our style, and follow the submission guidelines as closely as possible. We accept submissions only via e-mail."

⬛ ◻ ASCENT ASPIRATIONS

Ascent Aspirations Magazine, 1560 Arbutus Dr., Nanoose Bay BC C9P 9C8 Canada. E-mail: ascentaspirations@shaw.com. Web site: www.ascentaspirations.ca. **Contact:** David Fraser, editor. E-zine specializing in short fiction (all genres) and poetry, essays, visual art: 40 electronic pages; illustrations; photos. *Ascent* publishes two additional issues in print each year. "*Ascent Aspirations Magazine* publishes quarterly online and semi-annually in print. The print issues are operated as contests. Please refer to current guidelines before submitting. *Ascent Aspirations* is a quality electronic publication dedicated to the promotion and encouragement of aspiring writers of any genre. The focus however is toward interesting experimental writing in dark mainstream, literary, science fiction, fantasy and horror. Poetry can be on any theme. Essays need to be unique, current and have social, philosophical commentary." Quarterly online. Estab. 1997.

Needs Erotica, experimental, fantasy (space fantasy), feminist, horror (dark fantasy, futuristic, psychological, supernatural), literary, mainstream, mystery/suspense, New Age, psychic/supernatural/occult, science fiction (hard science/technological, soft/sociological). Receives 100-200 unsolicited mss/month. Accepts 40 mss/issue; 240 mss/year. Publishes ms 3 months after acceptance. **Publishes 10-50 new writers/year.** Recently published work by Taylor Graham, Janet Buck, Jim Manton, Steve Cartwright, Don Stockard, Penn Kemp, Sam Vargo, Vernon Waring, Margaret Karmazin, Bill Hughes. Length: 1,000 words or less. Publishes short shorts. Also publishes literary essays, literary criticism, poetry. Sometimes comments on rejected mss.

How to Contact "Query by e-mail with Word attachment." Include estimated word count, brief bio and list of publications. If you have to submit by mail because it is your only avenue, provide a SASE with either International Coupons or Canadian stamps only. Responds in 1 week to queries; 3 months to mss. Accepts simultaneous, multiple submissions, and reprints. Guidelines by e-mail or on Web site. Reviews fiction and poetry collections.

Payment/Terms "No payment at this time. Rights remain with author."

Advice "Short fiction should, first of all tell, a good story, take the reader to new and interesting imaginary or real places. Short fiction should use language lyrically and effectively, be experimental in either form or content and take the reader into realms where they can analyze and think about the human condition. Write with passion for your material, be concise and economical and let the reader work to unravel your story. In terms of editing, always proofread to the point where what you submit is the best it possibly can be. Never be discouraged if your work is not accepted; it may just not be the right fit for a current publication."

Ⓝ $☐ ⊚ Ⓒ ATOMJACK

Susurrus Press, 409 Alabama Street, Huntington WV 25704. (304)634-9867. E-mail: atomjackmagazine@yahoo.com. Web site: http://atomjackmagazine.com. **Contact:** Adicus Ryan Garton, editor. Online magazine. Contains illustrations. Includes photographs. "There are many online science fiction magazines, but they rarely combine a visual aesthetic with powerful stories. *Atomjack*, being a Susurrus publication, strives to achieve the prominence and quality of big print magazines in a free online publication. *Atomjack* is aimed at adults, as some stories have excessive violence or language unsuited for most children." Quarterly. Estab. 2006. Circ. 300-600 viewers per month.

Needs Comics/graphic novels, fantasy (space fantasy, science fantasy), horror (futuristic), science fiction (hard science/technological, soft/sociological). Does not want any stories that do NOT contain an element of science fiction. "*Atomjack* very rarely considers romance or erotic stories, though we do not entirely discount them." List of upcoming themes available for SASE, on Web site. Receives 200 mss/month. Accepts 8-12 mss/issue; 40 mss/year. Ms published 2 months after acceptance. **Publishes 10 new writers/year.** Published Lawrence Dagstine, Kristine Ong Muslim, Anthony Bernstein, Amanda Underwood, and Cameron Pierce. Length: 100-5,000 words. Average length: 3,500 words. Publishes short shorts. Average length of short shorts: 500 words. Also publishes literary criticism. Always comments on/critiques rejected mss.

How to Contact Send complete ms with cover letter. Accepts submissions by e-mail only. Include estimated word count, brief bio. Responds to queries in 2 weeks. Responds to mss in 3 months. Considers simultaneous submissions, previously published submissions, multiple submissions. Sample copy, guidelines available on Web site.

Payment/Terms Writers receive $10. Pays on publication. Acquires electronic rights. Sends galleys to author. Publication is not copyrighted.

Advice "Character development and plot are the most important aspect of an *Atomjack* story. We routinely publish stories that have great characters in unique situations in what may not be an original SF environment. We also reject many stories with an amazing concept but no story to reinforce it. *Atomjack* gives a curt, professional critique of all rejected work. Re-submit. *Atomjack* has published stories that were rewritten with the critique in mind and re-submitted."

BABEL, the Multilingual, Multicultural Online Journal and Community of Arts and Ideas

E-mail: submissions@towerofbabel.com. Web site: www.towerofbabel.com. **Contact**: Malcom Lawrence, Editor-in-Chief. Electronic zine. "Recognized by the United Nations as one of the most important social and human sciences online periodicals." Publishes "regional reports from international stringers all over the planet, as well as features, round table discussions, fiction, columns, poetry, erotica, travelogues, and reviews of all of the arts and editorials. We are an online community involving an extensive group of artists, writers, programmers and translators representing 250 of the world's languages."

Needs "There are no specifc categories of fiction we are not interested in. Possible exceptions: lawyers/vampires, different genders hailing from different planets, cold war military scenarios and things that go bump in the suburban night." Recently published work by Nicholas P. Snoek, Yves Jaques, Doug Williamson, A.L. Fern, Laura Feister, Denzel J. Hankinson, and Pete Hanson.

How to Contact Send queries/mss by email. "Please send submissions with a résumé/cover letter or biography attached to the email." Reviews novels and short story collections.

Advice "We would like to see more fiction with first-person male characters written by female authors, as well as more fiction first-person female characters written by male authors. We would also like to see that dynamic in action when it comes to other languages, cultures, races, classes, sexual orientations and ages. The best advice we could give to writers wanting to be published in our publication is simply to know what you are writing about and write passionately about it."

THE BARCELONA REVIEW

Correu Vell 12-2, Barcelona 08002 Spain. (00)34 93 319 15 96. E-mail: editor@barcelonareview.com. Web site: www.barcelonareview.com. **Contact:** Jill Adams, editor. *"TBR* is an international review of contemporary, cutting-edge fiction published in English, Spanish and Catalan. Our aim is to bring both new and established writers to the attention of a larger audience. Well-known writers such as Alicia Erian in the U.S., Michel Faber in the U.K., Carlos Gardini in Argentina, and Nuria Amat in Spain, for example, were not known outside their countries until appearing in *TBR*. Our multilingual format increases the audience all the more. Internationally known writers, such as Irvine Welsh and Douglas Coupland, have contributed stories that ran in small press anthologies available only in one country. We try to keep abreast of what's happening internationally and to present the best finds every two months. Our intended audience is anyone interested in high-quality contemporary fiction that often (but not always) veers from the mainstream; we assume that our readers are well read and familiar with contemporary fiction in general."

Needs Short fiction. "Our bias is towards potent and powerful cutting-edge material; given that general criteria, we are open to all styles and techniques and all genres. No slice-of-life stories, vignettes or reworked fables, and nothing that does not measure up, in your opinion, to the quality of work in our review, which we expect submitters to be familiar with." **Publishes 20 new writers/ year.** Recently published work by Niall Griffiths, Adam Haslett, G.K. Wuori, Adam Johnson, Mary Wornov, Emily Carter, Jesse Shepard and Julie Orringer.

How to Contact Send submissions by e-mail as an attached file. Hard copies accepted but cannot be returned. No simultaneous submissions.

Payment/Terms "In lieu of pay we offer a highly professional Spanish translation to English language writers and vice versa to Spanish writers."

Advice "Send top drawer material that has been drafted two, three, four times—whatever it takes. Then sit on it for a while and look at it afresh. Keep the text tight. Grab the reader in the first paragraph and don't let go. Keep in mind that a perfectly crafted story that lacks a punch of some sort won't cut it. Make it new, make it different. Surprise the reader in some way. Read the best of the short fiction available in your area of writing to see how yours measures up. Don't send anything off until you feel it's ready and then familiarize yourself with the content of the review/magazine to which you are submitting."

$ BLAZING! ADVENTURES MAGAZINE, THE PLACE WHERE PULP LIVES

OmenSpirites.com., New York, NY 11950. E-mail: blazingadventuresmagazine@gmail.com. Web site: www.blazingadventuresmagazine.com. **Contact:** Dash Courageous, editor/publisher. E-zine. "Within the mystery/crime genre, the idea of adventure and action has been lost to the exploits of writer platforms and crusades of moral injustices. These concepts are fine, but there was once a blance between what is the current trend, and what was. *Blazing! Adventures Magazine* was created for the balance in the genre with action, adventure, drama, the days when heroes roamed the pages of fiction, and kids read about fighter pilots, pirates and the fits of fantasy that entertained the populace. That's what is missing. Genre spoofs, genunine pulp crimes and adventures like in the days of fiction when variety was on the newsstands. *Blazing!* is here to fill that void." Semiannual. Estab. 2006.

Needs Fantasy, historical (20s-50s), mystery (private eye/hard-boiled), psychic/supernatural/occult, romance (suspense), science fiction (pulp style), thriller/espionage, western (frontier saga). Does not want serial killers, cozies, Asimov-type sci-fi, "fiction that doesn't have elements of thriller and suspense along with quick-paced action." Receives 15-20 mss/month. Accepts 10 mss/issue; 40 mss/year. Does not read late June to late August and late September to late November. Ms published 4 weeks after acceptance. **Publishes 2-3 new writers/year.** Published John Harper, TJ Glen, Keith Gilman, Andrew Salmon, Chris J. Wright, Ron Capshaw, Pat Lambe and Xavier Treadwell. Length: 2,500-5,000 words. Sometimes comments on/critiques rejected mss.

How to Contact Send complete ms with cover letter. Accepts submissions by e-mail. Include estimated word count, brief bio. Responds to queries in 1 week. Responds to mss in 2 weeks. Guidelines available on Web site.

Payment/Terms Writers receive $5-10. Pays on acceptance. Acquires one-time rights, electronic rights. Publication is copyrighted.

Advice "Fast pacing, high drama, thrilling adventure, these are the things *Blazing!* looks for in the stories we publish. Entertaining stories. Read pulp fiction from the past to learn about high adventure and how to build suspense in your fiction.''

$ BURST

Terra Media, LLC, P.O. Box 133, Kohler WI 53044. (920)331-4904. E-mail: burst@terra-media.us. Web site: www.terra-media.us/burst. **Contact:** Kevin Struck, editor. E-zine. ''*Burst* is a literary e-zine specifically designed for mobile devices, such as cell phones. Content must be short, entertaining, and get to the point. Material that is ambiguous and meaningful only to the writer is not for us. Specialize in flash fiction.'' Estab. 2006.

Needs Adventure, erotica, experimental, fantasy, humor/satire, mainstream, mystery, romance, science fiction. Accepts 35 mss/year. Ms published 3 months after acceptance. Length: 50-700 words.

How to Contact Send complete ms with cover letter. Accepts submissions only by e-mail. Responds to queries in 3 weeks. Responds to mss in 3 months. Considers simultaneous submissions, previously published submissions. Guidelines available on Web site.

Payment/Terms Acquires one-time rights. Pays flat rate of $10.

$ ▣ ▽ THE CAFE IRREAL, International Imagination

E-mail: editors@cafeirreal.com. Web site: www.cafeirreal.com. **Contact:** Alice Whittenburg, G.S. Evans, editors. E-zine: illustrations. ''*The Cafe Irreal* is a webzine focusing on short stories and short shorts of an irreal nature.'' Quarterly. Estab. 1998.

Needs Experimental, fantasy (literary), science fiction (literary), translations. ''No horror or 'slice-of-life' stories; no genre or mainstream science fiction or fantasy.'' Accepts 8-10 mss/issue; 30-40 mss/year. Recently published work by Ignacio Padilla, Charles Simic, Daniela Fisherova, Guido Eekhaut and Sharon Wahl. Length: 2,000 words (max). Publishes short shorts. Also publishes literary essays, literary criticism. Sometimes comments on rejected mss.

How to Contact Accepts submissions by e-mail. ''No attachments, include submission in body of e-mail. Include estimated word count.'' Responds in 2-4 months to mss. No simultaneous submissions. Sample copy online. Writer's guidelines online.

Payment/Terms Pays 1¢/word, $2 minimum. Pays on publication for first-time electronic rights. Sends galleys to author.

Advice ''Forget formulas. Write about what you don't know, take me places I couldn't possibly go, don't try to make me care about the characters. Read short fiction by writers such as Franz Kafka, Kobo Abe, Donald Barthelme, Mangnus Mills, Ana Maria Shua and Stanislaw Lem. Also read our Web site and guidelines.''

▣ CEZANNE'S CARROT, A Literary Journal of Fresh Observations

Spiritual, Transformational & Visionary Art, Inc., P.O. Box 6037, Santa Fe NM 87502-6037. E-mail: query@cezannescarrot.org. Web site: www.cezannescarrot.org. **Contact:** Barbara Jacksha and Joan Kremer, editors. Online magazine. ''*Cezanne's Carrot* publishes fiction, creative nonfiction, and art that explores spiritual, transformational, visionary, metaphysical or contemplative themes. We publish work that explores the higher, more expansive aspects of human nature, the integration of inner and outer worlds, and the exciting thresholds where the familiar meets the unknown.'' Quarterly. Estab. 2005.

Needs Experimental, fantasy (speculative), literary, new age, psychic/supernatural/occult, science fiction (soft/sociological), magical realism, irrealism, visionary, surrealism, metaphysical, spiritual. ''Does not want horror, gore, murder, serial-killers, abuse stories, drug stories, vampires or other monsters, political stories, war stories, stories written for children, stories that primarily promote an agenda or a particular religion. We're not interested in dogma in any form.'' Receives 100 mss/month. Accepts 10-15 mss/issue; 40-60 mss/year. Manuscript published 4-12 weeks after acceptance. **Publishes 1-5 new writers/year.** Published Bruce Holland Rogers, Tamara Kaye Sellman, Utahna Faith, Margaret Frey, Corey Mesler, Christine Boyka kluge, and Charles P. Ries. Length: 100-3,000 words. Average length: 1,800 words. Publishes short shorts.

How to Contact Send complete ms with cover letter. Accepts submissions by e-mail only. Include estimated word count, brief bio, list of publications. Responds to mss in 1-4 months. Considers simultaneous submissions, previously published submissions. Guidelines available on Web site.

Payment/Terms Acquires one-time rights, reprint rights.

Advice ''We only accept work with a strong tie to our journal's mission and theme. Read our guidelines and mission statement carefully. Read previous issues to understand the kind of work we're looking for. Only submissions sent to the correct e-mail address will be considered."

⊠ $⊡ ⊘ ◎ ⊻ CHIZINE, TREATMENT OF LIGHT AND SHADE IN WORDS

E-mail: savory@rogers.com. Web site: www.chizine.com. **Contact:** Brett Alexander Savory, editor-in-chief. E-zine. "Subtle, sophisticated dark fiction with a literary bent." Quarterly. Estab. 1997.

- Received Bram Stoker Award for Other Media in 2000.

Needs Experimental, fantasy, horror (dark fantasy, futuristic, psychological, supernatural), literary, mystery, science fiction (soft/sociological), Does not want "tropes of vampires, werewolves, mummies, monsters, or anything that's been done to death." Receives 100 mss/month. Accepts 3-4 mss/issue; 12-16 mss/year. Does not read July and August. Length: 4,000 words (max). Publishes short shorts. Average length of short shorts: 500 words. Also publishes poetry. Send to savory@rogers.com to query. Always comments on/critiques rejected mss.

How to Contact Send complete ms with cover letter. Accepts submissions by e-mail. Include estimated word count, brief bio. Responds to queries in 1 week. Responds to mss in 3 months. Considers simultaneous submissions. Guidelines available on Web site.

Payment/Terms Writers receive 7¢/word, with a $280 max. Pays on publication. Acquires all rights for 90 days, then archival rights for one year. Sends galleys to author. Publication is copyrighted. Sponsors the Chizine/Leisure Short Story contest. Guidelines posted on Web site around May. See entry in Contests & Awards section.

⊠ ⊛ ⊘ CONTE ONLINE, A JOURNAL OF NARRATIVE WRITING

E-mail: prose@conteonline.net. Web site: www.conteonline.net. **Contact:** Robert Lieberman, editor. Online magazine. "We aim to publish narrative writing of all kinds. Relating a sequence of events is a primary method of human communication; we are interested in the narrative form as a means of relating ideas, experiences, and emotions, and we love how the act of telling a story unites the perspectives of listeners and speakers. We are dedicated to the concept of disseminating fresh, stellar writing to as many people as possible, as quickly and as often as possible, hence our online basis. We are enthusiastic about publishing the latest works of writers from all backgrounds and of varying experience. We hope *Conte* will be a mechanism not only for publication, but communication among writers as well as between readers and authors, and above all that we continue the ancient and perhaps sacred tradition of telling a good yarn." Semiannual. Estab. 2005.

Needs "We'll consider fiction on essentially any topic; our primary focus is the effective use of narrative. We discourage fiction which does not present a clear (sequential or non-sequential) narrative progression; work without a distinctive and engaging plot of some form isn't what we are looking for. We tend to be frustrated by stories that merely raise questions but don't attempt to address them, or that end early without seeming complete." Receives 20-30 mss/month. Accepts 5-7 mss/issue; 10-14 mss/year. Manuscript published 2-3 months or less after acceptance. Agented fiction 5%. **Publishes 4 new writers/year.** Published Joanna Catherine Scott, Louis E. Bourgeois, Adam Sirois, Lyn Lifshin, Steve MacKinnon, James J. Cho, Jessica Murakami, Charles Rafferty, Kristin Berger, R.T. Castleberry and Bertha Rogers. Length: 8,000 words (max). Average length: 5,000 words. Publishes short shorts. Average length of short shorts: 1,000 words. Also publishes poetry. Sometimes comments on/critiques rejected mss.

How to Contact Send complete ms with cover letter. Accepts submissions by e-mail only. Include estimated word count, brief bio. Responds to queries in 3-4 weeks. Responds to mss in 8-10 weeks. Considers simultaneous submissions. Guidelines available via e-mail, on Web site.

Payment/Terms Acquires electronic rights. Sends galleys to author. Publication is not copyrighted.

Advice "We love to see stories that let us take something away—a fact, a perspective, a great bit of dialogue, some piece of the world you create we can keep with us after it's over. Writing that leads us somewhere unexpected is always a delight; immersive worlds and characters are the hallmarks of our favorite fiction. Stories that investigate the overlooked and show us the significance of something often missed are likely to grab our attention. In all, the clarity of the senses you lend us, the adroitness of your storytelling, and the joy we take in reading your tale are the primary barometers of our selection process. Tell your story completely; if you start us on a journey, we want to be taken all the way to the end. Details and imagery are what make a narrative come alive, but try not to lose momentum in them. Have the confidence to tell your story the way it needs to be told; we love reading, so we're already on your side to begin with."

▣ $⬙ CONTRARY

3114 S. Wallace Street, Suite 2, Chicago IL 60616-3299. E-mail: chicago@contrarymagazine.com. Web site: www.contrarymagazine.com. **Contact:** Jeff McMahon, editor. Online literary magazine/ journal. Contains illustrations. "*Contrary* publishes fiction, poetry, literary commentary, and prefers work that combines the virtues of all those categories. Founded at the University of Chicago, it now operates independently and not-for-profit on the South Side of Chicago. We like work that is not only contrary in content, but contrary in its evasion of the expectations established by its genre. Our fiction defies traditional story form. For example, a story may bring us to closure without ever delivering an ending. We don't insist on the ending, but we do insist on the closure. And we value fiction as poetic as any poem." Quarterly. Estab. 2003. Circ. 38,000 unique readers. Member CLMP.
Needs Literary. Receives 650 mss/month. Accepts 3 mss/issue; 12 mss/year. Ms published no more than 21 days after acceptance. **Publishes 1 new writer/year.** Published Thomas E. Kennedy, Andrew Coburn, Sarah Layden, Walter Cummins, Liz Prato, Laurence Davies, Edward McWhinney, and Amy Reed. Length: 2,000 words (max). Average length: 750 words. Publishes short shorts. Average length of short shorts: 750 words. Also publishes literary essays, poetry. Rarely comments on/critiques rejected mss.
How to Contact Accepts submissions through Web site only. www.contrarymagazine.com/Contrary/Submissions.html. Include estimated word count, brief bio, list of publications. Responds to queries in 2 weeks. Responds to mss in 3 months. Considers simultaneous submissions. Guidelines available on Web site.
Payment/Terms Pays $20-60. Pays on publication. Acquires first rights. Publication is copyrighted.
Advice "Beautiful writing catches our eye first. If we realize we're in the presence of unanticipated meaning, that's what clinches the deal. Also, we're not fond of expository fiction. We prefer to be seduced by beauty, profundity and mystery than to be presented with the obvious. We look for fiction that entrances, that stays the reader's finger above the mouse button. That is, in part, why we favor microfiction, flash fiction and short-shorts. Also, we hope writers will remember that most editors are looking for very particular species of work. We try to describe our particular species in our mission statement and our submission guidelines, but those descriptions don't always convey nuance. That's why many editors urge writers to read the publication itself; in the hope that they will intuit an understanding of its particularities. If you happen to write that particular species of work we favor, your submission may find a happy home with us. If you don't, it does not necessarily reflect on your quality or your ability. It usually just means that your work has a happier home somewhere else."

⬙ CONVERGENCE

E-mail: editor@convergence-journal.com. Web site: www.convergence-journal.com. **Contact:** Lara Gularte, editor. *Convergence* seeks to unify the literary and visual arts and draw new interpretations of the written word by pairing poems and flash fiction with complementary art. Quarterly. Estab. 2003. Circ. 400.
Needs Ethnic/multicultural, experimental, feminist, gay, lesbian, literary, regional, translations. Accepts 10 mss/issue. Publishes ms 3 weeks after acceptance. Recently published work by Andrena Zawinski, Grace Cavalieri, Lola Haskins, Molly Fisk, Renato Rosaldo. Publishes short shorts. Also publishes poetry. Sometimes comments on rejected mss.
How to Contact Send complete ms. E-mail submissions only. No simultaneous submissions. Responds in 2 weeks to queries; 4 months to mss. Writer's guidelines online.
Payment/Terms Acquires electronic rights.
Advice "We look for freshness and originality and a mastery of the craft of flash fiction."

⬙ ◎ THE COPPERFIELD REVIEW, A Journal for Readers and Writers of Historical Fiction

E-mail: info@copperfieldreview.com. Web site: www.copperfieldreview.com. **Contact:** Meredith Allard, executive editor. "We are an online literary journal that publishes historical fiction and articles, reviews and interviews related to historical fiction. We believe that by understanding the lessons of the past through historical fiction we can gain better insight into the nature of our society today, as well as a better understanding of ourselves." Quarterly. Estab. 2000.
Needs Historical (general), romance (historical), western (frontier saga, traditional). "We will consider submissions in most fiction categories, but the setting must be historical in nature. We don't want to see anything not related to historical fiction." Receives 30 unsolicited mss/month. Accepts

7-10 mss/issue; 28-40 mss/year. Responds to mss during the months of January, April, July and October. **Publishes "between 30 and 40 percent" new writers/year.** Publishes short shorts. Also publishes literary essays, literary criticism, poetry. Seldom comments on rejected mss.

How to Contact Send complete ms. Accepts submissions by e-mail. Responds in 6 weeks to queries. Accepts simultaneous, multiple submissions and reprints. Sample copy online. Writer's guidelines online. Reviews fiction.

Payment/Terms Acquires one-time rights.

Advice "We wish to showcase the very best in literary historical fiction. Stories that use historical periods and details to illuminate universal truths will immediately stand out. We are thrilled to receive thoughtful work that is polished, poised and written from the heart. Be professional, and only submit your very best work. Be certain to adhere to a publication's submission guidelines, and always treat your e-mail submissions with the same care you would use with a traditional publisher. Above all, be strong and true to your calling as a writer. It is a difficult, frustrating but wonderful journey. It is important for writers to review our online submission guidelines prior to submitting."

◎ DARGONZINE

E-mail: dargon@dargonzine.org. Web site: dargonzine.org. **Contact:** Ornoth D.A. Liscomb, editor. Electronic zine specializing in fantasy. "*DargonZine* is an electronic magazine that prints original fantasy fiction by aspiring Internet writers. The Dargon Project is a collaborative anthology whose goal is to provide a way for aspiring fantasy writers on the Internet to meet and become better writers through mutual contact and collaboration as well as contact with a live readership via the Internet."

Needs Fantasy. "Our goal is to write fantasy fiction that is mature, emotionally compelling, and professional. Membership in the Dargon Project is a requirement for publication." **Publishes 4-12 new writers/year.**

How to Contact Guidelines available on Web site. Sample copy online. Writer's guidelines online.

Payment/Terms "As a strictly noncommercial magazine, our writers' only compensation is their growth and membership in a lively writing community. Authors retain all rights to their stories."

Advice "The Readers and Writers FAQs on our Web site provide much more detailed information about our mission, writing philosophy and the value of writing for *DargonZine*."

N $ ▦ ◨ ◎ DARKER MATTER

6 Broad Piece, Soham, Ely, Cambs MB CB7 5EL, United Kingdom. E-mail: darkermatter06@gmail.com. Web site: www.darkermatter.com. **Contact:** Ben Coppin, editor. Online magazine. Contains illustrations. Includes photographs. "*Darker Matter* is an online science fiction magazine that is free for readers but pays professional rates to authors. It specializes in science fiction with a slight bias towards somewhat dark, melancholy stories (not horror)." Monthly. Estab. 2007.

Needs Science fiction (hard science/technological, soft/sociological). Does not want horror or fantasy. Receives 100 mss/month. Accepts 5 mss/issue; 55 mss/year. Ms published 3 weeks after acceptance. Published David D. Levine, Jerry Oltion, Bud Sparhawk and Edward M. Lerner. Length: 100-6,000 words. Average length: 2,500 words. Publishes short shorts. Average length of short shorts: 750 words. Also publishes book reviews. Send review copies to Ben Coppin, *Darker Matter*, at the address above. Rarely comments on/critiques rejected mss.

How to Contact Send complete ms with cover letter. Accepts submissions by e-mail *only*. Include estimated word count, brief bio, list of publications. Responds to mss in 6 weeks. Considers simultaneous submissions, multiple submissions. Guidelines available on Web site.

Payment/Terms Writers receive 5-10¢/word. Pays on acceptance. Acquires first serial rights, electronic rights. Sends galleys to author. Publication is copyrighted.

$ ▨ DEATHLINGS.COM, Dark Fiction for the Discerning Reader

130 E. Willamette Ave., Colorado Springs CO 80903-1112. E-mail: cvgelvin@aol.com. Web site: www.deathlings.com. **Contact:** CV Gelvin, editor. E-zine specializing in dark fiction. "Our wonderfully quirky themes for the short story contests have included "Frozen Smiles" (dolls), "Burbian Horrors," "Technology Run Amuck" and "Love Gone Bad." Quarterly. Estab. 2000.

Needs Horror (futuristic, psychological, supernatural). "No children's, fantasy, poetry or romance." List of upcoming themes available on Web site. Receives 20-30 unsolicited mss/month. Accepts 3-4 mss/issue. Publishes ms 1-2 months after acceptance. **Publishes 3-6 new writers/year.** Recently published work by David Ballard, Fiona Curnow, Denise Dumars, Jason Franks, dgk Golberg, Darren

O. Godfrey and CV Gelvin. Length: 4,000 words; average length: 3,000 words. Publishes short shorts. Sometimes comments on rejected mss.

How to Contact E-mail story attached in RTF. Include estimated word count, brief bio and list of publications with submission. Responds in 1-3 months to mss. Accepts simultaneous, multiple submissions and reprints. Guidelines free by e-mail or on Web site.

Payment/Terms Writers receive 3¢/word. Pays on publication for electronic rights. Sponsors awards/contests.

⬤ DIAGRAM, A Magazine of Art, Text, and Schematic

New Michigan Press, 648 Crescent NE, Grand Rapids MI 49503. E-mail: editor@thediagram.com. Web site: http://thediagram.com. **Contact:** Ander Monson, editor. "We specialize in work that pushes the boundaries of traditional genre or work that is in some way schematic. We do publish traditional fiction and poetry, too, but hybrid forms (short stories, prose poems, indexes, tables of contents, etc.) are particularly welcome! We also publish diagrams and schematics (original and found). Bimonthly. Estab. 2001. Circ. 200,000 + hits/month. Member CLMP.

Needs Experimental, literary. "We don't publish genre fiction, unless it's exceptional and transcends the genre boundaries." Receives 100 unsolicited mss/month. Accepts 2-3 mss/issue; 15 mss/year. **Publishes 5 new writers/year.** Average length: 250-2,000 words. Publishes short shorts. Also publishes literary essays, poetry. Often comments on rejected mss.

How to Contact Send complete ms. Accepts submissions by Web submissions manager; no e-mail please. Send SASE for return of the ms, or send disposable copy of the ms and #10 SASE for reply only. Responds in 2 weeks to queries; 1-2 months to mss. Accepts simultaneous submissions. Sample copy for $12 for print version. Writer's guidelines online.

Payment/Terms Acquires first, electronic rights.

Advice "We value invention, energy, experimentation and voice. When done very well, we like traditional fiction, too. Nearly all the work we select is propulsive and exciting."

⬤ DUCTS

P.O. Box 3203, Grand Central Station, New York NY 10163. (718)383-6728. E-mail: editor@ducts.org. Web site: http://ducts.org. **Contact:** Jonathan Kravetz. *DUCTS* is a Webzine of personal stories, fiction, essays, memoirs, poetry, humor, profiles, reviews and art. "*DUCTS* was founded in 1999 with the intent of giving emerging writers a venue to regularly publish their compelling, personal stories. The site has been expanded to include art and creative works of all genres. We believe that these genres must and do overlap. *DUCTS* publishes the best, most compelling stories and we hope to attract readers who are drawn to work that rises above." Semiannual. Estab. 1999. Circ. 12,000. CLMP.

Needs Ethnic/multicultural, humor/satire, literary, mainstream. "Please do not send us genre work, unless it is extraordinarily unique." Receives 50 unsolicited mss/month. Accepts 40 mss/issue; 80 mss/year. Publishes ms 1-6 months after acceptance. **Publishes 10-12 new writers/year.** Recently published work by Charles Salzberg, Mark Goldblatt, Richard Kostelanz, and Helen Zelon. Publishes short shorts. Also publishes literary essays, literary criticism, poetry. Sometimes comments on rejected mss.

How to Contact Reading period is January 1 through August 31. Send complete ms. Accepts submissions by e-mail to appropriate departments. Responds in 1-4 weeks to queries; 1-6 months to mss. Accepts simultaneous and reprints submissions. Writer's guidelines on ducts.org.

Payment/Terms Acquires one-time rights.

Advice "We prefer writing that tells a compelling story with a strong narrative drive."

Ⓝ ⬤ THE EXTERNALIST, A JOURNAL OF PERSPECTIVES

% Larina Warnock, Corvallis OR 97339-2052. E-mail: editor@theexternalist.com. Web site: www.the externalist.com. **Contact:** Larina Warnock, editor. Online magazine, PDF format, 45-60 pgs. "*The Externalist* embraces the balance between craft, entertainment and substance with a focus on subjects that are meaningful in human context. The externalist writer is the writer who is driven by a desire to write well while also writing in such a way that others can understand their perspective (even if they disagree or can't relate), and in this way, keeps an eye on the world outside of self. Externalism values craft and content equally. It recognizes there are still important lessons to be learned, there is still a need to understand and relate to the world around us, and differences are as important as similarities, and vice versa. The externalist believes there are significant human concerns across the globe and here in the United States, and that good literature has the power to create discussion around these concerns. The externalist also believes the multiplicity of perspectives found in today's quickly changing world can (and should) be valued as a means to comprehension—a way to change the things that do not work and give force to the things that do." Bimonthly. Estab. 2007. Circ. approx. 1,000 unique visitors a month.

- *The Externalist* has been nominated for "Best of the Web" and "Best of the Net."

Needs Adventure, ethnic/multicultural, family saga, fantasy, feminist, gay, historical, horror, humor/satire, lesbian, literary, mainstream, military/war, mystery, new age, psychic/supernatural/occult, religious, science fiction, thriller/espionage, and western, but "all fiction must have an externalist focus regardless of genre." Does not want children's or young adult literature, erotica or pornography, or standard romance. "We do not publish any work that is designed to inspire hate or violence against any population. Highly experimental work is strongly discouraged. Slice-of-life fiction that does not deal with a significant social issue will not be accepted." List of upcoming themes available on Web site. Receives 15-20 mss/month. Accepts 2-3 mss/issue; 12-18 mss/year. Ms published 4 months after acceptance. **Publishes 10-15 new writers/year.** Published Edward Rodosek, Miko Yanagisawa, Gary Beck and Bill Tietelbaum. Length: 500-5,000 words. Average length: 3,500 words. Publishes short shorts. Average length of short shorts: 750 words. Also publishes literary essays, literary criticism, poetry. Often comments on/critiques rejected mss.

How to Contact E-mail submissions only. Include estimated word count, brief bio. Responds to queries in 2-3 weeks. Responds to mss in 3-6 weeks. Considers simultaneous submissions, previously published submissions. Guidelines available on Web site.

Payment/Terms Contributor's link on Web page (see Web site for details). Acquires first North American serial rights. Sends galleys to author. Publication is copyrighted. "All work published in *The Externalist* is eligible for Editor's Choice (each issue) and our annual Best of *The Externalist* anthology."

Advice "The fiction that appears in *The Externalist* is well-crafted and speaks subtly about significant social issues in our world today. The more thought-provoking the story, the more likely we will accept it for publication. The editor has a soft spot for well written satire. However, read the work we publish before submitting. Familiarize yourself with externalism. This information is on our Web site free of charge, and even a brief look at the material we publish will improve your chances. Follow the guidelines! We do not open unsolicited attachments, and manuscripts that do not follow our e-mail formatting guidelines stand a good chance of hitting our junk mail folder and not being seen."

☑ ⦿ FAILBETTER.COM

Failbetter, 2022 Grove Avenue, Richmond VA 23221. E-mail: submissions@failbetter.com. Web site: www.failbtetter.com. **Contact:** Thom Didato, publisher. Andrew Day, managing editor. "We are a quarterly online magazine published in the spirit of a traditional literary journal—dedicated to publishing quality fiction, poetry, and artwork. While the Web plays host to hundreds, if not thousands, of genre-related sites (many of which have merit), we are not one of them." Quarterly. Estab. 2000. Circ. 50,000. Member CLMP.

Needs Literary, short stories, novel excerpts. "No genre fiction—romance, fantasy or science fiction." Always would like to see more "character-driven literary fiction where something happens!" Receives 175-200 unsolicited mss/month. Accepts 3-5 mss/issue; 12-20 mss/year. Publishes ms 4-8 months after acceptance. **Publishes 4-6 new writers/year.** Recently published work by Michael Martone, Daniel Alarcon, Jeffrey Lent, Elizabeth Crane, and Michael Kimball. Publishes short shorts. Often comments on rejected mss.

How to Contact Accepts submissions by e-mail. Include the word "submission" in the subject line. Responds in 3-4 months to email submissions; 4-6 month s to snail mail mss. Accepts simultaneous submissions. All issues are available online.

Payment/Terms Acquires one-time rights.

Advice "Read an issue. Read our guidelines! We place a high degree of importance on originality, believing that even in this age of trends it is still possible. We are not looking for what is current or momentary. We are not concerned with length: One good sentence may find a home here, as the bulk of mediocrity will not. Most importantly, know that what you are saying could only come from you. When you are sure of this, please feel free to submit."

☑ THE FAIRFIELD REVIEW

544 Silver Spring Rd., Fairfield CT 06824. (203)256-1960. Fax: (203)256-1970. E-mail: fairfieldreview @hpmd.com. Web site: www.fairfieldreview.org. **Contact:** Edward and Janet Granger-Happ, Pamela Pollak, editors. Electronic magazine. "Our mission is to provide an outlet for poetry, short stories and essays, from both new and established writers and students. We are accessible to the general public."

Needs Literary. Would like to see more stories "rich in lyrical imagery and those that are more humorous." **Publishes 20 new writers/year.** Recently published work by Nan Leslie (Pushcart nominee) and Richard Boughton.

How to Contact Strongly prefers submissions by e-mail. Replies by e-mail only. Right to retain publication in online archive issues, and the right to use in "Best of The Fairfield Review" anthologies. Sample copy online.

Payment/Terms Acquires first rights.

Advice "We encourage students and first-time writers to submit their work. In addition to the submission guidelines found in each issue on our Web site, we recommend reading the essay 'Writing Qualities to Keep in Mind' from our Editors and Authors page on the Web site. Keep to small, directly experienced themes; write crisply using creative, poetic images, avoid the trite expression."

Ⓝ ☑ ◎ FICKLE MUSES, An Online Journal of Myth and Legend

E-mail: fiction@ficklemuses.com. Web site: www.ficklemuses.com. **Contact:** Leslie Fox, fiction editor. Online magazine. Contains illustrations. Includes photographs. "We feature poetry and short stories that re-imagine old myths or reexamine mythic themes contemporarily." Weekly. Estab. 2007.

Needs Literary. "Stories may cross over into any genre as long as the story is based in a myth or legend. Does not want stories that treat myth as a false belief or stereotype (e.g. the myth of beauty). No pure genre (romance, horror, mystery, etc.)." Receives 13-15 mss/month. Accepts 12-24 mss/year. Ms published up to 3 months after acceptance. **Publishes approx 10% new writers/year.** Published Neil de la Flor, Maureen Seaton, Virginia Mohlere and M.M. De Voe. Length: 1,000-5,000 words. Average length: 2,000 words. Publishes short shorts. Average length of short shorts: 500 words. Also publishes literary essays, literary criticism, book reviews, poetry. Send review query to fiction@ficklemuses.com. Rarely comments on/critiques rejected mss.

How to Contact Send complete ms with cover letter. Accepts submissions by e-mail only. Include estimated word count and "a brief description of the myth or legend your story is based on if it is not standard knowledge." Responds to queries in 3 weeks. Responds to mss in 3 weeks. Considers simultaneous submissions, previously published submissions. Guidelines available on Web site.

Payment/Terms Acquires one-time rights. Publication is not copyrighted.

Advice "Originality. An innovative look at an old story. I'm looking to be swept away. Get a feel for our Web site."

5-TROPE

E-mail: editor.5trope@gmail.com. Web site: www.webdelsol.com/5_trope. **Contact:** Gunnar Benediktsson, editor. Online literary journal. "We aim to publish the new and original in fiction, poetry and new media. We are seeking writers with a playful seriousness about language and form." Quarterly. Estab. 1999. Circ. 5,000.

Needs Avant-garde prose, experimental, literary. "No religious, horror, fantasy, espionage." Receives 75 unsolicited mss/month. Accepts 6 mss/issue; 18 mss/year. Publishes ms 6-12 months after acceptance. **Publishes 5 new writers/year.** Recently published work by Cole Swensen, Carol Novack, Christopher Kennedy, Mike Topp, Norman Lock, Jeff Johnson, Peter Markus, Mandee Wright, and Jane Unrue. Length: 25-5,000 words; average length: 1,000 words. Publishes short shorts. Also publishes poetry. Sometimes comments on rejected mss.

How to Contact Accepts submissions by e-mail. Send complete mss electronically. Sample copy online.

Payment/Terms Acquires first rights. Sends galleys to author.

Advice "Before submitting, please visit our site, read an issue, and consult our guidelines for submission. Include your story within the body of an e-mail, not as an attachment. Include a descriptive subject line to get around spam filters. Experimental work should have a clarity about it, and should never be sentimental. Our stories are about the moment of rupture, not the moment of closure."

N $◻ FLASH ME MAGAZINE, THE ONLINE MAGAZINE EXCLUSIVELY FOR FLASH FICTION STORIES

Winged Halo Productions, Belleville IL. E-mail: info@wingedhalo.com. Web site: www.wingedhalo.com. **Contact:** Jennifer Dawson, Editor-in-Chief. Online magazine. "*Flash Me Magazine* is a quarterly magazine, accepting all genres of fiction, as long as the story is under 1,000 words. There are no restrictions on content, though we will not publish stories with excess gore, violence, profanity or sex." Quarterly. Estab. 2003. Circ. 1,000 visitors per month. Member Small Press Co-op.

Needs Fantasy (space fantasy, sword and sorcery), historical, horror (dark fantasy, futuristic, psychological, supernatural), humor/satire, literary, mainstream, military/war, mystery, romance (contemporary, futuristic/time travel, gothic, historical, regency, suspense), science fiction (soft/sociological). Receives 100 mss/month. Accepts 6-12 mss/issue; 24-48 mss/year. Ms published 3 months or less after acceptance. **Publishes 20 new writers/year.** Published Debbie Mumford, Bruce Holland Rogers, Angie Smibert and Amy Herlihy. Publishes short shorts only. Average length of short shorts: 750-max 1,000 words. Also publishes book reviews. Send review queries to reviews@wingedhalo.com. Always comments on/critiques rejected mss.

How to Contact Send complete ms with cover letter. Accepts submissions by e-mail. Include brief bio. Responds to queries in 3 months. Responds to mss in 3 months. Considers previously published submissions, multiple submissions. Guidelines available on Web site.

Payment/Terms Writers receive $5-20. Pays on publication. Acquires electronic rights. Sends galleys to author. Publication is copyrighted.

Advice "Anything well-written stands a chance, and anything with a good plot, as well. To really catch our eye though, a story has be unique and memorable. Read our guidelines carefully before submitting work."

$◻ FLASHQUAKE, An Online Journal of Flash Literature

River Road Studios, P.O. Box 2154, Albany NY 12220-0154. E-mail: dorton@flashquake.org. Web site: www.flashquake.org. **Contact:** Debi Orton, publisher. E-zine specializing in flash literature. "*flashquake* is a quarterly online literary journal featuring flash literature—flash fiction, flash nonfiction, and short poetry. Send us works that will leave readers thinking. We define flash as works less than 1,000 words, shorter pieces will impress us. Poetry can be up to 35 lines. We want the best story you can tell us in the fewest words you need to do it! Move us, engage us, give us a complete story with characters, plot, and a beginning, middle and end."

Needs Ethnic/multicultural (general), experimental, literary, flash literature of all types: fiction, memoir, creative nonfiction, poetry and artwork. "Not interested in romance, graphic sex, graphic violence, gore, vampires, or work of a religious nature." Receives 100-150 unsolicited mss/month. Accepts 30 mss/issue. Publishes ms 1-3 months after acceptance. Publishes only short shorts. Comments on rejected mss.

How to Contact Accepts submissions by e-mail (submit@flashquake.org) only. No land mail. Include brief bio, mailing address and e-mail address. Guidelines and submission instructions on Web site.

Payment/Terms Pays $5-25 plus CD copy of site. Pays within two weeks of publication for electronic rights. Sponsors occasional awards/contests.

Advice "Read our submission guidelines before submitting. Proofread your work thoroughly! We will instantly reject your work for spelling and grammar errors. Save your document as plain text and paste it into an e-mail message. We do not open attachments. We like experimental work, but that is not a license to forget narrative clarity, plot, character development or reader satisfaction."

◻ FLUENT ASCENSION

Fierce Concepts, P.O. Box 6407, Glendale AZ 85312. E-mail: submissions@fluentascension.com. Web site: www.fluentascension.com. **Contact:** Warren Norgaard, editor. Online magazine. Quarterly. Estab. 2003.

Needs Comics/graphic novels, erotica, ethnic/multicultural, experimental, gay, humor/satire, lesbian, literary, translations. Receives 6-10 unsolicited mss/month. Accepts 1-3 mss/issue. Publishes short shorts. Also publishes literary essays, literary criticism, poetry. Sometimes comments on rejected mss.

How to Contact Send complete ms. Accepts submissions by e-mail. Include estimated word count, brief bio and list of publications. Send SASE (or IRC) for return of ms or send disposable copy of ms and #10 SASE for reply only. Responds in 4-8 weeks to queries; 4-8 weeks to mss. Accepts simultaneous, multiple submissions. Sample copy online. Writer's guidelines online.

Payment/Terms Acquires electronic rights. Sponsors awards/contests.

N ☑ FRINGE MAGAZINE, THE NOUN THAT VERBS YOUR WORLD

8 Willow Ave, #2, Somerville MA 02144. (617)413-8674. E-mail: fringeeditors@gmail.com. Web site: www.fringemagazine.org. **Contact:** Katie Spencer, editor. Online magazine/E-zine specializing in literature. Contains illustrations and photographs. *"Fringe Magazine* is dedicated to political and experimental literature, and was founded to fight the homogenization of culture and the loss of revolutionary writing at the high literary and popular levels. Our audience is diverse, garnering more than 16,000 page views each month from more than 40 countries. *Fringe* is a 501(c)3 public charity organized under the laws of Delaware whose nonprofit purpose is to diversify the existing literary aesthetic, publish genres that other magazines do not print, and to give crucial early publication credits to young writers, particularly to writers of color and women writers. In each issue, *Fringe* features one artist per genre."* Bimonthly. Estab. 2006. Circ. over 16,000 page views per month. Member CLMP.

Needs Ethnic/multicultural (general), experimental, feminist, gay, humor/satire, lesbian, literary, mainstream. Special interest in experimental literature, cross-genre work, hypertext and flash-based literature. Does not want to see erotica or pornography, unless it has a higher literary purpose. "We enjoy stories that span cultures, but have recently received a lot of work in the genre of 'I went on vacation and got an exotic lover.' In general, we do not like work that is sentimental." The third anniversary issue, February 2009, will be themed. Submissions for this issue will open August 1, 2008 and close December 15, 2008. The theme will be announced at the end of July, 2008. List of upcoming themes available on Web site. Receives 30-60 mss/month. Accepts 1-2 mss/issue; 9-12 mss/year. Ms published 6-8 weeks after acceptance. **Publishes 5 new writers/year.** Published Sarah Sweeney, Amy Clark, Chris Siteman, Jasmin Saigal, TJ Dietderich, Kirstin Chen, and Chip Cheek. Length: 100-15,000 words. Average length: 3,000 words. Publishes short shorts. Average length of short shorts: 450 words. Also publishes literary essays, literary criticism, book reviews, poetry. Send review copies to Sarah Miles % the magazine address. "Reviews will not appear in the journal itself, but do appear on our blog." Often comments on/critiques rejected mss.

How to Contact Send complete ms with cover letter. Accepts submissions by e-mail. Include estimated word count, brief bio. Responds to queries in 3 weeks. Responds to mss in 3 months. Considers simultaneous submissions, multiple submissions. Guidelines available on Web site.

Payment/Terms Acquires first rights, electronic rights, archive rights.

Advice "We really enjoy fiction that takes risks, that dares to be off-beat, that experiments with form or content. Often, when we are torn between two pieces, we end up taking the one that seems 'more fringey,' or the one that engages with core political issues in the most complex and nuanced way. We are suckers for fiction that explores feminist themes in new, non-cliché, non-preachy manners. We love the postmodern. We drool over work that successfully engages with myth. Be careful with politics—they can add a lot to a work, but can also make it come across as preachy and flat. Do not summarize your story in your cover letter—it deprives us of whatever wonderful surprises your story has in store."

☑ FULLOSIA PRESS

Rockaway Park Philosophical Society, P.O. Box 280, Ronkonkoma NY 11779. E-mail: deanofrpps@aol.com. Web site: rpps_fullosia_press.tripod.com. **Contact:** J.D. Collins, editor; Geoff Jackson, assoc. editor. E-zine. "Part-time publisher of fiction and nonfiction. Our publication is right wing and conservative, leaning to views of Patrick Buchanan but amenable to the opposition's point of view. We promote an independent America. We are anti-global, anti-UN. Collects unusual news from former British or American provinces. Fiction interests include military, police, private detective, courthouse stories." Monthly. Estab. 1999. Circ. 175.

Needs Historical (American), military/war, mystery/suspense, thriller/espionage. Christmas, St. Patrick's Day, Fourth of July. Publishes ms 1 week after acceptance. **Publishes 10 new writers/ year.** Recently published work by Geoff Jasckson, 'Awesome' Dave Lawrence, Robert E.L. Nesbitt, MD, John Grey, Dr. Kelly White, James Davies, Andy Martin, Michael Levy, and Peter Vetrano's class. Length: 500-2,000 words; average length: 750 words. Publishes short shorts. Also publishes literary essays. Always comments on rejected mss.

How to Contact Query with or without published clips. Accepts submissions by e-mail. Include brief bio and list of publications. Mail submissions must be on 3¼ floppy disk. Responds in 1 month to mss. Please avoid mass mailings. Sample copy online. Reviews fiction.
Payment/Terms Acquires electronic rights.
Advice "Make your point quickly. If you haven't done so, after five pages, everybody hates you and your characters."

☐ THE FURNACE REVIEW

E-mail: editor@thefurnacereview.com. Web site: www.thefurnacereview.com. **Contact:** Ciara La-Velle, editor. "We reach out to a young, well-educated audience, bringing them new, unique, fresh work they won't find elsewhere." Quarterly. Estab. 2004.
Needs Erotica, experimental, feminist, gay, historical, humor/satire, lesbian, literary, mainstream, military/war. Does not want children's, science fiction, or religious submissions. Receives 50-60 unsolicited mss/month. Accepts 1-3 mss/issue; 5-8 mss/year. **Publishes 5-8 new writers/year.** Recently published work by Amy Greene, Dominic Preziosi, and Sandra Soson. Length: 7,000 words; average length: 4,000 words. Publishes short shorts. Also publishes poetry.
How to Contact Send complete ms. Accepts submissions by e-mail only. Responds in 4 month to queries. Accepts simultaneous submissions.
Payment/Terms Acquires first North American serial rights.

☑ THE GREEN HILLS LITERARY LANTERN

Published by Truman State University, Division of Language & Literature, Kirksville MO 63501. (660)785-4487. E-mail: adavis@truman.edu. Web site: http://ll.truman.edu/ghllweb. **Contact:** Fiction editor. "The mission of *GHLL* is to provide a literary market for quality fiction writers, both established and beginners, and to provide quality literature for readers from diverse backgrounds. We also see ourselves as a cultural resource for North Missouri. Our publication works to publish the highest quality fiction—dense, layered, subtle—and, at the same time, fiction which grabs the ordinary reader. We tend to publish traditional short stories, but we are open to experimental forms." Annual. Estab. 1990. The *GHLL* is now an online, open-access journal.
Needs Ethnic/multicultural, experimental, feminist, humor/satire, literary, mainstream, regional. "Our main requirement is literary merit. Wants more quality fiction about rural culture. No adventure, crime, erotica, horror, inspirational, mystery/suspense, romance." Receives 40 unsolicited mss/month. Accepts 15-17 mss/issue. Publishes ms 6-12 months after acceptance. **Publishes 0-3 new writers/year.** Recently published work by Karl Harshbarger, Mark Jacobs, J. Morris, Gary Fincke, Dennis Vannatta. Length: 7,000 words; average length: 3,000 words. Publishes short shorts. Also publishes poetry. Sometimes comments on rejected mss.
How to Contact SASE for return of ms. Responds in 4 months to mss. Accepts simultaneous, multiple submissions. Electronic submissions in .doc or .txt format also acceptable from writers living outside North America, but our manuscript readers still prefer hardcopy. E-mail attachment to adavis@truman.edu.
Payment/Terms No payment. Acquires one-time rights.
Advice "We look for strong character development, substantive plot and theme, visual and forceful language within a multilayered story. Make sure your work has the flavor of life, a sense of reality. A good story, well crafted, will eventually get published. Find the right market for it, and above all, don't give up."

Ⓝ $☑ IDEOMANCER

Web site: www.ideomancer.com. **Contact:** Marsha Sisolak, Publisher. Online magazine. Contains illustrations. "Ideomancer publishes science fiction, fantasy, horror, slipstream and poetry. We look for stories that explore the edges of ideas, stories that subvert, refute and push the limits. We want unique pieces from authors willing to explore non-traditional narratives, take chances with tone, structure and execution, and take risks. Our aim is to showcase speculative stories in all categores which provoke, reflect and marry ideas to resonance and character." Quarterly. Estab. 2001.
Needs Fantasy (mythic, urban, historical, low), horror (dark fantasy, futuristic, psychological, supernatural), science fiction (hard science/technological, soft/sociological). Special interests: slipstream and poetry. Does not want fiction without a speculative element. Receives 200 mss/month. Accepts 3-4 mss/issue; 9-12 mss/year. Does not read February, May, August and November. Ms published

within 12 months of acceptance. **Publishes 1-2 new writers/year.** Published Sarah Monette, Ruth Nestvold, Astrid Atkinson, Becca de la Rosa, January Mortimer, Yoon Ha Lee and David Kopaska-Merkel. Length: 7,000 words (max). Average length: 4,000 words. Publishes short shorts. Average length of short shorts: 1,000 words. Also publishes book reviews, poetry. Requests only to have a novel or collection reviewed should be sent to the publisher. Often comments on/critiques rejected mss.

How to Contact Send complete ms with cover letter. Accepts submissions by e-mail only. Include estimated word count. Responds to queries in 3 weeks. Responds to mss in 6 weeks. Guidelines available on Web site.

Payment/Terms Writers receive 3¢ per word, max of $40. Pays on acceptance. Acquires electronic rights. Publication is copyrighted.

Advice "Beyond the basics of formatting the fiction as per our guidelines, good writing and intriguing characters and plot, where the writer brings depth to the tale, make a manuscript stand out. We receive a number of submissions which showcase good writing, but lack the details that make them spring to life for us. Visit our Web site and read some of our fiction to see if we're a good fit. Read our submission guidelines carefully and use rtf formatting as requested. We're far more interested in your story than your cover letter, so spend your time polishing that."

◪ ◎ KENNESAW REVIEW

Kennesaw State University, Dept. of English, Building 27, 1000 Chastain Rd., Kennesaw GA 30144-5591. (770)423-6346. Web site: www.kennesawreview.org. **Contact:** Robert W. Hill, editor. Online literary journal. "Just good literary fiction, all themes, for an eclectic audience." Ongoing updates to Web site. Estab. 1987.

Needs Short stories and flash fiction. "No formulaic genre fiction." Receives 25 unsolicited mss/month. Accepts 2-4 mss/issue. Publishes ms 2-4 months after acceptance. Recently published work by Ellen Lundquist, Michael Cadnum, and Robert Philips.

How to Contact Send complete ms. Include previous publications. Responds in 2 months to mss. Accepts simultaneous, multiple submissions. Writer's guidelines online.

Payment/Terms Acquires first rights.

Advice "Use the language well and tell an interesting story."

$◪ THE KING'S ENGLISH

(503)709-1917. E-mail: thekingsenglish@comcast.net. Web site: www.thekingsenglish.org. **Contact:** Benjamin Chambers, editor. "We're an online publication only. Our focus is long literary fiction, especially if it's stuffed with strong imagery and gorgeous prose. Novellas 11,000-48,000 words (150 double-spaced pages). In very rare instances, we'll include detective fiction or sci-fi/fantasy, as long as there's a strong element of suspense, the setting is unusual, and the writing first-rate." Estab. 2003.

● Three-time winner of the Million Writers Award for Best Publisher of Novella-Length Fiction.

Needs Experimental, historical, literary, mainstream, mystery/suspense (private eye/hardboiled), thriller/espionage, translations. No horror, religious or heartwarming tales of redemption. Accepts 3 mss/issue; 12 mss/year. Also publishes literary essays, poetry.

How to Contact Send complete ms. Electronic submissions only. Responds in 2 weeks to queries; 1-2 months to mss. Accepts simultaneous, multiple submissions. Writer's guidelines by e-mail or on the Web site.

Payment/Terms Pays $20/story or essay, $10/poem. Acquires one-time, non-exclusive rights to anthologize and archive on the Web site.

Advice "Surprise us. With language, mostly, though concept and execution can do just as well or better. If your first page makes us long for a rainy day and a cozy armchair in which to curl up with your manuscript, you'll get our attention. Make sure your story deserves to be a long one. Write what you'd like to read. Save yourself some heartbreak and read our guidelines before submitting."

$● ◪ LONE STAR STORIES, SPECULATIVE FICTION AND POETRY

E-mail: submissions@erictmarin.com. Web site: www.lonestarstories.com. **Contact:** Eric T. Marin, editor. Online magazine. Contains illustrations and photographs. "*Lone Star Stories* publishes quality speculative fiction and poetry." Bimonthly. Estab. 2004.

Needs Speculative fiction (fantasy, dark fantasy, science fiction, and interstitial). Receives 100+

mss/month. Accepts 3 mss/issue; 18 mss/year. Manuscript published 2 months after acceptance. Average length: 5,000 words. Publishes short shorts. Average length of short shorts: 500 words. Also publishes poetry.

How to Contact Send complete ms with cover letter. Accepts submissions by e-mail. Include estimated word count. Responds to queries in 1 weeks. Responds to mss in 1 week. Considers simultaneous submissions, previously published submissions. Guidelines available on Web site.

Payment/Terms Writers receive $20 per story; $10 per poem. **Pays on acceptance.** Publication is copyrighted.

Advice "The standard advice applies: Read the current issue of *Lone Star Stories* to get a feel for what is likely to be published."

ℕ 🖉 🖨 MAD HATTERS' REVIEW: Edgy and Enlightened Art, Literature and Music in the Age of Dementia

E-mail: madhattersreview@gmail.com. Web site: www.madhattersreview.com. **Contact:** Carol Novack, Publisher/Editor-in-Chief. Online magazine. *"Mad Hatters' Review* is a socially aware/progressive, multi-media/literary journal, featuring original works of fiction, flash fiction, poetry, creative/literary nonfiction, whatnots, drama, collages, audios, book reviews, columns, contests and more. We also feature cartoons and comic strips, including the 'The Perils of Patriotic Polly' and 'Coconuts.' All of our contributing authors' writings are accompanied by original art created specifically for the material, as well as original, custom made music or recitations by authors. We are proud of our spectacular featured artists' galleries, as well as our mini-movies, parodies, and featured foreign sections. Our staff musicians and visual artists are wonderful. Webdelsol took us on board (the first and only multimedia) in 2006 and hosts our site." Semiannual. Estab. 2005. Member CLMP.

- Mad Hatters' Review has received an Artistry Award from Sixty Plus Design, 2006-7 Web Design Award from Invision Graphics, and a Gold Medal Award of Excellence for 2006-7 from ArtSpace2000.com.

Needs Experimental works, mixed media, translations, humor, literary prose and poetry that demonstrate a unique, unconventional, intellectual, sophisticated and emotional perspective on the world and a delight in craft. Does not want mainstream prose/story that doesn't exhibit a love of language and a sophisticated mentality. No religious or inspirational writings, confessionals, boys sowing oats, sentimental and coming of age stories. Accepts 3-6 mss/issue. Submissions are open briefly for each issue: check guidelines periodically for dates or subscribe free to newsletter. Ms published 5-6 months after acceptance. **Publishes 1 new writer/year.** Published Alastair Gray, Kass Fleisher, Vanessa Place, Elizabeth Block, Laura Marney, Vernon Frazer, Raymond Federman, Sam Witt, Rochelle Ratner, Michael Neff, David Meltzer, Stephanie Strickland, and Juan Jose Millas (translated from the Spanish). Length: 3,000 words (max). Average length of fictions: 1,500-2,500 words. Publishes short shorts. Average length of short shorts: 500-800 words. Also publishes literary essays, literary criticism, book reviews, and interviews. Send review queries to madhattersreview@gmail.com. Rarely comments on/critiques rejected mss.

How to Contact Accepts submissions by e-mail only. Include estimated word count, brief bio. Now has a submission form. Responds to queries in 1 week. Responds to mss in 1-6 weeks. Considers simultaneous submissions. Guidelines available on Web site.

Payment/Terms Acquires first rights. Sends galleys to author. "We have a new contest every issue where writers are asked to write a short short or poem inspired by a specific work of art." Entry fee is $6, prize is $50 and publication. See Web site for details.

Advice "Imagination, skill with and appreciation of language, inventiveness, rhythm, sense of humor/irony/satire and compelling style make a manuscript stand out. Read the magazine. Don't follow the rules you've been taught in the usual MFA program or workshop."

TIMOTHY MCSWEENEY'S INTERNET TENDENCY

826 Valencia Street, San Francisco CA 94110. E-mail: websubmissions@mcsweeneys.net. Web site: www.mcsweeneys.net. **Contact:** Dave Eggers, John Warner, Christopher Monks, editors. Online literary journal. *"Timothy McSweeney's Internet Tendency* is an offshoot of *Timothy McSweeney's Quarterly Concern,* a journal created by nervous people in relative obscurity, and published four times a year." Daily.

Needs Literate humor, sestinas. Sometimes comments on rejected mss.

How to Contact Accepts submissions by e-mail. "For submissions to the Web site, paste the entire piece into the body of an e-mail. Absolute length limit of 1,500 words, with a preference for pieces significantly shorter (700-1,000 words)." Sample copy online. Writer's guidelines online.

Advice "Do not submit your work to both the print submissions address and the Web submissions address, as seemingly hundreds of writers have been doing lately. If you submit a piece of writing intended for the magazine to the Web submissions address, you will confuse us, and if you confuse us, we will accidentally delete your work without reading it, and then we will laugh and never give it another moment's thought, and sleep the carefree sleep of young children. This is very, very serious."

MICROHORROR, SHORT STORIES. ENDLESS NIGHTMARES

5300 Merceron Ave, Baltimore, MD 21207. (443)670-6133. E-mail: microhorror@gmail.com. Web site: www.microhorror.com. **Contact:** Nathan Rosen, editor. Online magazine. "*MicroHorror* is not a magazine in the traditional sense. Instead, it is a free online archive for short-short horror fiction. With a strict limit of 666 words, *MicroHorror* showcases the power of the short-short horror to convey great emotional impact in only a few brief paragraphs." Estab. 2006.

• Golden Horror Award from Horrorfind.com in 2007.

Needs Horror (dark fantasy, futuristic, psychological, supernatural), young adult/teen (horror). Receives 25 mss/month. Accepts 300 mss/year. Ms published 1-3 days after acceptance. **Publishes 50 new writers/year.** Published D.W. Green, Michael A. Kechula, Oonah V. Joslin, Kevin Sweeney, James Lacey, Jeff Ryan, Sean Ryan, R. K. Gemienhardt, K. A. Patterson, Andrew JM Stone, Rod Drake, Yuichi Mendez, and Santiage Eximeno. Length: 666 words (max). Publishes short shorts. Average length of short shorts: 500 words. Often comments on/critiques rejected mss.

How to Contact Send complete ms with cover letter. Accepts submissions by e-mail. Include estimated word count, brief bio. Responds to queries in 1 week. Responds to mss in 1 week. Send either SASE (or IRC) for return of ms or disposable copy of ms and #10 SASE for reply only. Considers simultaneous submissions, previously published submissions, multiple submissions. Guidelines available on Web site.

Payment/Terms Acquires one-time rights. Publication is copyrighted.

Advice "This is horror. Scare me. Make shivers run down my spine. Make me afraid to look behind the shower curtain. Pack the biggest punch you can into a few well chosen sentences. Read all the horror you can, and figure out what makes it scary. Trim away all the excess trappings until you get right to the core, and use what you find."

MIDNIGHT TIMES

1731 Shadwell Dr., Barnhart MO 63012. E-mail: editor@midnighttimes.com. Web site: www.midnighttimes.com. **Contact:** Jay Manning, editor. *Midnight Times* is an online literary magazine dedicated to publishing quality poetry and fiction by both previously unpublished as well as published writers. The primary theme is darkness, but this doesn't necessarily mean evil. There can be a light at the end of the tunnel. Quarterly. Estab. 2003.

Needs Fantasy (sword and sorcery), horror (dark fantasy, futuristic, psychological, supernatural), literary, mainstream, psychic/supernatural/occult, science fiction, vampires. No pornography. Accepts 5-9 mss/issue; 20-36 mss/year. Publishes ms 3-9 months after acceptance. **Publishes many new writers/year.** Length: 500-10,000 words; average length: 4,000 words. Publishes short shorts. Also publishes poetry. Sometimes comments on rejected mss.

How to Contact Send complete ms. Prefers submissions by e-mail. Send SASE (or IRC) for return of the ms, or send disposable copy of the ms and #10 SASE for reply only. Responds in 2 weeks to queries; 1 month to mss. Accepts simultaneous, multiple submissions and reprints. Writer's guidelines for SASE or by e-mail or on Web site.

Payment/Terms No payment. Acquires one-time, electronic rights.

Advice "Please read the submission guidelines on MidnightTimes.com before submitting your work!"

MIDWAY JOURNAL

P.O. Box 14499, St. Paul MN 55114. (612)825-4811. E-mail: editors@midwayjournal.com. Web site: www.midwayjournal.com. **Contact:** Raph Pennel, fiction editor. Online magazine. "*Midway Journal* accepts submissions of aesthetically ambitious work that occupies the realms between the experimental and trasitional. Midway, or its position is midway, is a place of boundary crossing, where work complicates and even questions the boundaires between forms, binaries and genres." Bi-monthly. Estab. 2006. Member CLMP.

Needs Comics/graphic novels, ethnic/multicultural (general), experimental, feminist, gay, historical (general), humor/satire, lesbian, literary, science fiction (soft/sociological), translations. Does not want new age, young adult/teen, children/juvennile or erotica. "Writers should visit current and back issues to see what we have or have not published in the past." Receives 30 mss/month. Accepts 3-4 mss/issue; 18-24 mss/year. Does not read June 1-Nov 30. Ms published 4-12 months after acceptance. Agented fiction 1%. **Publishes 2-5 new writers/year.** Published Harrison Bas Wein, Frank Miller, Richard Hollinger and Noelle Sickels. Length: 250-25,000 words. Average length: 3,000 words. Publishes short shorts. Average length of short shorts: 600 words. Also publishes literary essays, poetry. Sometimes comments on/critiques rejected mss.

How to Contact Send complete ms with cover letter. Accepts international submissions by e-mail. Include estimated word count, brief bio, list of publications. Responds to queries in 1-2 weeks. Responds to mss in 3-6 months. Send either SASE (or IRC) for return of ms or disposable copy of ms and #10 SASE for reply only. Considers simultaneous submissions, previously published submissions. Guidelines available on Web site.

Payment/Terms Acquires one-time rights. Publication is copyrighted.

Advice "An interesting story with engaging writing, both in terms of style and voice, make a manuscript stand out. Round characters are a must. Writers who take chances either with content or with form grab an editor's immediate attention. Spend time with the words on the page. Spend time with the language. The language and voice are not vehicles, they, too, are tools."

Ⓝ $◻ ◎ MINDFLIGHTS

Double-Edged Publishing, 9618 Misty Brook Cove, Cordova TX 38016. (901)213-3768. E-mail: editor @mindflights.com. Web site: http://www.Mindflights.com. **Contact:** Selena Thomason, Managing Editor. Magazine/E-zine. "Publishes science fiction, fantasy, and all genres of speculative fiction and poetry. We want work that is grounded in a Christian or Christian-friendly worldview, without being preachy. Please see our vision and guidelines page for details. *MindFlights* is the merging of two established magazines: *The Sword Review* and *Dragons, Knights, & Angels.*" Monthly ezine, quarterly print edition. Estab. 2008.

Needs Fantasy (space fantasy, sword and sorcery), religious (fantasy), science fiction (hard science/technological, soft/sociological), special interests: speculative fiction and poetry with Christian themes. Does not want to see work "that would be offensive to a Christian audience. Also, we are a family-friendly market and thus do not want to see explicit sex, illicit drug use, gratuitous violence or excessive gore." Receives 30 mss/month. Accepts 6 mss/issue; 72 mss/year. Ms published 2 months after acceptance. **Publishes 6-12 new writers/year.** Length: 500-5,000 words. Average length: 3,000 words. Publishes short shorts. Average length of short shorts: 700 words. Also publishes poetry. Always comments on/critiques rejected mss.

How to Contact Send complete ms via online form. Include estimated word count. Responds to queries in 2 weeks. Responds to mss in 4 weeks. Considers previously published submissions, multiple submissions. Guidelines available on Web site.

Payment/Terms Writers receive ½¢/word, $5 min and $25 max, 1 contributor's copy if selected for print edition. Additional copies $6.49. Pays on acceptance. Acquires first rights, first North American serial rights, one-time rights, electronic rights. Sends galleys to author. Publication is copyrighted. Occasional contests. "Details and entry process would be on our Web site when contest is announced."

Advice "We look for speculative fiction that entertains, enlightens, and uplifts. We also prefer work that is family-friendly and grounded in a Christian world-view. We especially seek work that successfully melds the speculative with Christian themes. Please read our guidelines and proof your work carefully. (It is helpful to also have someone else proof your work as writers often miss typos in their own work.) Please do not submit work that is clearly inappropriate for our magazine and/or is full of typos, misspellings, and grammar errors."

Ⓝ $◻ ◎ MOUTH FULL OF BULLETS

P.O. Box 138, Mathews LA 70375. (985)532-3186. E-mail: editor@mouthfullofbullets.com. Web site: www.mouthfullofbullets.com. **Contact:** BJ Bourg, Owner & Acquisitions Editor. Online magazine. "I'm dedicated to offering writers a place where they can showcase their writing talent to as wide an audience as possible. To that end, I provide both a print and an online edition of the magazine. All original works appear exclusively in the print publication for a three-month period. After the exclusivity period has lapsed, the original works are then archived in the online edition, offering exposure to a much larger reading audience. In order to reach as many readers as possible, I don't require that readers subscribe or sign up in order to read the online content, and I make it available for free. *Mouth of Bullets* was started by a mystery writer to help other mystery writers, and I'm dedicated to doing everything I can to promote their work—at no cost to them. I strive to publish the best short stories, flash fiction and poems from some of the best new and vetren voices in the business." Quarterly. Estab. 2006. Circ. 1,000 + hits per month.

- A story published in MFOB was a finalist in the 2007 Deffinger Awards

Needs Children's/juvenile (mystery), mystery (amateur sleuth, cozy, police procedural, private eye/hard-boiled), religious (mystery/suspense), romance (suspense), young adult/teen (mystery/suspense). Does not want erotica or anything that does not contain a crime. Receives 20-50 mss/month. Accepts 20-25 mss/issue; 85-90 mss/year. Does not read January, April, July and October. Ms published 6 months after acceptance. **Publishes 12 new writers/year.** Published Jillian Berg, John M. Floyd, Herschel Cozine, SF Johnston, Stephen D. Rogers, Anita Page and Kimberly Brown. Length: 1,000-3,000 words. Average length: 2,000 words. Publishes short shorts. Average length of short shorts: 700 words. Also publishes book reviews, poetry. Send review copies to Kevin R. Tipple (kevin_tipple@att.net). Rarely comments on/critiques rejected mss.

How to Contact Send complete ms with cover letter. Accepts submissions by e-mail. Include estimated word count, brief bio, list of publications, mailing address, email address. Responds to mss in 1-3 months. Considers previously published submissions. Guidelines available on Web site. Sample copy for $6 (US funds only, check or money order).

Payment/Terms Writers receive $3-20. Pays on publication. Acquires first North American serial rights and anthology rights. Publication is copyrighted.

Advice "I want stories that feature believable characters who speak naturally, realistic situations that bleed conflict and surprise endings that stay with me long after I reach the final period. I love to be surprised. I hate it when I can figure out the ending halfway through a story. Now, while I love to be surprised, the twist at the end has to be plausible. Read and adhere to submission guidelines. I'm surprised by the number of writers who fail to follow this elementary rule of writing. Check your work for errors or omissions. Everyone's entitled to a few mistakes, but too many detract from the story. Be courteous. Above all else, surprise me!"

N $⊕ ◑ ◎ NEW CERES

Twelfth Planet Press, P.O. Box 3027, Yokine, Perth, Australia 6060. E-mail: ceressubs@gmail.com. Web site: www.newceres.com. **Contact:** Alisa Krasnostein, Editor. Online magazine. Contains illustrations. "*New Ceres* features fiction, articles and artwork inspired by the mysterious and elegant planet of New Ceres. During the war that left Earth uninhabitable, refugees from the doomed planet fled to the outer colonies. Many of them found their way to New Ceres, a planet that embraced the Age of Enlightenment almost two hundred years ago, and has not yet let go. The water may be green and spaceships may be landing on a regular basis, but New Ceres is a planet firmly entrenched in Eighteenth Century culture. Offworld technology is strictly forbidden to anyone outside the government, and powdered wigs are in fashion." Semiannual. Estab. 2006.

Needs Ethnic/multicultural, experimental, family saga, fantasy (space fantasy, sword and sorcery), feminist, gay, horror (dark fantasy, futuristic, psychological), humor/satire, lesbian, literary, mainstream, mystery, psychic/supernatural/occult, romance (futuristic/time travel, regency), science fiction (hard science/technological, soft/sociological), thriller/espionage, young adult/teen. Receives 5-10 mss/month. Accepts 4 mss/issue; 8 mss/year. Reads only during set readings periods, dates on Web site. Ms published 3-6 months after acceptance. **Publishes one or two new writers/year.** Published Stephen Dedman, Lucy Sussex, Jay Lake, Cat Sparks, and Alexandra Pierce. Length: 2,000-8000 words. Average length: 3,000-5,000 words. Rarely comments on/critiques rejected mss.

How to Contact Send complete ms with cover letter. Accepts submissions by e-mail only. Include estimated word count. Responds to queries in 1 weeks. Responds to mss in 2-4 weeks. Considers multiple submissions. Guidelines available on Web site.

Payment/Terms Writers receive 5¢ per word. Additional copies AUS $5. Pays on publication. Acquires first rights, electronic rights. Sends galleys to author. Publication is copyrighted.

Advice "Fiction must fit within the conceit of the shared world as clearly established on the Web site. High standard of quality fiction is sought. Read the Web site fully. Take notice of the world as set up in Issue 1. Subscribe to other issues to see where writers have taken various background elements and characters.''

NEW WORKS REVIEW

520 10th Street, Tell, City IN 47586. (812)547-6787. E-mail: brettalansanders@gmail.com. Web site: www.new-works.org. **Contact:** Brett Alan Sanders, managing editor. Online magazine. Contains illustrations and photographs. ''Our philosphy is to publish outstanding work suitable for all readers. All genres are published.'' Quarterly. Estab. 1998.

Needs Adventure, family saga, humor/satire, literary, mainstream, military/war, peace studies, mystery/suspense (amateur sleuth, cozy, police procedural, private eye/hard-boiled), thriller/espionage, translations, western. Does not want porn, anti-religious, erotica, or use of obscenities. Receives 30 mss/month. Accepts 10 mss/issue; 40 mss/year. Manuscript published 3 months after acceptance. **Publishes 5-10 new writers/year.** Published Irving Greenfield, Lynn Strongin, Tom Sheehan, Michael Corrigan, Brett Alan Sanders and Diane Sawyer. Average length: 3,000 words. Also publishes literary essays, literary criticism, poetry, and book reviews. Often comments on/ critiques rejected manuscripts.

How to Contact Send complete ms with cover letter. E-mail submissions preferred. Include estimated word count. Responds to queries in 1 week. Does not consider simultaneous submissions, previously published submissions, multiple submissions. Guidelines available on Web site.

Payment/Terms All rights retained by author. Sends galleys to author. Publication is copyrighted.

Advice ''Read established writers, edit and re-edit your stories, follow the guidelines.''

NUVEIN ONLINE

(626)401-3466. Fax: (626)401-3460. E-mail: editor@nuvein.com. Web site: www.nuvein.com. **Contact:** Enrique Diaz, editor. Online magazine published by the Nuvein Foundation for Literature and the Arts. ''We are open to short fiction, poetry and essays that explore topics divergent from the mainstream. Our vision is to provide a forum for new and experienced voices rarely heard in our global community.''

• *Nuvein Online* has received the Visionary Media Award.

Needs Fiction, poetry, plays, movie/theatre reviews/articles and art. Wants more ''experimental fiction, ethnic works, and pieces dealing with the exploration of gender and sexuality, as well as works dealing with the clash of cultures.'' **Publishes 20 new writers/year.** Recently published work by J. Knight, Paul A. Toth, Rick Austin, Robert Levin and Scott Essman, as well as interviews with film directors Guillermo Del Toro, Alejandro Gonzalez Iñarritu and Frank Darabont.

How to Contact Query. Accepts submissions by e-mail. Send work as attachment. Sample copy online.

Advice ''Read over each submission before sending it, and if you, as the writer, find the piece irresistible, e-mail it to us immediately!''

$ ON THE PREMISES, A GOOD PLACE TO START

On The Premises, LLC, 4323 Gingham Court, Alexandria VA 22310. (202)262-2168. E-mail: questions @onthepremises.com. Web site: www.OnThePremises.com. **Contact:** Tarl Roger Kudrick or Bethany Granger, Co-Publishers. E-zine. ''Stories published in *On the Premises* are winning entries in contests that are held every four months. Each contest challenges writers to produce a great story based on a broad premise that our editors supply as part of the contest. *On the Premises* aims to promote newer and/or relatively unknown writers who can write what we feel are creative, compelling stories told in effective, uncluttered and evocative prose. Entrants pay no fees, and winners recieve cash prizes in addition to publication.'' Triannual. Estab. 2007. Member Small Press Promotions.

Needs Adventure, ethnic/multicultural (general), experimental, family saga, fantasy, feminist, historical (general), horror, humor/satire, literary, mainstream, military/war, mystery, new age, psychic/supernatural/occult, romance, science fiction, thriller/espionage, western. Does not want young adult fiction, children's fiction, x-rated fiction. ''In general, we don't like stories that were written solely to make a social or political point, especially if the story seems to assume that no intelligent person could possibly disagree with the author. Save the idealogy for editorial and opinion pieces, please. But above all, we NEVER EVER want to see stories that do not use the contest premise! Use the premise, and make it 'clear' and 'obvious' that you are using the premise.'' Themes are announced the day each contest is launched. List of past and current premises available on Web site. Receives 10-40 mss/month. Accepts 3-6 mss/issue; 9-18 mss/year. Does not read February, June and October. Ms published a month or less after acceptance. **Publishes 3-6 new writers/year.** Published A'llyn Ettien, Cory Cramer, Mark Tullius, Michael Van Ornum, Ken Liu and K. Stodard Hayes. Length: 1,000-5000 words. Average length: 3,500 words. Sometimes comments on/critiques rejected mss.

How to Contact Send complete ms with cover letter. "We are a contest-based magazine and we strive to judge all entries 'blindly.' We request that an author's name and contact information be in the body of the email." Accepts submissions by e-mail only. Responds to mss in 2 weeks after contest deadline. Guidelines available on Web site.

Payment/Terms Writers receive $25-140. Pays on acceptance. Acquires electronic rights. Sends galleys to author. Publication is copyrighted.

Advice "Make sure you use the premise, not just interpret it. If the premise is 'must contain a real live dog,' then think of a creative, compelling way to use a real dog. Revise you draft, then revise again and again. Remember, we judge blindly, so craftmanship and creativety matter, not how well known you are."

▢ OPIUM MAGAZINE
Literary Humor for the Deliriously Captivated, 166 Albion St., San Francisco CA 94110. (347)229-2443. E-mail: todd@opiummagazine.com. Web site: www.opiumden.org. **Contact:** Todd Zuniga, editor-in-chief. Biannual magazine. Contains illustrations and photographs. *"Opium Magazine* displays an eclectic mix of stories, poetry, reviews, cartoons, interviews and much more. It features 'estimated reading times' that precede each piece. While the focus is often humorous literature, we love to publish heartbreaking, serious work. Our rule is that all work must be well written and engaging. While we publish traditional pieces, we're primarily engaged by writers who take risks." Updated daily. Estab. 2001. Circ. 25,000 hits/month. Member CLMP.

Needs Comics/graphic novels, experimental, humor/satire, literary, mainstream. "Vignettes and first-person 'look at what a whacky time I had going to Spain' stories aren't going to get past first base with us." Receives 200 mss/month. Accepts 60 mss/year. Manuscript published 4 months after acceptance. Agented fiction 10%. **Publishes 10-12 new writers/year.** Published Etgar Keret, Dennis Cooper, Jack Handey, Terese Svoboda. Length: 50-1,200 words. Average length: 700 words. Publishes short shorts. Average length of short shorts: 400 words. Also publishes literary essays, literary criticism, poetry. Sometimes comments on/critiques rejected mss.

How to Contact Send complete ms with cover letter by e-mail only. Ms received via snail mail will not be read. Include estimated word count, brief bio, list of publications, and your favorite book. Responds to queries in 1 week. Responds to mss in 10 weeks. Considers simultaneous submissions. Guidelines available via e-mail or on Web site.

Payment/Terms Acquires first North American serial rights. Publication is copyrighted.

Advice "If you don't strike out in that first paragraph to expose something definitive or new, then you better by the second. We get scores of stories, and like the readers we want to attract, we demand to be engaged immediately. Tell us it's your first time, we'll be gentle, and our editors usually give thoughts and encouragement if a piece has promise, even if we reject it."

◎ OUTER ART, the worst possible art in world
The University of New Mexico, 200 College Road, Gallup NM 87301. (505)863-7647. Fax: (505)863-7532. E-mail: smarand@unm.edu. Web site: www.gallup.unm.edu/ ~ smarandache/a/outer-art.htm. **Contact:** Florentin Smarandache, editor. E-zine. Annual. Estab. 2000.

Needs Experimental, literary, outer-art. Publishes ms 1 month after acceptance. Publishes short shorts. Also publishes literary essays, literary criticism.

How to Contact Accepts submissions by e-mail. Send SASE (or IRC) for return of the ms. Responds in 1 month to mss. Accepts simultaneous submissions and reprints. Writer's guidelines online.

▢ ✉ OXFORD MAGAZINE
Bachelor Hall, Miami University, Oxford OH 45056. (513)529-1279. E-mail: oxmagfictioneditor@mu ohio.edu. Web site: www.oxfordmagazine.org. **Contact:** Fiction editor. Annual. Estab. 1985. Circ. 1,000.

- *Oxford* has been awarded two Pushcart Prizes.

Needs Wants quality fiction and prose, genre is not an issue but nothing sentimental. Receives 150 unsolicited mss/month. **Publishes some new writers/year.** Recently published work by Stephen Dixon, Andre Dubus and Stuart Dybek. Publishes short shorts. Also publishes poetry.

How to Contact Responds in 2 months, depending upon time of submissions; mss received after December 31 will be returned. Accepts simultaneous submissions if notified. Sample copy for $5.

Payment/Terms Acquires one-time rights.

Advice ''*Oxford Magazine* accepts fiction, poetry, and essays (this last genre is a catch-all, much like the space under your couch cushions, and includes creative nonfiction, critical work exploring writing, and the like). Appearing once a year, *OxMag* is a Web-based journal that acquires first North American serial rights, one-time anthology rights and online serial rights. Simultaneous submissions are okay if you would kindly let us know if and when someone beats us to the punch.''

PAPERPLATES, a magazine for fifty readers

Perkolator Kommunikation, 19 Kenwood Ave., Toronto ON M6C 2R8 Canada. (416)651-2551. E-mail: magazine@paperplates.org. Web site: www.paperplates.org. **Contact:** Bethany Gibson, fiction editor. Electronic magazine. Quarterly. Estab. 1990.

Needs Condensed novels, ethnic/multicultural, feminist, gay, lesbian, literary, mainstream, translations. ''No science fiction, fantasy or horror.'' Receives 12 unsolicited mss/month. Accepts 2-3 mss/issue; 6-9 mss/year. Publishes ms 6-8 months after acceptance. Recently published work by Lyn Fox, David Bezmozgis, Fraser Sutherland and Tim Conley. Length: 1,500-3,500 words; average length: 3,000 words. Publishes short shorts. Also publishes literary essays, literary criticism, poetry.

How to Contact Accepts submissions by e-mail and land mail. Responds in 6 weeks to queries; 6 months to mss. Accepts simultaneous submissions. Sample copy online. Writer's guidelines online.

Payment/Terms No payment. Acquires first North American serial rights.

THE PAUMANOK REVIEW

E-mail: submissions@paumanokreview.com. Web site: www.paumanokreview.com. **Contact:** Katherine Arline, editor. Online literary magazine. ''*TPR* is dedicated to publishing and promoting the best in world art and literature.'' Quarterly. Estab. 2000.

- J.P. Maney's *Western Exposures* was selected for inclusion in the *E2INK Best of the Web Anthology*.

Needs Mainstream, narrative, experimental, historical, mystery, horror, western, science fiction, slice-of-life vignette, serial, novel excerpt. Receives 100 unsolicited mss/month. Accepts 6-8 mss/issue; 24-32 mss/year. Publishes ms 6 weeks after acceptance. **Publishes 4 new writers/year.** Recently published work by Patty Friedman, Elisha Porat, Barry Spacks and Walt McDonald. Length: 1,000-6,000 words; average length: 3,000 words. Publishes short shorts. Also publishes literary essays, poetry. Usually comments on rejected mss.

How to Contact Send complete ms as attachment (Word, RTF, HTML, TXT) or pasted in body of e-mail. Include estimated word count, brief bio, two ways to contact you, list of publications, and how you discovered *TPR*. Responds in 1 week to queries; 1 month to mss. Accepts simultaneous submissions and reprints. No multiple submissions. Sample copy online. Writer's guidelines online.

Payment/Terms Acquires one-time, anthology rights. Galleys offered in HTML or PDF format.

Advice ''Though this is an English-language publication, it is not US-or UK-centric. Please submit accordingly. *TPR* is a publication of Wind River Press, which also publishes *Critique* magazine and select print and electronic books.''

PBW

513 N. Central Ave., Fairborn OH 45324. (937)878-5184. E-mail: rianca@aol.com. Electronic disk zine; 700 pages, specializing in avant-garde fiction and poetry. ''*PBW* is an experimental floppy disk (CD-Rom) that prints strange and 'unpublishable' in an above-ground-sense writing.'' Twice per year. Estab. 1988.

How to Contact ''Manuscripts are only taken if they are submitted on disk or by e-mail.'' Send SASE for reply, return of ms. Sample copy not available.

Payment/Terms All rights revert back to author. Not copyrighted.

⊡ $⊠ THE PEDESTAL MAGAZINE

Pedestal Enterprises, Inc., 6815 Honors Court, Charlotte NC 28210. (704)643-0244. E-mail: pedmagaz ine@carolina.rr.com. Web site: www.thepedestalmagazine.com. **Contact:** Nathan Leslie, editor; John Amen, editor-in-chief. Online literary magazine/journal. "We publish poetry, fiction, reviews and interviews. We are committed to the individual voice and publish an eclectic mix of high-quality work." Bimonthly. Estab. 2000. Member CLMP.

Needs Adventure, ethnic/multicultural, experimental, family saga, fantasy, feminist, gay, glitz, historical, horror, humor/satire, lesbian, literary, mainstream, military/war, mystery, new age, psychic/supernatural/occult, romance, science fiction, thriller/espionage. Receives 100-150 mss/month. Accepts 3-5 mss/issue; 18-24 mss/year. Closed to submissions at the following times: January, March, May, July, September, November: from the 12th-19th; February, April, June, August, October, December: from the 14th-28th. Ms published 1-3 weeks after acceptance. **Publishes 1-2 new writers/year.** Published Grant Tracy, Mary Grabar, Karen Heuler, James Scott Iredell, Don Shea, Mary Carroll-Hackett, R.T. Smith and Richard Peabody. Publishes short shorts. Also publishes book reviews, poetry. Send review query to pedmagazine@carolina.rr.com. Rarely comments on/critiques rejected mss.

How to Contact Submit via the online form provided on the Web site. Include brief bio, list of publications. Responds to queries in 2-3 days. Responds to mss in 4-6 weeks. Considers simultaneous submissions, multiple submissions. Guidelines available on Web site.

Payment/Terms Writers receive 5¢/word. Pays on publication. Acquires first rights. Sends galleys to author. Publication is copyrighted.

Advice "Strong characterization, imagery and a distinct voice are always important. Also, we always look for startling or unusual themes and content. Writers we publish should be willing to push their readers and themselves into unfamiliar terrain. We read too many generic stories that read like bad television. Read the magazine to get a sense of what we publish. Polish your work as much as possible before submitting. Be professional."

⊡ ⊠ ◎ PERSIMMON TREE, AN ONLINE LITERARY MAGAZINE BY OLDER WOMEN

1534 Campus Drive, Berkeley CA 94708. (510)486-2332. E-mail: editor@persimmontree.org. Web site: www.persimmontree.org. **Contact:** Nan Gefen, Editor. Online magazine. "*Persimmon Tree* is a showcase for the talent and creativity of women over sixty, but the magazine appeals to readers of all ages." Quarterly. Estab. 2007. Member Council of Literary Magazines.

Needs Ethnic/multicultural (general), experimental, family saga, feminist, gay, historical (general), humor/satire, lesbian, literary, mainstream. Receives 80-100 mss/month. Accepts 2-3 mss/issue; 8-12 mss/year. Ms published 3-6 months after acceptance. **Publishes 2-3 new writers/year.** Published Grace Paley, Paula Gunn Allen, Daphne Muse, Carole Rosenthal and Sandy Boucher. Length: 1,200-3,000 words. Average length: 2,000 words. Publishes short shorts. Also publishes literary essays, literary criticism, book reviews, poetry.

How to Contact Send complete ms with cover letter. Accepts submissions by e-mail only. Include estimated word count, brief bio, list of publications. Responds to mss in 3-6 months. Considers simultaneous submissions, multiple submissions. Guidelines available on Web site.

Payment/Terms Acquires one-time rights. Sends galleys to author. Publication is copyrighted.

Advice "High quality of writing, an interesting or unique point of view, make a manuscript stand out. Make it clear that you're familiar with the magazine. Tell us why the piece would work for our audience."

THE PINK CHAMELEON

E-mail: dpfreda@juno.com. Web site: http://www.geocities.com/thepinkchameleon/index.html. **Contact:** Mrs. Dorothy Paula Freda, editor/publisher. Family-oriented electronic magazine. Annual. Estab. 2000. Reading period from January to April and September to October.

Needs Short stories, adventure, family saga, fantasy, humor/satire, literary, mainstream, mystery/suspense, religious/inspirational, romance, science fiction, thriller/espionage, western, young adult/teen, psychic/supernatural. "No violence for the sake of violence." Receives 20 unsolicited mss/month. Publishes ms within 1 year after acceptance. **Publishes 50% new writers/year.** Recently published work by Deanne F. Purcell, Martin Green, Albert J. Manachino, James W. Collins, Ken Sieben, Doris and Bob Papenmeyer, Thomas J. Misuraca, and Denise Noe. Length: 500-2,500 words;

average length: 2,000 words. Publishes short shorts. No novels or novel excerpts. Also publishes literary essays, poetry. Sometimes comments on rejected mss.

How to Contact Send complete ms in the body of the e-mail. No attachments. Responds in 1 month to mss. Accepts reprints. No simultaneous submissions. Sample copy online. Writer's guidelines online.

Payment/Terms "Non-profit. Acquires one-time rights for one year but will return rights earlier on request."

Advice "Simple, honest, evocative emotion, upbeat submissions that give hope for the future; well-paced plots; stories, poetry, articles, essays that speak from the heart. Read guidelines carefully. Use a good, but not ostentatious, opening hook. Stories should have a beginning, middle and end that make the reader feel the story was worth his or her time. This also applies to articles and essays. In the latter two, wrap your comments and conclusions in a neatly packaged final paragraph. Turnoffs include violence, bad language. Simple, genuine and sensitive work does not need to shock with vulgarity to be interesting and enjoyable."

ℕ $◨ ◎ PSEUDOPOD, THE SOUND OF HORROR

Escape Artists, Inc., P.O. Box 1538, Stone Mountain GA 30086. (678)389-6700. Fax: (206)666-3763. E-mail: editor@pseudopod.org. Web site: http://pseudopod.org. **Contact:** Ben Phillips, Editor. Online magazine. 25-40 min weekly episode, 5-10 min for sporadic specials like flash fiction or movie/book reviews. "*Pseudopod* is a genre magazine in audio form. We're looking for horror: dark, weird fiction. We run the spectrum from grim realism or magic-realism to blatantly supernatural dark fantasy. We publish highly literary stories reminiscent of Poe or Lovecraft, as well as vulgar, innovative, and/or shock-value-focused pulp fiction. We don't split hairs about genre definitions, and we don't have any hard and fast taboos about what kind of content can appear in our stories. Originality demands that you're better off avoiding vampires, zombies, and other recognizable horror tropes unless you have put a very original spin on them. (Ghosts are currently somewhat more smiled upon, mainly because they haven't settled into such predictably canonical treatment; you don't know what a ghost can do until the author establishes it, so fear of the unknown is intact - which is the real lesson here.) What matters most is just that the stories are dark and entertaining." Weekly. Estab. 2006. Circ. 5,500.

- Episode 27 was a finalist nominee for the 2007 Parsec (podcasting) award for Best SF Story (short form)

Needs Horror (dark fantasy, futuristic, psychological, supernatural, sentimental, literary, erotic, splatterpunk, romantic, humorours). Does not want archetypical vampire, zombie, or werewolf fiction. Receives 100 mss/month. Accepts 1 mss/issue; 70 mss/year. Manuscript published 1 month after acceptance. **Publishes 20 new writers/year.** Published Joel Arnold, Kevin J. Anderson, Richard Dansky, Scott Sigler, Paul Jessup, Nicholas Ozment, and Stephen Gaskell. Length: 2,000-6,000 words. Average length: 3,000 words. Publishes short shorts. Average length of short shorts: 800 words. Often comments on/critiques rejected manuscripts.

How to Contact Send complete ms with cover letter. Accepts submissions by e-mail. Include estimated word count, brief bio, brief list of publications. Responds to queries in 2 weeks. Responds to mss in 2 months. Considers simultaneous submissions, previously published submissions. Sample copy, guidelines available on Web site.

Payment/Terms Writers receive $20 under 2,000 words, $50 over 2,000 words. Pays on acceptance. "*Pseudopod* is released under a Creative Commons Attribution-Noncommercial-No Derivative Works 3.0 License—see http://creativecommons.org for more info."

Advice "Fast pacing is very important for audio listeners, but we forgive a lot in the name of literary value for outstanding stories. Be original, disturbing, and preferably character-focused. Have it critiqued first by a local writer's group (horror-oriented or not, it shouldn't matter—you want to tell a good story by conventional standards as well as have appeal for horror fans), or barring that, by an online critique group such as critters.org."

ℕ $◎ RAVING DOVE

E-mail: editor@ravingdove.org. Web site: www.ravingdove.org. **Contact:** Jo-Ann Moss, Editor. Online literary magazine. "*Raving Dove* publishes original poetry, nonfiction essays, fiction, photography, and art with (universal) anti-war, anti-violence, peace-related, and human rights themes." Triannual. Estab. 2004.

Needs Literary, mainstream. "*Raving Dove* is not a political publication. Material for or against one specific person or entity will not be considered, nor will lobbying of any kind. The pain of war and the vision of peace—in all their manifestations and in all their appearances throughout time—are our primary themes." Ms published up to 4 months after acceptance. Length: 3,000 words (max). Also publishes poetry.

How to Contact Accepts submissions by e-mail only. Include brief bio, submission genre, i.e., fiction, nonfiction, poetry, etc., in the e-mail subject line. Responds to mss in 3 months. Considers simultaneous submissions. Guidelines available on Web site.

Payment/Terms Writers receive $10. (May increase based on funding. Check Web site for current pay scale.) Pays on publication. Acquires first North American serial rights, electronic rights.

☑ REALPOETIK, A Little Magazine of the Internet

E-mail: salasin@scn.org. Web site: RealPoetik.blogspot.com. **Contact:** Fiction Editor. "We publish the new, lively, exciting and unexpected in vernacular English. Any vernacular will do." Weekly. Estab. 1993.

Needs "We do not want to see anything that fits neatly into categories. We subvert categories." Publishes ms 2-4 months after acceptance. **Publishes 20-30 new writers/year.** Average length: 250-500 words. Publishes short shorts. Also publishes literary essays, literary criticism, poetry. Sometimes comments on rejected mss.

How to Contact Query with or without published clips or send complete ms. Accepts submissions by e-mail. Responds in 1 month to queries. Sample copy online.

Payment/Terms Acquires one-time rights. Sponsors awards/contests.

Advice "Be different but interesting. Humor and consciousness are always helpful. Write short. We're a post-modern e-zine."

Ⓝ ☑ ◎ RESIDENTIAL ALIENS, Speculative Fiction from the Seven Stars

ResAliens, 6572 E. Central, Suite 102, Wichita KS 67206. (316)871-1200. E-mail: lyngperry@yahoo.com. Web site: http://residentialaliens.blogspot.com. **Contact:** Lyn Perry, Founding Editor. Online magazine/E-zine. "Because reading and writing speculative fiction is a strong interest of mine, I thought I'd contribute to the genre of faith-informed spec fic by offering other writers and readers of science fiction, fantasy, spiritual and supernatural thrillers a quality venue in which to share their passion. You could say *ResAliens* is speculative fiction with a spiritual thread." Monthly. Estab. 2007.

Needs Fantasy (space fantasy, sword and sorcery), horror (supernatural), science fiction (soft/sociological). Does not want horror, gore, erotica. Will publish a *Space Opera Anthology* summer of 2009, deadline for subs by June 1, 2009. List of upcoming themes available for SASE, on Web site. Receives 20 mss/month. Accepts 5-6 mss/issue; 65-75 mss/year. Ms published 1-2 months after acceptance. **Publishes 25 new writers/year.** Published George L. Duncan (author of novel *A Cold and Distant Memory*), Patrick G. Cox (author of novel *Out of Time*), Merrie Destefano (editor of *Victorian Homes Magazine*), Brandon Barr (co-author of upcoming novel *When the Sky Fell*), Ilaria Dal Brun (short story "Foul Breath"), Alex Moisi (short story "Up or Down"), Curtis Schweitzer (short story "Colossus"), and Glyn Shull (short story "Demonic Intent"). Length: 500-5,000 words. Average length: 3,500 words. Publishes short shorts. Average length of short shorts: 900 words. Will take serial novellas of 2-5 installments (up to 20,000 words). Also publishes book reviews. Send review copies to lyngperry@yahoo.com. Often comments on/critiques rejected mss.

How to Contact Send complete ms with cover letter. Accepts submissions by e-mail. Include estimated word count, brief bio. Responds to queries in 2-5 days; to mss in 1-2 weeks. Considers simultaneous submissions, previously published submissions, multiple submissions. Sample copy and guidelines available on Web site.

Payment/Terms Writers receive PDF file as their contributor's copy. Acquires one-time rights, electronic rights, 6 month archive rights. Sends galleys to author. Publication is copyrighted. "Occasionally sponsors contests."

Advice "We want stories that read well and move quickly. We enjoy all sorts of speculative fiction, and 'tried and true' forms and themes are fine as long as the author has a slightly different take or a fresh perspective on a topic. For example, time machine stories are great—how is yours unique or interesting?"

⬛ ⬛ THE ROSE & THORN LITERARY E-ZINE, Showcasing Emerging and Established Writers and A Writer's Resource

E-mail: BAQuinn@aol.com. Web site: www.theroseandthornezine.com. **Contact:** Barbara Quinn, fiction editor, publisher, managing editor. E-zine specializing in literary works of fiction, nonfiction, poetry and essays. "We created this publication for readers and writers alike. We provide a forum for emerging and established voices. We blend contemporary writing with traditional prose and poetry in an effort to promote the literary arts." Quarterly. Circ. 120,000.

Needs Adventure, ethnic/multicultural, experimental, fantasy, historical, horror (dark fantasy, futuristic, psychological, supernatural), humor/satire, literary, mainstream, mystery/suspense, New Age, regional, religious/inspirational, romance (contemporary, futuristic/time travel, gothic, historical, regency, romantic suspense), science fiction, thriller/espionage, western. Receives "several hundred" unsolicited mss/month. Accepts 8-10 mss/issue; 40-50 mss/year. **Publishes many new writers/year.** Publishes short shorts. Also publishes literary essays, poetry. Sometimes comments on rejected mss.

How to Contact Query with or without published clips or send complete ms. Accepts submissions by e-mail. Include estimated word count, 150-word bio, list of publications and author's byline. Responds in 1 week to queries; 1 month to mss. Accepts simultaneous submissions and reprints. Sample copy free. Writer's guidelines online. Length: 2,000 word limit.

Payment/Terms Writer retains all rights. Sends galleys to author.

Advice "Clarity, control of the language, evocative stories that tug at the heart and make their mark on the reader long after it's been read. We look for uniqueness in voice, style and characterization. New twists on old themes are always welcome. Use all aspects of good writing in your stories, including dynamic characters, strong narrative voice and a riveting original plot. We have eclectic tastes, so go ahead and give us a shot. Read the publication and other quality literary journals so you'll see what we look for. Always check your spelling and grammar before submitting. Reread your submission with a critical eye and ask yourself, 'Does it evoke an emotional response? Have I completely captured my reader?' Check your submission for 'it' and 'was' and see if you can come up with a better way to express yourself. Be unique."

⬛ ◎ THE SITE OF BIG SHOULDERS, Chicago Writing, Art and Photography

Chicago IL. E-mail: submissions@sobs.org. Web site: sobs.org. **Contact:** Justin Kerr, editor-in-chief. Online magazine. "*The Site of Big Shoulders* features original content with a connection to the greater Chicago area by virtue of authorship or subject matter. *SOBS* is a 501(c) (3) not-for-profit organization and a non-commercial community publishing effort that focuses on high editorial quality, aesthetics and production value without regard to commercial need or mass appeal." Estab. 1996. Circ. 150,000+ page views/month.

- This site has won the 2003 Community Arts Assistance Program Grant, the Bronze Trophy for Exceptional Creativity from the Chicago Internet Review (1998); the Artis Hot Site Award (1998) and the Juno Silver Award (1998).

Needs Regional (greater Chicago). "We do not publish fiction that does not have a connection to the greater Chicagoland region (northeast Illinois, northwest Indiana, southeast Wisconsin)." Receives 1-5 unsolicited mss/month. Accepts 4-8 mss/year. Publishes ms 2-12 months after acceptance. **Publishes 4-8 new writers/year.** Recently published work by James Ogle, Jack Lowe, Phil Brody and Li Young-Lee. Length: 200-3,000 words; average length: 1,000 words. Publishes short shorts. Also publishes literary essays, literary criticism, poetry.

How to Contact Send complete ms. Accepts submissions by e-mail. Include brief bio. Responds in 3 months to queries. Accepts simultaneous and reprints, multiple submissions. Sample copy online. Writer's guidelines online.

Payment/Terms Non-exclusive right to feature the submitted content within the Internet domain.

Advice "We are very open to the idea of publishing hypertext or other experimental fiction. Please submit clean, edited copy."

⬛ SLOW TRAINS LITERARY JOURNAL

P.O. 4741, Denver CO 80155. E-mail: editor@slowtrains.com. Web site: www.slowtrains.com. **Contact**: Susannah Indigo. Quarterly. Estab. 2000.

Needs Literary. No romance, sci-fi, or other specific genre-writing. Receives 100+ unsolicited mss/month. Accepts 10-15 mss/issue; 40-50 mss/year. Publishes ms 3 months after acceptance. **Pub-**

lishes 20- 40 new writers/year. Length: 1,000-5,000 words; average length: 3,500 words. Publishes short shorts. Also publishes literary essays, poetry. Rarely comments on rejected mss.

How to Contact Accepts submissions by e-mail. Responds in 4-8 weeks to mss. Accepts simultaneous and reprints submissions. Sample copy online. Writer's guidelines online.

Payment/Terms Pays 2 contributor's copies. Acquires one-time, electronic rights.

Advice "The first page must be able to pull the reader in immediately. Use your own fresh, poetic, compelling voice. Center your story around some emotional truth, and be sure of what you're trying to say."

☐ SNREVIEW, Starry Night Review—A Literary E-Zine

197 Fairchild Ave., Fairfield CT 06825-4856. (203)366-5991. E-mail: editor@snreview.org. Web site: www.snreview.org. **Contact:** Joseph Conlin, editor. E-zine specializing in literary short stories, essays and poetry. "We search for material that not only has strong characters and plot but also a devotion to imagery." Quarterly. Estab. 1999.

Needs Literary, mainstream. Receives 200 unsolicited mss/month. Accepts 40+ mss/issue; 150 mss/year. Publishes ms 6 months after acceptance. **Publishes 50 new writers/year.** Recently published work by Frank X. Walker, Adrian Louis, Barbara Burkhardt, E. Lindsey Balkan, Marie Griffin and Jonathan Lerner. Length: 1,000-7,000 words; average length: 4,000 words. Also publishes literary essays, literary criticism, poetry.

How to Contact Accepts submissions by e-mail only. Include 100 word bio and list of publications. Responds in 3 months to mss. Accepts simultaneous and reprints submissions. Sample copy online. Writer's guidelines online. A printed edition of SNReview is now available from an on-demand printer.

Payment/Terms Acquires first electronic and print rights.

ℕ $☐ SOUTHERN GOTHIC

WordArts, Inc., 7746 Newfound Gap Rd, Memphis TN 38125. E-mail: wordartsinc@yahoo.com. Web site: www.southerngothic.org. **Contact:** Jeff Crook, Editor. E-zine. "*Southern Gothic* is the only magazine on the market today dedicated solely to the unique subgenre known as Southern Gothic. Southern Gothic was made famous by such writers as William Faulkner, Flannery O'Connor, Tennessee Williams, Barry Hannah and others. We look for stories that cross genre boundaries and welcome tales with supernatural elements as well as more traditional literary stories." Estab. 2005.

● Two stories published in *Southern Gothic* were Notable Stories recognized by the *StorySouth* Million Writers Award in 2005 and 2006, and one was a top ten finalist in 2006.

Needs Adventure, experimental, fantasy (space fantasy, sword and sorcery), feminist, gay, historical (general), horror (dark fantasy, futuristic, psychological, supernatural), humor/satire, lesbian, literary, mainstream, military/war, mystery, science fiction (hard science/technological). Receives 60 mss/month. Accepts 12 mss/year. Ms published 1 month after acceptance. Published Phillip Hamrick, Corey Mesler, Mark MacNamara, Lucious Vaughn, Robert Morris Kennedy, Kathryn Krotzer Laborde, Traci O. Connor, Stephen Roger Powers and Jason Sanford. Length: 7,500 words (max). Average length: 4,000 words. Publishes short shorts. Average length of short shorts: 1,000 words.

How to Contact Send complete ms with cover letter. Accepts submissions by e-mail. Include estimated word count, brief bio, list of publications. Responds to mss in 4 months. Considers simultaneous submissions. Guidelines available on Web site.

Payment/Terms Acquires first North American serial rights, one-time rights, electronic rights. Publication is copyrighted.

Advice "A great story is paramount. Without story, there is no fiction. Brilliant language without a story is next to useless. But a great story must also be written well, in words that have a life of their own. I'm looking for stories that makes the top of my head come off, stories that make me laugh, cringe or swear out loud."

ℕ $☐ SPACESUITS AND SIXGUNS

Voidgunner Creative Studios, 716 22nd Ave NW, Minot ND 58703. E-mail: submissions@spacesuitsandsixguns.com. Web site: http://www.spacesuitsandsixguns.com. **Contact:** Editor at editor@spacesuitsandsixguns.com. Online magazine. "*Spacesuits and Sixguns* is a magazine of contemporary pulp fiction—simple, straightforward storytelling with an emphasis on action. We're not looking for Lovecraft or Howard pastiches, or stories set in the 1930's. Read a dozen pulp fiction stories, soak it all up, then ask yourself: what if this happened in my hometown today? Write close to home, write about what you love, and follow Elmore Leonard's maxim: leave out the parts people skip. All genres accepted—detective, horror, mystery, adventure, SF, sword and sorcery. We love them all. Give us about 4,000 words. Shorter is fine. We're flexible. If it's longer and it's good, no problem. Rule number one—be fun!" Quarterly. Estab. 2007. Circ. 2,500. Member SLF Small Press co-op.

Needs Fantasy (space fantasy), horror (dark fantasy, futuristic, psychological, supernatural), humor/satire, mystery (amateur sleuth, police procedural, private eye/hard-boiled), science fiction (space opera). Does not want erotica. List of upcoming themes available for SASE, on Web site. Receives 500 mss/month. Accepts 4-6 mss/issue; 16-24 mss/year. Ms published 1-3 months after acceptance. **Publishes few new writers/year.** Published Mike Wiecek, Lucy Snyder, Andrew Nicolle. Length: 4,000 words (max). Average length: 3,000 words. Publishes short shorts. Average length of short shorts: 1,000 words. Sometimes comments on/critiques rejected mss.

How to Contact Send complete ms with cover letter. Accepts submissions by e-mail. Include estimated word count, brief bio. Sample copy and guidelines available on Web site.

Payment/Terms Writers receive 3¢-$100. Pays on publication. Acquires first North American serial rights. Sends galleys to author. Publication is copyrighted.

Advice "Originality and authenticity stand out. The easiest way to accomplish this is to follow James Magnuson's dictum: find the most powerful experience in your life and write about it. Read well and exhaustively. If you decide to write a story about robots rebelling against their human masters, be aware of the enormous body of work already concerned with that subject. Read it all, then evaluate your own idea."

� $◻ ◻ ◎ ◿ SPACEWESTERNS, THE E-ZINE OF THE SPACE WESTERN SUB-GENRE

P.O. Box 93, Parker Ford PA 19457. (610)410-7400. E-mail: submissions2018@spacewesterns.com. Web site: www.spacewesterns.com. **Contact:** N.E. Lilly, Editor-in-chief. E-zine. "Aside from strictly short stories we also like to see stage plays, screen plays, comics, audio files of stories, short form videos and animation." Weekly. Estab. 2007.

Needs Adventure, comics/graphic novels, ethnic/multicultural, fantasy (space fantasy), horror (dark fantasy, futuristic, psychological, supernatural), humor/satire, mystery, science fiction (hard science/technological, soft/sociological), western (frontier saga, traditional), but it *must be space western*, science fiction western. List of upcoming themes available on Web site. Receives 12 mss/month. Accepts 52 mss/year. Ms published within 6 months after acceptance. **Publishes 12 new writers/year.** Published G. Richard Bozarth, Ben Jonjak, David B. Riley, James S. Dorr, Stanly G. Weinbaum and Steve Logan. Length: 2,500-7,500 words. Average length: 4,000-5,000 words. Also publishes literary essays, literary criticism, book reviews, poetry. Send review copies to N. E. Lilly. Often comments on/critiques rejected mss.

How to Contact Send complete ms with cover letter. Accepts submissions by e-mail only. Include estimated word count. Responds to queries in 2 weeks. Responds to mss in 4 weeks. Considers previously published submissions, multiple submissions. Guidelines available on Web site.

Payment/Terms Writers receive 1/2¢ per word, $25 max. Pays on publication. Publication is copyrighted.

Advice "First of all, have a well-crafted manuscript (no spelling or grammar errors). Secondly, a good idea—many errors will be forgiven for a solid concept and fresh idea. Be yourself. Write what you love. Familiarize yourself with the scope of the Universe."

◿ STEEL CITY REVIEW: A PITTSBURGH-BASED MAGAZINE OF SHORT FICTION

E-mail: editor@steelcityreview.com. Web site: www.steelcityreview.com. **Contact:** Julia LaSalle & Stefani Nellen, co-editors. Online magazine and publishing an annual print edition based on the Web content. "We seek short fiction dealing with technology, industry, work, and how these issues intersect with individuals' lives. We also seek stories set in Pittsburgh and illuminating the "feel" of living there. Finally, we seek science fiction stories. We are open to all topics, but strive to maintain a local flavor." Quarterly. Estab. Jan. 2007. Circ. 1,200 reads per month.

Needs Literary, mainstream, regional (Pittsburgh/Allegheny County area), science fiction (hard science/technological, soft/sociological). Does not want religious/inspirational, mystery, romance or children's stories. No erotica please. Receives about 30 mss/month. Accepts about 6 mss/issue; about 24 mss/year. Manuscript published 3-6 months after acceptance. Agented fiction 0%. **Publishes at least 4 new writers/year.** Published GK Wuon, Steve Fellner, Vanessa Gebbie, Claudia

Smith, Nathan Leslie, William R. Hamilton, JP Briggs. Length: 500-6,000 words. Average length: 3,500 words. Often comments on/critiques rejected mss.

How to Contact Send complete ms with cover letter. Accepts submissions by e-mail only. Include estimated word count, brief bio, list of publications. Responds to mss in 8 weeks. Considers simultaneous submissions. Guidelines available via e-mail, on Web site.

Payment/Terms Acquires one-time electronic rights and one-time anthology rights for inclusion in the annual print edition. Sends mock-up of Web page to author pre-publication for their approval. Publication is copyrighted.

Advice "We want polished, confident manuscripts related to our themes/aesthetic. We want readable, original fiction that makes us forget we're reading. Don't try too hard. Dare to be funny, but don't force it. Read past issues before submitting. Please make sure your submission is grammatically clean and typo-free."

🅽 ☑ ◎ STILL CRAZY, AN ONLINE LITERARY MAGAZINE

(614)746-0859. E-mail: editor@crazylitmag.com. Web site: www.crazylitmag.com. **Contact:** Barbara Kussow, editor. Online magazine. "*Still Crazy* publishes writing by people over age 50 and writing by people of any age if the topic is about people over 50. The editor is particularly interested in material that challenges the stereotypes of older people and that portrays older people's inner lives as rich and rewarding." Semiannual. Estab. 2007.

Needs Feminist. Special interests: seniors (over 50). "Does not want material that is too sentimental or inspirational." Accepts 6-8 mss/issue; 12-16 mss/year. Manuscript published 6-12 months after acceptance. Length: 2,500 words (max). Publishes short shorts. Also publishes poetry and short nonfiction. Sometimes comments on/critiques rejected mss.

How to Contact Submit via e-mail form on Web site. Attach MS Word doc or cut and paste into text of email. Include estimated word count, brief bio, age of writer. Responds to mss in 6 months. Considers simultaneous submissions, previously published submissions (please indicate when and where), multiple submissions. Guidelines available on Web site.

Payment/Terms Acquires one-time rights. Publication is not copyrighted.

Advice Looking for "interesting characters and interesting situations. Humor and Lightness welcome."

☑ STORY BYTES, Very Short Stories

E-mail: editor@storybytes.com. Web site: www.storybytes.com. **Contact:** M. Stanley Bubien, editor. Electronic zine. "We are strictly an electronic publication, appearing on the Internet in three forms. First, the stories are sent to an electronic mailing list of readers. They also get placed on our Web site, both in PDF and HTML format."

Needs "Stories must be very short—having a length that is the power of 2, specifically: 2, 4, 8, 16, 32, etc." No sexually explicit material. "Would like to see more material dealing with religion—not necessarily 'inspirational' stories, but those that show the struggles of living a life of faith in a realistic manner." **Publishes 33% new writers/year.** Recently published work by Richard K. Weems, Joseph Lerner, Lisa Cote and Thomas Sennet.

How to Contact Please query first. Query with or without published clips or send complete ms. Accepts submissions by e-mail. "I prefer plain text with story title, authorship and word count. Only accepts electronic submissions. See Web site for complete guidelines." Sample copy online. Writer's guidelines online.

Advice "In Story Bytes the very short stories themselves range in topic. Many explore a brief event—a vignette of something unusual, unique and at times something even commonplace. Some stories can be bizarre, while others quite lucid. Some are based on actual events, while others are entirely fictional. Try to develop conflict early on (in the first sentence if possible!), and illustrate or resolve this conflict through action rather than description. I believe we'll find an audience for electronic published works primarily in the short story realm."

☑ STORYSOUTH, THE BEST FROM NEW SOUTH WRITERS

898 Chelsea Ave., Columbus OH 43209. (614)545-0754. E-mail: storysouth@yahoo.com. Web site: www.storysouth.com. **Contact:** Jason Sanford, editor. "*storySouth* is interested in fiction, creative nonfiction, and poetry by writers from the New South. The exact definition *New South* varies from

person to person and we leave it up to the writer to define their own connection to the southern United States." Quarterly. Estab. 2001.

Needs Experimental, literary, regional (south), translations. Receives 70 unsolicited mss/month. Accepts 5 mss/issue; 20 mss/year. Publishes ms 1 month after acceptance. **Publishes 5-10 new writers/year.** Average length: 4,000 words. Publishes short shorts. Also publishes literary essays, literary criticism, poetry. Often comments on rejected mss.

How to Contact Send complete ms. Accepts e-mailed submissions only. Responds in 2 months to mss. Accepts simultaneous, multiple submissions. Writer's guidelines online.

Payment/Terms Acquires one-time rights.

Advice "What really makes a story stand out is a strong voice and a sense of urgency—a need for the reader to keep reading the story and not put it down until it is finished."

ℕ $◻ ◎ STRANGE HORIZONS

Strange Horizons, Inc., P.O. Box 1693, Dubuque IA 52004-1693. E-mail: fiction@strangehorizons.com. Web site: http://strangehorizons.com. **Contact:** Susan Groppi, Editor-in-Chief. Online magazine. "We're a science fiction magazine dedicated to showcasing new voices in the genre." Weekly. Estab. 2000.

Needs Fantasy (space fantasy, sword and sorcery), feminist, science fiction (hard science/technological, soft/sociological). Does not want horror; see Web site. Receives 300 mss/month. Accepts 48 or 50 mss/year. Does not read December. Ms published 2-4 months after acceptance. **Publishes 5-10 new writers/year.** Published Liz Williams, Charlie Anders, Elizabeth Bear, Carrie Vaughn, Benjamin Rosenbaum and Ruth Nestvold. Length: 2,000-8,000 words. Average length: 3,600 words. Publishes short shorts rarely. Also publishes literary essays, literary criticism, book reviews, poetry. Send review queries to reviews@strangehorizons.com. Rarely comments on/critiques rejected mss.

How to Contact Accepts submissions by e-mail. Responds to queries in 1 week. Responds to mss in 3 months. Guidelines available on Web site.

Payment/Terms Writers receive 5¢ per word. Pays on acceptance. Acquires first rights.

$◻ THE SUMMERSET REVIEW

25 Summerset Dr., Smithtown NY 11787. E-mail: editor@summersetreview.org. Web site: www.summersetreview.org. **Contact:** Joseph Levens, editor. Magazine: illustrations and photographs. "Our goal is simply to publish the highest quality literary fiction and essays intended for a general audience. This is a simple online literary journal of high quality material, so simple you can call it unique." Periodically releaseses print issues. Quarterly. Estab. 2002.

● Several editors-in-chief of very prominent literary publications have done interviews for *The Summerset Review*: M.M.M. Hayes of *StoryQuarterly*, Gina Frangello of *Other Voices*, Jennifer Spiegel of *Hayden's Ferry Review*.

Needs Literary. No sci-fi, horror, or graphic erotica. Receives 100 unsolicited mss/month. Accepts 4 mss/issue; 18 mss/year. Publishes ms 2-3 months after acceptance. **Publishes 5-10 new writers/year.** Length: 8,000 words; average length: 3,000 words. Publishes short shorts. Also publishes literary essays. Usually critiques on mss that were almost accepted.

How to Contact Send complete ms. Accepts submissions by e-mail. Responds in 1-2 weeks to queries; 4-12 weeks to mss. Accepts simultaneous and reprints submissions. Writer's guidelines online.

Payment/Terms $25 per story/essay. Acquires no rights other than one-time publishing, although we request credit if first published in *The Summerset Review*. Sends galleys to author.

Advice "Style counts. We prefer innovative or at least very smooth, convincing voices. Even the dullest of premises or the complete lack of conflict make for an interesting story if it is told in the right voice and style. We like to find little, interesting facts and/or connections subtly sprinkled throughout the piece. Harsh language should be used only if/when necessary. If we are choosing between light and dark subjects, the light will usually win."

ℕ $◻ ◎ SUSURRUS, THE LITERATURE OF MADNESS

Susurrus Press, 535 4th Ave Suite 3, Huntington WV 25701-1248. (304)622-9434. E-mail: susrrusmagazine@gmail.com. Web site: www.susurrusmagazine.com. **Contact:** Brian Worley, James Maddox, Fiction Editors. Online magazine. "*Susurrus* is a highly experimental venue for fiction that deals with the human condition in speculative situations. We publish fiction that shows that to be human is to be at least a little bit crazy. (Keeping this in mind, we publish very few insane asylum/psychiatric ward stories. We know crazy people are crazy. We want stories that show the rest of us are, too.)'' Quarterly. Estab. 2005. Circ. 1,000 unique hits a month.

Needs Adventure, experimental, horror (dark fantasy, futuristic, psychological, supernatural), humor/satire, literary, science fiction (soft/sociological). Special interests: cross-genre, slipstream, magical realism, surreal. Does not want serial killers, goth vampires, stories that turn out to be delusions by a person in an asylum, or stories that only detail a murder/suicide. Receives 50-100 mss/month. Accepts 6-8 mss/issue; 24-32 mss/year. Ms published 1-3 months after acceptance. **Publishes 5-10 new writers/year.** Published Cameron Pierce, Ashley Kaufman, James Swingle, Chris Pritchard, Tamara Kaye Sellman and Laura Sanger Kelly. Length: 25-5,000 words. Average length: 2,000 words. Publishes short shorts. Average length of short shorts: 500 words. Also publishes literary essays, literary criticism, book reviews, poetry. Send review copies to Brian Worley or James Maddox. Often comments on/critiques rejected mss.

How to Contact Send complete ms with cover letter. Accepts submissions by e-mail. Include estimated word count, brief bio. Responds to queries in 1-2 weeks. Responds to mss in 1-3 months. Considers simultaneous submissions, previously published submissions, multiple submissions. Guidelines and sample available on Web site.

Payment/Terms Pays on publication. Acquires electronic rights. Publication is copyrighted.

Advice ''As an online publisher, we have to remember that our readers are only three clicks away from seeing their house from outer space. Therefore, we like fiction that is paced for short attention spans. Beautiful, detailed description is great, but don't let it weigh down your story. Know both the genre you're writing in, and the magazine to which you're submitting. In other words, read the magazine, read from the section of the bookstore that's like what you write, then read some more.''

▣ TATTOO HIGHWAY, a Journal of Prose, Poetry & Art

E-mail: submissions@tattoohighway.org. Web site: www.tattoohighway.org. **Contact:** Sara McAulay, editor. *Tattoo Highway* publishes high quality literary prose, both experimental and mainstream, including hypertext and Flash media. Each issue has a theme, and subject matter generally spins off from that. The journal is visually handsome, with unusual graphics. ''We have no taboos except weak, hackneyed writing. Intended audience: grown-ups who appreciate well-crafted fiction and don't mind an occasional touch of the absurd.'' Semiannual. Estab. 1998.

Needs Experimental, gay, lesbian, literary, mainstream. ''Please no predictable 'formula' stories. No lectures, no tracts, no sermons (on the Mount or otherwise). Graphic sex and/or violence had better be absolutely necessary to the story and had better be exceptionally well written!'' Accepts 5-8 mss/ issue; 10-16 mss/year. Publishes ms 1 month after acceptance. Recently published work by D.S. Richardson, Susan Moon, Elizabeth Wray, Stephen D. Guitierrez, Daniel Olivas, Angela Costi, Stephen Newton, Yvonne Chism-Peace, Robert D. Vivian and Richard Holeton. Length: 2,500 words; average length: 1,000 words. Publishes short shorts. Also publishes literary essays, poetry. Sometimes comments on rejected mss.

How to Contact Accepts submissions by e-mail (ONLY). Send complete ms with cover letter. Responds in 1 week to queries; 1-3 months to mss. Accepts simultaneous, multiple submissions. Sample copy online.

Payment/Terms Acquires first electronic rights rights. Sponsors awards/contests.

Advice ''Look at past issues online, then bring us your best stuff.''

▣ TEKKA

Eastgate Systems, 134 Main St., Watertown MA 02472. (617)924-9044. Fax: (617)924-9051. E-mail: editor@tekka.net. Web site: www.tekka.net. **Contact:** Mark Bernstein, editor. ''*Tekka* is about enjoying new media and creating beautiful software. The future of serious writing lies on the screen, we're interested in real ideas, catchy hyper texts, articles and reviews as well as sci-fi.'' Quarterly. Estab. 2003.

Needs Comics/graphic novels, fantasy (space fantasy), science fiction (hard science/technological, soft/sociological). Publishes short shorts. Also publishes literary essays, literary criticism, poetry. Often comments on rejected mss.

How to Contact Send complete ms. Accepts submissions by e-mail, disk. Accepts simultaneous submissions. Writer's guidelines online.

⊠ ◪ TERRAIN.ORG, A Journal of the Built & Natural Environments

Terrain.org, P.O. Box 19161, Tucson AZ 19161. (520)241-7390. E-mail: review@terrain.org. Web site: www.terrain.org. **Contact:** Simmons Buntin, Editor/Publisher. E-zine. "*Terrain.org* is searching for that interface-the integration-among the built and natural environments, that might be called the soul of place. The works contained within Terrain.org ultimately examine the physical realm around us, and how those environments influence us and each other physically, mentally, emotionally and spiritually." Semiannual. Estab. 1998.

• PLANetizen Top 50 Web site 2002 & 2003.

Needs Adventure, ethnic/multicultural, experimental, family saga, fantasy, feminist, gay, glitz, historical, horror, humor/satire, lesbian, literary, mainstream, military/war, mystery, new age, psychic/supernatural/occult, science fiction, thriller/espionage, translations, western. Special interests: environmental. Does not want erotica. All issues are theme-based. List of upcoming themes available on Web site. Receives 10 mss/month. Accepts 3-5 mss/issue; 6-10 mss/year. Does not read June 1-August 1 and December 1-February 1. Manuscript published five weeks to 18 months after acceptance. Agented fiction 5%. **Publishes 1-3 new writers/year.** Published Al Sim, Jacob MacAurthur Mooney, T.R. Healy, Deborah Fries, Andrew Wingfield, Martin Ott, Scott Spires and Tiel Aisha Ansari. Length: 1,000-8,000 words. Average length: 5,000 words. Publishes short shorts. Average length of short shorts: 750 words. Also publishes literary essays, literary criticism, book reviews, poetry. Send review copies to Simmon Buntin. Sometimes comments on/critiques rejected mss.

How to Contact Send complete ms with cover letter. Accepts submissions by e-mail. Include brief bio. Responds to queries in 2 weeks. Responds to mss in 4 weeks. Considers simultaneous submissions, previously published submissions. Guidelines available on Web site.

Payment/Terms Acquires one-time rights. Sends galleys to author. Publication is copyrighted.

Advice "We have three primary criteria in reviewing fiction: 1) The story is compelling and well-crafted. 2) The story provides some element of surprise; i.e., whether in content, form or delivery we are unexpectedly delighted in what we've read. 3) The story meets an upcoming theme, even if only peripherally. Read fiction in the current issue and perhaps some archived work, and if you like what you read—and our overall environmental slant—then send us your best work. Make sure you follow our submission guidelines (including cover note with bio), and that your manuscript is as error-free as possible."

◪ THE 13TH WARRIOR REVIEW

Asterius Press, P.O. Box 5122, Seabrook NJ 08302-3511. E-mail: theeditor@asteriusonline.com. Web site: www.13thwr.org. **Contact:** John C. Erianne, publisher/editor. Online magazine. Estab. 2000.

Needs Literary/mainstream, erotica, experimental, magical realism, meta-fiction. Receives 500 unsolicited mss/month. Accepts 4-8 mss/issue; 10-15 mss/year. Publishes ms 6 months after acceptance. **Publishes 1-2 new writers/year.** Recently published work by Cindy Rosmus, Jeff Blechle, Elizabeth Farren, and Andrew Hellem. Length: 500-6,000 words; average length: 1,800 words. Publishes short shorts. Also publishes literary essays, literary criticism, poetry, and book reviews. Sometimes comments on rejected mss.

How to Contact Send complete ms. Include estimated word count, brief bio and address/e-mail. Send SASE or IRC for return of ms or send a disposable copy of ms and #10 SASE for reply only. Accepts submissions by e-mail (text is in message body only, no file attachments). Responds in 1 week to queries; 1-2 months to mss. Accepts simultaneous submissions. Sample copy online atwww.13thwr.org. Reviews fiction.

Payment/Terms Acquires first rights, Internet archival rights.

⊠ ◪ THREE-LOBED BURNING EYE

Legion Press, Portland OR. Web site: http://www.owlsoup.com/3LBE. **Contact:** Andrew S. Fuller, editor. Online magazine with an annual print anthology measuring $5^{1}/_{2} \times 8^{1}/_{2}$ and 180 pages, illustrated. Estab. 1999. Circ. 200 visitors per week.

Needs Horror (dark fantasy, futuristic, psychological, supernatural, other), literary, and science fiction (soft/sociological, magical realism). Publishes annual print anthology. Receives 50 unsolicited fiction mss/month. Accepts 6/issue or 18/year. Manuscript published within 1 year after acceptance. Agented fiction 20%. **Publishes 3 new writers/year.** Recently published work by Gemma Files, DF

Lewis, Laird Barron, Brenden Connell, Amy Grech, Neil Ayres, Tim Waggoner. Length: 1,000-7,000 words maximum; average length: 4,000 words. Publishes short shorts. Often comments on rejected mss.

How to Contact Submit online only via site's online form. Include estimated word count, list of publications. "Be brief, with nothing but the story itself." Responds to queries in 1 week; 1-3 months for mss. Accepts previously published submissions (query first). Sample copy and writer's guidelines on Web site.

Payments/Terms Pays $13 honorarium and 1 copy of annual print anthology. Additional copies $12 each. Payment is made upon publication for one-time, electronic, and electronic archival options. Publication is copyrighted.

Advice "Ours is a magazine of quality speculative fiction. We seek professional stories that expand the genre(s) by valuing originality in character, narrative, and plot. We want only your best fiction, distinct and remarkable tales that the reader cannot forget. We tend more towards horror, dark fantasy, and magical realism, maybe suspense or even western, though the story must contain some speculative element. Read some issues of *3LBE* to understand what we publish. Write something as good, or better. Read and know good fiction in the field. Avoid the clichés, the hackneyed plots and language, and the cheap thrills. There is nothing inherently wrong with genre mainstays (vampires, werewolves, ghosts, serial killers, faeries, and aliens), but *3LBE* is only interested in new explorations of these ideas. Be original, I cannot be more clear than this. Beware cleverness. Writers such as O Henry, Richard Matheson, and Robert Bloch were masters of the twist ending. Such structures are difficult to do well, and we are not interested in instant gratification stories of 1,000 words whose brief and empty narrative serves as a ramp to a final trick. We are not interested in glaring devices. We are looking for depth, texture, and imagination. Know what is gratuitous in sex, violence, gore, racism, sexism. Extremity belongs in a story only if it is relevant to the narrative."

◻ TOASTED CHEESE

E-mail: editors@toasted-cheese.com. Web site: www.toasted-cheese.com. **Contact:** submit@toasted-cheese.com. E-zine specializing in fiction, creative nonfiction, poetry and flash fiction. "*Toasted Cheese* accepts submissions of previously unpublished fiction, flash fiction, creative nonfiction and poetry. Our focus is on quality of work, not quantity. Some issues will therefore contain fewer/more pieces than previous issues. We don't restrict publication based on subject matter. We encourage submissions from innovative writers in all genres." Quarterly. Estab. 2001.

Needs Adventure, children's/juvenile, ethnic/multicultural, fantasy, feminist, gay, historical, horror, humor/satire, lesbian, literary, mainstream, mystery/suspense, New Age, psychic/supernatural/occult, romance, science fiction, thriller/espionage, western. "No fan fiction. No chapters or excerpts unless they read as a stand-alone story. No first drafts." Receives 70 unsolicited mss/month. Accepts 1-10 mss/issue; 5-30 mss/year. **Publishes 15 new writers/year.** Publishes short shorts. Also publishes poetry.

How to Contact Send complete ms in body of e-mail; no attachments. Accepts submissions by e-mail. Responds in 4 months to mss. No simultaneous submissions. Sample copy online. Writer's guidelines online.

Payment/Terms Acquires electronic rights. Sponsors awards/contests.

Advice "We are looking for clean, professional writing from writers of any level. Accepted stories will be concise and compelling. We are looking for writers who are serious about the craft: tomorrow's literary stars before they're famous. Take your submission seriously, yet remember that levity is appreciated. You are submitting not to traditional 'editors' but to fellow writers who appreciate the efforts of those in the trenches."

Ⓝ $◻ ◎ TOWER OF LIGHT FANTASY FREE ONLINE

9701 Harford Road, Carney MD 21234. (410)661-3362. E-mail: tol@tolfantasy.com. Web site: www.tolfantasy.com. **Contact:** Michael Southard, editor. Online magazine. "To publish great fantasy stories, especially the genre-blending kind such as dark fantasy, urban, science, and superhero fantasy. Romantic fantasy (not erotic, however) is also acceptable. And *Tower of Light* would very much like to showcase new work by beginning writers." Quarterly. Estab. 2007.

Needs Fantasy (space fantasy, sword and sorcery), horror (dark fantasy, futuristic, supernatural), psychic/supernatural/occult, religious (fantasy), romance (fantasy). Does not want erotic fantasy, or anything that does not have a mystical or supernatural element. List of upcoming themes available on Web site. Receives 15-30 mss/month. Accepts 5 mss/issue; 20 mss/year. Reading period: Jan 1-Mar 31; July 1-Aug 31. Ms published 6-12 months after acceptance. Published Ian Whates, Christopher Heath, Tom Williams, Daniel Henderson, Alice M. Roelke, Matthew Baron, Eric S. Brown, Ryder Patzuk-Russell and Mischell Lyne. Length: 500-4,000 words. Average length: 3,500 words. Publishes short shorts. Also publishes book reviews. Send review copies to Michael Southard. Sometimes comments on/critiques rejected mss.

How to Contact Send ms as email attachment. Responds to mss in 6-12 weeks. Considers previously published submissions, multiple submissions. Guidelines, sample copy available on Web site.

Payment/Terms Writers receive $5. Pays on publication. Acquires one-time rights, electronic rights. Sends galleys to author. Publication is not copyrighted.

Advice "Strong, well-developed characters that really elicit an emotional response, good writing, original plots and world-building catch my attention. Send me a good story, and make sure to check your spelling and grammar. I don't mind a couple of errors, but when there's more than half a dozen, it gets really irritating. Make sure to study the guidelines thoroughly; I'm looking for character-driven stories, preferably in third person limited point-of-view."

[N] ◯ [C] UGLY ACCENT, A Literary Adversaria Brought to You by the Midwest

P.O. Box 57301, Washington DC 20037-7301. E-mail: fiction@uglyaccent.com. Web site: www.uglyaccent.com. **Contact:** Juli Obudzinski, Fiction Editor. Online and print literary magazine: 8.5 × 11; 40 pages; newsprint paper; contains illustrations, photographs. "*Ugly Accent* is an emerging literary journal out of Madison, Wisconsin. The focus of our journal is not only to publish exceptional writing, but also to glorify the cesspool of talent this region breeds. We put forth a challenge to our submitters to find that inherent degree of separation from the good ole heartland." Semiannual. Estab. 2006. Circ. 2,000.

Needs Experimental, feminist, gay, humor/satire, lesbian, literary, regional (midwest). Does not want pieces containing unnecessary violence or those that are sexist, racist or homophobic in nature. Receives 10 mss/month. Accepts 2-7 mss/issue; 15-20 mss/year. Ms published 6 months after acceptance. **Publishes 5-10 new writers/year.** Published Susan Yount, Brian Nealon, C.J. Krueger, Joseph Fronczak, Ryan Chapman, Shanley Erin Kane, Bayard Godsave, Erica Goodkind, Louis Bourgeois, Erin Pringle, and Nicolette Kittinger. Length: 1,000-6,000 words. Average length: 3,000 words. Publishes short shorts. Average length of short shorts: 1,000 words. Also publishes literary essays, literary criticism, book reviews, poetry. Send review copies to Juli Obudzinski. Often comments on/critiques rejected mss.

How to Contact Send complete ms with cover letter. Include estimated word count, brief bio, list of publications. Responds to queries in 2-4 weeks; mss in 4-6 months. Send disposable copy of ms and #10 SASE for reply only. Considers simultaneous submissions, previously published submissions. Sample copy available on Web site. Guidelines available on Web site.

Payment/Terms Writers receive contributor's copies. Pays on publication. Acquires one-time rights, electronic rights. Publication is not copyrighted.

Advice "We are looking for writers with subtlety and a predilection for experimentation with language and form. We believe that prose should test the elasticity of language and utilize the form for all its worth. We seek literary pieces that challenge everything else that ends up filling the shelves of chain stores littered across the country. Those looking for fame need not apply. Instead, those whose writing challenges the mold, works against the metaphorical grain. We like good writing, who doesn't, but it also has to catch our attention somehow. Satires, absurdity, form stretching free style prose are all goodies for us. We like when you bend the rules a little and things become messy and a little strange."

[C] VERBSAP.COM, Concise Prose. Enough Said.

E-mail: editor@verbsap.com. Web site: www.verbsap.com. **Contact:** Laurie Seider, editor. Online magazine. "Verbsap showcases an eclectic selection of the finest in concise prose by established and emerging writers." Published quarterly. Estab. 2005.

Needs Literary, mainstream. Does not want violent, racist or pornographic content. Accepts 200 mss/year. Ms published 2-4 weeks after acceptance. Length: 3,000 words (max). Average length: 2,000 words. Publishes short shorts. Average length of short shorts: 900 words. Also publishes literary essays, author and artist interviews, and book reviews. Always comments on/critiques rejected mss.

How to Contact Follow online guidelines. Accepts submissions by e-mail. Responds to mss in 1-3 weeks. Considers simultaneous submissions. Guidelines available on Web site.

Payment/Terms Sends galleys to author. Publication is copyrighted.

Advice "We're looking for stark, elegant prose. Make us weep or make us laugh, but move us. You might find our 'Editor's Notebook' essays helpful."

✑ WILD VIOLET

Wild Violet, P.O. Box 39706, Philadelphia PA 19106-9706. E-mail: wildvioletmagazine@yahoo.com. Web site: www.wildviolet.net. **Contact:** Alyce Wilson, editor. Online magazine: illustrations, photos. "Our goal is to make a place for the arts: to make the arts more accessible and to serve as a creative forum for writers and artists. Our audience includes English-speaking readers from all over the world, who are interested in both 'high art' and pop culture." Quarterly. Estab. 2001.

Needs Comics/graphic novels, ethnic/multicultural, experimental, fantasy (space fantasy, sword and sorcery), feminist, gay, horror (dark fantasy, futuristic, psychological, supernatural), humor/satire, lesbian, literary, New Age, psychic/supernatural/occult, science fiction. "No stories where sexual or violent content is just used to shock the reader. No racist writings." Receives 30 unsolicited mss/month. Accepts 5 mss/issue; 20 mss/year. **Publishes 30 new writers/year.** Recently published work by Deen Borok, Wayne Scheer, Jane McDonald and Eric Brown. Length: 500-6,000 words; average length: 3,000 words. Also publishes literary essays, literary criticism, poetry. Sometimes comments on rejected mss.

How to Contact Send complete ms. Accepts submissions by e-mail. Include estimated word count and brief bio. Send SASE for return of ms or send a disposable copy of ms and #10 SASE for reply only. Responds in 1 week to queries; 3-6 months to mss. Accepts simultaneous, multiple submissions. Sample copy online. Writer's guidelines by e-mail.

Payment/Terms Writers receive bio and links on contributor's page. Request limited electronic rights, for online publication and archival only. Sponsors awards/contests.

Advice "We look for stories that are well-paced and show character and plot development. Even short shorts should do more than simply paint a picture. Manuscripts stand out when the author's voice is fresh and engaging. Avoid muddying your story with too many characters and don't attempt to shock the reader with an ending you have not earned. Experiment with styles and structures, but don't resort to experimentation for its own sake."

✑ WORD RIOT, A Communication-Breakdown Production

Word Riot Press, P.O. Box 414, Middletown NJ 07748-3143. (732)706-1272. Fax: (732)706-5856. E-mail: wr.submissions@gmail.com. Web site: www.wordriot.org. **Contact:** Jacki Corley, publisher; Timmy Waldron and Kevin O'cuinn, fiction editors; Charles P. Ries, poetry editor. Online magazine. Monthly. Estab. 2002. Member, CLMP.

Needs Humor/satire, literary, mainstream. "No fantasy, science fiction, romance." Accepts 20-25 mss/issue; 240-300 mss/year. Publishes ms 1-2 months after acceptance. Agented fiction 5%. Publishes 8-10 new writers/year. Length: 300-6,000 words; average length: 2,700 words. Publishes flash fiction, short stories, creative nonfiction and poetry. Also publishes literary essays, poetry. Often comments on rejected mss.

How to Contact Accepts submissions by e-mail. Include estimated word count and brief bio. Responds in 4-6 weeks to mss. Accepts multiple submissions. Sample copy online. Writer's guidelines online.

Payment/Terms Acquires electronic rights. Not copyrighted. Sponsors awards/contests.

Advice "We're always looking for something edgy or quirky. We like writers who take risks."

✑ WORDS ON WALLS

3408 Whitfield Ave. Apt 4, Cincinnati OH 45220. (513)961-1475. E-mail: editor@wordsonwalls.net. Web site: http://wordsonwalls.net. **Contact:** Kathrine Wright; Ariana-Sophia Kartsonis. Quarterly. Estab. 2003.

Needs Experimental, feminist, gay, literary. Receives 25-35 unsolicited mss/month. Accepts 2-3 mss/issue; 6-12 mss/year. Responds to mss in 12 weeks. Publishes ms 3-4 months after acceptance. Publishes short shorts. Also publishes literary essays, poetry. Often comments on rejected mss.

How to Contact Accepts submissions by e-mail. Accepts simultaneous, multiple submissions and reprints. Writer's guidelines online.

Payment/Terms Writer retains all rights.

Advice "We like work that is edgy, beautifully written with a strong sense of voice and music."

Consumer Magazines

In this section of *Novel & Short Story Writer's Market* are consumer magazines with circulations of more than 10,000. Many have circulations in the hundreds of thousands or millions. And among the oldest magazines listed here are ones not only familiar to us, but also to our parents, grandparents and even great-grandparents: *The Atlantic Monthly* (1857); *The New Yorker* (1925); *Esquire* (1933); and *Ellery Queen's Mystery Magazine* (1941).

Consumer periodicals make excellent markets for fiction in terms of exposure, prestige and payment. Because these magazines are well known, however, competition is great. Even the largest consumer publications buy only one or two stories an issue, yet thousands of writers submit to these popular magazines.

Despite the odds, it is possible for talented new writers to break into print in the magazines listed here. Your keys to breaking into these markets are careful research, professional presentation and, of course, top-quality fiction.

TYPES OF CONSUMER MAGAZINES

In this section you will find a number of popular publications, some for a broad-based, general-interest readership and others for large but select groups of readers—children, teenagers, women, men and seniors. There are also religious and church-affiliated magazines, publications devoted to the interests of particular cultures and outlooks, and top markets for genre fiction.

SELECTING THE RIGHT MARKET

Unlike smaller journals and publications, most of the magazines listed here are available at newsstands and bookstores. Many can also be found in the library, and guidelines and sample copies are almost always available by mail or online. Start your search by reviewing the listings, then familiarize yourself with the fiction included in the magazines that interest you.

Don't make the mistake of thinking that just because you are familiar with a magazine, their fiction is the same today as when you first saw it. Nothing could be further from the truth. Consumer magazines, no matter how well established, are constantly revising their fiction needs as they strive to expand their audience base.

In a magazine that uses only one or two stories an issue, take a look at the nonfiction articles and features as well. These can give you a better idea of the audience for the publication and clues to the type of fiction that might appeal to them.

If you write genre fiction, look in the Category Index beginning on page 594. There you will find a list of markets that say they are looking for a particular subject.

FURTHERING YOUR SEARCH

See You've Got a Story (page 2) for information about the material common to all listings in this book. In this section in particular, pay close attention to the number of submissions a magazine receives in a given period and how many they publish in the same period. This will give you a clear picture of how stiff your competition can be.

While many of the magazines listed here publish one or two pieces of fiction in each issue, some also publish special fiction issues once or twice a year. When possible, we have indicated this in the listing information. We also note if the magazine is open to novel excerpts as well as short fiction, and we advise novelists to query first before submitting long work.

The Business of Fiction Writing, beginning on page 65, covers the basics of submitting your work. Professional presentation is a must for all markets listed. Editors at consumer magazines are especially busy, and anything you can do to make your manuscript easy to read and accessible will help your chances of being published. Most magazines want to see complete manuscripts, but watch for publications in this section that require a query first.

As in the previous section, we've included our own comments in many of the listings, set off by a bullet (●). Whenever possible, we list the publication's recent awards and honors. We've also included any special information we feel will help you in determining whether a particular publication interests you.

The maple leaf symbol (🍁) identifies our Canadian listings. You will also find some English-speaking markets from around the world. These foreign magazines are denoted with 🌐 at the beginning of the listings. Remember to use International Reply Coupons rather than stamps when you want a reply from a country other than your own.

Periodicals of Interest

For More Info

For more on consumer magazines, see issues of *Writer's Digest* (F+W Publications) and other industry trade publications available in larger libraries.

For news about some of the genre publications listed here and information about a particular field, there are a number of magazines devoted to genre topics, including *The Drood Review of Mystery; Science Fiction Chronicle; Locus* (for science fiction); and *Romance Writers' Report* (available to members of Romance Writers of America).

$⬛ AIM MAGAZINE

Aim Publishing Co., P.O. Box 390, Milton WA 98354-0390. (253)815-9030. Fax: (206)543-2746. Web site: aimmagazine.org. **Contact:** Ruth Apilado, associate editor. Magazine: $8^1/_2 \times 11$; 48 pages; slick paper; photos and illustrations. Publishes material "to purge racism from the human bloodstream through the written word—that is the purpose of *Aim Magazine*." Quarterly. Estab. 1975. Circ. 10,000.

Needs Ethnic/multicultural, historical, mainstream, suspense. Open. No "religious" mss. Published special fiction issue last year; plans another. Receives 25 unsolicited mss/month. Accepts 15 mss/issue; 60 mss/year. Publishes ms 3 months after acceptance. **Publishes 40 new writers/year.** Recently published work by Christina Touregny, Thomas Lee Harris, Michael Williams and Jake Halpern. Publishes short shorts. Sometimes comments on rejected mss.

How to Contact Send complete ms. Accepts submissions by e-mail. Include SASE with cover letter and author's photograph. Responds in 2 months to queries; 1 month to mss. Accepts simultaneous submissions. Sample copy and writer's guidelines for $4 and 9×12 SAE with $1.70 postage or online.

Payment/Terms Pays $25-35. Pays on publication for first, one-time rights.

Advice "Search for those who are making unselfish contributions to their community and write about them. Write about your own experiences. Be familar with the background of your characters. Known for stories with social significance, proving that people from different ethnic, racial backgrounds are more alike than they are different."

$⬛ ▣ ANALOG SCIENCE FICTION & FACT

Dell Magazine Fiction Group, 475 Park Ave. S., 11th Floor, New York NY 10016. (212)686-7188. Fax: (212)686-7414. E-mail: analog@dellmagazines.com. Web site: www.analogsf.com. **Contact:** Stanley Schmidt, editor. Magazine: 144 pages; illustrations; photos. Monthly. Estab. 1930. Circ. 50,000.

• Fiction published in *Analog* has won numerous Nebula and Hugo Awards.

Needs Science fiction (hard science/technological, soft/sociological). "No fantasy or stories in which the scientific background is implausible or plays no essential role." Receives 500 unsolicited mss/month. Accepts 6 mss/issue; 70 mss/year. Publishes ms 10 months after acceptance. Agented fiction 5%. **Publishes 3-4 new writers/year.** Recently published work by Ben Bova, Stephen Baxter, Larry Niven, Michael F. Flynn, Timothy Zahn, Robert J. Sawyer, and Joe Haldeman. Length: 2,000-80,000 words; average length: 10,000 words. Publishes short shorts. Sometimes comments on rejected mss.

How to Contact Send complete ms with a cover letter. Accepts queries for serials and fact articles only; query by mail. Include estimated word count. Send SASE for return of ms or send a disposable copy of ms and #10 SASE for reply only. Responds in 1 month to queries. Accepts multiple submissions. No simultaneous submissions. Sample copy for $5. Writer's guidelines online. Reviews fiction.

Payment/Terms Pays 4¢/word for novels; 5-6¢/word for novelettes; 6-8¢/word for shorts under 7,500 words; $450-600 for intermediate lengths. Pays on acceptance for first North American serial, nonexclusive foreign serial rights. Sends galleys to author. Not copyrighted.

Advice "I'm looking for irresistibly entertaining stories that make me think about things in ways I've never done before. Read several issues to get a broad feel for our tastes, but don't try to imitate what you read."

$⬛ ART TIMES, Commentary and Resources for the Fine and Performing Arts

P.O. Box 730, Mount Marion NY 12456-0730. (914)246-6944. Fax: (914)246-6944. Web site: www.art timesjournal.com. **Contact:** Raymond J. Steiner, fiction editor. Magazine: 12×15; 24 pages; Jet paper and cover; illustrations; photos. "*Art Times* covers the art fields and is distributed in locations most frequented by those enjoying the arts. Our copies are distributed throughout the Northeast region as well as in most of the galleries of Soho, 57th Street and Madison Avenue in the metropolitan area; locations include theaters, galleries, museums, cultural centers and the like. Our readers are mostly over 40, affluent, art-conscious and sophisticated. Subscribers are located across U.S. and abroad (Italy, France, Germany, Greece, Russia, etc.)." Monthly. Estab. 1984. Circ. 28,000.

Needs Adventure, ethnic/multicultural, fantasy, feminist, gay, historical, humor/satire, lesbian, literary, mainstream, science fiction, contemporary. "We seek quality literary pieces. Nothing violent, sexist, erotic, juvenile, racist, romantic, political, etc." Receives 30-50 unsolicited mss/month. Accepts 1 mss/issue; 10 mss/year. Publishes ms 3 years after acceptance. **Publishes 6 new writers/ year.** Publishes short shorts.

How to Contact Send complete ms with SASE. Responds in 6 months to mss. Accepts simultaneous, multiple submissions. Sample copy for 9×12 SAE and 6 first-class stamps. Writer's guidelines for #10 SASE or on Web site.

Payment/Terms Pays $25 maximum (honorarium) and 1 year's free subscription. Pays on publication for first North American serial, first rights.

Advice "Competition is greater (more submissions received), but keep trying. We print new as well as published writers."

$ 🖉 ⊙ 🖳 ASIMOV'S SCIENCE FICTION

Dell Magazine Fiction Group, 475 Park Ave. S., 11th Floor, New York NY 10016. (212)686-7188. Fax: (212)686-7414. E-mail: asimovs@dellmagazines.com. Web site: www.asimovs.com. **Contact:** Sheila Williams, editor. Magazine: 5¼×8¼ (trim size); 144 pages; 30 lb. newspaper; 70 lb. to 8 pt. C1S cover stock; illustrations; rarely photos. Magazine consists of science fiction and fantasy stories for adults and young adults. Publishes "the best short science fiction available." Estab. 1977. Circ. 50,000.

• Named for a science fiction "legend," *Asimov's* regularly receives Hugo and Nebula Awards. Editor Gardner Dozois has received several awards for editing including Hugos and those from *Locus* magazine.

Needs Fantasy, science fiction (hard science, soft sociological). No horror or psychic/supernatural. Would like to see more hard science fiction. Receives approximately 800 unsolicited mss/month. Accepts 10 mss/issue. Publishes ms 6-12 months after acceptance. Agented fiction 10%. **Publishes 6 new writers/year.** Recently published work by Ursula LeGuin and Larry Niven. Publishes short shorts. Sometimes comments on rejected mss.

How to Contact Send complete ms with SASE. Responds in 2 months to queries; 3 months to mss. Accepts reprints submissions. No simultaneous submissions. Sample copy for $5. Writer's guidelines for #10 SASE or online. Reviews fiction.

Payment/Terms Pays 5-8¢/word. Pays on acceptance. Buys first North American serial, nonexclusive foreign serial rights; reprint rights occasionally. Sends galleys to author.

Advice "We are looking for character stories rather than those emphasizing technology or science. New writers will do best with a story under 10,000 words. Every new science fiction or fantasy film seems to 'inspire' writers—and this is not a desirable trend. Be sure to be familiar with our magazine and the type of story we like; workshops and lots of practice help. Try to stay away from trite, clichéd themes. Start in the middle of the action, starting as close to the end of the story as you possibly can. We like stories that extrapolate from up-to-date scientific research, but don't forget that we've been publishing clone stories for decades. Ideas must be fresh."

$ BACKROADS, Motorcycles, Travel & Adventure

Backroads, Inc., P.O. Box 317, Branchville NJ 07826. (973)948-4176. Fax: (973)948-0823. E-mail: editor@backroadsusa.com. Web site: www.backroadsusa.com. "*Backroads* is a motorcycle tour magazine geared toward getting motorcyclists on the road and traveling. We provide interesting destinations, unique roadside attractions and eateries, plus Rip & Ride Route Sheets. We cater to all brands. If you really ride, you need *Backroads*." Monthly. Estab. 1995. Circ. 50,000.

Needs Travel, motorcycle-related stories. Publishes ms 3 months after acceptance. Articles must be motorcycle-related and include images of motorcycles to accompany story. It helps if you actually ride a motorcycle.

How to Contact Query. Accepts submissions by e-mail. Sample copy for $5. Writer's guidelines on Web site.

Payment/Terms Pays 5¢/word. Pays on publication for one-time rights.

$ 🖉 BOMB MAGAZINE

80 Hanson Place, Suite 703, Brooklyn NY 11217. (718)636-9100. Fax: (718)636-9200. E-mail: generali nquiries@bombsite.com. Web site: www.bombsite.com. Magazine: 11×14; 104 pages; 70 lb. glossy cover; illustrations; photos. Written, edited and produced by industry professionals and funded by those interested in the arts. Publishes writing which is unconventional and contains an edge, whether it be in style or subject matter. Quarterly. Estab. 1981. Circ. 36,000.

Needs Experimental, novel excerpts, contemporary. No genre: romance, science fiction, horror, western. Receives 200 unsolicited mss/month. Accepts 6 mss/issue; 24 mss/year. Publishes ms 3-6 months after acceptance. Agented fiction 70%. **Publishes 2-3 new writers/year.** Recently published work by Lynne Tillman, Dennis Cooper, Susan Wheeler, and Laurie Sheck.

How to Contact SASE. Responds in 3-5 months to mss. Accepts multiple submissions. Sample copy for $7, plus $2.13 postage and handling. Writer's guidelines in FAQ on Web site.

Payment/Terms Pays $100, and contributor's copies. Pays on publication for first, one-time rights. Sends galleys to author.

Advice "We are committed to publishing new work that commercial publishers often deem too dangerous or difficult. The problem is, a lot of young writers confuse difficult with dreadful. Read the magazine before you even think of submitting something."

$🖉 📧 BOSTON REVIEW

35 Medford St., Suite 302, Sommerville, MA 02143. E-mail: review@bostonreview.net. Web site: www.bostonreview.net. **Contact:** Junot Diaz, fiction editor. Magazine: $10^3/4 \times 14^3/4$; 60 pages; newsprint. "The editors are committed to a society and culture that foster human diversity and a democracy in which we seek common grounds of principle amidst our many differences. In the hope of advancing these ideals, the *Review* acts as a forum that seeks to enrich the language of public debate." Bimonthly. Estab. 1975. Circ. 20,000.

• *Boston Review* is the recipient of a Pushcart Prize in poetry.

Needs Ethnic/multicultural, experimental, literary, regional, translations, contemporary, prose poem. Receives 150 unsolicited mss/month. Accepts 4-6 mss/year. Publishes ms 4 months after acceptance. Recently published work by Dagberto Gilb, Charles Johnson, Deb Olin Unferth, T.E. Holt, and Yvonne Woon. Length: 1,200-5,000 words; average length: 2,000 words. Occasionally comments on rejected mss.

How to Contact Send complete ms. Responds in 4 months to queries. Accepts simultaneous submissions if noted. Sample copy for $5 or online. Writer's guidelines online. Reviews fiction. "The editors are looking for fiction in which a heart struggles against itself, in which the messy unmanageable complexity of the world is revealed. Sentences that are so sharp they cut the eye."

Payment/Terms Pays $300, and 3 contributor's copies. Acquires first North American serial, first rights.

$🖉 BOYS' LIFE

Boy Scouts of America, 1325 W. Walnut Hill Lane, Irving TX 75015-2079. (972)580-2366. Fax: (972)580-2079. Web site: www.boyslife.org. Managing Editor: Michael Goldman. Senior Writer: Aaron Derr. Fiction Editor: Paula Murphey. Monthly magazine. Estab. 1911. Circ. 1,300,000. *Boys' Life* is "a 4-color general interest magazine for boys 8 to 18 who are members of the Cub Scouts, Boy Scouts or Venturers."

Needs Young readers, middle readers, young adults: adventure, animal, contemporary, history, humor, multicultural, nature/environment, problem-solving, sports, science fiction, spy/mystery. Does not want to see animals and adult reminiscence." Buys only 12-16 mss/year. Average word length: 1,000-1,500. Byline given.

How to Contact Send complete ms with cover letter and SASE to fiction editor. Responds to queries/ mss in 2 months.

Payment/Terms Pays on acceptance. Buys first rights. Pays $750 and up. Sample copies for $3.95 plus 9×12 SASE. Writer's guidelines available for SASE.

Tips "We strongly urge you to study at least a year's issues to better understand the type of material published. Articles for Boys' Life must interest and entertain boys ages 8 to 18. Write for a boy you know who is 12. Our readers demand crisp, punchy writing in relatively short, straightforward sentences. The editors demand well-reported articles that demonstrate high standards of journalism. We follow *The New York Times* manual of style and usage. All submissions must be accompanied by SASE with adequate postage."

🖉 📧 BRAIN, CHILD, The Magazine for Thinking Mothers

March Press, P.O. Box 5566, Charlottesville VA 22905. (434)977-4151. E-mail: editor@brainchildmag .com. Web site: www.brainchildmag.com. **Contact:** Jennifer Niesslein and Stephanie Wilkinson, co-editors. Magazine: $7^1/4 \times 10$; 60-100 pages; 80lb. matte cover; illustrations; photos. "*Brain, Child* reflects modern motherhood—the way it really is. We like to think of *Brain, Child* as a community, for and by mothers who like to think about what raising kids does for (and to) the mind and soul. *Brain, Child* isn't your typical parenting magazine. We couldn't cupcake-decorate our way out of a paper bag. We are more 'literary' than 'how-to,' more *New Yorker* than *Parents*. We shy away from expert advice on childrearing in favor of first-hand reflections by great writers (Jane Smiley, Barbara Ehrenreich, Anne Tyler) on life as a mother. Each quarterly issue is full of essays, features, humor, reviews, fiction, art, cartoons, and our readers' own stories. Our philosophy is pretty simple: Motherhood is worthy of literature. And there are a lot of ways to mother, all of them interesting. We're proud to be publishing articles and essays that are smart, down to earth, sometimes funny, and sometimes poignant." Quarterly. Estab. 2000. Circ. 30,000. Member, IPA, ASME.

• *Brain, Child* has either won or been nominated for the *Utne* Independent Prss Award each year it has been in existence.

Needs Literary, mainstream, literary. No genre fiction. Receives 200 unsolicited mss/month. Accepts 1 mss/issue; 4 mss/year. Publishes ms 6 months after acceptance. Recently published work by Anne Tyler, Barbara Lucy Stevens and Jane Smiley. Length: 800-5,000 words; average length: 2,500 words. Also publishes literary essays. Sometimes comments on rejected mss.

How to Contact Send complete ms. Accepts submissions by e-mail (be sure to copy and paste the ms into the body of the e-mail). Include estimated word count, brief bio and list of publications. Send SASE (or IRC) for return of ms or send a disposable copy of ms and #10 SASE for reply only. Responds in 1 month to queries; 1-3 months to mss. Accepts simultaneous and reprints, multiple submissions. Sample copy online. Writer's guidelines online. Reviews fiction.

Payment/Terms Payment varies. Pays on publication for first North American serial, electronic rights. *Brain, Child* anthology rights Sends galleys to author.

Advice "We only publish fiction with a strong motherhood theme. But, like every other publisher of literary fiction, we look for well-developed characters, a compelling story, and an ending that is as strong as the rest of the piece."

$ ⬛ ◎ BUGLE

Rocky Mountain Elk Foundation, P.O. Box 8249, 5705 Grant Creek Rd., Missoula MT 59808. (406)523-4538. Fax: (406)543-7710. E-mail: bugle@rmef.org. Web site: www.elkfoundation.org. **Contact:** P J DelHomme, hunting/human interest editor bugle@rmef.org. Paul Queneau, conservation editor pquenea@rmef.org. Magazine: 114-172 pages; 55 lb. Escanaba paper; 80 lb. Steriling cover, b&w, 4-color illustrations; photos. *Bugle* is the membership publication of the Rocky Mountain Elk Foundation, a nonprofit wildlife conservation group. "Our readers are predominantly hunters, many of them conservationists who care deeply about protecting wildlife habitat." Bimonthly. Estab. 1984. Circ. 155,000.

Needs Adventure, children's/juvenile, historical, humor/satire, novel excerpts, slice-of-life vignettes, western, human interest, natural history, conservation. "We accept fiction and nonfiction stories pertaining in some way to elk, other wildlife, hunting, habitat conservation, and related issues. We would like to see more humor." Upcoming themes: "Bowhunting for Elk"; "Lost: Stories of Disorientation"; "Bears" . Receives 20-30 unsolicited mss/month. Accepts 3-4 mss/issue; 18-24 mss/year. Publishes ms 1-36 months after acceptance. **Publishes 12 new writers/year.** Recently published work by Rick Bass and Susan Ewing. Length: 1,500-4,500 words; average length: 2,500 words. Publishes short shorts. Also publishes literary essays, poetry.

How to Contact Query with or without published clips or send complete ms. Prefers submissions by e-mail. Send SASE for reply, return of ms or send a disposable copy of ms. Responds in 1 month to queries; 3 months to mss. Accepts reprints, multiple submissions. Sample copy for $5. Writer's guidelines online.

Payment/Terms Pays 20¢/word. Pays on acceptance for one-time rights.

Advice "Hunting stories and essays should celebrate the hunting experience, demonstrating respect for wildlife, the land, and the hunt. Articles on elk behavior or elk habitat should include personal observations and entertain as well as educate. No freelance product reviews or formulaic how-to articles accepted. Straight action-adventure hunting stories are in short supply, as are "Situation Ethics" manuscripts."

$ ⬛ ◎ CADET QUEST MAGAZINE

P.O. Box 7259, Grand Rapids MI 49510-7259. (616)241-5616. Fax: (616)241-5558. E-mail: submissions@calvinistcadets.org. Web site: www.calvinistcadets.org. **Contact:** G. Richard Broene, editor. Magazine: $8^{1}/_{2} \times 11$; 24 pages; illustrations; photos. "*Cadet Quest Magazine* shows boys 9-14 how God is at work in their lives and in the world around them." Estab. 1958. Circ. 10,000.

Needs Adventure, children's/juvenile, religious/inspirational (Christian), spiritual, sports, comics. "Need material based on Christian perspective and articles on Christian role models. Avoid long dialogue and little action." No fantasy, science fiction, fashion, horror or erotica. List of upcoming themes available for SASE or on Web site in February. Receives 60 unsolicited mss/month. Accepts 3 mss/issue; 18 mss/year. Publishes ms 4-11 months after acceptance. **Publishes 0-3 new writers/year.** Length: 900-1,500 words; average length: 1,200 words. Publishes short shorts.

How to Contact Send complete ms by mail or send submissions in the body of the e-mail. Not as an attachment. Responds in 2 months. No queries. Accepts simultaneous, multiple submissions and reprints. Sample copy for 9×12 SASE. Writer's guidelines for #10 SASE.

Payment/Terms Pays 4-6¢/word, and 1 contributor's copy. Pays on acceptance for first North American serial, one-time, second serial (reprint), simultaneous rights. Rights purchased vary with author and material.

Advice "On a cover sheet, list the point your story is trying to make. Our magazine has a theme for each issue, and we try to fit the fiction to the theme. All fiction should be about a young boy's interests—sports, outdoor activities, problems—with an emphasis on a Christian perspective. No simple moralisms. Best time to submit material is February-April."

$🖂 CALLIOPE, Exploring World History

Cobblestone Publishing Company, 30 Grove St., Peterborough NH 03458. (603)924-7209. Fax: (603)924-7380. Web site: www.cobblestonepub.com. Editorial Director: Lou Waryncia. Co-editors: Rosalie Baker and Charles Baker. Magazine published 9 times/year. "*Calliope* covers world history (East/West), and lively, original approaches to the subject are the primary concerns of the editors in choosing material."

- Calliope themes for 2005-2006 include the Aztecs, Medieval Japan, the Spice Trade, Rembrandt, the Irish Potato Famine, Charles Dickens. For additional themes and time frames, visit their Web site.

Needs Middle readers and young adults: adventure, folktales, plays, history, biographical fiction. Material must relate to forthcoming themes. Word length: up to 800.

How to Contact "A query must consist of the following to be considered (please use nonerasable paper): a brief cover letter stating subject and word length of the proposed article; a detailed one-page outline explaining the information to be presented in the article; an bibliography of materials the author intends to use in preparing the article; a self-addressed stamped envelope. Writers new to Calliope should send a writing sample with query. In all correspondence, please include your complete address as well as a telephone number where you can be reached. A writer may send as many queries for one issue as he or she wishes, but each query must have a separate cover letter, outline and bibliography as well as a SASE. Telephone and e-mail queries are not accepted. Handwritten queries will not be considered. Queries may be submitted at any time, but queries sent well in advance of deadline may not be answered for several months. Go-aheads requesting material proposed in queries are usually sent five months prior to publication date. Unused queries will be returned approximately three to four months prior to publication date."

Payment/Terms Buys all rights for mss and artwork. Pays 20-25¢/word for stories/articles. Pays on an individual basis for poetry, activities, games/puzzles. Sample copy for $5.95 and SAE with $2 postage. Writer's guidelines for SASE.

🖂 CANADIAN WRITER'S JOURNAL

P.O. Box 1178, New Liskeard ON P0J 1P0 Canada. (705)647-5424. Fax: (705)647-8366. Web site: www.cwj.ca. Accepts well-written articles by all writers. Bimonthly. Estab. 1984. Circ. 350.

Needs Requirements being met by annual contest. Send SASE for rules, or see guidelines on Web site. "Does not want gratuitous violence, sex subject matter." Publishes ms 9 months after acceptance. **Publishes 40 new writers/year.** Also publishes poetry. Rarely comments on rejected mss.

How to Contact Accepts submissions by e-mail. Responds in 2 months to queries. Writer's guidelines online.

Payment/Terms Pays on publication for one-time rights.

$CAPPER'S

Ogden Publications, Inc., 1503 SW 42nd St., Topeka KS 66609-1265. (785)274-4300. E-mail: tsmith@ cappers.com. Web site: www.cappers.com. *"Capper's* is upbeat, focusing on the homey feelings people like to share, as well as hopes and dreams." Monthly. Estab. 1879. Circ. 200,000.

Needs Historical, mainstream, mystery/suspense, romance, serialized novels, western. Absolutley no sex, violence, profanity, or alcohol use. Publishes ms 2-24 months after acceptance. Send query lettr first.

How to Contact Responds in 2-3 months to queries; 6 months to mss. No simultaneous submissions. Sample copy online. Writer's guidelines online.

Payment/Terms Pays $100-400. Pays for poetry and fiction on acceptance; articles on publication. Acquires first North American serial rights.

$◎ CICADA MAGAZINE

Cricket Magazine Group, 70 East Lake, Suite 300, Chicago IL 60601. (312)701-1720. Fax: (312)701-1728. E-mail: dvetter@caruspub.com. Web site: www.cricketmag.com. **Contact:** Deborah Vetter, executive editor; John Sandfor, art director. Literary magazine: 128 pages; some illustrations. *"Cicada,* for ages 14 and up, publishes original short stories, poems, artwork and first-person essays written for teens and young adults." Bimonthly. Estab. 1998. Circ. 18,000.

Needs Adventure, fantasy, historical, humor/satire, mainstream, mystery/suspense, romance, science fiction, western, young adult/teen, sports. "Our readership is age 14-21. Submissions should be tailored for high school and college-age audience, not junior high or younger. We especially need humor and fantasy. We are also interested in first-person, coming-of-age nonfiction (life in the Peace Corps, significant first jobs, etc.)." Accepts 10 mss/issue; 60 mss/year. Publishes ms 1 year after acceptance. Length: 3,000-15,000 words; average length: 5,000 words. Also publishes poetry. Sometimes comments on rejected mss.

How to Contact Send complete ms. Send SASE for return of ms or send a disposable copy of ms and #10 SASE for reply only. Responds in 6 months to mss. Accepts simultaneous and reprints submissions. Sample copy for $8.50. Writer's guidelines for SASE and on Web site. Reviews fiction.

Payment/Terms Pays 25¢/word, plus 6 contributor's copies. Pays on publication. Rights vary.

Advice "Quality writing, good literary style, genuine teen sensibility, depth, humor, good character development, avoidance of stereotypes. Read several issues to familiarize yourself with our style."

$◙ ◎ CLUBHOUSE MAGAZINE

Focus on the Family, 8605 Explorer Dr., Colorado Springs CO 80920. (719)531-3400. Web site: www.clubhousemagazine.com. **Contact:** Joanna Lutz, editorial assistant. Magazine: 8×11; 24 pages; illustrations; photos. *"Clubhouse* readers are 8-12 year old boys and girls who desire to know more about God and the Bible. Their parents (who typically pay for the membership) want wholesome, educational material with Scriptural or moral insight. The kids want excitement, adventure, action, humor, or mystery. Your job as a writer is to please both the parent and child with each article." Monthly. Estab. 1987. Circ. 90,000.

Needs Adventure, children's/juvenile (8-12 years), humor/satire, mystery/suspense, religious/inspirational, holiday. Avoid contemporary, middle-class family settings (existing authors meet this need), stories dealing with boy-girl relationships. "No science fiction." Receives 150 unsolicited mss/month. Accepts 1 mss/issue. Publishes ms 6-12 months after acceptance. Agented fiction 15%. **Publishes 8 new writers/year.** Recently published work by Sigmund Brower and Nancy Rue.

How to Contact Send complete ms. Send SASE for reply, return of ms or send a disposable copy of ms. Responds in 2 months to mss. Sample copy for $1.50 with 9×12 SASE. Writer's guidelines for #10 SASE.

Payment/Terms Pays $200 and up for first time contributor and 5 contributor's copies; additional copies available. Pays on acceptance for non-exclusive license.

Advice Looks for "humor with a point, historical fiction featuring great Christians or Christians who lived during great times; contemporary, exotic settings; holiday material (Christmas, Thanksgiving, Easter, President's Day); parables; avoid graphic descriptions of evil creatures and sorcery; mystery stories; choose-your-own adventure stories. No contemporary, middle-class family settings (we already have authors who can meet these needs) or stories dealing with boy-girl relationships."

$◎ DISCIPLESWORLD, A Journal of News, Opinion, and Mission for the Christian Church
DisciplesWorld, Inc., 6325 N. Guilford Ave., Dyr. 213, Indianapolis IN 46202. E-mail: editor@disciple sworld.com. Web site: www.disciplesworld.com. "We are the journal of the Christian Church (Disciples of Christ) in North America. Our denomination numbers roughly 800,000. Disciples are a mainline Protestant group. Our readers are mostly laity, active in their churches, and interested in issues of faithful living, political and church news, ethics, and contemporary social issues." Monthly. Estab. 2002. Circ. 14,000.
Needs Ethnic/multicultural, mainstream, religious/inspirational, slice-of-life vignettes. "We're a religious publication, so use common sense! Stories do not have to be overtly 'religious,' but they should be uplifting and positive." Publishes ms 6 months after acceptance.
How to Contact Send complete ms. Accepts submissions by e-mail (editor@disciplesworld.com). Responds in 2 weeks to queries; 2 months to mss. Accepts simultaneous submissions. Sample copy for #10 SASE. Writer's guidelines online.
Payment/Terms Pays 16¢/word. Pays on publication for first North American serial rights.

$◎ FIFTY SOMETHING MAGAZINE
Linde Graphics Co., 1168 S. Beachview Rd., Willoughby OH 44094. (440)951-2468. Fax: (440)951-1015. "We are focusing on the 50-and-better reader." Quarterly. Estab. 1990. Circ. 10,000.
Needs Adventure, confessions, ethnic/multicultural, experimental, fantasy, historical, humor/satire, mainstream, mystery/suspense, novel excerpts, romance, slice-of-life vignettes, suspense, western. No erotica or horror. Receives 150 unsolicited mss/month. Accepts 5 mss/issue. Publishes ms 6 months after acceptance. **Publishes 20 new writers/year.** Recently published work by Gail Morrisey, Sally Morrisey, Jenny Miller, J. Alan Witt, and Sharon McGreagor. Length: 500-1,000 words; average length: 1,000 words. Publishes short shorts.
How to Contact Send complete ms. Responds in 3 months to queries; 3 months to mss. Accepts simultaneous submissions and reprints. Sample copy for 9 × 12 SAE and 4 first-class stamps. Writer's guidelines for #10 SASE.
Payment/Terms Pays $10-100. Pays on publication for one-time, second serial (reprint), simultaneous rights.

$ FLAUNT MAGAZINE
1422 North Highland Avenue, Los Angeles CA 90028. (323)836-1000. E-mail: info@flauntmagazine.com. Web site: www.flaunt.com. **Contact:** Andrew Pogany, senior editor. Magazine. "10 times a year *Flaunt* features the bold work of emerging photographers, writers, artists, and musicians. The quality of the content is mirrored in the sophisticated, interactive format of the magazine, using advanced printing techniques, fold-out articles, beautiful papers, and inserts to create a visually stimulating, surprisingly readable, and intelligent book that pushes the magazine into the realm of art-object. *Flaunt* magazine has for the last eight years made it a point to break new ground, earning itself a reputation as an engine and outlet for the culture of the cutting edge. *Flaunt* takes pride in reinventing itself each month, while consistently representing a hybrid of all that is interesting in entertainment, fashion, music, design, film, art, and literature." Estab. 1998. Circ. 110,000.
Needs Experimental, urban, academic. We publish 3 fiction peices a year. Length: 500-5,000 words.
How to Contact Guidelines available via e-mail.
Payment/Terms Acquires one-time rights and first option to reprint. Pays one-time flat-rate to be determined upon correspondence.

$ ⬛ ◎ ⬛ HIGHLIGHTS FOR CHILDREN
Manuscript Submissions, 803 Church St., Honesdale PA 18431-1824. (570)253-1080. Fax: (570)251-7847. Web site: www.highlights.com. **Contact:** Joelle Dujardin, associate editor. Magazine: 8½ × 11; 42 pages; uncoated paper; coated cover stock; illustrations; photos. "This book of wholesome fun is dedicated to helping children grow in basic skills and knowledge, in creativeness, in ability to think and reason, in sensitivity to others, in high ideals, and worthy ways of living—for children are the world's most important people. We publish stories for beginning and advanced readers. Up to 500 words for beginners (ages 3-7), up to 800 words for advanced (ages 8-12)." Monthly. Estab. 1946. Circ. about 2,000,000.
  • *Highlights* has won the Parent's Guide to Children's Media Award, Parent's Choice Award, and Editorial Excellence Awards from the Association of Educational Publishers.
Needs Adventure, children's/juvenile (up to age 12), fantasy, historical, humor/satire, animal, con-

temporary, folktales, multi-cultural, problem-solving, sports. "No war, crime or violence." Unusual stories appealing to both girls and boys; stories with good characterization, strong emotional appeal, vivid, full of action. "Needs stories that begin with action rather than description, have strong plot, believable setting, suspense from start to finish." Receives 600-800 unsolicited mss/month. **Publishes 30 new writers/year.** Recently published work by Eileen Spinelli, James M. Janik, Joy Cowley, Marilyn Kratz, Lissa Rovetch. Occasionally comments on rejected mss.

How to Contact Send complete ms Responds in 4 to 6 weeks. Responds in 2 months to queries. Accepts multiple submissions. Sample copy free. Writer's guidelines for SASE or on Web site.

Payment/Terms Pays $150 minimum, plus 2 contributor's copies. **Pays on acceptance.** Sends galleys to author.

Advice "We accept a story on its merit whether written by an unpublished or an experienced writer. Mss are rejected because of poor writing, lack of plot, trite or worn-out plot, or poor characterization. Children *like* stories and learn about life from stories. Children learn to become lifelong fiction readers by enjoying stories. Feel passion for your subject. Create vivid images. Write a child-centered story; leave adults in the background."

$HORIZONS: FOR TODAY'S JEWISH WOMAN

Targum Press, 22700 W. Eleven Mile Rd., Southfield MI 48034. Fax: (888)298-9992. E-mail: horizons @targum.com. Web site: www.targum.com. **Contact:** Suri Brand, chief editor. "We include fiction and nonfiction, memoirs, essays, historical, and informational articles, all of interest to the Orthodox Jewish Woman." Quarterly. Estab. 1994. Circ. 5,000.

Needs Historical, humor/satire, mainstream, slice-of-life vignettes. Nothing not suitable to Orthodox Jewish values. Receives 4-6 unsolicited mss/month. Accepts 2-3 mss/issue; 10-12 mss/year. Publishes ms 6 months after acceptance. **Publishes 15- 20 new writers/year.** Length: 1,000-3,000 words; average length: 1,500 words. Also publishes poetry.

How to Contact Send complete ms. Accepts submissions by e-mail, fax. Responds in 1 week to queries; 2 months to mss. Accepts simultaneous submissions. Writer's guidelines available.

Payment/Terms Pays 5¢/word. Pays 4-6 weeks after publication. Acquires one-time rights.

Advice "Study our publication to make certain your submission is appropriate to our target market."

$⬜⬜⬜⬜ IGNITE YOUR FAITH

(formerly Campus Life) Christianity Today, Inc., 465 Gundersen Dr., Carol Stream IL 60188. (630)260-6200. Fax: (630)480-2004. E-mail: iyf@igniteyourfaith.com. Web site: www.igniteyourfaith.com. **Contact:** Chris Lutes, editor. Magazine: 8¼×11¼; 72 pages; 4-color and b&w illustrations; 4-color and b&w photos. "*Ignite Your Faith* is a magazine for high-school students. Our editorial slant is not overtly religious. The indirect style is intended to create a safety zone with our readers and to reflect our philosophy that God is interested in all of life. Therefore, we publish 'message stories' side by side with general interest, humor, etc. We are also looking for stories that help high school students consider a Christian college education." Bimonthly. Estab. 1942. Circ. 100,000.

• *Ignite Your Faith* regularly receives awards from the Evangelical Press Association.

Needs "All fiction submissions must be contemporary, reflecting the teen experience in the new milllennium. We are a Christian magazine but are *not* interested in sappy, formulaic, sentimentally religious stories. We *are* interested in well-crafted stories that portray life realistically, stories high school and college youth relate to. Writing must reflect a Christian world view. If you don't understand our market and style, don't submit." Accepts 5 mss/year. Reading and response time slower in summer. **Publishes 3-4 new writers/year.**

How to Contact Query. Responds in 8 weeks to queries. Sample copy for $3 and 9½×11 SAE with 3 first-class stamps. Writer's guidelines online.

Payment/Terms Pays 20-25¢/word, and 2 contributor's copies. Pays on acceptance for first, one-time rights.

Advice "We print finely-crafted fiction that carries a contemporary teen (older teen) theme. First person fiction often works best. Ask us for sample copy with fiction story. We want experienced fiction writers who have something to say to young people without getting propagandistic."

⬜ JEWISH CURRENTS MAGAZINE

45 E. 33rd Street, New York NY 10016-1919. (845)626-2427. E-mail: lawrencebush@earthlink.net. **Contact:** Lawrence Bush. Magazine: 8½×11; 48 pages. A secular, progressive, independent Jewish

bimonthly, printing fiction, poetry articles and reviews on Jewish politics and history. Holocaust/ Resistance; Mideast peace process, Black-Jewish relations; labor struggles, women's issues. Audience is secular, left/progressive, Jewish, mostly urban. Bimonthly. Estab. 1946. Circ. 16,000.

Needs Ethnic/multicultural, feminist, historical, humor/satire, translations, contemporary. ''No no porn or hard sex, no escapist stuff. Go easy on experimentation, but we're interested.'' Must be well written! We are interested in *authentic* experience and readable prose; humanistic orientation. Jewish themes. '' Receives 6-10 unsolicited mss/month. Accepts 0-1 mss/issue; 8-10 mss/year. Publishes ms 2-24 months after acceptance. Recently published work by Elizabeth Swados, Esther Cohen, Lawrence Bush, Ralph Seliger, David Rothenberg. Length: 1,000-3,000 words; average length: 1,800 words. Publishes short shorts. Also publishes literary essays, literary criticism, poetry.

How to Contact Send complete ms with cover letter. ''Writers should include brief biographical information, especially their publishing histories.'' SASE. Responds in 2 months to mss. Sample copy for $3 with SAE and 3 first class stamps. Reviews fiction.

Payment/Terms Pays complimentary one-year subscription and 6 contributor's copies. ''We readily give reprint permission at no charge.'' Sends galleys to author.

$ ⬛ ◎ ⬛ KALEIDOSCOPE, Exploring the Experience of Disability Through Literature and the Fine Arts

Kaleidoscope Press, 701 S. Main St., Akron OH 44311-1019. (330)762-9755. Fax: (330)762-0912. Web site: www.udsakron.org. **Contact:** Gail Willmott, editor-in-chief. Magazine: $8\frac{1}{2} \times 11$; 64 pages; non-coated paper; coated cover stock; illustrations (all media); photos. Subscribers include individuals, agencies, and organizations that assist people with disabilities and many university and public libraries. Open to new writers but appreciates work by established writers as well. Especially interested in work by writers with a disability, but features writers both with and without disabilities. ''Writers without a disability must limit themselves to our focus, while those with a disability may explore any topic (although we prefer original perspectives about experiences with disability).'' Semiannual. Estab. 1979. Circ. 1,000.

- *Kaleidoscope* has received awards from the American Heart Association, the Great Lakes Awards Competition and Ohio Public Images.

Needs ''We look for well-developed plots, engaging characters and realistic dialogue. We lean toward fiction that emphasizes character and emotions rather than action-oriented narratives. No fiction that is stereotypical, patronizing, sentimental, erotic, or maudlin. No romance, religious or dogmatic fiction; no children's literature.'' Receives 20-25 unsolicited mss/month. Accepts 10 mss/year. Agented fiction 1%. **Publishes 2 new writer/year.** Recently published work by Kelly John Kalousdian, Beverly Lauderdale, and Paul Perry. Also publishes poetry.

How to Contact Accepts submissions by fax. Query first or send complete ms and cover letter. Include author's education and writing background and, if author has a disability, how it influenced the writing. SASE. Responds in 3 weeks to queries; 6 months to mss. Accepts simultaneous, multiple submissions and reprints. Sample copy for $6 prepaid. Writer's guidelines online.

Payment/Terms Pays $10-125, and 2 contributor's copies; additional copies $6. Pays on publication for first rights, reprints permitted with credit given to original publication. Rights revert to author upon publication.

Advice ''Read the magazine and get submission guidelines. We prefer that writers with a disability offer original perspectives about their experiences; writers without disabilities should limit themselves to our focus in order to solidify a connection to our magazine's purpose. Do not use stereotypical, patronizing and sentimental attitudes about disability.''

$ ◎ KENTUCKY MONTHLY

Vested Interest Publications, 213 St. Clair St., Frankfort KY 40601. (502)227-0053. Fax: (502)227-5009. E-mail: amanda@kentuckymonthly.com. Web site: www.kentuckymonthly.com. **Contact:** Amanda Hervy, associate editor. ''We publish stories about Kentucky and by Kentuckians, including stories written by those who live elsewhere.'' Monthly. Estab. 1998. Circ. 40,000.

Needs Adventure, historical, mainstream, novel excerpts. Publishes ms 3 months after acceptance.

How to Contact Query with published clips. Accepts submissions by e-mail, fax. Responds in 3 weeks to queries; 1 month to mss. Accepts simultaneous submissions. Sample copy online. Writer's guidelines online.

Payment/Terms Pays $50-100. Pays within 3 months of publication. Acquires first North American serial rights.

$◎ LAKE SUPERIOR MAGAZINE

Lake Superior Port Cities, Inc., P.O. Box 16417, Duluth MN 55816-0417. (218)722-5002. Fax: (218)722-4096. E-mail: edit@lakesuperior.com. Web site: www.lakesuperior.com. Bimonthly. Estab. 1979. Circ. 20,000.

Needs Ethnic/multicultural, historical, humor/satire, mainstream, novel excerpts, slice-of-life vignettes, ghost stories. "All stories must be Lake Superior related." Receives 5 unsolicited mss/month. Accepts 1-3 mss/year. Publishes ms 10 months after acceptance. **Publishes 1-6 new writers/year.** Length: 300-1,500 words; average length: 1,000 words. Publishes short shorts. Also publishes literary essays, poetry. Often comments on rejected mss.

How to Contact Query with published clips. Discourages submissions by e-mail. Responds in 3 months to queries. Sample copy for $3.95 and 5 first-class stamps. Writer's guidelines for #10 SASE or go online.

Payment/Terms Pays $1-125. Pays on publication for first North American serial, second serial (reprint) rights.

$◻ 🎖 LIGUORIAN

One Liguori Dr., Liguori MO 63057-9999. (636)464-2500. Fax: (636)464-8449. E-mail: liguorianeditor @liguori.org. Web site: www.liguorian.org. **Contact**: Richard Potts, C.Ss.R, editor-in-chief. Magazine: 10⅝×8; 40 pages; 4-color illustrations; photos. "Our purpose is to lead our readers to a fuller Christian life by helping them better understand the teachings of the gospel and the church and by illustrating how these teachings apply to life and the problems confronting them as members of families, the church, and society." Estab. 1913. Circ. 145,000.

- *Liguorian* received Catholic Press Association awards for 2006 including Honorable Mention for General Excellence.

Needs Religious/inspirational, young adult/teen, senior citizen/retirement. "Stories submitted to *Liguorian* must have as their goal the lifting up of the reader to a higher Christian view of values and goals. We are not interested in contemporary works that lack purpose or are of questionable moral value." Receives 25 unsolicited mss/month. Accepts 10 mss/year. **Publishes 8-10 new writers/year.**

How to Contact Send complete ms. Accepts submissions by e-mail, fax, disk. Responds in 3 months to mss. Sample copy for 9×12 SASE with 3 first-class stamps or online. Writer's guidelines for #10 SASE and on Web site.

Payment/Terms Pays 10-15¢/word and 5 contributor's copies. Pays on acceptance. Buys first rights.

Advice "First read several issues containing short stories. We look for originality and creative input in each story we read. Since most editors must wade through mounds of manuscripts each month, consideration for the editor requires that the market be studied, the manuscript be carefully presented and polished before submitting. Our publication uses only one story a month. Compare this with the 25 or more we receive over the transom each month. Also, many fiction mss are written without a specific goal or thrust, i.e., an interesting incident that goes nowhere is *not a story*. We believe fiction is a highly effective mode for transmitting the Christian message and also provides a good balance in an unusually heavy issue."

$📁 ◎ LIVE, A Weekly Journal of Practical Christian Living

Gospel Publishing House, 1445 N. Boonville Ave., Springfield MO 65802-1894. (417)862-2781. Fax: (417)862-6059. E-mail: rl-live@gph.org. Web site: www.radiantlife.org. **Contact:** Richard Bennett, editor. "*LIVE* is a take-home paper distributed weekly in young adult and adult Sunday school classes. We seek to encourage Christians to live for God through fiction and true stories which apply Biblical principles to everyday problems." Weekly. Estab. 1928. Circ. 60,000.

Needs Religious/inspirational, inspirational, prose poem. No preachy fiction, fiction about Bible characters, or stories that refer to religious myths (e.g., Santa Claus, Easter Bunny, etc.). No science fiction or Biblical fiction. No controversial stories about such subjects as feminism, war or capital punishment, "Inner city, ethnic, racial settings." Accepts 2 mss/issue. Publishes ms 18 months after acceptance. **Publishes 75-100 new writers/year.** Recently published work by Rick Barry, Amy Steiner, Marie Latta, and Sarah Gitlin.

How to Contact Send complete ms. Accepts submissions by e-mail, fax. Responds in 2 weeks to queries; 6 weeks to mss. Accepts simultaneous submissions. Sample copy for #10 SASE. Writer's guidelines for #10 SASE.

Payment/Terms Pays 7-10¢/word. Pays on acceptance for first, second serial (reprint) rights.

Advice "Write good, inspirational stories that will encourage people to become all they can be as Christians. Stories should go somewhere! Action, not just thought life; interaction, not just insights. Heroes and heroines, suspense and conflict. Avoid simplistic, pietistic, preachy, or critical conclusions or moralizing. We don't accept science fiction or Biblical fiction. Stories should be encouraging, challenging, humorous. Even problem-centered stories should be upbeat. Reserves the right to change the titles, abbreviate length and clarify flashbacks for publication."

$⊘◎⊻ THE MAGAZINE OF FANTASY & SCIENCE FICTION

Spilogale, Inc., P.O. Box 3447, Hoboken NJ 07030. (201)876-2551. E-mail: fandsf@aol.com. Web site: www.fsfmag.com. **Contact**: Gordon Van Gelder, editor. Magazine: 5×8; 160 pages; groundwood paper; card stock cover; illustrations on cover only. "For almost sixty years, we have been one of the leading publishers of fantastic fiction (which includes fantasy stories, science fiction, and some horror fiction). Our vision has changed little over six decades—we remain committed to publishing great stories without regard for whether they're classified as sf or fantasy. *The Magazine of Fantasy and Science Fiction* publishes various types of science fiction and fantasy short stories and novellas, making up about 80% of each issue. The balance of each issue is devoted to articles about science fiction, a science column, book and film reviews, cartoons, and competitions." Monthly. Estab. 1949. Circ. 30,000.

- The *Magazine of Fantasy and Science Fiction* won a Nebula Award for Best Novelet for "Two Hearts" by Peter S. Beagle and a Nebula Award for Best Short Story for "Echo" by Elizabeth Hand in 2007. Also won the 2007 World Fantasy Award for Best Short Story for "Journey into the Kingdom" by M. Rickert. Winner of the Locus Award for Best Magazine, 2001-2007. Editor Van Gelder won the Hugo Award for Best Editor (short form), 2007.

Needs Adventure, fantasy (space fantasy, sword and sorcery), horror (dark fantasy, futuristic, psychological, supernatural), psychic/supernatural/occult, science fiction (hard science/technological, soft/sociological), young adult/teen (fantasy/science fiction, horror). "We're always looking for more science fiction." Receives 600-900 unsolicited mss/month. Accepts 5-10 mss/issue; 60-100 mss/year. Publishes ms 6-9 months after acceptance. **Publishes 3-6 new writers/year.** Agented fiction 5%. Recently published work by Peter S. Beagle, Ursula K. Le Guin, Alex Irvine, Pat Murphy, Joyce Carol Oates, Gene Wolfe, Ted Chiang, S.L. Gilbow and Robert Silverberg. Length: Up to 25,000 words; average length: 7,500 words. Publishes short shorts. Send book review copies to Gordon Van Gelder. Sometimes comments on rejected mss.

How to Contact Send complete ms with SASE (or IRC). Include list of publications, estimated word count. No electronic submissions. Responds in 2 months to queries, 6-8 weeks to mss. Accepts reprint submissions. Sample copy for $5. Writer's guidelines for SASE or on Web site.

Payment/Terms Pays 6-9¢/word, 2 contributor's copies; additional copies $2.70. Pays on acceptance for first North American serial rights. Sends galleys to author. Publication is copyrighted.

Advice "Good storytelling makes a submission stand out. Regarding manuscripts, a well-prepared manuscript (i.e., one that follows the trafitional format, like that describted here: http://www.sfwa.org/writing/vonda/vonda.htm) stands out more than any gimmicks. Read an issue of the magazine before submitting. New writers should keep their submissions under 15,000 words—we rarely publish novellas by new writers."

$⊘◎ MATURE YEARS

The United Methodist Publishing House, 201 Eighth Ave. S., Nashville TN 37202-0801. (615)749-6292. Fax: (615)749-6512. E-mail: matureyears@umpublishing.org. **Contact:** Marvin Cropsey, editor. Magazine: 8½×11; 112 pages; illustrations; photos. Magazine "helps persons in and nearing retirement to appropriate the resources of the Christian faith as they seek to face the problems and opportunities related to aging." Quarterly. Estab. 1954. Circ. 55,000.

Needs Humor/satire, religious/inspirational, slice-of-life vignettes, retirement years issues, intergenerational relationships. "We don't want anything poking fun at old age, saccharine stories or anything not for older adults. Must show older adults (age 55 plus) in a positive manner." Accepts 1 mss/issue; 4 mss/year. Publishes ms 1 year after acceptance. **Publishes some new writers/year.** Recently published work by Harriet May Savitz, Donita K. Paul and Ann Gray.

How to Contact Send complete ms. Responds in 2 weeks to queries; 2 months to mss. No simultaneous submissions. Sample copy for $6 and 9×12 SAE. Writer's guidelines for #10 SASE or by e-mail.

Payment/Terms Pays $60-125. Pays on acceptance for first North American serial rights.

Advice "Practice writing dialogue! Listen to people talk; take notes; master dialogue writing! Not easy, but well worth it! Most inquiry letters are far too long. If you can't sell me an idea in a brief paragraph, you're not going to sell the reader on reading your finished article or story."

$ ⊞ ◎ MSLEXIA, For Women Who Write

Mslexia Publications Ltd., P.O. Box 656, Newcastle Upon Tyne NE99 1PZ United Kingdom. (00)44-191-2616656. Fax: (00)44-191-2616636. E-mail: postbag@mslexia.co.uk. Web site: www.mslexia.co.uk. **Contact**: Daneet Steffens, editor. Magazine: A4; 6 8 pages; some illustrations; photos. "*Mslexia* is for women who write, who want to write, who have a specialist interest in women's writing or who teach creative writing. *Mslexia* is a blend of features, articles, advice, listings, and original prose and poetry. Many parts of the magazine are open to submission from any women. Please request contributors ' guidelines prior to sending in work." Quarterly. Estab. 1999. Circ. 20,000.

Needs No work from men accepted, except on letters' page. Prose and poetry in each issue is to a specific theme (e.g. sins, travel, rain). Send SASE for themes. Publishes ms 1-2 months after acceptance. **Publishes 40-50 new writers/year**. Length: 3,000 words; average length: 2,000 words. Publishes short shorts to a specific theme and autobiography (800 words). Also publishes poetry.

How to Contact Accepts submissions by post, and by e-mail from overseas only (postbag@mslexia.co.uk). See www.mslexia.co.uk to read Contributors' Guidelines before submitting. Responds in 3 months to mss. Guidelines for SAE, e-mail, fax or on Web site.

Payment/Terms Pays £25 per poem; £15 per 1,000 words prose; features by negotiation. Plus contributors' copies.

Advice "Well structured, short pieces preferred. We look for intelligence and a strong sense of voice and place. Consider the obvious interpretations of the theme—then try to think of a new slant. Dare to be different. Make sure the piece is strong on craft as well as content. Extracts from novels are unlikely to be suitable."

$◎ NEW MOON, The Magazine for Girls & Their Dreams

New Moon Publishing, Inc., 2 W. First St. #10 1, Duluth MN 55802. (218)728-5507. Fax: (218)728-0314. E-mail: girl@newmoon.org. Web site: www.newmoon.org. "In general, all material should be pro-girl and feature girls and women as the primary focus. *New Moon* is for every girl who wants her voice heard and her dreams taken seriously. *New Moon* celebrates girls, explores the passage from girl to woman, and builds healthy resistance to gender inequities. The *New Moon* girl is true to herself and *New Moon* helps her as she pursues her unique path in life, moving confidently into the world." Bimonthly. Estab. 1992. Circ. 30,000.

Needs Adventure, fantasy, historical, humor/satire, slice-of-life vignettes. Publishes ms 6 months after acceptance.

How to Contact Send complete ms. Accepts submissions by e-mail. Responds in 2 months to mss. Accepts simultaneous submissions. Sample copy for $7 or online. Writer's guidelines for SASE or online.

Payment/Terms Pays 6-12¢/word. Pays on publication.

$NEWWITCH

BBI, Inc., P.O. Box 687, Forest Grove OR 97116. (503)430-8817. E-mail: meditor@newwitch.com. Web site: www.newwitch.com. **Contact:** Kenaz Filan, managing editor. Magazine. "*newWitch* is dedicated to Witches, Wiccans, Neo-Pagans, and various other earth-based, ethnic, pre/post-christian, shamanic and magical practitioners. We hope to reach not only those already involved in what we cover, but also the curious and completely new as well." Quarterly. Estab. 2002. Circ. 15,000.

Needs Adventure, erotica, ethnic/multicultural, fantasy, historical, horror, humor/satire, mainstream, mystery, religious, romance. Special interests: Pagan/Earth Religion material. Does not accept "faction"—fictionalized retellings of real events. Avoid gratuitous sex and violence: in movie rating terms think PG-13. Also avoid gratuitous sentimentality and Pagan moralizing: don't beat our readers with the Rede or the Threefold Law. Accepts 3-4 mss/year. Length: 1,000 words (min)-5,000 words (max).

How to Contact Send complete ms with cover letter. Accepts submissions by e-mail. Responds to queries in 1-2 weeks. Responds to mss in 1 month. Sample copy available for. Guidelines available on Web site.

Advice "Read the magazine, do your research, write the piece, send it in. That's really the only way to get started as a writer: Everything else is window dressing."

N $ OCEAN MAGAZINE

P.O. Box 84, Rodanthe, NC 27968. (252)256-2296. E-mail: diane@oceanmag.com. Web site: www.oceanmag.org. **Contact:** Diane Buccheri, editor. Magazine. "*Ocean Magazine* serves to celebrate and protect the greatest, most comprehensive resource for life on earth, our world's ocean. Ocean publishes articles, stories, poems, essays, and photography about the ocean—observations, experiences, scientific and environmental discussions—written with fact and feeling, illustrated with images from nature." Quarterly. Estab. 2003. Circ. 10,000.

Needs Adventure, fantasy, historical, romance. Accepts 1-2 mss/year. Length: 100-2,000 words.
How to Contact Query first. Accepts submissions by e-mail. Responds to queries in 2 weeks. Responds to mss in 1 month. Considers simultaneous submissions, previously published submissions.
Payment/Terms Pays on publication. Acquires one-time rights. Pays $75-200.

$ OUTLOOKS

#1B, 1230A 17th Avenue SW, Calgary AB T2T 0B8 Canada. (403)228-1157. Fax: (403)228-7735. E-mail: main@outlooks.ca. Web site: www.outlooks.ca. **Contact:** Roy Heale, editor. Magazine. "National lifestyle publisher for Canada's Gay and Lesbian community." Monthly. Estab. 1997. Circ. 37,500.

Needs Adventure, erotica, humor/satire. Accepts 10 mss/year. Manuscript published 2 months after acceptance. Length: 1,200-1,600 words.
How to Contact Query with clips of published work. Responds to queries in 2 weeks. Guidelines available on Web site.
Payment/Terms Acquires first rights. Pays between $120-$160 for fiction. Publication is copyrighted.

N $ PAKN TREGER

National Yiddish Book Center, 1021 West Street, Amherst MA 01002. (413)256-4900. Fax: (413)256-4700. E-mail: aatherley@bikher.org. Web site: www.yiddishbookcenter.org. **Contact:** Anne Atherly, editor's assistant. Literary magazine/journal. "*Pakn Treger* is looking for high-quality writing for a secular audience interested in Yiddish and Jewish history, literature, and culture." Triannual. Estab. 1980. Circ. 30,000.

Needs Historical, humor/satire, mystery. Accepts 2 mss/year. Manuscript published 4 months after acceptance. Length: 1,200-5,000 words.
How to Contact Query first. Accepts submissions by e-mail. Responds to queries in 2 weeks; mss in 2 months. Sample copy available via e-mail. Guidelines available via e-mail.
Payment/Terms Acquires one-time rights.
Advice "Read the magazine and visit Web site."

$ PENTHOUSE VARIATIONS

Penthouse Media Group, 2 Penn Plaza, Suite 1125, New York NY 10121. (212)702-6000. E-mail: variations@pmgi.com. Monthly. Estab. 1978. Circ. 60,000.

Needs Erotica. Publishes ms 6-14 months after acceptance.
How to Contact Responds in 1 month to queries; 2 months to mss. Writer's guidelines for #10 SASE or by E-mail.
Payment/Terms Buys all rights and pays $400 maximum for a 3,500 word manuscript on acceptance.
Advice "Variations publishes first person, sex-positive narratives in which the author fully describes sex scenes squarely focused within 1 of the magazine's usual categories, in highly explicit erotic detail. To submit material to Variations you must be eighteen years of age or older."

$ POCKETS

The Upper Room, 1908 Grand Ave., P.O. Box 340004, Nashville TN 37203-0004. (615)340-7333. Fax: (615)340-7267. E-mail: pockets@upperroom.org. Web site: www.pockets.org. **Contact:** Lynn W. Gilliam, editor. Magazine: 7×11; 48 pages; some photos. "Pockets is a Christian, inter-denominational publication for children 6-11 years of age. Each issue reflects a specific theme." Estab. 1981. Circ. 96,000.

• *Pockets* has received honors from the Educational Press Association of America.

Needs Adventure, ethnic/multicultural, historical (general), religious/inspirational, slice-of-life vignettes. No fantasy, science fiction, talking animals. "All submissions should address the broad theme of the magazine. Each issue is built around one theme with material which can be used by children in a variety of ways. Scripture stories, fiction, poetry, prayers, art, graphics, puzzles and activities are included. Submissions do not need to be overtly religious. They should help children experience a Christian lifestyle that is not always a neatly-wrapped moral package, but is open to the continuing revelation of God's will. Seasonal material, both secular and liturgical, is desired. No violence, horror, sexual, racial stereotyping or fiction containing heavy moralizing." Receives 200 unsolicited mss/month. Accepts 3-4 mss/issue; 33-44 mss/year. Publishes ms 1 year to 18 months after acceptance. **Publishes 15 new writers/year.** Length: 600-1,400 words; average length: 1,200 words.

How to Contact Send complete ms. Cover letter not required. Responds in 6 weeks to mss. Accepts one-time reprints, multiple submissions. For a sample copy, themes and/or guidelines send 9×12 SASE with 4 first-class stamps. Writer's guidelines, themes, and due dates available online.

Payment/Terms Pays 14¢/word, plus 2-5 contributor's copies. Pays on acceptance for first North American serial rights. Sponsors an annual fiction-writing contest.

Advice "We receive many inappropriate maunscripts. Study guidelines and themes before submitting. Many manuscripts we receive are simply inappropriate. New themes published in December of each year. We strongly advise sending for themes or reading them on the Web site before submitting." Include SASE with all submissions.

$☑ ◎ PORTLAND MONTHLY, Maine's City Magazine

722 Congress St., Portland ME 04102. (207)775-4339. Fax: (207)775-2334. E-mail: editor@portlandm onthly.com. Web site: www.portlandmagazine.com. **Contact:** Colin Sargent, editor. Magazine: 200 pages; 60 lb. paper; 100 lb. cover stock; illustrations; photos. "City lifestyle magazine—fiction, style, business, real estate, controversy, fashion, cuisine, interviews and art relating to the Maine area." Monthly. Estab. 1986. Circ. 100,000.

Needs Contemporary, literary (Maine connection). Query first. Receives 20 unsolicited mss/month. Accepts 1 ms/issue; 10 mss/year. **Publishes 50 new writers/year.** Recently published work by Rick Moody, Ann Hood, C.D.B Bryan, Joan Connor, Mameve Medwed, Jason Brown, Sarah Graves, Tess Gerritsor and Sebastian Junger.

How to Contact Send complete ms. SASE.

Payment/Terms Pays on publication for first North American serial rights.

Advice "We publish ambitious short fiction featuring everyone from Rick Moody to newly discovered fiction by Edna St. Vincent Millay."

$◎ ☑ ELLERY QUEEN'S MYSTERY MAGAZINE

Dell Magazines Fiction Group, 475 Park Ave. S., 11th Floor, New York NY 10016. (212)686-7188. Fax: (212)686-7414. E-mail: elleryqueen@dellmagazines.com. Web site: www.themysteryplace.c om. **Contact**: Janet Hutchings, editor. Magazine: 5¼×8⅓, 144 pages with special 240-page combined March/April and September/October issues. "*Ellery Queen's Mystery Magazine* welcomes submissions from both new and established writers. We publish every kind of mystery short story: the psychological suspense tale, the deductive puzzle, the private eye case, the gamut of crime and detection from the realistic (including the policeman's lot and stories of police procedure) to the more imaginative (including "locked rooms" and "impossible crimes"). *EQMM* has been in continuous publication since 1941. From the beginning, three general criteria have been employed in evaluating submissions: We look for strong writing, an original and exciting plot, and professional craftsmanship. We encourage writers whose work meets these general criteria to read an issue of *EQMM* before making a submission." Magazine for lovers of mystery fiction. Estab. 1941. Circ. 180,780 readers.

• *EQMM* has won numerous awards and sponsors its own award yearly for the best EQMM stories nominated by its readership.

Needs Mystery/suspense. No explicit sex or violence, no gore or horror. Seldom publishes parodies or pastiches. "We accept only mystery, crime, suspense and detective fiction." 2,500-8,000 words is the preferred range. Also publishes minute mysteries of 250 words; novellas up to 20,000 words from established authors. Publishes ms 6-12 months after acceptance. Agented fiction 50%. **Pub-**

lishes 10 new writers/year. Recently published work by Jeffery Deaver, Joyce Carol Oates and Margaret Maron. Sometimes comments on rejected mss.

How to Contact Send complete ms. Responds in 3 months to mss. Accepts simultaneous, multiple submissions. Sample copy for $5.50. Writer's guidelines for SASE or online.

Payment/Terms Pays 5-8¢/ a word, occasionally higher for established authors. Pays on acceptance for first North American serial rights.

Advice "We have a Department of First Stories and usually publish at least one first story an issue, i.e., the author's first published fiction. We select stories that are fresh and of the kind our readers have expressed a liking for. In writing a detective story, you must play fair with the reader, providing clues and necessary information. Otherwise you have a better chance of publishing if you avoid writing to formula."

$⊘ ◎ SEEK

Standard Publishing, 8805 Governor's Hill Drive, Suite 400, Cincinnati OH 45239. (513)728-6822. Fax: (513)931-0950. E-mail: seek@standardpub.com. Web site: www.standardpub.com. Magazine: 5½×8½; 8 pages; newsprint paper; art and photo in each issue. "Inspirational stories of faith-in-action for Christian adults; a Sunday School take-home paper." Quarterly. Estab. 1970. Circ. 27,000.

Needs Religious/inspirational, Religious fiction and religiously slanted historical and humorous fiction. No poetry. List of upcoming themes available online. Accepts 150 mss/year. Publishes ms 1 year after acceptance.

How to Contact Send complete ms. Accepts submissions by e-mail. Prefers submissions by e-mail. Writer's guidelines online.

Payment/Terms Pays 7¢/word. Pays on acceptance for first North American serial, pays 5¢ for second serial (reprint) rights.

Advice "Write a credible story with a Christian slant—no preachments; avoid overworked themes such as joy in suffering, generation gaps, etc. Most manuscripts are rejected by us because of irrelevant topic or message, unrealistic story, or poor charater and/or plot development. We use fiction stories that are believable."

$⊘ ◎ ☒ SHINE BRIGHTLY

GEMS Girls' Clubs, P.O. Box 7259, Grand Rapids MI 49510. (616)241-5616. Fax: (616)241-5558. E-mail: sara@gemsgc.org. Web site: www.gemsgc.org. **Contact:** Sara Hilton, Senior Editor. Magazine: 8½×11; 24 pages; 50 lb. paper; 50 lb. cover stock; illustrations; photos. "Our purpose is to lead girls into a living relationship with Jesus Christ and to help them see how God is at work in their lives and the world around them. Puzzles, crafts, stories and articles for girls ages 9-14." Monthly. Estab. 1971. Circ. 18,000.

• *SHINE* brightly has received awards for fiction and illustrations from the Evangelical Press Association.

Needs Adventure (that girls could experience in their hometowns or places they might realistically visit), children's/juvenile, ethnic/multicultural, historical, humor/satire, mystery/suspense (believable only), religious/inspirational (nothing too preachy), romance (stories that deal with awakening awareness of boys are appreciated), slice-of-life vignettes, suspense (can be serialized). Write for upcoming themes. Each year has an overall theme and each month has a theme to fit with yearly themes. Receives 50 unsolicited mss/month. Accepts 3 mss/issue; 30 mss/year. Publishes ms 1 year after acceptance. **Publishes some new writers/year.** Recently published work by A.J. Schut. Length: 400-1,000 words; average length: 800 words.

How to Contact Send complete ms. Responds in 2 months to queries. Accepts simultaneous and reprints submissions. Sample copy for 9×12 SAE with 3 first class stamps and $1. Writer's guidelines online.

Payment/Terms Pays 3¢/word. Pays on publication for first North American serial, second serial (reprint), simultaneous rights.

Advice "Check out our Web site. We are passionate about teaching girls to be world changers. We are looking for articles and stories that teach and inspire girls to reach outside of themselves to make change in the world. We are currently involved in Zambia and would like to see articles and stories about Africa."

$⊘ ◎ ⬇ ST. ANTHONY MESSENGER

28 W. Liberty St., Cincinnati OH 45202-6498. (513)241-5615. Fax: (513)241-0399. E-mail: patm@ame
ricancatholic.org. Web site: www.americancatholic.org. **Contact:** Father Pat McCloskey, O.F.M.,
editor. Magazine: 8×10¾; 60 pages; illustrations; photos. "*St. Anthony Messenger* is a Catholic
family magazine which aims to help its readers lead more fully human and Christian lives. We
publish articles which report on a changing church and world, opinion pieces written from the
perspective of Christian faith and values, personality profiles, and fiction which entertains and
informs." Estab. 1893. Circ. 308,884.

● This is a leading Catholic magazine, but has won awards for both religious and secular journalism and writing from the Catholic Press Association, the International Association of Business
Communicators, and the Society of Professional Journalists.

Needs Mainstream, religious/inspirational, senior citizen/retirement. "We do not want mawkishly
sentimental or preachy fiction. Stories are most often rejected for poor plotting and characterization;
bad dialogue—listen to how people talk; inadequate motivation. Many stories say nothing, are
'happenings' rather than stories." No fetal journals, no rewritten Bible stories. Receives 60-70 unsolicited mss/month. Accepts 1 mss/issue; 12 mss/year. Publishes ms 1 year after acceptance. **Publishes 3 new writers/year.** Recently published work by Geraldine Marshall Gutfreund, John Salustri,
Beth Dotson, Miriam Pollikatsikis and Joseph Pici. Sometimes requests revisions before acceptance.
How to Contact Send complete ms. Accepts submissions by e-mail, fax. "For quickest response
send self-addressed stamped postcard with choices: "Yes, we're interested in publishing; Maybe,
we'd like to hold for future consideration; No, we've decided to pass on the publication." Responds
in 3 weeks to queries; 2 months to mss. No simultaneous submissions. Sample copy for 9×12 SASE
with 4 first-class stamps. Writer's guidelines online. Reviews fiction.
Payment/Terms Pays 16¢/word maximum and 2 contributor's copies; $1 charge for extras. Pays on
acceptance for first North American serial, electronic rights.
Advice "We publish one story a month and we get up to 1,000 a year. Too many offer simplistic
'solutions' or answers. Pay attention to endings. Easy, simplistic, deus ex machina endings don't
work. People have to feel characters in the stories are real and have a reason to care about them
and what happens to them. Fiction entertains but can also convey a point and sound values."

$⊘ ◎ STANDARD

Nazarene Publishing House, 2923 Troost, Kansas City MO 64109. (816)931-1900. Fax: (816)412-
8306. E-mail: clyourdon@wordaction.com. Web site: www.wordaction.com. **Contact:** Charlie L.
Yourdon, editor; Everett Leadingham, senior editor. Magazine: 8½×11; 8 pages; illustrations; photos. Inspirational reading for adults. "In *Standard* we want to show Christianity in action, and we
prefer to do that through stories that hold the reader's attention." Weekly. Estab. 1936. Circ. 130,000.
Needs "Looking for stories that show Christianity in action." Accepts 200 mss/year. Publishes ms
14-18 months after acceptance. **Publishes some new writers/year.**
How to Contact Send complete ms. Accepts submissions by e-mail. SASE. Accepts simultaneous
submissions But pays at reprint rates. Writer's guidelines and sample copy for SAE with 2 first-class
stamps or available by e-mail request.
Payment/Terms Pays 3½¢/word for first rights; 2¢/word for reprint rights, and contributor's copies.
Pays on acceptance for one-time rights, whether first or reprint rights.
Advice "Be conscientious in your use of Scripture; don't overload your story with quotations. When
you quote the Bible, quote it exactly and cite chapter, verse, and version used. (We prefer NIV.)
Standard will handle copyright matters for Scripture. Except for quotations from the Bible, written
permission for the use of any other copyrighted material (especially song lyrics) is the responsibility
of the writer. Keep in mind the international audience of *Standard* with regard to geographic references and holidays. We cannot use stories about cultural, national, or secular holidays. Do not
mention specific church affiliations. *Standard* is read in a variety of denominations. Do not submit
any manuscripts which has been submitted to or published in any of the following: *Vista, Wesleyan
Advocate, Holiness Today, Preacher's Magazine, World Mission, Women Alive,* or various teen and
children's publications produced by WordAction Publishing Company. These are overlapping markets."

$⊙ ◎ THE STRAND MAGAZINE

P.O. Box 1418, Birmingham MI 48012-1418. (248)788-5948. Fax: (248)874-1046. E-mail: strandmag
@strandmag.com. Web site: www.strandmag.com. **Contact:** A.F. Gulli, editor. "After an absence

of nearly half a century, the magazine known to millions for bringing Sir Arthur Conan Doyle's ingenious detective, Sherlock Holmes, to the world has once again appeared on the literary scene. First launched in 1891, *The Strand* included in its pages the works of some of the greatest writers of the 20th century: Agatha Christie, Dorothy Sayers, Margery Allingham, W. Somerset Maugham, Graham Greene, P.G. Wodehouse, H.G. Wells, Aldous Huxley and many others. In 1950, economic difficulties in England caused a drop in circulation which forced the magazine to cease publication." Quarterly. Estab. 1998. Circ. 50,000.

Needs Horror, humor/satire, mystery/suspense (detective stories), suspense, tales of the unexpected, tales of terror and the supernatural "written in the classic tradition of this century's great author's. "We are NOT interested in submissions with any sexual content." Stories can be set in any time or place, provided they are well written and the plots interesting and well thought out." Publishes ms 4 months after acceptance.

How to Contact SASE (IRCs if outside the US). Query first. Responds in 1 month to queries. Sample copy not available. Writer's guidelines for #10 SASE.

Payment/Terms Pays $50-175. Pays on acceptance for first North American serial rights.

$WASHINGTON RUNNING REPORT

13710 Ashby Rd, Rockville MD 20853. (301)871-0006. Fax: (301)871-0005. E-mail: kathy@runwashington.com. Web site: www.runwashington.com. **Contact:** Kathy Freedman, editor. Magazine. "Written by runners for runners, *Washington Running Report* covers the running and racing scene in metropolitan Washington DC. Features include runner rankings, training tips and advice, feature articles on races, race results, race calendar, humor, product reviews and other articles of interest to runners." Bimonthly. Estab. 1984. Circ. 35,000.

Needs Adventure, fantasy, historical, humor/satire, mainstream, mystery. Accepts 1-2 mss/year. Manuscript published 2-4 months after acceptance. Length: 750-1,500 words.

How to Contact Send complete ms with cover letter. Accepts submissions by e-mail. Responds to queries in 2-3 weeks. Responds to mss in 1-2 months. Considers simultaneous submissions, previously published submissions. Sample copy free upon request.

Payment/Terms Acquires first rights, one-time rights, electronic rights.

$ WOMAN'S WEEKLY

IPC Magazines, The Blue Fin Building, 110 Southward Street, London SE1 0SU United Kingdom. **Contact:** Gaynor Davies. Publishes 1 serial and at least 2 short stories/week.

Needs "Short stories can be on any theme, but must have depth. No explicit sex or violence. Serials need not be written in installments. They are submitted as complete manuscripts and we split them up, or send first installment of serial (4,000 words) and synopsis of the rest."

How to Contact Send an sae for Writers' Guidelines.

Payment/Terms Short story payment starts at £100 and rises as writer becomes a more regular contributor. Serial payments start at around £600/installment. Writers also receive contributor's copies.

Advice "Read the magazine and try to understand who the publication is aimed at."

$WRITERS' JOURNAL, The Complete Writer's Magazine

Val-Tech Media, P.O. Box 394, Perham MN 56573-0394. (218)346-7921. Fax: (218)346-7924. E-mail: editor@writersjournal.com. Web site: www.writersjournal.com. "*WRITERS' Journal* is read by thousands of aspiring writers whose love of writing has taken them to the next step: Writing for money. We are an instructional manual giving writers the tools and information necessary to get their work published. We also print works by authors who have won our writing contests." Bimonthly. Estab. 1980. Circ. 26,000.

Needs "We only publish winners of our fiction contests—16 contests/year." Receives 200 contest entries mss/month. Publishes 5-7 mss/issue; 30-40 mss/year. **Publishes 100 new writers/year.** Also publishes poetry.

How to Contact Accepts contest submissions by postal mail only. Responds in 6 weeks to queries; 6 months to mss. Accepts unpublished simultaneous submissions. Sample copy for $6.

Payment/Terms Pays prize money on publication for one-time rights.

Book Publishers

I n this section, you will find many of the "big name" book publishers. Many of these publishers remain tough markets for new writers or for those whose work might be considered literary or experimental. Indeed, some only accept work from established authors, and then often only through an author's agent. Although having your novel published by one of the big commercial publishers listed in this section is difficult, it is not impossible. The trade magazine *Publishers Weekly* regularly features interviews with writers whose first novels are being released by top publishers. Many editors at large publishing houses find great satisfaction in publishing a writer's first novel.

On page 549, you'll find the publishing industry's "family tree," which maps out each of the large book publishing conglomerates' divisions, subsidiaries and imprints. Remember, most manuscripts are acquired by imprints, not their parent company, so avoid submitting to the conglomerates themselves. (For example, submit to Dutton or Berkley Books, not their parent Penguin.)

Also listed here are "small presses" publishing four or more titles annually. Included among them are independent presses, university presses and other nonprofit publishers. Introducing new writers to the reading public has become an increasingly important role of these smaller presses at a time when the large conglomerates are taking fewer chances on unknown writers. Many of the successful small presses listed in this section have built their reputations and their businesses in this way and have become known for publishing prize-winning fiction.

These smaller presses also tend to keep books in print longer than larger houses. And, since small presses publish a smaller number of books, each title is equally important to the publisher, and each is promoted in much the same way and with the same commitment. Editors also stay at small presses longer because they have more of a stake in the business—often they own the business. Many smaller book publishers are writers themselves and know firsthand the importance of a close editor-author or publisher-author relationship.

TYPES OF BOOK PUBLISHERS

Large or small, the publishers in this section publish books "for the trade." That is, unlike textbook, technical or scholarly publishers, trade publishers publish books to be sold to the general consumer through bookstores, chain stores or other retail outlets. Within the trade book field, however, there are a number of different types of books.

The easiest way to categorize books is by their physical appearance and the way they are marketed. Hardcover books are the more expensive editions of a book, sold through bookstores and carrying a price tag of around $20 and up. Trade paperbacks are soft-bound books, also sold mostly in bookstores, but they carry a more modest price tag of usually around $10 to $20. Today a lot of fiction is published in this form because it means a lower financial risk than hardcover.

Mass market paperbacks are another animal altogether. These are the smaller "pocket-size" books available at bookstores, grocery stores, drug stores, chain retail outlets, etc. Much genre or category fiction is published in this format. This area of the publishing industry is very open to the work of talented new writers who write in specific genres such as science fiction, romance and mystery.

At one time publishers could be easily identified and grouped by the type of books they produce. Today, however, the lines between hardcover and paperback books are blurred. Many publishers known for publishing hardcover books also publish trade paperbacks and have paperback imprints. This enables them to offer established authors (and a very few lucky newcomers) hard-soft deals in which their book comes out in both versions. Thanks to the mergers of the past decade, too, the same company may own several hardcover and paperback subsidiaries and imprints, even though their editorial focuses may remain separate.

CHOOSING A BOOK PUBLISHER

In addition to checking the bookstores and libraries for books by publishers that interest you, you may want to refer to the Category Index at the back of this book to find publishers divided by specific subject categories. The subjects listed in the Index are general. Read individual listings to find which subcategories interest a publisher. For example, you will find several romance publishers listed, but read the listings to find which type of romance is considered—gothic, contemporary, regency or futuristic. See You've Got a Story on page 2 for more on how to refine your list of potential markets.

The icons appearing before the names of the publishers will also help you in selecting a publisher. These codes are especially important in this section, because many of the publishing houses listed here require writers to submit through an agent. The 🅐 symbol indicates that a publisher accepts agented submissions only. A �',' icon identifies those that mostly publish established and agented authors, while a 🔾 points to publishers most open to new writers. See the inside front cover of this book for a complete list and explanations of symbols used in this book.

IN THE LISTINGS

As with other sections in this book, we identify new listings with a 🅽 symbol. In this section, most with this symbol are not new publishers, but instead are established publishers who were unable or decided not to list last year and are therefore new to this edition.

In addition to the 🅽 symbol indicating new listings, we include other symbols to help you in narrowing your search. English-speaking foreign markets are denoted by a 🌐 . The maple leaf symbol 🍁 identifies Canadian presses. If you are not a Canadian writer but are interested in a Canadian press, check the listing carefully. Many small presses in Canada receive grants and other funds from their provincial or national government and are, therefore, restricted to publishing Canadian authors.

We also include editorial comments set off by a bullet (●) within listings. This is where we include information about any special requirements or circumstances that will help you know even more about the publisher's needs and policies. The star 🟏 signals that this market is an imprint or division of a larger publisher. The 🟡 symbol identifies publishers who have recently received honors or awards for their books. The 🅖 denotes publishers who produce comics and graphic novels.

Each listing includes a summary of the editorial mission of the house, an overarching principle that ties together what they publish. Under the heading **Contact** we list one or more editors, often with their specific area of expertise.

Book editors asked us again this year to emphasize the importance of paying close attention to the **Needs** and **How to Contact** subheads of listings for book publishers. Unlike magazine editors who want to see complete manuscripts of short stories, most of the book publishers listed here ask that writers send a query letter with an outline and/or synopsis and several chapters of their novel. The Business of Fiction Writing, beginning on page 65 of this book, outlines how to prepare work to submit directly to a publisher.

There are no subsidy book publishers listed in *Novel & Short Story Writer's Market*. By subsidy, we mean any arrangement in which the writer is expected to pay all or part of the cost of producing, distributing and marketing his book. We feel a writer should not be asked to share in any cost of turning his manuscript into a book. All the book publishers listed here told us that they *do not charge writers* for publishing their work. **If any of the publishers listed here ask you to pay any part of publishing or marketing your manuscript, please let us know**. See our Complaint Procedure on the copyright page of this book.

A NOTE ABOUT AGENTS

Some publishers are willing to look at unsolicited submissions, but most feel having an agent is in the writer's best interest. In this section more than any other, you'll find a number of publishers who prefer submissions from agents. That's why we've included a section of agents open to submissions from fiction writers (page 103). For even more agents along with a great deal of helpful articles about approaching and working with them, refer to *Guide to Literary Agents* (Writer's Digest Books).

If you use the Internet or another resource to find an agent not listed in this book, be wary of any agents who charge large sums of money for reading a manuscript. Reading fees do not guarantee representation. Think of an agent as a potential business partner and feel free to ask tough questions about his or her credentials, experience and business practices.

Periodicals of Interest

For More Info

Check out issues of *Publishers Weekly* for publishing industry trade news in the U.S. and around the world or *Quill & Quire* for book publishing news in the Canadian book industry.

For more small presses see the *International Directory of Little Magazines and Small Presses* published by Dustbooks. To keep up with changes in the industry throughout the year, check issues of two small press trade publications: *Small Press Review* (also published by Dustbooks) and *Independent Publisher* (Jenkins Group, Inc.).

⋈ ○ ABERDEEN BAY

Champion Writers, 5676 Ridge View Drive, Alexandria VA 22310. Web site: www.aberdeenbay.com. **Contact:** Andy Zhang, principal editor (mainstream fiction and memoirs). Estab. 2007. "We're a small independent publisher who publishes trade paperback originals with outstanding quality." Publishes paperback originals, paperback reprints, e-books. Format: POD printing. **Published 1 new writer last year.** Plans 5 debut novels this year. Averages 20 total titles/year; 15 fiction titles/year. Distributes/promotes titles through various retailers.

Needs Ethnic/multicultural (Asian), family saga, feminist, gay, glitz, historical, lesbian, literary, mainstream, young adult/teen (adventure, easy-to-read, historical, mystery/suspense, problem novels, romance, series, sports, western). Published *Memories of an Eastern Sky.*

How to Contact Query with outline/synopsis and 3 sample chapters. Accepts queries by snail mail. Include brief bio, list of publishing credits. Send disposable copy of ms and SASE for reply only. Responds to queries in 8 weeks. Accepts unsolicited mss. Considers simultaneous submissions. Sometimes critiques/comments on rejected mss. Responds to mss in 12 weeks.

Terms Ms published 6 months after acceptance. Writer's guidelines on Web site. Pays royalties 10%, 2 author's copies. Book catalogs on Web site.

Advice "We strongly encourage new writers to submit exceptional manuscripts. Be sure your manuscript is ready to be published as we do not consider drafts, or manuscripts with grammar issues and typos. Be ready to show your enthusiasm in participating in marketing and developing as an author."

HARRY N. ABRAMS, INC.

La Martiniere Groupe, Attn: Managing Editor, 115 West 18th St., New York NY 10011. (212)206-7715. Fax: (212)645-8437. Web site: www.abramsbooks.com. **Contact:** Managing editor. Estab. 1949. Publishes hardcover and "a few" paperback originals. Averages 150 total titles/year.

Imprint(s) Abrams Books; Stewart, Tabori & Chang; Abrams Books for Young Readers (including Amulet Books for Middle Grade and Young Adult); Abrams Gifts and Stationery.

How to Contact Responds in 6 months to queries. No simultaneous submissions, electronic submissions.

Terms Pays royalty. Average advance: variable. Publishes ms 2 years after acceptance. Book catalog for $5.

◪ ABSEY & CO.

23011 Northcrest Drive, Spring TX 77389. (281)257-2340. E-mail: abseyandco@aol.com. Web site: www.absey.com. **Contact:** Edward E. Wilson, publisher. "We are interested in book-length fiction of literary merit with a firm intended audience." Publishes hardcover, trade paperback and mass market paperback originals. **Published 3-5 debut authors within the last year.** Averages 6-10 total titles, 6-10 fiction titles/year.

Needs Juvenile, mainstream/contemporary, short story collections. Published *Where I'm From,* by George Ella Lyon; *Blast Man Standing,* by Robert V. Spelleri.

How to Contact Accepts unsolicited mss. Query with SASE. Responds in 3 months to queries; 9 months to mss. No simultaneous submissions, electronic submissions.

Terms Royalty and advance vary. Publishes ms 1 year after acceptance. Ms guidelines online.

Advice "Since we are a small, new press looking for good manuscripts with a firm intended audience, we tend to work closely and attentively with our authors. Many established authors who have been with the large New York houses have come to us to publish their work because we work closely with them."

◪ ACADEMY CHICAGO PUBLISHERS

363 W. Erie St., Suite 7E., Chicago IL 60610-3125. (312)751-7300. Fax: (312)751-7306. E-mail: info@academychicago.com. Web site: www.academychicago.com. **Contact:** Anita Miller, senior editor. Estab. 1975. Midsize independent publisher. Publishes hardcover originals and trade paperback reprints. Averages 15 total titles/year.

Needs Historical, mainstream/contemporary, military/war, mystery. "We look for quality work, but we do not publish experimental, avant-garde novels." Biography, history, academic and anthologies. Only the most unusual mysteries, no private-eyes or thrillers. No explicit sex or violence. Serious fiction, no romance/adventure. "We will consider historical fiction that is well researched. No science fiction/fantasy, no religious/inspirational, no how-to, no cookbooks. In general, we are very conscious of women's roles. We publish very few children's books." Published *Clean Start*, by Patricia Margaret Page (first fiction); *Cutter's Island: Caesar in Captivity*, by Vincent Panella (first fiction, historical); *Murder at the Paniomic Games*, by Michael B. Edward.

How to Contact Accepts unsolicited mss. Do not submit by e-mail. Submit 3 sample chapter(s), synopsis. Accepts queries by mail. Include cover letter briefly describing the content of your work. Send SASE or IRC. "Manuscripts without envelopes will be discarded. *Mailers* are a *must* even from agents." Responds in 3 months to queries. No electronic submissions.

Terms Pays 7-10% royalty on wholesale price. Average advance: modest. Publishes ms 18 months after acceptance. Ms guidelines online.

Advice "At the moment we are swamped with manuscripts and anything under consideration can be under consideration for months."

★ ◨ ◎ ACE SCIENCE FICTION AND FANTASY

The Berkley Publishing Group, Penguin Group (USA), Inc., 375 Hudson St., New York NY 10014. (212)366-2000. Web site: www.penguin.com. **Contact:** Susan Allison, editor-in-chief; Anne Sowards, editor. Estab. 1953. Publishes hardcover, paperback and trade paperback originals and reprints. Averages 75 total titles, 75 fiction titles/year.

Needs Fantasy, science fiction. No other genre accepted. No short stories. Published *Iron Sunrise*, by Charles Stross; *Neuromancer*, by William Gibson; *King Kelson's Bride*, by Katherine Kurtz.

How to Contact Does not accept unsolicited mss. Submit 1-2 sample chapter(s), synopsis. Send SASE or IRC. Responds in 2-3 months to queries. Accepts simultaneous submissions.

Terms Pays royalty. Offers advance. Publishes ms 1-2 years after acceptance. Ms guidelines for #10 SASE.

Advice "Good science fiction and fantasy are almost always written by people who have read and loved a lot of it. We are looking for knowledgeable science or magic, as well as sympathetic characters with recognizable motivation. We are looking for solid, well-plotted science fiction: good action adventure, well-researched hard science with good characterization, and books that emphasize characterization without sacrificing plot. In fantasy we are looking for all types of work, from high fantasy to sword and sorcery." Submit fantasy and science fiction to Anne Sowards.

◨ ◎ AGELESS PRESS

3759 Collins St., Sarasota FL 34232. E-mail: irishope@comcast.net. Web site: http://irisforrest.com. **Contact:** Iris Forrest, editor. Estab. 1992. Independent publisher. Publishes paperback originals. Books: acid-free paper; notched perfect binding; no illustrations. Averages 1 total title/year.

Needs Experimental, fantasy, humor, literary, mainstream/contemporary, mystery, new age/mystic, science fiction, short story collections, thriller/espionage. Looking for material "based on personal computer experiences." Stories selected by editor. Published *Computer Legends, Lies & Lore*, by various (anthology); and *Computer Tales of Fact and Fantasy*, by various (anthology).

How to Contact Does not accept unsolicited mss. Query with SASE. Accepts queries by e-mail, fax, mail. Responds in 1 week to queries; 1 week to mss. Accepts simultaneous submissions, electronic submissions, submissions on disk. Sometimes comments on rejected mss.

Terms Average advance: negotiable. Publishes ms 6-12 months after acceptance.

Advice "Query! Don't send work without a query!"

★ ALGONQUIN BOOKS OF CHAPEL HILL

Workman Publishing, P.O. Box 2225, Chapel Hill NC 27515-2225. (919)967-0108. Web site: www.alg onquin.com. **Contact:** Editorial Department. Publishes hardcover originals. Averages 24 total titles/year.

Needs Literary fiction and nonfiction, cookbooks and lifestyle books (about family, animals, food, flowers, adventure, and other topics of interest). No poetry, genre fiction (romance, science fiction, etc.) or children's books. Recently published *Saving the World*, by Julia Alvarez; *Which Brings Me to You*, by Steve Almond and Julianna Baggott; *Hope and Other Dangerous Pursuits*, by Laila Lalami.

How to Contact Send a 20-page sample of your work, along with a cover letter, SASE, and a check for return postage (if you wish to have your mss returned). No phone, e-mail or fax queries or submissions.

Terms Ms guidelines online.

◎ AMERICAN ATHEIST PRESS

P.O. Box 5733, Parsippany NJ 07054-6733. (908)276-7300. Fax: (908)276-7402. E-mail: info@atheists .org. Web site: www.atheists.org. **Contact:** Frank Zindler, editor. Estab. 1963. Publishes trade paperback originals and reprints. Publishes quarterly journal, *American Atheist*, for which are needed articles of interest to atheists. **Published 40-50% debut authors within the last year.** Averages 12 total titles/year.

Imprint(s) Gustav Broukal Press.

Needs Humor (satire of religion or of current religious leaders), anything of particular interest to atheists. ''We rarely publish any fiction. But we have occasionally released a humorous book. No mainstream. For our press to consider fiction, it would have to tie in with the general focus of our press, which is the promotion of atheism and free thought.''

How to Contact Submit outline, sample chapter(s). Responds in 4 months to queries. Accepts simultaneous submissions.

Terms Pays 5-10% royalty on retail price. Publishes ms within 2 years after acceptance. Ms guidelines for 9×12 SAE.

Advice ''We will need more how-to types of material—how to argue with creationists, how to fight for state/church separation. etc. We have an urgent need for literature for young atheists.''

N ◳ AMIRA PRESS

(443)421-6831. E-mail: yvette@amirapress.com. Web site: www.amirapress.com. **Contact:** Yvette A. Lynn, CEO (sensual romance and mainstream fiction); Deborah Herald, managing editor—erotica (erotica, westerns, nonfiction). Estab. 2007. ''We are a small press which likes to publish works from all backgrounds and groups. Our authors and stories are diverse. Our slogan is 'Fiction that is Coloring the World,' which means we are bringing all types of people together with our books.'' Publishes paperback originals, e-books. POD printing. **Published 30 new writers last year.** Averages 50 fiction titles/year. Member EPIC. Distributes/promotes titles through Amazon, Mobipocket, Fictio nwise, BarnesandNoble.com, Target.com, Amirapress.com, and Ingrams.

Needs Adventure, erotica, ethnic/multicultural, fantasy, historical, horror, mainstream, mystery/ suspense, science fiction, psychic/supernatural, romance (contemporary, futuristic/time travel, historical, regency period, romantic suspense), short story collections, western, young adult/teen (adventure, fantasy/science fiction, mystery/suspense, problem novels). Special interests: interracial, sensual romance, fantasy. Anthologies in the works, please check Web site. Published *A Choice Between Two*, by Tressie Lockwood (erotica/sensual romance); *Mining Evermore*, by Kathleen Rowland (sensual paranormal romance); *No Matter What*, by Jordan Ryan (contemporary romance).

How to Contact Submit complete ms with cover letter. Accepts queries by e-mail. Include estimated word count, brief bio, list of publishing credits. Accepts unsolicited mss. Considers simultaneous submissions, submissions on CD or disk. Sometimes critiques/comments on rejected mss. Responds to mss in 3 months.

Terms Ms published 1-4 months after acceptance. Writer's guidelines on Web site. Pays royalties, 15% net (print)-50% net (e-books). Book catalogs on Web site.

Advice ''Please read our submission guidelines thoroughly and follow them when submitting. We do not consider a work until we have all the requested information and the work is presented in the format we outline.''

◪ ◳ ◎ ANNICK PRESS LTD.

15 Patricia Ave., Toronto ON M2M 1H9 Canada. (416)221-4802. Fax: (416)221-8400. E-mail: annickpress @annickpress.com. Web site: www.annickpress.com. Publisher of children's books. Publishes hardcover and trade paperback originals. Average print order; 9,000. First novel print order: 7,000. Plans 18 first novels this year. Averages 25 total titles/year. Distributes titles through Firefly Books Ltd.

Needs Juvenile, young adult. fiction, and nonfiction.

How to Contact Query with SASE. Responds in 1 month queries; 3 months to mss. No simultaneous submissions, electronic submissions. Sometimes comments on rejected mss. Does not accept unsolicited mss.

Terms Publishes ms 2 years after acceptance. Ms guidelines online.

• Does not accept unsolicited mss.

▨ ◪ ◎ ANVIL PRESS

278 East First Avenue, Vancouver BC V5T 1A6 Canada. (604)876-8710. Fax: (604)879-2667. E-mail: info@anvilpress.com. Web site: www.anvilpress.com. **Contact:** Brian Kaufman, publisher. Estab. 1988. "Three-person operation with volunteer editorial board." Publishes trade paperback originals. Canadian authors *only*. Books: offset or web printing; perfect bound. **Published some debut authors within the last year.** Averages 8-10 total titles/year.

Needs Experimental, literary, short story collections. Contemporary, modern literature—no formulaic or genre. Published *Stolen*, by Annette Lapointe (novel); *Suburban Pornography*, by Matthew Firth (stories); *A Small Dog Barking*, by Robert Strandquist (stories); *Cusp/Detritus*, by Catherine Owen and Karen Moe (poetry/photographs).

How to Contact Accepts unsolicited mss, or query with SASE. Include estimated word count, brief bio. Send SASE for return of ms or send a disposable ms and SASE for reply only. Responds in 2 months to queries; 6 months to mss. Accepts simultaneous submissions.

Terms Pays 15% royalty on net receipts. Average advance: $500. Publishes ms 8 months after acceptance. Book catalog for 9×12 SAE with 2 first-class stamps. Ms guidelines online.

Advice "We are only interested in writing that is progressive in some way—form, content. We want contemporary fiction from serious writers who intend to be around for a while and be a name people will know in years to come. Read back titles, look through our catalog before submitting."

Ⓐ ◪ ARCADE PUBLISHING

116 John St., Suite 2810, New York NY 10038. (212)475-2633. **Contact:** Richard Seaver, Jeannette Seaver, Cal Barksdale, Casey Ebro, James Jayo, and Tessa Ayel. Estab. 1988. Independent publisher. Publishes hardcover originals, trade paperback reprints. Books: 50-55 lb. paper; notch, perfect bound; illustrations. **Published some debut authors within the last year.** Averages 35 total titles, 10 fiction titles/year. Distributes titles through Hachette Book Group USA.

Needs Literary, mainstream/contemporary, short story collections. Published *Trying to Save Piggy Sneed*, by John Irving; *It Might Have Been What He Said*, by Eden Collinsworth; *Music of a Life*, by Andrei Makine; *The Last Song of Dusk*, by Siddharth Dhanvant Shanghvi; *Bibliophilia*, by Michael Griffith.

How to Contact Does not accept unsolicited mss. *Agented submissions only.* Agented fiction 100%. Responds in 1 month to queries; 4 months to mss.

Terms Pays royalty on retail price, 10 author's copies. Offers advance. Publishes ms within 18 months after acceptance. Ms guidelines for #10 SASE.

◪ ARIEL STARR PRODUCTIONS, LTD.

P.O. Box 17, Demarest NJ 07627. E-mail: darkbird@aol.com. **Contact:** Cynthia Soroka, president. Estab. 1991. Publishes paperback originals. **Published 2 debut authors within the last year.**

How to Contact Submit outline, 1 sample chapter. Accepts queries by e-mail, mail. Include brief bio. Send SASE or IRC. Responds in 6 weeks to queries; 4 months to mss. Sometimes comments on rejected mss.

Terms Publishes ms one year after acceptance.

▨ ◪ ◎ ARSENAL PULP PRESS

341 Water Street, Suite 200, Vancouver BC V6B 1B8 Canada. (604)687-4233. Fax: (604)687-4283. Web site: www.arsenalpulp.com. **Contact:** Bethanne Grabham, Editorial Asst. Estab. 1980. Literary press. Publishes hardcover and trade paperback originals, and trade paperback reprints. **Published some debut authors within the last year.** Plans 1,500 first novels this year. Plans 2 first novels this year. Averages 20 total titles/year. Distributes titles through Whitecap Books (Canada) and Consortium (U.S.). Promotes titles through reviews, excerpts and print advertising.

Needs Gay/lesbian, literary fiction and nonfiction, multicultural, regional (British Columbia), cultural studies, pop culture, political/sociological issues, cookbooks. No poetry.

How to Contact Accepts unsolicited mss. Submit outline, 2-3 sample chapter(s), synopsis. Include list of publishing credits. Send copy of ms and SASE (or with International Reply Coupons if sent from outside Canada) OR include e-mail address if manuscript does not need to be returned. Agented fiction 10%. Responds in 2 months to queries; 4 months to mss. Accepts simultaneous submissions. Sometimes comments on rejected mss.

Terms Publishes ms 1 year after acceptance. Book catalog and submission guidelines on Web site.

Advice Please consult Web site before submitting to ensure your manuscript is appropriate for our list. No fax or e-mail submissions, please.

☑ ◎ ARTE PUBLICO PRESS

University of Houston, 452 Cullen Performance Hall, Houston TX 77204-2004. Fax: (713)743-3080. Web site: www.artepublicopress.com. **Contact:** Dr. Nicolas Kanellos, editor. Estab. 1979. "Small press devoted to the publication of contemporary U.S.-Hispanic literature." Publishes hardcover originals, trade paperback originals and reprints. Averages 36 total titles/year.

- Arte Publico Press is the oldest and largest publisher of Hispanic literature for children and adults in the United States.

Imprint(s) Pinata Books featuring children's and young adult literature by U.S.-Hispanic writers.

Needs Ethnic, literary, mainstream/contemporary, written by U.S.-Hispanic authors. Published *Project Death*, by Richard Bertematti (novel, mystery); *A Perfect Silence*, by Alba Ambert; *Song of the Hummingbird*, by Graciela Limón; *Little Havana Blues: A Cuban-American Literature Anthology*.

How to Contact Accepts unsolicited mss. Query with SASE or submit 2 sample chapter(s), synopsis or submit complete ms. Agented fiction 1%. Responds in 2-4 months to queries; 3-6 months to mss. Accepts simultaneous submissions. Sometimes comments on rejected mss.

Terms Pays 10% royalty on wholesale price. Provides 20 author's copies; 40% discount on subsequent copies. Average advance: $1,000-3,000. Publishes ms 2 years after acceptance. Ms guidelines online.

Advice "Include cover letter in which you 'sell' your book—why should we publish the book, who will want to read it, why does it matter, etc."

Ⓝ ◻ ASPEN MOUNTAIN PRESS

P.O. Box 473543, Aurora CO 80047-3543. E-mail: submissions@aspenmountainpress.com. Web site: www.AspenMountainPress.com. **Contact:** Sandra Hicks, editor-in-chief (gay, mystery, erotica, science fiction, fantasy); Nikita Gordyn (paranormal romance, science fiction romance). Estab. 2006. "We are a small electronic press that specializes in e-books. A few outstanding stories are considered for print. We currently encourage newer, outstanding writers to take their craft to the next level. The bulk of our stories are romantic with varying degrees of sensuality/sexuality. We encourage romances between consenting adults. We encourage discussion among our authors; we frequently discuss marketing, we take author input into covers seriously, we pay every month royalties are earned." Publishes paperback originals, e-books. Format: POD printing; perfect bound. Average print order: 250-500. Debut novel print order: 250. **Published 30 debut writers last year**. Plans 25-30 debut novels this year. Averages 65 fiction titles/year. Member CIPA. Distributes/promotes titles through Fictionwise, AllRomance Ebooks, Mobipocket, Amazon, Ingrams, and Baker and Taylor.

Needs Adventure, erotica, fantasy (space fantasy, sword and sorcery), gay, historical (erotic regency), horror (dark fantasy, futuristic, psychological, supernatural), lesbian, military/war, mystery/suspense (amateur sleuth, cozy, police procedural, private eye/hardboiled), psychic/supernatural, romance (contemporary, futuristic/time travel, gothic, historical, regency, romantic suspense), science fiction (hard science/technological, soft/sociological), short story collections, thriller/espionage, western (frontier saga, traditional, gay). Special interests: "military/paramilitary with heroes the reader can identify with and science fiction romance—No first person!" Published *Cold Warriors*, by Clare Dargin (science fiction romance); *Del Fantasma: Texas Tea*, by Maura Anderson (erotic paranormal romance); and *Soul Sacrifice*, by Elisabeth Jason (erotic paranormal romance).

How to Contact Query with outline/synopsis and 2-4 sample chapters. Accepts queries by e-mail only. Include estimated word count, brief bio, list of publishing credits, and indicate whether the ms is finished. Responds to queries in 1 month. Accepts unsolicited mss. Often critiques/comments on rejected mss. Responds to mss in 2-3 months.

Terms Sends pre-production galleys to author. Ms published 3-12 months after acceptance. Writer's guidelines on Web site. Pays royalties of 8% min for print, 35-40% max for e-books.

Advice "Gay romances and erotica are very popular in e-books. Well-written science fiction and fantasy are also doing well. Eliminate dialogue tags when possible. Have someone outside your family read your submission and check for continuity errors, typing mistakes, and pacing. Follow the submission guidelines. Have a Web site and a blog. Have some idea on how you are going to market your book and let people know about it. Think outside the box. Traditional marketing, such as book marks, does not make sense in our industry."

⚎ ◎ ⚑ ATHENEUM BOOKS FOR YOUNG READERS

Simon & Schuster, 1230 Avenue of the Americas, New York NY 10020. (212)698-7000. Fax: (212)698-2796. Web site: www.simonsayskids.com. **Contact:** Caitlyn Dlouhy, executive editor; Ginee Seo, VP, editorial director, Books; Anne Schwartz, vice president and editorial director; Anne Schwartz Books. **Manuscript Acquisitions:** Carol Chou, editorial assistant. **Art Acquisitions:** Ann Bobco, executive art director. Estab. 1960. Atheneum Books for Young Readers is a hardcover imprint with a focus on literary fiction and fine picture books for preschoolers through young adults. Publishes special interest, first novels and new talent. Publishes 20-30 picture books/year; 20-25 middle readers/year; 15-25 young adult titles/year.

- In recent years, three books by Atheneum have received awards: *House of the Scorpion*, by Nancy Farmer, National Book Award; *Clever Beatrice*, by Margaret Willey, Charlotte Zolotow Award; and *Silent Night*, by Sandy Turner, Ragazzi Award.

Needs Adventure, ethnic, experimental, fantasy, gothic, historical, horror, humor, mainstream/contemporary, mystery, science fiction, sports, suspense, western, animal. "We have few specific needs except for books that are fresh, interesting and well written. Fad topics are dangerous, as are works you haven't polished to the best of your ability. (The competition is fierce.) Other things we don't need at this time are safety pamphlets, ABC books, coloring books and board books. In writing picture book texts, avoid the coy and 'cutesy,' such as stories about characters with alliterative names." Published *Ben Franklin's Almanac*, by Candace Fleming (nonfiction); *If I were a Lion*, by Sarah Weeks and Heather Soloman; *Seadogs*, by Lisa Wheeler; *Friction*, by E.R. Frank (YA novel); and *Audrey and Barbara*, by Janet Lawson (picture book fiction; debut author).

How to Contact Send query letters w/ SASE for picture books; send synopsis and first 3 chapters or first 30 pages w/ SASE for novels. Responds to queries in 1-2 months; requested mss in 3-4 months. Publishes a book 24-36 months after acceptance. Will consider simultaneous queries from previously unpublished authors and those submitted to other publishers, "though we request that the author let us know it is a simultaneous query." Please do not call to query or follow up.

Terms Pays 10% royalty on retail price. Average advance: $5,000-6,500. Publishes ms 18 months after acceptance. Ms guidelines for #10 SASE.

Advice "Write about what you know best. We look for original stories, unique and flavor-filled voices, and strong, evocative characters with whom a reader will readily embark on a literary journey. *Query letter only is best.* We do not accept unsolicited mss."

⚎ ◎ AUNT LUTE BOOKS

P.O. Box 410687, San Francisco CA 94141. (415)826-1300. Fax: (415)826-8300. E-mail: books@auntlute.com. Web site: www.auntlute.com. **Contact:** Shahara Godfrey, first reader. Small feminist and women-of-color press. Publishes hardcover and paperback originals. Averages 4 total titles/year.

Needs Ethnic, feminist, lesbian.

How to Contact Accepts unsolicited mss. Query with SASE or submit outline, sample chapter(s), synopsis. Send SASE or IRC. Responds in 4 months to mss.

Terms Pays royalty.

Advice "We seek manuscripts, both fiction and nonfiction, by women from a variety of cultures, ethnic backgrounds and subcultures; women who are self-aware and who, in the face of all contradictory evidence, are still hopeful that the world can reserve a place of respect for each woman in it. We seek work that explores the specificities of the worlds from which we come, and which examines the intersections between the borders which we all inhabit."

⚑ ⚎ AUTUMN HOUSE PRESS

87 ½ Westwood Street, Pittsburgh PA 15211. (412)381-4261. E-mail: info@autumnhouse.org. Web site: http://autumnhouse.org. **Contact:** Sharon Dillworth, fiction editor. Estab. 1998. "We are a non-profit literary press specializing in high-quality poetry and fiction. Our editions are beautifully designed and printed, and they are distributed nationally. Approximately one-third of our sales are to college literature and creative writing classes." Publishes hardcover originals, paperback originals. Format: acid-free paper; offset printing; perfect and casebound (cloth) bound; sometimes contains illustrations. Average print order: 1,500. Debut novel print order: 1,500. **Published 2 new writers last year.** Plans 2 debut novels this year. Averages 6 total titles/year; 2 fiction titles/year. Member CLMP, AWP, Academy of American Poets. "We distribute our own titles. We do extensive national promotion through ads, web-marketing, reading tours, book fairs and conferences."

Needs "We are open to all genres. The quality of writing concerns us, not the genre. We are looking for well-crafted prose fiction." Published *New World Order*, by Derek Green (collection of stories).
How to Contact Send query letter. Reads submissions Jan 1-June 30. Accepts queries by snail mail, e-mail, phone. See Web site for official guidelines. Responds to queries in 2 days. Accepts unsolicited mss. Never critiques/comments on rejected mss. Responds to mss by August.
Terms Sends pre-production galleys to author. Ms published 9-12 months after acceptance. Writer's guidelines on Web site. Pays royalties 7%, advance average of $2,500. Book catalogs free upon request, on Web site.
Advice "The competition is very tough—we received over 700 manuscripts in 2007. Send only your best work."

AVALON BOOKS

Thomas Bouregy & Co., Inc., 160 Madison Ave., 5th Floor, New York NY 10016. (212)598-0222. Fax: (212)979-1862. E-mail: editorial@avalonbooks.com. Web site: www.avalonbooks.com. **Contact:** Faith Black, associate editor. Estab. 1950. Publishes hardcover originals. **Published some debut authors within the last year.** Averages 60 total titles/year. Distributes titles through Baker & Taylor, libraries, Barnes&Noble.com and Amazon.com. Promotes titles through *Library Journal*, *Booklist*, *Publishers Weekly* and local papers.
Needs Historical (romance), mystery, contemporary romance, western. "We publish wholesome contemporary romances, mysteries, historical romances and westerns. Our books are read by adults as well as teenagers, and the characters are all adults. All mysteries are contemporary. We publish contemporary romances (four every two months), historical romances (two every two months), mysteries (two every two months) and westerns (two every two months). Submit first 3 sample chapters, a 2-3 page synopsis and SASE. The manuscripts should be between 40,000 to 70,000 words. Manuscripts that are too long will not be considered. Time period and setting are the author's preference. The historical romances will maintain the high level of reading expected by our readers. The books shall be wholesome fiction, without graphic sex, violence or strong language." Published *Death Superior*, by Matthew Williams (mystery); *A Matter of Motive*, by Michael Williams (mystery); *Christmas in Carol*, by Sheila Robins (romantic comedy); *Night Calls*, by Holly Jacobs (romantic comedy).
How to Contact Does not accept unsolicited mss. Query with SASE or IRC. Responds in 1 month to queries; 6-10 months to mss.
Terms Average advance: $1,000. Publishes ms 8-12 months after acceptance. Ms guidelines online.

AVON BOOKS

Harper Collins Publishers, 10 E. 53 Street, New York NY 10022. Web site: www.harpercollins.com. **Contact:** Michael Morrison, publisher. Estab. 1941. Publishes hardcover and paperback originals and reprints. Averages 400 total titles/year.
Imprint(s) Avon, EOS.
Needs Historical, literary, mystery, romance, science fiction, young adult, health, pop culture.
How to Contact Does not accept unsolicited mss. Query with SASE. Send SASE or IRC.
Terms Varies.

⚡ ◢ ◎ B & H PUBLISHING

LifeWay Christian Resources, 127 Ninth Ave. N., Nashville TN 37234. (615)251-2438. Fax: (615)251-3752. Web site: www.bhpublishinggroup.com/Fiction. **Contact:** David Webb, executive editor. Estab. 1934. Publishes hardcover and paperback originals. B & H is the book division of LifeWay, the world's largest publisher of Christian materials. Averages 90 total titles, 20 fiction titles/year. Member: ECPA.
Needs Religious/inspirational (contemporary women's fiction, suspense, romance, thriller, historical romance). Engaging stories told from a Christian worldview. Published *Elvis Takes a Back Seat*, by Leanna Ellis (contemporary); *Snow Angel*, by Jamie Carie (romance); *The Moon in the Mango Tree*, by Pamela Binnings Ewin (historical); *Shade*, by John B. Olson (thriller); and *Forsaken*, by James David Jordan (suspense).
How to Contact Does not accept unsolicited mss. Query with SASE. Accepts queries by e-mail.

Include synopsis, estimated word count, brief bio, list of publishing credits. Agented fiction 75%. Responds in 3 months to queries. Accepts simultaneous submissions.

Terms Pays negotiable royalty. Publishes ms 10-12 months after acceptance. Ms guidelines for #10 SASE.

☑ ◎ BAEN PUBLISHING ENTERPRISES

P.O. Box 1403, Riverdale NY 10471-0671. (718)548-3100. E-mail: info@baen.com. Web site: www.baen.com. **Contact:** Toni Weisskopf, publisher. Estab. 1983. "We publish books at the heart of science fiction and fantasy." Publishes hardcover, trade paperback and mass market paperback originals and reprints. **Published some debut authors within the last year.** Plans 2-3 first novels this year. Averages 120 total titles, 120 fiction titles/year. Distributes titles through Simon & Schuster.

Imprint(s) Baen Science Fiction and Baen Fantasy.

Needs Fantasy, science fiction. Interested in science fiction novels (based on real science) and fantasy novels "that at least strive for originality." Length: 110,00-150,000 words. Published *In Fury Born*, by David Weber; *Music to My Sorrow*, by Mercedes Lackey and Rosemary Edghill; *Ghost*, by John Ringo.

How to Contact Submit synopsis and complete ms. "Electronic submissions are strongly preferred. Attach manuscript as a Rich Text Format (.rtf) file. Any other format will not be considered." Additional submission guidelines online. Include estimated word count, brief bio. Send SASE or IRC. Responds in 9-12 months. No simultaneous submissions. Sometimes comments on rejected mss.

Terms Pays royalty on retail price. Offers advance. Ms guidelines online.

Advice "Keep an eye and a firm hand on the overall story you are telling. Style is important but less important than plot. Good style, like good breeding, never calls attention to itself. Read *Writing to the Point*, by Algis Budrys. We like to maintain long-term relationships with authors."

☑ ◎ BAKER BOOKS

Baker Book House Company, P.O. Box 6287, Grand Rapids MI 49516-6287. (616)676-9185. Fax: (616)676-2315. Web site: www.bakerbooks.com. **Contact:** Jeanette Thomason, special projects editor (mystery, literary, women's fiction); Lonnie Hull DuPont, editorial director (all genres); Vicki Crumpton, acquisitions editor (all genres). Estab. 1939. "Midsize publisher of work that interests Christians." Publishes hardcover and trade paperback originals and trade paperback reprints. Books: web offset print. Plans 5 first novels this year. Averages 200 total titles/year. Distributes titles through Ingram and Spring Arbor into both CBA and ABA markets worldwide.

Needs Literary, mainstream/contemporary, mystery, picture books, religious. "We are mainly seeking fiction of two genres: contemporary women's fiction and mystery." Published *Praise Jerusalem!* and *Resting in the Bosom of the Lamb*, by Augusta Trobaugh (contemporary women's fiction); *Touches the Sky*, by James Schaap (western, literary); and *Face to Face*, by Linda Dorrell (mystery); *Flabbergasted*, by Ray Blackston; *The Fisherman*, by Larry Huntsberger.

How to Contact Does not accept unsolicited mss.

Terms Pays 14% royalty on net receipts. Offers advance. Publishes ms within 1 year after acceptance. Ms guidelines for #10 SASE.

Advice "We are not interested in historical fiction, romances, science fiction, biblical narratives or spiritual warfare novels. Do not call to 'pass by' your idea."

Ⓐ ☑ ♈ BANCROFT PRESS

P.O. Box 65360, Baltimore MD 21209-9945. (410)358-0658. Fax: (410)764-1967. Web site: www.bancroftpress.com. **Contact:** Bruce Bortz, publisher (health, investments, politics, history, humor); Fiction Editor (literary novels, mystery/thrillers, young adult). "Small independent press publishing literary and commercial fiction, often by journalists." Publishes hardcover and trade paperback originals. Also packages books for other publishers (no fee to authors). **Published 2 debut authors within the last year.** Plans several first novels this year. Averages 4 total titles, 2-4 fiction titles/year.

● *The Re-Appearance of Sam Webber*, by Scott Fugua is an ALEX Award winner.

Needs Ethnic (general), family saga, feminist, gay/lesbian, glitz, historical, humor, lesbian, literary, mainstream/contemporary, military/war, mystery (amateur sleuth, cozy, police procedural, private eye/hard-boiled), new age/mystic, regional, science fiction (hard science/technological, soft/sociological), thriller/espionage, young adult (historical, problem novels, series. "Our No. 1 priority is publishing books appropriate for young adults, ages 10-18. All quality books on any subject that fit that category will be considered." Published *Those Who Trespass*, by Bill O'Reilly (thriller); *The Re-Appearance of Sam Webber*, by Scott Fugua (literary); and *Malicious Intent*, by Mike Walker (Hollywood).

How to Contact Accepts unsolicited mss. Query with SASE or submit outline, 2 sample chapter(s), synopsis, by mail or e-mail or submit complete ms. Accepts queries by e-mail, fax. Include brief bio, list of publishing credits. Send SASE for return of ms or send a disposable ms and SASE for reply only. Agented fiction 100%. Responds in 6-12 months to mss. Accepts simultaneous submissions. Sometimes comments on rejected mss.

Terms Pays various royalties on retail price. Average advance: $750. Publishes ms up to 3 years after acceptance. Ms guidelines online.

Advice "Be patient, send a sample, know your book's audience."

Ⓐ ⊠ BANTAM DELL PUBLISHING GROUP

Random House, Inc., 1745 Broadway, New York NY 10019. (212)782-9000. Fax: (212)782-8890. Web site: www.bantamdell.com. Estab. 1945. "In addition to being the nation's largest mass market paperback publisher, Bantam publishes a select yet diverse hardcover list." Publishes hardcover, trade paperback and mass market paperback originals; mass market paperback reprints. Averages 350 total titles/year.

Imprint(s) Bantam Hardcover; Bantam Trade Paperback; Bantam Mass Market; Crimeline; Dell; Delta; Domain; DTP; Delacorte Press; The Dial Press; Fanfare; Island; Spectra.

Needs Adventure, fantasy, horror.

How to Contact Agented submissions only.

Terms Offers advance. Publishes ms 1 year after acceptance.

Ⓒ BARBOUR PUBLISHING, INC.

P.O. Box 719, Uhrichsville OH 44683. (740)922-6045. Fax: (740)922-5948. E-mail: fictionsubmit@bar bourbooks.com. Web site: www.barbourpublishing.com. **Contact:** Rebecca Germany, senior editor (fiction). Estab. 1981. Publishes hardcover, trade paperback and mass market paperback originals and reprints. **Published 40% debut authors within the last year.** Averages 250 total titles/year.

Imprint(s) Heartsong Presents; Barbour Books and Heartsong Presents Mysteries.

Needs Historical, contemporary, religious, romance, western, mystery. All submissions must be Christian mss. "Heartsong romance is 'sweet'—no sex, no bad language. All stories must have Christian faith as an underlying basis. Common writer's mistakes are a sketchy proposal, an unbeliev-able story, and a story that doesn't fit our guidelines for inspirational romances." Published *A Sister's Secret*, by Wanda E. Brunstetter (fiction).

How to Contact Submit 3 sample chapter(s), synopsis by e-mail. Responds in 6 months to mss. Accepts simultaneous submissions.

Terms Pays 8-16% royalty on net price. Average advance: $1,000-8,000. Publishes ms 1-2 years after acceptance. Book catalog online or for 9×12 SAE with 2 first-class stamps; ms guidelines for #10 SASE or online.

Advice "Audience is evangelical/Christian conservative, non-denominational, young and old. We're looking for *great concepts*, not necessarily a big name author or agent. We want to publish books with mass appeal."

Ⓒ BAREFOOT BOOKS

2067 Massachusetts Avenue, Cambridge MA 02140. Web site: www.barefootbooks.com. **Contact:** Submissions editor. Publishes hardcover and trade paperback originals. **Published 35% debut au-thors within the last year.** Averages 30 total titles/year.

Needs Juvenile. Barefoot Books only publishes children's picture books and anthologies of folktales. "We do not publish novels." Published *The Prince's Bedtime*, by Joanne Oppenheim (picture book); *The Barefoot Book of Fairy Tales*, by Malachy Doyle (illustrated anthology).

How to Contact "We do accept query letters but prefer to receive full manuscripts." Include SASE. Responds in 4 months to mss. Accepts simultaneous submissions. No phone calls or e-mails, please.

Terms Pays 2½-5% royalty on retail price. Offers advance. Publishes ms 2 years after acceptance. Ms guidelines online.

Advice "Our audience is made up of children and parents, teachers and students of many different ages and cultures. Since we are a small publisher and we definitely publish for a 'niche' market, it is helpful to look at our books and our Web site before submitting, to see if your book would fit into our list.''

BARRON'S EDUCATIONAL SERIES, INC.

250 Wireless Blvd., Hauppauge NY 11788. (631)434-3311. Fax: (631)434-3394. E-mail: waynebarr@b arronseduc.com. Web site: barronseduc.com. **Contact:** Wayne Barr, director of acquisitions. Estab. 1941. Publishes hardcover, paperback and mass market originals and software. **Published 10% debut authors within the last year.** Averages 400 total titles/year.
Needs Middle grade, YA.
How to Contact Accepts simultaneous submissions. E-mail queries only, no attachments.
Terms Pays 12-13% royalty on net receipts. Average advance: $3-4,000. Publishes ms 18 months after acceptance. Ms queries online.
Advice "The writer has the best chance of selling us a book that will fit into one of our series. Children's books have less chance for acceptance because of the glut of submissions. SASE must be included for the return of all materials. Please be patient for replies."

FREDERIC C. BEIL, PUBLISHER, INC.

609 Whitaker St., Savannah GA 31401. (912)233-2446. Fax: (912)233-6456. Web site: www.beil.com. **Contact:** Frederic C. Beil III, president; Mary Ann Bowman, editor. Estab. 1982. "Our objectives are (1) to offer to the reading public carefully selected texts of lasting value; (2) to adhere to high standards in the choice of materials and bookmaking craftsmanship; (3) to produce books that exemplify good taste in format and design; and (4) to maintain the lowest cost consistent with quality." Publishes hardcover originals and reprints. Books: acid-free paper; letterpress and offset printing; Smyth-sewn, hardcover binding; illustrations. Plans 3 first novels this year. Averages 10 total titles, 4 fiction titles/year.
Imprint(s) The Sandstone Press, Hypermedia.
Needs Historical, literary, biography. Published *Dancing by The River*, by Marlin Barton; *Joseph Jefferson*, by Arthur Bloom (biography); *The Invisible Country*, by H.E. Francis (fiction).
How to Contact Does not accept unsolicited mss. Query with SASE. Responds in 2 weeks to queries. Accepts simultaneous submissions.
Terms Pays 7$\frac{1}{2}$% royalty on retail price. Publishes ms 20 months after acceptance.
Advice "Hope for a good harvest, but keep on hoeing."

BELLEVUE LITERARY PRESS

Dept. of Medicine, NYU School of Medicine, 550 First Avenue, OBV A-640, New York NY 10016. (212)263-7802. Fax: (212)263-7803. E-mail: egoldman@blreview.org. Web site: http://blpress.org. **Contact:** Erika Goldman, editorial director (literary fiction); Leslie Hodgkins, editor (literary fiction). Estab. 2005. "We're a small literary press that publishes nonfiction and fiction that ranges the intersection of the sciences (or medicine) and the arts." Publishes hardcover originals, paperback originals. Debut novel print order: 3000. Plans 2 debut novels this year. Averages 8 total titles/year; 2 fiction titles/year. Member CLMP. Distributes/promotes titles through Consortium.
Needs literary. Published *The Cure*, by Varley O'Connor (literary); *The Leper Compound*, by Paula Nangle (literary).
How to Contact Send query letter or query with outline/synopsis and 3 sample chapters. Accepts queries by snail mail, e-mail. Include estimated word count, brief bio, list of publishing credits. Send disposable copy of ms and SASE for reply only. Agented fiction: 75%. Responds to queries in 2 weeks. Accepts unsolicited mss. Considers simultaneous submissions. Rarely critiques/comments on rejected mss. Responds to mss in 6 weeks.
Terms Sends pre-production galleys to author. Manuscript published 8-12 months after acceptance. Writer's guidelines not available. Pays royalties 6-15%, advance $1,000. Book catalogs on Web site.

BEN BELLA BOOKS

6440 N. Central Expy., Suite 503, Dallas TX 75206. (214)750-3600. Fax: (214)750-3645. E-mail: leah@benbellabooks.com. Web site: www.benbellabooks.com. **Contact:** Leah Wilson, editor. Estab. 2001. Small, growing independent publisher specializing in popular culture, smart nonfiction and science fiction; our fiction is largely reprints or by established authors. Publishes hardcover and paperback originals and paperback reprints. Averages 30 total titles.

Needs Currently not accepting fiction submissions.

⬛ ✖ THE BERKLEY PUBLISHING GROUP

Penguin Putnam, Inc., 375 Hudson St., New York NY 10014. (212)366-2000. E-mail: online@penguin putnam.com. Web site: www.penguinputnam.com. Estab. 1954. ''Berkley is proud to publish in paperback some of the country's most significant best-selling authors.'' Publishes paperback and mass market originals and reprints. Averages approximately 800 total titles/year.

Imprint(s) Ace Books, Berkley Books, HP Books, Perigee, Riverhead Books.

Needs Adventure, historical, literary, mystery, romance, spiritual, suspense, western, young adult.

How to Contact Does not accept unsolicited mss.

Terms Pays 4-15% royalty on retail price. Offers advance. Publishes ms 2 years after acceptance.

⬛ ◎ BETHANY HOUSE PUBLISHERS

11400 Hampshire Ave. S., Minneapolis MN 55438. (952)829-2500. Fax: (952)996-1304. Web site: www.bethanyhouse.com Estab. 1956. ''The purpose of Bethany House Publisher's publishing program is to relate biblical truth to all areas of life—whether in the framework of a well-told story, of a challenging book for spiritual growth, or of a Bible reference work.'' Publishes hardcover and trade paperback originals, mass market paperback reprints. Averages 90-100 total titles/year.

Needs Adventure, children's/juvenile, historical, young adult. Published *The Still of Night*, by Kristen Heitzmann (fiction).

How to Contact Does not accept unsolicited mss. Accepts queries only by fax. Accepts simultaneous submissions. Query guidelines online.

Terms Pays negotiable royalty on net price. Average advance: negotiable. Publishes ms 1 year after acceptance.

⬛ ◎ BILINGUAL REVIEW PRESS

Hispanic Research Center, Arizona State University, P.O. Box 875303, Tempe AZ 85287-5303. (480)965-3867. Fax: (480)965-0315. E-mail: brp@asu.edu. Web site: www.asu.edu/brp. **Contact:** Gary Keller, publisher. Estab. 1973. ''University affiliated.'' Publishes hardcover and paperback originals and reprints. Books: 60 lb. acid-free paper; single sheet or web press printing; perfect-bound.

Needs Ethnic, literary, short story collections. Always seeking Chicano, Puerto Rican, Cuban-American or other U.S. Hispanic themes with strong and serious literary qualities and distinctive and intellectually important themes. Does *not* publish children's literature or trade genres such as travelogues and adventure fiction. Novels set in a pre-Columbian past are not likely to be published. Published *Moving Target: A Memoir of Pursuit*, by Ron Arias; *Contemporary Chicano and Chicana Art: Artists, Works, Culture, and Education*, Gary Keller, et al; *Triumph of Our Communities: Four Decades of Mexican American Art*, Gary Keller et al; *Assumption and Other Stories*, by Daniel A. Olivas; *Renaming Ecstasy: Latino Writings on the Sacred*, edited by Orlando Ricardo Menes.

How to Contact Accepts unsolicited mss. Query with SASE or submit 2-3 sample chapter(s). Accepts queries by email, mail. Include brief bio, list of publishing credits. Send SASE or IRC. Responds in 6 weeks to queries; 2-6 months to mss.

Terms Pays 10% royalty. Average advance: $500. Publishes ms 2 years after acceptance. Ms guidelines by email.

Advice ''Writers should take the utmost care in assuring that their manuscripts are clean, grammatically impeccable, and have perfect spelling. This is true not only of the English but the Spanish as well. All accent marks need to be in place as well as other diacritical marks. When these are missing its an immediate first indication that the author does not really know Hispanic culture and is not equipped to write about it. We are interested in publishing creative literature that treats the U.S Hispanic experience in a distinctive, creative, revealing way. The kind of books that we publish we keep in print for a very long time irrespective of sales. We are busy establishing and preserving a U.S. Hispanic canon of creative literature.''

◎ BIRCH BROOK PRESS

P.O. Box 81, Delhi NY 13753. Fax: (607)746-7453. Web site: www.birchbrookpress.info. **Contact:** Tom Tolnay, publisher. Estab. 1982. Small publisher of popular culture and literary titles in mostly handcrafted letterpress editions. Specializes in fiction anthologies with specific theme, and an occasional novella. "Not a good market for full-length novels." Publishes hardcover and trade paperback originals. Books: 80 lb. vellum paper; letterpress printing; wood engraving illustrations. Averages 6 total titles, 2 fiction titles/year. Member, Small Press Center, Publishers Marketing Association, Academy of American Poets. Distributes titles through Baker and Taylor, Barnes&Noble.com, Amazon.com, Gazelle Book Services in Europe, Multicultural Books in Canada. Promotes titles through Web site, catalogs, direct mail and group ads.

Imprint(s) Birch Brook Press, Persephone Press and Birch Brook Impressions.

Needs Literary, regional (Adirondacks), popular culture, special interest (flyfishing, baseball, books about books, outdoors). "Mostly we do anthologies around a particular theme generated inhouse. We make specific calls for fiction when we are doing an anthology." Published *Magic and Madness in the Library* (fiction collection); *Life & Death of a Book*, by William MacAdams; *Kilimanjaro Burning*, by John B. Robinson; *A Punk in Gallows America*, by P.W. Fox; *White Buffalo*, by Peter Skinner; *The Suspense of Loneliness* (anthology); *Tales for the Trail* (anthology); *Sexy Sixties*, by Harry Smith; *Human/Nature*, by Lance Lee; *Jack's Beans*, by Tom Smith; *The Alchemy of Words*, by Edward Francisco; *Where Things Are When You Lose Them*, by Martin Golan; *The Sea-Crossing of St. Brendan*, by Matthew Brennan; *Woodstoves & Ravens*, by Robert Farmer.

How to Contact Query with SASE or submit sample chapter(s), synopsis. Responds in 2 months to queries. Accepts simultaneous submissions. Sometimes comments on rejected mss.

Terms Modest flat fee on anthologies. Usually publishes ms 10-18 months after acceptance. Ms guidelines for #10 SASE.

Advice "Write well on subjects of interest to BBP, such as outdoors, flyfishing, baseball, music, literary novellas, books about books."

BKMK PRESS

University of Missouri-Kansas City, 5101 Rockhill Rd., Kansas City MO 64110-2499. (816)235-2558. Fax: (816)235-2611. E-mail: bkmk@umkc.edu. Web site: www.umkc.edu/bkmk. Estab. 1971. Publishes trade paperback originals. Averages 4 total titles/year.

Needs Literary, short story collections. Not currently acquiring novels.

How to Contact Query with SASE or submit 2-3 sample stories. Responds in 8 months to mss. Accepts simultaneous submissions.

Terms Pays 10% royalty on wholesale price. Publishes ms 1 year after acceptance. Ms guidelines online.

◙ ▼ BLACK HERON PRESS

P.O. Box 13396, Mill Creek WA 98145. Web site: www.blackheronpress.com. **Contact:** Jerry Gold, publisher. Estab. 1984. Two-person operation; no immediate plans to expand. "We're known for literary fiction. We've done several Vietnam titles and several surrealistic fictions." Publishes hardcover and trade paperback originals. **Published 1-2 debut authors within the last year.** Averages 4 total titles, 4 fiction titles/year.

• Ten books published by Black Heron Press have won regional or national awards.

Needs Experimental, humor, literary, mainstream/contemporary, science fiction (surrealism), war novels (literary). Published *Infinite Kindness*, by Laurie Blauner (historical fiction); and *Moses in Sinai*, by Simone Zelitch (historical fiction).

How to Contact Query letter with first 30 pages of completed manuscript, and SASE with SASE. Responds in 3 months to queries; 6 months to mss. Accepts simultaneous submissions.

Terms Pays 8% royalty on retail price.

Advice "A query letter should tell me: 1) number of words; 2) number of pages; 3) if ms is available on disk; 4) if parts of novel have been published; 5) if so, where? And at least scan some of our books in a bookstore or library. Most submissions we get have come to the wrong press."

Ⓝ ◯ ◎ BLACK LYON PUBLISHING, LLC

P.O. Box 567, Baker City OR 97814. (541)523-5173. Fax: (541)523-5173. E-mail: info@blacklyonpublishing.com. Web site: www.blacklyonpublshing.com. **Contact:** The Editors (romance & general fiction love stories). Estab. 2007. "Black Lyon Publishing is a small, independent publisher. We produce 1-2 romance or general fiction novels each month in both 5×8 trade paperback and PDF e-books formats. We are very focused on giving new novelists a launching pad into the industry." Publishes paperback originals, e-books. **Published 4 new writers last year.** Plans 12 debut novels this year. Averages 15-20 fiction titles/year. Distributes/promotes titles through Web site, Ingram and Baker & Taylor, bookstores, and major online retailers.

Needs romance (contemporary, futuristic/time travel, gothic, historical, regency period, romantic suspense). Special interests: ancient times. Published *Cast in Stone*, by Kerry A. Jones (paranormal romance); *The Medallion of Solaus*, by Kimberly Adkins (paranormal romance); *Maya's Gold*, by Mary Vine (contemporary romance).

How to Contact Send query letter. Query with outline/synopsis and sample chapters. Accepts queries by e-mail. Include estimated word count, brief bio, list of publishing credits. Send SASE or IRC for return of ms or disposable copy of ms and SASE/IRC for reply only. Responds to queries in 2 weeks. No unsolicited mss. Considers simultaneous submissions, submissions on CD or disk, e-mail submissions. Often critiques/comments on rejected mss. Responds to mss in 1 week.

Terms Sends pre-production galleys to author. Ms published within 6 months after acceptance. Writer's guidelines on Web site. Pays royalties and author's copies. Book catalogs on Web site.

Advice "Write a good, solid romance with a setting, premise, character or voice just a little 'different' than what you might usually find on the market. We like unique books-but they still need to be romances."

◐ BLEAK HOUSE BOOKS

923 Williamson St., Madison WI 53703. (608)467-0133. Web site: www.bleakhousebooks.com. Benjamin LeRoy, publisher Alison Janssen, editor. Estab. 1995. Publisher hardcover and paperback originals. Averages 15-20 titles annually.

Needs Mysteries and literary fiction. "We aren't looking for big budget special effects and car chases. The best part of the story isn't in the distractions, it's in the heart. Characters need to be well drawn. We don't want formula fiction. We don't want rehashes of CSI. We don't want unqualified 'experts' writing books with plot holes. We don't want authors who are so married to their words that they can't see when something doesn't work." Published *Head Games*, by Craig Mcdonald; *Soul Patch*, by Reed Farrel Coleman; *Chicago Blues*, edited by Libby Fischer Hellmann; *In the Light of You*, by Nathan Singer; *Yellow Medicine*, by Anthony Neil Smith.

How to Contact Does not accept unsolicited mss. Any unsolicited mss we receive will be recycled without ever being read. Query with SASE. Include estimated word count, brief bio, list of publishing credits. Agented fiction 75%. "Responds as fast as we can to queries. Depending on when we receive them, it may take awhile. Same holds true for submitted manuscripts, but we'll keep you abreast of what's going on when we know it." Responds in 3 weeks to queries; 2 months to mss. Accepts simultaneous submissions. No electronic submissions. Check Web site for up-to-date guidelines.

Terms All contracts negotiable depending on author, market viability, etc. Our average royalty rate is somewhere between 7.5-15% depending on hardcover/paperback, print run, and many other factors. Advances range from $500-$10,000. Publishes ms 12-18 months after acceptance.

Advice "We've grown from a two book a year publishing house to doing 20-25 books a year. We're still willing to take a chance on first-time authors with extraordinary books. We're still willing to take a chance on offbeat fiction. We are very busy in our office and sometimes our response time isn't as fast as we'd like it to be. But, between working with the books in house or looking at submissions, we feel it's very important to take care of our family of authors first. Please, if you value your work and you are serious about being published, do not send out first drafts. Edit your book. Then edit it again. Please also understand that for a book to be successful, the author and the publisher (and sometimes the agent) have to work together as a team. Good publishers need good writers as much as good writers need good publishers. It's a two-way street. Best of luck and keep writing."

✲ ∅ ◎ BOREALIS PRESS, LTD.

8 Mohawk Crescent and Tecumseh Press Ltd., Nepean ON K2H 7G6 Canada. (613)829-0150. Fax: (613)798-9747. E-mail: drt@borealispress.com. Web site: www.borealispress.com. **Contact:** David Tierney, editor; Glenn Clever, editor. Estab. 1972. "Publishes Canadiana, especially early works that have gone out of print, but also novels of today and shorter fiction for young readers." Publishes hardcover and paperback originals and reprints. Books: standard book-quality paper; offset printing; perfect bound. **Published some debut authors within the last year.** Averages 10-20 total titles/year. Promotes titles through web site, catalogue distribution, fliers for titles, ads in media.

• Borealis Press has a "New Canadian Drama," with 10 books in print.
Imprint(s) *Journal of Canadian Poetry*, Tecumseh Press Ltd., Canadian Critical Editions Series.
Needs Adventure, ethnic, historical, juvenile, literary, mainstream/contemporary, romance, short story collections, young adult. "Only material Canadian in content and dealing with significant aspects of the human situation." Published *Blue: Little Cat Come Home to Stay*, by Donna Richards (young adult); *Biography of a Beagle*, by Gail MacMillan (novel); *The Love of Women*, by Jennifer McVaugh (comic novel).
How to Contact Query with SASE or submit 1-2 sample chapter(s), synopsis. Accepts queries by email, fax. Responds in 2 months to queries; 4 months to mss. No simultaneous submissions.
Terms Pays 10% royalty on net receipts. 3 free author's copies. Ms guidelines online.
Advice "Have your work professionally edited. Our greatest challenge is finding good authors, i.e., those who submit innovative and original material."

☑ BRANDEN PUBLISHING CO., INC.

P.O. Box 812094, Wellesley MA 02482. Phone-Fax; (781)235-3634. Web site: www.brandenbooks.com. **Contact:** Adolph Caso, editor. Estab. 1909. Publishes hardcover and trade paperback originals, reprints and software. Books: 55-60 lb. acid-free paper; case—or perfect-bound; illustrations. Averages 15 total titles, 5 fiction titles/year.
Imprint(s) I.P.L; Dante University Press; Four Seas; Branden Publishing Co., Branden Books.
Needs Ethnic (histories, integration), historical, literary, military/war, religious (historical-reconstructive), short story collections. Looking for "contemporary, fast pace, modern society." Published *I, Morgain*, by Harry Robin; *The Bell Keeper*, by Marilyn Seguin; and *The Straw Obelisk*, by Adolph Caso; *Priest to Mafia Don* by Father Bascio.
How to Contact Does not accept unsolicited mss. Query with SASE. Responds in 1 month to queries.
Terms Pays 5-10% royalty on net receipts. 10 author's copies. Average advance: $1,000 maximum. Publishes ms 10 months after acceptance.
Advice "Publishing more fiction because of demand. *Do not make phone, fax or e-mail inquiries.* Do not oversubmit; single submissions only; do not procrastinate if contract is offered. Our audience is well-read general public, professionals, college students and some high school students. We like books by or about women."

☑ BRIDGE WORKS PUBLISHING CO.

Box 1798, 221 Bridge Lane, Bridgehampton NY 11932. (631)537-3418. Fax: (631)537-5092. **Contact:** Barbara Phillips, editorial director. Estab. 1992. "We are very small, doing only 1-6 titles a year. We publish quality fiction. Our books are routinely reviewed in major publications." Publishes hardcover originals and reprints. **Published some debut authors within the last year.** Distributes titles through National Book Network.
Needs Humor, literary, mystery, short story collections. "Query with SASE before submitting ms. First-time authors should have manuscripts vetted by freelance editors before submitting. We do not accept or read multiple submissions." Recent publications include *Blackbelly* and *Mineral Spirits*, by Heather Sharfeddin.
How to Contact Write to address above, including synopsis and estimated word count. Responds in one month to query and 50 pages, two months to entire ms. Sometimes comments on rejected mss.
Terms Pays 8% of net received from wholesalers and bookstores. Average advance: $1,000. Publishes ms 1 year after acceptance. Book catalog and ms guidelines for #10 SASE.
Advice "We are interested in discovering new writers and we work closely with our authors in both the editorial and marketing processes."

☑ ⚡ BROADWAY BOOKS

Doubleday Broadway Publishing Group, Random House, Inc., 1745 Broadway, New York NY 10019. (212)782-9000. Fax: (212)782-9411. Web site: www.broadwaybooks.com. **Contact:** William Thomas, editor-in-chief. Estab. 1995. Broadway publishes general interest nonfiction and fiction for adults. Publishes hardcover and trade paperback originals and reprints.
Needs Publishes a limited list of commercial literary fiction. Published *Freedomland*, by Richard Price.
How to Contact *Agented submissions only.*

▦ ◎ BROWN SKIN BOOKS

Pentimento, Ltd., P.O. Box 57421, London England E5 0ZD United Kingdom. E-mail: info@brownski nbooks.co.uk. Web site: www.brownskinbooks.co.uk. Estab. 2002. Publishes trade paperback originals. Averages 7 total titles/year.

Needs Erotica. "We are looking for erotic short stories or novels written by women of color, or sensual crime thrillers."

How to Contact Submit proposal package including 2 sample chapter(s), synopsis. Responds in 2 months to queries; 3 months to mss. Accepts simultaneous submissions.

Terms Pays 5-50% royalty or makes outright purchase. Publishes ms 18 months after acceptance. Ms guidelines online.

◪ CALAMARI PRESS

E-mail: derek@calamaripress.com. Web site: www.calamaripress.com. **Contact:** Derek White, editor. Estab. 2003. "Calamari Press is a small, one-person operation on a part-time basis that devotes special attention to creating book objects of literary text and art. It has no preconceived notions of what exactly that means and tastes are admittedly whimsical." Publishes paperback originals. Format: 60 lb. natural finch opaque paper; digital printing; perfect or saddle-stitched bound. Average print order: 300. Debut novel print order: 200. Averages 5 total titles/year; 4 fiction titles/year.

Needs Adventure, comics/graphic novels, ethnic/multicultural, experimental, literary, short story collections. Published *Land of the Snow Men*, by George Belden (Norman Lock) (fictional literary canard with illustrations); *The Singing Fish*, by Peter Markus (prose poem/short fiction collection); *The Night I Dropped Shakespeare On The Cat*, by John Olson; *The Revisionist*, by Miranda Mellis; *Part of the World*, by Robert Lopez.

How to Contact Query with outline/synopsis and 3 sample chapters. Accepts queries by e-mail only. Include brief bio. Send SASE or IRC for return of ms. Responds to queries in 2 weeks. Accepts unsolicited mss. Considers e-mail submissions only. Sometimes critiques/comments on rejected mss. Responds to mss in 2 weeks.

Terms Sends pre-production galleys to author. Manuscript published 2-6 months after acceptance. Writer's guidelines on Web site. Pays in author's copies. Book catalogs free upon request.

Advice "Research a press before you submit to them."

◪ ◎ CALYX BOOKS

P.O. Box B, Corvallis OR 97339-0539. (541)753-9384. Fax: (541)753-0515. **Contact:** M. Donnelly, director. Estab. 1986 for Calyx Books; 1976 for Calyx, Inc. "Calyx exists to publish women's literary and artistic work and is committed to publishing the works of all women, including women of color, older women, lesbians, working-class women, and other voices that need to be heard." Publishes fine literature by women, fiction, nonfiction and poetry. Publishes hardcover and paperback originals. Books: offset printing; paper and cloth binding. **Published 1 debut author within the last year.** Averages 1-2 total titles/year. Distributes titles through Consortium Book Sale and Distribution. Promotes titles through author reading tours, print advertising (trade and individuals), galley and review copy mailings, presence at trade shows, etc.

Needs Ethnic, experimental, feminist, gay/lesbian, lesbian, literary, mainstream/contemporary, short story collections. Published *Forbidden Stitch: An Asian American Women's Anthology; Women and Aging: Present Tense; Writing and Art by Young Women*; and *A Line of Cutting Women*.

How to Contact Closed to submissions until further notice.

Terms Pays 10-15% royalty on net receipts. Average advance: depends on grant support. Publishes ms 2 years after acceptance. Ms guidelines for #10 SASE.

◎ ▧ CANDLEWICK PRESS

2067 Massachusetts Ave., Cambridge MA 02140. (617)661-3330. Fax: (617)661-0565. E-mail: bigbear @candlewick.com. Web site: www.candlewick.com. **Contact:** Joan Powers, editor-at-large; Deb Wayshak Noyes, senior editor; Liz Bicknell, editorial director/associate publisher (poetry, picture books, fiction); Mary Lee Donovan, executive editor (picture books, fiction); Sarah Ketchersid, editor (board, toddler); Hilary Breed Van Dusen, acquisitions editor. Estab. 1991. "We are a truly child-centered publisher." Publishes hardcover originals, trade paperback originals and reprints. Averages 200 total titles/year.

- The Tale of Despereaux, by Kate DiCamillo won the 2004 Newbery Medal. *The Astonishing Life of Octavian Nothing, Traitor to the Nation, Volume One: The Pox Party*, by M.T. Anderson won the 2007 National Book Award.

Needs Juvenile, picture books, young adult. Published *The Tale of Despereaux*, by Kate DiCamillo; the Judy Moody series, by Megan McDonald, illustrated by Peter Reynolds; *Feed*, by M.T. Anderson; *Fairieality*, by David Ellwand.

How to Contact Does not accept unsolicited mss.

☐ CAROLINA WREN PRESS

120 Morris St., Durham NC 27701. (919)560-2738. E-mail: carolinawrenpress@earthlink.net. Web site: www.carolinawrenpress.org. **Contact:** Andrea Selch, president. Estab. 1976. "We publish poetry, fiction, nonfiction, biography, autobiography, literary nonfiction work by and/or about people of color, women, gay/lesbian issues, health and mental health topics in children's literature." Books: 6×9 paper; typeset; various bindings; illustrations. **Published 2 debut authors within the last year.** Distributes titles through Amazon.com, Barnes & Noble, Borders, Ingram and Baker & Taylor and on their Web site.

Needs "Though we accept unsolicited manuscripts of fiction and nonfiction September-December, we very rarely accept any. We suggest you submit to our Doris Bakwin Award for Writing by a Woman; contests is held in fall of odd-numbered years" Does not publish genre fiction or religious texts or self-help books. Published *Downriver* by Jeanne Leiby in 2007.

How to Contact Accepts unsolicited mss. Accepts queries by e-mail, mail. Include brief bio. Send SASE or IRC. Responds in 3 months to queries; 6 months to mss. "Please query before you send or else plan to enter one of our contests. The Doris Bakwin Award for Writing by a Woman accepts entries in odd-numbered years, with a deadline of December 1, 2009, 2011, etc; entry fee is required. Guidelines on our Web site in summer."

Terms Publishes ms 2 year after acceptance. Ms guidelines online.

Advice "Please read our mission statement online before submitting."

☒ ◎ CAROLRHODA BOOKS, INC.

A Division of Lerner Publishing Group, 241 First Ave. N., Minneapolis MN 55401. Fax: (612)332-7615. Web site: www.lernerbooks.com. Estab. 1959. Publishes hardcover originals. Acquisitions: Zelda Wagner, submission editor.

Needs Historical, juvenile, multicultural, picture books, young reader, middle grade and young adult fiction. "We continue to add fiction for middle grades and 8-10 picture books per year. Not looking for folktales or anthropomorphic animal stories." Recently published *The Perfect Shot*, by Elaine Marie Alphin; *Noel*, by Tony Johnston.

How to Contact No unsolicited submissions. "We will continue to seek targeted solicitations at specific reading levels and in specific subject areas. The company will list these targeted solicitations on our Web site and in national newsletters, such as the SCBWI Bulletin."

Terms Pays royalty on wholesale price or makes outright purchase. Negotiates payments of advance against royalty. Average advance: varied. Book catalog for 9×12 SAE with $3.50 postage.

Ⓐ ☒ ◙ CARROLL & GRAF PUBLISHERS, INC.

Avalon Publishing Group, 245 W. 17th St. 11th floor, New York NY 10011. (212)981-9919. Fax: (646)375-2571. Web site: www.avalonpub.com. **Contact:** Will Balliett, publisher; Phillip Turner, editor-in chief; Don Weise, senior editor. Estab. 1982. Publishes hardcover and trade paperback originals. Averages 120 total titles, 50 fiction titles/year.

Needs Literary, mainstream/contemporary, mystery, science fiction, suspense, thriller. Published *The Woman Who Wouldn't Talk*, by Susan McDougal.

How to Contact Does not accept unsolicited mss. *Agented submissions only.*

Terms Pays 10-15% royalty on retail price for hardcover, 6-7½% for paperback. Offers advance commensurate with the work. Publishes ms 9-18 months after acceptance.

◎ CAVE BOOKS

277 Clamer Rd., Trenton NJ 08628-3204. (609)530-9743. E-mail: pddb@juno.com. Web site: www.cavebooks.com. **Contact:** Paul Steward, managing editor. Estab. 1980. Small press devoted to books on caves, karst and speleology. Fiction: novels about cave exploration only. Publishes hardcover

and trade paperback originals and reprints. Books: acid-free paper; offset printing. Averages 2 total titles, 1 fiction title/year.

Needs Adventure, historical, literary, caves, karst, speleology. Recently published *Cave Geology*, by Arthur N. Palmer.

How to Contact Accepts unsolicited mss. Query with SASE or submit complete ms. Accepts queries by e-mail. Send SASE for return of ms or send a disposable ms and SASE for reply only. Responds in 2 weeks to queries; 3 months to mss. Accepts simultaneous submissions, electronic submissions. Sometimes comments on rejected mss.

Terms Pays 10% royalty on retail price. Publishes ms 18 months after acceptance.

Advice "In the last 3 years we have received only 3 novels about caves, and we have published one of them. We get dozens of inappropriate submissions. We only print books about caves."

CHARLESBRIDGE PUBLISHING

85 Main St., Watertown MA 02472. Web site: www.charlesbridge.com/school. Estab. 1980. Publishes hardcover and paperback nonfiction and fiction children's books and transitional books. Averages 36 total titles/year.

Needs Multicultural, nature, science, social studies, bedtime, math, etc. Recently published *A Mother's Journey*, by Sandra Markle; *Aggie and Ben*, by Lori Ries.

How to Contact Submit complete ms with SASE.

Terms Royalty and advance vary. Publishes ms 2 years after acceptance. Ms guidelines online.

CHRONICLE BOOKS

Adult Trade Division, 680 Second St., San Francisco CA 94107. (415)537-4200. Fax: (415)537-4440. Web site: www.chroniclebooks.com. **Contact:** Editorial Dept., Adult Trade Division. Estab. 1966. Publishes hardcover and trade paperback originals. Averages 175 total titles/year.

Needs Novels and story collections. No genre fiction.

How to Contact Submit complete ms and SASE. Responds in 3 months to mss. Accepts simultaneous submissions.

Terms Publishes ms 18 months after acceptance. Ms guidelines online.

⊠ ◎ CHRONICLE BOOKS FOR CHILDREN

680 Second St., San Francisco CA 94107. (415)537-4400. Fax: (415)537-4415. E-mail: kided@chroniclebooks.com. Web site: www.chroniclekids.com. **Contact:** Victoria Rock, founding publisher and editor-at-large; Traci Todd, editor; Andrea Menotti, editor; Julie Romeis, editor; Melissa Manlove, assistant editor. Publishes hardcover and trade paperback originals. **Published 5% debut authors within the last year.** Averages 50-60 total titles/year.

Needs Mainstream/contemporary, multicultural, young adult, picture books, middle grade fiction, young adult projects. Published *Wave*, by Suzy Lee (all ages, picture book); Ivy and Bean series, by Annie Barrows, illustrated by Sophie Blackwell (ages 6-11, chapter book); *Grandma Calls Me Beautiful*, by Barbara Joosse and Barbara Lavallee (ages 4-8, picture book).

How to Contact Submit complete ms (picture books); submit outline synopsis and 3 sample chapters (for older readers). Responds to queries in 1 month; will not respond to submissions unless interested. Do not send SASE; send SASP to confirm receipt. No electronic submissions, submissions on disk or fax.

Terms Royalty varies. Average advance: variable. Publishes ms 18-24 months after acceptance. Ms guidelines online.

Advice "We are interested in projects that have a unique bent to them—be it in subject matter, writing style or illustrative technique. As a small list, we are looking for books that will lend our list a distinctive flavor. Primarily, we are interested in fiction and nonfiction picture books for children ages up to 8 years, and nonfiction books for children ages up to 12 years. We publish board, pop-up and other novelty formats as well as picture books. We are also interested in early chapter books, middle grade fiction and young adult projects."

◎ ⍰ CIRCLET PRESS, INC.

39 Hurlbut Street, Cambridge MA 02138. (617)864-0492. E-mail: ctan@circlet.com. Web site: www.circlet.com. **Contact:** Cecilia Tan, publisher. Estab. 1992. Small, independent specialty book publisher. "We are the only book publisher specializing in science fiction and fantasy of an erotic nature."

Publishes hardcover and trade paperback originals. Books: perfect binding; illustrations sometimes. **Published 2 debut authors within the last year.** Averages 4 titles/year. Distributes titles through SCB Distribution in the US/Canada, Turnaround UK in the UK, and Bulldog Books in Australia. Promotes titles through reviews in book trade and general media, mentions in *Publishers Weekly*, *Bookselling This Week* and regional radio/TV.

- "Our titles were finalists in the Independent Publisher Awards in both science fiction and fantasy."

Imprint(s) The Ultra Violet Library (non-erotic lesbian/gay fantasy and science fiction).

Needs Short stories only. "Fiction must combine both the erotic and the fantastic. The erotic content needs to be an integral part of a science fiction story, and vice versa. Writers should not assume that any sex is the same as erotica." All books are anthologies of short stories. Published *Nymph*, by Francesca Lia Block; *The Darker Passions*, by Amarantha Knight.

How to Contact Accepts unsolicited mss only between April 15 and August 15. Check Web site for anthology topics which change annually. Query with SASE. Include estimated word count, brief bio, list of publishing credits. Send SASE for return of ms or send a disposable ms and SASE for reply only. Agented fiction 5%. Responds in 1 month to queries; 6-18 months to mss. Accepts simultaneous submissions, electronic submissions only from overseas authors. Always comments on rejected mss.

Terms Pays 4-12% royalty on retail price or makes outright purchase. Also pays in books, if author prefers. Publishes ms 18 months after acceptance. Ms guidelines online.

Advice "Read what we publish, learn to use lyrical but concise language to portray sex positively. No horror. Make sex and erotic interaction integral to your plot. Stay away from genre stereotypes. Use depth of character, internal monologue and psychological introspection to draw me in."

✪ ◎ ☑ CLARION BOOKS

Houghton Mifflin Co., 215 Park Ave. S., New York NY 10003. Web site: www.houghtonmifflinbooks. com. **Contact:** Dinah Stevenson, vice-president and publisher (YA, middle-grade, chapter book); Jennifer B. Greene, senior editor (YA, middle-grade, chapter book); Jennifer Wingertzahn, editor (YA, middle-grade, chapter book); Lynne Polvino, associate editor (YA, middle-grade, chapter book). Estab. 1965. "Clarion is a strong presence in the fiction market for young readers. We are highly selective in the areas of historical and contemporary fiction. We publish chapter books for children ages 7-10 and middle-grade novels for ages 9-12, as well as picture books and nonfiction." Publishes hardcover originals for children. Averages 50 total titles/year.

Needs Adventure, historical, humor, mystery, suspense, strong character studies. Clarion is highly selective in the areas of historical fiction, fantasy and science fiction. A novel must be superlatively written in order to find a place on the list. Mss that arrive without an SASE of adequate size will *not* be responded to or returned. Accepts fiction translations. Published *The Great Blue Yonder*, by Alex Shearer (contemporary, middle-grade); *When My Name Was Keoko*, by Linda Sue Park (historical fiction); *Dunk*, by David Lubar (contemporary YA).

How to Contact Submit complete ms. Responds in 2 months to queries. Prefers no multiple submissions of mss.

Terms Pays 5-10% royalty on retail price. Average advance: minimum of $4,000. Publishes ms 2 years after acceptance. Ms guidelines for #10 SASE.

◪ ☑ COFFEE HOUSE PRESS

27 N. Fourth St., Suite 400, Minneapolis MN 55401. Fax: (612)338-4004. **Contact:** Chris Fischbach, senior editor. Estab. 1984. "Nonprofit publisher with a small staff. We publish literary titles: fiction and poetry." Publishes trade paperback originals. Books: acid-free paper; cover illustrations. **Published some debut authors within the last year.** Averages 12 total titles, 6 fiction titles/year.

- This successful nonprofit small press has received numerous grants from various organizations including the NEA, the McKnight Foundation and Target.

Needs Ethnic, experimental, literary, mainstream/contemporary, short story collections, novels. Publishes anthologies, but they are closed to unsolicited submissions. Published *Miniatures*, by Norah Labiner (novel); *Circle K Cycles*, by Karen Yamashita (stories); *Little Casino*, by Gilbert Sorrentino (novel).

How to Contact Accepts unsolicited mss. Query with SASE. Agented fiction 10%. Responds in 1 month to queries; up to 4 months to mss. No electronic submissions.

Terms Pays 8% royalty on retail price. Provides 15 author's copies. Publishes ms 18 months after acceptance. Book catalog and ms guidelines for #10 SASE with 2 first-class stamps. Ms guidelines for #10 SAE with 55¢ first-class stamps.

COTEAU BOOKS

AKA Thunder Creek Publishing Co-operative Ltd., 2517 Victoria Ave., Regina SK S4P 0T2 Canada. (306)777-0170. Fax: (306)522-5152. E-mail: coteau@coteaubooks.com. Web site: www.coteaubooks .com. **Contact:** Nik L. Burton, managing editor. Estab. 1975. "Coteau Books publishes the finest Canadian fiction, poetry, drama and children's literature, with an emphasis on western writers." Publishes trade paperback originals and reprints. Books: 20 lb. offset or 60 lb. hi-bulk paper; offset printing; perfect bound; 4-color illustrations. Averages 16 total titles, 4-6 fiction titles/year. Distributes titles through Fitzhenry & Whiteside.

Needs Ethnic, fantasy, feminist, gay/lesbian, historical, humor, juvenile, literary, mainstream/contemporary, multicultural, multimedia, mystery, regional, short story collections, spiritual, sports, young adult. Canadian authors *only*. Published *God of the Plains*, by Gail Robinson (fiction); *Morningstar: A Warrior's Spirit*, by Morningstar Mercedi (memoir); *Peacekeepers*, by Dianne Linden (young adult).

How to Contact Accepts unsolicited mss. Submit complete manuscript, or 3-4 sample chapter(s), author bio. Responds in 2-3 months to queries; 6 months to mss. No simultaneous submissions. Sometimes comments on rejected mss.

Terms Pays 10% royalty on retail price. "We're a co-operative and receive subsidies from the Canadian, provincial and local governments. We do not accept payments from authors to publish their works." Publishes ms 1-2 years after acceptance. Ms guidelines online.

Advice "We publish short-story collections, novels, drama, nonfiction and poetry collections. Canadian authors only! This is part of our mandate. The work speaks for itself! Be bold. Be creative. Be persistent!"

COUNTERPOINT

The Perseus Books Group, 387 Park Avenue South, 12th Fl, New York NY 10016. Web site: www.cou nterpointpress.com. Estab. 1995. Publishes paperback and hardcover originals.

Needs Literary, short story collections. Published *Appetites*, by Caroline Knapp (literary/nonfiction); *Why Did I Ever*, by Mary Robinson (novel).

How to Contact Accepts unsolicited mss. *Agented submissions only.* Submit outline, 1 sample chapter(s), author bio. Accepts queries by mail. Agented fiction 98%. Responds in 3 months to queries; 3 months to mss. Accepts simultaneous submissions. No electronic submissions, submissions on disk.

Terms Pays royalty. Average advance: Negotiable. Publishes ms 24 months after acceptance.

COVENANT COMMUNICATIONS, INC.

920 E. State Rd., American Fork UT 84003-0416. (801)756-9966. E-mail: info@covenant-lds.com. Web site: www.covenant-lds.com. Averages 80+ total titles/year.

Needs Historical fiction, suspense, mystery, romance, children's; all submissions must have strong LDS (Church of Jesus Christ of Latter-day Saints, or "Mormons") content.

How to Contact Follow submission guidelines on web site at www.covenant-lds.com. Requires electronic submission. Responds in 4 months to mss.

Terms Pays 6½-15% royalty on retail price. Generally publishes ms 6-12 months after acceptance. Ms guidelines online.

Advice Our audience is exclusively LDS (Latter-Day Saints, "Mormon"). We do not accept manuscripts.

CRICKET BOOKS

Carus Publishing, 70 E. Lake St. Suite 300, Chicago IL 60601. E-mail: cricketbooks@caruspub.net. Web site: www.cricketbooks.net. **Contact:** Submissions editor. Estab. 1999. "Small, independent publisher able to integrate publishing with related Cricket and Cobblestone magazine groups. We publish children's fiction and nonfiction, from picture books to high young adult." Publishes hardcover and paperback originals. Distributes titles through PGW. Promotes titles through in-house marketing.

Imprint(s) Cricket Books, picture books to young adults.

Needs Children's/juvenile (adventure, animal, easy-to-read, fantasy, historical, mystery, preschool/picture book, sports), juvenile, young adult (adventure, easy-to-read, fantasy/science fiction, historical, horror, mystery/suspense, problem novels, romance, sports, western), Early chapter books and middle grade fiction. Plans anthologies for Christmas, dragons, poetry, and Cricket Magazine's anniversary edition. Editors select stories. Published *Seek*, by Paul Fleischman (YA fiction); *Robert and the Weird and Wacky Facts*, by Barbara Seuling (chapter book); and *Scorpio's Child*, by Kezi Matthews (fiction, ages 11-14).

How to Contact Currently only accepting submissions by authors previously published in Cricket magazine. Does not accept unsolicited mss. Submit complete ms. Include estimated word count, list of publishing credits. Send SASE for return of ms or send a disposable ms and SASE for reply only. Agented fiction 20%. Responds in 4 months to queries; 6 months to mss. Accepts simultaneous submissions. No electronic submissions, submissions on disk. Sometimes comments on rejected mss.

Terms Pays 10% royalty on net receipts. Open to first-time and unagented authors. Pays up to 10% royalty on retail price. Average advance: $1,500 and up. Publishes ms 18 months after acceptance. Ms guidelines online.

CROSSQUARTER PUBLISHING GROUP

P.O. Box 23749, Santa Fe NM 87502. (505)438-9846. Web site: www.crossquarter.com. **Contact:** Anthony Ravenscroft. Publishes case and trade paperback originals and reprints. **Published 90% debut authors within the last year.** Averages 1-2 total titles/year.

We are no longer accepting fiction manuscripts. We do continue to have the annual science fiction short story contest.

How to Contact Query with SASE. Responds in 3 months to queries. Accepts simultaneous submissions.

Terms Pays 8-10% royalty on wholesale or retail price. Publishes ms 1 year after acceptance. Book catalog for $1.75. Ms guidelines online.

Advice "Audience is earth-conscious people looking to grow into balance of body, mind, heart and spirit."

✪ ⬙ ⬙ CROSSTIME

Crossquarter Publishing Group, P.O. Box 86, Crookston MN 56716. (218)281-8065. Fax: (218)975-9715. E-mail: info@crossquarter.com. Web site: www.crossquarter.com. **Contact:** Anthony Ravenscroft. Estab. 1985. Small Publisher. Publishes paperback originals. Books: recycled paper; docutech or offset printing; perfect bound. **Published 2 debut authors within the last year.** Plans 2 first novels this year. Member SPAN, PMA.

Needs Mystery (occult), new age/mystic, psychic/supernatural, romance (occult), science fiction, young adult (fantasy/science fiction). Plans an anthology of Paul B. Duquette Memorial Short Science Fiction contest winners. Guidelines on Web site. Recently published *Many Voices, One Song*, by Barbara Percival; *When Dharma Fails Its King*, by Spencer Johnson; *Swamp Poet*, by Ben Goodridge; *CrossTIME Science Fiction Anthology Vol VI*.

How to Contact Currently closed to submissions unless for CrossTime Science Fiction Contest (see separate listing).

Terms Pays 6-10% royalty. Publishes ms 6-9 months after acceptance. Ms guidelines online.

✪ ⬙ ◎ CROSSWAY BOOKS

Division of Good News Publishers, 1300 Crescent St., Wheaton IL 60187-5800. (630)682-4300. Fax: (630)682-4785. Web site: www.crossway.com. **Contact:** Jill Carter. Estab. 1938. " 'Making a difference in people's lives for Christ' as its maxim, Crossway Books lists titles written from an evangelical Christian perspective." Midsize evangelical Christian publisher. Publishes hardcover and trade paperback originals. Averages 85 total titles, 1 fiction titles/year. Member ECPA. Distributes titles through Christian bookstores and catalogs. Promotes titles through magazine ads, catalogs.

Needs *Currently not accepting fiction manuscripts.*

How to Contact Does not accept unsolicited mss. Agented fiction 5%.

Terms Pays negotiable royalty. Average advance: negotiable. Publishes ms 18 months after acceptance. Ms guidelines online.

Advice "With so much Christian fiction on the market, we are carefully looking at our program to see the direction we wish to proceed. Be sure your project fits into our guidelines and is written from an evangelical Christian worldview. 'Religious' or 'Spiritual' viewpoints will not fit.''

☐ DAN RIVER PRESS

Conservatory of American Letters, P.O. Box 298, Thomaston ME 04861-0298. (207)226-7528. E-mail: cal@americanletters.org. Web site: www.americanletters.org. **Contact:** Richard S. Danbury, III, fiction editor. Estab. 1977. "Small press publisher of fiction and biographies owned by a non-profit foundation." Publishes hardcover and paperback originals. Books: paperback; offset or digital printing; perfect and cloth binding; illustrations. Averages 3-4 fiction titles/year, plus the annual (since 1984) *Dan River Anthology*. Promotes titles through the author's sphere of influence. Distributes titles by mail order to libraries and bookstores, as well as by Amazon, Barnesandnoble.com, Baker & Taylor, Ingram, 10 UK distributors, and author's influence.

Needs Adventure, family saga, fantasy (space fantasy, sword and sorcery), historical (general), horror (dark fantasy, futuristic, psychological, supernatural), humor, literary, mainstream/contemporary, military/war, mystery (amateur sleuth, police procedural, private eye/hard-boiled), new age/mystic, psychic/supernatural, religious (general religious, inspirational, religious mystery/suspense, religious thriller, religious romance), romance (contemporary, futuristic/time travel, gothic, historical, romantic suspense), science fiction (hard science/technological, soft/sociological), short story collections, thriller/espionage, western (frontier saga, traditional), young adult, outdoors/fishing/hunting/camping/trapping. Accepts anything but porn, sedition, evangelical, and children's literature. Publishes poetry and fiction anthology (submission guidelines to Dan River Anthology on the Web, or send #10 SASE).

How to Contact Accepts unsolicited mss. Accepts queries by mail. Include estimated word count, brief bio, list of publishing credits. Send SASE for return of ms or send a disposable ms and SASE for reply only. Responds in 2-3 days to queries; 1-2 weeks to mss. Accepts simultaneous submissions. No electronic submissions. Do not submit until you've read our guidelines.

Terms Pays 10-15% royalty and 5 author's copies. Average advance: occasional. Publishes ms 3-4 months after acceptance. Book catalog for 6×9 SASE with 68¢ postage affixed. Ms guidelines online or by #10 SASE.

Advice "Spend some time developing a following."

☑ JOHN DANIEL AND CO.

Daniel & Daniel, Publishers, Inc., P.O. Box 2790, McKinleyville CA 95519. (707)839-3495. Fax: (707)839-3242. E-mail: dandd@danielpublishing.com. Web site: www.danielpublishing.com. **Contact:** John Daniel, publisher. Estab. 1980. "We publish small books, usually in small editions, but we do so with pride." Publishes hardcover originals and trade paperback originals. Publishes poetry, fiction and nonfiction. Averages 4 total titles/year. Distributes through SCB Distributors. Promotes through direct mail, reviews.

Needs Literary, short story collections. Publishes poetry, fiction and nonfiction; specializes in belles letters, literary memoir. Published *Windstorm and Flood*, by Rosalind Brackenbury (novel); *Silence of Parents*, by Susan Geroe (novel); *Flight into Egypt*, by Julian Stamper (novel).

How to Contact Currently closed to fiction submissions.

Terms Pays 10% royalty on wholesale price. Average advance: $0-500. Publishes ms 1 year after acceptance. Ms guidelines online.

Advice "Having downsized from small to tiny, we can't publish as many books as before, and must be very selective. So it's a long shot. Never the less, we do consider all submissions."

☑ ◎ MAY DAVENPORT, PUBLISHERS

26313 Purissima Rd., Los Altos Hills CA 94022. (650)947-1275. Fax: (650)947-1373. E-mail: mdbooks @earthlink.net. Web site: www.maydavenportpublishers.com. **Contact:** May Davenport, editor/publisher. Estab. 1976. "We prefer books which can be *used* in high schools as supplementary readings in English or creative writing courses. Reading skills have to be taught, and novels by humorous authors can be more pleasant to read than Hawthorne's or Melville's novels, war novels, or novels about past generations. Humor has a place in literature." Publishes hardcover and paperback originals. Averages 4 total titles/year. Distributes titles through direct mail order.

Imprint(s) md Books (nonfiction and fiction).

Needs Humor, literary. "We want to focus on novels junior and senior high school teachers can share with the reluctant readers in their classrooms." Published *Charlie and Champ*, by Allyson Wagoner; *Senioritis*, by Tate Thompson; *A Life on The Line*, by Michael Horton; *Matthew Livingston & The Prison of Souls*, by Marco Conelli.

How to Contact Query with SASE. Responds in 1 month to queries.

Terms Pays 15% royalty on retail price. Publishes ms 1 year after acceptance. Ms guidelines for #10 SASE.

Advice "Just write humorous novels about today's generation with youthful, admirable, believable characters to make young readers laugh. High tech-oriented youth need role models in literature. Don't lecture! Rivet youthful readers to read and to relate to your fictional characters' creative doings. Can't? Try it anyway!"

⊠ ☐ ◎ DAW BOOKS, INC.

Penguin Group, Inc., 375 Hudson St., 3rd Floor, New York NY 10014-3658. (212)366-2096. Fax: (212)366-2090. E-mail: daw@us.penguingroup.com. Web site: www.dawbooks.com. **Contact:** Peter Stampfel, submissions editor. Estab. 1971. Publishes hardcover and paperback originals and reprints. Averages 60-80 total titles/year.

Needs Fantasy, science fiction. "We are interested in science fiction and fantasy novels. We are also interested in paranormal romantic fantasy. We like character-driven books. We accept both agented and unagented manuscripts. Long books are not a problem. We are not seeking short stories or ideas for anthologies. We do not want any nonfiction manuscripts."

How to Contact Submit complete ms with SASE. Do not submit your only copy of anything. Responds within 3 months to mss.

Terms Pays in royalties with an advance negotiable on a book-by-book basis. Ms guidelines online.

Advice "We strongly encourage new writers. Research your publishers and submit only appropriate work."

Ⓐ ⊠ ◎ DEL REY BOOKS

The Random House Publishing Group, Random House, Inc., 1745 Broadway, 18th Floor, New York NY 10019. (212)782-9000. Web site: www.delreybooks.com. **Contact:** Betsy Mitchell, editor-in-chief; Chris Schluep, senior editor, Liz Scheier, senior editor. Estab. 1977. "We are a long-established imprint with an eclectic frontlist. We're seeking interesting new voices to add to our best-selling backlist. Publishes hardcover, trade paperback, and mass market originals and mass market paperback reprints. Averages 120 total titles, 80 fiction titles/year.

Imprint(s) Imprints: Del Rey Manga, managed by Dallas Middaugh, publishes translations of Japanese comics as well as original graphic novels.

Needs Fantasy (should have the practice of magic as an essential element of the plot), science fiction (well-plotted novels with good characterizations and interesting extrapolations), alternate history. Published *Un Lun Dun*, by China Mieville; *His Majesty's Dragon*, by Naomi Novik; *Victory Conditions*, by Elizabeth Moon; *Dragon's Kin*, by Anne McCaffrey and Todd McCaffrey; *Star Wars: Death Star*, by Michael Reaves and Steve Perry.

How to Contact Does not accept unsolicited mss. *Agented submissions only.*

Terms Pays royalty on retail price. Average advance: competitive. Publishes ms 1 year after acceptance. Ms guidelines online.

Advice Has been publishing "more fiction and hardcovers, because the market is there for them. Read a lot of science fiction and fantasy, such as works by Anne McCaffrey, David Eddings, China Mieville, Arthur C. Clarke, Terry Brooks, Richard K. Morgan, Elizabeth Moon. When writing, pay particular attention to plotting (and a satisfactory conclusion) and characters (sympathetic and well rounded) because those are what readers look for."

⊠ ☻ DELACORTE BOOKS FOR YOUNG READERS

Random House Children's Books, 1540 Broadway, New York NY 10036. (212)782-900. Web site: www.randomhouse.com/kids. Distinguished literary fiction and commercial fiction for the middle grade and young adult categories.

Terms Ms guidelines online.

✪ ◎ DIAL BOOKS FOR YOUNG READERS

Penguin Group USA, 345 Hudson St., 14th Floor, New York NY 10014. (212)366-2000. Web site: www.us.penguingroup.com. **Contact:** Submissions Editor. Estab. 1961. Trade children's book publisher. Publishes hardcover originals. Averages 50 total titles/year.

Needs Adventure, fantasy, juvenile, picture books, young adult. Especially looking for "lively and well-written novels for middle grade and young adult children involving a convincing plot and believable characters. The subject matter or theme should not already be overworked in previously published books. The approach must not be demeaning to any minority group, nor should the roles of female characters (or others) be stereotyped, though we don't think books should be didactic, or in any way message-y. No topics inappropriate for the juvenile, young adult and middle grade audiences. No plays." Published *A Year Down Yonder*, by Richard Peck; *The Missing Mitten Mystery*, by Steven Kellog.

How to Contact Accepts unsolicited mss. "Submit entire picture book manuscript or the first three chapters of longer works. Please include a cover letter with brief bio and publication credits. Please note that, unless interested in publishing your book, Dial will not respond to unsolicited submissions. Please do NOT include a SASE. If Dial is interested, expect a reply from us within four months."

Terms Pays royalty. Average advance: varies.

✪ ◎ DOUBLEDAY BOOKS FOR YOUNG READERS

Random House Children's Books, 1540 Broadway, New York NY 10036. (212)782-9000. Web site: www.randomhouse.com/kids.

Ⓐ ✪ ◎ DOUBLEDAY RELIGIOUS PUBLISHING

Doubleday Broadway Publishing Group, Random House, Inc., 1745 Broadway, New York NY 10019. (212)782-9000. Web site: www.randomhouse.com. **Contact:** Eric Major, vice president, religious division; Trace Murphy, executive editor; Andrew Corbin, editor. Estab. 1897. Publishes hardcover and trade paperback originals and reprints. Averages 45-50 total titles/year.

Imprint(s) Image Books, Anchor Bible Commentary, Anchor Bible Reference, Galilee, New Jerusalem Bible.

Needs Religious.

How to Contact *Agented submissions only.* Accepts simultaneous submissions.

Terms Pays 7¹/₂-15% royalty. Offers advance. Publishes ms 1 year after acceptance. Book catalog for SAE with 3 first-class stamps.

◐ ◎ DOWN EAST BOOKS

Down East Enterprise, Inc., P.O. Box 679, Camden ME 04843-0679. Fax: (207)594-7215. **Contact:** Michael Steere, managing editor. Estab. 1967. "We are primarily a regional publisher concentrating on Maine or New England." Publishes hardcover and trade paperback originals, trade paperback reprints. First print order: 3,000. Averages 20-24 total titles/year.

Needs Juvenile, mainstream/contemporary, regional. "We publish 1-2 juvenile titles/year (fiction and nonfiction), and 1-2 adult fiction titles/year." See bookshelf on our Web site: www.downeast.com.

How to Contact Query with SASE. Responds in 3 months to queries. Accepts simultaneous submissions.

Terms Pays 10-15% royalty on net receipts. Average advance: $500 average. Publishes ms 18 months-2 years after acceptance. Ms guidelines for 9×12 SAE with 2 first-class stamps.

♣ ◯ ◎ DRAGON MOON PRESS

3521 43A Ave, Red Deer AB T4N 3W9 Canada. E-mail: publisher@dragonmoonpress.com. Web site: www.dragonmoonpress.com. **Contact:** Gwen Gades, publisher. Estab. 1994. "Dragon Moon Press is dedicated to new and exciting voices in science fiction and fantasy." Publishes trade paperback and electronic originals. Books: 60 lb. offset paper; short run printing and offset printing. Average print order: 250-3,000. **Published several debut authors within the last year.** Plans 5 first novels this year. Averages 4-6 total titles, 4-5 fiction titles/year. Distributed through Baker & Taylor. Promoted locally through authors and online at leading retail bookstores like Amazon, Barnes & Noble, Chapters, etc.

Imprint(s) Dragon Moon Press, Gwen Gades publisher (fantasy and science fiction).

Needs Fantasy, science fiction (soft/sociological). No horror or children's fiction, short stories or poetry. "We seek out quality manuscripts and authors who are eager to participate in the marketing of their book.

How to Contact Please visit our Web site at www.dragonmoonpress.com for submission guidelines. Accepts simultaneous submissions. No submissions on disk. "All submissions are requested electronically—do not mail submissions, as we will not respond. All mailed submissions are shredded and recycled."

Terms Pays 8-15% royalty on retail price. Publishes ms 2 years after acceptance.

Advice "First, be patient. Read our guidelines. Not following our submission guidelines can be grounds for automatic rejection. Second, be patient, we are small and sometimes very slow as a result, especially during book launch season. Third, we view publishing as a family affair. Be ready to participate in the process and show some enthusiasm and understanding in what we do. Remember also, this is a business and not about egos, so keep yours on a leash! Show us a great story with well-developed characters and plot lines, show us that you are interested in participating in marketing and developing as an author, and show us your desire to create a great book and you may just find yourself published by Dragon Moon Press."

⬛ ✒ ◎ DREAMCATCHER PUBLISHING

55 Canterbury St., #8 &9 Saint John NB E2L 2C6. (506)632-4008, Fax:(506)632-4009 E-mail: info@dreamcatcherpublishing.ca. Web site: www.dreamcatcherpublishing.nb.ca. Established in 1998. **Contact:** Elizabeth Margaris, Publisher. **Description of Company**: Publishes mainstream fiction, with first consideration to Atlantic Canadian writers. Especially interested in green themes, hope & inspiration (including autobiographies) with a humorous twist. **Imprints**: Magi Press (vanity press). **Submission Guidelines:** Unsolicited manuscripts, please send an inquiry first. Make you query letter businesslike, include synopsis and short bio.

Ⓐ ✪ ◯ DUTTON (ADULT TRADE)

Penguin Putnam, Inc., 375 Hudson St., New York NY 10014. (212)366-2000. Web site: www.penguinputnam.com. **Contact:** Editor-in-Chief: Brian Tart. Estab. 1852. Publishers hardcover originals. Averages 40 total titles/year.

Needs Adventure, historical, literary, mainstream/contemporary, mystery, short story collections, suspense. Published *The Darwin Awards II*, by Wendy Northcutt (humor); *Falling Angels*, by Tracy Chevalier (fiction); *The Oath*, by John Lescroart (fiction).

How to Contact *Agented submissions only*. Responds in 6 months to queries. Accepts simultaneous submissions.

Terms Pays royalty. Average advance: negotiable. Publishes ms 12-18 months after acceptance.

Advice "Write the complete manuscript and submit it to an agent or agents. They will know exactly which editor will be interested in a project."

✪ ✒ ◎ DUTTON CHILDREN'S BOOKS

Imprint of Penguin Group (USA), inc. 345 Hudson St., New York NY 10014. (212)4143700. Fax:(212)414-3397. Web site: www.penquin.com/youngreaders and www.DuttonWritersRoom.com. **Contact**: Stephanie Owens Lurie, president and publisher (picture books and fiction); Maureen Sullivan, executive editor (books for all ages with distinct narrative style); Lucia Monfried, senior editor (picture books and middle grade fiction); Julie Strauss-Gabel, associate editorial director (literary contemporary young adult fiction); Sarah Shumway, editor (commercial young adult fiction). Estab.1852. Dutton Children's Books publishes fiction and nonfiction for readers ranging from preschoolers to young adults on a variety of subjects. Publishes hardcover originals as well as novelty formats Averages 75 titles/year. 10% of books form first-time authors.

Needs Dutton Children's Books has a diverse, general-interest list that includes picture books, and fiction for all ages, from "middle grade" books to young adult readers. Published *Big Chickens Fly the Coop*, by Leslie Helakoski, illustrated by Henry Cole (picture book); *Antsy Does Time*, by Neal Shusterman (middle-grade novel); *Paper Towns*, by John Green (young adult novel).

How to Contact Query letter only; include SASE

Terms Pays royalty on retail price. Offers advance

Ⓝ ✒ DZANC BOOKS

2702 Lillian, Ann Arbor MI 48104. E-mail: info@dzancbooks.org. Web site: http://www.dzancbooks.org. **Contact:** Steve Gillis, editor (literary fiction); Dan Wickett, editor (literary fiction); Keith Taylor, editor (literary fiction). "We're an independent non-profit publishing literary fiction. We also set up writer-in-residence programs and help literary journals develop their subscription bases." Publishes paperback originals. **Published some debut authors within the last year.** Averages 6 fiction titles/year, 20 titles/year when imprints are included.

Imprint(s) OV Books, Gina Frangello/Stacy Bierlein, editors (literary fiction); Black Lawrence Press, Colleen Ryor/Diane Goettel, editors (literary fiction/nonfiction/poetry).

Needs Literary. Plans anthology *The Best of the Web*, in which online journal editors nominate stories and poems—series and press editors select from that list and selected reading. Published *All Over*, by Roy Kesey (short story collection).

How to Contact Query with outline/synopsis and 35 sample pages. Accepts queries by e-mail. Include brief bio. Agented fiction: 3%. Accepts unsolicited mss. Considers simultaneous submissions, submissions on CD or disk. Rarely critiques/comments on rejected mss. Responds to mss in 5 months.

Terms Sends pre-production galleys to author. Manuscript published 12-24 months after acceptance. Writer's guidelines on Web site.

Advice "Every word counts—it's amazing how many submissions have poor first sentences or paragraphs and that first impression is hard to shake when it's a bad one."

EAKIN PRESS/SUNBELT MEDIA, INC.

P.O. Box 90159, Austin TX 78709-0159. (512)288-1771. Fax: (512)288-1813. Web site: www.eakinpress.com. **Contact:** Virginia Messer, publisher. Estab. 1978. Eakin specializes in Texana and Western Americana for juveniles and adults. Publishes hardcover and paperback originals and reprints. Averages 60 total titles/year.

Imprint(s) Nortex; Sunbelt/Eakin; Eakin Press, Penpoint Press.

Needs Historical, juvenile. Juvenile fiction for grades K-12, preferably relating to Texas and the Southwest or contemporary. Nonfiction adult with Texas or Southwest theme. *Inside Russia*, by Inez Jeffry.

How to Contact Accepts unsolicited mss. Agented fiction 5%. Responds in 3 months to queries. Accepts simultaneous submissions.

Terms Pays royalty. Pays 10-12-15% royalty on net sales. Publishes ms 18 months after acceptance. Book catalog for $1.25. Ms guidelines online.

Advice "Only fiction with strong Southwest theme. We receive around 1,200 queries or unsolicited mss a year."

ECW PRESS

2120 Queen St. E., Suite 200, Toronto ON M4E 1E2 Canada. (416)694-3348. Fax: (416)698-9906. E-mail: info@ecwpress.com. Web site: www.ecwpress.com. **Contact:** Jack David, publisher. Estab. 1979. Publishes hardcover and trade paperback originals. Averages 40 total titles/year.

Needs Only Canadian authored fiction, specializes in mystery.

How to Contact Accepts simultaneous submissions.

Terms Pays 8-12% royalty on net receipts. Average advance: $300-5,000. Publishes ms 18 months after acceptance. Book catalog and ms guidelines free. Ms guidelines online.

Advice "Be sure to include return postage (SASE, IRC if outside of Canada) it you wish your material to be returned."

EDGE SCIENCE FICTION AND FANTASY PUBLISHING

Box 1714, Calgary AB T2P 2L7 Canada. (403)254-0160. Fax: (403)254-0456. E-mail: publisher@hadespublications.com. Web site: www.edgewebsite.com. **Contact:** Anita Hades, acquisitions manager (science fiction/fantasy). Estab. 1996. "We are an independent publisher of science fiction and fantasy novels in hard cover or trade paperback format. We produce high-quality books with lots of attention to detail and lots of marketing effort. We want to encourage, produce and promote thought-provoking and fun-to-read science fiction and fantasy literature by 'bringing the magic alive: one world at a time' (as our motto says) with each new book released." Publishes hardcover and trade paperback originals. Books: natural offset paper; offset/web printing; HC/perfect binding; b&w illustration only. Average print order: 2,000-3,000. Plans 20 first novels this year. Averages 16-20 total titles/year. Member of Book Publishers Association of Alberta (BPAA), Independent Publishers Association of Canada (IPAC), Publisher's Marketing Association (PMA), Small Press Center.

Imprint(s) Tesseract Books, Dragon Moon Press, Alien Vistas, Riverbend.

Needs Fantasy (space fantasy, sword and sorcery), science fiction (hard science/technological, soft/sociological). "We are looking for all types of fantasy and science fiction, horror except juvenile/young adlut, erotica, religious fiction, short stories, dark/gruesome fantasy, or poetry." Published *Stealing Magic*, by Tanya Huff; *Forbidden Cargo*, by Rebecca K. Rowe, The Hounds of Ash and other tales of Fool Wolf by Greg Keyes.

How to Contact Accepts unsolicited mss. Submit first 3 chapters and synopsis, Check Web site for guidelines (http:www.edgewebsite.com/authors.html) or send SAE & IRCs for same. Include estimated word count. Responds in 4-5 months to mss. No simultaneous submissions, electronic submissions. Rarely comments on rejected mss.

Terms Pays 10% royalty on wholesale price. Average advance: negotiable. Publishes ms 18-20 months after acceptance. Ms guidelines online.

Advice "Send us your best, polished, completed manuscript. Use proper manuscript format. Take the time before you submit to get a critique from people who can offer you useful advice. When in doubt, visit our Web site for helpful resources, FAQs and other tips."

⚝ EERDMANS BOOKS FOR YOUNG READERS

William B. Eerdmans Publishing Co., 2140 Oak Industrial Dr. NE, Grand Rapids MI 49505. (616)459-4591. Fax: (616)776-7683. E-mail: youngreaders@eerdmans.com. Web site: www.eerdmans.com/youngreaders. **Contact:** Judy Zylstra, editor. Publishes picture books and middle reader and young adult fiction and nonfiction. Averages 12-15 total titles/year.

Needs Juvenile, picture books, young adult, middle reader. Published *Going for The Record*, by Julie Swanson; *Dancing With Elvis,* by Lynda Stephenson.

How to Contact Responds in 6 weeks to 3 months to queries. Accepts exclusive submissions.

Terms Pays 5-7½% royalty on retail price. Publishes middle reader and YA books in 1-2 years; publishes picture books 2-4 years after acceptance.

▨ ◎ � WILLIAM B. EERDMANS PUBLISHING CO.

2140 Oak Industrial Dr. NE, Grand Rapids MI 49505. (616)459-4591. Fax: (616)459-6540. E-mail: info@eerdmans.com. Web site: www.eerdmans.com, www.eerdmans.com/submit.htm and http://www.eerdmans.com/youngreaders/submit.htm. **Contact:** Jon Pott, editor-in-chief, fiction editor (adult fiction); Shannon White, fiction editor (children). Estab. 1911. "Although Eerdmans publishes some regional books and other nonreligious titles, it is essentially a religious publisher whose titles range from the academic to the semi-popular. We are a midsize independent publisher. We publish the occasional adult novel, and these tend to engage deep spiritual issues from a Christian perspective." Publishes hardcover and paperback originals and reprints. **Published some debut authors within the last year.** Averages 120-130 total titles, 6-8 (mostly for children) fiction titles/year.

 • Eerdman's titles have won awards from the American Library Association and The American Bookseller's Association.

Imprint(s) Eerdmans Books for Young Readers.

Needs Religious (children's, general, fantasy). Published *I Wonder as I Wander*, by Gwenyth Swain, illustrated by Ronald Himler; *Gilgamesh the Herd*, by Geraldine McCaughrean, illustrated by David Parkins; *The Enemy Has a Face*, by Gloria D. Miklowitz (young adult); *Down in the Piney Woods* and *Mariah's Pond*, by Ethel Footman Smothers.

How to Contact Accepts unsolicited mss. Submit outline, 2 sample chapter(s), synopsis. Include brief bio, list of publishing credits. Send SASE for return of ms or send a disposable ms and SASE for reply only. Agented fiction 5%. Responds in 6 weeks to queries. true across the board for general submissions, children's department only responds to exclusive submissions.

Terms Pays royalty. Average advance: occasional. Publishes ms usually within 1 year after acceptance.

Advice "Our readers are educated and fairly sophisticated, and we are looking for novels with literary merit."

THE EIGHTH MOUNTAIN PRESS

624 SE 29th Ave., Portland OR 97214. E-mail: ruth@eighthmountain.com. Estab. 1985. Publishes original trade paperbacks. Averages 1 total title/year.

How to Contact No longer accepts unsolicited mss.
Terms Pays 7% royalty.

◎ ELLORA'S CAVE PUBLISHING, INC.

1056 Home Avenue, Akron OH 44310-3205. E-mail: submissions@ellorascave.com. Web site: www.
ellorascave.com and www.cerridwenpress.com. Estab. 2000. Publishes trade paperback and electronic originals and reprints. Averages 300 total titles/year.
Needs Erotic romance and erotica in all subgenres. For Cerridwen Press, all mainstream fiction
genres (mystery/suspense, scifi/futuristic, fantasy/paranormal, horror, women's fiction, romance
[non-erotic]).
How to Contact Submit proposal package including detailed full synopsis, first three chapters, last
chapter via e-mail. No paper submissions. Responds in 3-12 months to mss. Accepts simultaneous
submissions.
Terms Pays royalty of 37.5% of cover price for digital, 7.5% of cover for print. Ms guidelines online.

◙ ◎ EMPIRE PUBLISHING SERVICE

P.O. Box 1344, Studio City CA 91614-0344. Estab. 1960. Midsize publisher with related imprints.
Publishes hardcover reprints and trade paperback originals and reprints. Book: paper varies; offset
printing; binding varies. Average print order: 5,000-10,000. First novel print order: 2,500-5,000.
Published 4 debut authors within the last year. Averages 60 total titles, 5 fiction titles/year.
Distributes and promotes titles by "Sales & Marketing Distribution offices in five countries."
Imprint(s) Paul Mould Publishing, Paul Mould, editor (historical); Gaslight Publications (Sherlock
Holmes); Collectors Publications (erotica).
Needs Historical (pre-18th century), mystery (Sherlock Holmes). Plans anthology of Sherlock Holmes
short stories. Published *Gods Hammer*, by Eric Shumacher.
How to Contact Does not accept unsolicited mss. Query with SASE. Include estimated word count,
brief bio, list of publishing credits, general background. Send SASE for return of ms or send a
disposable ms and SASE for reply only. Agented fiction 2%. Responds in 1 month to queries; up to
1 year to mss. No simultaneous submissions, electronic submissions, submissions on disk.
Terms Pays 6-10% royalty on retail price. Average advance: variable. Publishes ms 6 months to 2
years after acceptance. Ms guidelines for $1 or #10 SASE.
Advice "Send query with SASE for only the type of material we publish, historical and Sherlock
Holmes."

◙ EMPYREAL PRESS

P.O. Box 1708, Champlain, NY 12919-9998. E-mail: empyrealpress@hotmail.com. Web site: www.sk
arwood.com. **Contact:** Colleen B. McCool. "Our mission is the publishing of literature which doesn't
fit into any standard 'mold'—writing which is experimental yet grounded in discipline, imagination."
Publishes trade paperback originals. **Published no debut authors within the last year.** Averages
0-1 total titles/year.
Needs "Empyreal Press is not currently accepting unsolicited manuscripts due to extremely limited
resources."

◙ ◎ EROS BOOKS

463 Barlow Ave., Staten Island NY 10308. (718)317-7484. E-mail: marynicholaou@aol.com. Web
site: www.eros.thecraze.com. **Contact:** Mary Nicholaou, fiction editor. Estab. 2000. "Small independent publisher of postmodern romance, short fiction and translations." Publishes paperback originals, e-books. Format: 20 lb. paper; offset printing. Average print order: 500. Debut novel print
order: 500. **Published 5 new writers last year.** Plans 10 debut novels this year. Averages 5 total
titles/year; 4 fiction titles/year.
Needs Postmodern, short, romance fiction, translations. Published *Cracks*, by Mary Nicholaou (postmodern romance); *Chimera*, by Clara Smith (postmodern romance).
How to Contact Query with outline/synopsis. Reads submissions June-September. Accepts queries
by snail mail, e-mail. Include social security number. Send SASE or IRC for return of ms or disposable
copy of ms and SASE/IRC for reply only. Agented fiction: 10%. Responds to queries in 2 weeks.
Considers simultaneous submissions, submissions on CD or disk. Always critiques/comments on
rejected mss. Responds to mss in 2 months.

Terms Pays in author's copies. Manuscript published 12 months after acceptance. Writer's guidelines available for SASE. Book catalogs available for SASE.

FANTAGRAPHICS BOOKS

7563 Lake City Way NE, Seattle WA 98115. Fax: (206)524-2104. E-mail: fbicomix@fantagraphics.com. Web site: www.fantagraphics.com. **Contact:** Michael Dowers (all genres). Estab. 1976. "Fantagraphics Books has been a leading proponent of comics as a legitimate form of art and literature since it began publishing the critical trade magazine *The Comics Journal* in 1976. By the early 1980s, Fantagraphics found itself at the forefront of the burgeoning movement to establish comics as a medium as eloquent and expressive as the more established popular arts of film, literature, poetry, et al. Fantagraphics quickly established a reputation as an advocacy publisher that specialized in seeking out and publishing the kind of innovative work that traditional comics corporations who dealt almost exclusively in superheroes and fantasy either didn't know existed or wouldn't touch: serious, dramatic, historical, journalistic, political and satirical work by a new generation of alternative cartoonists , as well as many artists who gained prominence as part of the seminal underground comix movement of the '60s. Fantagraphics has since gained an international reputation for its literate and audacious editorial standards and its exacting production values." Publishes hardcover originals, paperback originals, hardcover reprints, paperback reprints. Average print run: 3,000 (debut writer). **Publishes 3-4 debut writers/year.** Publishes 60 titles/year. Titles promoted/distributed by W.W. Norton & Co. Awards: Harvey Awards, Eisner Awards, Ignatz Awards, Quills nomination.
Needs All categories. Does not want superheros. Anthologies: MOME, Comic Books, Hotwire, Blab. Editors select stories.
How to Contact Prefers submissions from writer-artists. Detailed submission guidelines at www.fantagraphics.com/submissions.html. Agented submissions: less than 5%. Responds to queries and ms/art packages in 4 months. Often comments on rejected manuscripts.
Terms Creators paid royalty. Sends pre-publication galleys to author. Writer's and artist's guidelines on Web site. Book catalog free upon request.

FARRAR, STRAUS & GIROUX BOOKS FOR YOUNG READERS

Farrar Straus Giroux, Inc., 18 West 18th Street., New York NY 10011. (212)741-6900. **Contact:** Margaret Ferguson, editorial director (children's); Wesley Adams, executive editor (children's); Janine O'Malley, senior editor (children's). Estab. 1946. "We publish original and well-written materials for all ages." Publishes hardcover originals and trade paperback reprints. **Published some debut authors within the last year.** Averages 75 total titles/year.
Imprint(s) Frances Foster Books, edited by Frances Foster (children's); Melanie Kroupa Books, edited by Melanie Kroupa (children's).
Needs Children's/juvenile, picture books, middle grade, young adult, nonfiction. "Do not query picture books; just send manuscript. Do not fax queries or manuscripts." Published *So Sleepy Story*, by Uri Shulevitz; *Alabama Moon*, by Watt Key.
How to Contact Query with SASE. Include brief bio, list of publishing credits. Agented fiction 50%. Responds in 2 months to queries; 4 months to mss. Accepts simultaneous submissions. No electronic submissions or submissions on disk.
Terms Pays 2-6% royalty on retail price for paperbacks, 3-10% for hardcovers. Average advance: $3,000-25,000. Publishes ms 18 months after acceptance. Book catalog for 9×12 SAE with $1.87 postage. Ms guidelines for #10 SASE.
Advice "Study our list to avoid sending something inappropriate. Send query letters for long manuscripts; don't ask for editorial advice (just not possible, unfortunately); and send SASEs!"

FC2

Dept. of English, FSU, Tallahassee FL 32306. E-mail: FictionCollective2@gmail.com. Web site: http://fc2.org. **Contact:** Brenda L. Mills, executive editor. Estab. 1974. Publisher of innovative fiction. Publishes hardcover and paperback originals. Books: perfect/Smyth binding; illustrations. Average print order: 2,200. **Published some debut authors within the last year.** Plans 2 first novels this year. Averages 6 total titles, 6 fiction titles/year. Titles distributed through University of Alabama Press. No open submissions except through Ronald Sukenick Innovative Fiction Prize.
Needs Experimental, feminist, gay/lesbian, innovative; modernist/postmodern; avant-garde; anarchist; minority; cyberpunk. Published *Book of Lazarus*, by Richard Grossman; *Is It Sexual Harassment*

Yet?, by Cris Mazza; *Liberty's Excess*, by Lidia Yuknavitch; *The Wavering Knife*, by Brian Evenson.
How to Contact Does not accept unsolicited mss. See Web site (http://fc2.org/Sukenick%20prize.h tm) for contest info. Agented fiction 5%. Responds in 3 weeks to queries; 2-6 months to mss. Accepts simultaneous submissions.
Terms Pays 10% royalty. Publishes ms 1-3 years after acceptance. Ms guidelines online.
Advice "Be familiar with our list."

THE FEMINIST PRESS AT THE CITY UNIVERSITY OF NEW YORK

365 Fifth Ave., Suite 5406, New York NY 10016. (212)817-7917. Fax: (212)817-1593. E-mail: aroy@gc .cuny.edu. Web site: www.feministpress.org. **Contact:** Anjoli Roy. Estab. 1970. Small, nonprofit literary and educational publisher. The Feminist Press publishes mainly fiction reprints by classic American women authors and translations of distinguished international women writers. Publishes hardcover and trade paperback originals and reprints. Publishes original fiction occasionally; exceptions are anthologies and international works. We use acid-free paper and cloth for library sales; we produce four-color covers, perfect bind our books, and shoot from the original text when possible. We always include a scholarly and literary afterword, since we are introducing a text to a new audience. Average print run: 2,500. Averages 15-20 total titles, 4-8 fiction titles/year. Member: CLMP, Small Press Association, AAP. Distributes titles through Consortium Book Sales and Distribution. Promotes titles through author tours, advertising, exhibits and conferences. Charges permission fees (reimbursement).
Needs Ethnic, feminist, gay/lesbian, literary, short story collections, women's. The Feminist Press publishes mainly fiction reprints by classic women authors and imports and translations of distinguished international women writers. Very little original fiction is considered. Needs fiction by U.S. women of color writers from 1920-1970 who have fallen out of print. Published *Apples From the Desert*, by Savyon Liebrecht (short stories, translation); *The Parish and the Hill*, by Mary Doyle Curran (fiction reprint); *Allegra Maud Goldman*, by Edith Konecky (fiction, reprint); and *Still Alive*, by Ruth Kluger (memoir).
How to Contact Does not accept unsolicited mss. Email Anjoli Roy with the word "submission" in the subject heading. Describe in no more than 200 words the type of book you are proposing and who you are. If we wish to see a portion of the manuscript or other materials, we will reply to your email requesting that you send those. Before writing, please consult our Web site to research if your book project fits the Feminist Press's publishing line. Usually responds within 6 weeks to queries. Accepts simultaneous submissions, electronic submissions.
Terms Pays 10% royalty on net receipts. Pays 5-10 author's copies. Average advance: $1,000. Publishes ms 18-24 months after acceptance. Ms guidelines online.

FLORIDA ACADEMIC PRESS

P.O. Box 540, Gainesville FL 32602. (352)332-5104. Fax: (352)331-6003. E-mail: fapress@gmail.com. **Contact:** Florence Dusek, assistant editor (fiction). Publishes hardcover and trade paperback originals. **Published 50% debut authors within the last year.** Averages 10 total titles/year.
Needs Serious fiction and scholarly social science manuscripts.
How to Contact Submit complete ms. Responds in 4-12 weeks to mss.
Terms Pays 5-8% royalty on retail price, depending if paperback or hardcover. Publishes ms 3-5 months after acceptance.
Advice Considers complete mss only. "Manuscripts we decide to publish must be re-submitted in camera-ready form."

FORT ROSS INC. RUSSIAN-AMERICAN PUBLISHING PROJECTS

26 Arthur Place, Yonkers NY 10701. (914)375-6448. E-mail: fortross@optonline.net. Web site: www. fortrossinc.com. **Contact:** Dr. Vladimir P. Kartsev. Estab. 1992. "We welcome Russia-related manuscripts as well as books from well-established fantasy and romance novel writers who would like to have their novels translated in Russia by our publishing house in cooperation with the local publishers." Publishes hard cover and paperback originals. **Published 2 debut authors within the last year.** Averages 20 total titles/year.
Needs Adventure, fantasy (space fantasy, sword and sorcery), horror, mainstream/contemporary, mystery (amateur sleuth, police procedural, private eye/hard-boiled), romance (contemporary, regency), science fiction (hard science/technological, soft/sociological), suspense, thriller

How to Contact Does not accept unsolicited mss. Query with SASE. Include estimated word count, brief bio, list of publishing credits. Send SASE for return of ms or send a disposable ms and SASE for reply only. Responds in 1 month to queries; 3 months to mss. Accepts simultaneous submissions. **Terms** Pays 5-10% royalty on wholesale price or makes outright purchase of $500-1,500. Average advance: $500-$1,000; negotiable.

N ⚫ ◐ FREYA'S BOWER

Wild Child Publishing, P.O. Box 4897, Culver City CA 90231. E-mail: mbaun@freyasbower.com. Web site: http://www.freyasbower.com. **Contact:** Marci Baun, editor-in-chief; Faith Bicknell-Brown, managing editor. Estab. 2006. "Freya's Bower is a small, independent press that started out in March 2006. We are known for working with newer/unpublished authors and editing to the standards of NYC publishers. We respond promptly to submissions." Publishes paperback originals, e-books. Average print order: 50-200. Debut novel print order: 50. **Published over 30 new writers last year.** Plans 10-15 debut novels this year. Averages 75 total titles/year; 75 fiction titles/year. Member EPIC. Distributes/promotes titles through Ingram, All Romance eBooks, Fictionwise, Mobipocket and Web site.

Needs Adventure, erotica, ethnic/multicultural, experimental, fantasy, feminist, gay, historical, horror, humor/satire, lesbian, literary, mainstream, military/war, mystery/suspense, new age/mystic, psychic/supernatural, romance, science fiction, short story collections, thriller/espionage, western, young adult (fantasy/science fiction). Anthologies planned include Faeries, Dreams & Desires, vol. 2, M/M. Published *Dreams & Desires: A Collection of Romance & Erotic Tales* (romance/erotica); *Conspiracy of Angels*, by Zinnia Hope (contemporary romance/erotica); *Dragon Queen: Book 1 & Book 2*, by Emily Ryan-Davis (paranormal/contemporary erotica).

How to Contact Query with outline/synopsis and 1 sample chapter. Accepts queries by e-mail. Include estimated word count, brief bio. Writers submit material per submissions guidelines. See Web site for details. Responds to queries in 2-4 weeks. Accepts unsolicited mss. Often critiques/comments on rejected mss. Responds to mss in 2-4 weeks.

Terms Sends pre-production galleys to author. Ms published 2-5 months after acceptance. Writer's guidelines on Web site. Pays royalties 10-40%. Book catalogs on Web site.

Advice "We look for good stories. While we accept material that is popular, we are more focused on quality. Do your homework. Read our submission guidelines thoroughly. Read a few of our books. Study your craft. While we are willing to work with newer authors, we expect them to be willing to revise and eager to learn. A good attitude goes a long way . . . on both sides."

◐ ◎ ◐ FRONT STREET

An imprint of Boyds Mills Press, Inc., 815 Church St., Honesdale PA 18431. Web site: www.frontstreetbooks.com. **Contact:** Manuscript Submissions. Estab. 1994. "High-quality fiction for children and young adults." Publishes hardcover originals and trade paperback reprints. Books: coated paper; offset printing; case binding; 4-color illustrations. Averages 15 fiction titles/year. Distributes titles through independent sales reps, wholesalers, and via order line directly from Front Street. Promotes titles through sales and professional conferences, sales reps, reviews, catalogs, web site, and direct marketing.

Needs Adventure, ethnic, historical, humor, juvenile, literary, picture books, young adult (adventure, fantasy/science fiction, historical, mystery/suspense, problem novels, sports). "We look for fresh voices for children and young adults. Titles on our list entertain, challenge, or enlighten, always employing novel characters whose considered voices resonate." Published *Keturah and Lord Death*, by Martine Leavitt; *The Big House*, by Carolyn Coman; *I'm being Stalked by a Moonshadow*, by Doug MacLeod.

How to Contact Accepts unsolicited and international mss. Query with outline/synopsis, 3 sample chapters, and SASE and label the package "Manuscript Submission." Agented fiction 30%. Responds in 3 months to mss. Accepts simultaneous submissions.

Terms Pays royalty on retail price. Offers advance.

Advice "Read through our recently published titles and review our Web site. Check to see what's on the market and in our catalog before submitting your story. Feel free to query us if you're not sure."

Ⓐ ✖ ◎ LAURA GERINGER BOOKS

HarperCollins Children's Books, 1350 Avenue of the Americas, New York NY 10019. (212)261-6500. Web site: www.harperchildrens.com. **Contact:** Laura Geringer, senior vice president/publisher. "We look for books that are out of the ordinary, authors who have their own definite take, and artists who add a sense of humor to the text." Publishes hardcover originals. **Published some debut authors within the last year.** Averages 15-20 total titles/year.

Needs Adventure, fantasy, historical, humor, juvenile, literary, picture books, young adult. Recently published *So B. It,* by Sarah Weeks, *Down the Rabbit Hole,* by Peter Abrahams, *If You Give a Pig a Party,* by Laura Numeroff, illustrated by Felicia Bond.

How to Contact Does not accept unsolicited mss. Agented fiction 90%.

Terms Pays 10-12½% royalty on retail price. Average advance: variable.

Advice "A mistake writers often make is failing to research the type of books an imprint publishes, therefore sending inappropriate material."

◙ GERTRUDE PRESS

P.O. Box 83948, Portland OR 97283. Web site: www.gertrudepress.org. **Contact:** Justus Ballard (all fiction). Estab. 2005. "Gertrude Press is a nonprofit organization developing and showcasing the creative talents of lesbian, gay, bisexual, trans, queer-identified and allied individuals. We publish limited-edition fiction and poetry chapbooks plus the biannual literary journal, *Gertrude.*" Format: 60 lb. paper; high-quality digital printing; perfect (lit mag) or saddle-stitch (chapbook) bound. Average print order: 350. Published 5-10 new writers last year. Averages 4 total titles/year; 1 fiction title/year.

Needs Ethnic/multicultural, experimental, feminist, gay, humor/satire, lesbian, literary, mainstream, short story collections.

How to Contact Submit complete ms with cover letter. Submissions accepted year-round. Accepts queries by snail mail, e-mail. Include estimated word count, brief bio, list of publishing credits. Send disposable copy of ms and SASE for reply only. Responds to queries in 3-4 weeks; mss in 3-6 months. Accepts unsolicited mss. Considers simultaneous submissions, e-mail submissions. Sometimes critiques/comments on rejected mss.

Terms Manuscript published 3 months after acceptance. Writer's guidelines on Web site. Pays in author's copies (1 for lit mag, 50 for chapbook). Book catalogs not available.

Advice Sponsors poetry and fiction chapbook contest. Prize is $50 and 50 contributor's copies. Submission guidelines and fee information on Web site. "Read the journal and sample published work. We are not impressed by pages of publications; your work should speak for itself."

◖ GIVAL PRESS

P.O. Box 3812, Arlington VA 22203. (703)351-0079. E-mail: givalpress@yahoo.com. Web site: www. givalpress.com. **Contact:** Robert L. Giron, publisher. Estab. 1998. A small, award-winning independent publisher that publishes quality works by a variety of authors from an array of walks of life. Works are in English, Spanish and French and have a philosophical or social message. Publishes paperback originals and reprints and e-books. Books: perfect-bound. Average print order: 500. **Publishes established and debut authors.** Plans 2 first novels this year. Member AAP, PMA, Literary Council of Small Presses and Magazines. Distributes books through Ingram and BookMasters, Inc.

Needs Literary, ethnic, gay/lesbian. "Looking for French books with English translation." The Annual Gival Press Novel Award contest deadline is May 30th. The Annual Gival Press Short Story Award contest deadline is August 8th. Guidelines on Web site. Recently published *Fiction: The Spanish Teacher*, by Barbara De La Cuesta and Boys; *Lost & Found*, by Charles Casillo.

How to Contact Does not accept unsolicited mss. Query by e-mail first. Include description of project, estimated word count, brief bio, list of publishing credits. Agented fiction 5%. Responds by e-mail within 2 weeks. Rarely comments on rejected mss.

Terms Pays 20 contributor's copies. Offers advance. Publishes ms 1 year after acceptance. For book catalog send SASE and on Web site. Ms guidelines by SASE or on Web site.

Advice "Study the types of books we have published—literary works with a message of high quality."

◖ ◎ THE GLENCANNON PRESS

P.O. Box 1428, El Cerrito CA 94530. (510)528-4216. Fax: (510)528-3194. E-mail: merships@yahoo.c om. Web site: www.glencannon.com. **Contact:** Bill Harris (maritime, maritime children's). Estab.

1993. "We publish quality books about ships and the sea." Publishes hardcover and paperback originals and hardcover reprints. Books: Smyth: perfect binding; illustrations. Average print order: 1,000. First novel print order: 750. Averages 4-5 total titles, 1 fiction titles/year. Member PMA, BAIPA. Distributes titles through Quality Books, Baker & Taylor. Promotes titles through direct mail, magazine advertising and word of mouth.

Imprint(s) Palo Alto Books (any except maritime); Glencannon Press (merchant marine and Navy).

Needs Adventure, children's/juvenile (adventure, fantasy, historical, mystery, preschool/picture book), ethnic (general), historical (maritime), humor, mainstream/contemporary, military/war, mystery, thriller/espionage, western (frontier saga, traditional maritime), young adult (adventure, historical, mystery/suspense, western). Currently emphasizing children's maritime, any age. Recently published *Good Shipmates*, by Ernest F. Imhoff (anthology, merchant marine); *Fort Ross*, by Mark West (Palo Alto Books, western).

How to Contact Accepts unsolicited mss. Submit complete ms. Include brief bio, list of publishing credits. Send SASE for return of ms or send a disposable ms and SASE for reply only. Responds in 1 month to queries; 2 months to mss. Accepts simultaneous submissions. Often comments on rejected mss.

Terms Pays 10-20% royalty. Publishes ms 6-24 months after acceptance.

Advice "Write a good story in a compelling style."

Ⓐ DAVID R. GODINE, PUBLISHER, INC.

9 Hamilton Place, Boston MA 02108. (617)451-9600. Fax: (617)350-0250. E-mail: info@godine.com. Web site: www.godine.com. **Contact:** David R. Godine, president. Estab. 1970. Small independent publisher (5-person staff). Publishes hardcover and trade paperback originals and reprints. Averages 35 total titles/year.

Imprint(s) Nonpareil Books (trade paperbacks), Verba Mundi (translations), Imago Mundi (photography).

Needs Children's/juvenile, historical, literary. *No unsolicited mss.*

How to Contact Does not accept unsolicited mss. Query with SASE.

Terms Pays royalty on retail price. Publishes ms 3 years after acceptance.

Advice "Have your agent contact us. Please no phone queries."

✂ Ⓒ ◎ GOOSE LANE EDITIONS

500 Beaverbrook Court, Suite 330, Fredericton NB E3B 5X4 Canada. (506)450-4251. Fax: (506)459-4991. Web site: www.gooselane.com. **Contact:** Susanne Alexander, publisher. Estab. 1954. Publishes hardcover and paperback originals and occasional reprints. Books: some illustrations. Average print order: 3,000. First novel print order: 1,500. Averages 16-18 total titles, 6-8 fiction titles/year. Distributes titles through University of Toronto Press (UTP).

Needs Literary (novels), mainstream/contemporary, short story collections. "Our needs in fiction never change: substantial, character-centered literary fiction." Published *We Are Not in Pakistan*, by Shauna Singh Baldwin.

How to Contact Accepts unsolicited mss. Query with SASE. Responds in 6 months to mss. No simultaneous submissions.

Terms Pays 8-10% royalty on retail price. Average advance: $200-1,000, negotiable. Ms guidelines online.

Advice "We do not consider submissions from outside Canada."

◎ GOTHIC CHAPBOOK SERIES

Gothic Press, 2272 Quail Oak, Baton Rouge LA 70808-9023. E-mail: gothicpt12@aol.com. Web site: www.gothicpress.com. **Contact:** Gary W. Crawford, editor (horror, fiction, poetry and scholarship). Estab. 1979. "One person operation on a part-time basis." Publishes paperback originals. Books: printing or photocopying. Average print order: 150-200. Distributes titles through direct mail and book dealers.

Needs Horror (dark fantasy, psychological, supernatural). Need novellas and short stories.

How to Contact Accepts unsolicited mss. Query with SASE. Accepts queries by e-mail, phone. Include estimated word count, brief bio, list of publishing credits. Send SASE for return of ms or send a disposable ms and SASE for reply only. Responds in 2 weeks to queries; 2 months to mss. Sometimes comments on rejected mss.

Terms Pays 10% royalty. Ms guidelines for #10 SASE.

Advice "Know gothic and horror literature well."

⊌ GRAYWOLF PRESS

2402 University Ave., Suite 203, St. Paul MN 55114. E-mail: wolves@graywolfpress.org. Web site: www.graywolfpress.org. **Contact:** Polly Carden, editorial assistant. Estab. 1974. Growing independent literary press, nonprofit corporation. Publishes trade cloth and paperback originals. Books: acid-free quality paper; offset printing; hardcover and soft binding. Average print order: 3,000-10,000. First novel print order: 3,000-7,500. Averages 25 total titles, 5-7 fiction titles/year. Distributes titles nationally through Farrar, Straus and Giroux.

Needs Literary novels, short story collections. "Familiarize yourself with our list before submitting your work." Published Out *Stealing Horses*, by Per Petterson; *Refresh, Refresh*, by Benjamin Percy; *Snow, Ashes*, by Alyson Hagy; *The Water Cure*, by Percival Everett.

How to Contact Send query letter including SASE/IRC, estimated word count, brief bio, list of publishing credits. Agented fiction 90%. Responds in 3 months to queries. Accepts simultaneous submissions.

Terms Pays royalty on retail price, author's copies. Average advance: $2,500-15,000. Publishes ms 18-24 months after acceptance. Ms guidelines online.

Advice "Review our catalog and submission guidelines before submitting your work. We rarely publish story collections or novels by authors who have not published work previously in literary journals or magazines."

🄰 ◎ GREENE BARK PRESS

P.O. Box 1108, Bridgeport CT 06601. (610)434-2802. Fax: (610)434-2803. Web site: www.greenebark press.com. **Contact:** Tara Maroney, associate publisher. Estab. 1991. "We only publish children's fiction—all subjects, but usually reading picture book format appealing to ages 3-9 or all ages." Publishes hardcover originals. **Published some debut authors within the last year.** Averages 1-6 total titles/year. Distributes titles through Baker & Taylor and Quality Books. Promotes titles through ads, trade shows (national and regional), direct mail campaigns.

Needs Juvenile. Published *Edith Ellen Eddy*, by Julee Granger.

How to Contact Submit complete ms. Responds in 3 months to queries; 6 months to mss. Accepts simultaneous submissions. No electronic submissions.

Terms Pays 10-15% royalty on wholesale price. Publishes ms 1 year after acceptance. Ms guidelines for SASE or e-mail request.

Advice Audience is "children who read to themselves and others. Mothers, fathers, grandparents, godparents who read to their respective children, grandchildren. Include SASE, be prepared to wait, do NOT inquire by telephone, fax or e-mail."

✪ ⊘ GREENWILLOW BOOKS

HarperCollins Publishers, 1350 Avenue of the Americas, New York NY 10019. (212)261-6500. Web site: www.harperchildrens.com. Estab. 1974. Publishes hardcover originals and reprints. Averages 50-60 total titles/year.

Needs Children's books: fantasy, humor, literary, mystery. *Criss Cross*, by Lynne Rae Perkins, 2006 Newbery Medal Winner; *Deadline*, by Cris Crutcher; *Ida B*, by Katherine Hannigan.

How to Contact Does not accept unsolicited mss. "Unsolicited mail will not be opened and will not be returned."

Terms Pays 10% royalty on wholesale price for first-time authors. Average advance: variable. Publishes ms 2 years after acceptance.

🄽 ⊘ 🏆 HADLEY RILLE BOOKS

P.O. Box 25466, Overland Park KS 66225. E-mail: info@hadleyrillebooks.com. Web site: http://www.hadleyrillebooks.com. **Contact:** Eric T. Reynolds, Editor (science fiction, fantasy). Estab. 2005. "Small publisher, one to two person operation. The first seven titles are anthologies, mostly science fiction, with a little fantasy (in two titles). We've published new works by well-know authors (for example, new works by Sir Arthur C. Clarke, Mike Resnick, Stephen Baxter, Jay Lake, G. David Nordley, Robert Sheckley, Terry Bisson) as well as up-and-coming and new authors. At present time, about half of our anthologies are by invitation only, the other half are open to unsolicited submissions. We publish the kind of innovative anthologies that are generally not considered by larger publishers (somewhat common in the SF genre). Some of our anthologies are experimental, for example, the first title (*Golden Age SF*) had well-known authors write 'Golden Age' SF stories as if they were living during that time. The second title, *Visual Journeys*, asked each contributing author to choose a work of space art and write a story based on it. We included color plates of the art with each story. We're currently in the middle of a Ruins anthology series with stories that are set in or are about ruins. An anthology in 2008 will feature stories that deal with the consequences of global warming. Well-known futurists and SF writers are writing for this.'' Publishes hardcover originals, paperback originals. Format: Offset and POD printing. Published 30 new writers last year. Averages 5 fiction titles/year. Distributes/promotes titles via distributors, promotes at conventions, online advertising and by reviews.

- One story from *Golden Age SF: Tales of a Bygone Future* (2006) selected for David Hartwell and Kathryn Cramer's *Year's Best SF* #12, another selected for Rich Horton's *Space Opera 2007*. Four stories were included for honorable mention in Gardner Dozois' *The Year's Best Science Fiction #24*.

Needs Science fiction, fantasy, short story collections. Check Web site for current needs. Some anthologies are and will be open to unsolicited submissions, and will be announced on Web site. Published *Golden Age SF: Tales of a Bygone Future* (science fiction), *Visual Journeys: A Tribute to Space* (science fiction), *Ruins Terra* (SF/fantasy/horror).

How to Contact Send query letter. Accepts queries by e-mail. Include estimated word count, brief bio. Agented fiction: less than 5%. Accepts unsolicited mss. Often critiques/comments on rejected mss.

Terms Sends pre-production galleys to author. Ms published generally 6 months after acceptance. Writer's guidelines on Web site. Pays royalties of $1/2$ of the ratio of 1 to the number of stories in the book, advance of $30 for unsolicited work. Book catalogs on Web site.

Advice "We aim to produce books that are aligned with current interest in the genres. Anthology markets are somewhat rare in SF these days, we feel there aren't enough good anthologies being published each year and part of our goal is to present the best that we can. We like stories that fit well within the guidelines of the particular anthology for which we are soliciting manuscripts. Aside from that, we want stories with strong characters (not necessarily characters with strong personalities, flawed characters are welcome). We want a sense of wonder and awe. We want to feel the world around the character and so scene description is important (however, this doesn't always require a lot of text, just set the scene well so we don't wonder where the character is). We strongly recommend workshopping the story or having it critiqued in some way by readers familiar with the genre. We prefer clichés be kept to a bare minimum in the prose and avoid re-working old story lines.''

◻ HARBOR HOUSE

111 Tenth St., Augusta GA 30901. (706)738-0354. Fax: (706)823-5999. E-mail: harborhouse@harbor housebooks.com. Web site: www.harborhousebooks.com. **Contact:** Peggy Cheney, editorial director and assistant publisher. Estab. 1997. Harbor House seeks to publish the best in original fiction (southern, thrillers, horror) and current events/social issue nonfiction. Publishes hardcover originals and paperback originals. Average print order: 5,000. **Published 8 debut authors within the last year.** Member: Publishers Association of the South. Distribution with Ingram; Baker & Taylor; Anderson; and American Wholesale.

- Received a Golden Eye Literary Award.

Imprint(s) Batwing Press, Southern Winds, Savannah River Press.

Needs Horror, thriller, Civil War, new age/mystic, unsolved mysteries.

How to Contact Accepts queries by mail. Does not accept phone queries or proposals by e-mail. Accepts unsolicited mss or send outline, 3 sample chapter(s). Include estimated word count, brief bio, list of publishing credits, marketing plans, SASE. Agented fiction 10%. Responds in 4 weeks to queries; 2 months to mss. Accepts simultaneous submissions. Does not accept previously published works. Sometimes comments on rejected mss.

Terms Royalty rates vary, depending on hardcover or paperback. Minimum advance: $500.

Advice "We strongly encourage authors to consult our Web site before submitting material. We are particularly interested in developing unpublished authors.''

Ⓐ HARCOURT CHILDREN'S BOOKS

Imprint of Houghton Mifflin Harcourt Children's Book Group, 215 Park Ave South, New York, NY 10003. Web site: www.harcourtbooks.com. **Senior Vice President and Publisher:** Betsy Groban. **Associate Publisher:** Jennifer Haller. 20% of books by first-time authors; 50% of books from agented writers. "Harcourt Children's Books publishes hardcover picture books and fiction only."

- Harcourt Children's Books no longer accepts unsolicited manuscripts, queries, or illustrations. Recent Harcourt titles:*Tails*, by Matthew Van Fleet; *Leaf Man*, by Lois Ehlert; *The Great Fuzz Frenzy*, by Janet Stevens and Susan Steven Crummel; *How I Became a Pirate* and *Pirates Don't Change Diapers*, by Melinda Long, illustrated by David Shannon; and *Frankenstein Makes a Sandwich*, by Adam Rex, are all New York Times bestsellers. Other Harcourt titles include *Evil Genius*, by Catherine Jinks; and *Each Little Bird That Sings*, by Deborah Wiles, a 2005 finalist for the National Book Award

How to Contact Only interested in agented material.

Terms Pays authors royalty based on retail price. Sends preproduction galleys to authors.

Ⓐ ⚒ HARPERCOLLINS CHILDREN'S BOOKS

1350 Avenue of the Americas, New York NY 10019. (212)261-6500. Web site: www.harperchildrens.com. Book publisher. President and Publisher: Susan Katz. Associate Publisher/Editor-in-Chief: Kate Morgan Jackson. Associate Publisher, Fiction: Elise Howard. Editorial Directors: Margaret Anastas, Barbara Lalicki, Maria Modugno, Phoebe Yeh.

- HarperCollins Children's Books is not accepting unsolicited and/or unagented manuscripts or queries. "Unfortunately, the volume of these submissions is so large that we cannot give them the attention they deserve. Such submissions will not be reviewed or returned."

Imprints HarperTrophy, HarperTeen, EOS, HarperFestival, Greenwillow Books, Joanna Cotler Books, Laura Geringer Books, Katherine Tegen Books.

Needs Publishes picture, chapter, novelty, board and TV/movie books.

How to Contact Only interested in agented material.

Ⓐ ◎ HARVEST HOUSE PUBLISHERS

990 Owen Loop N., Eugene OR 97402. (541)343-0123. Fax: (541)302-0731. Web site: www.harvesthousepublishers.com. **Contact:** Acquisitions. Estab. 1974. "Our mission is to glorify God by providing high-quality books and products that affirm biblical values, help people grow spiritually strong, and proclaim Jesus Christ as the answer to every human need." Publishes hardcover originals and reprints, trade paperback originals and reprints, and mass market paperback originals and reprints. Books: 40 lb. ground wood paper; offset printing; perfect binding. Average print order: 10,000. First novel print order: 10,000-15,000. **Published 20 debut authors within the last year.** Averages 175 total titles, 15-20 fiction titles/year.

Needs Harvest House no longer accepts unsolicited manuscripts, proposals, or artwork.

How to Contact Does not accept unsolicited mss.

Advice "Attend a writer's conference where you have an opportunity to pitch your book idea to an editor face to face. We also look at fiction represented by a reputable agent."

▢ HELICON NINE EDITIONS

Subsidiary of Midwest Center for the Literary Arts, Inc., P.O. Box 22412, Kansas City MO 64113. (816)753-1016. E-mail: helicon9@aol.com. Web site: www.heliconnine.com. **Contact:** Gloria Vando Hickok. Estab. 1990. Small not-for-profit press publishing poetry, fiction, creative nonfiction and anthologies. Publishes paperback originals. Also publishes one-story chapbooks called *feuillets*, which come with envelope, 250 print run. Books: 60 lb. paper; offset printing; perfect bound; 4-color cover. Average print order: 1,000-5,000. **Published 1 debut author within the last year.** Distributes titles through Baker & Taylor, Brodart, Ingrams, Follet (library acquisitions), and booksellers. Promotes titles through reviews, readings, radio and television interviews.

How to Contact Does not accept unsolicited mss.

Terms Pays royalty. Author's copies. Offers advance. Publishes ms 12-18 months after acceptance.

Advice "We accept short story collections, welcome new writers and first books. Submit a clean, readable copy in a folder or box—paginated with title and name on each page. Also, do not pre-design book, i.e., no illustrations, unless they are an integral part of the book. We'd like to see books that will be read 50-100 years from now."

◎ HENDRICK-LONG PUBLISHING CO., INC.

10635 Toweroaks D., Houston TX 77070. (832)912-7323. Fax: (832)912-7353. E-mail: hendrick-long@worldnet.att.net. Web site: hendricklongpublishing.com. **Contact:** Michael Long. Estab. 1969. Only considers manuscripts with Texas theme. Publishes hardcover and trade paperback originals and hardcover reprints. Averages 4 total titles/year.

Needs Juvenile, young adult.

How to Contact Submit outline, 2 sample chapter(s), synopsis. Responds in 3 months to queries. No simultaneous submissions.

Terms Pays royalty on selling price. Offers advance. Publishes ms 18 months after acceptance. Book catalog for $8^{1}/_{2} \times 11$ or 9×12 SASE with 4 first-class stamps. Ms guidelines online.

Ⓐ ⊕ HESPERUS PRESS

4 Rickett Street, London England SW6 1RU United Kingdom. 44 20 7610 3331. Fax: 44 20 7610 3217. Web site: www.hesperus press.com. Estab. 2001. Hesperus is a small independent publisher mainly of classics and literary fiction. Publishes paperback originals. Books: munken paper; traditional printing; sewn binding. Average print order: 5,000. Distributes titles through Trafalgar Square in the US, Grantham Book Services in the UK.

Needs Literary. Published *Carlyle's House*, by Virginia Woolf (rediscovered modern classic); *No Man's Land*, by Graham Greene (rediscovered modern classic); *The Princess of Mantua*, by Marie Ferranti (award-winning fiction in translation); *The Maytrees*, by Annie Dillard (new fiction).

How to Contact Does not accept unsolicited mss. *Agented submissions only.* Query with SASE. Accepts queries by mail. Include estimated word count, brief bio, list of publishing credits. Agented fiction 100%. Responds in 8-10 weeks to queries; 8-10 weeks to mss. Accepts simultaneous submissions. No electronic submissions, submissions on disk.

Advice Find an agent to represent you.

Ⓝ ◌ Ⓦ HIGHLAND PRESS PUBLISHING

P.O. Box 2292, High Springs FL 32655. (386)454-3927. Fax: (386)454-3927. E-mail: The.Highland.Press@gmail.com. Web site: http://www.highlandpress.org. **Contact:** Leanne Burroughs, CEO (fiction)—she will forward all mss to appropriate acquiring editor. Estab. 2005. "Currently Highland Press Publishing is known for our focus on historical romances and our award-winning anthologies. Many people have told us that they can once again delight in reading with the anthologies, since they don't have to feel guilty about reading and then putting a book down before it's finished. With the short stories/novellas, they can read a heart-warming story, yet still get back to the demands of today's busy lives. As for our historicals, we publish historical novels like many of us grew up with and loved. History is a big part of the story and is tactfully woven throughout the romance." Publishes paperback originals, paperback reprints. Format: off set printing; perfect bound. Average print order: 1,000. Debut novel print order: 1,000. **Published 31 new writers last year.** Plans 25 debut authors this year. Averages 13 total titles/year; 12 fiction titles/year. Distributes/promotes titles through Ingram, Baker & Taylor, Nielsen, Powells.

- *Highland Wishes* was a Finalist, 2005 Readers' and Booksellers' Best and 2006 Winner, Reviewers' International Award of Excellence. *Faery Special Romances* was a nominee for 2007 Night Owl Romances. *Blue Moon Enchantment* won the 2007 P.E.A.R.L. Award (two separate stories). *Christmas Wishes* had several stories nominated for the 2007 P.E.A.R.L. Award and received the 2007 Linda Howard Award of Excellence. *Her Highland Rogue* received the 2006 Reviewer's International Award, the 2006 National Readers' Choice Award, and was a 2007 finalist for Readers' and Booksellers' Best. *Cat O'Nine Tales* had several stories as finalists or win the 2007 P.E.A.R.L. Award, 2007 Linda Howard Award of Excellence, and the 2007 Reviewers International Organization Award of Excellence.

Imprint(s) A Wee Dram (short stories/novellas), The Wee Ones (children's illustrated), Regency Royale (regency/romance), Thistle (Scottish historicals), Grace (inspirationals), Eire (Irish historicals), Pandora (young adult), Western (western/romance).

Needs Children's/juvenile (adventure, animal, easy-to-read, fantasy, historical, mystery, preschool/picture book, series), family saga, fantasy (space fantasy), historical, horror (dark fantasy, futuristic, supernatural), mainstream, military/war, mystery/suspense (amateur/sleuth, cozy, police procedural, private eye/hardboiled), religious (children's, general, inspirational, fantasy, mystery/suspense, thriller, romance), romance (contemporary, futuristic/time travel, gothic, historical, regency period, suspense), short story collections, thriller/espionage, western (frontier saga, traditional), young adult/teen (adventure, fantasy/science fiction, historical, horror, mystery/suspense, romance, series, western). Special interests: Children's ms must come with illustrator. "We will always be looking for good historical manuscripts. In addition, we are actively seeking inspirational romances and Regency period romances." Numerous romance anthologies are planned. Topics are posted on the Web site. Writers should query with their proposal. After the submission deadline has passed, editors select the stories. Published *The Sense of Honor*, by Ashley Kath-Bilsky (regency/ romance); *Faery Special Romances*, by Jacquie Rogers (short story collection/romance); *Cat O' Nine Tales*, by Deborah MacGillivray (short story collection/romance).

How to Contact Send query letter. Query with outline/synopsis and sample chapters. Accepts queries by snail mail, e-mail. Include estimated word count, target market. Send disposable copy of ms and SASE for reply only. Agented fiction: 10%. Responds to queries in 3 weeks. Accepts unsolicited mss. Considers simultaneous submissions, e-mail submissions. Sometimes critiques/comments on rejected mss. Responds to mss in 3-6 months.

Terms Sends pre-production galleys to author. Ms published within 12 months after acceptance. Writer's guidelines on Web site. Pays royalties 7.5-8%. Book catalogs on Web site.

Advice "I don't publish based on industry trends. We buy what we like and what we believe readers are looking for. However, often this proves to be the genres and time-periods larger publishers are not currently interested in. Be professional at all times. Present your manuscript in the best possible light. Be sure you have run spell check and that the manuscript has been vetted by at least one critique partner, preferably more. Many times we receive manuscripts that have wonderful stories involved, but would take far too much time to edit to make it marketable."

◎ HOLIDAY HOUSE INC.

425 Madison Ave., New York NY 10017. (212)688-0085. Fax: (212)421-6134. Web site: www.holiday house.com. Estab. 1935. Book publisher. **Vice President/Editor-in-Chief:** Mary Cash. **Acquisitions:** Acquisitions Editor. Publishes 35 picture books/year; 3 young readers/year; 15 middle readers/year; 8 young adult titles/year. 20% of books by first-time authors; 10% from agented writers. Mission Statement: "To publish high-quality books for children."

Needs All levels of young readers: adventure, contemporary, fantasy, folktales, ghost, historical, humor, literary, multicultural, school, suspense/mystery, sports. Recently published *Jazz*, by Walter Dean Myers, illustrated by Christopher Myers; *Keeper of Soles*, by Teresa Bateman, illustrated by Yayo; *Freedom Walkers*, by Russell Freedman.

How to Contact Send queries only to editor. Responds to queries in 3 months; mss in 4 months. "If we find your book idea suits our present needs, we will notify you by mail." Once a ms has been requested, the writers should send in the exclusive submission, with a SASE, otherwise the ms will not be returned.

Terms Pays authors an advance against royalties. Book catalog, ms guidelines available for a SASE.

Advice "We need books with strong stories, writing and art. We do not publish board books or novelties. No easy readers."

★ ◢ ◎ HOUGHTON MIFFLIN BOOKS FOR CHILDREN

Houghton Mifflin Company, 222 Berkeley St., Boston MA 02116. (617)351-5959. Fax: (617)351-1111. E-mail: children's_books@hmco.com. Web site: www.houghtonmifflinbooks.com. **Contact:** Submissions coordinator; Kate O'Sullivan senior editor; Ann Rider, senior editor; Margaret Raymo, editorial director. "Houghton Mifflin gives shape to ideas that educate, inform and, above all, delight." Publishes hardcover originals and trade paperback originals and reprints. **Published 12 debut authors within the last year.** Averages 100 total titles/year. Promotes titles through author visits, advertising, reviews.

Imprint(s) Clarion Books, New York City, Graphia Boston; Sand Pipers, Boston.

Needs Adventure, ethnic, historical, humor, juvenile (early readers), literary, mystery, picture books, suspense, young adult, board books. Published *Trainstop*, by Barbara Lehman; *The Willowbys,* by Lois Lowry; *Just Grace Walker the Dog*, by Cherise Mericle Harper.

How to Contact Accepts unsolicited mss. Responds only if interested. Do not send SASE. Accepts simultaneous submissions. No electronic submissions.

Terms Pays 5-10% royalty on retail price. Average advance: variable. Publishes ms 18-24 months after acceptance. Book catalog for 9×12 SASE with 3 first-class stamps. Ms guidelines online.

⚡ ⊘ IMAGES SI, INC

Imprint of Images Publishing, 109 Woods of Arden Rd., Staten Island NY 10312. (718)966-3964. Fax: (718)966-3695. Web site: www.imagesco.com/publishing/index.html. **Contact:** Acquisitions Editor. Estab. 1990. Publishes 2 audio books a year.

Needs Hard science fiction for audiocassettes and CDs. Published *Centauri III*, by George L. Griggs (science fiction print book); *Nova-Audio, Issues 1-3*, by Hoyt, Franklin, Schoen, Wild, Silverberg and Catelli (science fiction audio).

How to Contact Closed to submissions until 2008.

Terms Pays 10-20% royalty on wholesale price. Publishes stories 6 months-2 years after acceptance.

⊘ IMAJINN BOOKS

P.O. Box 545, Canon City CO 81212-0545. (719)275-0060. Fax: (719)276-0746. E-mail: editors@imaji nnbooks.com. Web site: www.imajinnbooks.com. **Contact:** Linda J. Kichline, editor. Estab. 1998. "ImaJinn Books is a small independent print-on-demand publishing house that specializes in Regency Romance, Urban Fantasy, and paranormal romances with story lines involving psychics or psychic phenomena, witches, vampires, werewolves, space travel, the future." Publishes trade paperback originals. Books: print-on-demand; perfect binding; no illustrations. **Published 3-4 debut authors.** Member: SPAN. Distributes titles through Ingram Books and imajinnbooks.com. Promotes titles through advertising and review magazines.

Needs Fantasy (romance), horror (romance), psychic/supernatural (romance), all Urban Fantasy story lines, and all Regency romance story lines. "We look for specific story lines based on what the readers are asking for and what story lines in which we're short. We post our current needs on our Web site." Published *Dancing with The Devil*, by Keri Arthur (horror romance); *Half Past Hell*, by Jay Roycraft (Urban Fantasy); and *Marry Me, Millie*, by J.A. Ferguson (Regency romance).

How to Contact Query with SASE. Prefers queries by email. Include estimated word count, brief bio, list of publishing credits. Unless otherwise requested prefers e-mail submissions. Agented fiction 20%. Responds in 3 months to queries; 9-12 months to mss. Often comments on rejected mss.

Terms Pays 6-10% royalty on retail price. Average advance: 100-200. Publishes ms 1-3 years after acceptance. Book catalog and ms guidelines for #10 SASE or online. Ms guidelines online.

Advice "Carefully read the author guidelines, and read books published by ImaJinn Books. Do not submit manuscript without querying first."

⊘ INGALLS PUBLISHING GROUP, INC

197 New Market Center, #135, Boone NC 28607. (828)297-7127. Fax: (828)297-1057. E-mail: sales@i ngallspublishinggroup.com. Web site: www.ingallspublishinggroup.com. **Contact:** Wendy Dingwall, Operations and Sales Manager. Estab. 2001. "We are a small regional house focusing on popular fiction and memoir. At present, we are most interested in regional fiction, historical fiction and mystery fiction." Publishes hardcover originals, paperback originals and paperback reprints. Books: 60# paper; offset printing; b&w illustrations. Average print order: 1,500-5,000. First novel print order: 1,500-3,000. **Published 1 debut author within the last year.** Plans 3 first novels this year. Member PMA, PAS, SIBA. Distributes titles through Biblio Distribution, sister company of NBN books.

Needs Historical, mystery (amateur sleuth, cozy, police procedural, private eye/hard-boiled), regional (southern Appalachian), romance (contemporary, historical, romantic suspense adventure), young adult (historical, mystery/suspense). Published *Murder At Blue Falls*, by Maggie Bishop (regional mystery); *Pelican Watch*, by Rose Senehi (romance suspense); *Getorix*, by Judith Geary (young adult historical); *Secret of the Lonely Grave* (juvenile mystery).

How to Contact Accepts unsolicited mss. Query with SASE or submit outline, 3 sample chapter(s). Reading period open from July to October. Accepts queries by e-mail, mail. Include estimated word count, brief bio, list of publishing credits. Send copy of ms and SASE. Agented fiction 10%. Responds in 6 months to queries; 6 months to mss. Accepts simultaneous submissions, electronic submissions. No submissions on disk. Often comments on rejected mss.

Terms Pays 10% royalty. Publishes ms 6 months-2 years after acceptance. Ms guidelines online.

⚡ INSOMNIAC PRESS

192 Spadina Ave., Suite 403, Toronto ON M5T 2C2 Canada. (416)504-6270. Fax: (416)504-9313. E-mail: mike@insomniacpress.com. Web site: www.insomniacpress.com. Estab. 1992. "Midsize independent publisher with a mandate to produce edgy experimental fiction." Publishes trade paper-

back originals and reprints, mass market paperback originals, and electronic originals and reprints. First novel print order: 3,000. **Published 15 debut authors within the last year.** Plans 4 first novels this year. Averages 20 total titles, 5 fiction titles/year.

Needs Comic books, ethnic, experimental, gay/lesbian, humor, literary, mainstream/contemporary, multicultural, mystery, suspense. We publish a mix of commercial (mysteries) and literary fiction. Published *Pray For Us Sinners*, by Patrick Taylor (novel).

How to Contact Accepts unsolicited mss. Accepts queries by email. Include estimated word count, brief bio, list of publishing credits. Send SASE for return of ms or send a disposable ms and SASE for reply only. Agented fiction 5%. Responds in 1 week to queries; 2 months to mss. Accepts simultaneous submissions. Sometimes comments on rejected mss.

Terms Pays 10-15% royalty on retail price. Average advance: $500-1,000. Publishes ms 6 months after acceptance. Ms guidelines online.

Advice "Visit our Web site, read our writer's guidelines."

INTERLINK PUBLISHING GROUP, INC.

46 Crosby St., Northampton MA 01060. (413)582-7054. Fax: (413)582-7057. E-mail: editor@interlink books.com. Web site: www.interlinkbooks.com. **Contact:** Michel Moushabeck, publisher; Pam Thompson, editor. Estab. 1987. "Midsize independent publisher specializing in world travel, world literature, world history and politics." Publishes hardcover and trade paperback originals. Books: 55 lb. Warren Sebago Cream white paper; web offset printing; perfect binding. Average print order: 5,000. **Published new writers within the last year.** Averages 50 total titles, 2-4 fiction titles/year. Distributes titles through Baker & Taylor. Promotes titles through book mailings to extensive, specialized lists of editors and reviews; authors read at bookstores and special events across the country.

Imprint(s) Interlink Books and Olive Branch Press.

Needs Ethnic, international. "Adult—We are looking for translated works relating to the Middle East, Africa or Latin America." Recently published *Everything Good Will Come*, by Sefi Atta (first novel); *The Gardens of Light*, by Amin Maalouf (novel translated from French); *War in the Land of Egypt*, by Yusef Al-Qaid (novel translated from Arabic).

How to Contact Does not accept unsolicited mss. Query with SASE and a brief sample. Responds in 3 months to queries. Accepts simultaneous submissions. No electronic submissions.

Terms Pays 6-8% royalty on retail price. Average advance: small. Publishes ms 18 months after acceptance. Ms guidelines online.

Advice "Our Interlink International Fiction Series is designed to bring writers who have achieved wide acclaim at home to North America."

▣ INVERTED-A

P.O. Box 267, Licking MO 65542. E-mail: amnfn@well.com. **Contact:** Aya Katz, chief editor (poetry, novels, political); Nets Katz, science editor (scientific, academic). Estab. 1985. Publishes paperback originals. Books: offset printing. Average print order: 1,000. Average first novel print order: 500. Distributes through Baker & Taylor, Amazon, Bowker.

Needs Utopian, political. Needs poetry submission for our newsletter, *Inverted-A Horn*.

How to Contact Does not accept unsolicited mss. Query with SASE. Reading period open from January 2 to March 15. Accepts queries by e-mail. Include estimated word count. Responds in 1 month to queries; 3 months to mss. Accepts simultaneous submissions. Sometimes comments on rejected mss.

Terms Pays in 10 author's copies. Publishes ms 1 year after acceptance. Ms guidelines for SASE.

Advice "Read our books. Read the Inverted-A Horn. We are different. We do not follow industry trends."

▣ ION IMAGINATION PUBLISHING

Ion Imagination Entertainment, Inc., P.O. Box 210943, Nashville TN 37221-0943. Fax: (615)646-6276. E-mail: ionimagin@aol.com. Web site: www.flumpa.com. **Contact:** Keith Frickey, editor. Estab. 1994. Small independent publisher of science-related children's fiction, multimedia and audio products. Publishes hardcover and paperback originals. Average first novel print order: 10,000. Member SPAN and PMA.

- Received the Parents' Choice, National Parenting Centers Seal of Approval, Dr. Toy, Parent Council.

Needs Children's/juvenile (adventure, animal, preschool/picture book, science).

How to Contact Does not accept unsolicited mss. Query with SASE. Include brief bio, list of publishing credits. Responds in 1 month to queries. Accepts simultaneous submissions. Sometimes comments on rejected queries.
Terms Pays royalty.

☑ ◎ ITALICA PRESS

595 Main St., Suite 605, New York NY 10044-0047. (212)935-4230. Fax: (212)838-7812. E-mail: inquiries@italicapress.com. Web site: www.italicapress.com. **Contact:** Ronald G. Musto and Eileen Gardiner, publishers. Estab. 1985. Small independent publisher of Italian fiction in translation. "First-time translators published. We would like to see translations of Italian writers who are well-known in Italy who are not yet translated for an American audience." Publishes trade paperback originals. Books: 50-60 lb. natural paper; offset printing; illustrations. Average print order: 1,500. Averages 6 total titles, 2 fiction titles/year. Distributes titles through Web site. Promotes titles through Web site.
Needs Translations of 20th century Italian fiction. Published *Eruptions*, by Monica Sarsini; *The Great Bear*, by Ginevra Bompianai; *Sparrow*, by Giovanni Verga.
How to Contact Accepts unsolicited mss. Query with SASE. Accepts queries by e-mail, fax. Responds in 1 month to queries; 2 months to mss. Accepts simultaneous submissions, electronic submissions, submissions on disk.
Terms Pays 7-15% royalty on wholesale price. Pays author's copies. Publishes ms 1 year after acceptance. Ms guidelines online.
Advice "Remember we publish *only* fiction that has been previously published in Italian. A *brief* call saves a lot of postage. 90% of proposals we receive are completely off base—but we are very interested in things that are right on target. Please send return postage if you want your manuscript back."

☑ ◎ JIREH PUBLISHING COMPANY

P.O. Box 1911, Suisun City CA 94585-1911. E-mail: jireh_subms@yahoo.com. Web site: www.jirehpublishing.com. Estab. 1995. Small independent publisher. "We have just begun our fiction line." Publishes hardcover, trade paperback and electronic originals. Books: paper varies; digital and offset printed; binding varies. Average print order: varies. First novel print order: varies. Plans 2 first novels this year. Averages 2-5 total titles, 1-2 fiction titles/year. Distributes titles through online bookstores and booksellers (retailers).
Needs Mystery/suspense, religious (Christian e-books, general religious, mystery/suspense, thriller, romance). "We are looking for Christian values in the books that we publish."
How to Contact Accepts unsolicited mss. Query by e-mail only. Include brief bio, list of publishing credits. Go to Web site for guidelines. Responds in 2 months to queries; 8 months to mss. Accepts simultaneous submissions, electronic submissions. No submissions on disk. Sometimes comments on rejected mss.
Terms Pays 10-12% royalty on wholesale price. Publishes ms 9-12 months after acceptance. Ms guidelines online.

⬥ ☑ ◎ JOURNEYFORTH

BJU Press, 1700 Wade Hampton Blvd., Greenville SC 29614-0001. (864)242-5100, ext. 4350. E-mail: jb@bjupress.com. Web site: www.bjupress.com. **Contact:** Nancy Lohr, acquisitions editor (juvenile fiction). Estab. 1974. "Small independent publisher of excellent, trustworthy novels for readers pre-school through high school. We desire to develop in our children a love for and understanding of the written word, ultimately helping them love and understand God's word." Publishes paperback originals and reprints. Books: 50 lb. white paper; Webb lithography printing; perfect binding. Average print order: 5,000. **Published some debut authors within the last year.** Averages 20-24 total titles. Distributes titles through Genesis Marketing, Spring Arbor and Appalachian.
Needs Adventure (children's/juvenile, young adult), historical (children's/juvenile, young adult), juvenile (animal, easy-to-read, series), mystery (children's/juvenile, young adult), sports (children's/juvenile, young adult), suspense (young adult), western (young adult), young adult (series). "Our fiction is all based on a moral and Christian wolrdview." Published *Susannah and the Secret Coins*, by Elaine Schulte (historical children's fiction); *Arby Jenkins Meets His Match*, by Sharon Hambrick (contemporary children's fiction); *Over the Divide*, by Catherine Farnes (young adult fiction).

How to Contact Accepts unsolicited mss. Query with SASE or submit outline, 5 sample chapters or submit complete ms. Include estimated word count, brief bio, social security number, list of publishing credits. Send SASE for return of ms or send a disposable ms and SASE for reply only. Responds in 1 month to queries; 3 months to mss. Accepts simultaneous submissions.

Terms Pays royalty. Publishes ms 12-18 months after acceptance. Ms guidelines online.

Advice "Study the publisher's guidelines. Make sure your work is suitable or you waste time for you and the publisher."

JUNO BOOKS

Wildside Press. (301)762-1305. Fax: (301)762-1306. E-mail: editor@juno-books.com. Web site: www.juno-books.com. **Contact:** Paula Guran, Editor (fantasy). Estab. 2006; Wildside 1989. "Juno Books is a small independent, but professional, publisher of a wide range of fantasy featuring strong female protagonists." Publishes hardcover originals, paperback originals, paperback reprints, e-books. Format: offset printing; mass market paperback or trade paperback bound. Average print order: mass market paperback first printing 10,000-25,000, trade 2000-5000. Debut novel print order: mass market paperback 10,000, trade 2000. **Published 6 new writers last year.** Plans 3 debut novels this year. Averages 14-18 fiction titles/year. Distributes/promotes titles nationally through Diamond Book Distribution. Promotion includes Web contests, conventions, print samplers, print ads, etc.

Needs "We welcome a cross-genre mix of contemporary and traditional FANTASY with mystery, thriller, paranormal romance, sf, adventure, historical fiction, detective, sensual, etc. Right now we're looking for contemporary and urban fantasy featuring strong female protagonists with 'kickassitude.' " Annually publishes *Best New Romantic Fantasy,* which features reprints of short stories from the previous year. Published *Matters of the Blood,* by Maria Lima (urban fantasy/paranormal romance); *The Eternal Rose,* by Gail Dayton (fantasy with romantic element); *Blood Magic,* by Matthew Cook (fantasy).

How to Contact Query with outline/synopsis and 3 sample chapters. Accepts queries by e-mail only. Include estimated word count, brief bio, list of best publishing credits. Agented fiction: 20%. Responds to queries in 3 months. Accepts unsolicited mss. Considers simultaneous submissions. Sometimes critiques/comments on rejected mss.

Terms Sends pre-production galleys to author. Ms published 6-24 months after acceptance. Writer's guidelines on Web site. Pays 6-10% royalties, average $1000 advance, author's copies. Advance is negotiable. Book catalog on Web site.

Advice "Women, in general, buy more books than men and display more author-loyalty than men. We feel fantasy that appeals to women—with a strong female protagonist and some sort of relationship involved—is a strong category and will continue to be so. As with any publisher, read our guidelines, please."

JUST US BOOKS, INC.

356 Glenwood Ave 3rd FL, East Orange NJ 07017. (973)672-7701. Fax: (973)677-7570. E-mail: info@justusbooks.com. Web site: www.justusbooks.com. Estab. 1988. Small independent publisher of children's books that focus on Black history, culture, and experiences (fiction and nonfiction). Publishes hardcover originals, paperback originals, hardcover reprints and paperback reprints (under its Sankofa Books imprint for previously published titles). Averages 4-8 total titles, 2-4 fiction titles/year. Member, Small Press Association; Children Book Council.

Needs Ethnic (African American), young adult (adventure, easy-to-read, historical, mystery/suspense, problem novels, series, sports). Published *Path to my African Eyes,* by Ermila Moodley.

How to Contact Does not accept unsolicited mss. Query with SASE, ms synopsis and pitch letter by mail only. Include brief bio, list of publishing credits. Send SASE for reply. Responds to queries in 10-12 weeks. Accepts simultaneous submissions.

Terms Pays royalty. Ms guidelines for SASE or on Web site.

Advice "We are looking for realistic, contemporary characters; stories and interesting plots that introduce both conflict and resolution. We will consider various themes and story-lines, but before an author submits a query we urge them to become familiar with our books."

JUSTIN, CHARLES & CO., PUBLISHERS

236 Huntington Ave., Ste 311, Boston MA 02115. (617)536-8601. E-mail: info@justincharlesbooks.com. Web site: www.justincharles.com. **Contact:** Stephen Hull, publisher (general fiction, mystery).

Estab. 2002. Publishes hardcover originals and paperback originals. **Published 4 debut authors within the last year.** Plans 2 first novels this year. Distributes in the U.S. and Canada through the National Book Network.

Imprint(s) Kate's Mystery Books.

Needs Humor, popular culture, mystery (amateur sleuth, police procedural, private eye/hard-boiled). Published *Las Vegas Little Black Book*, by David Demontmollin and Hiram Todd Norman (nonfiction); *Boyos*, by Richard Marinick (hard-boiled); *Second Sight*, Philip Craig and William Tapply (private eye); *The White Trilogy*, by Ken Bruen (mystery/police procedural).

How to Contact Accepts unsolicited mss. Query with SASE or submit 3-4 sample chapter(s), synopsis. Accepts queries by mail. Include brief bio, list of publishing credits. Send SASE for return of ms or send a disposable ms and SASE for reply only. Agented fiction 90%. Responds in 2 months to queries; 2-3 months to mss. Accepts simultaneous submissions. No electronic submissions, submissions on disk. Rarely comments on rejected mss.

Terms Publishes ms 1-2 years after acceptance. Ms guidelines online.

Advice "Please look at the types of books we have on our Web site and our writers guidelines."

KAEDEN BOOKS

P.O. Box 16190, Rocky River, OH 44116-6190. E-mail: lstenger@kaeden.com. Web site: www.kaeden.com. **Contact:** Lisa Stenger, Editor. Kaeden Books produces high-quality children's books for the educational market.

Needs Stories with humor, surprise endings and interesting characters suitable for the education market. "Must have well-developed plots with clear beginnings, middles and endings. No adult or religious themes." Word count range: 25-2,000.

How to Contact Submit complete ms; include SASE. Do not send originals. Respond within 1 year. For complete guidelines see www.kaeden.com. No phone calls please.

Terms Work purchased outright from authors. Pays royalties to previous authors.

Advice "We are particularly interested in humorous stories with surprise endings and beginning chapter books."

KEARNEY STREET BOOKS

P.O. Box 2021, Bellingham WA 98227. (360)738-1355. E-mail: garyrmc@mac.com. Web site: http://kearneystreetbooks.com. **Contact:** Gary McKinney, managing editor. Estab. 2003. "Books that rock—written by or about musicians or music." Publishes paperback originals. Perfect bound. Average print order: 200-2,000. Debut novel print order: 200. Plans 1 debut novel this year. Averages 1-2 total titles/year; 1-2 fiction titles/year. Member PMA, BPNW, PNBA. Distributes/promotes titles "marginally."

Needs Only publishes books about music or musicians. Published *Such a Killing Crime*, Robert Lopresti (mystery); *Tribute to Orpheus* (short story collection).

How to Contact Send query letter. Accepts queries by e-mail. Send disposable copy of ms and SASE for reply only. Responds to queries in 1 week. Accepts unsolicited mss. Responds to mss in 6-10 months. Considers simultaneous submissions, submissions on CD or disk. Never critiques/comments on rejected mss. Does not return rejected mss.

Terms Sends pre-production galleys to author. Manuscript published 18 months after acceptance. Pays "after expenses, profits split 50/50."

Advice "We publish very few titles. Nobody makes any money. This is all about the love of good fiction shunned by the corporations."

KENSINGTON PUBLISHING CORP.

850 Third Ave., 16th Floor, New York NY 10022. (212)407-1500. Fax: (212)935-0699. Web site: www.kensingtonbooks.com. **Contact:** John Scognamiglio, editor in chief (Kensington); Kate Duffy, editorial director (romance); Selena James, executive editor (African American fiction, Dafina Books); Audrey LaFehr, editorial director (women's fiction). Michaela Hamilton, executive editor. Estab. 1975. Full service trade commercial publisher, all formats. Publishes hardcover and trade paperback originals, mass market paperback originals and reprints. Averages over 500 total titles/year.

Imprint(s) Kensington; Dafina (Selena James, executive editor); Brava (Kate Duffy, editorial director); Aphrodisia; Kensington; Pinnacle; Zebra.

Needs Ethnic, gay/lesbian, historical, horror, mainstream/contemporary, multicultural, mystery, occult, romance (contemporary, historical, paranormal), suspense, thriller/espionage, western (epic), thrillers; women's. Published *Lost Souls*, by Lisa Jackson.

How to Contact Accepts unsolicited and unagented mss. Responds in 1 month to queries; 4 months to mss. Accepts simultaneous submissions.

Terms Pays 8-15% royalty on retail price or makes outright purchase. Average advance: $2,000 and up. Publishes ms 9-12 months after acceptance.

○ KOMENAR PUBLISHING

1756 LaCassie Ave., Ste. #202, Walnut Creek CA 94596. (510)444-2261. E-mail: komenar@komenarp ublishing.com. Web site: www.komenarpublishing.com. **Contact:** Charlotte Cook, president. Estab. 2005. "Komenar Publishing believes that a novel should be a compelling read. Readers are entitled to stories with strong forward momentum, engaging and dynamic characters, and evocative settings. The story must begin in the first chapter." Publishes hardcover originals. Averages 2-4 total titles/year.

Needs Well-written mss by first-time novelists.

How to Contact Send first 10 pages of ms, bio, and a cover letter. Responds to queries in 1-3 months. Considers simultaneous submissions. Responds to mss in 1-3 months. Proposal package must not exceed 12 total pages.

Terms Manuscript published 12 months after acceptance. Pays royalties. Book catalogs on Web site.

N ○ L&L DREAMSPELL

P.O. Box 1984, Friendswood TX 77546. E-mail: Administrator@lldreamspell.com. Web site: http://www.lldreamspell.com. **Contact:** Lisa René Smith, editor (fiction). "L&L Dreamspell is a micro publishing company based in the Houston, Texas area, publishing both fiction and nonfiction. Run by two gusty women, Linda Houle and Lisa Rene' Smith, we believe in making new author's dreams come true! We are a standard royalty paying publisher, and accept submissions for consideration through our Web site. We want to read outstanding mysteries, romance novels, and anything paranormal. Check our Web site for more information. We're still a young company—our nonfiction line was added in 2008. Linda and Lisa encourage all authors to follow their dreams . . . "Publishes paperback originals, e-books. Debut novel print order: 150. **Published 12 new writers last year.** Plans 12 debut novels this year. Averages 12 total titles/year; 12 fiction titles/year. Member PMA, SPAN. Distributes/promotes titles via Lightningsource, in addition to using a local printer (we also distribute our titles).

Needs adventure, erotica, fantasy, horror, mainstream, mystery/suspense, new age/mystic, romance. "We have MANY anthologies open for submission—too many to list! Writers may submit stories per our Web site's guidelines." Published *The Key*, by Pauline Baird Jones (mainstream romance/sci fi); *Cold Tears*, by John Foxjohn (mystery); *Dance on His Grave*, by Sylvia Dickey Smith (mystery).

How to Contact Query with outline/synopsis and 1 sample chapter. Accepts queries, submissions by e-mail only. Include estimated word count, list of publishing credits. Responds to queries in 2 weeks. Accepts unsolicited mss. Considers simultaneous submissions. Often critiques/comments on rejected mss. Responds to mss in 3 months.

Terms Sends pre-production galleys to author. Ms published 8 months after acceptance. Writer's guidelines on Web site. Pays royalties min 15%. Book catalogs not available.

Advice "We do pay attention to trends, but a great manuscript will always find an audience. Please follow our Web site submission guidelines if you want us to read your work."

N ⊠ ○ LACHESIS PUBLISHING

1787 Cartier Court, RR 1, Kingston, Nova Scotia B0P 1R0. Fax: (902)242-2178. E-mail: publisher@lac hesispublishing.com. Web site: www.lachesispublishing.com. **Contact:** Giovanna Lagana, senior editor (children's, romance, thriller/suspense); Louise Bohmer, editor-in-chief (horror /speculative); Dave Field, senior editor (western, science fiction); David Lee Summers, senior editor (science fiction, fantasy, paranormal). Estab. 2005. "Midsize independent publisher. Will assess all fiction but no poetry or collections of short stories." Publishes paperback originals, paperback reprints, e-books. Format: POD printing; some illustrations. Debut novel print order: 150. **Published 5 new writers last year.** Plans 6 debut novels this year. Averages 12 fiction titles/year.

Imprint(s) LBF Books.

Needs Adventure, children's/juvenile (fantasy, mystery, series), erotica, family saga, fantasy, gay, historical, horror, lesbian, mainstream, military/war, mystery/suspense, regional, romance, science fiction, thriller/espionage, western, young adult/teen. need erotica, gay and lesbian, and all types of romance

How to Contact Query with outline/synopsis and 3 sample chapters. Accepts queries by e-mail. Include estimated word count, brief bio, list of publishing credits, any connection with a writer's association. Responds to queries in 2 weeks. Accepts unsolicited mss. Considers simultaneous submissions. Always critiques/comments on rejected mss. Responds to mss in 3-5 months.

Terms Ms published 18 months after acceptance. Writer's guidelines on Web site. Pays royalties 10% min for print, 40% max for e-book.

Advice "Adhere to the guidelines on the Web site. Do not submit when house is closed to new submissions."

LAST KNIGHT PUBLISHING COMPANY

P.O. Box 270006, Fort Collins CO 80527. (970)391-6857. Fax: (720)596-6778. E-mail: ckaine@lastknightpublishing.com. Web site: www.LastKnightPublishing.com. **Contact:** Charles Kaine, publisher/owner. "Small independent publisher changing focus to narrow in on science fiction and fantasy. We are interested in making high quality books, both by the words written and how it is printed." Publishes paperback originals. Books: 70 lb. Vellum opaque paper; offset printed; perfect bound. Average print order: 1,500-4,000. Average first novel print order: 1,500. **Published 1 debut author within the last year.** Plans 2-3 first novels this year.

Needs Fantasy (space fantasy, sword and sorcery), magical realism, speculative fantasy, science fiction of all forms. Published *Ace on The River*, by Barry Greenstein, *The Breach*, by Brian Kaufman (historical fiction).

How to Contact Accepts unsolicited mss. Query with SASE or submit 3 sample chapter(s), synopsis. Accepts submissions by mail only. We do not respond to e-mail queries. Include estimated word count, brief bio, explanation of "why people will want to read the work." Send SASE for return of ms or send a disposable ms and SASE for reply only. Responds in 6 weeks to queries; 2-3 months to mss. Accepts simultaneous submissions. Often comments on rejected mss.

Terms Pays royalty. Average advance: negotiable. Publishes ms 9 months after acceptance. Ms guidelines online.

N LAVENDER ISIS PRESS

Lavender Isis Publishing, P.O. Box 47654, Tampa FL 33647. (602)703-8513. Fax: (602)795-8204. E-mail: info@lavenderisis.com. Web site: www.lavenderisis.com. **Contact:** Rae Lindley, publisher; Melissa Wathington, publisher. Estab. 2007. "We're a small independent publisher and writing community showcasing electronic and paperback books." Publishes paperback originals, e-books. **Published 4 new writers last year.** Plans 8 debut novels this year. Averages 26 fiction titles/year. Distributes/promotes titles via the Internet.

Imprint(s) Olympus Haven, Rae Lindley (sci-fi/fantasy); Praizes, Melissa Wathington (inspirational); Generations, Melissa Wathington (sci-fi/fantasy and inspirational).

Needs Fantasy, inspirational, science fiction. Published *The Dream King*, by Tara Newlands (urban fantasy/romance); *The Red Storm*, by Zinnia Hope (speculative romantic mystery); *The Eve of Alloria*, by Rae Lindley (illustrated spec fic).

How to Contact Accepts queries by snail mail, e-mail, fax. Responds to queries in 2 weeks, mss 1 month.

Terms Ms published within 6 months after acceptance. Pays royalties of 25-50%. Writer's guidelines on Web site.

Advice "Please double check your manuscript to make sure it is free of errors. Send your best creative work and even if we don't accept your submission, don't feel discouraged and by all means keep writing!"

LEAPFROG PRESS

Box 2110, Teaticket, MA 02536. E-mail: rana@leapfrogpress.com. Web site: www.leapfrogpress.com. **Contact:** Rana Hijrog, acquisitions editor. Estab. 1996. "We search for beautifully written literary titles and market them aggressively to national trade and library accounts. We also sell film, translation, foreign, and book club rights.'' Publishes paperback originals. Books: acid-free paper; sewn binding. Average print order: 5,000. First novel print order: 3,000-5,000 (average). Member, Publishers Marketing Association, PEN. Distributes titles through Consortium Book Sales and Distribution, St. Paul, MN. Promotes titles through all national review media, bookstore readings, author tours, Web site, radio shows, chain store promotions, advertisements, book fairs.

The Devil and Daniel Silverman by Theodore Rosak was nominated for the American Library Association Stonewall Award and was a San Francisco Chronicle best seller. *The German Money* by Lev Raphael was a Booksense 76 pick.

Needs ''Genres often blur; look for good writing. We are most interested in works that are quirky, that fall outside of any known genre, and of course are well written and finely crafted. We are most interested in literary fiction.'' Published *The War at Home*, by Nora Eisenberg; *Junebug*, by Maureen McCoy; *Paradise Dance*, by Michael Lee; *Waiting for Elvis*, by Toni Graham; and *Losing Kei*, by Suzanne Kamata. See web site for more recent titles.

How to Contact Query letter and first 5 to 10 ms pages. Prefers queries by e-mail. No attachments. Send SASE for return of ms or send a disposable ms and SASE for reply only. No response to e-mail queries unless we are interested. Responds in 3-6 months to queries by letter or e-mail; 6 months to mss. May consider simultaneous submissions.

Terms Pays 4-8% royalty on net receipts. Average advance: negotiable. Publishes ms 1-2 years after acceptance.

Advice ''We like anything that is superbly written and genuinely original. We like the idiosyncratic and the peculiar. We rarely publish nonfiction. Send only your best work, and send only completed work that is ready. That means the completed ms has already been through extensive editing and is ready to be judged. We consider submissions from both previously published and unpublished writers. We are uninterested in an impressive author bio if the work is poor; if the work is excellent, the author bio is equally unimportant.''

LEAPING DOG PRESS

P.O. Box 90473, Raleigh NC 27675-0473. (877)570-6873. Fax: (877)570-6873. E-mail: editor@leaping dogpress.com. Web site: www.leapingdogpress.com. **Contact:** Jordan Jones, editor and publisher.

🖪 🎯 LEE & LOW BOOKS INC.

95 Madison Ave., New York NY 10016-7801. (212)779-4400. Fax: (212)683-1894. E-mail: info@leean dlow.com. Web site: www.leeandlow.com. **Acquisitions:** Louise May, editor-in-chief; Jennifer Fox, senior editor. Publishes 12-14 children's books/year. 25% of books by first-time authors. Lee & Low Books publishes books with diverse themes. ''One of our goals is to discover new talent and produce books that reflect the diverse society in which we live.

- Lee & Low Books is dedicated to publishing culturally authentic literature. The company makes a special effort to work with writers and artists of color and encourages new voices.

Needs Picture books, young readers: anthology, contemporary, history, multicultural, poetry. ''We are not considering folktales or animal stories.'' Picture book, middle reader: contemporary, history, multicultural, nature/environment, poetry, sports. Average word length: picture books—1,000-1,500 words. Recently published Jazz Baby by Carol Boston Weatherford, illustrated by Laura Freeman; Home at Last by Susan Middleton Elya, illustrated by Felipe Davalos.

How to Contact Submit complete ms. No e-mail submissions. Responds in 4 months. Publishes a book 1-2 years after acceptance. Will consider simultaneous submissions. Guidelines on Web site. No SASE; Writer will be notified within 6 months if we have interest in the work. Manuscripts will not returned.

Terms Pays authors advances against royalty. Pays illustrators advance against royalty. Photographers paid advance against royalty. Book catalog available for 9×12 SAE and $1.65 postage; ms and art guidelines available via Web site or with SASE.

Advice ''We strongly urge writers to visit our Web site and familiarize themselves with our list before submitting. Materials will only be returned with SASE.''

🔀 🖪 LEISURE BOOKS

Dorchester Publishing Co., 200 Madison Ave., Suite 2000, New York NY 10016. (212)725-8811. Fax: (212)532-1054. Web site: www.dorchesterpub.com. **Contact:** Alissa Davis, editorial assistant. Estab. 1970. Publishes mass market paperback originals and reprints. Publishes romances, westerns, horrors, chick lit and thrillers only. Books: newsprint paper; offset printing; perfect bound. Average print order: variable. First novel print order: variable. Plans 25 first novels this year. Averages 255 total titles/year. Promotes titles through national reviews, ads, author readings, promotional items and on the Web site.

Imprint(s) Leisure Books.

Needs Horror, romance, western, thrillers, chick lit. "We strongly back first time writers. All historical romance should be set pre-1900. Horrors and westerns are growing as well. No sweet romance, science fiction, cozy mysteries." Published *The Price of Pleasure*, by Connie Mason (historical romance); *The Last Twilight*, by Marjorie M. Liu (paranormal romance); *Cuts*, by Richard Laymon (horror).

How to Contact Accepts unsolicited mss. Query with SASE or submit outline, first 3 sample chapters, synopsis. Agented fiction 70%. Responds in 6-8 months to queries. No simultaneous submissions, electronic submissions.

Terms Pays royalty on retail price. Average advance: negotiable. Publishes ms 12 months after acceptance. Book catalog for free (800)481-9191. Ms guidelines online.

Advice Encourage first novelists "if they are talented and willing to take direction and write the kind of genre fiction we publish. Please include a brief synopsis if sample chapters are requested."

⊘ LERNER PUBLISHING GROUP

241 First Ave. N., Minneapolis MN 55401. (612)332-3344. Fax: (612)332-7615. E-mail: info@lernerbo oks.com. Web site: www.lernerbooks.com. **Manuscript Acquisitions:** Jennifer Zimian, nonfiction submissions editor; Zelda Wagner, fiction submissions editor. Primarily publishes books for children ages 7-18. List includes titles in geography, natural and physical science, current events, ancient and modern history, high interest, sports, world cultures, and numerous biography series.

- Starting in 2007, Lerner Publishing Group no longer accepts submission in any of their imprints except for Kar-Ben Publishing.

How to Contact/Writers "We will continue to seek targeted solicitations at specific reading levels and in specific subject areas. The company will list these targeted solicitations on our Web site and in national newsletters, such as the SCBWI *Bulletin*."

⊠ LIFETIME BOOKS

Barclay Road Inc., 5005 Jean Talon #200, Montreal QC H3S 1G2 Canada. (514)807-5245. Fax: (206)350-5392. E-mail: pub@barclayroad.com. Web site: www.barclayroad.com. **Contact:** Barb Leonard, editor. Estab. 1998. Publishes hardcover originals, paperback originals, hardcover reprints, paperback reprints, e-books. Averages 5 total titles/year.

Needs Adventure, historical, juvenile, military, short story collections, sports, western, young adult.

How to Contact Submit complete ms with cover letter by e-mail only to subs@barclayroad.com. Responds to queries in 6 weeks. Considers simultaneous submissions. Responds to mss in 8 months.

Terms Manuscript published 18 months after acceptance. Writer's guidelines on Web site. Pays royalties, 3%-15%.

⊠ ◯ ◎ ⊠ LINDEN BAY ROMANCE, LLC

3529 Greenglen Circle, Palm Harbor FL 34684. E-mail: service@lindenbayromance.com. Web site: www.lindenbayromance.com. **Contact:** Barbabra Perfetti, managing editor (romance); Stephanie Wardall-Gaw, editor (romance). Estab. 2005. "Linden Bay Romance is an independent small press that publishes romance in electronic format and trade paperback. Our catalogue contains short stories, novellas and novels ranging in length from 10,000-80,000 words in all the usual romance sub-genres. We publish strictly romance, and do not publish drama or comedies whose main focus is not on the relationship of the main characters. Linden Bay is a royalty paying publisher, with no fees paid by authors." Publishes paperback originals, e-books. Format: POD printing. **Published 4 new writers last year.** Plans 3-4 debut novels this year. Averages 36 total titles/year; 36 fiction titles/year. Member AIPD, NYCIP. Distributes/promotes print titles with Baker & Taylor, then distributes through Amazon.com, Borders.com, Waldenbooks.com, and Target.com as well as from Web site. E-books are distributed through Allromancebooks.com, Mobipocket.com, Fictionwise.com, and Lightnightsource.com as well as through their affiliates. Between Your Sheets is the publicist for Linden Bay Romance and they conduct new release promotion.

• Linden Bay title *Ransom*, by Lee Rowan, won an EPPIE for Best GLBT Romance

Needs Romance (all sub-genres). "Trilogy" line, 3 short stories written by the same or different authors packaged together, is ongoing. Writers may submit directly when submissions are open. Otherwise, only agented and referred material will be accepted. Published *Walking Wounded*, by Lee Rowan (GLBT romance); *Forbidden: The Awakening*, by Samantha Sommersby (paranormal romance/urban fantasy); *Hiring Cupid*, by Jane Beckenham (contemporary romance).

How to Contact Query with outline/synopsis and 3 sample chapters. Accepts queries by e-mail. Include estimated word count, brief bio, list of publishing credits. Agented fiction: less than 5%. Responds to queries in 2-6 weeks. Accepts unsolicited mss. Considers simultaneous submissions, e-mail submissions. Always critiques/comments on rejected mss. Responds to mss in 2-4 weeks.

Terms Sends pre-production galleys to author. Ms published 3-6 months after acceptance. Writer's guidelines on Web site. Pays royalties. Book catalog on Web site.

Advice "We look for novels that focus on the developing relationship between a central pair of adult male and female characters as they discover their attraction to each other. Passion is paramount, and stories that contain a high level of unresolved sexual tension are given particular attention. Sex scenes can range from mildly erotic to very erotic, and can be as graphic as the story and the author's style deem appropriate. Please note: Sex between consenting adults only. We do not accept any submissions containing sex with minors (under 18). Also note that we require a 'happy ever after' type of ending."

ⒶⓍⓒ LITTLE, BROWN AND CO. BOOKS FOR YOUNG READERS

Division of Hachette Book Group USA (formerly AOL Time Warner Book Group), Time Life Building, 237 Park Avenue, New York NY 10169. (212)522-8700. Web site: www.twbookmark.com/children/index.html. Contact: Submissions editor. Estab. 1837. "We are looking for strong writing and presentation but no predetermined topics." Publishes hardcover originals, trade paperback reprints. Averages 100-150 total titles/year.

Imprint(s) Back Bay Books; Megan Tingley Books (Megan Tingley, VP publisher).

Needs Adventure, ethnic, fantasy, historical, humor, juvenile, mystery, picture books, science fiction, suspense, young adult. "We are looking for strong fiction for children of all ages in any area, including multicultural. We always prefer full manuscripts for fiction."

How to Contact *Agented submissions only.*

Terms Pays royalty on retail price. Average advance: negotiable. Publishes ms 2 years after acceptance. Ms guidelines online.

LIVINGSTON PRESS

University of West Alabama, Station 22, Livingston AL 35470. E-mail: jwt@uwa.edu. Web site: www.livingstonpress.uwa.edu. **Contact:** Joe Taylor, literary editor; Tina Jones, literary editor; Debbie Davis, literary editor. Estab. 1984. "Small university press specializing in offbeat and/or Southern literature." Publishes hardcover and trade paperback originals. Books: acid free; offset; some illustrations. Average print order: 2,500. First novel print order: 2,500. Plans 5 first novels this year. Averages 10 fiction titles/year.

Imprint(s) Swallow's Tale Press.

Needs Experimental, literary, short story collections, off-beat or southern. "We are interested in form and, of course style." Published *The Gin Girl*, by River Jordan (novel); *Pulpwood*, by Scott Ely (stories); *Live Cargo*, by Paul Toutonghi (stories).

How to Contact Query with SASE. Include estimated word count, brief bio, list of publishing credits. Send SASE for return of ms or send a disposable ms and SASE for reply only. Responds in 1 month to queries; 1 year to mss. Accepts simultaneous submissions. Send only in June and July.

Terms Pays 10% of 1,500 print run, 150 copies; thereafter pays a mix of royalties and books. Publishes ms 18 months after acceptance. Book catalog for SASE. Ms guidelines online.

ⓒ LLEWELLYN PUBLICATIONS

Llewellyn Worldwide, Ltd., 2143 Wooddale Drive, Woodbury MN 55125. (651)291-1970. Fax: (651)291-1908. E-mail: acquisitions@llewellyn.com. Web site: www.llewellyn.com, www.midnightinbooks.com, www.fluxnow.com. **Contact:** Barbara Moore, acquisitions editor (mystery: Midnight Ink imprint); Andrew Karre (young adult: flux imprint) Estab. 1901. The Llewellyn imprint specializes in New Age and Mind/Body/Spirit non-fiction. Two ficiton imprints, Midnight Ink (mystery) and Flux (young adult) accept novel submissions. Publishes trade paperback originals. **Published 30% debut authors within the last year.** Averages 100 total titles/year.

Needs Cozy mysteries, wide variety of young adult (teen, not middle grade).

How to Contact Responds in 3 months to queries. Accepts non-agented, simultaneous submissions.

Terms Pays 10% royalty on wholesale price or retail price. Submission guidelines online.

☑ ◎ LOST HORSE PRESS

105 Lost Horse Lane, Sandpoint ID 83864. (208)255-4410. Fax: (208)255-1560. E-mail: losthorsepress @mindspring.com. Web site: www.losthorsepress.org. **Contact:** Christine Holbert, publisher. Estab. 1998. Publishes hardcover and paperback originals. Books: 60-70 lb. natural paper; offset printing; b&w illustration. Average print order: 1,000-2,500. First novel print order: 500. **Published 2 debut authors within the last year.** Averages 4 total titles/year. Distributed by Eastern Washington University Press.

- *Woman on the Cross*, by Pierre Delattre, won the *ForeWord Magazine's* 2001 Book of the Year Award for literary fiction.

Needs Literary, regional (Pacific NW), short story collections, poetry. Published *Tales of a Dalai Lama*, by Pierre Delattre (literary fiction); *Love*, by Valerie Martin (short stories); *Hiding From Salesmen*, by Scott Poole; *Woman on the Cross*, by Pierre Delattre (magical realism); *Composing Voices*, by Robert Pack.

Terms Publishes ms 1-2 years after acceptance. Please check submission guidelines on Web site before submitting ms.

⋆ ☑ ◎ LOVE SPELL

Dorchester Publishing Co., Inc., 200 Madison Ave., 20th Floor, New York NY 10016. (212)725-8811. Fax: (212)532-1054. Web site: www.dorchesterpub.com. **Contact:** Alissa Davis, Editorial Assistant. Love Spell publishes the quirky sub-genres of romance: time-travel, paranormal, futuristic. "Despite the exotic settings, we are still interested in character-driven plots." Publishes mass market paperback originals. Books: newsprint paper; offset printing; perfect bound. Average print order: varies. First novel print order: varies. Averages 48 total titles/year.

Needs Romance (futuristic, time travel, paranormal, historical), whimsical contemporaries. "Books industry-wide are getting shorter; we're interested in 90,000 words." Published *Deep Magic*, by Joy Nas (historical romance); *Immortals: The Calling*, by Jennifer Ashley (paranormal romance).

How to Contact Accepts unsolicited mss. Query with SASE or submit 3 sample chapter(s), synopsis. Send SASE or IRC. Agented fiction 70%. Responds in 6-8 months to mss. No simultaneous submissions.

Terms Pays royalty on retail price. Average advance: varies. Publishes ms 1 year after acceptance. Book catalog for free (800)481-9191. Ms guidelines online.

Advice "The best way to learn to write a Love Spell Romance is by reading several of our recent releases. The best-written stories are usually ones writers feel passionate about—so write from your heart! Also, the market is very tight these days so more than ever we are looking for refreshing, standout original fiction."

◎ MARINE TECHNIQUES PUBLISHING, INC.

126 Western Ave., Suite 266, Augusta ME 04330-7249. (207)622-7984. Fax: (207)621-0821. E-mail: marinetechniques@midmaine.com. Web site: www.MarineTechPublishing.com. **Contact:** James L. Pelletier, president/CEO (commercial marine or maritime international); Christopher S. Pelletier, vice president operations; Jenelle M. Pelletier, editor in chief (national and international maritime related properties). **Published 15% debut authors within the last year.** Averages 3-5 total titles/ year.

Needs Must be commercial maritime/marine related.

How to Contact Submit complete ms. Responds in 2 months to queries; 6 months to mss. Accepts simultaneous submissions.

Terms Pays 25-43% royalty on wholesale or retail price. Publishes ms 6-12 months after acceptance.

Advice "Audience consists of commercial marine/maritime firms, persons employed in all aspects of the marine/maritime commercial and recreational fields, persons interested in seeking employment in the commercial marine industry, firms seeking to sell their products and services to vessel owners, operators and mangers in the commercial marine industry worldwide, etc."

☑ ◎ MCBOOKS PRESS

ID Booth Building, 520 N. Meadow St., Ithaca NY 14850. (607)272-2114. Fax: (607)273-6068. E-mail: jackie@mcbooks.com. Web site: www.mcbooks.com. **Contact:** Jackie Swift. Estab. 1979. Small independent publisher; specializes in historical fiction, American publisher of Alexander Kent's Richard Bolitho series and Julian Stockwin's Kydd novels. Also publishes John Biggins, James Duffy, Douglas W. Jacobson. Publishes trade paperback and hardcover originals and reprints. Averages 20 total titles, 14 fiction titles/year. Distributes titles through Independent Publishers Group.

Needs General historical, military historical.

How to Contact Does not accept unsolicited mss. Submission guidelines available on Web site. Query with SASE or via email. Include list of publishing credits. Responds in 3 months to queries. Accepts simultaneous submissions.

Terms Pays 5-10% royalty on retail price. Average advance: $1,000-5,000.

Advice "We are small and do not take on many unpublished writers. Looking for historical action-adventure stories that appeal to men, with a secondary appeal to women. Historical and military accuracy is a must. We are moving away from nautical fiction to some degree. Especially looking for stories with at least one strong female character."

❎ ◎ ☑ MARGARET K. MCELDERRY BOOKS

Simon & Schuster Children's Publishing Division, Simon & Schuster, 1230 Sixth Ave., New York NY 10020. (212)698-7605. Fax: (212)698-2797. Web site: www.simonsayskids.com. **Contact:** Emma D. Dryden, vice president/publisher. Estab. 1971. Publishes quality material for preschoolers to 18-year-olds. Publishes hardcover and paperback originals. Books: high quality paper; offset printing; three piece and POB bindings; illustrations. Average print order: 15,000. First novel print order: 10,000. **Published some debut authors within the last year.** Averages 35 total titles/year.

- Books published by Margaret K. McElderry Books have received numerous awards, including the Newbery and Caldecott Medals.

Needs Adventure, fantasy, historical, mainstream/contemporary, mystery, picture books, young adult (or middle grade). All categories (fiction and nonfiction) for juvenile and young adult. "We will consider any category. Results depend on the quality of the imagination, the artwork and the writing." Published *Dr. Ted*, by Andrea Beaty; illustrated by Pascal LeMaitre and *Bear Feels Sick* by Karma Wilson; Illustrated by Jane Chapeman (picture books); *Sight*, by Adrienne Maria Vrettos (middle-grade fiction); *City of Bones* and *City of Ashes* by Cassandra Clare (teen fiction), by *OOPS!* by Alan Kaatz; illustrated by Edward Koren (poetry).

Terms Average print order is 10,000-15,000 for a first middle grade or young adult book; 7,500-20,000 for a first picture book. Pays royalty on hardcover retail price: 10% fiction; 5% author, 5% illustrator (picture book). Offers $5,000-8,000 advance for new authors. Publishes ms up to 3 years after acceptance. Ms guidelines for #10 SASE.

Advice "Imaginative writing of high quality is always in demand; also picture books that are original and unusual. Keep in mind that McElderry is a very small imprint, so we are very selective about the books we will undertake for publication. We try not to publish any 'trend' books. Be familiar with our list and with what is being published this year by all publishing houses."

☑ MEDALLION PRESS, INC.

P.O. Box 48889, Tampa, Fl 33646. Web site: www.medallionpress.com. **Contact:** Kerry Estevez, acquisitions editor. Estab. 2003. "We are an independent publisher looking for books that are outside of the box. Please do not submit to us if you are looking for a large advance. We reserve our funds for marketing the books." Publishes paperback originals. Average print order: 5,000. **Published 20+ debut authors within the last year.**

Imprint(s) Platinum/Hardcover; Gold/Mass Market; Silver/Trade Paper; Bronze/Young Adult; Jewel/Romance; Amethyst/Fantasy, Sci-Fi, Paranormal; Emerald/Suspense; Ruby/Contemporary; Sapphire/Historical.

Needs Adventure, ethnic, fantasy (space fantasy, sword and sorcery), glitz, historical, horror (dark fantasy, futuristic, psychological, supernatural), humor, literary, mainstream/contemporary, military/war, mystery (amateur sleuth, police procedural, private eye/hard-boiled), romance, science fiction (hard science/technological, soft/sociological), thriller/espionage, western (frontier saga), young adult. Published *Siren's Call*, by Mary Ann Mitchell (horror); *Grand Traverse*, by Michael Beres (mainstream fiction); *Memories of Empire*, by Django Wexler (epic fantasy).

How to Contact Does not accept unsolicited mss. "Minimum word count 80K for adult fiction, 55K for YA, no exceptions." No poetry, anthologies, erotica or inspirational. Submit first 3 consecutive chapters and a chapter-by-chapter synopsis. "Without the synopsis, the submission will be rejected." Accepts queries only by mail. No e-mail queries. Include estimated word count, brief bio, list of publishing credits. Send SASE or IRC. Responds in 4-8 months to mss. Accepts simultaneous submissions. Sometimes comments on rejected mss.

Terms Offers advance. Publishes ms 1-2 years after acceptance. Ms guidelines online.

Advice "We are not affected by trends. We are simply looking for well crafted, original, grammatically correct works of fiction. Please visit our Web site for the most current guidelines prior to submitting anything to us."

◎ MERIWETHER PUBLISHING, LTD.

885 Elkton Dr., Colorado Springs CO 80907-3557. (719)594-4422. Fax: (719)594-9916. Web site: www.meriwetherpublishing.com; www.contemporarydrama.com. **Contact:** Rhonda Wray, associate editor (church plays); Ted Zapel, editor (school plays, comedies, books). Estab. 1969. "Mid-size, independent publisher of plays. We publish plays for teens, mostly one-act comedies, holiday plays for churches and musical comedies. Our books are on the theatrical arts." Publishes paperback originals and reprints. Books: quality paper; printing house specialist; paperback binding. Average print order: 5,000-10,000. **Published 25-35 debut authors within the last year.**

Needs Mainstream/contemporary, comedy, religious (children's plays and religious Christmas and Easter plays), suspense—all in playscript format. Published *Pirates and Petticoats*, by Pat Cook (a two-act pirate comedy); *Let Him Sleep Until it's Time for His Funeral*, by Peg Kehret (two-act play).

How to Contact Accepts unsolicited mss. Query with SASE. Accepts queries by e-mail. Include list of publishing credits. Send SASE for return of ms or send a disposable ms and SASE for reply only. Responds in 3 weeks to queries; 2 months to mss. Accepts simultaneous submissions. Sometimes comments on rejected mss.

Terms Pays 10% royalty on retail price or makes outright purchase. Publishes ms 6-12 months after acceptance. Book catalog and ms guidelines for $2 postage.

Advice "If you're interested in writing comedy/farce plays, we're your best publisher."

◿ MILKWEED EDITIONS

1011 Washington Ave. S., Suite 300, Minneapolis MN 55415. (612)332-3192. Fax: (612)215-2550. E-mail: editor@milkweed.org. Web site: www.milkweed.org. **Contact:** Daniel Slager, Publisher; The Editors, first reader. Estab. 1984. Nonprofit publisher. Publishes hardcover originals and paperback originals and reprints. Books: book text quality—acid-free paper; offset printing; perfect or hardcover binding. Average print order: 4,000. First novel print order depends on book. **Published some debut authors within the last year.** Averages 15 total titles/year. Distributes through Publisher's Group West. Each book has its own marketing plan involving print ads, tours, conferences, etc.

Needs Literary. Novels for adults and for readers 8-13. High literary quality. For adult readers: literary fiction, nonfiction, poetry, essays; for children (ages 8-13): literary novels. Translations welcome for both audiences. Published *The Blue Sky*, by Galsan Tschinag (translation); *Visigoth*, by Gary Amdahl (first fiction, short stories); *The Farther Shore*, by Matthew Eck.

How to Contact Submit complete ms. Responds in 2 months to queries; 6 months to mss. Accepts simultaneous submissions.

Terms Variable royalty on retail price. Average advance: varied. Publishes ms 1-2 years after acceptance. Book catalog for $1.50 postage. Ms guidelines online.

Advice "Read good contemporary literary fiction, find your own voice, and persist. Familiarize yourself with our list before submitting."

✬ ◎ MILKWEED FOR YOUNG READERS

Milkweed Editions, 1011 Washington Ave. S., Suite 300, Minneapolis MN 55415. (612)332-3192. Fax: (612)215-2550. Web site: www.milkweed.org. **Contact:** Daniel Slager, Publisher; Children's reader. Estab. 1984. "Milkweed for Young Readers are works that embody humane values and contribute to cultural understanding." Publishes hardcover and trade paperback originals. Averages 1-2 total titles/year. Distributes titles through Publishers Group West. Promotes titles individually through print advertising, Web site and author tours.

• *Perfect*, by Natasha Friend, was chosen as a Book Sense 76 Children's Book selection. **Needs** Adventure, historical, humor, mainstream/contemporary, animal, environmental. For ages 8-13. Published *The Cat*, By Jutta Richter, and *The Linden Tree* by Ellie Mathews.
How to Contact Query with SASE. Agented fiction 30%. Responds in 2 months to queries. Accepts simultaneous submissions.
Terms Pays 6% royalty on retail price. Average advance: variable. Publishes ms 1 year after acceptance. Book catalog for $1.50. Ms guidelines for #10 SASE or on the Web site.
Advice "Familiarize yourself with our books before submitting. You need not have a long list of credentials—excellent work speaks for itself."

▦ ◪ MONSOON BOOKS

52 Telok Blangah Road, #03-05 Telok Blangah House, 098829 Singapore. (+65)63776272. Fax: (+65)62761743. E-mail: sales@monsoonbooks.com.sg. Web site: www.monsoonbooks.com.sg. **Contact**: Philip Tatham (all fiction). Estab. 2002. "Monsoon Books is a small independent publisher of fiction and memoirs, based in Asia with worldwide distribution." Publishes paperback originals, paperback reprints. Books: Mungken 80 gram paper; offset printing; threadsewn binding. Average print order: 3,000. First novel print order: 3,000. **Published 7 new writers last year**. Plans 10 first novels this year. Averages 20 total titles/year; 12 fiction titles/year. Distributes titles through Worldwide Distribution and promotes through Freelance Publicists for USA and Asia.
Needs erotica, ethnic/multicultural, family saga, gay, historical, horror (supernatural), humor satire, literary, mainstream, military/war, mystery/suspense (police procedural, private eye/hard-boiled), regional (Asia), thriller/espionage, translations, young adult (romance). Special interests: Southeast Asia. Published *Rouge Raider*, by Nigel Barley (historical fiction); *In Lust We Trust*, by Gerrie Lim (new journalism); *Private Dancer*, by Stephen Leather (general fiction/international relationships).
How to Contact Query with outline/synopsis and submit complete ms with cover letter. Accepts queries by snail mail, fax and e-mail. Please include estimated word count, brief bio, list of publishing credits, and list of three comparative titles. Send SASE or IRC for return of ms. Agented fiction 20%. Responds in 1 week to queries; 12 weeks to manuscripts. Accepts simultaneous submissions, submissions on CD or disk. Rarely comments on rejected manuscripts.
Terms Pays 7-10% royalty. Advance is negotiable. Publishes ms 6-12 months after acceptance. Guidelines online.
Advice "Due to the difficulty of getting published in New York and London, Monsoon represents a more viable option and is attracting new writers from USA, UK and Australia."

◪ ◎ MOODY PUBLISHERS

Moody Bible Institute, 820 N. LaSalle Blvd., Chicago IL 60610. E-mail: acquisitions@moody.edu. **Contact:** Acquistions Coordinator (all fiction). Estab. 1894. Small, evangelical Christian publisher. "We publish fiction that reflects and supports our evangelical worldview and mission." Publishes hardcover, trade and mass market paperback originals. Averages 70 total titles, 10-12 fiction titles/year. Member, CBA. Distributes and promotes titles through sales reps, print advertising, promotional events, Internet, etc.
Needs contemporary, historical, literary, mystery, suspense, science fiction. Recently published *My Hands Came Away Red*, by Lisa McKay (suspense novel); *Feeling for Bones*, by Bethany Pierce (contemporary/literary).
How to Contact Accepts unsolicited mss. proposal with SASE and two chapters. Accepts queries by mail and e-mail. Include estimated word count, brief bio, list of publishing credits. Send SASE for return of ms or send a disposable ms and SASE for reply only. Agented fiction 75%. Responds in 4-5 months to queries. Accepts electronic submissions.
Terms Royalty varies. Average advance: $1,000-10,000. Publishes ms 9-12 months after acceptance. Ms guidelines for SASE and on Web site.
Advice "Get to know Moody Publishers and understand what kinds of books we publish. We will decline all submissions that do not support our evangelical Christian beliefs and mission."

◎ MOUNTAIN STATE PRESS

2300 MacCorkle Ave. SE, Charleston WV 25304-1099. (304)357-4767. Fax: (304)357-4715. E-mail: msp1@mountainstatepress.org. Web site: www.mountainstatepress.org. **Contact:** Rhonda Thomas. Estab. 1978. "A small nonprofit press run by a volunteer board. We specialize in books about West

Virginia or by authors from West Virginia. We strive to give a voice to Appalachia." Publishes paperback originals and reprints. Plans 2 first novels this year. Distributes titles through bookstores, distributors, gift shops and individual sales (Amazon.com and Barnes & Noble online carry our titles). Promotes titles through newspapers, radio, mailings and book signings.

Needs Family saga, historical (West Virginia), military/war, new age/mystic, religious. Currently compiling an anthology of West Virginia authors. Published *Lucinda's Mountain*, by Adda Leah Davis; *Family Spirit*, by Jill Thompson Decker .

How to Contact Accepts unsolicited mss. Query with SASE or submit complete ms. Accepts queries by e-mail, fax. Include estimated word count, brief bio. Send SASE for return of ms or send a disposable ms and SASE for reply only. Responds in 6 months to mss. Often comments on rejected mss.

Terms Pays royalty.

Advice "Topic of West Virginia is the best choice for our press. Send your manuscript in and it will be read and reviewed by the members of the Board of Mountain State Press. We give helpful suggestions and critique the writing."

MOYER BELL, LTD.

549 Old North Rd., Kingston RI 02881. (401)783-5480. Fax: (401)284-0959. E-mail: moyerbellbooks@ yahoo.com. Web site: www.moyerbellbooks.com. Averages 15 total titles/year.

Imprint(s) Asphodel Press.

Needs Literary.

How to Contact Query with SASE.

Terms Pays 6-10% royalty on retail price.

☑ NBM PUBLISHING

40 Exchange Pl., Ste. 1308, New York NY 10005. Web site: www.nbmpub.com. **Contact:** Terry Nantier, editor/art director. Estab. 1976. "One of the best regarded quality graphic novel publishers. Our catalog is determined by what will appeal to a wide audience of readers." Publishes hardcover originals, paperback originals. Format: offset printing; perfect binding. Average print order: 3,000-4,000; average debut writer's print order: 2,000. Publishes 1-2 debut writers/year. Publishes 30 titles/year. Member: PMA, CBC. Distributed/promoted "ourselves." Imprints: ComicsLit (literary comics), Eurotica (erotic comics).

Needs Children's/juvenile (especially fairy tales, classics), creative nonfiction (especially true crime), erotica, ethnic/multicultural, fantasy, historical, horror (dark fantasy, psychological), humor (satire), literary, manga, mystery/suspense, romantic suspense, science fiction, translations, young adult/teen. Does not want superhero or overly violent comics.

How to Contact Prefers submissions from writer-artists, creative teams. Send a one-page synopsis of story along with a few pages of comics (copies NOT originals) and a SASE. Attends San Diego Comicon. Agented submissions: 2%. Responds to queries in 1 week; to ms/art packages in 3-4 weeks. Sometimes comments on rejected manuscripts.

Terms Royalties and advance negotiable. Publishes ms 6 months to 1 year after acceptance. Writer's guidelines on Web site. Artist's guidelines on Web site. Book catalog free upon request.

☑ ◎ THOMAS NELSON, INC.

Box 141000, Nashville TN 37214-1000. (615)889-9000. Web site: www.thomasnelson.com. **Contact:** Acquisitions Editor. "Largest Christian book publisher." Publishes hardcover and paperback orginals. Averages 100-150 total titles/year.

Needs Publishes commercial fiction authors who write for adults and teens 12 and up from a Christian worldview. Published *A Time to Dance*, by Karen Kingsbury; *Saint*, by Ted Dekker; and *Hood*, by Stephen Lawhead.

How to Contact Does not accept unsolicited mss or queries.

Terms Pays royalty on net receipts. Rates negotiated for each project. Offers advance. Publishes ms 1-2 years after acceptance. Ms guidelines online.

Advice "We publish stories that are written form a Christian worldview. The authors must be Christians, but the stories do not need to have an overt Christian message. We're interested in publishing the best stories to the broadest audiences."

◪ ◎ ◿ NEW VICTORIA PUBLISHERS

P.O. Box 13173, Chicago IL 60613-0173. (773)793-2244. E-mail: newvicpub@aol.com. Web site: www.newvictoria.com. **Contact:** Patricia Feuerhaken, president. Estab. 1976. "Publishes mostly lesbian fiction—strong female protagonists. Most well known for Stoner McTavish mystery series." Publishes trade paperback originals. Averages 2-3 total titles/year. Distributes titles through Bookworld (Sarasota, FL) and Bulldog Books (Sydney, Australia). Promotes titles "mostly through lesbian feminist media."

- *Mommy Deadest*, by Jean Marcy, won the Lambda Literary Award for Mystery.

Needs Lesbian, feminist fiction including adventure, erotica, fantasy, historical, humor, mystery (amateur sleuth), or science fiction. "Looking for strong feminist, well drawn characters, with a strong plot and action. We will consider any original, well written piece that appeals to the lesbian/feminist audience." Publishes anthologies or special editions. Published *Killing at the Cat*, by Carlene Miller (mystery); *Queer Japan*, by Barbara Summerhawk (anthology); *Skin to Skin*, by Martha Miller (erotic short fiction); *Talk Show*, by Melissa Hartman (novel); *Flight From Chador*, by Sigrid Brunel (adventure); *Owl of the Desert*, by Ida Swearingen (novel).

How to Contact Accepts unsolicited mss. Submit outline, sample chapter(s), synopsis. Accepts queries by e-mail, fax. Send SASE or IRC. No simultaneous submissions.

Terms Pays 10% royalty. Publishes ms 1 year after acceptance. Ms guidelines for SASE.

Advice "We are especially interested in lesbian or feminist novels, ideally with a character or characters who can evolve through a series of books. Stories should involve a complex plot, accurate details, and protagonists with full emotional lives. Pay attention to plot and character development. Read guidelines carefully."

◳ ◎ NEWEST PUBLISHERS LTD.

201, 8540-109 St., Edmonton AB T6G 1E6 Canada. (780)432-9427. Fax: (780)433-3179. E-mail: info@newestpress.com. Web site: www.newestpress.com. **Contact:** Lou Morin, General Manager. Estab. 1977. Publishes trade paperback originals. **Published some debut authors within the last year.** Averages 11-14 total titles/year. Promotes titles through book launches, media interviews, review copy mailings.

Imprint(s) Prairie Play Series (drama); Writer as Critic (literary criticism); Nunatak New Fiction.

Needs Literary. "Our press is interested in Western Canadian writing." Published *Icefields*, by Thomas Wharton (novel); *Blood Relations and Other Plays*, by Sharon Pollock (drama); *A Thirst to Die For*, by Ian Waddell (mystery, debut author).

How to Contact Accepts unsolicited mss. Submit complete ms. Send SASE or IRC. Responds in 9-12 months to queries. Accepts simultaneous submissions.

Terms Pays 10% royalty. Publishes ms 24-30 months after acceptance. Book catalog for 9 × 12 SASE. Ms guidelines online.

Advice "We publish western Canadian writers only or books about western Canada. We are looking for excellent quality and originality."

ℕ ◿ NOW COMICS

Now Media Group, Inc. (815)919-2586. E-mail: info@nowcomics.com. Web site: www.nowcomics.com. **Contact:** Tony Caputo and Barry Peterson. Estab. 2003. "Small independent publisher of graphic novels, trade paperbacks, and comic books." Publishes paperback originals, hardcover reprints, paperback reprints. Format: matte/gloss paper; offset/digital printing; perfect bound. **Published 1 new writer last year.** Averages 3 total titles/year.

Needs Adventure, children's/juvenile, experimental, family saga, fantasy, historical, horror, humor, manga, mystery/suspense, psychic/supernatural, religious, romance, science fiction, thriller espionage, translations, young adult/teen. Does not want superhero stories. Published *Vespers*, by Tony C. Caputo (horror); *Vinny The Bug Man*, by Chet Spelwak (children's); *Doctor Gordon*, by Marc Hansen (humor).

How to Contact Responds to queries in 1 week. Considers simultaneous submissions, submissions on CD or disk, e-mail submissions. Always critiques/comments on rejected mss.

◻ ◿ OAK TREE PRESS

140 E. Palmer St., Taylorville IL 62568. (217)824-6500. Fax: (217)824-2040. E-mail: oaktreepub@aol.com. Web site: www.oaktreebooks.com. **Contact:** Billie Johnson, publisher (mysteries, romance,

nonfiction); Sarah Wasson, acquisitions editor (all); Barbara Hoffman, senior editor (children's, young adult, educational). Estab. 1998. "Small independent publisher with a philosophy of author advocacy. Welcomes first-time authors, and sponsors annual contests in which the winning entries are published." Publishes hardcover, trade paperback and mass market paperback originals and reprints. Books: acid-free paper; perfect binding. First novel print order: 1,000. **Published 4 debut authors within the last year.** Plans 8 first novels this year. Averages 12 total titles, 8 fiction titles/year. Member: SPAN, SPAWN. Distributes through Ingram, Baker & Taylor and Amazon.com. Promotes through Web site, conferences, PR, author tours.

● *Affinity for Murder*, by Anne White, was an Agatha Award finalist. *Timeless Love*, by Mary Montague Sikes, received a Prism Award.

Imprint(s) Oak Tree Press, Dark Oak Mysteries, Timeless Love, Coptales, Acorn Books for Children (children's, YA).

Needs Adventure, confession, ethnic, fantasy (romance), feminist, humor, mainstream/contemporary, mystery (amateur sleuth, cozy, police procedural, private eye/hard-boiled), new age/mystic, picture books, romance (contemporary, futuristic/time travel, romantic suspense), suspense, thriller/espionage, young adult (adventure, mystery/suspense, romance). Emphasis on mystery and romance novels. Recently published *The Poetry of Murder*, by Bernadette Steele (mystery); *A Lesson in Murder,* by Augustus Cileone(mystery); *Feild of Destiny*, by Patricia Sheehy (romance); *Eagle Rising*, by Mary Montague Sikes (paranormal romance); *Code Two °N° a Half,* by William Wilhelm (memoir-police officer), and Burning Questions, by Elaine Busby(contemporary romance).

How to Contact Does not accept or return unsolicited mss. Query with SASE. Accepts queries by e-mail. Include estimated word count, brief bio, list of publishing credits, brief description of ms. Send SASE for return of ms or send a disposable ms and SASE for reply only. Agented fiction 5%. Responds in 4-6 weeks to queries; 2 months to proposals; 3-6 months to mss. Accepts simultaneous submissions, electronic submissions. No submissions on disk. Rarely comments on rejected mss.

Terms Pays 10-20% royalty on wholesale price. Average advance: negotiable. Publishes ms 9-18 months after acceptance. Book catalog for SASE or on Web site www.oaktreebooks.com. Ms guidelines for SASE or on Web site.

Advice "Understand the business and be eager and enthusiastic about participating in the marketing and promotion of the title."

N ⊠ ⊘ ⊙ OBRAKE BOOKS

Obrake Canada, Inc., 3401 Dufferin Street, P.O. Box 27538, Toronto, ON M6A3B8. Fax: (416)907-5734. E-mail: editors@obrake.com. Web site: www.obrake.com. **Contact:** Echez Godoy, acquisitions editor (fiction-suspense, thriller, multicultural, science fiction, literary, romance, short story collection, mystery, ethnic, African based novels, African American characters and interest). Estab. 2006. "We're a small independent publisher of hardcover and trade-paper fiction and nonfiction books. We publish mainly thriller, suspense, romance, mystery, multicutural, and ethnic novels and short story collections." Publishes hardcover originals, paperback originals, paperback reprints. Average print order: 1,500. Debut novel print order: 1,500. **Published 1 new writer last year.** Plans 3 debut novels this year. Averages 10 total titles/year; 7 fiction titles/year. Member Independent Publishers Association PMA (USA), Canadian Booksellers Association (CBA), Book Promoters Association of Canada (BPAC). Distributes/promotes titles through national distributors in USA and Canada, Library Suppliers/Buyers, Chain bookstores (e.g. Barnes and Nobles [USA], Chapters/Indigo Bookstore [Canada]), Indigo Books & Music, Online (Amazon), worldwide distribution.

Needs Adventure, children's/juvenile (adventure, fantasy, historical, mystery), comics/graphic novels, erotica, ethnic/multicultural, feminist, gay, historical (general), horror (psychological, supernatural), lesbian, literary, mainstream, mystery/suspense, psychic/supernatural, regional, religious (mystery/suspense, thriller, romance), romance (contemporary, historical, romantic suspense), short story collections, thriller/espionage, young adult/teen (adventure, fantasy/science fiction, historical, horror, romance). Published *Corrupted Ambition*, by Obi Orakwue (thriller/suspense); *The Terrorist Creed*, by Obi Orakwue (suspense); *Overqualified Labourer*, by Obi Orakwue (mystery).

How to Contact Send query letter. Query with outline/synopsis and 3 sample chapters, 50 pages max. Accepts queries by snail mail, e-mail. Include estimated word count, brief bio. Send SASE or IRC for return of ms or disposable copy of ms and SASE/IRC for reply only. Agented fiction: 5%. Responds to queries in 3-6 weeks. Accepts unsolicited mss. Considers simultaneous submissions,

submissions on CD or disk. Rarely critiques/comments on rejected mss. Responds to mss in 3-6 months.

Terms Sends pre-production galleys to author. Ms published 10 months after acceptance. Writer's guidelines available for SASE, on Web site. Pays royalties 8-15%, advance $350 average. Book catalogs free upon request.

Advice "Follow our submission guidelines."

OMNIDAWN PUBLISHING

Omnidawn Corporation, P.O. Box 5224, Richmond CA 94805-5224. (510)237-5472. E-mail: submissions@omnidawn.com. Web site: www.omnidawn.com. **Contact:** Rusty Morrison and Ken Keegan, editors. Estab. 2001. Omnidawn is a small independent publisher run by two part-time editors. "We specialize in new wave fabulist and fabulist fiction and innovative poetry. See Web site for complete description." Publishes primarily paperback originals. Books: archival quality paper; offset printing; trade paperback binding. Average print order: 3,000. Plans 1 first novel this year. Distributes titles through Independent Publishers Group.

Needs New wave fabulist and fabulist.

How to Contact See Web site for details regarding submission policies and contact procedures, which are subject to change. No electronic or disk submissions.

Terms Publishes ms 6-12 months after acceptance. Ms guidelines online.

Advice "Check our Web site for latest information."

ORCA BOOK PUBLISHERS

P.O. Box 5626, Victoria BC V8R 6S4 Canada. (250)380-1229. Fax: (250)380-1892. E-mail: orca@orcabook.com. Web site: www.orcabook.com. **Contact:** Christi Howes, children's book editor. Estab. 1984. Only publishes Canadian authors. Publishes hardcover and trade paperback originals, and mass market paperback originals and reprints. Books: quality 60 lb. book stock paper; illustrations. Average print order: 3,000-5,000. First novel print order: 3,000-5,000. Plans 3-4 first novels this year. Averages 50 total titles/year.

Needs Hi-lo, juvenile (5-9 years), literary, mainstream/contemporary, young adult (10-18 years). "Ask for guidelines, find out what we publish." Looking for "children's fiction."

How to Contact Query with SASE or submit proposal package including outline, 2-5 sample chapter(s), synopsis, SASE. Agented fiction 20%. Responds in 1 month to queries; 1-2 months to mss. No simultaneous submissions. Sometimes comments on rejected mss.

Terms Pays 10% royalty. Publishes ms 12-18 months after acceptance. Book catalog for 8½×11 SASE. Ms guidelines online.

Advice "We are looking to promote and publish Canadians."

OUR CHILD PRESS

P.O. Box 4379, Philadelphia PA 19118-8379. (610)308-8988. E-mail: ourchldpress@aol.com. Web site: www.ourchildpress.com. **Contact:** Carol Perrott, CEO. Estab. 1984. Publishes hardcover and paperback originals and reprints.

• Received the Ben Franklin Award for *Don't Call Me Marda*, by Sheila Welch.

Needs Especially interested in books on adoption or learning disabilities. Published *Things Little Kids Need to Know*, by Susan Uhlig.

How to Contact Does not accept unsolicited mss. Query with SASE. Responds in 2 weeks to queries; 2 months to mss. Accepts simultaneous submissions. Sometimes comments on rejected mss.

Terms Pays 5% royalty. Publishes ms 6 months after acceptance.

OUTRIDER PRESS, INC.

2036 North Winds Drive, Dyer IN 46311. (219)322-7270. Fax: (219)322-7085. E-mail: outriderpress@sbcglobal.net. Web site: www.outriderpress.com. **Contact:** Whitney Scott, editor. Estab. 1988. Small literary press and hand bindery; publishes many first-time authors. Publishes paperback originals. Books: 70 lb. paper; offset printing; perfect bound. Average print order: 2,000. **Published 25-30 debut authors within the last year.** Distributes titles through Baker & Taylor.

• Was a *Small Press Review* "Pick" for 2000.

Needs Ethnic, experimental, family saga, fantasy (space fantasy, sword and sorcery), feminist, gay/lesbian, historical, horror (psychological, supernatural), humor, lesbian, literary, mainstream/contemporary, mystery (amateur sleuth, cozy, police procedural, private eye/hard-boiled), new age/ mystic, psychic/supernatural, romance (contemporary, futuristic/time travel, gothic, historical, regency period, romantic suspense), science fiction (soft/sociological), short story collections, thriller/ espionage, western (frontier saga, traditional). Published *Telling Time*, by Cherie Caswell Dost; *If Ever I Cease to Love*, by Robert Klein Engler.

How to Contact Accepts unsolicited mss. Query with SASE. Accepts queries by mail. Include estimated word count, brief bio, list of publishing credits. Agented fiction 10%. Responds in 3 weeks to queries; 4 months to mss. Accepts simultaneous submissions, electronic submissions, submissions on disk. Sometimes comments on rejected mss. In affiliation with Tallgrass Writers Guild, publishes an annual anthonlogy with cash prizes. 2009 themes is: "Fearsome Fascinations: Vampires, Zombies. Artificial Intelligence (with hostile intent) and other frights. As always, broadly interpreted." Deadline is February 27, 2009. For details and complete guidelines, e-mail outriderpress@sbcglobal.net.

Terms Pays honorarium. Publishes ms 6 months after acceptance. Ms guidelines for SASE.

Advice "It's always best to familiarize yourself with our publications. We're especially fond of humor/irony."

◙ PANTHER CREEK PRESS

104 Plum Tree Terrace #115, Houston TX 77077. E-mail: panthercreek3@hotmail.com. Web site: www.panthercreekpress.com. **Contact:** Guida Jackson, publisher; Ted Walthen, editor (literary); Jerry Cooke, assistant editor (mystery). Estab. 1999. "Mid-size publisher interested in Merchant-Ivory type fiction." Publishes paperback originals. Books: 60 lb. white paper; docutech-printed; perfect bound. Average print order: 1,500. **Published 4 debut authors within the last year.** Distributes titles through Baker & Taylor, Amazon.

Imprint(s) Enigma Books, Jerry Cooke, editor (mystery); Claredon House, Guida Jackson (literary).

Needs Ethnic, experimental, humor, literary, mainstream/contemporary, multicultural, mystery (amateur sleuth), regional (Texana), short story collections. Published *The Caballeros of Ruby, Texas*, by Cynthia Leal Massey (literary); *Salvation and Other Stories*, by Terry Dalrymple (collection); *Sue Ellen Learns to Dance*, by Judy Alter (collection).

How to Contact Will not read unsolicited mss. Query with SASE. Accepts queries only by e-mail. Include estimated word count, brief bio, list of publishing credits. Send SASE for return of ms or send a disposable ms and SASE for reply only. Responds in 3 weeks to queries; 2 months to mss. Accepts simultaneous submissions.

Terms Pays 10% royalty, 5 author's copies. Publishes ms 1 year after acceptance. Guidelines and catalog available on Web site.

Advice "We would enjoy seeing more experimental work. We don't want to see thrillers, fantasies, horror. The small, thoughtful literary story that large publishers don't want to take a chance on is the kind that gets our attention."

◙ ◎ ◪ PAPERCUTZ

40 Exchange Pl., Ste. 1308, New York NY 10005. Fax: (212)643-1545. E-mail: salicrup@papercutz.com. Web site: www.papercutz.com. **Contact:** Jim Salicrup (material aimed at the tween and teen market). Estab. 2004. "Independent publisher of graphic novels based on popular existing properties aimed at the teen and tween market." Publishes hardcover originals, paperback originals. Format: glossy white 100 lb. paper; offset four-color printing; perfect bound; full-color comics illustrations. Publishes 10+ titles/year. Distributed by Holtzbrinck Publishers.

Publishes Licensed characters/properties aimed at a tween and teen market. Not looking for original properties at this point. "Looking for professional comics writers able to write material for tweens and teens without dumbing down their work. Also looking for comic book artists able to work in animated or manga styles." Published *Nancy Drew, Girl Detective #1* "The Demon of River Heights," by Stefan Petrucha (tween/teen mystery); *The Hardy Boys #1* "The Ocean of Osyria," by Scott Lobdell (tween/teen mystery/adventure); *Zorro #1* "Scars!," by Don McGregor (tween/teen action/ adventure). Series projects: Nancy Drew, Girl Detective; The Hardy Boys; Tales from the Crypt, etc.

How to Contact Prefers submissions from writers, artists. Accepts unsolicited submissions. Send low res files of comic art samples or a link to samples on artist's Web site. Attends New York comic book conventions, as well as the San Diego Comic-Con, and will review portfolios if time allows. Agented submissions: 0%. Responds to queries and ms/art packages in 1-2 weeks. Considers simultaneous submissions, e-mail submissions, submissions on disk. Never comments on rejected manuscripts.

Terms Pays a page rate. Writer's and artist's guidelines not available. Book catalog free upon request.
Advice "Be familiar with our titles—that's the best way to know what we're interested in publishing. If you are somehow attached to a successful tween or teen property and would like to adapt it into a graphic novel, we may be interested."

◻ ◎ PARADISE CAY PUBLICATIONS, INC.

P.O. Box 29, Arcata CA 95518-0029. (707)822-9063. Fax: (707)822-9163. E-mail: mattm@humboldt1. com. Web site: www.paracay.com. **Contact:** Matt Morehouse, publisher. Publishes hardcover and trade paperback originals and reprints. Books: 50 lb. paper; offset printing; perfect bound and hardcover; illustrations. Average print order: 10,000. Average first novel print order: 3,000. **Published 3 debut authors within the last year.** Averages 5 total titles.
Needs Adventure (nautical, sailing). All fiction must have a nautical theme.
How to Contact Query with SASE or submit 2-3 sample chapters, synopsis. Responds in 1 month to queries; 2 months to mss.
Terms Pays 10-15% royalty on wholesale price or makes outright purchase of $1,000-$10,000. Average advance: $0-2,000. Publishes ms 6 months after acceptance. Book catalog and ms guidelines on Web site.
Advice "Must present in a professional manner. *Must* have a strong nautical theme."

◻ ◙ PATHWISE PRESS

2311 Broadway St., New Orleans, LA 70125. E-mail: pathwisepress@hotmail.com. Web site: www.p athwisepress.com. **Contact:** Christopher Harter. Estab. 1997. Small independent publisher interested in work that is neither academic or Bukowski. "We publish chapbooks only." Publishes paperback originals. Books: 20 lb. white linen paper; laser printing; saddle-stitch bound; illustrations. Average print order: 200-300.
Needs Experimental, literary, short story collections.
How to Contact "Pathwise Press currently on hiatus. Interested parties should e-mail or check Web site for updates."
Terms Pays 10-20% royalty. Publishes ms 6 months after acceptance. Ms guidelines online.
Advice "Proofread your work. Finished book should be 48-60 pages, including front and back matter, so consider length before submitting."

◙ PAYCOCK PRESS

3819 No. 13th St., Arlington VA 22201. (703)525-9296. E-mail: hedgehog2@erols.com. Web site: www.gargoylemagazine.com. **Contact:** Lucinda Ebersole and Richard Peabody. Estab. 1976. "Too academic for underground, too outlaw for the academic world. We tend to be edgy and look for ultra-literary work." Publishes paperback originals. Books: POD printing. Average print order: 500. Averages 1 total title/year. Member CLMP. Distributes through Amazon and Web site.
Needs Experimental, literary, short story collections.
How to Contact Accepts unsolicited mss. Accepts queries by e-mail. Include brief bio. Send SASE for return of ms or send a disposable ms and SASE for reply only. Agented fiction 5%. Responds in 1 month to queries; 4 months to mss. Accepts simultaneous submissions, electronic submissions. Rarely comments on rejected mss.
Terms Publishes ms 12 months after acceptance.
Advice "Check out our Web Site. Two of our favorite writers are Paul Bowles and Jeanette Winterson."

✖ ◙ ◎ PEACHTREE CHILDREN'S BOOKS

Peachtree Publishers, Ltd., 1700 Chattahoochee Avenue, Atlanta GA 30318-2112. (404)876-8761. Fax: (404)875-2578. E-mail: hello@peachtree-online.com. Web site: www.peachtree-online.com. **Contact:** Helen Harriss, acquisitions editor. "We publish a broad range of subjects and perspectives, with emphasis on innovative plots and strong writing." Publishes hardcover and trade paperback originals. Averages 30 total titles, 20-25 fiction titles/year.
Needs Juvenile, picture books, young adult. Looking for very well written middle grade and young

adult novels. No adult fiction. No short stories. Published *Sister Spider Knows All*; *Shadow of A Doubt*; *My Life and Death*, by Alexandra Canarsie.

How to Contact Submit 3 sample chapter(s) or submit complete ms. Responds in 6 months to queries; 6 months to mss. Accepts simultaneous submissions.

Terms Pays royalty on retail price; advance varies. Publishes ms 1 year or more after acceptance. Book catalog for 6 first-class stamps. Ms guidelines online.

◎ PEACHTREE PUBLISHERS, LTD.

1700 Chattahoochee Ave., Atlanta GA 30318-2112. (404)876-8761. Fax: (404)875-2578. E-mail: hello @peachtree-online.com. Web site: www.peachtree-online.com. **Acquisitions:** Helen Harriss. Publishes 30-35 titles/year.

Needs Picture books, young readers: adventure, animal, concept, history, nature/environment. Middle readers: adventure, animal, history, nature/environment, sports. Young adults: fiction, mystery, adventure. Does not want to see science fiction, romance.

How to Contact Submit complete ms (picture books) or 3 sample chapters (chapter books) by postal mail only. Responds to queries/mss in 6-7 months. Publishes a book 1-2 years after acceptance. Will consider simultaneous submissions.

Terms "Manuscript guidelines for SASE, visit Web site or call for a recorded message. No fax or e-mail submittals or queries please."

⚡ ⊘ ◎ PEDLAR PRESS

P.O. Box 26, Station P, Toronto ON M5S 2S6 Canada. (416)534-2011. E-mail: feralgrl@interlog.com. **Contact:** Beth Follett, owner/editor. Publishes hardcover and trade paperback originals. **Published 50% debut authors within the last year.** Averages 7 total titles/year. Distributes in Canada through LitDistCo.; in the US distributes directly through publisher.

Needs Experimental, feminist, gay/lesbian, literary, picture books, short story collections. Canadian writers only. Published Black Stars in a White Night Sky, by Jonarno Lawson, illustrated by Sherwin Tjia.

How to Contact Query with SASE, sample chapter(s), synopsis.

Terms Pays 10% royalty on retail price. Average advance: $200-400. Publishes ms 1 year after acceptance. Ms guidelines for #10 SASE.

Advice "I select manuscripts according to my taste, which fluctuates. Be familiar with some if not most of Pedlar's recent titles."

◖ ◎ ⚡ PELICAN PUBLISHING CO.

1000 Burmaster St., Gretna LA 70053. (504)368-1175. Web site: www.pelicanpub.com. **Contact:** Nina Kooij, editor-in-chief. Estab. 1926. "We seek writers on the cutting edge of ideas. We believe ideas have consequences. One of the consequences is that they lead to a best-selling book." Publishes hardcover, trade paperback and mass market paperback originals and reprints. Books: hardcover and paperback binding; illustrations sometimes. Buys juvenile mss with illustrations. Averages 65 total titles/year. Distributes titles internationally through distributors, bookstores, libraries. Promotes titles at reading and book conventions, in trade magazines, in radio interviews, print reviews and TV interviews.

• *The Warlord's Puzzle*, by Virginia Walton Pilegard, was #2 on *Independent Bookseller's Book Sense 76* list. *Dictionary of Literary Biography* lists; *Unforgotten*, by D.J. Meador, as "one of the best of 1999."

Needs Historical, juvenile (regional or historical focus). "We publish maybe one novel a year, usually by an author we already have. Almost all proposals are returned. We are most interested in historical Southern novels." Published Jubal, by Gary Penley (novel); Toby Belfer Visits Ellis Island, by Gloria Teles Pushker (young reader).

How to Contact Does not accept unsolicited mss. Query with SASE or submit outline, 2 sample chapter(s), synopsis. Responds in 1 month to queries; 3 months to mss. No simultaneous submissions. Rarely comments on rejected mss.

Terms Pays royalty on actual receipts. Average advance: considered. Publishes ms 9-18 months after acceptance. Book catalog for SASE. Writer's guidelines for SASE or on Web site.

Advice "Research the market carefully. Check our catalog to see if your work is consistent with our list. For ages 8 and up, story must be planned in chapters that will fill at least 90 double-spaced manuscript pages. Topic for ages 8-12 must be Louisiana related and historical. We look for stories that illuminate a particular place and time in history and that are clean entertainment. The only original adult work we might consider is historical fiction, preferably Civil War (not romance). Please don't send three or more chapters unless solicited. Follow our guidelines listed under 'How to Contact.''

PEMMICAN PUBLICATIONS

150 Henry Ave., Main Floor RM 12, Winnipeg MB R3B 0J7 Canada. (204)589-6346. Fax: (204)589-2063. E-mail: rmcilroy@pemmican.mbc.ca. Web site: www.pemmican.mb.ca. **Contact:** Randal McIlroy, managing editor. Estab. 1980. Metis adult and children's books. Publishes paperback originals. Books: stapled-bound smaller books and perfect-bound larger ones; 4-color illustrations, where applicable. Average print order: 1,500. First novel print order: 1,000. **Published some debut authors within the last year.** Averages 6 total titles/year. Distributes titles through press releases, Web site, fax, catalogues, and book displays.

Needs Stories by and about the Canadian Metis experience, especially from a modern adult or young-adult perspective. Recently published *Cries from a Metis Heart*, by Lorraine Mayer (adult nonfiction); *Goose Girl*, by Joe and Matrine McClellan(children's fiction); and *The Bannock Book,* by Linda Ducharme (children's fiction).

How to Contact Accepts unsolicited mss by conventional mail only. Submit samples and synopsis. Send SASE for return of ms or send a disposable ms and SASE for reply only. Accepts simultaneous submissions.

Terms Pays 10% royalty. Provides 10 author's copies. Average advance: $350.

THE PERMANENT PRESS/SECOND CHANCE PRESS

4170 Noyac Rd., Sag Harbor NY 11963. (631)725-1101. Fax: (631)725-8215. Web site: www.thepermanentpress.com. **Contact:** Judith and Martin Shepard, publishers. Estab. 1978. Mid-size, independent publisher of literary fiction. "We keep titles in print and are active in selling subsidiary rights." Publishes hardcover originals. Average print order: 1,500. Averages 12 total titles, 11 fiction titles/year. Distributes titles through Ingram, Baker & Taylor and Brodart. Promotes titles through reviews.

Needs Literary, mainstream/contemporary, mystery. Especially looking for high-line literary fiction, "artful, original and arresting." Accepts any fiction category as long as it is a "well-written, original full-length novel." Published *The Last Refuge, Two Time and Head Wounds* by Chris Knopf; *The Contractor*, by Charles Holdefer; *The Night Battles*, by M.F. Bloxam; *A Richer Dust*, by Amy Boaz.

How to Contact Accepts unsolicited mss. Send SASE for return of ms or send a disposable ms and SASE for reply only. Responds in 12 weeks to queries; 8 months to mss. Accepts simultaneous submissions.

Terms Pays 10-15% royalty on wholesale price. Offers $1,000 advance for Permanent Press books; royalty only on Second Chance Press titles. Publishes ms 18 months after acceptance. Ms guidelines for #10 SASE.

Advice "We are looking for good books; be they 10th novels or first ones, it makes little difference. The fiction is more important than the track record. Send us the first 25 pages, it's impossible to judge something that begins on page 302. Also, no outlines—let the writing present itself."

PIÑATA BOOKS

Arte Publico Press, University of Houston, 452 Cullen Performance Hall, Houston TX 77204-2004. (713)743-2841. Fax: (713)743-3080. Web site: www.artepublicopress.com. **Contact:** Nicolas Kanellos, director. Estab. 1994. Piñata Books is dedicated to the publication of children's and young adult literature focusing on U.S. Hispanic culture by U.S. Hispanic authors. Publishes hardcover and trade paperback originals. **Published some debut authors within the last year.** Averages 10-15 total titles/year.

Needs Adventure, juvenile, picture books, young adult. Published *Trino's Choice*, by Diane Gonzales Bertrand (ages 11-up); *Delicious Hullabaloo/Pachanga Deliciosa*, by Pat Mora (picture book); and *The Year of Our Revolution*, by Judith Ortiz Cofer (young adult).

How to Contact Does not accept unsolicited mss. Query with SASE or submit 2 sample chapter(s), synopsis, SASE. Responds in 1 month to queries; 6 months to mss. Accepts simultaneous submissions.

Terms Pays 10% royalty on wholesale price. Average advance: $1,000-3,000. Publishes ms 2 years after acceptance. Book catalog and ms guidelines available via Web site or with #10 SASE.

Advice "Include cover letter with submission explaining why your manuscript is unique and important, why we should publish it, who will buy it, relevance to the U.S. Hispanic culture, etc."

◪ ◎ PINEAPPLE PRESS, INC.

P.O. Box 3889, Sarasota FL 34230. (941)739-2219. Fax: (941)739-2296. E-mail: info@pineapplepress. com. Web site: www.pineapplepress.com. **Contact:** June Cussen, editor. Estab. 1982. Small independent trade publisher. Publishes hardcover and trade paperback originals. Books: quality paper; offset printing; Smyth-sewn or perfect bound; illustrations occasionally. Averages 25 total titles/year. Distributes titles through Pineapple, Ingram and Baker & Taylor. Promotes titles through reviews, advertising in print media, direct mail, author signings and the World Wide Web.

Needs Will only consider fiction set in Florida.

How to Contact Does not accept unsolicited mss. Query with sample, SASE. Responds in 2 months to queries. Accepts simultaneous submissions.

Terms Pays 6^{1}/$_{2}$-15% royalty on net receipts. Average advance: rare. Publishes ms 18 months after acceptance. Book catalog for 9×12 SAE with $1.29 postage.

Advice "Quality first novels will be published, though we usually only do one or two novels per year and they must be set in Florida. We regard the author/editor relationship as a trusting relationship with communication open both ways. Learn all you can about the publishing process and about how to promote your book once it is published. A query on a novel without a brief sample seems useless."

◪ POCOL PRESS

6023 Pocol Drive, Clifton VA 20124. (703)830-5862. E-mail: chrisandtom@erols.com. Web site: www.pocolpress.com. **Contact:** J. Thomas Hetrick, editor (baseball history and fiction). Pocol Press publishes first-time, unagented authors. Our fiction deals mainly with single author short story collections from outstanding niche writers. Publishes paperback originals. Books: 50 lb. paper; offset printing; perfect binding. Average print order: 500. **Published 2 debut authors within the last year.** Averages 4-6 total titles, 3 fiction titles/year. Member: Small Press Publishers Association. Distributes titles through Web site, authors, e-mail, word-of-mouth and readings.

Needs Horror (psychological, supernatural), literary, mainstream/contemporary, short story collections, baseball. Published *Believers*, by Nathan Leslie (short fiction); *A Collection of Friends*, by Thomas Sheehan (memoir); *Journeymen*, by Michael Rychlik (baseball fiction).

How to Contact Does not accept or return unsolicited mss. Query with SASE or submit 1 sample chapter(s). Accepts queries by mail. Include estimated word count, brief bio, list of publishing credits. Responds in 2 weeks to queries; 2 months to mss. No simultaneous submissions, submissions on disk. Sometimes comments on rejected mss.

Terms Pays 10-12% royalty. Publishes ms 1 year or less after acceptance. Book catalog for SASE or on Web site. Ms guidelines for SASE or on Web site.

Advice "Pocol Press is unique; we publish good writing and great storytelling. Write the best stories you can. Read them to you friends/peers. Note their reaction. Publishes some of the finest fiction by a small press."

◪ ◎ ◪ POISONED PEN PRESS

6962 E. 1st Ave. #103, Scottsdale AZ 85251. (480)945-3375. Fax: (480)949-1707. E-mail: info@poison edpenpress.com. Web site: www.poisonedpenpress.com. **Contact:** editor@poisonedpenpress.com (mystery, fiction). Estab. 1997. Publishes hardcover originals and paperback reprints. Books: 60 lb. paper; offset printing; hardcover binding. Average print order: 3,500. First novel print order: 3,000. **Published 4 debut authors within the last year.** Plans 5 first novels this year. Member Publishers Marketing Associations, Arizona Book Publishers Associations, Publishers Association of West. Distributes through Ingram, Baker & Taylor, Brodart.

- Was nominated in 2002 for the *LA Times* Book Prize. Also the recipient of several Edgar and Agatha Awards.

Needs Mystery (amateur sleuth, cozy, police procedural, private eye/hard-boiled, historical). Published *The Heat of The Moon*, by Sandra Parshall (mystery/fiction); *Impulse*, by Frederick Ramsay (mystery/fiction); *The Do-Re-Mi*, by Ken Kuhlken (mystery/fiction); *Drive*, by James Sallis (mystery/fiction).

How to Contact Accepts unsolicited mss. Query with SASE. Accepts queries by e-mail to editor@pois onedpenpress.com. Responds in 1 week to queries; 6-9 months to mss. Only accepts electronic submissions. No simultaneous submissions. Often comments on rejected mss.

Terms Pays 9-15% royalty. Average advance: $1,000. Publishes ms 12-15 months after acceptance. Ms guidelines online.

☑ THE POST-APOLLO PRESS

35 Marie St., Sausalito CA 94965. (415)332-1458. Fax: (415)332-8045. E-mail: postapollo@earthlink. net. Web site: www.postapollopress.com. **Contact:** Simone Fattal, publisher. Estab. 1982. Specializes in writers published in Europe or the Middle East who have been translated into English for the first time. Publishes trade paperback originals and reprints. Books: acid-free paper; lithography printing; perfect-bound. Average print order: 1,000. **Published some debut authors within the last year.** Averages 4 total titles/year. Distributes titles through Small Press Distribution, Berkley, California. Promotes titles through advertising in selected literary quarterlies, SPD catalog, ALA and ABA and SF Bay Area Book Festival participation.

Needs Experimental, literary (plays), spiritual. "Many of our books are first translations into English." Published *Some Life*, by Joanne Kyger; *In/Somnia*, by Etel Adnan; *9:45*, by Kit Robinson; and *Happily*, by Lyn Hejinian.

How to Contact Submit 1 sample chapter(s). Responds in 3 months to queries.

Terms Pays 5-7% royalty on wholesale price. Publishes ms 1½ years after acceptance. Book catalog and ms guidelines for #10 SASE.

Advice "We want to see serious, literary quality, informed by an experimental aesthetic."

⬆ ◻ ☑ PRAIRIE JOURNAL PRESS

Prairie Journal Trust, P.O. Box 61203, Brentwood Postal Services, Calgary AB T2L 2K6 Canada. E-mail: prairiejournal@yahoo.com. Web site: www.geocities.com/prairiejournal/. **Contact:** Anne Burke, literary editor. Estab. 1983. Small-press, noncommercial literary publisher. Publishes paperback originals. Books: bond paper; offset printing; stapled binding; b&w line drawings. **Published some debut authors within the last year.** Distributes titles by mail and in bookstores and libraries (public and university). Promotes titles through direct mail, reviews and in journals.

- Prairie Journal Press authors have been nominees for The Journey Prize in fiction and finalists and honorable mention for the National Magazine awards.

Needs Literary, short story collections. Published *Prairie Journal Fiction, Prairie Journal Fiction II* (anthologies of short stories); *Solstice* (short fiction on the theme of aging); and *Prairie Journal Prose*.

How to Contact Accepts unsolicited mss. Sometimes comments on rejected mss.

Terms Pays 1 author's copy; honorarium depends on grant/award provided by the government or private/corporate donations. SAE with IRC for individuals. No U.S. stamps please.

Advice "We wish we had the means to promote more new writers. We look for something different each time and try not to repeat types of stories if possible. We receive fiction of very high quality. Short fiction is preferable although excerpts from novels are considered if they stand alone on their own merit."

⬆ ☑ ☑ PUFFIN BOOKS

Penguin Group (USA), Inc., 345 Hudson St., New York NY 10014. (212)366-2000. Web site: www.pen guinputnam.com. **Contact:** Sharyn November, senior editor; Kristin Gilson, editorial director. Puffin Books publishes high-end trade paperbacks and paperback reprints for preschool children, beginning and middle readers, and young adults. Publishes trade paperback originals and reprints. Averages 175-200 total titles/year.

Needs Young adult, middle grade; easy-to-read grades 1-3. "We publish paperback reprints and original titles. We do not publish original picture books." Published *Looking for Alaska*, by John Green.

How to Contact Does not accept unsolicited mss. Send SASE or IRC. Responds in 3 months to mss. No simultaneous submissions.

Terms Royalty varies. Average advance: varies. Publishes ms 1 year after acceptance. Book catalog for 9×12 SAE with 7 first-class stamps; send request to Marketing Department.

Advice "Our audience ranges from little children 'first books' to young adult (ages 14-16). An original idea has the best luck."

◯ ◎ � **PUREPLAY PRESS**

11353 Missouri Ave., Los Angeles CA 90025. (310)479-8773. Fax: (310)473-9384. E-mail: editor@pur eplaypress.com. Web site: www.pureplaypress.com. **Contact:** David Landau. "We are a small, niche publisher devoted to Cuba's history and culture. We publish high-quality books that people will want to read for years to come." Books are in English, Spanish and bilingual formats. Publishes hardcover and paperback originals. Ms guidelines online.

▣ **G.P. PUTNAM'S SONS**

Penguin Putnam Books For Young Readers, 345 Hudson St., New York NY 10014. (212)414-3610. Web site: www.penguinputnam.com. **Manuscript Acquisitions:** Susan Kochan, associate editorial director; John Rudolph, senior editor; Timothy Travaglini, senior editor; Stacey Barney, editor. **Art Acquisitions:** Cecilia Yung, art director, Putnam and Philomel. Publishes 25 picture books/year; 15 middle readers/year; 5 young adult titles/year. 5% of books by first-time authors; 50% of books from agented authors.

- G. Putnam's Sons 2007 titles *Slam*, by Nick Hornby and *The Three Snow Bears*, by Jan Brett were #1 on the New York Times Bestseller List.

Needs Juvenile picture books: animal, concept, contemporary, humor, multicultural. Young readers: adventure, contemporary, history, humor, multicultural, special needs, suspense/mystery. Middle readers: adventure, contemporary, history, humor, fantasy, multicultural, problem novels, sports, suspense/mystery. Young adults: contemporary, history, fantasy, problem novels, special needs. Does not want to see series. Average word length: picture books—200-1,000; middle readers—10,000-30,000; young adults—40,000-50,000. Recently published Leaves, by David Ezra Stein (ages 4-8); *Faeries of Dreamdark: Blackbringer*, by Lainie Taylor (ages 10 and up).

How to Contact Accepts unsolicited mss. No SASE required, as will only respond if interested. Picture books: send full mss. Fiction: Query with outline/synopsis and 10 manuscript pages. Responds to mss within 4 months if interested. Will consider simultaneous submissions.

Terms Pays authors royalty based on retail price. Sends prepublication galleys to authors.

Advice "Study our catalogs and get a sense of the kind of books we publish, so that you know whether your project is likely to be right for us."

▦ ◯ ◎ **RANSOM PUBLISHING LTD.**

51 Southgate Street, Winchester, SO23 9EH United Kingdom. (+44)01962 862307. Fax: (+44)05601 148881. E-mail: rebecca@ransom.co.uk. Web site: www.ransom.co.uk. **Contact:** Jenny Ertie, editor; Rebecca Pash, Marketing Editor. Estab. 1995. Independent UK publisher with distribution in English speaking markets throughout the world. Specializes in books for reluctant and struggling readers. One of the few English language publishers to publish books with very high interest age and very low reading age. Has a developing list of children's books for home and school use. Specializes in phonics and general reading programs. Publishes paperback originals. **Published 5 debut authors within the last year.** Member BESA (UK), IPG (UK).

Needs Easy reading for young adults. Books for reluctant and struggling readers.

How to Contact Accepts unsolicited mss. Query with SASE or submit outline/proposal. Prefers queries by e-mail. Include estimated word count, brief bio, list of publishing credits. Responds in 3-4 weeks to queries. Accepts simultaneous submissions, electronic submissions, submissions on disk. Never comments on rejected mss.

Terms Pays 10% royalty on net receipts. Ms guidelines by e-mail.

RED HEN PRESS

P.O. Box 3537, Granada Hills CA 91394. (818)831-0649. Fax: (818)831-6659. E-mail: editor@redhen. org. Web site: www.redhen.org. **Contact:** Mark E. Cull, publisher/editor (fiction); Kate Gale, poetry editor (poetry, literary fiction). Estab. 1993. Publishes trade paperback originals. **Published 10% of books from debut authors within the last year.** Averages 22 total titles, 10 fiction titles/year.

Needs Ethnic, experimental, feminist, gay/lesbian, historical, literary, mainstream/contemporary, short story collections. "We prefer high-quality literary fiction." Published *The Misread City: New Literary Los Angeles*, edited by Dana Gioia and Scott Timberg; *Rebel*, by Tom Hayden.

How to Contact Query with SASE. Agented fiction 10%. Accepts simultaneous submissions.

Terms Publishes book 1 year after acceptance of ms. Publishes ms 1 year after acceptance. Book catalog and ms guidelines available via Web site or free.

Advice "Audience reads poetry, literary fiction, intelligent nonfiction. If you have an agent, we may be too small since we don't pay advances. Write well. Send queries first. Be willing to help promote your own book."

RENAISSANCE HOUSE

465 Westview Ave, Englewood, NJ .07631. (800)547-5113. Web site: www.renaissancehouse.net. **Contact:** Sam Laredo, publisher; Raquel Benatar, editor. Publishes hardcover and trade paperback originals. **Published 25-30% debut authors within the last year.** Averages 30 total titles/year. **Needs** Fantasy, juvenile, multicultural, picture books, legends, fables. Recently published *The Spirits of the Mountain*, by Raquel Benatar. **How to Contact** Query with SASE. Agented fiction 25%. Responds in 2 months to queries; 2 months to mss. Accepts simultaneous submissions.
Terms Pays 5-10% royalty on net receipts. Ms guidelines online.

REVELL PUBLISHING

Subsidiary of Baker Book House, P.O. Box 6287, Grand Rapids MI 49516-6287.
Web site: www.bakerbooks.com.
How to Contact Does not accept unsolicited mss.

RIVER CITY PUBLISHING

River City Publishing, LLC, 1719 Mulberry St., Montgomery AL 36106. (334)265-6753. Fax: (334)265-8880. E-mail: jgilbert@rivercitypublishing.com. Web site: www.rivercitypublishing.com. **Contact:** Jim Gilbert, editor. Estab. 1989. Midsize independent publisher (10-20 books per year). "We publish books of national appeal, with an emphasis on Southern writers and Southern stories." Publishes hardcover and trade paperback originals. Averages 6 total titles, 2 fiction titles/year.
• Had three nominees to *Foreword* fiction book of the year awards (2002); won Ippy for Short Fiction (2005).
Needs Ethnic, historical, literary, multicultural, regional (southern), short story collections. No poetry or children's books. Published *Murder Creek*, by Joe Formichella (true crime); *Breathing Out the Ghost*, by Kirk Curnutt (novel); *The Bear Bryant Funeral Train*, by Brad Vice (short story collection).
How to Contact Accepts unsolicited submissions and submissions from unagented authors, as well as those from established and agented writers. Submit 5 consecutive sample chapters or entire manuscript for review. "Please include a short biography that highlights any previous writing and publishing experience, sales opportunities the author could provide, ideas for marketing the book, and why you think the work would be appropriate for River City." Send appropriate-sized SASE or IRC, "otherwise, the material will be recycled." Also accepts queries by e-mail. "Please include your electronic query letter as inline text and not an as attachment; we do not open unsolicited attachments of any kind. Please do not include sample chapters or your entire manuscript as inline text. We do not field or accept queries by telephone." Agented fiction 25%. Responds in three to nine months; "please wait at least 3 months before contacting us about your submission." Accepts simultaneous submissions. No multiple submissions. Rarely comments on rejected mss.
Terms Pays 10-15% royalty on retail price. Average advance: $500-5,000. Publishes ms 1 year after acceptance.
Advice "Only send your best work after you have received outside opinions. From approximately 1,000 submissions each year, we publish no more than 8 books and few of those come from unsolicited material. Competition is fierce, so follow the guidelines exactly. All first-time novelists should submit their work to the Fred Bonnie Award contest."

RONSDALE PRESS

3350 W. 21st Ave., Vancouver BC V6S 1G7 Canada. (604)738-4688. Fax: (604)731-4548. E-mail: ronsdale@shaw.ca. Web site: www.ronsdalepress.com. **Contact:** Ronald B. Hatch, president/editor; Veronica Hatch, editor (YA historical). Estab. 1988. Ronsdale Press is "dedicated to publishing books that give Canadians new insights into themselves and their country." Publishes trade paperback originals. Books: 60 lb. paper; photo offset printing; perfect binding. Average print order: 1,500.
Published some debut authors within the last year. Averages 10 total titles, 3 fiction titles/year.
Sales representation: Literary Press Group. Distribution: LitDistco. Promotes titles through ads in *BC Bookworld* and *Globe & Mail* and interviews on radio.

Needs Literary, short story collections, novels. Canadian authors *only*. Published *The City in the Egg*, by Michel Tremblay (novel); *Jackrabbit Moon*, by Sheila McLeod Arnopoulos (novel); and *What Belongs*, by F.B. André (short story collection).

How to Contact Accepts unsolicited mss. Accepts queries by e-mail. Send SASE or IRC. Responds in 2 weeks to queries; 2 months to mss. Accepts simultaneous submissions. Sometimes comments on rejected mss.

Terms Pays 10% royalty on retail price. Publishes ms 1 year after acceptance. Ms guidelines online.

Advice "We publish both fiction and poetry. Authors *must* be Canadian. We look for writing that shows the author has read widely in contemporary and earlier literature. Ronsdale, like other literary presses, is not interested in mass-market or pulp materials."

ⓃⒶ RTMC ORGANIZATION, LLC

P. O. Box 15105, Baltimore MD 21282. E-mail: submissions@rtmc.org. Web site: http://www.rtmc.o rg. **Contact:** G. Levine (fiction). Estab. 2006. "Small independent publisher of new novels by previously unpublished authors who are committed to learning and practicing the craft of written storytelling. We accept mainstream genre commercial novels. The kind of thing you would not mind your mother knowing you have written, nor mind your spouse reading. If it makes you blush more than twice during the entire novel, then submit it elsewhere." Publishes hardcover originals, paperback originals. Format: 55-60 lb. offwhite paper; offset printing; hard and perfect bound; chapter headings illustrations. Average print order: 5,000. Debut novel print order: 5,000. **Published 2 new writers last year.** Plans 6 debut novels this year. Averages 12 fiction titles/year. Member PMA, SPAN. Distributes titles through Baker & Taylor, uses an internal publicist.

Needs Adventure, fantasy, historical, literary, mystery/suspense, romance, thriller/espionage, young adult/teen. Published *Arnie Carver and the Plague of Demeverde*, by Kenneth R. Besser (YA fiction); *Pay the Piper*, by Raymond Abraham (legal thriller). Ongoing series: YA Adventures.

How to Contact Send query letter. Accepts queries by e-mail. Include estimated word count, brief bio, list of publishing credits. Send SASE or IRC for return of ms. Responds to queries in 6 weeks. No unsolicited mss. Considers simultaneous submissions. Sometimes critiques/comments on rejected mss.

Terms Sends pre-production galleys to author. Ms published within 2 years after acceptance. Writer's guidelines available for SASE. Pays royalties 10-15% retail. Advance is negotiable. Book catalogs not available.

Advice "Craft a great story, wonderfully written. Have a marketing plan in mind for how you will develop a following of readers."

Ⓐ SALVO PRESS

P.O. Box 9736, Beaverton, OR 97007. Web site: www.salvopress.com. **Contact:** Scott Schmidt, publisher (mystery, suspense, thriller & espionage). Estab. 1998. "We are a small press specializing in mystery, suspense, espionage and thriller fiction. Our press publishes in trade paperback and e-book format." Publishes hardcover, trade paperback originals and e-books in most formats. Books: $5^{1}/_{2} \times 8^{1}/_{2}$; or 6×9 printing; perfect binding. **Published 3 debut authors within the last year.** Averages 3 total titles, 3 fiction titles/year.

Needs Adventure, literary, mystery (amateur sleuth, police procedural, private/hard-boiled), science fiction (hard science/technological), suspense, thriller/espionage. "Our needs change. Check our Web site." Published *The Cold Edge*, by Trevor Scott (espionage/thriller); *The Great Planet Robbery*, by Craig DiLouie (Sci-Fi); and *Perfectly Healthy Man Drops Dead*, by Bruce Hartman (mystery).

How to Contact Query by e-mail only at query@salvopress.com. Please place the word "Query" as the subject. Include estimated word count, brief bio, list of publishing credits, "and something to intrigue me so I ask for more." Agented fiction 15%. Responds in 1 month to queries; 2 months to mss. No simultaneous submissions. Sometimes comments on rejected mss.

Terms Pays 10% royalty. Publishes ms 9 months after acceptance. Book catalog and ms guidelines online.

ⓃⒶⓋ SAMHAIN PUBLISHING, LTD

577 Mulberry Street, Suite 1520, Macon GA 31201. (478)929-7001. Fax: (478)929-8311. E-mail: books @samhainpublishing.com. Web site: www.samhainpublishing.com. **Contact:** Angela James, executive editor (fiction). Estab. 2005. "A small, independent publisher, Samhain's motto is 'It's all about

the story.' We look for fresh, unique voices who have a story to share with the world. We encourage our authors to let their muse have its way and to create tales that don't always adhere to current trends. One never knows what the next 'hot genre' will be or when it will start, so write what's in your soul. These are the books that, whether the story is based on 'formula' or is an 'original,' when written from the heart will earn you a life-time readership." Publishes paperback originals, e-books. Format: POD/offset printing; line illustrations. **Published 20-30 new writers last year.** Plans 20 or more debut novels this year. Averages 240 fiction titles/year. Distributes/promotes titles through Ingrams Publisher Services and through a variety of media outlets both online and offline.

• Preditor and Editors Best Publisher 2006

Needs Erotica, fantasy (space fantasy, sword and sorcery), gay, glitz, historical, horror (dark fantasy, futuristic, pyschological, supernatural), lesbian, mainstream, military/war, mystery/suspense, psychic/supernatural, religious, romance (contemporary, futuristic/time travel, gothic, historical, paranormal, regency period, romantic suspense), science fiction, thriller/espionage, western (frontier saga, traditional), young adult/teen (problem novel). "Samhain is looking to expand outside the romance genre and appreciates submissions of fantasy, science fiction, horror and mainstream/women's fiction. Within the romance genre we are actively seeking unique paranormals, futuristics and non-erotic books. However, all genres of fiction are currently accepted." Anthologies planned include a 2008 untitled Christmas anthology and a 2008 untitled annual Samhain anthology. Open call for submissions is placed on Web site. Full manuscript is required for special anthologies and the editor in charge of anthology selects final stories. Published *Steelflower*, by Lilith Saincrow (fantasy); *Annabell's Courtship*, by Lucy Monroe (historical romance); *Blackmailed*, by Annmarie McKenna (erotic romance).

How to Contact Query with outline/synopsis and 3 sample chapters. Accepts queries by e-mail. Include estimated word count, brief bio, list of publishing credits and "how an author is working to improve craft: association, critique groups, etc." Responds to queries in 10-12 weeks. Accepts unsolicited mss. Sometimes critiques/comments on rejected mss. Responds to mss in 10-12 weeks.

Terms Sends pre-production galleys to author. Ms published 6-18 months after acceptance. Writer's guidelines on Web site. Pays royalties 30-40% for e-books, average of 8% for tradepaper, an advance and author's copies (quantity varies). Book catalogs on Web site.

Advice "Because we are an e-publisher first, we do not have to be as concerned with industry trends and can publish less popular genres of fiction if we believe the story and voice are good and will appeal to our customers. Please follow submission guidelines located on our Web site, include all requested information and proof your query/manuscript for errors prior to submission."

⬛ ◎ ⬛ SARABANDE BOOKS, INC.

2234 Dundee Rd., Suite 200, Louisville KY 40205. (502)458-4028. Fax: (502)458-4065. E-mail: info@sarabandebooks.org. Web site: www.sarabandebooks.org. **Contact:**Sarah Gorham, editor-in-chief; Kirby Gann, managing editor. Estab. 1994. "Small literary press publishing poetry, short fiction and literary nonfiction." Publishes hardcover and trade paperback originals. **Published some debut authors within the last year.** Averages 12 total titles, 2-3 fiction titles/year. Distributes titles through Consortium Book Sales & Distribution. Promotes titles through advertising in national magazines, sales reps, brochures, newsletters, postcards, catalogs, press release mailings, sales conferences, book fairs, author tours and reviews.

• Marjorie Sander's story collection Portrait of My Mother Who Posed Nude in Wartime won the 2004 National Jewish Book Award. *When It Burned to the Ground* by Yolanda Barnes won the 2006 Independent Publisher Award for Best Multicultural Fiction.

Needs Literary, novellas, short novels, 250 pages maximum, 150 pages minimum. Submissions to Mary McCarthy Prize in Short Fiction accepted January through February. Published *Other Electricities*, by Ander Monson; *More Like Not Running Away*, by Paul Shepherd.

How to Contact See Web site for McCarthy Contest entry form. Accepts simultaneous submissions.

Terms Pays royalty of 10% on actual income received. Publishes ms 18 months after acceptance. Ms guidelines for #10 SASE.

Advice "Make sure you're not writing in a vacuum, that you've read and are conscious of contemporary literature. Have someone read your manuscript, checking it for ordering, coherence. Better a lean, consistently strong manuscript than one that is long and uneven. We like a story to have good narrative, and we like to be engaged by language."

Ⓐ 🔀 ⊘ ◎ **SCHOLASTIC CANADA LTD.**

604 King St. West, ON M5V 1E1 Canada. (416)915-3500. Fax: (416)849-7912. Web site: www.scholas tic.ca; for ms/artist guidelines: www.scholastic.ca/aboutscholastic/manuscripts.htm. **Acquisitions:** Editor, children's books. Publishes hardcover and trade paperback originals. Imprints: Scholastic Canada; North Winds Press; Les Editions Scholastic. Publishes 70 titles/year; imprint publishes 4 titles/year. 3% of books from first-time authors; 50% from unagented writers. Canadian authors, theme or setting required.

- At presstime Scholastic Canada was not accepting unsolicited manuscripts. For up-to-date information on their current submission policy, call their publishing status line at (905)887-7323, ext. 4308 or view their submission guidelines on their Web site.

Needs Juvenile picture books, young readers, young adult. Average word length: picture books—under 1,000; young readers—7,000-10,000; middle readers—15,000-30,000; young adult—25,000-40,000.

How to Contact Query with synopsis, 3 sample chapters and SASE. Nonfiction: Query with outline, 1-2 sample chapters and SASE (IRC or Canadian stamps only). Responds in 3 months. Publishes book 1 year after acceptance.

Terms Pays authors royalty of 5-10% based on retail price. Offers advances. Book catalog for $8^{1}/_{2} \times 11$ SAE with $2.55 postage stamps (IRC or Canadian stamps only).

Ⓐ ◎ **SCHOLASTIC PRESS**

Scholastic Inc., 557 Broadway, New York NY 10012. (212)343-6100. Fax: (212)343-4713. Web site: www.scholastic.com. **Contact:** David Saylor, editorial director (picture books) David Levithan, editorial director, middle grade, young adult; Dianne Hess, executive editor (picture books, early chapter books, middle grade, YA); Tracy Mack, executive editor (picture books, middle grade, young adult); Kara LaReau, executive editor; Anamika Bhatnager, senior editor (picture books, early chapter books, middle grade). Publishes hardcover originals. **Published some debut authors within the last year.** Averages 30 total titles/year. Promotes titles through trade and library channels.

Needs Juvenile, picture books, novels. Wants "fresh, exciting picture books and novels—inspiring, new talent." Published *Chasing Vermeer*, by Blue Balliet; *Here Today*, by Ann M. Martin; *Detective LaRue*, by Mark Teague.

How to Contact Does not accept unsolicited mss. *Agented submissions and submissons by published authors only.* No simultaneous submissions.

Terms Pays royalty on retail price. Average advance: variable. Publishes ms 18-24 months after acceptance.

Advice "Be a big reader of juvenile literature before you write and submit!"

SCIENCE & HUMANITIES PRESS

P.O. Box 7151, Chesterfield MO 63006-7151. (636)394-4950. E-mail: publisher@sciencehumanitiespr ess.com. Web site: www.sciencehumanitiespress.com. **Contact:** Dr. Bud Banis, publisher. Publishes trade paperback originals and reprints, and electronic originals and reprints. **Published 25% of books from debut authors within the last year.** Averages 20-30 total titles/year.

Imprint(s) Science & Humanities Press; BeachHouse Books; MacroPrintBooks (large print editions); Heuristic Books; Early Editions Books.

Needs Adventure, historical, humor, literary, mainstream/contemporary, military/war, mystery, regional, romance, science fiction, short story collections, spiritual, sports, suspense, western, young adult. "We prefer books with a theme that gives a market focus. Brief description by e-mail."

How to Contact Responds in 3 months to queries; 3 months to solicited mss. Do not send unsolicited mss. Accepts simultaneous submissions.

Terms Pays 8% royalty on retail price. Publishes ms 6-12 months after acceptance. Ms guidelines online.

Advice Sales are primarily through the Internet, outlets such as amazon.com, special orders, reviews in specialized media, direct sales to libraries, special organizations and use as textbooks. "Our expertise is electronic publishing for continuous short-run-in-house production rather than mass distribution to retail outlets. This allows us to commit to books that might not be financially successful in conventional book store enviroments and to keep books in print and available for extended periods of time. Books should be types that would sell steadily over a long period of time, rather than those that require rapid rollout and bookstore shelf exposure for a short time. We consider the nurture of new talent part of our mission but enjoy experienced writers as well. We are proud that many or our books are second, third and fourth books from authors who were once first-time authors. A good book is not a one-time accident.''

◐ ◎ SERENDIPITY SYSTEMS

P.O. Box 140, San Simeon CA 93452. (805)927-5259. E-mail: bookware@thegrid.net. Web site: www.s-e-r-e-n-d-i-p-i-t-y.com. **Contact:** John Galuszka, publisher. Estab. 1986. Electronic publishing only. ''We publish on disks, the Internet and CD-ROMs in Adobe PDF format. **''Published some debut authors within the last year.** Averages 6-12 total titles, 15 fiction titles/year.

Imprint(s) Books-on-Disks; Bookware.

Needs ''We want to see *only* works which use (or have a high potential to use) hypertext, multimedia, interactivity or other computer-enhanced features. We cannot use on-paper manuscripts. We only publish book-length works, not individual stories.'' Published *The Blue-Eyed Muse*, by John Peter (novel).

How to Contact Submit complete ms. Accepts queries by e-mail. Send SASE or IRC. Responds in 1 month to mss. Accepts simultaneous submissions, submissions on disk. Often comments on rejected mss.

Terms Pays 33% royalty on wholesale price or on retail price, depending on how the books goes out. Publishes ms 2 months after acceptance. Ms guidelines online.

Advice ''We are interested in seeing multimedia works suitable for Internet distribution. Would like to see: more works of serious literature—novels, short stories, etc. Would like to not see: right wing adventure fantasies from 'Tom Clancy' wanna-be's.''

Ⓐ SIMON & SCHUSTER

1230 Avenue of the Americas, New York NY 10020. (212)698-7000. Web site: www.simonsays.com.

Imprint(s) Simon & Schuster Adult Publishing Group: Simon & Schuster; Scribner (Scribner, Lisa Drew, Simple Abundance Press); The Free Press; Atria Books; Kaplan; Touchstone; Scribner Paperback Fiction; S&S Libros en Espanol; Simon & Schuster Source; Wall Street Journal Books; Pocket Books (Pocket Star; Washington Square Press; MTV Books; Sonnet Books; Star Trek; The New Fogler Shakespeare; VH-1 Books; WWF Books). Simon & Schuster Children's Publishing: Aladdin Paperbacks; Atheneum Books for Young Readers (Richard Jackson Books); Little Simon (Simon Spotlight; Rabbit Ears Books & Audio); Margaret K. McElderry Books, (Archway Paperbacks; Minstreal Books); Simon & Schuster Books for Young Readers (Paula Wiseman Books).

How to Contact Agented submissions only. **Terms** Pays royalty. Offers advance. Ms guidelines online.

◪ ◐ SKYSONG PRESS

35 Peter St. S, Orillia ON L3V 5A8 Canada. (705)329-1770. E-mail: skysong@bconnex.net. Web site: www.bconnex.net/ ~ skysong/. **Contact:** Steve Stanton. Estab. 1988. Skysong Press is a small independent Christian publisher. **Published 3 debut authors within the last year.**

Imprint(s) Dreams & Visions.

Needs Short stories 2,000-6,000 words: Ethnic, experimental, fantasy, literary, mainstream/contemporary, religious, romance, science fiction.

How to Contact Accepts unsolicited mss. Submit complete ms and SASE. Accepts queries by e-mail. Include estimated word count, list of publishing credits. Responds in 2-6 weeks to queries; 2-6 months to mss. Accepts simultaneous submissions. Rarely comments on rejected mss.

Terms Average advance: 1 cent/word. Publishes ms 6-12 months after acceptance. Ms guidelines online.

◐ ◪ SMALL BEER PRESS

150 Plesant St., #306, Easthampton MA 01017. (413)203-1636. Fax: (413)203-1636. E-mail: info@lcrw.net. Web site: www.lcrw.net. **Contact:** Gavin J. Grant. Estab. 2000. Averages 3-6 fiction titles/year.

● Small Beer Press also publishes the zine *Lady Churchill's Rosebud Wristlet*. SBP's books have been Hugo and Locus Award winners, as well as BookSense Picks and finalists for The Story Prize.

Needs Literary, experimental, speculative, story collections. Recently published *Generation Loss: A*

Novel, by Elizabeth Hand (post-punk lit thriller); *Interfictions: An Anthology of Interstitial Writing*, Delia Sherman and Theodora Goss, editors; *Skinny Dipping in the Lake of the Dead*, by Alan DeNiro (story collection); *Mothers & Other Monsters*, by Maureen F. McHugh (story collection); *Magic for Beginners*, by Kelly Link.

How to Contact "We do not accept unsolicited novel or short story collection manuscripts. Queries are welcome. Please send queries with an SASE by mail."

Advice "Please be familiar with our books first to avoid wasting your time and ours, thank you."

⊿ SOHO PRESS, INC.

853 Broadway, New York NY 10003. (212)260-1900. Fax: (212)260-1902. E-mail: soho@sohopress.com. Web site: www.sohopress.com. **Contact:** Laura Hruska, editor-in-chief (literary novels, mysteries with foreign or exotic settings); Katie Herman, editor (literary novels, mysteries with foreign or exotic settings). Estab. 1986. "Independent publisher known for sophisticated fiction, mysteries set abroad, women's interest (no genre) novels and multicultural novels." Publishes hardcover and trade paperback originals and reprint editions. Books: perfect binding; halftone illustrations. First novel print order varies. **Published 7 debut authors within the last year.** Averages 70 total titles, 65 fiction titles/year. Distributes titles through Consortium Book Sales & Distribution in the US and Canada, Turnaround in England.

Imprint(s) Soho Crime: procedural series set abroad.

Needs Adventure, ethnic, feminist, historical, literary, mainstream/contemporary, mystery (police procedural), suspense, multicultural. Published *Thirty-Three Teeth*, by Colin Cotterill; *When Red is Black*, by Qiu Xiaolong; *Murder on the Ile Saint-Louis*, by Cara Black; *The Farming of Bones*, by Edwidge Danticat; *The Darkest Child*, by Delores Phillips; *The First Wave*, by James R. Benn.

How to Contact Send first three chapters. Include estimated word count, brief bio, list of publishing credits. Send SASE for return of ms or send a disposable ms and SASE for reply only. Agented fiction 85%. Responds in 3 months to queries; 3 months to mss. Accepts simultaneous submissions. No electronic submissions. Sometimes comments on rejected mss.

Terms Pays 10-15% royalty on retail price for harcovers, 7.5% on trade paperbacks. Offers advance. Publishes ms 18-24 months after acceptance. Ms guidelines online.

Ⓐ ⊠ SOURCEBOOKS LANDMARK

Sourcebooks Inc, P.O. Box 4410, Naperville IL 60567-4410. Web site: www.sourcebooks.com "Our fiction imprint, Sourcebooks Landmark, publishes a variety of titles. We are interested first and foremost in books that have a story to tell."

How to Contact Submit through agent only. Agented fiction: 100. Responds to queries in 6-8 weeks.

☑ ◎ SPIRE PRESS

532 LaGuardia Place, Suite 298, New York NY 10012. E-mail: editor@spirepress.org. Web site: www.spirepress.org. **Contact:** Shelly Reed. Publishes 5-6 books/year. **Publishes 1-2 new writers/year.**

Needs Literary story collections. Also publishes memoir, poetry. No novels. No horror, romance, or religious work. Length: 30,000+ words. Recently published work by Richard Weems.

How to Contact Send first 15 pages and synopsis in August only. Send disposable copy and #10 SASE for reply only. Responds in 3 months. Accepts simultaneous submissions. Rarely comments on rejected queries. Writer's guidelines online.

Terms Pays in advance copies and 15% royalty.

Advice "You should have published short stories and/or essays in established literary journals before querying us."

⊿ SPOUT PRESS

P.O. Box 581067, Minneapolis MN 55458. (612)782-9629. E-mail: editors@spoutpress.org. Web site: www.spoutpress.org. **Contact:** Chris Watercott, fiction editor. Estab. 1989. "Small independent publisher with a permanent staff of five—interested in experimental fiction for our magazine and books." Publishes paperback originals. Books: perfect bound; illustrations. Average print order: 1,000. **Published 1 debut author within the last year.** Distributes and promotes books through the Web site, events and large Web-based stores such as Amazon.com.

Needs Ethnic, experimental, literary, short story collections. Published *I'm Right Here*, by Tony

Rauch. Runs annual fiction of the year story contest for Spout magazine. First prize is cash. Accepts submissions fall through spring. See Web site for specific dates and details.

How to Contact Does not accept unsolicited mss. Query with SASE. Accepts queries by mail. Include estimated word count, brief bio, list of publishing credits. Send SASE for return of ms or send a disposable ms and SASE for reply only. Responds in 1 month to queries; 3-5 months to mss. Accepts simultaneous submissions. Rarely comments on rejected mss.

Terms Individual arrangement with author depending on the book. Publishes ms 12-15 months after acceptance. Ms guidelines for SASE or on Web site.

Advice "We tend to publish writers after we know their work via publication in our journal, *Spout Magazine.*"

🅰 ST. MARTIN'S PRESS

175 Fifth Ave., New York NY 10010. (212)674-5151. Fax: (212)420-9314. Web site: www.stmartins.com. Estab. 1952. General interest publisher of both fiction and nonfiction. Publishes hardcover, trade paperback and mass market originals. Averages 1,500 total titles/year.

Imprint(s) Bedford Books; Buzz Books; Thomas Dunne Books; Forge; Minotaur; Picador USA; Stonewall Inn Editions; TOR Books; Griffin.

Needs Fantasy, historical, horror, literary, mainstream/contemporary, mystery, science fiction, suspense, western (contemporary), general fiction; thriller.

How to Contact *Agented submissions only.*

Terms Pays royalty. Offers advance. Ms guidelines online.

STARCHERONE BOOKS

P.O. Box 303, Buffalo NY 14201-0303. (716)885-2726. E-mail: publisher@starcherone.com. Web site: www.starcherone.com. **Contact:** Ted Pelton, publisher. Estab. 2000. Non-profit publisher of literary and experimental fiction. Publishes paperback originals and reprints. Books: acid-free paper; perfect bound; occasional illustrations. Average print order: 1,000. Average first novel print order: 1,000. **Published 2 debut authors within the last year.** Member CLMP. Titles distributed through Web site, Small Press Distribution, Amazon, independent bookstores.

Needs Experimental, literary. Published *Quinnehtokqut,* by Joshua Harmon (debut author, novel); *Hangings*, by Nina Shope (debut author, short stories); *My Body in Nine Parts*, by Raymond Federman (experimental).

How to Contact Accepts queries by mail or e-mail during August and September of each year. Include brief bio, list of publishing credits. Always query before sending ms. Responds in 2 months to queries; 6-10 months to mss. Accepts simultaneous submissions.

Terms Pays 10-12.5% royalty. Publishes ms 9-18 months after acceptance. Guidelines and catalog available on Web site.

Advice "Become familiar with our interests in fiction. We are interested in new strategies for creating stories and fictive texts. Do not send genre fiction unless it is unconventional in approach."

🅰 🅼 SYNERGEBOOKS

32700 River Bend Rd. #5 P.O. Box 685, Chiloquin OR 97624. (541)783-7512. E-mail: synergebooks@aol.com. Web site: www.synergebooks.com. **Contact:** Debra Staples, editor. Estab. 1999. Small press publisher, specializing in quality e-books from talented new writers in a myriad of genres, including print-on-demand. SynergEbooks "works together" with the author to edit and market each book. Publishes paperback originals and e-books. Books: 60 lb. paper; print-on-demand; perfect bound. Average first novel print order: 30. **Published 10-20 debut authors within the last year.** Averages 50 total titles, 15 fiction titles/year.

• Authors have received EPPIES and other awards.

Needs Adventure, business, family saga, fantasy (space fantasy, sword and sorcery), historical, horror, humor, mainstream/contemporary, mystery, new age/mystic, religious (children's religious, inspirational, religious fantasy, religious mystery/suspense, religious thriller, religious romance), romance (contemporary, futuristic/time travel, historical, regency period, romantic suspense), science fiction, short story collections, western (frontier saga, traditional), young adult (adventure, fantasy/science fiction, historical, horror, mystery/suspense, romance), native american. Welcomes series books (1-9 in a series, with at least 1 title completed at time of submission.) Published *A Talent to Deceive: Who REALLY Killed the Lindberg Baby?*, by William Norris (nonfiction); *Liberated* *in the Valley of the Kings,* by Mary Lukes Stamoulis (fiction); *A Traveler's Highway to Heaven: History on the Hoof* series, by William J. Bonville (travel).

How to Contact Accepts unsolicited mss. Query via e-mail or snail mail, email preferred, 3 sample chapter(s), synopsis via attached mail in .doc format. Include estimated word count, brief bio, list of publishing credits, and e-mail address. Agented fiction 1%. Responds in 3 weeks to queries; 3 months to mss. Accepts simultaneous submissions, submissions on disk. Sometimes comments on rejected mss.

Terms Pays 15-40% royalty. Publishes ms 3-6 months after acceptance. Ms guidelines online.

Advice "We do not care if you've ever been published. If your work is unique in some way, and you are willing to work together to market your book, there is a good chance you will be accepted. Unedited manuscripts will no longer be considered. Keep in mind that we are first and foremost a digital publisher, so if you are not willing to market your work online, we suggest you submit to a different publisher."

◎ THIRD WORLD PRESS

P.O. Box 19730, 7822 S. Dobson Ave., Chicago IL 60619. (773)651-0700. Fax: (773)651-7286. E-mail: TWPress3@aol.com. Web site: www.thirdworldpressinc.com. **Contact:** Gwendolyn Mitchell, editor. Estab. 1967. Black-owned and operated independent publisher of fiction and nonfiction books about the black experience throughout the Diaspora. Publishes hardcover and trade paperback originals and reprints. Averages 20 total titles/year. Distibutes titles through Independent Publisher Group.

Needs Materials for literary, ethnic, contemporary, juvenile and children's books. "We publish nonfiction, primarily, but will consider fiction." Published *The Covenant with Black America*, with an introduction by Tavis Smiley; *1996,* by Gloria Naylor.

How to Contact Accepts unsolicited mss. Submit outline, 5 sample chapter(s), synopsis. Responds in 8 weeks to queries; 5 months to mss. Accepts simultaneous submissions.

Terms Pays royalty on net revenues. Individual arrangement with author depending on the book, etc. Publishes ms 18 months after acceptance. Ms guidelines for #10 SASE.

Ⓐ ◑ TIN HOUSE BOOKS

2601 NW Thurman St., Portland OR 97210. (503)219-0622. Fax: (503)222-1154. E-mail: meg@tinhouse.com. Web site: www.tinhouse.com. **Contact:** Lee Montgomery, editorial director; Michelle Wildgen, editor; Meg Storey, associate editor; Tony Perez, assistant editor. Estab. 2005. "We are a small independent publisher dedicated to nurturing new, promising talent as well as showcasing the work of established writers. Our Tin House New Voice series features work by authors who have not previously published a book." Publishes hardcover originals, paperback originals, paperback reprints. **Plans 3 debut novels this year.** Averages 6-8 total titles/year; 4-6 fiction titles/year. Distributes/promotes titles through Publishers Group West.

Needs Literary, novels, short story collections, poetry, translations. Publishes A New Voice series.

How to Contact Agented mss only. Accepts queries by snail mail, e-mail, phone. Include brief bio, list of publishing credits. Send SASE or IRC for return of ms or disposable copy of ms and SASE/IRC for reply only. Agented fiction 80%. Responds to queries in 2-3 weeks. Responds to mss in 2-3 months. Considers simultaneous submissions. Sometimes critiques/comments on rejected mss.

Terms Sends pre-production galleys to author. Manuscript published approximately one year after acceptance. Writer's guidelines on Web site. Advance is negotiable. Book catalogs not available.

◑ TITAN PRESS

PMB 17897, Encino CA 91416. E-mail: titan91416@yahoo.com. Web site: www.calwriterssfv.com. **Contact:** Stefanya Wilson, editor. Estab. 1981. Publishes hardcover originals and paperback originals. Books: recycled paper; offset printing; perfect bound. Average print order: 2,000. Average first novel print order: 1,000. **Published 3 debut authors within the last year.** Averages 12 total titles, 6 fiction titles/year. Distributed at book fairs and through the Internet and at Barnes & Noble.

Needs Literary, mainstream/contemporary, short story collections. Published *Orange Messiahs,* by Scott Alixander Sonders (fiction).

How to Contact Does not accept unsolicited mss. Query with SASE. Include brief bio, social security number, list of publishing credits. Agented fiction 50%. Responds in 3 months to mss. Accepts simultaneous submissions. Sometimes comments on rejected mss.

Terms Pays 20-40% royalty. Publishes ms 1 year after acceptance. Ms guidelines for #10 SASE.
Advice "Look, act, sound and *be* professional."

TORQUERE PRESS

P.O. Box 2545, Round Rock TX 78680. (512)586-6921. Fax: (866)287-4860. E-mail: torquere@torquer epress.com. Web site: www.torquerepress.com. **Contact:** Shawn Clements, submission editor (homoerotica, suspense) and Lorna Hinson, senior editor (gay and lesbian romance, historical). Estab. 2003. "We are a gay and lesbian press focusing on romance. We particularly like paranormal and western romance." Publishes paperback originals. Averages 140 total titles/year.
Imprint(s) Top Shelf—Shawn Clements, editor; Screwdrivers—M. Rode, editor; Single Shot—Jane Davitt, editor.
Needs All categories gay and lesbian themed. Adventure, erotica, historical, horror, mainstream, multicultural, mystery, occult, romance, science fiction, short story collections, suspense, western. Published *Broken Road*, by Sean Michael (romance); *Soul Mates: Bound by Blood*, by Jourdan Lane (paranormal romance).
How to Contact Query with outline/synopsis and 3 sample chapters. Responds to queries in 2 months; mss in 3-4 months. Electronic submissions preferred. Send query to submissions@torquerep ress.com.
Terms Manuscript published 6 months after acceptance. Pays royalties. Book catalogs on Web site.
Advice "Our audience is primarily persons looking for a familiar romance setting featuring gay or lesbian protagonists. Clean manuscripts and strong plots receive priority."

Ⓝ ⓦ ◪ TOTAL-E-BOUND PUBLISHING

Total-e-Ntwined Limited, 1 Faldingworth Road, Spridlington, Market Rasen, Lincolnshire, UK LN8 2DE. E-mail: info@total-e-bound.com. Web site: http://www.total-e-bound.com; http://www.foru m.totalebound.com. **Contact:** Claire Siemaszkiewicz, editor; Michele Paulin, editor; Janice Bennett, editor. Estab. 2006. "The team at Total-e-bound came together to provide a unique service to our authors and readers. We are a royalty paying, full-service e-publisher. This means that there are no fees to the author to

become published with us. Brought together by a mutual love of outstanding erotic fiction, we offer a mass of business experience in the form of editors, artists, marketeers, IT technicians and support staff to meet all of your needs. We love what we do and are totally dedicated, committed and loyal to providing the best service that we can to our authors and our readers. TEB publishes, markets and promotes top quality erotic romance e-books and paperback books. Publishes paperback originals, e-books. Averages 100 fiction titles/year. Distributes/promotes titles through the Total-e-bound shop and through channel partners/distributors.
Needs Erotic romance, action/adventure, bondage/BDSM, comedy/humour, contemporary, fantasy/fairytale, futuristic/sci-fi, gay/lesbian, historical (Rubenesque), menage-a-trois, new age/mystic, paranormal/timetravel, thriller/crime, shapeshifters/morphers, vampire/werewolf, western. Anthologies are released every quarter—each with a distinctive theme. "We produce a series of four anthologies per year, six short stories in each. Published Campus Cravings Series, by Carol Lynne (gay/contemporary); *Sink or Swim*, by Alexis Fleming (paranormal); and *Wild in the Country*, by Portia Da Costa (contemporary/erotica). Current and planned series include Campus Cravings (M/M), Good-time Boys (M/M), Cattle Valley (M/M), Horsemen of Apocalypse Island (fantasy), Wives R Us (contemporary), The Goddess Grind (contemporary/paranormal), Sons of Olympus (paranormal), Psychic Detective (paranormal), and The Watchers (paranormal/fantasy).
How to Contact Query with outline/synopsis and first 3 and last chapters. Accepts queries by e-mail. Include estimated word count, brief bio, list of publishing credits. Agented fiction: 10%. Responds to queries in 1-2 weeks. Accepts unsolicited mss. Often critiques/comments on rejected mss. Responds to mss in 2-8 weeks.
Terms Ms published 2-6 months after acceptance. Pays royalties 40% e-book, 10% print. Book catalogs on Web site.
Advice "First impressions are important. Send in a good intro letter with your synopsis and manuscript, giving details of what you will do yourself to promote your work. Always read and follow the submission guidelines."

⬩ ◎ TRADEWIND BOOKS

202-1807 Maritime Mews, Vancouver BC V6H 3W7 Canada.(604)662-4405. Fax: (604)730-0454. E-mail: tradewindbooks@yahoo.com. Web site: www.tradewindbooks.com. **Manuscript Acquisitions:** Michael Katz, publisher. **Senior Editor:** R. David Stephens. Publishes 2 picture books; 3 young adult titles/year; 1 book of poetry. 15% of books by first-time authors.

Needs Juvenile. Picture books: adventure, multicultural, folktales. Average word length: 900 words. Recently published *The Heretic's Tomb*, by Simon Rose; *ShuLi and Tamara*, by Paul Yee; *Baaaad Animals*, by Tiffany Stone.

How to Contact Picture books: submit complete ms. YA novels by Canadian authors only. Chapter books by US authors considered. Will consider simultaneous submissions. Do not send query letter. Responds to mss in 12 weeks. Unsolicited submissions accepted only if authors have read a selection of books published by Tradewind Books. Submissions must include a reference to these books.

Terms Royalties negotiable. Offers advances against royalties. Catalog available on Web site.

◪ ⬓ TRICYCLE PRESS

P.O. Box 7123, Berkeley CA 94707. (510)559-1600. Web site: www.tricylepress.com. **Contact:** Nicole Geiger, publisher. Estab. 1993. "Tricycle Press is a children's book publisher that publishes picture books, board books, chapter books, and middle grade novels and early young adult novels. As an independent publisher, Tricycle Press brings to life kid-friendly books that address the universal truths of childhood in an off-beat way." Publishes hardcover and trade paperback originals. **Published 3 debut authors within the last year.** Averages 20-24 total titles, 17-21 fiction titles/year.

• Received a 2007 notable children's book citation from the American Library Association for middle grade novel *Hugging the Rock* by Susan Taylor Brown.

Needs Children's/juvenile (adventure, historical, board book, preschool/picture book), preteen. "One-off middle grade novels—quality fiction, tween fiction." Published *Hugging The Rock*, by Susan Taylor Brown (middle grade); *Time Bomb*, by Nigel Hinton (middle grade); *Girl Wonders*, by Karen Salmansohn (middle grade) *Shify* by Lynn E. Hazen (young adult).

How to Contact Accepts unsolicited mss. Include three chapters and outline, brief bio, list of publishing credits, e-mail address. Send SASE for return of ms or send a disposable ms and SASE for reply only. Agented fiction 60%. Responds in 4-6 months to mss. Accepts simultaneous submissions.

Terms Pays 15-20% royalty on net receipts. Average advance: $0-9,000. Publishes ms 1-2 years after acceptance. Book catalog and ms guidelines for 9×12 SASE with 3 first-class stamps, or visit the Web site.

◪ TWILIGHT TIMES BOOKS

P.O. Box 3340, Kingsport TN 37664. (423)323-0183. Fax: (423)323-2183. E-mail: publisher@twilighttimesbooks.com. Web site: www.twilighttimesbooks.com. **Contact:** Ardy M. Scott, managing editor. Estab. 1999. "We publish compelling literary fiction by authors with a distinctive voice." Publishes hardcover and paperback originals and paperback reprints and e-books. Book: 60 lb. paper; offset and digital printing; perfect bound. Average print order: 1500. **Published 3 debut authors within the last year.** Averages 50 total titles, 12 fiction titles/year. Member: AAP, PAS, SPAN, SLF. Nationally distributed by Midpoint Trade Books.

Needs Historical, literary, mystery, nonfiction, science fiction, and young adult. Published *Hudson Lake*, by Laura Toops; *The New Bedford Samurai*, by Anca Vlaspolos; *Valley of the Raven*, By Ken Ramirez.

How to Contact Accepts unsolicited mss. Query with SASE or submit 2 sample chapter(s). Do not send complete mss. Accepts queries by e-mail, mail. Include estimated word count, brief bio, list of publishing credits, marketing plan. Send copy of ms and SASE. Agented fiction 10%. Responds in 4 weeks to queries; 2 months to mss. Accepts electronic submissions, submissions on disk. Rarely comments on rejected mss.

Terms Pays 8-15% royalty. Ms guidelines online.

Advice "The only requirement for consideration at Twilight Times Books is that your novel must be entertaining and professionally written."

⬓ ◪ UNCIAL PRESS

GCT, Inc., 2550 SW 204th Ave., Aloha OR 97996. E-mail: administrator@uncialpress.com. Web site: www.uncialpress.com. **Contact:** E. Star Conrad, publisher (fiction: mainstream, all genres except horror & erotica; nonfiction: humor, personal naratives); Judith B. Glad, senior editor (fiction: mainstream, all genres except horror & erotica; poetry). Estab. 2006. "Uncial Press is an electronic publisher, primarily of genre fiction, but open to both nonfiction and unusual fiction that does not fit in any particular genre or category. We buy what appeals to us and our tastes are eclectic. At present ours is a two-person operation. We release two full-length e-books a month, or one full-length and two short stories." Publishes e-books. Plans 1 debut novel this year. Averages 30 fiction titles/year. Member AIDP. Distributes/promotes titles through Uncial Web site, Fictionwise.com, Mobipocket.com, Allromancebooks.com and through Lightning Source which distributes to a variety of e-book retail sites.

Needs Fantasy, historical, humor/satire, mainstream, mystery/suspense (amateur sleuth, police procedural, private eye/hardboiled, cozy), psychic/supernatural, romance (contemporary, futuristic/time travel, gothic, historical, regency period, romantic suspense), science fiction (hard science/technological, soft/sociological), thriller/espionage, western (frontier saga, traditional). "We are actively seeking traditional and historical Regency romances, fantasy, science fiction and nonfiction humor." Also accepts short stories over 5,000 words. Published *The Beggarmaid*, by Lesley-Anne McLeod (Regency romance); *Zygeradon*, by Michelle I. Levine (fantasy); *Her Best Man*, by, Jana Richards (contemporary romance).

How to Contact Accepts submissions by e-mail only. Include estimated word count and a short synopsis (under 1,000 words). Responds to queries in 2 weeks. Accepts unsolicited mss. Considers simultaneous submissions. Rarely critiques/comments on rejected mss. Responds to mss in 2 weeks.

Terms Sends pre-production galleys to author. Ms published within 18 months after acceptance. Pays royalties. Book catalog on Web site.

Advice "We believe that electronic publishing is a growing field and will continue to devote ourselves to publishing extraordinary books. Write a good, tight story and follow our submission guidelines."

UNIVERSITY OF IOWA PRESS

119 W. Park Rd, Iowa City IA 52242-1000. (319)335-2000. Fax: (319)335-2055. E-mail: uipress@uiowa.edu. Web site: www.uiowapress.org. **Contact:** Holly Carver, director; Joe Parsons, acquisitions editor. Estab. 1969. Publishes paperback originals. Average print run for a first book is 1,000-1,500. Averages 35 total titles/year.

Needs Currently publishes the Iowa Short Fiction Award selections.

How to Contact Responds in 6 months to queries. See Web site for details .

Terms Pays 7-10% royalty on net receipts. Publishes ms 1 year after acceptance. Ms guidelines online.

UNIVERSITY OF MICHIGAN PRESS

839 Greene St., Ann Arbor MI 48106. (734)764-4388. Fax: (734)615-1540. E-mail: ump.fiction@umich.edu. Web site: www.press.umich.edu. **Contact:** Chris Hebert, editor (fiction). Midsize university press. Publishes hardcover originals. Member AAUP.

Imprint(s) Sweetwater Fiction Originals (literary/regional).

Needs Literary, short story collections, novels.

How to Contact Accepts unsolicited mss. Query with SASE or submit outline, 3 sample chapter(s). Accepts queries by mail. Include brief bio, list of publishing credits. Responds in 4-6 weeks to queries; 6-8 weeks to mss. Accepts simultaneous submissions. No electronic submissions, submissions on disk. Sometimes comments on rejected mss.

Terms Ms guidelines online.

Advice "Aside from work published through the Michigan Literary Fiction Awards, we seek only fiction set in the Great Lakes region."

UNIVERSITY OF NEVADA PRESS

MS 166, Reno NV 89557. (775)682-7393. Fax: (775)784-6200. Web site: www.unpress.nevada.edu. **Contact:** Margaret Dalrymple (fiction). Estab. 1961. "Small university press. Publishes fiction that primarily focuses on the American West." Publishes hardcover and paperback originals. Averages 25 total titles, 2 fiction titles/year. Member: AAUP

• *Strange White Male*, by Gerald Haslam won the WESTAF Award for Fiction in 2000 and *Foreword Magazine's* second place winner for Book of the Year.

Needs "We publish in Basque Studies, Gambling Studies, Western literature, Western history, Natural science, Environmental Studies, Travel and Outdoor books, Archeology, Anthropology, and Political Studies, all focusing on the West''.

How to Contact Submit outline, 2-4 sample chapter(s), synopsis. Include estimated word count, brief bio, list of publishing credits. Send SASE or IRC. Responds in 2 months to queries. No simultaneous submissions.

Terms Publishes ms 18 months after acceptance. Book catalog and ms guidelines free Ms guidelines online.

Advice We loo for literary ficition that focuses on the contemporary West.

WALKER AND CO.

Walker Publishing Co., 175 Fifth Ave., New York NY 10010. Web site: www.walkeryoungreaders.com. **Contact:** Emily Easton, publisher (picture books, middle grade & young adult novels); Stacy Cantor, Associate editor; Mary Kate Castellani, assistant editor. Estab. 1959. Midsize publisher. Publishes hardcover trade originals. Average first novel print order: 5,000-7,500. Averages 25 total titles/year.

Needs Juvenile (fiction, nonfiction), picture books (juvenile). Published *Stolen Car*, by Patrick Jones; *Skinny*, by Ibi Kaslik

How to Contact Accepts unsolicited mss. Query with SASE. Include ''a concise description of the story line, including its outcome, word length of story, writing experience, publishing credits, particular expertise on this subject and in this genre. Common mistake: not researching our publishing program and forgetting SASE.'' Agented fiction 50%. Responds in 3 months to queries. Sometimes comments on rejected mss. Send SASE for our reponse to your submission. We do not return manuscripts and proposals.

Terms Pays 5%- 10% on . Average advance: competitive. Publishes ms 1 year after acceptance.

◪ ◎ ⯑ THE WATERBROOK MULTNOMAH PUBLISHERS GROUP

The WaterBrook Multnomah Publishing Group, 12265 Oracle Blvd, Suite 200, Colorado Springs, Colorado 80921. Phone: (719)590-4999 Fax: (719)590-8977. Web site: www.mpbooks.com. **Contact:** Editorial department. Estab. 1987. Midsize independent publisher of evangelical fiction and nonfiction. Publishes hardcover and trade paperback originals. Books: perfect binding. Average print order: 15,000. Averages 75 total titles/year.

- Multnomah Books has received several Gold Medallion Book Awards from the Evangelical Christian Publishers Association.

Imprint(s) Multnomah Books (''Christian living and popular theology books''); Multnomah Fiction (''Changing lives through the power of story''); Multnomah Gift (''Substantive topics with beautiful, lyrical writing'').

Needs Adventure, historical, humor, literary, mystery/suspense, religious, romance, western. Published *The Rescuer*, by Dee Henderson (romance/suspense); *Diary Of a Teenage Girl* series, by Melody Carlson (YA); and *Sisterchicks Do the Hula*, by Robin Jones Gunn (contemporary).

How to Contact Does not accept unsolicited mss. *Agented submissions only.* Accepts simultaneous submissions.

Terms Pays royalty on wholesale price. Provides 100 author's copies. Offers advance. Publishes ms 1-2 years after acceptance. Ms guidelines online.

Advice ''Looking for moral, uplifting fiction. We're particularly interested in contemporary women's fiction, historical fiction, superior romance and mystery/suspense.''

◪ ◎ WHITE MANE KIDS

White Mane Publishing, P.O. Box 708, Shippensburg PA 17257. (717)532-2237. Fax: (717)532-6110. E-mail: marketing@whitemane.com. Web site: www.whitemane.com. Publishes hardcover orginals and paperback originals.

Needs Children's/juvenile (historical), young adult (historical). Published *Anybody's Hero: Battle of Old Men & Young Boys*, by Phyllis Haslip; *Crossroads at Gettysburg*, by Alan Kay.

How to Contact Accepts unsolicited mss. Query with SASE. Accepts queries by fax, mail. Include estimated word count, brief bio, summary of work and marketing ideas. Send SASE for return of ms or send a disposable ms and SASE for reply only. Responds in 1 month to queries; 3-4 months to mss. Accepts simultaneous submissions. Rarely comments on rejected mss.

Terms Pays royalty. Publishes ms 12-18 months after acceptance. Ms guidelines for #10 SASE.
Advice "Make your work historically accurate."

N ☐ WILD CHILD PUBLISHING

P.O. Box 4897, Culver City CA 90231. E-mail: mgbaun@wildchildpublishing.com. Web site: http://www.wildchildpublishing.com/. **Contact:** Marci Baun, editor-in-chief (genres not covered by other editors); Faith Bicknell-Brown, managing editor (horror and romance); S.R. Howen, editor (science fiction and nonfiction). Estab. 2006. Wild Child Publishing is a small, independent press that started out as a magazine in September 1999. We are known for working with newer/unpublished authors and editing to the standards of NYC publishers. Publishes paperback originals, e-books. Format: POD printing; perfect bound. Average print order: 50-200. Debut novel print order: 50. **Published 12 new writers last year.** Plans 10 debut novels this year. Averages 12 fiction titles/year. Member EPIC. Distributes/promotes titles through Ingrams and own Web site, Mobipocket Kindle, Amazon, and soon with Fictionwise. Freya's Bower already distributed with through Fictionwise.

• Was named a Top 101 Writers' Web sites in 2005.

Imprint(s) Freya's Bower.

Needs Adventure, children's/juvenile, erotica for Freya's Bower only, ethnic/multicultural, experimental, fantasy, feminist, gay, historical, horror, humor/satire, lesbian, literary, mainstream, military/war, mystery/suspense, New Age/mystic, psychic/supernatural, romance, science fiction, short story collections, thriller/espionage, western, young adult/teen (fantasy/science fiction). Multiple anthologies planned. Writers should submit material per our submissions guidelines. Published *Fade to Pale*, by James Cheetham (horror/psychological thriller); *Iron Horse Rider*, by Adelle Laudan (biker fiction/romance); *Quits: Book 2: Devils*, by M.E. Ellis (horror, psychological thriller, paranormal).

How to Contact Query with outline/synopsis and 1 sample chapter. Accepts queries by e-mail only. Include estimated word count, brief bio. Responds to queries in 2-4 weeks. Often critiques/comments on rejected mss. Responds to mss in 2-4 weeks.

Terms Sends pre-production galleys to author. Ms published 2-4 months after acceptance. Pays royalties 10-40%. Book catalogs on Web site.

Advice "Read our submission guidelines thoroughly. Send in entertaining, well-written stories. Be easy to work with and upbeat."

N ☐ ◎ THE WILD ROSE PRESS

P.O. Box 708, Adams Basin NY 14410. E-mail: rpenders@thewildrosepress.com. Web site: http://www.thewildrosepress.com. **Contact:** Diana Carlile, senior editor (Scarlet Rose-erotic romance); Nicole D'Arienzo, senior editor (historical department-Cactus Rose [Westerns], English Tea rose [Regency] and American Historicals); Kathy Cottrell, senior editor (Last Rose of Summer-contemporary romance for older heroines, second time around type of love stories); Nicola Martinez, senior editor (White Rose-inspirational romance); Jill Williamson, senior editor, Climbing Roses (Climbing Roses-Y/A Line); Anna Darclon, senior editor (Vintage Rose-stories set in the 1920's-1970's); Ami Russell, senior editor (Faery Rose-paranormals that include faeries, elves, sprites, etc.); CallieLynn Wolfe, senior editor (Black Rose-dark paranormals that include werewolves, vampires, etc.); Stacy Holmes/Spencer Pape, editorial team (Yellow Rose-cowboys, ranch setting romances); Leanne Morgena, senior editor (Sweetheart Rose-sweet romance); Lori Graham, senior editor (Crimson Rose-mystery and suspense); Roseann Armstrong, senior editor(Champagne Rose-contemporary romance). Estab. 2006." The Wild Rose Press is considered a small press. Our company is owned by RJ Morris and Rhonda Penders. The company is run out of upstate, NY and is a full-time operation, although 99% of the staff works from their home offices in the US, Canada, and in Australia. We have authors in several different countries including of course the U.S. What makes The Wild Rose Press unique is our down to earth approach to writing. We are writers ourselves and know what it means to submit a manuscript. Therefore, we opened our 'garden' with the mission of being a kinder and gentler publisher; a publishing house by writers for writers. There are no form rejection letters allowed. Every writer will get constructive criticism on his/her manuscript and if its rejected, the author will get a detailed, personalized rejection letter. We have a writers resource section on the Web site called 'The Greenhouse' which is full of articles on the craft of writing as well as promotion. We have loops and chats and several different venues for author education. We believe in 'growing writers,' not just publishing them." Publishes paperback originals, paperback reprints, e-books. Average print order: POD. **Published over 100 new writers last year.** "Plans are to continue in the same for this year.'' Averages approximately 300 fiction titles/year. Member of EPIC, also an RWA Recognized Publisher. Distributes/promotes titles through all major distribution channels such as Barnes & Noble, Amazon.com, fictionwise.com, coffeetimeromance.com, allaboutromance.com, Borders, in addition to Bakers & Taylor or Ingram.

Needs Only publishes romance. Does not want gay/lesbian romance, or ''anything that does not have romance as a central part of the story (although exceptions are made for the YA line). We would like to see more historicals, particularly American historicals, good time travels. Also seeking submissions for our Black Rose Line (dark paranormal), Climbing Roses Line (YA), in particular. All lines in the company are currently open and accepting submissions. We would also encourage and like to see multicultural romances and stories about people of different ethnic backgrounds in every line.'' Anthologies planned include a romance anthology in 2008 in which the authors were selected by the editors to contribute. Short story series in several of the lines are also planned. One such series is set in the Yellow Rose Line—WayBack, Texas. All stories are under 40,000 words and feature a small fictional town and the local rodeo that happens every Saturday night. *Published Nothing to Fear*, by Alicia Dean (romantic suspense); *Beauty and the Geek*, by Roni Adams (contemporary romance); *Shane's Hideaway*, by Sheridon Smythe (romantic suspense).

How to Contact E-mail Queries are preferred although snail mail queries will be accepted as well. Query with outline/synopsis (up to 5 pages) and sample chapters. Include estimated word count, brief bio, list of publishing credits, and ''anything the author considers important that we know when considering the manuscript.'' Send disposable copy of ms and SASE for reply only. Responds to queries in 4 weeks. Accepts unsolicited mss. Considers simultaneous submissions, submissions on CD or disk, e-mail submissions preferred. Always critiques/comments on rejected mss. Responds to mss on average 12 weeks.

Terms Sends pre-production galleys to author. Ms published within 12 months after acceptance. Writer's guidelines on Web site. Pays royalties 7-30%.

Advice ''We have grown very fast in just under two years but we will continue to stick to our mission of caring about our writers and authors. They are our number one priority. Our editors work very hard to give every writer the best possible service we can. However, once you submitted, please be patient. I know you hear that a lot. The editors are doing everything they can to get to your particular manuscript. However, if there is ever a question or a concern about your manuscript, you can come directly to me (rpenders@thewildrosepress.com) and I am always interested in getting you the information you need. We have a huge staff of editors on board and they really do a remarkable job at getting to manuscripts on a timely basis. My other piece of advice is simply to keep writing. Work on something else. Push yourself to try a category you haven't tried before. If you always write for contemporary, maybe try a historical piece. If you always write fantasy try a straight contemporary. It's always good to stretch your skills and see what you can do with them.''

🗒 ◎ WILSHIRE BOOK CO.

9731 Variel Ave., Chatsworth, CA 92311-4315. (818)700-1522. Fax: (818)700-1527. E-mail: mpowers @mpowers.com. Web site: www.mpowers.com. **Contact:** Melvin Powers, publisher; editorial department (adult fables). Estab. 1947. ''You are not only what you are today, but also what you choose to become tomorrow.'' Looking for adult fables that teach principles of psychological growth. Publishes trade paperback originals and reprints. **Published 7 debut authors within the last year.** Averages 25 total titles/year. Distributes titles through wholesalers, bookstores and mail order. Promotes titles through author interviews on radio and television.

Needs Adult allegories that teach principles of psychological growth or offer guidance in living. Minimum 25,000 words. Published *The Princess Who Believed in Fairy Tales*, by Marcia Grad; *The Knight in Rusty Armor*, by Robert Fisher; *The Dragon Slayer With a Heavy Heart*, by Marcia Powers.

How to Contact Accepts unsolicited mss. Query with SASE or submit 3 sample chapter(s), synopsis or submit complete ms. Accepts queries by e-mail. Responds in 2 months to queries. Accepts simultaneous submissions.

Terms Pays standard royalty. Offers advance. Publishes ms 6 months after acceptance. Ms guidelines online.

Advice ''We are vitally interested in all new material we receive. Just as you hopefully submit your manuscript for publication, we hopefully read every one submitted, searching for those that we believe will be successful in the marketplace. Writing and publishing must be a team effort. We need you to write what we can sell. We suggest that you read the successful books mentioned above or others that are similar: *Greatest Salesman in the World, Illusions, Way of the Peaceful Warrior, Celestine Prophecy*. Analyze them to discover what elements make them winners. Duplicate those elements in your own style, using a creative new approach and fresh material, and you will have written a book we can successfully market."

◑ WIND RIVER PRESS

E-mail: submissions@windriverpress.com. Web site: www.windriverpress.com. **Contact:** Katherine Arline, editor (mainstream, travel, literary, historical, short story collections, translations). Estab. 2002. Publishes full and chapbook length paperback originals and reprints and electronic books. "Wind River Press works closely with the author to develop a cost-effective production, promotion and distribution strategy."

Needs Historical, literary, mainstream/contemporary, short story collections. Plans anthology of works selected from Wind River Press's magazines (*Critique* and *The Paumanok Review*). Recently published books by Elisha Porat, Gaither Stewart and Rochelle Mass.

How to Contact Accepts unsolicited mss. Accepts queries by e-mail. Include estimated word count, brief bio, list of publishing credits. Agented fiction 5%. Responds in 3 weeks to queries; 2 months to mss. Accepts simultaneous submissions. Always comments on rejected mss.

Terms Individual arrangement depending on book formats and target audience. Publishes ms 6 months after acceptance. Guidelines and book catalog available on Web site.

WINDRIVER PUBLISHING, INC.

72 N. Windriver Road, Silverton ID 83867-0446. (208)752-1836. Fax: (208)752-1876. E-mail: info@windriverpublishing.com. Web site: www.windriverpublishing.com. Estab. 2003. Publishes hardcover originals and reprints, trade paperback originals, mass market originals. Averages 8 total titles/year.

Needs Adventure, fantasy, historical, humor, juvenile, literary, military/war, mystery, religious, science fiction, spiritual, suspense, young adult.

How to Contact Responds in 2 months to queries; 4-6 months to mss. Accepts simultaneous submissions.

Terms Pays 8-15% royalty on wholesale price. Publishes ms 12-18 months after acceptance. Ms guidelines online.

◎ WOODLEY MEMORIAL PRESS

English Dept., Washburn University, Topeka KS 66621. (785)670-1908. E-mail: karen.barron@washburn.edu. Web site: www.washburn.edu/reference/woodley-press. **Contact:** K.L. Barron, corresponding editor. Estab. 1980. "Woodley Memorial Press is a small, nonprofit press which publishes novels and fiction collections by Kansas writers only; by 'Kansas writers' we mean writers who reside in Kansas or have a Kansas connection." Publishes paperback originals.

Needs Literary, mainstream/contemporary, short story collections. Published KS Notable Book winner *Great Blues*, by Steve Semken; *The Trouble With Campus Security*, by G.W. Clift; and *Loading The Stone*, by Harley Elliot.

How to Contact Accepts unsolicited mss. Accepts queries by e-mail. Responds in 2 weeks to queries; 6 months to mss. Often comments on rejected mss.

Terms Publishes ms 1 year after acceptance. Ms guidelines online.

Advice "We only publish one to three works of fiction a year, on average, and those will definitely have a Kansas connection. We seek authors who are dedicated to promoting their works."

WORD WARRIORS PRESS

3808 Blaisdell Ave. S. #309, Minneapolis MN 55409. Web site: www.wordwarriorpress.com. **Contact:** Gail Cerridwen, managing editor Publishes paperback originals. Averages 1-2 total titles/year.

Terms Pays royalties.

◐ YELLOW SHOE FICTION SERIES

Louisiana State University Press, P.O. Box 25053, Baton Rouge LA 70894-5053. Web site: www.lsu.edu/lsupress. **Contact:** Michael Griffith, editor. Estab. 2004. Literary fiction series. Averages 2 titles/year.

Needs Literary. "Looking first and foremost for literary excellence, especially good manuscripts that have fallen through the cracks at the big commercial presses. I'll cast a wide net.'' Published *The Animal Girl*, by John Fulton.

How to Contact Does not accept unsolicited mss. Accepts queries by mail, Attn: John Easterly. No electronic submissions.

Terms Pays royalty. Offers advance. Ms guidelines online.

✅ ◎ ZONDERVAN

HarperCollins Publishers, 5300 Patterson Ave. Se, Grand Rapids MI 49530-0002. (616)698-6900. Manuscript submission line (616)698-3447. **Contact**: Submissions accepted only by email and only for certain types of manuscripts. See Web site for current submission guidelines and email address: www.zondervan.com. Estab. 1931. ''Our mission is to be the leading Christian communications company meeting the needs of people with resources that glorify Jesus Christ and promote biblical principles.'' Large evangelical Christian publishing house. Published some debut authors within the last year. Averages 120 trade books per year.

Needs See Web site: www.zondervan.com. **Format in which to submit**: Include a vita, tentative title of the book, description of the book with strong case for why the book must be written and published (2-4 pages), plot outline or table of contents, and one or two sample chapters. DO NOT SEND ENTIRE MANUSCRIPT. Manuscripts should be typed in Microsoft Word in $8\frac{1}{2} \times 11$'' portrait format, double-spaced with one-inch margins on all sides. Number pages consecutively through the entire manuscript. Do not have separate pagination for each chapter. Place your ''footnotes'' after each chapter as endnotes. Book proposals should be single-spaced with one-inch margins on all sides.

Terms Normally pays royalties based on net amount received from sales.

Advice Almost no unsolicited manuscripts are published.

Contests & Awards

I n addition to honors and, quite often, cash prizes, contests and awards programs offer writers the opportunity to be judged on the basis of quality alone without the outside factors that sometimes influence publishing decisions. New writers who win contests may be published for the first time, while more experienced writers may gain public recognition of an entire body of work.

Listed here are contests for almost every type of fiction writing. Some focus on form, such as short stories, novels or novellas, while others feature writing on particular themes or topics. Still others are prestigious prizes or awards for work that must be nominated, such as the Pulitzer Prize in Fiction. Chances are, no matter what type of fiction you write, there is a contest or award program that may interest you.

SELECTING AND SUBMITTING TO A CONTEST

Use the same care in submitting to contests as you would sending your manuscript to a publication or book publisher. Deadlines are very important, and where possible, we've included this information. At times contest deadlines were only approximate at our press deadline, so be sure to write, call or look online for complete information.

Follow the rules to the letter. If, for instance, contest rules require your name on a cover sheet only, you will be disqualified if you ignore this and put your name on every page. Find out how many copies to send. If you don't send the correct amount, by the time you are contacted to send more, it may be past the submission deadline. An increasing number of contests invite writers to query by e-mail, and many post contest information on their Web sites. Check listings for e-mail and Web site addresses.

One note of caution: Beware of contests that charge entry fees that are disproportionate to the amount of the prize. Contests offering a $10 prize, but charging $7 in entry fees, are a waste of your time and money.

If you are interested in a contest or award that requires your publisher to nominate your work, it's acceptable to make your interest known. Be sure to leave the publisher plenty of time, however, to make the nomination deadline.

[N] [⊕] AEON AWARD

Albedo One/Aeon Press, % 8 Bachelor's Walk, Dublin 1, Ireland. Fax: +353 (1)8730177. E-mail: fraslaw@yahoo.co.uk. Web site: www.albedo1.com. **Contact:** Frank Ludlow, Event Coordinator. "We aim to encourage new writers into the genre and to encourage existing writers to push at their boundaries" Annual. Competition/award for short stories. Prize: First prize €1,000, second €200 and third €100. The top three stories are guaranteed publication in *Albedo One*. Categories: any speculative genre, "i.e. fantasy, SF horror or anything in between or unclassifiable (like slipstream)." A short list is drawn up by the *Albedo One* editorial team and the final decision is made by renowned author Ian Watson. Entry Fee: € 7. Pay via Web site. Guidelines available in December. Accepts inquiries by fax, e-mail. The best stories of each submission period are shortlisted for the grand prize. **The competition is run in four quarterly periods with probable deadlines of the end of March, June, September and November.** Check the Web site for definite dates. Entries should be unpublished. Award open to "anyone with € 7 and a burning desire to be the best." Length: under 8,000 words. Cover letter should include name, address, e-mail, word count, novel/story title. It is essential the story is marked so it can be identified with its author. Writers may submit own work. "As the contest is initially judged by the editorial staff of *Albedo One*, I think it is fair to say that choices will be influenced by the individual tastes of these people. You can see what they like in *Albedo One* on a regular basis. I wish I could say there is a certain formula, but we pick the best stories submitted to us and although there can often be little evidence of genre influence visible on the page, we always feel that the stories are informed by the author's genre sensibilities. In other words, we like stories by authors who used to like/write science fiction. Confused? Pick up an issue of the magazine and check it out." Results announced within two months of the final deadline. Winners notified by e-mail, and at event/banquet. Winners in 2007 were announced at Eurocon in Copenhagen. Results made available to entrants on Web site.

[N] [⊕] [◎] AHWA FLASH & SHORT STORY COMPETITION

AHWA (Australian Horror Writers Association), %Post Office, Elphinstone, Victoria 3448, Australia. E-mail: competitions@australianhorror.com. Web site: http://www.australianhorror.com. **Contact:** David Carroll, Competitions Officer. "To showcase the diversity and talent of writers of horror fiction." Annual. Competition/award for short stories and flash fiction. The writers of the winning story in each category will receive an engraved plaque, plus the stories will be published (TBA) at paying rates. There are 2 categories: short stories (1,500 to 8,000 words) and flash fiction (less than 1,000 words). Last year, we received close to 110 entries in total, split approximately 40-60%. Writers may submit to one or both categories, but entry is limited to 1 story per author per category. There will be a panel of 3 judges who will announce a shortlist of 5 stories prior to the announcement of the winners. Entry free for AHWA members; for non-members, $5 for flash, $10 for short story. Payment can be made via our secure Paypal option using ahwa@australianhorror.com. Alternatively, contact us and we can arrange other payment methods (e.g., direct debit). Checks will not be accepted due to the cost associated with banking them. Guidelines available in January. Accepts inquiries by e-mail. **Entry deadline is May 31.** Entries should be unpublished. Anyone may enter the contest by submitting a story to competitions@australianhorror.com as an attached doc or rtf. Please do not send the story in the body of the email. Alternatively, contact us to arrange postal submissions. Cover letter should include name, address, e-mail, word count, novel/story title. Please do not include your name, address, or email on the ms as we hand the entries to the judges blind to remove any possible bias. Only include the title and word count at the start, plus title and page number on each page. "We're after horror stories, tales that frighten, yarns that unsettle us in our comfortable homes. All themes in this genre will be accepted, from the well-used (zombies, vampires, ghosts etc) to the highly original, so long as the story is professional and well written. No previously published entries will be accepted—all tales must be an original work by the author. Stories can be as violent or as bloody as the storyline dictates, but those containing gratuitous sex or violence will not be considered. Please check your entries for spelling and grammar mistakes and follow standard submission guidelines (eg, 12 point font, Ariel, Times New Roman, or Courier New, one and a half spacing between lines, with title and page number on each page." Results announced July/August. Winners notified at national convention in Australia. Results made available to entrants on Web site.

⬚ AIM MAGAZINE SHORT STORY CONTEST

P.O. Box 390, Milton WA 98354-0390. (253)815-9030. E-mail: apiladoone@aol.com. Web site: www.aimmagazine.org. **Contact:** Ruth Apilado, associate editor. $100 prize offered to contest winner for best unpublished short story (4,000 words maximum) "promoting brotherhood among people and cultures." Judged by staff members. No entry fee. Deadline: August 15. Competition receives 20 submissions per category. Guidelines available anytime. Accepts inquiries by e-mail and phone. Winners are announced in the autumn issue and notified by mail on September 1. List of winners available for SASE. Open to any writer.

◎ ALABAMA STATE COUNCIL ON THE ARTS INDIVIDUAL ARTIST FELLOWSHIP

201 Monroe St., Montgomery AL 36130-1800. (334)242-4076, ext. 224. Fax: (334)240-3269. E-mail: randy.shoults@arts.alabama.gov. Web site: www.arts.state.al.us. **Contact:** Randy Shoults, literature program manager. "To recognize the achievements and potential of Alabama writers." Judged by independent peer panel. Guidelines available in January. For guidelines, fax, e-mail, visit Web site. Accepts inquiries by fax, e-mail and phone. "Two copies of the following should be submitted: a résumé and a list of published works with reviews, if available. A minimum of 10 pages of poetry or prose, but no more than 20 pages. Please label each page with title, artist's name and date. If published, indicate where and the date of publication." Winners announced in June and notified by mail. List of winners available for SASE, fax, e-mail or visit Web site. No entry fee. Deadline: March. Competition receives 25 submissions annually. Two-year residency required.

⬚ NELSON ALGREN SHORT FICTION CONTEST

Chicago Tribune, Nelson Algren Awards, 435 N. Michigan Ave., Chicago IL 60611. E-mail: efigula@tribune.com. Web site: http://www.chicagotribune.com/about/custom/events/chi-csliteraryprizes-htmlstory,0,4283547.htmlstory?coll = chi-eventnavigation-fea. **Contact:** Erin Figula, senior marketing specialist. "Honors excellence in short story writing by previously unpublished authors." Prize: $5,000 grand prize, $1,500 runners-up prizes (3). Judged by a group of *Chicago Tribune* editors and contributors. No entry fee. Cover letter should include name, address, phone, e-mail, word count, title. "No info on manuscript besides title and page numbers." Results announced October. Winners notified by mail or phone in September. For contest results, visit Web site. Deadline: February 15. Entries must be unpublished and written by a U.S. citizen. Competition for short stories. Open to any writer. Guidelines also available by e-mail and on Web site. Accepts inquiries by e-mail.

Ⓝ ⬚ ALLIGATOR JUNIPER'S NATIONAL WRITING CONTEST

Alligator Juniper, 220 Grove Ave, Prescott AZ 86301. (928)350-2012. Fax: (928)776-5137. E-mail: aj@prescott.edu. Web site: http://www.prescott.edu/highlights/alligator_juniper/index.html. **Contact:** Rachel Yoder, managing editor. Annual. Competition/award for short stories. Prize: Winner receives $500 and publication. Finalists are published and receive copies. Categories: fiction, creative nonfiction, poetry. "All entries are read and discussed by advanced writing students at Prescott College enrolled in the *Alligator Juniper* practicum class. This class is overseen by two faculty members, each of whom is a working writer in the genres of poetry, fiction and creative nonfiction. All entrants receive a personal letter from one of our staff regarding the status of their submission. We usually inform in late January. The individual attention we devote to each manuscript takes time. We appreciate your patience." Entry fee: $10 (includes copy of issue). Make checks payable to *Alligator Juniper*. Accepts inquiries by fax, e-mail, phone. **Submission period is May 1-October 1.** Entries should be unpublished. Deadline: **December 1, 2008.** Anyone may enter contest. Length: Prose should be under 30 pages; poetry 5 poems or less. Cover letter should include name, address, phone, e-mail, word count, novel/story title. Writers may submit own work. "Send us your best work; we often don't know what we're looking for until we read it. Historically, winning work has grappled poetically and honestly with issues of race, sexuality, patriotism, politics, the environment, and language itself. We publish work that is both long and short, traditional and experimental in its approaches. Our editorial staff is composed of savvy, college-aged readers; do your best to wow us." Results announced January. Winners notified by phone, by e-mail. Winners announced December. Results made available to entrants with SASE, by fax, by e-mail, on Web site.

◎ AMERICAN ASSOCIATION OF UNIVERSITY WOMEN AWARD IN JUVENILE LITERATURE

North Carolina Literary and Historical Association, 4610 Mail Service Center, Raleigh NC 27699-4610. (919)807-7290. Fax: (919)733-8807. E-mail: michael.hill@ncmail.net. **Contact:** Michael Hill, awards coordinator. Award's purpose is to "select the year's best work of literature for young people by a North Carolina writer." Annual award for published books. Award: cup. Competition receives 10-15 submissions per category. Judged by three-judge panel. No entry fee. **Deadline: July 15.** Entries must be previously published. Contest open to "residents of North Carolina (three-year minimum)." Guidelines available July 15. For guidelines, send SASE, fax, e-mail or call. Accepts inquiries by fax, e-mail, phone. Winners announced October 15. Winners notified by mail. List of winners available for SASE, fax, e-mail.

AMERICAN LITERARY REVIEW SHORT FICTION AWARD

American Literary Review, P.O. Box 311307, University of North Texas, Denton TX 76203-1307. (940)565-2755. Web site: www.engl.unt.edu/alr. "To award excellence in short fiction." Prize: $1,000 and publication. Judged by rotating outside writer. Past judges have included Marly Swick, Antonya Nelson and Jonis Agee. Entry fee: $15. For guidelines, send SASE or visit Web site. Accepts inquiries by fax and phone. Deadline: September 1. Entries must be unpublished. Contest open to anyone not affiliated with the University of North Texas. "Only solidly crafted, character-driven stories will have the best chance for success." Winners announced and notified by mail and phone in February. List of winners available for SASE.

☐ AMERICAN MARKETS NEWSLETTER SHORT STORY COMPETITION

American Markets Newsletter, 1974 46th Ave., San Francisco CA 94116. E-mail: sheila.oconnor@juno.com. Award is "to give short story writers more exposure." Accepts fiction and nonfiction up to 2,000 words. Entries are eligible for cash prizes and all entries are eligible for worldwide syndication whether they win or not. Send double-spaced manuscripts with your story/article title, byline, word count and address on the first page above your article/story's first paragraph (no need for separate cover page). There is no limit to the number of entries you may send. Prize: 1st Place: $300; 2nd Place: $100; 3rd Place: $50. Judged by a panel of independent judges. Entry fee: $12 per entry; $20 for 2; $25 for 3; $30 for 4; $5 each entry thereafter. For guidelines, send SASE, fax or e-mail. **Deadline: June 30 and December 31.** Contest offered biannually. Published and unpublished stories are actively encouraged. Add a note of where and when previously published. Open to any writer. "All kinds of fiction are considered. We especially want women's pieces—romance, with a twist in the tale—but all will be considered." Results announced within 3 months of deadlines. Winners notified by mail if they include SASE.

◎ AMERICAN SCANDINAVIAN FOUNDATION TRANSLATION PRIZE

American Scandinavian Foundation, 58 Park Ave., New York NY 10016. (212)879-9779. Fax: (212)686-2115. E-mail: info@amscan.org. Web site: www.amscan.org. **Contact:** Valerie Hymas. Award to recognize excellence in fiction, poetry and drama translations of Scandinavian writers born after 1800. Prize: $2,000 grand prize; $1,000 prize. No entry fee. Cover letter should include name, address, phone, e-mail and title. Deadline: June 1. Entries must be unpublished. Length: no more than 50 pages for drama, fiction; no more than 35 pages for poetry. Open to any writer. Guidelines available in January for SASE, by fax, phone, e-mail or on Web site. Accepts inquiries by fax, e-mail, phone. Results announced in November. Winners notified by mail. Results available for SASE or by fax, e-mail, Web site.

N ☐ AMERICAN SHORT FICTION SHORT STORY CONTEST

American Short Fiction, P.O. Box 301209, Austin TX 78703. (512)5538-1305. Fax: (512)5538-1306. E-mail: editors@americanshortfiction.org. Web site: www.americanshortfiction.org. **Contact:** Stacey Swann, editor. "To reward the best short fiction being written with prize money and publication in *American Short Fiction*." Annual. Competition/award for short stories. Prize: $1,000 and publication for first place, $500 for second place. Receives about 300 entries per category. The first round of judging is a blind read by *American Short Fiction* editorial staff. Ten stories are sent to guest judge for final blind judging. The guest judge changes every year. Entry fee: $20. Make checks payable to *American Short Fiction*. Guidelines available in August. Accepts inquiries by e-mail. **Contest submission period is September 15th through December 1st.** Entries should be unpublished. Anyone may enter contest. Length: 6,000 max. Cover letter should include name, address, phone, e-mail, word count, novel/story title. Title only on ms. Writers may submit own work. "Familiarize yourself with our journal and aesthetic." Results announced mid to late March. Winners notified by e-mail. Results made available to entrants with SASE, by e-mail, on Web site.

◙ THE SHERWOOD ANDERSON FOUNDATION FICTION AWARD

The Sherwood Anderson Foundation, 216 College Rd., Richmond VA 23229. (804)289-8324. Fax: (804)287-6052. E-mail: mspear@richmond.edu. Web site: www.sherwoodandersonfoundation.o rg. **Contact:** Michael M. Spear, foundation co-president. Contest is to honor, preserve and celebrate the memory and literary work of Sherwood Anderson, American realist for the first half of the 20th century. Annual award to support developing writers of short stories and novels. Entrants must have published at least one book of fiction or have had several short stories published in major literary and/or commercial publications. Self-published stories do not qualify. Award: $15,000 grant. Judged by a committee established by the foundation. Entry fee: $20 application fee (payable to The Sherwood Anderson Foundation). Deadline: April 1. Send a detailed résumé that includes a bibliography of your publications. Include a cover letter that provides a history of your writing experience and your future plans for writing projects. Also, submit 2 or 3 examples of what you consider to be your best work. Do not send manuscripts by e-mail. Only mss in English will be accepted. Open to any writer who meets the qualifications listed above. Accepts inquiries by e-mail. Mail your application to the above address. No mss or publications will be returned.

⚟ ◎ ANNUAL ATLANTIC WRITING COMPETITION

Writer's Federation of Nova Scotia, 1113 Marginal Road, Halifax NS B3H 4P7 Canada. (902)423-8116. Fax: (902)422-0881. E-mail: talk@writers.ns.ca. Web site: www.writers.ns.ca. **Contact:** Susan Mersereau, program officer. Award's purpose is "to provide feedback to emerging writers and create a venue for their work to be considered against that of other beginning authors. Annual award to residents of Atlantic Canada for short stories, poetry, and novels as well as children's literature, YA novels, poetry and essay." Prize: In Canadian money: $200, $150, $100 for adult novel; $150, $75, $50 for children's literature and YA novel; $100, $75, $50 for short stories and essay/magazine article. Judged by a jury of professionals from the writing/literature field—authors, librarians, publishers, teachers. Entry fee: $25 per novel entry ($20 for WFNS members); $15 per entry in other categories ($10 members). **Deadline: first Friday in December of each year.** Entries must be unpublished. Length: story 3,000 words maximum; novel 100,000 words maximum; children's writing 20,000 words maximum, YA novel 75,000 words maximum. Writers must use pseudonym; use $8^{1}/_{2} \times 11$ white paper (one side only); and format entry typed and double-spaced. To be eligible, writers must be residents of Atlantic Canada, older than 16 and not extensively published in the category they are entering. Guidelines available by SASE or on Web site. Accepts inquiries by e-mail, phone. Winners announced in August. List of winners available on Web site.

◎ ANNUAL BOOK COMPETITION

Washington Writers' Publishing House, Elisavietta Ritchie, P.O Box 298, Broomes Island MD 20615. E-mail: megan@bcps.org. Web site: www.wwph.org. **Contact:** Moira Egan, president. "To award literary excellence in the greater Washington DC-Baltimore area." Annual. Competition/award for novels, story collections. Prize: $500, publication, and 50 copies of book. Categories: fiction (novel or collection of short stories). Receives about 50 entries per category. Judged by members of the press. Entry fee: $25. Make checks payable to WWPH. Guidelines available all year with SASE, on Web site. Accepts inquiries by e-mail. Deadline: Nov. 1. Entries should be unpublished. "Individual stories or excerpts may have been published in journals and anthologies." Open to fiction writers living within 60 miles of the Capitol (Baltimore area included). Length: no more than 350 pages, double or $1^{1}/_{2}$ spaced. Cover letter should include name, address, phone, e-mail, novel/collection title, place(s) where stories/excerpts were previously published. None of this information should appear on the actual manuscript. Writers may submit own work. Results announced January of each year. Winners notified by phone, by e-mail. Results made available to entrants on Web site.

◻ ANNUAL FICTION CONTEST

Women in the Arts, P.O. Box 2907, Decatur IL 62524. (217)872-0811. **Contact:** Vice President. Annual competition for essays, fiction, fiction for children, plays, rhymed poetry, unrhymed poetry. Prize: $50, $35, $15 in all categories. Categories: Essay (up to 1,500 words); fiction (up to 1,500 words); fiction for children (up to 1,500 words); play (one act, 10-page limit); rhymed and unrhymed poetry (up to 32 lines). Judged by published, professional writers who live outside the state of Illinois. All entries will be subject to blind judging. Entry fee: $2 per entry, unlimited entries. Deadline: November 1. Do not submit drawings for any category. Double-space prose. Entries must be typed on 8½×11 paper and must be titled. Do not put your name on any page of the ms. Do put your name, address, telephone number, e-mail and titles of your entries on a cover sheet. Submit one cover sheet and one check, with all entries mailed flat in one envelope. Do not staple. No entries published by WITA, author retains rights. Open to any writer. Results announced March 15 annually. Winners notified by mail. "Send a perfect manuscript—no typos, Liquid Paper or holes from 3-ring binders."

⊚ ANNUAL JUVENILE FICTION CONTEST

Women in the Arts, P.O. Box 2907, Decatur IL 62524. (217)872-0811. **Contact:** Vice President. Annual competition for essays, fiction, fiction for children, plays, rhymed poetry, unrhymed poetry. Prize: $15-$50. Judged by anonymous judges who are published, professional writers who live outside Illinois. Entry fee: $2 per entry. Word length: 1,500 maximum for fiction, essay, fiction for children; one act for plays; up to 32 lines for poetry. Deadline: November 1. Entries must be original work of the author. Entries must be typed on 8½×11 white paper and must be titled. Do not put your name on any page of the entry. Instead, put your name, address, telephone number, e-mail and titles of your entries on a cover sheet. Submit one cover sheet and one check. Mail all entries flat in a single envelope. Do not staple. Open to any writer. "Entrants must send for contest rules and follow the specific format requirements."

ℕ ◻ ANNUAL POETRY & FICTION COMPETITIONS

Inkwell, Manhattanville College, 2900 Purchase St., Box 1379, Purchase NY 10577. (914)323-7239. E-mail: inkwell@mville.org. Web site: www.inkwelljournal.org. **Contact:** Editor. Annual. Competition/award for short stories. Prize: $1,500 for fiction, $1,000 for poetry. Categories: fiction and poetry. Receives about 500 (fiction) and 1,000 (poetry) entries per category. Judged by different judges every year. Entry fee: $15 per story. Make checks payable to Manhattanville—Inkwell. Guidelines available in May/June on Web site. Accepts inquiries by e-mail. Submission period: August 1-October 31. Entries should be unpublished. Length: 6,000 words (fiction). Cover letter should include name, address, phone, e-mail, word count, novel/story title. None of this information should appear on the manuscript. Writers may submit own work. Winners notified by mail, by phone, by e-mail, on Web site. Results made available to entrants with SASE, on Web site.

ANNUAL POETRY/FICTION CONTEST

Rambunctious Press, Inc., 1221 Pratt Blvd., Chicago IL 60626. (773)338-2439. **Contact:** E. Hausler, editor. Annual competition for short stories. Prize: $100, $75, $50. Entry fee: $4 per story or $15 subscription. For guidelines send SASE. Deadline: December 31. Entries must be unpublished. Length: 12 pages. Open to any writer. "Follow the theme with creativity. Each contest has a theme. Examples: Courage, Color and Milestones." Winners announced three months after contest deadline. "All contestants will receive a list of winners."

◻ ANTIETAM REVIEW ANNUAL LITERARY AWARD

Antietam Review, 14 West Washington Street, Hagerstown MD 21740. (301)791-3132. Fax: (240)420-1754. E-mail: antietamreview@washingtoncountyarts.com (for queries only). Web site: www.washingtoncountyarts.com. **Contact:** Philip Bufithis, executive editor. Review estab. 1982. Circ. 1,000. To encourage and give recognition to excellence in short fiction and poetry. Prize: $150 for selected prose and $100 for selected poem. Both categories receive two copies of magazine. Categories: "Fiction: Contributors may submit only 1 entry with fewer than 5,000 words. Editors seek high quality, well-crafted work with significant character development and shift. A manuscript stands out because of its energy and flow. Short stories are preferred; however, novel excerpts are considered if they work as independent pieces. Poetry: Up to three poems with no more than 30 lines. No haiku, religious or rhyme." Entry fee: $15 for fiction (three poems considered one fee); check, credit card and money orders accepted. Entries must be unpublished. Open to any writer.

⊚ ARROWHEAD REGIONAL ARTS COUNCIL INDIVIDUAL ARTIST CAREER DEVELOPMENT GRANT

Arrowhead Regional Arts Council, 1301 Rice Lake Rd., Suite 111, Duluth MN 55811. (218)722-0952 or (800)569-8134. Fax: (218)722-4459. E-mail: info@aracouncil.org. Web site: www.aracouncil.org.

Award to "provide financial support to regional artists wishing to take advantage of impending, concrete opportunities that will advance their work or careers." Prize: up to $1,000. Categories: novels, short stories, story collections and translations. Judged by ARAC Board. No entry fee. Guidelines available by phone, e-mail or on Web site. **See Web site for 2009 deadlines.** Entries must be unpublished. Award is offered 3 times per year. Applicants must live in the seven-county region of Northeastern Minnesota. Results announced approximately 6 weeks after deadline. Winners notified by mail. List of winners available by phone.

THE ART OF MUSIC ANNUAL WRITING CONTEST

Piano Press, P.O. Box 85, Del Mar CA 92014-0085. (619)884-1401. Fax: (858)755-1104. E-mail: pianopress@pianopress.com. Web site: www.pianopress.com. **Contact:** Elizabeth C. Axford. Offered annually. Categories are: essay, short story, poetry and song lyrics. All writings must be on music-related topics. The purpose of the contest is to promote the art of music through writing. Acquires one-time rights. All entries must be accompanied by an entry form indicating category and age; parent signature is required of all writers under age 18. Poems may be of any length and in any style; essays and short stories should not exceed five double-spaced, typewritten pages. All entries shall be previously unpublished (except poems and song lyrics) and the original work of the author. Guidelines and entry form for SASE, on Web site or by e-mail. Prize: Cash, medal, certificate, publication in the biannual anthology/chapbook titled *The Art of Music: A Collection of Writings*, and copies of the book. Judged by a panel of published poets, authors and songwriters. Entry fee: $20 fee. Inquiries accepted by fax, e-mail, phone. **Deadline: June 30.** Short stories should be no longer than five pages typed and double spaced. Open to any writer. "Make sure all work is fresh and original. Music-related topics only." Results announced October 31. Winners notified by mail. For contest results, send SASE or visit Web site.

ARTIST TRUST/ WASHINGTON STATE ARTS COMMISSION FELLOWSHIP AWARDS

Artist Trust, 1835 12th Ave, Seattle WA 98122. (209)467-8734 ext 9. Fax: (206)467-9633. E-mail: info@artisttrust.org. Web site: http://artisttrust.org. **Contact:** Heather Helback-Olds, Director of Programs. "Artist Trust/ Washington State Arts Commission Fellowship awards practicing professional Washington State artists of exceptional talent and demonstrated ability." Annual. Prize: $6,500. "The Fellowship awards are multidisciplinary awards. The categories for 2009 are Literary, Music, Media and Craft. Accepted genres for Literary are: poetry, fiction, graphic novels, experimental works, creative nonfiction, screen plays, film scripts and teleplays." Receives about 175 entries per category. Entries are judged by work samples as specified in the guidelines. Winners are selected by a multidisciplinary panel of artists and arts professionals. No entry fee. Guidelines available in April. Accepts inquiries by e-mail, phone. April-June is the submission period. **Deadline is approximately the 4th Friday of June.** Web site should be consulted for the exact date. Entries can be unpublished or previously published. Washington State residents only. Length: up to 15 pages for poetry, fiction, graphic novels, experimental works and creative nonfiction, and up to 20 pages for screen plays, film scripts and teleplays. All mss must be typed with a 12-pnt font size or larger and cannot be single spaced (except for poetry). Include artist statement and resume with name, address, phone, e-mail, and novel/story title. "The Fellowship awards are highly competitive. Please follow guidelines with care." Results announced October. Winners notified by mail. Results made available to entrants on Web site.

ASTED/GRAND PRIX DE LITTERATURE JEUNESSE DU QUEBEC-ALVINE-BELISLE

Association pour l'avancement des sciences et des techniques de la documentation, 3414 Avenue du Parc, Bureau 202, Montreal QC H2X 2H5 Canada. (514)281-5012. Fax: (514)281-8219. E-mail: info@asted.org. Web site: www.asted.org. **Contact:** Brigitte Moreau and Olivia Marleau, co-presidents. "Prize granted for the best work in youth literature edited in French in the Quebec Province. Authors and editors can participate in the contest." Offered annually for books published during the preceding year. Prize: $1,000. No entry fee. Deadline: June 1. Entries must be previously published. Open to editors and authors with books published during the preceding year.

THE ATHENAEUM LITERARY AWARD

The Athenaeum of Philadelphia, 219 S. Sixth St., Philadelphia PA 19106-3794. (215)925-2688. Fax: (215)925-3755. E-mail: erose@PhilaAthenaeum.org. Web site: www.PhilaAthenaeum.org. **Contact:**

Ellen L. Rose. Annual award to recognize and encourage outstanding literary achievement in Philadelphia and its vicinity. Prize: a certificate bearing the name of the award, the seal of the Athenaeum, the title of the book, the name of the author and the year. Categories: The Athenaeum Literary Award is granted for a work of general literature, not exclusively for fiction. Judged by a committee appointed by the Board of Directors. No entry fee. Deadline: December. Entries must be previously published. Nominations shall be made in writing to the Literary Award Committee by the author, the publisher, or a member of the Athenaeum, accompanied by a copy of the book. Open to work by residents of Philadelphia and its vicinity. Guidelines available for SASE, by fax, by e-mail and on Web site. Accepts inquiries by fax, e-mail and phone. Juvenile fiction is not included. Results announced in Spring. Winners notified by mail. For contest results, see Web site.

N AUTUMN HOUSE FICTION PRIZE

Autumn House Press, 87 ½ Westwood Street, Pittsburgh PA 15211. (412)381-4261. E-mail: info@autumnhouse.org. Web site: http://autumnhouse.org. **Contact:** Michael Simms, executive editor. "To identify and publish the best fiction manuscripts we can find" Annual. Competition/award for short stories, novels, story collections, translations. Prize: $2,500 and book publication. Only one category: all genres of fiction (short stories, short-shorts, novellas, and novels, or any combination of genres) are eligible. Entries are judged by Sharon Dillworth, who is assisted by an able team of experienced, published writers. Entry fee: $25. Make checks payable to Autumn House Press. Accepts inquiries by e-mail, phone. **Entry deadline is June 30, 2009.** Entries should be unpublished. Open to all writers over the age of 18. Length: approx 200-300 pgs. Cover letter should include name, address, phone, e-mail, novel/story title. The mss are judged blind, so please include two cover pages, one with contact information and one without. "The competition is tough, so submit only your best work!" Results announced September. Winners notified by mail, by phone, by e-mail. Results made available to entrants with SASE, by fax, by e-mail, on Web site.

◪ AWP AWARD SERIES IN THE NOVEL, CREATIVE NONFICTION AND SHORT FICTION

The Association of Writers & Writing Programs, Mail Stop 1E3, George Mason University, Fairfax VA 22030. (703)993-4301. Fax: (703)993-4302. E-mail: awp@awpwriter.org. Web site: www.awpwriter.org. **Contact:** Supriya Bhatnagar, director of publications. The AWP Award Series was established in cooperation with several university presses in order to publish and make fine fiction and nonfiction available to a wide audience. Offered annually to foster new literary talent. Guidelines for SASE and on Web site. Categories: novel ($2,000), Donald Hall Prize in Poetry ($4,000), Grace Paley Prize in Short Fiction ($4,000), and creative nonfiction ($2,000). Entry fee: $25 for nonmembers, $10 for members. Entries must be unpublished. **Mss must be postmarked between January 1-February 28.** Cover letter should include name, address, phone number, e-mail and title. "This information should appear in cover letter only." Open to any writer. Guidelines available on Web site in November. No phone calls, please. Manuscripts published previously in their entirety, including self-publishing, are not eligible. No mss returned. Results announced in August. Winners notified by mail or phone. For contest results send SASE, or visit Web site. No phone calls, please.

▢ ◎ AWP INTRO JOURNALS PROJECT

Dept. of English, Bluffton University, 1 University Drive, Bluffton OH 45817-2104. E-mail: awp@gmu.edu. Web site: www.awpwriter.org. **Contact:** Jeff Gundy. "This is a prize for students in AWP member university creative writing programs only. Authors are nominated by the head of the creative writing department. Each school may nominate no more than one work of nonfiction, one work of short fiction and three poems." Prize: $100 plus publication in participating journal. 2006 journals included *Puerto del Sol, Quarterly West, Mid-American Review, Willow Springs, Tampa Review, Controlled Burn, Artful Dodge, Colorado Review,* and *Hayden's Ferry Review.* Categories: Short stories, nonfiction and poetry. Judged by AWP. No entry fee. Deadline: December 3. Entries must be unpublished. Open to students in AWP Member University Creative Writing Programs only. Accepts inquiries by e-mail, fax and phone. Guidelines available for SASE or on Web site. Results announced in Spring. Winners notified by mail in Spring. For contest results, send SASE or visit Web site.

N BAKELESS PRIZE

Bread Loaf Writers' Conference/Middlebury College and Houghton Mifflin Bakeless Prize, Bread Loaf Writers' Conf., Middlebury College, Middlebury VT 05753. (802)443-2018. E-mail: jbates@midd lebury.edu. Web site: http://www.bakelessprize.org. **Contact:** Jennifer Bates, Contest Coordinator. "To promote first books of the highest caliber." Annual. Prize: Publication by Houghton Mifflin and fellowship to attend Bread Loaf Writers' Conference. Categories: One award each for Fiction (average 500 entries), Poetry (average 700 entries) and Creative Nonfiction (average 100 entries). Judges and guidelines announced on web site in June. Entry fee: $10. Make checks payable to Middlebury College. Accepts inquiries by e-mail. **Submission period is September 15 to November 1.** Entries should be unpublished. Anyone writing in English may enter contest. Cover letter should include name, address, phone, e-mail, novel/story title. No identifying information on ms. Writers may submit own work. "Make sure your manuscript is ready." Results announced May. Winners notified by phone in April. Results made available to entrants with SASE, on Web site.

☑ ◎ BARD FICTION PRIZE

Bard College, P.O. Box 5000, Annandale-on-Hudson NY 12504-5000. (845)758-7087. Fax: (845)758-7043. E-mail: bfp@bard.edu. Web site: www.bard.edu/bfp. **Contact:** Irene Zedlacher. The Bard Fiction Prize is intended to encourage and support young writers of fiction to pursue their creative goals and to provide an opportunity to work in a fertile and intellectual environment. Prize: $30,000 cash award and appointment as writer-in-residence at Bard College for 1 semester. Judged by committee of 5 judges (authors associated with Bard College). No entry fee. Cover letter should include name, address, phone, e-mail and name of publisher where book was previously published. Guidelines available by SASE, fax, phone, e-mail or on Web site. Deadline: July 15. Entries must be previously published. Open to US citizens aged 39 and below. Accepts inquiries by fax, e-mail and phone. Results announced by October 15. Winners notified by phone. For contest results, e-mail or visit Web site.

☑ ◎ MILDRED L. BATCHELDER AWARD

Association for Library Service to Children, 50 E. Huron St., Chicago IL 60611. (800)545-2433 ext. 2163. Fax: (312)944-7671. E-mail: alsc@ala.org. Web site: www.ala.org/alsc. **Contact:** ALSC, attn: Batchelder Award. Award is to "encourage international exchange of quality children's books by recognizing US publishers of such books in translation." Prize: Citation. Judged by Batchelder Award selection committee. No entry fee. Deadline: December 31. Books should be US trade publications for which children, up to and including age 14, are the potential audience. Previously published translations only. Accepts inquiries by fax, e-mail and phone. Guidelines available in February for SASE, by fax, phone, e-mail or on Web site. Results announced at ALA Midwinter Meeting. Winners notified by phone. Contest results by phone, fax, for SASE or visit Web site.

◎ THE BEACON CONTEST

First Coast Romance Writers, ℅ Maria Connor, 11567 Kelvyn Grove Place, Jacksonville FL 32225. E-mail: theconnorfamily@msn.com. Web site: www.firstcoastromancewriters.com/beacon.html. **Contact:** Maria Connor, contest coordinator. Award "to provide published authors with a chance for greater success." Prize: Beacon lapel pin. Categories: Historical, Traditional Regency, Long Contemporary (over 70,000 words), Short Contemporary (up to 70,000 words), Inspirational, Paranormal/Fantasy/Sci Fi, Single Title Mainstream, Romantic Suspense Chick Lit, First Book. Judged by finalists are read by book retailers. Entry fee: $25 per category (make checks payable to FCRW). 2006 entries should be published (romance genre; send 3 autographed copies of the entry novel). Deadline: March 1. Entries must be previously published. Must be copyright 2005. Open to writers of all romance categories. Guidelines available on Web site, for SASE or by e-mail. Accepts inquiries by e-mail. Results announced in June. Winners notified by mail. For contest results, send SASE. "Make certain to autograph the 3 copies sent in, as well as verify publication year."

Ⓝ BELLEVUE LITERARY REVIEW GOLDENBERG PRIZE FOR FICTION

Bellevue Literary Review, NYU Dept of Medicine, 550 First Ave. OBV-A612, New York NY 10016. (212)263-3973. E-mail: info@blreview.org. Web site: www.blreview.org. **Contact:** Stacy Bodziak, Managing Editor. "The BLR prizes award outstanding writing related to themes of health, healing, illness, the mind and the body." Annual. Competition/award for short stories. Prize: $1,000 and publication. Receives about 200-300 entries per category. *BLR* editors select semi-finalists to be read by an independent judge who chooses the winner. Previous judges include Ray Gonzalez (2006), Amy Hempel (2007) and Rick Moody (2008). Entry fee: $15, or $20 to include one year subscription.

Send credit card information or make checks payable to *Bellevue Literary Review*. Guidelines available in March. Accepts inquiries by e-mail, phone. Submissions open in March. **Entry deadline is August 1st**. Entries should be unpublished. Anyone may enter contest. Length: no minimum, maximum of 5,000 words. Cover letter should include name, address, phone, e-mail, story title. Title and word count should appear on ms. Writers may submit own work. Results announced December. Winners notified by mail, by e-mail. Results made available to entrants with SASE, by e-mail, on Web site.

☐ GEORGE BENNETT FELLOWSHIP

Phillips Exeter Academy, 20 Main St., Exeter NH 03833-2460. Web site: www.exeter.edu. Annual award for fellow and family "to provide time and freedom from material considerations to a person seriously contemplating or pursuing a career as a writer. Applicants should have a manuscript in progress which they intend to complete during the fellowship period." Duties: To be in residency for the academic year; to make oneself available informally to students interested in writing. Guidelines for SASE or on Web site. The committee favors writers who have not yet published a book with a major publisher. Residence at the Academy during the fellowship period required. Prize: $10,000 stipend, room and board. Judged by committee of the English department. $10 application fee. Application form and guidelines for SASE and on Web site. Deadline: December 1. Results announced in March. Winners notified by letter or phone. List of winners available in March. All entrants will receive an announcement of the winner. "Stay within a few pages of the limit. (We won't read more anyway.) Trust us to recognize that what you are sending is a work in progress. (You have the chance to talk about that in your statement.) Hope, but don't expect anything. If you don't win, some well-known writers have been in your shoes—at least as many as have won the fellowship."

◎ BEST LESBIAN EROTICA

Cleis Press, P.O. Box 395, Greenville NY 12083. E-mail: tristan@puckerup.com. **Contact:** Tristan Taormino, series editor. Categories: Novel excerpts, short stories, other prose; poetry will be considered but is not encouraged. No entry fee. Include cover page with author's name, title of submission(s), address, phone, fax, e-mail. All submissions must be typed and double-spaced. Also number the pages. Length: 5,000 words. You may submit a maximum of 3 different pieces of work. Submit 2 hard copies of each submission. No e-mail submissions will be accepted; accepts inquiries by e-mail. Accepts both previously published and unpublished material. Open to any writer. All submissions must include SASE or an e-mail address for response. No mss will be returned.

◎ "BEST OF OHIO WRITER" CONTEST

Ohio Writer Magazine, 2570 Superior, #203, Cleveland OH 44114. (216)694-0000. Fax: (216)694-0004. E-mail: pwlgc@yahoo.com. Web site: www.pwlgc.com. **Contact:** Judith Mansour-Thomas, executive director. Award "to promote and encourage the work of writers in Ohio." Prize: $150, $50. Judged by "a selected panel of prominent Ohio writers." Entry fee: $15, which includes 1-yr. subscription to the magazine. **Deadline: July 31.** Entries must be unpublished. Ohio residents only. Guidelines available after January 1 for SASE or e-mail. Accepts inquiries by e-mail and phone. Length: 2,500 words, "No cliché plots; we're looking for fresh unpublished voices." Results announced November 1. Winners notified by mail. For contest results, send SASE or e-mail after November 1.

◙ BINGHAMTON UNIVERSITY JOHN GARDNER FICTION BOOK AWARD

Binghamton Center for Writers, State University of New York, P.O. Box 6000, Binghamton NY 13902. (607)777-2713. Fax: (607)777-2408. E-mail: cwpro@binghamton.edu. Web site: english.binghamton.edu/cwpro. **Contact:** Maria Mazziotti Gillan, director. Award's purpose is "to serve the literary community by calling attention to outstanding books of fiction." Prize: $1,000. Categories: novels and short story collections. Judged by "rotating outside judges." No entry fee. Entry must have been published in book form with a minimum press run of 500. Each book submitted must be accompanied by an application form, available online or send SASE to above address. Submit three copies of the book; copies will not be returned. Publishers may submit more than one book for prize consideration. **Deadline: March 1.** Entries must have appeared in print between January 1 and December 31 of the year preceding the award. Open to any writer. Results announced in Summer. Winners notified by e-mail or phone. For contest results, send SASE or visit Web site.

⊻ ◎ IRMA S. AND JAMES H. BLACK AWARD

Bank Street College of Education, 610 W. 112th St., New York NY 10025. (212)875-4450. Fax: (212)875-4558. E-mail: lindag@bnkst.edu. Web site: streetcat.bnkst.edu/html/isb.html. **Contact:** Linda Greengrass, award director. Offered annually for a book for young children, for excellence of both text and illustrations. Entries must have been published during the previous calendar year. Prize: press function and scroll and seals by Maurice Sendak for attaching to award winner's book run. Judged by adult children's literature experts and children 6-10 years old. No entry fee. Guidelines for SASE, fax, e-mail or on Web site. Accepts inquiries by phone, fax, e-mail. Deadline: December 15. Entries must be previously published. "Write to address above. Usually publishers submit books they want considered, but individuals can too. No entries are returned." Winners notified by phone in April and announced in May. A list of winners will be available on Web site.

⊕ ⊻ JAMES TAIT BLACK MEMORIAL PRIZES

Department of English Literature, University of Edinburgh, David Hume Tower, George Square, Edinburgh Scotland EH8 9JX United Kingdom. (44-13)1650-3619. Fax: (44-13)1650-6898. E-mail: s.strathdee@ed.ac.uk. Web site: www.englit.ed.ac.uk/jtbinf.htm. **Contact:** Sheila Strathdee, Department of English Literature. "Two prizes each of £10,000 are awarded: one for the best work of fiction, one for the best biography or work of that nature, published during the calendar year January 1 to December 31." Judged by the professor of English Literature. No entry fee. Accepts inquiries by fax, e-mail, phone. **Deadline: December 1.** Entries must be previously published. "Eligible works are those written in English and first published or co-published in Britain in the year of the award. Works should be submitted by publishers." Open to any writer. Winners notified by phone, via publisher. Contact department of English Literature for list of winners or check Web site.

◖ BLACK WARRIOR REVIEW FICTION CONTEST

Black Warrior Review, P.O. Box 862936, Tuscaloosa AL 35486. Web site: www.webdelsol.com/bwr. **Contact:** Fiction Contest. Prize: $1,000 and publication in Spring issue. All entrants receive 1-yr subscription to journal. Entry fee: $15 per short story. Make checks payable to the University of Alabama. Send name, phone number, e-mail, SASE and reading fee with ms. Deadline: October 1. Entries must be unpublished. Open to any writer. Winners announced in December.

⊕ ⊻ ◎ THE BOARDMAN TASKER AWARD FOR MOUNTAIN LITERATURE

The Boardman Tasker Charitable Trust, Pound House, Llangennith, Swansea Wales SA3 1JQ United Kingdom. Phone/fax: (44-17)9238-6215. E-mail: margaretbody@lineone.net. Web site: www.board mantasker.com. **Contact:** Margaret Body. "The award is to honor Peter Boardman and Joe Tasker, who disappeared on Everest in 1982." Offered annually to reward a work of nonfiction or fiction, in English or in translation, which has made an outstanding contribution to mountain literature. Books must be published in the UK between November 1 of previous year and October 31 of year of the prize. Writers may obtain information, but entry is by publishers only. "No restriction of nationality, but work must be published or distributed in the UK." Prize: £3,000. Judged by a panel of 3 judges elected by trustees. No entry fee. "May be fiction, nonfiction, poetry or drama. Not an anthology. Subject must be concerned with a mountain environment. Previous winners have been books on expeditions, climbing experiences, a biography of a mountaineer, novels." Guidelines available in January for SASE, by fax, e-mail or on Web site. Deadline: August 1. Entries must be previously published. Publisher's entry only. Open to any writer. Results announced in November. Winners notified by phone or e-mail. For contest results, send SASE, fax, e-mail or visit Web site. "The winning book needs to be well written to reflect a knowledge of and a respect and appreciation for the mountain environment."

BOULEVARD SHORT FICTION CONTEST FOR EMERGING WRITERS

Boulevard Magazine, 6614 Clayton Rd., PMB #325, Richmond Heights MO 63117. (314)862-2643. Fax: (314)781-7250. E-mail: ballymon@hotmail.com. Web site: www.richardburgin.com. **Contact:** Richard Burgin, editor. Offered annually for unpublished short fiction to award a writer who has not yet published a book of fiction, poetry or creative nonfiction with a nationally distributed press. "We hold first North American rights on anything not previously published." Open to any writer with no previous publication by a nationally known press. Guidelines for SASE or on Web site. Prize: $1,500, and publication in 1 of the next year's issues. Judged by editors of *Boulevard*. Entry fee: $15 fee/story; includes 1-year subscription to *Boulevard*. Guidelines available in April for SASE, e-mail, on Web site and in publication. Accepts inquiries by e-mail, phone. Deadline: December 15. Open to any writer. Author's name, address, phone, e-mail, story title, word count and "Boulevard Emerging Writers Contest" should appear on page 1; last name on each page is helpful. Include a 3×5 index card with your name, address and title of your submission(s). Results announced in Spring issue. Winners notified by mail or phone usually during February/March.

☐ THE BRIAR CLIFF POETRY, FICTION & CREATIVE NONFICTION COMPETITION

The Briar Cliff Review, Briar Cliff University, 3303 Rebecca St., Sioux City IA 51104-0100. (712)279-5321. Fax: (712)279-5410. E-mail: curranst@briarcliff.edu. Web site: www.briarcliff.edu/bcreview. **Contact:** Tricia Currans-Sheehan, editor. Award "to reward good writers and showcase quality writing." Offered annually for unpublished poem, story and essay. Prize: $1,000, and publication in Spring issue. All entrants receive a copy of the magazine with winning entries. Judged by editors. "We guarantee a considerate reading." Entry fee: $20. Guidelines available in August for SASE. Inquiries accepted by e-mail. **Deadline: Submissions between August 1 and November 1.** No mss returned. Entries must be unpublished. Length: 6,000 words maximum. Open to any writer. Results announced in December or January. Winners notified by phone or letter around December 20. For contest results, send SASE with submission. "Send us your best. We want stories with a plot."

☐ THE BRIDPORT PRIZE

P.O. Box 6910, Bridport, Dorset DT6 6QB United Kingdom. (01308)428333. E-mail: frances@bridport prize.org.uk. Web site: www.bridportprize.org.uk. **Contact:** Frances Everitt, administrator. Award to "promote literary excellence, discover new talent." Prize: £5,000 sterling; £1,000 sterling; £500 sterling, plus various runners-up prizes and publication of approximately 13 best stories and 13 best poems in anthology. Categories: short stories and poetry. Judged by 1 judge for fiction (in 2008, Helen Simpson) and 1 judge for poetry (in 2008, David Harsent). Entry fee: £6 sterling for each entry. **Deadline: June 30.** Entries must be unpublished. Length: 5,000 maximum for short stories; 42 lines for poetry. Open to any writer. Guidelines available in January for SASE or visit Web site. Accepts inquiries by fax, e-mail, phone. Results announced in November of year of contest. Winners notified by phone or mail in October. For contest results, send SASE.

☐ BURNABY WRITERS' SOCIETY CONTEST

Burnaby Writers' Society, 6584 Deer Lake Ave., Burnaby BC V5G 3T7 Canada. E-mail: info@bws.bc. ca. Web site: www.bws.bc.ca. Offered annually for unpublished work. Open to all residents of British Columbia. Categories vary from year to year. Send SASE for current rules. Purpose is to encourage talented writers in all genres. Prize: 1st Place: $200; 2nd Place: $100; 3rd Place: $50; and public reading. Entry fee: $5. Guidelines available by e-mail, for SASE or on Web site. Accepts inquiries by e-mail. Deadline: May 31. Results announced in September. Winners notified by mail, phone, e-mail. Results available for SASE or on Web site.

☐ BUSH ARTIST FELLOWS PROGRAM

Bush Foundation, 332 Minnesota St., Suite E-900, St. Paul MN 55101. Fax: (651)297-6485. E-mail: BAFinfo@bushfoundation.org. Web site: www.bushfoundation.org. **Contact:** Julie Dalgliesh, program director. Award to "provide artists with significant financial support that enables them to further their work and their contributions to their communities. Fellows may decide to take time for solitary work or reflection, engage in collaborative or community projects, or embark on travel or research." Prize: $48,000 for 12-24 months. Categories: fiction, creative nonfiction, poetry. Judged by a panel of artists and arts professionals who reside outside of Minnesota, South Dakota, North Dakota or Wisconsin. No entry fee. Applications available in August. Accepts inquiries by fax and e-mail. Applicants must be at least 25 years old, U.S. citizens or Permanent Residents, and residents of Minnesota, South Dakota, North Dakota or Western Wisconsin. Students not eligible. Must meet certain publication requirements. Results announced in Spring. Winners notified by letter. List of winners available in May and sent to all applicants.

☐ BYLINE MAGAZINE AWARDS

P.O. Box 111, Albion NY 14411. (585)355-8172. E-mail: robbi@bylinemag.com. Web site: www.byli nemag.com. **Contact:** Robbi Hess, award director. Several monthly contests, open to anyone, in various categories that include fiction, nonfiction, poetry and children's literature; a semi-annual poetry chapbook award which is open to any poet; and an annual *ByLine* Short Fiction and Poetry Award open only to our subscribers. For chapbook award and subscriber awards, publication constitutes part of the prize; winners grant first North American rights to *ByLine*. Prize: for monthly contests, cash and listing in magazine; for chapbook award, publication of chapbook, 50 copies and $200; for *ByLine* Short Fiction and Poetry Award, $250 in each category, plus publication in the magazine. Entry fee: $3-5 for monthly contests and $15 for chapbook contest. Deadline: varies. Entries must be unpublished.

⊕ ☑ ◎ THE CAINE PRIZE FOR AFRICAN WRITING

51a Southwark St., London England SE1 1RU United Kingdom. E-mail: info@caineprize.com. Web site: www.caineprize.com. **Contact:** Nick Elam, administrator. Annual award for a short story (3,000-15,000 words) by an African writer. "An 'African writer' is normally taken to mean someone who was born in Africa, who is a national of an African country, or whose parents are African, and whose work has reflected African sensibilities." Entries must have appeared for the first time in the 5 years prior to the closing date for submissions, which is January 31 each year. Publishers should submit 6 copies of the published original with a brief cover note (no pro forma application). Prize: £10,000. Judged by a panel of judges appointed each year. No entry fee. Cover letter should include name, address, phone, e-mail, title and publication where story was previously published. Deadline: January 31. Entries must be previously published. Word length: 3,000-15,000 words. Manuscripts not accepted. Entries must be submitted by publishers not authors. Results announced in mid-July. Winners notified at event/banquet. For contest results, send fax, e-mail or visit our Web site.

◎ CALIFORNIA BOOK AWARDS

Commonwealth Club of California, 595 Market St., San Francisco CA 94105. (415)597-6703. Fax: (415)597-6729. E-mail: bookawards@commonwealthclub.org. Web site: www.commonwealthclub.org/features/caBookAwards/. **Contact:** Gina Baleria, literary director. Award to honor excellence in literature written by California residents. Prize: $2,000, gold medal; $300, silver medal. Categories: fiction, first work of fiction, nonfiction, juvenile, young adult, poetry, Californiana, contribution to publishing. Judged by jury. No entry fee. **Deadline: Friday, December 19, 2009 by 5pm.** Entries must be previously published. California residents only. Writer or publisher may nominate work. Guidelines available in January on Web site. Results announced in Spring. Winners notified by phone. For contest results, send e-mail.

☑ JOHN W. CAMPBELL MEMORIAL AWARD FOR BEST SCIENCE FICTION NOVEL OF THE YEAR

Center for the Study of Science Fiction, English Department, University of Kansas, Lawrence KS 66045. (785)864-3380. Fax: (785)864-1159. E-mail: jgunn@ku.edu. Web site: www.ku.edu/~sfcent er. **Contact:** James Gunn, professor and director. Award to "honor the best science fiction novel of the year." Prize: Trophy. Winners receive an expense-paid trip to the university to receive their award. Their names are also engraved on a permanent trophy. Categories: novels. Judged by a jury. No entry fee. Deadline: see Web site. Entries must be previously published. Open to any writer. Accepts inquiries by e-mail and fax. "Ordinarily publishers should submit work, but authors have done so when publishers would not. Send for list of jurors." Results announced in July. For contest results, send SASE.

◻ THE ALEXANDER PATTERSON CAPPON FICTION AWARD

New Letters, 5101 Rockhill Rd., Kansas City MO 64110. (816)235-1168. Fax: (816)235-2611. Web site: www.newletters.org. Offered annually for unpublished work to discover and to reward new and upcoming writers. Buys first North American serial rights. Prize: 1st place: $1,500 and publication in a volume of *New Letters*; 1 runner-up will receive a copy of a recent book of poetry or fiction from affiliate BkMk Press. All entries will be given consideration for publication in future issues of *New Letters*. Judged by renowned writers. Previous judges have included Philip Levine, Charles Simic, Joyce Carol Oates, Rosellen Brown, Phillip Lopate, Maxine Kumin. Entry fee: $15 (includes a 1-year subscription to New Letters); $10 for each entry after first. Entries in fiction are not to exceed 8,000 words. Send two cover sheets—the first with complete name, address, e-mail/phone, category and title(s); the second with category and title(s) only. Personal information should not appear anywhere else on the entry. Also enclose a stamped, self-addressed postcard if you would like notification of receipt and entry number and an SASE for list of winners. Note that manuscripts will not be returned. Deadline: May 18. Entries must be unpublished. Simultaneous and multiple submissions welcome. Winners announced mid-September. Open to any writer.

Ⓝ $CHIZINE/LEISURE SHORT STORY CONTEST

Dorchester Publications, 200 Madison Ave, Suite 2000, New York NY 10016. Web site: www.dorchest erpub.com. **Contact:** Brett Alexander Savpry, senior editor. Held annually "to find the top three dark fiction stories." Competition/award for short stories. Prize: 7¢/word, up to 4,000 words, plus a choice of selected Leisure horror titles. Judged by a revolving panel of writers and editors of dark fiction selected by the Editor-in-Chief of Chizine. No entry fee. Guidelines available in May. Accepts inquiries by e-mail. **Submissions accepted June 1st through 30th.** Entries should be unpublished. Contest open to anyone. Cover letter and ms should include name, address, e-mail, word count, novel/story title. Writers may submit own work. Results announced end of July. Winners notified by e-mail. Results made available to entrants on Web site.

Ⓒ Ⓘ THE CHRISTOPER AWARDS

The Christophers, 12 E. 48th St., New York NY 10017-1091. (212)759-4050. Fax: (646)843-1547. E-mail: awardsinfo@christophers.org. Web site: www.christophers.org. **Contact:** Judith Trojan, program director. Award "to encourage authors and illustrators to continue to produce works which affirm the highest values of the human spirit in adult and children's books." Prize: bronze medallion. Categories: Adult nonfiction and young adult novels and nonfiction. Judged by a panel of juvenile reading and subject experts. Juvenile titles are "children tested." No entry fee. Submission period: June 1 through November 1 every year. Entries must be previously published. Potential winners are nominated and reviewed throughout the year by juvenile book professionals, members of the Christopher staff, and by specially supervised children's reading groups. Open to any writer. For guidelines send 6×9 SASE, e-mail or visit Web site. Inquiries accepted by letter, fax, e-mail and phone. Winners chosen in early January and notified by mail in late January. Awards are presented annually in March at a black-tie gala in New York City. For contest results, send SASE, fax or visit Web site. Example of book award: *The Miraculous Journey of Edward Tulane*, by Kate DiCamillo; illustrated by Bagram Ibatoulline (children's book category 2006). "Publishers generally submit fiction/nonfiction books for young people. Authors and illustrators should familiarize themselves with our awards criteria and encourage their publishers to submit applicable titles."

ⓒ Ⓘ CITY OF TORONTO BOOK AWARDS

City of Toronto, 100 Queen St. West, City Hall, 10th Floor, West Tower, Toronto ON M9W 3X3 Canada. (416)392-8191. Fax: (416)392-1247. Web site: www.toronto.ca/book_awards. **Contact:** Bev Kurmey, protocol officer. "The Toronto Book Awards honor authors of books of literary or artistic merit that are evocative of Toronto." Categories: short stories, novels, story collections, translations. Judged by committee. No entry fee. Guidelines available by e-mail, on Web site. Accepts inquiries by phone, fax, e-mail. Writers may submit their own fiction. Cover letter should include name, address, phone, e-mail, title. Deadline: Feb. 28. Entries must be previously published. Books must have been published during the year prior to the award (i.e. in 2008 for the 2009 deadline). Open to any writer. Results announced in Sept., short list in June. Winners notified by mail, e-mail. Results available on Web site.

Ⓒ CNW/FFWA ANNUAL FLORIDA STATE WRITING COMPETITION

%CNW Publishing, Florida Freelance Writers Association, P.O. Box A, North Stratford NH 03590-0167. E-mail: contest@writers-editors.com. Web site: www.writers-editors.com. **Contact:** Dana K. Cassell, executive director. Annual award "to recognize publishable talent." Divisions & Categories: Nonfiction (previously published article/essay/column/nonfiction book chapter; unpublished or self-published article/essay/column/nonfiction book chapter); Fiction (unpublished or self-published short story or novel chapter); Children's Literature (unpublished or self-published short story/ nonfiction article/book chapter/poem); Poetry (unpublished or self-published free verse/traditional). Prize: 1st Place: $100, plus certificate; 2nd Place: $75, plus certificate; 3rd Place: $50, plus certificate. Honorable Mention certificates will be awarded in each category as warranted. Judged by editors, librarians and writers. Entry fee: $5 (active or new CNW/FFWA members) or $10 (nonmembers) for each fiction/nonfiction entry under 3,000 words; $10 (members) or $20 (nonmembers) for each entry of 3,000 words or longer; and $3 (members) or $5 (nonmembers) for each poem. Guidelines for SASE or on Web site. Accepts inquiries by e-mail, phone and mail. Deadline: March 15. Open to any writer. Results announced May 31. Winners notified by mail and posted on Web site. Results available for SASE or visit Web site.

CONSEIL DE LA VIE FRANCAISE EN AMERIQUE/PRIX CHAMPLAIN

Conseil de la Vie Francaise en Amerique, Faculté des lettres, DKN-3219, Univesité Laval, Quebec City QC G1K 7P4 Canada. (418)806-23021. Fax: (418)644-7670. E-mail: cvfa@cvfa.ca. Web site: www.cvfa.ca. **Contact:** Director General. Award to encourage literary work in novel or short story in French by Francophiles living outside Quebec, in the US or Canada. Prize: $1,500 Canadian. Judged by 3 different judges each year. No entry fee. Deadline: December 31. Entries must be previously published. "There is no restriction as to the subject matter. If the author lives in Quebec, the subject matter must be related to French-speaking people living outside of Quebec." Submissions must have been published no more than 3 years before award. Open to any writer. Guidelines for SASE or IRC or on Web site. Author must furnish 4 examples of work, curriculum vitae, address and phone number.

CRAZYHORSE FICTION PRIZE

College of Charleston, Dept. of English, 66 George St., Charleston SC 29424. (843)953-7740. E-mail: crazyhorse@cofc.edu. Web site: http://crazyhorse.cofc.edu. **Contact:** Editors. Prize: $2,000 and publication in *Crazyhorse*. Judged by anonymous writer whose identity is disclosed when the winners are announced in April. Past judges: Charles Baxter (2002), Michael Martone (2003), Diana Abu-Jaber (2004), T.M. McNally (2005), Dan Chaon (2006), Antonya Nelson (2007). Entry fee: $16 (covers 1-yr subscription to *Crazyhorse*; make checks payable to *Crazyhorse*). To enter, please send up to 25 pages of prose. Include a detachable cover sheet with your name, address and telephone number; please do not include this information on the ms itself. Send SASE or see Web site for additional details. **Deadline: December 16th of each year**; see Web site. Open to any writer.

CROSSTIME SHORT SCIENCE FICTION CONTEST

Crossquarter Publishing Group, P.O. Box 23749, Santa Fe NM 87502. (505)438-9846. Web site: www.crossquarter.com. **Contact:** Therese Francis, owner. Original short (up to 8,500 words) science fiction stories that demonstrate the best of the human spirit. Stories may be science fiction, fantasy or urban fantasy. No horror. No dystopia. Prize: 1st place: $250 plus publication in next volume of *CrossTIME Anthology*; 2nd place: $125 plus publication in the anthology; 3rd place: $75 plus publication in the anthology; 4th place: $50 plus publication in the anthology; 5th through 15th places: a distinctive certificate honoring their accomplishment plus publication in the anthology. Judges are not required to award all 15 positions; ties are possible. Each entrant will receive one copy of the resulting anthology highlighting the 1st through 15th place winners. Entry fee: $15 for first submission, $10 for each additional submission. The official entry form is required (available online), along with entry fee (check, money order, Visa, MasterCard, American Express). If you are entering more than one ms, you may mail all entries in the same envelope and write one check for the total entry fee. Submission should be typewritten on $8^{1}/_{2} \times 11$ white paper. Your name, address, phone number and word count must appear in the upper left-hand corner of the first page. Staple or paperclip the pages together. Team writing is acceptable, but only one copy of the anthology will be sent. The "team leader" should complete the official entry form. Deadline: January 15. Entries must be unpublished. Your entry must be original, unpublished and unproduced, not accepted by any other publisher or producer at the time of submission. However, stories previously printed for copies only or for less than $25 are acceptable, provided all rights have reverted to you. (Example would be school newspapers. Include information on where and when previously published.) Open to any writer. Byline given. Publisher buys all rights for five years (early buy-out negotiable). To receive notification of the receipt of your ms, include self-addressed, stamped postcard.

THE CRUCIBLE POETRY AND FICTION COMPETITION

Crucible, Barton College, College Station, Wilson NC 27893. (252)399-6456. E-mail: tgrimes@barton.edu. **Contact:** Terrence L. Grimes, editor. Offered annually for unpublished short stories. Prize: $150 (1st Prize); $100 (2nd Prize) and publication in *Crucible*. Competition receives 300 entries. Categories: Fiction should be 8,000 words or less. Judged by in-house editorial board. No entry fee. Guidelines available in January for SASE, e-mail or in publication. Deadline: April. Open to any writer. "The best time to submit is December through April." Results announced in July. Winners notified by mail. For contest rules, send e-mail.

N DANAHY FICTION PRIZE

University of Tampa Press, Tampa Review, 401 West Kennedy Blvd., Tampa FL 33606. E-mail: utpress@ut.edu. Web site: http://tampareview.ut.edu. **Contact:** Richard Mathews, Editor. "To recognize, promote, and publish outstanding previously unpublished short fiction." Annual. Competition/award for short stories. Prize: $1,000 and publication in *Tampa Review*. All entries are considered for publication in *Tampa Review*. All entrants receive a complimentary one-year subscription to *Tampa Review*. Receives about 350 entries per category. Entries are judged by the editors of *Tampa Review*. Entry fee: $15. Make checks payable to *Tampa Review*. Accepts inquiries by e-mail. **Entries must be postmarked no later than Nov. 1st.** Entries should be unpublished. Anyone may enter contest. Length: Submissions between 500 and 5,000 words preferred; mss. slightly outside this range will also be considered. Cover letter should include name, address, phone, e-mail, word count, novel/story title. All this information should also be on first page of ms. Writers may submit own work. Results announced March. Winners notified by mail, phone, e-mail. Results made available to entrants with SASE.

DOROTHY DANIELS ANNUAL HONORARY WRITING AWARD

Simi Valley Branch of the National League of American Pen Women, Inc., P.O. Box 1485, Simi Valley CA 93062. E-mail: cdoering@adelphia.net. **Contact:** Carol E. Doering, vice president and contest chairperson. Award for short stories. Prize: $100. Judged by NLAPW members. Entry fee: $5 per entry; make checks payable to NLAPW-SV Branch. Guidelines available in January for SASE. Accepts inquiries by e-mail. Deadline: July 30. Entries must be unpublished. Length: 2,000 words maximum. Open to any writer. Cover letter should include name, address, phone, word count, title and category; name and address must not appear on ms, entry must be titled. Results announced November 5. Winners notified by mail. For contest results, send SASE.

☐ DEAD OF WINTER

E-mail: editors@toasted-cheese.com. Web site: www.toasted-cheese.com. **Contact:** Stephanie Lenz, editor. The contest is a winter-themed short fiction contest with a new topic each year. Topic and word limit announced Nov. 1. The topic is usually geared toward a supernatural theme. Prize: Amazon gift certificates in the amount of $20, $15 and $10; publication in *Toasted Cheese*. Also offers honorable mention. Categories: short stories. Judged by two *Toasted Cheese* editors who blind judge each contest. Each judge uses her own criteria to rate entries. No entry fee. Cover letter should include name, address, e-mail, word count and title. **Deadline: December 21.** Entries must be unpublished. Word limit varies each year. Open to any writer. Guidelines available in November on Web site. Accepts inquiries by e-mail. "Follow guidelines. Write a smart, original story. We have further guidelines on the Web site." Results announced January 31. Winners notified by e-mail. List of winners on Web site.

☐ ◎ DELAWARE DIVISION OF THE ARTS

820 N. French St., Wilmington DE 19801. (302)577-8278. Fax: (302)577-6561. Web site: www.artsdel .org. **Contact:** Kristin Pleasanton, art & artist services coordinator. Award "to help further careers of emerging and established professional artists." For Delaware residents only. Prize: $10,000 for masters; $5,000 for established professionals; $2,000 for emerging professionals. Judged by out-of-state, nationally recognized professionals in each artistic discipline. No entry fee. Guidelines available after January 1 on Web site. Accepts inquiries by e-mail, phone. Expects to receive 25 fiction entries. Deadline: August 15. Open to any writer. Results announced in December. Winners notified by mail. Results available on Web site. "Follow all instructions and choose your best work sample."

N RICK DEMARINIS SHORT FICTION PRIZE

Cuthroat, A Journal of the Arts, P.O. Box 2414, Durango CO 81302. (970)903-7914. E-mail: cutthroatm ag@gmail.com. Web site: http://www.cutthroatmag.com. **Contact:** Pamela Uschuk, editor-in-chief. "To recognize a fine piece of fiction by giving the author an honorarium and a venue for publication." Annual. Competition/award for short stories. $1,250 plus publication for First Prize; $250 plus publication for Second Prize. Receives about 250 plus entries. Magazine staff chooses 20-25 finalists, and a different nationally known fiction writer is selected each year as the final judge. Entry fee: $15. Make checks payable to Raven's Word Writers Center. Guidelines available in January. **Entries postmark deadline is October 10, 2009.** Entries should be unpublished. Anyone writing anywhere in English may enter contest. Length: 5,000 word limit. Cover letter should include name, address, phone, e-mail, novel/story title. No identifying information may appear anywhere on the ms. "Our criteria is excellence" Results announced December. Winners notified by phone. Results made available to entrants with SASE.

DOBIE/PAISANO FELLOWSHIPS

Dobie Paisano Fellowship Program. The University of Texas at Austin, Graduate School, 1 University Station (G0400), Austin, TX 78712-0531. ((512)471-8528. Fax (512)471-7620. E-mail: adameve@mail .utexas.edu. Web site: www.utexas.edu/orgs/Paisano. **Contact:** Michael Adams, Director. Two fellowship awards for writers of fiction, poetry, and nonfiction: one for four months with a stipend of $5,000 a month. Requires previous publication; one for six months with a stipend of $3,000 a month (previous publication not required but permitted. Fellow lives (rent and bills free) at Paisano ranch southwest of Austin, Texas. Judged by committee from Texas Institute of Letters and the University of Texas. Entry fee: $20 Deadline: January 15. Entries must be unpublished. Open to writers with a Texas connection—native Texans, people who have lived in Texas at least three years, or writers with published significant work on Texas." Winners announced early May. List of winners available at Web site.

JACK DYER FICTION PRIZE

Crab Orchard Review, Dept. of English, Faner Hall, Southern Illinois University Carbondale, Carbondale IL 62901-4503. Web site: www.siu.edu/~crborchd. **Contact:** Jon Tribble, managing editor. Offered annually for unpublished short fiction. Crab Orchard Review acquires first North American serial rights to all submitted work. Open to any writer. Prize: $1,500 and publication. Judged by editorial staff (pre-screening); winner chosen by genre editor. Entry fee: $15/entry (can enter up to 3 stories, each story submitted requires a separate fee and can be up to 6,000 words), which includes a 1-year subscription to Crab Orchard Review. Guidelines available after January for SASE or on Web site. Deadline: Reading period for entries is February 1 through April 1. Entries must be unpublished. Length: 6,000 words maximum. U.S. citizens only. "Please note that no stories will be returned." Results announced by end of October. Winners notified by mail. Contest results on Web site or send SASE. "Carefully read directions for entering and follow them exactly. Send us your best work. Note that simultaneous submissions are accepted for this prize, but the winning entry must NOT be accepted elsewhere. No electronic submissions."

DZANC PRIZE

Dzanc Books, 2702 Lillian, Ann Arbor MI 48104. E-mail: info@dzancbooks.org. Web site: http://www.dzancbooks.org. **Contact:** Dan Wickett, executive director. "Our goal is to help authors find means of producing their work and doing community service." Annual. Prize: $5,000. Single category of a combination of work in progress and literary community service. Entries are judged by Dzanc editors (Steve Gillis, Dan Wickett and Keith Taylor). No entry fee. Accepts inquiries by e-mail. **Entry deadline is Nov. 1, 2008.** Entries should be unpublished. Any author with a work of literary fiction in progress, and community service that is based in the United States, may enter contest. Writers may submit own work. "Have a good idea of what we're looking for in terms of literary community service (see Web site)" Results announced in December. Winners notified by e-mail. Results made available to entrants via email, and on Web site.

EATON LITERARY AGENCY'S ANNUAL AWARDS PROGRAM

Eaton Literary Agency, P.O. Box 49795, Sarasota FL 34230. (941)366-6589. Fax: (941)365-4679. E-mail: eatonlit@aol.com. Web site: www.eatonliterary.com. **Contact:** Richard Lawrence, vice president. Offered biannually for unpublished mss. Prize: $2,500 (over 10,000 words); $500 (under 10,000 words). Judged by an independent agency in conjunction with some members of Eaton's staff. No entry fee. Guidelines available for SASE, by fax, e-mail, or on Web site. Accepts inquiries by fax, phone and e-mail. **Deadline: March 31 (mss under 10,000 words); August 31 (mss over 10,000 words).** Entries must be unpublished. Open to any writer. Results announced in April and September. Winners notified by mail. For contest results, send SASE, fax, e-mail or visit Web site.

◢ EMERGING VOICES ROSENTHAL FELLOWSHIP

PEN USA, % Antioch University, 400 Corporate Pointe, Culver City CA 90230. (310)862-1555. Fax: (310)862-1556. E-mail: ev@penusa.org. Web site: www.penusa.org. **Contact:** Christine Lanoie-New-man, program director. "To serve up-and-coming writers who in some way lack access to traditional writing and publishing opportunities. To help these not-yet-published authors gain the creative and professional skills needed to flourish in the literary world." Annual. Prize: $1,000 and 8 month mentorship with established author, plus classes and workshops and the opportunity to meet au-thors, agents, editors and publishers. Categories: fiction, poetry, creative nonfiction. Receives about 100 entries per category. Entries judged by EV selection committee composed of EV Program Director, former EV fellows and prominent local authors. Entry fee: $10. Make checks payable to PEN USA. Guidelines available in February by phone, on Web site, in publication. Accepts inquiries by e-mail, phone. **Deadline: September 2009.** "Candidates are chosen based on writing talent and lack of access to traditional writing and publishing opportunities." Those with a graduate degree in writing or significant publication credits are not eligible. Length: 20 pages max. Entrants must complete EV application, which is available on PEN's Web site. Writers may submit own work. "Utilize EV application. Follow all instructions. Don't wait until the last minute to assemble letters of recommen-dation." Results announced November. Winners notified by mail, phone, e-mail. Results made available to entrants on Web site.

EMERGING WRITERS NETWORK SHORT FICTION CONTEST

Emerging Writers Network, 1334 Woodbourne Street, Westland MI 48186.E-mail: wickettd@yahoo.com. Web site: www.emergingwriters.typepad.com. **Contact:** Dan Wickett, president. Purpose to "find an excellent short story, get it published in *Storyglossia*, and award the author." Annual. Competition/award for short stories. Prize: $1,000, publication on EWN Blog, publication in spring issue of *Storyglossia*. Judging: All stories initially read by Dan Wickett. Top 20 go without author names to guest judge who chooses winner. 2007 guest judge was Alyson Hagy. Entry fee: $15. Make checks payable to Dan Wickett. Guidelines available in April on Web site. Accepts inquiries by e-mail. Submission period: January 1 through July, 1 2009. Entries should be unpublished. Open only to authors who have had, or will have had, less than 3 books published by December prior to contest. Length: 3,000-8,000 words. Cover letter should include name, address, e-mail, word count, story title. Writers may submit own work. "Have an idea of the type of fiction the Emerging Writers Network supports and is generally excited about by reading the Web site." Results announced during the month of December. Winners notified by mail, e-mail. Results made available to entrants on Web site.

◎ THE EMILY CONTEST

West Houston Chapter Romance Writers of America, 5603 Chantilly Lane, Houston TX 77092. E-mail: emily@whrwa.com. Web site: www.whrwa.com. **Contact:** Ellen Watkins, Emily Contest chair. Award "to help people writing romance novels learn to write better books and to help them make contacts in the publishing world." Prize: first place entry in each category receives the Emily brooch; all finalists receive certificates. Judged by authors and experienced critiquers in the first round; final round judges are editors at a major romance publishing house. Entry fee: $20 for WHRWA members; $30 for non-members. Deadline: October 1. Entries must be unpublished. Length: first 35 pages of a novel. Open to all unpublished romance writers. Guidelines available in July for SASE, by e-mail or on Web site. Accepts inquiries by e-mail. "We look for dynamic, interesting romance stories with a hero and heroine readers can relate to and love. Hook us from the beginning and keep the level of excitement high." Results announced in February. Winners notified by mail or phone. For contest results, send SASE or visit Web site.

◢ ◎ THE VIRGINIA FAULKNER AWARD FOR EXCELLENCE IN WRITING

Prairie Schooner, 201 Andrews Hall, P.O. Box 880334, Lincoln NE 68588-0334. (402)472-0911. Fax: (402)472-9771. E-mail: jengelhardt2@unl.edu. Web site: www.unl.edu/schooner/psmain.htm. **Contact:** Hilda Raz, editor. Offered annually for work published in *Prairie Schooner* in the previous year. Prize: $1,000. Categories: short stories, essays, novel excerpts and translations. Judged by Editorial Board. No entry fee. Guidelines for SASE or on Web site. Accepts inquiries by fax and e-mail. "We only read mss from September 1 through May 1." Winning entry must have been published in *Prairie Schooner* in the year preceding the award. Results announced in the Spring issue. Winners notified by mail in February or March.

⊕ ❑ FISH ONE PAGE PRIZE

Fish Publishing, Durrus, Bantry, County Cork Ireland. E-mail: info@fishpublishing.com. Web site: www.fishpublishing.com. **Contact:** Clem Cairns, editor. Prize: 1st prize: 1,000 Euro (approx. $1,300). Nine runners up get 100 Euro (approx. $130). The authors of the 10 best works of short-short fiction will be published in the Fish Short Story Prize Anthology. Entry fee: $15 per story. Enter online. **Deadline: March 19.** Entries must be unpublished. Stories must fit on one A4 page. Entries can be in any style or format and can be on any subject. The competition is open to writers from all countries, but entries must be written in English. Guidelines on Web site or by e-mail.

⊕ ❑ FISH SHORT STORY PRIZE

Fish Publishing, E-mail: info@fishpublishing.com. Web site: www.fishpublishing.com. **Contact:** Clem Cairns, editor. Purpose is to "find and publish new and exciting short fiction from all over the world; to support the short story and those who practice it." Offered annually for unpublished fiction mss. Prize: 1st Prize: 2,500 Euros (approx. $5,000); 2nd Prize: 1 week at Anam Cara Writers' Retreat in the west of Ireland plus 250 Euros; third prize is 250 Euros. The top 15 stories will be published in Fish's anthology, which is launched at the West Cork Literary Festival in June. Judged by a panel of international judges which changes every year. Entry fee: $30 per story. Guidelines available in July by e-mail, on Web site or in publication. Enter online at www.fishpublishing.com. **Deadline: November 30.** Length: 5,000 words maximum. Open to any writer except those who have won before or who have been a runner-up twice. "Don't be afraid to write with your own voice. We value originality. Do make sure that your story is as good as you can get it. Don't try to please a judge or judges. Make sure it is neat and easy to read." Results announced March 17 every year. Winners notified by mail, phone or e-mail and at prize ceremony book launch in Bantry, County Cork, last Saturday in June. For contest results, e-mail, or visit Web site. See Web site for additional contests, including "One Page Story Prize," "Short Fiction Prize," "Short Histories Prize," and "Fish-Knife Award."

❑ FLORIDA FIRST COAST WRITERS' FESTIVAL NOVEL, SHORT FICTION, PLAYWRITING & POETRY AWARDS

Writers' Festival & Florida Community College at Jacksonville, FCCJ North Campus, 4501 Capper Road, Jacksonville FL 32218-4499. (904)766-6760. E-mail: dathomas@fccj.edu. Web site: www.fccj.edu/wf. **Contact:** Dr. Dana Thomas, festival contest director. Conference and contest "to create a healthy writing environment, honor writers of merit and find a novel manuscript to recommend to New York publishers for 'serious consideration.'" Judged by university faculty and freelance and professional writers. Entry fee: $39 (novels); $30 (plays); $15 (short fiction); $7 (poetry). **Deadline: November 1 for novels, plays and short fiction; December 1 for poetry.** Entries must be unpublished. Word length: no limit for novel; 6,000 words for short fiction; 30 lines for poetry. Open to any writer. Guidelines available on the Web site or in the fall for SASE. Accepts inquiries by fax and e-mail. "For stories and novels, make the opening pages sparkle. For plays, make them at least two acts and captivating. For poems, blow us over with imagery and insight and avoid clichés and wordiness." Results announced on the Web site and at FCCJ's Florida First Coast Writers' Festival held in the spring.

❑ FLORIDA STATE WRITING COMPETITION

Florida Freelance Writers Association, P.O. Box A, North Stratford NH 03590-0167. (603)922-8338. E-mail: contest@writers-editors.com. Web site: www.writers-editors.com. **Contact:** Dana K. Cassell, executive director. Award "to offer additional opportunities for writers to earn income and recognition from their writing efforts." Prize: varies from $50-100. Categories: novels and short stories; also children's lit and nonfiction. Judged by authors, editors and librarians. Entry fee: $5-20. **Deadline: March 15.** Entries must be unpublished or self-published; except for one previously published nonfiction category. Open to any writer. Guidelines are revised each year and are subject to change. New guidelines are available in summer of each year. Accepts inquiries by e-mail. Results announced May 31. Winners notified by mail and posted on the Web site. For contest results, send SASE marked "winners" or visit Web site.

❑ H.E. FRANCIS SHORT STORY AWARD

The Ruth Hindman Foundation, University of Alabama English Dept., Department of English, Huntsville AL 35899. E-mail: MaryH71997@aol.com. Web site: http://www.uah.edu/colleges/liberal/engl

ish/hefranciscontest/. **Contact:** Patricia Sammon. Offered annually for unpublished work not to exceed 5,000 words. Acquires first time publication rights. Prize: $1,000. Judged by a panel of nationally recognized, award-winning authors, directors of creative writing programs, and editors of literary journals. Entry fee: $15 reading fee (make check payable to the Ruth Hindman Foundation). Deadline: December 31.

🎖 JOHN GARDNER FICTION BOOK AWARD

Binghamton Center for Writers, State University of New York, P.O. Box 6000, Binghamton NY 13902. (607)777-2713. E-mail: cwpro@binghamton.edu. Web site: http://english.binghamton.edu/cwpro. **Contact:** Maria Mazziotti Gillan, director. "To recognize the strongest novel or collection of short stories published the preceding year." Annual. Competition/award for novels, story collections. Prize: $1,000. Entries are judged by a rotating guest judge. Entry fee: send 3 copies of the book. Guidelines available in June. Accepts inquiries by e-mail, phone. **Entry deadline is March 1st.** Entries should be previously published, with a min press run of 500. Author or publishers may submit. Publishers may submit as many as their authors published that year as they would like. Winners notified by e-mail. Winners announced by mid-summer. Results made available to entrants with SASE, on Web site.

🎖 ☑ GEORGETOWN REVIEW PRIZE

Georgetown Review, 400 East College St, Box 227, Georgetown KY 40324. E-mail: gtownreview@geor getowncollege.edu. Web site: http://georgetownreview.georgetowncollege.edu. **Contact:** Steven Carter, editor. "Contest for short stories, poetry and creative nonfiction." Annual. Competition/ award for short stories. Prize: $1,000 and publication; runners-up receive publication. Receives about 400 entries for each category. Entries are judged by the editors. Entry fee: $10 for first entry, $5 for each one thereafter. Make checks payable to *Georgetown Review*. Guidelines available in July. Accepts inquiries by e-mail. **Entry deadline is Nov. 15th, 2009.** Entries should be unpublished. Contest open to anyone except family, friends of the editors. Cover letter, ms should include name, address, phone, e-mail, novel/story title. Writers may submit own work. "We're just looking to publish quality work. Sometimes our contests are themed, so check the Web site for details." Results announced Feb or March. Winners notified by e-mail. Results made available to entrants with SASE.

☐ GIVAL PRESS NOVEL AWARD

Gival Press LLC, P.O. Box 3812, Arlington VA 22203. (703)351-0079. E-mail: givalpress@yahoo.com. Web site: www.givalpress.com. **Contact:** Robert L. Giron, publisher. "To award the best literary novel." Annual. Prize: $3,000 (USD), publication and author's copies. Categories: literary novel. Receives about 60-80 entries per category. Final judge for 2007 was Kim Roberts. Entries read anony-mously. Entry fee: $50 (USD). Make checks payable to Gival Press, LLC. Guidelines with SASE, by phone, by e-mail, on Web site, in journals. Accepts inquiries by e-mail. **Deadline: May 30 of each year.** Entries should be unpublished. Open to any author who writes original work in English. Length: 30,000-100,000 words. Cover letter should include name, address, phone, e-mail, word count, novel title. Only the title and word count should appear on the actual ms. Writers may submit own work. "Review the types of mss Gival Press has published. We stress literary works." Results announced late fall of same year. Winners notified by phone. Results made available to entrants with SASE, by e-mail, on Web site.

☐ GIVAL PRESS SHORT STORY AWARD

Gival Press, P.O. Box 3812, Arlington VA 22203. (703)351-0079. E-mail: givalpress@yahoo.com. Web site: www.givalpress.com. **Contact:** Robert L. Giron, publisher. "To award the best literary short story." Annual. Prize: $1,000 and publication on Web site. Category: literary short story. Receives about 60-80 entries per category. Entries are judged anonymously. Entry fee: $25. Make checks payable to Gival Press, LLC. Guidelines available online, via e-mail, or by mail. Deadline: Aug. 8th of every year. Entries must be unpublished. Open to anyone who writes original short stories in English. Length: 5,000-15,000 words. Include name, address, phone, e-mail, word count, title on cover letter. Only the title and word count should be found on ms. Writers may submit their own fiction. "We publish literary works." Results announced in the fall of the same year. Winners notified by phone. Results available with SASE, by e-mail, on Web site.

☑ THE GLASGOW PRIZE FOR EMERGING WRITERS

Washington and Lee University/*Shenandoah*, Mattingly House, 2 Lee Ave., Lexington VA 24450-2116. (540)458-8765. Fax: (540)458-8461. E-mail: lleech@wlu.edu. Web site: shenandoah.wlu.edu. **Contact**: Lynn Leech, managing editor. Award for writer with only one published book in genre being considered. (Genre alternates: 2008, short story; 2009, poetry.) Prize: $2,500, publication of new work in *Shenandoah*. Judged by anonymous writer/editor, announced after prize winner is selected. Entry fee: $25 (includes 1-yr subscription to *Shenandoah*; send credit card information or make checks payable to *Shenandoah*). To apply send first book, one unpublished story or 5 poems, SASE, and vita, along with check for $25 (from either author or publisher). Cover letter should include name, address, phone and e-mail. Books submitted for consideration will not be returned and will be donated to the University library after the contest. Guidelines available on Web site. Accepts inquiries by e-mail. Results announced on Web site and winners notified by mail or e-mail in May. Deadline: post-marked between March 15-31. Open to any writer.

☒ GLIMMER TRAIN'S FAMILY MATTERS

Glimmer Train Stories, 1211 NW Glisan St. Suite 207, Portland OR 97209. (503)221-0836. Fax: (503)221-0837. Web site: www.glimmertrain.org. **Contact:** Susan Burmeister-Brown, co-editor. Offered quarterly for unpublished stories about family. Prize: 1st place: $1,200, publication in *Glimmer Train Stories*, and 20 copies of that issue; 1st/2nd runners up receive $500/$300, respectively, and possible publication. Entry fee: $15. **Contest open the months of January, April, July, and October.** Entries should be unpublished. Length: 1,200-12,000 words. Make your submissions online at www.glimmertrain.org. Winners will be notified and results will be posted three months after the close of each competition.

☐ GLIMMER TRAIN'S FICTION OPEN

Glimmer Train Press, Inc., 1211 NW Glisan St., Suite 207, Portland OR 97209. (503)221-0836. Fax: (503)221-0837. Web site: www.glimmertrain.org. **Contact:** Susan Burmeister-Brown, co-editor. Offered quarterly for unpublished stories on any theme. Open to all writers. Word count: 2,000-20,000. Prize: 1st place: $2,000, publication in *Glimmer Train Stories*, and 20 copies of that issue; 1st/2nd runners-up: $1,000/$600 respectively, and possible publication in *Glimmer Train Stories*. Entry fee: $20/story. **Contest open the months of March, June, September and December.** Make your submissions online (www.glimmertrain.org). Winners will be called and results announced three months after the close of each contest.

☐ GLIMMER TRAIN'S SHORT STORY AWARD FOR NEW WRITERS

Glimmer Train Press, Inc., 1211 NW Glisan St., Suite 207, Portland OR 97209. (503)221-0836. Fax: (503)221-0837. Web site: www.glimmertrain.org. Contact: Susan Burmeister-Brown, co-editor. Offered for any writer whose fiction hasn't appeared in a nationally-distributed publication with a circulation over 5,000. Word limit: 1,200-12,000 words. Stories must be previously unpublished. Entry fee: $15/story. Contest open in the months of May and November. Make your submissions online at www.glimmertrain.org. Prize: Winner receives $1,200, publication in *Glimmer Train Stories*, and 20 copies of that issue. First/second runners-up receive $500/$300, respectively, and possible publication. Winners will be called and results announced three months after the close of each contest.

☐ GLIMMER TRAIN'S VERY SHORT FICTION AWARD

Glimmer Train Press, Inc., 1211 NW Glisan St., Suite 207, Portland OR 97209. (503)221-0836. Fax: (503)221-0837. Web site: www.glimmertrain.org. **Contact:** Susan Burmeister-Brown, co-editor. Award to encourage the art of the very short story. "We want to read your original, unpublished, very short story—word count not to exceed 3,000 words." Prize: $1,200 and publication in *Glimmer Train Stories* and 20 author's copies (1st place); First/Second runners-up: $500/$300 respectively and possible publication. Entry fee: $15/story. Contest open in the months of February and August. Open to any writer. Make your submissions online at www.glimmertrain.org. Winners will be called and results announced three months after the close of each contest.

GOLDENBERG PRIZE FOR FICTION

Bellevue Literary Review, NYU School of Medicine, 550 First Avenue, New York NY 10016.(212)263-3973. Fax: (212)263-3206. E-mail: info@blreview.org. Web site: www.blreview.org. **Contact:** Stacy

Bodziak, Managing Editor. "Prize is created to honor outstanding writing related to themes of health, healing, illness, the mind and the body." Annual. Competition/award for short stories. Prize: $1,000 and publication in the Spring issue of *Bellevue Literary Review*. Fiction prizes have been judged by Ray Gonzalez (2006 prize), Amy Hempel (2007 prize) and Rick Moody (2008 prize). Entry fee: $15. Send credit card information through Web site. Make checks payable to *Bellevue Literary Review*. Guidelines available in February. Accepts inquiries by e-mail, phone. **Deadline is August.** Entries should be unpublished. Length: Maximum 5,000 words. Writers may submit own work. Winners notified by e-mail. Winners announced November-December.

THE GOODHEART PRIZE FOR FICTION

Shenandoah: The Washington and Lee University Review, Mattingly House, 2 Lee Ave., Lexington VA 24450-2116. (540)458-8765. Fax: (540)458-8461. E-mail: shenandoah@wlu.edu. Web site: shena ndoah.wlu.edu. **Contact:** Lynn Leech, managing editor. Awarded to best story published in *Shenandoah* during a volume year. Prize: $1,000. Judged by writer whose identity is revealed after the prize winner has been selected. No entry fee. All stories published in the review are automatically considered for the prize. Winners are notified by mail or e-mail each Spring. Results are available on Web site. "Read *Shenandoah* to familiarize yourself with the work we publish."

🅽 🌒 🅖 GRANTS FOR ARTIST'S PROJECTS

Artist Trust, 1835 12th Ave, Seattle, WA 98122. (206)467-8734 x9. Fax: (206)467-9633. E-mail: info@artisttrust.org. Web site: www.artisttrust.org. **Contact:** Heather Helbach-Olds, Director of Programs. "The GAP Program provides support for artist-generated projects, which can include (but are not limited to) the development, completion or presentation of new work." Annual. Prize: maximum of $1,500 for projects. Accepted are poetry, fiction, graphic novels, experimental works, creative nonfiction, screen plays, film scripts and teleplays. Entries are judged by work sample as specified in the guidelines. Winners are selected by a multidisciplinary panel of artists and artist professionals. No entry fee. Guidelines available in December. Accepts inquiries by mail, phone. Submission period is Dec-Feb.**Deadline is approximately the 4th Friday of Feb.** Web site should be consulted for exact date. Entries can be unpublished or previously published. *Washington state residents only.* Length: 8 pages max for poetry, fiction, graphic novels, experimental work and creative nonfiction; up to 12 pages for screen plays, film scripts and teleplays. All mss must be typed with a 12-point font size or larger and cannot be single-spaced (except for poetry). Include application with project proposal and budget, as well as resume with name, address, phone, e-mail, and novel/story title. "GAP awards are highly competitive. Please follow guidelines with care." Results announced June. Winners notified by mail. Results made available to entrants by mail and on Web site.

🗀 THE GREAT BLUE BEACON SHORT-SHORT STORY CONTEST

The Great Blue Beacon: The Newsletter for Writers of All Genres and Skill Levels, 1425 Patriot Drive, Melbourne FL 32940-6881. (321)253-5869. E-mail: a byers2@cfl.rr.com. **Contact:** A.J. Byers; editor/publisher. Award to "recognize outstanding short-short stories." Prize: $50 (first prize), $25 (second prize), $10 (third prize) and publication of winning entry in *The Great Blue Beacon*. Judged by outside panel of judges. Entry fee: $5 ($4 for subscribers). Make checks out to A.J. Byers. Guidelines available periodically when announced. Length: 1,000 words or fewer. Cover letter and first page of ms should include name, address, phone, e-mail, word count and title. **Deadline: TBA**. Entries must be unpublished. Open to any writer. Two-three contests a year for short-short stories. Receives 50-75 entries per contest. For guidelines, send SASE or e-mail. Accepts inquiries by e-mail and phone. Results announced two months after contest deadline. Winners notified by SASE or e-mail. For contest results, send SASE or e-mail.

🔃 🎯 GREAT CANADIAN STORY CONTEST

Storyteller, Canada's Short Story Magazine, 3687 Twin Falls Place, Ottawa ON K1V 1W6 Canada. (613)822-9734. E-mail: info@storytellermagazine.com. Web site: www.storytellermagazine.com. **Contact:** Terry Tyo, publisher/managing editor. "Purpose of competition is to publish great Canadian stories. Stories must have a uniquely Canadian element (theme, setting, history, institution, politics, social phenomenon, etc.)." Prize: Varies from year to year. Short list determined by editors; readers choose from short list. Entry fee: $5 Canadian (make check or money order payable to TYO Communications). Deadline: varies. Entries must be unpublished. Canadian citizens or residents only. Guidelines available in February by SASE or on Web site. Length: 2,000-6,000 words. No simultaneous submissions or e-mail submissions. *Storyteller* cannot return mss unless accompanied by SASE. "Read the magazine. The short list comprises our summer issue, so all stories must be suitable for publication in *Storyteller* to qualify. Results announced on or around July 1st. Winners notified by phone or e-mail. For contest results, send SASE or visit Web site.

GREAT LAKES COLLEGES ASSOCIATION NEW WRITERS AWARD

Great Lakes Colleges Association Inc., 535 W. William, Suite 301, Ann Arbor MI 48103. (734)661-2350. Fax: (734)661-2349. E-mail: shackelford@glca.org. **Contact:** Greg Wegner. Award for first publication in fiction, creative nonfiction or poetry. Writer must be nominated by publisher or can submit work if self-published. Prize: Winners are invited to tour the GLCA colleges. An honorarium of $500 will be guaranteed the author by each GLCA member college they visit. Judged by professors from member colleges. No entry fee. **Deadline: June.** Open to any writer. Submit 4 copies of the book to Greg Wegner. Guidelines available early 2009. Accepts inquiries by fax and e-mail. Results announced in winter. Letters go to publishers who have submitted.

THE GRUB STREET BOOK PRIZE IN FICTION

Grub Street, 160 Boylston Street, Boston MA 02116. (617)695-0075. Fax: (617)695-0075. E-mail: info@grubstreet.org. Web site: http://www.grubstreet.org. **Contact:** Sonya Larson, program coordinator. "To support writers who are publishing beyond their first or second, third, fourth (or beyond . . .) book, and who are living outside of New England." Annual. Competition/award for short story collections, novels. Prize: Each winner receives a $1,000 honorarium and a Friday night reading/book party at Grub Street's event space in downtown Boston. The reading and party are co-sponsored by a local independent bookstore, which will sell books at the event. Saturday morning, winners will lead a two-hour "craft class" on a topic of their choice for a small group of aspiring Grub Street writers. Grub Street will provide accommodations for one night in Boston and cover all travel and meal expenses. Categories: Fiction, Poetry, and Non-fiction. Different deadlines apply for each category. Entries are judged by a guest judge and committee of readers drawn from the Grub Street staff. Committee members negotiate their top picks at a meeting facilitated by the guest judge. Entry fee: $10. Send credit card information or make checks payable to Grub Street. Guidelines available in June. Accepts inquiries by fax, e-mail, phone. **Entry deadline is October 15th.** Entries should be previously published. "The publication date must be in 2008 or 2009, and the hardcover or paperback original must be available to booksellers by the time of the winner's visit to Boston. The book submitted for entry must not be self-published. Galleys may be submitted for the contest as long as the first edition is published by May 2010." All applicants must have at least one previously published novel or short story collection (self-publication not eligible), and must not primarily reside in the following states: Massachusetts, Vermont, Maine, Connecticut, New Hampshire or Rhode Island. Cover letter should include name, address, phone, e-mail, novel/story title. Also include a curriculum vitae and a 500-word synopsis of the proposed craft class. Writers may submit own work. "Though Grub Street's top criterion is the overall literary merit of the work submitted, the award committee especially encourages writers publishing with small presses, writers of short story collections, and writers of color to apply. We also want the award to benefit writers for whom a trip to Boston will likely expand their readership in a meaningful way. Please give careful thought to your proposal for the craft class, and please plan it as a 3-hour class for a group of 15 adult writers of mixed experience." Results announced 2-3 months after submission deadline.

HAMMETT PRIZE

Internatonal Association of Crime Writers/North American Branch, P.O. Box 8674, New York NY 10116-8674. Fax: (815)361-1477. E-mail: mfrisque@igc.org. Web site: www.crimewritersna.org. **Contact:** Mary A. Frisque, executive director, North American Branch. Award established "to honor a work of literary excellence in the field of crime writing by a U.S. or Canadian author." Award for novels, story collections, nonfiction by one author. Prize: trophy. Judged by committee. "Our reading committee seeks suggestions from publishers and they also ask the membership for recommendations. Eligible books are read by a committee of members of the organization. The committee chooses five nominated books, which are then sent to three outside judges for a final selection. Judges are outside the crime writing field." No entry fee. For guidelines, send SASE or e-mail. Accepts inquiries by e-mail. **Deadline: December 1.** Entries must be previously published. To be eligible "the book must have been published in the U.S. or Canada during the calendar year." The author must be a U.S. or Canadian citizen or permanent resident. Nominations announced in January, winners announced in fall. Winners notified by mail, phone and recognized at awards ceremony. For contest results, send SASE or e-mail.

N WILDA HEARNE FLASH FICTION CONTEST

Big Muddy: A Journal of the Mississippi River Valley, WHFF Contest, Southeast Missouri State Univ., MS 2650, One University Plaza, Cape Girardeau MO 63701. (573)651-2044. Fax: (573)651-5188. E-mail: upress@semo.edu. Web site: http://www6.semo.edu/universitypress/hearne.htm. **Contact:** Dr. Susan Swartwout, Publisher/Editor. "We're searching for the best short-short story of any theme." Annual. Prize: $200 and publication in *Big Muddy*. Semi-finalists will be chosen by a regional team of published writers. The final ms will be chosen by Susan Swartwout, publisher of Southeast Missouri State University Press. Entry fee: $15 (includes a copy of *Big Muddy* in which the winning story appears). Make checks payable to SEMO UP—WHFF. Guidelines available in January. Accepts inquiries by e-mail, phone. **Submission period is Jan 1— Aug 1.** Entries should be unpublished. Anyone may enter contest. Length: 500 words max. Cover letter should include name, address, phone, e-mail, story title. The title and page numbers should appear on each page of the ms. Writers may submit own work. Results announced fall. Winners notified by mail, by phone, by e-mail. Results made available to entrants with SASE.

◎ DRUE HEINZ LITERATURE PRIZE

University of Pittsburgh Press, 3400 Forbes Ave., 5th Floor, Eureka Building, Pittsburgh PA 15260. (412)383-2492. Fax: (412)383-2466. E-mail: press@pitt.edu. Web site: www.pitt.edu/~press. Award to "support the writer of short fiction at a time when the economics of commercial publishing make it more and more difficult for the serious literary artist working in the short story and novella to find publication." Prize: $15,000 and publication by the University of Pittsburgh Press. No entry fee. "It is imperative that entrants review complete rules of the competition before submitting a manuscript." Deadline: Submissions received only during the months of May and June. Competition for story collections. No previously published collections. Manuscripts must be unpublished in book form. Length: 150-300 typed pages. The award is open to writers who have published a book-length collection of fiction or three short stories or novellas in commercial magazines or literary journals of national distribution. On-line publication does not count toward this requirement. Cover letter should include name, address, phone, e-mail, title, name of publications where work was originally published. This information should not appear on the ms. Results announced in December or January. Winners notified by phone. For contest results, send SASE with manuscript.

◻ LORIAN HEMINGWAY SHORT STORY COMPETITION

P.O. Box 993, Key West FL 33041-0993. (305)294-0320. E-mail: shortstorykw@aol.com. Web site: www.shortstorycompetition.com. **Contact:** Carol Shaughnessy, co-director. Award to "encourage literary excellence and the efforts of writers who have not yet had major-market success." Competition for short stories. Prize: $1,000 (first prize), $500 (second prize), $500 (third prize), honorable mentions. Judged by a panel of writers, editors and literary scholars selected by author Lorian Hemingway. Guidelines available in January for SASE, by e-mail or on Web site. Accepts inquiries by SASE, e-mail or visit Web site. **Deadline: May 15.** Entries must be unpublished. Length: 3,000 words maximum. "Open to all writers whose work has not appeared in a nationally distributed publication with a circulation of 5,000 or more." Entry fee is $12 for each story postmarked by May 1, and $15 for stories postmarked between May 1 and May 15. "We look for excellence, pure and simple—no genre restrictions, no theme restrictions. We seek a writer's voice that cannot be ignored." Results announced at the end of July during Hemingway Days festival. Winners notified by phone prior to announcement. For contest results, send e-mail or visit Web site. "All entrants will receive a letter from Lorian Hemingway and a list of winners, via mail or e-mail, by October 1."

◻ ◎ HIGHLIGHTS FOR CHILDREN FICTION CONTEST

Highlights for Children, 803 Church St., Honesdale PA 18431-1824. (570)253-1080. Fax: (570)251-7847. E-mail: eds@highlights-corp.com. Web site: www.highlights.com. **Contact:** Marileta Robinson, senior editor. Award "to honor quality stories (previously unpublished) for young readers and to encourage children's writers." Offered for stories for children ages 2-12; category varies each year. No crime or violence, please. Specify that ms is a contest entry. Prize: $1,000 to 3 winners, plus publication in *Highlights*. Categories: Short stories. Judged by *Highlights* editors, with input given by outside readers. No entry fee. "There is a different contest theme each year. We generally receive about 1,400 entries." Cover letter should include name, address, phone, e-mail, word count and title. "We prefer that these things appear on the first page of the manuscript as well." **Deadline: January 1-31 (postmarked).** Entries must be unpublished. Length: 500 words maximum for stories for beginning readers (to age 8) and 800 words for more advanced readers (ages 9-12). No minimum word count. Open to anyone 16 years of age or older. Results announced in June. Winners notified by mail or phone. For contest results, send SASE. See www.highlights.com for current theme and guidelines or send a SASE to *Highlights for Children*.

TONY HILLERMAN MYSTERY SHORT STORY CONTEST

Tony Hillerman Writers Conference and *Cowboys & Indians* magazine, 128 Grant Ave., Santa Fe NM 87501. E-mail: wordharvest@wordharvest.com. Web site: www.wordharvest.com. **Contact:** Anne Hillerman, contest administrator. "Purpose is to encourage mystery short stories set in the West or Southwest in the tradition of Tony Hillerman." Annual. Competition/award for short stories. Prize: $1,500 cash and publication in *Cowboys & Indians* magazine, a successful glossy national publication; signed Hillerman books; and tickets to the award banquet held in conjunction with the Tony Hillerman Writers Conference: Focus on Mystery in Albuquerque the first weekend of November. Category: mystery short story set in West or Southwest with at least one Native American or cowboy character. Receives about 260 entries per year. Entries are judged by a professional writer/editor with connections to both the conference and *Cowboys & Indians* magazine. Entry fee: $15; critiques available for $100. Make checks payable to Wordharvest. Guidelines available in June on Web site, in publication. Accepts inquiries by e-mail. **Deadline: September 15, 2009.** Entries should be unpublished. Open to all, as long as the entry is a previously unpublished mystery story that meets the guidelines. Length: 2,500 words. Cover letter should include name, address, phone, e-mail, word count, story title. Include only title on ms. Writers may submit own work. "Look at previous year's winner (published in March issue) for reference and info about the contest. Know that next year's winner must be different in terms of setting, plot and characters. Look at the magazine for info about the readers. Humor is a plus! Graphic sex, violence and four-letter words do not fit the magazine's tone." Winners notified by phone in October. Results made available to entrants on Web site.

THE HILLERMAN PRIZE

Wordharvest & St. Martin's Press, 304 Calle Oso, Santa Fe NM 87501. (505)471-1565. E-mail: wordharvest@wordharvest.com. Web site: www.hillermanconference.com. **Contact:** Anne Hillerman, Co-organizer; Jean Schaumberg, Co-organizer. "To honor the contributions made by Tony Hillerman to the art and craft of the mystery." Annual competition/award for novels. Prize: $10,000 advance and publication by Thomas Dunne Books/St. Martin's Minotaur imprint. Categories: unpublished mystery novels set in the southwest, written by a first-time author in the mystery genre. One entry per author. Nominees will be selected by judges chosen by the editorial staff of St. Martin's Press, with the assistance of organizers of the Tony Hillerman Writers Conference (Wordharvest), and the winner will be chosen by St. Martin's editors. No entry fee. Accepts inquiries by e-mail, phone. **Entry deadline is July 1, 2008.** Entries should be unpublished. All first-time writers of an unpublished mystery set in the American southwest may enter contest. Length: no less than 220 typewritten pages or approx. 60,000 words. Cover letter should include name, address, phone, e-mail, list of publishing credits. Please include SASE for response. Writers may submit their own work. "Make sure murder or another serioius crime or crimes is at the heart of the story, and emphasis is on the solution rather than the details of the crime. The story's primary setting should be the southwest US, which includes AZ, CO, NV, NM, OK, TX, and UT." Results announced at the Tony Hillerman Writers Conference. St. Martin's Press notifies the winner by phone or by e-mail 2-3 weeks prior to the conference. Results made available to entrants on Web site.

PEARL HOGREFE FELLOWSHIP

The Pearl Hogrefe Fund and Department of English, 203 Ross Hall, Iowa State University, Ames IA 50011. (515)294-2477. Fax: (515)294-6814. E-mail: englgrad@iastate.edu. Web site: www.engl.iastate.edu. **Contact:** Helen Ewald, graduate studies coordinator. Award "to provide new Iowa State MA students with writing time." Competition for manuscript sample of 25 pages, any genre. Prize: $1,200/month for 9 months and full payment of tuition and fees. Judged by the creative writing staff at Iowa State University. No entry fee. Deadline: January 15. Open to published and unpublished manuscripts. "No restrictions, except the applicant cannot hold or expect to receive a master's degree in English or creative writing during the current year." Open to any writer. Guidelines available by e-mail. Accepts inquiries by fax, e-mail, phone. Results announced April 1. Winners notified by phone.

☐ TOM HOWARD/JOHN H. REID SHORT STORY CONTEST

Tom Howard Books, Mail to: Winning Writers, 351 Pleasant St., PMB 222, Northampton MA 01060-3961. (866)946-9748. Fax: (413)280-0539. E-mail: johnreid@mail.qango.com. Web site: www.winningwriters.com/tomstory. **Contact:** John H. Reid, award director. "Established in 1993, this award honors the best short stories, essays and other works of prose being written today." Annual. Prize: $2,000 (first prize), $1,000 (second prize), $500 (third prize), $250 (fourth prize). There will also be five High Distinction Awards of $200 each and five Most Highly Commended Awards of $100 each. The top fourteen entries will be published on the Winning Writers Web site and announced in Tom Howard Contest News and the Winning Writers Newsletter. Categories: All entries are judged in one category. "We received 1,510 entries for the 2007 contest." Judged by a former journalist and magazine editor, John H. Reid. Mr. Reid has judged literary contests for over 15 years. He has published several novels, a collection of poetry, a guide to winning literary contests, and 15 books of film criticism and movie history. He is assisted by Dee C. Konrad, a leading educator and published author, who served as Associate Professor of English at Barat College of DePaul University and dean of Liberal Arts and Sciences for the year 2000-2001. Entry fee: $12 per entry. Make checks payable to Winning Writers. (U.S. funds only, please.) Guidelines available in Sept. on Web site. Prefers inquiries by e-mail. **Deadline: March 31, 2009.** "Both published and unpublished works are accepted. In the case of published work, the contestant must own the online publication rights." Open to all writers. Length: 5,000 words max per entry. Cover letter should include name, address, phone, e-mail, story title, place(s) where story was previously published (if any). Only the title should be on the actual ms. Writers may submit own work. "Read past winning entries at www.winningwriters.com/contests/tomstory/ts_pastwinners.php." Results announced May 15. Winners notified by e-mail. Results made available to entrants on Web site.

THE JULIA WARD HOWE/BOSTON AUTHORS AWARD

The Boston Authors Club, 79 Moore Rd., Wayland MA 01778. (617)783-1357. E-mail: bostonauthors@aol.com. Web site: www.bostonauthorsclub.org. **Contact:** Alan Lawson. This annual award honors Julia Ward Howe and her literary friends who founded the Boston Authors Club in 1900. It also honors the membership over 108 years, consisting of novelists, biographers, historians, governors, senators, philosophers, poets, playwrights, and other luminaries. There are 2 categories: trade books and books for young readers (beginning with chapter books through young adult books). Works of fiction, nonfiction, memoir, poetry, and biography published in current year (2008 for 2009 prize) are eligible. Authors must live or have lived (college counts) within a 100-mile radius of Boston. Subsidized books, cook books and picture books are not eligible. No fee. **Deadline: January 15.** Prize: $1,000 in each category.

☐ ◎ L. RON HUBBARD'S WRITERS OF THE FUTURE CONTEST

Author Services Inc., P.O. Box 1630, Los Angeles CA 90078. (323)466-3310. Fax: (323)466-6474. E-mail: contests@authorservicesinc.com. Web site: www.writersofthefuture.com. **Contact:** Joni, contest director. Established in 1983. Foremost competition for new and amateur writers of unpublished science fiction or fantasy short stories or novelettes. Offered "to find, reward and publicize new speculative fiction writers so they may more easily attain professional writing careers." Open to new and amateur writers who have not professionally published a novel or short novel, more than 1 novelette, or more than 3 short stories. Eligible entries are previously unpublished short stories or novelettes (under 17,000 words) of science fiction or fantasy. Guidelines for SASE or on Web site. Accepts inquiries by fax, e-mail, phone. Prize: awards quarterly: 1st place: $1,000; 2nd place: $750; and 3rd place: $500. Annual grand prize: $5,000. "Contest has four quarters. There shall be 3 cash prizes in each quarter. In addition, at the end of the year, the 4 first-place, quarterly winners will have their entries rejudged, and a grand prize winner shall be determined." Judged by K.D. Wentworth (initial judge), then by a panel of 4 professional authors. **Deadline: December 31, March 31, June 30, September 30.** Entries must be unpublished. Limit one entry per quarter. No entry fee; entrants retain all rights to their stories. Open to any writer. Manuscripts: white paper, black ink; double-spaced; typed; each page appropriately numbered with title, no author name. Include cover page with author's name, address, phone number, e-mail address (if available), as well as estimated word count and the title of the work. Results announced quarterly in e-newsletter. Winners notified by phone.

◎ INDIANA REVIEW ½ K (SHORT-SHORT/PROSE-POEM) CONTEST

Indiana Review, Ballantine Hall 465/Indiana University, 1020 E. Kirkwood Ave., Bloomington IN 47405-7103. (812)855-3439. Fax: (812)855-4253. E-mail: inreview@indiana.edu. Web site: www.ind iana.edu/~inreview. **Contact:** Abdel Shakur, editor. Competition for fiction and prose poems no longer than 500 words. Prize: $1,000 plus publication, contributor's copies and a year's subscription. All entries considered for publication. Judged by *Indiana Review* staff and outside judges. Entry fee: $15 fee for no more than 3 pieces (includes a year's subscription, two issues). Make checks payable to *Indiana Review*. **Deadline: June 9.** Entries must be unpublished. Guidelines available in March for SASE, by phone, e-mail, on Web site, or in publication. Length: 500 words, 3 mss per entry. Open to any writer. Cover letter should include name, address, phone, e-mail, word count and title. No identifying information on ms. "We look for command of language and form." Results announced in August. Winners notified by mail. For contest results, send SASE or visit Web site.

◻ INDIANA REVIEW FICTION CONTEST

Indiana Review, BH 465/Indiana University, 1020 E. Kirkwood Ave., Bloomington IN 47405-7103. (812)855-3439. Fax: (812)855-4253. E-mail: inreview@indiana.edu. Web site: www.indiana.edu/~inreview. **Contact:** Abdel Shakur, editor. Contest for fiction in any style and on any subject. Prize: $1,000, publication in the *Indiana Review* and contributor's copies. Judged by *Indiana Review* staff and outside judges. Entry fee: $15 fee (includes a year's subscription). Deadline: Mid-October. Entries must be unpublished. Mss will not be returned. No previously published work, or works forthcoming elsewhere, are eligible. Simultaneous submissions accepted, but in the event of entrant withdrawal, contest fee will not be refunded. Length: 15,000 words (about 40 pages)maximum, double spaced. Open to any writer. Cover letter must include name, address, phone number and title of story. Entrant's name should appear only in the cover letter, as all entries will be considered anonymously. Results announced January. Winners notified by mail. For contest results, send SASE. "We look for a command of language and structure, as well as a facility with compelling and unusual subject matter. It's a good idea to obtain copies of issues featuring past winners to get a more concrete idea of what we are looking for."

◎ INDIVIDUAL ARTIST FELLOWSHIP/MINI FELLOWSHIP

Kansas Arts Commission, 700 SW Jackson St., Suite 1004, Topeka KS 66603-3761. (785)296-3335. Fax: (785)296-4989. E-mail: kac@arts.state.ks.us. Web site: www.arts.state.ks.us. **Contact:** Tom Klocke, program consultant. "Awards are based on artistic merit and recognize sustained achievement and excellence." Fellowships awarded every other year in fiction, poetry and playwriting. Prize: $5,000 for fellowship; $500 for mini-fellowship. Judged by Kansas professionals in the field—generally, the panel meets in January. No entry fee. Deadline: October 13, 2009. Entries may be previously published or unpublished; do not submit work completed prior to 2001. Open to Kansas residents only. Undergraduate or graduate degree-seeking students are ineligible. Guidelines on Web site. Accepts inquiries by fax, e-mail, phone. Length: 30 pages mss for fiction and playwriting; 20 pages/mss for poetry. Competition receives 40-50 fellowship submissions; 10-15 mini-fellowship submissions. "Follow guidelines for application explicitly." Results announced in February each year. Winners notified by mail or phone.

Ⓝ ◎ INDIVIDUAL EXCELLENCE AWARDS

Ohio Arts Council, 727 E. Main St., Columbus OH 43205-1796. (614)466-2613. Fax: (614)466-4479. E-mail: ken.emerick@oac.state.oh.us. Web site: www.oac.state.oh.us. **Contact:** Ken Emerick, director, Individual Creativity. "An award of excellence for completed work for Ohio residents who are not students." Annual. Competition/award for short stories, novels, story collections. Prize: $5,000 or $10,000, determined by review panel. Categories: fiction/nonfiction, poetry, criticism, playwriting/

screenplays. Receives about 125 poetry, 125 fiction/nonfiction, 10-15 criticism, 25-30 playwriting entries per year. Judged by three-person panel of out-of-state panelists, anonymous review. No entry fee. Guidelines available in June on Web site. Accepts inquiries by e-mail, phone. Deadline: September 1. Open to Ohio residents living and working in the state for at least one year prior to the deadline who are also not students. Length: 20-30 pages fiction/nonfiction, 10-15 pages poetry, 30-50 pages criticism, 1 play or 2 short 1-act plays. Cover letter should include name, address, title of work. None of this information should appear on the actual manuscript. Writers may submit own work. "Submit concise bodies of work or sections, not a sampling of styles." Results announced Jan. Winners notified by mail. Results made available to entrants on Web site.

ⓝ INKWELL SHORT FICTION CONTEST

Inkwell Literary Magazine, Manhattanville College, 2900 Purchase Street, Purchase NY 10577. (914)323-7239. Fax: (914)323-3122. E-mail: inkwell@mville.edu. Web site: http://www.inkwelljournal.org. **Contact:** Competition fiction editor. Annual. Competition/award for short stories. Prize: $1,500. Entries are judged by editorial staff. Finalists are picked by a celebrity judge. Brian Morton judging 2008 contest. Entry fee: $15. Make checks payable to Inkwell-Manhattanville College. Guidelines available in June. Accepts inquiries by fax, e-mail, phone.**Entry deadline is October 30.** Entries must be unpublished. Anyone may enter contest. Length: 5,000 words max. Cover letter should include name, address, phone, e-mail, word count, novel/story title. Only title on ms. Writers may submit own work. "Follow the guidelines. Proofread your work. Don't write for editors, teachers, or critics; write for you, and for your readers." Results announced December. Winners notified by phone, by e-mail. Results made available to entrants with SASE, by e-mail.

INTERNATIONAL READING ASSOCIATION CHILDREN'S BOOK AWARDS

International Reading Association, P.O. Box 8139, 800 Barksdale Rd., Newark DE 19714-8139. (302)731-1600, ext. 221. E-mail: exec@reading.com. "This award is intended for newly published authors of children's books who show unusual promise in the children's book field." Offered annually for an author's first or second published book in fiction and nonfiction in 3 categories: primary (preschool-age 8), intermediate (ages 9-13), and young adult (ages 14-17). Guidelines and deadlines for SASE. Prize: 6 awards of $1,000 each, and a medal for each category. Categories: fiction and nonfiction. No entry fee. Entries in a language other than English must include a one-page abstract in English and a translation into English of one chapter or similar selection that in the submitter's estimation is representative of the book. **Deadline: November 1.** Entries must be previously published. Books from any country and in any language copyrighted during the previous calendar year will be considered. For guidelines with specific information write to Executive Office, International Reading Association, P.O. Box 8139, Newark DE 19714-8139.

ⓞ THE IOWA SHORT FICTION AWARD

Iowa Writers' Workshop, 102 Dey House, 507 N. Clinton St., Iowa City IA 52242-1000. (319)335-2000. Fax: (319)335-2055. Web site: www.uiowapress.org. **Contact:** Holly Carver, director. Award "to give exposure to promising writers who have not yet published a book of prose." Prize: publication by University of Iowa Press. Judged by Senior Iowa Writers' Workshop members who screen manuscripts; published fiction author of note makes final selections. No entry fee. Submission period: Aug. 1-Sept. 30. Entries must be unpublished, but stories previously published in periodicals are eligible for inclusion. "The manuscript must be a collection of short stories of at least 150 word-processed, double-spaced pages." Open to any writer. No application forms are necessary. Do not send original ms. Include SASE for return of ms. Announcement of winners made early in year following competition. Winners notified by phone.

◻ ⓞ JOSEPH HENRY JACKSON AWARD

The San Francisco Foundation, Administered by Intersection for the Arts, 446 Valencia St., San Francisco CA 94103. (415)626-2787. Fax: (415)626-1636. Web site: www.theintersection.org. **Contact:** Kevin B. Chen, program director. Award "to encourage young, unpublished writers." Offered annually for unpublished, work-in-progress fiction (novel or short story), nonfiction or poetry by an author age 20-35, with 3-year consecutive residency in northern California or Nevada prior to submission. Prize: $2,000 and certificate. Categories: short stories, novels and short story collections, and poetry. No entry fee. Deadline: March 31. Entries must be unpublished. Work cannot exceed

40 double-spaced, typed pages. Entry form and rules available in mid-January for SASE. "Submit a serious, ambitious portion of a book-length manuscript." Results announced September. Winners will be announced in letter mailed to all applicants.

JAMES JONES FIRST NOVEL FELLOWSHIP

Wilkes University, English Department, Kirby Hall, Wilkes-Barre PA 18766. (570)408-4530. Fax: (570)408-7829. E-mail: english@wilkes.edu. Web site: www.wilkes.edu/humanities/jones.asp. **Contact:** J. Michael Lennon, English department professor. Offered annually for unpublished novels, novellas and closely-linked short stories (all works in progress). "The award is intended to honor the spirit of unblinking honesty, determination and insight into modern culture exemplified by the late James Jones." The competition is open to all American writers who have not previously published novels. Prize: $10,000; $250 honorarium (runner-up). Categories: novel, novella, collected short stories. Entry fee: $20 fee. Make checks payable to Wilkes University. Deadline: March 1. Entries must be unpublished. Open to any previously unpublished writer. Guidelines available after June 1 by e-mail, for SASE and on Web site. Accepts inquiries by e-mail. Word length: 50 double-spaced pages and a two-page thematic outline. Title page should include name, address, phone and e-mail address if available. Results announced on or near September 30. For contest results see Web site, e-mail or send SASE marked 'winner's list.'

JUST DESERTS SHORT-SHORT FICTION PRIZE

Passages North, NMU 1401 Presque Isle Ave, Marquette MI 49855. (906)227-1203. E-mail: passages@nmu.edu. Web site: http://myweb.num.edu/~passages. Annual. Prize: $1,000 First Prize and 2 honorable mentions. Entry fee: $10 for up to 2 stories; includes contest issue. Make checks payable to Northern Michigan University. **Submission period is Oct 15th-Jan 31st.** Entries should be unpublished. Anyone may enter contest. Length: max of 1,000 words. Cover letter should include name, address, phone, e-mail. Writers may submit own work. Winners notified by e-mail. Results made available to entrants with SASE.

EZRA JACK KEATS/KERLAN COLLECTION MEMORIAL FELLOWSHIP

Ezra Jack Keats Foundation, University of Minnesota, 113 Andersen Library, 222 21st Ave. S., Minneapolis MN 55455. (612)624-4576. Fax: (612)625-5525. E-mail: clrc@tc.umn.edu. Web site: special.lib.umn.edu/clrc/. Competition for books of children's literature. The Ezra Jack Keats/Kerlan Memorial Fellowship from the Ezra Jack Keats Foundation provides $1,500 to a "talented writer and/or illustrator of children's books who wishes to use the Kerlan Collection for the furtherance of his or her artistic development." This fellowship is intended to provide financial assistance for writers and illustrators who wish to use the original manuscripts, illustrations, and books of the Kerlan Collection in course of their professional development. Special consideration will be given to those who would find it difficult to finance a visit to the Kerlan Collection. The Ezra Jack Keats Fellowship recipient will receive funds for travel expenses and a per diem allotment. Applications for 2009 must be postmarked by December 31, 2008. The winner will be notified by April 30, 2009. Study and written report must be completed during the 2009 calendar year. The application may be downloaded at www.special.lib.umn.edu/clrc/kerlan/2008_Keats_app.pdf. For paper copies of the application send a request including a large size (6×9 or 9×12) self-addressed, 97¢ postage paid envelope.

THE KIRIYAMA PACIFIC RIM BOOK PRIZE

Kiriyama Pacific Rim Institute, 650 Delancey St., Suite 101, San Francisco CA 94107. (415)777-1628. Fax: (415)777-1646. Web site: www.kiriyamaprize.org. Offered for work published during the previous year to promote books that will contribute to greater mutual understanding and increased cooperation throughout all areas of the Pacific Rim and South Asia. Guidelines and entry form on request or may be downloaded from the prize Web site. Books must be submitted for entry by the publisher. Proper entry forms must be submitted. Contact the administrators of the prize for complete rules and entry forms. Prize: $30,000 to be divided equally between the author of 1 fiction and of 1 nonfiction book. No entry fee. Deadline: October.

E.M. KOEPPEL SHORT FICTION AWARD

Writecorner Press, P.O. Box 140310, Gainesville FL 32614-0310. Web site: www.writecorner.com. **Contact:** Mary Sue Koeppel, editor. Award for short stories. Prize: $1,100 first prize, and $100 for

Editors' Choices. Judged by award-winning writers. Entry fee: $15 first story, $10 each additional story. Make checks payable to Writecorner Press. Send 2 title pages: One with title only and one with title, name, address, phone, e-mail, short bio. Place no other identification of the author on the ms that will be used in the judging. Guidelines available for SASE or on Web site. Accepts inquiries by e-mail and phone. Expects 300+ entries. **Deadline: October 1-April 30.** Entries must be unpublished. Open to any writer. Results announced in Summer. Winners notified by mail, phone in July (or earlier). For results, send SASE or check Web site.

✉ ◎ THE LAWRENCE FOUNDATION AWARD

Prairie Schooner, 201 Andrews Hall, P.O. Box 880334, Lincoln NE 68588-0334. (402)472-0911. Fax: (402)472-9771. E-mail: jengelhardt2@unl.edu. Web site: http://prairieschooner.unl.edu. **Contact:** Hilda Raz, editor-in-chief. Offered annually for the best short story published in *Prairie Schooner* in the previous year. Prize: $1,000. Judged by editorial staff of *Praire Schooner*. No entry fee. Only work published in *Prairie Schooner* in the previous year is considered. Work is nominated by editorial staff. Results announced in the Spring issue. Winners notified by mail in February or March.

◎ LAWRENCE FOUNDATION PRIZE

Michigan Quarterly Review, 3574 Rackham Building, Ann Arbor MI 48109-1070. (734)764-9265. E-mail: mqr@umich.edu. Web site: www.umich.edu/~mqr. **Contact:** Vicki Lawrence, managing editor. Competition for short stories. Prize: $1,000. Judged by editorial board. No entry fee. No deadline. "An annual cash prize awarded to the author of the best short story published in *Michigan Quarterly Review* each year. Stories must be already published in *Michigan Quarterly Review*. This is not a competition in which manuscripts are read outside of the normal submission process." Guidelines available for SASE or on Web site. Accepts inquires by e-mail and phone. Results announced in December. Winners notified by phone or mail.

⊡ ◎ STEPHEN LEACOCK MEMORIAL MEDAL FOR HUMOUR

Stephen Leacock Association, Box 854, Orrillia ON L3V 6K8 Canada. (705)835-3218 or (705)835-3408. Fax: (705)835-5171 or (705)835-3689. E-mail: drapson@encode.com or wayne@rural-roots.com. Web site: www.leacock.com. **Contact:** Judith Rapson, award chair. Award for humorous writing by a Canadian, given in memory of Stephen B. Leacock, Canada's best-known writer of humorous fiction. Prize: silver medal and $10,000 given by TD Financial Group. Categories: novels, short story collections, drama, poetry, translations. Judged by five judges from across Canada, plus a local reading committee which has one vote. Entry fee: $100; make checks payable to Stephen Leacock Association. Entry must be a book published in the year prior to the presentation of the award and must be accompanied by a short biographical sketch and photograph of the author. Cover letter should include publisher's name, address, e-mail and name of contact person. Deadline: December 31. Authors must be Canadian citizens or landed immigrants; no more than two authors permitted for any given entry. Guidelines available in August for fax or on Web site. Book may be nominated by author or publisher. Books are judged primarily on humorous content but also on literary merit and general appeal. Results announced in April at luncheon in Orillia; winner required to attend Award Dinner in Orillia in June and deliver address. Results available for SASE, by fax, e-mail or on Web site.

◎ LEAGUE OF UTAH WRITERS CONTEST

League of Utah Writers, P.O. Box 460562, Leeds UT 84746. (435)313-4459. Fax: (435)879-8190. E-mail: justwrite@numucom.com or reelsweetjustwrite@juno.com. Web site: www.luwrite.com. **Contact:** Dorothy Crofts, membership chair. "The LUW Contest has been held since 1935 to give Utah writers an opportunity to get their works read and critiqued. It also encourages writers to keep writing in an effort to get published." Competition for short stories and novels. Prize: $30/$20/$10 in children's book category; $50/$25/$15 full-length teen book category; $100/$50/$25 full-length book category. Categories: 34 total categories. "We do have separate categories for speculative fiction, children's and teens' besides our full-length book category on any subject." Judged by professional judges who are paid for their services. Entry fee: $3-6, short story; $5-20 full-length book. Guidelines available after February for SASE or on Web site. Accepts inquiries by fax, e-mail and phone. Deadline: June 16. Entries must be unpublished. Open to any writer. "Read the contest rules and guidelines. Don't skim over them. Rules change and are revised from year to year. Don't forget to enclose your entry fee when mailing your entries." Winners announced at the Annual Writers Round-Up in September. List of winners available at Round-Up or for SASE.

N ⊚ LESBIAN WRITERS FUND

Astraea Lesbian Foundation for Justice, 116 E. 16th St., 7th Floor, New York NY 10003. (212)529-8021. E-mail: grants@astraeafoundation.org. Web site: www.astraeafoundation.org. "This award is to support the work of emerging lesbian writers, and to acknowledge the contributions of established writers to our movement and culture." Annual. Competition/award for short stories, novels, story collections and poetry. Prize: First place awardees and two runners-up in the poetry and fiction categories will receive cash awards ($10,000 for awardee; $1,500 for runners-up). Each year a new set of judges reviews applications. An independent team of two judges in each genre selects the winners unanimously. The names of applicants will not be known to the judges until the decisions are made and all applicants have been notified by mail. All applications will be reviewed by a panel of lesbian writers who will remain anonymous until after the process has been completed. Entry fee: $5. Make checks payable to Astraea Lesbian Foundation for Justice. Accepts inquiries by e-mail, phone. **Entry deadline is June 30, 2009.** Entries may be pubilshed or unpublished. "To be eligible for an award from the Lesbian Writers Fund, you must satisfy all of the following: You are a lesbian-identified writer of poetry and/or fiction. Your submission is a poetry or fiction sample in English (nonfiction, screenplays, or playsare ineligible). You reside in the United States. Your submitted work includes some lesbian content (e.g. lesbian desire, identity, and/or perspective). You have published at least one piece of your writing (in any genre) in a newspaper, magazine, journal, anthology, or professional web publication (excluding personal or selfproducedhomepages). You have not published more than one book, including a chapbook, in any subject or genre with a publisher. If a second book has been accepted by a publisher, but has not been published yet, you are not eligible to apply. Published books or anthologies you have edited do not count towards the maximum. If awarded, you agree to be acknowledged publicly as a lesbian writer and agree to have your work publicized as Astraea sees fit. This may include an announcement or profile in our Web site and newsletter. All previous finalists, except for first place winners are eligible to apply. Past judges are excluded. Current staff and Board members of the Astraea Foundation are ineligible to apply." Write to grants@astraeafoundation.org for complete guidelines and application instructions. Submit up to 20 pages from a novel or a collection of short stories. Mss must be double spaced. "While there is no minimum page limit for fiction submissions, we recommend that you submit at least 10 pages, so that the judges gain a deeper understanding of your work." Name should not appear on ms; all pages must have identification number provided with application. Writers must submit own work. Results announced January 2010. Winners notified by mail.

LITERAL LATTÉ FICTION AWARD

Literal Latté, 200 East 10th St., Suite 240, New York NY 10003. (212)260-5532. E-mail: litlatte@aol.com. Web site: www.literal-latte.com. **Contact:**Edward Estlin, contributing editor. Award "to provide talented writers with three essential tools for continued success: money, publication and recognition." Offered annually for unpublished fiction. Guidelines for SASE or on Web site. Open to any writer. Prize: $1,000 and publication in Literal Latté (first prize), $300 (second prize), $200 (third prize), up to 7 honorable mentions. Judged by the editors. Entry fee: $10/story. Guidelines available for SASE, by e-mail or on Web site. Accepts inquiries by e-mail. Deadline: January 15. Entries must be unpublished. Length: 6,000 words maximum. Guidelines available for SASE, by e-mail or on Web site. Accepts inquiries by e-mail or on Web site. "The first-prize story in the first annual Literal Latté Fiction Awards has been honored with a Pushcart Prize." Winners notified by phone. List of winners available in late April for SASE or by e-mail.

⊕ ◻ LONG STORY CONTEST, INTERNATIONAL

White Eagle Coffee Store Press, P.O. Box 383, Fox River Grove IL 60021. (847)639-9200. E-mail: wecspress@aol.com. Web site: http://members.aol.com/wecspress. **Contact:** Frank E. Smith, publisher. Offered annually since 1993 for unpublished work to recognize and promote long short stories of 8,000-14,000 words (about 30-50 pages). Sample of previous winner: $6.95, including postage. Open to any writer, no restrictions on materials. Prize: (A.E. Coppard Prize) $1,000 and publication, plus 25 copies of chapbook and 10 press kits. Categories: No limits on style or subject matter. Entry fee: $15 fee, $10 for second story in same envelope. Guidelines available in April by SASE, e-mail or on Web site. Accepts inquiries by e-mail. Length: 8,000-14,000 words (30-50 pages double-spaced) single story; may have multiparts or be a self-contained novel segment. **Deadline: December 15.** Accepts previously unpublished submissions, but previous publication of small parts with acknowledgment is okay. Simultaneous submissions okay. Send cover with name, address, phone; second title page with title only. Submissions are not returned; they are recycled. "SASE for most current information." Results announced in late spring. Winners notified by phone. For contest results, send SASE or visit Web site in late spring. "Write with richness and depth. This has become the premiere competition in the world for long stories, giving many winners and finalists the opportunity to move to the next level of publishing success."

◎ THE HUGH J. LUKE AWARD

Prairie Schooner, 201 Andrews Hall, P.O. Box 880334, Lincoln NE 68588-0334. (402)472-0911. Fax: (402)472-9771. E-mail: jengelhardt2@unl.edu. Web site: prairieschooner.unl.edu/. **Contact:** Hilda Raz, editor-in-chief. Offered annually for work published in *Prairie Schooner* in the previous year. Prize: $250. Judged by editorial staff of *Prairie Schooner*. No entry fee. Only work published in *Prairie Schooner* in the previous year is considered. Work is nominated by the editorial staff. Guidelines for SASE or on Web site. Results announced in the Spring issue. Winners notified by mail in February or March.

LUMINA

Sara Lawrence College, Sara Lawrence College Slonim House 1 Mead Way, Bronxville NY 10708. E-mail: lumina@slc.edu. Web site: http://pages.slc.edu/ ~ lumina/contest.html. **Contact:** Lani Scozzari, director. "We accept submissions from anyone who is not a Sarah Lawrence student. We are seeking short unpublished fiction, up to 5,000 words." Annual. Competition/award for short stories. Prize: First prize: $500; Second prize: $100; Third prize: $50. Plus publication and 2 copies of the journal. Initial reading done by Sarah Lawrence College MFA candidates and final decision to be made by Margot Livesey. Entry fee: $10. Cover letter should include e-mail.**Deadline:** December 1

⊕ ◎ THE MAN BOOKER PRIZE

The Man Group, Middlesex House, 34-42 Cleveland Street, London England W1T 4JE United Kingdom. 020 7631 2666. Fax: 020 7631 2699. Web site: www.themanbookerprize.com. "The Booker Prize for Fiction was set up in 1968 as a result of discussions between Booker plc and the Publishers Association about the need for a significant literary award in Britain, along the lines of the Prix Goncourt and similar awards in France. In 2002 the sponsorship of the Prize was awarded to The Man Group, and the prize is now known as The Man Booker Prize." Books are only accepted through UK publishers. However, publication outside the UK does not disqualify a book once it is published in the UK. Open to any full-length novel written by a citizen of the Commonwealth or the Republic of Ireland. No novellas, collections of short stories, translations, or self-published books. Prize: The winner receives £50,000, and the short-listed authors receive £2,500. Judged by Ireland's finest critics, writers and academics. No entry fee. Deadline: July. Open to citizens of the Commonwealth or Republic of Ireland.

⊕ ◎ MARSH AWARD FOR CHILDREN'S LITERATURE IN TRANSLATION

Marsh Christian Trust, The English-Speaking Union, Dartmouth House, 37 Charles Street, London, W1J 5ED United Kingdom. E-mail: education@esu.org.. **Contact:** Elizabeth Stokes. Award "to promote the publication of translated children's books in the UK." Biennial award for children's book translations. Judged by Patricia Crampton, Caroline Horn, Wendy Cooling, Elizabeth Hammill. No entry fee. Entries must be previously published. Entries should be translations into English first published in the UK. Entries must be nominated by publishers. Open to any writer. Guidelines available for SASE. Cover letter should include name, address, phone, e-mail and title. Accepts inquiries by e-mail. Results announced in January. Winners notified by mail and at presentation event.

◎ WALTER RUMSEY MARVIN GRANT

Ohioana Library Association, 274 E. First Ave., Suite 300, Columbus OH 43201. (614)466-3831. Fax: (614)728-6974. E-mail: ohioana@sloma.state.oh.us. Web site: www.ohioana.org. **Contact:** Linda Hengst. Award "to encourage young, unpublished writers 30 years of age or younger." Competition for short stories. Prize: $1,000. No entry fee. Up to 6 pieces of prose may be submitted; maximum 60 pages, minimum 10 pages double-spaced, 12-point type. Deadline: January 31. Entries must be unpublished. Open to unpublished authors born in Ohio or who have lived in Ohio for a minimum of five years. Must be 30 years of age or younger. Guidelines for SASE. Winner notified in May or June. Award given in October.

☐ MASTERS LITERARY AWARDS

Titan Press, P.O. Box 17897, Encino CA 91416-7897. Web site: www.calwrierstv.com. Offered annually and quarterly for work published within 2 years (preferred) and unpublished work (accepted). Fiction, 15-page maximum; poetry, 5 pages or 150-lines maximum; and nonfiction, 10 pages maximum. "A selection of winning entries may appear in our national literary publication." Winners may also appear on the Internet. Titan Press retains one-time publishing rights to selected winners. Prize: $1,000, and possible publication in the *Titan Press Internet* journal. Judged by 3 literary professionals. Entry fee: $15. Deadline: Ongoing (nominations made March 15, June 15, September 15, December 15). Any submission received prior to an award date is eligible for the subsequent award. Submissions accepted throughout the year. All entries must be in the English language. Guidelines for #10 SASE. "Be persistent, be consistent, be professional."

◎ MEMPHIS MAGAZINE FICTION AWARDS

Memphis Magazine, P.O. Box 1738, Memphis TN 38101. (901)521-9000. E-mail: sadler@memphisma gazine.com. Web site: www.memphismagazine.com. **Contact:** Marilyn Sadler, senior editor/contest coordinator. Annual. Competition/award for short stories. Prize: $1,000 grand prize and publication in *Memphis*; two $500 honorable mention awards. Judged by a panel of five, all with fiction writing experience and publications. Entry fee: $10/story. Guidelines available in April by phone, on Web site, in publication. Accepts inquiries by fax, e-mail, phone. Deadline: Aug. 1. Entries should be unpublished. "Manuscripts may be previously published as long as previous publication was not in a national magazine with over 20,000 circulation or in a regional publication within Shelby County." Open to all authors who live within 150 miles of Memphis. Length: 3,000-4,500 words. Cover letter should include name, address, phone, story title. Do not put your name anywhere on the ms itself. Writers may submit own work. "Each story should be typed, double-spaced, with unstapled, numbered pages. Stories are not required to have a Memphis or Southern theme, but we do want a compelling story and first-rate writing." Winners contacted in late September.

N DAVID NATHAN MEYERSON FICTION PRIZE

Southwest Review, P.O. Box 750374, Dallas TX 75275-0374. (214)768-1037. Fax: (214)768-1408. E-mail: swr@mail.smu.edu; tlewers@mail.smu.edu. Web site: www.smu.edu/southwestreview. **Contact:** Jennifer Cranfill, managing editor. Prize will consist of $1,000 and publication in the *Southwest Review*. Open to writers who have not yet published a book. Submissions must be no longer than 8,000 words. $25 reading fee must accompany each submission. Work should be printed without the author's name. Name and address should appear only on the cover letter. Submissions will not be returned. For notification of the winning submission, include a S.A.S.E. Postmarked deadline for receipt is May 1, 2009.

◎ MICHIGAN LITERARY FICTION AWARDS

University of Michigan Press, 839 Greene St., Ann Arbor MI 48104. Fax: (734)615-1540. E-mail: ump.fiction@umich.edu. Web site: www.press.umich.edu/fiction. Prize: $1,000 advance and publication. Categories: novels. No entry fee. Guidelines for SASE or on Web site. Accepts inquiries by e-mail. Deadline: July 1. Entries must be unpublished. Contest open to writers who have previously published at least one literary novel or story collection. Cover letter should include name, address, phone, e-mail and title; title only on every page of ms. Results announced in November. Winners notified by mail. For contest results, send SASE or visit Web site.

◎ A MIDSUMMER TALE

E-mail: editors@toasted-cheese.com. Web site: www.toasted-cheese.com. **Contact:** Theryn Fleming, editor. A Midsummer Tale is a summer-themed creative nonfiction contest. Topic changes each year. Check Web site for current focus and word limit. "We usually receive around 20 entries." Prize: First prize: $20 Amazon gift certificate, publication; Second prize: $15 Amazon gift certificate, publication;

Third prize: $10 Amazon gift certificate, publication. Some feedback is often given to entrants. Categories: creative nonfiction. Judged by two Toasted Cheese editors who blind-judge each contest. Each judge has her own criteria for selecting winners. No entry fee. Guidelines, including the e-mail address to which you should send your entry and instructions for what to include and how to format, are available May 1 on Web site. Accepts inquiries by e-mail. **Deadline: June 21.** Entries must be unpublished. Open to any writer. Results announced July 31 on Web site. Winners notified by e-mail.

Ⓝ MIGHTY RIVER SHORT STORY CONTEST

Big Muddy: A Journal of the Mississippi River Valley, MRSS Contest, Southeast Missouri State Univ., MS 2650, One University Plaza, Cape Girardeau MO 63701. (573)651-2044. Fax: (573)651-5188. E-mail: upress@semo.edu. Web site: http://www6.semo.edu/universitypress/mrss.htm. **Contact:** Dr. Susan Swartwout, publisher/editor. "We're searching for the best short story relating in some way to the Mississippi River, the River Valley, or a sister River: its landscape, people, culture, history, current events, or future." Annual. Competition/award for short stories. Prize: $500 and publication in *Big Muddy*. Semi-finalists will be chosen by a regional team of published writers. The final ms will be chosen by Susan Swartwout, publisher of Southeast Missouri State University Press. Entry fee: $15 (includes a copy of *Big Muddy* in which the winning story appears). Make checks payable to SEMO UP-MRSS. Guidelines available in January. Accepts inquiries by phone and by e-mail. **Submission period is Jan 1-Aug 1.** Entries should be unpublished. Anyone may enter contest. Length: up to 30 pages, double-spaced. Cover letter should include name, address, phone, e-mail, story title. The title and page numbers should appear on each page of the ms. Writers may submit own work. Results announced Fall. Winners notified by mail, by phone, by e-mail. Results made available to entrants with SASE.

◖ MILKWEED EDITIONS NATIONAL FICTION PRIZE

Milkweed Editions, 1011 Washington Ave. S., Suite 300, Minneapolis MN 55415. (612)332-3192. Fax: (612)215-2550. E-mail: editor@milkweed.org. Web site: www.milkweed.org. **Contact:** The Editors. Annual award for unpublished works. "Looking for a novel, novella, or a collection of short stories. Manuscripts should be of high literary quality and must be double-spaced and between 150-400 pages in length. Writers who need their work returned must include a SAS book mailer. Manuscripts not accompanied by a SAS book mailer will be recycled." Winner will be chosen from the mss Milkweed accepts for publication each year. All mss submitted to Milkweed will automatically be considered for the prize. Submission directly to the contest is no longer necessary. Must be written in English. Writers should have previously published a book of fiction or 3 short stories (or novellas) in magazines/journals with national distribution." Catalog available on request for $1.50. Guidelines for SASE or online. Prize: Publication by Milkweed Editions, and a cash advance of $5,000 against royalties agreed upon in the contractual arrangement negotiated at the time of acceptance. Judged by Milkweed Editions. No entry fee. Deadline: rolling. Entries must be unpublished. Previous winners: *The Father Shore*, by Matthew Eck; *Visigoth*, by Gary Amdahl; *Crossing Bully Creek*, by Margaret Erhart; *Ordinary Wolves*, by Seth Kantner; *Roofwalker*, by Susan Power—this is the caliber of fiction we are searching for." Winners are notified by phone and announced in November.

◎ MILLION WRITERS AWARD

StorySouth, 898 Chelsea Ave., Columbus OH 43209. (614)545-0754. E-mail: storysouth@yahoo.com. Web site: www.storysouth.com. **Contact:** Jason Sanford, editor. Contest "to honor and promote the best fiction published annually in online journals and magazines. The reason for the Million Writers Award is that most of the major literary prizes for short fiction (such as the O. Henry Awards) ignore Web-published fiction. This award aims to show that world-class fiction is being published online and to promote this fiction to the larger reading and literary community." Prize: Cash prize and publicity for the author and story. Categories: short stories. Judged by *StorySouth* judges. No entry fee. Cover letter should include e-mail address, word count, title and publication where story was previously published. Guidelines available in December on Web site. Deadline: January. Entries must be previously published. All stories must be 1,000 words or longer. Open to any writer. Results announced in March on Web site. Winners notified by e-mail.

◎ THE MILTON CENTER POSTGRADUATE FELLOWSHIP

The Milton Center at *Image*, 3307 Third Ave. West, Seattle WA 98119. (206)281-2988. E-mail: miltonc
enter@imagejournal.org. Web site: www.imagejournal.org/Milton. **Contact:** Gregory Wolfe, director. Award "to bring emerging writers of Christian commitment to the Center, where their primary
goal is to complete their first book-length manuscript in fiction, poetry or creative nonfiction." $25
application fee. Guidelines on Web site. Deadline: March 15. Open to any writer.

MISSISSIPPI REVIEW PRIZE

Mississippi Review, 118 College Dr., #5144, Hattiesburg MS 39406. (601)266-4321. Fax: (601)266-
5757. E-mail: reif@mississippireview.com. Web site: www.mississippireview.com. **Contact:** Rie Fortenberry, managing editor. Award "to reward excellence in new fiction and poetry and to find new
writers who are just beginning their careers." Offered annually for unpublished fiction and poetry.
Guidelines available online. Accepts inquiries by e-mail or phone. Prize: $1,000 plus publication for
fiction and poetry winners; publication for all runners up. Entry fee: $15. Deadline: October 1. Entries
must be unpublished. Length: 50,000 words or less. Cover letter should include author's name,
address, phone, e-mail, word count and title of story. No mss returned. Winners notified in January.
For contest results, visit Web site.

◯ THE MISSOURI REVIEW EDITORS' PRIZE CONTEST

Missouri Review, 1507 Hillcrest Hall, Columbia MO 65211. (573)882-4474. Fax: (573)884-4671. Web
site: www.missourireview.org. **Contact:** Richard Sowienski, managing editor. Prize: $3,000 for fic-
tion, poetry, essay and publication in *The Missouri Review*. Judged by *The Missouri Review* editors.
Entry fee: $20; make checks payable to *Missouri Review*. Each fee entitles entrant to a one-year
subscription to the journal, an extension of a current subscription, or a gift subscription. Guidelines
and inquiries accepted on Web site. Expects to receive 1,800 entries. Deadline: October 1. Entries
must be unpublished. Page length restrictions: 25 typed, double-spaced for fiction and essays; 10
for poetry. Open to any writer. Guidelines available in June for SASE. Outside of envelope should
be marked "fiction" or "essay" or "poetry." On first page of submission include the author's name,
address, e-mail address and telephone number. Results announced in January. Winners notified by
phone and mail. For contest results, send SASE. "Send only fully realized work with a distinctive
voice, style and subject."

◫ MONTANA PRIZE IN FICTION

Cutbank Literary Magazine, English Dept., LA 133, UMT, Missoula MT 59812. Fax: (406)243-6156.
E-mail: cutbank@umontana.edu. Web site: www.cutbankonline.org. **Contact:** fiction editor. "Since
CutBank was founded in 1973, we have watched as the landscape for literary and 'little' magazines
has broadened considerably, resulting in more quality short stories, essays, and poems finding their
way to an audience each year. Occasionally, we come across a submission that seems to stand above
the already impressive work being published in its genre, the sort of piece that serves to credit the
wide field of literary publications generally. The goal of *CutBank*'s annual contests it to provoke,
identify, and reward work of that caliber." Annual. Competition/award for short stories. Prize: $500
and publication in the summer issue of *CutBank*. Entries are narrowed down to a pool of five to ten
submissions which are then submitted to a guest judge for selection of the winner. The judge of the
2007-2008 Montana Prize in Fiction was Aimee Bender. Entry fee: $13 (includes a one-year, two-
issue subscription to *CutBank*). Limit of one work of fiction per submitter (though writers may also
submit work to our contests in other genres). Make checks payable to *Cutbank Literary Magazine*.
Guidelines available in November. Accepts inquiries by e-mail. **Submission period is December 1,
2008-February 28, 2009.** Entries should be unpublished. Anyone may enter contest. Please submit
no more than 40 double-spaced pages. Cover letter should include name, address, phone, e-mail,
novel/story title. Only name and title on ms. Writers may submit own work. "Read the magazine
and get a sense of our style. We are seeking work that showcases an authentic voice, a boldness of
form, and a rejection of functional fixedness." Results announced June. Winners notified by e-mail.
Results made available to entrants on Web site.

◫ ◎ BRIAN MOORE SHORT STORY AWARDS

Creative Writers Network, 109-113 Royal Ave., Belfast 6T1 1FF Ireland. E-mail: info@creativewriters
network.org. Web site: www.creativewritersnetwork.org. **Contact:** Administrator. Award to promote

the short story form. Prize: £500, £300, £200 and publication in *Ulster Tatler* and *Ulla's Nib*. Judged by established UK fiction writer. Entry fee: £5. **Deadline: January 31, 2009.** Entries must be unpublished. Open to writers of Irish descent. Guidelines available in August/September 2008 by e-mail or on Web site. Accepts inquiries by e-mail. Results announced in April/May 2009. Winners notified by mail in March. List of winners available on Web site.

MUNICIPAL CHAPTER OF TORONTO IODE JEAN THROOP BOOK AWARD

Municipal Chapter of Toronto IODE (Imperial Order of the Daughters of the Empire), 40 St. Clair Ave., Suite 200, Toronto ON M4T 1M9 Canada. (416)925-5078. Fax: (416)925-5127. **Contact:** Jennifer Werry, education officer. To acknowledge authors and/or illustrators in the Greater Toronto Area. Prize: $1,000 to author and/or illustrator. Categories: short stories, novels, story collections. Judged by committee comprised of IODE education officer, president and other officers (approx. 5). No entry fee. Accepts inquiries by fax, phone. Cover letter should include name, address, phone, e-mail, title, place of original publication. Deadline: Nov. 1. Entries must be previously published. Open to books geared toward 6-12 year olds. Must be Canadian citizens. Authors/illustrators may submit their own work. "Submit books directly to the attention of Theo Heras at the Lillian Smith Library, Toronto. She compiles submissions and short lists them." Results announced in February and available by fax. Award given at annual dinner meeting in March.

NATIONAL READERS' CHOICE AWARDS

E-mail: NRCAcontest@hotmail.com. Web site: www.okrwa.com. **Contact:** Donnell Epperson, coordinator. Contest "to provide writers of romance fiction with a competition where their published novels are judged by readers." Prize: "There is no monetary award; just an awards banquet hosted at the Annual National Romance Writers Convention." Categories: The 12 categories include traditional series (50-60,000 words); short contemporary series (fewer than 70,000 words); long contemporary series (more than 70,000 words); single title contemporary (novel or novella of at least 25,000 words); historical (25,000+ words); Regency (25,000+ words); romantic suspense (25,000+ words); inspirational (25,000+ words); young adult (25,000+ words); paranormal (25,000+ words); romantic (erotic novel or novella of 25,000+ words); mainstream with romantic elements (25,000+ words). Entry fee: $25; make checks payable to NRCA. See Web site for entry address and contact information. All entries must have an original copyright date the current contest year. (See Web site for details.) Entries will be accepted from authors, editors, publishers, agents, readers, whoever wants to fill out the entry form, pay the fee and supply the books. Deadline: Fee deadline: November; book deadline: January. (See Web site for exact dates.) No limit to the number of entries, but each title may be entered only in one category. Open to any writer. For guidelines, send SASE, e-mail or visit Web site. Entry form required—available on Web site. Deadline for entry forms is November 20 (send to above address). Five copies of each entry must be mailed to the category coordinator; contact information for coordinator will be provided by December 1. Results announced in July. Winners notified by phone, if not at the awards ceremony, in July. List of winners will be mailed; also available by e-mail.

NATIONAL WRITERS ASSOCIATION NOVEL WRITING CONTEST

The National Writers Association, 10940 S. Parker Rd #508, Parker CO 80134. (303)841-0246. Fax: (303)841-2607. E-mail: authorsandy@hotmail.com. Web site: www.nationalwriters.com. **Contact:** Sandy Whelchel, director. Annual contest "to help develop creative skills, to recognize and reward outstanding ability, and to increase the opportunity for the marketing and subsequent publication of novel manuscripts." Prize: 1st place: $500; 2nd place: $300; 3rd place: $200. Judges' evaluation sheets sent to each entry with SASE. Categories: Open to any genre or category. Judged by editors and agents. Entry fee: $35. **Deadline: April 1.** Entries must be unpublished. Length: 20,000-100,000 words. Open to any writer. Entry form and information available on Benefits section of Web site.

NATIONAL WRITERS ASSOCIATION SHORT STORY CONTEST

The National Writers Association, 10940 S. Parker Rd. #508, Parker CO 80134. (303)841-0246. Fax: (303)841-2607. E-mail: authorsandy@hotmail.com. Web site: www.nationalwriters.com. **Contact:** Sandy Whelchel, director. Annual contest "to encourage writers in this creative form and to recognize those who excel in fiction writing." Prize: 1st place: $200; 2nd place: $100; 3rd place: $50. Entry fee: $15. **Deadline: postmarked by July 1.** Entries must be unpublished. Length: 5,000 words maximum. Entry form and information available in January on Benefits section of Web site. Accepts inquiries by fax, phone and e-mail. Evaluation sheets sent to each entrant if SASE is provided. Results announced at the NWAF Summer Conference in June. Winners notified by phone or e-mail. List of winners available in *Authorship* or on Web site.

NELLIGAN PRIZE FOR SHORT FICTION

Colorado Review and the Center for Literary Publishing, 9105 Campus Delivery, Colorado State University, Fort Collins CO 80523. (970)491-5449. E-mail: creview@colostate.edu. Web site: http://nelliganprize.colostate.edu. **Contact:** Stephanie G'Schwind, Editor/Director. "The Nelligan Prize for Short Fiction was established in memory of Liza Nelligan, a writer, editor, and friend of many in Colorado State University's English Department, where she received her master's degree in literature in 1992. By giving an award to the author of an outstanding short story each year, we hope to honor Liza Nelligan's life, her passion for writing, and her love of fiction." Annual. Competition/award for short stories. Prize: $1,000 plus publication in *Colorado Review*. Receives approximately 900 stories. All entries are read blind by *Colorado Review*'s editorial staff. Fifteen entries are selected to be sent on to a final judge. Entry fee: $10. Send credit card information or make checks payable to *Colorado Review*. Guidelines available in August 2008. Accepts inquiries by e-mail, phone. **Entry deadline March 13, 2009.** Entries should be unpublished. Anyone may enter contest. Cover letter should include name, address, phone, e-mail, and novel/story title. "Authors should provide two cover sheets: one with name, address, phone, e-mail, and title of story, and a second with only the title of the story. Manuscripts are read 'blind,' so authors' names should not appear anywhere else in the manuscript." Writers may submit own work. "Successful short story writers are those who are reading contemporary short fiction (short story collections, literary magazines, annual prize anthologies), reading about the craft, and actively engaging in the practice of writing." Results announced in July of each year. Winners notified by phone. Results made available to entrants with SASE.

NEVADA ARTS COUNCIL ARTIST FELLOWSHIPS

716 N. Carson St., Suite A, Carson City NV 89701. (702)687-6680. Fax: (775)687-6688. Web site: www.nevadaculture.org. **Contact:** Fran Morrow, artist service coordinator. Award "to honor Nevada individual artists and their artistic achievements and to support artists' efforts in advancing their careers." Prize: $5,000 ($4,500 immediately and $500 after public service event completed). Categories: fiction, nonfiction, poetry, playwriting and writing for children. Judged by peer panels of professional artists. No entry fee. Deadline: April. Open to Nevada residents only. Guidelines available by phone, e-mail or on Web site. Results announced in June. Winners notified by mail and phone. Entrants receive list of recipients. "Inquire about jackpot grants for Nevada residents' projects, up to $1,000."

NEW LETTERS LITERARY AWARDS

New Letters, 5101 Rockhill Rd., Kansas City MO 64110-2499. (816)235-1168. Fax: (816)235-2611. E-mail: newletters@umkc.edu. Web site: www.newletters.org. Award to "find and reward good writing from writers who need the recognition and support." Award has 3 categories (fiction, poetry and creative nonfiction) with 1 winner in each. Offered annually for previously unpublished work. Prize: 1st place: $1,500, plus publication; all entries are considered for publication. Judged by 2 rounds of regional writers (preliminary judging). Winners picked by an anonymous judge of national repute. Entry fee: $15/entry (includes year's subscription). Make checks payable to *New Letters* or send credit card information. Deadline: May 18. Entries must be unpublished. Open to any writer. Guidelines available in January for SASE, e-mail, on Web site and in publication. Cover letter should include name, address, phone, e-mail and title. Results announced in September. Winners notified by phone. For contest results, send SASE, e-mail or visit Web site.

NEW MILLENNIUM WRITING AWARDS

New Millennium Writings, Room M2, P.O. Box 2463, Knoxville TN 37901. (423)428-0389. Fax: (865)428-2302. E-mail: DonWilliams7@charter.net. Web site: www.newmillenniumwritings.com/awards.html. **Contact:** Don Williams, editor. Award "to promote literary excellence in contemporary fiction." Offered twice annually for unpublished fiction, poetry, essays or nonfiction prose to encourage new fiction writers, poets and essayists and bring them to attention of publishing industry.

Entrants receive an issue of *NMW* in which winners appear. Prize: $1,000 (fiction, poetry, nonfiction and short-short fiction, 1,000 words or less); winners published in *NMW* and on Web site. Judged by novelists and short story writers. Entry fee: $17 for each submission. Deadline: November 17 and June 17. Entries must be unpublished. Biannual competition. Length: 1,000-6,000 words. Guidelines available year round for SASE and on Web site at www.writingawards.com. "Provide a bold, yet organic opening line, sustain the voice and mood throughout, tell an entertaining and vital story with a strong ending. *New Millennium Writings* is a forward-looking periodical for writers and lovers of good reading. It is filled with outstanding poetry, fiction, essays and other speculations on subjects both topical and timeless about life in our astonishing times. Our pages brim with prize-winning essays, humor, full-page illustration, writing advice and poetry from writers at all stages of their careers. First-timers find their work displayed alongside such well-known writers as Shel Silverstein, Khaled Hosseini, Ted Kooser, Lucille Clifton, John Updike, Sharyn McCrumb, Lee Smith, Norman Mailer, Madison Smartt Bell and Cormac McCarthy." Results announced October and April. Winners notified by mail and phone. All entrants will receive a list of winners, plus a copy of the annual anthology. Send letter-sized SASE with entry for list.

⬚ NEW SOUTH WRITING CONTEST

(Formerly *GSU Review* Writing Contest) *New South*, Georgia State University, Campus Box 1894, MSC 8R0322, Unit 8, Atlanta GA 30303-3083. E-mail: new_south@langate.gsu.edu. Web site: www.r eview.gsu.edu. **Contact:** Editor. To promote quality work of emerging writers. Prize: $1,000 first prize; $250 second prize; publication for winners. Categories: fiction, poetry; receives more than 250 entries each. Judged by staff at *New South* (finalists); 2007 winners were chosen by Keith Lee Morris (fiction) and Jake Adam York (poetry). Entry fee: $15, includes copy of Spring /Summer issue with contest results. Make checks payable to GSU. **Deadline: March 4.** Entries must be unpublished. Length: should not exceed 7,500 words. Address fiction submissions to Prose Editor; and poetry submissions Poetry Editor. Mss must be typed or letter-quality printed. On the first page of the ms include name, address, phone, e-mail, word count. Limit each submission to one short story/three poems. Guidelines available by SASE or on Web site. Contest open to all except faculty, staff, students of Georgia State University. US residents only. Winners notified by e-mail. "We look for engagement with language and characters we care about."

⬚ NEW YORK STORIES FICTION PRIZE

New York Stories, English Department, E-103, LaGuardia Community College/CUNY, 31-10 Thomson Ave., Long Island City NY 11101. E-mail: nystories@lagcc.cuny.edu. Web site: www.newyorkstories .org. **Contact:** Daniel Caplice Lynch, editor-in-chief. Offered annually for unpublished work to showcase new, quality short fiction. Stories must not exceed 6,000 words. Prize: 1st place: $500 and publication; 2nd place: $250 and consideration for publication. Judged by the editor. Entry fee: $15. Each submission should be accompanied by a separate, non-refundable check for $15, payable to *New York Stories*. Mss are not returned. Please write "New York Stories Fiction Prize" on the outer envelope and the title page. Deadline: September 15. Entries must be unpublished. Open to any writer. Guidelines on Web site and in publication. Accepts inquires by e-mail. Cover letter should include name, address, phone, e-mail, word count and title. "Also include this information on the manuscript." Winners notified by phone or e-mail. For contest results, send SASE or visit Web site.

� ◎ JOHN NEWBERY AWARD

American Library Association (ALA), Association for Library Service to Children, 50 E. Huron St., Chicago IL 60611. (312)280-2163. Fax: (312)944-7671. E-mail: alsc@ala.org. Web site: www.ala.org/ alsc. **Contact:** ALSC, Attn: Newbery Medal. Prize: Medal. Judged by Newbery Award Selection Committee. No entry fee. Deadline: December 31. Entries must be previously published. Only books for children published in the U.S. during the preceeding year are eligible. Entry restricted to U.S. citizens, residents. Guidelines available on Web site, by fax, phone or e-mail. Accepts inquiries by fax and e-mail. Results announced at the ALA Midwinter Meeting. Winners notified by phone. For contest results, visit Web site in February or contact via phone, fax, e-mail or SASE.

⊕ ▣ ◎ THE NOMA AWARD FOR PUBLISHING IN AFRICA

P.O. Box 128, Witney, Oxon OX8 5XU. United Kingdom. E-mail: maryljay@aol.com. Web site: www.n omaaward.org. **Contact:** Mary Jay. Sponsored by Kodansha Ltd. Award "to encourage publication of works by African writers and scholars in Africa, instead of abroad as is still too often the case at present." Categories: scholarly or academic; books for children; literature and creative writing, including fiction, drama and poetry. Judged by a committee of African scholars and book experts and representatives of the international book community. Chairman: Walter Bgoya. No entry fee. **Deadline: February 28.** Entries must be previously published. Guidelines and entry forms available in December by fax, e-mail or on Web site. Submissions are through publishers only. "Publisher must complete entry form and supply six copies of the published work." Maximum number of entries per publisher is three. Results announced in October. Winners notified through publisher. List of winners available from Secretariat or on Web site. "The award is for an outstanding book. Content is the overriding criterion, but standards of publication are also taken into account."

◎ NORTH CAROLINA ARTS COUNCIL WRITERS' RESIDENCIES

109 E. Jones St., Raleigh NC 27601. (919)807-6512. Fax: (919)807-6532. E-mail: debbie.mcgill@ncmail.net.. Web site: www.ncarts.org. **Contact:** Deborah McGill, literature director. Awards encourage and recognize North Carolina's finest creative writers. Every year we offer a 2-month residency for 1 writer at Headlands Center for the Arts (California) and a 1-month residency for 1 writer at Vermont Studio Center. Judged by panels of writers and editors convened by the residency centers. No entry fee. Deadline: early June; see Web site for details. Writers must be over 18 years old, not currently enrolled in a degree-granting program on undergraduate or graduate level, must have been a resident of North Carolina for 1 full year as of application deadline and must plan to remain a resident for the following year. Please see Web site for other eligibility requirements. Guidelines available after March 1 by phone or online. Accepts inquiries by fax and e-mail. Results announced in the fall. Winners notified by phone. Other applicants notified by mail.

◎ NORTHERN CALIFORNIA BOOK AWARDS

Northern California Book Reviewers Association, % Poetry Flash, 1450 Fourth St. #4, Berkeley CA 94710. (510)525-5476. Fax: (510)525-6752. E-mail: editor@poetryflash.org. Web site: www.poetryflash.org. **Contact:** Joyce Jenkins, executive director. "Award is to celebrate books published by Northern California authors in poetry, fiction, nonfiction, translation and children's literature." Annual. Competition/award for novels, story collections, translations. Prize: awards publicity from a professional publicist, $100 cash award, and reading at awards ceremony. Awards $1,000 for lifetime achievement award. Categories: novels and short story collections. Judged by members of the association, active book reviewers, and book editors. No entry fee. **Deadline: Dec. 1** for books published in that calendar year. Entries should be previously published. Open to authors living in Northern California. Winners announced in April. Results made available to entrants with SASE, by fax, by e-mail, on Web site.

◯ NOVEL MANUSCRIPT CONTEST

Writers' League of Texas, 611 S. Congress Ave., Suite 130, Austin TX 78704. (512)499-8914. Fax: (512)499-0441. E-mail: wlt@writersleague.org. Web site: www.writersleague.org. **Contact:** Kristy Bordine. Prize: First place winners meet individually with an agent at the Writers' League of Texas Agents Conference in June. Categories: mainstream fiction, mystery, thriller/action adventure, romance, science fiction/fantasy/horror, historical/western, narrative nonfiction, and children's long and short works. Judged by preliminary judges (first round), then agent or editor reads finalists' ms. Entry fee: $50 for score sheet with comments. Send credit card information or make check payable to Writer's League of Texas. Cover letter should include name, address, phone, e-mail, title. Entries must be unpublished. Submit first 10 pages of novel, double-spaced. Open to any writer. Guidelines available in January for by e-mail or on Web site. Accepts inquiries by e-mail. Results announced at the June conference. Results available on Web site.

◎ NOVELLO LITERARY AWARD

Novello Festival Press, 310 N. Tryon St., Charlotte NC 28202. (704)432-0153. Web site: www.novellopress.org. **Contact:** A. Rogers, executive editor. "To recognize a writer of a book-length work of literary fiction or nonfiction who resides in North Carolina or South Carolina." Annual. Competition/award for novels, story collections. Prize: $1,000 advance against royalties, publication, national distribution of the winning book. Categories: Literary fiction/nonfiction (including novel, short story collection, memoir, biography, history). Receives about 100 entries per year. Judged by the editor(s), staff, advisory committee of the press, and others in the literary arts community whom they may designate. No entry fee. Guidelines available in Nov. on Web site and in regional writers resources. Submission period: Nov.-May 1. Entries should be unpublished. "Portions may be previously published (e.g. a short story within a collection)." Open to writers over the age of 18 who reside in NC or SC. Length: 200-400 pages, typed and double-spaced. Cover letter should include name, address, phone, e-mail, word count, novel/collection title. Identifying information may or may not be included on the actual ms; "this is not a blind competition." Writers may submit own work. No agent submissions. "Do not send genre fiction, poetry, or work for children. Literary fiction and/or literary nonfiction only." Results announced Oct. during The Novello Festival of Reading. Winners notified by mail, by phone. Winners announced Oct. Results made available to entrants on Web site.

☐ ◎ THE FLANNERY O'CONNOR AWARD FOR SHORT FICTION

The University of Georgia Press, 330 Research Dr., Athens GA 30602-4901. Web site: www.ugapress. uga.edu. **Contact:** Andrew Berzanskis, coordinator. Does not return mss. Manuscripts must be 50,000-75,000 words (which is approximately 200-275 pages long). Authors do not have to be previously published. Prize: $1,000 and publication under standard book contract; selects two prize winners a year. Categories: Wants collections of short stories. Stories that have previously appeared in magazines or in anthologies may be included. Collections that include long stories or novellas (50-150 pages) are acceptable. However, novels or single novellas will not be considered. Stories previously published in a book-length collection of the author's own work may not be included. Entry fee: $20; checks payable to University of Georgia Press. Complete submission guidelines online. Submission Period: April 1-May 31. Open to all writers in English. "Manuscripts under consideration for this competition may be submitted elsewhere at the same time. Please notify us immediately, however, if your manuscript is accepted by another publisher while it is under review with our press. Authors may submit more than one manuscript to the competition as long as each submission is accompanied by a $20 entry fee, meets all eligibility requirements, and does not duplicate material sent to us in another manuscript." Winners are usually notified before the end of November. Entrants who have enclosed an SASE will receive a letter announcing the winners.

◎ FRANK O'CONNOR FICTION AWARD

descant, Texas Christian University, TCU Box 297270, Fort Worth TX 76129. (817)257-6537. Fax: (817)257-6239. E-mail: descant@tcu.edu. Web site: www.descant.tcu.edu. **Contact:** David Kuhne, editor. Annual award to honor the best published fiction in *descant* for its current volume. Prize: $500. No entry fee. Guidelines available for SASE or on Web site. **Deadline: April 1.** Entries must be previously published. Results announced in August. Winners notified by phone in July. For contest results, send SASE. Also offers the Gary Wilson Award for short fiction. Prize: $250. Send SASE for guidelines.

Ⓝ ⊕ FRANK O'CONNOR INTERNATIONAL SHORT STORY AWARD

The Munster Literature Centre, Frank O'Connor House, 84 Douglas Street, Cork, Ireland. (+)353-214312955. E-mail: Munsterlit@eircom.net. Web site: www.munsterlit.ie. **Contact:** Patrick Cotter, artistic director. "To reward the author of the best original short story collection published in English anywhere in the world in the previous year." Annual. Prize: On today's exchange rate US $51,300. Receives about 40-60 entries each year. Entries are judged by three judges at the longlist stage. Judges for 2008 are Bret Anthony Johnston (author), Eileen Battersby (Chief literary critic, *Irish Times*), and Rosalind Porter (associate fiction editor, *Granta* magazine). The shortlist is judged by these three and Patrick Cotter, artistic director of the Munster Literature Centre. No entry fee. Guidelines available in November. Accepts inquiries by e-mail. **Entry deadline is February.** Entries should be previously published. "Collections must be published between September 1st of the previous calendar year and the end of August in the year the award is made. Seven published or proof copies are acceptable as entries." Entries from known vanity presses are disqualified. Cover letter should include name, address, phone, e-mail, novel/story title. Writers may submit their own work. "Write world class short stories." Results announced the closing day of the Frank O'Connor International Short Story Festival during the third weekend in September. Results made available to entrants on Web site.

ⓃⒻ SEAN O'FAOLAIN SHORT STORY PRIZE

The Munster Literature Centre, Frank O'Connor House, 84 Douglas Street, Cork, Ireland. (+)353-214319255. E-mail: munsterlit@eircom.net. Web site: www.munsterlit.ie. **Contact:** Patrick Cotter, artistic director. "To reward writers of outstanding short stories" Annual. Prize: 1st prize €1500 (approx US $2,200); 2nd prize €500 (approx $730). Four runners-up prizes of €100 (approx $146). All six stories to be published in *Southword Literary Journal*. Receives about 500 entries. Guest judge reads each and every story anonymously. Judge in 2008 was Nuala Ni Chonchuir. Entry fee: $15. Make checks payable to Munster Literature Centre. Guidelines available in November. Accepts inquiries by e-mail, phone. **Entry deadline is July 31.** Entries should be unpublished. Anyone may enter contest. Length: 3,000 words max. Cover letter should include name, address, phone, e-mail, word count, novel/story title. No identifying information on ms. "Read previous winners in *Southword Journal*. "Results announced last day of Frank O'Connor International Short Story Festival in third weekend of September. Winners notified by mail or e-mail. Results made available to entrants on Web site.

Ⓒ THE OHIO STATE UNIVERSITY PRIZE IN SHORT FICTION

The Ohio State University Press and the MFA Program in Creative Writing at The Ohio State University, 1070 Carmack Rd., Columbus OH 43210-1002. (614)292-1462. Fax: (614)292-2065. Web site: ohiostatepress.org. Offered annually to published and unpublished writers. Submissions may include short stories, novellas or a combination of both. Manuscripts must be 150-300 typed pages; novellas must not exceed 125 pages. No employee or student of The Ohio State University is eligible. Prize: $1,500, publication under a standard book contract. Entry fee: $20. Deadline: Must be postmarked during the month of January.

◎ (ALICE WOOD MEMORIAL) OHIOANA AWARD FOR CHILDREN'S LITERATURE

Ohioana Library Association, 274 E. First Ave., Suite 300, Columbus OH 43201. (614)466-3831. Fax: (614)728-6974. E-mail: ohioana@sloma.state.oh.us. Web site: www.ohioana.org. **Contact:** Linda Hengst, executive director. Offered to an author whose body of work has made, and continues to make, a significant contribution to literature for children or young adults and through their work as a writer, teacher, or administrator, or through their community service, interest in children's literature has been encouraged and children have become involved with reading. Nomination forms for SASE. Recipient must have been born in Ohio or lived in Ohio at least 5 years. Prize: $1,000. No entry fee. Deadline: December 31. Guidelines for SASE. Accepts inquiries by fax and e-mail. Results announced in August or September. Winners notified by letter in May. For contest results, call or e-mail.

Ⓞ◎ OHIOANA BOOK AWARDS

Ohioana Library Association, 274 E. 1st Ave., Suite 300, Columbus OH 43201-3673. (614)466-3831. Fax: (614)728-6974. E-mail: ohioana@sloma.state.oh.us. Web site: www.ohioana.org. **Contact:** Linda Hengst, executive director. Offered annually to bring national attention to Ohio authors and their books, published in the last 2 years. (Books can only be considered once.) Categories: Fiction, nonfiction, juvenile, poetry, and books about Ohio or an Ohioan. Writers must have been born in Ohio or lived in Ohio for at least 5 years, but books about Ohio or an Ohioan need not be written by an Ohioan. Prize: certificate and glass sculpture. Judged by a jury selected by librarians, book reviewers, writers and other knowledgeable people. Each Spring the jury considers all books received since the previous jury. No entry fee. Deadline: December 31. Two copies of the book must be received by the Ohioana Library by December 31 prior to the year the award is given; literary quality of the book must be outstanding. No entry forms are needed, but they are available July 1 of each year. "We will be glad to answer letters or e-mails asking specific questions." Results announced in August or September. Winners notified by mail in May.

Ⓝ $Ⓒ ON THE PREMISES CONTEST

On The Premises, LLC, 4323 Gingham Court, Alexandria VA 22310. (202)262-2168. E-mail: questions @onthepremises.com. Web site: www.onthepremises.com. **Contact:** Tarl Roger Kudrick or Bethany Granger, Co-publishers. "*On the Premises* aims to promote newer and/or relatively unknown writers who can write what we feel are creative, compelling stories told in effective, uncluttered and evocative prose. Each contest challenges writers to produce a great story based on a broad premise that our editors supply as part of the contest.'' Competition/award for short stories. Prize: First prize is $140, Second prize $100, Third prize $70, and Honorable Mentions recieve $25. All prize winners are published in *On the Premises* magazine. Entries are judged blindly by the publishers Tarl Roger Kudrick and Bethany Granger. No entry fee. Accepts inquiries by e-mail only. The contest is held every four months. Check Web site for exact dates. Entries should be unpublished. Open to everyone. Length: min 1000 words, max 5000. Email should include name, address, e-mail, novel/story title, with ms attached. No contact info should be in ms. Writers may submit own work. ''Write something compelling, creative and well-crafted. Above all, USE THE PREMISE. If the premise is 'use a real live dog,' find a creative way to use a dog, don't create a character named Dog, or a spaceship, or something similar.'' Results announced within 2 weeks of contest deadline. Winners notified by e-mail. Winners announced with publication of *On the Premises*. Results made available to entrants on Web site, in publication.

◌ OPEN WINDOWS

Ghost Road Press, 5303 E. Evans Ave. #309, Denver CO 80222. (303)758-7623. Fax: (303)671-5664. E-mail: info@ghostroadpress.com. Web site: ghostroadpress.com. **Contact:** Sonya Unrein, editor. This anthology series showcases new and established voices in poetry, fiction and creative nonfiction. The 2005 edition was a finalist for the Coloradio Book Award. Prizes: $500 + 4 copies for best story, creative nonfiction piece, and poem; 3 copies for 2nd prize; 2 copies for 3rd prize (9 winners total). Categories will be judged separately. The contest submission period is January to July. (See Web site for 2008 dates.) Winners will be announced on September 15 on our Web site. Please do NOT send a SASE. There are two ways to enter. Send a labeled CD-ROM or an e-mail attachment (preferred) with the following items: The work(s) in a Word document with the title of the piece on every page in the right-hand corner—no author info on the work itself—double-spaced; a cover sheet with author name, address, phone number, and working e-mail address. The cover sheet should include a 30-40 word bio. If you are sending more than one poem, each poem should appear on its own page, as it should appear in its printed form. No 3.5 floppy disks; CDs only. For e-mail, please use an appropriate subject line, such as ''Open Windows contest entry.'' You may pay submission fee (1 story or essay, up to 3 poems per $15) by check or online with Paypal on our Web site. No entries will be processed until payment is received.

◌ ORANGE BLOSSOM FICTION CONTEST

The Oak, 1530 Seventh St., Rock Island IL 61201. (309)788-3980. **Contact:** Betty Mowery, editor. Award ''to build up circulation of publication and give new authors a chance for competition and publication along with seasoned writers.'' Prize: subscription to *The Oak*. Categories: short fiction. Judged by published authors. Entry fee: six 42¢ stamps. Deadline: April 1. ''May be on any subject, but avoid gore and killing of humans or animals.'' Open to any writer. Guidelines available for SASE. Prefers name, address, contest deadline and title on ms; no cover letter. Guidelines for other contests available for SASE. ''No reply will be made without SASE.'' Results announced a week after deadline. Winners notified by mail. ''Material is judged on content and tightness of writing as well as word lengths, since there is a 500-word limit. Always inclu de a SASE with submissions. Entries without six 42¢ stamps will not be judged.''

◎ OREGON BOOK AWARDS

Literary Arts, 224 NW 13th Ave., Ste. 306, #219, Portland OR 97209. (503)227-2583. E-mail: kristy@li terary-arts.org. Web site: www.literary-arts.org. **Contact:** Kristy Athens, program coordinator. The annual Oregon Book Awards celebrate Oregon authors in the areas of poetry, fiction, nonfiction, drama and young readers' literature published between April 1and March 31. Prize: Finalists are invited on a statewide reading tour and are promoted in bookstores and libraries across the state. Judged by writers who are selected from outside Oregon for their expertise in a genre. Past judges include Mark Doty, Colson Whitehead and Kim Barnes. Entry fee determined by initial print run; see Web site for details. Deadline: last Friday in May. Entries must be previously published. Oregon residents only. Guidelines available in February for SASE and on Web site. Accepts inquiries by phone and e-mail. Finalists announced in October. Winners announced at an awards ceremony in November. List of winners available in November.

◎ OREGON LITERARY FELLOWSHIPS

Literary Arts, Inc., 224 NW 13th Ave., Suite 306, Portland OR 97209. (503)227-2583. Fax: (503)243-1167. E-mail: susan@literary-arts.org. Web site: www.literary-arts.org. **Contact:** Susan Denning, Director of Programs and events. Annual fellowships for writers of fiction, poetry, literary nonfiction, young readers and drama. Prize: $2500 minimum award, for approximately 12 writers. Judged by out-of-state writers. No entry fee. Guidelines available in February for SASE. Accepts inquiries by e-mail, phone. **Deadline: last Friday in June.** Oregon residents only. Recipients announced in December.

◘ PATERSON FICTION PRIZE

The Poetry Center at Passaic County Community College, One College Blvd., Paterson NJ 07505-1179. (973)684-6555. Fax: (973 523-6085. E-mail: mgillan@pccc.edu. Web site: www.pccc.edu/poetry. **Contact:** Maria Mazziotti Gillan, executive director. Award "to encourage recognition of high-quality writing." Offered annually for a novel or collection of short fiction published the previous calendar year. Prize: $1,000. Judges rotate each year. No entry fee. Deadline: Submissions accepted after January 10. Open to any writer. Guidelines available for SASE, e-mail or on Web site. Accepts inquiries by e-mail or phone. Results announced in July. Winners notified by mail. For contest results, send SASE or visit Web site.

◘ PEARL SHORT STORY PRIZE

Pearl Magazine, 3030 E. Second St., Long Beach CA 90803-5163. (562)434-4523. E-mail: Pearlmag@aol.com. Web site: www.pearlmag.com. **Contact:** Marilyn Johnson, fiction editor. Award to "provide a larger forum and help widen publishing opportunities for fiction writers in the small press and to help support the continuing publication of Pearl." Prize: $250, publication in Pearl and 10 copies of the journal. Judged by the editors of Pearl: Marilyn Johnson, Joan Jobe Smith, Barbara Hauk. Entry fee: $10/story. Include a brief bio and SASE for reply or return of mss. Accepts simultaneous submissions, but asks to be notified if story is accepted elsewhere. **Submission period: April 1-May 31 (postmark).** Entries must be unpublished. "Although we are open to all types of fiction, we look most favorably on coherent, well-crafted narratives containing interesting, believable characters in meaningful situations." Length: 4,000 words maximum. Open to any writer. Guidelines for SASE or on Web site. Accepts queries by e-mail or fax. Results announced in September. Winners notified by mail. For contest results, send SASE, e-mail or visit Web site.

◎ WILLIAM PEDEN PRIZE IN FICTION

The Missouri Review, 1507 Hillcrest Hall, Columbia MO 65211. (573)882-4474. Fax: (573)884-4671. Web site: www.missourireview.com. **Contact:** Speer Morgan. Offered annually "for the best story published in the past volume year of the magazine. All stories published in *The Missouri Review* are automatically considered." Prize: $1,000, and reading/reception. No entry fee. Submissions must have been previously published in the volume year for which the prize is awarded. No application process: All fiction published in *The Missouri Review* is automatically entered.

◎ PEN CENTER USA ANNUAL LITERARY AWARDS

PEN Center USA, %Antioch University Los Angeles, 400 Corporate Pointe, Culver City CA 91030. (310)862-1555. Fax: (310)862-1556. E-mail: awards@penusa.org. Web site: www.penusa.org. Offered annually for fiction, creative nonfiction, poetry, children's/young adult literature, or translation published January 1-December 31 of 2007. Prize: $1,000 and honored at a ceremony in Los Angeles. Judged by panel of writers, editors and critics. Entry fee: $35. Guidelines available in July for SASE, fax, e-mail or on Web site. Accepts inquiries by fax, phone and e-mail. All entries must include 4 non-returnable copies of each submission and a completed entry form. **Deadline: December 15.** Entries must be professionally published or produced. Open to authors west of the Mississippi River, including all of Minnesota and Louisiana. Results announced in summer. Winners notified by phone and mail. For contest results, send SASE or visit Web site.

◐ ◎ PEN/FAULKNER AWARDS FOR FICTION

PEN/Faulkner Foundation, The Folger Shakespeare Library, 201 E. Capitol St., Washington DC 20003. (202)898-9063. Fax: (202)675-0363. E-mail: jneely@penfaulkner.org. Web site: www.penfaulkner.org. **Contact:** Jessica Neely, PEN/Faulkner Foundation Executive Director. Offered annually for best book-length work of fiction by an American citizen published in a calendar year. Prize: $15,000 (one winner); $5,000 (4 finalists). Judged by three writers chosen by the Trustees of the Award. No entry fee. **Deadline: October 31.** Open to US citizens only, but they need not be US residents. Writers and publishers submit four copies of eligible titles published during the current year. No juvenile or self-published books.

PHOEBE WINTER FICTION CONTEST

Phoebe, George Mason University, 4400 University Dr., Fairfax VA 22030-4444. (703)993-2915. E-mail: editor@phoebe@gmu.edu. Web site: www.gmu.edu/pubs/phoebe/. **Contact:** John Copen-haver, editor. To recognize new and exciting short fiction. Offered annually for unpublished work. Prize: $1,000 and publication. All entrants receive a free issue. Judged by outside judge—recognized fiction writer hired by *Phoebe*—who changes each year. The 2005 judge was Tom Franklin. Entry fee: $1 5/story. Send ms and cover letter, which should contain name, address, title of story and brief bio. Name and address should not appear on actual ms. Enclose SASE for contest results. Additional guidelines available after September for SASE or on Web site. Mss not returned. Deadline: December 1. Entries must be unpublished. Word length: 25 pages maximum. Open to any writer. Results announced in the Fall. Winners notified by mail. List of winners available. *"Phoebe* encourages experimental writing."

PLAYBOY COLLEGE FICTION CONTEST

Playboy, 730 Fifth Ave., New York NY 10019. Web site: www.playboy.com/on-campus/collegefiction/. **Contact:** Contest director. Prize: 1st prize: $3,000 US and publication in magazine; 2nd prize: $500 and year's subscription; 3rd prize: $200 and year's subscription. Categories: short stories. No entry fee. Guidelines available online and in magazine. Length: 25 double-spaced pages (max). Include 3×5 card with name, age, college affiliation, home address, phone, e-mail, title. Deadline: Feb. 15. Entries must be unpublished. Open to college students (including graduate students). No age limit. Closed to employees of *Playboy* and their families, agents, affiliates. Winners will be notified by mail. Results available for SASE.

POCKETS FICTION-WRITING CONTEST

Upper Room Publications, 1908 Grand Ave. AV, P.O. Box 340004, Nashville TN 37203-0004. (615)340-7333. Fax: (615)340-7267. E-mail: pockets@upperroom.org. Web site: www.pockets.org. *Pockets* is a devotional magazine for children between the ages of 6 and 11. Contest offered annually for unpublished work to discover new children's writers. Prize: $1,000 and publication in *Pockets*. Categories: short stories. Judged by *Pockets* staff and staff of other Upper Room Publications. No entry fee. Guidelines available for #10 SASE or on Web site. **Deadline: Must be postmarked between March 1-August 15.** Entries must be unpublished. Because the purpose of the contest is to discover new writers, previous winners are not eligible. No violence, science fiction, romance, fantasy or talking animal stories. Word length 1,000-1,600 words. Open to any writer. Winner announced November 1 and notified by U.S. mail. Contest submissions accompanied by SASE will be returned Nov. 1. *"Send SASE with 4 first-class stamps to request guidelines and a past issue, or go to www.pockets.org."*

KATHERINE ANNE PORTER PRIZE IN SHORT FICTION

The University of North Texas Press, Dept. of English, P.O. Box 311307, Denton TX 76203. (940)565-2142. Fax: (940)565-4590. E-mail: kdevinney@unt.edu. Web site: www.unt.edu/untpress. **Contact:** Karen DeVinney, managing editor. "Purpose is to encourage and promote short fiction." Annual. Competition/award for story collections. Prize: $1,000 and publication by UNT Press. Categories: short fiction, which may be a combination of short-shorts, short stories and novellas (single novellas and novels alone will not be accepted). Judged by anonymous judge (2006 was Dan Chaon). Entry fee: $20. Make checks payable to UNT Press. Guidelines available in Jan. with SASE, by fax, by phone, by e-mail, on Web site, in publication. Accepts inquiries by fax, e-mail, phone. **Submission period: July & August.** Entries should be unpublished in book format, but may include both unpublished and previously published stories. Open to all. Length: 27,500-50,000 words. Cover letter should include name, address, phone, e-mail, word count, ms title, place(s) where story or stories were previously published. Names should appear on the actual ms. Writers may submit their own work. "Simply follow the rules and do your best." Results announced in January. Winners notified by mail, by phone, by e-mail. Results made available to entrants with SASE, by fax, by e-mail, on Web site.

POSTROMANTIC POETRY AND SHORT STORY

2537 Hawthorne Way, Saline MI 48176. (734)944-7742. E-mail: postromanticism@aol.com. Web site: http://postromanticism.com. **Contact:** Claudia Moscovici, director. "Postromanticism began as a movement in art—painting and sculpture—and we would like to expand it to poetry and fiction. The purpose of the contest is to find and publish on postromanticism.com, the official Web site of the postromantic movement, quality poetry and short fiction that fits with our vision and complements the postromantic art. For short story contest, our standards are broad. We're looking for good writing that focuses on important aspects of the human condition—love, family, suffering. We're not seeking genre fiction or experimental fiction. We invite entries for mainstream writing with a lyrical feel, fresh outlook, interesting, believable characters and engaging plot." Competition/award for short stories. Prize: The first prize winner wins $100 and online publication of his or her short story on the official Web site of the postromantic movement, postromanticism.com. We will also publish online the fifteen most appropriate poems and ten most appropriate short stories for each of our two annual contests (October 15 and March 15). Entries are judged based on the quality of the writing and the compatibility of the writing and style with the ideals of the postromantic movement. Entry fee: $10. Make checks payable to Claudia Moscovici, Postromanticism.org. Guidelines available in January. Accepts inquiries by e-mail. Entries should be unpublished. Length: 3,000 word maximum. Cover letter should include name, address, phone, e-mail, word count, novel/story title. "Look at postromanticism.com before you submit to get a sense of what this movement is about. Ultimately, however, you'll be judged by similar standards to those used by literary agents and mainstream publishers: a compelling plot, believable and engaging characters, elegant prose. Touches of humor can also add a lot to a short story. Please include SASE if you desire a reply by mail or your submission returned." Winners notified by mail, e-mail.

PRAIRIE SCHOONER BOOK PRIZE SERIES

Prairie Schooner, 201 Andrews Hall, PO Box 880334, Lincoln NE 68588-0334. Web site: http://prairies chooner.unl.edu. **Contact:** Attn: Fiction. Annual. Competition/award for story collections. Prize: $3,000 and publication through the University of Nebraska Press for one book of short fiction and one book of poetry; one runner-up in each category will receive a $1,000 prize. Entry fee: $25. Make checks payable to *Prairie Schooner*. Deadline: Submissions were accepted between January 15 and March 15 for 2007 contest; check Web site for 2008 dates. Entries should be unpublished. Send full manuscript (the author's name should not appear anywhere on the ms). Send two cover pages: one listing only the title of the ms, and the other listing the title, author's name, address, telephone number, and e-mail address. Send SASE for notification of results. All mss will be recycled. You may also send an optional SAS postcard for confirmation of receipt of ms. Winners notified by phone, by e-mail. Results made available to entrants on Web site, in publication.

⊚ PRAIRIE SCHOONER GLENNA LUSCHEI AWARDS

Prairie Schooner, 201 Andrews Hall, P.O. Box 880334, Lincoln NE 68588-0334. (402)472-0911. Fax: (402)472-9771. E-mail: jengelhardt2@unl.edu. Web site: www.unl.edu/schooner/psmain.htm. **Contact:** Hilda Raz, editor-in-chief. Awards to honor work published the previous year in *Prairie Schooner*, including poetry, essays and fiction. Prize: $250 in each category. Judged by editorial staff of *Prairie Schooner*. No entry fee. For guidelines, send SASE or visit Web site. "Only work published in *Prairie Schooner* in the previous year is considered." Work nominated by the editorial staff. Results announced in the Spring issue. Winners notified by mail in February or March.

⊡ PRISM INTERNATIONAL ANNUAL SHORT FICTION CONTEST

Prism International, Creative Writing Program, UBC, Buch E462, 1866 Main Mall, Vancouver BC V6T 1Z1 Canada. (604)822-2514. Fax: (604)822-3616. Web site: prismmagazine.ca. Offered annually for unpublished work to award the best in contemporary fiction. Works of translation are eligible. Guidelines for SASE, by e-mail, or on Web site. Acquires first North American serial rights upon publication, and limited Web rights for pieces selected for Web site. Open to any writer except students and faculty in the Creative Writing Department at UBC, or people who have taken a creative writing course at UBC with the 2 years prior to the contest deadline. Prize: 1st Place: $2,000; Runners-up (3): $200 each; winner and runners-up published. Entry fee: $28/story, $7 each additional story (outside Canada pay US currency); includes subscription. **Deadline: January 31.**

◎ PUSHCART PRIZE

Pushcart Press, P.O. Box 380, Wainscott NY 11975. (516)324-9300. Web site: www.pushcartprize.com. **Contact:** Bill Henderson, president. Award to "publish and recognize the best of small press literary work." Prize: Publication in *Pushcart Prize: Best of the Small Presses* anthology. Categories: short stories, poetry, essays on any subject. No entry fee. Deadline: December 1. Entries must be previously published. Must have been published during the current calendar year. Open to any writer. Nomination by small press publishers/editors only.

◙ ◎ QUEBEC WRITERS' FEDERATION BOOK AWARDS

Quebec Writers' Federation, 1200 Atwater, Montreal QC H3Z 1X4 Canada. (514)933-0878. E-mail: admin@qwf.org. Web site: www.qwf.org. **Contact:** Lori Schubert, executive director. Award "to honor excellence in writing in English in Quebec." Prize: $2,000 (Canadian) in each category. Categories: fiction, poetry, nonfiction, first book and translation. Each prize judged by panel of 3 jurors, different each year. $20 entry fee. Guidelines for submissions sent to Canadian publishers and posted on Web site in March. Accepts inquiries by e-mail. Deadline: May 31, August 15. Entries must be previously published. Length: must be more than 48 pages. "Writer must have resided in Quebec for 3 of the previous 5 years." Books may be published anywhere. Winners announced in November at Annual Awards Gala and posted on Web site.

DAVID RAFFELOCK AWARD FOR PUBLISHING EXCELLENCE

National Writers Association, 10940 S. Parker Rd. #508, Parker CO 80134. (303)841-0246. Fax: (303)841-2607. E-mail: contests@nationalwriters.com. Web site: www.nationalwriters.com. **Contact:** Sandy Whelchel, executive director. Award to "assist published authors in marketing their work and promoting them." Prize: publicity tour, including airfare, and services of a publicist (valued at $5,000). Categories: novels and short story collections. Judged by publishers and agents. Entry fee: $100. Deadline: May 1. Published works only. Open to any writer. Guidelines for SASE, by e-mail or on Web site. Winners announced in June at the NWAF conference and notified by mail or phone. List of winners available for SASE or visit Web site.

◙ ◎ SIR WALTER RALEIGH AWARD

North Carolina Literary and Historical Association, 4610 Mail Service Center, Raleigh NC 27699-4610. (919)807-7290. Fax: (919)733-8807. **Contact:** Michael Hill, awards coordinator. "To promote among the people of North Carolina an interest in their own literature." Prize: statue of Sir Walter Raleigh. Categories: novels and short story collections. Judged by university English and history professors. No entry fee. Guidelines available in August for SASE. Accepts inquiries by fax. Deadline: July 15. Entries must be previously published. Book must be an original work published during the 12 months ending June 30 of the year for which the award is given. Writer must be a legal or physical resident of North Carolina for the 3 years preceding the close of the contest period. Authors or publishers may submit 3 copies of their book to the above address. Results announced in October. Winners notified by mail. For contest results, send SASE.

◖ RAMBUNCTIOUS REVIEW FICTION CONTEST

Rambunctious Review, 1221 W. Pratt Blvd., Chicago IL 60626. **Contact:** N. Lennon, Editor. Annual themed contest for unpublished stories. Acquires one-time publication rights. Open to any writer. "There are no stylistic limitations, but the story should reflect the writer's philosophy on the theme of the next issue." Last year's theme: Milestones. Prize: 1st prize: $100; 2nd prize: $75; 3rd prize: $50; all winning stories will be published in future issues of *Rambunctious Review*. Judged by previous contest winners. Entry fee: $4/story. The writer's name and address must be on each page. Stories will not be returned. Entrants will be notified of contest results the following March. Guidelines available for SASE or in publication in September. Deadline: December 31. Entries must be unpublished. Looking for "originality; short, clear exposition; character-driven" stories.

◎ RANDOM HOUSE, INC. CREATIVE WRITING COMPETITION

Random House Inc., 1745 Broadway, New York NY 10019. (212)782-8319. Fax: (212)940-7590. E-mail: creativewriting@randomhouse.com. Web site: www.randomhouse.com/creativewriting/. **Contact:** Melanie Fallon Hauska, director. Offered annually for unpublished work to NYC public high school seniors. Three categories: poetry, fiction/drama and personal essay. Prize: 72 awards given in literary (3) and nonliterary (2) categories. Awards range from $500-10,000. Categories: short stories and poems. Judged by various city officials, executives, authors, editors. No entry fee. Guidelines available in October on Web site and in publication. **Deadline: February 8.** Entries must be unpublished. Word length: 2,500 words or less. Applicants must be seniors (under age 21) at a New York high school. No college essays or class assignments will be accepted. Results announced mid-May. Winners notified by mail and phone. For contest results, send SASE, fax, e-mail or visit Web site.

⚈ ◎ THE REA AWARD FOR THE SHORT STORY

Dungannon Foundation, 53 W. Church Hill Rd., Washington CT 06794. Web site: www.reaaward.org. **Contact:** Elizabeth Rea, president. "Sponsored by the Dungannon Foundation, the Rea Award was established in 1986 by Michael M. Rea to honor a living U.S. or Canadian writer who has made a significant contribution to the short story form." Prize: $30,000. Categories: short stories. Judged by 3 jurors (2006 jurors were Ann Beattie, Richard Ford, and Joyce Carol Oates). No entry fee. Award cannot be applied for. The recipient is selected by an annually appointed jury. Award announced in fall annually. List of winners available on Web site. 2006 winner was John Updike.

Ⓝ ◯ RED HEN SHORT FICTION AWARD

Red Hen Press, P.O. Box 3537, Granada Hills CA 91394. Web site: www.redhen.org. **Contact:** Mark E. Cull, publisher. "Purpose: to find new experimental fiction." Annual competition/award for short stories. Prize: $1,000 and publication. Categories: short fiction. Judged by a single rotating judge who is also the fiction editor of *The Los Angeles Review* for the issue the story will be included in. Entry fee: $20. Make checks payable to Red Hen Press. Guidelines available in January on Web site. Deadline: June 30. Entries should be unpublished. Open to all. Length: 25 pages max. Cover letter should include name, address, phone, e-mail, word count, story title. Nothing should appear on ms except title. Writers may submit own work. Results announced by October. Winners notified by phone. Results made available to entrants on Web site.

⊕ ◎ THE RED HOUSE CHILDREN'S BOOK AWARD

(formerly The Children's Book Award), owned and coordinated by the Federation of Children's Book Groups (Reg Charity No. 268289), 2 Bridge Wood View, Horsforth, Leeds, West Yorkshire LS18 5PE, UK. E-mail: info@rhcba.co.uk. Web site: www.redhousechildrensbookaward.co.uk. **Contact:** Andrea Goodall, national coordinator. Purpose of the award is to enable children choose the best works of fiction published in the UK. Prize: silver bowl, portfolio of children's letters and pictures. Categories: Books for Younger Children, Books for Younger Readers, Books for Older Readers. No entry fee. **Closing Date is December 31.** Either author or publisher may nominate title. Guidelines available on Web site. Accepts enquiries by email and phone. Shortlist announced in February and winners announced in June. Winners notified at award ceremony and dinner at the Hay Literary Festival and via the publisher. For contest results, visit the Web site.

◰ ◎ HAROLD U. RIBALOW AWARD

Hadassah Magazine, 50 W. 58th St., New York NY 10019. (212)451-6289. Fax: (212)451-6257. E-mail: tblunt@hadassah.org. **Contact:** Tom Blunt, Ribalow Prize Coordinator. Offered annually for English-language books of fiction (novel or short stories) on a Jewish theme published the previous calendar year. Books should be submitted by the publisher. "Harold U. Ribalow was a noted writer and editor who devoted his time to the discovery and encouragement of young Jewish writers." Prize: $3,000 and excerpt of book in *Hadassah Magazine*. No entry fee. Deadline: March 1. Book should have been published the year preceding the award.

◯ THE SCARS EDITOR'S CHOICE AWARDS

Scars Publications and Design, 829 Brian Court, Gurnee IL 60031-3155. E-mail: editor@scars.tv. Web site: http://scars.tv. **Contact:** Janet Kuypers, editor/publisher. Award "to showcase good writing in an annual book." Prize: publication of story/essay and 1 copy of the book. Categories: short stories. Entry fee: $18/short story. Deadline: revolves for appearing in different upcoming books as winners. Entries may be unpublished or previously published. Open to any writer. For guidelines, visit Web site. Accepts inquiries by e-mail. Length: "We appreciate shorter works. Shorter stories, more vivid and more real storylines in writing have a good chance. Results announced at book publication, online. Winners notified by mail when book is printed. For contest results, send SASE or e-mail or look at the contest page at Web site."

A. DAVID SCHWARTZ FICTION PRIZE

cream city review and funded by Harry W. Schwartz Bookshops. Dept. of English, University of Wisconsin-Milwaukee, P.O. Box 413, Milwaukee WI 53201. (414)229-4708. E-mail: creamcity@uwm .edu. Web site: http://www.uwm.edu/Dept/Engish/ccr. **Contact:** Jay P. Johnson, editor-in-chief. Purpose: "to recognize what the judge determines to be the most original, well-crafted work of previously unpublished short fiction. We are devoted to publishing memorable and energetic fiction, poetry, and creative nonfiction by new and established writers. *Cream city review* is particularly interested in publishing new voices; our reputation and long publishing history attracts well-known writers, often leading to unpublished writers appearing next to poet laureates. Our contest is open to all writers in all places, so long as the work is in English, original and previously unpublished." Annual. Competition/award for short stories. Prize: $1,000 plus publication in *cream city review*. Receives about 50-250 entries. Entries are judged by guest-judges; 2007: C.J. Hribal; 2008: Michael Martone. Entry fee: $15. Fee includes the award-winners issue. Make checks payable to *cream city review*. **Deadline: early December.** Guidelines available in Jan 2008. Anyone may enter contest. Length: A work of more than 30 pages would have to be particularly impressive. Cover letter should include name, address, phone, e-mail, novel/story title. Also include on first page of ms. Writers may submit own work. "See aesthetic statement; read previous issues of *cream city review* to gain an understanding of the work we are interested in publishing; familiarize yourself with the work of the judge." Results announced Feb/March. Winners notified by e-mail. Winners announced Feb/March. Results made available to entrants with SASE, on Web site.

SCIENCE FICTION WRITERS OF EARTH (SFWOE) SHORT STORY CONTEST

Science Fiction Writers of Earth, P.O. Box 121293, Fort Worth TX 76121-1293. E-mail: sfwoe@flash.n et. Web site: www.flash.net/ ~ sfwoe. **Contact:** Gilbert Gordon Reis, SFWoE administrator. Award to "promote the art of science fiction/fantasy short story writing." Prize: $200, $100, $50, $25. Also $75 paid to place the winning story on the SFWoE Web Site for 180 days. Categories: short story. Judged by author Edward Bryant. Entry fee: $5 for membership and first entry; $2 each for additional entries (make checks payable to SFWoE). Cover letter or entry form from Web site should include name, address, phone, e-mail address, word count and title. Same information should appear on ms title page. Deadline: October 30. Entries must be unpublished. The author must not have received payment for a published piece of fiction. Stories should be science fiction or fantasy, 2,000-7,500 words. Guidelines available for SASE, e-mail or on Web site. Accepts inquiries by e-mail and mail. "Visit our Web site and read the winning stories. Read our online newsletter to know what the judge looks for in a good story. Contestants enjoy international competition." Results announced after January 31. Winners notified by mail, phone or e-mail. "Each contestant is mailed the contest results, judge's report, and a listing of the top 10 contestants." Send separate SASE for complete list of the contest stories and contestants (or print from Web site).

SCRIPTAPALOOZA TELEVISION WRITING COMPETITION

7775 Sunset Blvd., PMB #200, Hollywood CA 90046. (323)654-5809. E-mail: info@scriptapalooza.c om. Web site: www.scriptapaloozatv.com. "Seeking talented writers who have an interest in American television writing." Prize: $500 to top winner in each category (total $1,500), production company consideration. Categories: sitcoms, pilots, one-hour dramas and reality shows. Entry fee: $40; accepts Paypal credit card or make checks payable to Scriptapalooza. **Deadline: April 15 and October 15 of each year.** Length: standard television format whether one hour, one-half hour or pilot. Open to any writer 18 or older. Guidelines available now for SASE or on Web Site. Accepts inquiries by e-mail, phone. "Pilots should be fresh and new and easy to visualize. Spec scripts should stay current with the shows, up-to-date story lines, characters, etc." Winners announced February 15 and August 15. For contest results, visit Web Site.

MICHAEL SHAARA AWARD FOR EXCELLENCE IN CIVIL WAR FICTION

Civil War Institute at Gettysburg College, 300 North Washington Street, Campus Box 435, Gettysburg, PA 17325. (717)337-6590. Fax: (717)337-6596. E-mail: civilwar@gettysburg.edu. Web site: http:// www.gettysburg.edu/civilwar. **Contact:** Tina Grim. Offered annually for fiction published January

1-December 31. Contest "to encourage examination of the Civil War from unique perspectives or by taking an unusual approach." All Civil War novels are eligible. Publishers should make nominations, but authors and critics can nominate as well. Prize: $5,000, which includes travel stipend. No entry fee. **Deadline: December 31.** Entries must be previously published. Judged for presentation of unique perspective, use of unusual approach, effective writing, contribution to existing body of Civil War literature. Competition open to authors of Civil War novels published for the first time in the year designated by the award (i.e. for 2008 award, only novels published in 2008 are eligible). Guidelines available on Web site. Accepts inquiries by fax, e-mail, and phone. Cover letter should include name, address, phone, e-mail, and title. Need 10 copies of novel. "Enter well before deadline. Results announced in July. Winners notified by phone. For contest results, visit Web site http://www.gettysburg.edu/civilwar.

SHORT GRAIN WRITING CONTEST

Grain Magazine, Box 67, Saskatoon SK S7K 3K1 Canada. (306)244-2828. Fax: (306)244-0255. E-mail: grainmag@sasktel.net. Web site: www.grainmagazine.ca. **Contact:** Kair McCrea, Business Administrator. Competition for postcard (flash) fiction, prose poems, dramatic monologues, nonfiction. Prize: 3 prizes of $500 in each category, plus publication. Entry fee: $30 fee for 2 entries in any additional categories, plus $8 for 3 additional entries; US and international entries $36, ($6 postage) in US funds (non-Canadian). Entrants receive a one-year subscription. Guidelines available by fax, e-mail, on Web Site or for SASE. **Deadline: February 28.** Contest entries must be either an original postcard story (narrative fiction in 500 words or less); prose poem (lyric poem written as a prose paragraph or paragraphs in 500 words or less); dramatic monologue (a self-contained speech given by a single character in 500 words or less); or essay or creative nonfiction piece (5,000 words or less). Cover document for each entry should include name, address, phone, e-mail, word count and title; title only on ms. Results announced in May. Winners notified by phone, e-mail, fax or mail. For contest results, send SASE, e-mail, fax or visit Web Site.

JOHN SIMMONS SHORT FICTION AWARD

University of Iowa Press, 102 Dey House, 507 N. Clinton St., Iowa City IA 52242-1000. (319)335-2000. Fax: (319)335-2055. Web site: www.uiowapress.org. **Contact:** Holly Carver, director. Award "to give exposure to promising writers who have not yet published a book of prose." Offered annually for a collection of short stories. Anyone who has not published a book of prose fiction is eligible to apply. Prize: Publication by the University of Iowa Press. Judged by Senior Iowa Writers' Workshops members who screen manuscripts; published fiction author of note makes final two selections. No entry fee. For guidelines, send SASE or visit Web site. Accepts inquiries by fax, phone. No application forms are necessary. A SASE must be included for return of ms. Submission period: August 1-September 30. "Individual stories can be previously published (as in journals), but never in *book* form." Stories must be in English. Length: "at least 150 word-processed, double-spaced pages; 8-10 stories on average for ms." Results announced early in year following competition. Winners notified by phone.

SKIPPING STONES HONOR AWARDS

P.O. Box 3939, Eugene OR 97403-0939. Phone/fax: (541)342-4956. E-mail: editor@skippingstones.org. Web site: www.skippingstones.org. **Contact:** Arun N. Toké, executive editor.

- Skipping Stones received the 2007 N.A.M.E. Award for outstanding contribution to multicultural education.

Annual awards since 1994 to "promote multicultural and/or nature awareness through creative writings for children and teens and their educators." Prize: honor certificates; seals; reviews; press release/publicity. Categories: short stories, novels, story collections, poetry and nonfiction. Judged by "a multicultural committee of teachers, librarians, parents, students and editors." Entry fee: $50 ($25 for small, low-income publishers/self-publishers). **Deadline: February 1**. Entries must be previously published. Open to published books and resources that appeared in print during a two year period prior to the deadline date. Guidelines for SASE or e-mail and on Web site. Accepts inquiries by e-mail, fax, phone. "We seek authentic, exceptional, child/youth friendly books that promote intercultural, international, intergenerational harmony and understanding through creative ways. Writings that come out of your own experiences and cultural understanding seem to have an edge." Results announced in May each year. Winners notified through personal notifications, press release and by publishing reviews of winning titles in the summer issue. For contest results, send SASE, e-mail or visit Web site.

SKIPPING STONES YOUTH AWARDS

Skipping Stones Magazine, P.O. Box 3939, Eugene OR 97403-0939. Phone/fax: (541)342-4956. E-mail: editor@skippingstones.org. Web site: www.skippingstones.org. **Contact:** Arun N. Toké, executive editor.

- Skipping Stones is a winner of the 2007 NAME award.

Annual awards to "promote creativity and multicultural and nature awareness in youth." Prize: publication in Autumn issue, honor certificate, subscription to magazine, plus 5 multicultural or nature books. Categories: short stories. Entry fee: $3/entry, make checks payable to *Skipping Stones*. Cover letter should include name, address, phone and e-mail. Deadline: June 20. Entries must be unpublished. Length: 1,000 words maximum. Open to any writer between 7 and 17. Guidelines available by SASE, e-mail or on Web site. Accepts inquiries by e-mail or phone. "Be creative. Do not use stereotypes or excessive violent language or plots. Be sensitive to cultural diversity." Results announced in the September-October issue. Winners notified by mail. For contest results, visit Web site. Everyone who enters receives the issue which features the award winners.

THE BERNICE SLOTE AWARD

Prairie Schooner, 201 Andrews Hall, P.O. Box 880334, Lincoln NE 68588-0334. (402)472-0911. Fax: (402)472-9771. E-mail: jengelhardt2@unlnotes.unl.edu. Web site: http://prairieschooner.unl.edu. **Contact:** Hilda Raz, editor-in-chief. Offered annually for the best work by a beginning writer published in *Prairie Schooner* in the previous year. Prize: $500. Categories: short stories, essays and poetry. Judged by editorial staff of *Prairie Schooner*. No entry fee. **Submissions should be postmarked between January 15 and March 15.** For guidelines, send SASE or visit Web site. "Only work published in the journal during the previous year will be considered." Work is nominated by the editorial staff. Results announced in the Spring issue. Winners notified by mail in February or March.

KAY SNOW WRITING AWARDS

Willamette Writers, 9045 SW Barbur Blvd., Suite 5A, Portland OR 97219. (503)452-1592. Fax: (503)452-0372. E-mail: wilwrite@teleport.com. Web site: www.willamettewriters.com. **Contact:** Pat MacAodha. Contest offered annually to "offer encouragement and recognition to writers with unpublished submissions." Acquires right to publish excerpts from winning pieces 1 time in their newsletter. Prize: 1st place: $300; 2nd place: $150; 3rd place: $50; excerpts published in Willamette Writers newsletter, and winners acknowledged at banquet during writing conference. Student writers win $50 in categories for grades 1-5, 6-8, and 9-12. $500 Liam Callen Memorial Award goes to best overall entry. Entry fee: $15 fee; no fee for student writers. **Deadline: April 23.** Guidelines for #10 SASE, fax, by e-mail or on Web site. Accepts inquires by fax, phone and e-mail. Winners notified by mail and phone. For contest results, send SASE. Prize winners will be honored at the two-day August Willamette Writers' Conference. Press releases will be sent to local and national media announcing the winners, and excerpts from winning entries may appear in our newsletter.

SOCIETY OF MIDLAND AUTHORS AWARD

Society of Midland Authors, P.O. Box 10419, Chicago IL 60610-0419. E-mail: writercc@aol.com. Web site: http://midlandauthors.com. **Contact:** Carol Jean Carlson, awards chairman. "Established in 1915, the Society of Midland Authors Award (SMA) is presented to one title in each of six categories 'to stimulate creative effort,' one of SMA's goals, to be honored at the group's annual awards banquet in May." Annual. Competition/award for novels, story collections (by single author). Prize: cash prize of at least $300 and a plaque that is awarded at the SMA banquet. Categories: children's nonfiction and fiction, adult nonfiction and fiction, adult biography, and poetry. Judging is done by a panel of three judges for each category that includes a mix of experienced authors, reviewers, book sellers, university faculty and librarians. No entry fee. Guidelines available in September-November with SASE, on Web site, in publication. Accepts inquiries by e-mail, phone. **Deadline: Feb. 1, 2009.** Entries must be published in the prior calendar year, e.g. 2007 for 2008 award. "The contest is open to any title with a recognized publisher that has been published within the year prior to the contest year." Open to authors or poets who reside in, were born in, or have strong ties to a Midland state, which includes Illinois, Indiana, Iowa, Kansas, Michigan, Minnesota, Missouri, Nebraska, North

Dakota, South Dakota, Ohio and Wisconsin. SMA only accepts published work accompanied by a completed award form. Writers may submit own work. Entries can also be submitted by the publisher's rep. "Write a great story and be sure to follow contest rules by sending a copy of the book to each of the three judges for the given category who are listed on SMA's Web site." Results announced at the SMA Awards Banquet each May. Other announcements follow in the media. Winners notified by mail, by phone. Results made available to entrants on Web site, in our monthly membership newsletter. Results will also go to local media in the form of press releases.

N ◎ SOUTH CAROLINA ARTS COMMISSION AND THE POST AND COURIER SOUTH CAROLINA FICTION CONTEST

1800 Gervais St., Columbia SC 29201. (803)734-8696. Web site: www.southcarolinaarts.com. **Contact:** Sara June Goldstein, program director for the literary arts. "This annual writing competition calls for previously unpublished short stories of 2,500 words or less. The stories do not need to be Southern, nor do they need to be set in South Carolina, although such stories are acceptable for consideration. Up to 12 short stories will be selected for publication; each writer whose work is selected will receive $500 from *The Post and Courier*, which purchases first publication rights. Stories will also be published electronically by posting them on *The Post and Courier*'s Web site, which links to the Art Commission's Web site. No entry fee. Deadline: January 15. Applicant must be a legal resident of South Carolina and be 18 years of age or older at the time of application. Guidelines and application available on the Arts Commission's Web site.

◎ SOUTH DAKOTA ARTS COUNCIL

711 E. Wells Avenue, Pierre SD 57501-3369. (605)773-3301. E-mail: sdac@state.sd.us. Web site: www.artscouncil.sd.gov. **Contact:** Dennis Holub, executive director. "Individual Artist Grants (up to $3,000) and Artist Collaboration Grants (up to $6,000) are planned for fiscal 2007." No entry fee. Deadline: March 1. Open to South Dakota residents only. Students pursuing an undergraduate or graduate degree are ineligible. Guidelines and application available on Web site or by mail. Applicants must submit application form with an original signature; current résumé no longer than 5 pages; appropriate samples of artistic work (see guidelines); up to 5 pages additional documentation; SASE with adequate postage for return of ms (if desired).

◻ SOUTHWEST WRITERS (SWW) CONTESTS

SouthWest Writers (SWW), 3721 Morris St. NE, Suite A, Albuquerque NM 87111-3611. (505)265-9485. E-mail: SW Writers@juno.com. Web site: www.southwestwriters.org. **Contact:** John Candelaria, chair. The SouthWest Writers (SWW) Contest encourages and honors excellence in writing. There are 16 categories, including Christian Novel. (Please see rules on Web site for more details.) Prizes: Finalists in all categories are notified by mail and are listed on the SWW Web site with the title of their entry. First, second and third place winners in each category also receive cash prizes of $150, $100, and $50 (respectively), as well as a certificate of achievement. First place winners also compete for the $1,000 Storyteller Award. Winners will be honored at a contest awards banquet (date and time TBA). Categories: Nine categories-broken down by genre-are for short story and novel writers. For novels: Mainstream and Literary; Mystery, Suspense, Thriller, or Adventure; Romance; Science Fiction, Fantasy, or Horror; Historical or American Frontier/Western; Middle Grade (4th-6th grade) or Young Adult (7th grade and up). For short stories: Middle Grade or Young Adult; Mainstream and Literary. Other Genres: Christian, Memoir, Screenplay, Poetry, etc; Middle Grade (4th-6th grade) or Young Adult (7th grade and up). Judged by editors and agents (most from New York publishing houses) who are chosen by the contest chairs. Screening panel sends top 10 entries in each category to judges. Judges rank and critique the top three entries in each category. All entries may receive an optional written critique by a qualified consultant. Entry fee: Early deadline with no critique, $20 for members; $30 for nonmembers; late deadline, an additional $5. Early deadline with critique, $45 for members; $55 for nonmembers; late deadline, an additional $5. Cash, check (made out to SouthWest Writers), money order or credit card. No cover letter is required; send copy of the SWW Contest Entry Form. Personal information should not appear anywhere on ms. Novels: The first 20 pages, beginning with the prologue and/or first chapter, plus a 2-page maximum synopsis. Short Stories: 5,000 words or less. Please follow detailed instructions for submission in Category Specific Guidelines on Web site. Deadline: May 1; late deadline: May 15. Entries must be unpublished. Open to all writers from around the world. All entries should be submitted in

English and follow standard ms format. "Entrants should read the SWW Contest Rules for complete information on the SWW Web site." Guidelines available in January by SASE, e-mail, on Web site or in SouthWest Sage SWW newsletter. Accepts inquiries by e-mail, phone. Mail SASE to receive rules, entry form in hard copy. Do not use certified mail to send submissions; enclose an SASP to verify receipt.

◎ SPUR AWARDS

Western Writers of America, Inc., 1080 Mesa Vista Hall, MSC06 3770, 1 University of New Mexico Albuquerque NM 87131. (505)277-5234. E-mail: wwa@unm.edu. Web site: www.westernwriters.org. **Contact:** Awards Coordinator. Purpose of award is "to reward quality in the fields of western fiction and nonfiction." Prize: Trophy. Categories: short stories, novels, poetry, songs, scripts and nonfiction. No entry fee. **Deadline: December 31.** Entries must be published during the contest year. Open to any writer. Guidelines available in Sept./Oct. for SASE, on Web site or by phone. Inquiries accepted by e-mail or phone. Results announced annually in Summer. Winners notified by mail. For contest results, send SASE.

Ⓝ ◯ ST. LOUIS SHORT STORY CONTEST

P.O. Box 9337, St. Louis MO 63117. (314)646-8515. Fax: (314)646-8515. E-mail: Form on Web site. Web site: http://stlshortstory.com. **Contact:** Brian Jones, contest administrator. Purpose: "to provide an opportunity and national platform for serious writers to showcase their talents." Annual. Competition/award for short stories. Prize: $5,000 to the 1st place winner. (This is a "winner take all" format.) The winner and the top 20 quarterfinalists will have their stories posted on the contest Web site as well as published in the 2007 St. Louis Short Story Anthology. Categories: short story (all-encompassing, not genre specific). Each entry will be judged by a panel of five judges who are professional writers from five separate fields: poetry, novel, short story, screenplay and technical writing. Entry fee: $10. Make checks payable to St. Louis Short Story Contest. Accepts inquiries by e-mail form on Web site. Deadline: May 18. Entries should be unpublished. Open to all. Length: 3,500 words. Cover letter should include name, address, phone, e-mail, word count, novel/story title. Only title should appear on actual ms. Writers may submit own work. "Be bold, be clear, and think outside the box with regards to story." Winners notified by phone, by e-mail. Winners announced Dec. 1. Results made available to entrants on Web site.

Ⓝ JOHN STEINBECK SHORT STORY AWARD

Reed Magazine. San Jose State University, Dept. of English, One Washington Square, San Jose CA 95192. (408)924-4458. E-mail: reed@email.sjsu.edu. Web site: www.sjsu.edu/reed. **Contact:** Nick Taylor, editor. "Award for an unpublished short story of up to 6,000 words." Annual. Competition/award for short stories. Prize: $1,000 prize and publication in *Reed Magazine*. Receives several hundred entries per category. Entries are judged by a prominent fiction writer; 2007 judge was Tobias Wolff. Entry fee: $15 (includes issue of *Reed*). Make checks payable to *Reed Magazine*. Guidelines available in April 2008. **Submission period is June 1-November 1, 2008.** Entries should be unpublished. Anyone may enter contest. Length: less than 6,000 words. Fill out submission form online: http://www.sjsu.edu/reed/form.HTM. Writers may submit own work. "Do not submit any pornographic material, science fiction, fantasy, or children's literature. The work must be your own, (no translations)." Results announced in April. Winners notified by mail. Results made available to entrants on Web site, in publication.

◎ STONY BROOK SHORT FICTION PRIZE

Department of English, State University of New York, Stony Brook NY 11794-5350. (631)632-7400. Web site: www.stonybrook.edu/fictionprize. **Contact:** John Westermann. Award "to recognize excellent undergraduate fiction." Prize: $1,000 and publication on Web site. Categories: Short stories. Judged by faculty of the Department of English & Creative Writing Program. No entry fee. Guidelines available on Web site. Inquiries accepted by e-mail. Expects 300 entries. Deadline: March 1. Word length: 7,500 words or less. "Only undergraduates enrolled full time in American or Canadian colleges and universities for the 2006-2007 academic year are eligible. Proof required. Students of all races and backgrounds are encouraged to enter. Guidelines for SASE or on Web site. Ms should include name, permanent address, phone, e-mail, word count and title. Winners notified by phone; results posted on Web site by June.

◐ ◎ THEODORE STURGEON MEMORIAL AWARD FOR BEST SHORT SF OF THE YEAR

Center for the Study of Science Fiction, English Department, University of Kansas, Lawrence KS 66045. (785)864-3380. Fax: (785)864-1159. E-mail: jgunn@ku.edu. Web site: www.ku.edu/~ sfcent er. **Contact:** James Gunn, professor and director. Award to "honor the best science fiction short story of the year." Prize: Trophy. Winners receive expense-paid trip to the University and have their names engraved on permanent trophy. Categories: short stories. Judged by jury. No entry fee. Entries must be previously published. Guidelines available in December by phone, e-mail or on Web site. Accepts inquiries by e-mail and fax. Entrants for the Sturgeon Award are by nomination only. Results announced in July. For contest results, send SASE.

◙ ◯ SUBTERRAIN ANNUAL LITERARY AWARDS COMPETITION: THE LUSH TRIUMPHANT

subTERRAIN Magazine, P.O. Box 3008 MPO, Vancouver BC V6B 3X5 Canada. (604)876-8710. Fax: (604)879-2667. E-mail: subter@portal.ca. Web site: www.subterrain.ca **Contact:** Jenn Farrell, managing editor. Offered annually to foster new and upcoming writers. Prize: $ 1000 (Canadian) cash prizes in each category, publication, and 1-year subscription to *subTERRAIN*. Categories: short stories, poetry, nonfiction. Judged by an editorial collective. Entry fee: $2 5. Entrants may submit as many entries in as many categories as they like. Guidelines on Web Site. **Deadline: May 15.** Entries must be unpublished. Length: Fiction: 3,000 words maximum; Poetry: a suite of 5 related poems (max 15 pages); creative nonfiction: max 4,000 words. Results announced on Web Site. "All entries must be previously unpublished material. Submissions will not be returned, so do not send originals. If submitting from outside Canada, please include International Reply Coupons to cover return postage."

Ⓝ RONALD SUKENICK AMERICAN BOOK REVIEW INNOVATIVE FICTION PRIZE

FC2, American Book Review University of Houston-Victoria School of Arts and Sciences, 3007 N. Ben Wilson, Victoria TX 77901.(850)644-2260. Fax: (850)644-6808. E-mail: fictioncollective2@gmail .com. Web site: http://fc2.org/Sukenick%20prize.htm. **Contact:** Brenda Mills, Executive Editor. "To discover new writers of experimental fiction, and to publish work by writers who have not previously published with FC2." Annual. Competition/award for novels, story collections. Prize: $1000 and publication. Entries are judged by Board of Directors. For the 2007 contest, the final judge was Michael Martone. Each year it will be a different member of the Board. Entry fee: $25. Make checks payable to American Book Review. Guidelines available in June. Accepts inquiries by e-mail. **Submission period is August 15-November 1.** Entries should be unpublished. Anyone who has not previously published with FC2 may enter contest. Cover letter should include name, address, phone, e-mail, novel/story title. Only the title should appear on the ms, since all mss are read blind by the judges. Writers may submit their own work. "Be familiar with our list." Results announced May. Winners notified by phone, by e-mail. Winners announced May.

◯ TALL GRASS WRITERS GUILD LITERARY ANTHOLOGY/CONTEST

2036 North Winds Drive, Dyer IN 46311. (219)322-7085. Fax: (219)322-7085. E-mail: outriderpress@ sbcglobal.net. Web site: www.outriderpress.com. **Contact:** Whitney Scott, senior editor. Competition to collect diverse writings by authors of all ages and backgrounds on the theme of "vacations" (spiritual as well as physical). Prize: publication in anthology, free copy to all published authors, $2,000 in cash prizes. Judge is Pulitzer Prize-winning author Robert Olen Butler. Categories: short stories, poetry and creative nonfiction. Entry fee: $16; $12 for members (make check payable to Tallgrass Writers Guild). Deadline: February 28. Word length: 2,500 words or less. Previously published and unpublished submissions accepted. Send SASE. Open to any writer. Guidelines and entry form available for SASE, by fax, e-mail and on Web site. Accepts inquiries by e-mail. Cover letter and ms should include name, address, phone, e-mail, word count and title. Results announced in May. "Must include e-mail address and SASE for response." For contest results, send e-mail.

◎ SYDNEY TAYLOR MANUSCRIPT COMPETITION

Association of Jewish Libraries, 204 Park St., Montclair NJ 07042. (973)744-3836. E-mail: stmacajl@a ol.com. Web site: www.jewishlibraries.org. **Contact:** Aileen Grossberg, coordinator. Award "to identify and encourage writers of fiction for ages 8-11 with universal appeal of Jewish content; story should deepen the understanding of Judaism for all children, Jewish and non-Jewish, and reveal positive aspects of Jewish life. No short stories or plays. Length: 64-200 pages." Judged by 5 AJL member librarians. Prize: $1,000. No entry fee. Guidelines available by SASE, e-mail or on Web site. **Deadline: December 15.** Entries must be unpublished. Cover letter should include name, address, phone, e-mail and title. Results announced April 15. Winners notified by phone or e-mail. For contest information, send e-mail or visit Web site. Check Web site for more specific details and to download release forms which must accompany entry.

☐ THE PETER TAYLOR PRIZE FOR THE NOVEL

Knoxville Writers' Guild and University of Tennessee Press, P.O. Box 2565, Knoxville TN 37901. Web site: www.knoxvillewritersguild.org. Offered annually for unpublished work to discover and publish novels of high literary quality. Guidelines for SASE or on Web site. Only full-length, unpublished novels will be considered. Short story collections, translations, or nonfiction cannot be considered. Prize: $1,000, publication by University of Tennessee Press (a standard royalty contract). Judged by a widely published novelist who chooses the winner from a pool of finalists. 2007 judge: Kelly Cherry. Entry fee: $25, payable to KWG. Multiple and simultaneous submissions okay. Manuscripts should be a minimum of 40,000 words and should be of letter-quality print on standard white paper. Text should be double-spaced, paginated and printed on one side of the page only. Please do not use a binder; use two rubber bands instead. Please use a padded mailer for shipping. The mss should be accompanied by two title pages: one with the title only; the other with the title and author's name, address and phone number. The author's name or other identifying information should not appear anywhere else on the ms. Manuscripts will not be returned. Each ms must be accompanied by a self-addressed, stamped postcard for confirmation of receipt, along with an SASE for contest results. No FedEx or UPS, please. Deadline: February 29. Entries must be unpublished. The contest is open to any U.S. resident writing in English. Members of the Knoxville Writers' Guild, current or former students of the judge, and employees and students of the University of Tennessee system are not eligible. Contest results will be announced in November.

◎ TEDDY CHILDREN'S BOOK AWARD

Writers' League of Texas, 611 S. Congress Ave., Suite 130, Austin TX 78704. (512)499-8914. Fax: (512)499-0441. E-mail: wlt@writersleague.org. Web site: www.writersleague.org. **Contact:** Kristy Bordine, program and membership administrator. Award established to "honor an outstanding book for children published by a member of the Writers' League of Texas." Prize: $1,000. Categories: long works and short works. Entry fee: $25. **Deadline: May 31.** Entries should be previously published children's books (during the period of January 1 to December 31, 2008) by Writers' League of Texas members. League members reside all over the U.S. and in some foreign countries. Persons may join the league when they send in their entries. Guidelines available in January for SASE, fax, e-mail, or visit Web site. Results announced in September. Winners notified at ceremony.

☐ THREE CHEERS AND A TIGER

E-mail: editors@toasted-cheese.com. Web site: www.toasted-cheese.com. **Contact:** Stephanie Lenz, editor. Purpose of contest is to write a short story (following a specific theme) within 48 hours. Prize: Amazon gift certificates and publication. Categories: short stories. Blind-judged by two *Toasted Cheese* editors. Each judge uses his or her own criteria to choose entries. No entry fee. Cover letter should include name, address, e-mail, word count and title. Information should be in the body of the e-mail. It will be removed before the judging begins. Entries must be unpublished. Contest offered biannually. Word limit announced at the start of the contest. Contest-specific information is announced 48 hours before the contest submission deadline. Open to any writer. Accepts inquiries by e-mail. "Follow the theme, word count and other contest rules. We have more suggestions at our Web site." Results announced in April and October. Winners notified by e-mail. List of winners on Web site.

THREE OAKS PRIZE FOR FICTION

Story Line Press, P.O. Box 1240, Ashland OR 97520-0055. (541)482-9363. E-mail: mail@storylinepress.com. Web site: www.storylinepress.com. **Contact:** Three Oaks Competition. Offered annually to find and publish the best work of fiction (novels or short story collections). Open to any writer. Prize: $1,500 advance and book publication by Story Line Press. Entry fee: $25. Guidelines for SASE or on Web site. Deadline: April 30. Entries must be unpublished. Results announced 6-8 weeks after deadline. Winners notified by phone. "A press release announcing the winner along with a letter from the publisher is sent to all entrants who supply SASE for contest results. If for some reason a contestant doesn't receive this, they may contact us by phone, e-mail or mail.''

☑ ◎ THE THURBER PRIZE FOR AMERICAN HUMOR

Thurber House, 77 Jefferson Ave., Columbus OH 43215. (614)464-1032. Fax: (614)280-3645. E-mail: mkendall@thurberhouse.org. Web site: www.thurberhouse.org. **Contact:** Missie Kendall, special events, media manager. Award ''to give the nation's highest recognition of the art of humor writing.'' Prize: $5,000. Judged by well-known members of the national arts community. Entry fee: $65 per title. Deadline: April. Published submissions or accepted for publication in U.S. for the first time. Primarily pictorial works such as cartoon collections are not considered. Word length: no requirement. Work must be nominated by publisher. Guidelines available for SASE. Accepts inquiries by phone and e-mail. Results announced in November. Winners notified in person at the Algonquin Hotel in New York City. For contest results, visit Web site.

☒ ◗ TICKLED BY THUNDER ANNUAL FICTION CONTEST

Tickled By Thunder, 14076-86A Ave., Surrey BC V3W 0V9 Canada. E-mail: info@tickledbythunder.com. Web site: www.tickledbythunder.com. **Contact:** Larry Lindner, editor. Award to encourage new writers. Prize: $150 Canadian, 4-issue subscription (one year) plus publication. Categories: short stories. Judged by the editor and other writers. Entry fee: $10 Canadian (free for subscribers but more than one story requires $5 per entry). Deadline: February 15. Entries must be unpublished. Word length: 2,000 words or less. Open to any writer. Guidelines available for SASE, e-mail, on Web site. Accepts inquiries by e-mail. Results announced in May. Winners notified by mail. For contest results, send SASE.

☒ THE TONKA FICTION CONTEST

Minnetonka Review, P.O. Box 386, Spring Park MN 55384. Web site: www.minnetonkareview.com. **Contact:** Troy Ehlers, Editor. ''We wish to seek out and publish the best literary short stories.'' Annual. Competition/award for short stories. Prize: First prize is $1,000, publication and plaque. Second prize is $100. Third prize is $50. 10 Honorable Mentions. Finalists are chosen by editorial staff and readers. Winners are chosen by guest judge. Judge in 2008 was Robin Lippincott. Entry fee: $10 and includes copy of award issue. Make checks payable to *Minnetonka Review*. Guidelines available in July. **Contest open Aug 15-Nov 30**. Entries should be unpublished. Open to all writers living in the USA. Length: Maximum 6000 words. Cover letter should include name, address, phone, e-mail, word count, novel/story title. Title only on ms. Writers may submit own work. ''Check our Web site for current guidelines and pay attention to the kind of work we have published, either through buying a sample issue or reading the samples online.'' Results announced February. Winners notified by mail, by phone, by e-mail. Results made available to entrants on Web site, in award issue.

☒ ◎ TORONTO BOOK AWARDS

Toronto Protocol, City Clerk's Office, 100 Queen St. West, City Hall, 10th Floor, West Tower, Toronto ON M5H 2N2 Canada. (416)392-8191. Fax: (416)392-1247. E-mail: bkurmey@toronto.ca. Web site: www.toronto.ca/book_awards. **Contact:** Bev Kurmey, protocol officer. The Toronto Book Awards honor authors of books of literary or artistic merit that are evocative of Toronto. Annual award for short stories, novels, poetry or short story collections. Prize: $15,000. Each short-listed author (usually 4-6) receives $1,000 and the winner receives the remainder. Categories: No separate categories—novels, short story collections, books of poetry, biographies, history, books about sports, children's books—all are judged together. Judged by jury of five who have demonstrated interest and/or experience in literature, literacy, books and book publishing. No entry fee. Cover letter should include name, address, phone, e-mail and title of entry. Six copies of the entry book are also required. Deadline: February 28. Entries must be previously published. Guidelines available in September on Web site. Accepts inquires by fax, e-mail, phone. Finalists announced in June; winners notified in September at a gala reception. More information and results available on Web site.

⊕ ◗ ◎ UPC SCIENCE FICTION AWARD

Technical University of Catalonia, Board of Trustees, Gran Capita 2-4, Edifici NEXUS 08034, Barcelona Spain. E-mail: consell.social@upc.edu. Web site: www.upc.edu/sciencefiction. **Contact:** Anna

Serra Hombravella, secretary. "The award is based on the desire for integral education at UPC, since it unifies the concepts of science and literature." Prize: £6,000 (about $16,000 US). Judged by professors of the university and science fiction writers. No entry fee. Submissions may be made in Spanish, English, Catalan or French. The author must sign his work with a pseudonym and enclose a sealed envelope with full name, personal ID number, address and phone. The pseudonym and title of work must appear on the envelope. Deadline: September 15. Entries must be unpublished. Length: 70-115 pages, double-spaced, 30 lines/page, 70 characters/line. Open to any writer. Guidelines available in January for SASE, e-mail, phone, or on Web site. Results announced in December. Winners notified by phone in November. List of winners sent to all entrants; also available for SASE and on Web site, or by e-mail.

◎ VIOLET CROWN BOOK AWARD

Writers' League of Texas, 611 S. Congress Ave., Suite 130, Austin TX 78704. (512)499-8914. Fax: (512)499-0441. E-mail: wlt@writersleague.org. Web site: www.writersleague.org. **Contact:** Kristy Bordine, program and membership administrator. Award "to recognize the best books published by Writers' League of Texas members from January 1 through December 31, 2008 in fiction, nonfiction, literary poetry and literary prose categories." Prize: three $1,000 cash awards and 3 trophies. Entry fee: $25. Send credit card information or make checks payable to Writers' League of Texas. "Anthologies that include the work of several authors are not eligible." **Deadline: May 31.** Entries must be previously published. "Entrants must be Writers' League of Texas members. League members reside all over the U.S. and in some foreign countries. Persons may join the League when they send in their entries." Publisher may also submit entry in author's name. Guidelines available after January for SASE, fax, e-mail or on Web site. Accepts inquiries by fax, e-mail or on phone. Results announced in September. Winners notified at awards ceremony. For contest results, send SASE or visit Web site. "Special citations are presented to finalists."

Ⓝ WAASMODE SHORT FICTION PRIZE

Passages North, NMU 1401 Presque Ilse Ave, Marquette MI 49855. (906)227-1203. E-mail: passages@nmu.edu. Web site: http://myweb.nmu.edu/~passages. Annual Competition/award for short stories. Prize: $1000 first prize; two honorable mentions. Entry fee: $10 per story, includes contest issue. Make checks payable to Northern Michigan University. **Submission period is Oct 15-Jan 31.** Entries should be unpublished. Anyone may enter contest. Length: 7500 word max. Writers may submit own work. Winners notified by e-mail. Results made available to entrants with SASE.

◎ EDWARD LEWIS WALLANT BOOK AWARD

Irving and Fran Waltman, 3 Brighton Rd., West Hartford CT 06117. (860)232-1421. **Contact:** Mrs. Fran Waltman, co-sponsor. To recognize an American writer whose creative work of fiction has significance for the American Jew. Prize: $500 and a scroll. Judged by panel of 3 judges. No entry fee. Accepts inquiries by phone. Writers may submit their own work. Deadline: Dec. 31. Entries must be previously published. Open to novels or story collections. Open to all American writers. Winner announced in Jan./Feb. and notified by phone.

◯ THE ROBERT WATSON LITERARY PRIZE IN FICTION AND POETRY

(formerly The Greensboro Review Literary Award in Fiction and Poetry) *The Greensboro Review*, 3302 Hall for Humanities and Research Administration, UNCG, P.O. Box 26170, Greensboro NC 27402-6170. (336)334-5459. E-mail: anseay@uncg.edu. Web site: www.uncg.edu/eng/mfa. **Contact:** Allison Seay, assistant editor. Offered annually for fiction (7,500 word limit) and poetry; the best work is published in the Spring issue of *The Greensboro Review*. Sample issue for $5. Prize: $500 each for best short story and poem. Judged by editors of *The Greensboro Review*. No entry fee. Guidelines for SASE or on Web site. Deadline: September 15. Entries must be unpublished. No simultaneous submissions or submissions by e-mail. Open to any writer. Winners notified by mail, phone or e-mail. List of winners published in Spring issue. "All manuscripts meeting literary award guidelines will be considered for cash award as well as for publication in the Spring issue of *The Greensboro Review*."

◯ WISCONSIN INSTITUTE FOR CREATIVE WRITING FELLOWSHIP

University of Wisconsin—Madison, Creative Writing/English Dept., 6195B H.C. White Hall, 600 N. Park St., Madison WI 53706. (608)263-3374. E-mail: rfkuka@wisc.edu. Web site: www.creativewriti

ng.wisc.edu. **Contact:** Ron Kuka, program coordinator. Fellowship provides time, space and an intellectual community for writers working on first books. Receives approximately 300 applicants a year for each genre. Prize: $25,000 for a 9-month appointment. Judged by English Department faculty and current fellows. Entry fee: $20, payable to the Department of English. Applicants should submit up to 10 pages of poetry or one story of up to 30 pages and a résumé or vita directly to the program during the month of February. An applicant's name must not appear on the writing sample (which must be in ms form) but rather on a separate sheet along with address, social security number, phone number, e-mail address and title(s) of submission(s). Candidates should also supply the names and phone numbers of two references. Accepts inquiries by e-mail and phone. Deadline: February. "Candidates must not yet have published, or had accepted for publication, a book by application deadline." Open to any writer with either an M.F.A. or Ph.D. in creative writing. Please enclose a SASE for notification of results. Results announced by May 1. "Send your best work. Stories seem to have a small advantage over novel excerpts."

TOBIAS WOLFF AWARD IN FICTION

Bellingham Review, Mail Stop 9053, Western Washington University, Bellingham WA 98225. (360)650-4863. E-mail: bhreview@cc.wwu.edu. Web site: www.wwu.edu/~bhreview. **Contact:** Fiction Editor. Offered annually for unpublished work. Guidelines for SASE or online. Prize: $1,000, plus publication and subscription. Categories: novel excerpts and short stories. Entry fee: $1 8 for 1st entry; $10 each additional entry. Guidelines available in September for SASE or on Web site. Deadline: Contest runs: Dec. 1-March 15. Entries must be unpublished. Length: 8,000 words or less per story or chapter. Open to any writer. Winner announced in August and notified by mail. For contest results, send SASE.

JOHN WOOD COMMUNITY COLLEGE ADULT CREATIVE WRITING CONTEST

1301 S. 48th St., Quincy IL 62305. Fax: (214)228-9483. E-mail: jmcgovern@jwcc.edu. Web site: www.jwcc.edu. **Contact:** Janet McGovern, education specialist. Award to "promote new writing." Prize: Cash prizes dictated by the number of entries received. Categories: Categories include traditional rhyming poetry, limerick or haiku, light or humorous poetry, nonfiction, fiction. Entry fee: $5/poem; $7/fiction or nonfiction. "No identification should appear on manuscripts, but send a separate 3×5 card for each entry with name, social security number (in order to print checks for cash prizes), address, phone number, e-mail address, word count, title of work and category in which each work should be entered. You may use one check or money order and place all entries in the same envelope." Guidelines available after July for SASE, fax, e-mail, phone or on Web site. Entries must be unpublished. Open to any writer. Winners notified by mail in late June. For contest results, send SASE, fax, e-mail or visit Web site www.jwcc.edu.Deadline: January 1 and April 2.

WORLD FANTASY AWARDS

World Fantasy Awards Association, P.O. Box 43, Mukilteo WA 98275-0043. E-mail: sfexecsec@gmail.com. Web site: www.worldfantasy.org. **Contact:** Peter Dennis Pautz, president. Awards "to recognize excellence in fantasy literature worldwide." Offered annually for previously published work in several categories, including life achievement, novel, novella, short story, anthology, collection, artist, special award-pro and special award-nonpro. Works are recommended by attendees of current and previous 2 years' conventions and a panel of judges. Prize: Bust of HP Lovecraft. Judged by panel. No entry fee. Guidelines available in December for SASE or on Web site. **Deadline: June 1.** Entries must be previously published. Published submissions from previous calendar year. Word length: 10,000-40,000 for novella, 10,000 for short story. "All fantasy is eligible, from supernatural horror to Tolkien-esque to sword and sorcery to the occult, and beyond." Cover letter should include name, address, phone, e-mail, word count, title and publications where submission was previously published, submitted to the address above and the panel of judges when they appear on the Web site. Results announced November 1 at annual convention. For contest results, visit Web site.

WRITER'S DIGEST ANNUAL SHORT SHORT STORY COMPETITION

Writer's Digest, 4700 E. Galbraith Rd., Cincinnati OH 45236. E-mail: short-short-competition@fwpubs.com. Web site: www.writersdigest.com. **Contact:** Terri Boes, contest administrator. Annual. Competition/award for short-shorts. Prize: 1st place receives $3,000 and option for free "Best Seller Publishing Package" from Trafford Publishing; 2nd place receives $1,500; 3rd place receives $500;

4th-10th place receive $100; 11th-25th place receive $50 gift certificate for Writer's Digest Books. The names and story titles of the 1st-10th place winners will be printed in the June issue of *Writer's Digest*, and winners will receive the latest edition of *Novel & Short Story Writer's Market*. Entry fee: $12/story. Make checks payable to Writer's Digest. Deadline: Dec. 1. Entries should be unpublished. "*Writer's Digest* reserves the one-time publication rights to the 1st-25th place winning entries to be published in a *Writer's Digest* publication." Open to all except employees of F+W Publications, Inc., and their immediate families and *Writer's Digest* contributing editors and correspondents as listed on the masthead. Length: 1,500 words or fewer. Type the word count on the first page of your entry, along with your name, address, phone number and e-mail address. All entries must be typewritten and double-spaced on one side of $8^{1}/_{2} \times 11$ A4 white paper. Mss will not be returned. Enclose a self-addressed, stamped postcard with your entry if you wish to be notified of its receipt. Write, see publication, or visit Web site for official entry form. Writers may submit own work. Results announced June. Winners notified in Feb. Results made available to entrants on Web site, in publication.

☐ WRITER'S DIGEST ANNUAL WRITING COMPETITION

Writer's Digest, 4700 E. Galbraith Rd., Cincinnati OH 45236. (513)531-2690, ext. 1328. E-mail: writing-competition@fwpubs.com. Web site: www.writersdigest.com. **Contact:** Terri Boes, contest administrator. Annual. Competition/award for short stories, articles, poems, scripts. Prize: Grand prize is $3,000 cash and an all-expenses-paid trip to New York City to meet with editors and agents. *Writer's Digest* will fly you and a guest to The Big Apple, where you'll spend 3 days and 2 nights in the publishing capital of the world. While you're there, a *Writer's Digest* editor will escort you to meet and share your work with four editors or agents. You'll also receive a free Diamond Publishing Package from Outskirts Press. First place in each category receives $1,000 cash, a ms critique and marketing advice from a *Writer's Digest* editor or advisory board member, and $100 worth of Writer's Digest Books. Second place in each category receives $500 cash, plus $100 worth of Writer's Digest Books. Third place in each category receives $250 cash, plus $100 worth of Writer's Digest Books. Fourth place in each category receives $100 cash, the latest editon of *Writer's Market Deluxe*, and a 1-yr subscription to *Writer's Digest*. Fifth place in each category receives $50 cash, the latest edition of *Writer's Market Deluxe*, and a 1-yr subscription to *Writer's Digest*. Sixth-tenth place in each category receives $25 cash. First through tenth place winners also receive a copy of *Writer's Market Deluxe* and a one-year subscription to Writer's Digest mgazine. All other winners receive distinctive certificates honoring their accomplishment. Categories: Inspirational Writing (spiritual/religious); Article: Memoir/Personal Essay; Article: Magazine Feature; Short Story: Genre; Short Story: Mainstream/Literary; Poetry: Rhyming; Poetry: Non-rhyming; Script: Stage Play; Script: TV/Movie; Children's Fiction. Judged by the editors of *Writer's Digest*. Entry fee: $10 for first poem, $5 each additional poem; all other entries are $15 for first ms, $10 each additional ms. Make checks payable to Writer's Digest. Accepts inquiries by e-mail. **Deadline: May 15.** Entries should be unpublished. "Entries in the Magazine Feature Article category may be previously published. *Writer's Digest* retains one-time publication rights to the grand prize and first place winning entries in each category to be published in a *Writer's Digest* publication." Open to all writers except employees of F+W Publications, Inc, and their immediate families, *Writer's Digest* contributing editors and correspondents as listed on the masthead, Writer's Online Workshops instructors, and Grand Prize winners from the previous three years. Length: 2,000 words max for Memoir/Personal Essay, Feature Article, and Children's Fiction; 2,500 words max for Insipirational Writing; 4,000 words max for Short Story categtories; 32 lines max for Poetry categories; 15 pages in standard format plus 1-pg synopsis for Script categories. Write, visit www.writersdigest.com/contests/annual/77th/entryform.asp, or see publication for official entry form. Your name, address, phone number, and competition category must appear in the upper left-hand corner of the first page, otherwise your entry is disqualified. See additional guidelines in publication or on Web site. Winners notified by mail. Winners notified by Oct. Results made available to entrants on Web Site after the issue has been published.

☐ WRITER'S DIGEST POPULAR FICTION AWARDS

Writer's Digest Magazine, 4700 East Galbraith Rd., Cincinnati OH 45236. (513)531-2690, ext. 1328. E-mail: popularfictionawards@fwpubs.com. **Contact:** Terri Boes, contest administrator. Annual. Competition/award for short stories. Prizes: Grand Prize is $2,500 cash, $100 worth of Writer's Digest Books, plus a ms critique and marketing advice from a *Writer's Digest* editor or advisory board member; First Prize in each of the five categories receives $500 cash, $100 worth of Writer's Digest Books, plus a ms critique and marketing advice from a *Writer's Digest* editor or advisory board member; Honorable Mentions receive promotion in *Writer's Digest* and the next edition of *Novel & Short Story Writer's Market*. Categories: Romance, Mystery/Crime, Sci-Fi/Fantasy, Thriller/Suspense, Horror. Judged by *Writer's Digest* editors. Entry fee: $12.50. Make checks payable to *Writer's Digest*. Accepts inquiries by mail, e-mail, phone. Deadline: Nov. 1. Entries should be unpublished. Open to all "except employees of F + W Publications, Inc., and their immediate family members, *Writer's Digest* contributing editors and correspondents as listed on our masthead, Writer's Online Workshops instructors, and Grand Prize Winners from the previous three years in any *Writer's Digest* competitions." Length: 4,000 words or fewer. Entries must be accompanied by an Official Entry Form or facsimile. Your name, address, phone number and competition category must appear in the upper left-hand corner of the first page of your manuscript, otherwise it is disqualified. Writers may submit own work. Results announced in the July issue of *Writer's Digest*. Winners notified by mail before March 1.

🎖 WRITERS' FELLOWSHIP

NC Arts Council, Department of Cultural Resources, Raleigh NC 27699-4632. (919)807-6512. Fax: (919)807-6532. E-mail: debbie.mcgill@ncmail.net. Web site: www.ncarts.org. **Contact:** Deborah McGill, literature director. Fellowships are awarded to support the creative development of NC writers and to stimulate the creation of new work. Prize: $10,000. Categories: short stories, novels, literary nonfiction, literary translation, spoken word. Work for children also invited. Judged by a panel of literary professionals appointed by the NC Arts Council, a state agency. No entry fee. **Deadline: November 1, 2008.** Mss must not be in published form. We receive approximately 300 applications. Word length: 20 double-spaced pages (max). The work must have been written within the past 5 years. Only writers who have been full-time residents of NC for at least 1 year as of the application deadline and who plan to remain in the state during the grant year may apply. Guidelines available in late August on Web site. Accepts inquiries by fax, e-mail, phone. Results announced in late summer. All applicants notified by mail.

🌐 ⬚ WRITERS' FORUM SHORT STORY COMPETITION

Writers International Ltd., P.O. Box 3229, Bournemouth BH1 1ZS United Kingdom. E-mail: editorial @writers-forum.com. Web site: www.writers-forum.com. **Contact:** Zena O'Toole, editorial assistant. "The competition aims to promote the art of short story writing." Prize: Prizes are £300 for 1st place, £150 for 2nd place and £100 for 3rd place. Categories: short stories. Judged by a panel who provides a short list to the editor. Entry fee: £10 or £7 for subscribers to *Writers' Forum*. Cover letter should include name, address, phone, e-mail, word count and title. Entries must be unpublished. "The competition is open to all nationalities, but entries must be in English." Length: 1,500-3,000 words. Open to any writer. Guidelines available for e-mail, on Web site and in publication. Accepts inquiries by fax, e-mail, phone. Make entry fee cheques payable to Writers International Ltd., or send credit card information. Winners notified by mail. List of winners available in magazine.

⬚ WRITERS' JOURNAL ANNUAL FICTION CONTEST

Val-Tech Media, P.O. Box 394, Perham MN 56573. (218)346-7921. Fax: (218)346-7924. E-mail: writersjournal@writersjournal.com. Web site: www.writersjournal.com. **Contact:** Leon Ogroske, editor (editor@writersjournal.com). Offered annually for previously unpublished fiction. Open to any writer. Prize: 1st Place: $500; 2nd Place: $200; 3rd Place: $100, plus honorable mentions. Prizewinning stories and selected honorable mentions published in *WRITERS' Journal*. Entry fee: $15 reading fee. Guidelines and entry forms available for SASE and on Web site. Accepts inquiries by fax, e-mail and phone. **Deadline: January 30.** "Writer's name must not appear on submission. A separate cover sheet must include name of contest, title, word count and writer's name, address, phone and e-mail (if available)." Results announced in July/August. Winners notified by mail. A list of winners is published in July/August issue and posted on Web site or available for SASE.

⬚ 🎖 WRITERS' JOURNAL ANNUAL HORROR/GHOST CONTEST

Val-Tech Media, P.O. Box 394, Perham MN 56573. (218)346-7921. Fax: (218)346-7924. E-mail: writersjournal@writersjournal.com. Web site: www.writersjournal.com. **Contact:** Leon Ogroske, editor. Offered annually for previously unpublished works. Open to any writer. Prize: 1st place: $250; 2nd place: $100; 3rd place: $75, plus honorable mentions. Prize-winning stories and selected honorable mentions published in *WRITERS' Journal*. Entry fee: $7. Guidelines available for SASE, by fax, phone, e-mail, on Web site and in publication. Accepts inquiries by e-mail, phone, fax. **Deadline: March 30.** Entries must be unpublished. Length: 2,000 words. Cover letter should include name, address, phone, e-mail, word count and title; just title on ms. Results announced in September annually. Winners notified by mail. For contest results, send SASE, fax, e-mail or visit Web site.

☐ ◎ WRITERS' JOURNAL ANNUAL ROMANCE CONTEST

Val-Tech Media, P.O. Box 394, Perham MN 56573. (218)346-7921. Fax: (218)346-7924. E-mail: writersjournal@writersjournal.com. Web site: www.writersjournal.com. **Contact:** Leon Ogroske, editor. Offered annually for previously unpublished works. Open to any writer. Prize: 1st place: $250; 2nd place: $100; 3rd place: $50, plus honorable mentions. Prize-winning stories and selected honorable mentions published in *WRITERS' Journal*. Entry fee: $7 fee. No limit on entries per person. Guidelines for SASE, by fax, phone, e-mail, on Web site and in publication. Accepts inquiries by fax, e-mail, phone. **Deadline: July 30.** Entries must be unpublished. Length: 2,000 words maximum. Open to any writer. Cover letter should include name, address, phone, e-mail, word count and title; just title on ms. Results announced in January/February issue. Winners notified by mail. Winners list published in *WRITERS' Journal* and on Web site. Enclose SASE for winner's list or send fax or e-mail.

☐ ◎ WRITERS' JOURNAL ANNUAL SHORT STORY CONTEST

Val-Tech Media, P.O. Box 394, Perham MN 56573. (218)346-7921. Fax: (218)346-7924. E-mail: writersjournal@writersjournal.com. Web site: www.writersjournal.com. **Contact:** Leon Ogroske. Offered annually for previously unpublished short stories less than 2,000 words. Open to any writer. Guidelines for SASE and online. Prize: 1st place: $350; 2nd place: $125; 3rd place: $75, plus honorable mentions. Prize-winning stories and selected honorable mentions published in *WRITERS' Journal* November/December issue. Winners notified by mail. Winners list published in *WRITERS' Journal* and on Web site. Entry fee: $10 reading fee. **Deadline: May 30.**

◙ ZOETROPE SHORT STORY CONTEST

Zoetrope: All-Story, 916 Kearny St., San Francisco CA 94133. (415)788-7500. Fax: (415)989-7910. E-mail: contests@all-story.com. Web site: www.all-story.com. **Contact:** Francis Ford Coppola, publisher. Annual contest for unpublished short stories. Prize: 1st place: $1,000; 2nd place: $500, 3rd place: $250; plus 7 honorable mentions. Judged by Joyce Carol Oates in 200 7. Entry fee: $15. Guidelines for SASE, by e-mail, in publication, or on Web site.**Deadline: October 1.** Entries must be unpublished. Word length: 5,000 words maximum. Open to any writer. "Please mark envelope clearly 'short fiction contest'." Winners notified by phone or e-mail December 1. Results announced December 1. A list of winners will be posted on Web site and published in spring issue.

Conferences & Workshops

Why are conferences so popular? Writers and conference directors alike tell us it's because writing can be such a lonely business—at conferences writers have the opportunity to meet (and commiserate) with fellow writers, as well as meet and network with publishers, editors and agents. Conferences and workshops provide some of the best opportunities for writers to make publishing contacts and pick up valuable information on the business, as well as the craft, of writing.

The bulk of the listings in this section are for conferences. Most conferences last from one day to one week and offer a combination of workshop-type writing sessions, panel discussions and a variety of guest speakers. Topics may include all aspects of writing from fiction to poetry to scriptwriting, or they may focus on a specific type of writing, such as those conferences sponsored by the Romance Writers of America (RWA) for writers of romance or by the Society of Children's Book Writers and Illustrators (SCBWI) for writers of children's books.

Workshops, however, tend to run longer—usually one to two weeks. Designed to operate like writing classes, most require writers to be prepared to work on and discuss their fiction while attending. An important benefit of workshops is the opportunity they provide writers for an intensive critique of their work, often by professional writing teachers and established writers.

Each of the listings here includes information on the specific focus of an event as well as planned panels, guest speakers and workshop topics. It is important to note, however, some conference directors were still in the planning stages for 2009 when we contacted them. If it was not possible to include 2009 dates, fees or topics, we have provided information from 2008 so you can get an idea of what to expect. For the most current information, it's best to check the conference Web site or send a self-addressed, stamped envelope to the director in question about three months before the date(s) listed.

FINDING A CONFERENCE

Many writers try to make it to at least one conference a year, but cost and location count as much as subject matter or other considerations when determining which conference to attend. There are conferences in almost every state and province and even some in Europe open to North Americans.

To make it easier for you to find a conference close to home—or to find one in an exotic locale to fit into your vacation plans—we've divided this section into geographic regions. The conferences appear in alphabetical order under the appropriate regional heading.

Note that conferences appear under the regional heading according to where they will be held, which is sometimes different from the address given as the place to register or send for information. The regions are as follows:

Northeast (page 493): Connecticut, Maine, Massachusetts, New Hampshire, New York, Rhode Island, Vermont

Midatlantic (page 503): Washington DC, Delaware, Maryland, New Jersey, Pennsylvania

Midsouth (page 506): North Carolina, South Carolina, Tennessee, Virginia, West Virginia

Southeast (page 510): Alabama, Arkansas, Florida, Georgia, Louisiana, Mississippi, Puerto Rico

Midwest (page 515): Illinois, Indiana, Kentucky, Michigan, Ohio

North Central (page 520): Iowa, Minnesota, Nebraska, North Dakota, South Dakota, Wisconsin

South Central (page 522): Colorado, Kansas, Missouri, New Mexico, Oklahoma, Texas

West (page 529): Arizona, California, Hawaii, Nevada, Utah

Northwest (page 537): Alaska, Idaho, Montana, Oregon, Washington, Wyoming

Canada (page 542)

International (page 546)

To find a conference based on the month in which it occurs, check out our Conference Index by Date at the back of this book.

LEARNING AND NETWORKING

Besides learning from workshop leaders and panelists in formal sessions, writers at conferences also benefit from conversations with other attendees. Writers on all levels enjoy sharing insights. Often, a conversation over lunch can reveal a new market for your work or let you know which editors are most receptive to the work of new writers. You can find out about recent editor changes and about specific agents. A casual chat could lead to a new contact or resource in your area.

Many editors and agents make visiting conferences a part of their regular search for new writers. A cover letter or query that starts with "I met you at the Green Mountain Writers Conference," or "I found your talk on your company's new romance line at the Moonlight and Magnolias Writer's Conference most interesting . . ." may give you a small leg up on the competition.

While a few writers have been successful in selling their manuscripts at a conference, the availability of editors and agents does not usually mean these folks will have the time there to read your novel or six best short stories (unless, of course, you've scheduled an individual meeting with them ahead of time). While editors and agents are glad to meet writers and discuss work in general terms, usually they don't have the time (or energy) to give an extensive critique during a conference. In other words, use the conference as a way to make a first, brief contact.

SELECTING A CONFERENCE

Besides the obvious considerations of time, place and cost, choose your conference based on your writing goals. If, for example, your goal is to improve the quality of your writing, it will be more helpful to you to choose a hands-on craft workshop rather than a conference offering a series of panels on marketing and promotion. If, on the other hand, you are a science fiction novelist who would like to meet your fans, try one of the many science fiction conferences or "cons" held throughout the country and the world.

Look for panelists and workshop instructors whose work you admire and who seem to be writing in your general area. Check for specific panels or discussions of topics relevant to what you are writing now. Think about the size—would you feel more comfortable with a small workshop of eight people or a large group of 100 or more attendees?

If your funds are limited, start by looking for conferences close to home, but you may want to explore those that offer contests with cash prizes—and a chance to recoup your expenses. A few conferences and workshops also offer scholarships, but the competition is stiff and writers interested in these should find out the requirements early. Finally, students may want to look for conferences and workshops that offer college credit. You will find these options included in the listings here. Again, send a self-addressed, stamped envelope for the most current details.

NORTHEAST (CT, MA, ME, NH, NY, RI, VT)

ⓝ ANNUAL NEW YORK ROUND TABLE WRITERS' CONFERENCE

20 West 44th Street, New York NY 10036. (212)764-7021. E-mail: smallpress@aol.com. Web site: www.writersconferencenyc.com. **Contact:** Karin Taylor, director. Estab. 2004. Annual. Next conference held in April, 2009. Conference duration: 2 days. Average attendance: 200. "The purpose is to educate writers about the business of getting published." Site: The conference takes place at the New York Center for Independent Publishing, based in Midtown Manhattan. Panels in 2008 included Birth of a Book, Memoir Writing, Writing Process and Fiction Writing. Speakers for 2008 included Brigid Hughes (*A Public Space*), Marjorie Braman (HarperCollins) and author Sharon Mesmer.
Costs In 2008, $250 (1 day) to $350 (2 days).
Accommodations Does not offer overnight accommodations. Provides list of area hotels or lodging options.
Additional Information Information available in January. For brochure, fax request, call, e-mail or visit Web site. Agents and editors participate in conference. "We try to provide writers with useful tools to help increase their chances of finding a literary agent or publisher."

ⓝ BIG APPLE WRITING WORKSHOPS, MEET THE AUTHORS/MEET THE AGENTS

IWWG, P.O. Box 810, Gracie Station NY 10028. (212)737-7536. Fax: (212)737-9469. E-mail: dirhahn @aol.com. Web site: www.iwwg.org. **Contact:** Hannalore Hahn, founder & executive director. Estab. 1980. Semi-annual. Oct 18-19, 2008 and April 2009. Conference duration: 2 days. Average attendance: 150. Workshop. "The three-fold purpose entails: 1) A full day writing workshop; 2) A panel discussion with 12 recently published IWWG members about how they became authors, found agents and publishers; 3) An open house with 8 agents for authors to meet." Site: Scandinavia House is the official building for Sweden, Norway, Finland, Iceland and Denmark. It is a modern building on Parl Avenue in midtown Manhattan. It offers two comfortable lecture halls and a cafeteria (with Scandinavian food). Previous panels include "Fiction and Nonfiction: Writing and Selling on Both Sides of the Aisle" and "The Writer at Work: Writing Adrift/Writing a Draft."
Costs $130 for members of IWWG/$160 for non-members for both days. Individual sections may be selected and paid for if not attending full conference.
Accommodations Does not offer overnight accommodations. Provides list of area hotels or lodging options.
Additional Information For brochure, send SASE, fax request, call, e-mail, visit Web site. Agents and editors participate in conference. "We've had over 50 Meet the Author/Meet the Agent events. Close to 4,000 books have been published by IWWG members since our inception in 1976."

BOOKEXPO AMERICA/WRITER'S DIGEST BOOKS WRITERS CONFERENCE

4700 East Galbraith Rd., Cincinnati OH 45236. (513)531-2690. Fax: (513)891-7185. E-mail: publicity @fwpubs.com. Web site: www.writersdigest.com/bea or www.bookexpoamerica.com/writersconfe rence. **Contact:** Greg Hatfield, publicity manager. Estab. 2003. Annual. Conference duration: one day, 2009's date is May 27. Average attendance: 600. "The purpose of the conference is to prepare writers hoping to get their work published. We offer instruction on the craft of writing, as well as advice for submitting their work to publications, publishing houses and agents. We provide breakout sessions on these topics, including expert advice from industry professionals, and offer workshops on fiction and nonfiction, in the various genres (literary, children's, mystery, romance, etc.). We also provide attendees the opportunity to actually pitch their work to agents." Site: The conference facility varies from year to year, as we are partnered with the BookExpo America trade show. The 2009 conference will take place in New York City. Themes and panels have included Writing Genre

Fiction, Children's Writing, Brutal Truths About the Book Publishing Industry, Crafting a Strong Nonfiction Book Proposal, Crafting Your Novel Pitch, and Secrets to Irresistible Magazine Queries. Past speakers included Jacquelyn Mitchard, Jodi Picoult, Jerry B. Jenkins, Jonathan Karp, Steve Almond, John Warner, Heather Sellers, Donald Maass and Michael Cader.

Costs The price in 2008 was $199, which included lunch and a copy of the 2008 *Writer's Market*.

Additional Information Information available in February. For brochure, visit Web site. Agents and editors participate in conference.

BREAD LOAF WRITERS' CONFERENCE

Middlebury VT 05753. (802)443-5286. Fax: (802)443-2087. E-mail: blwc@middlebury.edu. Web site: www.middlebury.edu/~blwc. **Contact:** Noreen Cargill, administrative manager. Estab. 1926. Annual. Last conference held August 13-24, 2008. Conference duration: 11 days. Average attendance: 230. For fiction, nonfiction, poetry. Site: Held at the summer campus in Ripton, Vermont (belongs to Middlebury College). 2007 faculty and staff included William Kittredge, Percival Everett, Sigrid Nunez, Joanna Scott, Susan Orlean.

Costs In 2007, $2,260 (included room and board). Fellowships available.

Accommodations Accommodations are at Ripton. Onsite accommodations included in fee.

Additional Information 2008 conference information available December 2007 on Web site. Accepts inquiries by fax, e-mail and phone.

CHILDREN'S LITERATURE CONFERENCE

239 Montauk Hwy, Southampton NY 11968-6700.(631)632-5030. Fax: (631)632-2578. Web site: www.stonybrook.edu/writers. Conference held mid-July. "Are you interested in writing or illustrating children's books? How about studying children's literature? We're inviting writers, illustrators, teachers, and readers to spend a few days in the Hamptons to analyze and celebrate books, plays, and television programs for children."

ENVIRONMENTAL WRITERS' CONFERENCE AND WORKSHOP

in honor of Rachel Carson, St. Thomas Aquinas College, 125 Route 340, Sparkill NY 10976. (845)398-4247. Fax: (845)398-4224. E-mail: info@new-cue.org. Web site: www.new-cue.org. **Contact:** Barbara Ward Klein, president. Estab. 1999. Biennial (on the "even" year). Last conference held June 10-13, 2008. Conference duration: Tuesday-Friday. Average attendance: 100. Featured speakers include Verlyn Klinkenborg of the NY Times, Alison Hawthorne Deming, John Elder, David Gessner and Linda Lear. In addition, Jennifer Sahn, editor of *Orion* magazine will be editor-in-residence. Program also includes accepted readings, workshops and guided outdoor activities. Site: The 2008 Environmental Writers' Conference and Workshops was held once again at The Spruce Point Inn in Boothbay Harbor, Maine. The Inn is one of the finest in New England and Boothbay Harbor is the largest boating harbor north of Boston. A call for submissions will be posted with registration information in early September, 2009.

Costs Registration costs for 2008 was $395 for returning participants and $440 for new participants and included most meals but did not include accommodations and travel.

Accommodations Rooms at the Spruce Point Inn are $99-150/night (dbl. occupancy); rooms nearby are $70-125/night (dbl. occupancy).

Additional Information Readings of papers accepted for presentation at the event are limited to 15 minutes and will be eligible for inclusion in archives housed at the Thoreau Institute Library at Walden Woods. Deadline for paper submissions in January 2010. "The event is interdisciplinary, encouraging participants from colleges and universities, governmental agencies, public and private organizations as well as amateur and published writers. This is an opportunity to participate and to enjoy the company of like-minded individuals in one of the most beautiful coastal locations on the eastern seaboard of the US."

GOTHAM WRITERS' WORKSHOP

WritingClasses.com (online division), 555 8th Avenue, Suite 1402, New York NY 10018. (212) 974-8377. Fax: (212) 307-6325. E-mail: dana@write.org. Web site: www.writingclasses.com. **Contact:** Dana Miller, director of student affairs. Estab. 1993. "Classes held throughout the year. There are four terms, beginning in January, April, June/July, September/October." Conference duration: 10-week, 6-week, 1-day, and online courses offered. Average attendance: approximately 1,300 students per term, 6,000 students per year. Offers craft-oriented creative writing courses in fiction writing, screenwriting, nonfiction writing, memoir writing, novel writing, children's book writing, playwriting, poetry, songwriting, mystery writing, science fiction writing, romance writing, television writing, documentary film writing, feature article writing, travel writing, creative writing, and business writing. Also, Gotham Writers' Workshop offers a teen program, private instruction and classes on selling your work. Site: Classes are held at various schools in New York City as well as online at www.writingclasses.com. View a sample online class on the Web site.

Costs 10-week and online courses—$420 (includes $25 registration fee); 6-week courses-$320 (includes $25 registration fee); 1-day courses—$150 (includes $25 registration fee). Meals and lodging not included.

Additional Information "Participants do not need to submit workshop material prior to their first class." Sponsors a contest for a free 10-week online creative writing course (value = $420) offered each term. Students should fill out a form online at www.writingclasses.com to participate in the contest. The winner is randomly selected. For brochure send e-mail, visit Web site, call or fax. Accepts inquiries by e-mail, phone, fax. Agents and editors participate in some workshops.

GREAT RIVER ARTS

33 Bridge Street, P.O. Box 48, Bellows Falls VT 05101. (802)463-3330. E-mail: grai@sover.net. Web site: www.greatriverarts.org. **Contact:** Tonia Fleming, administrator. Estab. 1999. Year-round workshops. Conference duration: 2-5 days. Average attendance: 6-8 per class. Master class and workshops in the visual and literary arts. Site: Classes are held in the Bellows Falls, Vermont/Walpole, New Hampshire region located on the shores of the Connecticut River. Classes are given in poetry, memoir, fiction and children's book arts.

Costs 2007 rates were $500-750. Does not include lodging or meals.

Accommodations Provides list of area hotels.

Additional Information Participants may need to submit material prior to arrival depending on course. Brochures for 2009 available in February/March 2008 by e-mail, phone, fax and on Web site. Accepts inquiries by e-mail, phone, fax.

GREEN MOUNTAIN WRITERS CONFERENCE

47 Hazel St., Rutland VT 05701. (802)236-6133. E-mail: ydaley@sbcglobal.net. Web site: www.verm ontwriters.com. **Contact:** Yvonne Daley, director. Estab. 1999. Annual. Check Web site for 2009 conference dates; last conference was July 28-August 1, 2008. Conference duration: 5 days. Average attendance: 40. "The conference is an opportunity for writers at all stages of their development to hone their skills in a beautiful, lakeside environment where published writers across genres share tips and give feedback." Site: Conference held at an old dance pavilion on a 5-acre site on a remote pond in Tinmouth, VT. Past features include Place in story: The Importance of Environment; Creating Character through Description, Dialogue, Action, Reaction, and Thought; The Collision of Real Events and Imagination. Previous staff has included Yvonne Daley, Ruth Stone, Verandah Porche, Grace Paley, David Huddle, Sydney Lea, Joan Connor, Tom Smith and Howard Frank Mosher.

Costs $500 before June 15, $525 after. Fee includes lunch, snacks, beverages, readings.

Accommodations Offers list of area hotels and lodging.

Additional Information Participants' mss can be read and commented on at a cost. Sponsors contests. Conference publishes a literary magazine featuring work of participants. Brochures available in January on Web site or for SASE, e-mail. Accepts inquiries by SASE, e-mail, phone. "We aim to create a community of writers who support one another and serve as audience/mentors for one another. Participants often continue to correspond and share work after conferences." Further information available on Web site, by e-mail or by phone.

◎ HIGHLIGHTS FOUNDATION WRITING FOR CHILDREN

814 Court St., Honesdale PA 18431. (570)253-1192. Fax: (570)253-0179. E-mail: contact@highlightsf oundation.org. Web site: www.highlightsfoundation.org. **Contact:** Kent Brown, executive director. Workshops geared toward those interested in writing for children; beginner, intermediate and advanced levels. Dozens of Classes include: Writing Poetry, Book Promotion, Characterization, Developing a Plot, Exploring Genres, The Publishing Business, What Makes a Good Book, and many more. Annual workshop. Held July 14-21, 2007, at the Chautauqua Institution, Chautauqua, NY. Registration limited to 100.

Costs Call for availability and pricing. Scholarships are available for first-time attendees. Phone, e-mail, or visit our Web site for more information or email contact@highlightsfoundation.org.

IWWG MEET THE AGENTS AND EDITORS: THE BIG APPLE WORKSHOPS

% International Women's Writing Guild, P.O. Box 810, Gracie Station, New York NY 10028-0082. (212)737-7536. Fax: (212)737-9469. E-mail: iwwg@iwwg.com. Web site: www.iwwg.com. **Contact:** Hannelore Hahn, executive director. Estab. 1976. Biannual. Workshops held the second weekend in April and the second weekend in October. Average attendance: 200. Workshops to promote creative writing and professional success. Site: Private meeting space of Scandinavia House, midtown New York City. Saturday: 1-day writing workshop. Sunday afternoon: open house/meet the agents, independent presses and editors.
Costs $130 for members; $155 for non-members for the weekend.
Accommodations Information on transportation arrangements and overnight accommodations available.
Additional Information Accepts inquiries by fax, e-mail, phone.

N © LEGAL FICTION WRITING FOR LAWYERS

SEAK Inc., P.O. Box 729, Falmouth MA 02541. (508)548-7023. Fax: (508)540-8304. E-mail: seakinc@aol.com. Web site: www.seak.com. **Contact:** Karen Babitsky, director of marketing. Estab. 2003. Annual. October 2008. Conference duration: 2 days. Average attendance: 150. Conference focuses on writing legal fiction. Site: Sea Crest Ocean Front Resort, Falmouth MA on Cape Cod. 2006 faculty included Lisa Scottoline and Stephen Horn, both from *Esquire*.
Costs $995 conference only.
Accommodations Provides list of area hotels and lodging options.
Additional Information A writing exercise will be mailed to attendees. Send in a sample of your work to be reviewed if you register before August. Accepts inquiries by e-mail, phone and fax.

N LESLEY UNIVERSITY WRITER'S CONFERENCE

29 Everett Street, Cambridge MA 02138. (617)349-8298. Fax: (617)349-8335. E-mail: jwadling@lesley.edu. Web site: www.lesley.edu/info/luwc. **Contact:** Joyce Wadlington, director continuing education. Estab. 2007. Annual. Last conference held July 27 through August 1, 2008. Conference duration: one week. Average attendance: 40-60 people. Workshop/residency. "We focus on fiction, nonfiction, children's book writing, and poetry." Workshop limit: 10. Site: Lesley University Campus, Cambridge, MA. 2008 faculty included Laurie Foos (*Before Elvis There Was Nothing*), Steven Cramer (*Goodbye to the Orchard*), Leah Hager Cohen (*House Lights*), and children's book writer David Elliot (*And Here's to You!*). Guest faculty included Lois Lowry (*The Giver*) and Frank Bidart (*Star Dust*).
Costs 2008: tuition $745 plus $30 registration fee.
Accommodations Participants stay in the residence halls, with alternate accommodations are available within walking distance. Meal plans, $115 (commuter) and $138 (resident). Parking available for a fee.
Additional Information Admission is selective and based on evaluation of applicant's work. For brochure, call or e-mail.

THE MACDOWELL COLONY

100 High St., Peterborough NH 03458. (603)924-3886. Fax: (603)924-9142. E-mail: admissions@macdowellcolony.org. Web site: www.macdowellcolony.org. **Contact:** Admissions Director. Estab. 1907. Open to writers and playwrights, composers, visual artists, film/video artists, interdisciplinary artists and architects. Site: includes main building, library, 3 residence halls and 32 individual studios on over 450 mostly wooded acres, 1 mile from center of small town in southern New Hampshire. Available up to 8 weeks year-round. Provisions for the writer include meals, private sleeping room, individual secluded studio. Accommodates variable number of writers, 10 to 20 at a time.
Costs "There are no residency fees. Grants for travel to and from the Colony are available based on need. The MacDowell Colony is pleased to offer grants up to $1,000 for artists in need of financial assistance during a residency at MacDowell. At the present time, only artists reviewed and accepted by the admissions panel are eligible for this grant." Application forms available. Application deadline: January 15 for summer (June 1-Sept. 30), April 15 for fall (Oct. 1-Jan. 31), September 15 for winter/spring (Feb. 1-May 31). Submit 6 copies of a writing sample, no more than 25 pages. Please

refer to work sample guidelines. Work in progress strongly recommended. Brochure/guidelines available; SASE required for return of work sample.

MARYMOUNT MANHATTAN COLLEGE WRITERS' CONFERENCE

Marymount Manhattan College, 221 E. 71st St., New York NY 10021. (212)774-4810. Fax: (212)774-4814. E-mail: lfrumkes@mmm.edu. **Contact:** Lewis Burke Frumkes or Selma Hernadez. Estab. 1993. Annual. June. Conference duration: "Actual conference is one day, and there is a three-day intensive preceding." Average attendance: 200. "We present workshops on several different writing genres and panels on publicity, editing and literary agents." Site: College/auditorium setting. 2008 conference featured 2 fiction panels, a children's book writing panel, a mystery/thriller panel and a literary agent panel. Keynote speaker for 2008 was Stuart Woods. The conference itself included more than 50 authors.

Costs $175, includes lunch and reception.

Accommodations Provides list of area lodging.

Additional Information 2009 conference information will be available in March by fax or phone. Also accepts inquiries by e-mail. Editors and agents sometimes attend conference.

◎ MEDICAL FICTION WRITING FOR PHYSICIANS

SEAK, Inc., P.O. Box 729, Falmouth MA 02541. (508)548-7023. Fax: (508)540-8304. E-mail: mail@seak.com. Web site: www.seak.com. **Contact:** Karen Babitsky, Director of Marketing. Estab. 2000. Annual. Last Conference: October 25-26, 2008. Conference Duration: 2 days. Average attendance: 150. Workshop focuses on writing medical fiction and is geared for physicians. Site: Sea Crest Ocean Front Resort, Falmouth MA on Cape Cod. 2007 speakers are Michael Palmer, MD; Tess Garritsen, MD; and 13 literary agents.

Accommodations Provides list of area hotels and lodging options.

Additional Information Accepts inquiries by e-mail, phone, fax. Agents and editors attend this conference.

NEW ENGLAND WRITERS CONFERENCE

P.O. Box 5, 151 Main St., Windsor VT 05089-0005. (802)674-2315. E-mail: newvtpoet@aol.com. Web site: www.newenglandwriters.org. **Contact:** Susan Anthony, Director. Estab. 1986. Annual. Conference held third Saturday in July. Conference duration: 1 afternoon. Average attendance: 100. The purpose is "to bring an affordable literary conference to any writers who can get there and to expose them to emerging excellence in the craft." Site: The Old South Church on Main St. in Windsor, VT. Offers panel and seminars by prominent authors, agents, editors or publishers; open readings, contest awards and book sales/signings. Featured guest speakers have included Reeve Lindbergh, Rosanna Warren and John Kenneth Galbraith.

Costs $20 (includes refreshments). No pre-registration required.

Accommodations Provides a list of area hotels or lodging options.

Additional Information Sponsors poetry and fiction contests as part of conference (Award announced at conference). Conference information available in May. For brochure send SASE or visit Web site. Accepts inquiries by SASE, e-mail, phone. "Be prepared to listen to the speakers carefully and to network among participants."

NY STATE SUMMER WRITERS INSTITUTE

Skidmore College, 815 N. Broadway, Saratoga Springs NY 12866. (518)580-5593. Fax: (518)580-5548. E-mail: cmerrill@skidmore.edu. Web site: www.skidmore.edu/summer. **Contact:** Christine Merrill, program coordinator. Estab. 1987. Annual. Conference duration: Two-week or four-week session. Average attendance: 80 per two-week session. This event features fiction, nonfiction, poetry and short story workshops. College credit is available for four-week attendees. Site: held on Skidmore campus—dorm residency and dining hall meals. "Summer in Saratoga is beautiful." Past faculty has included Amy Hempel, Nick Delbanco, Margot Livesey, Jay McInerney, Rick Moody and Lee K. Abbott. Visiting faculty has included Joyce Carol Oates, Russell Banks, Ann Beattie, Michael Cunningham and Michael Ondaatje.

Costs Tuition is $1,060 for 2 weeks and $2,120 for 4 weeks. Room and board is additional—$658 for 2 weeks and $1,316 for 4 weeks. "These are 2007 rates. Visit Web site for updated fees for our 2009 institute."

Additional Information "Writing samples are required with applications: fiction, 5-20 pages; poetry, 2-3 poems; nonfiction prose, 5-20 pages."

⊚ ODYSSEY FANTASY WRITING WORKSHOP

P.O. Box 75, Mont Vernon NH 03057-1420. Phone/fax: (603)673-6234. E-mail: jcavelos@sff.net. Web site: www.odysseyworkshop.org. **Contact:** Jeanne Cavelos, director. Estab. 1996. Annual. Last workshop held June 9 to July 18, 2008. Conference duration: 6 weeks. Average attendance: limited to 16. "A workshop for fantasy, science fiction and horror writers that combines an intensive learning and writing experience with in-depth feedback on students' manuscripts. The only six-week workshop to combine the overall guidance of a single instructor with the varied perspectives of guest lecturers. Also, the only such workshop run by a former New York City book editor." Site: conference held at Saint Anselm College in Manchester, New Hampshire. Previous guest lecturers included: George R.R. Martin, Harlan Ellison, Ben Bova, Dan Simmons, Jane Yolen, Elizabeth Hand, Terry Brooks, Craig Shaw Gardner, Patricia McKillip and John Crowley.

Costs In 2007: $1,700 tuition, $700 housing (double room), $1,400 (single room); $25 application fee, $500-600 food (approximate), $210 processing fee to receive college credit.

Accommodations "Workshop students stay at Saint Anselm College Apartments and eat at college."

Additional Information Students must apply and include a writing sample. Application deadline April 10. Students' works are critiqued throughout the 6 weeks. Workshop information available in October. For brochure/guidelines send SASE, e-mail, visit Web site, call or fax. Accepts inquiries by SASE, e-mail, fax, phone.

Ⓝ THE POWER OF WORDS

Goddard College, 123 Pitkin Rd., Plainfield VT 05667. (802)454-8311, x204. E-mail: TLAconference@goddard.edu. Web site: www.goddard.edu/powerofwords. **Contact:** Denise Whitesides-Skeeba, coordinator. Estab. 2003. Annual. Last conference held Sept. 12-15, 2008. Conference duration: 4 days. Average attendance: 150. "Purpose is to explore social and personal transformation through the spoken, written and sung word and to share resources for making a living using writing, storytelling, drama, etc. in local communities." Site: A small college campus nestled in the Green Mountains of Vermont; campus was once historic farm, and historic buildings still in use—features woodlands (with trails), dorms, meeting halls and offices. Keynoters for 2008: Walter Mosley, novelist; Bread and Puppet Theatre Company; Kelley Hunt, rhythm and blues singer; Rick Jarow, author of *Creating the Work You Love*; Sherry Reiter, poetry therapy pioneer; plus 25 other writers, storytellers and performers to be announced.

Costs $210 early bird registration/$240 afterwards/$270 at the door.

Accommodations Offers ride-sharing and taxi-sharing from airport via electronic boards. Offers overnight accommodations. $40 double/$60 single per night plus $12/meal.

Additional Information Submit workshop material prior to festival; deadline for proposals is January 15. Information available in March. For brochure, send SASE, call, e-mail, visit Web site. "Please visit www.goddard.edu/powerofwords for more information."

THE PUBLISHING GAME

Peanut Butter and Jelly Press, P.O. Box 590239, Newton MA 02459. E-mail: alyza@publishinggame.com. Web site: www.publishinggame.com. **Contact:** Alyza Harris, manager. Estab. 1998. Monthly. Conference held monthly, in different locales across North America: Boston, New York City, Philadelphia, Washington DC, Boca Raton, San Francisco, Los Angeles, Toronto, Seattle, Chicago. Conference duration: 9 a.m. to 4 p.m. Maximum attendance: 18 writers. "A one-day workshop on finding a literary agent, self-publishing your book, creating a publishing house and promoting your book to bestsellerdom!" Site: "Elegant hotels across the country. Boston locations alternate between the Four Seasons Hotel in downtown Boston and The Inn at Harvard in historic Harvard Square, Cambridge." Fiction panels in 2005 included Propel Your Novel from Idea to Finished Manuscript; How to Self-Publish Your Novel; Craft the Perfect Book Package; How to Promote Your Novel; Selling Your Novel to Bookstores and Libraries. Workshop led by Fern Reiss, author and publisher of The Publishing Game series.

Costs $195.

Accommodations "All locations are easily accessible by public transportation." Offers discounted conference rates for participants who choose to arrive early. Offers list of area lodging.

Additional Information Brochures available for SASE. Accepts inquiries by SASE, e-mail, phone, fax, but e-mail preferred. Agents and editors attend conference. "If you're considering finding a literary agent, self-publishing your novel or just want to sell more copies of your book, this conference will teach you everything you need to know to successfully publish and promote your work."

ROBERT QUACKENBUSH'S CHILDREN'S BOOK WRITING & ILLUSTRATING WORKSHOPS

460 E. 79th St., New York NY 10075-1443. (212)744-3822. Fax: (212)861-2761. E-mail: rqstudios@aol .com. Web site: www.rquackenbush.com. **Contact:** Robert Quackenbush, director. Estab. 1982. Annual. Workshop to be held during second week of July. Conference duration: Four days. Limited to 10 people. Workshops to promote writing and illustrating books for young readers. "Focus is generally on picture books, easy-to-read and early chapter books. Come prepared with stories and/ or illustrations to be developed into a finished state ready to present to a publisher and be ready to meet a lot of nice people to help you." Site: Held at the Manhattan studio of Robert Quackenbush, author and illustrator of more than 200 books for children. All classes led by Robert Quackenbush.
Costs $750 tuition covers all the costs of the workshop but does not include housing and meals. A $100 nonrefundable deposit is required with the $650 balance due three weeks prior to attendance.
Accommodations A list of recommended hotels and restaurants is sent upon receipt of deposit to applicants living out of the area of New York City.
Additional Information Class is for beginners and professionals. Critiques during workshop. Private consultations also available at an hourly rate. "Programs suited to your needs; individualized schedules can be designed. Write or phone to discuss your goals and you will receive a prompt reply." Conference information available 1 year prior to conference. For brochure, send SASE, e-mail, visit Web site, call or fax. Accepts inquiries by fax, e-mail, phone, SASE.

REMEMBER THE MAGIC IWWG ANNUAL SUMMER CONFERENCE

International Women's Writing Guild, P.O. Box 810, Gracie Station, New York NY 10028-0082. (212)737-7536. Fax: (212)737-9469. Web site: www.iwwg.org. **Contact:** Hannelore Hahn. Estab. 1978. Annual. Conference held in the summer. Conference duration: 1 week. Average attendance: 450. The conference features 65 workshops held every day on every aspect of writing and the arts. Site: Saratoga Springs, 30 minutes from Albany, NY, and 4 hours from New York City. Conference is held "on the tranquil campus of Skidmore College in Saratoga Springs, where the serene Hudson Valley meets the North Country of the Adirondacks."
Costs $1,085 single, $945 double (members); $1,130 single, $990 double (non-members). Five day, weekend and commuter rates are also available. Includes meals and lodging.
Accommodations Modern, air-conditioned and non-air-conditioned dormitories—single and/or double occupancy. Equipped with spacious desks and window seats for gazing out onto nature. Meals served cafeteria-style with choice of dishes. Variety of fresh fruits, vegetables and salads have been found plentiful, even by vegetarians. Conference information is available now. For brochure send SASE, e-mail, visit Web site or fax. Accepts inquiries by SASE, e-mail, phone or fax. "The conference is for women only."

SCBWI ANNUAL WINTER CONFERENCE ON WRITING AND ILLUSTRATING FOR CHILDREN

(formerly SCBWI Midyear Conference), Society of Children's Book Writers and Illustrators, 8271 Beverly Blvd., Los Angeles CA 90048. (323)782-1010. Fax: (323)782-1892. E-mail: conference@scbwi .org. Web site: www.scbwi.org. **Contact:** Stephen Mooser. Estab. 2000. Annual. Conference held in February. Average attendance: 800. Conference is to promote writing and illustrating for children: picture books; fiction; nonfiction; middle grade and young adult; network with professionals; financial planning for writers; marketing your book; art exhibition; etc. Site: Manhattan.
Costs See Web site for current cost and conference information.
Additional Information SCBWI also holds an annual summer conference in August in Los Angeles. See the listing in the West section or visit www.scbwi.org for details.

SCBWI/HOFSTRA CHILDREN'S LITERATURE CONFERENCE

University College for Continuing Education, Hofstra University, Hempstead NY 11549. (516)463-7600. Web site: www.hofstra.edu/ucce/childLitConf. **Contact:** Connie C. Epstein, Adrienne Betz and Judith Reed, co-organizers. Estab. 1985. Annual. Average attendance: 200. Conference to encourage good writing for children. "Purpose is to bring together various professional groups—writers, illustrators, librarians, teachers—who are interested in writing for children." Site: The conference takes place at the Student Center Building of Hofstra University, located in Hempstead, Long Island. "Each year we organize the program around a theme. This year's theme is "The Rhythm of the Book." We have two general sessions, an editorial panel and six break-out groups held in rooms in the Center." Previous agents/speakers have included: Paula Danziger and Anne M. Martin and a panel of children's book editors critique randomly selected first-manuscript pages submitted by registrants. Special interest groups are offered in picture books, nonfiction and submission procedures, with others in fiction.

Costs $82 (previous year) for SCBWI members; $87 for nonmembers. Lunch included.

SEACOAST WRITERS ASSOCIATION SPRING AND FALL CONFERENCES

59 River Road, Stratham NH 03885-2358. E-mail: patparnell@comcast.net. **Contact**: Pat Parnell, conference coordinator. Annual. Conferences held in May and October. Conference duration: 1 day. Average attendance: 60. "Our conferences offer workshops covering various aspects of fiction, nonfiction and poetry." Site: Chester College of New England in Chester, New Hampshire.

Costs Approximately $50.

Additional Information "We sometimes include critiques. It is up to the speaker." Spring meeting includes a contest. Categories are fiction, nonfiction (essays) and poetry. Judges vary from year to year. Conference and contest information available for SASE December 1, April 1, and September 1. Accepts inquiries by SASE, e-mail and phone. For further information, check the Web site www.seacoastwritersassociation.org.

THE SOUTHAMPTON WRITERS CONFERENCE

Stony Brook Southampton, 239 Montauk Highway, Southampton NY 11968. (631)632-5030. Fax: (631)632-2578. E-mail: southamptonwriters@stonybrook.edu. Web site: www.stonybrook.edu/writers. **Contact**: Adrienne Unger, administrative coordinator. Estab. 1975. Annual. Conference held in July. Conference duration: 12 days. Average attendance: 95. The primary work of the conference is conducted in writing workshops in the novel, short story, poem, play, literary essay and memoir. Site: The seaside campus of Stony Brook Southampton is located in the heart of the Hamptons, a renowned resort area only 70 miles from New York City. During free time, participants can draw inspiration from Atlantic beaches or explore the charming seaside towns. Faculty has included Frank McCourt, Billy Collins, Bharati Mukherjee, Roger Rosenblatt, Ursula Hegi, Alan Alda, and Jules Feiffer, Melissa Bank and Matt Klam.

Costs Application fee: $25; tuition, room and board: $2,100; tuition only: $1,500 (includes breakfast and lunch).

Accommodations On-campus housing-doubles and small singles with shared baths-is modest but comfortable. Housing assignment is by lottery. Supplies list of lodging alternatives.

Additional Information Applicants must complete an application form and submit a writing sample of unpublished, original work up to 20 pages (15 pages for poetry). See Web site for details. Brochures available in December by fax, phone, e-mail and on Web site. Accepts inquiries by SASE, e-mail, phone and fax. Editors and agents attend this conference.

Ⓝ THRILLERFEST

New York NY. (636)938-7163. E-mail: tfest@thrillerwriter.org. Web site: www.thrillerwriters.org. Estab. 2006. Annual. July 2009. Conference duration: 4 days. Average attendance: 650. Workshop/ conference/festival. "To promote thriller fiction and the thriller in general, to fans, aspiring writers, and established authors in an atmosphere that encourages casual mixing, accessibility and sharing." Previous years have focused on aspects of the thriller and writing the thriller from a creative as well as business/professionally-minded approach. The various subgenres are explores as well as the traits, advantages and disadvantages of each. In addition, the fist two days of the conference, made up of CraftFest, focus on workshops aimed toward the professional and would-be professional. 2008 guest speakers and panelists included David Morrell, Gayle Lynds, Sandra Brown, James Rollins, Kathy Reichs, Eric Van Lusbbader, Brad Thor, Vince Flynn, Joe Finder, Steve Barry, Tess Gerritsen, Heather Graham, Lee Child, James Patterson and Clive Cussler.

Costs $400-750 depending on specific event selection and available early-bird discounting. Some meals are included in some of the packages.

Accommodations Does not offer overnight accommodations. Provides list of area hotels or lodging options. Discounted room rate available at conference location.

Additional Information Information available in September. For brochure, call or e-mail. Agents and editors participate in conference. "AgentFest is a three hour event in which authors have the opportunity to 'speed pitch' their story to dozens of agents in a single setting. ThrillerFest boasts a very congenial, relaxed and friendly atmosphere in which the best and the brightest in our field can mix and interact comfortably with those dreaming of becoming just that."

◎ VERMONT COLLEGE POSTGRADUATE WRITERS' CONFERENCE

36 College St., Montpelier VT 05602. (802)223-2133. Fax: (802)828-8649. E-mail: roger.weingarten@ tui.edu. Web site: www.tui.edu/conferences. **Contact:** Roger Weingarten, director. Estab. 1995. Annual. August 8-14. Conference duration: 6 days. Average attendance: 65. This workshop covers the following areas of writing: novels, short stories, creative nonfiction, poetry, poetry manuscript and translation. Site: Union Institute & University's historic Vermont College campus in Montpelier. Workshops are centered on craft and often include exercises. 2008 faculty include Short Story: Michael Martone, and Antonya Nelson; Short-Short Story: Ander Monson; Novel: Ellen Lesser, and Clint McCown; Creative Nonfiction: Christopher Noel, and Sue William Silverman; Poetry Manuscript: Robin Behn, Richard Jackson, and Charles Harper Webb; Poetry: Leslie Ullman, Bruce Weigl, and Roger Weingarten.

Costs Tuition is $800-875; private dorm room: $330; shared dorm room is $180; meals: $140.

Accommodations Shuttles from airport available.

Additional Information Workshop material must be submitted 7 weeks prior to conference. Submit 25 pages of prose, 6 pages of poetry, 50 pages of poetry ms. Brochures available at Web site. "This conference is for advanced writers with postgraduate degrees or equivalent experience. Workshops are limited to 5-7 participants. Scholarship support available. Contact director."

VERMONT STUDIO CENTER

P.O. Box 613, Johnson VT 05656. (802)635-2727. Fax: (802)635-2730. E-mail: writing@vermontstudi ocenter.org. Web site: www.vermontstudiocenter.org. **Contact:** Gary Clark, writing program director. Estab. 1984. Ongoing residencies. Conference duration: From 2-12 weeks. "Most residents stay for 1 month." Average attendance: 53 writers and visual artists/month. "The Vermont Studio Center is an international creative community located in Johnson, Vermont, and serving more than 500 American and international artists and writers each year (50 per month). A Studio Center Residency features secluded, uninterrupted writing time, the companionship of dedicated and talented peers, and access to a roster of two distinguished Visiting Writers each month. All VSC Residents receive three meals a day, private, comfortable housing and the company of an international community of painters, sculptors, poets, printmakers and writers. Writers attending residencies at the Studio Center may work on whatever they choose—no matter what month of the year they attend." Visiting writers have included Ron Carlson, Donald Revell, Jane Hirshfield, Rosanna Warren, Chris Abani, Bob Shacochis, Tony Hoagland, and Alice Notley.

Costs "The cost of a 4-week residency is $3,750. Generous fellowship and grant assistance available.

Accommodations Provided.

Additional Information Conferences may be arranged with visiting writers of the resident's genre. If conference scheduled, resident may submit up to 15 pages of ms. "We have competitions for full fellowships three times a year. The deadlines are February 15, June 15 and October 1. Writers should submit manuscripts of 15 pages. Application fee is $25." Writers encouraged to visit Web site for more information. May also e-mail, call, fax.

WESLEYAN WRITERS CONFERENCE

Wesleyan University, 294 High St., room 207, Middletown CT 06459. (860)685-3604. Fax: (860)685-2441. E-mail: agreene@wesleyan.edu. Web site: www.wesleyan.edu/writers. **Contact:** Anne Greene, director. Estab. 1956. Annual. Conference held the third week of June. Average attendance: 100. For novel, short story, fiction techniques, poetry, short- and long-form nonfiction, memoir, multi-media work. Site: The conference is held on the campus of Wesleyan University, in the hills overlooking the Connecticut River. Meals and lodging are provided on campus. Features daily seminars, readings, lectures and workshops, mss consultations, publishing advice; faculty of award-winning writers and guest speakers.

Costs In 2007, day students' rate $1,050 (included tuition, meals), boarding students' rate of $1,250 (included tuition, meals and room for 5 nights).

Accommodations "Participants can fly to Hartford or take Amtrak to Meriden, CT. We are happy to help participants make travel arrangements." Overnight participants stay on campus or in hotels.

Additional Information "Award-winning faculty. Participants are welcome to attend seminars in a range of genres if they are interested. Scholarships and teaching fellowships are available, including the Joan Jakobson Scholarships for writers of fiction, poetry and nonfiction and the Jon Davidoff Scholarships for journalists." Accepts inquiries by e-mail, phone, fax.

THE "WHY IT'S GREAT" WRITING WORKSHOP & RETREAT

21 Aviation Road, Albany NY 12205. (518)453-0890. E-mail: workshop@whyitsgreat.com. Web site: www.whyitsgreat.com. **Contact:** David Vigoda, director. Estab. 2003. Annual. Conference held in July. Conference duration: 4 days. Average attendance: 30. The fundamental activity is the appreciation and understanding of what makes great writing great. The key insight is realizing that no analysis of technique alone can be sufficient. Great writing is the melding of great technique with great heart and each must be able to get out of the way of the other even as they complete each other. Technique without heart is meaningless; heart without technique is incoherent. There are workshops about one and workshops about the other, but this is the one about cultivating and resolving the struggle between them. Writers of fiction, poetry, nonfiction are full participants. Issues include thematic material, narration and voice. Examples are drawn from all types of writing. Site: World Fellowship Center is a secular educational camp founded in 1941 to promote peace, justice and freedom. The vacation resort is situated on 450 undeveloped acres of beautiful woods, wetlands and a large "forever wild" sanctuary pond in the New Hampshire Whithe Mountains. It is perfect for a writer's retreat and attracts singles, couples and families. There are always interesting conversations to join and lots of recreational choices, including swimming, boating and hiking. Themes are determined by participants, according to their preferences. David Vidoda, novelist and poet, directs the workshop.

Costs The workshop fee for 2006 was $185. The cost to stay at the World Fellowship Center ranges from $42-$81 per day per adult (less for children), including all meals, facilities and programs. Weekly rates are available.

Accommodations Guests arrange their own transportation. Shuttle service is available for those arriving by bus. Carpools may be available from Massachusetts and metro New York/New Jersey.

Additional Information Brochure available by phone, e-mail or on the Web site. "No proof of ability is required. It doesn't matter if someone has written three novels or is still trying to get the first one started—or wrote 30 pages and froze. The workshop is non-competitive so all participants can feel safe in a group setting as they share their own work, insights and experience."

WRITER'S VOICE OF THE WEST SIDE YMCA

5 West 63rd Street, New York NY 10023. (212)875-4124. Fax: (212)875-4198. E-mail: graucher@ymc anyc.org. **Contact:** Glenn Raucher. Estab. 1981. Workshop held 6 times/year. Conference duration: 8 weeks or 7 weeks; 2 hours, one night/week. Average attendance: 10. Workshop on "fiction, poetry, writing for performance, nonfiction, multi-genre, playwriting, screenwriting, children's fiction and memoir." Special one-day intensives throughout the year. Frequent Visiting Author readings, which are free and open to the public. Site: Workshop held at the Westside YMCA.

Costs $375/8-week workshop, $330/7-week workshops, $125/$112 for West Side Y members, $100/ $90 for older adult 65+ members.

Additional Information For workshop brochures or get e-mailing list. Accepts inquiries by SASE, e-mail, fax, phone. "The Writer's Voice of the Westside Y is the largest non-academic literary arts center in the U.S."

YADDO

Box 395, Saratoga Springs NY 12866-0395. (518)584-0746. Fax: (518)584-1312. E-mail: yaddo@yadd o.org. Web site: www.yaddo.org. **Contact:** Candace Wait, program director. Estab. 1900. Two seasons: large season is in mid-May-August; small season is late September-May (stays from 2 weeks to 2 months; average stay is 5 weeks). Average attendance: Accommodates approximately 32 artists in large season, 12-15 in the small season. "Those qualified for invitations to Yaddo are highly qualified writers, visual artists, composers, choreographers, performance artists and film and video artists who are working at the professional level in their fields. Artists who wish to work collaboratively are encouraged to apply. An abiding principle at Yaddo is that applications for residencies are judged on the quality of the artists' work and professional promise." Site: includes four small lakes, a rose garden, woodland.

Costs No fee is charged; residency includes room, board and studio space. Limited travel expenses are available to artists accepted for residencies at Yaddo.

Accommodations Provisions include room, board and studio space. No stipends are offered.

Additional Information To apply: Filing fee is $20 (checks payable to Corporation of Yaddo). Two letters of recommendation are requested. Applications are considered by the Admissions Committee and invitations are issued by March 15 (deadline: January 1) and October 1 (deadline: August 1). Information available for SASE (63¢ postage), by e-mail, fax or phone and on Web site. Accepts inquiries by e-mail, fax, SASE, phone.

MIDATLANTIC (DC, DE, MD, NJ, PA)

BAY TO OCEAN WRITERS' CONFERENCE
Chesapeake College, Wye Mills, MD 21679. (410)820-8822. E-mail: info@baytoocean.com. Web site: www.baytoocean.com. **Contact:** Carolyn Jaffe. Estab. 1998. Annual. Conference held last Saturday in February. Conference duration: 1 day. Average attendance: 130. Approximately 20 speakers conduct workshops on publishing, agenting, editing, marketing, craft, writing for television and movies, poetry, fiction, nonfiction and freelance writing. Site: Chesapeake College, Rt. 213 and Rt. 50, Wye Mills, on Maryland's historic Eastern Shore. Accessible to individuals with disabilities.

Costs $80 before January 15th; $90 from January 16th until conference date; students $55, includes sessions, continental breakfast and networking lunch.

Additional Information Mail-in registration form available on Web site in the fall prior to the conference. Conference is for writers of all levels, especially new to intermediate writers. This conference has sold out early the past two years.

GREATER LEHIGH VALLEY WRITERS GROUP 'THE WRITE STUFF' WRITERS CONFERENCE
P.O. Box 96, Nazareth PA 18064-0096. (908)479-6581. Fax: (908)479-6744. E-mail: write@glvwg.org. Web site: www.glvwg.org. **Contact:** JoAnn Dahan, chair. Estab. 1993. Annual. Last conference was March 28-29, 2008. Conference duration: 1 day. Average attendance: 140. This conference features workshops in all genres. Site: "The Four Points Sheraton is located in the beautiful Lehigh Valley. The spacious hotel has an indoor swimming pool where our keynote will address the conference over a wonderful, three-course meal. The hotel rooms are very inviting after a long day's drive. We try to offer a little bit of everything to satisfy all our attendees." 2006 keynote speaker was Stephen Fried, investigative journalist and essayist.

Costs In 2006, for members, $95, which includes all workshops, 2 meals and a chance to pitch your work to an editor or agent. Also a book fair with book signing. For non-members, cost is $115. Late registration: $130.

Additional Information For more information, see the Web site. Sponsors contest for conferees. The Writer's Flash contest is judged by conference participants. Write 100 words or less in fiction, creative nonfiction or poetry. Brochures available in March for SASE, or by phone, e-mail or on Web site. Accepts inquiries by SASE, e-mail, phone, fax. Agents and editors attend conference. "Be sure to refer to the Web site, as often with conferences things change. Greater Lehigh Valley Writers Group has remained one of the most friendly conferences and we give the most for your money. Breakout rooms offer craft topics, editor and agent panels, a 'chick lit' panel and more."

◎ HIGHLIGHTS FOUNDATION FOUNDERS WORKSHOPS
814 Court St., Honesdale PA 18431. (570)253-1192. Fax: (570)253-0179. E-mail: contact@highlightsf oundation.org. Web site: www.highlightsfoundation.org. **Contact:** Kent L. Brown Jr., executive director. Estab. 2000. Workshops held seasonally from March through November. Conference duration: 3-7 days. Average attendance: limited to 8-15. Conference focuses on children's writing: fiction, nonfiction, poetry, promotions, picture books, writing from nature, young adult novels, and much more. "Our goal is to improve, over time, the quality of literature for children by educating future generations of children's authors." Recent faculty/speakers have included Joy Cowley, Patricia Lee

Gauch, Carolyn Yoder, Sandy Asher, Rebecca Dotlich, Carolyn Coman, Jane Yolen, Rich Wallace and Peter Jacobi.

Costs Range from $695 and up, including meals, lodging, materials.

Accommodations "Participants stay in guest cabins on the wooded grounds surrounding Highlights Founders' home adjacent to the house/conference center, near Honesdale, PA."

Additional Information "Some workshops require pre-workshop assignment." Brochure available for SASE, by e-mail, on Web site, by phone, by fax. Accepts inquiries by phone, fax, e-mail, SASE. Editors attend conference. "Applications will be reviewed and accepted on a first-come, first-served basis. Applicants must demonstrate specific experience in writing area of workshop they are applying for—writing samples are required for many of the workshops."

◎ MONTROSE CHRISTIAN WRITER'S CONFERENCE

5 Locust Street, Montrose Bible Conference, Montrose PA 18801-1112. (570)278-1001 or (800)598-5030. Fax: (570)278-3061. E-mail: mbc@montrosebible.org. Web site: www.montrosebible.org. **Contact:** Donna Kosik, MBC Secretary/Registrar. Estab. 1990. Annual. Conference held in July 2007. Average attendance: 85. "We try to meet a cross-section of writing needs, for beginners and advanced, covering fiction, poetry and writing for children. It is small enough to allow personal interaction between conferees and faculty. We meet in the beautiful village of Montrose, Pennsylvania, situated in the mountains. The Bible Conference provides hotel/motel-like accommodation and good food. The main sessions are held in the chapel with rooms available for other classes. Fiction writing has been taught each year."

Costs In 2007 registration (tuition) was $150.

Accommodations Will meet planes in Binghamton, NY and Scranton, PA. On-site accommodations: room and board $255-300/conference; $55-65/day including food (2007 rates). RV court available.

Additional Information "Writers can send work ahead of time and have it critiqued for a small fee." The attendees are usually church related. The writing has a Christian emphasis. Conference information available April 2007. For brochure send SASE, visit Web site, e-mail, call or fax. Accepts inquiries by SASE, e-mail, fax, phone.

PENNWRITERS CONFERENCE

RR #2, Box 241, Middlebury Center PA 16935. E-mail: conferenceco@pennwriters.org. Web site: www.pennwriters.org. **Contact:**Vicky Fisher, conference coordinator. Estab. 1987. Annual. Conference held the third or fourth weekend of May. Average attendance: 100. "We encompass all genres and will be aiming for workshops to cover many areas, including fiction (long and short), nonfiction, etc." Site: Past workshops held in Harrisburg, Pittsburgh, Grantsville. Theme for 2006 was "Rekindling the Spark." Speakers included Anne Sowards and Evan Fogelman.

Costs Approximately $145 for members, $170 for nonmembers (2006 rate).

Accommodations See Web site for current information.

Additional Information Sponsors contest. Published authors judge fiction in 2 categories, short stories and Great Beginnings (novels). For conference information send SASE. Accepts inquiries by fax and e-mail. "Agent/editor appointments are available on a first-come, first serve basis."

PENN WRITERS CONFERENCE

3440 Market St., Suite 100, Philadelphia PA 19104. (215)898-6493. Fax: (215)573-2053. E-mail: writconf@sas.upenn.edu. Web site: www.pennwritersconference.org. **Contact:** Nadia Daniel, manager, non-credit programs. Estab. 1995. Annual. 2005 conference held in October. Conference duration: Two days. Average attendance: 300. Upcoming themes and speakers to be announced.

Costs Check Web site for 2006 costs.

Additional Information Brochures available in September.

◎ SANDY COVE CHRISTIAN WRITERS CONFERENCE

60 Sandy Cove Rd., North East MD 21901-5436. (800)234-2683. Fax: (410)287-3196. E-mail: info@sandycove.org or jim@jameswatkins.com. Web site: www.sandycovewriters.com. **Contact:** Jim Watkins, director of conference. Estab. 1982. Annual. Last conference held Sept. 29-Oct 2, 2008. Average attendance: 160. Focus is on "all areas of writing from a Christian perspective such as: periodicals, devotionals, fiction, juvenile fiction, Sunday School curriculum, screenwriting, self-publishing, Internet writing, etc." Site: "Sandy Cove is conveniently located mid-way between Baltimore and

Philadelphia, just off I-95." Located on 220 acres of Maryland woodland, near headwaters of the Chesapeake Bay. Visit Web site for current date and faculty.

Costs In 2007, costs were full package: $499 per person (single room occupancy) or $440 per person (double room occupancy)—includes lodging, meals, materials, seminars, sessions, private appointments and 2 ms evaluations. Add $15/night for bay-view room.

Accommodations No arrangements for transportation. "Hotel-style rooms, bay view available. Suites available for additional fee."

Additional Information "Manuscript critiques from editors and professional writers offered. See Web site for details. Also offers 1-day student training for high school and college age students."

N ⓒ ⓖ SPX (SMALL PRESS EXPO)

E-mail: stevec@spxpo.com. Web site: www.spxpo.com. **Contact:** Steve Conley, executive director. Estab. 1996. Annual. Last festival held October. Conference duration: 2 days. Average attendance: 2,000+. "North America's premier independent comics arts and cartooning festival, SPX brings together over 300 artists and publishers to meet their readers, booksellers, distributors and each other. In its tenth year, SPX now serves as the preeminent showcase for the exhibition of independent comic books and the discovery of new creative talent." Site: In 2008, Marriott Bethesda North Hotel & Conference Center in Bethesda, MD.

Costs $8/day or $15 for weekend pass. "As with every year, all profits from SPX will go to support the Comic Book Legal Defense Fund, protecting the First Amendment rights of comic book readers and professionals."

Accommodations Detailed directions and transportation options offered on Web site. The Marriott Bethesda North Hotel & Conference Center offers reduced rates for expo attendees at $119 per night.

Additional Information Sponsors contest. "The Ignatz Award is a festival prize awarded at SPX to recognize outstanding achievement in comics and cartooning. A panel of five cartoonists develop the ballot, which is then voted on by SPX attendees. You do not need to submit your comic for the panel to consider you for nomination to the Ignatz ballot. However, if you would like to guarantee that you are considered, you can send six (6) copies of your comic to Jeff Alexander, Ignatz Awards Coordinator, % Big Planet Comics, 426 Maple Avenue East, Vienna, VA 22180." Additional guidelines on Web site. For brochure, visit Web site. Editors participate in conference.

WASHINGTON INDEPENDENT WRITERS (WIW) WASHINGTON WRITERS CONFERENCE

1001 Connecticut Ave. NW, Ste. 701, Washington DC 20036. (202)775-5150. Fax: (202)775-5810. E-mail: info@washwriter.org. Web site: www.washwriter.org. **Contact:** Donald Graul Jr., executive director. Estab. 1975. Annual. Conference held in June. Conference duration: Saturday. Average attendance: 350. "Gives participants a chance to hear from and talk with dozens of experts on book and magazine publishing as well as meet one-on-one with literary agents." Site: George Washington University Conference Center. Past keynote speakers included Erica Jong, Diana Rehm, Kitty Kelley, Lawrence Block, John Barth, Stephen Hunter, Francine Prose. 200 Keynote Speaker, Larry Kishbaum.

Additional Information Send inquiries to info@washwriter.org.

WILLIAM PATERSON UNIVERSITY SPRING WRITER'S CONFERENCE

English Dept., Atrium 250, 300 Pompton Rd., Wayne NJ 07470-2103. (973)720-3567. Fax: (973)720-2189. E-mail: liut@wpunj.edu. Web site: http://euphrates.wpunj.edu/WritersConference. **Contact:** Timothy Liu, associate professor. Annual. Conference held in April. Conference duration: 1 day. Average attendance: 100-125. The 2005 conference focused on "writing the world." Several hands-on workshops were offered in many genres of creative writing, critical writing and literature. Included reading by nationally recognized author. Site: William Paterson University campus. 2005 keynote speaker: poet Linda Gregg. Past faculty has included Yusef Komunyakaa, Joyce Carol Oates, Susan Sontag and Jimmy Santiago Braca.

Costs $40 (2005) includes 2 workshops, plenary readings, meals.

Additional Information Conference information is available November/December. For brochure send e-mail, visit Web site, call or fax. Accepts inquiries by SASE, e-mail, phone and fax. Agents and editors participate in conference.

WINTER POETRY & PROSE GETAWAY IN CAPE MAY

18 North Richards Ave., Ventnor NJ 08406. (609)823-5076. E-mail: info@wintergetaway.com. Web site: www.wintergetaway.com. Established 1994. **Contact:** Peter E. Murphy, founder/director. An-

nual 4-day event. 2009 dates: January 16-19. Location: The Grand Hotel on the Oceanfront in Historic Cape May, NJ. Workshops offered include Writing New Stories, Revising a Short Story Toward Publication, Focusing Your Fiction, Finishing Your Novel, Flash Fiction, as well as workshops in Creative Nonfiction and Turning Memory into Memoir. Workshops meet from 9-4 Saturday & Sunday and 9-12 on Monday. The Getaway also features workshops in poetry writing, song writing, writing for children, painting and photography. Other special features include extra-supportive sessions for beginners. There are usually 10 or fewer participants in each workshop and fewer than 7 in each of the prose workshops. Previous staff has included Renee Ashley, Christian Bauman, Anndee Hochman, Laura McCullough, Sondra Perl, Carol Plum-Ucci, Mimi Schwartz, David Schwartz, Robbie Clipper Sethi, Richard K. Weems.

Costs $375 registration, including 2 lunches, 3 receptions, 3 days of workshops, and a 20-minute tutorial with one of the poets on staff.

Accommodations "The Grand Hotel on the Oceanfront in Historic Cape May, NJ. Participants stay in comfortable rooms, most with an ocean view, perfect for thawing out the muse. Hotel facilities include a pool, sauna, and whirlpool, as well as a lounge and disco for late evening dancing for night people."

Additional Information "Individual tutorials available." Brochure and registration form available by mail or on Web site. "The Winter Getaway is known for its challenging and supportive workshops that encourage imaginative risk-taking and promote freedom and transformation in the participants' writing."

MIDSOUTH (NC, SC, TN, VA, WV)

AMERICAN CHRISTIAN WRITERS CONFERENCES

P.O. Box 110390, Nashville TN 37222. (800)21-WRITE. Fax: (615)834-7736. E-mail: ACWriters@aol. com. Web site: www.ACWriters.com. **Contact:** Reg Forder, director. Estab. 1988. Annual. Conferences held throughout the year in over 2 dozen cities. Conference duration: 2 days. Average attendance: 30-80. Conference's purpose is to promote all forms of Christian writing. Site: Usually located at a major hotel chain like Holiday Inn.

Costs $109 for 1 day; $199 for 2 days. Plus meals and accommodations.

Accommodations Special rates available at host hotel.

Additional Information Conference information available for SASE, e-mail, phone or fax. Accepts inquiries by fax, e-mail, phone, SASE.

BLUE RIDGE "AUTUMN IN THE MOUNTAINS" NOVEL RETREAT

(800)588-7222. E-mail: ylehman@bellsouth.net. Web site: www.lifeway.com/autumninthemountains. **Contact:** Yvonne Lehman, director. Estab. 2007. Annual. Retreat held October 5-9, 2008. Limited attendance: 50 (register early). Requirements: previous attendance at a writers conference "somewhere" and have a novel in progress. Mornings: classes by established authors to take your novel to a higher level. Afternoons: Writing time. Late afternoon: Discussion/Brainstorming groups. Evening: Critique Groups in your particular novel category.

Costs $315 tuition, deluxe accommodations in Mountain Laurel on-campus hotel. See Web site for on-campus room rates.

BLUE RIDGE MOUNTAINS CHRISTIAN WRITERS CONFERENCE

(800)588-7222. E-mail: ylehman@bellsouth.net. Web site: www.lifeway.com/christianwriters. **Contact:** Yvonne Lehman, director. Estab. 1999. Annual. Last conference held May 20-24, 2007. Average attendance: 380. All areas of Christian writing including fiction, nonfiction, devotionals, women's fiction, romance, suspense, romance, craft of writing, etc. For beginning and advanced writers. Site: LifeWay/Ridgecrest Conference Center, 20 miles east of Asheville, NC. Companies represented May 18-22, 2008 include AMG Publications, B&H, Focus on the Family, Howard Books, The Upper Room, LifeWay Christian Resources, Christian Writers Guild, Living Ink Books, Hensley Publishing, Today's Christian Woman, Benrey Literary Agency, Les Stobbe Agency, Bethan House, Big Idea (Veggie Tales), MacGregor Literary Agency, The Nashville Group, WinePress, William K. Jensen Literary Agency, et al. Faculty includes professional authors, agents and editors.

Costs 2007: $315, which includes all sessions, breaks, and a special Wednesday evening Awards Ceremony. Additional on-campus meal package available for $98/person.

Accommodations LifeWay Ridgecrest Conference Center. See Web site for on-campus room rates.

Additional Information Sponsors contests for unpublished writers. Awards include trophy and $200 scholarship toward next year's conference. See Web site for critique service and daily schedule-offering keynote sessions, continuing classes and workshops.

HIGHLAND SUMMER CONFERENCE

Box 7014, Radford University, Radford VA 24142-7014. (540)831-5366. Fax: (540)831-5951. E-mail: dcichran@radford.edu. Web site: www.radford.edu/~arsc. **Contact:** Dana Cochran, assistant to director. Estab. 1978. Annual. Conference held first 2 weeks of June. Conference duration: 2 weeks. Average attendance: 25. Three hours graduate or undergraduate credits. Site: The Highland Summer Conference is held at Radford University, a school of about 9,000 students. Radford is in the Blue Ridge Mountains of southwest Virginia, about 45 miles south of Roanoke, VA. "The HSC features one (two weeks) or two (one week each) guest leaders each year. As a rule, our leaders are well-known writers who have connections, either thematic or personal or both, to the Appalachian region. The genre emphasis depends upon the workshop leader(s). In the past we have had as guest lecturers Nikki Giovanni, Sharyn McCrumb, Gurney Norman, Denise Giardinia, George Ella Lyon, Jim Wayne Miller, Wilma Dykeman and Robert Morgan."

Costs "The cost is based on current Radford tuition for 3 credit hours plus an additional conference fee. On-campus meals and housing are available at additional cost. 2008 conference tuition was $771 for in-state undergraduates, $837 for graduate students."

Accommodations "We do not have special rate arrangements with local hotels. We do offer accommodations on the Radford University Campus in a recently refurbished residence hall. (In 2007 cost was $26.09-36.08 per night.)"

Additional Information "Conference leaders typically critique work done during the two-week conference, but do not ask to have any writing submitted prior to the conference beginning." Conference information available after February for SASE. Accepts inquiries by e-mail, fax.

Ⓝ JAMES RIVER WRITERS CONFERENCE

James River Writers, Zero East 4th St. #24, Richmond VA 23224. (804)230-4575. Fax: (804)230-4576. E-mail: info@jamesriverwriters.com. Web site: http://jamesriverwriters.com. **Contact:** Anne Westrick, administrative director. Estab. 2003. Annual. October 10-11, 2008; October 9-10, 2009. Average attendance: 250. Conference. "The James River Writers Conference offers two days of cross-genre sessions to bring aspiring writers together with professionals to share the ups and downs of the writing life. By seeking to build and inspire the community of writers, the sessions address a myriad of topics related to the craft and business of writing fiction, nonfiction, poetry, fantasy/sci-fi, children's, magazine articles, short stories, memoir, biography, and romance. The purpose is to energize the creative literary community." Site: "The Library of Virginia provides a beautiful setting including a 250-seat lecture hall and four rooms seating 35-60 each for break-out sessions, all located in one wing of the Library, off the main front lobby. The site lends itself to an intimacy unusual for writers conferences." In 2007 the fiction-related panels included Stories of the South, Getting Graphic, Point of View, Say What?!, How to Thrill Your Readers, On the Dark Side, How to Make Your Settings Come to Life, Finding Your Voice, and Writing PG-13. In 2007, Pulitzer Prize-winning poet Claudia Emerson and NY Times bestselling authors Eric Van Lustbader, Kyle Mills, Sheri Reynolds, Sharyn McCrumb, HarperCollins editorial director Michael Stearns and editorial consultant Marcela Landres, plus 40 other writers, editors and agents participated in panel discussions. Past years' conference guests have included Tom Robbins, Edward P. Jones, Jeannette Walls, Mark Bowden, Rosalind Miles, Dennis McFarland, David L. Robbins, Dean King and Hampton Sides.

Costs In 2007 the cost was $140 early registration and $155 after September 1, 2007, which included a box lunch.

Accommodations Richmond is easily accessibly by air and train. Does not offer overnight accommodations. Provides list of area hotels or lodging options. "Each year we arrange for special conference rates at an area hotel."

Additional Information Workshop material is not required, however we have offered two options for submissions: (1) the first pages critique session in which submissions are read before a panel of agents and editors who are seeing them for the first time and are asked to react on the spot. No

508 **Conferences & Workshops**

additional fee. No guarantee that a particular submission will be read. Details posted on the Web site, jamesriverwriters.com; and (2) in 2007, for an additional $35 fee, participants submitted in advance ten pages which were critiqued by Marcela Landres, who then met with each writer for a 15 minute consultation during the conference. Information available in June. For brochure, visit Web site. Agents participate in conference. Editors participate in conference.

KILLER NASHVILLE

P.O. Box 680686, Franklin TN 37068-0686.(615)599-4032. E-mail: contact@killernashville.com. Web site: www.KillerNashville.com. **Contact:** Clay Stafford. Estab. 2006. Annual. Next event: August 2008. Conference duration: 4 days. Average attendance: 180+. "Conference designed for writers and fans of mysteries and thrillers, including authors (fiction and nonfiction), playwrights, and screenwriters. Sponsors include Middle Tennessee State University, Barnes & Noble Booksellers, Mystery Writers of America, Sisters in Crime, First Tennessee Bank, Landmark Booksellers, and The Nashville Scene. Law enforcement workshop partners include the Federal Bureau of Investigation (FBI), The Tennessee Bureau of Investigations (TBI), Alcohol, Tobacco, & Firearms (ATF), Franklin Police Department, Brentwood Police Department, and Wilson County Sheriff's Department. Agents, editors and industry professionals include Carey Nelson Burch (William Morris Agency), Donna Bagdasarian (Maria Carvainia Agency), Maryglenn McCombs (Oceanview Publishing), Kathyrn Knight (Dalmation Press), Janet Young (Ingram Books) and Helen Yu (literary attorney). Event includes book signings and panels." Past panelists included authors Michael Connelly, Carol Higgins Clark, Hallie Ephron, Chris Grabenstein, Rhonda Pollero, P.J. Parrish, Reed Farrel Coleman, Kathryn Wall, Mary Sums, Don Bruns, Bill Moody, Richard Helms, Alexandra Sokoloff and Steven Womack. **Costs** Signings events are free; current prices for events available on Web site.
Additional Information "Additional information about registration is provided at www.KillerNashvill e.com."

NORTH CAROLINA WRITERS' NETWORK FALL CONFERENCE

P.O. Box 954, Carrboro NC 27510-0954. (919)967-9540. Fax: (919)929-0535. E-mail: mail@ncwriters. org. Web site: www.ncwriters.org. **Contact:** Cynthia Barnett, executive director. Estab. 1985. Annual. Average attendance: 350. "The conference is a weekend full of classes, panels, readings and informal gatherings. The Network serves writers at all stages of development from beginning, to emerging, to established. We also encourage readers who might be considering writing. We have several genres represented. In the past we have offered fiction, nonfiction, poetry, screenwriting, writing for children, blogging, journalism and more. We always invite New York editors and agents for one-on-one sessions with authors and offer craft classes in editing, pitching and marketing." Site: "We hold the conference at a conference center with hotel rooms available."
Costs "Conference registration fee for NCWN members is approximately $250 and includes at least two meals."
Accommodations "Special conference hotel rates are available, but the individual makes his/her own reservations."
Additional Information For brochure, e-mail us or visit our Web site. Online secure registration available at www.ncwriters.org.

◎ OUTDOOR WRITERS ASSOCIATION OF AMERICA ANNUAL CONFERENCE

OWAA, 121 Hickory St., Suite 1, Missoula MT 59801. (406)728-7434. Fax: (406)728-7445. E-mail: rginer@montana.com. Web site: www.owaa.org. **Contact:** Robin Giner, meeting planner. Estab. 1927. Annual. Conference held June 21-24, 2008, in Bismarck, ND. Average attendance: 500. Conference concentrates on outdoor communications (all forms of media). Featured speakers have included Don Ranley, University of Missouri, Columbia; Richard Louv, author of *Last Child in the Woods*; Nina Leopold Bradley (daughter of Aldo Leopold); Secretary of the Interior, Gail Norton; Bill Irwin, the only blind man to hike the Appalachian Trail.
Costs $380 for nonmembers. Registration fee includes cost of most meals.
Accommodations List of accommodations available after February. Special room rates for attendees.
Additional Information Sponsors contests, "but all is done prior to the conference and you must be a member to enter them." Conference information available February 2008. For conference information, visit www.owaa.org/conf-2008/index.php, send e-mail, call or fax. Accepts inquiries by e-mail, fax.

SEWANEE WRITERS' CONFERENCE

735 University Ave., Sewanee TN 37383-1000. (931)598-1141. E-mail: cpeters@sewanee.edu. Web site: www.sewaneewriters.org. **Contact:** Cheri B. Peters, creative writing programs manager. Estab. 1990. Annual. 2008 conference held in July. Average attendance: 140. "We offer genre-based workshops in fiction, poetry and playwriting and a full schedule of readings, craft lectures, panel discussions, talks, Q&A sessions and the like." Site: "The Sewanee Writers' Conference uses the facilities of Sewanee: The University of the South. Physically, the University is a collection of ivy-covered Gothic-style buildings, located on the Cumberland Plateau in mid-Tennessee." Invited editors, publishers and agents structure their own presentations, but there is always opportunity for questions from the audience." 2008 faculty included fiction writers John Casey, Tony Earley, Randall Kenan, Margot Livesey, Jill McCorkle, Erin McGraw, Tim O'Brien, and Christine Schutt; and poets Daniel Anderson, Claudia Emerson, Andrew Hudgins, Mark Jarman, Mary Jo Salter, Alan Shapiro, Mark Strand, and Greg Williamson; and playwrights Romulus Linney and Arlene Hutton.

Costs Full conference fee (tuition, board and basic room) is $1,685.

Accommodations Participants are housed in university dormitory rooms. Motel or B&B housing is available but not abundantly so. The cost of dormitory housing is included in the full conference fee. Complimentary chartered bus service is available—on a limited basis—on the first and last days of the conference.

Additional Information "We offer each participant (excepting auditors) the opportunity for a private manuscript conference with a member of the faculty. These manuscripts are due one month before the conference begins." Conference information available beginning in Mid-January. The application season runs from February 1 to May 1, or until all spaces have been filled. Early application is encouraged. For brochure send address and phone number, e-mail, visit Web site or call. "The conference has available a limited number of fellowships and scholarships; these are awarded on a competitive basis."

SOUTH CAROLINA WRITERS WORKSHOP ANNUAL CONFERENCE

P.O. Box 7104, Columbia SC 29202. (803)794-0832. Web site: www.scwriters.com. Estab. 1990. Annual. Conference held in October. Conference duration: 3 days. Average attendance: 150. Conference theme varies each year. Hands-on and lecture-style sessions in both craft and the business of writing are featured for all major genres.

Additional Information Please check Web site for more information. Accepts inquiries by e-mail. Agents and editors attend this conference.

Ⓢ STELLARCON

Box I-1, Elliott University Center, UNCG, Greensboro NC 27412. E-mail: info@stellarcon.org. Web site: www.stellarcon.org. **Contact:** Mike Monaghan, convention manager. Estab. 1976. Annual. Last conference held March 14-16, 2008. Average attendance: 500. Conference focuses on "general science fiction and fantasy (horror also) with an emphasis on literature." Site: Downtown Radisson, High Point, NC. See Web site for 2008 speakers.

Costs See Web site for 2008 rates.

Accommodations "Lodging is available at the Radisson."

Additional Information Accepts inquiries by e-mail. Agents and editors participate in conference.

VIRGINIA FESTIVAL OF THE BOOK

145 Ednam Dr. , Charlottesville VA 22903 . (434)924-6890. Fax:(434)296-4714. E-mail: vabook@virginia.edu. Web site: www.vabook.org. **Contact**: Nancy Damon, programs director. Estab. 1995. Annual. Festival held in March. Average attendance: 22,000. Festival held to celebrate books and promote reading and literacy. Site: Held throughout the Charlottesville/Albemarle area.

Costs Most events are free and open to the public. 2009 Dates are March 18-22, 2009.

Accommodations Overnight accomodations available.

Additional Information "Authors must 'apply' to the festival to be included on a panel." Conference information is available on the Web site, e-mail, fax or phone. For brochure visit Web site. Accepts inquiries by e-mail, fax, phone. Authors, agents and editors participate in conference. "The festival is a five-day event featuring authors, illustrators and publishing professionals. The featured authors are invited to convene for discussions and readings or write and inquire to participate. All attendees welcome."

Conferences

WILDACRE WRITERS WORKSHOP

Mailing address: 233 S. Elm St., Greensboro NC 27401-2602. (336)370-9188. Fax: (336)370-9188. E-mail: judihill@aol.com. Web site: www.Wildacres.com. **Contact:** Judith Hill, director. Estab. 1985. Annual. Residential workshop held second week in July. Conference duration: 1 week. Average attendance: 110. Workshop focuses on novel, short story, poetry, creative nonfiction. Site: Beautiful retreat center on top of a mountain in the Blue Ridge Mountains of North Carolina. Faculty 2008: Ron Rash, Luke Whisnant, Janice Fuller, Quinn Dalton, Lee Zacharias, Jon Tuttle, Nancy Bartholomew, Phillip Gardner, and Jim Clark.

Costs $550 (everything is included: workshop, ms critique, double room, all meals).

Accommodations Vans available, $50 round trip.

Additional Information "New people must submit a writing sample to be accepted. Those attending send their manuscript one month prior to arrival." Workshop information is available on the Web site after November 30th. For information visit Web site. Accepts inquiries by e-mail and phone.

SOUTHEAST (AL, AR, FL, GA, LA, MS, PR [PUERTO RICO])

ALABAMA WRITERS' CONCLAVE

137 Sterline Dr., Hueytown AL 35023. E-mail: irene@irenelatham.com. Web site: www.alabamawritersconclave.org. Contact: Irene Latham, program chair; Don Johnson, treasurer. Estab. 1923. Last event held July 20-22, 2007. Average attendance: 80-100. Conference to promote all phases of writing. Also offers ms critiques and eight writing contests. Site: Four Points Sheraton at the University of Alabama campus in Tuscaloosa, Alabama.

Costs Fees for conference are $150 (member)/$175 (nonmember), includes 2 meals. Critique fee $25 (member)/$30 (nonmember). Membership $25.

Accommodations Special conference rate s.

Additional Information "We have major speakers and faculty members who conduct intensive, energetic workshops. Our annual writing contest guidelines and all other information is available at www.alabamawritersconclave.org."

ARKANSAS WRITERS' CONFERENCE

AR Penwomen Pioneer Branch of the National League of American Penwomen, 6817 Gingerbread Lane, Little Rock AR 72204. (501)565-8889. Fax: (501)565-7220. E-mail: pvining@aristotle.net. Web site: http://groups.yahoo.com/group/arpenwomen. **Contact:** Send SASE to: Peggy Vining, at the address listed above. Estab. 1944. Annual. Conference held first weekend in June. Average attendance: 175. "We have a variety of subjects related to writing. We have some general sessions, some more specific, but we try to vary each year's subjects."

Costs Registration: $15; luncheon: $19; banquet: $20; contest entry $10 (2006 rates).

Accommodations "We meet at a Holiday Inn Presidential in Little Rock. Rooms available at reduced rate." Holiday Inn has a bus to bring our attendees from the airport. Rooms average $79.

Additional Information "We have 36 contest categories. Some are open only to Arkansans, most are open to all writers. Our judges are not announced before the conference. All are qualified, many from out of state." Conference information available February 15. For brochures or inquiries send SASE with full mailing address, call or fax. "We have had 226 people attending from 12 states— over 2,000 contest entries from 40 states and New Zealand, Mexico and Canada."

AWP ANNUAL CONFERENCE AND BOOKFAIR

MS 1E3, George Mason University, Fairfax VA 22030. (703)993-4301 Fax: (703)993-4302. E-mail: awpconf@gmu.edu. Web site: www.awpwriter.org. **Contact:** Matt Scanlon, director of conferences. Estab. 1967. Annual. Conference held February 11-14, 2009, in New York City. Conference duration: 4 days. Average attendance: 4,000. The annual conference is a gathering of 4,000+ students, teachers, writers, readers and publishers. All genres are represented. Site: This year the conference will be held at Hilton New York. "We will offer 175 panels on everything from writing to teaching to critical analysis." In 2007, Lee Smith, John Barth, Kaye Gibbons, C.D. Wright, Ann Beattie, and Robert Olen Butler were special speakers.

Costs Early registration fees: $40 student; $140 AWP member; $160 non-member.

Accommodations Provide airline discounts and rental-car discounts. Special rate at Hilton.
Additional Information Check Web site for more information.

GEORGIA WRITERS ASSOCIATION'S SPRING FESTIVAL OF WORKSHOPS

1071 Steeple Run, Lawrenceville GA 30043. (678)407-0703. Fax: (678)407-9917. E-mail: festival2007 @georgiawriters.org. Web site: www.georgiawriters.org; link to festival page: www.georgiawriters. org/Festival-2007.htm. **Contact**: Geri Taran. Estab. 1995. Annual. Last conference held May 5, 2007. Average attendance: 200. Conference is comprehensive—all genres and business aspects of a writing career, and agents, publishers, editors. Approximately 20 workshops, 4 each hour running concurrently. Site: Smyrna Community Center (Atlanta vicinity), large main area, separate rooms for sessions. Presenters/speakers have included Bobbie Christmas, Michael Lucker, Peter Bowerman, Eric Haney, Barbara LeBey, David Fulmer and many others.
Costs 2007: $85 at the door; $75 in advance; $95 includes annual membership expiring on June 30, 2008 ($45 annual dues).

HOW TO BE PUBLISHED WORKSHOPS

P.O. Box 100031, Birmingham AL 35210-3006. E-mail: mike@writing2sell.com. Web site: www.writi ng2sell.com. **Contact:** Michael Garrett. Estab. 1986. Workshops are offered continuously year-round at various locations. Conference duration: 1 session. Average attendance: 10-15. Workshops to "move writers of category fiction closer to publication." Focus is not on how to write, but how to get published. Site: Workshops held at college campuses and universities. Themes include marketing, idea development and manuscript critique.
Costs $55-89.
Additional Information "Special critique is offered, but advance submission is not required." Workshop information available on Web site. Accepts inquiries by e-mail.

ℕ MONTEVALLO LITERARY FESTIVAL

Station 6420, University of Montevallo, Montevallo AL 35115.(205)665-6420. Fax: (205)665-6422. E-mail: murphyj@montevallo.edu. Web site: www.montevallo.edu/english. **Contact:** Dr. Jim Murphy, director. Estab. 2003. Annual. Last festival held: April 13-14, 2007. Average attendance: 60-100. "Readings, panels, and workshops on all literary genres and on literary editing/publishing. Workshops with manuscript critiques in fiction, poetry, and drama." Site: Several sites on a bucolic liberal arts university campus. 2007 fiction workshop leader was John Dufresne. Past fiction workshop faculty included Patricia Foster, Tom Franklin, Sheri Joseph, Sena Jeter Naslund, Brad Vice, Brad Watson. See Web site for 2008 dates and speakers.
Costs In 2007: $45 for festival, including meals; $95 for festival, including meals and workshop.
Accommodations Free on-campus parking. Offers overnight accommodations at Ramsay Conference Center on campus. Rooms $40/night. Call (205)665-6280 for reservations. Visit www.montevallo. edu/cont_ed/ramsay.shtm for information.
Additional Information Workshop participants submit up to 5 pages of poetry/up to 15 pages of prose; e-mail as Word doc to Jim Murphy (murphyj@montevallo.edu) at least 2 weeks prior to festival. Information for upcoming festival available in February. For brochure, visit Web site. Accepts inquiries by mail (with SASE), e-mail, phone, and fax. Editors participate in conference. "This is a friendly, relaxed 2-day festival dedicated to bringing literary writers and readers together on a personal scale."

MOONLIGHT AND MAGNOLIAS WRITER'S CONFERENCE

Georgia Romance Writers, 2173 Indian Shoals Drive, Loganville GA 30052. E-mail: info@georgiarom ancewriters.org. Web site: www.georgiaromancewriters.org. **Contact:** Pam Mantovani. Estab. 1982. Annual. Last conference held October 3-5, 2008, in the Westin Atlanta North Hotel in Atlanta, GA. Average attendance: 175. "Conference focuses on writing of women's fiction with emphasis on romance. Includes agents and editors from major publishing houses. Previous workshops have included: beginning writer sessions, research topics, writing basics and professional issues for the published author; plus specialty sessions on writing young adult, multi-cultural, inspirational and Regency. Speakers have included experts in law enforcement, screenwriting and research. Literary raffle and advertised speaker and GRW member autographing open to the public. Published authors make up 25-30% of attendees." Brochures available for SASE in June.

Costs $170 GRW member/$180 nonmember for conference registration. Check Web site for current conference fees, hotel rates and registration forms.

Additional Information Maggie Awards for excellence are presented to unpublished writers. The Maggie Award for published writers is limited to Region 3 members of Romance Writers of America. Deadline for published Maggie is May 2. Deadline for unpublished Maggies is June 1. Entry forms and guidelines available on Web site. Published authors judge first round, category editors judge finals. Guidelines available for SASE in Spring.

NATCHEZ LITERARY AND CINEMA CELEBRATION

P.O. Box 1307, Natchez MS 39121-1307. (601)446-1208. Fax: (601)446-1214. E-mail: carolyn.smith@ colin.edu. Web site: www.colin.edu/NLCC. **Contact:** Carolyn Vance Smith, co-chairman. Estab. 1990. Annual. Conference held February 20-24, 2008. Average attendance: 3,000. Conference focuses on "all literature, including film scripts." Site: 500-seat auditorium, various sizes of break-out rooms. Theme: "Southern Accents, Language in the Deep South." Scholars will speak on food and drink in history, literature, film and real life.

Costs "About $100, includes a meal, receptions, book signings, workshops. Lectures/panel discussions are free."

Accommodations "Groups can ask for special assistance. Usually they can be accommodated." Call 866-296-6522.

Additional Information "Participants need to read selected materials prior to attending writing workshops. Thus, pre-enrollment is advised." Conference information is available in Fall. For brochure send SASE, e-mail, visit Web site, call or fax. Accepts inquiries by SASE, e-mail, phone and fax. Agents and editors participate in conference.

OXFORD CONFERENCE FOR THE BOOK

Center for the Study of Southern Culture, The University of Mississippi, University MS 38677-1848. (662)915-5993. Fax: (662)915-5814. E-mail: aabadie@olemiss.edu. Web site: www.olemiss.edu/depts/south. **Contact:** Ann J. Abadie, associate director. Estab. 1993. Annual. Conference held in March or April. Average attendance: 300. "The conference celebrates books, writing and reading and deals with practical concerns on which the literary arts depend, including literacy, freedom of expression and the book trade itself. Each year's program consists of readings, lectures and discussions. Areas of focus are fiction, poetry, nonfiction and—occasionally—drama. We have, on occasion, looked at science fiction and mysteries. We always pay attention to children's literature." Site: University of Mississippi campus. Annual topics include Submitting Manuscripts/Working One's Way into Print; Finding a Voice/Reaching an Audience; The Endangered Species: Readers Today and Tomorrow. In 2007, among the more than 50 program participants were authors Laurie Halse Anderson, Rick Bass, Kevin Canty, Ellen Douglas, Andre Dubus III, Claude Edgerton, Thomas Sayers Ellis, Kimiko Hahn, Karen Hesse, Jill McCorkle, Jonathan Miles, and Steve Yarbrough. Also on the program were publisher Carlo Feltrinelli and editors Gary Fisketjon and Shannon Ravenel. The 2008 program, April 3-5, was dedicated to the author Zora Neale Hurston.

Costs "The conference is open to participants without charge."

Accommodations Provides list of area hotels.

Additional Information Brochures available in February by e-mail, on Web Site, by phone, by fax. Accepts inquiries by e-mail, phone, fax. Agents and editors participate in conference.

MARJORIE KINNAN RAWLINGS: WRITING THE REGION

P.O. Box 12246, Gainesville FL 32604. (888)917-7001. Fax: (352)373-8854. E-mail: SarahBewley@sarahbewley.com. Web site: www.writingtheregion.com. **Contact:**Sarah Bewley, Writers Programs Coordinator. Estab. 1997. Annual. July 23-27, 2008. Conference duration: 5 days. Average attendance: 120. Conference concentrates on fiction, writing for children, poetry, nonfiction, drama, screenwriting, writing with humor, setting, character, etc. Site: Conference held at historic building, formerly the Thomas Hotel.

Costs $395 for 5 days including meals; $375 "early bird" registration (breakfast and lunch); $145 single day; $95 half day.

Accommodations Special conference rates at area hotels available.

Additional Information Optional trip and dinner at Rawlings Home at Crosscreek offered. Evening activities and banquets also planned. Manuscript consultation on an individual basis by application only and $100 additional fee. Sponsors essay contest for registrants on a topic dealing with Marjorie Kinnan Rawlings. Call for brochures/guidelines. Accepts inquiries by fax, e-mail. Call toll free 888-917-7001.

◎ SCBWI SOUTHERN BREEZE FALL CONFERENCE

Writing and Illustrating for Kids '09, P.O. Box 26282, Birmingham AL 35260. E-mail: jskittinger@bell south.net. Web site: www.southern-breeze.org **Contact:** Jo Kittinger, co-regional advisor. Estab. 1992. Annual. Conference held the third Saturday in October. Average Attendance: 160. This conference is designed to educate and inspire creators of quality children's literature.

Costs About $125 for SCBWI members, $145 for non-members.

Accommodations: Nearby hotel offers a group rate to Southern Breeze conference attendees. The conference is held in a fabulous school.

Additional Information: This Southern Breeze conference offers an amazing lineup of 28 workshops on craft and the business of writing and illustrating. Tracks are included for the novice or professional. Speakers generally include editors, agents, authors, art directors, writers, and illustrators—all professionals in children's books. Come prepared to be WOWED! Manuscript and portfolio critiques available for an additional fee; manuscripts must be sent by deadline. Conference information is included in the Southern Breeze News, mailed in September. Visit Web site for details. Accepts inquiries by SASE or e-mail.

◎ SCBWI SOUTHERN BREEZE SPRINGMINGLE CONFERENCE

Springmingle '09, P.O. Box 26282, Birmingham AL 35260. E-mail: jskittinger@bellsouth.net. Web site: www.southern-breeze.org. **Contact:** Jo Kittinger, co-regional advisor. Estab. 1992. Annual. Conference held the last full weekend each February (Friday PM-Sunday AM). Average Attendance: 160. This is a seminar designed to educate and inspire creators of quality children's literature.

Site: Event is held in a hotel ballroom in the Atlanta, GA area. Speakers generally include editors, agents, authors, art directors—all professionals in children's books.

Costs: About $200; SCBWI non-members pay about $30 more. Some meals are included.

Accommodations: Individuals make their own reservations. Ask for the Southern Breeze group rate in the conference site's hotel.

Additional Information: Manuscript and portfolio critiques available for an additional fee. Mss must be sent ahead of time. Conference information is included in the Southern Breeze News, mailed in January. Visit Web site for details. Accepts inquiries by SASE, e-mail.

SOUTHEASTERN WRITERS ASSOCIATION

SWA, 161 Woodstone Dr., Athens GA 30605. E-mail: whyzz@bellsouth.net. Web site: www.southea sternwriters.com. **Contact:** Sheila Hudson, registrar. Estab. 1975. Annual. Conference held third week of June every year. Average attendance: 75 (limited to 100). Conference offers classes in fiction, nonfiction, juvenile, inspirational writing, poetry, etc. Site: Epworth-by-the-Sea, St. Simons Island, GA.

Costs 2007 costs: $359 early bird tuition, $399 after April 1, 2008 $125 daily tuition. Three days' tuition required for free manuscript conferences. Conference tuition includes $35 annual membership fee.

Accommodations Offers overnight accommodations. 2007 rates were approximately $650/single to $425/double and including motel-style room and 3 meals/day per person. Off site lodging also available.

Additional Information Sponsors numerous contests in several genres and up to 3 free ms evaluation conferences with instructors. Agents and editors participate in conference panels and/or private appointments. Complete information is available on the Web site in March of each year, including registration forms. E-mail or send SASE for brochure.

TENNESSEE WILLIAMS/NEW ORLEANS LITERARY FESTIVAL

938 Lafayette St., Suite 514, New Orleans LA 70113. (504)581-1144. E-mail: info@tennesseewilliams. net. Web site: www.tennesseewilliams.net. **Contact:** Paul J. Willis, executive director. Estab. 1987. Annual. Conference held in late March. Average attendance: "10,000 audience seats filled." Conferences focus on "all aspects of the literary arts including editing, publishing and the artistic process. Other humanities areas are also featured, including theater and music." Site: "The festival is based

at the Bourbon Orleans hotel and at historic Le Petit Theatre du Vieux Carré and other sites throughout the French Quarter.''

Costs ''Ticket prices range from $10 for a single event to $60 for a special event. Master classes are $35 per class. Theatre events are sold separately and range from $10-25.''

Accommodations ''Host hotel is Bourbon Orleans Hotel.''

Additional Information ''In conjunction with the University of New Orleans, we sponsor a one-act play competition. Entries are accepted from September 1 through December 15. There is a $25 fee, which must be submitted with the application form. There is a $1,000 cash prize and a staged reading at the festival, as well as a full production of the work at the following year's festival.'' Conference information is available in late January. For brochure send e-mail, visit Web site or call. Accepts inquiries by e-mail and phone. Agents and editors participate in conference.

WRITE IT OUT

P.O. Box 704, Sarasota FL 34230-0704. (941)359-3824. E-mail: rmillerwio@aol.com. Web site: www.writeitout.com. **Contact:** Ronni Miller, director. Estab. 1997. Workshops held 2-3 times/year in March, June, July and August. Conference duration: 5-10 days. Average attendance: 4-10. Workshops on ''fiction, poetry, memoirs. We also offer intimate, motivational, in-depth free private conferences with instructors.'' Site: Workshops in Italy in a Tuscan villa, in Sarasota at a hotel, and in Cape Cod at an inn. Theme: ''Feel It! Write It!'' Past speakers included Arturo Vivante, novelist.

Costs 2006 fees: Italy, $1,795; Cape Cod, $800. Price includes tuition, room and board in Italy. Cape Cod just tuition. Airfare not included.

Additional Information ''Critiques on work are given at the workshops.'' Conference information available year round. For brochures/guidelines e-mail, call or visit Web site. Accepts inquiries by phone, e-mail. Workshops have ''small groups, option to spend time writing and not attend classes, with personal appointments with instructors.''

Ⓝ WRITERS IN PARADISE

Eckerd College, 4200 54th Ave South, St. Petersburg FL 33711. (727)864-7994. Fax: (727)864-7575. E-mail: cayacr@eckerd.edu. Web site: www.writersinparadise.com. **Contact:** Christine Caya, conference coordinator. Estab. 2005. Annual. January 2009. Conference duration: 8 days. Average attendance: 84 max. Workshop. Offers college credit. ''Writers in Paradise Conference offer workshop classes in fiction (novel and short story), poetry and nonfiction. Working closely with our award-winning faculty, students will have stimulating opportunities to ask questions and learn valuable skills from fellow students and authors at the top of their form. Most importantly, the intimate size and secluded location of the Writers in Paradise experience allows you the time and opportunity to share your manuscripts, critique one another's work and discuss the craft of writing with experts and peers who can help guide you to the next level.'' Site: Located on 188 acres of waterfront property in St. Petersburg, Florida, Eckerd College is a private, coeducational college of liberal arts and sciences. In 2008, lectures were given on the craft of writing fiction by Ann Hood and Richard Price. Fiction faculty also led discussions during two mornings of informal roundtables. 2008 Faculty and Guest Faculty included: Lexy Bloom (Vintage/Anchor), Beth Ann Fennelly (*Unmentionables*), Marc Fitten (*The Chattahooche Review*), Lisa Gallagher (HarperCollins), Ann Hood (*The Knitting Circle*), Tom Franklin (*Smonk*), Dennis Lehane (*Gone, Baby, Gone* and *Mystic River*), Laura Lippman (*What the Dead Know*), Peter Meinke (*Unheard Music*), Roland Merullo (*Breakfast with Buddha*), Thisbe Nissen (*The Good People of New York*), Richard Price (*Clockers* and *Freedomland*), David Hale Smith (DHS Literary, Inc.), Les Standiford (*Last Train to Paradise*), and Sterling Watson (*Sweet Dream Baby*).

Costs 2008 tuition fee: $675.

Accommodations Does not offer overnight accommodations. Provides list of area hotels or lodging options.

Additional Information Application materials are required of all attendees. Acceptance is based on a writing sample and a letter detailing your writing background. Submit one short story (25 pages max) or the opening 25 pages of a novel-in-progress, plus a two-page synopsis of the book. Deadline for application materials is December 3rd. ''Writers in Paradise is a conference for writers of various styles and approaches. While admission is selective, the admissions committee accepts writers with early potential as well as those with strong backgrounds in writing.'' Sponsors contest. ''At the final Evening Reading Series Event, Co-directors Dennis Lehane and Sterling Watson will announce 'The

Best of' nominees of the Writers in Paradise Conference. Winners will be published in *Sabal—A Review Featuring the Best Writing of the Writers in Paradise Conference at Eckerd College*. One winner and one honorable mention will be selected from each workshop based on the material brought into the workshop for discussion. Selection will be made by the faculty member leading the workshop. There are no additional fees or entry forms needed.'' Information available in October 2008. For brochure, send SASE, call, e-mail. Agents participate in conference. Editors participate in conference. ''The tranquil seaside landscape sets the tone for this informal gathering of writers, teachers, editors and literary agents. After 8 days of workshopping and engagement with peers and professionals in your field, you will leave this unique opportunity with solid ideas about how to find an agent and get published, along with a new and better understanding of your craft.''

◎ WRITING STRATEGIES FOR THE CHRISTIAN MARKET
2712 S. Peninsula Dr., Daytona Beach FL 32118-5706. (386)322-1111. Fax: (386)322-1111. E-mail: rupton@cfl.rr.com. Web site: www.ruptonbooks.com. **Contact:** Rosemary Upton. Estab. 1991. Independent studies with manual. Includes Basics I, Marketing II, Business III, Building the Novel. Critique by mail with SASE. Question and answer session via e-mail or U.S. mail. Critique shop included once a month, except summer (July and August). Instructor: Rosemary Upton, novelist.
Costs $30 for manual and ongoing support.
Additional Information ''Designed for correspondence students as well as the classroom experience, the courses are economical and include all materials, as well as the evaluation assignments.'' Those who have taken Writing Strategies instruction are able to attend an on-going monthly critiqueshop where their peers critique their work. Manual provided. For brochures/guidelines send SASE, e-mail, fax or call. Accepts inquiries by fax, e-mail. Independent study by mail only offered at this time.

MIDWEST (IL, IN, KY, MI, OH)

ANTIOCH WRITERS' WORKSHOP
P.O. Box 494, Yellow Springs OH 45387. (937)475-7357. E-mail: info@antiochwritersworkshop.com. Web site: www.antiochwritersworkshop.com. **Contact:** Laura Carlson, director. Estab. 1986. Annual. Conference held July 12-18, 2008. Conference duration: 1 week. Average attendance: 80. Workshop concentration: poetry, nonfiction, fiction, personal essay, memoir, mystery. Site: Workshop located in the idyllic Glen Helen Nature Preserve and in locations around the charming village of Yellow Springs. Past faculty have included Sue Grafton, Natalie Goldberg, Sena Jeter Naslund, Ann Hagedorn, Katrina Kittle, Silas House, and Ralph Keyes.
Costs Tuition is $735 (regular) or $675 (alumni and local participants), which includes a nonrefundable $125 registration fee.
Accommodations Accomodations are available in local homes through the village host program ($150 for the week) or at area hotels and B&Bs.
Additional Information Intensive sessions for beginning and experienced writers, small group lunches with faculty, agent pitch sessions, optional ms critiques.

COLUMBUS WRITERS CONFERENCE
P.O. Box 20548, Columbus OH 43220. (614)451-3075. Fax: (614)451-0174. E-mail: AngelaPL28@aol.com. Web site: www.creativevista.com. **Contact:** Angela Palazzolo, director. Estab. 1993. Annual. Conference held in August. Average attendance: 250+. ''In addition to agent and editor consultations, the conference covers a wide variety of fiction and nonfiction topics presented by writers, editors and literary agents. Writing topics have included novel, short story, children's, young adult, poetry, historical fiction, science fiction, fantasy, humor, mystery, playwriting, working with an agent, working with an editor, screenwriting, magazine writing, travel, humor, cookbook, technical, queries, book proposals, and freelance writing.'' The Conference has included many writers and editors, including Chuck Adams, Tracy Bernstein, Sheree Bykofsky, Oscar Collier, Lisa Cron, Jennifer DeChiara, Tracey E. Dils, Hallie Ephron, Karen Harper, Scott Hoffman, Jeff Kleinman, Simon Lipskar, Noah Lukeman, Donald Maass, Lee Martin, Erin McGraw, Kim Meisner, Doris S. Michaels, Rita Rosenkrantz, and Nancy Zafris.
Costs To be announced.

Additional Information To receive a brochure, contact the conference by e-mail, phone, or postal mail, or visit www.creativevista.com.

◎ FESTIVAL OF FAITH AND WRITING

Calvin College/Department of English, 1795 Knollcrest Circle SE, Grand Rapids MI 49546. (616)526-6770. E-mail: ffw@calvin.edu. Web site: www.calvin.edu/festival. **Contact:** English Dept. Estab. 1990. Biennial. Conference usually held in April of even years. Conference duration: 3 days. Average attendance: 1,800. The Festival of Faith and Writing encourages serious, imaginative writing by all writers interested in the intersections of literature and belief. Site: The festival is held at Calvin College in Grand Rapids, MI, 180 miles north of Chicago. Focus is on fiction, nonfiction, memoir, poetry, drama, children's, young adult, literary criticism, film and song lyrics. Past speakers have included Annie Dillard, John Updike, Katherine Paterson, Elie Wiesel, Joyce Carol Oates, Leif Enger, Salman Rushdie, and Marilynne Robinson.

Costs Registration: consult Web site. Registration includes all sessions during the 3-day event but does not include meals, lodging or evening concerts.

Accommodations Shuttles are available to and from select local hotels. Consult festival Web site for a list of hotels with special conference rates.

Additional Information Some agents and editors attend the festival and consult with prospective writers.

GREEN RIVER NOVELS-IN-PROGRESS WORKSHOP

2011 Lauderdale Rd., Louisville KY 40205. (502)417-5514. E-mail: nipw@greenriverwriters.org. Web site: www.nipw.org. **Contact:** Jeff Yocom, workshop director. Estab. 1991. Annual. Conference usually held in March. Conference duration: 1 week. Average attendance: 50. Conference covers fiction writing in various genres. Site: Held on the urban campus of Spalding University; small dormitories and class rooms/meeting rooms. Features faculty-led breakout sessions on subjects such as character development, plot, contacting agents, etc. Includes individual mentoring and opportunities to pitch to editors and agents.

Costs $479 with personal instruction option, $329 without.

Accommodations $20 per night for private dorm room.

Additional Information See Web site for updates on conference information.

INDIANA UNIVERSITY WRITERS' CONFERENCE

464 Ballantine Hall, Bloomington IN 47405-7103. (812)855-1877. Fax: (812)855-9535. E-mail: writecon@indiana.edu. Web site: www.indiana.edu/~writecon. **Contact:** Amy Locklin, director. Estab. 1940. Annual. Conference/workshops held in June. Average attendance: 115. "The Indiana University Writers' Conference believes in a craft-based teaching of writing. We emphasize an exploration of creativity through a variety of approaches, offering workshop-based craft discussions, classes focusing on technique, and talks about the careers and concerns of a writing life." Site: Located on the campus of Indiana University, Bloomington. Participants in the week-long conference join faculty-led workshops in fiction, poetry and creative nonfiction; take classes on various aspects of writing; engage in one-on-one consultation with faculty members; and attend a variety of readings and social events. Previous faculty include: Raymond Carver, Gwendolyn Brooks, Andre Dubus, Kurt Vonnegut Jr., Mark Doty, Robert Olen Butler, Aimee Bender, Jean Thompson, Brenda Hillman, Li-Young Lee and Brigit Pegeen Kelly.

Costs Approximately $300 for all classes and $500 for all classes and a workshop; does not include food or housing. Scholarships and college credit options are available.

Additional Information "In order to be accepted in a workshop, the writer must submit the work they would like critiqued. Work is evaluated before accepting applicant. Scholarship awards are based on the quality of the manuscript and are determined by an outside judge." For brochures/guidelines send SASE, visit our Web site, e-mail or call. Deadline for scholarship application is April 15. Apply early, as workshops fill up quickly.

KENTUCKY WRITER'S WORKSHOP

Pine Mountain State Resort Park, 1050 State Park Rd., Pineville KY 40977. (606)337-3066. Fax: (606)337-7250. E-mail: dean.henson@ky.gov. Web site: http://parks.ky.gov. **Contact:** Dean Henson, event coordinator. Estab. 1995. Annual. Workshop held each March. Average attendance: 50-

65. "Focuses on writing in various genres, including fiction, mystery, poetry, novels, short stories, essays, etc." Site: Pine Mountain State Resort Park (a Kentucky State Park).

Costs Registration fee is $30 for non-package participants.

Accommodations Special all-inclusive event packages are available. Call for information.

Additional Information Brochures available 2 months in advance by e-mail or phone. Accepts inquiries by SASE, e-mail, phone, fax. "Our conference features successful and celebrated Kentucky authors speaking and instructing on various topics of the writing endeavor. This workshop is designed to help developing authors improve their writing craft."

KENYON REVIEW WRITERS WORKSHOP

The Kenyon Review, Kenyon College, Gambier OH 43022. (740)427-5207. Fax: (740)427-5417. E-mail: writers@kenyonreview.org. Web site: www.kenyonreview.org. **Contact:** Anna Duke Reach, director. Estab. 1990. Annual. Workshop held mid to late June. Conference duration: 8 days. Average attendance: 60-70. Participants apply in poetry, fiction or literary nonfiction, and then participate in intensive daily workshops which focus on the generation and revision of significant new work. Site: The conference takes place on the campus of Kenyon College in the rural village of Gambier, Ohio. Students have access to college computing and recreational facilities and are housed in campus housing. Workshop leaders have included David Baker, Ron Carlson, Rebecca McClanahan, Meghan O'Rourke, Rosanna Warren, and Nancy Zafris.

Costs $ 1,995 including room and board.

Accommodations The workshop operates a shuttle to and from Gambier and the airport in Columbus, Ohio. Offers overnight accommodations. Participants are housed in Kenyon College student housing. The cost is covered in the tuition.

Additional Information Application includes a writing sample. Admission decisions are made on a rolling basis. Workshop information is available November 1. For brochure send e-mail, visit Web site, call, fax. Accepts inquiries by SASE, e-mail, phone, fax.

LAMB'S SPRINGFED WRITING RETREAT

(formally Walloon Writer's Retreat), P.O. Box 304, Royal Oak MI 48068-0304. (248)589-3913. Fax: (248)589-9981. E-mail: johndlamb@ameritech.net. Web site: www.springfed.org. **Contact:** John D. Lamb, director. Estab. 1999. Annual. Last conference held September 27-30, 2007. Next conference is October 9-12, 2008. Average attendance: 75. Focus includes fiction, poetry, screenwriting and nonfiction. Site: The Birchwood Inn, Harbor Spring, MI. Attendees stay in comfortable rooms, and seminars are held in conference rooms with fieldstone fireplaces and dining area. Past faculty included Billy Collins, Michael Moore, Jonathan Rand, Jacquelyn Mitchard, Jane Hamilton, Thomas Lux, Joyce Maynard, Craig Holden, Chuch Pfarrer and Ivan Raimi.

Costs Single occupancy is $600, $535 (3 days, 2 nights, all meals included). $360 non-lodging.

Accommodations Shuttle rides from Traverse City Airport or Pellston Airport. Offers overnight accommodations. Provides list of area lodging options.

Additional Information Optional: Attendees may submit 3 poems or 5 pages of prose for conference with a staff member. Brochures available mid-June by e-mail, on Web site or by phone. Accepts inquiries by SASE, e-mail, phone.

MID-MISSISSIPPI WRITERS CONFERENCE

John Wood Community College, 1301 S. 48th St., Quincy IL 62305. (217)641-4903. Fax: (217)641-4900. E-mail: ssparks@jwcc.edu. **Contact:** Sherry Sparks. Estab. 2001. Conference in April. Conference duration: 1 weekend. Average attendance: 30-50. Workshop/conference covers all areas of writing, for beginners and more advanced. "We encourage and invite beginning-level writers." Site: John Wood Community College.

Costs $35-$50; some meals included.

Accommodations List of area hotels available.

Additional Information Sponsors contest. Brochures/registration forms available in February; send SASE, visit Web site, e-mail, fax or call. "Come ready to make new friends, see a beautiful city and be inspired to write!"

MIDWEST WRITERS WORKSHOP

Dept. of Journalism, Ball State University, Muncie IN 47306. (765)282-1055. Fax: (765)285-5997. E-mail: info@midwestwriters.org. Web site: www.midwestwriters.org. **Contact:** Jama Bigger. Estab.

1974. Annual. Workshops to be in July. Average attendance: 150. Site: Conference held at New Alumni Center, Ball State University.

Costs $275 for 3-day workshop; $90 for 1-day Intensive Session including opening reception, hospitality room and closing banquet.

Accommodations Special hotel rates offered.

Additional Information Manuscript evaluation for extra fee. Conference brochures/guidelines are available for SASE.

ON THE WRITE PATH

Seventh Annual Writers' Conference, Elgin Community College, 1700 Spartan Drive, Elgin IL 60123. (847)622-3036. Fax: (847)214-7815. E-mail: dnewberg@elgin.edu. Web site: www.elgin.edu. **Contact:** Donna Newberg. Estab. 1997. Annual. Conference usually held in March. Conference duration: 1 day. Average attendance: 60-80. Event focus changes every year. 2004 conference focused on publishing. Site: Held at Elgin Community College; keynote speaker presents in auditorium, smaller sessions held in breakout rooms, lunch buffet. 2004 topics included How Characters Converse and Planning the Storyline. Speakers for 2004 were Judy Snyder, Pat DiPrima, Rick Holinger and Dianne Helm.

Costs $109 includes full cost, including lunch.

Additional Information Participants need to register with social security number, name, address, birth date and year, and pay in advance. Brochure with registration form available in January by phone, e-mail and on Web site. Accepts inquiries by SASE, e-mail, phone and fax. Agents and editors attend conference.

OPEN WRITING WORKSHOPS

Creative Writing Program, Department of English, Bowling Green State University, Bowling Green OH 43403. (419)372-8370. Fax: (419)372-6805. E-mail: mnagel@bgnet.bgsu.edu. Web site: www.bgsu.edu/departments/creative-writing/. "Check our Web site for next workshop dates." Conference duration: 1 day. Average attendance: 10-15. Workshop covers fiction and poetry. Site: Workshops are held in a conference room, roundtable setting, on the campus of Bowling Green State University. Provides close reading and ms critique. 2005 faculty included fiction writer Wendell Mayo and poet/editor Karen Craigo.

Costs $50 for workshop; does not include lodging or other services; $35 for alums and students.

Accommodations Parking provided on campus.

Additional Information Participants need to submit workshop material prior to conference. Fiction or nonfiction: 1 story, 15 pages double-spaced maximum; send 2 copies. Poetry: 3 poems, a total of 100 lines for all 3; send 2 copies. "Deadlines are set about 3 weeks before the workshop. This gives us time to copy all the manuscripts and mail to all participants with detailed instructions." For brochure or inquiries, e-mail, visit Web site, call or fax. "These are no-nonsense workshops whose purpose is to 'open' doors for writers who are writing in comparative isolation. We provide guidance on preparation of manuscripts for publication as well."

Ⓝ THE RAGDALE FOUNDATION

1260 North Green Bay Road, Lake Forest IL 60045. (847)234-1036 ext. 206. Fax: (847)234-1063. E-mail: admissions@ragdale.org. Web site: www.ragdale.org. **Contact:** Director of the Artist-In-Residence Program. Estab. 1976. Conference duration: Residencies are 2-8 weeks in length, year-round. Average attendance: 12 artists, writers and composers at one time; nearly 200 residents per year. "Emerging and established artists, writers and composers from all over the world apply for residencies, in order to be awarded time and space to focus on their work and escape day-to-day distractions." Site: Ragdale is located 30 miles north of Chicago. Arts and crafts architect Howard Van Doren Shaw designed two of the main residency buildings. Twelve people are in residence at any given time. It is an historical, home-like setting adjacent to 55 acres of preserved prairie. Dinners are prepared and communal 6 nights a week.

Costs The application fee is $30. The residency fee is just $25/day even though the actual cost to Ragdale is $240/day. The fee includes food and a private room in which to work.

Additional Information "Interested people must submit materials according to application guidelines. Applications may be attained from the Web site, by e-mail or phone request. For brochure, send

SASE, call, e-mail, visit Web site. "The small group atmosphere is conducive to productivity, inspiration, interaction (if desired) and creative exploration."

READERS AND WRITERS HOLIDAY CONFERENCE

Central Ohio Fiction Writers (COFW), P.O. Box 1981, Westerville OH 43086-1981. E-mail: wadkins4 @woh.rr.com. Web site: www.cofw.org. **Contact:** Sheri Adkins, president. Estab. 1990. Annual. Conference held in Columbus, OH. 2007 Conference dates September 28-29. Average attendance: 120. COFW is a chapter of Romance Writers of America. The conference focuses on all romance subgenres and welcomes published writers, pre-published writers and readers. Conference theme: celebrates and fosters writers at every stage of their careers. Best-selling authors provide motivation and instruction; workshops, speakers, and materials cover a broad spectrum of topics. Two agents and two editors will speak and take short appointments. Appointments to early registrants who have completed at least one manuscript.

Costs Price will include Saturday lunch.

Accommodations See www.cofw.org for exact location. There will be a special conference rate for hotel rooms.

Additional Information Registration form and information available on Web site or by e-mail.

SPACE (SMALL PRESS AND ALTERNATIVE COMICS EXPO)

Back Porch Comics, P.O. Box 20550, Columbus OH 43220.E-mail: bpc13@earthlink.net. Web site: www.backporchcomics.com/space.htm. **Contact:** Bob Corby. Next conference/trade show to be held in the spring (see Web site for exact date). Conference duration: 2 days. "The Midwest's largest exhibition of small press, alternative and creator-owned comics." Site: 2007 held at the Aladdin Shrine Complex multipurpose room in Columbus, Ohio. 2007 special guests were Dave Sim and Gerhard.

Additional Information For 2009 brochure, visit Web site. Editors participate in conference.

TOUCH OF SUCCESS WRITER'S CONFERENCE

P.O. Box 59, Glendale KY 42740. (270)769-1823. Web site: www.touchofsuccess.com. **Contact:** Bill Thomas, author/director. Estab. 1978. Annual. Conference held from March to November. Conference duration: 2 days. Workshop focuses on journalism, nonfiction, fiction. Site: Oakbrook Farm Center for the Arts, 3 miles from historic railroad village of Glendale on family pioneer farm amidst Amish country. Workshops led by Bill Thomas, who has published hundreds of magazine articles, some poetry, and more than 25 books.

Costs $395, includes lunches (we have our own chef) and some local transportation including pickup and delivery from Louisville Regional Airport.

Additional Information Brochures available after January 1, 2007, by SASE or on Web site. Accepts inquiries by SASE and phone. "Submit letter of application giving background, purpose and goals for attending this event."

WESTERN RESERVE WRITERS & FREELANCE CONFERENCE

Lakeland Community College, 7700 Clocktower Dr., Kirtland OH 44094. (440)525-7000. Web site: www.deannaadams.com. E-mail: deencr@aol.com. **Contact:** Deanna Adams, co-coordinator. Estab. 1983. Biannual. Last conference held September 17, 2008. Conference duration: One day. Average attendance: 120. "The Western Reserve Writers Conferences are designed for all writers, aspiring and professional, and offer presentations in all genres-nonfiction, fiction, poetry, essays, creative nonfiction and the business of writing, including Web sites and successful freelance writing." Site: Located in the main building of Lakeland Community College, the conference is easy to find and just off the I-90 freeway. The Fall 2008 conference featured top notch presenters from newspapers such as the Cleveland Plain Dealer, magazines such as Ohio Magazine, along with successful authors and freelance writers. Presentations included how to draft a standout book proposal, creating credible characters, contracts/copyrights, public speaking, tips on completing your novel, and when and how to get an agent. Included throughout the day are editing consults, Q & A Panel, and book sale/ author signings.

Costs Fall conference, includes lunch: $95. Spring conference, no lunch: $69.

Additional Information Brochures for the conferences are available by February (for spring conference) and July (for fall). Also accepts inquiries by e-mail and phone, or see Web site. Editors and agents often attend the conferences.

⊚ WRITE-TO-PUBLISH CONFERENCE

9118 W Elmwood Dr., Suite 1G, Niles IL 60714-5820. (847)296-3964. Fax: (847)296-0754. E-mail: lin@writetopublish.com. Web site: www.writetopublish.com. **Contact:** Lin Johnson, director. Estab. 1971. Annual. Conference held June 4-7, 2008. Average attendance: 275. Conference on "writing all types of manuscripts for the Christian market." Site: Wheaton College, Wheaton, IL (Chicago).
Costs $425.
Accommodations In campus residence halls or discounted hotel rates. Cost $225-310.
Additional Information Optional ms evaluation available. College credit available. Conference information available in January. For brochures/guidelines, visit Web site, or e-mail: brochure@writetop ublish.com. Accepts inquiries by e-mail, fax, phone.

WRITERS ONLINE WORKSHOPS

F + W Publications, Inc., 4700 E. Galbraith Rd., Cincinnati OH 45236. (800)759-0963. Fax: (513)531-0798. E-mail: wdwowadmin@fwpubs.com. Web site: www.writersonlineworkshops.com. **Contact:** Joe Stollenwerk, educational services manager. Estab. 2000. Online workshop; ongoing. Conference duration: From 4-28 weeks. Average attendance: 10-15 per class. "We have workshops in fiction, nonfiction, memoir, poetry, proposal writing and more." Site: Internet-based, operated entirely on the Web site. Current fiction-related courses include Fundamentals of Fiction, Focus on the Novel, Focus on the Short Story, Advanced Novel Writing, Advanced Story Writing, Creating Dynamic Characters, Writing Effective Dialogue, Writing the Novel Proposal, Essentials of Mystery Writing, Essentials of Science Fiction & Fantasy Writing, Essentials of Romance Writing, Essentials of Writing to Inspire, Voice and Viewpoint, and Marketing Short Stories. New in 2008-2009: First Draft in 35 Days, What's My Genre?, and others.
Costs $119-579.
Additional Information Additional information always available on Web site. Accepts inquiries by e-mail and phone.

NORTH CENTRAL (IA, MN, NE, ND, SD, WI)

GREAT LAKES WRITERS FESTIVAL

Lakeland College, P.O. Box 359, Sheboygan WI 53082-0359. (920)565-1276. Fax: (920)565-1260. E-mail: elderk@lakeland.edu. Web site: www.greatlakeswritersfestival.org. **Contact:** Karl Elder, coordinator. Estab. 1991. Annual. Last conference held Nov. 1-2, 2007. Conference duration: 2 days. "Festival celebrates the writing of poetry, fiction and creative nonfiction." Site: Lakeland College is a small, 4-yr. liberal arts college of 235 acres, a beautiful campus in a rural setting, founded in 1862. No themes or panels, just readings and workshops. 2007 faculty included Philip Dacey and Margaret Dawe.
Costs Free and open to the public. Participants may purchase meals and must arrange for their own lodging.
Accommodations Does not offer overnight accommodations. Provides list of area hotels or lodging options.
Additional Information All participants who would like to have their writing considered as an object for discussion during the festival workshops must submit it to Karl Elder electronically by Oct. 15. Participants may submit material for workshops in one genre only (poetry, fiction or creative nonfiction). Sponsors contest. Contest entries must contain the writer's name and address on a separate title page, be in type, and be submitted as clear, hard copy on Friday at the festival registration table. Entries may be in each of three genres per participant, yet only one poem, one story, and/ or one nonfiction piece may be entered. There are two categories—high school students on one hand, all others on the other—of cash awards for first place in each of the three genres. The judges reserve the right to decline to award a prize in one or more of the genres. Judges will be the editorial staff of *Seems* (a.k.a. *Word of Mouth*), excluding the festival coordinator, Karl Elder. Information available in September. For brochure, visit Web site. Editors

GREEN LAKE CHRISTIAN WRITERS CONFERENCE

Green Lake Conference Center, W2511 State Road 23, Green Lake WI 54941. (920)294-3323. E-mail: janwhite@glcc.org. Web site: www.glcc.org. **Contact:** Jan White. "Come learn, write and celebrate with us!" Sunday afternoon-Friday morning, August 17-22, 2008, our 60th annual conference. In 2009: Sunday-Friday, August 23-28. Attendees may be well-published or beginners, may write for secular and/or Christian markets. Leaders are experienced writing teachers. Spend 11½ contact hours in the workshop of your choice: fiction, nonfiction, poetry, inspirational/devotional. Also take in as many seminars as you wish to enhance specific skills: marketing, humor, songwriting, writing for children, self-publishing, writing for churches, interviewing, memoir writing, the magazine market. Evening: panels of experts will answer your questions. Social and leisure activities. **Location:** GLCC is in south central WI, has 1,000 acres, 2 ½ mi of shoreline on WI's deepest lake, and offers a beautiful resort setting.
Accomodations Hotels, lodges and all meeting rooms are a/c. Affordable rates, excellent meals.
Additional Information Party & writers' showcase. Brochure and scholarship info from Web site or contact Jan White (920-294-7327). Call to register.

INTERNATIONAL MUSIC CAMP CREATIVE WRITING WORKSHOP

1930 23rd Ave. SE, Minot ND 58701. Phone/fax: (701)838-8472. E-mail: info@internationalmusiccamp.com. Web site: www.internationalmusiccamp.com. **Contact:** Dr. Timothy Wollenzien, camp director. Estab. 1956. Annual. Last conference held June 24-30, 2007. Average attendance: 35. "The workshop offers students the opportunity to refine their skills in thinking, composing and writing in an environment that is conducive to positive reinforcement. In addition to writing poems, essays and stories, individuals are encouraged to work on their own area of interest with conferencing and feedback from the course instructor." Site: International Peace Garden on the border between the US and Canada. "Similar to a university campus, several dormitories, classrooms, lecture halls and cafeteria provide the perfect site for such a workshop. The beautiful and picturesque International Peace Garden provides additional inspiration to creative thinking." 2006 instructor was Colin Kapelovitz, Dickinson State University, ND.
Costs $320, includes tuition, room and board. Early bird registration (postmarked by May 15) $295.
Accommodations Airline and depot shuttles are available upon request. Housing is included in the $295 fee.
Additional Information Conference information is available in September. For brochure visit Web site, e-mail, call or fax. Accepts inquiries by e-mail, phone and fax. Agents and editors participate in conference.

IOWA SUMMER WRITING FESTIVAL

C215 Seashore Hall, University of Iowa, Iowa City IA 52242-1802. (319)335-4160. E-mail: iswfestival @uiowa.edu. Web site: www.uiowa.edu/~iswfest. **Contact:** Amy Margolis, director. Estab. 1987. Annual. Festival held in June and July. Workshops are one week or a weekend. Average attendance: limited to 12/class—over 1,500 participants throughout the summer. "We offer workshops across the genres, including novel, short story, poetry, essay, memoir, humor, travel, playwriting, screenwriting, writing for children and more. All writers 21 and over are welcome. You need only have the desire to write." Site: University of Iowa campus. Guest speakers are undetermined at this time. Readers and instructors have included Lee K. Abbott, Marvin Bell, Lan Samantha Chang, Janet Desaulniers, Hope Edelman, Bret Anthony Johnston, and many more.
Costs $500-525 for full week; $250 for weekend workshop. Discounts available for early registration. Housing and meals are separate.
Accommodations Iowa House, $70/night; Sheraton, $88/night, Heartland Inn, $62/night (rates subject to change).
Additional Information Conference information available in February. Accepts inquiries by fax, e-mail, phone. "Register early. Classes fill quickly."

WISCONSIN REGIONAL WRITERS' ASSOCIATION CONFERENCES

N 4549 Cty Rd Y, Montello WI 53949. (608)297-9746. E-mail: registration@wrwa.net. Web site: www.wrwa.net. **Contact:** Nate Scholze, Fall Conference Chair; Roxanne Aehl, Spring Conference Chair. Estab. 1948. Annual. Conferences held in May and September "are dedicated to self-improvement through speakers, workshops and presentations. Topics and speakers vary with each event."

Average attendance: 100-150. "We honor all genres of writing. Fall conference is a two-day event featuring the Jade Ring Banquet and awards for six genre categories. Spring conference is a one-day event."

Costs $40-75.

Accommodations Provides a list of area hotels or lodging options. "We negotiate special rates at each facility. A block of rooms is set aside for a specific time period."

Additional Information Award winners receive a certificate and a cash prize. First place winners of the Jade Ring contest receive a jade ring. Must be a member to enter contests. For brochure, call, e-mail or visit Web site in March/July.

WRITERS INSTITUTE

610 Langdon St., Room 621, Madison WI 53703. (608)262-3447. Fax: (608)265-2475. Web site: www.dcs.wisc.edu/lsa/writing. **Contact:** Christine DeSmet. Estab. 1989. Annual. Conference usually held in April. Site: Pyle Center. Average attendance: 200.

Costs $215 includes materials, breaks.

Accommodations Provides a list of area hotels or lodging options.

Additional Information Sponsors contest. Submit 1-page writing sample and $10 entry fee. Conference speakers are judges. For brochure send e-mail, visit Web site, call, fax. Accepts inquiries by SASE, e-mail, phone, fax. Agents and editors participate in conference.

WRITING WORKSHOP

P.O. Box 65, Ellison Bay WI 54210. (920)854-4088. E-mail: clearing@theclearing.org. Web site: www.theclearing.org. **Contact:** Kathy Vanderhoof, registrar. Estab. 1935. Annual. Average attendance: 16. "General writing, journal, poetry as well as fiction and nonfiction." Held in a "quiet, residential setting in deep woods on the shore of Green Bay."

Costs $820 for double (2005); includes lodging, meals, tuition.

Accommodations "Two to a room with private bath in rustic log and stone buildings with meals served family-style."

SOUTH CENTRAL (CO, KS, MO, NM, OK, TX)

AGENTS & EDITORS CONFERENCE

Writers' League of Texas, 611 S. Congress Ave, Suite 130, Austin TX 78704. (512)499-8914. Fax: (512)499-0441. E-mail: wlt@writersleague.org. Web site: www.writersleague.org. **Contact:** Kristy Bordine, Program and Membership Coordinator. Estab. 1982. Conference held in June. Conference duration: Friday-Sunday. Average attendance: 300. "Each Summer the League holds its annual Agents & Editors Conference, which provides writers with the opportunity to meet top literary agents and editors from New York and the West Coast." Open to writers of both fiction and nonfiction. Topics include: Finding and working with agents and publishers; writing and marketing fiction and nonfiction; dialogue; characterization; voice; research; basic and advanced fiction writing/focus on the novel; business of writing; also workshops for genres. Agents/speakers have included Malaika Adero, Stacey Barney, Sha-Shana Crichton, Jessica Faust, Dena Fischer, Mickey Freiberg, Jill Grosjean, Anne Hawkins, Jim Hornfischer, Jennifer Joel, David Hale Smith and Elisabeth Weed. Agents and editors will be speaking and available for meetings with attendees.

Costs $295-345. Contests and awards programs are offered separately.

Additional Information Brochures/guidelines are available on request.

ANNUAL RETREATS, WORKSHOPS AND CLASSES

611 S. Congress Ave., Suite 130, Austin TX 78704. (512)499-8914. Fax: (512)499-0441. E-mail: wlt@writersleague.org. Web site: www.writersleague.org. **Contact:** Kristy Bordine, Program and Membership Coordinator. "Classes and workshops provide practical advice and guidance on various aspects of fiction, creative nonfiction and screenwriting." Site: Writers' League of Texas resource center or as indicated on Web site. Some classes are by e-mail. "Topics for workshops and classes have included E-publishing; Creative Nonfiction; Screenwriting Basics; Novel in Progress; Basics of Short Fiction; Technique; Writing Scenes; Journaling; Manuscript Feedback; Essays; Newspaper Columns." Instructors include Suzy Spencer, Barbara Burnett Smith, Scott Wiggerman, Diane Fanning,

Marion Winik, Emily Vander Veer, Annie Reid, Bonnie Orr, Jan Epton Seale, Susan Wade, Lila Guzman, Laurie Lynn Drummond, David Wilkinson, John Pipkin, Ann McCutchan and Dao Strom. **Costs** $45-$250.
Additional Information Available at www.writersleague.org.

ASPEN SUMMER WORDS WRITING RETREAT & LITERARY FESTIVAL

110 E. Hallam St., #116, Aspen CO 81611. (970)925-3122. Fax: (970)925-5700. E-mail: info@aspenwr iters.org. Web site: www.aspenwriters.org. **Contact:** Natalie Lacy, programs manager. Estab. 1976. Annual. 2008 conference held June 22-27. Conference duration: 6 days. Average attendance: writing retreat, 150; literary festival, 300+, 1,800 visitors. Retreat includes intensive workshops in fiction (beginning through advanced), creative nonfiction, poetry, writing for young readers, young writers' workshop, magazine writing and food writing, plus a "Readers' Retreat" which in 2008 focused on Indian Literature. Literary festival features approximately 18 events (craft talks, author readings, and interviews; publishing panel discussions; agent/editor meeting; and social gatherings) for readers and writers. Festival theme for 2008 was "Passage to India". Retreat faculty for 2008: Richard Bausch (Fiction); Jan Greenberg (Writing for Young Readers); William Loizeaux (Narrative Nonfiction); Sue Miller (Advanced Fiction); Pamela Painter (Fiction); Robert Pinsky (Poetry); Nic Pizzolatto (Beginning Ficiton); Douglas Bauer (Magazine Writing and Food Writing); Cerena Thomsen (Young Writers Workshop). Festival presenters for 2007: Ngugi Wa Thiong'o, Chimamanda Adiche, Wole Soyinka, Henry Louis Gates Jr., and Alaa Al Aswany.
Costs $475/retreat; $250/2 day symposia; $175/2-day reader's retreat. Tuition includes daily continental breakfast and lunch, plus one evening reception. $200 festival pass; retreat students receive a $50 discount when they sign up for the literary festival. Festival registration includes two wine and hors d'oeuvres receptions. $35/private meetings with agents and editors.
Accommodations Discount lodging at the conference site will be available. 2008 rates to be announced. 2006 room rates were $125/single room in a shared 2-bedroom condo or $165/1-bedroom condo. Free shuttle around town.
Additional Information Application deadline: April 1. Mss must be submitted by May 25th for review by faculty, for most workshops. 10-page limit for workshop application mss. A limited number of partial-tuition scholarships are available. Deadline for agent/editor meeting registration is May 25th. Brochures available for SASE, by e-mail and phone request, and on Web site.

EAST TEXAS CHRISTIAN WRITER'S CONFERENCE

East Texas Baptist University, School of Humanities, 1209 N. Grove, Marshall TX 75670. (903)923-2269. E-mail: jhopkins@etbu.edu or jcornish@etbu.edu. Web site: www.etbu.edu/News/cwc. **Contact:** Joy Cornish. Estab. 2002. Annual. Conference held first Friday and Saturday of June each year. Conference duration: 2 days (Friday & Saturday). Average attendance: 160. "Primarily we are interested in promoting quality Christian writing that would be accepted in mainstream publishing." Site: We use the classrooms, cafeterias, etc. of East Texas Baptist University. Past conference themes were Back to Basics, Getting Started in Fiction, Writers & Agents, Writing Short Stories, Writing for Newspapers, The Significance of Style, Writing Fillers and Articles, Writing Devotionals, Blogging for Writers, Christian Non-Fiction, Inspirational Writing, E-Publishing, Publishing on Demand, and Editor and Author Relations. Past conference speakers/workshop leaders were David Jenkins, Bill Keith, Pete Litterski, Joe Early, Jr., Mary Lou Redding, Marie Chapian, Denny Boultinghouse, Vickie Phelps, Michael Farris, Susan Farris, Pamela Dowd, Donna Walker-Nixon, Lexie Smith, Janet Crews, Kay Coulter, John Krueger, Jim Pence, Andrea Chevalier, Marie Bagnull, and Leonard Goss.
Costs $60 for individual; $40 students. Price includes meal.
Additional Information "We have expanded to include publishers, small presses, publish-on-demand opportunities, e-publishing and agents. A bookstore is provided with a variety of materials for writers."

EMINENCE AREA ARTS COUNCIL SHORT STORY WORKSHOP

P.O. Box 551, Eminence MO 65466-0551. (573)226-5655. E-mail: hilma@socket.net. **Contact:** Hilma Hughes, administrator. Estab. 1989. Annual. Last workshop held May 24-26, 2007. Conference duration: 3 days. Average attendance: 12. "The Short Story Workshop focuses on fiction of any genre." Workshop centers on the process of writing; participants leave with a finished short story. Site: Museum and Art Gallery conference room. We have large tables with chairs for participants. There

is already a large-screen TV and VCR for the leaders to use. The museum is accessible to the physically challenged. Workshop led by Dr. C.D. Albin.
Costs $45.
Accommodations EAAC provides list of area lodging.
Additional Information Accepts inquiries by e-mail or phone. "We are a small rural community on the scenic Riverways. The workshops are an excellent opportunity to rest, relax and get away from the rush of daily life. Many participants have valued this part of the experience as much as the learning and writing process."

FORT BEND WRITERS GUILD WORKSHOP

12523 Folkcrest Way, Stafford TX 77477-3529. E-mail: rogerpaulding@earthlink.net. Web site: www. fortbendwritersguild.com. **Contact:** Roger Paulding. Estab. 1997. Annual. Conference will be held in April. Conference duration: 1 day. Average attendance: 75. Focuses on fiction (novels) and screenwriting. Site: Held at Holiday Inn Southwest, Houston.
Costs $60 (including buffet lunch) before February 28; $65 thereafter; $75 at door on day of workshop. Check Web site for updated prices. Use PayPal if you wish for workshop or contest entries. Nonmembers add $10.
Additional Information Sponsors a contest. Submit for novel competition first 15 pages plus one-page synopsis, entry fee $20 plus $10 membership fee; for short story competition 10 pages complete, $10 each. "Judges are published novelists." First prize: $300, second place: $200, third place: $100. Deadline February 28, 2009. Not necessary to attend workshop in order to win. For brochure send SASE, e-mail or check Web site.

◎ THE GLEN WORKSHOP

Image, 3307 Third Avenue W, Seattle WA 98119. (206)281-2988. Fax: (206)281-2335. E-mail: glenwo rkshop@imagejournal.org. Web site: www.imagejournal.org. Estab. 1991. Annual. Workshop held in August. Conference duration: 1 week. Average attendance: 140-150. Workshop focuses on "fiction, poetry and spiritual writing, essay, memoir. Run by *Image*, a literary journal with a religious focus. The Glen welcomes writers who practice or grapple with religious faith." Site: 200 6 conference held in Santa Fe, NM in the first week of August and features "presentations and readings by the faculty." Faculty has included Erin McGraw (fiction), Lauren F. Winner (spiritual writing), Paul Mariani and Andrew Hudgins (poetry) and Jeanne Murray Walker (playwriting).
Costs $630-920, including room and board; $365-455 for commuters (lunch only).
Accommodations Arrange transportation by shuttle. Accommodations included in conference cost.
Additional Information Prior to arrival, participants may need to submit workshop material depending on the teacher. "Usually 10-25 pages." Conference information is available in February. For brochure send SASE, e-mail, visit Web site, call or fax. "Like *Image*, the Glen is grounded in a Christian perspective, but its tone is informal and hospitable to all spiritual wayfarers."

◎ GLORIETA CHRISTIAN WRITERS CONFERENCE

Glorieta Conference Center, 3311 Candelaria NE, Ste. I, Albuquerque NM 87107-1952. (800)433-6633. Fax: (505)899-9282. E-mail: info@classervices.com. Web site: www.glorietacwc.com. **Contact:** Linda Jewell, seminar manager. Estab. 1997. Annual. Conference held October 22-26, 2008. Conference duration: 5 days. Average attendance: 350. For "beginners, professionals, fiction, poetry, writing for children, drama, magazine writing, nonfiction books." To train Christian writers in their craft, provide them with an understanding of the industry, and give opportunities to meet with publishers. Site: "Located just north of historic Santa Fe, NM, conference center with hotels and dining hall with buffet-style meals." Plans "continuing course for fiction writers and numerous one-hour workshops."
Costs 2007 rates were $450 for early registration or $495 regular registration plus applicable tax; meals and lodging were additional and range from $200-500 depending on housing and meal plans. For lodging and meals contact Glorieta LifeWay Conference Center at 800/797-4222.
Additional Information "The craft of writing is universal, but attendees should be aware this conference has a Christian emphasis."

◎ TONY HILLERMAN WRITERS CONFERENCE

304 Calle Oso, Santa FE NM 87501. (505)471-1565. E-mail: wordharvest@yahoo.com. Web site: http://sfworkshops.com. **Contact:** Jean Schaumberg, co-director. Estab. 2004. Annual. November.

Conference duration: 4 days. Average attendance: 160. Site: Albuquerque Hyatt Regency. Previous faculty included Tony Hillerman, David Morrell, Michael McGarrity, and Jonathan and Faye Kellerman.

Costs Previous year's costs: $395 per-registration.

Accommodations Previous year $99 per night at the Hyatt Regency (plus parking).

Additional Information Sponsors on-site mini contest, $1,500 short story contest with *Cowboys & Indians Magazine* and a $10,000 first mystery novel contest with Thomas Dunne Books. Brochures available in July for SASE, by phone, e-mail, fax and on Web site. Accepts inquiries by SASE, phone, e-mail.

NATIONAL WRITERS ASSOCIATION FOUNDATION CONFERENCE

10940 S. Parker Rd. #508, Parker CO 80138. (303)841-0246. Fax: (303)841-2607. E-mail: conference@ nationalwriters.com. Web site: www.nationalwriters.com. **Contact:** Sandy Whelchel, executive director. Estab. 1926. Annual. Conference held in June. Conference duration: 3 days. Average attendance: 200-300. For general writing and marketing.

Costs $200 (approximately).

Additional Information Awards for previous contests will be presented at the conference. Conference information available annually in December. For brochures/guidelines send SASE, visit Web site, e-mail, fax or call.

THE NEW LETTERS WEEKEND WRITERS CONFERENCE

University of Missouri-Kansas City, College of Arts and Sciences Continuing Ed. Division, 5300 Rockhill Rd., Kansas City MO 64110-2499. (816)235-2736. Fax: (816)235-5279. Web site: www.newle tters.org. **Contact:** Robert Stewart. Estab. mid-'70s as The Longboat Key Writers Conference. Annual. Conference held in June. Conference duration: 3 days. Average attendance: 75. For "craft and the creative process in poetry, fiction, screenwriting, playwriting and journalism; but the program also deals with matters of psychology, publications and marketing. The conference is appropriate for both advanced and beginning writers." Site: "The conference meets at the beautiful Diastole conference center of The University of Missouri-Kansas City."

Costs Several options are available. Participants may choose to attend as a non-credit student or they may attend for 1-3 hours of college credit from the University of Missouri-Kansas City. Conference registration includes continental breakfasts, Saturday and Sunday lunch. For complete information, contact the university.

Accommodations Information on area accommodations is made available.

Additional Information Those registering for college credit are required to submit a ms in advance. Manuscript reading and critique are included in the credit fee. Those attending the conference for non-credit also have the option of having their ms critiqued for an additional fee. Accepts inquiries by phone, fax.

NIMROD ANNUAL WRITERS' WORKSHOP

University of Tulsa, 800 S. Tucker Dr., Tulsa OK 74104. (918)631-3080. Fax: (918)631-3033. E-mail: nimrod@utulsa.edu. Web site: www.utulsa.edu/nimrod. **Contact:** Eilis O'Neal, managing editor. Estab. 1978. Annual. Conference held in October. Conference duration: 1 day. Average attendance: 150-200. Workshop in fiction and poetry. "Prize winners (*Nimrod*/Hardman Prizes) conduct workshops as do contest judges." Past judges: Rosellen Brown, Stanley Kunitz, Toby Olson, Lucille Clifton, W.S. Merwin, Ron Carlson, Mark Doty, Anita Shreve and Francine Prose.

Costs Approximately $50. Lunch provided. Scholarships available for students.

Additional Information *Nimrod International Journal* sponsors *Nimrod*/Hardman Literary Awards: The Katherine Anne Porter Prize for fiction and The Pablo Neruda Prize for poetry. Poetry and fiction prizes: $2,000 each and publication (1st prize); $1,000 each and publication (2nd prize). Deadline: must be postmarked no later than April 30.

⊚ ROMANCE WRITERS OF AMERICA NATIONAL CONFERENCE

16000 Stuebner Airline Rd. Suite140, Spring TX 77379. (832)717-5200, ext. 121. Fax: (832)717-5201. E-mail: info@rwanational.com. Web site: www.rwanational.com. **Contact:** Nicole Kennedy, PR manager. Estab. 1981. Annual. Average attendance: 1,500. Over 100 workshops on writing, researching and the business side of being a working writer. Publishing professionals attend and accept appointments. Site: Conference will be held San Francisco in 2008 and Washington D.C in 2009. Keynote speaker is renowned romance writer.

Costs In 2008, early registration $425 for RWA members/$500 nonmembers; late registration, $475 for RWA members/$550 nonmembers.

Additional Information Annual RITA awards are presented for romance authors. Annual Golden Heart awards are presented for unpublished writers. Conference brochures/guidelines and registration forms are available for SASE and on Web site in January. Accepts inquiries by SASE, e-mail, fax, phone.

SAN JUAN WRITERS WORKSHOP

P.O. Box 841, Ridgeway CO 81432. (806)438-2385. E-mail: inkwellliterary@mac.com. Web site: http://homepage.mac.com/inkwellliterary. **Contact:** Jill Patterson, director. Estab. 2002. Annual. Workshop held July or August each year. Last conference was July 21-29, 2007. Conference duration: up to 10 days. Average attendance: 40 per session. Focuses on "fiction, poetry, creative nonfiction in each session. Sessions focus on generating new material, workshopping manuscripts, revising and submitting for publication. "The goal of the San Juan Workshops is to remove writers from the hectic pace of everyday life and give them the inspiration, space and quiet to attend to their writing." Site: "The Workshops are held for one week, each summer, in Ouray, CO,. Switzerland of America. In this cozy mountain village, everything is within walking distance, including the Ouray Hot Springs Pool, Cascade Falls, the local movie theater in the historical Wright Opera House, several fine restaurants, lodging and the Community Center where workshop events take place." 2007 panels included Generating New Material, Craft and Critique, Revising and Submitting for Publication. Panelists in 2007 included Emily Fox Gordon, Bob Hicok, Pamela Painter, Pam Houston, Gary Short, Philip Gerard, Scott Russell Sanders, Andrew Hudgins, and Robert Olen Butler.

Costs $350-475, includes workshop instruction, faculty readings, breakfast each day and admission to all receptions. "All sessions will require an additional, non-refundable application fee of $25. There are substantial discounts for attending multiple sessions. There are also $100 scholarships available."

Accommodations Offers shuttle to/from airport in Montrose, CO. Provides a list of hotels.

Additional Information Accepts inquiries by SASE, e-mail, phone. "There are social activities, including mountain cookout, concerts in the local park, the annual pub crawl, champagne brunch and readings." See Web site for more information.

SMALL PUBLISHERS MARKETING CONFERENCE AND TRADE SHOW

Small Publishers Association of North America, 1618 West Colorado Ave., Colorado Springs CO 80904. (719)475-1726. Fax: (719)471-2182. E-mail: info@spannet.org. Web site: www.spannet.org. **Contact:** Jennifer Quintana, coordinator. Estab. 1996. Annual. Last conference was October 2007. Conference duration: 3 days. Average attendance: 85. Conference/workshop and trade show for the self-publisher or independent/small press. Intensive one-on-one time with seven expert speakers and 27 industry leaders and vendors. Attendees learn how to sell more books, increase profits, create a more effective message and boost their professional standing. Site: East Coast in 2007.

Costs $345, early registration price for members. Marketing workbook and meals are included in registration fee. Hotel rooms discounted for attendees.

Additional Information Brochures available in June by fax, e-mail and on Web site. Accepts inquiries for SASE and by e-mail, phone and fax.

SOUTHWEST LITERARY CENTER OF RECURSOS DE SANTA FE

826 Camino de Monte Rey, Santa Fe NM 87505. (505)577-1125. Fax: (505)982-7125. Web site: www.santafewritersconference.com. **Contact:** Literary Center director. Estab. 1984. Annual. 2008 conference was held July 21-25, possible extension to include Santa Fe Spanish Market. Conference duration: 6 days. Average attendance: 50. This year's conference includes lectures, afternoon talks, and private conferences on fiction, and nonfiction. Faculty included Natalie Goldberg, Lisa Dale Norton, Sallie Bingham, Julie Shigekuni and Denise Chavez and more.

Costs $550. Scholarships may be available.

Additional Information Brochure available by e-mail, fax, phone and on Web site.

SOUTHWEST WRITERS CONFERENCE

3721 Morris NE Ste A, Albuquerque NM 87111. (505)265-9485. Fax: (505)265-9483. E-mail: swwriters@juno.com. Web site: www.southwestwriters.org. **Contact:** Conference Chair. Estab. 1983. Annual. Conferences held throughout the year. Average attendance: 50. "Conferences concentrate on all areas of writing and include appointments and networking." Workshops and speakers include writers, editors and agents of all genres for all levels from beginners to advanced.

Costs $99 and up (members); $159 and up (nonmembers); includes conference sessions and lunch.

Accommodations Usually have official airline and discount rates. Special conference rates are available at hotel. A list of other area hotels and motels is available.

Additional Information Sponsors an annual contest judged by authors, editors and agents from New York, Los Angeles, etc., and from other major publishing houses. Many categories. Deadline, fee structure on Web site. For brochures/guidelines send SASE, visit Web site, e-mail, call. "An appointment (10 minutes, one-on-one) may be set up at the conference with the editor/agent of your choice on a first-registered/first-served basis."

STEAMBOAT SPRINGS WRITERS GROUP

Steamboat Arts Council, P.O. Box 774284, Steamboat Springs CO 80477. (970)879-8079. E-mail: sswriters@cs.com. Web site: www.steamboatwriters.com. **Contact:** Harriet Freiberger, director. Estab. 1982. Annual conference. Group meets year-round on Thursdays, 12:00 to 2:00 at Arts Depot; guests welcome. Conference held in July. Conference duration: 1 day. Average attendance: 30. "Our conference emphasizes instruction within the seminar format. Novices and polished professionals benefit from the individual attention and camaraderie which can be established within small groups. A pleasurable and memorable learning experience is guaranteed by the relaxed and friendly atmosphere of the old train depot. Registration is limited." Site: Restored train depot.

Costs $45 before May 25, $55 after. Fee covers all conference activities, including lunch.

Accommodations Lodging available at Steamboat Resorts.

Additional Information Optional dinner and activities during evening preceding conference. Accepts inquiries by e-mail, phone, mail.

SUMMER WRITING PROGRAM

Naropa University, 2130 Arapahoe Ave., Boulder CO 80302. (303)245-4600. Fax: (303)546-5287. E-mail: swpr@naropa.edu. Web site: www.naropa.edu/swp. **Contact:** Corrina Lesser, registration manager. Estab. 1974. Annual. Workshops held: June 16-July 13, 2008. Workshop duration: 4 weeks. Average attendance: 250. Offers college credit. "With 14 workshops to choose from each of the four weeks of the program, students may study poetry, prose, hybrid/cross-genre writing, small press printing, or book arts." Site: All workshops, panels, lectures and readings are hosted on the Naropa University main campus. Located in downtown Boulder, the campus is within easy walking distance of restaurants, shopping and the scenic Pearl Street Mall. Prose-related panels include Ecology, Poetics of Prose, Telling Stories, The Informant "Other." Faculty has included Samuel Delany, David Antin, Amiri Baraka, Laird Hunt, Thomas Glave, Rebecca Brown, Chris Tysh, Brian Evenson, Bobbie Louise Hawkins, Fiona Templeton, David Levi Strauss, Tonya Foster, Richard Tuttle, Anne Waldman, Miguel Algarin, Sonia Sanchez, Robin Blaser.

Costs In 2006: $375/week, $1,500 for all four weeks (non-credit students); $900/week, $3,600 for all four weeks (BA students); $1,230/week, $4,920 for all four weeks (MFA students).

Accommodations Offers overnight accommodations. Dormitory housing is available at Sangha House. Large room is $50/night or $350/week, medium room is $45/night or $315/week, small room is $40/night or $280/week.

Additional Information If students would like to take the Summer Writing Program for academic credit, they must submit a visiting student application, transcripts, a letter of intent, and 5-10 pages of their creative work. Information available in April. For brochure, call, e-mail. Accepts inquiries by e-mail, phone. Editors participate in conference.

TAOS SUMMER WRITERS' CONFERENCE

Department of English Language and Literature MSC03 2170, 1 University of New Mexico, Albuquerque NM 87131-0001. (505)277-5572. Fax: (505)277-2950. E-mail: taosconf@unm.edu. Web site: www.unm.edu/~taosconf. **Contact:** Sharon Oard Warner, director. Estab. 1999. Annual. Held each year in July. Average attendance: 180. Workshops in novel writing, short story writing, screenwriting, poetry, creative nonfiction, publishing, and special topics such as yoga and writing. Master classes in novel, memoir and poetry. For beginning and experienced writers. "Taos itself makes our conference unique. We also offer daily visits to the D.H. Lawrence Ranch, the Harwood Museum and other local historical sites." Site: Workshops and readings are all held at the Sagebrush Inn Conference Center, part of the Sagebrush Inn, an historic hotel and Taos landmark since 1929.

Costs Weeklong workshop tuition is $600, includes a Sunday evening New Mexican buffet dinner, a Friday evening barbecue and other special events. Weekend workshop tuition is $300.

Accommodations We offer a discounted car rental rate through the Sagebrush Inn or the adjacent Comfort Suites. Conference participants receive special discounted rates $59-99/night. Room rates at both hotels include a full, hot breakfast.

Additional Information "We offer three Merit Scholarships, the Taos Resident Writer Award, the Hispanic Writer Award and one D.H. Lawrence Fellowship. Scholarship awards are based on submissions of poetry, fiction and creative nonfiction." They provide tuition remission; transportation and lodging not provided. To apply for a scholarship, submit 10 pages of poetry, nonfiction or fiction along with registration and deposit. Applicants should be registered for the conference. The Fellowship is for emerging writers with one book in print, provides tuition remission and cost of lodging. Brochures available late winter. "The conference offers a balance of special events and free time. If participants take a morning workshop, they'll have the afternoons free and vice versa. We've also included several outings, including a tour of the Harwood Arts Center and a visit to historic D.H. Lawrence Ranch outside Taos."

⊙ TEXAS CHRISTIAN WRITERS' CONFERENCE

First Baptist Church, 6038 Greenmont, Houston TX 77092. (713)686-7209. E-mail: marthalrogers@sb cglobal.net. **Contact:** Martha Rogers. Estab. 1990. Annual. Conference held in August. Conference duration: 1 day. Average attendance: 60-65. "Focus on all genres." Site: Held at the First Baptist Church fellowship center and classrooms. 2008 faculty: Susan Titus Osborne, Don Aycock, Terry Burns and Deb Raney as Keynote speaker. Additional faculty: Anita Highman, Janice Thompson, Kathleen Y'Barbo and Martha Rogers.

Costs $65 for members of IWA, $80 nonmembers, discounts for seniors (60+) and couples, meal at noon, continental breakfast and breaks.

Accommodations Offers list of area hotels or lodging options.

Additional Information Open conference for all interested writers. Sponsors a contest for short fiction; categories include articles, devotionals, poetry, short story, book proposals, drama. Fees: $8-15. Conference information available with SASE or e-mail to Martha Rogers. Agents participate in conference.

THUNDER WRITER'S RETREATS

Durango CO 81301-3408. (970)385-5884. Fax: (970)247-5327. E-mail: thunder@thunderforwriters.c om. Web site: www.thunderforwriters.com. **Contact:** Michael Thunder. Estab. 2000. On demand, per client's need. Conference duration: 1-2 weeks. Average attendance: 1 individual/session. Focus is on fiction and scriptwriting. Site: Durango, Colorado, "beautiful mountain environment."

Costs $1,000/week coaching fee. Meals and lodging are dependent on the writer's taste and budget.

Accommodations Provides a list of area hotels or lodging options.

Additional Information "These writer's retreats are geared toward concepting a project or project development. Usually writers stay one week and receive 10 hours of one-on-one coaching. The rest of their time is spent writing. One and sometimes two interviews are required to design a course of action adapted to the writer's needs." Please call, e-mail, fax or send SASE for more information.

MARK TWAIN CREATIVE WRITERS WORKSHOPS

University House, 5101 Rockhill Rd., Kansas City MO 64110-2499. (816)235-1168. Fax: (816)235-2611. E-mail: BeasleyM@umkc.edu. Web site: www.newletters.org. **Contact:** Betsy Beasley, administrative associate. Estab. 1990. Annual. Held 3 weeks of June, from 9:30 to 12:30 each weekday morning. Conference duration: 3 weeks. Average attendance: 40. "Focus is on fiction, poetry and literary nonfiction." Site: University of Missouri-Kansas City Campus. Panels planned for next conference include the full range of craft essentials. Staff includes Robert Stewart, editor-in-chief of *New Letters* and BkMk Press, and Michael Pritchett, creative writing professor.

Costs Fees for regular and noncredit courses.

Accommodations Offers list of area hotels or lodging options.

Additional Information Submit for workshop 6 poems/one short story prior to arrival. Conference information is available in March by SASE, e-mail or on Web site. Editors participate in conference.

◎ WRITERS WORKSHOP IN SCIENCE FICTION

Lawrence KS 66045-2115. (785)864-3380. Fax: (785)864-1159. E-mail: jgunn@ku.edu. Web site: www.ku.edu/~sfcenter. **Contact:** James Gunn, professor. Estab. 1984. Annual. Workshop held in late June to early July. Conference duration: 2 weeks. Average attendance: 10-14. The workshop is "small, informal and aimed at writers on the edge of publication or regular publication." For writing and marketing science fiction and fantasy. Site: "Housing is provided and classes meet in university housing on the University of Kansas campus. Workshop sessions operate informally in a lounge." Past guests included Frederik Pohl, SF writer and former editor and agent; John Ordover, writer and editor; George Zebrowski, Pamela Sargent, Kij Johnson and Christopher McKittrick, writers; Lou Anders, editor. A novel workshop in science fiction and fantasy is also available.

Costs $400 tuition. Housing and meals are additional.

Accommodations Several airport shuttle services offer reasonable transportation from the Kansas City International Airport to Lawrence. During past conferences, students were housed in a student dormitory at $14/day double, $28/day single.

Additional Information "Admission to the workshop is by submission of an acceptable story. Two additional stories should be submitted by the end of May. These three stories are distributed to other participants for critiquing and are the basis for the first week of the workshop; one story is rewritten for the second week. The workshop offers a 3-hour session manuscript critiquing each afternoon. The rest of the day is free for writing, study, consultation and recreation." Information available in December. For brochures/guidelines send SASE, visit Web site, e-mail, fax, call. The workshop concludes with The Campbell Conference, a round-table discussion of a single topic, and the presentation of the Campbell and Sturgeon Awards for the Best SF Novel and Short Story of the Year. "The Writers Workshop in Science Fiction is intended for writers who have just started to sell their work or need that extra bit of understanding or skill to become a published writer."

WEST (AZ, CA, HI, NV, UT)

◎ ☑ ALTERNATIVE PRESS EXPO (APE)

Comic-Con International, P.O. Box 128458, San Diego CA 92112-8458. (619)491-2475. Fax: (619)414-1022. E-mail: cci-info@comic-con.org. Web site: www.comic-con.org/ape/. **Contact:** Eddie Ibrahim, director of programming. Annual. Last conference held November 1-2, 2008, in San Francisco. Conference duration: 2 days. "Hundreds of artists and publishers converge for the largest gathering of alternative and self-published comics in the country." Includes panels on graphic novels, Web comics, how to pitch your comic to publishers, and the traditional APE 'queer cartoonists' panel. Site: Large conference or expo center in host city. Check Web site for 2008 location. 2007 special guests included Kevin Huizenga, Karl Christian Krumpholz, Hope Larson, Francoise Mouly, Art Spiegelman, Brian Lee O'Malley, Gene Yang.

Costs $7 single day; $10 both days.

Accommodations Does not offer overnight accommodations. Provides list of area hotels or lodging options on Web site.

Additional Information For brochure, visit Web site. Editors participate in conference.

BIG BEAR WRITER'S RETREAT

P.O. Box 1441, Big Bear Lake CA 92315-1441. (909)585-0059. Fax: (909)266-0710. E-mail: mike@writers-review.com. **Contact:** Mike Foley, director. Estab. 1995. Biannual. Conferences held in May or October. Conference duration: 3 days. Average attendance: 15-25. Past themes included Finding New Creativity, Character and Setting, Avoiding Common Errors, Character Depth, Embracing Yourself as a Writer. Site: "A small, intimate lodge in Big Bear, San Bernardino mountains of Southern California." Retreat is hosted annually by Mike Foley, editor of *Dream Merchant Magazine*, and Tom Foley, Ph.D., artistic psychologist.

Costs $499, includes meals and lodging.

Accommodations Offers overnight accommodations. On-site facilities included in retreat fee.

Additional Information Prior to arrival, submit a fiction or nonfiction sample, 10 double-spaced pages maximum. 2007 conference information is available March 2006. For brochure send SASE, e-mail, call or fax. Accepts inquiries by SASE, e-mail, phone and fax. Editors participate in conference. "This is unlike the standard writer's conference. Participants will live as writers for a weekend. Retreat includes workshop sessions, open writing time and private counseling with retreat hosts. A weekend of focused writing, fun and friendship. This is a small group retreat, known for its individual attention to writers, intimate setting and strong bonding among participants."

BLOCKBUSTER PLOTS FOR WRITERS WRITING WORKSHOPS

708 Blossom Hill Rd. #146, Los Gatos CA 95032. Fax: (408)356-1798. E-mail: contact@blockbusterplots.com. Web site: www.blockbusterplots.com. **Contact:** Martha Alderson M.A., instructor. Estab. 2000. Held four times per year. Conference duration: 2 days. Average attendance: 6-8. Workshop is intended to help writers create an action, character and thematic plotline for a screenplay, memoir, short story, novel or creative nonfiction. Site: a house.
Costs $135 per day.
Accommodations Provides list of area hotels and lodging options.
Additional Information Brochures available by fax, e-mail or on Web site. Accepts inquiries by SASE, e-mail and fax.

JAMES BONNET'S STORYMAKING: THE MASTER CLASS

P.O. Box 841, Burbank CA 91503-0841. (310)572-9410. E-mail: bonnet@storymaking.com. Web site: www.storymaking.com. **Contact:** James Bonnet. Estab. 1990. Conference held February, May, July, October. Conference duration: 2 days. Average attendance: 25. Conferences focus on fiction, mystery and screenwriting. Site: In 2007, Sportsmen's Lodge, Studio City, California and Nans Sous Ste. Anne, France. Topics for next conference include The High Concept Great Idea, The Creative Unconscious, Metaphor, The Archetypes, The Fundamentals of Plot, Structure, Genre, Character, Complications, Crisis, Climax, Conflict, Suspense and more. James Bonnet (author) is scheduled to participate as speaker.
Costs $350 per weekend.
Accommodations Provides a list of area hotels or lodging options.
Additional Information For brochure send SASE, e-mail, visit Web site, or call. Accepts inquiries by SASE, e-mail, phone and fax. "James Bonnet, author of *Stealing Fire From the Gods*, teaches a story structure and story-making seminar that guides writers from inspiration to final draft."

◎ BYU WRITING FOR YOUNG READERS WORKSHOP

348 HCEB, Brigham Young University, Provo UT 84602. (801)422-2568. E-mail: cw348@byu.edu. Web site: http://wfyr.byu.edu. **Contact:** Bill Kelly. Estab. 2000. Annual. Workshop held June or July each year. Average attendance: 150. Conference focuses on "all genres for children and teens." Site: Brigham Young University's Conference Center. Mornings feature small group workshop sessions with a published author. Afternoon breakout sessions on a variety of topics of interest to writers. Sessions for picture book, novel, illustration, fantasy, beginners, general writing. Two editors and an agent are in attendance. Past faculty has included Eve Bunting, Tony Johnston, Tim Wynne-Jones, John H. Ritter, Alane Ferguson, Lael Little, Laura Torres, Gloria Skurzynski, Claudia Mills.
Costs $399 conference fee and closing banquet.
Accommodations Provides list of area hotels.
Additional Information Brochures available in March by phone and on Web site. Accepts inquiries by SASE, e-mail, phone. Agents and editors participate in conference. "Bring the manuscript you are currently working on."

ℕ ◎ CLARION SCIENCE FICTION AND FANTASY WRITERS' WORKSHOP

UCSD 9500 Gilman Drive #0410, La Jolla CA 92097-0410. (858)534-2115. E-mail: clarion@ucsd.edu. Web site: http://clarion.ucsd.edu. **Contact:** Tania Mayer, Program Coordinator. Estab. 1968. Annual. Conference duration: Six-week residency in summer (late June-early Aug.). Average attendance: 18. Workshop. "Clarion is a short-story writing workshop focused on fundamentals particular to the writing of science fiction, fantasy and horror." Site: The workshop is held at the UC San Diego campus in the beautiful beach town of La Jolla. Participants reside in campus apartments and attend workshop sessions in a seminar room. Beaches and shopping are within easy reach by public transportation. Summer temperatures in San Diego are normally 70-80°F, dry and comfortable. The instructors for the summer 2008 workshop were Kelly Link, James Patrick Kelly, Mary Anne Mohanraj, Neil Gaiman, Nalo Hopkinson and Geoff Ryman.

Costs The fees for 2008 (application, tuition, room and board) were approximately $4,400. Financial aid is available.

Accommodations Participants make their own travel arrangements to and from the campus. Campus residency is required. Participants are housed in semi-private accommodations (private bedroom, shared bathroom) in student apartments. The room and board fee includes three meals a day at a campus dining facility. In 2008 the room and board fee for the six-week residency were approximately $2,500.

Additional Information "Workshop participants are selected on the basis of their potential for highly successful writing careers. Applications are judged by a review panel composed of the workshop instructors. Prospective students submit an application and two complete short stories, each between 2,500 words and 6,000 words in length. The application deadline (typically, March 1) is posted on the Clarion Web site." Information available in September. For brochure, visit Web site. Agents and editors frequently participate in Clarion as instructors or guest speakers.

◎ DESERT DREAMS CONFERENCE: REALIZING THE DREAM

P.O. Box 27407, Tempe AZ 85285. (623)910-0524. E-mail: desertdreams@desertroserwa.org. Web site: www.desertroserwa.org. **Contact:** Conference coordinator. Estab. 1986. Biennial. Last conference held April 4-6, 2008. Next conference Spring 2008. Average attendance: 250. Conference focuses on romance fiction. Site: Phoenix, AZ. Past panels included: Plotting, Dialogue, Manuscript Preparation, Web site Design, Synopsis, Help for the Sagging Middle. Keynote speakers in 2006 included Debbie Macomber, Lisa Gardner, Jennifer Cruise and Debra Dixon. Guest editors/agents from St. Martin's Press, Harlequin, Irene Goodman Literary Agency, Borders Group, Ellora's Cave, Spectrum Literary Agency and more.

Costs Vary each year; approximately $175-225 for full conference.

Accommodations Hotels may vary for each conference; it is always a resort location in the Phoenix area.

Additional Information Sponsors contest as part of conference, open to conference attendees only. For brochure, inquiries, contact by e-mail, phone, fax, mail or visit Web site. Agents and editors participate in conference.

Ⓝ ◎ Ⓖ INTERNATIONAL COMIC-CON

Comic-Con International, P.O. Box 128458, San Diego CA 92112-8458. (619)491-2475. Fax: (619)414-1022. E-mail: cci-info@comic-con.org. Web site: www.comic-con.org/cci/. **Contact:** Gary Sassaman, director of programming. Annual. Last conference held July 24-27, 2008. Conference duration: 4 days. Average attendance: 104,000. "The comics industry's largest expo, hosting writers, artists, editors, agents, publishers, buyers and sellers of comics and graphic novels." Site: San Diego Convention Center. "Nearly 300 programming events, including panels, seminars and previews, on the world of comics, movies, television, animation, art, and much more." 2006 special guests included Ray Bradbury, Forrest J. Ackerman, Sergio Aragones, John Romita Sr., J. Michael Straczynski, Daniel Clowes, George Perez.

Costs $50 by April 19, $55 by June 7, $65 at the door. Special discounts for children and seniors.

Accommodations Does not offer overnight accommodations. Provides list of area hotels or lodging options. Special conference hotel and airfare discounts available. See Web site for details.

Additional Information For brochure, visit Web site. Agents and editors participate in conference.

◎ IWWG EARLY SUMMER CONFERENCE

The International Women's Writing Guild, P.O. Box 810, Gracie Station, New York NY 10028. (212)737-7536. Fax: (212)737-9469. E-mail: iwwg@iwwg.org. Web site: www.iwwg.org. Established 1978. **Contact:** Hannelore Hahn, executive director. 2008 dates: June 13-20. Location: Skidmore College in Saratoga Springs, NY. Average attendance: 500 maximum. Purpose/Features Open to all women. Around 65 workshops offered each day. 2008 poetry staff includes Barbara Garro, Marj Hahne, D.H. Melhem, Myra Shapiro, and Susan Baugh.Costs/Accommodations 2006 cost: $1,085 (single), $945 (double) for IWWG members; $1,330 (single), $990 (double), $1,034 (single). Includes program and room and board for 7 nights, 21 meals at Skidmore College. Shorter conference stays available, such as 5 days or weekend. Commuters welcome.

Additional Information Post-conference retreat weekend also available. Information available for SASE, by e-mail, or on Web site.

LA JOLLA WRITERS CONFERENCE

P.O. Box 178122, San Diego CA 92177. (858)467-1978. Web site: www.lajollawritersconference.com. **Contact:** Jared Kuritz, director. Established 2001. Annual. 2008 Conference held November 7-9. Conference duration: 3 days. Maximum attendance limited to 200. The *La Jolla Writers Conference* welcomes writers of all levels of experience. This three-day event, now in its 8th year, always boasts exciting, interactive workshops, lectures, and presentations by an outstanding and freely accessible faculty comprised of best-selling authors, editors from major publishing houses, and literary agents, all of whom value meeting and working with a diverse group of creative people passionate about writing. The LJWC uniquely covers the art, craft, and business of writing for both fiction and nonfiction.

Costs $285 Early, $355 Regular, $400 Late, includes access to all classes, 3 keynotes, Friday night reception, and Saturday Lunch/Saturday Dinner.

Additional Information Private Read & Critiques for an additional fee.

LEAGUE OF UTAH WRITERS ROUND-UP

P.O. Box 460562, Leeds UT 84746. (435)313-4459 or (801)450-7310. E-mail: reelsweetjustwrite@juno.com. Web site: www.luwrite.com. **Contact:** Dorothy Crofts, membership chairman. Estab. 1935. Annual. Conference held September 12-13, 2008. Conference duration: 2 days, Friday and Saturday. Average attendance: 200. "The purpose of the conference is to award the winners of our annual contest as well as offer instruction in all areas of writing. Speakers cover subjects from generating ideas to writing a novel to working with a publisher. We have something for everyone." Site: Conference held at hotel conference rooms and ballroom facilities. 2005 themes included: Essays, Mystery, Writing for Magazines, Children's Nonfiction, Poetry, General Fiction. 2005 keynote speaker was Mary Higgins Clark.

Costs $125 for LUW members; $160 for nonmembers (fee includes 4 meals).

Accommodations St. George Hilton Garden Inn, 1731 Convention Center Drive, St. George, UT. Special hotel rate for conferees: $89/night.

Additional Information Opportunity for writers to meet one-on-one with literary agents from New York. Sponsors contests for 8 fiction categories, 3 open to nonmembers of League. Word limits vary from 1,500 to 90,000. Conference brochures/guidelines available for SASE, by fax and on Web site. Accepts inquiries by phone, fax, e-mail, SASE.

MENDOCINO COAST WRITERS CONFERENCE

College of the Redwoods, 1211 Del Mar Drive, Fort Bragg CA 95437. (707)962-2600 ext 2167. E-mail: info@mcwc.org. Web site: www.mcwc.org. **Contact:** Barbara Lee, registrar. Estab. 1989. Annual. Last conference held August 2008. Average attendance: 100. "We hope to encourage the developing writer by inviting presenters who are both fine writers and excellent teachers." Site: College of the Redwoods is a small community college located on the gorgeous northern California coast. Focuses are fiction, poetry, creative nonfiction, memoir. Special areas have included children's (2003), mystery (2002), social awareness (2007). In 2008 faculty included James D. Houston, Jody Gehrman, Michael Datcher, Daphne Gottlieb, Amy Stewart, Susan Wooldridge, Jenoyne Adams, Marianne Villaneuva.

Costs Before June 15, 200 8: $450.00; after June 15: $495.00

Additional Information Brochures for the conference will be available in March by SASE, phone, e-mail or on the Web site. Agents and editors participate in the conference. "The conference is small, friendly and fills up fast with many returnees."

◎ MORMON WRITERS' CONFERENCE

Association for Mormon Letters, P.O. Box 1315, Salt Lake City UT 84110-1315. (801)582-2090. E-mail: aml@mormonletters.org. Web site: www.mormonletters.org. **Contact:**Conference Chair. Estab. 1999. Annual. Conference held on a Saturday in late fall. Average attendance: 100. The conference usually covers anything to do with writing by, for or about Mormons, including fiction, nonfiction, theater, film, children's literature. Site: Last few years it has been in Orem, UT. "Plenary speeches, panels and instructional presentations by prominent authors and artists in the LDS artistic community."

Costs $15 for general public, $5 for AML members and for students who are not AML members, free to AML student members; catered lunch additional $15 with pre-registration.

Additional Information For brochures/guidelines send SASE, e-mail, visit Web site. Accepts inquiries by SASE, e-mail.

MOUNT HERMON CHRISTIAN WRITERS CONFERENCE

P.O. Box 413, Mount Hermon CA 95041-0413. (831)335-4466. Fax: (831)335-9413. E-mail: info@mhc amps.org. Web site: www.mounthermon.org/writers. **Contact:** David R. Talbott, director of adult ministries. Estab. 1970. Annual. Conference held March 14-18, 2008. Average attendance: 450. "We are a broad-ranging conference for all areas of Christian writing, including fiction, children's, poetry, nonfiction, magazines, books, educational curriculum and radio and TV scriptwriting. This is a working, how-to conference, with many workshops within the conference involving on-site writing assignments." Site: "The conference is sponsored by and held at the 440-acre Mount Hermon Christian Conference Center near San Jose, California, in the heart of the coastal redwoods. Registrants stay in hotel-style accommodations, and full board is provided as part of the conference fees. Meals are taken family style, with faculty joining registrants. The faculty/student ratio is about 1:6 or 7. The bulk of our faculty is editors and publisher representatives from major Christian publishing houses nationwide."

Costs Registration fees include tuition, conference sessions, resource notebook, refreshment breaks, room and board and vary from $735 (economy) to $1,100 (deluxe), double occupancy (2007 rates).

Accommodations Airport shuttles are available from the San Jose International Airport. Housing is not required of registrants, but about 95% of our registrants use Mount Hermon's own housing facilities (hotel-style double-occupancy rooms). Meals with the conference are required and are included in all fees.

Additional Information Registrants may submit 2 works for critique in advance of the conference. No advance work is required, however. Conference brochures/guidelines are available online only in December. Accepts inquiries by e-mail, fax. "The residential nature of our conference makes this a unique setting for one-on-one interaction with faculty/staff. There is also a decided inspirational flavor to the conference, and general sessions with well-known speakers are a highlight. Come rested, with plenty of business cards and samples of works in progress or just completed."

PIMA WRITERS' WORKSHOP

Pima Community College, 2202 W. Anklam Road, Tucson AZ 85709-0170. (520)206-6084. Fax: (520)206-6020. E-mail: mfiles@pima.edu. **Contact:** Meg Files, director. Estab. 1988. Annual. Conference held in May. Average attendance: 300. "For anyone interested in writing—beginning or experienced writer. The workshop offers sessions on writing short stories, novels, nonfiction articles and books, children's and juvenile stories, poetry, screenplays." Site: Sessions are held in the Center for the Arts on Pima Community College's West campus. Past speakers include Michael Blake, Ron Carlson, Gregg Levoy, Nancy Mairs, Linda McCarriston, Jerome Stern, Connie Willis, Larry McMurtry, Barbara Kingsolver and Robert Morgan.

Costs $80 (can include ms critique). Participants may attend for college credit, Meals and accommodations not included.

Accommodations Information on local accommodations is made available and special workshop rates are available at a specified motel close to the workshop site (about $70/night).

Additional Information Participants may have up to 20 pages critiqued by the author of their choice. Manuscripts must be submitted 3 weeks before the workshop. Conference brochure/guidelines available for SASE. Accepts inquiries by e-mail. "The workshop atmosphere is casual, friendly and supportive, and guest authors are very accessible. Readings, films and panel discussions are offered as well as talks and manuscript sessions."

SAN DIEGO STATE UNIVERSITY WRITERS' CONFERENCE

SDSU College of Extended Studies, 5250 Campanile Drive, San Diego CA 92182-1920. (619)594-2517. Fax: (619)594-8566. E-mail: brownz@mail.sdsu.edu. Web site: www.ces.sdsu.edu. **Contact:** Rose Brown, facilitator. Estab. 1984. Annual conference held in January. Conference duration: 2 days.

Average attendance: 375. Covers fiction, nonfiction, scriptwriting, and e-books. Held at the Doubletree Hotel in Mission Valley. Each year the conference offers a variety of workshops for beginning, intermediate, and advanced writers. This conference allows the individual writer to choose which workshop best suits his/her needs. In addition to the workshops, editor reading appointments and agent/editor consultation appointments are available for additional fees, so attendees can meet with editors and agents one-on-one to discuss specific issues. A reception is offered Saturday immediately following the workshops, offering attendees the opportunity to socialize with the faculty (editors, agents, speakers) in a relaxed atmosphere. Last year, about 70 faculty attended.

Costs In 2007: $365-485. (2008 cost will be published with fall update of Web site.) Includes lunch and reception Saturday evening.

Accommodations Doubletree Hotel, (800)222-TREE. Attendees must make their own travel arrangements.

Additional Information Complete conference information is available at www.ces.sdsu.edu/writers.

⊠ SAN FRANCISCO WRITERS CONFERENCE

1029 Jones St, San Francisco CA 94109. (415)673-0939 or (866)862-739. Fax: (415)673-0367. E-mail: sfwriters@aol.com. Web site: http://www.sfwriters.org. **Contact:** Elizabeth Pomada. Estab. 2004. Annual. February 15-17, 2008. Conference duration: 3 days. Average attendance: 450-500. "Focus is on WRITING and PUBLISHING. Attendees learn from bestselling authors, literary agents, and editors. The emphasis is on producing the best possible work and finding the most effective way to get it published from traditional (major publishers to specialty houses are always at the event) to self-publishing (iUniverse is a sponsor) and cutting edge venues (including Web sites/blogging)." The event is held at the Mark Hopkins Hotel in San Francisco. "It is an elegant and historic venue at the top of Nob Hill. General sessions, keynotes and luncheons are in the Ballroom with breakout sessions in smaller rooms at the hotel. Previous panels include A Conversation on Writing (Gail Tsukiyama and Karen Joy Fowler) and Writing for Children (Lemony Snickett). Previous topics include: Romance (Passion on the Page), How to Write a Fiction Query Letter, Workshops on Plot/Dialogue/Characterization, The Art of Literary Fiction, The Perfect Murder. The founders of SFWC are Elizabeth Pomada (nonfiction literary agent) and Michael Larsen (agent and author of many writing related books including *Guerrilla Marketing for Writers*). Presenters for 2008 included Sheldon Siegel (*The Confession*), April Sinclair (*Coffee Will Make You Black*), Daisy Maryles (*Publishers Weekly*), dozens of literary agents and editors from top publishing houses including St. Martin's, Simon & Schuster, Random House, John Wiley & Sons, and New World Library. (Nearly 100 presenters)

Costs 2008 fee is $595 (early sign-up discounts available).

Accommodations BART trains bring attendees arriving at SFO or Oakland airports to downtown San Francisco. Then use cable car or taxi from there to hotel. Does not offer overnight accommodations. "All sessions are held at the Mark Hopkins Hotel, so make reservations there or at a nearby hotel. Mark Hopkins is offering an attendee rate of just $152 a night rate (based on availability)!"

Additional Information No application needed. Sponsors contest. This contest is judged by literary agents. For brochure, visit Web site. Agents and editors participate in conference. "San Francisco Writers Conference has over 100 editors, agents, authors and book marketing professionals as its faculty each year! Additionally we limit our attendance to 300 for the best one-on-one interaction during the event. It is truly one of the best events for advancing writing careers."

SANTA BARBARA CHRISTIAN WRITERS CONFERENCE

P.O. Box 42429, Santa Barbara CA 93140. (805)682-0316. E-mail: opalmaebailey@aol.com. **Contact:** Opal Dailey, director. Estab. 1997. Conference held October 7, 2006. Conference duration: 1 day. Average attendance: 60-70. Site: Westmont College, "liberal arts Christian College. Beautiful campus in the Montecito Foothills at Santa Barbara.

Costs $89 for 2007. Includes continental breakfast, lunch and afternoon snack.

Additional Information Conference information available in May. For brochure, send SASE or call. Accepts inquiries by e-mail, SASE and phone. Agents and editors participate in conference.

◎ SCBWI ANNUAL SUMMER CONFERENCE ON WRITING & ILLUSTRATING FOR CHILDREN

(formerly SCBWI/International Conference on Writing & Illustrating for Children), Society of Children's Book Writers and Illustrators, 8271 Beverly Blvd., Los Angeles CA 90048. (323)782-1010.

Fax: (323)782-1892. E-mail: conference@scbwi.org. Web site: www.scbwi.org. **Contact**: Lin Oliver, executive director. Estab. 1972. Annual. Conference held in August. Conference duration: 4 days. Average attendance: 800. Writer and illustrator workshops geared toward all levels. Covers all aspects of children's magazine and book publishing.

Costs Approximately $400; includes all 4 days and one banquet meal. Does not include hotel room.

Accommodations Information on overnight accommodations made available.

Additional Information Ms and illustration consultations are available. Brochure/guidelines available on Web site. SCBWI also holds an annual winter conference in New York City. See the listing in the Northeast section or visit www.scbwi.org for details.

SQUAW VALLEY COMMUNITY OF WRITERS

P.O. Box 1416, Nevada City CA 95959-1416. (530)470-8440. E-mail: info@squawvalleywriters.org. Web site: www.squawvalleywriters.org. **Contact:** Brett Hall Jones, executive director. Estab. 1969. Annual. Conference held in August. Conference duration: 7 days. Average attendance: 124. "These writers workshops in fiction, nonfiction and memoir assist talented writers by exploring the art and craft as well as the business of writing." Offerings include daily morning workshops led by writer-teachers, editors, or agents of the staff, limited to 12-13 participants; seminars; panel discussions of editing and publishing; craft colloquies; lectures; and staff readings. Past themes and panels included Personal History in Fiction, Narrative Structure, Roots, and Anatomy of a Short Story. Past faculty and speakers included Dorothy Allison, Bill Barich, Max Byrd, Louis Edwards, Anne Lamott, Martin J. Smith, Anthony Swofford, Mark Childress, Janet Fitch, Richard Ford, Karen Joy Fowler, Lynn Freed, Dagoberto Gilb, Molly Giles, Glen David Gold, Sands Hall, James D. Houston, Louis B. Jones, Alice Sebold, Amy Tan, Al Young.

Costs Tuition is $750, which includes 6 dinners.

Accommodations The Community of Writers rents houses and condominiums in the Valley for participants to live in during the week of the conference. Single room (one participant): $550/week. Double room (twin beds, room shared by conference participant of the same sex): $350/week. Multiple room (bunk beds, room shared with 2 or more participants of the same sex): $200/week. All rooms subject to availability; early requests are recommended. Can arrange airport shuttle pickups for a fee.

Additional Information Admissions are based on submitted ms (unpublished fiction, one or two stories or novel chapters); requires $25 reading fee. Submit ms to Brett Hall Jones, Squaw Valley Community of Writers, P.O. Box 1416, Nevada City, CA 95959. Deadline: May 10. Notification: June 10. Brochure/guidelines available February by phone, e-mail or visit Web site. Accepts inquiries by SASE, e-mail, phone. Agents and editors attend/participate in conferences.

STEINBECK FESTIVAL

1 Main Street, Salinas CA 93901. (831)796-3833. Fax: (831)796-3828. Web site: www.steinbeck.org. Estab. 1980. Annual. Conference held August 7-10, 2008. Average attendance: 1,000 "over 4-day period." Conference focuses on the life and writings of John Steinbeck. Multi-day festival includes speakers, bus and walking tours, events and museum admission. Site: National Steinbeck Center, a museum with permanent, multimedia exhibition about John Steinbeck and changing art and cultural exhibits.

Costs Fees range from $17 to $75 per person, depending on the programs offered.

Accommodations Provides a list of area hotel and lodging options.

TMCC WRITERS' CONFERENCE

TMCC Workforce Development and Continuing Education Division, 5270 Neil Road Rm 216, Reno NV 89502. (775)829-9010. Fax: (775)829-9032. E-mail: wdce@tmcc.edu. Web site: www.wdce.tmcc writers.edu. Estab. 1990. Annual. 2009 conference held in April. Average attendance: 125. Conference focuses on strengthening mainstream/literary fiction and nonfiction works and how to market them to agents and publisher. Site: Truckee Meadows Community College in Reno, Nevada.

Cost: $89 for lectures; $29 for one-on-one appointment with an agent.

Accommodations: A wide range of affordable accommodations are available nearby.

Additional Information: Brochures are available the end of November through the Web site, e-mail or mail. Accepts inquires by phone or e-mail. Multiple agents, along with successful authors, participate in this event. "This conference features a supportive, informal atmosphere where questions are encouraged."

UCLA EXTENSION WRITERS' PROGRAM

10995 Le Conte Avenue, #440, Los Angeles CA 90024-2883. (310)825-9415 or (800)388-UCLA. Fax: (310)206-7382. E-mail: writers@UCLAextension.edu. Web site: www.uclaextension.edu/writers. **Contact:** Cindy Lieberman, program manager. Courses held year-round with one-day or intensive weekend workshops to 12-week courses. Writers Studio held in February. A 9-month master class is also offered every fall. "The diverse offerings span introductory seminars to professional novel and script completion workshops. The annual Writers Studio and a number of 1-, 2- and 4-day intensive workshops are popular with out-of-town students due to their specific focus and the chance to work with industry professionals. The most comprehensive and diverse continuing education writing program in the country, offering over 550 courses a year, including screenwriting, fiction, writing for the youth market, poetry, nonfiction, playwriting and publishing. Adult learners in the UCLA Extension Writers' Program study with professional screenwriters, fiction writers, playwrights, poets and nonfiction writers, who bring practical experience, theoretical knowledge and a wide variety of teaching styles and philosophies to their classes." Site: Courses are offered in Los Angeles on the UCLA campus and in the 1010 Westwood Center in Westwood Village, as well as online. **Costs** Vary from $95 for one-day workshops to about $475 for quarterly courses to $3,250 for the 9-month master class. **Accommodations** Students make own arrangements. The program can provide assistance in locating local accommodations. **Additional Information** Writers Studio information available October. For brochures/guidelines/ guide to course offerings, visit Web site, e-mail, fax or call. Accepts inquiries by e-mail, fax, phone. "Some advanced level classes have manuscript submittal requirements; instructions are always detailed in the quarterly UCLA Extension course catalog. The UCLA Extension Screenwriting Competition is now in its third year, featuring prizes and industry recognition to the top three winners. An annual fiction prize, The James Kirkwood Prize in Creative Writing, has been established and is given annually to one fiction writer who has produced outstanding work in a Writers' Program course."

🆉 🎯 🅖 WONDERCON

Comic-Con International, P.O. Box 128458, San Diego CA 92112-8458. (619)491-2475. Fax: (619)414-1022. E-mail: cci-info@comic-con.org. Web site: www.comic-con.org/wc/. **Contact:** Greg Sassaman, director of programming. Estab. 1986. Annual. Last conference held February 22-24, 2008, in San Francisco. Conference duration: 3 days. Average attendance: 14,500. "In addition to comics publisher panels, you can count on special spotlights on all of our guests. We're currently talking to many major Hollywood studios to once again present exclusive material and appearances at WonderCon. WonderCon offers a giant exhibit hall filled to the brim with the finest in old and new comics, books, original art, anime, manga, movie memorabilia, action figures and toys, DVDs, and much more. WonderCon also presents one of the best Artists' Alley sections in the country with some of the most popular artists in comics, past, present and future." Site: 2008 was held at Moscone West conference center in San Francisco. WonderCon 2008 programming featured Writing with J. Michael Straczynski, Finding Truth in Comic Books, TOKYOPOP Creator Panel, The Secret Origins of Good Readers, Secret History of Comics, and much more. Check Web site for 2009 guests and programming schedule. **Accommodations** Does not offer overnight accommodations. Provides list of area hotels or lodging options. Special hotel rates available for WonderCon attendees. Check Web site for details. **Additional Information** For brochure, visit Web site. Editors participate in conference.

WRITE FROM THE HEART

9827 Irvine Avenue, Upper Lake CA 95485. (707)275-9011. E-mail: Halbooks@HalZinaBennet.com. Web site: www.HalZinaBennet.com. **Contact:** HalZina Bennett. Offered 4 to 6 times a year. Conference duration: 3-5 days. Also, year-long mentorships. Average attendance: 15-30. "Open to all genres, focusing on accessing the author's most individualized sources of imagery, characterization, tensions, content, style and voice." Site: Varies; California's Mt. Shasta, Mendocino California coast, Chicago, Colorado. Panels include Creativity and Life Experiences: Sourcing Story and Character from What You Have Lived, Getting Happily Published, and more. Instructor: Hal Zina Bennett. **Costs** $350 and up. **Accommodations** No arrangements for transportation. Provides list of area hotels.

Additional Information Brochures available. Request by SASE, e-mail, phone, fax or on Web site. Editors participate in conference. "Hal is a personal writing coach with over 200 successfully published clients, including several bestsellers. His own 30 books include fiction, nonfiction, poetry."

WRITERS STUDIO AT UCLA EXTENTION

1010 Westwood Blvd., Los Angeles CA 90024. (310)825-9415. E-mail: writers@uclaextension.edu. Web site: www.uclaextension.edu/writers. **Contact:** Corey Campbell. Estab. 1997. Annual in February. Conference duration: 4 days; 10 a.m. to 6 p.m. Average attendance: 150-200. Intensive writing workshops in the areas of creative writing, screenwriting and television writing. Site: Conducted at UCLA Extension's 1010 Westwood Center.
Cost Fee is $775 after December 7, 2007.
Accommodations Information on overnight accommodations is available.
Additional Information For more information, call number (310)825-9415 or send an e-mail to writers @uclaextension.edu.

WRITING AND ILLUSTRATING FOR YOUNG READERS WORKSHOP

BYU, conferences and workshops, 348 HCEB, BYU, Provo UT 84602-1532. (801)422-2568. Fax: (801)422-0745. E-mail: cw348@byu.edu. Web site: http://wifyr.byu.edu. **Contact:** Conferences & Workshops. Estab. 2000. Annual. 5-day workshop held in June of each year. The workshop is designed for people who want to write or illustrate for children or teenagers. Participants focus on a single market during daily four-hour morning writing workshops led by published authors or illustrators. Afternoon workshop sessions include a mingle with the authors, editors and agents. Workshop focuses on fiction for young readers: picture books, book-length fiction, fantasy/science fiction, nonfiction, mystery, illustration and general writing. Site: Conference Center at Brigham Young University in the foothills of the Wasatch Mountain range.
Costs $450, full registration includes all workshops and breakout sessions plus a banquet on Thursday evening. $120, afternoon-only registration includes all afternoon workshop sessions plus the banquet on Thursday evening.
Accommodations Local lodging, airport shuttle. Lodging rates: $49-95/night.

NORTHWEST (AK, ID, MT, OR, WA, WY)

◎ BOUCHERCON

507 S. 8th Street, Philadelphia PA 19147. (215)923-0211. Fax: (215)923-1789. E-mail: registration@b ouchercon2007. Web site: www.bouchercon.com; www.bouchercon2007.com. Conference held October 9-12, 2008, in Anchorage, AK. The Bouchercon is "the world mystery and detective fiction event." Site: Anchorage Hilton Hotel. See Web site for details. Special guests include Ann Rule, Alexander McCall Smith.
Costs $200 (prior to July 1, 2007), $250 (after July 1) registration fee covers writing workshops, panels, reception, etc.
Additional Information Sponsors Anthony Award for published mystery novel; ballots due prior to conference. Information available on Web site.

CENTRUM'S PORT TOWNSEND WRITERS' CONFERENCE

P.O. Box 1158, Port Townsend WA 98368-0958. (360)385-3102. Fax: (360)385-2470. E-mail: info@ce ntrum.org. Web site: www.centrum.org. **Contact:** Jordan Hartt, program manager. Estab. 1974. Annual. Conference held mid-July. Average attendance: 180. Conference to promote poetry, fiction, creative nonfiction "featuring many of the nation's leading writers." Two different workshop options: "New Works" and "Works-in-Progress." Site: The conference is held at Fort Worden State Park on the Strait of Juan de Fuca. "The site is a Victorian-era military fort with miles of beaches, wooded trails and recreation facilities. The park is within the limits of Port Townsend, a historic seaport and arts community, approximately 80 miles northwest of Seattle, on the Olympic Peninsula." Guest speakers participate in addition to full-time faculty.
Costs Tuition $495, Room and board ranges from $200-$390, depending on the option you choose.
Accommodations "Modest room and board facilities on site." Also list of hotels/motels/inns/bed & breakfasts/private rentals available.

Additional Information Brochures/guidelines available for SASE or on Web site. "The conference focus is on the craft of writing and the writing life, not on marketing."

◎ CLARION WEST WRITERS' WORKSHOP

340 15th Avenue E, Suite 350, Seattle WA 98112-5156. (206)322-9083. E-mail: info@clarionwest.org. Web site: www.clarionwest.org. **Contact:** Leslie Howle, executive director. Estab. 1983. Annual. Workshop usually held in late June through July. Average attendance: 18. "Conference to prepare students for professional careers in science fiction and fantasy writing." Deadline for applications: March 1. Site: Conference held in Seattle's University district, an urban site close to restaurants and cafes, but not too far from downtown. Faculty: 6 teachers (professional writers and editors established in the field). "Every week a new instructor—each a well-known writer chosen for the quality of his or her work and for professional stature—teaches the class, bringing a unique perspective on speculative fiction. During the fifth week, the workshop is taught by a professional editor."

Costs Workshop tuition, dormitory housing and some meals: $3,200. ($100 discount if application received by February 1).

Accommodations Students stay on site in workshop housing at one of the University of Washington's sorority houses.

Additional Information "Students write their own stories every week while preparing critiques of all the other students' work for classroom sessions. This gives participants a more focused, professional approach to their writing. The core of the workshop remains science fiction, and short stories (not novels) are the focus." Conference information available in Fall 2008. For brochure/guidelines send SASE, visit Web site, e-mail or call. Accepts inquiries by e-mail, phone, SASE. Limited scholarships are available, based on financial need. Students must submit 20-30 pages of ms with $25 fee for applications sent by mail, $30 for e-mail applications by e-mail to qualify for admission.

Ⓝ ◎ Ⓒ EMERALD CITY COMICON

800 Convention Place, Seattle, WA 98037. E-mail: info@emeraldcitycomicon.com. Web site: www.e meraldcitycomicon.com. Estab. 2002. Annual. Next show: May 10-11, 2008. Conference duration: 2 days. "The premiere comic book convention of the Pacific Northwest. Includes comic creators and media guests, various creative and publishing panels, exhibitors, dealers and much more." Site: Washington State Convention & Trade Center. Guests include J. Michael Straczynski, Brian Michael Bendis, David Finch, Arthur Suydam, Tim Sale and many more, as well as Image Comics, Oni Press, Fantagraphics, Dark Horse, Top Shelf and others.

Costs $15/day or $25/weekend pre-sale, $20/Sat, $15/Sun or $30/weekend on-site.

Accommodations Offers overnight accommodations. Discounted rate at Roosevelt Hotel, Crowne Plaza and Red Lion in Seattle.

Additional Information For information, visit Web site. Editors participate in conference.

FLATHEAD RIVER WRITERS CONFERENCE

P.O. Box 7711, Kalispell MT 59904. E-mail: slimsmith@montanasky.net. **Contact:** Val Smith. Estab. 1990. Annual. Next conference: Intense workshops October 1-3, 2008, Conference October 4-5, 2008. Attendance limited to 100. Deals with all aspects of writing, including short and long fiction and nonfiction. Site: Kalilspell, MT. Past speakers includes Anne Rule, Linda Seger, Donald Maass.

Costs Cost of general weekend conference; $150 includes breakfast and lunch, not lodging.

Additional Information "We limit attendance to 100 in order to assure friendly, easy access to presentations."

◎ HEART TALK

Women's Center for Ministry, Western Seminary, 5511 SE Hawthorne Blvd., Portland OR 97215-3367. (503)517-1931 or (877)517-1800, ext. 1931. Fax: (503)517-1889. E-mail: wcm@westernsemina ry.edu. Web site: www.westernseminary.edu/women/. **Contact:**Kenine Stein, administrative associate. Estab. 1998. Every other year (alternates with speaker's conferences). March 12-15, 2008 will be a speakers conference with Carol Kent and team from Speak Up With Confidence. Original and mini-advanced seminars, with a writing workshop included in mini-advanced. Last writing conference was March 11-14, 2008. Conference duration: writing, 1 day; speaking, 2-4 days. Average attendance: 100 + . "Heart Talk provides inspirational training for women desiring to write for publication and/or speak publicly." Site: "Western Seminary has a chapel plus classrooms to accommodate various size groups. The campus has a peaceful park-like atmosphere with beautiful lawns, trees and flowers." Heart Talk 2009 will be the next conference, tentatively scheduled for March. Please check Web site for further details as they become available. (Topics in 2007 ranged from writing inspirational shorts, gift books, storyboarding, to book proposals, publishing alternatives, marketing, self-editing, being own publicist, and more. 2007 keynote speaker was Deborah Hedstrom-Page. Workshops by Athena Dean, Sue Miholer, Elizabeth Jones, Carla Williams, Maxine Marsolini, and Karla Dornacher. Editors available for 1:1 consultation included Rebekah Clark, Athena Dean, Elizabeth Jones, Renee Sanford, and Carla Williams.)

Costs $55 in 2007; box lunch can be ordered.

Additional Information Conference information available in January by e-mail, phone, fax and on Web site. For inquiries, contact by mail, e-mail, phone. Conference "is open to Christian women who desire to write for publication. Please view our Web site for Heart Talk 2009 Writer's Conference details. They will be posted as they become available. E-mail us to be added to our Heart Talk mailing list."

JACKSON HOLE WRITERS CONFERENCE

Jackson WY (307)766-2938. Fax: (307)766-3914. E-mail: jrieman@uwyo.edu. Web site: http://jacksonholewritersconference.com/. **Contact:** Jerimiah Rieman, coordinator. Annual. Last conference held June 26-29, 2008. Conference duration: 4 days. Average attendance: 100. The Jackson Hole Writers Conference draws a wide range of participants, from beginners to published writers. Site: Snow King Resort. The conference is directed toward fiction, screen writing and creative nonfiction, offering programs relevant to all 3 disciplines: story structure, character development, narrative thrust, work habits and business techniques. In addition, separate sessions deal with skills particular to each specialty.

Costs $325 conference pre-registration; $300 conference pre-registration for past participants; $75 spouse/guest registration; $50 ms evaluation; $75 extended ms evaluation. "You must register for conference to be eligible for manuscript evaluation."

Accommodations $135/night for single or double; $145/night triple; $155/night quadruple.

Additional Information The conference faculty's goal is to help our writers get published. Agent and editor roundtable discussions are geared specifically to teach you how your writing can be crafted, shaped and packaged for sale. Ms evaluations are also available. See Web site for details.

THE NOVEL WRITERS WORKSHOP

P.O. Box 392, Langley WA 98260. E-mail: bob@bobmayer.org. Web site: www.bobmayer.org. **Contact:** Bob Mayer. Estab. 2002. Conference duration: 4 days. Average attendance: limit of 8 attendees. Workshop. Site: Saratoga Inn, Whidbey Island, WA.

Costs $550 in 2007

Accommodations Does not include overnight accommodations. Provides list of area hotels or lodging options.

Additional Information Participants submit cover letter, one page synopsis, and first 15 pages of ms. For brochure, visit Web site.

PACIFIC NORTHWEST WRITERS CONFERENCE

P.O. Box 2016, Edmonds WA 98020-9516. (425)673-2665. Fax: (425)771-9588. E-mail: pnwa@pnwa.org. Web site: www.pnwa.org. **Contact:** Brenda Stav, association executive. Annual. 2008 conference held July 17-20. Average attendance: 450.

Accommodations Hotel shuttle to and from airport available. Offers discounted rate for overnight lodging; $129/night in 2005.

Additional Information Offers contest with 11 fiction categories: young writers, romance genre, screenwriting, adult genre novel, Jean M. Auel Mainstream Novel, Judine and Terry Brooks Juvenile/YA Novel, adult short story, juvenile short story/picture book, poetry, nonfiction book/memoir, adult article/essay/short memoir. Entry requirements vary with category. Guidelines for contest available on Web site; brochure for conference available on Web site in late February. Accepts inquiries by e-mail, phone, fax. Agents and editors participate in conference.

SAGEBRUSH WRITERS WORKSHOP

P.O. Box 1255, Big Timber MT 59011-1255. (406)932-4227. E-mail: sagebrsh@ttc-cmc.net. **Contact:** Gwen Petersen, director. Estab. 1997. Annual. Workshop usually held in April or May. Conference duration: 2½ days. Average attendance: 25-30. "Each year, the workshop has a different focus." Conference features "intensive personal instruction, good food, advance critiques, well-published authors/instructors, agents/editors, book sales and signings, readings." Site: American Legion, Carnegie Library or other venue, Big Timber, MT. Faculty consists of one writer/instructor and 2 guest speakers.

Costs $190 (2005), included Friday evening banquet dinner with guest speakers, all snacks at breaks.

Accommodations Offers shuttle from airport by arrangement with Sagebrush. Provides a list of area hotels and/or lodging options.

Additional Information "Submissions optional but encouraged—up to 10 pages." Workshop information is available February. For brochure send SASE, e-mail, call or fax. Accepts inquiries by SASE, e-mail, phone and fax. Agents and editors participate in conference.

SITKA CENTER FOR ART AND ECOLOGY

P.O. Box 65, Otis OR 97368. (541)994-5485. Fax: (541)994-8024. E-mail: info@sitkacenter.org. Web site: www.sitkacenter.org. **Contact:** Laura Young, program manager. Estab. 1970. "Our workshop program is open to all levels and is held annually from late May until late November. We also have a residency program from September through May." Average attendance: 10-16/workshop. A variety of workshops in creative process, including book arts and other media. Site: The Center borders a Nature Conservatory Preserve, the Siuslaw National Experimental Forest and the Salmon River Estuary, located just north of Lincoln City, OR.

Costs "Workshops are generally $50-300; they do not include meals or lodging."

Accommodations Does not offer overnight accommodations. Provides a list of area hotels or lodging options.

Additional Information Brochure available in February of each year by SASE, phone, e-mail, fax or visit Web site. Accepts inquiries by SASE, e-mail, phone, fax.

SITKA SYMPOSIUM

P.O. Box 2420, Sitka AK 99835-2420. (907)747-3794. Fax: (907)747-6554. E-mail: island@ak.net. Web site: www.islandinstitutealaska.org. **Contact:** Carolyn Servid, director. Estab. 1984. Annual. Conference held in June. Conference duration: 3-5 days. Enrollment limited to 60. Conference "to consider the relationship between writing and the ideas of selected theme focusing on social and cultural issues." Site: The Symposium is held in downtown Sitka, in the heart of southeast Alaska's striking coastal mountains and temperate rain forest. Many points of visitor interest are within walking distance. Guest speakers have included Alison Deming, Scott Russell Sanders, Rina Swentzell, Barry Lopez, William Kittredge, Gary Synder, Lorna Goodison, Terry Tempest Williams, Robert Hass, Wendell Berry and Linda Hogan.

Costs $350.

Accommodations Accommodation info is listed on Symposium brochure and Web site.

Additional Information Conference brochures/guidelines are available for SASE or online. Accepts inquiries by e-mail and fax.

SOUTH COAST WRITERS CONFERENCE

P.O. Box 590, 29392 Ellensburg Avenue, Gold Beach OR 97444. (541)247-2741. Fax: (541)247-6247. E-mail: scwc@socc.edu. Web site: www.socc.edu/scwriters. **Contact:** Janet Pretti, coordinator. Estab. 1996. Annual. Conference held President's Day weekend. Workshops held Friday and Saturday. Average attendance: 100. "We try to cover a broad spectrum: fiction, historical, poetry, children's, nature." Site: "Friday workshops are held at The Event Center on the Beach. Saturday workshops are held at the high school." 2008 keynote speaker will be David Oliver Relin. Other presenters Larry Brooks, Jim Coffee, Ann Cameron, Rory Miller, Jayel Gibson, Phil Hann, Jessica Bryan, Sylvia Tohill, Sue Lick, Dan Frechette, Sally Harrold, and Se-ah-dom Edmo.

Costs $55 before January 31; $65 after. Friday workshops are an additional $40. No meals or lodging included.

Accommodations Provides list of area hotels.

Additional Information Sponsors contest. Bob Simons Scholarship open to anyone. Contact SCWC for details.

◎ THUNDER ARM WRITING RETREAT WITH NORTH CASCADES INSTITUTE

North Cascades Institute, 810 Highway 20, Sedro-Wooley WA 98284-9394. (360)856-5700 ext. 209. Fax: (360)856-1934. E-mail: nci@ncascades.org. Web site: www.ncascades.org. Contact: Deb Martin, registrar. Estab. 1999. Annual. 2007 conference was held July 25-29. Conference duration: 4 days. Average attendance: 32. Led by three outstanding writers, the Institute's Thunder Arm Writing Retreat engages amateur and professional writers alike with lectures, discussions, readings and writing exercises centered on the natural world. "Nature writing, at its simplest, strives to explore basic principles at work in nature and to convey these in language that introduces readers to the facility and wonder of their own place in the world." Site: North Cascades Environmental Learning Center on Diablo Lake in North Cascades National Park. Past faculty includes: Barbara Kingsolver, Robert Michael Pyle, William Kittredge, Ann Zwinger, Gary Ferguson, Kathleen Dean Moore, and William Dietrich.

Costs 2007 costs were $325 (triple occupancy), $475 (double), $695 (single). All options include meals.

Additional Information For conference information, visit Web Site, e-mail or call.

TIN HOUSE SUMMER WRITERS WORKSHOP

P.O. Box 10500, Portland OR 97296. (503)219-0622. Fax: (503)222-1154. E-mail: cheston@tinhouse.com. Web site: www.tinhouse.com. **Contact:** Cheston Knapp, Director. Estab. 2003. Annual in July. Conference duration: 1 week. Average attendance: 100. A weeklong intensive of panels, seminars, workshops and readings led by the editors of *Tin House* magazine and Tin House Books, and their guests—prominent contemporary writers of fiction, nonfiction, poetry and film. Site: The workshop will be held at Reed College in scenic Portland, OR, just minutes from downtown and the airport. Facilities include bookstore, library, mail service, an art gallery, print shop and athletic facilities. Each afternoon agents, editors, writers and filmmakers will discuss ideas and offer a range of discussions on topics and issues concerning the craft and business of writing. See Web site for specifics. 2007 faculty included Charles Baxter, T.C. Boyle, Annie Proulx, Colson Whitehead, Aimee Bender, Dorothy Allison.

Costs 2006 tuition was $950; food and lodging $550. Application fee $35. Scholarships available.

Additional Information Attendees must submit writing sample and attend by invitation. Deadline: April 1, then rolling while space allows. Admission is based on the strength and promise of the writing sample—up to 15 pages of fiction. Brochures available in February for SASE, by fax, phone, e-mail and on Web site. Accepts inquiries by SASE, e-mail, phone, fax. Agents and editors attend conference.

WILLAMETTE WRITERS CONFERENCE

9045 SW Barbur Blvd., Suite 5-A, Portland OR 97219-4027. (503)452-1592. Fax: (503)452-0372. E-mail: wilwrite@willamettewriters.com. Web site: www.willamettewriters.com. **Contact:** Bill Johnson, office manager. Estab. 1981. Annual. Conference held in August. Conference duration: 3 days. Average attendance: 600. "Willamette Writers is open to all writers, and we plan our conference accordingly. We offer workshops on all aspects of fiction, nonfiction, marketing, the creative process, screenwriting, etc. Also we invite top-notch inspirational speakers for keynote addresses. Recent theme was 'The Writers Way.' We always include at least one agent or editor panel and offer a variety of topics of interest to both fiction and nonfiction writers and screenwriters." Recent editors, agents and film producers in attendance have included: Elise Capron; Jane Friedman; Laura Rennert; Angela Rinaldi; Tony Outhwaite.

Costs Cost for 3-day conference including meals is $395 members; $425 nonmembers.

Accommodations If necessary, these can be made on an individual basis. Some years special rates are available.

Additional Information Conference brochure/guidelines are available in May for catalog-size SASE, e-mail, fax, phone or on Web site. Accepts inquiries by fax, e-mail, phone, SASE.

WORKSHOPS WITH JESSICA PAGE MORRELL

P.O. Box 820141, Portland OR 97282-1141. E-mail: jesswrites@juno.com or jessica@spiritone.com. Web site: www.writing-life.com. **Contact:** Jessica P. Morrell. Estab. 1991. "I teach a variety of one-day and weekend workshops in the Pacific Northwest, Vancouver, B.C., the Oregon Coast and will begin teaching in Mexico in 2009. Subjects include Deep Fiction; Fiction Middles; Plot is a Verb The

First 50 Pages; Show, Don't Tell; Narrative Nonfiction; Between the Lines: the Subtler Aspects of Fiction Story People, The Final Edit and A Vivid Vision. I also lead fiction and nonfiction critique groups in Portland, OR. Please contact me for details about my schedule or subscribe to my newsletter. I generally teach about 12 workshops a year." Jessica Page Morrell is the author of *Writing Out the Storm, Between The Lines: Master the Subtle Elements of Fiction Writing, The Writer's I Ching,* and *Bullies, Bastards, & Bitches, How to Write the Bad Guys in Fiction,* and a book upcoming in 2009 for writers.

Costs for workshop ranges from $75-300. Provides a list of area hotels or lodging options.

Additional Information Available via e-mail or mail inquiries.

WRITE ON THE SOUND WRITERS' CONFERENCE

Edmonds Arts Commission, 700 Main Street, Edmonds WA 98020. (425)771-0228. Fax: (425)771-0253. E-mail: wots@ci.edmonds.wa.us. **Contact:** Kris Gillespie, conference organizer. Estab. 1986. Annual. Last conference held October 7-8 2007. Conference duration: 2.5 days. Average attendance: 180. "Conference is small—good for networking—and focuses on the craft of writing." Site: "Edmonds is a beautiful community on the shores of Puget Sound, just north of Seattle. View brochure at www.ci.edmonds.wa.us/artscommission/wpts.stm."

Costs $108 by Sept. 19, $130 after Sept. 19 for 2 days, $68 for 1 day (2007); includes registration, morning refreshments and 1 ticket to keynote lecture.

Additional Information Brochures available August 1. Accepts inquiries by phone, e-mail, fax.

THE WRITERS WORKSHOP

PO Box 329, Langley WA 98260.E-mail: bob@bobmayer.org. Web site: www.bobmayer.org. **Contact:** Bob Mayer. Estab: 2002. Held every 3 months. Last conference: November 2008. Conference duration: 4 days. Site: Held at the Saratoga Inn, Langley WA

Cost: $550 in 2007

Additional Information Limited to eight participants and focused on their novel.

WRITING IT REAL IN PORT TOWNSEND

(formerly the Colorado Mt. Writer's Workshop), 394 Colman Drive, Port Townsend, WA 98368. (360)385-7839. Web site: http://writingitreal.com/wirconference2007.htm. Established 1999. Annual. Last conference held in June. Conference duration: 4 days. Average Attendance: 35. Named one of the top retreats by *Personal Journaling Magazine,* this conference focuses on fiction, poetry and personal essay. The conference is designed to lift writers, novice or experienced, to the next level. Site: Held at a hotel (housing there or around town) in Port Townsend, WA. Features personal writing. Faculty includes Sheila Bender, Susan Reich, Jack Heffron.

Costs $475 ($425 if paid in full by April 1). Accommodations and meals separate. Daily activities include craft talks, small group manuscript workshop, hands-on exercises for creating new work, instructor and group responses, readings.

CANADA

◘ ◎ BLOODY WORDS MYSTERY CONFERENCE

Phone/fax: (416)497-5293. E-mail: soles@sff.net. Web site: www.bloodywords.com. **Contact:** Caro Soles, chair. Estab. 1999. Annual. Last conference held June 6-8, 2008. Average attendance: 300. Focus: Mystery/true crime/forensics, with Canadian slant. Purpose: To bring readers and writers of the mystery genre together in a Canadian setting. Site: Toronto, ON: Eaton Center Downtown Marriott. Conference includes two workshops and two tracks of panels, one on factual information such as forensics, agents, scene of the crime procedures, etc. and one on fiction, such as "Death in a Cold Climate," "Murder on the Menu," "Elementary, My Dear Watson," and a First Novelists Panel. Guests of honor in 2008 were Rosemary Aubert and Carolyn Hart.

Costs 2007 fee: $175 (Canadian)/$165 (US), included the banquet and all panels, readings, dealers' room and workshop.

Accommodations Offers block of rooms in hotel; list of optional lodging available. Check Web site for details.

Additional Information Sponsors short mystery story contest—5,000 word limit; judges are experienced editors of anthologies; fee is $5 (entrants must be registered). Conference information is available now. For brochure visit Web site. Accepts inquiries by e-mail and phone. Agents and editors participate in conference. "This is a conference for both readers and writers of mysteries, the only one of its kind in Canada. We also run 'The Mystery Cafe,' a chance to get to know 15 authors, hear them read and ask questions (half hour each)."

█ BOOMING GROUND

Buch E-462, 1866 Main Mall, Creative Writing Program, UBC, Vancouver BC V6T 121 Canada. (604)822-2469. Fax: (604)822-3616. E-mail: apply@boomingground.com. Web site: www.boominggr ound.com. **Contact:** Nancy Lee. Estab. 1998. Average attendance: 30 per session. Writing mentorships geared toward beginner, intermediate, and advanced levels in novel, short fiction, poetry, nonfiction and children's writing. Open to students. Online mentorship program-students work for 4-8 months with a mentor by e-mail, allowing up to 120-240 pages of material to be created. Site: Online and by e-mail.

Costs $780 (Canadian) for online mentorships; individual manuscript evaluation also available.

Additional Information Workshops are based on works-in-progress. Writers must submit ms with application. For guidelines visit Web site, e-mail, or call. Accepts inquiries by phone, fax, e-mail. "Classes are offered for writers at all levels—from early career to mid-career. All student work is evaluated by a jury. Our mentorships are ideal for long-form work such as novels, collections of poetry and short fiction."

█ HUMBER SCHOOL FOR WRITERS SUMMER WORKSHOP

Humber Institute of Technology and Advanced Learning, 3199 Lake Shore Blvd. West, Toronto ON M8V 1K8 Canada. (416)675-6622 ext. 3448. Fax: (416)251-7167. E-mail: antanas.sileika@humber.ca. Web site: www.humber.ca/creativeandperformingarts. **Contact:** Antanas Sileika, director. Annual. Workshop held July. Conference duration: 1 week. Average attendance: 100. Focuses on fiction, poetry, creative nonfiction. Site: Humber College's Lakeshore campus in Toronto. Panels cover success stories, small presses, large presses, agents. Faculty: Changes annually. 2007 included Andrea Levy, Nino Ricci, Miriam Toews, Guy Vanderhaeghe, Marsha Skrypuch, Erika de Vasconcelos, Alistair Macleod, David Bezmozgis, Joseph Boyden, Wayson Choy, Bruce Jay Friedman, Isabel Huggan, Kim Moritsugu, Olive Senior and others.

Costs Workshop fee is $950 Canadian ($800 US).

Accommodations Provides lodging. Residence fee is $350 Canadian ($280 US).

Additional Information Participants "must submit sample writing no longer than 15 pages approximately 4 weeks before workshop begins." Brochures available mid-February for e-mail, phone, fax. Accepts inquiries by e-mail, phone, fax. Agents and editors participate in conference.

█ MARITIME WRITERS' WORKSHOP

UNB Arts Centre, P.O. Box 4400, Fredericton NB E3B 5A3 Canada. Phone/fax: (506)453-4623. E-mail: atitus@unb.ca. Web site: http://extend.unb.ca/pers_cult/writers/index.php. **Contact:** Andrew Titus, coordinator. Estab. 1976. Workshop held annually in July. Average attendance: 50. "We offer small groups of 10, practical manuscript focus. Novice writers welcome. Workshops in fiction, poetry, mystery/suspense, and francophone literature. The annual Maritime Writers' Workshop is a practical, wide-ranging program designed to help writers develop and refine their creative writing skills. This weeklong program will involve you in small group workshops, lectures and discussions, public readings and special events, all in a supportive community of writers who share a commitment to excellence. Workshop groups consist of a maximum of 10 writers each. Instructors are established Canadian authors and experienced teachers with a genuine interest in facilitating the writing process of others. For over a quarter century, Maritime Writers' Workshop has provided counsel, encouragement and direction for hundreds of developing writers." Site: University of New Brunswick, Fredericton campus.

Costs 2006: $495 tuition.

Accommodations On-campus accommodations and meals.

Additional Information "Participants must submit 10-20 manuscript pages which form a focus for workshop discussions." Brochures available after March. No SASE necessary. Accepts inquiries by e-mail and fax.

☒ SAGE HILL WRITING EXPERIENCE

Box 1731, Saskatoon SK S7K 3S1 Canada. Phone: (306)652-7395. E-mail: sage.hill@sasktel.net. Web site: www.sagehillwriting.ca. **Contact:** Steven Ross Smith. Annual. Workshops held in July and May. Conference duration: 10-14 days. Average attendance: Summer, 30-40; Fall, 6-8. "Sage Hill Writing Experience offers a special working and learning opportunity to writers at different stages of development. Top quality instruction, low instructor-student ratio and the beautiful Sage Hill setting offer conditions ideal for the pursuit of excellence in the arts of fiction, poetry and playwriting." Site: The Sage Hill location features "individual accommodation, in-room writing area, lounges, meeting rooms, healthy meals, walking woods and vistas in several directions." Various classes are held: Introduction to Writing Fiction & Poetry; Fiction Workshop; Fiction Colloquium, Poetry Workshop; Poetry Colloquium; Playwriting Lab.

Costs Summer program, $1,095 (Canadian) includes instruction, accommodation, meals and all facilities. Fall Fiction Colloquium: $1,395 (Canadian).

Accommodations On-site individual accommodations for Summer and Fall programs located at Lumsden, 45 kilometers outside Regina.

Additional Information Application requirements for Introduction to Creative Writing: A 5-page sample of your writing or a statement of your interest in creative writing; list of courses taken required. For workshop and colloquium programs: A résumé of your writing career and a 12-page sample of your work-in-progress, plus 5 pages of published work required. Application deadline for the Summer Program is in April. Spring program deadline in March. Guidelines are available for SASE, e-mail, fax, phone or on Web site. Scholarships and bursaries are available.

☒ THE VICTORIA SCHOOL OF WRITING

1027 Pandora Ave., Victoria BC V8W 3P6 Canada. (250)595-3000. E-mail: info@victoriaschoolofwriting.org. Web site: www.victoriaschoolofwriting.org. Conference held the third week in July annually. "Five-day intensive workshop on beautiful Vancouver Island with outstanding author-instructors in fiction, poetry, nonfiction, memoir, work-in-progress and other genres."

Costs $500-600 (Canadian).

Accommodations On site.

Additional Information Workshop brochures available. Accepts inquiries by e-mail, phone, Web site or land mail.

☒ ☒ WIRED WRITING STUDIO

P.O. Box 1020, Banff AB T1L 1H5 Canada. (800)565-9989. E-mail: arts_info@banffcentre.ca; christie.rall@banffcentre.ca. Web site: www.banffcentre.ca. **Contact:** Office of the Registrar. Annual. Writing workshop. Program Dates: October 6 to 18, 2008 (2-week on-site residency in Banff); November 1, 2008 to March 31, 2009 (20-week online residency). Application deadline: June 16, 2008. "The Wired Writing Studio is a unique opportunity for poets and writers of fiction and other narrative prose to pursue their artistic visions and develop their voices through one-on-one editorial assistance from experienced writers/editors, as well as through involvement in a community of working writers, both on-site at The Banff Centre and online for five months following the residency. Intended specifically for those producing work of literary merit who are at an early stage in their careers, this program offers an extended period of writing time: 2 weeks in Banff and the remaining 20 weeks in the writer's own home or work space, working online. This balance is of special advantage to those with young families, demanding jobs, and other commitments that will not permit them to be away for longer periods. By delivering most of the program online, the Wired Writing Studio broadens a writer's understanding of the Internet's potential as a tool for artistic and professional development. Each participant is assigned to one faculty mentor and will continue with that mentor throughout the program. Online, the creative community is sustained by e-mail, by participation in an online discussion forum, and by readings posted on the Web site." Site: "The Banff Centre enables both emerging and established individuals to interact within a multidisciplinary and multicultural environment, allowing them to push boundaries, to experiment, to share knowledge, to create and showcase new work, and to develop new ideas and solutions for the present and the future."

Costs Workshop fee: please see Web site for up-to-date information, www.banffcentre.ca/writing/.

Accommodations please see Web site for up-to-date information. On-site only, hotel style which also serves as private work spaces. Computers should be brought along for private use. Public computers available on campus.

Additional Information "At time of application, writers must submit writing samples and statement of expectations. Application fee: $57 Canadian. Brochure currently available for e-mail and on Web site. For inquiries, contact by SASE, e-mail, phone, fax. Other writing programs are offered at The Banff Centre include: Banff International Translation Centre, Literary Journalism, Spoken Word, Science Communications, and Mountain Writing."

⬛ THE WRITERS' RETREAT

15 Canusa St., Stanstead QC J0B 3E5 Canada. (819)876-2065. E-mail: info@writersretreat.com. Web site: www.writersretreat.com. **Contact:** Micheline Cote, director. Estab. 2000. Year-round. The Writers' Retreat is designed to comprehensively implement, support, and promote residential retreats and literary services to writers of all literary genres. Residential retreats are open year-round and are located in Canada, Costa Rica, Mexico and the United States, coming soon in Europe. Site: The headquarters are located in Quebec on the Vermont/Quebec border with additional retreats located in Ouray, Colorado; Santa Cruz, California; Santa Fe, New Mexico; Prince Edward Island and New Brunswick, Canada. The Writers' Retreat workshops feature instruction in fiction and nonfiction writing and screenwriting. "Our sole purpose is to provide an ambiance conducive to creativity for career and emerging writers." Residency includes a private studio, breakfast, reference books, wireless Internet, critique, on site editor.
Costs Residency varies between $575-$1,200 per week depending on location. Workshop tuition varies from $195-$1,500, depending on the format.
Additional Information Accepts inquiries by e-mail and phone.

⬛ ⬛ WRITING STUDIO

P.O. Box 1020, Banff AB T1L 1H5 Canada. (800)565-9989. E-mail: arts_info@banffcentre.ca. Web site: www.banffcentre.ca. **Contact:** Office of the Registrar. Annual writing workshop. Program dates: April 28, 2008-May 31, 2008. Application deadline: November 15, 2007. "Writing Studio is a five-week program offering poets and writers of fiction and other narrative prose the time, space, and support they need to pursue a writing project, with the benefit of editorial consultation. Designed for literary writers at an early stage in their careers, the program offers an extended period of uninterrupted writing time, one-on-one editorial assistance from experienced writers/editors, and an opportunity to engage with a community of working writers. The Writing Studio is an ideal environment for artistic inspiration and growth. Situated in the majestic Canadian Rockies, The Banff Centre offers a unique natural setting for artists of all disciplines to realize their creative potential. All participants may work with at least 2 or, in the case of poets, 3 faculty mentors during the 5 weeks of the program. As part of the Banff Summer Arts Festival, Writing Studio participants and faculty offer a weekly reading series. To help writers develop their public reading skills, we offer one-on-one sessions with a voice and relaxation instructor. Activities other than the writer's individual work (i.e., guided hikes, social gatherings, concerts and performances) are voluntary, and participants are encouraged to structure their time to suit their own needs and goals." Site: The Banff Centre enables both emerging and established individuals to interact within a multidisciplinary and multicultural environment, allowing them to push boundaries, to experiment, to share knowledge, to create and showcase new work, and to develop new ideas and solutions for the present and the future.
Costs Workshop fee: please see Web site for up-to-date information, www.banffcentre.ca/writing/.
Accommodations Please see Web site for up-to-date information. On-site only, hotel-style, which also serve as private workspaces. Computers should be brought along for private use. Public computers available on campus.
Additional Information "At time of application, writers must submit writing samples and statement of expectations. Application fee: $57 Canadian. Brochure currently available for e-mail and on Web site. For inquiries, contact by SASE, e-mail, phone, fax. Other writing programs are offered at The Banff Centre include: Banff International Translation Centre, Literary Journalism, Spoken Word, Science Communications, and Mountain Writing."

⬛ ⬛ WRITING WITH STYLE

The Banff Centre, P.O. Box 1020, Banff AB T1L 1H5 Canada. (800)565-9989. E-mail: arts_info@banff centre.ca. Web site: www.banffcentre.ca. **Contact:** Office of the Registrar. Semiannual. Writing workshop. Program dates: Spring: April 21, 2008-April 26, 2008; Fall: September 15, 2008-September 20, 2008. Application deadline: February 01, 2008 (spring); May 15, 2008 (fall). Conference duration: 1

week. Average attendance: 30-40 participants. "Writing With Style is a unique opportunity for writers of all levels to participate in a week-long workshop at The Banff Centre, a setting for artists that is both inspiring and productive. Whether you have attended many writing workshops or this is your first, Writing With Style will be an intense and transformative experience. Amidst a diverse community of writers, you will encounter new ideas and gain confidence in your own style and voice, while shaping and editing your work-in-progress under the guidance of an experienced writer and editor. The program offers a variety of activities designed to maximize the artistic growth of each writer. Participants will enjoy morning group sessions led by a faculty member, in which their work is read and discussed by the other writers in the program. Afternoons are left free for writing and one-on-one meetings and consultations with faculty. Participants are also invited to take part in evening readings with faculty and fellow writers." Site: "The Banff Centre enables both emerging and established individuals to interact within a multidisciplinary and multicultural environment, allowing them to push boundaries, to experiment, to share knowledge, to create and showcase new work, and to develop new ideas and solutions for the present and the future." Genres include short fiction, memoir, poetry, travel writing, creative nonfiction and mystery writing.

Costs Workshop fee: please see Web site for up-to-date information, www.banffcentre.ca/writing/.

Accommodations On-site only, hotel style which also serve as private work spaces. Computers should be brought along for private use. Public computers available on campus. Please see Web site for up-to-date information, www.banffcentre.ca/writing/.

Additional Information "At time of application, writers must submit writing samples and statement of expectations. Application fee: $57 Canadian. Brochure currently available for e-mail and on Web site. For inquiries, contact by SASE, e-mail, phone, fax. Other more advanced writing programs are also offered at The Banff Centre."

INTERNATIONAL

⊕ ANNUAL WINCHESTER WRITERS' CONFERENCE, FESTIVAL AND BOOKFAIR

University of Winchester, Winchester, Hampshire S022 4NR UK. Telephone +44 (0)1962 827238. E-mail: Barbara.Large@winchester.ac.uk. Web site: www.writersconference.co.uk. The 28th Winchester Writers' Conference, Festival and Bookfair will be held on the weekend of June 27-29, 2008 and followed by the Weeklong Writing Workshops at the University of Winchester, Hampshire, UK Colin Dexter, internationally renowned for the Morse crime fiction books and television series will give the Plenary Address. This international conference offers all writers the opportunity to harness their creative ideas and to develop their technical skills under the guidance and instruction of 65 professional writers, literary agents, commissioning editors and book industry specialists during mini courses, workshops, seminars, lectures and 500 one to one appointments. Enter the fifteen writing competitions attached to this conference, even if you can't attend. Book online or print down the application and post. For further information contact Barbara Large, Conference Director, Winchester Writers' Conference, Faculty of Arts.

ART WORKSHOPS IN GUATEMALA

4758 Lyndale Ave. S, Minneapolis MN 55419-5304. (612)825-0747. E-mail: info@artguat.org. Web site: www.artguat.org. **Contact:** Liza Fourre, director. Estab. 1995. Annual. Workshops held year-round. Maximum class size: 10 students per class. Workshop titles include: Fiction Writing: Shaping and Structuring Your Story with Gladys Swan; New Directions in Travel Writing with Richard Harris; Poetry: Snapshots in Words with Rosanne Lloyd; and Creative Writing: Journey of the Soul with Sharon Doubiago.

Costs $1,695 (includes tuition, lodging in a lovely colonial style B&B, and ground transportation, and some pretty interesting field trips).

Accommodations All transportation and accommodations included in price of conference.

Additional Information Conference information available now. For brochure/guidelines visit Web site, e-mail, fax or call. Accepts inquiries by e-mail, phone.

⊕ DINGLE WRITING COURSES

Ballintlea, Ventry, Co Kerry Ireland. 353 66 9159815. E-mail: info@dinglewritingcourses.ie. Web site: www.dinglewritingcourses.ie. **Contact:** Abigail Joffe and Nicholas McLachlan. Estab. 1996.

Annual. Writing workshops held 3 or 4 weekends per year in September and October. Average attendance: 14. Creative writing weekends for fiction, poetry, memoir, novel, writing for children, etc. Site: '' Writer's Retreat on the Dingle Peninsula.'' Recent tutors included Niall Williams, Paula Meehan and Kate Thompson.

Costs 400€ for a weekend (Friday evening to Sunday evening) includes all meals, accommodation, tuition.

Accommodations ''We arrange taxis on request; cost not included in fee.'' Organizes overnight accommodations. ''Large communal eating facility and workroom; spectacular views.'' Also provides list of area lodging.

Additional Information Some workshops require material submitted in advance. Brochures available in May by e-mail, phone, fax or on Web site. Accepts inquiries by e-mail, phone, fax.

INTERNATIONAL READERS THEATRE WORKSHOPS

P.O. Box 17193, San Diego CA 92177. (619)276-1948. Fax: (858)581-3289. E-mail: wadams1@san.rr. com. Web site: www.readerstheatreinstitute.com. **Contact:** Bill Adams, director. Estab. 1974. Last workshop held July 20- August 2, 2008. Average attendance: 50-70. Workshop on ''all aspects of Readers Theatre with emphasis on script making.'' Site: Workshop held at Britannia Hotel in London.

Costs ''$1,795 includes housing for two weeks (twin accommodations), continental breakfast, complimentary mid-morning coffee break on class days, textbook (a $45 value) and all Institute fees.''

Additional Information ''One-on-one critiques available between writer and faculty (if members).'' Conference information available December. For brochures/guidelines visit Web site, e-mail, fax, call, send SASE. Conference offers ''up to 12 credits in theatre, theatre (speech) and/or education (6 credits) from the University of Southern Maine at $154/unit (subject to legislative change for 2006).''

KILLALOE HEDGE-SCHOOL OF WRITING

4 Riverview, Killaloe Co. Clare Ireland. (+353)61 375 217. Fax: (+353)61 375 487. E-mail: khs@killa loe.ie. Web site: www.killaloe.ie/khs. **Contact:** K.Thorne, secretary. Estab. 1999. Held every second weekend between January and May. Conference duration: 10 a.m. Saturday till 4 p.m. Sunday. Average attendance: 15-20. Holds workshops on 6 different topics: Get Started Writing; Start Your Novel; Writing a Nonfiction Book; Write for Magazines and Papers; Write Your Memoirs; Get Started Writing-Level Two. Speakers include David Rice, Catherine Thorne and others yet to be invited.

Costs 185 EURO per workshop. Includes midday meal each day. Does not include lodging.

Accommodations Runs a shuttle from Shannon Airport.

Additional Information ''Please check out our Web site.''

PARIS WRITERS WORKSHOP/WICE

20, Bd. du Montparnasse, Paris 75015 France. (331)45.66.75.50. Fax: (331)40.65.96.53. E-mail: pww @wice-paris.org. Web site: www.pariswritersworkshop.org. **Contact:** Marcia Lebre or John Baxter, co-directors. Estab. 1987. Annual. Last conference held July 1-11, 2008. Average attendance: 100. ''Conference concentrates on fiction, nonfiction, poetry, creativity and genre writing. Visiting lecturers speak on a variety of issues important to beginning and advanced writers.'' 2008 writers in residence: Nuala O'Faolain, Nahid Rachlin, Vijay Seshadri, Catherine Texier, Cole Swensen, Patrick McGilligan, Ann Snodgrass, Karen Weir-Jimerson,Toni Johnson-Woods, Susan Tiberghien, Gillian Reynolds, Kevin Jackson, Tina Daniell, Jon Fink. Located in the heart of Paris on the Bd. du Montparnasse, the stomping grounds of such famous American writers as Ernest Hemingway, Henry Miller and F. Scott Fitzgerald. The site consists of four classrooms, a resource center/library and private terrace.''

Costs Tuition varies depending on courses.

Additional Information ''Students submit 1 copy of complete manuscript or work-in-progress which is sent in advance to writer-in-residence. Each student has a one-on-one consultation with writer-in-residence.'' Conference information available late fall. For brochures/guidelines visit Web site, e-mail, call or fax. Accepts inquiries by SASE, phone, e-mail, fax. ''Workshop attracts many expatriate Americans and other English-language writers worldwide. We are an intimate workshop with an exciting mix of more experienced, published writers and enthusiastic beginners.''

Conferences

▓ TY NEWYDD WRITERS' CENTRE

Llanystumdwy, Cricieth Gwynedd LL52 0LW United Kingdom. 01766-522811. Fax: 01766 523095. E-mail: post@tynewydd.org. Web site: www.tynewydd.org. **Contact:** Sally Baker, director, Executive Director. Estab. 1990. Year-round. Regular courses held throughout the year. Every course held Monday-Saturday. Average attendance: 14. "To give people the opportunity to work side-by-side with professional writers, in an informal atmosphere." Site: Ty Newydd, large manor house, last home of the prime minister, David Lloyd George. Situated in North Wales, Great Britain—between mountains and sea.

Costs Single room, $834/£480, shared room, $954/£420 for Monday-Saturday (includes full board, tuition).

Accommodations Transportation from railway stations arranged. Accommodation in Ty Newydd (onsite).

Additional Information Course information available by mail, phone, e-mail, fax or visit Web site. Accepts inquiries by SASE, e-mail, fax, phone. "More and more people come to us from the U.S. often combining a writing course with a tour of Wales."

▓ WRITING, CREATIVITY AND THE JOURNEY OF SOUL, A Woman's Retreat

P.O. Box 536, Yorktown Heights NY 10598. (914)926-4432. E-mail: emily@emilyhanlon.com. Web site: www.awritersretreat.com. **Contact:** Emily Hanlon. Estab. 1998. Annual. Retreat held in Castlefiorentino, Italy, Sept. 5-15, 2008. Average attendance: 20 is the limit. Women only. "The multifaceted journey of creativity is not limited to the arts, but nurtures life at the most profound depths, those of soul. It is this we explore in Italy as we reclaim the intuitive wisdom of the Feminine. One of the most powerful ways we will experience this is through our writing. The retreat is open to anyone on the creative journey."

Costs Range from $2,800 to $3,550 depending on choice of room and payment schedule. 10 days, includes room, workshop materials, all meals, and sightseeing, including two days in Florence. Post retreat trip to Venice, September 16-20, 2008. See Web Site.

Additional Information Conference information free and available online. Accepts inquiries by e-mail, phone. Retreat leader, Emily Hanlon, is a best selling novelist. She has published for children and adults and has a book on writing, *The Art of Fiction Writing*, and has had articles published in *Writer's Digest*. Her Web sites are: www.thefictionwritersjourney.com and www.creativesoulworks. com. Please e-mail or call if you would like to be put on the mailing list.

ZOETROPE: ALL-STORY SHORT STORY WRITERS' WORKSHOP

916 Kearny St., San Francisco CA 94133. (415)788-7500. E-mail: info@all-story.com. Web site: www. all-story.com. **Contact:** Michael Ray, editor. Estab. 1997. Annual. Last workshop was August 18-25, 2007. Conference duration: 1 week. Average attendance: 20. Workshop focuses on fiction, specifically short stories. Site: Francis Ford Coppola's gorgeous Blancaneaux Lodge in Belize, on the banks of the Privassion River. Guests stay in luxurious private cabanas and villas, all with spa baths and decks with hammocks and river views. Past instructors include Philip Gourevitch, National Book Award finalist Susan Straight, Pulitzer Prize-winner Robert Olen Butler, and George Saunders.

Costs Ranges from $2,750 to $3,850, depending on accommodations. That fee is all-inclusive, including accommodations, food, workshop, day excursions, all transfers to and from Belize City, and a camp T-shirt.

Additional Information Please submit a completed application and an original work of short fiction less than 5,000 words by August 1. Application forms are available on the Web site. Accepts inquiries by phone, fax, e-mail and for SASE. Editors attend the conference.

Publishers and Their Imprints

The publishing world is in constant transition. With all the buying, selling, reorganizing, consolidating, and dissolving, it's hard to keep publishers and their imprints straight. To help make sense of these changes, here's a breakdown of major publishers (and their divisions)—who owns whom and which imprints are under each company umbrella. Keep in mind that this information changes frequently. The Web site of each publisher is provided to help you keep an eye on this ever-evolving business.

HARLEQUIN ENTERPRISES

www.eharlequin.com

Harlequin
Harlequin American Romance
Harlequin Bianca
Harlequin Blaze
Harlequin Deseo
Harlequin Everlasting Love
Harlequin Historical
Harlequin Intrigue
Harlequin Jazmin
Harlequin Julia
Harlequin Medical Romance
Harlequin NASCAR
Harlequin NEXT
Harlequin Presents
Harlequin Romance
Harlequin Superromance

HQN Books

LUNA

MIRA

Kimani Press
Kimani Press Arabesque
Kimani Press Kimani Romance

Kimani Press Kimani TRU
Kimani Press New Spirit
Kimani Press Sepia

Red Dress Ink

Silhouette
Silhouette Desire
Silhouette Nocturne
Silhouette Romantic Suspense
Silhouette Special Edition

SPICE
SPICE Books
SPICE Briefs

Steeple Hill
Steeple Hill Café
Steeple Hill Love Inspired
Steeple Hill Love Inspired Historical
Steeple Hill Love Inspired Suspense
Steeple Hill Women's Fiction

Worldwide Library
Rogue Angel
Worldwide Mystery

HARPERCOLLINS

www.harpercollins.com

HarperCollins Australia
Angus & Robertson
Collins
Fourth Estate
Harper Perennial
HarperCollins
HarperSports
Voyager

HarperCollins Canada
Collins Canada
HarperCollinsPublishers
HarperPerennial Canada
HarperTrophyCanada
Phyllis Bruce Books

HarperCollins Children's Books Group
Amistad
Bowen Press
Eos
Greenwillow Books
HarperCollins Children's Audio
HarperCollins Children's Books
HarperFestival
HarperEntertainment
HarperTeen
HarperTrophy
Joanna Cotler books
Julie Andrews Collection
Katherine Tegen Books
Laura Geringer Books
Rayo

HarperCollins General Books Group
Amistad
Avon
Avon A
Avon Inspire
Avon Red
Caedmon
Collins
Collins Design

Ecco
Eos
Harper Mass Market
Harper Paperbacks
Harper Perennial
Harper Perennial Modern
HarperAudio
HarperCollins
HarperCollins e-Books
HarperEntertainment
HarperLuxe
HarperOne
Morrow Cookbooks
Rayo
William Morrow

HarperCollins India

HarperCollins New Zealand

HarperCollins UK
Collins
Collins Education
Collins Languages
HarperFiction
  AVON
  Voyager
HarperNonfiction
  HarperSport
  HarperThorsons Harper Element
  Tolkien and Estates
HarperCollins Children's Books
Press Books
  FourthEstate
  HarperPerennial
  HarperPress

Zondervan
Vida
Zonderkidz
Zondervan

MACMILLAN US

http://us.macmillan.com

Bedford, Freeman & Worth Publishing Group
Bedford/St. Martin's
Hayden-McNeil
Pulgrave Macmillan
W.H. Freeman
Worth Publishers

Farrar, Straus & Giroux
Books for Young Readers
Faber & Faber, Inc.
Hill & Wang (division)
North Point Press

Feiwel & Friends

First Second

Henry Holt
Books for Young Readers
Christy Ottariano Books
Metropolitan Books
Owl Books

Times Books

Macmillan Audio

Picador

Priddy Books

Roaring Brook Press

Square Fish

St. Martin's Press
Griffin Books
Let's Go
Minotaur
St. Martin's Paperbacks
St. Martin's Press
Thomas Dunne Books
Truman Talley Books

Tom Doherty Associates
Forge
Tor Books

PENGUIN GROUP (USA), INC.

www.penguingroup.com

Penguin Adult Division
Ace
Alpha
Avery
Berkley
Dutton
Gotham
HPBooks
Hudson Street Press
Jeremy P. Tarcher
Jove
NAL
Penguin
Penguin Press
Perigree
Plume
Portfolio
Putnam
Riverhead
Sentinel
Viking

Young Readers Division
Dial
Dutton
Firebird
Frederick Warne
Grosset & Dunlap
Philomel
Price Stern Sloan
Puffin Books
Putnam
Razorbill
Speak
Viking

Resources

RANDOM HOUSE, INC.

www.randomhouse.com

Bantam Dell Publishing Group
Bantam Hardcover
Bantam Mass Market
Bantam Trade Paperback
Delacorte Press Hardcover
Dell Mass Market Paperback
Delta Trade Paperback
The Dial Press Hardcover
The Dial Press Trade Paperback
Spectra

Crown Publishing Group
Clarkson Potter
Crown
Crown Business
Crown Forum
Harmony
Potter Craft
Potter Style
Shaye Arehart Books
Three Rivers Press

Doubleday Broadway
Broadway Books
Currency
Doubleday
Doubleday Image
Doubleday Religious Publishing
Harlem Moon
Main Street Books
Morgan Road Books
Spiegel & Grau
Nan A. Talese

Knopf Publishing Group
Alfred A. Knopf
Anchor Books
Everyman's Library
Pantheon Books
Schocken Books
Vintage Books

Random House Publishing Group
Ballantine Books
Del Rey
Del Rey/Lucas Books
Fawcett

Ivy
The Modern Library
One World
Random House Trade Group
Random House Trade Paperbacks
Reader's Circle
Striver's Row Books
Villard Books
Wellspring

Random House Audio Publishing Group
Listening Library
Random House Audio
Random House Audio Assets
Random House Audio Dimensions
Random House Audio Price-less
Random House Audio Roads
Random House Audio Voices

Random House Children's Books
Bantam Delacorte Dell Books for Young Readers
Knopf/Crown Books for Young Readers
Wendy Lamb Book
Random House Books for Young Readers
Robin Corey Books
Schwartz & Waote Books

Random House Direct, Inc.
Bon Apétit
Gourmet Books
Pillsbury

Random House Information Group
Fodor's Travel Publications
Living Language
Prima Games
Princeton Review
Random House Español
Random House Puzzles & Games
Random House Reference Publishing

Random House International
Areté
McClelland & Stewart Ltd.

Plaza & Janés
Random House Australia
Random House Canada Ltd.
Random House Mondadori
Random House South Africa
Random House South America
Random House United Kingdom
Transworld UK

Verlagsgruppe Random House

Random House Large Print

Random House Value Publishing

Waterbrook Press
Fisherman Bible Study Guides
Shaw Books
Waterbrook Press

SIMON & SCHUSTER

www.simonsays.com

Simon & Schuster Adult Publishing
Atria Books
    Washington Square Press
Free Press
Howard Books
Pocket Books
Scribner
Simon & Schuster
Strebor
The Touchstone & Fireside Group

Simon & Schuster Audio
Pimsleur
Simon & Schuster Audioworks
Sound Ideas

Simon & Schuster Children's Publishing
Aladdin Paperbacks
Atheneum Books for Young Readers
Libros Para Niños
Little Simon®
Little Simon Inspirations
Margaret K. McElderry Books
Simon & Schuster Books for Young Readers
Simon Pulse
Simon Scribbles
Simon Spotlight®
Simon Spotlight Entertainment

Simon & Schuster International
Simon & Schuster Australia
Simon & Schuster Canada
Simon & Schuster UK

HACHETTE BOOK GROUP USA

www.hachettebookgroupusa.com

Center Street

FaithWords

Grand Central Publishing
Business Plus
5-Spot
Forever
Springboard Press
Twelve
Vision
Wellness Central

Hachette Book Group Digital Media
Hachette Audio

Little, Brown and Company
Back Bay Books

Little, Brown Books for Young Readers
LB Kids
Poppy

Orbit

Yen Press

Canadian Writers Take Note

While much of the information contained in this section applies to all writers, here are some specifics of interest to Canadian writers:

Postage: When sending an SASE from Canada, you will need an International Reply Coupon ($3.50). Also be aware, a GST tax is required on postage in Canada and for mail with postage under $5 going to destinations outside the country. Since Canadian postage rates are voted on in January of each year (after we go to press), contact a Canada Post Corporation Customer Service'Division (located in most cities in Canada) or visit www.canadapost.ca for the most current rates.

Copyright: For information on copyrighting your work and to obtain forms, write Canadian Intellectual Property Office, Industry Canada, Place du Portage I, 50 Victoria St., Room C-114, Gatineau, Quebec K1A 0C9 or call (866)997-1936. Web site: www.cipo.gc.ca.

The public lending right: The Public Lending Right Commission has established that eligible Canadian authors are entitled to payments when a book is available through a library. Payments are determined by a sampling of the holdings of a representative number of libraries. To find out more about the program and to learn if you are eligible, write to the Public Lending Right Commission at 350 Albert St., P.O. Box 1047, Ottawa, Ontario K1P 5V8 or call (613)566-4378 or (800)521-5721 for information. Web site: www.plr-dpp.ca/. The Commission, which is part of The Canada Council, produces a helpful pamphlet, *How the PLR System Works*, on the program.

Grants available to Canadian writers: Most province art councils or departments of culture provide grants to resident writers. Some of these, as well as contests for Canadian writers, are listed in our Contests and Awards section. For national programs, contact The Canada Council, Writing and Publishing Section, 350 Alberta St., P.O. Box 1047, Ottawa, Ontario K1P 5V8 or call (613)566-4414 or (800)263-5588 for information. Fax: (613)566-4410. Web site: www.canadacouncil.ca.

For more information: Contact The Writer's Union of Canada, 90 Richmond St. E, Suite 200, Toronto, Ontario M5C 1P1; call them at (416)703-8982 or fax them at (416)504-9090. E-mail: info@writersunion.ca. Web site: www.writersunion.ca. This organization provides a wealth of information (as well as strong support) for Canadian writers, including specialized publications on publishing contracts; contract negotiations; the author/editor relationship; author awards, competitions and grants; agents; taxes for writers, libel issues and access to archives in Canada.

Printing & Production

Terms Defined

I n most of the magazine listings in this book, you will find a brief physical description of each publication. This material usually includes the number of pages, type of paper, type of binding and whether or not the magazine uses photographs and/or illustrations.

Although it is important to look at a copy of the magazine to which you are submitting, these descriptions can give you a general idea of what the publication looks like. This material can provide you with a feel for the magazine's financial resources and prestige. Do not, however, rule out small, simply produced publications, as these may be the most receptive to new writers. Watch for publications that have increased their page count or improved their production from year to year. This is a sign the publication is doing well and may be accepting more fiction.

You will notice a wide variety of printing terms used within these descriptions. We explain here some of the more common terms used in our listing descriptions. We do not include explanations of terms such as Mohawk and Karma which are brand names and refer to the paper manufacturer.

PAPER

A5: An international paper standard; 148×210 mm or 5.8×8.3 in.

acid-free: Paper that has low or no acid content. This type of paper resists deterioration from exposure to the elements. More expensive than many other types of paper, publications done on acid-free paper can last a long time.

bond: Bond paper is often used for stationery and is more transparent than text paper. It can be made of either sulphite (wood) or cotton fiber. Some bonds have a mixture of both wood and cotton (such as "25 percent cotton" paper). This is the type of paper most often used in photocopying or as standard typing paper.

coated/uncoated stock: Coated and uncoated are terms usually used when referring to book or text paper. More opaque than bond, it is the paper most used for offset printing. As the name implies, uncoated paper has no coating. Coated paper is coated with a layer of clay, varnish or other chemicals. It comes in various sheens and surfaces depending on the type of coating, but the most common are dull, matte and gloss.

cover stock: Cover stock is heavier book or text paper used to cover a publication. It comes in a variety of colors and textures and can be coated on one or both sides.

CS1/CS2: Most often used when referring to cover stock, CS1 means paper that is coated only on one side; CS2 is paper coated on both sides.

newsprint: Inexpensive absorbent pulp wood paper often used in newspapers and tabloids.

text: Text paper is similar to book paper (a smooth paper used in offset printing), but it has been given some texture by using rollers or other methods to apply a pattern to the paper.

vellum: Vellum is a text paper that is fairly porous and soft.

Some notes about paper weight and thickness: Often you will see paper thickness described in terms of pounds such as 80 lb. or 60 lb. paper. The weight is determined by figuring how many pounds in a ream of a particular paper (a ream is 500 sheets). This can be confusing, however, because this figure is based on a standard sheet size and standard sheet sizes vary depending on the type of paper used. This information is most helpful when comparing papers of the same type. For example, 80 lb. book paper versus 60 lb. book paper. Since the size of the paper is the same it would follow that 80 lb. paper is the thicker, heavier paper.

Some paper, especially cover stock, is described by the actual thickness of the paper. This is expressed in a system of points. Typical paper thicknesses range from 8 points to 14 points thick.

PRINTING

There are many other printing methods but these are the ones most commonly referred to in our listings.

letterpress: Letterpress printing is printing that uses a raised surface such as type. The type is inked and then pressed against the paper. Unlike offset printing, only a limited number of impressions can be made, as the surface of the type can wear down.

offset: Offset is a printing method in which ink is transferred from an image-bearing plate to a "blanket" and from the blanket to the paper.

sheet-fed offset: Offset printing in which the paper is fed one piece at a time.

web offset: Offset printing in which a roll of paper is printed and then cut apart to make individual sheets.

BINDING

case binding: In case binding, signatures (groups of pages) are stitched together with thread rather than glued together. The stitched pages are then trimmed on three sides and glued into a hardcover or board "case" or cover. Most hardcover books and thicker magazines are done this way.

comb binding: A comb is a plastic spine used to hold pages together with bent tabs that are fed through punched holes in the edge of the paper.

perfect binding: Used for paperback books and heavier magazines, perfect binding involves gathering signatures (groups of pages) into a stack, trimming off the folds so the edge is flat and gluing a cover to that edge.

saddle stitched: Publications in which the pages are stitched together using metal staples. This fairly inexpensive type of binding is usually used with books or magazines that are under 80 pages.

Smythe-sewn: Binding in which the pages are sewn together with thread. Smythe is the name of the most common machine used for this purpose.

spiral binding: A wire spiral that is wound through holes punched in pages is a spiral bind. This is the binding used in spiral notebooks.

Glossary

Advance. Payment by a publisher to an author prior to the publication of a book, to be deducted from the author's future royalties.

Adventure story. A genre of fiction in which action is the key element, overshadowing characters, theme and setting. The conflict in an adventure story is often man against nature. A secondary plot that reinforces this kind of conflict is sometimes included. In Allistair MacLean's *Night Without End*, for example, the hero, while investigating a mysterious Arctic air crash, also finds himself dealing with espionage, sabotage and murder.

All rights. The rights contracted to a publisher permitting a manuscript's use anywhere and in any form, including movie and book club sales, without additional payment to the writer.

Amateur sleuth. The character in a mystery, usually the protagonist, who does the detection but is not a professional private investigator or police detective.

Anthology. A collection of selected writings by various authors.

Association of Authors' Representatives (AAR). An organization for literary agents committed to maintaining excellence in literary representation.

Auction. Publishers sometimes bid against each other for the acquisition of a manuscript that has excellent sales prospects.

Backlist. A publisher's books not published during the current season but still in print.

Biographical novel. A life story documented in history and transformed into fiction through the insight and imagination of the writer. This type of novel melds the elements of biographical research and historical truth into the framework of a novel, complete with dialogue, drama and mood. A biographical novel resembles historical fiction, save for one aspect: Characters in a historical novel may be fabricated and then placed into an authentic setting; characters in a biographical novel have actually lived.

Book producer/packager. An organization that may develop a book for a publisher based upon the publisher's idea or may plan all elements of a book, from its initial concept to writing and marketing strategies, and then sell the package to a book publisher and/or movie producer.

Cliffhanger. Fictional event in which the reader is left in suspense at the end of a chapter or episode, so that interest in the story's outcome will be sustained.

Clip. Sample, usually from a newspaper or magazine, of a writer's published work.

Cloak-and-dagger. A melodramatic, romantic type of fiction dealing with espionage and intrigue.

Commercial. Publishers whose concern is salability, profit and success with a large reader-ship.

Contemporary. Material dealing with popular current trends, themes or topics.

Contributor's copy. Copy of an issue of a magazine or published book sent to an author whose work is included.

Copublishing. An arrangement in which the author and publisher share costs and profits.

Copyediting. Editing a manuscript for writing style, grammar, punctuation and factual accuracy.

Copyright. The legal right to exclusive publication, sale or distribution of a literary work.

Cover letter. A brief letter sent with a complete manuscript submitted to an editor.

"Cozy" (or "teacup") mystery. Mystery usually set in a small British town, in a bygone era, featuring a somewhat genteel, intellectual protagonist.

Cyberpunk. Type of science fiction, usually concerned with computer networks and human-computer combinations, involving young, sophisticated protagonists.

Electronic rights. The right to publish material electronically, either in book or short story form.

E-zine. A magazine that is published electronically.

Electronic submission. A submission of material by e-mail or on computer disk.

Ethnic fiction. Stories and novels whose central characters are black, Native American, Italian-American, Jewish, Appalachian or members of some other specific cultural group. Ethnic fiction usually deals with a protagonist caught between two conflicting ways of life: mainstream American culture and his ethnic heritage.

Experimental fiction. Fiction that is innovative in subject matter and style; avant-garde, non-formulaic, usually literary material.

Exposition. The portion of the storyline, usually the beginning, where background information about character and setting is related.

Fair use. A provision in the copyright law that says short passages from copyrighted material may be used without infringing on the owner's rights.

Fanzine. A noncommercial, small-circulation magazine usually dealing with fantasy, horror or science-fiction literature and art.

Fictional biography. The biography of a real person that goes beyond the events of a person's life by being fleshed out with imagined scenes and dialogue. The writer of fictional biographies strives to make it clear that the story is, indeed, fiction and not history.

First North American serial rights. The right to publish material in a periodical before it appears in book form, for the first time, in the United States or Canada.

Flash fiction. See short short stories.

Galleys. The first typeset version of a manuscript that has not yet been divided into pages.

Genre. A formulaic type of fiction such as romance, western or horror.

Gothic. This type of category fiction dates back to the late 18th and early 19th centuries. Contemporary gothic novels are characterized by atmospheric, historical settings and feature young, beautiful women who win the favor of handsome, brooding heroes-simultaneously dealing successfully with some life-threatening menace, either natural or supernatural. Gothics rely on mystery, peril, romantic relationships and a sense of foreboding for their strong, emotional effect on the reader. A classic early gothic novel is Emily Bronte's Wuthering Heights. The gothic writer builds a series of credible, emotional crises for his ultimately triumphant heroine. Sex between the woman and her lover is implied rather than graphically detailed; the writer's descriptive talents are used instead to paint rich, desolate, gloomy settings in stark mansions and awesome castles. He composes slow-paced, intricate sketches that create a sense of impending evil on every page.

Graphic novel. A book (original or adapted) that takes the form of a long comic strip or heavily illustrated story of 40 pages or more, produced in paperback. Though called a novel, these can also be works of nonfiction.

Hard science fiction. Science fiction with an emphasis on science and technology.

Hard-boiled detective novel. Mystery novel featuring a private eye or police detective as the protagonist; usually involves a murder. The emphasis is on the details of the crime and the tough, unsentimental protagonist usually takes a matter-of-fact attitude towards violence.

High fantasy. Fantasy with a medieval setting and a heavy emphasis on chivalry and the quest.

Historical fiction. A fictional story set in a recognizable period of history. As well as telling the stories of ordinary people's lives, historical fiction may involve political or social events of the time.

Horror. Howard Phillips (H.P.) Lovecraft, generally acknowledged to be the master of the horror tale in the 20th century and the most important American writer of this genre since Edgar Allan Poe, maintained that "The oldest and strongest emotion of mankind is fear, and the oldest and strongest kind of fear is fear of the unknown. These facts few psychologists will dispute, and their admitted truth must establish for all time the genuineness and dignity of the weirdly horrible tale as a literary form." Lovecraft distinguishes horror literature from fiction based entirely on physical fear and the merely gruesome. "The true weird tale has something more than secret murder, bloody bones or a sheeted form clanking chains according to rule. A certain atmosphere of breathless and unexplainable dread of outer, unknown forces must be present; there must be a hint, expressed with a seriousness and portentousness becoming its subject, of that most terrible concept of the human brain-a malign and particular suspension or defeat of the fixed laws of Nature which are our only safeguards against the assaults of chaos and the daemons of unplumbed space." It is that atmosphere-the creation of a particular sensation or emotional level-that, according to Lovecraft, is the most important element in the creation of horror literature. Contemporary writers enjoying considerable success in horror fiction include Stephen King, Robert Bloch, Peter Straub and Dean Koontz.

Hypertext fiction. A fictional form, read electronically, which incorporates traditional elements of storytelling with a nonlinear plot line, in which the reader determines the direction of the story by opting for one of many author-supplied links.

Imprint. Name applied to a publisher's specific line (e.g. Owl, an imprint of Henry Holt).

Interactive fiction. Fiction in book or computer-software format where the reader determines the path the story will take by choosing from several alternatives at the end of each chapter or episode.

International Reply Coupon (IRC). A form purchased at a post office and enclosed with a letter or manuscript to a international publisher, to cover return postage costs.

Juveniles, Writing for. This includes works intended for an audience usually between the ages of 2 and 18. Categories of children's books are usually divided in this way: (1) picture books and storybooks (ages 2 to 8); (2) young readers or easy-to-read books (ages 5 to 8); (3) middle readers or middle grade (ages 9 to 11); (4) young adult books (ages 12 and up).

Libel. Written or printed words that defame, malign or damagingly misrepresent a living person.

Literary fiction. The general category of fiction which employs more sophisticated technique, driven as much or more by character evolution than action in the plot.

Literary fiction vs. commercial fiction. To the writer of literary, or serious, fiction, style and technique are often as important as subject matter. Commercial fiction, however, is written with the intent of reaching as wide an audience as possible. Commercial fiction is sometimes called genre fiction because books of this type often fall into categories, such as western, gothic, romance, historical, mystery and horror.

Literary agent. A person who acts for an author in finding a publisher or arranging contract terms on a literary project.

Mainstream fiction. Fiction which appeals to a more general reading audience, versus literary or genre fiction. Mainstream is more plot-driven than literary fiction and less formulaic than genre fiction.

Malice domestic novel. A mystery featuring a murder among family members, such as the murder of a spouse or a parent.

Manuscript. The author's unpublished copy of a work, usually typewritten, used as the basis for typesetting.

Mass market paperback. Softcover book on a popular subject, usually around 4×7, directed to a general audience and sold in drugstores and groceries as well as in bookstores.

Middle reader. Also called middle grade. Juvenile fiction for readers aged 9 to 11.

Ms(s). Abbreviation for manuscript(s).

Multiple submission. Submission of more than one short story at a time to the same editor. Do not make a multiple submission unless requested.

Mystery. A form of narration in which one or more elements remain unknown or unexplained until the end of the story. The modern mystery story contains elements of the serious novel: a convincing account of a character's struggle with various physical and psychological obstacles in an effort to achieve his goal, good characterization and sound motivation.

Narration. The account of events in a story's plot as related by the speaker or the voice of the author.

Narrator. The person who tells the story, either someone involved in the action or the voice of the writer.

New Age. A term including categories such as astrology, psychic phenomena, spiritual healing, UFOs, mysticism and other aspects of the occult.

Noir. A style of mystery involving hard-boiled detectives and bleak settings.

Nom de plume. French for "pen name"; a pseudonym.

Nonfiction novel. A work in which real events and people are written [about] in novel form, but are not camouflaged, as they are in the roman a' clef. In the nonfiction novel, reality is presented imaginatively; the writer imposes a novelistic structure on the actual events, keying sections of narrative around moments that are seen (in retrospect) as symbolic. In this way, he creates a coherence that the actual story might not have had. *The Executioner's Song*, by Norman Mailer, and *In Cold Blood*, by Truman Capote, are notable examples of the nonfiction novel.

Novella (also novelette). A short novel or long story, approximately 20,000-50,000 words.

#10 envelope. 4×9½ envelope, used for queries and other business letters.

Offprint. Copy of a story taken from a magazine before it is bound.

One-time rights. Permission to publish a story in periodical or book form one time only.

Outline. A summary of a book's contents, often in the form of chapter headings with a few sentences outlining the action of the story under each one; sometimes part of a book proposal.

Over the transom. A phrase referring to unsolicited manuscripts, or those that come in "over the transom."

Payment on acceptance. Payment from the magazine or publishing house as soon as the decision to print a manuscript is made.

Payment on publication. Payment from the publisher after a manuscript is printed.

Pen name. A pseudonym used to conceal a writer's real name.

Periodical. A magazine or journal published at regular intervals.

Plot. The carefully devised series of events through which the characters progress in a work of fiction.

Police procedural. A mystery featuring a police detective or officer who uses standard professional police practices to solve a crime.

Popular fiction. Generally, a synonym for category or genre fiction; i.e., fiction intended to appeal to audiences for certain kinds of novels. Popular, or category, fiction is defined as such primarily for the convenience of publishers, editors, reviewers and booksellers who must identify novels of different areas of interest for potential readers.

Print on demand (POD). Novels produced digitally one at a time, as ordered. Self-publishing through print on demand technology typically involves some fees for the author. Some authors use POD to create a manuscript in book form to send to prospective traditional publishers.

Proofreading. Close reading and correction of a manuscript's typographical errors.

Proofs. A typeset version of a manuscript used for correcting errors and making changes, often a photocopy of the galleys.

Proposal. An offer to write a specific work, usually consisting of an outline of the work and one or two completed chapters.

Protagonist. The principal or leading character in a literary work.

Psychological novel. A narrative that emphasizes the mental and emotional aspects of its characters, focusing on motivations and mental activities rather than on exterior events. The psychological novelist is less concerned about relating what happened than about exploring why it happened. The term is most often used to describe 20th-century works that employ techniques such as interior monologue and stream of consciousness. Two examples of contemporary psychological novels are Judith Guest's *Ordinary People* and Mary Gordon's *The Company of Women*.

Public domain. Material that either was never copyrighted or whose copyright term has expired.

Pulp magazine. A periodical printed on inexpensive paper, usually containing lurid, sensational stories or articles.

Query. A letter written to an editor to elicit interest in a story the writer wants to submit.

Reader. A person hired by a publisher to read unsolicited manuscripts.

Reading fee. An arbitrary amount of money charged by some agents and publishers to read a submitted manuscript.

Regency romance. A subgenre of romance, usually set in England between 1811-1820.

Remainders. Leftover copies of an out-of-print book, sold by the publisher at a reduced price.

Reporting time. The number of weeks or months it takes an editor to report back on an author's query or manuscript.

Reprint rights. Permission to print an already published work whose rights have been sold to another magazine or book publisher.

Roman à clef. French "novel with a key." A novel that represents actual living or historical characters and events in fictionalized form.

Romance novel. A type of category fiction in which the love relationship between a man and a woman pervades the plot. The story is often told from the viewpoint of the heroine, who meets a man (the hero), falls in love with him, encounters a conflict that hinders their relationship, then resolves the conflict. Romance is the overriding element in this kind of story: The couple's relationship determines the plot and tone of the book. The theme of the novel is the woman's sexual awakening. Although she may not be a virgin, she has never before been so emotionally aroused. Despite all this emotion, however, characters and plot both must be well developed and realistic. Throughout a romance novel, the reader senses the sexual and emotional attraction between the heroine and hero. Lovemaking scenes, though sometimes detailed, are not generally too graphic, because more emphasis is placed on the sensual element than on physical action.

Royalties. A percentage of the retail price paid to an author for each copy of the book that is sold.

SAE. Self-addressed envelope.

SASE. Self-addressed stamped envelope.

Science fiction [vs. fantasy]. It is generally accepted that, to be science fiction, a story must have elements of science in either the conflict or setting (usually both). Fantasy, on the other hand, rarely utilizes science, relying instead on magic, mythological and neomythological beings and devices and outright invention for conflict and setting.

Second serial (reprint) rights. Permission for the reprinting of a work in another periodical after its first publication in book or magazine form.

Self-publishing. In this arrangement, the author keeps all income derived from the book, but he pays for its manufacturing, production and marketing.

Sequel. A literary work that continues the narrative of a previous, related story or novel.

Serial rights. The rights given by an author to a publisher to print a piece in one or more periodicals.

Serialized novel. A book-length work of fiction published in sequential issues of a periodical.

Setting. The environment and time period during which the action of a story takes place.

Short short story. A condensed piece of fiction, usually under 1,000 words.

Simultaneous submission. The practice of sending copies of the same manuscript to several editors or publishers at the same time. Some editors refuse to consider such submissions.

Slant. A story's particular approach or style, designed to appeal to the readers of a specific magazine.

Slice of life. A presentation of characters in a seemingly mundane situation which offers the reader a flash of illumination about the characters or their situation.

Slush pile. A stack of unsolicited manuscripts in the editorial offices of a publisher.

Social fiction. Fiction written with the purpose of bringing about positive changes in society.

Soft/sociological science fiction. Science fiction with an emphasis on society and culture versus scientific accuracy.

Space opera. Epic science fiction with an emphasis on good guys versus bad guys.

Speculation (or Spec). An editor's agreement to look at an author's manuscript with no promise to purchase.

Speculative fiction (SpecFic). The all-inclusive term for science fiction, fantasy and horror.

Splatterpunk. Type of horror fiction known for its very violent and graphic content.

Subsidiary. An incorporated branch of a company or conglomerate (e.g. Alfred Knopf, Inc., a subsidiary of Random House, Inc.).

Subsidiary rights. All rights other than book publishing rights included in a book contract, such as paperback, book club and movie rights.

Subsidy publisher. A book publisher who charges the author for the cost of typesetting, printing and promoting a book. Also called a vanity publisher.

Subterficial fiction. Innovative, challenging, nonconventional fiction in which what seems to be happening is the result of things not so easily perceived.

Suspense. A genre of fiction where the plot's primary function is to build a feeling of anticipation and fear in the reader over its possible outcome.

Synopsis. A brief summary of a story, novel or play. As part of a book proposal, it is a comprehensive summary condensed in a page or page and a half.

Tabloid. Publication printed on paper about half the size of a regular newspaper page (e.g. *The National Enquirer*).

Tearsheet. Page from a magazine containing a published story.

Techno-Thriller. This genre utilizes many of the same elements as the thriller, with one major difference. In techno-thrillers, technology becomes a major character. In Tom Clancy's *The Hunt for Red October* for example, specific functions of the submarine become crucial to plot development.

Theme. The dominant or central idea in a literary work; its message, moral or main thread.

Thriller. A novel intended to arouse feelings of excitement or suspense. Works in this genre are highly sensational, usually focusing on illegal activities, international espionage, sex and violence. A thriller is often a detective story in which the forces of good are pitted against the forces of evil in a kill-or-be-killed situation.

Trade paperback. A softbound volume, usually around 5×8, published and designed for the general public, available mainly in bookstores.

Traditional fantasy. Fantasy with an emphasis on magic, using characters with the ability to practice magic, such as wizards, witches, dragons, elves and unicorns.

Unsolicited manuscript. A story or novel manuscript that an editor did not specifically ask to see.

Urban fantasy. Fantasy that takes magical characters such as elves, fairies, vampires or wizards and places them in modern-day settings, often in the inner city.

Vanity publisher. See subsidy publisher.

Viewpoint. The position or attitude of the first- or third-person narrator or multiple narrators, which determines how a story's action is seen and evaluated.

Western. Genre with a setting in the West, usually between 1860-1890, with a formula plot about cowboys or other aspects of frontier life.

Whodunit. Genre dealing with murder, suspense and the detection of criminals.

Work-for-hire. Work that another party commissions you to do, generally for a flat fee. The creator does not own the copyright and therefore cannot sell any rights.

Young adult. The general classification of books written for readers 12 and up.

Zine. Often one- or two-person operations run from the home of the publisher/editor. Themes tend to be specialized, personal, experimental and often controversial.

Genre Glossary

Definitions of Fiction Subcategories

The following were provided courtesy of The Extended Novel Writing Workshop, created by the staff of Writers Online Workshops (www.writersonlineworkshops .com).

MYSTERY SUBCATEGORIES

The major mystery subcategories are listed below, each followed by a brief description and the names of representative authors, so you can sample each type of work. Note that we have loosely classified "suspense/thriller" as a mystery category. While these stories do not necessarily follow a traditional "whodunit" plot pattern, they share many elements with other mystery categories. In addition, many traditional mysteries are marketed as suspense/thriller because of this category's current appeal in the marketplace. Since the lines between categories are frequently blurred, it seems practical to include them all here.

Classic Mystery (Whodunit). A crime (almost always a murder or series of murders) is solved. The detective is the viewpoint character; the reader never knows any more or less about the crime than the detective, and all the clues to solving the crime are available to the reader.

Amateur detective. As the name implies, the detective is not a professional detective (private or otherwise), but is almost always a professional something. This professional association routinely involves the protagonist in criminal cases (in a support capacity), gives him or her a special advantage in a specific case, or provides the contacts and skills necessary to solve a particular crime. (Jonathan Kellerman, Patricia Cornwell, Jan Burke)

Courtroom Drama. The action takes place primarily in the courtroom; the protagonist is generally a defense attorney out to prove the innocence of his or her client by finding the real culprit. (Scott Turow, Steve Martini, Richard North Patterson, John Grisham)

Cozy. A special class of the amateur detective category that frequently features a female protagonist. (Agatha Christie's Miss Marple stories are the classic example.) There is less on-stage violence than in other categories and the plot is often wrapped up in a final scene where the detective identifies the murderer and explains how the crime was solved. In contemporary stories, the protagonist can be anyone from a chronically curious housewife to a mystery-buff clergyman to a college professor, but he or she is usually quirky, even eccentric. (Susan Isaacs, Andrew Greeley, Lillian Jackson Braun)

Espionage. The international spy novel is less popular since the end of the cold war, but stories can still revolve around political intrigue in unstable regions. (John le Carré, Ken Follett)

Heists and Capers. The crime itself is the focus. Its planning and execution are seen in detail and the participants are fully-drawn characters that may even be portrayed sympathetically. One character is the obvious leader of the group (the "brains"); the other members are often brought together by the leader specifically for this job and may or may not have a previous association. In a heist, no matter how clever or daring the characters are, they are still portrayed as criminals and the expectation is that they will be caught and punished (but not always). A caper is more light hearted, even comedic. The participants may have a noble goal (something other than personal gain) and often get away with the crime. (Eric Ambler, Tony Kenrick, Leslie Hollander)

Historical. May be any category or subcategory of mystery, but with an emphasis on setting, the details of which must be diligently researched. But beyond the historical details (which must never overshadow the story), the plot develops along the lines of its contemporary counterpart. (Candace Robb, Caleb Carr, Anne Perry)

Juvenile/Young adult. Written for the 8-12 age group (Middle Grade) or the 12 and up age group (Young Adult), the crime in these stories may or may not be murder, but it is serious. The protagonist is a kid (or group of kids) in the same age range as the targeted reader. There is no graphic violence depicted, but the stories are scary and the villains are realistic. (Mary Downing Hahn, Wendy Corsi Staub, Cameron Dokey, Norma Fox Mazer)

Medical thriller. The plot can involve a legitimate medical threat (such as the outbreak of a virulent plague) or the illegal or immoral use of medical technology. In the former scenario, the protagonist is likely to be the doctor (or team) who identifies the virus and procures the antidote; in the latter he or she could be a patient (or the relative of a victim) who uncovers the plot and brings down the villain. (Robin Cook, Michael Palmer, Michael Crichton, Stanley Pottinger)

Police procedurals. The most realistic category, these stories require the most meticulous research. A police procedural may have more than one protagonist since cops rarely work alone. Conflict between partners, or between the detective and his or her superiors is a common theme. But cops are portrayed positively as a group, even though there may be a couple of bad or ineffective law enforcement characters for contrast and conflict. Jurisdictional disputes are still popular sources of conflict as well. (Lawrence Treat, Joseph Wambaugh, Ridley Pearson, Julie Smith)

Private detective. When described as "hard-boiled," this category takes a tough stance. Violence is more prominent, characters are darker, the detective—while almost always licensed by the state—operates on the fringes of the law, and there is often open resentment between the detective and law enforcement. More "enlightened" male detectives and a crop of contemporary females have brought about new trends in this category. (For female P.I.s—Sue Grafton, Sara Paretsky; for male P.I.s—John D. MacDonald, Lawrence Sanders, Robert Parker)

Suspense/Thriller. Where a classic mystery is always a whodunit, a suspense/thriller novel may deal more with the intricacies of the crime, what motivated it, and how the villain (whose identity may be revealed to the reader early on) is caught and brought to justice. Novels in this category frequently employ multiple points of view and have a broader scope than a more traditional murder mystery. The crime may not even involve murder—it may be a threat to global economy or regional ecology; it may be technology run amok or abused at the hands of an unscrupulous scientist; it may involve innocent citizens victimized for personal or corporate gain. Its perpetrators are kidnappers, stalkers, serial killers, rapists, pedophiles, computer hackers, or just about anyone with an evil intention and the means to carry it out. The protagonist may be a private detective or law enforcement official, but is just as likely to be a doctor, lawyer, military officer or other individual in a unique position to identify the villain and bring him or her to justice. (James Patterson, John J. Nance, Michael Connelly)

Technothriller. These are replacing the traditional espionage novel, and feature technology as an integral part of not just the setting, but the plot as well. (Tom Clancy, Stephen Coonts)

Woman in Jeopardy. A murder or other crime may be committed, but the focus is on the woman (and/or her children) currently at risk, her struggle to understand the nature of the danger, and her eventual victory over her tormentor. The protagonist makes up for her lack of physical prowess with intellect or special skills, and solves the problem on her own or with the help of her family (but she runs the show). Closely related to this category is the Romantic Suspense. But, while the heroine in a romantic suspense is certainly a "woman in jeopardy," the mystery or suspense element is subordinate to the romance. (Mary Higgins Clark, Mary Stewart, Jessica Mann)

ROMANCE SUBCATEGORIES
These categories and subcategories of romance fiction have been culled from the *Romance Writer's Sourcebook* (Writer's Digest Books) and Phyllis Taylor Pianka's *How to Write Romances* (Writer's Digest Books). We've arranged the "major" categories below with the subcategories beneath them, each followed by a brief description and the names of authors who write in each category, so you can sample representative works.

Category or Series. These are published in "lines" by individual publishing houses (such as Harlequin and Silhouette); each line has its own requirements as to word length, story content and amount of sex. (Debbie Macomber, Nora Roberts, Glenda Sanders)

Christian. With an inspirational, Christian message centering on the spiritual dynamic of the romantic relationship and faith in God as the foundation for that relationship; sensuality is played down. (Janelle Burnham, Ann Bell, Linda Chaikin, Catherine Palmer, Dee Henderson, Lisa Tawn Bergen)

Glitz. So called because they feature (generally wealthy) characters with high-powered positions in careers that are considered to be glamorous—high finance, modeling/acting, publishing, fashion—and are set in exciting or exotic (often metropolitan) locales such as Monte Carlo, Hollywood, London or New York. (Jackie Collins, Judith Krantz)

Historical. Can cover just about any historical (or even prehistorical) period. Setting in the historical is especially significant, and details must be thoroughly researched and accurately presented. For a sampling of a variety of historical styles try Laura Kinsell (*Flowers from the Storm*), Mary Jo Putney (*The Rake and the Reformer*) and Judy Cuevas (*Bliss*). Some currently popular periods/themes in historicals are:

Gothic: historical with a strong element of suspense and a feeling of supernatural events, although these events frequently have a natural explanation. Setting plays an important role in establishing a dark, moody, suspenseful atmosphere. (Phyllis Whitney, Victoria Holt)

Historical fantasy: with traditional fantasy elements of magic and magical beings, frequently set in a medieval society. (Amanda Glass, Jayne Ann Krentz, Kathleen Morgan, Jessica Bryan, Taylor Quinn Evans, Carla Simpson, Karyn Monk)

Early American: usually Revolution to Civil War, set in New England or the South, but "frontier" stories set in the American West are quite popular as well. (Robin Lee Hatcher, Elizabeth Lowell, Heather Graham)

Native American: where one or both of the characters are Native Americans; the conflict between cultures is a popular theme. (Carol Finch, Elizabeth Grayson, Karen Kay, Kathleen Harrington, Genell Dellim, Candace McCarthy)

Regency: set in England during the Regency period from 1811-1820. (Carol Finch, Elizabeth Elliott, Georgette Heyer, Joan Johnston, Lynn Collum)

Multicultural. Most currently feature African-American or Hispanic couples, but editors are looking for other ethnic stories as well. Multiculturals can be contemporary or historical, and fall into any sub-category. (Rochelle Alers, Monica Jackson, Bette Ford, Sandra Kitt, Brenda Jackson)

Paranormal. Containing elements of the supernatural or science fiction/fantasy. There are numerous subcategories (many stories combine elements of more than one) including:

Time travel: One or more of the characters travels to another time—usually the past—to find love. (Jude Devereaux, Linda Lael Miller, Diana Gabaldon, Constance O'Day Flannery)

Science fiction/Futuristic: S/F elements are used for the story's setting: imaginary worlds, parallel universes, Earth in the near or distant future. (Marilyn Campbell, Jayne Ann Krentz, J.D. Robb [Nora Roberts], Anne Avery)

Contemporary fantasy: From modern ghost and vampire stories to "New Age" themes such as extraterrestrials and reincarnation. (Linda Lael Miller, Anne Stuart, Antoinette Stockenberg, Christine Feehan)

Romantic Comedy. Has a fairly strong comic premise and/or a comic perspective in the author's voice or the voices of the characters (especially the heroine). (Jennifer Crusie, Susan Elizabeth Phillips)

Romantic Suspense. With a mystery or psychological thriller subplot in addition to the romance plot. (Mary Stewart, Barbara Michaels, Tami Hoag, Nora Roberts, Linda Howard, Catherine Coulter)

Single title. Longer contemporaries that do not necessarily conform to the requirements of a specific romance line and therefore feature more complex plots and nontraditional characters. (Mary Ruth Myers, Nora Roberts, Kathleen Gilles Seidel, Kathleen Korbel)

Young Adult. Focus is on first love with very little, if any, sex. These can have bittersweet endings, as opposed to the traditional romance happy ending, since first loves are often lost loves. (YA historical—Nancy Covert Smith, Louise Vernon; YA contemporary—Mary Downing Hahn, Kathryn Makris)

SCIENCE FICTION SUBCATEGORIES

Peter Heck, in his article "Doors to Other Worlds: Trends in Science Fiction and Fantasy," which appears in the 1996 edition of *Science Fiction and Fantasy Writer's Sourcebook* (Writer's Digest Books), identifies some science fiction trends that have distinct enough characteristics to be defined as categories. These distinctions are frequently the result of marketing decisions as much as literary ones, so understanding them is important in deciding where your novel idea belongs. We've supplied a brief description and the names of authors who write in each category. In those instances where the author writes in more than one category, we've included titles of appropriate representative works.

Hard science fiction. Based on the logical extrapolation of real science to the future. In these stories the scientific background (setting) may be as, or more, important than the characters. (Larry Niven)

Social science fiction. The focus is on how the characters react to their environments. This category includes social satire. (George Orwell's *1984* is a classic example.) (Margaret Atwood, *The Handmaid's Tale*; Ursula K. Le Guin, *The Left Hand of Darkness*; Marge Piercy, *Woman on the Edge of Time*)

Military science fiction. Stories about war that feature traditional military organization and tactics extrapolated into the future. (Jerry Pournelle, David Drake, Elizabeth Moon)

Cyberpunk. Characters in these stories are tough outsiders in a high-tech, generally near-future society where computers have produced major changes in the way that society functions. (William Gibson, Bruce Sterling, Pat Cadigan, Wilhelmina Baird)

Space opera. From the term "horse opera," describing a traditional good-guys-vs-bad-guys western, these stories put the emphasis on sweeping action and larger-than-life characters. The focus on action makes these stories especially appealing for film treatment. (The Star Wars series is one of the best examples, also Samuel R. Delany.)

Alternate history. Fantasy, sometimes with science fiction elements, that changes the accepted account of actual historical events or people to suggest an alternate view of history. (Ted Mooney, *Traffic and Laughter*; Ward Moore, *Bring the Jubilee*; Philip K. Dick, *The Man in the High Castle*)

Steampunk. A specific type of alternate history science fiction set in Victorian England in which characters have access to 20th-century technology. (William Gibson; Bruce Sterling, *The Difference Engine*)

New Age. A category of speculative fiction that deals with subjects such as astrology, psychic phenomena, spiritual healing, UFOs, mysticism and other aspects of the occult. (Walter Mosley, *Blue Light*; Neil Gaiman)

Science fantasy. Blend of traditional fantasy elements with scientific or pseudo-scientific support (genetic engineering, for example, to "explain" a traditional fantasy creature like the dragon). These stories are traditionally more character driven than hard science fiction. (Anne McCaffrey, Mercedes Lackey, Marion Zimmer Bradley)

Science fiction mystery. A cross-genre blending that can either be a more-or-less traditional science fiction story with a mystery as a key plot element, or a more-or-less traditional whodunit with science fiction elements. (Philip K. Dick, Lynn S. Hightower)

Science fiction romance. Another genre blend that may be a romance with science fiction elements (in which case it is more accurately placed as a subcategory within the romance genre) or a science fiction story with a strong romantic subplot. (Anne McCaffrey, Melanie Rawn, Kate Elliot)

Young Adult. Any subcategory of science fiction geared to a YA audience (12-18), but these are usually shorter novels with characters in the central roles who are the same age as (or slightly older than) the targeted reader. (Jane Yolen, Andre Norton)

FANTASY SUBCATEGORIES

Before we take a look at the individual fantasy categories, it should be noted that, for purposes of these supplements, we've treated fantasy as a genre distinct from science fiction. While these two are closely related, there are significant enough differences to warrant their separation for study purposes. We have included here those science fiction categories that have strong fantasy elements, or that have a significant amount of crossover (these categories appear in both the science fiction and the fantasy supplements), but "pure" science fiction categories are not included below. If you're not sure whether your novel is fantasy or science fiction, consider this definition by Orson Scott Card in *How to Write Science Fiction and Fantasy* (Writer's Digest Books):

> "Here's a good, simple, semi-accurate rule of thumb: If the story is set in a universe that follows the same rules as ours, it's science fiction. If it's set in a universe that doesn't follow our rules, it's fantasy.
> Or in other words, science fiction is about what could be but isn't; fantasy is about what couldn't be."

But even Card admits this rule is only "semi-accurate." He goes on to say that the real boundary between science fiction and fantasy is defined by how the impossible is achieved: "If you have people do some magic, impossible thing [like time travel] by stroking a talisman or praying to a tree, it's fantasy; if they do the same thing by pressing a button or climbing inside a machine, it's science fiction."

Peter Heck, in his article "Doors to Other Worlds: Trends in Science Fiction and Fantasy," which appears in the 1996 edition of the *Science Fiction and Fantasy Writer's Sourcebook* (Writer's Digest Books), does note some trends that have distinct enough characteristics to be defined as separate categories. These categories are frequently the result of marketing decisions as much as literary ones, so understanding them is important in deciding where your novel idea belongs. We've supplied a brief description and the names of authors who write in each category, so you can sample representative works.

Arthurian. Re-working of the legend of King Arthur and the Knights of the Round Table. (T.H. White, *The Once and Future King*; Marion Zimmer Bradley, *The Mists of Avalon*)

Contemporary (also called "urban") fantasy. Traditional fantasy elements (such as elves and magic) are incorporated into an otherwise recognizable modern setting. (Emma Bull, *War for the Oaks*; Mercedes Lackey, *The SERRAted Edge*; Terry Brooks, the Knight of the Word series)

Dark fantasy. Closely related to horror, but generally not as graphic. Characters in these stories are the "darker" fantasy types: vampires, witches, werewolves, demons, etc. (Anne Rice; Clive Barker, *Weaveworld, Imajica*; Fred Chappell)

Fantastic alternate history. Set in an alternate historical period (in which magic would not have been a common belief) where magic works, these stories frequently feature actual historical figures. (Orson Scott Card, *Alvin Maker*)

Game-related fantasy. Plots and characters are similar to high fantasy, but are based on a particular role-playing game. (Dungeons and Dragons; Magic: The Gathering; Dragonlance Chronicles; Forgotten Realms; Dark Sun)

Heroic fantasy. The fantasy equivalent to military science fiction, these are stories of war and its heroes and heroines. (Robert E. Howard, the Conan the Barbarian series; Elizabeth Moon, *Deed of Paksenarion*; Michael Moorcock, the Elric series)

High fantasy. Emphasis is on the fate of an entire race or nation, threatened by an ultimate evil. J. R. R. Tolkien's Lord of the Rings trilogy is a classic example. (Terry Brooks, David Eddings, Margaret Weis, Tracy Hickman)

Historical fantasy. The setting can be almost any era in which the belief in magic was strong; these are essentially historical novels where magic is a key element of the plot and/or setting. (Susan Schwartz, *Silk Road and Shadow*; Margaret Ball, *No Earthly Sunne*; Tim Powers, *The Anubis Gates*)

Juvenile/Young adult. Can be any type of fantasy, but geared to a juvenile (8-12) or YA audience (12-18); these are shorter novels with younger characters in central roles. (J.K. Rowling, C.S. Lewis)

Science fantasy. A blend of traditional fantasy elements with scientific or pseudo-scientific support (genetic engineering, for example, to "explain" a traditional fantasy creature like the dragon). These stories are traditionally more character driven than hard science fiction. (Anne McCaffrey, Mercedes Lackey, Marion Zimmer Bradley)

HORROR SUBCATEGORIES

Subcategories in horror are less well defined than in other genres and are frequently the result of marketing decisions as much as literary ones. But being familiar with the terms used to describe different horror styles can be important in understanding how your own novel might be best presented to an agent or editor. What follows is a brief description of the most commonly used terms, along with names of authors and, where necessary, representative works.

Dark Fantasy. Sometimes used as a euphemistic term for horror in general, but also refers to a specific type of fantasy, usually less graphic than other horror subcategories, that features more "traditional" supernatural or mythical beings (vampires, werewolves, zombies, etc.) in either contemporary or historical settings. (Contemporary: Stephen King, *Salem's Lot*; Thomas Tessier, *The Nightwalker*. Historical: Brian Stableford, *The Empire of Fear*; Chelsea Quinn Yarbro, *Werewolves of London*.)

Hauntings. "Classic" stories of ghosts, poltergeists and spiritual possessions. The level of violence portrayed varies, but many writers in this category exploit the reader's natural fear of the unknown by hinting at the horror and letting the reader's imagination supply the details. (Peter Straub, *Ghost Story*; Richard Matheson, *Hell House*)

Juvenile/Young Adult. Can be any horror style, but with a protagonist who is the same age as, or slightly older than, the targeted reader. Stories for middle grades (eight to 12 years old) are scary, with monsters and violent acts that might best be described as "gross," but stories for young adults (12-18) may be more graphic. (R.L. Stine, Christopher Pike, Carol Gorman)

Psychological horror. Features a human monster with horrific, but not necessarily supernatural, aspects. (Thomas Harris, *The Silence of the Lambs*, *Hannibal*; Dean Koontz, *Whispers*)

Splatterpunk. Very graphic depiction of violence—often gratuitous—popularized in the 1980s, especially in film. (*Friday the 13th*, *Halloween*, *Nightmare on Elm Street*, etc.)

Supernatural/Occult. Similar to the dark fantasy, but may be more graphic in its depiction of violence. Stories feature satanic worship, demonic possession, or ultimate evil incarnate in an entity or supernatural being that may or may not have its roots in traditional mythology or folklore. (Ramsey Campbell; Robert McCammon; Ira Levin, *Rosemary's Baby*; William Peter Blatty, *The Exorcist*; Stephen King, *Pet Sematary*)

Technological horror. "Monsters" in these stories are the result of science run amok or technology turned to purposes of evil. (Dean Koontz, *Watchers*; Michael Crichton, *Jurassic Park*)

Professional Organizations

AGENTS' ORGANIZATIONS

Association of Authors' Agents (AAA), 20 John St., London WC1N 2DR, United Kingdom. (44)(20)7405-6774. E-mail: aaa@apwatt. Web site: www.agentsassoc.co.uk.

Association of Authors' Representatives (AAR), 676A 9th Ave., #312, New York NY 10036. (212)840-5777. E-mail: aarinc@mindspring.com. Web site: www.aar-online.org.

Association of Talent Agents (ATA), 9255 Sunset Blvd., Suite 930, Los Angeles CA 90069. (310)274-0628. Fax: (310)274-5063. E-mail: shellie@agentassociation.com. Web site: www.agentassociation.com.

WRITERS' ORGANIZATIONS

Academy of American Poets, 584 Broadway, Suite 604, New York NY 10012-5243. (212)274-0343. Fax: (212)274-9427. E-mail: academy@poets.org. Web site: www.poets.org.

American Crime Writers League (ACWL), 17367 Hilltop Ridge Dr., Eureka MO 63205. Web site: www.acwl.org.

American Medical Writers Association (AMWA), 40 W. Gude Dr., Suite 101, Rockville MD 20850-1192. (301)294-5303. Fax: (301)294-9006. E-mail: amwa@amwa.org. Web site: www.amwa.org.

American Screenwriters Association (ASA), 269 S. Beverly Dr., Suite 2600, Beverly Hills CA 90212-3807. (866)265-9091. E-mail: asa@goasa.com. Website: www.asascreenwriters.com.

American Translators Association (ATA), 225 Reinekers Lane, Suite 590, Alexandria VA 22314. (703)683-6100. Fax: (703)683-6122. E-mail: ata@atanet.org. Web site: www.atanet.org.

Education Writers Association (EWA), 2122 P St. NW, Suite 201, Washington DC 20037. (202)452-9830. Fax: (202)452-9837. E-mail: ewa@ewa.org. Web site: www.ewa.org.

Garden Writers Association (GWA), 10210 Leatherleaf Ct., Manassas VA 20111. (703)257-1032. Fax: (703)257-0213. Web site: www.gardenwriters.org.

Resources

Horror Writers Association (HWA), 244 5th Ave., Suite 2767, New York NY 10001. E-mail: hwa@horror.org. Web site: www.horror.org.

The International Women's Writing Guild (IWWG),P.O. Box 810, Gracie Station, New York NY 10028-0082. (212)737-7536. Fax: (212)737-9469. E-mail: dirhahn@iwwg.org. Web site: www.iwwg.com.

Mystery Writers of America (MWA), 17 E. 47th St., 6th Floor, New York NY 10017. (212)888-8171. Fax: (212)888-8107. E-mail: mwa@mysterywriters.org. Web site: www.mysterywriters.org.

National Association of Science Writers (NASW), P.O. Box 890, Hedgesville WV 25427. (304)754-5077. Fax: (304)754-5076. E-mail: diane@nasw.org. Web site: www.nasw.org.

National Association of Women Writers (NAWW), 24165 IH-10 W., Suite 217-637, San Antonio TX 78257. Web site: www.naww.org.

Organization of Black Screenwriters (OBS). Web site: www.obswriter.com.

Outdoor Writers Association of America (OWAA), 121 Hickory St., Suite 1, Missoula MT 59801. (406)728-7434. Fax: (406)728-7445. E-mail: krhoades@owaa.org. Web site: www.owaa.org.

Poetry Society of America (PSA), 15 Gramercy Park, New York NY 10003. (212)254-9628. Web site: www.poetrysociety.org.

Poets & Writers, 72 Spring St., Suite 301, New York NY 10012. (212)226-3586. Fax: (212)226-3963. Web site: www.pw.org.

Romance Writers of America (RWA), 16000 Stuebner Airline Rd., Suite 140, Spring TX 77379. (832)717-5200. E-mail: info@rwanational.org. Web site: www.rwanational.org.

Science Fiction and Fantasy Writers of America (SFWA), P.O. Box 877, Chestertown MD 21620. E-mail: execdir@sfwa.org. Web site: www.sfwa.org.

Society of American Business Editors & Writers (SABEW), University of Missouri, School of Journalism, 385 McReynolds, Columbia MO 65211. (573)882-7862. Fax: (573)884-1372. E-mail: sabew@missouri.edu. Web site: www.sabew.org.

Society of American Travel Writers (SATW), 1500 Sunday Dr., Suite 102, Raleigh NC 27607. (919)861-5586. Fax: (919)787-4916. E-mail: satw@satw.org. Web site: www.satw.org.

Society of Children's Book Writers & Illustrators (SCBWI), 8271 Beverly Blvd., Los Angeles CA 90048. (323)782-1010. Fax: (323)782-1892. E-mail: scbwi@scbwi.org. Web site: www.scbwi.org.

Washington Independent Writers (WIW), 1001 Connecticut Ave. NW, Suite 701, Washington DC 20036. (202)775-5150. Fax: (202)775-5810. E-mail: info@washwriter.org. Web site: www.washwriter.org.

Western Writers of America (WWA). E-mail: wwa@unm.edu. Web site: www.westernwriters.org.

INDUSTRY ORGANIZATIONS

American Booksellers Association (ABA), 200 White Plains Rd., Tarrytown NY

10591. (914)591-2665. Fax: (914)591-2720. E-mail: info@bookweb.org. Web site: www.bookweb.org.

American Society of Journalists & Authors (ASJA), 1501 Broadway, Suite 302, New York NY 10036. (212)997-0947. Fax: (212)937-2315. E-mail: execdir@asja.org. Web site: www.asja.org.

Association for Women in Communications (AWC), 3337 Duke St., Alexandria VA 22314. (703)370-7436. Fax: (703)370-7437. E-mail: info@womcom.org. Web site: www.womcom.org.

Association of American Publishers (AAP), 71 5th Ave., 2nd Floor, New York NY 10003. (212)255-0200. Fax: (212)255-7007. Or, 50 F St. NW, Suite 400, Washington DC 20001. (202)347-3375. Fax: (202)347-3690. Web site: www.publishers.org.

The Association of Writers & Writing Programs (AWP), The Carty House, Mail stop 1E3, George Mason University, Fairfax VA 22030. (703)993-4301. Fax: (703)993-4302. E-mail: services@awpwriter.org. Web site: www.awpwriter.org.

The Authors Guild, Inc., 31 E. 32nd St., 7th Floor, New York NY 10016. (212)563-5904. Fax: (212)564-5363. E-mail: staff@authorsguild.org. Web site: www.authorsguild.org.

Canadian Authors Association (CAA), Box 419, Campbellford ON K0L 1L0 Canada. (705)653-0323. Fax: (705)653-0593. E-mail: admin@canauthors.org. Web site: www.canauthors.org.

Christian Booksellers Association (CBA), P.O. Box 62000, Colorado Springs CO 80962-2000. (800)252-1950. Fax: (719)272-3510. E-mail: info@cbaonline.org. Web site: www.cbaonline.org.

The Dramatists Guild of America, 1501 Broadway, Suite 701, New York NY 10036. (212)398-9366. Fax: (212)944-0420. Web site: www.dramaguild.com.

National League of American Pen Women (NLAPW), 1300 17th St. NW, Washington DC 20036-1973. (202)785-1997. Fax: (202)452-8868. Website: www.americanpenwomen.org.

National Writers Association (NWA), 10940 S. Parker Rd., #508, Parker CO 80134. (303)841-0246. Fax: (303)841-2607. E-mail: anitaedits@aol.com. Web site: www.nationalwriters.com.

National Writers Union (NWU), 113 University Place, 6th Floor, New York NY 10003. (212)254-0279. Fax: (212)254-0673. E-mail: nwu@nwu.org. Web site: www.nwu.org.

PEN American Center, 588 Broadway, Suite 303, New York NY 10012-3225. (212)334-1660. Fax: (212)334-2181. E-mail: pen@pen.org. Web site: www.pen.org.

The Playwrights Guild of Canada (PGC), 54 Wolseley St., 2nd Floor, Toronto ON M5T 1A5 Canada. (416)703-0201. Fax: (416)703-0059. E-mail: info@playwrightsguild.ca. Web site: www.playwrightsguild.com.

Volunteer Lawyers for the Arts (VLA), One E. 53rd St., 6th Floor, New York NY 10022. (212)319-2787. Fax: (212)752-6575. Web site: www.vlany.org.

Women in Film (WIF), 8857 W. Olympic Blvd., Suite 201, Beverly Hills CA 90211. (310)657-5144. E-mail: info@wif.org. Web site: www.wif.org.

Women in the Arts Foundation (WIA), 32-35 30th St., D24, Long Island City NY 11106. (212)941-0130. E-mail: reginas@anny.org. Web site: www.anny.org/2/orgs/womeninarts/.

Women's National Book Association (WNBA), 2166 Broadway, #9-E, New York NY 10024. (212)208-4629. Web site: www.wnba-books.org.

Writers Guild of Alberta (WGA), 11759 Groat Rd., Edmonton AB T5M 3K6 Canada. (780)422-8174. Fax: (780)422-2663. E-mail: mail@writersguild.ab.ca. Web site: writersguild.ab.ca.

Writers Guild of America-East (WGA), 555 W. 57th St., Suite 1230, New York NY 10019. (212)767-7800. Fax: (212)582-1909. Web site: www.wgaeast.org.

Writers Guild of America-West (WGA), 7000 W. Third St., Los Angeles CA 90048. (323)951-4000. Fax: (323)782-4800. Web site: www.wga.org.

Writers Union of Canada (TWUC), 90 Richmond St. E., Suite 200, Toronto ON M5C 1P1 Canada. (416)703-8982. Fax: (416)504-9090. E-mail: info@writersunion.ca. Web site: www.writersunion.ca.

Literary Agents Category Index

Agents listed in this edition of *Novel & Short Story Writer's Market* are indexed below according to the categories of fiction they represent. Use it to find agents who handle the specific kind of fiction you write. Then turn to those listings in the alphabetical Literary Agents section for complete contact and submission information.

Action/Adventure

Erotica

Ethnic

Experimental

Glitz

Hi-Lo

Historical

Horror

Humor/Satire

Juvenile

Literary

Mainstream/Contemporary

Agents Category Index

Agents Category Index

Agents Category Index

Translation

Westerns/Frontier

Women's

Young Adult

Conference Index by Date

Our conference index organizes all conferences listed in this edition by the month in which they are held. If a conference bridges two months, you will find its name and page number under both monthly headings. If a conference occurs multiple times during the year (seasonally, for example), it will appear under each appropriate monthly heading. Turn to the listing's page number for exact dates and more detailed information.

August

September

Category Index

Our category index makes it easy for you to identify publishers who are looking for a specific type of fiction. Publishers who are not listed under a fiction category either accept all types of fiction or have not indicated specific subject preferences. Also not appearing here are listings that need very specific types of fiction, e.g., "fiction about fly fishing only."

To use this index to find markets for your work, go to category title that best describes the type of fiction you write and look under either Magazines or Book Publishers (depending on whom you're targeting). Finally, read individual listings *carefully* to determine the publishers best suited to your work.

For a listing of agents and the types of fiction they represent, see the Literary Agents Category Index beginning on page 575.

ADVENTURE

Magazines

Book Publishers

Book Publishers

EXPERIMENTAL

Magazines

Book Publishers

Book Publishers

FEMINIST

Magazines

Book Publishers

HORROR
Magazines

Book Publishers

Humor/Satire

Magazines

Category Index

LESBIAN

Magazines

Book Publishers

LITERARY
Magazines

Book Publishers

MAINSTREAM/ CONTEMPORARY

Magazines

Book Publishers

Category Index

MILITARY/WAR

Magazines

Book Publishers

MYSTERY/SUSPENSE

Magazines

Book Publishers

NEW AGE/MYSTIC/ SPIRITUAL
Magazines

Book Publishers

PSYCHIC/SUPERNATURAL/ OCCULT
Magazines

Book Publishers

REGIONAL

Magazines

RELIGIOUS/INSPIRATIONAL

Magazines

Book Publishers

Book Publishers

SHORT STORY COLLECTIONS
Book Publishers

THRILLER/ESPIONAGE
Magazines

Book Publishers

General Index

General Index

General Index